A HISTORY OF ENGLISH DRAMA 1660–1900

A HISTORY OF ENGLISH DRAMA

1660–1900

BY

ALLARDYCE NICOLL

VOLUME V

LATE NINETEENTH CENTURY DRAMA

1850–1900

CAMBRIDGE
AT THE UNIVERSITY PRESS
1967

Published by the Syndics of the Cambridge University Press
Bentley House, 200 Euston Road, London, N.W. 1
American Branch: 32 East 57th Street, New York, N.Y. 10022

First Edition 1946
Reprinted 1949
Second Edition 1959
Reprinted 1962
1967

Issued as Vol. V of
A History of English Drama 1600–1900

Printed in Great Britain
at the University Printing House, Cambridge
(Brooke Crutchley, University Printer)

CONTENTS

Chapter Six

Jones and Pinero: Plays of the Eighties

Chapter Seven

Wilde and Shaw: Plays of the Nineties

Appendix A

The Theatres: 1850–1900

Appendix B

CHAPTER I

THE THEATRE

I. *Introductory*

WITHIN the half-century covered by this survey the modern drama, with all its essential conditions and conventions, was born. The theatre of the eighteen-fifties, even although it may be vaguely within human memory, seems far distant from the theatre of the nineteen-thirties; the theatre of the nineties—and that not only in matter of time—appears to be part of ourselves. In 1850 Tom Robertson was as yet only a touring actor, dreaming perhaps, like Arthur Gower in *Trelawney of the "Wells"*, of dramatic work to come, but still thoroughly immersed in the older stock traditions; Charles Kean was just starting his extraordinary antiquarian experiments at the Princess's; the popular playhouses were rejoicing in eminently moral, but aesthetically unadventuresome, "domestic dramas", of which maybe the titles—*Adam Winter; or, Dark Deeds of Old London* (Brit. 1850), *Pure as Driven Snow; or, Tempted in Vain* (Brit. 1869) and *Faithful under Peril; or, A Father's Dishonour and a Daughter's Shame* (Pav. 1873)—sufficiently illustrate the calibre. When we step into the world of the nineties we seem to have traversed countless ages. Sir Arthur Pinero and Henry Arthur Jones have now definitely established themselves; men are talking freely of, and animatedly discussing, the work of Ibsen, whose *Ghosts* and *A Doll's House* make Robertson's once realistic *Caste* and *School* seem artificial and antiquated; Oscar Wilde is rousing London society by the effervescent play of his wit; and George Bernard Shaw is stepping from the ranks of the musical and theatrical critics to prove himself the dramatic force of the century.

Not often are contemporaries enabled to trace with any surety of appreciation the changing tastes and tendencies of their own age, but the theatrical current was running so strong during those years that none could escape an awareness of its force. A veritable revolution occurred between 1850 and 1900; some deplored it and others praised, but all were conscious of the fact, and the intensity of the revolution may perhaps best be realised by the way in which it stamped itself thus upon the consciousness both of those who in that period were merely spectators and of those who were actively immersed in the practical business of the theatre.

The revolution gathered impetus as it advanced through the decades. From 1850 to 1870 its movement, though sure, was comparatively slight, and in the year 1871 a writer in *The Saturday Review* was reluctantly forced to cast a melancholy eye over the dramatic prospect. Many new theatres, he saw, had been erected in London, but in his opinion these had "been built beyond the possibilities of finding either plays to act in them or audiences to witness the performances". When he wrote, adaptations from the novels of Charles Dickens were still the rage, but "What", he enquired dismally, "What will become of the English stage when the public has grown weary, if it ever does grow weary, of dramatic versions of the stories of the late Mr Dickens? The number of new theatres increases, but the number of these stories must always remain the same."[1]

A bare seventeen years later in the same journal another critic was writing on the same theme, and "Undoubtedly", he said,

> the theatres today fill a more important place in the national life, at any rate in London, than ever. Their number has of late years multiplied some three-fold, and plans for still further increasing them are constantly reaching us. The popular interest in the stage is no longer content with the criticisms on plays and players furnished by such daily and weekly papers as deal with general news, but has called into existence numerous publications, of which the drama, either alone or in conjunction with sport, is the *raison d'être*. The monthly magazines have caught the infection, and deal largely in theatrical topics, while even in the *Annual*

[1] xxxi, Jan. 14, 1871, 50–1.

Register, which used to restrict its notice of the contemporary stage to at most a few lines, we now find ample reference, not only to the pieces running from night to night in the London theatres, but even to the more notable of those produced at special matinée performances.

There is no denying the fact that the stage has become more fashionable and more popular.[1]

And by 1895 *The Era* could definitely pronounce its judgment:

The drama in England never was in a better condition than at the present time. The tone of criticism, the ideals of the actor and the actress, and the aims of the dramatist, have all been elevated.... The drama is taking its proper place amongst the arts; and we may expect in the next ten or twenty years to find our progress even more gratifying and astonishing than that which we have made since the fifties.[2]

The preceding paragraphs may perhaps give the impression that all was accomplished within a brief space of thirty years, but such an assumption would be far from the truth. That the movement which led through Tom Robertson to Sir Arthur Pinero, H. A. Jones and G. B. Shaw was not without its embryonic beginnings in the period 1800–50 has been sufficiently indicated in the volumes of this history devoted to that time.[3] Indeed, it may well be correct to state that the theatre of 1900 represents the final and assured culmination of an organic growth which may be traced back at least to the stage of the Restoration. The picture-frame stage is the last achievement of a desire at which we have seen men vaguely grasping for two centuries, and the realistic problem-play is the ultimate realisation of something which has similarly been adumbrated for generations. This essentially is the truth. On the other hand, we may be permitted to suggest that, while man's stature can be traced back in a line of continuous progress to the most primitive of cellular forms, yet we cannot

[1] *The Renaissance of the Drama* (lxvi, Dec. 8, 1888, 76).

[2] *Dramatic Progress* (lvii, Jan. 26, 1895, 17).

[3] In addition to the authorities cited there, see Ernest Reynolds, *Early Victorian Drama* (1830–70) (Cambridge, 1936) and L. Waitzkin, *The Witch of Wych Street: A Study of the Theatrical Reforms of Madame Vestris* (Cambridge, U.S.A., 1933).

speak of man, as an independent and recognisable being, until a particular stage of development has been reached. No doubt in the theatre of the forties, alongside the relics of the old romantic melodrama and the still primitive but potentially progressive domestic dramas, one may discern fresh tendencies which presage the coming of other and more vital forms of dramatic art, but it is not until the seventies that these vital forms take definite shape and are consciously exploited.

Any examination, however cursory, of theatrical literature during the second half of the nineteenth century must make apparent the truly extraordinary alteration in attitude and accomplishment which came after the year 1870. Fundamentally that alteration is to be explained, not as the result of any one man's effort or as the consequence of any single change in social life, but as a necessary natural outgrowth dependent upon a series of movements which, though separate and diverse, at this time met and harmonised. As is usual in the sphere of the drama, the theatre led the way. The new plays could not have been had there not come, in previous years, a fresh orientation among those specifically concerned with the stage. Histrionic method suffered a complete mutation between these years. We start with the "classic" school of J. P. Kemble and Mrs Siddons; we end with the naturalistic ease of an Alexander and with the romantic vigour of an Irving. In 1800 the playhouses were lighted precisely as playhouses had been lit since the sixteenth century; in 1870 gas illumination, with all its accompanying flexibility in manipulation, was well-nigh universal. When Hazlitt watched Edmund Kean, the antique apron stage had not quite vanished and proscenium doors still obtruded themselves upon the attention of spectators; when Fechter came to London in the sixties he was experimenting with sectional stages and cycloramas. Most important of all is the fact that during this period the conception of the stage-manager, producer or director was born. In 1800, as in the preceding years, plays, like Topsy, "just growed"; the chief player, no doubt, took command of the rehearsals, but these rehearsals were comparatively few in number and from them little more seems to have been hoped for than acquainting the actors with their parts and in general terms settling their movements and business. It is only when we reach the mid-nineteenth century that we begin to encounter the directorial principle and, with it, the conception of a unified performance. To several men has been given the credit of initiating this conception; some say Robertson and Bancroft, some say Gilbert, some say Boucicault. The probability is that no single individual was responsible. This was not a thing invented by a peculiar genius with revolutionary views; it was the result of a general desire. Only when a director, or "stage-manager" according to contemporary theatrical parlance, could take control, was anything in the nature of a genuinely realistic production possible.

Compared with this active growth, the drama seemed for long to lag behind. Robertson had tried to discover a literary medium adequate to harmonise with these new stage ideals, but his steps were but halting and his vision more than half obscured. Sir Arthur Pinero and H. A. Jones carried on the search more surely and with a greater sense of set and deliberate purpose; but the final achievement of their aims came not until near the close of the century. This delayed development was due to a variety of causes. Primarily, perhaps, must be taken into account the fact that only in the last years were these various progressive movements in the theatre brought to fulfilment and harmony; basically most important was the attitude of the audience. A new audience was growing from the year 1840, but it took long before that audience reached self-expression and, consequently, before there could be a co-ordination of forces before and behind the curtain. A definite change in attitude is apparent with the coming of Queen Victoria. Towards the end of the year 1848 Charles Kean was appointed to supervise what soon came to be known as the "Windsor theatricals"—performances at court of successful plays taken from the London theatres. Three years later the young queen engaged a special box at the Princess's Theatre, "which she has retained annually ever since, and still more satisfactorily marked her approbation of the theatre by constant personal attendance".[1] The encouragement of these theatricals and the royal visits to privileged London playhouses soon convinced the aristocracy that what for years had been regarded as an almost entirely popular amusement might be tolerated by society. This influence, however, did not produce any sudden and immediately appreciable difference in the nature of the audience; that Charles Kean made appeal, in his early performances at the Princess's, to at least a certain section of cultured persons is clear, but it was not until the seventies and eighties that we find a definite turning of the managers from the type of fare suitable for the more popular audiences of 1830 to that fit for the more representative audiences which had taken their place.

This representative audience, while no doubt it was mainly responsible for the rapid development in dramatic style at the close of the century, would not itself have produced so great an effect had it not coalesced with other forces. Extremely important was the fresh opportunity offered to the dramatists of obtaining really adequate financial awards for their labours. Between 1830 and 1860 little could be made by a practising playwright unless he were prepared to sacrifice all his literary ambitions and devote himself to hack-work—turning out hurriedly written farces and melodramas, monthly, to order. The breakdown in the old stock company system, however, and the consequent development of long runs introduced fresh conditions. The substitution of royalties for outright purchases, combined with the protection afforded by the law of copyright, came to guarantee to the author of a successful play an income which compared favourably with the remuneration received by a popular novelist or essayist. Art in its higher reaches may be independent of sordid monetary conditions, yet even playwrights must live. The majority of authors seek for at least a share of jam and honey; and the development of a new drama in the last decades of

[1] J. W. Cole, *The Life and Theatrical Times of Charles Kean* (1859), ii, 13.

the century is by no means unconnected with the larger financial rewards offered to the dramatists.

Only by an adequate appreciation of all these tendencies can we seek to understand that truly extraordinary "Renascence of the English drama", as H. A. Jones has styled it—extraordinary because, in spite of the gradual approach which we, standing on our historical vantage ground, are able clearly to distinguish, of its apparent suddenness and of the changes immediately consequent upon its coming. So complex are the conditions which made for this renascence that such a summary as has been given above is a necessary basis for adequate appreciation, but no mere summary can provide a satisfactory picture of the social and theatrical circumstances which wrought the miracle. It will be necessary now to examine in greater detail the factors which conspired together to provide a platform, strongly and stoutly enough built to bear the stalwart band of dramatic reformers who established what we know as the modern drama.

II. *The Audience*

The period which we are now about to examine opens with the glittering splendours of the Great Exhibition. Like a fairy palace of comfortably solid proportions grew the crystal halls, and men could not tire of wandering through them. The Great Exhibition was the symbol of an age that was passing away and the premonition of an age that was to come. It stood representative of early Victorianism, secure, industrious, pacific; what made it possible was a force destined to shatter that security.[1]

This Great Exhibition was the self-expression of a metropolis which had multiplied its inhabitants mightily within a short span of years. In 1801 London had some 865,000 citizens; these had grown to one and a half millions by 1831, and the following twenty years witnessed a vast increase. It was these who were the originators and first supporters of

[1] R. H. Mottram, *Town Life*, in *Early Victorian England*, ed. by G. M. Young (1934), i, 212–22.

the Exhibition. With their help alone, however, the project could not have hoped to succeed; it required the attendance of many thousands from all parts of Britain, required too the visits of other thousands from France and Germany. In 1800 such visits would have been an impossibility, but by 1850 practical scientific development had provided means of transport undreamed of in the past. Before 1830 London had miserably inadequate methods of conveying its inhabitants from one part of the city to another; twenty years later suburbia was in full process of growth. The first railway (between Manchester and Liverpool) did not come until 1828; by 1843 the foundations at least of the present railroad system had been definitely laid.

The very means of conveyance which brought the Great Exhibition from a dream to realisation were the same which wrought a complete change in the world theatrical. Up to the middle of the nineteenth century the potential playgoing public was exceedingly small. Although London might be increasing annually, the fact that no suitable provision was made whereby the ordinary citizens might traverse its extending area automatically cut off many of these from possible attendance—save on rare and festive occasions—at the metropolitan theatres. When, however, the railway and the omnibus became common and familiar, at once the circumstances were altered. The whole of the suburban area, west, north and south, was brought into easy association with the theatrical district and quantitatively the number of likely ticket buyers was increased a hundredfold.

The conditions rendered it possible for great masses of the middle class, resident in the outlying quarters, to come to the playhouse if they wished; but other causes must be sought to explain how these middle-class people obtained the desire to enter the theatres. The stage in the early part of the century was largely a "popular" affair, and for the most part bourgeois opinion regarded its delights with cringing disapproval.[1] Typical audiences were composed mainly of

[1] See *A History of Early Nineteenth Century Drama* (1930), i, 7–22. This book is referred to subsequently as *E.N.D.*

lower-class citizens with a sprinkling of representatives from the gayer and more libertine section of the aristocracy. The staid middle class and the respectable, dignified nobility tended to look upon the stage as a thing not to be supported in an active manner. Some advance towards a changed orientation is to be discerned during the forties; for this a few individuals, such as Macready and Phelps, may be regarded as responsible. The great alteration, however, does not come until after the middle of the century, and perhaps no single individual did more to effect its realisation than Queen Victoria.

Victoria and the theatre do not commonly associate themselves in our minds, yet the queen's encouragement of the royal "theatricals" not only instituted something fresh and significant but, as contemporaries realised, something destined to yield a rich harvest in the future.[1] "But now", lilts J. R. Planché,[2]

> But now a fresh start's given the Drama to,
> By royal patronage. "The play's the thing",
> And goes to Court.

"If the patronage by Royalty," writes a commentator in 1853, "which appears to be increasing with every year, is a sign of the Drama's palmy days, then most assuredly may it be said to be 'looking up'."[3] Four years earlier than that a critic in *The Times*[4] guessed rightly at the effect which would result from this royal interest. "When the highest personage in the land", he deemed,

> considers that an English dramatic performance is such an entertainment as to merit the construction of a stage in her own drawing room, with all the appurtenances of a regular theatre, the opinion that the native drama is unfashionable receives an

[1] On these royal theatricals see J. W. Cole, *op. cit.* i, 346–8 and 351; B. Webster, *The Series of Dramatic Entertainments performed by Royal Command at Windsor Castle, 1848–9* (1849); and J. K. Chapman *A Complete History of Theatrical Entertainments, Dramas, Masques, and Triumphs, at the English Court* (1849).

[2] *Mr Buckstone's Ascent of Mount Parnassus* (H. 1853).

[3] *The Dramatic Register for 1853* (Lacy, 1854), p. 33.

[4] Jan. 26, 1849.

authoritative rebuke. The plays that are acted at Windsor Castle are the same that may be seen at the Haymarket and Lyceum, the actors in the Rouben's Room are precisely the same individuals as those who appear on the public boards and it would be absurd to say that an entertainment which acquired a high rank at Windsor loses that rank when it comes to the metropolis.

That this critic was justified is amply proved by later events; he was even correct in what must then have seemed his fanciful guess that "a new stock of dramatists, worthy to compete with those of the Elizabethan era, may spring into evidence from the effect of the Windsor Theatricals". Nor was Victoria content to honour the stage in this way only. As has been indicated above, until the death of the Prince Consort in 1861 she pursued her interest in the stage and, through her visits to the Haymarket, the Princess's and the St James's, encouraged the managers and stimulated enthusiasm for the drama. As Henry Elliott put it in 1896,

Acting, as a profession, now has the direct sanction and approval of the fount of honour in these islands; and it owes that recognition to the gracious sympathy and appreciation of the present wielder of the sceptre.[1]

That a complete alteration was not effected is but natural, and naturally, too, complaints continued to be made regarding popular taste—such are perennial things and were as common in the days of *Hamlet* as in those of *Abie's Irish Rose*. In 1871 Thomas Purnell took a melancholy view:

The chief supporters of our theatres are country people... those of the nobility afflicted with *ennui*...busy professional men who come at fixed intervals with their families...men who go to the theatres from habit, just as they smoke tobacco, and a large number of green grocers and other shop keepers, who have received orders for displaying play-bills in their windows.... At one time the most intellectual and scholarly people habitually visited the playhouse,

but these, in his opinion, now kept away, since

[1] *The Stage under Victoria* (*The Theatre*, N.S. xxviii, Nov. 1896, 242–3). Further remarks on this subject will be found in J. Knight, *The History of the English Stage during the Reign of Victoria* (1901), A. Filon, *The English Stage: an Account of the Victorian Drama* (1897) and R. F. Sharp, *A Short History of the English Stage to 1908* (1909).

their field of intellectual recreation is widened, and the social changes of our time provide them with other and more profitable means of mental excitement.[1]

"Though theatres have multiplied of late," complained F. C. Broughton seven years later, "it cannot be said that audiences have vastly increased."[2] At a time when even pessimists could no longer deny that many more persons than before were attending performances regularly, the complaints, keyed to a different pitch, were still to be heard. Some averred that the new public was responsible for the success of meretricious productions—*A Gaiety Girl*, *The Prisoner of Zenda* and *The Sign of the Cross*;[3] others blamed their constant seeking for amusement (as though that were not the object of all playgoers).[4] "Within the last two or three years", declares W. Winter in *The Theatre* for 1887,

although noble and beautiful works have been shown, and several important advance steps have been taken—a complete avalanche of trash has been cast upon our stage, and our people have accepted it and they have, practically, approved it. Why? For the reason, partly, that scarcely a voice among public censors has been raised against this flagrant abuse of the theatre....It was unfortunate that the custom of viewing the stage as an "amusement" ever came to prevail; for the stage is an institution far higher and finer than any amusement, and it possesses at the present epoch an influence upon society second only to that of the hearthstone and the altar. But even viewing it as one of the amusements, no man has a right to degrade its character or impair its usefulness.... There is more than common need of wholesome censure, as well of the public taste as of the pernicious doctrine that it is the province and policy of thinkers, writers and managers to follow the people instead of leading them.[5]

[1] *Dramatists of the Present Day by "Q"* (i.e. Thomas Purnell) (1871), pp. 14–16. This essay was reprinted from *The Athenaeum*.

[2] *Modern Audiences* (*The Theatre*, N.S. i, Aug. 1878, 36).

[3] W. Davenport Adams, *What is the Theatrical Public?* (*The Theatre*, N.S. xxix, April 1897, 198–200).

[4] H. A. Jones, *The Renascence of the English Drama* (1895), p. 3. This essay first appeared in *The Nineteenth Century* for 1883.

[5] *The Theatre*, N.S. x, Sept. 1887, 159. This is quoted from *The New York Tribune*, but *The Theatre*'s editor comments that these "pertinent remarks...apply, unfortunately, to the English as well as the American stage".

Those who looked to the "hearthstone and the altar" thus vented their dissatisfaction, and here joined hands with the reformers, for whom otherwise they had but little sympathy. "Half a dozen visits in the year", thought G. B. Shaw in 1896,

> serve all the purposes of those respectably literate citizens who are...anxious to see whatever is good in the theatre. Let me turn to the index of William Archer's *Theatrical World of 1895*, and try to pick out 52 new plays that would have justified such a citizen in going once a week to the theatre,

and the effort, he imagines, would be in vain.[1] Taste in appreciation of acting, too, was taxed:

> Perhaps the greatest difficulty that faces the British dramatist, at any rate one of the more important obstacles to his success, is to be found in the histrionic taste of the public. We by no means intend to insinuate that it is deficient or unsound, or that even at times it does not assert itself in an advantageous and a commendable manner; but we think our readers will be with us when we affirm that too often the judgment of an audience is uncertain and its favour capricious. Triumph and failure do not always depend upon the merit and shortcomings of author or actor.... The intellectual acumen and force that are brought to the judgment of an opera, a sonata, a picture, or a poem will surely be found sufficient in the encouragement of the highest aspirations of the Drama. In the meanwhile, however, the public should seek to stimulate its theatrical taste, define and improve it.[2]

Opposed to these more gloomy denunciations, and more valid because seizing on the essential qualities of change which differentiated the theatre of 1890 from that of 1850, come the optimistic views of those who recognised in the new audience a power and a force apt to introduce a great era of dramatic productivity. The general growth of an intellectual public was noted even in the seventies.[3] The subject

[1] *On Nothing in Particular and the Theatre in General* (*The Saturday Review*, lxxxi, March 14, 1896, 273).

[2] *Taste and the Drama* (*The Era*, xli, Jan. 26, 1879, 12). There is an interesting article on *The English Stage* in *The Quarterly Review*, clv, April 1883, 354–88, in which the writer, after quoting William Archer's dictum that "modern Englishmen cannot be got to take the drama seriously", compares the audiences of his own time with those of the Elizabethan age.

[3] *Our Stage: Its Present and its probable Future* (*The Theatre*, N.S. i, Aug. 1878, 1–7).

of regenerating the stage, wrote one man in 1879, "is now taken up as a stock text by editors and their leader-writers in the leading daily journals, whereas a very short time ago it would have been felt that a leader on such a topic in the *Daily News* or *Daily Telegraph*, to say nothing of *The Times*, was a matter for a nine days' wonder".[1] By the nineties the increase of interest taken in the drama had become incontrovertible. "The theatre", it was said in 1898, "is growing in importance as a social organ. Modern civilisation is rapidly multiplying the class to which the theatre is both school and church, and when the dramatic art is practised rightly...The national importance of the theatre will be as unquestioned as that of the army, the fleet, the Church, the law and the schools."[2] In spite of his shortcomings as a critic, H. A. Jones proved himself a clear-sighted observer when he looked on the spectators of his own time. The first thing, he imagined, that would strike a stranger visiting the London theatres would be the enormous popularity of the playhouse among all classes;[3] "the material prosperity of the English drama was never so great as at the present moment", he declared in 1891;[4] and he was eager in his defence of at least one section of the audience:

> We have on our first nights, interspersed with perhaps a few ticklish but easily quieted elements of mischief, that serried pack of bright earnest intelligent faces in the first row of the pit, lovers of the drama for the drama's sake, whose self-appointed duty it is to give a loud and unmistakable verdict of approval or condemnation.[5]

Of one thing everyone was assured—that audiences were

[1] *Regenerating the Stage* (*id.* N.S. iii, Nov. 1879, 181–4). This article calls attention to the discussion on the theatre at the Art Section of the Social Science Congress, presided over by the Bishop of Manchester.

[2] *The Stage and its Critics* (*Blackwood's Edinburgh Magazine*, clxiii, June 1898, 871–4).

[3] *The Renascence of the English Drama* (1895), p. 154; essay first printed in *The English Illustrated Magazine*, Jan. and Feb. 1885, pp. 280 and 341.

[4] *Id.* p. 96; essay first printed in *The New Review*, July 1891, p. 86.

[5] *Id.* pp. 18–19; essay first printed in *The Nineteenth Century*, Sept. 1883, p. 452. These remarks, of course, are to be qualified by Jones's other strictures on theatrical taste in general.

more decorous and better-mannered than they had been in the past. Even in 1859 J. W. Cole could comment on the fact that

> modern audiences are less easily worked up to strong demonstration than they were at the beginning of the present century.... Audiences now-a-days are more numerous than ever; but they sit, for the most part, in silent admiration....The stalls, boxes, and even the pit, are too genteel to clap their hands; and the Olympian deities are awed into silence by their isolation, and the surrounding chill.[1]

The wild riots have disappeared;[2] and the disturbances which had been so common on first nights have given way to a new tolerance. In 1892, indeed, Alfred Berlyn was impelled to enquire whether contemporary audiences were not too patient.[3] Some writers might object that on these first nights the stall seats were now mostly filled with paper and that claques, organised by authors, managers and actors, were part of the ordinary theatre routine;[4] but such views were sternly rebutted by others.[5]

This new respectability in the playhouse was due partly to the fact that many of the potentially rowdy elements were being catered for in the music halls, but partly, at least, it was the result of a rather surprising alliance between church and stage. While an uncompromising Reverend John Robertson in Glasgow might still repeat the same arguments as had been employed by his predecessors, bitterly attacking Irving

[1] *Op. cit.* i, 92. It is true that lack of courtesy among spectators was noted in *The Theatre*, N.S. xiv, July 1889, 10–13, but no serious examples were there listed. The subject is also touched upon, *id.* N.S. iv, Aug. 1884, 91–2.

[2] Cf. those noted in *A History of Early Eighteenth-Century Drama* (Cambridge, 1937; referred to hereafter as *E.E.D.*), pp. 5–10, *A History of Late Eighteenth-Century Drama* (Cambridge, 1929; referred to hereafter as *L.E.D.*), p. 12, and *E.N.D.* i, 7–11. Some of the relatively rare disturbances chronicled during this period are listed by Wyndham Albery, *The Dramatic Works of James Albery* (1939) i, xcvii–cii.

[3] *The Theatre*, N.S. xix, Mar. 1892, 140–2.

[4] J. F. Nisbet, *The Composition of London Audiences* (*id.* N.S. xxx, Nov. 1897, 226–9).

[5] A. W. à Beckett, "*Organised Disturbance*" *Criticised* (*id.* N.S. xxix, Feb. 1897, 74–8).

for his supposed delinquencies,[1] that sort of thing was becoming rare. Since the days of the Church Fathers ecclesiastical opinion had been opposed to the playhouse, yet now, as Alfred Halstead noted in 1897, even the Non-Conformists were losing their old hatred of the stage.[2] The Reverend H. C. Dimsdale, we learn, who was "spiritual pastor of the Eton Mission, Hackney", in 1889 "produced a pantomime called *Dick Whittington and his Cat* at his Mission Hall",[3] and was not immediately blasted therefore either by heaven or by his superiors. A dozen years earlier, the Reverend J. Panton Ham, a Unitarian minister, in lecturing on the theatre,

> denied that there was a very great deal to reform on our Stage; that it was constantly watched by vigilant and honest critics, and that there were many noble-minded managers who, like Macready, were only too anxious to elevate the tone of the Drama. He called on religious people to aid them in their work.[4]

A few months before this, the Bishop of Manchester delivered addresses to audiences of actors and actresses from the stages of Drury Lane and the Prince's, when he emphasised that "he did not want to abolish the Theatre, but to purify it".[5] "Socially", said the Reverend H. R. Haweis in a sermon delivered at St James's, Marylebone, "we have reached a critical time in the history of the Stage; a time when prelates and play-actors shake hands."[6] The cue was taken by many in the seventies. The Reverend C. C. Coe referred to "the desire to give the player the social status which his calling, if properly pursued, most justly demanded".[7] "Shall a man

[1] *Id.* N.S. xxv, Jan. 1895, 61–2. For the church-and-stage controversy see J. Macdonald, *What is the Theatre?* (Edinburgh, 1851) and *The Theatre* (1866); W. Keddie, *The Theatre: Its Pernicious Tendency* (Glasgow, 1853); A. J. Baxter, *The Theatre a Religious Institution* (1865); R. B. Drummond, *The Theatre, its Bearings on Morals* (Edinburgh, 1875). On the Bishop of London's views see Frank Marshall, *The Stage and its Detractors* (*The Theatre*, N.S. vi, Nov. 1885, 233–40).

[2] *Id.* N.S. xxx, Aug. 1897, 78–80; N.S. xxix, June 1897, 308–9.

[3] *The Church on the Stage* (*The Era*, li, Jan. 26, 1889, 13).

[4] *The Pulpit and the Stage* (*id.* xl, Oct. 21, 1877, 12). This was in America; see note, p. 11 *infra*.

[5] *A Bishop on the Stage* (*id.* xxxix, Feb. 11, 1877, 7); *The Theatre*, i, Feb. 1877, 21.

[6] *The Era*, xli, Oct. 19, 1879, 5.

[7] *The Theatre*, i, Feb. 1877, 34.

go to the Theatre?" enquired another, and gave the answer: "Yes, if only as a reformer....Go...as you ought to go anywhere, to enjoy the good, encourage actors and Managers in their strife for that.....Help the art to climb and re-establish itself."[1] Men took pains to point out the essential morality of the theatre now:

Be it remembered this vital influence for good is not a thing of late existence; in all the struggles that the Stage has had with intolerance; in spite of the temptation that a certain number of people in every crowded city may offer to Managers to seek advantage by pandering to the vicious impulse of our nature...and even with the desire of the audiences of so-called minor Theatres to have their entertainment highly spiced, the English dramatist has for the most part kept the principle of his work sound.... The stale contrivance of the penitence and confession of many a heavy villain at the end of Transpontine melodramas...might be cited as further evidence of the truly moral teaching with which the English Stage was instinct.[2]

The more liberal ideas thus naïvely expressed were destined to win their way. Professor Blackie in Edinburgh added his weight to the new movement[3] and various churchmen, sensing the tendencies of the time, hastened to disassociate themselves from former ecclesiastical condemnatory remarks. In 1878 the Church Congress, meeting at Sheffield, found that "the discussion which aroused most interest" concerned the stage. A few years later, at another Church Congress held at Leicester, the Reverend H. C. Shuttleworth declared his opinion that "of all the influences upon Society, the Drama" had "ever been one of the most powerful. The dramatic instinct", he thought, was "natural to mankind, and the Stage will never cease to be an instrument of tremendous power for good or evil. Church and Stage should go hand in hand", he added, and concluded his comments by turning upon the church and flaying it for its former attitude towards

[1] *The Era*, xxxiii, March 12, 1871, 10. This was part of a lecture delivered in Baltimore, but the sentiments are akin to those encountered in England.

[2] *The Stage as a Teacher of Morality* (*id.* xxxix, Jan. 14, 1877, 12).

[3] *The Theatre*, i, April 1877, 119.

the theatre.[1] From this changed orientation ultimately came the Church and Stage Guild, organised "to promote religious and social sympathy between the members of the Church and Stage".[2]

No doubt this movement was largely responsible for the imposition of a stricter and more formal "morality" in the drama. A review in *The Theatre* of a play in which conjugal infidelity was dealt with amusingly opined that this drama could

> only be regarded as a direct hindrance to those who are just now striving by every means in their reach to win for the acted drama its recognition as a high moral influence, a social power, and an intellectual instrument, worthy of the strongest support which the culture of the nation can afford.[3]

On the same grounds, this journal displayed considerable nervousness when it learned that the National Sunday League was thinking of pleading for theatrical representations on the sabbath; in the writer's opinion such a move would result only in giving argumentative material to the enemy and in estranging new friends.[4] The danger, may be, was a real one; for after all, there was something in the remark of a contemporary that "the young clergymen on the council" of the Church and Stage Guild might "not realize that their *penchant* for the conversion of young actresses" was "open, to say the least of it, to misconception".[5]

The approval of the Church, whatever disadvantages and misconceptions might arise, was of immense value to the theatre; without it the audience could not have become truly representative of the community. In the seventies the discussions in congresses and the sermons from the pulpit were beginning to draw back to the auditorium certain sections of the community which had refrained from attendance at dramatic representations or attended seldom and in mental

[1] *The Era*, xliii, Oct. 10, 1880, 7.

[2] *The Church and Stage Guild* (*id.* xlii, Jan. 25, 1880, 4); *The Theatre*, N.S. iii, Oct. 1878, 183–5.

[3] *The Theatre*, i, May 1877, 183–4.

[4] *Id.* N.S. i, Oct. 1878, 182–5.

[5] *Id.* N.S. iii, Dec. 1879, 247.

perturbation. A decade later all was assured. When in 1897 Henry Irving received his knighthood, gave a reading of *Becket* in Canterbury Cathedral and unveiled a statue in Paddington Green to the memory of Mrs Siddons—the first statue to a player erected in London—he demonstrated in himself the result of a new tolerance which had brought the stage and those associated with it into an entirely fresh realm.[1] The player was now received into society; he was recognised as an artist worthy of distinguished remembrance; he was even accepted within the walls of that church which, save for temporary encouragement of religious plays in the Middle Ages, had severely frowned on him and on his profession.

Gradually, the tone of the public attitude towards the stage thus altered, and various elements, physical and spiritual, in the theatre altered accordingly. Marie Wilton provided a carpet for the stalls at the Prince of Wales's in 1865,[2] and her action was symbolic. The old front rows of the severely benched pit were becoming refined. The dress circle, referred to in a letter of February 18, 1869,[3] rapidly assumed a new importance. The theatre had become fashionable. A novel significance now was attached to the dinner hour, which had not worried the high-tea and supper partakers on whom Sadler's Wells and the Adelphi had previously subsisted. During these years the formal hour of dinner was being advanced, and when eventually it reached seven o'clock it had the effect of completely revolutionising playhouse programmes.[4] In earlier days popular audiences had demanded their full money's worth. A performance which started at 6.30 might close about midnight and was expected to include a farce, a tragedy or comedy, a pantomime and a few other divertisements. The new patrons had chaster predilections; coming to the theatre decorously at eight o'clock, they were

[1] *The Progress of the Player* (*The Theatre*, N.S. xxx, July 1897, 1–4); cf. *id.* N.S. xxvi, July 1895, 1–9.

[2] Bradlee Watson, *Sheridan to Robertson* (1926). See also M. St C. Byrne, *Stalls and Places in the Orchestra* (*The Times Literary Supplement*, June 29, 1933).

[3] Frank Archer, *An Actor's Notebooks* (1912), p. 66.

[4] On the dinner hour see Mrs C. S. Peel, *Homes and Habits* (*Early Victorian England, 1830–1865* (1934), i, 98).

content to depart homeward about eleven, and soon showed themselves completely satisfied with the presentation of one long play.[1] Charles Kean seems to have started the fashion for one major play preceded by a curtain-raiser; even the curtain-raiser was abandoned by the Bancrofts. Perhaps it were not too much to say that the characteristic modern dramatic performance was created by a change in society's dinner hour. Created by this society, too, was the modern matinée. Matinées would have been impossible in 1830; but the presence within the new audience of numerous leisured persons able to attend the theatres in the morning or the afternoon had made such performances all the rage in 1880. Inaugurated about 1869, they gradually increased in number until a correspondent of 1889 could refer to "these days of endless matinées".[2] The significance of this innovation must be reserved for later discussion.[3]

The presence of more intelligent and sophisticated spectators in the playhouses made inevitably for the opening up of dramatic realms forbidden by law or social taboo in the past. Sydney Grundy in his reactionary age might see seeds of disaster in this extension of theme. In 1896 he felt sure the stage was "marching to its doom" because the serious drama was in the hands of "a coterie of enthusiastic eccentrics".[4] Now, looking back, we realise that the "enthusiastic eccentrics", both behind and before the curtain, were preparing fresh soil for tillage. The office of the Licenser of Plays, reflecting the tastes of the new audience, was slowly becoming more liberal. True, the scrutiny of texts was still severe. "Omit all oaths" is a common rubric in the manuscripts of plays preserved in the custody of the Lord Chamber-

[1] *The Theatre*, N.S. xxiii, Jan. 1894, 19; *The Era*, xxxiii, Oct. 23, 1870, 10. In 1871 T. Purnell (*op. cit.* p. 70) noted that "the late dinner-hour of our day, combined with the increasing disposition of cultured people to show no emotion, is inimical to farce".

[2] *The Theatre*, N.S. xiv, July 1889, 12. S. J. Adair Fitz-Gerald has an interesting note on *The Matinée Question* (*id.* N.S. xviii, Oct. 1891, 159–60).

[3] *Infra*, pp. 59–60.

[4] *The Theatre*, N.S. xxvii, March 1896, 131. For Grundy's position see also William Archer, *What does the Public want?* (*id.* N.S. v, June 1885, 269–75).

lain.[1] "However she persists in saying, there is something more between us than meets the naked eye" was cut; "Jael had but a nail for a weapon, Delilah her scissors" was cut; throughout the entirety of Browning's *Colombe's Birthday* (H. 1853) "Heaven" was substituted for "God"; in a version of *Hard Times* (Str. 1854) objection was taken to "Lord! I do give thee humble and hearty thanks for this my deliverance". The later attitude to these oaths is well displayed in a comment on *Our Wives* (Eastbourne, 1885):

> Omit the frequent swearing, which, it should be understood, is no longer usual in these days in respectable drawing rooms, and in the company of ladies, and is calculated to give offence to any intelligent and respectable audience.

Not only oaths, of course, were regarded as reprehensible; topical references, too, were frequently lined out. "Proclamation—BEARBAITING! This Act is not licensed by the Lord Chamberlain" was duly censored in a pantomime, *Harlequin Hudibras* (D.L. 1852), and in a burlesque, *William Tell* (Str. 1857), the reader of plays found occasion to object to a piece of dialogue:

—Tell me of something that will make one sad.
—See Kean play Hamlet, that will do it, lad.
—Oh! dear! that remedy's much too severe:
My nerves would never stand the shock, I fear.

When Sergeant Towner and Frank Beaumont submitted their drama, *Called to the Front* (Brit. 1885), they were informed that the villain of the piece must positively not be described as belonging to the Guards.

The whole question of the censorship was much discussed in these years,[2] praise or blame being awarded in accordance with the beliefs of the critical camp to which the particular writer belonged. Again, it is in the seventies that we first encounter the development of conscious likes and dislikes.

[1] The references to deletions ordered by the Lord Chamberlain are taken from an examination of the copies officially deposited at St James's Palace.

[2] On the censorship generally see G. M. G. *The Stage Censor* (1905) and W. Nicholson, *The Struggle for a Free Stage* (1906).

The censoring of some French plays called forth a protest in *The Athenaeum* in 1873,[1] and this perhaps occasioned the writing of a long article on the licensing laws in *The Era* for 1874.[2] Then came a growl from Sydney Grundy five years later,[3] which in turn led to a general series of complaints from the company of younger writers during the last decades of the century. This "theatrical anachronism" was attacked in *The Pall Mall Gazette* in 1880;[4] William Archer never ceased denouncing the iniquities of the censor's office;[5] and finally G. B. Shaw came forward with caustic pen to scourge and lacerate.[6] In spite of such attacks, however, there can be no doubt but that the censorship had grown in those years more tolerant and that it displayed a willingness to permit the public representation of dramas which would have shocked earlier society into convulsions.

The force of the new audience in the theatre is to be seen nowhere more clearly than in the widespread periodical discussions which, as has been noted above, occupied considerable space in the newspapers and journals of the time—especially clearly is this indicated in the broad lines of demarcation between two powerful groups of critics and essayists, the groups themselves being characteristic of a split among the spectators. The two schools of thought were described by W. A. Lewis Bettany in 1892 as "the Ancients and the Moderns";[7] the description is apt, for the one represented

[1] No. 2372, April 12, 1873, 482. Cf. *The Lord Chamberlain and the Drama* (*The Era*, xxxiv, Jan. 14, 1872, 12); in the same issue is a letter from the Licenser of Plays, W. B. Donne.

[2] *The Examiner of Stage Plays* (xxxvi, July 26, 1874, 9).

[3] *The Theatre*, N.S. ii, March 1879, 99–103. An article entitled *Theatrical Fenianism* in *The Saturday Review* (xli, Jan. 15, 1876, 76) also has a close bearing on this subject. Cf. "*A False Step*" *towards discrediting the Censorship* (*The Theatre*, N.S. i, Nov. 1878, 259–62) and *The Censorship on its Trial* (*id.* N.S. i, Dec. 1878, 332–5).

[4] xxxi, May 13, 1880, 11.

[5] *Mr Archer and the Censorship* (*The Era*, liv, March 21, 1892, 15); *The Pall Mall Gazette*, lx, March 23, 1895, 3. See also Arthur Goodrich, *The Dramatic Censorship* (*The Theatre*, N.S. xix, May 1892, 232–7) and Robert Buchanan, *The Ethics of Play-Licensing* (*id.* N.S. xxvii, May 1896, 254–7).

[6] *The Saturday Review*, lxxix, March 2, 1895, 280–2.

[7] *Criticism and the Renascent Drama* (*The Theatre*, N.S. xix, June 1892, 277–83).

the great mass of stolid, respectable, middle-class opinion and the other reflected the tastes of the younger intellectuals who, sensing the change in the theatre, had come to look upon it as a place where high aspirations and daring thought might find scope. "The present controversy between these rival schools", Bettany informs us, "has been simmering ever since 1880, and long before the production of 'A Doll's House' in 1889 there had been signs of the coming clash.... Nevertheless, it may be fairly said that up to the year 1889, 'the new criticism' had but a solitary champion—Mr William Archer. Since then, however, several younger writers have rallied to Mr Archer's support." Before 1892, "the dispute had mainly consisted in an occasional difference of opinion between the opposing leaders, caused by the production now of Mr Pinero's 'Lords and Commons', now of Mr Grundy's 'Clito', and now of Mr Jones's 'The Noble Vagabond'. The events of the past three years have tended to make the struggle much more bitter and much more personal. Ibsen has been thrown like an apple of discord...and over every important new play the battle has been fiercely renewed, Mr Archer ably championing the cause of modernity, and being stoutly backed up by his adroit guerilla lieutenant 'Spectator', of the *Star*."

The recognised leader of the Ancients was the redoubtable Clement Scott. In him, thought a writer in *Blackwood's Edinburgh Magazine*,[1] "our English theatre has found... precisely the critic which it deserved". The immense personal esteem in which he was held by the public at large was merely the reflection of a tendency which produced a Henry Irving and a Beerbohm Tree. "Other men", said Shaw in 1896,[2]

may have hurried from the theatre to the newspaper office to prepare, red hot, a notice of the night's performance for the morning's paper; but nobody did it before him with the knowledge that the notice was awaited by a vast body of readers conscious of his personality and anxious to hear his opinion, and that the

[1] clxvii, Jan. 1900, 98–108. For a penetrating study of Scott see W. L. Courtney, *The Passing Hour* (n.d.), pp. 213–20.

[2] *The Saturday Review*, lxxxi, May 30, 1896, 548–9.

editor must respect it, and the sub-editor reserve space for it, as the most important feature of the paper. This strong position Mr Scott has made for himself. His opportunity has of course been made by circumstance—by the growth of mammoth newspapers like the *Daily Telegraph*, the multiplication of theatres, and the spread of interest in them.

The real secret of Clement Scott's popularity lay, as Shaw readily divined, in the superabundance of his sympathy and the impression of heartfelt integrity which he introduced into his writings. His critiques

> are alive: their admiration is sincere and moving: their sentiment is vivid and genuine....The public believes in Mr Scott because he interprets the plays by feeling with the actor or author...and giving his feeling unrestrained expression in his notices.

There can be no question concerning Scott's ability, but he applied that ability to discredit the new drama. What appealed to his sentimental heart he praised; what aimed at appealing to his mind he was incapable of appreciating. In *Ghosts* he viewed, not a work calculated to penetrate deeply into a serious social problem, but a sociological pamphlet which introduced topics about which he was resolutely determined to keep grim silence in public. That his own defence was justified we may agree:

> We who are entrusted with the difficult and delicate task of criticising our fellow men and women, write, we are proud to say, unbiassed, unfettered, at the dictates of our own impressions, and fortified by an experience that justifies us in speaking—[1]

but it cannot be denied that he did his best to kill the rising spirit of a renascent drama. In his youth he was among the revolutionaries who rallied around the teacup-and-saucer comedy; in his age he was a likable and vigorous reactionary.

Among his followers may be noted J. F. Nisbet, of *The Times*, less emotional than he, one who, although he welcomed Jones, Pinero and Grundy, took but a pessimistic view of the newer drama and constantly pleaded for old-time conventionality. To the same group belonged Alfred Watson,

[1] *The Theatre*, N.S. xvii, Feb. 1891, 86.

of *The Standard*, Wedmore, "most self-satisfied of critics", and Edward Morton, "most rollicking of dramatic Philistines".

The Moderns found their earliest and, in many respects, their most stalwart champion in William Archer. Despite a certain woodenness, Archer showed himself the farthest-seeing and the most broad-minded of the younger group. In method he was the direct opposite of Scott. Where the one judged by emotion, the other always judged by reason. Coldly analytical in his appreciations, he yet at times could summon a glow of mental vigour hardly less inspiring than Scott's most impassioned outbursts. The pair met, indeed, in an arena of dramatic fanaticism, for both were champions. That Archer was wrong in condemning entirely the conventional drama of the past seems now clear to most of us; but his service to the theatre in acclaiming Ibsen and in welcoming younger writers of the naturalistic school can in no way be minimised.[1]

Those who rallied to his standard, men who followed a new set of commandments, by which the critic

> should praise Ibsen, Maeterlinck, and Zola...should slate melodrama, "the well-made play", farce, and burlesque...should pooh-pooh Messrs Pinero and Jones...should regard Mr Irving with a wondering pity...should occasionally conceal his contempt for the actor...should support the Independent Theatre at least with praises...should condemn Clement Scott and all his *Telegraph*-ese notes and criticism; and...should write his critiques on Impressionist principles,

were, although at first few in numbers, soon an influential group. A. B. Walkley, of *The Star* and *The Times*, became noted for his apt combination of scholarly exactitude and witty style. In *The Sunday Sun* and *The Gentleman's Magazine* young Justin McCarthy made himself a noted controversialist, while Addison Bright, of *The Lady's Pictorial*, won admiration by his acute judgment of acting and by his critical analysis

[1] Cf. Sydney Grundy, *Marching to our Doom* (*The Theatre*, N.S. xxvii, April 1896 196–200) and Oliver Bluff, *Critics? and Criticism* (*id.* N.S. xviii, Oct. 1891, 153–7).

of contemporary drama. Vigour characterised the writing of E. F. Spence in *The Pall Mall Gazette*, scholarship that of Joseph Knight in *The Athenaeum*, and chastened enthusiasm that of the anonymous reviewers of *The Daily Graphic* and *Sporting Life*.

Quite naturally, a few critical authors gave no formal allegiance to either contrasted party, but for the most part these men suffered from the spinelessness which Dante pilloried in the *Inferno*. Timidity, as was pointed out by a contemporary, prevented their joining the new school, while conviction forbade their adopting the stereotyped formulae of Scott. Among these, most notable were Davenport Adams of *The Globe*, Malcolm Watson of *The Saturday Review*, Pollock of *The St James's Gazette* and Jope Slade of *The Echo*.[1]

As we survey this varied array of regular critics, we realise with absolute clarity how far theatrical interest had progressed by the end of the nineteenth century. Criticism now was no longer a perfunctory thing, nor was it an affair which appealed in the main only to the intellectuals; it had become part of the public's interest, and the Parnassian controversies were followed eagerly even by the common mortals on the plains beneath. Not many save authors and actors had been actively concerned with the charming delinquencies of Mr Puff, but now the shortcomings of criticism were matters of fundamental importance. Special articles on the functions of the critic appear in the journals of the time;[2] the weaknesses of the minor reviews are alternately attacked and defended; the tendency towards greater kindliness of tone finds comment:

> That theatrical criticism is stingless is a complaint now generally heard. One has, indeed, only to compare the utterances of men

[1] Interesting individualists among the critics were W. S. Gilbert (*Fun*), Frank Burnand (*Punch*) and Lewis Wingfield, "Whyte Tyghe" (*The Globe*).

[2] In addition to those cited above, see S. J. A. Fitz-Gerald, *The True Power of Criticism* (*The Theatre*, N.S. xxvii, Jan. 1896, 29–31), A.J.D., *The Degeneracy of Dramatic Criticism* (*id.* N.S. xv, May 1890, 253–6), W. Davenport Adams, *Dramatic Criticism* (*id.* N.S. xvi, Aug. 1890, 55–9).

of judgment such as Leigh Hunt and Hazlitt, to say nothing of prejudiced and vituperative writers such as Theodore Hook, with those of the modern press, to see how far we have gone in the direction of "respective lenity". The idea that failure in ambitious effort is offence seems to have been dismissed.[1]

Dion Boucicault, in a letter to Charles Reade, attributed the "decline" of the drama, partly at least, to "the mischievious influence of the press".[2] The playwrights regularly uttered their "growls" against the critics of the time. One such[3] complained of the gradual disappearance of the old "first night" review, bringing to his aid tortuous arguments:

At a time when it was considered that a notice of a new play should appear in the morrow's paper as a piece of actual *news* which the reader had a right to expect, such notices were naturally written under great disadvantages, and, knowing this, the critics, as a rule, wielded their midnight pens with a certain air of kindly reservation. But recently theatrical matters have assumed a prominence altogether remarkable, and dramatic criticisms are looked for with eagerness, not only in the London papers, but in all the principal provincial ones, several of these latter receiving "criticisms" wired by telegraph "after the play"....I maintain that in most cases new plays, of any importance at all, should be seen a second time by the critic before he ventures to give any elaborate comment upon their merits, or upon the manner of their representation.

This question of first-night criticism attracted much attention during the period, and there was a great deal of somewhat acrimonious controversy devoted to it in the journals.[4] Other writers drew attention to the arduous labours of the ordinary dramatic reviewer, declaring that too many enter the theatre "already weary and *distrait*"—which is "altogether unfair, alike to managers, playwrights, and players".[5] The problem

[1] *The Athenaeum*, No. 3287, Oct. 25, 1890, 557–8.

[2] *The Theatre*, i, Sept. 1877, 141–2.

[3] H. J. Byron, *Growls from a Playwright* (*id.* N.S. i, Jan. 1880, 20–24).

[4] "*First Night*" *Criticisms* (*The Era*, xxxii, April 10, 1870, 9); *First Night Audiences* (*id.* xli, April 13, 1879, 14); *A Cry in the Wilderness* (*The Theatre*, N.S. xxi, May 1893, 255–9); Clement Scott, *The First Night Criticism* (*id.* N.S. xxiv, Sept. 1894, 100–5); *The Saturday Review*, lxxxix, Jan. 6, 1900, 13.

[5] *The Theatre*, N.S. xxvi, Dec. 1895, 340–3.

of whether a dramatist might justifiably discuss, as a critic, the productions of his fellow-dramatists was another frequent subject of discussion,[1] and the gentle art of puffing still called for attention.[2] Some said the critics were not cultured enough;[3] others declared with equal enthusiasm that their main fault was their inability to see through the eyes of ordinary uncultured spectators.[4]

These discussions are typical of the time. No age hitherto had shown itself so deeply interested in such problems. Schools of Criticism, Censorship, and, as we shall see, Dramatic Academies, National Theatres—these had become matters of general interest to thousands who previously would have dismissed them as unimportant or sinful. The theatre had become an institution of universal appeal.

III. *The Theatre*

In 1843 the stage had been freed from the monopoly which weighed heavily upon it since the days of Charles II;[5] but for some years it hardly grasped the full significance of its liberty. Samuel Phelps, it is true, was enabled by the new Act to put on his notable series of productions at Sadler's Wells from 1844 to 1862,[6] but the true start in a fresh direction was not taken until, on September 28, 1850, Charles Kean opened the Princess's with the first of his classic revivals.

During the decade 1843–53 there was practically no theatre-building in London, and for a time it looked as though this

[1] *The Critic-Dramatist: Old Type and New* (*The Theatre*, N.S. xxvi, Oct. 1895, 187–90); *Should Dramatic Critics write Plays?* (*id.* N.S. xxvi, Dec. 1895, 317–24); and see *The Saturday Review*, lxxx, Nov. 16, 1895, 650.

[2] *The Theatre*, iii, June 1878, 318–19.

[3] *Id.* N.S. xxii, July 1893, 3–8.

[4] Evelyn Ballantyne, *The Stalls, the Pit, and the Critic* (*id.* N.S. xvi, July 1890, 20–4); Charles Dickens, *The Public's Point of View* (*id.* N.S. xxiv, Nov. 1894, 220–6).

[5] See *E.N.D.* i, 22–3 and Ernest Reynolds, *Early Victorian Drama* (*1830–70*) (Cambridge, 1936), pp. 26–9.

[6] On his activities see John Coleman, *Memoirs of Samuel Phelps* (1886) and W. M. Phelps and John Forbes-Robertson, *The Life and Life-Work of Samuel Phelps* (1886).

Act, so long struggled for, was not to be of any practical assistance to the stage. Then suddenly there came an awakening. The new audiences which were arising both in the metropolis and in the provinces demanded new theatres—demanded, too, that many of the older theatres should be remodelled in accordance with the spirit of a later age. Between 1860 and 1870 came the rebuilt *Royalty*, *The Gaiety*, *The Charing Cross*, *The Globe*, *The Holborn*, *The Queen's* and *The Prince of Wales's*;[1] between 1870 and 1880 *The Court*, *The Opera Comique*, *The Vaudeville*, *The Criterion*, *The Philharmonic* and *The Imperial*; the following decade saw *The Comedy*, *The Savoy*, *The Avenue*, *The Novelty*, *Terry's*, *The Lyric*, *The Shaftesbury*, *The Prince's*, *The Empire* and *The Garrick*; while in the last ten years of the century were opened *The Duke of York's*, *Daly's*, *Her Majesty's* and *Wyndham's*. This brief list, which does not include any of the music halls or of the important suburban houses, amply testifies to the awakened and steadily increasing interest in the stage. The West End playhouses could now easily be reached, by means of omnibus or railroad, by an increasing population and those in the new suburban districts catered for such individuals as, because of lack of means or energy, preferred to take their pleasures nearer home.

"During the summer of 1851", noted J. W. Cole,[2] "there were nineteen theatres open in London, exclusive of the two Italian operas and the St James's, devoted entirely to French tragedy and comedy." The year 1851 was exceptional, for the great Exhibition had attracted thousands of country visitors and of foreigners to London; but even then there was less than a score of playhouses functioning in the metropolis. Barely half a century later, in 1899, London boasted sixty-one theatres—thirty-eight in the West End and twenty-three in the nearby suburban districts. Nor could these regular theatres by any means supply all the dramatic and semi-dramatic entertainment sought for by the public. Cer-

[1] Important reconstructions are noted here as well as the erection of entirely new theatres.

[2] *Op. cit.* ii, 10–11.

tainly in the fifties there were numerous houses which presented "dioramas, waxworks, pyrotechnics, astronomical and scientific experiments, Chinese villages, *poses plastiques* and aquatic performances",[1] but these were as nothing compared with the thirty-nine music halls which flourished at the end of the century. Quite apart from the fact that these music halls occasionally produced short plays, their influence on the general fortunes of the theatre and their significance as centres of entertainment was enormous. In some respects, the music hall was as characteristic a growth of Victorian England as the plays of Robertson, Pinero and Jones.[2]

Architecturally, the playhouse of this time reached a form after which men had been vaguely groping for two hundred years. That tendency which, beginning at the close of the seventeenth century, gradually cut away the old Restoration apron and its attendant stage-doors, now attained its culmination. The apron vanished entirely and the picture-frame stage, apt for realistic and spectacular experiments, was established. Percy Fitzgerald, commenting on the new Haymarket, drew attention to a "novel arrangement" introduced by Bancroft:

> A rich and elaborate gold border, about two feet broad, after the pattern of a picture frame, is continued all round the proscenium, and carried even below the actor's feet—There can be no doubt the sense of illusion is increased, and for the reason just given; the actors seem cut off from the domain of prose; there is no borderland or platform in front; and, stranger still, the whole has the air of a picture projected on a surface.[3]

Here the picture-frame stage is not only recognised but consciousness of its function and significance is clearly expressed. With this picture-frame effect, far more could be achieved scenically than had ever been dreamed of before. True, the old conventional devices clung tenaciously to the boards of the stage and for long impeded the development of fresh theatrical ideals. Managers still made use of antiquated customs, and some of them showed not the slightest

[1] Ernest Reynolds, *op. cit.* p. 74.
[2] M. Willson Disher, *Winkles and Champagne* (1938).
[3] *The World behind the Scenes* (1881), pp. 20–1.

appreciation of what might be done with the instruments now at their command.

An interesting example of this is provided by the front curtain. Even as late as 1881 Percy Fitzgerald found himself compelled to call attention to the fact that the use of this curtain was but sparing. "What", he enquires sarcastically,

> can be more absurd or ludicrous than to see a table and two chairs moving on the scene, of themselves apparently, but drawn on by a cord? or, more singular still, to see, on the prompter's whistle being heard, the table hurrying off at one side, the sofa and chairs at the other? After all, the invariable law that each scene can only be terminated by another taking its place, seems unmeaning. If a curtain fell for a moment or two while the change was made, it would be as logical as letting the "drop" fall at the end of each act.[1]

Although Charles Kean had employed "folding curtains of magnificent velvet"[2] to conceal scenic changes in his production of *Henry VIII*, the ancient methods of altering the sets persisted until the eighties.[3] Thus audiences might see a "canvas landscape" ascend "as though it were a vast window-blind, its wooden lath swinging below", and "the average representation of 'a bridge breaking down'" must have been but a clumsy picture when spectators could "distinctly see the 'broken' portion working smoothly on a hinge."[4]

The eighties, however, saw the new take the place of the old. Had Fitzgerald been penning his work in 1891 instead of in 1881 its comments would have been vastly different. Two things are here to be observed—first, the definite improvement in scenic discipline, and, second, the definite change in orientation, from conventionalism to naturalistic effect.

[1] *Op. cit.* p. 35. Already, however, the familiar modern iron curtain (or "asbestos") had been introduced at the Apollo.

[2] *The Illustrated London News*, June 2, 1855.

[3] *Between the Acts* (*The Saturday Review*, lxvi, Sept. 15, 1888, 321–2).

[4] Percy Fitzgerald, *op. cit.* p. 3; cf. Bradlee Watson, *op. cit.* p. 276 (with references from *The Theatrical Journal*, Feb. 6, 1859). It is interesting to note that Irving used the device of darkening the theatre in order to conceal scene-changes (Mrs Alec Tweedie, *Behind the Footlights* (1904), p. 223).

It was in this period that the modern producer or director—stage-manager, he was called then—was born. Up to the seventies things theatrical were often chaotic and confused. Some managers attempted to supervise and control, but there was in general no real endeavour to establish co-ordination and co-operative effort among the many workers back-stage. Murray of Edinburgh was considered peculiar because he "insisted upon every member of his company *acting* at rehearsal exactly as they intended to do at night".[1] The condition of the theatre "in 1865 was absolutely disheartening", declared a writer twenty years later,[2] and that in spite of the fact that we recognise now how much had already been done to prepare the way for a fresh conception. When *King John* was reclothed under the direction of Planché in 1828 a move was made towards the securing of unity in visual effect; only externals were influenced, it is true, but we may readily see how this innovation might lead to others. A further development came when, in the fifties, Charles Kean set forth his versions of Shakespeare. No doubt little was done towards controlling the styles of individual actors or towards building up mass effects by strict attention to detail, but unquestionably his productions were heavily stamped with the impress of a single mind. More significant still was the work of Bancroft at his little theatre in Tottenham Court Road. "Decency and order" were demanded there[3] and an ideal was set up for a unified realism in stage presentation.[4] Now a clear line of progress was set towards the concept of an art theatre, wherein many workers should contribute to secure a pre-designed effect. With the Bancrofts "the star system was revoked in favour of the individual merit system" and the stage-manager definitely had control of the rehearsals.

The Bancrofts used this method to produce a greater

[1] This was before 1850: J. C. Dibdin, *The Annals of the Edinburgh Stage* (Edinburgh, 1888), p. 423.

[2] *The Theatre*, N.S. vi, July 1885, 49.

[3] *Id.* p. 50.

[4] A. W. à Beckett, *Is Realism on the Stage overdone?* (*The Theatre*, N.S. xxviii, Sept. 1896, 132–6).

illusion of the real; Dion Boucicault adopted it chiefly in order to obtain more "theatrical" and more thrilling effects. He has been claimed as the inaugurator of the directorial idea, but a clearer view discerns him as one among many in whose minds the age had implanted this vision. Boucicault paid minute attention to the working of stage tricks, to the controlling of the lights and to the placement of his actors. In these ways he proved the forerunner of Sir Augustus Harris who was noted by A. W. à Beckett to have "worked a reformation on the stage" both in the *mise-en-scène* and in the direction of performers participating in the production.[1] His Drury Lane spectacles attained their perfection from his personal managerial care and ability.

Among the innovators, too, was W. S. Gilbert, who acknowledged a considerable debt to the activities of the Bancrofts and of Robertson. In no uncertain terms the author of the Savoy operas declared that Robertson

> invented stage-management. It was an unknown art before his time. Formerly, in a conversation scene, for instance, you simply brought down two or three chairs from the flat and placed them in a row in the middle of the stage, and the people sat down and talked, and when the conversation was ended the chairs were replaced. Robertson showed how to give life and variety and nature to the scene by breaking it up with all sorts of little incidents and delicate by-play.[2]

Similar "life and variety" Gilbert injected into his own productions by taking complete control. Edmond Rickett recalls that

> he was probably the most dreaded director in London—for he invariably directed personally and autocratically the production of his own plays and operas. Nor does this apply merely to the spoken word. He planned the scenery, the lighting and ordered not only the groupings of the chorus but practically every inflection

[1] *Green-Room Recollections* (1896), p. 35. Attention may be called to a short article in *The Theatre*, N.S. xiii, May 1889, 260–1, where the new functions of the producer are discussed; a clear distinction is drawn here between the old "stage manager" and this novel official in the theatre.

[2] Sidney Dark and Rowland Grey, *W. S. Gilbert: his Life and Letters* (1923), p. 59.

of the voice and every gesture of the actors. And there was no argument and no appeal from his decision.[1]

It is important to remember that all these varied approaches towards a fresh conception were being made from the middle of the century onwards, although at the same time the fact must fully be recognised that the final establishment of new principles in the English theatre, while it was largely the result of native endeavour, owed much to the visits of foreign artists. In 1880 Londoners were enabled to see the performances of a Rotterdam company which aroused much admiration on account of "the completeness of their performances" and because "considerations of general effect" were "not subordinated to the pretensions of a 'star' actor or actress"; the players' "extreme clearness, significance and decision" in gesture also won critical esteem.[2] The troupe paved a way for the visit of the Saxe-Meiningen company (opening at Drury Lane, May 30, 1881). All that had been admired in the work of the Rotterdam players was here found in even greater perfection. To the English theatre, as to theatres in many other lands, they immediately provided a model.[3] Under their director Chronegk they "taught a lesson in the management of stage crowds",[4] and lessons in many other things besides. Their magnificent co-operation, their attention to detail and their archaeological accuracy brought to the age precisely what it had been seeking.

Thus, out of varied needs and influences was the producer brought into being. Old-stagers, of course, might look back through rosy spectacles into the past and declare that not

[1] *Certain Recollections of W. S. Gilbert* (*The New York Times*, April 1, 1934).

[2] *The Saturday Review*, xlix, June 19, 1880, 790; Joseph Knight, *Theatrical Notes* (1893), viii; *The Theatre*, N.S. ii, July 1880, 28–35.

[3] For their influence on Russia, see C. Stanislavski, *My Life in Art* (1924), pp. 196–206, and on their activities in general, C. Weiser, *Zehn Jahre Meininger: Ein Beitrag zur Theatergeschichte* (*Archiv für Theatergeschichte*, i, 1904, 118–26).

[4] Philip Beck, *Realism* (*The Theatre*, N.S. vii, Sept. 1883, 127–31; Sir Theodore Martin, *The Meiningen Company and the London Stage* (*Blackwood's Edinburgh Magazine*, cxxx, Aug. 1881, 248–63); *Die Meininger* (*The Theatre*, N.S. iv, Aug. 1881, 102–5).

so much, after all, had been accomplished. In 1891 Lady Martin, writing of the production of Browning's *Strafford* in 1837, asserted that that play had been "mounted in all matters with great care. Modern critics", she said, "seem to have little knowledge of the infinite pains bestowed in all respects before their day upon the representation of historical and Shakespearian plays."[1] Such statements, however, cannot be accepted at their face value. Unquestionably, with our perspective in time, we can now see how, between the time when *Strafford* was produced and the end of the century, opinion had moved forward and created the ideal of a producer who, without subordinating all to one particular part, engaged himself to obtain order and harmony from the manifold efforts of all those taking part in a performance.

During the period the producer's main task was to secure an impression of reality on the stage. This tendency towards naturalism proved to be the most determined and the most persistent of its age; indeed, by it may these fifty years of theatrical endeavour best be tested and understood. To grasp fully its significance one must bear in mind the fact that the romantic movement of the early nineteenth century had contained within itself the seeds both of a creative idealism and of a creative realism—both of these being in direct opposition to the ideals of the eighteenth-century Augustans.

Typical form was what the Augustans aimed at; class characters, alike in tragedy and in comedy, formal and conventional settings, acting that depended mainly upon relatively fixed gestures—these were the things upon which the eighteenth-century theatre was based. The critics might stalwartly clamour for verisimilitude, but audiences as a whole accepted the playhouse as a place where the exact representation of life had no business. With the coming of romanticism men started to explore—on the one hand, the realms of unreal, imaginative wonder, and, on the other, the forms of life immediately around them. *The Lyrical Ballads* demonstrates both these tendencies—Wordsworth aiming at the close and detailed observation of life and at the use of familiar

[1] Sir Theodore Martin, *Helena Faucit* (*Lady Martin*) (1900), p. 244.

speech, Coleridge seeking escape in the fantastic dream world of *The Ancient Mariner*. For a time, particularly in poetry, idealism triumphed; but gradually, and especially in the novel and in the drama, the gropings toward naturalistic expression took greater and greater hold of the public.

As early as 1827 Boaden could declare that, in his opinion, "the modern stage affects reality infinitely beyond the proper objects of dramatic representation",[1] and deplore a tendency which made audiences forget they were in a theatre, watching persons who were, after all, merely actors making pretence. From this time on, the movement toward the extreme of naturalism was constant. "The almost universal craving for Realism", thought an observer in 1883, "just now is one of the most curious signs of the times."[2] The public, he felt sure, would not then rest content with Vincent Crummles's real pump and two washing-tubs; it would demand "entire rows of real tubs, with real suds, real soap, real thumb blue, real washing-powder, and real hot water for the mutual drenching of two real irate females". It is not uninteresting to observe that, in this period when the public was clamorous in demanding these naturalistic effects, many of those most intelligently interested in the theatre divined the dangers inherent in the new style. "Extreme confidence in the practical worth of stage accessories naturally leads to carelessness in dramatic construction" decided the critic of *The Graphic* in 1869,[3] and in other articles, principally one on "The Limits of Scenic Effect",[4] gave arguments to justify his position. "While play-maker, play-actor, and play-goer admit reluctantly that there is something wrong in the British drama," he wrote,

> they can point triumphantly to what has done the mischief—the glories of British scenery. This, at least, flourishes; and has almost reached perfection....Set scenes, perfect structures that

[1] *Memoirs of Mrs Siddons* (1827), ii, 355; cf. pp. 292–3.

[2] Philip Beck, *Realism* (*The Theatre*, N.S. ii, Sept. 1883, 127–31). Three years earlier Walter Gordon, in an article on *Realism* (*id.* N.S. ii, Nov. 1880, 283–5) found the stage fully gripped by the prevailing fashion.

[3] i, 31, Dec. 11, 1869.

[4] i, 11, Dec. 4, 1869.

have to be "built", have taken the place of the old "flats"; side scenes have given way to regular enclosures; and drawing-rooms and boudoirs appear ready furnished with hangings, buhl, clocks, etc.; in short, as the bills are careful to inform us, "the furniture in Act IV by Messrs —— and ——, of Oxford Street".

"This mimicry," he opines,

once begun, is endless; it becomes gigantic and insupportable. Whole houses and streets have to be built up with infinite toil and cost; mountains have to be constructed, bridges thrown across....Yet still we are not in the least beguiled; we may venture to say that the skilfully, effectively painted flat scene is far more welcome to the eye, has more illusion, and has certainly no points of weakness or make-shift, which the most careful eye can detect....Once we descend into archaeological minuteness, the eye is disturbed, criticism is challenged, or we become pledged to a minuteness of detail which the play does not require, and which is an insufferable burden to those who get up the play.

Fundamentally the same attitude was adopted by Henry Labouchere, of *Truth*. "The new mechanical machinery", he thought,[1] "is far more unnatural than the old full and front sets." Imagination, in his opinion, was being thrust aside; the time was come "to relieve the stage from the thraldom of the stage carpenter" who long enough had had "his wicked way". Labouchere added to his argument regarding the unimaginative quality of realistic scenery another respecting its cost and confusing characteristics when applied to any kind of play other than the familiar "domestic drama". Writers of more romantic plays, he stated,

must reconsider their tactics. They are overlaying their plays with unnecessary scenery, and burdening the action with superfluous characters. The manager whose treasury is sufficiently taxed already by vexatiously costly productions and extravagant salaries, would...welcome any reform that tended towards theatrical economy.

And that reform must lie either in the re-introduction of frankly conventional settings or in simplification. As things stood,

[1] *Truth*, xviii, Nov. 12, 1885.

all nature, repose, and reality are lost. Lights are lowered and raised again so frequently that the spectators are as worried as passengers are in a railway train passing through innumerable tunnels on a bright summer day. Midnight death-scenes change into Buckinghamshire lanes, homesteads whirl into Thames Embankments, Egyptian sphinxes and Cleopatra needles become village-pumps, moonlit spinnies resolve themselves into flash drinking-houses in squalid London.[1]

Labouchere was even prepared to defend and demand the retention of ancient conventions. In reviewing a revival of *The Iron Chest* at the Lyceum in 1879,[2] he expressed regret at the disappearance of that green carpet which for generations had been the familiar accompaniment of the serious drama. This "floor-covering", he thought, was "as necessary to the proper consideration of tragedy as is the extinction of all gas when a ghost story is told in a country house". Some years later, a still more redoubtable warrior tilted his lance against the naturalistic enemy; in 1890 Henry Arthur Jones, despite his interest in the domestic problem-play, saw cause to deplore the loss of imaginative reality through the over great emphasis upon realistic trappings:

The uneducated playgoer goes to a theatre and sees a real lamp-post and a real London street. He goes to another theatre and hears a gentleman in antique dress soliloquising in blank verse. He recognises certain features of the lamp-post and certain features of the London street, but soliloquies in blank verse are palpable and egregious impossibilities. He thinks that the lamp-post and the London street are "real life" and that Hamlet is not.[3]

That these men had ample reason innumerable instances persuade us. Ellen Terry describes how Charles Reade introduced into *Rachel the Reaper* (Qns. 1874) "*real* pigs, *real* sheep, a *real* goat, and a *real* dog" with "*real* litter...strewn all over the stage".[4] A real steam-launch on real water drew spectators to Leonard Grover's *Lost in New York* (Olym. 1896), and the whirligig of fashion could bring a judgment

[1] *Truth*, xviii, Aug. 27, 1885.
[2] *Id.* vi, Oct. 2, 1879, 416.
[3] *The Renascence of the English Drama* (1895), p. 86. This article appeared originally in *The New York Dramatic Mirror*, April 19, 1890.
[4] Ellen Terry, *The Story of my Life* (1908).

that Sarcey was behind the times precisely because he did not believe in historical realism.[1]

For realism, of course, could be interpreted in terms both historical and contemporary. While on the one hand it led towards a closer approach in dialogue to ordinary conversational usage, in setting to a more faithful simulating of nature's three-dimensional forms and in acting to a more restrained and less conventional method of delivery, the same tendency effected a vast alteration in the production of earlier classics and of original plays written about past themes. When W. G. Wills's *Charles I* was presented at the Lyceum in 1872, "the Scenery and Appointments", we are informed, were "prepared with the intention of giving reality to a reproduction of the actual period during which the incidents are supposed to have taken place"—and this statement succinctly expresses the ideal which most managers kept strictly before them in their efforts.

Of these managers, the most representative is Charles Kean. Not only did his work come early in the period but his enunciation of aim was uncompromising and extreme. At a banquet given in his honour at the conclusion of the 1859 season he rose to acknowledge the toast. "I may safely assert", he said, "that in no single instance have I ever permitted historical truth to be sacrificed to theatrical effect."[2] That assertion, so strangely opposed to modern conceptions, gives us the clue for an understanding of his work and that of his companions. Kean was as proud of being an F.S.A. as of being a distinguished producer. His playbills soon extended themselves into miniature essays in which his own learning was set forth and ample indication given of the scholarly assistance which his enthusiasm had evoked. The historical plays of Shakespeare were his delight, but even those dramas, such as *A Midsummer Night's Dream* and *A Winter's Tale*, which were set in fantastic realms came to be treated in a similar manner. Kean's biographer, J. W. Cole,[3] recognised that *A Midsummer Night's Dream* did not

[1] *The Theatre*, N.S. xxi, Jan. 1895, 62.
[2] J. W. Cole, *op. cit.* ii, 382.
[3] *Op. cit.* ii, 197–8.

offer much "scope for that illustrative and historical accuracy, or for that classical research, so peculiarly identified with Mr Kean's system of management";

nevertheless, he availed himself of the few opportunities afforded by the subject, of carrying out his favourite plan. So little is known of Greek manners and architecture in the time of Theseus, twelve hundred years before the Christian era, and so probable is it that the buildings were of the rudest form, that any attempt to represent them on the stage would have failed in the intended object of profitable instruction. Holding himself, for these reasons, "unfettered with regard to chronology", Mr Kean presented ancient Athens to us, in the opening scene, at the culminating period of its magnificence, "as it would have appeared to one of its own inhabitants at a time when it had attained its greatest splendour in literature and art". His scholastic taste took advantage of the specified scene of action, to place before the eyes of the spectators, on the rising of the curtain, a restored view of the famous city, "standing in its pride and glory", which excited the spontaneous sympathy, and called up some of the earliest and deepest impressions of every educated mind. We saw, on the hill of the Acropolis, the far-famed Parthenon, the Erichtheum, and the statue of the tutelary goddess Minerva, or Athena; by its side the theatre of Bacchus; in advance, the temple of Jupiter Olympus, partially hiding the hall of the Museum; and on the right, the temple of Theseus. The view also included the summit of that memorable eminence, "from whence the words of sacred truth were first promulgated to the Athenian citizens by apostolic inspiration".[1]

We must not, of course, allow ourselves to be misled by these accounts into assuming that historical accuracy stood separate from all other considerations. No doubt Kean felt sincere in his declaration which he made to the guests at the banquet of 1859, but a clue to another object is to be found in one phrase of the above account. Even if, says Cole, Kean had been able to obtain reliable information concerning prehistoric Athens, he would probably have found "that the buildings were of the rudest form". The implication

[1] An excellent conception of Charles Kean's care and method is to be gained from an examination of the volumes (preserved in the Victoria and Albert Museum) wherein are bound the scene designs and property drawings for several of his productions.

is obvious; all this research and historical endeavour was designed, not simply to depict the past accurately, but to choose from the past that which made a goodly show. While Planché was honest enough in his encouraging of the historical costuming of Shakespeare's plays, while Phelps and Kean trotted forth their "records of antiquity" and their "authorities" for this or that production, the historical aim was generally confused with, and at times even lost in, the desire to present a richly coloured spectacle. Propriety, too, and the dictates of Victorian fashion might disturb severest accuracy. A Roman-clad Antony might stalwartly stand beside a very demure and much petticoated Cleopatra. Even Mrs Kean, for all her husband's devotion to archaeology, persisted in wearing her hair in her own individual manner—drawn straight down from her forehead "in curtains" and twisted curiously round her ears. As Hermione in *A Winter's Tale* she donned underskirt after underskirt in true contemporary style and posed by her pedestal a most un-Grecian statue.

Fundamentally, then, Kean's productions depended upon show; the antiquarian "correctness" was a sop to public taste and to his own vanity. The ideal of correctness, of course, was always insisted upon, until eventually (in 1907) a critic could condemn Tree's production of *Antony and Cleopatra* precisely because of the accurately designed Egyptian garments worn by Cleopatra's court—Cleopatra, this critic pointed out, was of a Greek dynasty and probably would have introduced Athenian fashions to the élite of Alexandria. Never for a moment, however, was the passion for spectacle lost. Kean's explanation of his aims in producing *A Midsummer Night's Dream* may sound like the combination of a sermon and a text-book, but once we proceed to practical matters of the stage we find ourselves in a different world. "The Scenery", we read, is

under the Direction of Mr GRIEVE, and Painted by Mr GRIEVE, Mr W. GORDON, Mr F. LLOYDS, Mr CUTHBERT, Mr DAYES, Mr MORRIS, and numerous Assistants. The Music under the Direction of Mr J. L. HATTON. The Dances and Action by Mr OSCAR BYRN. The Decorations and Appointments by Mr E. W.

BRADWELL. The Dresses by Mrs and Miss HOGGINS. The Machinery by Mr G. HODSON.

With these in charge, we are carried, first, to "A Terrace adjoining the Palace of Theseus overlooking the City of Athens". In the second scene comes the "Workshop of Quince the Carpenter", where, we are relieved to discover, all "the Furniture and Tools...are Copied from Discoveries at Herculaneum". Then, in Act 2, comes "A Wood near Athens (Moonlight)", which gives way to a "Moving Diorama, Exhibiting Another Part of the Wood" and "Titania's Shadow Dance". The third act is ejaculatingly labelled "THE WOOD!" and brings on a general "Dance of Fairies". In the fourth act we have "Titania's Bower", "Athens. Interior of Quince's House" and "The Wood (Sunrise)", while for the final scene is reserved, in largest capitals,

ATHENS

INTERIOR OF THE PALACE OF THESEUS

These are the indications on the playbill. J. W. Cole adds some further details:

the introduction to the haunt of the supernatural beings; the first appearance of *Oberon* and *Titania*, with their attendant trains; the noiseless footsteps of the dance on the moonlit greensward, with the shadowed reflection of every rapid and graceful movement; the wood peopled with its innumerable fairy legions, whose voices lull their queen to sleep upon a bank of flowers; the melodious music composed by Mendelssohn to the words of the author.... The perpetual change of scene and incident; the shifting diorama; the beams of the rising sun glittering on the leaves; the gradual dispersion of the mist, discovering the fairy guardians, light and brilliant as gossamer, grouped around the unconsciously sleeping mortals; the dazzling magnificence of the palace of Theseus at the close, thronged on every staircase, balustrade and corridor, with myriads of aerial beings—

indeed, "an endless succession of skilfully-blended, pictorial, mechanical, and musical effects".[1]

[1] *Op. cit.* ii, 199. On Kean's activities in this direction see H. M. Cundall, *Charles Kean, F.S.A. and Theatrical Scenery* (*The Art Journal*, 1903, pp. 199–206), Edward F. Strange, *The Scenery of Charles Kean's*

Thus went realism and spectacle hand in hand. Who would profess to say which was which in *The Merchant of Venice*, where

> the gradual illumination of the lighthouse and various mansions, in almost every window, the moon slowly rising and throwing her silver light upon the deep blue waters of the Mediterranean, were managed with imposing reality?[1]

Or who could tell for which purpose were introduced many of the mechanical devices of these years? The gauze that simulated mist in *A Midsummer Night's Dream* served both, as did the panoramic and dioramic effects. It was instructive to go up the Thames by barge and see, passing by, the various edifices of Henry VIII's time, but this formed also a rich and thrilling show. Even Pepper's Ghost may be regarded as a device calculated to excite with wonder, to raise scientific curiosity and to make the supernatural more "naturalistic". To cause a ghost to move laboriously over a creaking stage-floor and cast dark shadows on the scenery is clearly conventional; Pepper's Ghost simply made disembodied creatures look more like disembodied creatures, while at the same time succeeding in providing a novel spectacle.[2]

Pepper's Ghost does not seem to have been much utilised in ordinary dramatic productions, but its counterpart appeared in Fechter's presentation of *Hamlet*, wherein the ghost delivered his long speech, standing in an archway, apparently in the full light of the moon. "As he began to scent the early

Plays and the Great Scene-Painters of his Day (*The Magazine of Art*, 1901–2, pp. 454–9 and 514–18), *The English Stage* (*The Quarterly Review*, clv, April 1883, 354–88). Further notes on *mise-en-scène* will be found in *Scenery and Scene-Painters* (*The Era Almanack*, 1871, pp. 35–40) and Georges Bourdon, *Les théâtres anglais* (*Revue de Paris*, 1900, pp. 859–94).

[1] J. W. Cole, *op. cit.* ii, 333.

[2] Percy Fitzgerald, *The World Behind the Scenes* (1881), pp. 65–6, gives an account of this device: "Just behind the footlights a portion of the stage was raised; an enormous sheet of plate-glass, such as would be used for a great shop-window, was placed on the stage, slightly inclined forwards. It was thus that a person below the stage, in the pit made under the footlights, was reflected, unseen himself, to the audience from the glass." Dion Boucicault, writing on *The Decline of the Drama* (*The North American Review*, cxxv, Sept. 1877, 239), notes that "ghosts are now secured by patent and produced by machinery by Professor Pepper".

morning air, he began to fade, without any motion on his part or any darkening of the stage and grew dimmer by degrees until he vanished altogether. This was about as spectral a bit of business as could be imagined. It was brought about as follows: The ghost stood behind a large concealed wheel which, when started, caught up, at each revolution, a fresh piece of some almost transparent stuff, artfully tinted to match the background, until the requisite thickness was obtained. The ghost apparently melted into thin air."[1]

The built-up sets which became commoner after 1870 served the same double purpose.[2] In 1875 the Bancrofts, impelled by the desire for realism and intent upon spectacular display, caused "elaborate capitals of enormous weight" to be "cast in plaster" for a production of *The Merchant of Venice*, even although part of the wall of the theatre had to be cut away to find room for them "to be moved by means of trucks, on and off the small stage".[3] It was about the same time that the box-set came definitely to supplant the conventional wings and back-cloths which had been handed down from the period of the Restoration, although it is to be noted that, even after its introduction, it long left much to be desired. A critic in 1879,[4] noticing the production of *Fernande* at the Court, draws attention to a "happy innovation which, it is to be hoped, will be widely copied. In this representation of an interior, the two sides of the room come completely down to the proscenium. There are not those gaps through which people in the private boxes and in some of the stalls can see prompters, scene-shifters, and actors waiting for their cues, to the great detriment of all stage illusion."[5] Stage illusion, interpreted as naturalistic illusion,

[1] *The New York Evening Post Magazine*, Dec. 20, 1919.

[2] An appeal for a more conventional attitude towards scenic backgrounds is made by Percy Fitzgerald, *Thoughts on Scenery* (*The Theatre*, N.S. i, Oct. 1878, 201–4). See *supra*, p. 36.

[3] Sir Squire and Lady Bancroft, *Recollections of Sixty Years* (1909), p. 205.

[4] *The Saturday Review*, xlviii, Sept. 27, 1879, 386–7.

[5] On the introduction of the box-set see also Percy Fitzgerald, *Theatrical Anecdotes* (1874), p. 71, and on the exactitude of interiors, A. W. Bean, *Artistic Stage Interiors* (*The Theatre*, N.S. xviii, July 1891, 16–20).

is now the final ideal. That ideal is served by the complete box-set for interiors, while for exteriors the cyclorama—described as a "semicircular" background "with a coved ceiling"—provided both spectacular effect and the simulation of a real sky.[1]

Throughout the period continual experimentation was being carried out in the devising of new scenic effects. When Planché introduced in *The Golden Branch* (Lyc. 1847) a

ACT II.—SCENE 1. A Room in Ballyraggett House, in 1st groove. SCENE 2. Father Dolan's (repeat of Scene 4, Act I.), full set. SCENE 3. The Barrack Room, in 1st groove. SCENE 4. Mrs. O'Kelly's Cabin, in 1st groove. SCENE 5. The Gate Tower, full set.

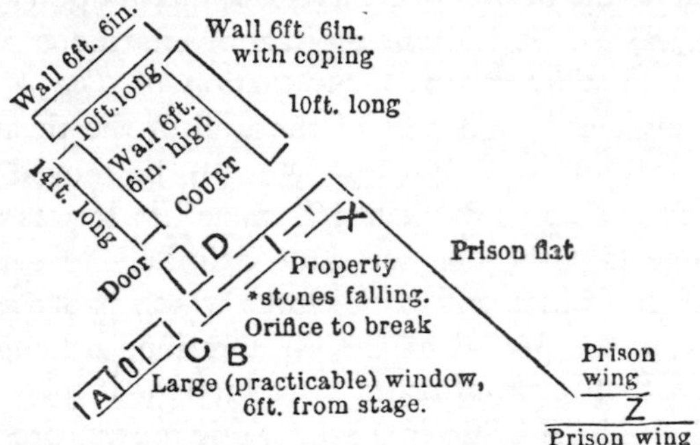

Fig. 1. *The Shaughraun*: scene-plot for Act II, scene 5, "The Gate Tower".

scene showing the "Spirit vaults beneath the Enchanter's Castle" and then made this "whole scene, together with the personages in it", vanish to reveal "The Brown Study of KING BROWN", he inaugurated the transformation so dear to later pantomimic tastes. Responsible for the carrying out of the device was William Beverley, "an ingenious machinist, as well as an admirable painter", according to the testimony of the author. New methods of scene change were being

[1] Percy Fitzgerald, *The World Behind the Scenes* (1881), p. 27. Fitzgerald, in *The Art of Acting* (1892), p. 162, notes that when the Paris Opera was being built "one M. Raymond submitted models of a kind of panoramic structure which filled the back of the stage in a semi-circular fashion, thus doing away with side scenes. The sky was formed by a hemisphere, so that the whole had the appearance of the apse of a cathedral."

substituted for the ancient use of grooves. Particularly interesting in this connection is the second act of Boucicault's *The Shaughraun* (D.L. 1875). The fifth scene of this act shows "The interior of a prison; large window, R., old fireplace, R.C., small window, C., door, L. Through window R. is seen exterior and courtyard." Robert, in prison, works to effect his escape while Conn assists him from without; part of the wall is broken when

> The Scene moves—pivots on a point at the back. The prison moves off and shows the exterior of tower, with CONN clinging to the walls, and ROBERT creeping through the orifice. The walls of the yard appear to occupy three-fourths of stage.

How this was effected is shown in a scene-plot printed with the text of the play. It is explained that a man "inside boxed wall at A" moves that piece of scenery, which is pivoted at C;

> when it gets square home at B a man at D pushes big boxed wall, the whole moves slowly, till smaller wall piece enters and disappears off at Z. The larger wall piece having pivoted on X will now be close to prison flat, the three walls of court will be drawn after it, and occupy the stage.

As an example of the way in which the stage of the seventies was breaking with earlier principles hardly anything better could have been found. Almost equally significant is the scene-plot for the last scene of the act, showing "The Ruins of St Bridget's Abbey". It will be noted in this that, while built-up scenery is freely employed, flat side-wings are still preserved. The set is midway between those of 1800 and those of 1900 and thus harmonises with the spirit and technique of the play for which it was designed. One may add that the five full-stage scenes in *The Shaughraun* are divided by others set in the familiar "grooves".

Boucicault, who was one of the greatest experimenters in this direction, was also an active experimenter in the manipulation of light effects—and these light effects proved possibly the most serviceable instrument in the realisation of those fresh aims which were animating the age. "All the great triumphs of modern stage effect", deemed Fitzgerald justly, date from the introduction of a strong light. When gas was introduced, it was found that a more gaudy display of colours could be effected; but it was the application of the lime-light that really threw open the realms of glittering fairyland to the scenic artist.[1]

In 1826 the whole theatre remained in an even glare of light, with no attempt made to concentrate the illuminant;[2] by 1849 the gas had been put "wholly under the control of the prompter",[3] the auditorium was darkened during the performance and endeavours were made, particularly by Charles Kean, to secure adequate direction and shading of the lights.

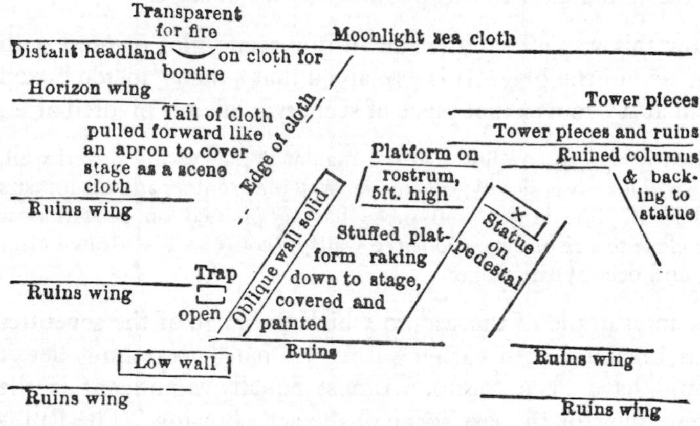

Fig. 2. *The Shaughraun*: scene-plot for Act II, scene ii, "Ruins of St Bridget's Abbey".

Limelight seems to have been tentatively employed by Macready, but it was Kean who first made it a definite and necessary part of theatre equipment; he was using it regularly in his productions of the fifties. Twenty years later came the invention of arclight, and the introduction of the incandescent mantle in 1890 brought further possibilities, possibilities immeasurably increased when electricity came to take the

[1] *The World behind the Scenes* (1881), p. 41.
[2] *The Theatrical Observer*, Sept. 15, 1826.
[3] *The Theatrical Journal*, Dec. 13, 1849.

place of gas illumination.[1] Independent research in spectacular devices was soon brought into association with the stage. In New York Steele MacKaye opened his Spectatorium in 1893;[2] in 1896 E. L. Bruce exhibited his "aerial graphoscope" at Kensington; and about the same time Professor Herkomer was experimenting independently with projected cloud effects.[3] In all of these show and illusion travelled together.

Sometimes, of course, one prevailed, sometimes the other. Often unadorned realism held such charms that but to see reproduced upon the stage what anyone might see without effort on the streets outside the theatre was very ecstasy and bliss. A real cow could make the success of a play, not because it was a strange cow or a prize cow or a sagacious cow—simply because it, a cow of cows, was made to appear in a faithfully imitated farmyard scene. A real lamp-post on the stage was a wonder, and a real hansom cab the realisation of a dream. Men began to pay attention now to things they had never heeded before. Alfred Wigan, for example, observed that, if an interior set had a mirror placed facing the audience, this mirror could reflect part of the auditorium, which, according to the new creed, was as absurd as any absurdity tantalisingly demonstrated by Euclid. Accordingly, he introduced a mirror which, instead of a silvered surface, was covered with a piece of wallpaper similar to that on the rest of the scenery; in other words, the mirror was made to simulate a reflection of the invisible fourth wall.[4]

Peculiarly enough—and yet not peculiarly when one considers aright the philosophic principles at work—this very same tendency towards naturalism which incidentally en-

[1] E. Ack, *Machinerie électrique du théâtre de Drury Lane à Londres* (*Genie civil*, xxxiv, Jan. 28, 1899, 204–5) and W. W. Davies, *Electric Light in the Theatre* (*Notes and Queries*, viii, 8, 1895, 288–9).

[2] Percy MacKaye, *Epoch: The Life of Steele MacKaye* (New York, 1927), ii, 345–8.

[3] An early use of the magic lantern for the projection of a scene is recorded in connection with *The Flying Dutchman* by E. Fitzball, *Thirty-Five Years of a Dramatic Author's Life* (1859), ii, 13–14.

[4] Godfrey Turner, *Show and its Value* (*The Theatre*, N.S. iii, May 1884, 234).

couraged the elaborately spectacular productions of Shakespeare's plays was responsible for experimentation in the highly conventional manner of Elizabethan staging. Charles Kean applied the realistic method for the purpose of making Lear look like an ancient British monarch and Hamlet seem a genuine melancholy Dane; others, employing an identical method, demanded that Shakespeare's stage be reproduced in all exactitude and his characters be costumed as they might have appeared in the original productions. Thus was the historical-real sponsored and guided by William Poel. Founding an Elizabethan Reading Society, that innovator first produced the early *Hamlet* at St George's Hall in April 1887 and followed that by performances of a series of Elizabethan plays. Webster's *The Duchess of Malfi* appeared at the Opera Comique in October 1892, Marlowe's *Doctor Faustus* at St George's Hall in July 1896, *Arden of Feversham* at the same place in July 1897, Beaumont and Fletcher's *The Coxcomb* at the Inner Temple Hall in February 1898, Middleton and Rowley's *The Spanish Gipsy* at St George's Hall in April 1898, Ford's *The Broken Heart* in June of that year, and Ben Jonson's *The Sad Shepherd* in July—a truly remarkable series of experiments.[1] Such experiments could not have been conducted before this time, for during these years only had there come the desire and the knowledge; hitherto there had been but slight understanding of the true features exhibited by an Elizabethan playhouse. At the beginning of the century Edmund Malone had groped blindly towards the truth, but not till De Witt's famous sketch of The Swan was published (in 1888) could men obtain any adequate conception of what a playhouse of 1600 looked like. Once this conception had been gained, the ideal might be realised of reconstructing that playhouse and of performing Shakespeare's dramas in their original manner. In 1893 a bare "Elizabethan" stage of this kind was used for a production of *Twelfth Night* and in 1896 for a production of *The Two Gentlemen of Verona*.

In these ways an age of invention and materialism affected

[1] *William Poel and his Stage Productions* (privately printed for the William Poel Portrait Committee, 1933).

the theatre, and amid the conflicting manifestations of a single aim we must tread in our path towards an understanding of the nineteenth-century playhouse. On the one hand there is the unadorned Elizabethan stage companioned by the rather drab and barren middle-class interior, reproduced with painstaking exactness; on the other there is that scenic splendour by which both poet and actor "were subordinated to the antiquary" while "the costumier helped still further to debauch the public taste".[1]

IV. *Actors, Managers and Authors*

The audience changed; the theatre changed; and with them the actor, too, altered his methods and, chameleon-like, assumed the colouring of his age. In spite of all Garrick's efforts, the chief histrionic tendency at the beginning of the century was that which may be described as "classical". J. P. Kemble and Mrs Siddons were the leaders of a school which recognised acting as a conventional art and strove to exhibit skill rather than simulate real life.[2] For them and for their audiences plays and dramatic characters existed mainly for the opportunities they provided to the performer. Typical is the scene at Mrs Siddons's farewell in 1812 as narrated by Cole. The play was *Macbeth* and, we are informed, "her friends insisted on having" it "terminated when she made her final exit, in the sleeping scene".[3] The tragedy and its persons mattered little; the artistry of the actress alone had significance. That continual "playing for points", so characteristic of these theatres, tells the same tale, for in the "point", made or lost, the character depicted had perforce to be forgotten.

[1] *The Drama in England* (*The Quarterly Review*, cxxxii, Jan. 1872, 1–26).

[2] By far the finest account of the various styles of acting in the early nineteenth century appears in Bradlee Watson, *Sheridan to Robertson* (Cambridge, U.S.A. 1926). See also C. F. Armstrong, *A Century of Great Actors: 1750–1850* (1912), H. B. Baker, *Our Old Actors* (1881), H. Simpson and C. Brown, *A Century of Famous Actresses, 1750–1850* (1913). Information regarding the Kembles will be found in Percy Fitzgerald, *The Kembles* (2 vols. 1871), J. Boaden, *Memoirs of the Life of John Philip Kemble* (2 vols. 1825) and J. Boaden, *Memoirs of the Life of Mrs Siddons* (2 vols. 1827).

[3] *Op. cit.* i, 33.

Opposed to this highly intellectualised "classic" model, Edmund Kean established, in the second decade of the century, a highly romantic method, and for years his passionate and perfervid style, suited to the mood of an age which produced a Byron and a Shelley, continued to flourish.[1] Flamboyant in the hands of Kean himself, of G. F. Cooke,[2] of G. V. Brooke, it reflected now the satanic idealism of the one poet and now the rapturous ecstasies of the other. In the sphere of comedy a like absence of restraint proved popular. Burlesque methods were by no means confined to extravaganza; they coloured vividly the interpretation of both farce and comedy. Here, too, the "idealism" inherent in the romantic mould found clear (if somewhat strange and perverse) expression.

Romanticism, however, as has been seen, contained within itself the seeds of realism and it is consequently not surprising to find, in the period when domestic melodrama flourished and Lytton essayed his first experiments in the comedy of manners, the arising of more naturalistic styles. Macready[3] and Samuel Phelps[4] were more colloquial than Kean; Kean's son, Charles, brought a "gentlemanly" air to melodrama and Alfred Wigan strained towards reality. In comedy Madame Vestris[5] and Charles Mathews[6] set new standards which provided a foundation for what was to come; the low comedian who had been so popular in the days of Charles Lamb gave place to performers of a more refined, more "genteel" and more versatile sort.

Thus was the way being paved for the theatre of the sixties and seventies. On April 15, 1865, Squire Bancroft made his debut in London under the management of Marie Wilton,

[1] The best account of his work is H. M. Hillebrand, *Edmund Kean* (New York, 1933).

[2] William Dunlap, *Memoirs of George Fred. Cooke* (2 vols. 1813).

[3] See *Macready's Reminiscences*, ed. Sir Frederick Pollock (2 vols. 1875) and W. Archer, *W. C. Macready* (1890).

[4] John Coleman, *Memoirs of Samuel Phelps* (1886), W. M. Phelps and J. Forbes-Robertson, *The Life and Life-work of Samuel Phelps* (1886).

[5] L. Waitzkin, *The Witch of Wych Street. A Study of the Reforms of Madame Vestris* (Cambridge, U.S.A. 1933).

[6] *Memoirs of Charles Mathews, Comedian* (4 vols. 1838–9).

who was later to become his wife, and with their conjunction a new era of comedy acting began.[1] This was recognised by contemporaries. "The new school of acting", writes one critic in the year 1888,[2]

> dates from the early days of the Bancrofts at the Prince of Wales's Theatre, and was the result of a most praiseworthy stand against the absurd artificialities and conventionalities then in vogue on the stage....How delighted fashionable audiences were with a system which replaced the grossest caricature of themselves, their manners and customs, with the closest and most faithful reproduction was at once proved by the rapid bounds by which the theatre at which that system first saw the light progressed in public esteem. The managers of the other houses, bewildered by the success which attended this new competition for public favour, at first attempted to explain it away, but ended by copying much of their rivals' method; and the new school thus spread from the stage of the Prince of Wales's to the other theatres of London. Still as the popularity of the Prince of Wales's flourished unabated, so also flourished and increased the new school of actors. That its efforts are uniformly successful from an artistic point of view can hardly be averred by any who desire to see on the stage any more lively display of the passions or humours of life than they can witness for nothing in their own houses....The dread of over-accentuating any display of the feelings has led to a diluted method of playing what should be strong scenes, and a half-hearted handling of strong characters, which have so long prevailed throughout the London Theatres that it is now impossible to expect a full-bodied performance, instinct with life and passion, save from a few players of the old regime.

This critic divined an essential truth. There can be no doubt but that the Bancrofts succeeded in banishing many follies and absurdities which had encrusted themselves upon the stage. Typical is Sir Squire Bancroft's account of the preparations for *Caste* (P.W. 1867).[3] Fred Younge was given the role of D'Alroy and Bancroft took that of Hawtree. The former was "amazed" when the latter "asked if he would mind being the fair man";

[1] Marie and Squire Bancroft, *The Bancrofts* (1909) and *Mr and Mrs Bancroft on and off the Stage* (1889).

[2] *The Saturday Review*, lxvi, Dec. 22, 1888, 741–2.

[3] *Mr and Mrs Bancroft on and off the Stage* (1889), p. 110.

he said how on earth could he do such a thing! He was the sentimental hero, and of course was intended to be dark; while, as what he described as the comic dandy or fop, I was equally compelled to be fair, and wear long flaxen whiskers.

Such things the Bancrofts put to shame, and in doing so inevitably they lost much of the old ranting vigour of the old-timers. Actors now, coming into society, were afraid to express their passions freely. Edmund Kean may have been lionised by lords and ladies in his day, but at a fashionable dinner-table he was rather an eccentric oddity than a genuinely honoured guest; his son, Charles Kean, was master of theatrical ceremonies to Queen Victoria and mingled freely with society. By the end of the century men did not gasp with indignant amazement when an actor was formally knighted by the crown—not for his contributions to charity, but because of his eminence on the stage. The contemporary change in histrionic method, observed the same critic in *The Saturday Review*,[1] was "founded essentially on the manners of the politer classes of society...as a protest against the exaggeration of which the old school of actors was continually guilty", and these politer classes could now be studied at first hand.[2] In place of "the stilted and declamatory style of an earlier generation" there was substituted a "suppressed emotion" and a "reserved force" which, when carried to excess, resulted in underacting. True, the most prominent member of the profession during those years, Sir Henry

[1] lxvi, Sept. 1, 1888, 266.

[2] Numerous books are concerned with the activities of actors during this period; among these may be mentioned Frank Archer, *An Actor's Notebooks* (1912); J. H. Barnes, *Forty Years on the Stage* (1914); A. H. Calvert, *Sixty-eight Years on the Stage* (1911); Mrs Patrick Campbell, *My Life and Some Letters* (1922); J. Coleman, *Players and Playwrights I have Known* (2 vols. 1888); C. and E. Compton, *Memoirs of Henry Compton* (1879); Dutton Cook, *Hours with the Players* (2 vols. 1881), *Nights at the Play* (2 vols. 1883) and *On the Stage* (2 vols. 1883); W. A. Donaldson, *Recollections of an Actor* (1865); A. Ellerslie, *The Diary of an Actress* (1885); D. Frohman, *Memories of a Manager* (1911); J. K. Jerome, *On the Stage—and Off* (1885); J. W. Marston, *Our Recent Actors* (2 vols. 1888); T. E. Pemberton, *The Kendals* (1900); A. J. Smythe, *The Life of William Terriss* (1898); J. L. Toole, *Reminiscences of J. L. Toole* (2 vols. 1889); C. M. Younge, *A Memoir of Charles Mayne Younge* (2 vols. 1891); A. E. W. Mason, *Sir George Alexander and the St James' Theatre* (1935).

Irving, did not accept the restraint and persisted in his own particular style of romantic interpretation; but Irving's method was a kind of *tour de force* and is not strictly typical of the dominant forces of the age.[1]

Unquestionably the English actors of this generation were considerably aided in their efforts by foreign example. On November 3, 1860, Fechter first performed in England and his influence may readily be traced on others. Although we might not now recognise his style as realistic, it contributed something to the new school. The Rotterdam and Saxe-Meiningen companies, even although—or perhaps precisely because—they included no star players, later made their influence felt. Nor must one forget the successive visits of Augustin Daly's actors from 1884 until, in 1893, Daly's Theatre was formally opened in London. The original visit, with the opening of Toole's Theatre on July 19, 1884, marks an historic occasion. From the time when, about the year 1700, Tony Aston sailed across the Atlantic, many English players had toured to America or had settled down there. For long, however, the passage was an arduous and difficult one. Even when Charles Kean crossed the ocean in 1833 the voyage lasted forty days. This, remarks his biographer, "was before the broad Atlantic had been spanned by steamers as with a bridge, reducing to hours what had formerly occupied days", so that the three thousand mile journey took about as long as "it took our ancestors a few generations back to rumble in a lumbering *diligence* from Edinburgh to London".[2]

[1] On Irving see E. Gordon Craig, *Henry Irving* (1930); W. Archer, *Henry Irving, Actor and Manager* (1883); A. Brereton, *The Life of Henry Irving* (1908) and *The Lyceum and Henry Irving* (1903); W. Calvert, *Sir Henry Irving and Miss Ellen Terry* (1897); H. A. Clapp, *Reminiscences of a Dramatic Critic. With an Essay on the Art of Henry Irving* (1902); P. Fitzgerald, *Henry Irving* (1893) and *Sir Henry Irving* (1906); C. Hiatt, *Henry Irving* (1899); F. Marshall, *Henry Irving, Actor and Manager* (1883); Clement Scott, *From The Bells to King Arthur* (1896). W. Archer and R. W. Lowe have a (now rare) satire, *The Fashionable Tragedian* (Edinburgh, 1877). On Ellen Terry see Clement Scott, *Ellen Terry* (N.Y., revised edition, 1900); Ellen Terry, *The Story of My Life* (1908) and *Memoirs* (1933); C. Hiatt, *Ellen Terry and her Impersonations* (1898); T. E. Pemberton, *Ellen Terry and her Sisters* (1902). On Tree see Max Beerbohm, *Herbert Beerbohm Tree* (1921).

[2] J. W. Cole, *op. cit.* i, 203.

Up to this time, hardly anyone thought of a reciprocal movement of actors to England, but, with the greater facilities for travel and with the rapid growth of the American stage, at last the time was reached when Daly could dare to bring over an entire American company—incidentally meeting with critical acclaim for his excellent stage management and for the performances of Ada Rehan and John Drew.[1]

With the introduction of new histrionic ideals and with the closer co-operation between stage and society, when it became no shame for persons "of gentle birth and education" to tread the boards,[2] many things which before had been passed over in indifference aroused public interest. In 1877 a "Dramatic Reform Association" is formally promulgated, its aim being to introduce a "higher standard of taste".[3] The question of child performers—hitherto undiscussed—becomes "a serious one", not lightly to be dismissed.[4] The schoolboards begin to take an interest in boys "who attended school in the morning, and in the afternoon and evening personified a Colorado Beetle and a French soldier" for a salary of 9*s*. weekly.[5] The actors come to take themselves more seriously, and in 1891 is held the first meeting of the Actors' Association, "an event", says *The Era*, "which may well be regarded with joy and triumph by the whole of the theatrical profession".[6]

By far the most sweeping change in conditions, however, effected by this new movement in the theatre was the complete dissolution of the stock company and the establishment of the long run. In the good old days a perfectly normal system was universally recognised. London had a number of theatres, in each of which was established a stock company

[1] J. F. Daly, *The Life of Augustin Daly* (New York, 1917). It is to be observed that from the very first Daly broke away from the traditional "lines of business" (*op. cit.* p. 90).

[2] *The Saturday Review*, lxvi, Dec. 15, 1888, 710.

[3] *The Theatre*, ii, Dec. 1877, 298–9.

[4] *The Era*, xl, Feb. 17, 1878, 12; *id.* xlix, May 21, 1887, 13.

[5] *The School Board and the Theatres* (*id.* xl, Feb. 10, 1878, 7); cf. *The Theatre*, N.S. xxv, March 1895, 140–3.

[6] *The Era*, liv, March 3, 1892, 13; cf. *id.* Dec. 3, 1892, 11; *id.* lv, July 22, 1893, 13; *The Athenaeum*, No. 3327, Aug. 1, 1891, p. 172.

or at least a company engaged for the season. When any deficiencies had to be made up, the managers looked for fresh talent among the scores of other stock companies which could be found either stationed in the larger provincial cities or else working the various circuits of smaller towns. It was recognised that, in ordinary circumstances, any young man or woman who intended to follow the profession had to put in a few years of training at these provincial schools; only rarely could a genius or a child of good fortune make his debut in London and be accepted into the Drury Lane or Covent Garden companies. Even when the days of stardom dawned and a Kean or a Macready went to glitter for a space in Birmingham or in Edinburgh, the troupe with which he played was the ordinary stock troupe of the town. Thus the "good stock company was a kind of histrionic nursery, the young actors and actresses of which were literally in a dramatic school", gaining excellent experience both by reason of the constant variation in the repertoire and by their occasional conjunction with visiting stars.[1]

Then arose the new public in London and the resultant long run. Actors became social personalities and were sought after by admiring audiences; the audiences had increased and found easy means of reaching the theatres; foreign visitors, because of accelerated Channel crossings, more frequently appeared in the auditoriums—for these and a dozen other reasons the long run became inevitable in London.[2] Starting tentatively in the abnormal days of the Great Exhibition of 1851, the movement rapidly gained in impetus as the years advanced. Charles Kean created a record with the hundred nights of his *Henry VIII* (P'cess, 1855), beat that record by fifty with *A Midsummer Night's Dream* (P'cess, 1856) and was easily outdistanced in a few years by Sothern's production of Taylor's *Our American Cousin* (H. 1861), and by Robertson's *Caste* (P.W. 1867). Instead of a constant change of bill, necessitating the maintenance of a salaried group of performers chosen for their recognised skill in portraying

[1] *The Stock Company Question* (*The Era*, lii, Dec. 14, 1889, 13).
[2] *The Theatre*, iii, Feb. 1878, 76.

type parts, the theatres subsisted on plays which ran for hundreds of nights, plays which were becoming increasingly naturalistic and hence demanded an interpretation of characters, not according to type parts but according to individualities. Naturally, the managers found that their most profitable plan was to get their play, study the *dramatis personae*, and engaged such performers as might best suit the requirements of the script.

This system established in London, the managers soon discovered a new additional source of income. The provincial cities were, like the metropolis, rapidly increasing and there too a vast audience was arising. Speedier methods of communication brought to them news of London's latest successes and inevitably was born a desire to see these successes reproduced. As a result, the metropolitan managers gathered a first, a second and even a third touring company and sent these out over the country.[1] Of necessity, because of this competition, the provincial stock companies disappeared and the old Theatres Royal, instead of being managed by men qualified in repertory work, passed into the hands of directors interested in nothing but profitable "bookings". Since these provincial theatres could now be hired or contracted for on a sharing basis, still another development occurred, for London managers came to find it convenient to produce a play first in the provinces and then bring it, polished after the "try-out", to the metropolis.[2]

[1] Considerable doubt exists concerning the origin of this practice. Ernest Reynolds, in *Early Victorian Drama (1830–70)* (Cambridge, 1936), pp. 67–8, declares that the earliest professional company touring with a single play was that of *Caste* in 1867. This tour was anticipated by the distinguished amateurs who, inspired by Dickens, took Lytton's *Not so bad as we seem* to the provinces in 1851. In 1892 it was noted (by Walter Baynham, in *The Glasgow Stage* (1892), p. 209) that "Mr Boucicault has been considered the first to introduce the present system of travelling companies, although the Haymarket company had... appeared with almost the full corps in 1849....The present system of bringing down a play with a complete cast was then but in perspective. The members of travelling corps eight and twenty years ago (i.e. in 1864) had to depend upon aid from those of the stock resident company."

[2] On this subject and on the growth of the suburban theatres see Robert Buchanan, *An Interesting Experiment* (*The Theatre*, N.S. xxviii, July 1896, 9–11), Henry Elliott, *The Suburban Theatre* (*id.* N.S. xxix, April 1897, 202–5) and John Hollingshead, *The Theatrical Radius* (*id.* N.S. xxx, Dec. 1897, 302–6).

The establishment of the long run produced many changes in the theatrical world. One result was that the young actor found himself without an adequate opportunity for training; another was that, instead of being able to see a fairly extensive collection of old and new plays presented in repertoire, audiences now were regaled either with long-run successes or occasional and elaborate revivals; from this generated decreasing opportunities for the young author and the inception of the commercial manager. These may occupy our attention for a moment.

An apprentice actor might obtain a part in a touring company but, if he were successful in gaining this role, he might "easily go round the provinces for eighteen months perseveringly playing the same part", without having any chance of acquiring versatility. So serious was this that in 1898 Beerbohm Tree declared that "nothing in these days is more destructive of true theatrical art than the long run".[1] This was the first problem that the stage had to settle. The second concerned the disappearance of the old repertory. "What is wanted in London", declared a writer in *The Pall Mall Gazette*,[2]

> is a theatre where it would be possible from time to time to play single performances of some of the plays that were once applauded as masterpieces and that now lie untroubled on the shelves by all save a few persistent students.... Such a work could, of course, only be done by private enterprise, by private enthusiasm. The revival of an old comedy at a regular theatre would not do, because it could not appeal to a public who would support it for a run.... The old tragedies, the old comedies, are not very expensive pieces to mount, and the chance of interpreting them now and then might be of no small advantage to young actors and to young actresses. The number of persons in London who would go sometimes to see a Restoration comedy or an Elizabethan tragedy is not in all probability very large, but also, in all probability, is larger than many would imagine.

[1] *The Pall Mall Gazette*, lxvi, June 16, 1898, 3. There is an important article on this subject, *The Provinces as a Dramatic School*, in *The Saturday Review*, lxvi, Oct. 13, 1888, 433–4. See also *id.* Nov. 3, 1888, 522–3 and *The Era*, xl, April 14, 1878, 7.

[2] lvi, Sept. 19, 1893, 4–5

If the public, or a part of it, were deprived of their old favourites, so that Jonson and others who had long held the stage were now theatrically forgotten, the playwrights had equally valid grounds for complaint. The long-run system had conduced to the establishment in London of two types of manager—the star actor, like Irving or Tree, who controlled the fortunes of a company, and the purely business man who, choosing what he considered to be a likely play, proceeded to finance its production. "The ease with which a man may become a manager without adequate equipment in money or knowledge of his business"[1] was a common theme of complaint. Against the actor-manager was preferred the accusation that he either subsisted on a series of revivals which cost him no royalties or else selected new plays which contained one fat part for himself.[2] That this objection was not without justification is easily demonstrated by a glance at the productions of Charles Kean at the Princess's and of Henry Irving at the Lyceum. So far as the commercial manager was concerned, the complaint most commonly expressed was that, in his want of knowledge and in his purely financial aims, he persisted in leaning upon the plays written by a limited number of already tried and recognised authors. His objection to the perusal of outsiders' manuscripts, his delay in returning these, his fondness for conventionality, his dread of novel ventures, and his profound belief in the value of a successful name on his playbill were all duly pilloried.[3] A letter written by W. Allingham to *The Athenaeum* demonstrates some of the difficulties and dangers associated with this attitude of the managers. "Your dramatic critic", he writes,

[1] *The Athenaeum*, No. 2394, Sept. 13, 1873, 347–8.

[2] *Dramatic Revivals* (*The Era*, xxxviii, July 9, 1876, 10). See on this subject *Dramatic Authors vs. Actor-Managers* (*The Saturday Review*, lxx, Aug. 9, 1890, 168–9) and Sydney Grundy, *The Dearth of Originality* (*The Theatre*, N.S. i, Nov. 1878, 274–7). Further discussions of this problem will be found in *The Fortnightly Review*, liii, April 1890, 499–516, June 1890, 922–36, liv, July 1890, 1–19, and in *The Nineteenth Century*, xxvii, June 1890, 1040–58.

[3] *The Theatre*, iii, no. 57, Feb. 27, 1878, pp. 74, 75; *The Era*, xxxix, Jan. 14, 1877, 4; *id.* xli, Sept. 22, 1878, 6; *The Pall Mall Gazette*, xxxi, May 14, 1880, 12; *The Athenaeum*, No. 3613, Jan. 23, 1897, 114.

having mentioned my play "Ashby Manor" in connexion with "The Lord Harry" at the Princess's Theatre, I am emboldened to send you a brief statement which seems to me to raise a not unimportant question. In 1883 I sent my play in print to Mr Wilson Barrett, and had, at his request, an interview with that gentleman, and a second one in 1884. He said he was "much struck" with "Ashby Manor", but it was not suitable for his company, and in any case would require "a great deal of pulling about". He made no proposal but asked if I had anything else to show him. Since then I have heard nothing. Mr Barrett has now produced "The Lord Harry", not only the germ of which is unquestionably in "Ashby Manor", though there has been extensive "pulling about" and much addition of sensational incident and scenery, unconnected with any plot—but also the personages in each are essentially identical.

The question, of some importance to the English drama, is this, How shall a writer outside theatrical circles bring a play under the eyes of managers without the risk that, should it contain anything of value for stage purposes, this will be appropriated without the smallest acknowledgement?[1]

One dramatic author in 1870 gave it as his belief that a play "from an unknown writer, although as brilliant as Sheridan or profound as Shakespeare" would stand little chance of being "accepted by a Manager for representation".[2] The existence of a "Dramatic Ring", due to "the cowardice of English managers" and "none the less effectual although not organised", was generally admitted.[3] "The cry that English authorship is dead", declared Grundy, "ought to be, rather, that English dramatic authorship has been murdered....The pressing requirement of the theatre is a manager who has the courage to avail himself of the wealth of dramatic genius which lies outside the Ring."

As a slight attempt to find a solution for these conditions came the matinée. The matinée system, whereby an author could hire a theatre for an afternoon or morning and present his untried play, served a useful purpose in mitigating the

[1] *The Athenaeum*, No. 3045, March 6, 1886, 338.
[2] *The Era*, xxxii, Jan. 23, 1870, 6.
[3] Sydney Grundy, *The Dramatic Ring* (*The Theatre*, N.S. iii, Dec. 1879, 273–7); H. A. Jones, *op. cit.* 163 (article first printed in *The English Illustrated Magazine*, Jan.–Feb. 1885); *The Era*, xxxix, Jan. 14, 1877, 4.

force of the established ring. No doubt the system brought with it many disadvantages, making "every third person one meets" consider himself a born dramatist, insistent "on putting his efforts before the public",[1] but the virtues of the device are apparent. It is true that the matinée soon ceased to present merely new plays and became an occasion for the addition of two weekly performances of popular productions, but throughout the greater part of this period it preserved its other functions.

The independent matinée, however, was not enough. Those with vision realised that to meet the needs of the time co-operative action was essential; the matinée idea might be used, but in a resolute and determined manner. Hence the growth of an element entirely new to the theatre—the stage society. Typical is the organisation known as The Dramatic Students, founded in 1886. Of it *The Saturday Review* has this to say:

> The Dramatic Students are a society of young professional actors, who, finding that the long runs now common in successful plays give them scant occasion to gain variety of skill in their art, have determined to bring out, in single morning performances, the less known masterpieces of English dramatic literature. They eschew such plays as are included in the ordinary repertory.... We follow their efforts with great interest, for we believe that these form the nucleus of a very wholesome revival of interest in the best theatrical writing....By-and-bye this seed will, we do not doubt, bear fruit, and the public will insist on seeing more of these interesting pieces, and on seeing them repeated. It is a sheer absurdity that our seventeenth century dramatic literature should be without dispute one of the richest ornaments of our language and yet that none of it, except three or four plays of Shakespeare's, should ever be seen, even for a moment on the stage.[2]

William Poel's activities[3] had a similar object and there were other ventures of the kind during the period. Akin to these was the Independent Theatre Society. Started by a few audacious and vigorous enthusiasts in 1891, it eventually

[1] *The Theatre*, N.S. xiv, July 1889, 12.
[2] lxi, Jan. 23, 1886, 116.
[3] *Supra*, p. 48.

passed on its mantle to The Stage Society eight years later. Perhaps it did not do all it set out to accomplish. In reviewing one of the plays presented under its auspices, the critic of *The Theatre*, at any rate, opined that it was sufficient to say "Independent Theatre play" in order "to indicate that its construction is amateurish and its theme unpleasant".[1] But, whatever its shortcomings, it undoubtedly achieved a great deal. "The Independent Theatre", wrote G. B. Shaw in 1895,

is an excellent institution, simply because it is independent. The lisparagers ask what it is independent of.... It is, of course, independent of commercial success.... If Mr Grein had not taken the dramatic critics of London and put them in a row before "Ghosts" and "The Wild Duck", with a certain small but inquisitive and influential body of enthusiasts behind them, we should be far less advanced today than we are. The real history of the drama for the last ten years is not the history of the prosperous enterprises of Mr Hare, Mr Irving, and the established West-end theatres, but of the forlorn hopes led by Mr Vernon, Mr Charrington, Mr Grein, Messrs Henly and Stevenson, Miss Achurch, Miss Robins and Miss Lea, Miss Farr and the rest of the Impossibilists.[2]

One danger of the Independent Theatre was that it might become a highbrow society, extolling commercial failure as an artistic virtue. "No author", notes Shaw, "whose play strikes, or is aimed at, the commercially successful pitch will give it to Mr Grein", and consequently he pleads for the presentation of one marketable play each year. Thus, in his opinion, the London managers might be persuaded to

help and cherish the Independent Theatre as a sort of laboratory in which they can have experiments tried on the public from time to time without the cost and responsibility incurred by, for example, Mr Beerbohm Tree in the experiments he made at the Haymarket with "Beau Austin" and "An Enemy of the People".

Another danger, commented on boldly by Antoine,[3] lay in

[1] *The Theatre*, N.S. xxv, Feb. 1895, 107.

[2] *The Saturday Review*, lxxix, Jan. 26, 1895, 126; cf. an article in *The Athenaeum*, No. 3557, Dec. 28, 1895, 912.

[3] See *The Pall Mall Gazette*, lxv, Sept. 28, 1897, 7.

the fact that this association directed its attention to the production of foreign plays rather than to the cultivation of native talent; but that, no doubt, was natural when Ibsen had swum into the horizon of the younger writers but was still looked on as a cloudy and rather ominous symbol by the over-respectable audiences in the commercial theatres.

Most important of all these movements were those which aimed at the establishment either of permanent endowed theatres or of dramatic schools. In the year 1875, the annual birthday exercises at Stratford were marked by "the inauguration of a Shakespearian scheme on a far grander scale than any which has preceded it". "It is contemplated", we are informed, "to build a Shakespeare Theatre in Shakespeare's native town, and it is considered feasible that a School, or University of Dramatic Art, can be established there, with its libraries, class-rooms, houses for instructors, scholarships for students, and special chairs for Professors."[1] This concept by many was combined with another—that of setting up in London a dramatic academy which might serve as a training school for young players and be to the theatre what the Royal Academy was to the world of art. In recording the Stratford proposals, *The Era* seized the opportunity to plead this cause:

> We would, at the outset, implore the prime movers in the scheme to decide definitely, and once for all, if the Shakespeare Memorial is intended as a tribute to mere sentiment, or is destined to have some sound and practical outcome....There is but one place in England which should be the headquarters of dramatic art—in London. Only in one place can a Shakespeare Theatre be erected—in London....For years and years we have talked of the institution of an Academy of [Dramatic] Art. Over and over again in these columns it has been urged that either Government aid or generous private enterprise would establish a dramatic mutual society like the Comedie Francaise of Molière in Paris, or an art school like the Parisian Conservatoire. Here at last is the foundation of one or other such scheme....Where...can Shakespeare's plays be better acted than in London, where we have the very pick of the Dramatic Profession?[2]

[1] *The Era*, xxxvii, May 2, 1875, 13. See also W. A. Chevalier, *A Tribute to the Shakespeare Memorial at Stratford-on-Avon. Outlines of a Scheme for Reforming the Stage* (1875). [2] *Id.* 13.

The prominence given to this subject in the newspapers of the time may not be overlooked. Dramatic academies of a sort had, of course, existed in earlier years, but they were trivial or private institutions. The Restoration "Nursery"[1] was one such; another, later, was the Musical and Dramatic Academy started by Glover and his wife at 21*a* Soho Square in 1848.[2] This new movement pointed to something on a larger, more ambitious scale, and, moreover, called into being a controversy which, not yet dead, indicated by its acrimony and persistence the widespread general interest in the subject. A serious attempt to start such a Dramatic College was made in 1876,[3] but objections were brought forward to its institution as "false in principle and useless in practice". "The radical mistake", it was thought, "was made in erecting such a building without the prospect of an endowment, and in believing that the housing of a few old pensioners of indifferent fame was the outcome of the theatrical revolution in this country."[4] A year later the chairman of the governors, Lord William Lennox, commented on the same subject. "The first stone of the Royal Dramatic College", he stated,

> was laid by the late Prince Consort. It was opened by his Royal Highness the Prince of Wales, and, therefore, we would suppose that, under such distinguished auspices, the Royal Dramatic College would not have had to do—what it does today—appeal to the public for funds to carry it on.[5]

The performances given by the students of the College met with some approval, but apparently it soon ceased to function for lack of support; at any rate a new plea was being made in 1879 for "an academy of acting",[6] followed again by a

[1] *A History of Restoration Drama* (1928), pp. 280–1.

[2] *The Theatrical Journal* Feb. 24, 1848.

[3] Already on Jan. 12, 1859, a meeting had been called at the Adelphi Theatre for the purpose of discussing the establishment of a Royal Dramatic College; Charles Kean, Benjamin Webster, Charles Dickens and W. M. Thackeray were made trustees of this venture. See H. Dodd, *Royal Dramatic College: Correspondence respecting proposed gift of land* (1859).

[4] *The Era*, xxxviii, July 30, 1876, 10; cf. also *id.* July 23, 1876, 10.

[5] *Id.* xxix, Feb. 25, 1877, 12.

[6] *The Theatre*, N.S. iii, Sept. 1879, 61–4.

proposal to establish a Royal Academy of Dramatic Art. This met with the unqualified approval of W. E. Henley.[1] For it he envisaged many useful functions:

It might sit as a jury on unpublished plays and unknown playwrights....In time it might build a theatre...and the National Theatre would be the issue...it would create, organise, and control a complete system of instruction.

and, he thought, if the instructors "did but half their duty, they would make technical incapacity far rarer on the English stage than it is". In 1882 the question was still being debated. Hamilton Aidé then launched a fresh plea, arguing the case rather more fully than his predecessors had done:

It is rather singular that, of all the arts, the one which is perhaps the most popular, judging by the crowds that flock nightly to an increasing number of theatres, is the only one for which, up to the present time, no school or organised system of education upon any considerable scale has been provided. There was a time when the want of such definite routine of instruction was supplied by means no longer at our command—the constant variety of practice in country theatres, and the stream of tradition unbroken for several generations, simultaneously training and exercising the capacities of actors, and maintaining a standard whereby their efforts might be gauged. But the stream of tradition is dry, and country theatres have no longer stock companies. The system of long runs in London, and of importing the pieces which have enjoyed them into the provinces, is disastrous to the true interests of the Drama. That the performances must suffer after a time, and that the best artists in the world must unconsciously exaggerate or flag, after the weary iteration of months, is self-evident. What the audience is less likely to remember is, how this condition of things on the stage necessarily affects the beginners in the profession....It is with the view of raising the standard of education on the stage, and, by offering some obstacles to indolent incompetency, of clearing the ground for the more active and industrious, that an association has lately been formed in the hope of creating a School of Dramatic Art. Other schemes of a like character have in past years been projected; but, for some cause or another, they have all of them collapsed before they reached maturity....

[1] *A Corporation of Actors* (*The Theatre*, N.S. ii, Nov. 1880, 274–9).

The present association, however, is formed under exceptional conditions.[1]

The committee of this new venture included Lytton, Tennyson, Mathew Arnold, Henry Morley and Wilkie Collins. Tentatively an academy was opened in October 1882, but was forced to close in 1885. *The Quarterly Review* in 1883 had a long article dealing with the disappearance of the old stock companies,[2] and five years later *The Saturday Review* was still commenting on the imperative need of a dramatic school in London.[3] "The supplanting of the stock companies by casts engaged for the run of the piece in town and by touring companies in the country" was here again noted as having effected a revolution. "The provinces, theatrically considered," it was found, "have in fact so completely surrendered their importance and independence to the preponderating influence of the metropolis, and have for so many years been content to take their dramatic supply at second-hand from that fountain-head, that it is useless to expect the origination of any important change except in town." The method, as this writer saw it, was to arouse the self-seeking London managers to some kind of disinterested effort.[4]

About this time, several articles were published, complaining of the want of proper theatrical instruction and proposing a revival of ancient traditions. In 1890, however, B. W. Findon, in a general survey of the whole subject, decided that nothing could be done towards a resuscitation of the old provincial stock companies. That solution, he believed, was hopeless. Although he fully realised that something positive had to be done, he feared, on the other hand, that "a State-aided school would quickly become fossilized, and produce nothing but dramatic dummies". Hence followed an interesting suggestion that "the future School of

[1] *A Dramatic School* (*The Theatre*, N.S. v, Feb. 1882, 73–6). See also, *A Dramatic School of Art* (*Truth*, xi, June 1, 1882, 756), *A Subventioned Theatre* (*id.* iii, March 21, 1878, 361) and *A Dramatic Academy* (*id.* vii, Jan. 22, 1880, 109).

[2] clv, April 1883, 354–88.

[3] lxvi, Nov. 17, 1888, 581–2.

[4] Cf. *id.* lxvi, Nov. 24, 1888, 615.

Dramatic Art is the amateur dramatic club". With this idea in mind, Findon proposed "the formation of a Grand Central Club"—the British Drama League of to-day—"to which all amateur clubs" should "have the right to be affiliated on payment of an annual subscription". The whole movement, he thought, should be initiated and controlled by professionals, for it

> must, above all things, have the active support of the theatrical manager. It must be clearly and distinctly understood that he will regard it as his recruiting ground, and that it shall be to the stage what our great military schools are to the army.[1]

So the various efforts proceeded. In 1895 S. J. Adair Fitzgerald was pleading once more for a Royal Academy of Dramatic Art[2]—"a sort of dramatic Athenaeum and Museum combined, containing a theatre, lecture rooms, galleries, and a library". And when we leave this half-century, in 1900, a writer in *The Era* is still proclaiming that

> it would be the grandest thing of all if the committee which is to be formed by, or for, the Actor's Association could permanently establish an academy of acting—the "Royal Academy of the Drama" would follow after.[3]

That but little success attended the efforts of the several sponsors counts as nothing compared with the vast amount of public interest involved and with the fact that eventually out of all this discussion grew the present Royal Academy of Dramatic Art. Similarly, the failure to establish a National Theatre should not blind our eyes to the immense publicity which the idea of a permanent home for the classic drama received between 1870 and 1900. A scheme for such a national theatre had been promulgated as early as 1848, but once more the seventies witnessed the first determined effort in that direction, Tom Taylor arguing in favour[4] and Thomas Purnell

[1] *The Amateur Club as a Stepping-Stone to the Stage* (*The Theatre*, N.S. xvi, Aug. 1890, 63–7).

[2] *Id.* N.S. xxv, June 1895, 344–6.

[3] lxiii, April 14, 1900, 11.

[4] See the series of letters contributed by him to *The Echo* on June 7, 1871, and subsequent dates.

against.[1] The controversy proceeded apace. H. J. Byron, George Godwin and others took various sides in *The Theatre* during the years 1878 and 1879.[2] On October 8, 1879, Mrs Pfeiffer restimulated interest in the subject by a letter contributed to *The Times*, and an offer of £100 towards its accomplishment was announced towards the end of that month.[3] Ten years later, in *A Plea for an Endowed Theatre*, William Archer went over again the same old arguments,[4] receiving the critical and enthusiastic support of *The Saturday Review*.[5] William Poel discussed *The Functions of a National Theatre* in 1893;[6] Sir Edward Russell put forward another plan in 1897;[7] and Sir Henry Irving, in an address delivered in 1894, discussed the desirability of having subsidised municipal theatres.[8] As we reach the end of the period, we find that the seemingly interminable discussion results in a prospectus issued for a National Theatre Company, Limited.[9]

The space devoted to these projects is justified in that nothing could present a clearer picture of the atmosphere amid which authors and actors worked and of the definite needs of the time. If, however, the authors complained and felt that only subsidised theatres could provide alleviation for the abuses of the time, it is to be noted that their fortunes, during the last two decades of the century, had markedly

[1] *Op. cit.* pp. 13–17. A plea for a national theatre was separately put forward by Henry Neville in *The Stage: Its Past and Present in Relation to Fine Art*, an address delivered in 1871 and published in 1875.

[2] *A Subsidised Theatre for London* (*The Theatre*, N.S. i, Aug. 1878, 7–11), H. J. Byron, *The Other Side of the Question* (*id.* Sept. 1878, 109–12), George Godwin, *The National Theatre Question* (*id.* Dec. 1878, 346–52), Henry Peat, *Objections to State Aid* (*id.* N.S. ii, Feb. 1879, 28–31), *A National Theatre* (*id.* April 1879, 147–50), *A National Theatre* (*Truth*, v, Feb. 6, 1879, 160).

[3] *The Era*, xli, Oct. 26, 1879, 5. For other contemporary comments see *The Era*, xxxiii, July 23, 1871, 12; xxxvii, Jan. 10, 1875, 11; xli, Nov. 2, 1879, 12; xli, Oct. 12, 1879, 12; *The Quarterly Review*, cxxxii, No. 263, Jan. 1872, 1–26.

[4] *The Fortnightly Review*, xlv, May 1889, 610–26.

[5] lxvii, May 11, 1889, 567.

[6] *The Theatre*, xxii, Sept. 1893, 164–6.

[7] *Id.* xxx, July 1897, 10–14.

[8] *The Pall Mall Gazette*, lix, Sept. 27, 1894, 8.

[9] *Id.* lxxi, July 21, 1900.

improved. In the seventies Dion Boucicault could still complain of low income from playwriting and of French competition. As an example he narrates how some thirty years before he had been offered £100 for a new drama and how, on his protesting, the manager had replied: "I can go to Paris and select a first-class comedy; having seen it performed, I feel certain of its effect. To get this comedy translated will cost me £25. Why should I give £300 or £500 for your comedy, of the success of which I cannot feel so assured?"[1] There was no wonder that Boucicault bitterly pilloried this type of man who, "in most instances, received his education in a bar room, possibly on the far side of the counter". About the same time, Frank Marshall[2] declared that "the difficulties which beset the path of a dramatist nowadays who would give us original plays of real literary merit are almost insuperable". Among his reasons for making this statement he adduces the popularity of French adaptations, the small fame and profits accruing from dramatic composition and the fact that plays could not be printed without the loss of acting rights.

Yet even then, in the seventies, a revolution had occurred which was destined to transform the entire profession of playwriting. In 1847, or thereabouts, Boucicault had been offered £100 for an original play.[3] This was a fairly normal recompense. Charles Reade and Tom Taylor received a total of £150 for *Masks and Faces* (H. 1852) and £100 for *Two Loves and a Life* (Adel. 1854).[4] The latter's *Our American Cousin* (H. 1861), which netted the management over £20,000, brought the author only £150.[5] A few privileged writers might expect a trifle more; Charles Kean paid G. W. Lovell £400 for *The Wife's Secret* (H. 1848), gave Douglas Jerrold

[1] *The Theatre*, i, Sept. 1877, 141–2; cf. *The Era*, xxxix, June 3, 1877, 12 and *id.* xli, April 13, 1879, 7–8.

[2] *The Drama of the Day in its Relation to Literature* (*The Theatre*, N.S. i, Aug. 1878, 23–6).

[3] No mention is made in this reference to benefits. The change in stage economics is to be seen in the attack made, during the seventies, on the benefit system (*The Athenaeum*, No. 2394, Sept. 13, 1873, 347–8).

[4] Malcolm Elwin, *Charles Reade* (1931), pp. 85 and 101.

[5] *The Theatre*, N.S. iii, Dec. 1879, 265.

£300 each for *A Heart of Gold* (P'cess, 1854) and *St Cupid* (P'cess, 1853), and even went so far as to offer Knowles £1000 for a new play;[1] but the ordinary author could not look for more than a maximum of about £50 per act. For this reason many of them were willing to hire themselves out as stock-dramatists at annual salaries; for a time Morton and Boucicault wrote exclusively for the Princess's,[2] MacDermott for the Grecian, Hazlewood for the Britannia, à Beckett for the St James's, W. Brough for the Lyceum and Faucit for the Victoria.[3] All this was before a startling revolution casually introduced by Boucicault. In the year 1860, when he took his *Colleen Bawn* (Adel. 1860) to Webster, he made a novel proposal; instead of asking for a lump sum, he suggested sharing terms—and found himself eventually the richer by £10,000.[4] At first the full significance of this was not recognised. Some of the astuter authors—such as Burnand who, by making similar arrangements, cleared £2000 for his *Ixion* (Roy. 1863) and as much for *Black-eyed Susan* (Roy. 1866)—eagerly followed Boucicault's example, but the practice did not become universal until the eighties. Even in 1879 F. C. Burnand found it necessary to remind his fellows that every playwright ought to demand 10% of the gross receipts of the production;[5] it is known that James Albery received a flat sum of only £3 a performance for *Two Roses* (Vaud. 1870) and of £2 a performance for *Tweedie's Rights* (Vaud. 1871).[6] The general adoption of the new plan brought considerable changes; instead of a bevy of hack authors there came into being the privileged members of the "Dramatic Ring". "It is easier to make a fortune than to earn a livelihood by

[1] J. W. Cole, *op. cit.* i, 343 and 323.

[2] Townsend Walsh, *The Career of Dion Boucicault* (New York, 1915), p. 42; J. W. Cole, *op. cit.* ii, 133.

[3] Errol Sherson, *London's Lost Theatres of the Nineteenth Century* (1925), p. 97.

[4] Arthur à Beckett, *The Earnings of Playwrights and Players* (*The Theatre*, N.S. xxvi, Oct. 1895, 209–13). In 1874 Boucicault asked Augustin Daly for a 12% royalty (to be divided between himself and Bret Harte) for a play (J. F. Daly, *op. cit.* p. 173).

[5] *Authors and Managers* (*The Theatre*, N.S. ii, Feb. 1879, 14–17).

[6] *The Dramatic Works of James Albery*, ed. by W. Albery (1939), i, xxviii.

writing plays" had become a just judgment by the year 1896.[1]

The possibility of making their fortunes had the result of attracting to the theatre many men who in previous years would have devoted themselves entirely to the novel. G. B. Shaw, despite his vivid theatricality, almost certainly would have joined Thackeray and Dickens had he flourished in 1840.[2] For a time, it is true, one other thing served to hold back these authors from the stage. The Copyright Act of 1833 had brought the work of the dramatists alongside the work of other literary artists, but some doubts and difficulties remained.[3] One was of a practical kind, for stage copyright was based on actual performance of the play. To comply with the law, authors and managers turned to the provinces, where many "copyright performances" were presented, or else made use of the newly developing matinee for a similar purpose. Many of these productions seem to have been little more than perfunctory readings, and consequently induced complaints.[4] More serious was the problem of American copyrights. The United States had now become a great theatrical centre, and much additional income, it was seen, might accrue from the successful performance of new dramas there. But no law prevented a manager in New York from taking the printed text of such a drama and presenting it without payment of a single cent. Of this a moving testimony remains in Lacy's edition of *Maud's Peril* (Adel. 1867); this

[1] Leopold Wagner, *Playwriting: Past and Present* (*The Theatre*, N.S. xxviii, Aug. 1896, 66–8). It should be noted that, in addition to London royalties, additional sums could now be made from "country royalties". Morton, it is said, drew over £500 a year from this source, the money being collected by the Dramatic Authors' Society (A. W. à Beckett, *Green-Room Recollections* (1896), p. 254).

[2] This movement of literary men to the theatre, because of increased returns, is emphasised by Mrs Alec Tweedie, *Behind the Footlights* (1904), pp. 95–7.

[3] *Dramatic Copyright* (*The Era*, xlvi, Aug. 30, 1884, 7–8); *Dramatic Copyright* (*The Athenaeum*, Nov. 21, 1874). The conditions of 1873 are fully outlined in J. Coryton's *Stage Right. A Compendium of the Law relating to Dramatic Authors* (1873). See also *A Handy-book on the Law of the Drama and Music* (1864) and B. W. Weller, *Stage Copyright at Home and Abroad* (1912).

[4] Mrs Alec Tweedie, *Behind the Footlights* (1904), pp. 95–7.

is dedicated by Watts Phillips, "with feelings of deep disgust, to the Thief of Thieves, who, by means of shorthand, or other petty larceny devices, caused a mutilated copy of the work to be circulated in America, to the detriment of the Author". Hoping that such "petty larceny devices" would not be successful, the English dramatist frequently found that it was to his advantage to keep his play unpublished, and the careful guarding of manuscript became almost an echo of a similar treasuring of precious prompt-books in the days of Elizabeth. By the eighties, however, this state of affairs had attracted sufficient attention to call for immediate action. An international copyright agreement was signed in 1887;[1] this covered most of the European countries. Much more important was the American copyright bill which came at the beginning of the last decade of the century.[2] Quite apart from the additional incomes it now offered to successful dramatists, it established an entirely new set of conditions. Already in its first comment on the agreement, *The Era* hinted at its possible influence:

> There is...one ray of hope for English authors in the act. It has been often suggested that they should more frequently publish their plays for reading purposes. As is well known, this is done to a great extent in France, and the French dramatists reap no inconsiderable rewards from this source. On this side of the Channel, Mr W. S. Gilbert is, we believe, almost the only modern author who has published his works; but we understand that the experiment has not been unprofitable to him. If the English authors, indeed, would take the trouble—as the French dramatists do—to prepare their plays for the press in a readable form, and not present them in the "acting edition" shape, with its irritating stage directions, and with the names of the speakers at the side of the page, we believe that the best works of such authors as Mr H. A. Jones and Mr Pinero would be perused by no small section of the British public....We are never likely to have a native drama of much literary merit without the practice of publication to emphasise conscientious finish and rebuke slovenly writing.[3]

[1] *The Era*, i, Dec. 10, 1887, 9.

[2] See *A Petition to the Senate...for the Amendment of the Copyright Law...from the Dramatists, Theatrical Managers and other Members of the Dramatic Profession* (New York, 1891).

[3] *The Era*, liii, Jan. 10, 1891, 15. H. A. Jones's comments on this Act in the preface to *Saints and Sinners* (Vaud. 1884) are well known.

The hope expressed by the editor of *The Era* was carried to realisation. From the year when this Act was passed a complete change came to the printed drama. Samuel French still continues to issue his "acting plays", but the more ambitious authors turn now to address their works to a reading public. Stage directions are completely revolutionised; instead of the old L.C. and P.S. and R.C., intelligible only to those versed in theatrical abbreviations and designed for the guidance of acting groups, there are introduced ever lengthier and lengthier descriptions of the set, of the characters, of the movements until the descriptive material has sometimes come to assume equal importance with the dialogue. Dramatically, of course, these new stage directions have little interest for us; carried to excess, they have led some authors seriously astray; but they serve to demonstrate the fresh appeal which was being made by the modern drama.

In every way now men of literary genius could be attracted to the theatre; they were tempted by the possibility of great material rewards and they knew that their work, if worthy, would no longer be forced to remain in guarded manuscript or, at best, be issued in cheap series of stage texts, but were likely to appear in dignified form apt to appeal to the ordinary reading public.

CHAPTER II

CONTEMPORARY DRAMATIC CONDITIONS

THE stage was thus set in the seventies for the dramatic renascence. The audience had increased and become more representative of all classes in the nation; the theatre had found a new ideal which, if ridiculous when carried to excess, had vitality and inspiration in it; the dramatic author suddenly discovered that he had walked into a realm, spiritually and materially different from that inhabited by the melodramatists and extravaganza writers who, fifty years before, had been compelled to turn out hundreds upon hundreds of plays if they were to hope that the howling wolf might be directed from their doors.

That this revival may be traced back evenly in the evolution of the English stage is obvious; equally obvious is the fact that it was not confined to England. Indeed, such progressive strides had been taken during the nineteenth century by the French, Russian and Scandinavian theatres that there has been a tendency among some writers on this subject to explain the awakening of dramatic interest in London by reference to outside influences. Such an interpretation of events is unquestionably false, yet it is impossible to pass to another extreme and attempt to deny those influences. The truth lies between the two positions. The English stage was independently moving towards this "renascence", but, when conditions were favourable, various European developments certainly stimulated and strengthened the movement of youth in London.

Even the most cursory glance at the fortunes of the European stage during the nineteenth century makes clear the fact that the revolutions already described had their counterparts abroad and also that generally these revolutions reached fulfilment at a considerably earlier period than they did in London. Work of a genuinely modern character does not proceed from the pens of English dramatists till the eighties and nineties; indeed, one might go further and say that plays of this sort are hardly to be found before the year 1895. Yet by 1868 Henri Becque, a man responsible for developing a strong and vital naturalism in the playhouse, had produced *Le prodigue*, and by 1882, with *Les corbeaux*, had reached his full maturity.[1] Partly through the influence of Becque's naturalism, the Théâtre Libre was established by Antoine in 1887, and with the stimulus provided by this organisation came into being a group of notable dramatists—François de Curel, Villiers de l'Isle Adam, Georges Ancey, Léon Hennique, Jean Jullien, Georges de Porto-Riche, Pierre Wolff, Georges Courteline and Eugène Brieux. To compare the work that these men were doing in the eighties and nineties with the contemporary repertoire of London playhouses brings an immediate realisation of the relatively fettered expression exhibited by the English stage. Realism may seem to us now an outworn ideal; in following its paths the dramatists of this time may appear to be following idols false because uninspired with any imaginative glow; but undoubtedly we are forced to admit that the playwrights in Paris were more successful than their English confrères in attaining what they sought. These French dramatists wanted a realistic approach and

[1] On the "advance" movement in Europe during this time see Anna Irene Miller, *The Independent Theatre in Europe: 1887 to the Present* (1931) and S. M. Waxman, *Antoine and the Théâtre Libre* (1926). There are many studies of the major dramatists; of these may be mentioned Storm Jameson, *Modern Drama in Europe* (1920), L. Lewisohn, *The Modern Drama* (1915), A. Henderson, *European Dramatists* (1914), E. E. Hale, *Dramatists of Today* (1911), J. G. Huneker, *Iconoclasts: A Book of Dramatists* (1905), Ashley Dukes, *Modern Dramatists* (1912) and G. Brandes, *Creative Spirits of the XX Century* (1903). A useful survey is Barrett H. Clark's *A Study of the Modern Drama* (1925). On the French theatre of the time see Brander Matthews, *French Dramatists of the Nineteenth Century* (New York, 1924), F. W. Chandler, *The Contemporary Drama of France* (1920), N. C. Arvin, *Eugene Scribe and the French Theatre, 1815–1860* (1924), H. A. Smith, *Main Currents of Modern French Drama* (1925), J. A. Hart, *Sardou and the Sardou Play* (1913) and Barrett H. Clark, *Contemporary French Dramatists* (1915).

they found it; most of the English dramatists obviously wished to build their plays out of the common stuff of life, but only too frequently they permitted the old conventionalism to distract them and thwart them in their aims. That occasionally these old conventions, because they were born of an essentially popular theatre, gave a kind of melodramatic vigour to the English plays is certainly true; nevertheless, such vigour proved often but a poor compensation for the loss of unity and harmony attendant upon this confusion of spirit.

Germany displayed a similar energy and forcefulness. There, far off in the days when London was subsisting on extravaganza and melodramatic excitement, Friedrich Hebbel was writing in a strain definitely "modern" because of its intensity and technical brilliance, while Otto Ludwig with *Der Erbförster* (1849) explored the possibilities of the naturalistic method in a manner hitherto untried.[1] By the year 1889 the Freie Bühne had been founded in Berlin; during that year came the production of Hauptmann's *Vor Sonnenaufgang*. *Die Weber*, a play far in advance of anything the London theatres had then to offer, was written three years later, in 1892. Hermann Sudermann's dramatic debut occurred contemporaneously, his *Die Ehre* being presented in 1889 and *Die Heimat* in 1893; the year 1889 saw the appearance of Frank Wedekind's *Die junge Welt*, and two years later *Frühlings Erwachen* was given to the public. While this movement was thus progressing in Berlin, Vienna remained by no means inactive. By 1887 Hermann Bahr had started to experiment with his ironic social comedy; Anton Schnitzler in 1893 first displayed his peculiarly brilliant and mordant genius; in 1891 Hugo von Hofmannsthal presented the earliest of a series of plays in which to dramaturgic skill was united a literary grace unique in its individuality.

During the time when France and Germany were thus awakening to a new spirit in the theatre, other countries,

[1] Georg Witkowski, *The German Drama of the Nineteenth Century* (1909), C. von Klenze, *From Goethe to Hauptmann* (1926) and M. Martersteig, *Das deutsche Theater im neunzehnten Jahrhundert* (Leipzig, 1924).

even the most remote, experienced a similar renascence. To have said in a London greenroom of the eighties that any drama of worth might be discovered in the land of the almighty Tsar would, no doubt, have aroused a burst of jeering merriment; yet Russia was at that time building up a stage whereon were displayed a fine sense of character delineation, an appreciation of subtle dramatic values and an enthusiasm far surpassing anything yet accomplished in England.[1] Leo Tolstoi's *The Nihilist* was written as early as 1863, some years before Tom Robertson's initial efforts in social comedy; *The Power of Darkness*, which, whatever we may think of its dramatic quality, displays a vigour and an intransigent spirit unrecognisable in any English plays of the time, appeared in 1886. Two years before that, in 1884, Anton Chekhov completed *On the High Road*, while the year 1889 brought *The Swan Song* and 1896 *The Sea-Gull*.[2] Not until the twentieth century was this Russian drama appreciated in the rest of Europe, yet its worth and its vision could have caused no surprise in the minds of those able to compare such a play as A. S. Griboiedov's *The Misfortune of Being Clever*, written in 1823, with any work of a similar kind contemporaneously presented in the London theatres.

The most extraordinary and significant development, however, came from a land even more distant from men's minds than Russia. Henrik Ibsen was born at Skien, Norway, in 1828.[3] His first play, *Catiline*, was written when he was twenty-two years of age and ushered in a series of historical romances. From *The Warrior's Barrow* of 1854 to *Emperor and Galilean* his dramas were historical or legendary in subject-matter and idealistically lyrical in mood. Then came *Pillars*

[1] Leo Wiener, *The Contemporary Drama of Russia* (1924), Oliver M. Sayler, *The Russian Theater* (1922), Alexander Bakshy, *The Path of the Modern Russian Stage* (1916). *The Russian Theatre* (1930) by René Fülöp-Miller and Joseph Gregor presents a well-illustrated survey with special attention to the Soviet playhouse.

[2] Anton Chekhov, *Literary and Theatrical Reminiscences*, translated by S. S. Koteliansky (1923) and C. Stanislavski, *My Life in Art* (1924).

[3] H. Koht, *The Life of Ibsen* (1931), E. Gosse, *Henrik Ibsen* (1908), H. Rose, *Henrik Ibsen* (1913), O. Heller, *Henrik Ibsen, Plays and Problems* (1912), M. J. Moses, *Henrik Ibsen: the Man and his Plays* (1908), and H. J. Weigand, *Modern Ibsen: A Reconsideration* (1925).

of Society in 1877, followed by *A Doll's House* (1879), *Ghosts* (1881), *An Enemy of the People* (1882), and *The Wild Duck* (1884). In *The Wild Duck* a new mood entered; the barer realism shaded into symbolism, with a definite progression from *Rosmersholm* (1886), through *The Lady from the Sea* (1888), *Hedda Gabler* (1890), *The Master Builder* (1892), *Little Eyolf* (1894) and *John Gabriel Borkman* (1894), to *When We Dead Awaken* (1899). It is truly extraordinary to think that Ibsen's work was completed ere Shaw's had barely begun—completed when the English stage was still struggling to secure its freedom. Nor was Ibsen alone in the Scandinavian countries. Bjørnstjerne Bjørnson was born only four years later than he, and, after a kindred series of experiments in historical drama, also turned, with *The Newly-married Couple* (1865), to realistic treatment of ordinary life. *A Gauntlet*, perhaps his best play, was produced in 1883.[1] Then, strangest and in some respects strongest figure of all, came August Strindberg, whose *The Father* (1887), *Comrades* (1888) and *Miss Julie* (1888) provide a stark penetration into life and a piercing psychological analysis unique in their uncompromising vigour.[2]

Although many of the more revolutionary plays did not come to English authors' notice until the twentieth century, there is no need of trying to demonstrate that this widespread European movement did not contribute largely to London's dramatic renascence; all we may do is to emphasise, first, that the London theatres assumed a fresh vitality quite independently of the continental movement, secondly, that this fresh vitality is to be easily traced back to the melodramatic theatre of the forties, and thirdly, that even when we reach the last years of the century we can see the popular interest in the stage often battling against instead of alongside the newer continental ideals. When the half-century opened, we are in the midst of a free filching from the French—a filching, moreover, which, with a monotonous regularity, selected only

[1] W. M. Payne, *Bjørnstjerne Bjørnson* (1903).

[2] V. J. McGill, *August Strindberg, the Bedeviled Viking* (1930) and L. Lind-af-Hageby, *August Strindberg, the Spirit of Revolt* (1913).

the lesser, the least thoughtful and technically the most conservative of plays. "At this moment", remarks Percy Fitzgerald as late as 1881,

> it may be said that the English stage is virtually subsisting on the French. What a contrast this to the old days of exuberant native production, when Dibdin, dying so lately as 1841, was stated to be the author of 200 pieces, and Mr Planché of over 100!—[1]

forgetting the wholesale borrowing from Paris in these good old times. The complaints continued down to the end of the century; in 1897 Edward Morton lamented that

> the theatrical entertainment offered by the capital of the greatest empire of the world includes one play, and only one, by an English dramatist of repute.[2]

The rest were merely "versions" of Gallic dramas.

This was the usual kind of adaptation; only in the last decade of the century did there arise any real appreciation either of new technical methods or of the fresh ideals exemplified in the plays of Ibsen and his companions. To William Archer belongs the credit of preaching Ibsen's worth and of introducing him to the English public[3]—a task in which he received considerable aid from J. T. Grein and G. B. Shaw. This task was an uphill one. Even such a "modern" as Max Beerbohm could not find sympathy for "Mr Shaw's desire to Ibsenise the English stage from footlights to flies",[4] although he recognised the eminence of the Norwegian dramatist.[5] In 1893 Joseph Knight declared that his influence was "not as yet far-reaching",[6] even among the more progressive writers. The plays, in English dress, started to come before the public in the eighties, but it was not until the next decade that the fame of the author became promulgated. *Quicksands;*

[1] *Op. cit.* p. 289.

[2] *The French Invasion* (*The Theatre*, N.S. xxx, July 1897, 27–9); see also *French Authors and English Adapters* (*id.* N.S. i, Dec. 1878, 329–32).

[3] On Ibsen in England see Robert Huber, *Ibsens Bedeutung für das englische Drama* (Marburg, 1914), G. B. Shaw, *The Quintessence of Ibsenism* (1913) and Miriam A. Franc, *Ibsen in England* (1919).

[4] *The Saturday Review*, lxxxv, April 9, 1898, 482.

[5] *Id.* lxxxviii, July 1899, 102.

[6] *Theatrical Notes* (1893), xv.

or, The Pillars of Society appeared at the Gaiety as early as 1880, but *Rosmersholm* had to wait until 1891[1] for production. When they eventually arrived they were met by a blast of sometimes good-natured but more frequently embittered abuse. Burlesques like *Rosmer of Rosmersholm* (1891) and *Jerry-Builder Solness* (St G. 1893) made fun of their novel features, while critics and correspondents reviled their ideas in the press. An open letter addressed to William Archer in 1897 described Ibsen as

> a dramatist who, apart from the non-construction of his alleged plays, deliberately selects his subjects from the most sordid, abject, even the most revolting corners of human life, relieving the crushing effect of their hideous monotony only by a mechanical joyless mirth like the crackling of thorns.[2]

"Go out from the moral leper house", trumpeted Clement Scott,

> and hospital and society dissecting room, reeking with the smell of dissolution, and tell us something of the cleanliness that is next to Godliness; something of the trials and struggles of the just, the sorely-tried, the tempted, and the pure.[3]

"Candidly," wrote another critic of an "Ibsenite" play,

> this continued harping upon nauseous topics is becoming something more than tiresome, and it is high time an emphatic protest were made against the growing custom of turning the theatre into a social lazar-house.[4]

Ibsen, then, was introduced with much difficulty to the stage, and many heartburning controversies had to be indulged in before he became accepted by all as a master undoubted and supreme. Throughout this period his influence was less than that of many another continental author—such as Scribe—who, less daring, tried pathos made familiar by the tread of unadventuresome feet.

Among the influences on the drama of this time must be

[1] *Rosmersholm* (Vaud. 1891) and *Beata* (Glo. 1892).
[2] *The Theatre*, N.S. xxx, July 1897, 7.
[3] *The Modern Society Play* (*The Theatre*, N.S. xxv, Jan. 1895, 6–10).
[4] *Id.* p. 46.

reckoned that of contemporary fiction, both native and foreign. Scott and Dickens had already provided founts of inspiration for the melodramatists of the preceding half-century, and still their works continued to be used for plot material. It is instructive to note that no less than eight versions of *Ivanhoe* are recorded between 1850 and 1900,[1] and five of *The Heart of Midlothian.*[2] New novels by Dickens were eagerly seized upon and old ones were redramatised. There were at least eight versions of *Bleak House*;[3] from *David Copperfield* Andrew Halliday took *Little Emily* (Olym. 1869) and E. H. Brooke *Little Em'ly's Trials* (S.W. 1871), while B. Ellis's *Poor Em'ly* appeared at Southampton in 1870 and G. Hamilton's *Emily* at the Albion in 1877. Other early novelists, too, had their writings seized upon. There were, for example, four versions of *Jane Eyre* and a burlesque.[4] But naturally it was the contemporary writers of fiction who most appealed. Thus, when Ouida brought out *Moths*, there was a general rush to bring its excitements to the stage. Three adaptations were written in 1882, three in 1883, while two burlesques were soon on the boards.[5] These few examples may serve to stand for many hundreds. To record here the various adaptations from fiction made during these fifty years would indeed be a lengthy task.

In passing, however, we must note one thing. The contemporary fiction was developing a style different from that

[1] Anonymous (Ast. 1859), L.C. licensed for Queen's 1859, Queen's 1863 and Garrick 1872, R. Cowie (Dundee, 1875), J. Sturgis (R.E.O.H. 1891), E. Stevens (Grand, Glasgow, 1896), R. Edgar (Amphi. L'pool, 1871); a burlesque by H. J. Byron appeared at the Strand in 1862.

[2] D. Boucicault (Ast. 1863), J. Bennett (Lyc. Edinburgh, 1894), L.C. licensed for Albion 1877, Standard 1862 and Pavilion 1863.

[3] Anonymous (M'Bone, 1853), Elphinstone and Neale (C.L. 1853), anonymous (Str. 1854), P. Burnett (P.W. L'pool, 1875), G. Lander (Pav. 1876), Eliza Thorne (Alex. Sheffield, 1876), and Grand, Walsall, 1892.

[4] L.C. licensed for Coventry 1877, T. H. Paul (Adel. Oldham, 1879), W. G. Wills (Glo. 1882); J. Willing's *Poor Relations; or, Jane Eyre*, appeared at the Park in 1879.

[5] H. Hamilton (Glo. 1882), John Chute (Croydon, 1882), anonymous (S.W. 1882), W. F. Lyon (Peterborough, 1883), A. M. Seaton (L'pool, 1883), Mervyn Dallas (Str. 1884). The first burlesque was D. W. Edgar's *Moth Quitoes; or, Ouida's Moths* (Middlesbrough, 1882), the second F. H. Herbert's *Moths à la Mode* (P'cess, Edinburgh, 1883).

of the early nineteenth century. Love of incident and grotesque characterisation had appealed in the past; now a deeper psychological note and a franker treatment of intimate domestic life became the fashion. How much the imitation of this on the stage contributed to the development of the characteristic problem-play may readily be realised.

CHAPTER III

BOUCICAULT AND TAYLOR: PLAYS OF THE FIFTIES

I. *Domestic and Historical Drama*

To survey in detail the dramatic fare between 1850 and 1860 would be, largely, to cover ground so similar to that already traversed between 1840 and 1850 that it would seem common and familiar. For this section of the theatrical highway, accordingly, we may walk without taking intimate stock of the road surface or of the surrounding landscape. That both were slightly different from what immediately preceded them is true, but the difference is but slight. Farce, extravaganza, melodrama and comic opera flourish now as they flourished in the earlier years.

From J. R. Planché's *The Camp at the Olympic* (Olym. 1853) we may obtain a good bird's-eye view of prevailing conditions. This skit, written for Alfred Wigan when he took over the Olympic Theatre, imagines the manager and his wife totally at a loss to know what they should present to the public. Suddenly Fancy, attired in a jester's costume, pounces up through a trap. By means of her magic the scene becomes "*the Camp of the Combined British Dramatic Forces*". Tragedy enters first and is soon joined by Comedy. The former, we learn, is now superannuated and the latter's spirit has grown dull—

> Wit! oh, my dear, don't mention such a thing!
> Wit on the stage what wit away would fling?
> There are so few who know it when they hear it,
> And half of those don't like so much as fear it.

Dramatic taste is both low and fickle:

> O mercy! Tell me, pray.
> What horse will win the Derby, sir? You may,

I'm sure, as easily as I tell you
What the dear British public will come to!
Just what they like—whatever that may be—
Not much to hear, and something strange to see.

Popular are Burlesque—"a vice of kings! a king of shreds and patches!"—English Opera "with a foreign band", Ballet, Melodrama, Pantomime, Hippo-Drame and Spectacle. "Immortal Shakespeare!" cries the last ironically, echoing a remark made by Tragedy,

Immortal Shakespeare! come, the less you say
The better on that head. There's not a play
Of his for many a year the town has taken,
If I've not buttered preciously his bacon.

The playlet ends on a characteristic note. "I am completely bothered," confesses Wigan, "that's a fact, And, like some actors, don't know how to act!"

TRAGEDY. But screw your courage to the sticking place!
MR WIGAN. I have—and stuck quite fast—that's just my case.
MRS WIGAN. I'll tell you what to do.
MR WIGAN. I wish you would.
MRS WIGAN. In each of them there's something that is good.
Without committing ourselves here to fix 'em,
Let's take the best and mix 'em.
MR WIGAN. Mix 'em!
MRS WIGAN. Mix 'em.
MR WIGAN. Like pickles? or like physic? what a notion!
D'ye think the town will swallow such a potion?
Why, Tragedy's a black dose of itself!
MRS WIGAN. Who talks of taking *all*, you silly elf?
I mean an extract of each spirit—Tragic,
Comic, Satiric, Operatic, Magic,
Romantic, Pantomimic, Choreographic,
Spectacular, Hip-
MR WIGAN. Spare that tongue seraphic
Such vain exertion—for they would but call
Your mixture melo-drama, after all.
MRS WIGAN. With all my heart, I say, I don't care what
It's called.

This satiric picture is by no means untrue to the spirit of

the time. Mixed forms were what the public desired. In 1868 Dion Boucicault told Mrs Bancroft that although the audience might pretend it wanted pure comedy, it really sought for other things. "What they want", he opined, "is *domestic drama*, treated with broad comic character." "A sentimental, pathetic play, comically rendered", was their desire.[1] These words are as valid for 1858 as they were for ten years later. The public wanted nothing pure except its heroines.

In spite of this, we do recognise that the tread of the dramatists is unquestionably firmer, and that the movement towards surer and franker delineation of life begins to wring a changed form out of the antique melodrama. In this period perhaps the most original and influential of dramatists was Dion Boucicault, who had already associated himself with the new spirit in comedy by the writing of *London Assurance* (C.G. 1841).[2] *London Assurance* and its companion plays of the forties marked, however, only a beginning, and Boucicault first definitely found his footing when he produced *The Corsican Brothers* at the Princess's in 1852. From this time on, his most characteristic pieces were plays wherein were mingled elements taken from all worlds—of sentimentalism much, a flash or two of broad wit and above all a series of exciting incidents recalling the familiar technique of early melodrama. Boucicault's importance as a dramatist rests on two things—his uncanny sense of theatrical values and his keenly observant eye. No man knew better than he just what would appeal on the stage. The construction of his plays, if we make allowance for their frankly melodramatic framework, is excellent; and of countless theatrical devices he was the

[1] *Mr and Mrs Bancroft on and off the Stage* (1889), p. 118.

[2] See T. Walsh, *The Career of Dion Boucicault* (New York, 1915) and article on *Mr Boucicault and Mr Barnum* (*The Saturday Review*, lxi, May 1886, 607–8). On the drama of this period generally see J. W. Cunliffe, *Modern English Playwrights: A Short History of the English Drama from 1825* (1927), A. E. Morgan, *Tendencies of Modern English Drama* (1924), P. M. A. Filon, *The English Stage* (1897), Mario Borsa, *The English Stage of To-day* (1908), Ernst L. Stahl, *Das englische Theater im 19. Jahrhundert* (Munich, 1914) and C. F. Armstrong, *Shakespeare to Shaw* (1913).

eager inventor. From revolving towers to sham locomotives he sounded the whole range of scenic sensationalism. Yet his plays do not derive their interest entirely from this exciting incident. Crude as many of his effects may seem to us, he had an acute eye for oddity in real life, and many of his best scenes rely, not on scenic splendour, but on the depiction, through laughter or tears, of domestic interiors. It was this—the cultivation of naturalistically conceived scenes allied to melodramatic excitement—which gave him his contemporary importance. *The Streets of London* (P'cess, 1864) may appear merely amusing to modern audiences, but, since realism in art is no fundamental or static method, it appealed in its own day as a truthful picture of social events. The atmosphere of the later Irish dramas may seem absurd, but they were to Victorian spectators what the plays of Sean O'Casey are to audiences of to-day.

That in 1882 Boucicault was a "dramatist of yesterday" as William Archer styled him[1] is unquestionably true, but our concern is with the development of dramatic art during this whole period and, in our endeavour to assess Boucicault's value right, it is our business to place ourselves imaginatively in his own time and thus judge him in relation to contemporary moods and desires. It is also true that he was a skilful adaptor, taking much from sources diverse in their scope;[2] but no one can deny that he gave theatrical quality to what he borrowed, that he surpassed every other playwright of the time in sensing the wishes of the public and that to his alien material he added much that came from his own observation of life.

Boucicault's career, of course, carries us well beyond the fifties, just as its beginnings carry us to the other side of this half-century, but we shall not be far wrong in saying that the decade 1850 60 exhibited his most characteristic and influential work. With his sure appreciation of public taste he divined that romantic supernaturalism was what the audiences

[1] *English Dramatists of Today* (1882), pp. 38–48.

[2] Cf. Thomas Purnell, *op. cit.* pp. 58–68; A. H. Thorndike, *English Comedy* (New York, 1929), pp. 519–20.

most desired in the early fifties; and the result was *The Corsican Brothers* (P'cess, 1852). This drama immediately received "the stamp of current fashion", so that it led the van in a sweeping rush of dramatisations of the same theme. For a time, says Cole,[1] "the subject became a perfect mania". His success naturally induced Boucicault to exploit for a time further romantic possibilities of adventurous and supernatural action. In *The Vampire* (P'cess, 1852), *Geneviève; or, The Reign of Terror* (Adel. 1853) and *Louis XI* (P'cess, 1855) he freely exploited a flamboyant dramatic style which corresponded to the romantically melodramatic acting method rendered fashionable by Charles Kean. The last-mentioned play, an adaptation from the French of Casimir de la Vigne, gained a run of sixty-two nights and that largely because of the complete harmony between the spirit of the drama and its histrionic interpretation. Audiences were in raptures. "The enthusiastic feeling of the house on the first night", declares Cole,[2]

> reminded us of the excitement we had witnessed during the best days of his father's *Othello*. Even when the play was over, and the principal character lay dead before the audience, they trembled lest he should start up again, and work fresh mischief with the revivified influence of a ghoul or a vampire....The success of "Louis the Eleventh" established a decisive period in Mr C. Kean's career as an actor.

No doubt can remain that this combination was thoroughly representative of at any rate one mood of the time; Kean's romantic impersonations were as typical as was Boucicault's flamboyant, yet decisively refined, melodramatic method.

By the close of the fifties, however, Boucicault was sensing the necessity of a change, if not in theme at least in outward semblance. Out of these historical or pseudo-historical romances grew the plays which, after all, form his most characteristic contribution to the theatre of his day. With *The Octoroon; or, Life in Louisiana* (New York, 1859; Adel. 1861) and *The Colleen Bawn; or, The Brides of Garryowen* (New York, 1860; Adel. 1860) a definite approach was made

[1] *Op. cit.* ii, 32. [2] *Id.* pp. 124–5.

towards reproducing the conditions of real life; in that life Boucicault discovered new material to exploit, new appeals which he might make to the public. Cleverly, however, he chose spheres of interest where he might freely introduce a flavour of romance, a dash of patriotic sentiment, a certain semblance of the real allied to a richness of spectacle. *The Colleen Bawn*, with its musical accompaniments, is thus obviously related to the older melodrama. In the printed text and in the original play-bills the scenic show is fully advertised; that was part of the appeal. At the same time this melodramatic basis and this pleasing spectacle are subtly related to actual existence; instead of wizards' caverns and vampires' dens *The Colleen Bawn* introduces us to the familiar made rosy and imaginative. Those prospective playgoers who read the original list of scenes would have appreciated this to the full:

Act I

LAKE OF KILLARNEY (MOONLIGHT)

The Signal Light!

Gap of Dunloe

Cottage on Muckross Head

The Irish Fireside—The Cruiskeen Lawn—The Oath!

Act II

Torc Cregan

COTTAGE OF THE COLLEEN BAWN

"The Pretty Girl Milking Her Cow"

Mac Gillicuddy's Reeks

The O'Donoghue's Stables

The Water Cave

Act III

THE HUT CASTLE CHUTE

THE CASTLE GARDENS

Illuminated Hall and Garden in Castle Chute

From romantic moonlight on the fair Lake of Killarney through the splendour of the castle gardens to the lonely cottage; from the thrilling signal light through the oath to the pretty girl milking her cow—Boucicault sounds the gamut of a particular style. The plot fully accords with the scenery; it is full of exciting incidents and of dramatic suspense. Hardress Cregan has secretly married Eily O'Connor, but finds himself faced with ruin unless he marries Anne Chute. The dilemma for him is a terrible one; and the confusion in which the characters are placed is rendered greater by the fact that Anne, loving Kyrle Daly, is led to believe that he, not Cregan, is Eily's husband. Cregan has a faithful devoted servant in Danny Mann; to relieve his master he attempts to slay Eily, but she is saved by Myles-na-Coppalean, the stock, pathetically dog-like lover. It is all very exciting and not for one moment is the attention of the audience permitted to flag. But if it is exciting, it is also very appealing in its apparent realism. The Irish dialect employed has a kind of double effect—it gives a pleasing air of wild romantic remoteness to the action and at the same time creates the illusion that all these events are definitely related to life.

A similar combination of elements appears in *The Octoroon*. No one could fail to be impressed by the author's rich vitality and dramatic inventiveness. The love of George Peyton for Zoe, the octoroon; the poverty threatening Mrs Peyton; the villainies of McClosky; the apparent disasters and the ultimate triumph of good—all these keep the plot moving swiftly. And again theatrical use is made of the life known to the audience. To us this use of material things may seem more than a trifle absurd and forced; but the sense of novelty which would accompany their original introduction must have amply compensated for any dim feeling of dissatisfaction. Take the camera episode. McClosky is the brutal villain of the regular melodramatic tradition, and in Act II he murders Paul, thinking that no eye has seen his crime. Unfortunately for him, however, a camera belonging to Scudder has been standing facing him all the time, and, as he is muttering "What a find! this infernal letter would have saved all", the stage direction declares that "*he remains nearly motionless under the focus of camera*". The result of this becomes apparent in the last scene. McClosky is accusing the Indian Wahnotee of killing Paul, while Scudder endeavours to plead for him:

Scudder. I appeal against your usurped authority; this Lynch law is a wild and lawless proceeding. Here's a pictur' for a civilized community to afford; yonder, a poor ignorant savage, and round him a circle of hearts, white with revenge and hate, thirsting for his blood; you call yourselves judges—you ain't—you're a jury of executioners. It is such scenes as these that bring disgrace upon our Western life.

M'Closky. Evidence! Evidence! give us evidence, we've had talk enough; now for proof.

Omnes. Yes, yes! Proof, proof.

Scudder. Where am I to get it? the proof is here, in my heart!

Pete (*who has been looking about the camera*). Top sar! top a bit! Oh, laws-a-mussey, see dis, here's pictur I found sticking in that yar telescope machine, sar! look sar!

Scudder. A photographic plate. (Pete *holds lantern up*) What's this, eh? two forms! the child—'tis he! dead—and above him—Ah, ah! Jacob McClosky—'twas you murdered that boy!

M'Closky. Me?

Scudder. You! You slew him with that tomahawk, and as you stood over his body with the letter in your hand, you thought that no witness saw the deed, that no eye was on you, but there was, Jacob McClosky, there was—the eye of the Eternal was on you—the blessed sun in heaven, that looking down struck upon this plate the image of the deed. Here you are, in the attitude of your crime!

Thus is the villain foiled. The means may be ridiculous and we may permit ourselves to smile superiorly, but Boucicault is sure of his business and recognises that the utilisation of this new invention (about which both the audience and he know little) will be exciting and thrilling. Things like these thrilled contemporary audiences on both sides of the Atlantic: Boucicault was able to write to a friend that "the sensation produced in New York" by this drama was "intense", the houses being "crammed to suffocation".[1]

The same skill is shown throughout the entirety of Boucicault's dramatic career. *Arrah-na-Pogue; or, The Wicklow*

[1] Letter to G. W. Riggs, formerly in the possession of the late Father Riggs of New Haven, U.S.A. The source of this play was a story written by Hezekiah L. Hosmer, editor of *The Toledo Daily Blade*.

Wedding (Dublin, Nov. 1864; P'cess, March 1865) presents, in an Irish setting, a kindred mixture of diverse elements. Against a background of nationalist sentiment and revolutionary ardour Beamish MacCoul stages a robbery, for which the honest Shaun is arrested. Love, of course, has to play its part here and its path has to be duly crossed; Fanny Power, who adores and is adored by Beamish, comes to believe that Arrah is his mistress. Complications and complexities ensue, with frantic efforts made by O'Grady to save poor Shaun. At last Beamish, having given himself up, is about to be condemned, when a kind-hearted and liberal-souled Secretary decides to save him. *Arrah-na-Pogue* is no less thrilling than *The Octoroon*, and its hair-raising excitements are cleverly interspersed with a variety of comic business. Perhaps Boucicault's importance may best be gauged when we regard him as one of the masters—for such in a way he is—of George Bernard Shaw. Amid Boucicault's realms of sensation and laughter and propaganda the young Shaw wandered, and the result is to be viewed, not only in the melodramatic *Devil's Disciple*, but in *Arms and the Man*, *Caesar and Cleopatra*, *The Man of Destiny* as well. Nor is this indebtedness one merely of a general sort. "Technically", says Shaw in his preface to *Three Plays for Puritans*,

I do not find myself able to proceed otherwise than as former playwrights have done. True, my plays have the latest mechanical improvements; the action is not carried on by impossible soliloquys and asides; and my people get on and off the stage without requiring four doors to a room which in real life would have only one. But my stories are the old stories; my characters are the familiar harlequin and columbine, clown and pantaloon (note the harlequin's leap in the third act of Caesar and Cleopatra); my stage tricks and suspenses and thrills and jests are the ones in vogue when I was a boy, by which time my grandfather was tired of them.

How true this statement is may be realised by glancing at two scenes from *Arrah-na-Pogue* and *The Devil's Disciple* respectively. The former presents a court-martial scene. There is a severe Major and a kindly Colonel O'Grady; the prisoner is Shaun, who has allowed himself to be arrested in the stead of another:

MAJOR. Your name?
SHAUN. Is it my name, sir? Ah, you're jokin'! Sure there's his honour beside ye can answer for me, long life to him!
MAJOR. Will you give the Court your name, fellow?
SHAUN. Well, I'm not ashamed of it.
O'GRADY. Come, Shaun, my man.
SHAUN. There, didn't I tell ye! he knows me well enough.
MAJOR. Shaun (*writing*)... What is your other name?
SHAUN. My mother's name?
MAJOR. Your other name.
SHAUN. My other name? D'ye think I've taken anybody else's name? Did ye ever know me, boys, only as Shaun?...
O'GRADY. He is called Shaun the Post.
SHAUN. In regard of me carrying the letter-bag by the car, yer honour.
MAJOR. Now prisoner, are you guilty or not guilty?
SHAUN. Sure, Major, I thought that was what we'd all come here to find out.

Contrast this with the court-martial scene in Shaw's play. There is here too a severe Major (Swindon) and a good-humoured General (Burgoyne); the prisoner (Richard) has allowed himself to be arrested in the place of Anthony Anderson:

SWINDON. Your name, sir?
RICHARD. Come: you don't mean to say that you've brought me here without knowing who I am?
SWINDON. As a matter of form, sir, give me your name.
RICHARD. As a matter of form, then, my name is Anthony Anderson, Presbyterian minister in this town....
BURGOYNE. Any political views Mr Anderson?
RICHARD. I understand that that is just what we are here to find out.

The same situation; the same fundamental types; even in part the same expressions.

Throughout his dramatic career Boucicault displayed a rich theatrical exuberance and a keen appreciation of stage values. As Joseph Knight observed of *The Shaughraun* (New

York, 1874; D.L. Sept. 1875), he found the ordinary conditions of life in England "prosaic and commonplace" and consequently turned to the richer material discoverable amidst the romantically rebel Irish folk;[1] good fun abounds in all his dramas; and in all is the effective utilisation of exciting escapades, often with distinctively novel circumstances connected therewith. In *The Shaughraun* there was "a revolving tower" which showed, "from the inside first, and then from the outside, the escape of the hero";[2] in *The Poor of New York* (New York, 1857) occurred a scene showing two adjoining rooms[3] and a most exciting conflagration:

Stage dark. The exterior of the tenement house, No. 19½ *Cross Street, Five Points—the shutters of all the windows are closed. A light is seen through the round holes in the shutters of the upper windows—presently a flame rises—it is extinguished—then revives. The light is seen to descend as the bearer of it passes down the staircase, the door opens cautiously—*BLOODGOOD, *disguised, appears—he looks round—closes the door again—locks it.*

BLOOD. (*aloud*). In a few hours, this accursed house will be in ruins. The receipt is concealed there—and it will be consumed in the flames. (*The glow of fire is seen to spread from room to room*) Now Badger—do your worst—I am safe! (*Exit*) *The house is gradually enveloped in fire, a cry outside is heard "Fi-er!" "Fi-er!"; it is taken up by other voices more distant. The tocsin sounds—other churches take up the alarm—bells of Engines are heard. Enter a crowd of persons. Enter* BADGER, *without coat or hat—he tries the door—finds it fast; seizes a bar of iron and dashes in the ground floor window, the interior is seen in flames. Enter* DAN.

DAN (*seeing* BADGER *climbing into the window*). Stop! Stop!

BADGER *leaps in and disappears. Shouts from the mob;* DAN *leaps in—another shout.* DAN *leaps out again black and burned, staggers forward and seems overcome by the heat and smoke. The shutters of the garret fall and discover* BADGER *in the upper floor. Another cry from the crowd, a loud crash is heard,* BADGER *disappears as if falling with the inside of the building. The shutters of the windows fall away, and the inside of the house is seen, gutted by the fire; a cry of horror is uttered by the mob.* BADGER *drags himself from the ruins, and falls across the sill of the lower window.* DAN *and two of the mob run to help him forward but recoil before the heat; at length*

[1] *Theatrical Notes* (1893), pp. 56–9.

[2] See *supra*, p. 44.

[3] Act v, Scene 2.

they succeed in rescuing his body—which lies C. LIVINGSTONE, PAUL and PUFFY *rush on.* DAN *kneels over* BADGER *and extinguishes the fire which clings to parts of his clothes.*

That is the entirety of the scene, and a very thrilling one it must have been, brought the nearer to the spectators as it was by the fact that here Boucicault was treating of the great financial crash of 1837, still a vivid reality in men's memories. His merit ever consisted in this ability to give thrilling form to material which seemed to be the material of life and yet was always material of the theatre. Sometimes he achieved his end by visual means; sometimes, as in *The O'Dowd* (Adel. Oct. 1880), by skilful arrangement of the incidents. In this last-mentioned play Mike O'Dowd is first shown in London, embarrassed by a debt of £20,000. His friends rally round him, but even their efforts fail to stave off disaster. Emigrating to America, he at length succeeds in amassing wealth and returns to Europe. The play ends with a thrilling scene in which he saves a ship by guiding her through a channel of which only he and his father are aware. Inventiveness was always Boucicault's greatest gift and if the inventions were not always his own he proved felicitous in adapting the ideas of others. A semi-realistic "problem-play", for example, he transforms and makes interesting by devising a special framework. *Dot* (New York, 1859; Adel. April, 1862), based on *The Cricket on the Hearth*, is introduced by Oberon and Titania, conceived as wretched, poverty-stricken wanderers, forgotten by the modern world; their place is taken by Home, and this provides an opportunity for emphasising that poetry must now be sought in the quiet domestic interior.

Boucicault's knowledge of the stage and its possibilities was completer than that possessed by any of his contemporaries, and unlike so many of these he had a keen eye for whatsoever in real life might provide him with opportunities for the building up of melodramatic incident. The invention of the camera, a great financial failure, the problem of the octoroon, the conflict between Yankee and Virginian or between Irish and English—all were vigorously seized on and easily assimilated. His plays may lack literary finish; but at least they present in a bold way that theatrical effectiveness and that theatrical interest which are the primal demands we must make of a dramatist. Readily may we ridicule much of his work, but, when we seriously consider his accomplishment in terms of contemporary stage practice, it is hard indeed to deny him praise and esteem.

But few writers in this time vied with him in this combination of diverse interests. Most of the melodramas followed the time-worn lines laid down by the authors of the forties. *The Writing on the Wall* (H. Aug. 1852), by Thomas and J. M. Morton,[1] may be taken as representative of a thousand others. In this play the serious plot deals with Richard Oliver, who has murdered Walter Elton and who endeavours to cast the blame on the dead man's brother, Everhard Elton. This Everhard hovers round the side-wings in the disguise of Tobias the Blind Man. Not content with the slaying of one Elton and the traducing of another, Oliver proceeds darkly with his attempt to encompass the total destruction of the Elton family. With the horrid chuckle of the melodramatic villain, he purchases Elton Hall—only to discover there that the murdered man had scrawled upon a wall, in his own blood, the name of his slayer. Alongside of this story runs one of more comic import, introducing Lotty Smithers, famous in circus-land as Carlotta Smitherini, Gammon and Walker, two bucolic farmers, and Fergusson Trotter, a philanthropist who tries to start a model farm. Everything here is planned according to ancient formula. Oliver, in the first act, is asked why he hates the Eltons, and his reply is characteristic:

> My hatred is at least honest, because open. I hate the Eltons because—but my hatred owns responsibility to no man: I hate them—because I hate them.

Which is a very correct sentiment in the mouth of a stage villain. The revealing of the murderer's identity is planned in similar wise:

[1] See C. Scott, *John Maddison Morton* (*London Society*, xlix, 1886).

Oliver. We've still clear time enough, and we'll make the most of it.

Smithers. What are you going to do?

Oliver (*seizing crow-bar*). To grind to dust, those damned and damning words—the Writing on the Wall!

Smithers. You dare not—sure—

Oliver. Dare not?—look here! (*advances to door, a loud crash is heard within followed by piercing shriek, twice or thrice repeated; falls back*) What's that? (*desperately*) Ah, the legend! Spite of all the legends of Hell, I'll enter! (*he batters the door, which at last falls forward with a heavy crash;* MARGARET *is discovered within, in white robe and dishevelled hair;* OLIVER *staggers back to front of stage;* SMITHERS *falls on his knees; the noise brings on* SIR PHILIP, LADY ELTON *and* JOSEPH, R.; GUESTS *and* SERVANTS, L.).

Margaret. Richard Oliver! (*she utters the name with peculiar solemnity, and they all start in recognition of the legend*) Are you come to claim your bride? Enter then: my father's spirit is here, to join our hands.

Sir Philip. (R.C.) Sister!

Lady Elton. (R.) Margaret, beloved child, come from that dreadful chamber.

Margaret (*waves them back*). Not till I discharge my father's will. In this room of horror, I took refuge from worse horror. Here, where my father's spirit flew to heaven, I invoked his aid to save me: at that moment, a huge oaken screen broke through the mouldering floor, and by the beams of light that streamed in radiant floods upon the wall, he sent his answer—look! (*points*) 'tis there!—"RICHARD OLIVER MY MURDERER!"

If another example of the kind be desired, it may be found in J. E. Carpenter's *Love and Honour, or Soldiers at Home—Heroes Abroad* (Surrey, Nov. 1855), wherein Captain Melville, the villain, forges a will to defraud his younger brother and aims at seducing Jessie Gray the miller's daughter. Strange how persistently the motif utilised by Thomas Southerne in *The Fatal Marriage* (D.L. 1694) and carried on through Schiller's *Die Raüber* continued to make its appeal. This particular evil brother is shot at by George St Clair, who is consequently court-martialled. The escape of St Clair is engineered by Jessie and, some evidence coming to light, Melville is dismissed. Finally, at the close of the drama, we find ourselves in Sebastopol, where St Clair is a colonel and

Melville a spy. The latter is shot and, dying, recognises in St Clair his much-injured brother. Typical, not only of this play but of many akin to it, is the close of the first act. The scene is a cottage exterior and Melville is addressing Briefwrit:

Melville. Cease your ill-timed and assumed mannerism. See! there is a light in the cottage—she has not retired to rest. I will try what persuasion can do first. 'Tis I—Melville!

(*He taps at the window—St Clair is seen at an upper window of the inn.*)

Jessie (*At the window*). Why do you seek me at this untimely hour?

Melville. Dearest Jessie, this moment is one of life or death to me. For your sake I have applied for my discharge from my regiment—I am about to put your love to the test: consent to fly with a friend I can trust; to-morrow I will join you, and, all necessary forms over, we can return, and claim your father's forgiveness.

Jessie. Do I dream! no! The soldier spoke the truth, and you are a villain. Leave me, sir: this secret flight were unnecessary, if your intentions are honourable. Your impetuosity reveals the baseness of your purpose. Leave me, I say again, or I will alarm the neighbours!

Melville. I expected such an answer from you, and am prepared. Resistance is vain;—you must comply with my desires.

Jessie. Father! Father! Where are you? Save your daughter.

Melville. Nay! before he can return, you will be far from hence. You are mine, and thus I gain you.

(*He jumps in at the window, and carries her out through the door, passing her to Briefwrit.*)

St Clair (*At the upper window of the Inn*). Hold, Captain! Unless your companion releases the girl, I fire—

Melville. Distraction! you dare not! (*Gets in front of them.*) Now, then, fire, if you dare—I am your superior officer.

St Clair. Stand aside.

Melville. Forward!

(*St Clair fires—the Captain falls—St Clair jumps from the window, and rescues Jessie—Stephen Gray rushes in—others enter from the house and at the back, form picture, and the drop descends.*)

This passage, strained and ridiculous, is no extreme example of the common melodramatic style of the period. To obtain an idea of the true depth to which the popular dramatists could descend we must turn to such plays as C. H. Hazlewood's *Waiting for the Verdict; or, Falsely Accused* (C.L. Jan. 1859). Compared with this, *Love and Honour* seems a masterpiece.

Out of these plays, however, something was germinating—something that promised a richer and a more plentiful harvest for the future. Boucicault's main tendencies were towards the sensational and the comic, but others were endeavouring to give more of vital content to the serious matter which formed a main part in the melodramatic mélange. Thus Charles Selby, one trained in the realm of the minor drama, penned *The Marble Heart; or, The Sculptor's Dream* (Adel. May 1854), calling it "A Romance of Real Life" and definitely making an experiment along novel lines.[1] This, although it springs from the melodramatic, is not an ordinary melodrama; rather might it be styled an essay in genuine tragic matèrial. The first act opens in Athens and shows us the sculptor Phidias rejected, in favour of wealth, by the marble hearts of his time. The next scene carries us to the modern world and there we are confronted by a series of persons who are the counterparts or descendants of the ancient denizens of Athens—Ferdinand Volage (Diogenes), Raphael Duchatlet (Phidias), Mons. Veaudoré (Gorgias), Mlle Marco (Lais) and Marie (the Slave Thea). At the conclusion of the play the sculptor goes mad and dies. If only for the experimentation in the treatment *The Marble Heart* would be a notable drama for the year 1854.

Of all the dramatists who endeavoured to develop this popular drama into more profitable paths, perhaps Tom Taylor is the most interesting. That he borrowed many of his plots is unquestioned,[2] but, like Boucicault, he was a man

[1] It must be confessed that this play is adapted from *Les filles de marbre* of Barrière and Thiboust. Its French derivation ought not, however, to cause us to overlook the importance of this play's production in the fifties. The way in which the new movement in the French theatre might influence the English is to be seen in such a play as *The Barrister* (Surrey, March 1852), adapted from Emile Augier, with its interesting treatment of domestic friction.

[2] T. Purnell, *op. cit.* pp. 94–126. See J. Sheehan, *Tom Taylor* (*Dublin University Magazine*, xc, 1877, pp. 142–58) and T. Hughes, *In Memoriam Tom Taylor* (*Macmillan's Magazine*, xlii, 1880, pp. 298–301).

who understood his theatre perfectly and always transformed what he utilised. Taylor's dramatic work, which extends in time from the forties to the seventies, is perplexing in its variety, but he is sufficiently a man of his time to recognise the desirability of mingling freely his humour and his pathos. In many of his plays he indicated a distinct leaning towards the historic theme; indeed, part of his merit consisted in reviving the costume play, which had been so popular during the Scott period, and in dealing with that in a bolder and more realistic technique. In *Plot and Passion* (Olym. Oct. 1853) he turns to the Napoleonic régime for his subject-matter, introducing the intrigues of Fouché, the loves of de Neuville and Madame de Fontanges, the belated honesty of the villain's accomplice, Desmarets. The Monmouth rebellion forms the subject-matter for *A Sheep in Wolf's Clothing* (Olym. Feb. 1857) which narrates how Anne Carew conceals her husband, Jasper, from the authorities. To facilitate this she permits Colonel Percy Kirke to make love to her and is nearly involved in disaster through the impertinent busybody, Keziah Mapletoft. At the conclusion Lord Churchill arrives *ex machina*, cashiers Kirke and allows Jasper to escape. For *The Fool's Revenge* (S.W. Oct. 1859) he takes Victor Hugo's *Le roi s'amuse* as his basis,[1] and in writing *The Hidden Hand* (Olym. Nov. 1864) he turns to *L'aïeule* of Dennery and Edmond. The date of the action here is 1685, and the characters are drawn so as to show the hatred of the Welsh towards the English. A sentimental conclusion mars a play otherwise rendered thrillingly exciting by its passion, intrigue and poison. This period of the late seventeenth century clearly fascinated Taylor, and once more he deals with it melodramatically in *Lady Clancarty: or, Wedded and Wooed. A Tale of the Assassination Plot 1696* (Olym. March 1874).

Besides these plays, Taylor wrote a few other historical dramas of a more ambitious kind. Based on Charlotte Birch-Pfeiffer's *Elizabeth von England*, *'Twixt Axe and Crown; or, The Lady Elizabeth* (Queen's, Jan. 1870) attempts a higher

[1] See an article by T.T., *Mr Phelps and The Fool's Revenge* (*The Theatre*, N.S. i, Dec. 1878, 338–44).

flight with its blank verse dialogue and indicates a desire to give to the theatre something more of literary grace. That his effort was a worthy one may readily be allowed; but that he failed to reach true success in these more ambitious plays cannot be denied.

All these dramas, the literary and the melodramatic, must, however, cede place to the few historical plays which Taylor wrote in association with Charles Reade. Taylor himself was inclined towards the sentimental, and perhaps that sentimentality had to be tempered by the greater robustness and even brutality of Reade's talent.[1] *Two Loves and a Life* (Adel. March 1854) was one of the earliest of their collaborative efforts; in turning to it we recognise a greater firmness in the handling and a surer delineation of character than are to be found in Taylor's unaided efforts. Here we are introduced to Sir Gervase Rokewood and Father Radcliffe, who are organising the men at Morecombe Bay in support of Prince Charlie. Ruth Ravenscar, really the daughter of Radcliffe, saves the Duke of Cumberland and his men from disaster, while Anne, Rokewood's beloved, is forced by her father Musgrave to betray the conspirators. Rokewood is arrested, but is eventually saved by Ruth, who pleads to the Duke of Cumberland for his life. Comedy scenes introducing John Daw, the schoolmaster, and Potts, the barber, give the necessary relief to a well-planned, if melodramatic and occasionally sentimental, plot. Interesting, too, is *The King's Rival; or, The Court and the Stage* (St J. Oct. 1854), another collaborative venture. Here Charles II is the hero, and Miss Stewart the heroine. The former, ever captivated by a pretty face, becomes enamoured of the latter who, for her part, loves and is loved by the Duke of Richmond. The attentions of the Merry Monarch are proving somewhat of an embarrassment for the fair Stewart when kind-hearted Nell Gwynne steps in to set everything to rights. Perhaps Charles II, like Shakespeare, forms a kind of sociological thermometer. In the mid-eighteenth century a Georgian damsel wished she were

[1] See Malcolm Elwin, *Charles Reade* (1931) and E. G. Sutcliffe, *The Stage in Reade's Novels* (*Studies in Philology*, xxvii, Oct. 1930, 654–88).

back in good King Somebody's days.[1] About 1820 a Charles II drama endeavoured to demonstrate that affairs of the heart at Whitehall were of the purest and most honourable; a little flirtation, perhaps, but positive evil, never. Fifty years later come Taylor and Reade, interpreting the period sentimentally it is true, but honestly prepared to admit that Charles did have his mistresses and that there might be danger for a young girl in his court. Fifty years later came *And So To Bed*, which provided for the nineteen-twenties what *The King's Rival* and *Rochester* did for the mid-nineteenth century. Finally we reach G. B. Shaw's philosophic and political treatment of the good old days when the Merry Monarch reigned—a reflection of the interests of 1939.

Not all Taylor's dramas were of the historical kind. A link between these and his plays on domestic themes may be found in *Retribution* (Olym. May 1856), based on Charles de Bernard's novel, *La loi du talion*. Here Oscar de Beaupré is shown as having seduced the wife of Rodolphe. The latter, in the guise of Count Priuli, seeks revenge by attempting to seduce Madame de Beaupré, who is loved by Victor de Mornac, his brother. This play ends tragically with the deaths of both Victor and Oscar. There is here a slight flavour of the romantic drama, but the theme is one of more immediate contemporary interest and has a distinct "domestic" tone in spite of its romantic proclivities. Based on another French novel, *Le Gendre* (by the same author), *Still Waters Run Deep* (Olym. May 1855) introduces us to what was perhaps Taylor's greatest contribution to the theatre of his time. The plot of this play deals mainly with Mildmay, a man who has been married but a year and who has adopted an attitude of *laissez faire* while his wife's aunt, Mrs Sternhold, domineers over his household. His wife herself indulges in a flirtation with the rascally Captain Hawksley, a gentleman of fortune who had previously had an affair with Mrs Sternhold. Coming to learn of his attempt to seduce her niece, Mrs Sternhold tries to hinder him, but is silenced when he threatens to publish a number of her letters, addressed to him. Disaster

[1] See *E.E.D.* p. 160 and *E.N.D.* i, 16–17.

threatens, but is prevented by Mildmay's sudden change of front. Taking command of the situation, he succeeds in extracting the letters from Hawksley and in getting that disturber of the peace (or piece) sentenced for a forgery committed by him four years previously. In this play the most important thing is not the plot or the technique; it is the frankness with which the affairs of sex are discussed. In *The King's Rival* Charles, it is admitted, had mistresses; in *Still Waters Run Deep* is the equally important admission that illicit love was a fact of life. The scene wherein Mrs Sternhold confronts Hawksley may be lacking in vigour and intellectual honesty if we view it from our position in the twentieth century, but for its own age it marks a very deliberate break with convention. The way is being prepared for the dramas of the last decade of the century; the scope of the domestic play is being extended to include subjects and characters which before were taboo.

This greater intimacy and this application of the dramatist to contemporary material is marked clearly in what, after all, is Taylor's most interesting play, *The Ticket-of-Leave Man* (Olym. May 1863). Starting with an interesting crowd scene set in a restaurant (an innovation in itself), we are immediately introduced to the London underworld. The provincial Bob Brierly is taken in by Dalton (The Tiger) and is sent to prison. Released thence, he marries the little orphan, May Edwards, whom he had befriended, and secures honourable employment. Discovered by his former associates, he is threatened by them until he pretends to join them in their schemes. Actually, however, he works against them and aids the police in securing their capture. *The Ticket-of-Leave Man* is one of the first melodramas to deal with the criminal life of London, to take as a hero a man who had suffered imprisonment for association with these criminals, to introduce a detective (Hawkshaw) on the stage, and to break away from the familiar domestic interior sets in an attempt (as in the restaurant scene) to treat of the teeming world of contemporary social life. Marred by hopeless coincidences though it may be, this play definitely marks a stage in the development of the nineteenth-century stage. It springs from the old melodrama; it borrows from the adaptations of Dickens' novels which had been and still were so popular; but, in spite of these things, it has a quality of its own which must induce us to rate Taylor as one of the more noteworthy dramatic authors of the century.

Perhaps it may not be unprofitable to glance at one or two other plays which, either by reason of their intrinsic merits or by reason of their authorship, deserve some particular attention. Of the historical plays, W. R. Markwell's *Louis XI* (D.L. Feb. 1853) merits mention. Melodramatic it is with its hero, Nemours, and its heroine, Marie de Comine, and melodramatically bombastic is its dialogue. On the other hand, Markwell, like Taylor, is here aiming at something beyond what the minor writers of the forties indulged in; his *Louis XI* indicated, albeit but crudely, how that minor theatre was to become amalgamated with the literary. While displaying a full consciousness of what the public wanted, and while manifestly prepared to satisfy that want, Markwell has a decidedly ambitious aim here and succeeds in striking a note higher and more significant. Thrills there are, but the thrills are subordinated to the building up of a serious atmosphere and the delineation of character. C. S. Cheltnam's *Edendale* (Charing Cross, June 1869) might be taken as representing the further development of this new note. Choosing the American Civil War as a background, the author concentrates his attention on the loves of a Northerner, Fairholt, and a Southerner, Ada Vandeleur. Whereas Markwell had not learned how adequately to modulate his instrument, Cheltnam shows a power of moving from the easy flippant conversation of the early familiar scenes to the torment of passion in which his persons are later involved. Still more inclining towards the literary are the plays of Westland Marston, who was regarded by Thomas Purnell in 1871 as "with the possible exception of Lord Lytton, the sole living representative of the legitimate drama".[1] This author's *Patri-*

[1] *Op. cit.* pp. 31–44. See R. H. Horne, *A New Spirit of the Age* (World's Classics edition, pp. 358–78).

cian's Daughter, originally produced in 1842, is his best-known play, but he continued his theatrical career over two clear decades. The quality of living character he gives to his persons is probably his most noteworthy virtue. Thus in *A Hard Struggle* (Lyc. Feb. 1858) he contrives to make real a poor and improbable story by the vitality with which he delineates the noble lover, Reuben Holt, the passionate young doctor, Fergus Graham, and the distressed girl, Lilian Trevor. In Marston's plays clearly another step is being taken towards that union of popular and literary elements out of which the new drama was to grow.

More sentimentally inclined is J. Palgrave Simpson, an author whose work covers three decades. *Second Love* (H. July 1856) is fairly typical of his style. The serious here outweighs the comic. Knowing that she has been left a large sum of money, Colonel Dangerfield makes passionate advances to the blind girl Elinor. This Elinor has a devoted lover in the person of Ralph Thornhill, who is prepared to make any sacrifice to secure her happiness. Just when the villain seems about to win the day, Elinor is luckily cured of her affliction, literally sees Dangerfield's duplicity and the wedding bells ring out on her marriage to Ralph. Of similar tone is *Daddy Hardacre* (Olym. March 1857), featuring Daddy Hardacre himself (a miser), Esther (his lovable daughter) and Mary (the honest maid). To Hardacre comes his brother-in-law's son, Charles, with a letter stating that the writer, being on the brink of ruin, proposes to blow his brains out. Noble Esther hears of this, steals her father's money and sends it to London by Adolphus Jobling, her comic suitor. Of course Charles and Esther fall in love; and of course Charles's father is saved in the nick of time—the conventions of the Simpsonian drama could not have permitted anything else. All of the characters in these plays are stock types; of this a note to the list of dramatis personae in *Alone* (Court, Oct. 1873), in which Simpson collaborated with Herman C. Merivale, is characteristic. Of Stratton Strawless in this play Simpson observes that "the part does not belong to the line of the 'Old Man' but of the 'Eccentric Comedian'". His figures thus have a marked sameness, and this sameness intrudes into the plots as well. In *Alone* it is Colonel Challice, not the heroine, who is blind. Cruelly, this gentleman has thrown off his daughter years before, but she returns and reads *Lear* to him so prettily that he relents and takes her once more to his heart. *Shadows of the Past* (Brighton, Nov. 1867) shows Simpson approaching the problem drama, and *Broken Ties* (Olym. June 1872) reveals to perfection his strong sentimental leanings. In the latter, the happiness of the hero, Warner, is nearly destroyed by the fact that his wife is pursuing a career of her own. Disaster almost threatens when suddenly the wife decides that home, after all, is best—and throws herself sobbingly into her husband's arms.

II. *Comedy-Dramas and Farces*

Nearly all of the authors mentioned above aimed at the introduction of laughter as well as tears into their plays; the peculiar atmosphere of Boucicault's dramas, as we have seen, arises precisely from the skilful juxtaposition of these two elements. Sometimes, too, the use of historical material was designed, not to illustrate past events but to provide colour for a farcical situation; W. J. Sorrell's *A Border Marriage* (Adel. Nov. 1856) and Douglas Jerrold's *St Cupid; or, Dorothy's Fortune* (P'cess, Jan. 1853) may be mentioned as examples. On the whole, however, the historical plays were mainly tragic in theme or sensationally adventuresome, and in the domestic dramas comedy was subordinated to serious purpose. Now it is necessary to turn for a moment to that field of play-writing wherein the comic elements preponderated.

Tom Taylor was responsible for one of the most popular of all such pieces—*Our American Cousin* (New York, Oct. 1858; H. Nov. 1861), a comedy long remembered for the Dundreary of Sothern.[1] Structureless and indulgent of much farcial business, this play is nowise to be condemned. True, it seems that the spirit in which its performance was conceived

[1] See G. A. H. Sala, *Breakfast in Bed* (1863), pp. 7–32.

deviated markedly from that in which it was written. "From a comedy of a heavy type—in fact, a domestic drama," Arthur à Beckett declares, "it became a roaring farce."[1] The set of eccentric types, however, are well conceived—kind-hearted Asa Trenchard, foppish Lord Dundreary, "interesting" Georgina, gay Florence Trenchard, villainous Coyle—and equally well conceived is the series of ridiculous situations in which these characters are involved. With this comedy Taylor set a new fashion and stimulated many imitators.

As in the realm of melodrama, so in this of comedy-farce we may trace, if but vaguely, the signs of things to come. Thus *Victims* (H. July 1857), where Mrs Merryweather, who thinks herself persecuted, is flattered and fluttered by the attentions of the poetaster Fitzherbert and where the husband proves himself the magnanimous hero, presents a faint suspicion of the atmosphere which later produced *How He Lied to Her Husband*. One could not suggest, naturally, that Taylor is a neglected genius in whose works lies buried a comic talent equal to that of Shaw; but potentially *Victims* contains the material out of which the Shavian comedy was wrought. The same spirit animates *To Oblige Benson* (Olym. March 1854).[2] Here Mrs Benson is engaged in a flirtation with Meredith. A friend, Mrs Southdown, anxious to awaken Mrs Benson's mind to an appreciation of the dangers in her path, suggests to the husband that he make pretence at jealousy. This course the good man adopts, but only too rapidly passes from feigned to real passion. In vain Mrs Southdown, who imagines he is overacting just a little, endeavours to restrain him. The conception and the dialogue here have both a certain ease and style. Then there is the famous *Masks and Faces* (H. Nov. 1852) written in collaboration with Charles Reade. The treatment of Peg Woffington, if somewhat sentimental, has a decided lightness and delicacy and the character of Triplet is well managed. Taylor's worth may be gauged by the fact that *Masks and Faces* still gives pleasure in revival.

In connection with Taylor's *Victims* and *To Oblige Benson*

[1] *Green-Room Recollections* (1896), pp. 16–17.
[2] Adapted from *Un service à Blachard* by Vande.

it may be worthy of remark that the theme of married boredom was one which attracted much attention during this time. The theme itself may owe its popularity to French example (as in Augier), but so frequently is it exploited that we must believe it somehow in accordance with popular predilections. Sometimes the playwright will deal with it seriously, more often he will give it a humorous turn, as in Ben Webster's *A Novel Expedient* (H. June 1852) or George Henry Lewes' *A Cozy Couple* (Lyc. April 1854). In the former it is the wife who is dissatisfied; taking advice, she pretends to make love to Harry Damon who, playing up to her, succeeds in nearly scaring her out of her wits. The husband, Mr Dormouse, in the latter is the person bored and weary. When an old friend, Tom Russelton, appears and tells him of his adventures, he nearly breaks his chains and is prevented from doing so only by the fact that the wandering Tom, sensing the felicity of a domestic fireside, agrees to stay and keep him company. Similar in tone is Felix Dale's *Six Months Ago* (Olym. July 1867), wherein Edwin, rather bored, welcomes Jack Deedes, an old friend of his bachelor days, and so angers his wife that she decides to sue for a divorce. This course of action is prevented only by Edwin's sudden realisation that he loves her truly and cannot bear the thought of parting. Ben Webster, author of *A Novel Expedient*, may be noted as among the more prolific comic writers of his time: witness his *Giralda; or, The Miller's Wife* (H. Sept. 1850) with its gay Spanish intrigue and its management of a confusing set of criss-cross affections.

Another writer who deserves some attention is J. B. Buckstone. His career, of course, falls mainly in the first half of the century,[1] but he carried on his activities into the fifties. In *Leap Year; or, The Ladies' Privilege* (H. Jan. 1850) Flora Flowerdew is a widow who has to take a second husband if she is not to lose her late spouse's money. Her friend, Miss O'Leary, tries hard to get her suited, bringing forward in turn Sir Solomon Solus, Captain Mouser and Mr Dimple; the buxom Flora, however, discovers that she really loves

[1] See *E.N.D.* i, 116–17.

her manservant, William Walker—and he turns out to be the very relative to whom her money would have gone had she remained single. By their marriage it is accordingly kept, most conveniently, in the family. *Good for Nothing* (H. Feb. 1851) displays the more sentimental side of Buckstone's writing. The heroine here is Nan, a hoyden befriended by soft-hearted Tom and Harry. In spite of the fact that she has acquired a most unenviable reputation in the neighbourhood, she succeeds in demonstrating that her heart is kindly and generous; the curtain falls just as she comes in from having saved a poor little child from a watery death in the canal. Equally sentimental, but rather more skilful in technique, is Leicester Vernon's *The Lancers* (P'cess, Nov. 1853) with its fresh treatment of an old theme—the meeting of an aristocrat (Victor de Courcy), disguised as a commoner, with a well-born girl (Estelle Duvernay), dressed as a country lass. Where sentiment is not the dramatist's object, most of these plays veer towards the farcical. J. M. Morton's *The Three Cuckoos* (H. March 1850), in this style, presents a typical example. Set in the year 1691, it deals uproariously with the confusions arising from Pertyn Postlethwaite's entering of Colonel Cranky's house in order to visit the maid, Polly.

This style of play perhaps offers but little to attract us; yet we may recognise the importance, for the building up of the later drama, of this sentimentally humane spirit and of these risible low-comedy elements. In some of the plays written in a kindred manner occasionally there is struck out a really appealing situation or a genuinely comic idea. *The Waiter at Cremorne* (Sur. March 1855) may be trivial in theme, but genuinely comic is the way in which W. E. Suter deals with the distress of Mr and Mrs Muddlebank when, by mischance, they engage a waiter whom both recognise as a familiar servitor at some entertainment gardens and who, they fear, knows of their peccadilloes. A *Meg's Diversion* (Roy. Oct. 1866), by H. T. Craven, may be mostly dull, even though it contains a merry Meg and a comically solemn Jasper Pidgeon. We are, however, in the true realm of laughter when Jasper, the uneducated, proudly boasts that he has been studying in order to make himself worthy of Meg. "Ah! your remarks are French polished—a cut above me that", he says, and then adds with feigned indifference, "though this morning I partly translated a Scotch song into Latin." Pressed to produce his effort, he explains:

Well, I saw in a book that *corpus* was Latin for "body", so it immediately occurred to me to adopt it to music. (*sings*)

"Gin a corpus meet a corpus, coming through the rye,
Gin a corpus kiss a corpus, need a corpus cry."

CHAPTER IV

ROBERTSON AND BYRON: PLAYS OF THE SIXTIES

I. *The Old School*

THROUGHOUT the whole of this period these earlier styles remained. They had proved popular in 1840, they still proved popular in 1860, and even in 1900 they still maintained their appeal with certain audiences. Before the sixties, however, there had been no formal opposition; sometimes an individual author such as Boucicault wrested an interest from material which, in the hands of others, was but imitatively conventional, sometimes another playwright caught a glimpse of wit lighter in texture and more spiritually vivid than familiarly appeared in the rough-handled farce which was his model; beyond this, melodrama, burlesque, sentimental comedy and low buffoonery ruled without a rival. The importance of this decade lies in the facts that for the first time in the nineteenth century a clear split is discernible between two distinct schools of playwrights and that, even before 1870, the influence of the younger group had made itself widely felt. In thus speaking of older and younger, no suggestion is made that this contest was one between aged dramatists and more youthful competitors; indeed, some of the most conservative were the least advanced in years. The Old School is simply the school of play-writing which looked to the theatre of 1830–60 for its inspiration; in its ranks it included both a number of veterans whose greatest achievements belonged to previous decades and several younger men, recent recruits, who were prepared to march under the same standard.

How closely the sixties had adopted the popular styles of the preceding decade is realisable when we compare Planché's survey of dramatic tastes in *The Camp at the Olympic* (Olym. 1853)[1] with H. J. Byron's similar bird's-eye view in *1863; or, The Sensations of the Past Season* (St J. Dec. 1863). The latter starts in an author's study; the writer is in despair until Fancy "enters suddenly through the panelling" and summons forth the popular successes of the year. First arrives "the Adelphi Ghost of Haunted Man" from *Robert the Devil*, in which the device of Pepper's Ghost was used to add to the thrilling effect.[2] Other supernatural figures are adduced to testify to the popularity of kindred shows at the time. Next comes Bel Domonio and Manfred, the latter of whom complains about the "fickle town":

> Conceived in poet's brain not to be acted,
> It's most extraordinary, I attracted.
> Remorse at heart, dark fancies in my skull,
> Could I be anything but very dull?
> My long soliloquies, though, seldom tired;
> The crowded audience listened and perspired:
> Though 'twas two hours full ere I'd talking done,
> I still had breath for a tremendous *run*.
> My scenery drew too, which the fact denotes,
> The public must be *canvassed* for their votes.

"At the time when *Society* was performed"—two years later than this, in 1865—wrote T. Edgar Pemberton,[3] "the English theatrical world...was in a parlous state." At Drury Lane Phelps was appearing in a short-lived production of *King John*; the Princess's had Reade's *It's Never too Late to Mend*; at the Adelphi Jefferson was acting in *Rip Van Winkle* and Fechter was at the Lyceum in *The Watch Cry*. The plays were most poor in workmanship and antiquated in technique; the playgoers were apathetic.

During these years, the ancient uniform settled with a not uneasy grace on the shoulders of Byron,[4] an author as prolific as the older Planchés and Dibdins. Byron's efforts were various. Farce, sentimental comedy, extravaganza, burlesque

[1] *Supra*, p. 82. [2] *Supra*, p. 42.
[3] *John Hare, Comedian, 1865–95* (1895), pp. 10–15.
[4] P. Wrey, *H. J. Byron* (*London Society*, xxvi, 1874).

—all came readily from his pen, and this very variety renders his work thoroughly representative of the popular tastes in his time. He never reached very high, but he did succeed in descending to almost unbelievable depths. Perhaps at the start it may be convenient to select two characteristic pieces, one typical of the lower levels and the other of his more ambitious flights. *The Garibaldi "Excursionists"* (P'cess, Nov. 1860) may stand for a number of one-act farces, based on simple themes and depending entirely on absurd situation. Here the absurdities arise from the quandary of Fitzbosh and Poldoody when, forced to join the militia, they fancy they are being shipped off to Italy for the purpose of aiding Garibaldi's insurrection. There is no wit here and no idea behind the plot.

In other plays, however, Byron aimed at something more. When this mood comes to him, an almost problem-drama atmosphere is called into being and sentimentalism rules. Of this kind is *Cyril's Success* (Glo. Nov. 1868). Therein Byron very deliberately tried to accomplish more than the writing of a merely popular piece. Clearly, in the dedication to Shirley Brooks, does he indicate his desire to reach beyond the farcical and the melodramatic. "I have endeavoured", he says,

in *Cyril's Success* to write a Play that would be effective in performance, and not altogether unworthy perusal; and, although it is to a certain extent "classy", I can assure those critics who think London and provincial audiences care only for coarse sensation and extravagance, that having been played a hundred nights in London it "went" (to use an actor's phrase) with very remarkable effect, both as regards interest and applause, in some small provincial towns, where the audiences were principally of the humbler classes, and it entirely eclipsed in attraction two of my melodramas which were played during my country tour.

And now you naturally ask—why write and print this? Simply because I am somewhat tired of being termed a "droll", a "punster", and so on; and, as a mere piece of self-justification—self-assertion it may be termed—beg to remind any one who may care to recollect the fact, that *Cyril's Success* is original, and a comedy—and, even in these vicious dramatic days—in five acts! *There!*

The main character in the drama is Cyril Cuthbert, a novelist, who, because of his success, comes to neglect his wife. She believes that he has been unfaithful to her and leaves him. His success, however, proves but a bubble reputation, and, himself neglected by the world, he remains in abject loneliness until the wife, touched by pity, returns and comforts him. Comedy is provided, alongside this serious theme, by Titeboy, Pincher and Miss Grannett (a schoolmistress, really Pincher's wife). Read in the light of present-day standards, *Cyril's Success* may seem rather a poor production, spiritually separated by aeons from the work of, say, Strindberg though chronologically removed therefrom only by some twenty years. Yet, far-off though it may be in conception of character and plot, such a play as this is to the sixties in England what *Comrades* was to the Scandinavian eighties.

Where Byron most lamentably fails in his serious plays is in creation of character and inventive power. His dramatic figures are all marred by artificiality of treatment, and a general tendency towards self-repetition becomes painfully apparent to any reader of his work. Thus, for example, the sympathetically conceived aristocratic fool whose heart is pure as gold boringly intrudes into play after play. Sir Simon Simple of *Not Such a Fool as He Looks* (Manchester, Dec. 1868; Glo. Oct. 1869) has many brothers. Sir Simon is a young knight who has been reared by the money-lender Murgatroyd. The latter has a niece, Felicia Craven, and for her Murgatroyd has, as it were, nourished this supposed scion of a noble race. Unfortunately for his hopes, however, Felicia shows herself to be a lady of individual spirit; loving, and being determined to marry, a certain Frederick Grantley, she takes Simon into her confidence. Poor Simon now finds himself in an awkward position; deeply stirred by Felicia's story, he takes upon himself the burden of telling Murgatroyd he will not wed her. An enraged outburst from the money-lender and a throwing out-of-doors for Simon are the result; and, more important still, the latter is crudely informed that, far from having aristocratic blood in his veins, his mother is Mrs Mould, the washerwoman. Eventually, in act 5, the wretched youth in search of a mother discovers that to Mrs Mould, also, he owes no filial obedience and that his genuine parents are a certain Mrs Merton and Murgatroyd himself. In this position he stays put; but one has the uneasy suspicion that his stability is the result, not of a preconceived climax in the plot, but simply of the fact that Byron, having exhausted the permitted number of acts, found himself compelled to abandon his riot of shifting paternities.

A type much akin to Sir Simon appears in *Old Soldiers* (Str. Jan. 1873) and *Old Sailors* (Str. Oct. 1874). He does not boast aristocratic birth or upbringing, but in his noble simplicity he shows spiritual affinity to the other. *Old Soldiers* thus introduces a faithful Cassidy who heroically tends the somewhat stupid but honest-hearted Lionel Leveret and aids this gentleman, after he has been nearly cheated by Captain McTavish, to woo, successfully, the desirable Mary Moss. In *Old Sailors*, the faithful servant is Joe Grill, attending Lieutenant Lamb, a retired naval officer, and his functions are the same as those of Cassidy. With these persons associate, fitly enough, several other purely theatrical types—a brewer Pollard who loves a wealthy young Millicent Tremaine, an innocuous gentleman Frank who loves and is loved by an equally harmless Clara Mayfield, and a rich but caddish Ravenbill.

The stock roles became even more strongly marked in *Partners for Life* (Glo. Oct. 1871) which presents, as its main figures, Emily and Ernest, a devoted pair who occasionally indulge in a domestic quarrel, and, alongside of these, Horace Mervyn, a gentleman under the thumb of the villainous Muggles, Sir Archibald Drelincourt, a selfish philanthropist, and the old maid Priscilla. More skilfully, similar figures are moulded into the framework of *Our Boys* (Vaud. Jan. 1875)—perhaps Byron's best play—but types there too they remain. Sir Geoffry Champneys, the "County Magnate", Talbot his son, Perkyn Middlewick, "a retired Butterman", Kempster and Poodles, the menservants, Violet Melrose, the "heiress", and Mary Melrose, "her poor Cousin", are as utterly innocent of individuality as any of the persons in Byron's other plays.

That the public enjoyed such type characterisations, however, is proved by the extraordinary success of this comedy-drama; opening on January 16, 1875, it ran continuously for four years and three months, finally ending its run on April 18, 1879. This popular success alone would make Byron's work worthy of our attention; he had caught better than any of his contemporaries the tastes of the public and in so far stands forward as the most representative dramatist of the sixties and even of the seventies.

Apart from the general weakness in character delineation a manifest paucity of plot material is immediately apparent in his plays. Wealth versus birth, selfishness versus honesty—these form his stock themes. They come into *Weak Woman* (Str. May 1875) which a contemporary critic thought "one of his happiest efforts",[1] and they provide the main theme of *Courtship; or, The Three Caskets* (Court, Oct. 1879). In the latter the principal person is Millicent Vivian, a lady who is pursued by two suitors—Claude de Courcy, a pretended aristocrat in dire financial straits, and Phineas Gubbins, a business man who seeks for a well-born bride. This pair is strongly reminiscent of the similar couple in *Old Sailors*. Millicent's heart goes out to neither of these, for a rather saturnine gentleman farmer, one Edward Trentham, has attracted her attention. Since he is full of the most noble and exalted pride and since the other suitors pester her, she pretends that she has lost all her money. True to contemporary theatrical traditions, Courcy and Gubbins instantly veer off and the fair Millicent is left happily nestling in Trentham's manly arms. Villain and heroine, both cast in conventional patterns, dominate in *The Lancashire Lass; or, Tempted, Tried and True* (Alex. Liverpool, Oct. 1867). This play, cast in the form of a dramatic prologue and three acts (a style inaugurated by Douglas Jerrold), is technically similar to *Blow for Blow* (Holborn, Sept. 1868). The latter first shows us Josiah Craddock arrested for forgery, mainly because of testimony brought forward by John Drummond, a man whose actions are motivated by his unsuccessful love for

[1] J. Knight, *Theatrical Notes* (1893), p. 35.

a fair heroine, Mildred. Thence we move to the main action. Mildred is dead, but Drummond remains filled with bitter thoughts of revenge on his enemies and is barely thwarted as the curtain falls. Sentiment rules here; it rules, too, in the theatrically set *Prompter's Box* (Adel. March 1870) and in the rustic *Daisy Farm* (Olym. May 1871). The whole plot of *Daisy Farm* is governed by the desire and determination of all concerned to keep a certain item of information from the heroine, Bridget. Bridget has found a happy second mate in Andrew Armstrong, when suddenly a Tramp appears posing as her long-lost former spouse. Armstrong gives him £400 to go off, but the son of Bridget's first marriage, Charley Burridge, a wastrel with a few good elements to his character, robs and thinks that he has killed the Tramp. This, of course, is the moment for the appearance of a *deus ex machina*—here a Mr Craven, who, persuading Charley to emigrate to Australia, generally tidies things up. Equally sentimentally are circus folk dealt with in *Fine Feathers* (Glo. April 1873), a play in which Byron returns to a fond and familiar theme—the lost heir. At first it seems that Harry Greville is heir to the vast Gaisford estates—Madame Rumbalino assures him he is the true claimant; then Ethel Carlingford appears as the favoured of fortune; and finally the dark horse comes home in the modest person of Ruth, supposed daughter of Madame. More vital and original is *Bow Bells* (Roy. Oct. 1880). Even if the characters in this comedy-drama are stock figures, the plot at least has an individual theme. After a long and busy career within the sound of Bow Bells, Twinklehorn decides to retire and enjoy the peace of a rustic existence at Sloshington-le-Willows; he will have with him only his well-beloved nieces, Effie and Bessie. The country, however, does not present him with the joys he sought. His butler is rightly named Boozer, boon companion to Sloggs, the gardener, while his house is haunted by the adventurer Captain Basil Bagot and his designing sister, Mrs Percival. Aid has to come from the city ere poor Twinklehorn is released from their clutches. As a final example of this particular style of Byronian drama, which, despite melodramatic incidents and rather poor comedy scenes, reveals potentialities of higher worth, his *Married in Haste* (H. Oct. 1875) may be selected. The main theme here concerns Ethel Grainger who has married Augustus Vere, an artist spoiled by having been made entirely dependent on his uncle Percy Pendragon. Cast off, this couple are shown living in abject poverty. While Augustus amuses himself with another lady, he refuses to allow Ethel to sell the pictures she has painted because he is professionally jealous (again an adumbration of the *Comrades* motif). Eventually Ethel decides to leave him, when suddenly a *deus ex machina* plumps heavily down in the person of Gibson Greene. A reading of this play certainly must convince us that Byron possessed, potentially at least, a real dramatic talent; taking *Married in Haste* and *Cyril's Success* alone, we are inevitably forced to a considerably higher appreciation of his talents than one might form from a perusal either of *Old Soldiers* or of the critiques on his work by Archer and Knight. For Archer, Byron is his "*bête noir* in the dramatic world".[1] These plays, in Archer's opinion, "do not contain a thought worth thinking, a lesson worth learning, a scene worth remembering, or a character worth loving or hating".[2] A more kindly tone pervades the criticism of Joseph Knight, but even he finds very little of value either in this drama, *Married in Haste*, or in Byron's work as a whole:

> When first heard...it leaves the impression of being a clever and almost a good play. Reflection is required before we perceive that the story is artificial and improbable as well as flimsy.[3]

Flimsy, improbable and artificial it may be, but a man who could suggest in 1876 the discussion of two fundamental problems—hasty marriage with its possible consequence and artistic jealousy between husband and wife—is not to be entirely dismissed; and this conviction is strengthened when we recall that Byron, trite as many of his "comic" scenes may be, sometimes brings forth a witty jest almost worthy of Wilde. "I never make mistakes," says Greene, "I could rise to crime, if required; but descend to a mistake—never!"

[1] *English Dramatists of To-day* (1882), p. 121.
[2] *Ib.* p. 147. [3] *Op. cit.* pp. 71–3.

This lighter side of Byron's talent was, of course, much obscured and vitiated by the crudely popular humour of his burlesque. In these he punned and over-punned in a frantic effort to keep funny; in these too he filched unmercifully from his predecessors. *1863; or, The Sensations of the Past Season* (St J. Dec. 1863) takes its conception and even some of its dialogue from Planché's *The Camp at the Olympic* (Olym. Oct. 1853); and it by no means stands alone. Popular as Byron's burlesques proved, they do not show the inventive faculty, the delicacy and the grace so apparent in the work of others. What Planché tries to make fantastic and extravagant, Byron is content merely to debase. His puns are innumerable, but he hardly ever succeeds in striking off an example of this type of humour which seems unpremeditated and yet to the point. The really good pun is a play both on word and on idea; Byron generally is content to dwell merely on a similarity in sound. Where William Brough, in *The Field of the Cloth of Gold* (Str. April 1868), makes Henry VIII, on his return to England after a stormy channel crossing, remark sadly that

> Yesterday all was fair—a glorious Sunday,
> But this *sick transit* spoils the *glory o' Monday*,

Byron rests satisfied with a constant crackling of forced wit which lacks vitality and ease; where Planché's wit soars aloft amid a multitude of fiery sparks, Byron's splutters like a damp squib. His usual style finds fairly typical expression in the following lines from *Aladdin: or, The Wonderful Scamp!* (Str. April 1861):

> Such trifles, perhaps as lace, you might just wring out,
> But good *loud*-pattern'd gowns would make you sing out;
> Plain cotton dresses too would make you wince,
> Fancy a *Princess* scrubbing at the *prints*.
> Talk not of washing, or I fain must scold,
> Remember I'm cast in an *iron mould*;
> Therefore obey your *ryal* father, child.
> —Don't be more vexed, and don't get *father riled*.

or these from *Eurydice; or, Little Orpheus and his Lute* (Str. April 1871):

He aims so sure, he kills all birds that fly,
Brings down the heron with un-*heron* eye.

That contempt is commonly expressed for the pun may partly be attributed to Byron's bad example.

Of Byron's companions there were many. Extravaganzas, full of similar puns, were common, in both senses of the word. Fairly typical is *Leatherlungos the Great, how he storm'd, reigned and mizzled* (Adel. July 1872), by C. S. Cheltnam, where occur many such passages as:

Placidorus. I hope you think our ballet-girls are pretty?
Decollatessa. Their legs, I dare say, are extremely witty;
For more than dancing, nothing, on the whole,
Leads to such elevation of the *sole.*

Alongside of the extravaganzas came the familiar mixed comedies. The setting forth of fixed types in a serio-comic setting, as in Wybert Reeve's *Won at Last!* (Ch. X. Oct. 1869), proved the easiest of dramatic tasks, and most dramatists took the path of least resistance. In these "straight" plays a purely conventional view of life was (with a few exceptions) adopted; this too was the easiest way, for interpretation and criticism imply the exercise of thought. Of such plays, Thomas J. Williams' *Who's to Win Him?* (Lyc. Jan. 1868) is typical. Here Cyril Dashwood is shown in search of a wife; Sylvia, Minuetta, Musidora and Arabella all seek to capture his fancy, but in the end he chooses poor little modest innocent Rose. We are bound to suppose, one must believe, that contemporary audiences did not stop to consider the implications of the last words spoken by this blushing maid:

Arabella (*aside*). My deep-laid scheme entirely thrown away! (*to girls*) To think that Mr Dashwood should have preferred a *little girl.*

Sylvia (*angrily*). Bewildering!

Minuetta (*ditto*). Unheard of!

Musidora (*ditto*). Incomprehensible!

Rose (*to girls*). Nay, not so, my dear friends, 'tis easily explained; young as I am, I know that we all disdain that which is within our reach, and prize most that which is most difficult to obtain;

so, (*to audience*) young ladies, whenever you fall in love with a gentleman, pray don't *tell* him so; let him alone; and ten to one, he'll fall in love with *you*—a too evident partiality only defeats its own object, while maidenly reserve cannot fail, in the long run, safely to decide the all important question,

"Who's to Win Him?"

A merciful "*curtain*" hereupon descends on this nineteenth-century Pamela.

Farcical situations pleased others. J. P. Wooler uses a highly improbable device in *A Winning Hazard* (P.W. April 1865) and drags out his piece with impossible lies and intrigues, based on the idea that, to win a legacy, it is the object of Dudley and Jack to get Aurora and/or Coralie to accept their hands in marriage. The familiar *deus ex machina* (here a Du Graylock) appears in the same author's *Laurence's Love Suit* (Str. Jan. 1865) which deals with the time-honoured theme of a dependent ward (Eva Carlton) who rejects a young gentleman (Laurence Vane) because he is rich. So far as plays of this kind are concerned it would seem as if half the women pursued men on account of their wealth and the other half occupied their leisure in refusing them for the same reason. Absurd caricatures of various kinds fill these pieces. For many it was sufficient to invent the most flimsy of situations and build upon that foundation a ridiculous series of situations. In *A Return Ticket* (St J. Aug. 1862) by George Spencer and Walter James (it actually required two authors to compose this one-act piece) the authors conceive of an old gentleman, a *virtuoso*, who is so infatuated by recent mechanical devices that he will have none but inventors for his sons-in-law; the way in which two lovers disguise and make fools of themselves provides the questionable fun of the farce. This for its absurdity of situation and, say, C. S. Cheltnam's *Mrs Green's Snug Little Business* (Str. Jan. 1865) for its absurdity in characterisation (Mrs Green, Bung the Beadle and Mr Rapps the Policeman) may serve as representative of a thousand others.

II. *The Reform of Robertson*

Against work of this kind Tom Robertson rebelled. The position that Robertson occupies in the history of the English drama is, of course, one a trifle difficult to define exactly. That he was an innovator is certain; yet it is equally sure that his work found its basis in the efforts of his predecessors and that he made free use of melodramatic devices. "Robertson", wrote Boucicault in 1868, "differs from me, not fundamentally, but scenically; his action takes place in lodgings and drawing-rooms—mine has a more romantic scope",[1] and his judgment is absolutely just. Indeed, he might have gone further, for he himself had already experimented in the dramatic treatment of real life; and even before his time Lytton had made a plea for a serious comedy which should be a mirror of contemporary conditions. In presenting to the public a volume of his *Dramatic Works* in 1841 the author of *Money* clearly showed that he realised the needs of his age. "The comedy of a time", he wrote,

> must be faithful to the character of the time itself. In our age men are more earnest than in that of the old artificial comedy. No matter in what department, the essence of the drama is still the faithful though idealising representation of life; and in 1840 we know that all life at least is *not* a jest. In the old comedy there is a laugh at everything most serious. But in that day...the fashion in real life ran in the same direction. In Shakespeare the dishonour of a husband is the material for revenge and tragedy; in Congreve and Wycherley it is the most fruitful food for ridicule and burlesque. But these last writers as artists have their excuse; they are not writing for the pulpit or the academy, but for the stage, and they must embody the manners and morals that they observe around them. It is precisely because the present age is more thoughtful, that Comedy, in its reflection of the age, must be more faithful to the chequered diversities of existence and go direct to its end through humours to truth, no matter whether its path lie through smiles or tears. All that can fairly be asked of comedy for the maintenance of its genuine character is, that the pathos it admits of should not be derived from tragical sources—that it should spring naturally from the comic incidents and comic agencies in which its general spirit must exist.

[1] *Mr and Mrs Bancroft on and off the Stage* (1889), p. 118.

The kind of comedy here adumbrated is tentatively tried in Lytton's own *Money*; an approach is made to it, with melodramatic trappings, in some of Boucicault's plays; Tom Taylor has it in his mind when he writes on themes taken from contemporary life; even Byron endeavours to find expression for it in *Cyril's Success* and *Married in Haste*. Others, such as Edmund Falconer, one of Robertson's most interesting predecessors, went even further. Sometimes this author writes cheaply and shallowly. *Next of Kin* (Lyc. April 1860) may be taken as an example of his more mediocre efforts; this, although styled a comedy-drama, deals farcically with a certain Timothy Chump, who is found to be heir to a great fortune, and with a rascally lawyer named Grubton. Equally poor is the comedy entitled *Does He Love Me?* (H. June 1860) which presents an old-fashioned story of Miss Vandeleur, the heiress, who changes places with her cousin, Miss Melrose, and of Lord Mowbray, who similarly exchanges identity with Everton Leigh. The only vitality visible here is in the creation of the amusing "Physical and Mental" Bubble. In *Extremes; or, Men of the Day* (Lyc. Aug. 1858), however, Falconer displays more interesting material. Though sentimental, this is a well-written serious comedy in the Lytton style; and, in view of its realism, there is interest in observing that the play has been dedicated to the author's "Lancashire Friends"—indeed, we might perhaps say that this is the first of the long line of local dramas which, half a century later, introduced as material the provincial life of England; Falconer thus becomes a true ancestor of Stanley Houghton. His main theme, certainly, is an old one, involving the use of the heavily barnacled will, through which Lucy Vavasour and Frank Hawthorne find themselves forced to marry if they are to hope for an inheritance—a convention of which time must be weary. Yet Falconer does succeed in giving this ancient theme life. Interestingly he develops his duel of love and pride, until, when Frank refuses to marry her, Lucy decides to give him her hand. Low comedy is provided by such doubtful comedy matter as the slippery aspirates of James, the butler, but the main object—the writing of a genuine serious (or sentimental) comedy of character—has been realised.

What, then, we may ask, did Robertson really bring to the theatre? Lytton's critical remarks might almost have been framed as a preface for the *Dramatic Works* of Robertson himself, and about 1860 such a man as Falconer was producing plays which bore a marked resemblance to the genuine Robertsonian comedies. In seeking an answer to this question, we must, it seems, look both within and without; for Robertson's contribution consists both in the spirit of his drama and in his stage reforms.[1] To interpret this contribution aright we must bear in mind that, when Robertson came to write, "realism", in the words of Thomas Purnell, was "wanted".[2] Now, various approaches had been made towards that realism, but the steps taken had been somewhat hesitant and faltering. The introduction of a real lamp-post and a real cab may have been thrilling; such procedure may have made a distinct break with the conventional tradition of the past; yet little attempt had been made to harmonise these real objects with the spirit of the plays or with the methods of production.[3] Boucicault thus mixes freely in his dramas matter of a purely artificial kind and material gathered directly from life. What Robertson did was to emphasise clearly the necessity of securing a complete harmony in performance, and of emphasising what may be termed spiritual reality. In this he was aided by the support of Marie Wilton (Lady Bancroft). Under her management of the Prince of Wales's Theatre, which opened in 1865, an endeavour was made so to polish and refine the performances as to make them artistic unities instead of merely virtuoso entertainments. Sharing his ideals,

[1] Konrad Grein, *Thomas William Robertson (1829–1871). Ein Beitrag zur Geschichte des neueren englischen Dramas* (Marburg, 1911).

[2] *Op. cit.* pp. 80–93.

[3] On this see F. Rahill, *A Mid-Victorian Regisseur* (*Theatre Arts Monthly*, xiii, 1929, 838–44); D. Harrison, *Tom Robertson* (*The Contemporary Review*, cxxxv, March 1929, 356–61); T. E. Pemberton, *The Life and Writings of T. W. Robertson* (1893); *The Principal Works of T. W. Robertson. With a Memoir by his Son* (2 vols. 1889); *Thomas William Robertson and the Modern Theatre* (*Temple Bar*, xliv, 1875); W. Wilding Jones, *Robertson as a Dramatist* (*The Theatre*, N.S. ii, July 1879, 355–60).

Marie Wilton allowed Robertson to direct his own plays, and the care which he devoted to this is amply indicated even in the abbreviated acting texts of his comedies.

It is not, of course, that Robertson was a revolutionary from the beginning of his career. In *The Star of the North* he demonstrates that he was simply carrying on accepted forms. All the persons in this silly treatment of Catherine and Peter are cast in the stock terms hallowed by time; the "Lead, Light Comedian, Character Role, Walking Gentleman, Juvenile and Soubrette", as listed in the printed text, strut and fret their shadowy parts on an uninspired stage. Knowing Robertson's later achievements, one finds surprise and interest in such early works as *The Half Caste; or, The Poisoned Pearl* and *Birds of Prey; or, A Duel in the Dark*. Both of these are melodramas, and at first glance we might say that they offer nothing which might remove them from the familiar run of similar contemporary pieces. Awareness of what Robertson was later to accomplish, however, leads us to detect in both elements of a prophetic kind. In *The Half Caste* the eccentric wit of Lord Falconer and the Hon. Augustus Fitznoddleton suggests later comedy scenes, while the general theme of *Birds of Prey*, vaguely suggesting the mood of *Les corbeaux*, gives a faint suggestion of the purposeful flavour which appears in his more familiar plays. This sketch of pretended aristocrats battening upon fools provides a serious outline to what otherwise would have been merely a play of exciting incident.

Robertson's efforts in realism are adumbrated in *David Garrick* (P.W. Birmingham, April 1864; H. April 1864). The apparatus which accompanies the printed text is revealing. First comes a section on the scenery, with plans for two sets and elaborate description of the arrangements in the rooms. "Closed in", we read,

> Curtains to window, L. 2 E., and open doorway (wide), R. 2 E.; door, L. 1 E., practicable. A is a lacquer-work sideboard; B, B, B. are large China jars on stands; L. side there are smaller vases, and East Indian curiosities, arranged for effect, C. is a backing to R.U.E. opening; pictures on flat are, among others (all very

dingy), a pair of portraits, lady and gentleman, period James I or Charles II; hearth-rug; carpet down; statuette on table, L.C., front, with small books; books on table, R., with one folio Shakespeare. All the furniture having chintz cloths on; bell-pull, R. 1 E.; picture on set, R. 1 E.; high up, looking-glass over mantel; fire in fireplace, to burn; ornaments on mantel.

This is followed by an equally elaborate description of the costumes. Throughout the play itself, moreover, Robertson has indicated, in precise manner, both the gestures of his characters and their relative positions on the stage. These directions naturally become still more extended in the plays which he later penned for the same management. Thus, in *Society* (P.W. Liverpool, May 1865; P.W. Nov. 1865), the space devoted in Act II to the setting and action at the "Owl's Roost" is almost as great as that devoted to the dialogues. That Robertson did not confine himself entirely to "door-knobs" is already proved by contemporary record. Certainly, he wanted a room to look like a room, and he was determined to see that it should contain the kind of furniture and ornament which such a room would have in real life; but more important for him was the sense of spiritual reality to be conveyed by means of his actors. "I look upon stage management, as now understood," declared W. S. Gilbert, "as having been absolutely invented by him."[1]

This reform Robertson was able to undertake at the Prince of Wales's, partly because of the sympathetic direction of that theatre, partly also because social conditions had so altered as to allow an evening's performance to be made up with one single play and to permit that play to run for many weeks.[2] So long as three pieces had to be given on one night and so long as there was constant change in repertoire, there could be but little hope of securing such attention to detail as Robertson demanded. The long-run system may have done much harm, but for Robertson's work it was indispensable; only by time and care might his effects be realised. Spectators could now come to the theatre and feel that they were looking on a genuine domestic interior; many indeed expressed some

[1] See *supra*, p. 32. [2] See *supra*, pp. 55.

surprise that audiences would pay to hear "what they hear in their own houses".[1]

This reference to "hearing" brings us to the inner contribution of Robertson. When care could thus be devoted to the set and the actors, opportunity was offered for a greater realism in dialogue and in theme. Robertson made us, as a contemporary noted, carry "our fire-side concerns to the theatre with us".[2] So far as dialogue is concerned, Robertson, while perhaps not adding anything to what had already appeared in the work of his predecessors, contrived to get a more even flow, a greater semblance to reality, than any of his predecessors had done. Sentimentality there is in his plays, and his moral purpose makes him indulge in passages which are obviously far removed from common parlance. These artificial passages undoubtedly fix themselves more firmly upon our minds than they once did, and, as a result, we are sometimes inclined to overlook the genuine ease and skill of his style. When, however, we are able to shake ourselves free, we realise that, not only has he been sufficiently skilful to adapt his language to the requirements of his several persons but he has the power of evoking a comic spirit distinct from the farcical and burlesque experiments of his companions. It is peculiar, and perhaps unfortunate, that Robertson's deliberately expressed jokes are often trite, obvious and futile, while his plays abound in sly little hits and comments which, because of their appositeness, are excellent theatre. "I would have existence all like Tennyson," sighs a young lady in *Play* (P.W. Feb. 1868), "instead of which, it's nothing but butchers' bills!"

This varied and skilfully modulated dialogue accompanies a fresh treatment of dramatic characters. The drama of the period 1800–60, both serious and comic, had been dominated by type portraits. These type portraits were either of conventionally conceived figures (such as hero and villain in melodrama) or of grotesque eccentricities so absurd as to be utterly impossible. The range of parts was thus definitely

[1] Thomas Purnell, *op. cit.* p. 93.
[2] M. Morris, *op. cit.* pp. 165–87.

limited, and any deviation from the commonly accepted roles was rare and unfavourably frowned upon. It is to Robertson's credit that he restored once more the individually conceived character, and that this was the result of conscious effort and deliberate aim is shown by his continued progress as a dramatist. Such an early play as *David Garrick* (H. 1864) contained a collection of types—Ingot, the familiar old "father", Squire Chivy, the equally familiar "huntsman" with his "Yoicks", Araminta, the typical "bluestocking". Something of this style still remains in *Society* (P.W. 1865); it has practically vanished in *Caste* (P.W. April 1867).

On one other thing does Robertson's reputation rest. In spite of its propensity for sentimental moralisings, English comedy prior to 1860 was largely innocent of any larger sense of purpose. Lytton's *Money* is one of the very few plays of the early nineteenth century wherein may be discerned a desire to introduce something more than a mere collection of type characters involved in a conventional series of intrigues. Put in another way, we may declare that these plays rarely, if ever, paid thought to theme as distinct from plot. This conception of theme value, it is true, is apparent in some of Byron's dramas, but, with hardly an exception, such plays belong to a date after and not before the production of Robertson's *Society*. There can be no doubt that Robertson it was who first in the modern English drama realised the desirability of introducing a central purpose into his comedy dramas. Of this realisation testimony remains in the titles he gave to his plays—*Society*, *Caste*, *Play*, *School* and *War*. Still further, Robertson's aim lay, not merely in presenting a problem or a moral truth, but in surveying this problem impartially. Looking at the Chodds in *Society*, one may be tempted to aver that it was Robertson's aim to ridicule the vulgarities of common life; but a deeper glance shows us that Lady Ptarmigant and her aristocratic companions are correspondingly ridiculed. It was Robertson's virtue that he endeavoured to present a view of the whole life of his time—its complete *Society*. Instead of Byron's rude juxtaposition of well-born pride and the vulgar honesty of the middle-classes, Robertson welded a unified whole from the teeming life of his day.

His skill in plot construction hardly need be insisted upon. It is apparent even in *David Garrick* (H. 1864); indeed, this quality alone gives distinction to that improbable tale of the eighteenth-century actor's noble magnanimity. The same skill carries him successfully through the complexities of the plot used in *Society* (P.W. 1865). Sentimentality rules in both of these, a sentimentality interspersed with patches of comic matter in the "Tom and Jerry" style; but such sentimentality is atoned for by the directness and firmness of the "Owl's Roost" scene in the latter play. Here Robertson displays both a keen power of observation and an acute sense of the theatre. To us its effect may be somewhat cheapened by imitation, but the "five-shillings" episode is cleverly designed:

SIDNEY (L.). I find I've nothing in my portmonnaie but notes. I want a trifle for a cab. Lend me five shillings.

TOM. I haven't got it; but I can get it for you.

SIDNEY. There's a good fellow, do. (*Returns to seat.*)

TOM (*to* MAC USQUEBAUGH, *after looking round*). Mac, (*whispering*) lend me five bob.

MAC U. My dear boy, I haven't got so much.

TOM. Then don't lend it.

MAC U. But I'll get it for you. (*Crosses to* BRADLEY*—whispers*) Bradley, lend me five shillings.

BRAD. I haven't it about me; but I'll get it for you. (*Crosses to* O'SULLIVAN*—whispers*) O'Sullivan, lend me five shillings.

O'SULL. I haven't got it; but I'll get it for you. (*Crossing to* SCARGIL*—whispers*) Scargil, lend me five shillings.

SCARG. I haven't got it, but I'll get it for you. (*Crossing to* MAKVICZ*—whispers*) Doctor, lend me five shillings.

DR M. I am waiting for chaange vor a zoveren; I'll give it you when de waiter brings it me.

SCARG. All right! (*To* O'SULLIVAN) All right!

O'SULL. All right! (*To* BRADLEY) All right!

BRAD. All right! (*To* MAC USQUEBAUGH) All right!

MAC U. All right! (*To* TOM) All right!

TOM (*to* SIDNEY). All right!

Similarly does *Caste* (P.W. 1867), in spite of its Victorian sentiment, make theatrical use of life. The results of George

D'Alroy's marriage to Esther Eccles, the haughty disdain of the Marquise de St Maur, the jollity of Polly Eccles, the honesty of her jo, Sam Gerridge, and the charming kindliness of Captain Hawtree—all are combined to create a definite whole. Even in our modern days, when *Caste* was revived at the Old Vic, its sentimentalities were forgotten in the genuine interest it aroused.

Play (P.W. Feb. 1868) is less entertaining—perhaps because Robertson was a trifle out of his depth in his delineation of the rascally Chevalier Browne, the romantic Rosie and the fervent Frank Price. In passing it may be noted how prone Robertson was to linking his plot up with some legendary narrative material. Here it is a German myth; in *School* (P.W. Jan. 1869) it is the familiar tale of Cinderella. The first act of the latter play starts with a retelling of the fairy tale by Bella, while the other girls listen and pass comments, these comments finally destroying the narration as the ever-important theme of love is introduced:

NAOMI. Go on, Bella, The prince fell in love.
CLARA. What is love?
MILLY. You stupid thing!
TILLY. Such ignorance!
HETTY. That stupid Clara!
CLARA. I don't believe any of you know; not even you big girls.
TILLY. Everybody knows what love is.
CLARA. Then what is it?
NAOMI. Who's got a dictionary? You're sure to find it there.
TILLY. My eldest sister says it's the only place in which you can find it.
HETTY. Then she's been jilted.
MILLY. My pa says love is moonshine.
NAOMI. Then how sweet and mellow it must be.
MILLY. Particularly when the moon is at the full.
NAOMI. And there's no eclipse.
TILLY. It seems that nobody knows what love is.
HETTY. I despise such ignorance.
CLARA. Then why don't they teach it us? We've a music master to teach music, why not a love master to teach love?
NAOMI. You don't suppose love is to be taught like geography or the use of the globes, do you? No, love is an extra.

And it is Robertson's business in the play to show how little Naomi discovers this extra and meets her prince. In a similar fashion, the second scene of *Play* introduces Rosie's retelling the legend "of the beautiful lady in Grey"—a legend which also has its bearing on the action of the comedy. While the device is fairly obvious, it does aid in giving to Robertson's plays a broader foundation and in early focusing the attention of the audience upon the main theme.

School in many respects is a much more interesting and a better written comedy than *Play*. With a fairly deft touch Robertson treats of the love of Lord Beaufoy for Bella and that of Jack Poyntz for Naomi Tighe, and he succeeds in giving individual life to Dr Sutcliffe and his schoolma'am wife. The end is frankly artificial, but we must not condemn it unless we are prepared to condemn a precisely similar device in the last act of Shaw's *Heartbreak House*:

FARINTOSH. A true lady.
DR SUTCLIFFE. So many things are required for the composition of the real thing. One wants nobility of feeling.
FARINTOSH. A kind heart.
DR SUTCLIFFE. A noble mind.
FARINTOSH. Modesty.
DR SUTCLIFFE. Gentleness.
FARINTOSH. Courage.
DR SUTCLIFFE. Truthfulness.
FARINTOSH. Birth.
DR SUTCLIFFE. Breeding.
MRS SUTCLIFFE (*coming between them*). And above all—School.

As a final example of Robertson's work, we may select his *War* (St J. Jan. 1871). No better understanding, perhaps, may be gained of his ability than a comparison of this play with Carpenter's *Love and Honour* (Sur. 1855), written on a similar theme.[1] In the latter is an entirely melodramatic plot; there is a pure heroine; an equally pure hero finds himself confronted by a black and cowardly villain. Robertson's play has a different cast. A melodramatic tinge colours its action, certainly; and the situations are frequently dealt with in a sentimental manner. On the other hand, we

[1] See *supra*, p. 95.

recognise immediately that the dialogue here has a naturalistic ease which sharply differentiates it from Carpenter's effort. The very first lines strike a novel note:

BLANCHE (*heard without*). Never mind; I'll find her in the garden.

JESSIE (*heard outside*). Don't trouble yourself; I'll find them.

(*Enter* BLANCHE *from* D. *in flat, and* JESSIE *from* D. *at back. They look about the stage as if searching for someone. Suddenly they meet each other face to face, and start.*)

BLANCHE. Oh!

JESSIE. Oh!

BLANCHE. Jessie!

JESSIE. Blanche!

BLANCHE } JESSIE } (*together*). Is that you?

BLANCHE. You took away my breath.

JESSIE. And you've made my heart beat.

BLANCHE. Did you think I was a young man?

JESSIE. No, but—

BLANCHE. But what?

JESSIE. I—I don't know.

This opening gives the tone of the whole play:

KATIE. I know all about it. The fact is, that because Lotte's papa is a German—

BLANCHE. Now, don't tell us that, because we know that as well as you.

JESSIE. Yes, we all know as well as each other.

BLANCHE. Girls, I have an idea. As we all know, and all want to tell, let's all tell each other.

THE GIRLS. Yes, yes, yes, yes!

BLANCHE. Well, you know, in Germany it is the custom to call a young lady a bride—

JESSIE. As soon as she is engaged.

AGNES. Just so; and everybody congratulates them—I mean the bride and bridegroom, just the same as if they were married.

JESSIE. How nice! I should like to be a bride.

BLANCHE. And I should like to be a bridegroom.

KATIE. And I should like to be both bride and bridegroom, too.

JESSIE. Oh, how selfish!

AGNES. Katie wants everything.

BLANCHE. And what a bridegroom!

JESSIE. An officer.

AGNES. A soldier.
KATIE. More—a horse soldier.
BLANCHE. And more—a French horse soldier.

This may be regarded merely as a dramatist's trick, a convenient method of concealing the provision of necessary information; but, even though it be a trick, the device is novel and indicates in itself one of Robertson's contributions to the playwright's craft.

A second matter attracts our attention. *Love and Honour* was a pure melodrama, evil brother and all. *War* may occasionally recall the transpontine thrills, but it lacks the familiar vulgar trappings, and, in particular, we note that the villain has vanished. Robertson essays to write, not in terms of theatrical black and white, but in those of life where grey is the predominant shade. The conflicts in his plays are not so much conflicts of moral opinions as the clash and confusion of social forces. Impartially he views *Society*; and with unprejudiced judgment he delineates the racial hatred of French and Germans.

This introduces us to the final and essential difference between *War* and *Love and Honour*. *Love and Honour* exists for a story and its component situations; *War* exists for an idea. It is the very theme of war which dominates the dramatist's mind as he traces the love of Oscar de Rochevaunes and Lotte Hartmann, as he dwells sympathetically on the peace-loving German father. At one step we have moved from an old world into a new, from an exploiting of sensationalism to a deliberate attempt, through the medium of art, at dealing significantly with the major problems of the day. Antiquated though *War* may be to-day, it is definitely and demonstrably modern in its essential conception.

"Of the playwrights of yesterday," says William Archer, "the first in point of merit and influence is undoubtedly Mr T. W. Robertson."[1] A more reasoned view of dramatic development during the nineteenth century must be forced to place Tom Robertson not first in merit among the playwrights of the past but first in time among the dramatic writers of the present.

[1] *English Dramatists of To-Day* (1882), p. 21.

CHAPTER V

GILBERT AND ALBERY: PLAYS OF THE SEVENTIES

I. *The Fantastic and Satiric Comedy*

DURING the gradual but determinedly certain progress of this naturalistic style a few men murmured of revolt. The forces of rebellion, however, were weak and ill-armed; nor may we feel surprised that, confronted at once by the naturalistic pioneers and by the popular exponents of melodrama, they failed to achieve either immediate power or future influence. Among their ranks only one attained a position of pre-eminence, and that rather because of his association with a composer than because of his own unaided dramatic efforts.

William Schwenk Gilbert is a peculiar but a by no means unexplainable figure in the grey shadows of the Victorian stage.[1] Born in 1836, he started his dramatic career at the

[1] On this period generally see *The Eighteen-Seventies* (1929), with an article by Sir A. W. Pinero, *The Theatre of the Seventies*. Gilbert's relations with the drama of his time are dealt with by M. Ellehauge, *The Initial Stages in the Development of the English Problem-Play* (*Englische Studien*, lxvi, March 1932, 373–401). On Gilbert generally see Sidney Dark and Rowland Grey, *William Schwenk Gilbert, his Life and Letters* (1923), A. C. Wilson, *W. S. Gilbert* (*Manchester Quarterly*, li, 1925, 277–97) and Peyton Wray, *Mr W. S. Gilbert* (*London Society*, No. 157, Jan. 1875). An excellent bibliography has been prepared by T. Searle (1931). There are, of course, many books and articles on the operas: see particularly P. Fitzgerald, *The Savoy Opera* (1894), F. A. Cellier and C. Bridgeman, *Gilbert, Sullivan and D'Oyly Carte* (1914), H. Walbrook, *The Gilbert and Sullivan Opera* (1922), H. A. Lytton, *The Secrets of a Savoyard* (1922), A. H. Godwin, *Gilbert and Sullivan* (1926), I. Goldberg, *The Story of Gilbert and Sullivan* (1929), E. A. Browne, *W. S. Gilbert* (1907). Of special interest are C. Lambton, *Gilbertian Characters, and a Discourse on W. S. Gilbert's Philosophy* (1931). On Gilbert's 'philosophy' and on the type of comedy he made his own, particularly interesting are the following: A. F. Marshall, *The Spirit of Gilbert's Comedies* (*The Month*, lv, 1885, 254–62), Max Beerbohm, *Mr Gilbert's Rentrée* (*The Saturday*

age of thirty with a piece called *Dulcamara* (St J. Dec. 1866) and proceeded prolifically to turn out a series of farces and extravaganzas which, although marked by a neater turn of phrase and a more delicate wit, are akin to scores of similar pieces produced between 1830 and 1860. The school to which he belongs is clearly shown; from Planché he derives his original inspiration and thus he stands as the boon companion of the brothers Brough and of H. J. Byron.[1] This indebtedness to Planché was noted in his own time, and has been duly emphasised by both Harley Granville-Barker[2] and Dougald MacMillan.[3] There can be no doubt about it; Gilbert would not have been, had Planché not turned out his long series of pleasant extravaganzas. Again and again may we demonstrate—demonstrate specifically with due citation of act and scene—how many witticisms, quips and cranks the author of *Patience* filched from the author of *Success*. Yet Gilbert's genius was not merely an imitative one. From Planché he may derive much, but he both gives new use to what he borrows and informs his plays with a spirit distinctively his own. As Davenport Adams noted, he "was the first to apply systematically to extravaganza the spirit and method of Topsy-turveydom".[4] That spirit and method found its earliest clear expression in *The Palace of Truth* (H. Nov. 1870).

The Palace of Truth is a blank verse "fairy comedy", a new type of play which we must associate directly with Gilbert's name. The fairy comedy that Gilbert exploited was no pretty-pretty piece peopled by tripping Oberons and

Review, xcvii, May 1904, 619–20), W. Sichel, *The English Aristophanes* (*The Fortnightly Review*, N.S. xc, Oct. 1911, 681–704), H. Rowland Brown, *The Gilbertian Idea* (*The Cornhill Magazine*, lii, April 1922, 503–12), Edith Hamilton, *W. S. Gilbert* (*Theatre Arts Monthly*, xi, Oct. 1927, 781–90), and A. E. du Bois, *W. S. Gilbert, Practical Classicist* (*The Sewanee Review*, xxxvii, Jan.–March 1929, 94–107).

[1] W. Davenport Adams, *The Silence of Mr Gilbert* (*The Theatre*, N.S. xxiv, Dec. 1894, 286–9).

[2] H. Granville-Barker, *Exit Planché—Enter Gilbert* (*The London Mercury*, xxv, March and April 1932, 457–66, 558–73).

[3] *Planché's Early Classical Burlesques* (*Studies in Philology*, xxv, July 1928, 340–5) and *Some Burlesques with a Purpose* (*Philological Quarterly*, viii, July 1929, 255–63).

[4] *Loc. cit.*

coquettish Titanias; indeed, the term "fairy" hardly does true justice to the form. A more just title would be "fantastic comedy", and this would have the advantage of being applicable to those many plays of Gilbert's which, while not introducing the fairy characters, share in the general atmosphere of poetic fancy which was peculiarly his own. *Engaged*, though written in prose about contemporaries, is intimately related to *The Palace of Truth*.

Gilbert's Palace of Truth is a mysterious mansion entering which all persons are compelled, without realising what they are doing, to utter aloud their inmost thoughts. Thither go King Phanor and his court, with the result that the seeming cold Princess Zeolide becomes passionate, the gushing Prince Philamir grows blasé and cold, the Diogenes-like Aristaeus develops into quite a genial gentleman. Perhaps the atmosphere of the play may best be represented by the scene where the artful coquette Azema tries to entrap Prince Philamir, revealing as she does so all the tricks of her trade:

AZEMA. Are you Prince Philamir?
CHRYSAL. (C.). Not I, indeed, fair lady. This is he—
The most conceited coxcomb in the world.
(*With an elaborate bow to* PHILAMIR, *who starts angrily*).
No thanks—indeed 'tis true.
AZEMA (*to* CHRYSAL). Then go your way—
I don't want you! I only want the prince.
'Twas Philamir I came to captivate.
CHRYSAL. Here's candour, if you like!
AZEMA. Oh, leave us, sir!
Find some excuse to go, that he and I
May be alone together.
PHILAMIR. Leave me, sir.
I'll give your tongue a lesson ere the night!
CHRYSAL. How has my tongue offended?—Oh, I see—
Exactly—don't explain! (*Aside*) Poor Zeolide!
Exit, L.U.E.
PHILAMIR. Insolent scoundrel! (*following him*).
AZEMA. (R.). Oh, don't follow him.
I want you here alone. You can begin—
I am not shy, thou I appear to be.

Indeed, I entered here ten minutes since;
Because I heard from those outside the gates,
That you, Prince Philamir, had just arrived.

PHILAMIR. (L.). Then you're a stranger here?

AZEMA. I am, indeed!
The people told me any one was free
To enter.

PHILAMIR. Yes, quite right. Did they say more?

AZEMA. Oh, yes, much more. They told me, then, that you
Received but sorry treatment at the hands
Of Princess Zeolide. They told me too,
That your betrothal might ere long collapse;
(*With extreme modesty*), So, thought I, as I am beyond dispute
The fairest maid for many a mile around—
And as, moreover, I possess the gift
Of feigning an enchanting innocence,
I possibly may captivate the Prince,
And fill the place once filled with Zeolide.
(*Sits* R.—*her dress is disarranged.*)

PHILAMIR. The Princess has a candid enemy!
I beg your pardon, but the furniture
Has caught your dress.

AZEMA (*re-arranging her dress hastily*).
Oh, I arranged it so;
That you might see how truly beautiful
My foot and ankle are.
(*As if much shocked at the expose.*)

PHILAMIR. I saw them well,
They're very neat.

AZEMA. I now remove my glove
That you may note the whiteness of my hand.
I place it there (*near* PHILAMIR) in order that you may
Be tempted to enclose it in your own.

PHILAMIR. To that temptation I at once succumb.
(*Taking her hand—she affects to withdraw it angrily.*)

AZEMA (*struggling to release herself*).
Go on! If you had any enterprise
You'd gently place your arm around my waist
And kiss me.

PHILAMIR. It might anger you!

AZEMA. Oh, no!
It's true that I should start with every show

Of indignation, just in order to
Maintain my character for innocence—
But that is all.

PHILAMIR (*puts his arm round her and kisses her*).
There, then—'tis done!

AZEMA (*starting, with a great show of rage*).
How, sir?
I think it's time that I should take my leave.
(*Very indignantly*) I shall be in the Avenue of Palms
At ten o'clock tonight. I mention this
That you may take the hint and be there, too.

The spirit of *The Palace of Truth* is ironic and satiric, but in his next important poetic play, *Pygmalion and Galatea* (H. Dec. 1871), Gilbert showed that his fancy could move as easily in serious as in comic realms. The irony may still be there, but it is now an irony which approaches the tragic impression. Bringing Galatea to life, Pygmalion is cursed with blindness by his jealous wife, Cynisca. Greatly loving, Galatea, in a spirit of self-sacrifice, voluntarily turns herself once more to stone. Such is the bare theme of the piece; this, however, is enriched, not only by the introduction of several subsidiary characters such as the wealthy patron Chrysos and his wife Daphne, but by a tremulous poetic expression which shows Gilbert capable of greater and more serious things than one might, judging from his other works, have imagined. In this play, inspired though it may have been by *Les filles de marbre*,[1] he proves himself something more than the jester and indicates that his genius contained an emotional as well as an intellectual quality. This seriousness is reflected in a different way in *Randall's Thumb* (Court, Jan. 1871), a peculiar drama amidst this fantasy. The thumb of the title is one under which Buckthorpe is firmly held. Forced to serve the villain's purposes, this hero is saved only by the love of a sentimentally conceived heroine. Such a milieu, however, could not hold Gilbert long. More typical of his genius is the "musical fairy tale" entitled *Creatures of Impulse* (Court, April 1871) which, with the score of Alberto Randegger, anticipates the Savoy operas to come. The witch who

[1] See *supra*, p. 97.

has power to charm and ensnare is characteristic, and even some of the verse reads as if it came, not from this early work, but from one of the famous later series:

Sergeant. A soldier of the King's Hussars,
Although a gallant son of Mars;
To no one may he be gall*ant*,
Except his mother and his aunt!
Pipette. A very proper rule indeed,
And one that surely should succeed.
Peter. But don't you find it rather slow—
Monotonous, in fact?
Sergeant. Oh no!
Each warrior who joins our corps,
Can count his mothers by the score;
And as for aunts—as I'm alive—
Each grenadier has thirty-five!
Peter. I shouldn't like to serve with him,
One's aunt's are elderly and grim.
Pipette. One's mothers too, as facts will show,
Are always aged dames.
Sergeant. Oh no!
The grimmest aunt in all our corps,
Is seventeen—or little more;
The oldest mother's age may be,
A little short of twenty-three!

The intellectually serious predominates once more in *The Wicked World* (H. Jan. 1873), and a comparison of the tone of this play with that of *Pygmalion* is not uninstructive. Sometimes we get the impression in Gilbert's work that he is genuinely afraid of life. He has the seeing eye of the artist, and what he sees makes him terrified. To conceal that terror and to find escape he turns to his topsy-turvy fantasy. In *The Wicked World*, lightly as the theme is dealt with, this is amply apparent. The fairy world here is a replica, in refined form, of a human world below. From the latter, two men, Sir Ethais and Sir Phyllon, are drawn upwards, and through them love is introduced into the fairy realms. At first this love intrigues the gossamer creatures of the upper air, but gradually horror and dismay enter their hearts. In fear they banish the two humans, and banishing them, they cast off the emotion of love. Nature, as Gilbert sees her, is a monster of fair proportions and awesomely cruel spirit. Gilbert himself is the jester who mocks and grimaces lest his own being break under the strain of life and lest his hatred of worldly vices issue forth in terms anti-social and lunatic.

Another aspect of his cynicism, thus born of his peculiarly individual conception of human existence, is to be traced in *Sweethearts* (P.W. Nov. 1874). The first act of this takes place in the year 1844. Here we see an ardent lover, Spreadbarrow, vowing eternal devotion to Jenny Northcott. Brokenhearted at her apparent indifference, he leaves for India after having planted a small sapling before her drawing-room window. In the second act the scene is unchanged, save that thirty years have passed by. The old house is there, but no longer as a solitary mansion, for the city has spread its octopus arms around it; and the tiny sapling has now become a great spreading tree. Spreadbarrow enters, an elderly man, and meets Jenny without recognising her. In an adroit piece of dialogue it is made clear that while he has come to regard his boyish passion as a mere folly, while he even makes a mistake in Jenny's name, she, who had affected indifference, has all this time been living devotedly on his memory. This is sentimentalism, if you like; but it is sentimentalism worn with an intellectual difference. *Sweethearts* is as clever a bit of play-making and as atmospheric a drama as the nineteenth century had, so far, produced.

The quiet sorrows of life, against which naught may prevail, dominate throughout *Broken Hearts* (Court, Dec. 1875). The scene is a lonely island, where dwell in seclusion a group of girls who, injured by the world, have fled here for safety and rest. The only man in their company is a servant, Mousta, an ill-shapen dwarf. The essential tone of the play Gilbert suggests in his very first lines, "*A tropical landscape*" forms the setting, "*in the distance, a calm sea*". Quietly a fountain plays and in the foreground is "*an old sun-dial formed of the upper part of a broken pillar, round the shaft of which some creeping flowers are trained*".

MOUSTA, *a deformed ill-favoured dwarf, hump-backed and one-eyed, is discovered seated* R. *of fountain, reading a small black-letter volume.*

MOUSTA (*reads*). "*To move a mountain.*" That will serve me not,
Unless, indeed, 'twill teach me how to lift
This cursed mountain from my crippled back!
"*To make old young.*" Humph! I'm but forty-two—
But still, I'll mark that page—the day will come
When I shall find it useful. Ha! What's this?
"*To make the crooked straight; to heal the halt;*
And clothe unsightly forms with comeliness."
At last! At last!

The contrast of physical misshapenness and natural beauty, made the more poignant by the entry, immediately afterwards, of the lovely young Vavir, is typical Gilbert's mood. The book which Mousta has is a magic volume belonging to Prince Florian who, possessing the power to make himself invisible, has succeeded in landing on the island. There he finds these broken-hearted girls, each of whom has taken some object on which she may lavish her pitiful devotion—one adores the sun dial, another the fountain. And as the play thus opens with Mousta's pain, so it ends with Vavir's death:

VAVIR (*very feebly*). Weep not; the bitterness of death is past.
Kiss me, my sister. Florian, think of me.
I loved thee very much! Be good to her.
Dear Sister, place my hand upon my dial.
Weep not for me; I have no pain indeed.
Kiss me again; my sun has set. Good night!
Good night!

Without possessing that sternness of character out of which the tragic dramatist is made, without showing any tendency towards that self-superiority from which the satirist takes his being, Gilbert assumes certain qualities of each and frames them in a mood of abject hopelessness. His world is the world of the world-weary and of the disillusioned. "Years afterward, Gilbert told Miss Anderson there was 'more of me' in *Broken Hearts* than anywhere else."[1]

[1] Sidney Dark and Rowland Grey, *op. cit.* p. 54.

In *Broken Hearts* he reaches the most poignant expression of this temper. Joseph Knight's criticism was just when he said that whereas in *The Wicked World* Gilbert was a satirist and in *Pygmalion* a humorist, in this he proved himself a poet.[1] But having become a tragic poet, he suddenly throws off his despair and seeks with a laugh to see the universe, not as a cruel prison and torture-chamber, but as a hall of most ridiculous folly. From this mood spring *Tom Cobb* (St J. April 1875) and, more importantly, *Engaged* (H. Oct. 1877). *Engaged* is a light comedy and it deals with persons who, outwardly at least, are ordinary humans; but in essence its spirit belongs to the spirit which produced the pathetically serious poetic dramas of imaginary characters. From them it takes its pervasive colouring; from them is derived that peculiar laughter which, free though it may be and based on incidents of an almost farcical kind, yet assumes at times a poetic flavour and remains always beyond the reach of farce. Gilbert's own preliminary note is important. "It is absolutely essential to the success of this piece", he says,

> that it should be played with the most perfect earnestness and gravity throughout. There should be no exaggeration in costume, make-up, or demeanour; and the characters, one and all, should appear to believe, throughout, in the perfect sincerity of their words and actions. Directly the actors show that they are conscious of the absurdity of their utterances the piece begins to drag.

Technically, this is the cleverest thing which Gilbert had yet done. It starts with a new device, the surprise exposition, a device which has so frequently been employed by more recent dramatists. The play opens with what seems a perfectly simple bucolic love scene between Angus and Maggie. Then enters Maggie's mother, Mrs Macfarlane:

MRS MACFARLANE. Why, Angus—Maggie, what's a' this!

ANGUS. Mistress Macfarlane, dinna be fasht wi'me; dinna think worse o'me than I deserve. I've loved your lass honestly these fifteen years, but I never plucked up the hairt to tell her so until now; and when she answered fairly, it was not in human

[1] *Theatrical Notes* (1893), pp. 83–8.

nature to do aught else but hold her to my hairt and place one kiss on her bonnie cheek.

MRS MACFARLANE (R.). Angus, say nae mair. My hairt is sair at losing my only bairn; but I'm nae fasht wi' ee. Thou'rt a gude lad, and it's been the hope of my widowed auld heart to see you twain one. Thou'lt treat her kindly—I ken that weel. Thou'rt a prosperous, kirk-going man, and my Meg should be a happy lass indeed. Bless thee, Angus; bless thee!

Immediately after this apparently sentimental-emotional opening comes the shock of the following:

ANGUS (C., *wiping his eyes*). Dinna heed the water in my 'ee—it will come when I'm over glad. Yes, I'm a fairly prosperous man. What wi' farmin' a bit land, and gillieing odd times, and a bit o' poachin' now and again; and what wi' my illicit whusky still—and throwin' trains off the line, that the poor distracted passengers may come to my cot, I've mair ways than one of making an honest living—and I'll work them a' nicht and day for my bonnie Meg!

MRS MACFARLANE (*seated*, R.). D'ye ken, Angus, I sometimes think that thou'rt losing some o' thine auld skill at upsetting railway trains. Thou hast not done sic a thing these sax weeks, and the cottage stands sairly in need of sic chance custom as the poor delayed passengers may bring.

MAGGIE. Nay, mither, thou wrangest him. Even noo, this very day, has he not placed twa bonnie braw sleepers across the up-line, ready for the express from Glaisgie, which is due in twa minutes or so.

This clever device gives the tone to what follows. Ingeniously Gilbert proceeds with the fortunes of Maggie and her Angus, and pursues the susceptible Cheviot Hill through his amazing jungle of amatory adventures, getting him into and out of engagements with extraordinary dexterity until, in the end, he abandons him to the arms of Miss Treherne with whom, it is discovered, he has unwittingly contracted a Scots marriage.

Already, however, by the time when *Engaged* was written Gilbert had discovered another medium of expression—one which was destined to bring him and his collaborator, Arthur Sullivan, endless fame, but which, precisely because of its success, served to deviate his attention from the ordinary drama. With *Trial by Jury* (Roy. March 1875), we may say, the Savoy operas were born; and the realm of poetic drama and of irresponsible comedy lost one of its most promising supporters. These Savoy operas, of course, do not mark any radical change in Gilbert's attitude or in his fundamental method; they too are "fairy comedies". Topsy-turvydom is as prominent here as in the earlier plays; satire at human follies, an undercurrent of pathetic seriousness and an inimitable fund of wit have combined to give them their peculiar popularity, and just such a combination rules in *The Palace of Truth.* In *Trial by Jury* we are introduced to a world in appearance like our own but unlike in thought. The Judge brings to a fitting conclusion the lyrical case:

All the legal furies seize you!
No proposal seems to please you,
I can't stop up here all day,
I must shortly go away,
Barristers, and you, attorneys,
Set out on your homeward journeys;
Gentle, simple-minded Usher,
Get you, if you like, to Russ*her*;
Put your briefs upon the shelf,
I will marry her myself!

Even more alike to *The Palace of Truth* is *The Sorcerer* (O.C. Nov. 1877), with its eccentric Sir Marmaduke Pointdextre and Lady Sangazure confronted by John Wellington Wells, of J. W. Wells and Co., Family Sorcerers. So soon as this last-mentioned character speaks we recognise, too, how closely Gilbert is allied to one who, had he not been stopped by an officious censorship and so forced to write *Tom Jones*, might have been the Gilbert of the eighteenth century. Gilbert is another Henry Fielding with less robustness and a greater wealth of poetic expression. Compare, for instance, these words of Wells with the auction in *The Historical Register* (H.[2] 1737):

MR WELLS. Yes sir, we practise Necromancy in all its branches. We've a choice assortment of wishing-cups, divining-rods, amulets, charms, and counter-charms....Our penny Curse—one of the cheapest things in the trade—is considered infallible. We have some very superior Blessings, too, but they're very little asked for. We've only sold one since Christmas—to a gentleman who bought it to send to his mother-in-law but it turned out that he was afflicted in the head, and it's been returned on our hands. But our sale of penny Curses, especially on Saturday nights, is tremendous. We can't turn 'em out fast enough.

Thus speaks Mr Wells; and here is Fielding's Mr Hen:

Gentlemen and Ladies, this is Lot 1. A most curious Remnant of Political Honesty. Who puts it up, Gentlemen? It will make you a very good Cloke, you see its both Sides alike, so you may turn it as often as you will—Come, five Pounds for this curious Remnant; I assure you, several great Men have made their Birthday Suits out of the same Piece—It will wear for ever, and never be the worse for wearing—Five Pounds is bid—no Body more than five Pounds for this curious Piece of Political Honesty, five Pound, no more—(*knocks*) Lord *Both-Sides*. Lot 2, a most delicate Piece of Patriotism, Gentlemen, who bids? Ten Pounds for this Piece of Patriotism?...I assure you, several Gentlemen at Court have worn the same; its a quite different thing within to what it is without....You take it for the old Patriotism, whereas it is indeed like that in nothing but the Cut, but alas! Sir, there is a great Difference in the Stuff. But, Sir, I don't propose this for a Town-Suit, this is only proper for the Country; Consider, Gentlemen, what a Figure this will make at an Election—Come, five Pound—one Guinea—Put Patriotism by.

The one passage may owe nothing directly to the other, but the operation of mind is the same and the technical means used for securing the satirical effect are almost identical.

A slightly different field Gilbert turned to conquer in *H.M.S. Pinafore; or, The Lass that Loved a Sailor* (O.C. May 1878). Here the whole navy is upside down and the Captain greets his crew in recitative:

CAPTAIN. My gallant crew, good morning.
ALL (*saluting*). Sir, good morning!
CAPTAIN. I hope you're all quite well.
ALL (*as before*). Quite well; and you, sir?
CAPTAIN. I am in reasonable health, and happy
To meet you all once more.
ALL (*as before*). You do us proud, sir!

A still greater verve, a still easier flow of ridiculous rimes and eccentric ideas, have come to the author; nothing quite so good as Sir Joseph's "When I was a lad I served a term" had he introduced into any of his work. Perhaps striving to capitalise on his success Gilbert's next effort was again a sea story, *The Pirates of Penzance; or, The Slave of Duty* (O.C. April 1880), but this suffers from the comparison. Ruth's "When Frederick was a little lad" is not so fine as Sir Joseph's frank self-revelations.

With *Patience; or Bunthorne's Bride* (O.C. April 1881) a new door is opened. The caricature of certain poetic tendencies of the time is magnificently done, and an even cleverer use of rhythmic devices becomes evident:

If you're anxious for to shine in the high aesthetic line as a man of culture rare,
You must get up all the germs of the transcendental terms, and plant them everywhere.
You must lie upon the daisies and discourse in novel phrases of your complicated state of mind,
The meaning doesn't matter if it's only idle chatter of a transcendental kind.
  And everyone will say,
  As you walk your mystic way,
"If this young man expresses himself in terms too deep for *me*.
Why, what a singularly deep young man this deep young man must be!"

Patience was followed by *Iolanthe; or, The Peer and the Peri* (Savoy, Nov. 1882), in its title indicating the close connection which bound Gilbert to earlier writers of extravaganza, and in its settings—"An Arcadian Landscape" and "Palace Yard, Westminster"—showing how equally close was its connection with his own fairy plays. In *Princess Ida; or, Castle Adamant* (Savoy, Jan. 1884) the fantastic spirit has taken complete command, only to suffer a transmutation in *The Mikado; or, The Town of Titipu* (Savoy, March 1885). Deservedly *The Mikado* has become a favourite among the Gilbert and Sullivan operas. A free fancy riots here in a maze of intricated and varied measures. From the lyric movement of "A wandering minstrel I" through the grotesque narrative of "Our great Mikado, virtuous man" and the satirically lively "As some day it may happen that a victim must be found" to the delightfully inane "On a tree by a river" and the grotesquely ridiculous "There is a beauty in the bellow of the blast" the author moves with undiminishing ease and skill.

The manner in which Gilbert sought to avoid self-imitation is indicated by the production of *Ruddigore; or, The Witch's Curse* (Savoy, Jan. 1887) and *The Yeomen of the Guard; or, The Merryman and his Maid* (Savoy, Oct. 1888). The latter, too, shows clearly enough the serious element which, given the slightest excuse, was prepared to rise above Gilbert's eccentric jesting. The figure of Jack Point may be related thus to little Vavir in *Broken Hearts*; Vavir's dying speech has a definite relationship to Point's last song ere he falls, insensible, on the stage:

> It is sung to the moon
> By a love-lorn loon
> Who fled from the mocking throng, O!
> It's the song of a merryman, moping mum,
> Whose soul was sad, and whose glance was glum
> Who sipped no sup and who craved no crumb,
> As he sighed for the love of a ladye!

Jack Point may be a jester and his words may have a comic ring; but again the merriment is born of a universal sadness.

The Gondoliers; or, The King of Barataria (Savoy, Dec. 1889) came next, and here the laughter has regained its sway in a world where

> Lord Chancellors were cheap as sprats,
> And Bishops in their shovel hats
> Were plentiful as tabby cats—
> In point of fact, too many.

Then once more a return in *Utopia Limited; or, The Flowers of Progress* (Savoy, Oct. 1893), an opera in which Gilbert reveals clearly what may be called the philosophic basis of his work. The state where "a Despotism tempered by

Dynamite provides—the most satisfactory description of a ruler" is not merely a joke; it is the logical creation of Gilbert's thoughts on humanity. "Properly considered," says the King, "what a farce life is, to be sure!

First you're born—and I'll be bound you
Find a dozen strangers round you.
"Hallo," cries the new-born baby,
"Where's my parents? which may they be?"
  Awkward silence—no reply—
  Puzzled baby wonders why!
Father rises, bows politely—
Mother smiles (but not too brightly)—
Doctor mumbles like a dumb thing—
Nurse is busy mixing something—
  Every symptom tends to show
  You're decidedly *de trop*—

You grow up and you discover
What it is to be a lover.
Some young lady is selected—
Poor, perhaps, but well-connected,
  Whom you hail (for Love is blind)
  As the Queen of fairy kind.
Though she's plain—perhaps unsightly,
Makes her face up—laces tightly,
In her form your fancy traces
All the gifts of all the graces.
  Rivals none the maiden woo,
  So you take her and she takes you!

Ten years later—Time progresses—
Sours your temper—thins your tresses;
Fancy, then, her chain relaxes;
Rates are facts and so are taxes.
  Fairy Queen's no longer young—
  Fairy Queen has got a tongue.
Twins have probably intruded—
Quite unbidden—just as you did—
They're a source of care and trouble—
Just as you were—only double.
  Comes at last the final stroke—
  Time has had his little joke!

Like this King, Gilbert, who saw so clearly the follies and the miseries of the world, always liked "to look on the humorous side of things".

With *Utopia Limited*, as expressing the inner mood from which Gilbert's fantastic conceptions proceeded, we may take our leave of him—by far the greatest writer whom the English stage had attracted throughout the entire course of the nineteenth century. That his genius was a peculiar one, that he stands apart from the prevailing realistic movement of his time and that he abandoned the ordinary stage for the stage of comic opera, cannot in any wise take from his importance. His influence, if directly it proved but slight, indirectly was enormous. From his work sprang the new comedy of manners, and in particular the eccentric Wildian comedy, during the last ten years of the century. Nor has his power entirely waned. New York, in *Of Thee I Sing*, *As Thousands Cheer* and *Let 'Em Eat Cake*, recently witnessed a revival of musical satire which owed not a trifle to Gilbert's example.

II. *The Continuance of the Realistic Drama*

During the years that Gilbert was thus opening up fresh vistas for the comic dramatist, the realistic movement continued on its steady course towards an impossible goal. A very few authors, mostly members of the earlier extravaganza school, endeavoured to vie with him in producing comedies, but, lacking his grace and wit, they all miserably failed. One example here will suffice. Gilbert à Beckett[1] essays a fairly clever theme in *The Last of the Legends; or, The Baron, the Bride, and the Battery* (Ch. X. Sept. 1873). Introducing a number of characters supposed to belong to the Middle Ages, he contrasts these with another person who is a tourist of the year 2100 come to view some medieval ruins. The story is quite in the Gilbertian manner (and since this play appeared two years before *Trial by Jury* we get another indication of the way in which Gilbert was influenced by his contemporaries), but the ingenuity both in intrigue and in

[1] On him see Arthur à Beckett, *Gilbert Abbott à Beckett as a Dramatist* (*The Theatre*, N.S. ix, March 1887, 146–53), A. W. à Beckett, *The à Becketts of Punch* (1903).

juxtaposition of conflicting thoughts is almost entirely absent. Where Gilbert's work has the immediate touch of authentic genius, à Beckett's is laboured and forced. All we may say is that, in such works as *In the Clouds: A Glimpse of Utopia* (Alex. Dec. 1873), à Beckett proved himself a link uniting the extravagant world of Planché and the fantastic realm of Gilbertian opera.

Within these ten years from 1870 to 1880 the old melodrama still continued to make its pristine appeal, and the lesser houses of entertainment revelled in their bold bad villains and their impossibly virtuous heroines. How incredibly poverty-stricken in style were many of those pieces cannot be appreciated save by those who have waded through the volumes of *Lacy's Acting Edition* or the manuscripts in the Lord Chamberlain's collection of plays, many of which never saw the light of day in printed form. At the Grecian, audiences revelled in such dismalities as Paul Meritt's *Glin Gath; or, The Man in the Cleft* (Grec. April 1872); in the provinces spectators groaned under works such as T. A. Palmer's *East Lynne* (Nottingham, Nov. 1874). The latter is interesting both for its wretchedness of dialogue and for its method of adaptation; Palmer has seen fit to put in brackets after many of his speeches page references to the novel, from which, of course, his plot is taken, as thus:

LEVINSON (*leaning over her chair*). His wife, ah, Isabel, there is the bitterness in reflection, that you *are his*; had we listened to our hearts in those days we might have been happier now, you and I were created to love each other, and (ISABEL *rises*) I would have declared the love that was consuming me, but—....I know the fault was mine, I might then have won you and been happy. (165).[1]

Many of the plays, even those given at more important theatres, were, like G. C. Herbert's *Our Bitterest Foe: An Incident of 1870* (Glo. April 1874), incredibly stupid in theme and execution. Even at the Court, where Gilbert was serving his apprenticeship, audiences could delight in such a work as H. T. Craven's *Coals of Fire* (Court, Nov. 1871), a silly

[1] Act I, scene ii.

drama which tells how Wilfred Jormal jilts Ella for Edith, how his father is discovered to be a swindler, how Edith falls in love with Ella's brother and how Ella thus has her revenge. We may remember, too, that it was this decade which produced Leopold Lewis's famous melodrama of *The Bells* (Lyc. Nov. 1871), for long Irving's most famous instrument.

This kind of drama, on the other hand, was, in the main, moving towards newer things. In such a play as *Gilded Youth* (T.R. Brighton, Sept. 1872) by Sir C. L. Young, although the basis is melodrama, it is melodrama chastened and striving towards a fresh goal. The tone is modern, and the actions are provided with a psychological basis. Still further, the farcical underplot which was the almost constant accompaniment of the older plays of this type has here been replaced by a tone of bantering light comedy. The same development may be observed in other works by this writer, such as the "dramatic sketch" *Yellow Roses* (High Wycombe, Jan. 1878), and the comedietta *Petticoat Perfidy* (Court, May 1885). The latter is particularly interesting since it carries a stage further the social comedy element introduced into *Gilded Youth* and achieves some real success in character-drawing with its Mrs Montrevor and its Mrs Jones. The latter, suspecting that the former has robbed her of the affections of Lord Fabian, dupes her into sitting in an opera-box with a tailor. To gain vengeance, Mrs Montrevor causes her maid Juliette to pose as a Russian princess and so puts Mrs Jones completely to shame. In the end both are discomfited, for it is discovered that Juliette is the real flame of Lord Fabian.

The work of Sir Charles Young, although forgotten to-day, has considerable historical interest. In *Shadows* (P'cess, May 1871), for example, he tries an interesting experiment. The action is contemporary, but in order to demonstrate the links which connect generation with generation the author has introduced a prologue set in 1660. The device is similar to that used in reverse wise by John Drinkwater in *Mary Queen of Scots*. Of all this writer's work only one play is at all remembered now. In *Jim the Penman* (H. April 1886) is told the story of apparently respectable and philanthropic James Ralston, who in reality is a swindler leagued with Baron Hauteville. This rogue's security is threatened by the arrival of Louis Percival, a former dupe, and shattered by the testimony of his wife. *Jim the Penman* is a purposeful melodrama not unworthy to stand beside Taylor's *The Ticket-of-Leave Man* and Jones's *The Silver King*.

The old melodramatic devices might remain, but the essential spirit, as here, was changing. C. H. Hazlewood was thus impelled, in *The Lost Wife; or, A Husband's Confession* (Brit. Aug. 1871), to introduce, amidst a series of improbable adventures which end among the bushrangers of New South Wales, a fully motivated villain similar to Luke the Labourer.[1] Jonas Fletcher here pursues Sir Michael Saxilby with his vengeance, but he has been sufficiently wronged to become more than a stock evildoer. Thus, too, in George Roberts's *Behind the Curtain* (Holb. April 1870), although the technique is old, a certain freshness of spirit is evident in the handling of the subject. The author shows his indebtedness to the past by falling back, at the close of his play, upon those lengthy stage directions which had so pleased a Fitzball and a Dibdin:

BOLTON *makes a feint of taking notes from his pocket, while* TWIST *does the same with respect to will, when* BOLTON *suddenly turns upon him, and after a short struggle throws him,* L.—*as* BOLTON *is kneeling on* TWIST *and takes will,* OLIVE *rushes forward and snatches it from* BOLTON—*picture*—ALL *advance from doorway*—BOLTON *turns upon* OLIVE—*short struggle*—OLIVE *throws* BOLTON *off,* C.—POLICE *enter down steps whom* D'ARCY *has called on—they seize* BOLTON—*he struggles, throws them off and rushes into chamber,* R. 3 E. *followed by* OLIVE—*a pause—report of pistol heard,* R.—GRACE *and* POLLY *scream—music throughout.*

In spite of this, the theme has a certain vitality and the choice of a stage world for milieu is something new.[2]

[1] *E.N.D.* i, 116–17.

[2] Incidentally may be noted the popularity of stage material during this time, as in *Behind a Mask* (Roy. March 1871) by B. H. Dixon and A. Wood, and of police themes, as in Wybert Reeve's *The Dead Witness; or, Sin and its Shadow* (Sheffield, Nov. 1863). *Masks and Faces* and *The Ticket-of-Leave Man* no doubt had much to do with the exploitation of these themes.

During this time the more important works of the contemporary realists in Paris were gradually becoming known, and through this influence the already awakening spirit of the English drama was being impelled still further along fresh lines. Campbell Clarke proved in this sphere an able intermediary. In *Awaking* (Gai. Dec. 1872) he takes the *Marcel* of J. Sandeau and C. A. de Courcelle, and, even though he does alter, succeeds in retaining the more important elements of the original play. The general idea has been preserved intact and the drama remains, what it was, a study in psychology, not without its adumbrations of Pirandellesque methods. The story tells how Victor Tremaine, who has accidentally killed his child several years before, suffers from an obsession, believing that his wife hates him bitterly. The wife, Dr Merridew and his brother Harold decide on an experiment. They bring Victor back secretly to his house and surround him with newspapers and other objects belonging to the time when the accident occurred. The endeavour has for its object, of course, the preparing of the man's mind for the quiet reception of his wife. Less successful was Clarke's version of the *Monsieur Alphonse* by Dumas *fils*. In this play, which he entitled *Love and Honour* (T.R. Birmingham, June 1875; Glo. Aug. 1875), the English adapter, no doubt influenced by contemporary popular taste, has completely altered the essential theme of the French play. In the hands of Dumas, *Monsieur Alphonse* essays to do what Kotzebue tried in *Menschenhass und Reue*—the preparing of such a plot and the creation of such characters as might render a plea for forgiveness of adultery appreciated by an ordinary audience. Clarke, however, evidently feeling that this would not be immediately palatable in a London theatre, has taken away all guilt from the heroine through the introduction of a sham-marriage episode. As a result, the essential basis of its action is completely cut away and any interest we might have had in the plot vanishes. Unquestionably, this version is a failure; but it did serve to introduce something new, and the very cause of its failure gives it considerable historical interest.

The development of the new note in drama is, perhaps, to be seen most clearly in the change almost everywhere observable throughout the realm of light comedy. Already this new note has been commented on in connection with the work of Sir C. L. Young, but to him it is by no means confined. Fred W. Broughton shows something of it in *Withered Leaves* (Sheffield, April 1875) while *Ruth's Romance*, albeit somewhat hackneyed in theme, captures the same mood. The heroine here is a bright and sprightly Ruth, a young lady of fashion who has been forced by her father's will to spend some weeks in the country engaged in farm pursuits. With her lives her sister and her brother-in-law, but this pair, because of the brother-in-law's (Captain Wilton's) debts, remain incognito and as obscure as may be. With Ruth, Jack Dudley falls in love, but, ere the course of his passion may run smooth, he has to surmount various obstacles—the most important being due to the fact that, hearing Ruth and Wilton in private conversation, he believes they are lovers and imagines the worst. The easy dalliance of Broughton's dialogue, though William Archer failed to see it, was to be of profound value for the later theatre.[1]

The increased technical skill of these dramatists of the seventies is shown, too, by such a play as Walter Lisle's *The Love Test* (Gai. June 1873) where a half-hour of badinage is kept up, uninterruptedly and without action, by two characters only. For a playwright of 1830 such a task would have been a hard one, but Lisle succeeds here in keeping our interest intent on his lively Mrs Leslie and his honest Captain Beaumont. *The Love Test* is only one of many such single-act comediettas which, introducing only two characters, sought to concentrate attention on character and dialogue instead of on action. Most of them, certainly, like S. Theyre Smith's *Happy Pair* (St J. March 1868), simply ring the changes on domestic infelicities;[2] but the commonness of themes and persons should not conceal from us the very important training ground they provided for those later dramatists who,

[1] See W. Archer, *English Dramatists of To-day* (1882), pp. 87–94.
[2] On Smith see W. Archer, *op. cit.* pp. 328–33.

abandoning the swift movement of the melodramatic stage, were determined to evoke dramatic excitement out of ordinary thoughts and commonplace motives. In two respects particularly did these plays thus give assistance towards the building up of a new drama. When only two characters appear on the stage throughout the course of a play, obviously that play, if it is to have any hope of success, must be dominated by an idea. It may be simply the idea of a wife's revolt, as in *Happy Pair*, or that of elderly love-making, as in *The Love Test*; but, however vague and however trite, there has to be introduced something of which most of the earlier farces were entirely innocent. Secondly, in such plays the dramatist must concentrate on style. His dialogue has to have verve, logical development and point. Again, when we turn for comparison to the older plays, we find that frequently a playwright, feeling his dialogue grow weak, took the easiest course and allowed horse-play to make up for his lack of wit. Of this expedient the new dramatists refuse themselves permission to make use; they are willing to restrict themselves to a bare interior, a couple of chairs and two persons who, if they move at all, do so only to settle in their chairs again. The light easy style, as exemplified in the plays mentioned above, in C. M. Rae's *Follow the Leader* (Ch. X. April 1873) or in J. W. Jones's *On an Island* (Bradford, March 1879), where Jack and Mildred, accidentally abandoned on an island in Windermere, patch up an old quarrel, has triumphed over farcical incident.

As yet, of course, comedy had not been able to cast over the sentimentally rosy colouring which had rouged its cheeks since the eighteenth century. A new light comedy was unquestionably coming into existence; but so far it remained heavily trammelled by that sickly emotionalism which had been passed down from Cumberland and Kelly. The union of the two qualities is well to be seen in the work of James Albery.[1] Everyone knows the title at least of his most famous play, *Two Roses* (Vaud. June 1870), a drama second to none

[1] See *The Dramatic Works of James Albery*, ed. by Wyndham Albery (2 vols. 1939).

in this period both for influence and for popularity. So far as plot is concerned, Albery here is content to follow along time-worn lines. The central figure, if not the hero, is Digby Grant, a decayed gentleman who has not been too proud to accept presents from Jenkins and loans from Jack Wyatt. Suddenly, however, he finds himself—or thinks he finds himself—the possessor of an income totalling £10,000 a year, and at once he breaks off the engagement between Jack and his daughter Lotty. Fortune in comedy has usually a trick in store for persons who act in this wise, and, by the time the third act is reached, Grant discovers to his dismay that the £10,000 a year income really belongs to the poor, rejected Caleb Deecie, a blind youth who has been passionately devoted to Grant's other daughter, Ida. The story, as will be realised, is a tissue of episodes, each one of which had been consecrated by frequent use; any claim Albery may have cannot rest on his theme. This theme, however, has associated with it a number of figures interestingly drawn. Digby Grant has personality, even if that personality is of a somewhat unenviable sort. Similar characters have been introduced in a variety of plays from 1870 on to our own day—sometimes, as here, he is a decayed gentleman living on his social position, sometimes he is an impoverished artist, living on his reputation for genius—but, whatever his actual status may be, he displays the familiar contempt of money and willingness to sponge on others. Save when such a character is presented in a new light, we have become a trifle tired of his eccentricities now, but again we must remember that in 1870, so far as the stage was concerned, he had all the virtues of novelty. He represented an entirely fresh comic type, and it must be confessed that Albery has succeeded in wresting from him a number of scenes which, even to-day, still possess comic vitality. Jenkins, too, is an individuality and a creation; while, if the one lover, Jack Wyatt, is somewhat conventional, the other, Caleb Deecie, has an engaging and sympathetic presence. One of Albery's great assets clearly lay in his power of drawing character.

In addition to this, he shared with others of his time a new skill in the writing of dialogue. When Mrs Cupps, Grant's landlady, presents him with her bill, that gentleman airily waves her aside. "And yet", says Mrs Cupps, "you pay away money without occasion. Last night you gave my potman sixpence to fetch you a cab—but I must go without!" To this Grant replies:

Mrs Cupps, you do not understand the feelings of a gentleman. I cannot be under obligations to a potman—absurd! Your case is different. There's your account—I acknowledge the debt—I do not dispute it, or attempt to deduct overcharges, or take off a discount for cash like a common cad. If you bring it to me next year, I shall still acknowledge it; I can do no more—I am a gentleman, I can do no less.

There is evident here a nice sense of values—character values as well as those that appertain to dramatic rhythm and comic purpose. A disciple of Robertson, Albery makes marked advances and definitely leads the comic stage towards the plays of Wilde.

With these two essential qualities, it may seem strange that Albery did not succeed in doing more for the stage than he actually succeeded in accomplishing. The reason of his failure lay, first of all, in that weakness of plot-constructing power to which reference has been made. Throughout the whole of his dramatic career this weakness is evident and possibly because of it Albery turned so freely to the French for his later themes. *The Spendthrift; or, The Scrivener's Daughter* (Olym. May 1875) thus might have been a really good comedy had it not been marred by the introduction of a series of utterly impossible and improbable situations. The second defect lay in the lack of unity in Albery's aims. Throughout Gilbert's writings we may trace a consistent progress; pathos may predominate in one, satire in another, light jesting in a third—but the pathos, the satire and the jesting are all demonstrably the varied expressions of one man's personality. Personality it was that Albery lacked. At one moment he is penning sentimental comedy of *Two Roses* type; next he is trying to pursue Gilbert with poetic fantasies like *Oriana* (Glo. Feb. 1873) and *The Will of Wise King Kino* (P'cess,

Sept. 1873), showing in this how far he fell below Gilbert's easily attained eminence; next he turns to French sources and out of *Les dominos roses* he fashions that play, *The Pink Dominos* (Crit. March 1877) which seemed so *risqué* to the society of its day, and in which the sentimental comedy is laid aside in favour of a rather mawkish cynicism; next again wc have him turning to the serious plays of Sardou and Augier, making a *Crisis* (H. Dec. 1878) out of *Les Fourchambault*. Lack of a central purpose and not creative versatility explains this strange variety. "Most undisciplined" of the better dramatists of his day, Joseph Knight considered him,[1] and the criticism is just. William Archer expressed a similar opinion about his work. "I should like," he wrote,

> in conclusion, to sum up Mr Albery's literary character in a neatly rounded paragraph, but it somehow does not lend itself readily to neatly-rounded treatment. It is too full of contradictions and paradoxes. His mind has so many different veins and strata that a whole case-full of specimens would be necessary to present an adequate sample of it.[2]

In this his talent proved but a reflex of the spirit of his age. The theatre was in a state of transition. New ideas were germinating; new devices were being tried out; new experiments were being made in choice of theme and of character; but so far there was but little sense of conscious direction. The audiences had increased and, as all contemporaries noted, fresh interest was being taken in things theatrical, but the spectators' tastes were mixed and no one could clearly diagnose what they would desire. The raw material, as it were, had been prepared for the modern drama, but the modern spirit had not yet come to form that raw material into the finished fabrics, the comfortable and uncomfortable woollens of the problem play, the delicate silks of the new comedy of manners.

[1] *Theatrical Notes* (1893), p. 37.
[2] *English Dramatists of To-day* (1882), pp. 85–6.

CHAPTER VI

JONES AND PINERO: PLAYS OF THE EIGHTIES

I. *The Turn of the Tide*

In the year 1882 appeared a remarkable volume. William Archer was at that time a young enthusiast for the theatre and *English Dramatists of To-day* was his first published book. So many works of kindred sort have succeeded this essay of 1882 that maybe we shall be apt to overlook its real significance unless we bear firmly in our minds the thought that it was the only study up to that date which deliberately attempted to provide a critical survey of contemporary dramatic writing. There had been, of course, hundreds of volumes written on stage affairs, but almost all of these were either biographical and anecdotal (lives of actors and the like) or historical. The only predecessors of Archer's series of critical estimates were the collected reviews of men like Hazlitt and Leigh Hunt, and those, while they succeeded in presenting a clear and vivid picture of the contemporary stage, did not have the same comprehensive aim as he held before himself in the composition of his work.

The publication of *English Dramatists of To-day*, therefore, marks a distinct level reached by the theatre of the early eighties; it reflects the new living interest which had been awakened among thinking people in the fortunes of the English drama. This living interest may be amply traced, too, in the periodical writings of the day. From 1850 to 1870 the newspapers and journals had tended monotonously to echo those complaints concerning dramatic decline which had been so piteous in earlier years.[1] In 1871 Tom Taylor was engaged in shedding many tears over the poor dejected stage

[1] *E.N.D.* i, 58–77.

of his time.[1] Long runs, show and machinery induced his severest comments and, characteristically, he contrasted present with past unfavourably. "Till the present generation", he opined, "the theatre was pre-eminent among amusements, and commanded attention and interest from all classes, the most instructed and cultivated, as well as the most high-bred." Even at the very close of this decade there were men still prepared to praise the "palmy" days of English drama between 1800 and 1825.[2] "With the rapidity of a whirlwind," wrote another, forgetting earlier complaints, "and with much of its wildness, a sudden passion has arisen, to run down our English Theatres, our Managers, and our actors in a breath."[3] H. F. Hyde, a few years later, referred to the repeated "remarks on the dearth of dramatic authors",[4] a fact accepted as unchallenged in *The Theatre* for 1877.[5]

Archer's book and the periodical writings of the eighties introduce us to something new, to an entirely fresh approach. For Archer the terms "yesterday" and "to-day" mean, not "flourishing" and "moribund", as they had done for earlier critics, but "outworn" and "vital" respectively. Suddenly men came to the realisation that the dramatist's worth was beginning to be appreciated and that "men of the mightiest intellect" were coming to devote themselves to the stage.[6] That "the attitude of Literature towards the stage" was "now more friendly than it used to be" was recognised by Henry Morley in 1880,[7] and, speaking thus at University College, London, he drew attention to the fact that, on the

[1] Article by Tom Taylor in *Dark Blue*, discussed in *The Era*, xxxiii, Aug. 27, 1871, 11.

[2] *The Theatre*, N.S. ii, June 1879, 296–300.

[3] *The Era*, xxxiii, Aug. 20, 1871, 12.

[4] *Id.* xxxvii, May 2, 1875.

[5] N.S. i, July 1877, 343–4, where the long run is held responsible. Other references of a similar kind may be found *id.* N.S. ii, Feb. 1879, 1–4 and 14–17; March 1879, 71–5 and 107–8; *The Era*, xli, Jan. 26, 1879, 12–13.

[6] *The Era*, xli, Feb. 9, 1879, 12; xlii, Nov. 2, 1879, 12. W. S. Gilbert, in a letter to *The Times* (Feb. or March 1879) declared that it was "most unfair" to require authors of established reputation to submit their plays "in a complete form" (that is to say, in a matinée production). A new attitude is apparent in his remarks.

[7] Cf. *The Era*, xlii, Jan. 11, 1880, 3.

night of his lecture, there were nine original plays being acted in London as against six taken from the French. This, he observed, was "a change and an improvement upon the state of things two years ago".[1] As yet, of course, there was no general agreement concerning a genuine dramatic revival, and some persons continued to murmur either against the literary men of the time or against the supposedly unfair conditions which prevented these literary men from giving their best to the stage. Writing to *The Times* in January 1880, Henry Irving deemed the "dearth of good dramatists" to be "unquestionable", proposing as the reason that "although many people are anxious to write for the stage, few will take the trouble to study the technique which is essential to an acting play".[2] In this judgment he was supported by J. Palgrave Simpson who thought that "it is not dramatists who are needed...but dramatists who...know their business",[3] but countered by F. C. Burnand who declared that

> there's no dearth of authors, but there's a deuce of a difficulty in getting them to write. Those who get their living by it...are all hard at work from year's end to year's end, not only at plays, mind you, but at half-a-hundred other things—essays, articles, magazines, books. The current literature of the day takes it out of them, so to speak, and leaves them small time for really important work.

By 1883, however, the "remarkable improvement in the condition of the English drama", the beginnings of which had been traced by Henry Morley, had become indisputable.[4] "The British Drama," he said,

> is no longer written by Frenchmen; and no longer are plays presented as New and Original which are not adapted, only taken, from the French.... It seems as though the English dramatist instead of stealing the Frenchman's plays ready-made, has rather

[1] In the same year (*The Era*, xlii, Aug. 22, 1880, 3) Frank Freeland took up Gilbert's complaint and emphasised the fact that while managers were prepared to take the work of known authors, the untried dramatist (unless he had money to put his play into matinée performance) was doomed to silence. See *supra*, pp. 59.

[2] See *The Theatre*, N.S. i, Jan. 1880, 1–11.

[3] *Id.*

[4] *The Saturday Review*, lxi, Nov. 3, 1883, 364.

awakened to the greater advantage of borrowing the Frenchman's tools and of using them to make his own. The recent raising of the general level of the contemporary British drama is due to the adoption of French methods and customs.

The passing of but a few seasons during these adventurous years wrought strange marvels. "The extraordinary number of new plays produced" was noted by *The Saturday Review* in its comprehensive survey of the season 1887–8;[1] this was regarded as evidence of an increased "dramatic literary industry", warranting employment of the phrase "Renaissance of the Drama".[2]

In viewing this advance, of course, we must bear in mind two facts—first, that, while a fresh technique was entering in and while some revolutionary experiments were being made, the old guard continued to hold its own with the greater public, and, secondly, that many critics, championed by Clement Scott, did their best to stem the rising tide.[3] The results of a competition organised by *Truth* in the summer of 1884 are, in this connection, highly illuminating. The popular favourites were duly graded, and the voting provided the following list. Three men came in the "50" class—H. J. Byron (57), T. W. Robertson (56) and W. S. Gilbert (51); four were in the 40's—W. G. Wills (48), Tom Taylor (47), Lord Lytton and Dion Boucicault (both 45); two in the 30's—G. R. Sims (36) and Charles Reade (33); and two in the 20's—J. Albery (24) and F. C. Burnand (23). Nothing could indicate more clearly the general tastes of the public. On the other hand, the playbills of these years tell the story of advance. The season 1887–8 saw the appearance of Mrs Beere's productions of F. C. Grove's *As in a Looking Glass* and Mrs Praed's *Ariane*, and of Olga Nethersole's production of *The Dean's Daughter* by Sydney Grundy and F. C. Philips.[4] The following years witnessed the appearance of A. W. Pinero's *The Profligate* (Gar. 1889), H. A. Jones's *Wealth* (H. 1889), and *The People's Idol* (Olym. 1890), wherein

[1] *The Saturday Review*, lxvi, Aug. 4, 1888, 147.
[2] *Id.* lxvi, Dec. 8, 1888, 676.
[3] See *supra*, p. 23.
[4] On these see *The Theatre*, N.S. xxiii, May 1894, 239–47.

W. Barrett and V. Widnell dealt with the question of capital and labour, a theme likewise taken up by W. Bourne in *Work and Wages* (Hanley, 1890; Pav. 1890) and by W. J. Patmore in *Capital and Labour* (Pav. 1891).[1] About the same time L. N. Parker treated the theme of illicit love tragically in *The Sequel* (Vaud. 1891) and W. Jones discussed hereditary insanity in *The Scapegoat* (Glo. 1891). It was all of this which made Clement Scott feel it his bounden duty to speak out boldly. "I can see no value", he said,

> in a play that only provokes disgust—no pity, no love, no charity, no mercy, no tenderness, no nobility—only cowardice, meanness, and horror.[2]

Such plays, he thought, were ruining the stage.

II. *Henry Arthur Jones*

If we refer back to the *Truth* competition, it will be observed that of the eleven favourites recorded there William Archer dismissed five in a single chapter devoted to the "dramatists of yesterday"—Robertson, Taylor, Lytton, Boucicault and Reade. His own catalogue includes sixteen playwrights, among whom appear the other six from the 1884 competition. This leaves ten whom, although not voted for heavily by the readers of *Truth*, Archer would place among the "dramatists of to-day". Some of these we have already encountered as representative dramatists of the seventies—Broughton, Meritt and Smith; the others are Sydney Grundy, Bronson Howard, H. A. Jones, H. C. Merivale, A. W. Pinero, Robert Reece, Alfred Tennyson and W. G. Wills.

Whatever shortcomings Archer may have had as a critic, his youthful acumen is ably demonstrated by his inclusion of Jones and Pinero among his company of major writers, for neither had, before 1882, done much to merit such a choice. Cleverly and keenly Archer sensed their potentialities.

[1] On this subject of labour and strikes see *The Theatre*, N.S. xxi, Feb. 1893, 99. George Moore's *The Strike at Arlingford* appeared at the Opera Comique in 1893.

[2] *Why do we go to the Play?* (*The Theatre*, N.S. xi, March 1888, 117–26).

"Though neither long nor eventful," he wrote, "the career of Mr Jones as a dramatist has been promising",[1] and this promise gave him hope for the future. Up to that time Jones had given to the stage *Hearts of Oak* (Exeter, May 1879), *Harmony Restored* (Grand, Leeds, Aug. 1879), *Elopement* (Oxford, Aug. 1879), *It's Only Round the Corner* (Exeter, Dec. 1879), *A Clerical Error* (Court, Oct. 1879), *An Old Master* (P'cess, Nov. 1880), *His Wife* (S.W. April 1881), and *Home Again* (Oxford, Sept. 1881).[2] Of these, Archer knew only three—a couple of comediettas and the dramatisation of a novel by Anthony Hope; yet, from such limited knowledge, he divined what we, with our advantage in time, recognise as among Jones's most valuable assets—"a good deal of culture and a great deal of earnest aspiration".[3]

Two forces moulded Jones's apprentice efforts—the influence of Robertson and the less tangible influence of contemporary melodrama, and of these perhaps the latter is the more important. Throughout the whole of his career he found that the serious theme provided him with the greatest opportunity for the expression of his dramatic interests. True, he could on occasion turn out a comedy-farce like *The Deacon* (Shaft. Aug. 1890) and a comedy of manners such as *The Liars* (Crit. Oct. 1897), but these were not his most characteristic plays; his early work is best represented in *The Silver King* (P'cess, Nov. 1882) and his later in *Michael and his Lost Angel* (Lyc. Jan. 1896).

In his youth Jones was thus trained in the melodramatic tradition. *Hearts of Oak* (Exeter, May 1879) moves along a path trodden by countless feet since the beginning of the nineteenth century. The large legacy concealed in an ancient manor had served many another dramatist, and Jones makes no more startling use of it than his companions had done.

[1] *Op. cit.* p. 220.

[2] On Jones's dramatic work see R. A. Cordell, *Henry Arthur Jones and the Modern Drama* (1932), D. A. Jones, *The Life and Letters of Henry Arthur Jones* (1930), P. Shorey, *Henry Arthur Jones* (1925), and W. A. L. Bettany, *The Drama of Modern England as viewed by Mr H. A. Jones* (*The Theatre*, N.S. xxii, 1893, 203–9). His plays are, of course, discussed in all volumes dealing with the "dramatic renaissance".

[3] *Op. cit.* p. 225.

Grandfather Prettyjohn, cynically wise though he be, is a stock character; the love of Kitty Prettyjohn for the ne'er-do-well Ned Devenish runs roughly in conventional manner; and the villain, Mr Cornelius, differs from other villains in nothing save that he has the grace to show faint twinges of conscience. *The Silver King*, written in collaboration with Henry Herman, belongs to the same school; it certainly would never have been composed had Tom Taylor not penned *The Ticket-of-Leave Man* in 1863. This, of course, does not mean that *The Silver King* possesses no merit. It is, indeed, a well-constructed and interesting play of its kind; but its kind is that of melodrama. Wilfred Denver, like the hero of Taylor's play, is cast among evil companions and barely succeeds in escaping the clutches of the law. Eventually he finds himself in America and returns to England as a wealthy man to wreak vengeance on his foes and relieve the distress of his poverty-stricken wife. Dark villainy, sentimental pathos and a dash of comedy are employed here to build up an atmosphere which, although it bears the semblance of reality, is demonstrably theatrical.

The Silver King presents to us two of the qualities destined to be the most clearly marked in Jones's later writings—a desire to treat certain social problems seriously and a tendency to infuse into this treatment much of an artificial and melodramatic flavour. Of these, *Saints and Sinners* (Margate, Sept. 1884; Vaud. Sept. 1884) may be taken as an example. The preface to this play clearly indicates the author's desire to enlarge the sphere of dramatic material and to bring to the drama of his time a sense of artistic and philosophic purpose. In so far, Jones was doing, earlier than Pinero, what the latter accomplished in *The Second Mrs Tanqueray* (St J. 1893). Indeed, he went further, for whereas Pinero restricted himself to purely social problems and to the delineation of character, Jones here made a plea for the introduction into the theatre of larger problems still, of questions not concerned with man's relation to man but of those where man's relation to God was the object of enquiry. Bold as this endeavour was, however, Jones failed in two ways. First of all, here as elsewhere, he was apt to interpret religious problems in a material way. His interest is not in faith and pious rapture but in sectarian conventions and the outward manifestations of piety. The beliefs of a particular church concern him little; his mind is mightily occupied with the social results of the clash between church and chapel. Secondly, because of his training in melodrama, Jones constantly falsifies and makes artificial both his situations and his characters. *Saints and Sinners*, which, to be effective, ought to have been etched in delicate shades, becomes monotonously crude with its violent contrasts. The story tells of Jacob Fletcher, Minister of the Bethel Chapel, Steepleford. This man's daughter, Letty, a good-natured girl weary of her daily round of dull respectability, is entrapped by the villain, Captain Eustace Fanshawe. With the aid of George Kingsmill, Letty's faithful lover, Jacob succeeds in releasing her; but in the meantime rumours of her escapade have been bruited abroad. At his chapel Samuel Hoggard, a sanctimonious money-grabber, stands out against Jacob and gets him hounded out of his position. The last scene shows Letty miserably dying. The play is unquestionably an interesting one, but its effect becomes weakened because of its emphasis on social conventions and because of its sentimentally melodramatic colouring. "If ever there was a devil on the face of this earth," says Leeson, Fanshawe's servant, "it's Captain Eustace Fanshawe!" and that gentleman himself thus soliloquises:

> And I might have been a good man, I suppose—if I could have chosen my own father and mother, and if everything and every creature I've met, from my cradle upwards hadn't pushed me to the bad. If, instead of meeting that other woman ten years ago, I had met with Letty Fletcher—What's the good of wishing? After all, there's a great comfort in being out-and-out wicked—it's like being soaked through, you can defy the elements.

No black-whiskered villain of 1830 could have expressed himself with greater assurance. Indeed, had we met with this speech out of its context, we should hardly have guessed that it came from a play which may be regarded as one of the first of modern English problem dramas.

The sentimentalism which underlies *Saints and Sinners* finds even clearer expression in a number of plays written about this time—notably in *Sweet Will* (New Club, C.G. March 1887). Here Will Darbyshire loves Judith Loveless, but refuses to reveal his adoration because he has to go to a fever-infested district of the Orient in order to provide an income for his old mother. Just as our feelings are at the point of being hopelessly harrowed, a *deus ex machina* (in the shape of a Chicago friend) makes a gesture, if not an appearance, by sending him a present of 50,000 dollars. Joy in his heart, sweet Will tells Judith he loves her and wedding bells begin to peal in the distance. It is all very pretty and all very absurd.

But if one part of *Saints and Sinners* finds exaggerated expression in *Sweet Will*, another, and a more important part, is carried to extremes in Jones's strangest play, *The Tempter* (H. Sept. 1893)—a still more courageous effort to establish a new verse drama. The effort proved futile and even disastrous, yet nevertheless by making it Jones showed that he had a vision beyond that of Pinero. Where the latter reached a culmination of artistic striving in the naturalistic social drama, Jones, in spite of his often petty and querulous girding at Ibsen, proved himself anxious to get further than mere naturalism might carry him and devise a medium of expression richer and more profound than the imitation of real life could offer. The very setting of *The Tempter* is interesting—fourteenth-century life with the Devil in a physical embodiment drawing Prince Leon from the love of Lady Avis to that of Lady Isobel. The attempt was surely a noble one for the year 1893, and the attack on realism in the critical preface sounded a note rarely heard in those years. Again, however, Jones failed—failed partly because he was not poet enough to master such a theme, partly because his mind was too little to grasp the implications of that theme, partly because of his own overweening self-confidence. A very great leader he might have been; instead of which he made himself an exceedingly lonely figure. Striving to bring religion into drama, he professed to despise religion; striving to get beyond a narrower naturalism, he turned foolishly and besottedly against Ibsen; striving to reform the stage, he bitterly attacked William Archer. "For many years", he wrote in answer to some of Archer's criticisms, "I have been in great peace about the future of my soul. I am in equal peace about the quite minor question of my future place in the English drama." By the narrowness of his outlook and the pettiness of his nature, Jones ruined whatever chances he had of guiding the drama of his time in new directions.

That is not to say he did not do important work; it implies only that he might have done greater. His own mind could not keep pace with his dreams. In concept he imagined the theatre of Strindberg and Andreev; in actuality he could do little more than write unsuccessful essays like *The Tempter* or pursue the common path of contemporary realism, with a strong flavour of sentimental ideality. Of the latter style *The Masqueraders* (St J. April 1894) provides a good example. Dulcie Larondie is his heroine here—a girl of breeding who, having lost her money, is forced to serve as a barmaid. At the inn, a kiss from her is auctioned and Sir Brice Skene gains it against her true, if somewhat morose, lover David Remon. Sir Brice proposes marriage and she accepts; but soon their domestic felicity is ruined by the fact that Brice runs through all his money. Remon aids her and at last gambles for her against her husband. After he has won, he confronts her, but goes off on a scientific expedition in sentimental exaltation, leaving her unstained and "pure". The story here is a rather foolish one, and, although Jones has succeeded in making a fair portrait of Remon, his characters generally do not have sufficient life to conceal from us the violent creaking of his plot.

Passionate adoration of an ideal sort fascinated Jones. He would have been in his true element had he been born a companion of Dryden and so been permitted to pen dramas in the Almanzor style. Perhaps his leaning towards melodrama is the result of this, for melodrama was the nineteenth-century bastard of seventeenth-century love-and-honour tragedy.

The Physician (Crit. March 1897) displays him essaying another plot not dissimilar to that of *The Masqueraders*. Dr Carey is a famous nerve specialist who, when the curtain rises, is in the uncomfortable mood of feeling that nothing matters simply because his friend Lady Valerie Camville has light-heartedly thrown him over. A new vision, however, comes to him when Edana Hinde steps into his consulting room. Not for herself has she come; her business is to beg him to cure her fiancé Walter Amphiel, a temperance reformer. For her sake Carey consents and to his horror discovers that the temperance reformer is in reality a secret drunkard subject to violent attacks of delirium tremens. What he is to do, is the question. Magnanimously he conceals from Edana both the fact that he loves her and the fact that Amphiel is a drunkard. Of course, she succeeds in penetrating to the truth, Amphiel conveniently dies and the curtain eventually falls as Edana sinks gracefully and lachrymosely into the doctor's arms. His great self-sacrifice is being suitably rewarded. Again we recognise here the attempt at something genuinely significant, and again we realise that the something significant has become of little account precisely because of Jones's lack of subtlety. His play professes to be a play of character, but his persons are all stock types—the familiar clergyman's daughter, the drunken villain who has ruined a village maiden, the noble hero, one after another they thrust their familiar visages across the footlights. Everything is old and tawdry except perhaps Carey's appreciation of suffering as the basis of self-knowledge, and that intrudes as a kind of extraneous conception imposed on, instead of developing from, his personality.

More interesting in many ways, since less pretentious, is *The Rogue's Comedy* (Gar. April 1896). Had the treatment been a trifle lighter, this might have proved an excellent play. The main character is a certain Bailey Prothero, a rogue who finds it lucrative to pretend to occult powers. Aided materially by his wife, "Miss Jenison" (who gives him necessary information), he hoodwinks many persons in society by revealing to them supposed secrets of their past, and luck aids him by leading him to make excellent prophecies regarding several stocks which rise in value. Gradually he is surrounded by a flock of believers, with only two dissentients, Lady Clarabut and George Lambert, a barrister. Lambert, although he does not know it, is really Prothero's son and his opposition to the latter is dictated largely by the fact that he dotes on Nina Clarabut. Gradually Prothero rises in power till eventually he heads a great South African company. At this moment an old companion of his named Robert Cushing makes his appearance. Vainly his wife counsels him to leave London; instead he sets up palatial quarters in Park Lane. Inevitably disaster overtakes him, and, forced by Cushing and by his own son Lambert, he is compelled to abandon his projects. Many artificialities there are in this play, but on the whole it shows excellent treatment. The drawing-room scene in Act I and the dramatic climax of Act III when Prothero points out to his restive dupes that they must sink or swim with him are boldly managed. *The Rogue's Comedy*, in one way, displays Jones at his best, for, when he forgot his philosophic purposes, he manifested a theatrical skill superior to almost anything which his period had to offer.

Michael and his Lost Angel (Lyc. 1896) presents his serious style at its best. Ambitious in scope, it aims at setting forth fundamental principles in dramatic form, and we must agree, with some necessary qualifications, that in this aim Jones has succeeded. In Michael, the clergyman who falls from grace through his love of Audrie, he presents a study bolder and more complex than anything he had hitherto attempted. To take as dramatic hero a man of the church who, after forcing a girl to confess her sin publicly before the congregation, finds himself seized by an all-consuming love and actually declares that he feels no sorrow for his defection, was an endeavour sufficiently temerarious in the nineties, and the choice of theme indicates how determined Jones was to permit no outside considerations to thwart him in his aims. Yet *Michael and his Lost Angel* somehow fails to convince us. The weakness may be due to the fact that Jones by inclination would have been a tragic dramatist whereas in talent he was capable of giving expression only to the serious problem note. The utter disaster of *The Tempter* tells its own tale; Jones had not the slightest spark of poetry in his nature, and something of poetic abandon is, perhaps, necessary if such a theme as he had here chosen were to find adequate dialogue. In reading *Michael and his Lost Angel* we ache for an infusion of that trembling rhythm, that unsought vision, which, even in translation, is never absent from Ibsen's scenes. Bernard Shaw imagined that the play required a different ending, that Michael ought to have trumpeted abroad his new-found glory of love; maybe some such conclusion might have been given to the plot, but it is not from this that our inner dissatisfaction arises. That dissatisfaction comes from a discrepancy between the essential aim of the drama and its actual execution.

An indication of those qualities which Jones lacked is provided by an earlier play, *The Dancing Girl* (H. Jan. 1891). Popular in its own time because it gave all the thrill of novelty without raising those awkward thoughts which the plays of Ibsen persisted in raising, it reveals itself to us as a prime example of dramatic falsity. Fundamentally it is untrue, because the author is incapable of rising to the level of thought he desires to attain. This story of a young Quaker girl (Drusilla Ives) who goes to London, becomes famous as a dancer, lives with the Duke of Guisebury as his mistress, and finally suffers poetic justice by dying miserably in New Orleans was intended to be a kind of problem plot, but the poverty of Jones's intellect forbade it from being anything save a rather tawdry tale of *The Girl's Friend* variety. Jones, of course, declared that he was not writing here a play with a moral, but the declaration rings false; in this, as in so many other of his dramas, his whole conception was based on a moral idea, and the treatment of his characters was determined by a definite point of view, not of a theatrical but of a social kind. Unfortunately, much as he thought about life and much as he prided himself upon the importance of his own ideas, his mind was narrow and conventional; "I am still in favour of what is called bourgeois morality", he stated once, and the confession is self-revealing. His interpretation of Drusilla Ives and of her adventures rises not one whit above the commonest opinions of the most common among the many persons who flocked to see *The Dancing Girl* in 1891. In a pure melodrama we do not seek for anything beyond common standards; our dissatisfaction with Jones arises from the fact that he considers himself somewhat superior to this level and consequently raises expectations which, because of his intellectual inferiority, he cannot satisfy.

So far as the new drama is concerned, Jones's contribution was therefore indirect rather than direct. He awakened the desire for something that should stimulate thought even although his own plays remained bound by a middle-class morality innocent of thought or vision. For this we may be grateful to him, and in this tendency we may readily see the beginnings of that movement which later produced such social plays as those of Galsworthy on the one hand and, on the other, of Somerset Maugham. Besides this, Jones proved himself an able craftsman. *The Dancing Girl* owed its success partly at least to a most effective situation handled with genuine theatrical skill at the close of the second last act. The same skill gives life to many of his plays, and in its finest expression provides the magnificent cross-examination scene in *Mrs Dane's Defence* (Wyndham's, Oct. 1900). This scene we could not imagine treated in any more adroit manner; every line has its purpose and we are held breathless watching the conflict of forces in an episode essentially theatrical. *Mrs Dane's Defence* has the same weakness as *The Dancing Girl*, but that it is magnificently planned we cannot deny.

In addition to this power of creating impressive and dramatically thrilling scenes, Jones possessed one other quality which, although somewhat obscured by his over-serious aims, gives to his plays a genuine value. He was—strangely enough when we consider his solemn demeanour and his melodramatic training—a master of a certain kind of satirical humour, blunt but occasionally very effective. The best parts of *The Rogue's Comedy* are those wherein the whims of society are depicted; even more markedly is this power of humour exhibited in *The Triumph of the Philistines, and how Mr Jorgan preserved the Morals of Market Pewbury under very trying Circumstances* (St J. May 1895). In Jones resided something of the spirit of Dickens; much as he fancied himself as a seriously minded contemplator of life, his best work was done when he remained contented with the grotesque delineation of common follies. His touch, perhaps, may be somewhat heavy, but, however broadly his colours are laid on, he was clearly fashioning here the body of a new comedy. A vicious attack on the "smug and banal ideals" of the English forms a rather unsatisfactory preface for this play; after all, Jones was the last person on earth to indulge in criticism of ideals of such a kind. No doubt the comedy springs from a recognition of the absurdities consequent upon the intrusion of a liberated morality into a sphere of conventional existence; but whatever of virtue there is in *The Triumph of the Philistines* arises, not from a sense of conscious purpose, but essentially from the merely observing and recording eye of the dramatist. The attitude of Jorgan and his associates when they endeavour to banish Alma Suleny from their community is dealt with vividly and vivaciously; Sally Lebrune is drawn to the life; and the complications which ensue when the amoral Sally winks to Sir Valentine Fellowes and maliciously entangles Jorgan are followed through with a genuine sense of fun.

The same good humour gives grace to *The Liars* (Crit. Oct. 1897), wherein Jones presents a real contribution to the newly developing comedy of manners. At times the dialogue takes on the refinement of real wit as when, in the first act, Dolly addresses her husband:

> Oh, my dear, you don't expect me to remember *all* the things that are inconvenient to you. Besides, other people don't wrap up. Jessica is out on the river with absolutely nothing on her shoulders—

and Mrs Crespin replies:

> Is it not a physiological fact that when our hearts reach a certain temperature our shoulders may be, and often are, safely left bare?

But the special flavour of this play is formulated, not by witty conversation, but by a delicate treatment of character and of situation. The story of Falkner's love of Lady Jessica, wife to Gilbert Nepean, becomes informed by a true sense of humorous observation. The serious purpose which, because not profound enough, marred Jones's other plays is here avoided and all his best qualities—his theatric skill and his ability to see and, seeing, to depict—are permitted free play.

Jones's contributions to the stage of his time are important, and that importance we must duly recognise even while we discern that his value as a dramatist is considerably less than was once imagined. That he failed to introduce any deep thought is certain, for deep thought was beyond him; but his very attempt to produce plays in which an idea—particularly an idea of a religious kind—assumed a major role aided the stage in shaking itself free from the innocuous and stupid farces which hitherto had been the rage. Jones undoubtedly did much to assist the audience towards the rediscovery of fields of dramatic interest long left barren and neglected. During the Elizabethan period all that interested man was material for the playwright, but, during the later centuries, the subject-matter permitted to the dramatist had become narrowed down to a few set themes. Jones showed, in *Saints and Sinners*, in *The Tempter* and in *Michael and his Lost Angel*, that religious convention, if not religious conviction, might form as effective a theme as wooing and marriage; in *The Physician* he presented what was a real problem, however sentimentally he himself dealt with it; while in *The Liars* he pointed out the way for a new social comedy. For these things unquestionably he deserves to be remembered. Just is the summary of Richard Cordell:

> Henry Arthur Jones found the contemporary English drama insignificant, puerile; he left it respected, flourishing, and mature. That he alone is responsible for the renascence is contrary to fact and reason; that to him belongs a generous share of the credit for restoring the drama in England to its rightful position as a civilized and civilizing art is indisputable.[1]

[1] *Op. cit.* p. 253.

III. *Sir Arthur Pinero*

In his criticism of Jones, William Archer had but two or three plays on which to build a judgment; hardly more had been provided by Arthur Pinero by the year 1882.[1] Available for Archer, indeed, were only a few short pieces—*The Money-Spinner* (P's, Manchester, Nov. 1880; St J. Jan. 1881), *Imprudence* (Folly, July 1881) and *The Squire* (St J. Dec. 1881)—all plays which, although they may contain work potentially interesting, can hardly be rated as masterpieces.[2] In each one of these Pinero was clearly trying his hand at dramatic composition, and the prentice touch is often painfully apparent. Even then, however, such apprentice efforts indicated a certain primitive originality, and Archer, again acutely, recognised that his

> manner is not that of Mr T. W. Robertson, nor of Mr Gilbert, nor of Mr Byron, nor of Mr Burnand. His style is his own, and his effects, if not in themselves novel, are procured in a more or less original fashion. Even his construction, though it is his weakest point, shows an effort at something better than the ordinary invertebrate pulpiness of "original comedies".[3]

Already, too, a decided versatility had been shown in these early adventures. *Imprudence* was a farce, *The Money-Spinner* a kind of melodrama, and *The Squire* an essay in a real study of character. To select a theme which definitely posed a problem such as is introduced into the last-mentioned play indicates at once how sincere Pinero was at the start of his dramatic career and how determined he was to relate the characters of his imagination to the social life of his day. *The Squire* points forward unmistakably to *The Second Mrs*

[1] On Pinero see Hamilton Fyfe, *Arthur Wing Pinero* (1902) and *Sir Arthur Pinero's Plays and Players* (1930); W. Stöcker, *Pineros Dramen. Studien über Motive, Charaktere und Technik* (Marburg, 1911); Dutton Cook, *The Case of Mr Pinero* (*The Theatre*, N.S. v, 1882, 202–4); R. F. Sharp, *A. W. Pinero and Farce* (*id.* N.S. xx, 1892, 154–7); *Mr Pinero and Literary Drama* (*id.* N.S. xxii, 1893, 3–8).

[2] Before this date Pinero had also written *Two Hundred a Year* (Glo. Oct. 1877), *Two can play at that Game* (Lyc. 1878), *La Comète* (Croydon, April 1878), *Daisy's Escape* (Lyc. Sept. 1879), *Hester's Mystery* (Folly, June 1880) and *Bygones* (Lyc. Sept. 1880).

[3] *Op. cit.* p. 277.

Tanqueray (St J. 1893) and to *Mid-Channel* (St J. Sept. 1909). As Archer observes:

> In the course of the very curious and interesting controversy which raged for some time after the production of "The Squire", Mr Pinero published the memorandum in his note-book which formed the germ of the drama. It ran as follows: "The notion of a young couple secretly married—the girl about to become a mother—finding that a former wife is still in existence. The heroine amongst those who respect and love her. The fury of a rejected lover who believes her to be a guilty woman. Two men face to face at night-time. Qy—Kill the first wife?"[1]

By this we realise the essential problem from which Pinero's conception of plot and character was evolved. His play differs from the majority of contemporary efforts in its purpose; and, as it were, he goes back to the stage which Robertson had reached, resolute to advance still further than that dramatist had done. For this he was qualifying himself excellently. Not only had he the advantage denied to Robertson of many models provided by the newer school of French playwrights, he showed himself possessed of a power over both the realm of serious emotional situation and that of light comedy. In the one Robertson was restricted by prevailing standards in melodrama and in the sentimental play, and in the other by lack of experience in handling light social conversation. Being a pioneer, he was forced to create his own medium; Pinero came at a time when, through the efforts of men such as Gilbert, Albery, Theyre Smith and Young, the requisite medium had been shaped and adjusted to dramatic requirements.

How far this medium as it was applied to light comedy aided Pinero is to be seen when we glance at the farces and comedies which he wrote between *The Squire* (St J. 1881) and the problem plays of the nineties. Of these *The Magistrate* (Court, March 1885) proves one of the most interesting. Here the weakness in construction, which Archer had seen as one of his greatest faults, has disappeared. In a series of growing crises Pinero carries us onward from one ridiculous

[1] *Op. cit.* pp. 282–3.

situation to another, indulging in the impossible certainly—for such is the way of farce—but retaining always a lively sense of theatrical values. The magistrate who gives his title to the play is one Posket, married to a widow who, in order to conceal her age, declares that her nineteen-year-old son Cis is really only fourteen. To her dismay news comes that the lad's godfather, Lukyn, is arriving home from India and off she proceeds to warn him of her deception. Meanwhile, in her absence the mice (Posket and Cis) decide they can safely play. They, too, set off on a jaunt and by farcical coincidence all find themselves in the same hotel. Fortunately for the plot, there is a police raid, in the course of which Lukyn and Mrs Posket are arrested. This pair are then brought up in court before Posket himself, who is so utterly dazed that he permits his clerk to persuade him into giving them seven days hard. A solution is finally reached when a brother magistrate, Bellamy, reopens the case and releases the prisoners with an admonition.

Not so skilfully constructed as *The Magistrate*, but none the less interesting as a specimen of the work through which Pinero gained his training, *The Schoolmistress* (Court, March 1886) deals with adventures in the Volumnia College for Daughters of Gentlemen, managed by a certain Miss Dyott who has married an impoverished gentleman, Queckett. To obtain money for the satisfying of his somewhat luxurious tastes, she plans to take part in an opera bouffe planned for the Christmas vacation. During her absence, the girls and Queckett decide to have a spree, the main object of which is to celebrate the secret marriage of Dinah Rankling to Reginald Paulover. Admiral Rankling, by an error, arrives at this party and, as one may imagine, there are many confusions, until in the end Miss Dyott returns home and proceeds to exercise her authority.

One other specimen of this farce may be mentioned—*Dandy Dick* (Court, Jan. 1887)—perhaps, on the whole, the best of them all. The Very Rev. Augustin Jedd is the chief figure in this; arrested in suspicious circumstances, this poor gentleman suffers a series of doleful adventures. Easily and with dramatic interest the plot develops, while the characters are well conceived and nicely balanced. The horsy Georgiana Tidman is thus well contrasted with the Dean, and an air of liveliness is provided by means of Jedd's precocious daughters, Salome and Sheba, who succeed in marrying Major Tarver and Mr Darbey. An excellent comic butler, Blore, completes a group skilfully blended to draw the last ounce of merriment from a ridiculous situation.

The value of these farces for the development of Pinero's art rests in the experience they gave him in the building of plot and the requirements of stage speech. That they make no pretence to mirroring life naturalistically matters not at all; their importance is definitely theatrical. Through them Pinero learned the use of his chosen instrument.

In the midst of this world of laughter, however, Pinero did not forget the serious purpose which had inspired him to write *The Squire*, and in *The Hobby-Horse* (St J. Oct. 1886) he turned aside to pen a social comedy. The general atmosphere here was one which he was to exploit in a number of plays—the satirising of social follies without the vigour and intellectual passion of the pure satirist. Philanthropy in *The Hobby-Horse* gains Pinero's contempt, and this he exposes in the scheme of Spencer Jermyn for a decayed jockeys' home and in that of his wife for an orphanage. In the interests of her cause Mrs Jermyn goes off as "Miss Moxon" to the East End of London, and there the Rev. Noel Brice falls deeply in love with her. She and her husband are shown thoroughly rid of their philanthropic predilections by the fall of the final curtain. This play well illustrates a weakness which mars much of Pinero's work during the eighties and nineties. First of all, he often mixes his styles in these plays, so that unity of impression is hopelessly lost. When Jermyn is conversing with the unregenerate Shattock and Pews we are wholly in the realm of farce; when Brice is making love to "Miss Moxon" we are in that of the lachrymose drama. Shattock is a figure who might have appeared in *Dandy Dick*; Brice is the familiar unhappy lover who, his day's work ended, is allowed to fade away into a melancholy gloom. This in itself, however, is not the chief failing of *The Hobby-Horse.* Satire springs from an intellectual disgust at human stupidities. The satirist thus laughs at and lacerates the miser or the astrologer's dupe because intellectually he views their actions as being beneath human dignity. Pinero's satire is not of this kind; it does not build itself out of a feeling of superiority. The true satirist never sneers, for a sneer implies that the object sneered at is subconsciously conceived of as a superior object. Jonson satirises follies beneath him; the lesser man simply sneers at those above. *The Hobby-Horse* and some of its companion pieces might, then, more reasonably be called sneering comedies than comedies of satire. No high intellectual ideal inspires them and drives them forward.

This judgment is true of many plays by Pinero. In *The Weaker Sex* (Manchester, Sept. 1888; Court, March 1889) he turns on the movement for women's rights just as he had turned on philanthropy in the other drama. Technically this comedy-drama is good; but its theme is handled in a manifestly shallow manner. The story deals mainly with Lady Vivash who had loved and quarrelled with Philip Lyster. Lyster has since made a great name for himself as Ira Lee, the poet, and, meeting Lady Vivash's daughter, Sylvia, has fallen madly in love with her. On discovering who Sylvia really is he departs out of their lives. Into this circle the author thrusts Mrs Boyle-Chewton, the leader of the women's movement. With rather futile sneering, he makes her farcically believe that a member of Parliament, Mr Bargus (who has associated himself with her cause only to serve his own ambition), is making her a proposal of marriage when in reality he is sueing for her daughter's hand. The treatment here seems as weak as that of *The Hobby-Horse.* The struggle for women's rights was one that might have been dealt with in an entirely farcical manner for the sake of such merriment as it might provide or in an entirely serious manner. Between these two there could be no dramatically effective middle course.

A third example of this style appears in *The Times* (Terry's,

Oct. 1891). The object against which Pinero here tilts is social aspiration, and again we recognise that his method is spiritually lacking in power and in sympathy. The scheming of a self-made parvenu to enter the sacred portals of society may quite legitimately lead towards farcical episode; equally legitimately it may be dealt with seriously, either from the point of view of society as a whole or from that of the individual. Pinero again contents himself with sneering. Percy Egerton-Bompas he presents as a man who, grown wealthy, dreams of naught save higher social life; quite naturally this man is overjoyed when he learns that his daughter Beryl has become engaged to Lord Lurgashall, and quite naturally, too, he is dismayed when he discovers that his son, Howard, has been inveigled into marrying his landlady's daughter. Trimble, a social tout who, for considerations, aids him in his social advances, advises him to conceal the *mésalliance*, to educate his son's wife and her mother and to bring them before society under changed names. Various complications arise, and in the end Egerton-Bompas has to confess, broken-heartedly, that he has lost. The treatment of this theme, however, leaves Beryl and Lord Lurgashall in the air, and that, of course, would never do, so, after the latter has departed from the parvenu's house, back he comes to whisper sentimentally in Beryl's ear that he loves her still, that he will overlook her father's vulgarity and marry her just the same. The combination of this sneering and this sentimentality takes from *The Times* any virtue it might otherwise have possessed.

Happily, however, Pinero by no means confined his attention to themes of this kind and to this atmosphere. Pure sentimentality he exploited in *Sweet Lavender* (Terry's, March 1888) where, as one reviewer enthusiastically declared, he gave

> an admirable retort witty to the disciples of Zola and "*naturalisme*" who think a play cannot be healthy without being insipid. In "Sweet Lavender" the dramatist introduces us to good women and honest men, and withal the play is as brilliant as a flash of light.[1]

[1] *The Theatre*, N.S. xi, May 1888, 263.

Even if we cannot share in this enthusiastic acclamation, we may admit that *Sweet Lavender's* sentimentality provides more pleasing theatrical qualities than the sneers of *The Times*.

Something of the same mood he introduced into *Lady Bountiful* (Gar. March 1891), wherein Camilla Brent is shown maintaining her uncle Roderick Heron and his son Dennis, whom she loves. The latter thinks of nothing but hunting, and this much distresses Camilla, but when he learns that he and his father have been living on her bounty he immediately leaves the house and takes a job as riding-master at the stables of honest John Veale. There Margaret Veale falls in love with him and out of pity he marries her. Later she dies and Dennis returns to find Camilla just about to wed old Sir Richard Philliter. On seeing Dennis she faints and the wedding is postponed. The plot is a trifle stupid, but Pinero's sincerity of purpose may be acknowledged.

In these plays love acts a major role, love that is faithful and true and devoted, love that is tortured and misled and weak. Sentimentally it is dealt with, yet the sentimentalism has a quality of its own which may be genuinely esteemed. Here Pinero was on surer ground than when he was writing his sneering comedies. And out of these sentimental pieces grew one drama of real significance—*Trelawny of the "Wells"* (Court, Jan. 1898). In *Trelawny* may be viewed a symbol of the renascent English drama. Something of the refashioned farce had gone to its making, something too of the newer sentimentalism. It is a period piece in which an endeavour is made to present a picture of the young Tom Robertson and his times; Robertson becomes viewed partly as a figure of the past, partly as the master of the then modern style. Thirty years have gone by since he was stirring theatrical audiences by his revolutionary methods, and those methods, like many things revolutionary, have settled down to become common practice and daily convention. The people talk, not as Robertson would have made his own characters talk, but in the manner of 1890, which simply means that their dialogue is nearer to the real green-room chatter of the sixties than to the more formal (and yet for its time naturalistic) speech put into the mouths of Robertson's own stage figures. Here the style of *Caste* is seized upon, fondly analysed and made more vivacious in content.

That Pinero had a gift for the writing of comedy *Trelawny* amply testifies; additional testimony comes from *The Princess and the Butterfly; or, The Fantastics* (St J. March 1897) which is a truly excellent sentimentalised comedy of manners. The Princess Pannonia has here returned to London after the death of her old husband. Middle age is beginning to creep upon her and upon a friend of hers, Sir George Lamorant, whom she is about to marry. Suddenly, however, she falls violently in love with a serious-minded youth named Edward Oriel, and Sir George experiences an equally violent infatuation for the Princess's adopted child, the bright-spirited Fay Zuliani. Through the mazes of this situation the characters drift in a whirl of fashionable gaiety. Their artificiality and the contrast between that artificiality and natural impulse provide Pinero with material of which he makes good use. Nearly does he succeed in his attempt to enter that dream world which Charles Lamb saw in the comedy of Congreve. "Are you sane, all of you—any of you?" cries Lady Ringstead at the close of the play. "Are you real? To me, you appear like dream people—fantastic creatures", and the answer to her questions comes in the form of a Hungarian dance, "Love is Ever Young". *The Princess and the Butterfly* has the theme of *The Vinegar Tree* presented without the sophistication of that modern comedy and with a delicate sense of fantastic values.

Through these plays Pinero made many important contributions to the stage of his time; but their historical value becomes of minor importance when they are placed beside *The Second Mrs Tanqueray* (St J. May 1893). "On May 27, 1893," wrote a reviewer in *The Theatre*,[1] "a day long to be remembered in the annals of the English stage, *The Second Mrs Tanqueray* was produced at the St James's Theatre, and Mr Pinero was hailed unanimously not only as one of the

[1] N.S. xxii, July 1893, 3–8.

greatest of living dramatists, but as the author of a play which is also a piece of literature." With this drama, as *The Theatre* reviewer recognised, the long-desired union of literary excellence and of dramatic skill had become an accomplished fact; and from that union he prophesied not only the further cultivation of the theatre by men of letters but the arising of a new style in theatrical criticism. "In the days to come when the production of a new play by a leading dramatist shall be regarded not as a theatrical fixture, but as an important event in the world of art and letters, masterpieces will not be dismissed in hastily scribbled paragraphs, but will be discussed soberly and thoughtfully by men of culture and intelligence." "I wonder", wrote William Archer,[1] "if Mr Pinero himself quite realises what an immeasurable advance he has made in *The Second Mrs Tanqueray* on all his former works?...It is not merely the seriousness of the subject that distinguishes this play from its predecessors.... Here we have a positively good play. Here, without raving, we can praise almost without reservation....In brief, the play is modern and masterly." By modern Archer meant that this drama aimed at the closest possible approach to naturalism. In it, Archer imagined, the author had "thrown to the winds all extrinsic considerations, compromises, superstitions, and...set himself, for his own personal satisfaction, to do the best work that was in him". From it Archer looked for the inauguration of a new period of creative productivity, and rightly he prognosticated that after times would find it "epoch-making".

To-day, of course, we see the weaknesses of this drama more clearly than contemporaries saw them. We recognise in it a certain sentimentalism; we detect a spurious literary quality in the dialogue; we are not so rapturously prepared to recognise in the characters masterpieces of psychological delineation. Yet, with all this recognition of its failings, none of us may deny the fact that in *The Second Mrs Tanqueray* the English drama at the close of the nineteenth century first surely found itself. It did not spring full-formed like Minerva

[1] *The Theatrical "World"* for 1893, p. 128.

out of Jove's forehead; much work in the theatre had gone to its making. It did not face facts so boldly as many imagined. It did not even provide such a fine technical model as some other plays of the same period. To it more than to any other drama of its time, however, the English stage owed its later prevailing tendency towards the naturalism of daily life. The fantasy of Gilbert was forgotten; the artificiality of Wilde was neglected; and the strange poetic quality of Ibsen's work was interpreted in terms of common daily life.

With *The Second Mrs Tanqueray* and with *The Notorious Mrs Ebbsmith* (Gar. March 1895)[1] Pinero succeeded in doing something more important than all Henry Arthur Jones had accomplished. His theatrical skill is as assured as Jones's; and he brings to his themes some at least of those qualities which make for tragedy—conviction, deeper thought and fine sympathy. Here the sneering tone which vitiated the spirit of his other plays has been laid aside and he re-introduces to the stage that noble pity which had found hardly any exponent since the seventeenth century. It is a strange fact that whereas Jones, brought up in the melodramatic tradition, seemed to reach his finest achievement in *The Rogue's Comedy* and in *The Liars*, Pinero, whose training had been in farce, discovered his real strength in a kind of tragic drama.

IV. *Other Dramatists of the Eighties*

Necessarily, in dealing with the work of Pinero and of Jones, we have carried our survey to the end of the century. Most of their important work, as will be realised, came after and not before the year 1890, and consequently the influence of their styles is but little to be traced in this particular decade which is at present under our consideration. Apart from their plays, these ten years have not much to offer us. Farce of a violently exaggerated and almost unbelievably inane kind mightily pleased the public. Charles Hawtrey's *The Private Secretary*, based on *Der Bibliotheker* of von

[1] See H. Schutz Wilson, *The Notorious Mrs Ebbsmith, A Study* (1895).

Moser, appeared obscurely at the Theatre Royal in Cambridge, was brought to the Prince's in March 1884 and settled down to an extraordinary run. This piece, coldly regarded in the script, seems utterly beneath contempt, although, as may be realised by its success, it formed a not entirely despicable medium for farcical interpretation. That such was its only object is shown by dialogue and stage direction:

CATTERMOLE. Oh dear! oh dear! (*he turns chair round with a howl. She shrieks and runs away*). My good woman, go and play! go and run up and down! (*gag*).

MRS STEAD. And he never goes out—always, etc. etc.

It is these "gags" and "etceteras" rather than the actual written dialogue which give interest to this piece in the theatre. Of like kind is *Charley's Aunt* (Bury St Edmunds, Feb. 1892; Roy. Dec. 1892) by Brandon Thomas; and only a trifle more foolish are the American farces of Harry Pleon. *Dutch Justice; or, Up before the Magistrate* (Gai. Birmingham, July 1888) may be taken as a fair specimen. Described as "A Funny Melange of Magisterial Errors", it utterly baffles us in its unbelievable stupidity. Only the fact that audiences of to-day roar with merriment over the sillinesses of the Ritz Brothers can make us credit the following as having once been laughable:

Well, here's a go! I was standing where I was, and running as fast as I could, and all of a sudden I slipped and fell over myself, and slipped, just as a fourwheeled hansom cab run over me. I shouted hands off, and he nearly took my feet off. But anyhow I found this note (*Shows one*) And it says the beak is too ill to go to court to-day. So I'm going to take his place and lock everybody up, and cop all the fines myself. I shan't know what to say, but I suppose it will be all right. Whatever foolish things I say it will be in my favour, because then I shall be like a many of our Judges, full of silly and unfair sentences.

(*Song, if required, and exit.*)

The song, I fancy, we do not require. Equally poor are all Pleon's works—*Muldoon's Picnic* (M'bone, Nov. 1886), and *Peck's Bad Boy* (Brit. June 1891) are both "nonsensical pieces of absurdity" without the slightest grain of true wit or humour. Some farces, it is true, reach a trifle higher, but the trifle must be duly emphasised. J. Wear Gifford's *Supper for Two; or, The Wolf and the Lamb* (P'cess, Glasgow, Nov. 1883) is fairly representative of such plays. This shows Quilldriver, an attorney, coming to an inn and there meeting one Horatio Blazer. Blazer, to display his courage, wishes to pick a quarrel with someone not very formidable, and poor Quilldriver finds himself in an awkward predicament. Happily, however, the waiter, Joseph, endeavours to make capital out of the two of them; overstepping himself, he finds Blazer and Quilldriver leagued against him. The theme, though slight, is at least superior to that of any among Pleon's pieces. Similar in character are the farces of Alfred Maltby, once noted as a prolific writer of burlesque, extravaganza and would-be amusing sketches; *Taken by Storm* (Aven. Nov. 1884) in which "Dick" (Captain Richard Shye) captures his Gertrude, presents a fair specimen of his style.

The eighties abound also in melodramas which rarely proceed beyond the forms established earlier in the century. G. R. Sims and Henry Pettitt turned out a variety of these. *The Harbour Lights* (Adel. Dec. 1885), written in collaboration, may be selected for mention here. The hero is a bold and frank-faced lieutenant; the villain a wicked squire who ruins an innocent girl and then attempts to steal the fair heroine's money. Through trial and torment move the good characters until, just before the final curtain, the squire is shot by the honest lover of the girl whom he had dishonoured. Plays of this kind, mostly with domestic settings, flourished, for spectators were still attracted by melodramatic simplification of human character and emotion. Stories could please such as that presented in Brandon Thomas's *The Colour-Sergeant* (P'cess, Feb. 1885), where we are told how a retired sergeant has disowned his son and sits at home all alone and desolate, when suddenly the son returns—dressed up all gloriously in a sergeant's uniform too. Even a man like Westland Marston could traffic in these things. His *Under Fire* (Vaud. April 1885) deals mainly with a stereotyped Lady Fareham who has a dread secret known only to a Mrs Naylor.

Lady Fareham's daughter Carrie is truly loved by Guy Morton who is forced to resign his pretentions in favour of a more showy Charles Wolverley. In the end, of course, Wolverley's worthlessness is demonstrated and Guy, the hero, returns in triumph. To proceed more deeply into the niceties of the plot were needless.

At the same time, various efforts were being made in the direction of the newer drama and, although few of them reached even a faint measure of literary success or escaped, even temporarily, from sentimental mawkishness, these demonstrate that the forces of the "moderns" were increasing. In *Human Nature* (D.L. Sept. 1885), for example, by Henry Pettitt and Augustus Harris, we can easily trace the infiltration of the new style of ideas into the melodramatic form. The old type villain is here, in the person of a rascally lawyer, and by his side is the stock villainess, a wily scheming woman. This pair, acting in concert, poison Captain Temple's mind and make him doubt his wife's virtue. The villainy is antiquated, but the application of the villainy is new. Melodramas of this sort come fairly close in spirit to the mood of the English adaptations of such French problem-dramas as Octave Feuillet's *Péril en la demeure*[1] and Victorien Sardou's *La maison neuve*. The latter was rendered into an English form, as *Mayfair* (St J. Oct. 1885), by A. W. Pinero. Although condemned by some contemporaries because, in their opinion, its theme of a wife tempted by a lord's advances after she hears of the infidelities of her husband was not "British", *Mayfair* comes within approachable distance of *Human Nature*, an essentially British production.

Some of the melodramas, too, developed a kind of propagandist tone—another straw in the rising wind. G. R. Sims's *The Last Chance* (Adel. April 1885), in spite of its confused Russian adventures among impossible Nihilists, thus has a certain serious note, as has Mark Quinton's *In His Power* (Alex. L'pool, Sept. 1884; Olym. Jan. 1885), a drama which

[1] In the version by G. W. Godfrey as *The Opal Ring* (Court, Jan. 1885). An earlier adaptation had been made by Tom Taylor as *The House or the Home?* (Adel. May 1859).

mingles a theme of bigamous marriage unwittingly entered into with another theme of diplomatic secrets and devious espionage.

Besides such plays, of course, there were other more determined efforts in the direction of the newer styles; sometimes these were accomplished with a faint measure of success, more commonly the play of ideas and the posing of problems were dealt with in a spirit mawkish and uninspired. Jerome K. Jerome, for example, shows himself impelled towards the modernist movement in *Sunset* (Com. Feb. 1888). Based on Tennyson's *The Sisters*, this one-act piece has value in demonstrating the increased skill which the dramatic renaissance had brought with it. The story is a simple one—telling how Lois loves Lawrence, how Lawrence has become infatuated with her sister Joan whom he has met while on holiday without knowing who she is, and how Lois, in self-renunciation, gives him up—sentimental unquestionably, yet revealing a poignancy of which the old sentimentalism was utterly ignorant. Just as the one-act comedies of manners demonstrated the growing power of the dramatists in their handling of character, situation and dialogue, so such a play as *Sunset* shows clearly how much deeper these dramatists could strike at the basis of human emotion and how infinitely more skilful they were in dealing with episodes in which the dramatic interest arose, not from an outer conflict as in the melodrama, but from the clash of nature with nature, or of thought with thought.

CHAPTER VII

WILDE AND SHAW: PLAYS OF THE NINETIES

I. *The Success of the Reformers*

THE eighties had achieved something quite definite, but only in the last decade of the century was absolute surety reached. These ten years opened well. Between 1890 and 1891 audiences were able to witness the first productions of *The Pharisee* (Shaft. 1890) by M. Watson and Mrs Wallis, H. A. Jones's *The Dancing Girl* (H. 1891), C. Haddon Chambers's *The Idler* (St J. 1891), A. W. Pinero's *Lady Bountiful* (Gar. 1891) and *Beau Austin* (H. 1890) by W. E. Henley and R. L. Stevenson. Apart from these—all notable plays—the works of Ibsen came freely before the public. *A Doll's House*, which had been originally presented at the Novelty in 1889, was revived at Terry's in 1891, and English audiences saw for the first time *Rosmersholm* (Vaud. 1891), *Ghosts* (Roy. 1891), *Hedda Gabler* (Vaud. 1891) and *The Lady from the Sea* (Terry's, 1891). While the season of 1891–2 was, perhaps, not so satisfactory, it counted in its repertoire J. M. Barrie's *Walker, London* (Toole's, 1892) and Oscar Wilde's *Lady Windermere's Fan* (St J. 1892), besides welcoming the early performances of the Independent Theatre Society and a number of revivals at the Olympic and the Lyceum—notably Irving's *Henry VIII*. The great event of the next season was the production of Pinero's *The Second Mrs Tanqueray* (St J. 1893), an enormous success; less popular in appeal but of no less importance were the performances of George Moore's *The Strike at Arlingford* (O.C. 1893) and G. B. Shaw's *Widowers' Houses* (Roy. 1892). The old melodrama and comic opera, as contemporaries observed, were ceasing to have their earlier appeal; the public was now clamouring for realism. So great had been the progress that one writer, in comparing conditions in 1894 with those in 1878, could speak of the latter as "prehistoric".[1]

A lull came in the years 1894–5, causing some to lose heart. Malcolm Watson noted that playwrights were falling into ruts and that there was a boring run of dramas dealing with women of whose pasts public opinion was doubtful.[2] The annual review of the stage presented by *The Theatre* in 1897 was despairing.[3] Musical farce, it was noted, had taken a new lease of life and "no new playwright" had "been discovered to help on that 'renascence' of which we heard so much two years ago, and those with established reputations" had "done little or nothing to add to them". The only encouraging feature seemed to be "the revival of interest...in the romantic drama, and especially in Shakspere".[4] Once more the pessimists seized their chance to complain. The managers were attacked for their "shrinking from anything new" and for their "timidity as to incurring any chance of failure".[5] "The efforts made in the past to stimulate the production of original plays", notes *The Theatre*,

> have been extremely feeble, and have had poor results. The Independent Theatre is practically the only working organisation that has professed such an aim, and the original English pieces which it gave were in about the same proportion to its foreign productions as was Jack Falstaff's halfpenny worth of bread to his "intolerable deal of sack". The Dramatic Students' Society contented itself with the revival of old plays....The British Society of Dramatic Art declared a part of its mission to be the affording to young and deserving authors a chance of getting their feet upon the ladder, but it went the wrong way to work, and came to an untimely end.[6]

[1] *Our Stage To-day* (*The Theatre*, N.S. xxiv, Sept. 1894, 89–96); cf. *id.* N.S. xxi, Feb. 1893, 115. On this period generally see Holbrook Jackson, *The Eighteen-Nineties* (1923).

[2] *The Turn of the Tide* (*The Theatre*, N.S. xxvii, Sept. 1895, 134–7).

[3] N.S. xxix, Jan. 1897, 1–3.

[4] On the revivals sponsored by Forbes-Robertson, Beerbohm Tree, Irving and Alexander see *A Boom in Shakespere* (*The Theatre*, N.S. xxx, Sept. 1897, 115–17).

[5] *Id.* N.S. xxix, April 1897, 205–10.

[6] *The Dearth of Dramatists* (*id.* N.S. xxix, May 1897, 268–74).

It is interesting to observe that these were the years that saw the appearance of Pinero's *The Notorious Mrs Ebbsmith* (Gar. 1895) and *Trelawny of the "Wells"* (Court, 1898), H. A. Jones's *The Masqueraders* (St J. 1894), *The Triumph of the Philistines* (St J. 1895), *Michael and his Lost Angel* (Lyc. 1896) and *The Liars* (Crit. 1897), all of Oscar Wilde's brilliant comedies, C. Haddon Chambers's *The Tyranny of Tears* (Crit. 1899), J. M. Barrie's early plays, and Shaw's *Arms and the Man* (Aven. 1894), *Candida* (S. Shields, 1895), *The Devil's Disciple* (Bijou, 1897), *The Man of Destiny* (Grand, Croydon, 1897), and *Caesar and Cleopatra* (Newcastle, 1899).

A decade which gave birth to all of these—especially when we compare it with any decade since those wonderful opening years of the seventeenth century—need not feel ashamed of itself. Looking back, we can only smile now at such a statement as that which appeared in *The Pall Mall Gazette* for 1893:[1] "at present," wrote the critic, "English dramatic art is sick unto death, and the signs of her rejuvenescence attenuated to the dimensions of the mathematical point". Thus does time have his revenges.

It was, of course, still an age of transition, so that the poor dramatist stood, as Robert Buchanan said, "bewildered... certain of execration from one side or the other, sure that if he secures the approval of Mr Bernard Shaw he will earn the contempt of Mr Clement Scott" until he drifted "aimlessly from one experiment to another" or sat "paralysed at his desk".[2] To one who truly recognised the spirit of the time, however, there could be no doubt. Max Beerbohm divined aright that the main dramatic current of the time was that "of realistic modern comedy and tragedy".

> Regret it as you may, modern realism is the only direction in which our drama can really progress....Every decade has brought us perceptibly nearer to something fine.[3]

He thought "that in sixty years at the present rate of progress", the theatre should have achieved its final aims in this kind.

[1] lii, April 8, 1893, 3.

[2] *A Word on the Defunct Drama* (*The Theatre*, N.S. xxviii, Oct. 1896, 208–10).

[3] *The Saturday Review*, xc, July 28, 1900, 112.

II. *The New Comedy of Wit*

The two plays which Oscar Wilde wrote in the eighties—*Vera; or, The Nihilists* (printed 1880) and *The Duchess of Padua* (printed 1883)—could hardly have led anyone to presage the later contributions to the stage which this author was to make. *Salomé* (Paris, 1896) belongs to their tradition, but not that exquisite set of four dramas—*Lady Windermere's Fan* (St J. Feb. 1892), *A Woman of No Importance* (H. April 1893), *An Ideal Husband* (H. Jan. 1895) and *The Importance of Being Earnest* (St J. Feb. 1895). With these entered into the theatre once more a grace and a refinement which long it had lacked. Jones was usually too serious; Pinero, if sincere, wanted polish; Wilde brought to the drama qualities distinct from each. "I took the drama," he declared in *De Profundis*, "the most objective form known to art, and made of it as personal a mode of expression as the lyric or the sonnet; at the same time I widened its range and enriched its characterisation"—and the self-judgment bears with it an element of truth. Jones and Pinero both wrote of society, but society they had come to know only after they had won a certain measure of success. Wilde was of the élite from the very start, and all his career is coloured by his passion for style; an attitude for him was more important than a moral truth. No external considerations prevented his appreciation of mannered gesture; indeed, the mannered gesture became for him the most desirable thing in life. He did not need to sneer, as Pinero did; he permitted others to do the sneering. He felt no call to preach, as Jones did; for preaching to him remained hopelessly outside the sphere of art. It is this quality of fashionable ease which represents his greatest contribution to the stage.[1]

Lady Windermere's Fan has at first sight a definite kinship

[1] See Frank Harris, *Oscar Wilde, His Life and Confessions* (2 vols. 1916); Arthur Ransome, *Oscar Wilde* (1912); Stuart Mason, *Oscar Wilde, Art and Morality* (1912); André Gide, *Oscar Wilde, a Study* (1905); L. C. Ingleby, *Oscar Wilde* (1907). For his writings consult Stuart Mason, *A Bibliography of Oscar Wilde* (1914).

with *Mrs Dane's Defence* and *The Second Mrs Tanqueray*; this "play about a good woman" seems as obvious an essay in the delineation of social life as any of the other plays about women not so good. A further glance, however, soon convinces us of the falsity of such a judgment. Wilde takes delight in choosing a theme which may be likely to interest contemporary audiences, but in the moral implications of the theme he has simply no interest. Many an episode to which Pinero and Jones would have devoted infinite care, endeavouring to make them as life-like as possible, are hastily hurried over. A good example comes at the end of the first act, where Lady Windermere thus soliloquises:

How horrible! I understand now what Lord Darlington meant by the imaginary instance of the couple not two years married. Oh! It can't be true—she spoke of enormous sums of money paid to this woman. I know where Arthur keeps his bank book—in one of the drawers of that desk. I might find out by that. I *will* find out. (*Opens drawer.*) No, it is some hideous mistake. (*Rises and goes* C.) Some silly scandal! He loves *me*! He loves *me*! But why should I not look? I am his wife, I have a right to look! (*Returns to bureau, takes out book and examines it, page by page, smiles and gives a sigh of relief.*) I knew it, there is not a word of truth in this stupid story. (*Puts book back in drawer. As she does so, starts and takes out another book.*) A second book—private—locked! (*Tries to open it, but fails. Sees paper knife on bureau, and with it cuts cover from book. Begins to start at the first page.*) Mrs Erlynne—£600—Mrs Erlynne—£700—Mrs Erlynne—£400. Oh! it is true! it is true! How horrible! (*Throws book on floor.*)

Here Wilde is using an old technique—a technique, moreover, which he, skilled as he was, must have known to be antiquated and which easily he could have replaced by another. The fact seems to be that he simply did not wish to make this scene more life-like; he has chosen his theme, not in order to create a sense of illusion, but simply as a basis for something else. That something else was his wit. The value of *Lady Windermere's Fan* does not rest in its story but in its dialogue. Finely polished, his prose has a metallic ring lacking in the less refined accents of Jones and Pinero. Once more Wilde carries us into the realm once dominated by Etherege when gentlemen conversed in epigram and gaily tossed similes to one another as in some spiritual battledore and shuttlecock.

This style reaches its finest expression in *The Importance of Being Earnest*. No inharmonious thoughts of life and morality intrude here, for the plot is given the same filigree grace as the language itself. Shot through with the best flowers of Wildian epigram, it maintains easily its settled plan and style. "My dear Algy, you talk exactly as if you were a dentist. It is very vulgar to talk like a dentist when one isn't a dentist. It produces a false impression"—"The amount of women in London who flirt with their own husbands is perfectly scandalous. It looks so bad. It is simply washing one's clean linen in public"—"You don't seem to realise that in married life three is company and two is none"—"Algy, you always adopt a strictly immoral attitude towards life. You are not quite old enough to do that"—one after another these epigrams keep crowding in upon us, harmonising in their artificiality with the wholly artificial spirit of this eccentric comedy. From the first interlude with Lane, the butler, to Jack's final "Gwendolen, it is a terrible thing for a man to find out suddenly that all his life he has been speaking nothing but the truth. Can you forgive me?" we are in a world of delightful make-believe where effervescent wit and swift surprise in situation keep us constantly in mental alertness.

This perhaps is the only comedy written by Wilde wherein he fully achieves complete harmony in aim and achievement. *A Woman of No Importance* is serious without conviction and *An Ideal Husband* seems to veer between the problem note of Pinero and the delicately absurd. That the latter play has a successfully developed and interesting plot cannot be denied; but there may be experienced a slight sense of dissatisfaction when Lord Goring throws off his air of polite inefficacy and becomes a business-like and energetic man of the world. It is as if Earnest suddenly revealed himself as a capable stockbroker or Algernon displayed a dully solemn interest in stamp-collecting. On the other hand, here as in *Lady Windermere's Fan* Wilde showed how the fashionable society of his time could be used for the purposes of comedy and in so far he re-established a true comedy of manners which, during the twentieth century, was to develop in the hands of Somerset Maugham and of Noel Coward. His success stimulated others in his own time—Pinero and Jones particularly; and we recognise that, quite apart from his own plays, the English theatre of the last few years of the century would have proved much less lively and much less stimulating had Wilde not been there to give it ease and grace.

III. *George Bernard Shaw*

To emphasise the importance of Bernard Shaw were obviously otiose; that has been done sufficiently by himself and by others.[1] This importance derives from the fact that here a great genius, with an essentially dramatic talent, came to the stage and seized from each of the various forces of his time those elements which were of greatest value and significance. To compare Shakespeare and Shaw may be a trifle foolish, for such comparisons of persons far removed in time from one another savour of the purely academic; but, provided we maintain our sense of proportion and balance, the parallel may yield material for critical evaluation. Shakespeare was born in 1564 and came to the theatre in the early nineties of the sixteenth century; Shaw was born in 1856 and had his first play produced in 1892. When Shakespeare joined a company of London players he found a renaissant drama which as yet had not realised its own destiny. Lyly had provided a new model in mythological fantastic comedy; Gascoigne had experimented in translations from the Italian *commedia erudita*; a strange romantic style was being exploited by Greene and a peculiar romantic revenge drama had attracted the attention of Kyd; above all, Marlowe was plumbing

[1] The library of critical works on Shaw has not yet assumed the proportions of the Shakespeare library; but then Shakespeare died over three hundred years ago. The standard biography is that of Archibald Henderson (new edition, 1933). The studies by Holbrook Jackson, H. L. Mencken, G. K. Chesterton, Edward Shanks, John Palmer, Joseph McCabe, A. Hamon and D. A. Lord survey various aspects of his work.

the depths of a new tragedy and displaying the full powers of blank verse rhetoric. Shakespeare's virtue it was, not merely to bring a still further outstanding genius to the stage, but to seize from Lyly and Greene and Kyd and Gascoigne and Marlowe just such material as might be regarded most valuable and to weld these into one harmonious whole. Marlowe's verse and high tragic conception he made his own, and combined with that the subtlety of *The Spanish Tragedy*; to the Italian wit as reflected in Gascoigne he added Lyly's over-delicate grace and Greene's romantic robustiousness.

Shaw's position is by no means dissimilar. From Jones and Pinero he learned much, and still more did he learn from Ibsen. To Wilde he went for some of his skill in quip and epigram, and many a device he borrowed from dramatists whose very names maybe are now forgotten. In our excitement over all that seemed so novel and so startlingly thrilling in Shaw, we often forget that when he was a young man of twenty or thirty he frequented the theatres and eagerly watched performances of all the good old plays from earliest melodramas to Jones's *The Silver King*, from Lytton's *Money* to Robertson's comedies and Byron's latest successes. His dramas, so far from being new, are a tissue of reminiscences of earlier work; just as Shakespeare's plays are broadly based upon the foundations laid by his predecessors. One of the most surprising things about drama is that greatness does not really spring from complete originality. "The thief of all thieves was the Warwickshire thief" sang David Garrick in *The Jubilee* (D.L. 1769), and almost the same might be lilted of every dramatic genius. Molière found inspiration for his work in the *commedia dell' arte* as Wycherley found inspiration in Molière.

Already[1] an example has been given of the way in which Shaw has seized material from a play by Boucicault; and this example must be regarded, not as a solitary one, but as representative of much in the plays pleasant and unpleasant. Other melodramas find themselves reflected in his work; there are reminiscences of Lytton's *Money* and of comedies by

[1] See *supra*, pp. 90–1.

Jerrold and Robertson and Byron. This does not, however, by any means imply that Shaw's dramatic genius, any more than Shakespeare's, was merely imitative. The appearance of *Widowers' Houses* in 1892 marked the beginning of a new epoch even as did the appearance of *Love's Labour's Lost* almost exactly three centuries previously.

Shaw's genius consisted in his fusing of different elements in the theatre of his day and in looking towards the future instead of towards the immediate present. Jones's plays were frequently powerful dramatically, but they were apt to be a trifle dull; Wilde's were gay enough but proved, on examination, to be but flimsy things at the best; Pinero could laugh farcically, or superiorly sneer, or write pathetically of the woman with a past, but he had not the all-embracing ability to do more than one of these things at one time. Shaw takes the whole of theatrical emotion as his province and can move easily from one mood to the other while keeping all subordinate to one universal aim. Where Jones and Pinero were single-minded pioneers, he was the accomplished master benefiting from their adventures.

The great Shavian epoch, of course, does not come until the beginning of the twentieth century, but already before 1900 Shaw had fully displayed the extent of his powers. Ten plays in all he wrote in the course of these eight years—*Widowers' Houses* (Roy. Dec. 1892), *Arms and the Man* (Aven. April 1894), *Candida* (S. Shields, March 1895; H.M. Aberdeen, July 1897), *The Devil's Disciple* (Bijou, April 1897), *The Man of Destiny* (Grand, Croydon, July 1897; Com. March 1901), *The Philanderer* (published 1898), *Mrs Warren's Profession* (published 1898), *You Never Can Tell* (published 1898; Roy. Nov. 1899), *Caesar and Cleopatra* (Newcastle, March 1899; Sav. Nov. 1907) and *Captain Brassbound's Conversion* (licensed 1899; Str. Dec. 1900; Court, March 1906). Not one of these before 1900 proved a popular success, yet even in the nineties Shaw's influence was far-spread. Both by these plays and by his dramatic criticisms in *The Saturday Review* he had made himself one of the most dominant theatrical forces in London.

One thing must be realised if ever we are to understand Shaw rightly; he is not a philosopher, but a dramatist. He himself, of course, has constantly reiterated that the theatre is being used by him merely as a platform, and his reiterations have been taken seriously by most of his critics; but Shaw is no more a prophet than were Shakespeare and Molière. "I am convinced that fine art is the subtlest, the most seductive, the most effective means of propagandism in the world," he declares, and would have us believe that his only interest in the stage lies in the fact that the drama gives him an opportunity of appealing to thousands; "prophet" he styles himself and wishes (or pretends to wish) us to regard him as a purveyor of ideas and not of episodes. Perhaps, so often has he repeated this, Shaw has become convinced in his own mind; but it is certain that the power of keeping his plays alive will be, not their prophetic ideas, but their sheer dramaturgic skill. Essentially a playwright, his comedies are instinct with the life of the theatre.

This, of course, is not to say that he has no literary aim; rather that he, more than any other man of his time, sought for and achieved a significant and harmonious union of literary and theatrical qualities. With a boldness rivalled by none save perhaps Oscar Wilde, Shaw made claim to the appreciation of the literary connoisseur. His plays he issued in a form which made them appeal to a reading public; his prefaces were intended to stimulate this appeal, and by means of his elaborate stage directions he aimed at creating in the study the atmosphere of the stage. From many other literary dramatists, however, Shaw separated himself by frankly accepting those elements in the playhouse which make for popularity; and not a single writer has shown a surer knowledge of stagecraft and of the desires of the audience, or a more subtle and effective use of these elements. He was willing and eager to make full and free employment of physical action on the stage—the eternally exciting appeal of melodrama—and to utilise boldly those conceptions which made the burlesque, the farce and the extravaganza once so popular. Again we realise how much akin he was in 1890 to the young

Shakespeare of 1590. When the latter came to London, he found the playhouses in the hands of crude dramatists who courted attention by rough, tempestuous, melodramatic action or by vulgar and unpolished jests. Instead of condemning these and striving to evolve something new, Shakespeare laid his hands on whatsoever was likely to be of service to him—plots, situations, characters, dialogue—transforming all by the magic of his skill, yet retaining that which formed the basic strength and theatrical value of the material he had chosen. In a manner precisely similar Shaw turned for guidance to the dramatists who were his immediate predecessors and laid heavy toll upon them.

That Shaw's plays are not merely reproductions of popular melodrama and farce is obvious; like Shakespeare he created out of what he took from others an art expression individual and distinct. This introduces the question of the kind of theatre which Shaw has produced. Tragedy and gloomily serious drama such as *The Second Mrs Tanqueray* and *Mrs Dane's Defence* he completely avoided; the sphere of comedy it was which he made his own. Shaw's comedy, however, was of a peculiar kind, and clearly our first task should be to determine the precise aim which he had in view when composing, say, *Arms and the Man* or *Androcles and the Lion.* To be continually seeking for elaborate classifications in art, of course, may become a very definite critical fault; but, whatever disdain we may experience when we encounter such formal criticism carried to excess, we cannot escape from the fact that some sort of classification is necessary; we could not deal with *Twelfth Night* by comparing it with Sean O'Casey's *The Silver Tassie*. We all recognise, that is to say, certain clearly differentiated types of drama—tragedy, comedy, melodrama, farce. Beyond this, however, we must go. Within the one sphere of dramatic endeavour which we call "comedy", we have to distinguish many diverse forms; indeed, there are some comedies which aim at conveying to an audience impressions which are more nearly allied to the impressions conveyed by some kinds of tragedy than to those aroused, say, by *As You Like It* or *The Way of the World.*

There is a vast measure of difference between the spirit of Jonson's *The Alchemist*, classically bitter, and the enchanted fancies of *A Midsummer Night's Dream*.

Looking at English drama as a whole, it seems that we may trace four main forms within this comic sphere. The first is Shakespeare's comedy of romance, distinguished by its all-pervading humour—a humour which permits the dramatist to mingle together the most strangely varied elements, which allows him to put his fairies alongside his human lovers, to make his clown strut with his kings. In addition to this quality of humour, there is always in Shakespeare's comedy the overshadowing presence of a kindly and dominant Nature. It is Nature that leads the lovers out of the mazy wildernesses of the fairy-haunted forest; it is Nature that makes Don John's machinations, which have hoodwinked the clever, superior and self-conscious aristocrats, revealed through the agency of the dull-witted Dogberry. When Dogberry triumphs, Nature smiles. This, then, is one type of comedy; the second is that of Ben Jonson. Here the aim is directly satirical—satirical, not of social manners but of individual follies. Jonson seizes on particular eccentricities or errors or vices peculiar to certain men, and by the creation of type characters such as his Sir Epicure or his Volpone, throws lurid light on human duplicity. In the comedy of Congreve there is another, and a distinct, aim. Here the dramatist is no longer concerned with individual follies. He has deliberately restricted himself to one small section of society—the courtly circle—a section of society highly conscious of its own rules, conventions and manners, anxious to preserve intact the refinement of social graces and to reveal its intellectually brilliant wit. If Shakespeare is preoccupied with humour, and Jonson with satiric bitterness, Congreve is concerned, above all other things, with a wit that is airy, delicate and flimsily brittle. Finally, we reach what, for want of a better term, we may style the sentimental comedy. In this once more the whole of social life is taken within the playwright's sphere of observation, and his endeavour is to delineate and to discuss certain problems or difficulties which confront man as a social animal. At first, perhaps, only the most immediately obvious problems will be dealt with—duelling, gambling and the like; in the beginning, too, these problems will be discussed, not in a rationalistic and realistic manner, but in a spirit of vague emotional sympathy; but gradually a deeper note will enter in and the purely sentimental comedy will become the comedy of serious purpose.

When we turn from these four major forms of comic endeavour to the plays of Bernard Shaw, we recognise that many of their characteristics are to be found reflected in his work as well. Something of Shakespeare's humour is here. The atmosphere of *Measure for Measure* and, more particularly, of *All's Well that Ends Well*, seems very close to that of *Man and Superman*. Shaw's Life Force is simply Shakespeare's Nature. Many of Shaw's characters are conceived intellectually as types in the Jonsonian manner; yet his comedy as a whole does not reflect the mood established in *Volpone* and *Bartholomew Fair*. To other scenes we turn and find there a pure wit, as delicately expressed as the wit of Congreve; viewing this we feel we are in the presence of comedies cast in the Restoration mould. Yet immediately other scenes attract our attention, scenes in which we discern something of that aim to which, crudely, the sentimental dramatists were seeking to give expression.

This does not imply, however, that Shaw's plays are made up merely by a mingling of devices and moods exploited by earlier dramatists. From his first comedies to his latest, Shaw has exhibited a characteristic quality which has made his work essentially and uniquely individual. Perhaps the clue to this quality is provided by himself. In a conversation some time ago, someone spoke of his wit and humour. "My plays contain," he said, "not so much humour and wit, as fun." This self-judgment gives us our clue. His comedies, as distinct from all the others mentioned above, are comedies of purposeful fun. Herein lies one of his great contributions to the modern theatre. His fun is something peculiar to himself: an effervescing, bubbling-up, eternally youthful and joyous exuberance of spirit. He is continually inverting ideas and poking fun—poking fun at us, at his audiences, at his characters, at ideas. He will take the popular conceptions of certain historic figures—a Napoleon, a Caesar—and, turning them topsy-turvy, will smile good-naturedly at our set ideas. In *Caesar and Cleopatra* he will introduce a secretary for Caesar, a British slave, and he will make this Briton declare to Cleopatra:

Blue is the colour worn by all Britons of good standing. In war we stain our bodies blue; so that though our enemies may strip us of our clothes and our lives, they cannot strip us of our respectability.

He will make Apollodorus approach Caesar with "Hail, Caesar! I am Apollodorus the Sicilian, an artist." The Briton cries "An artist! Why have they admitted this vagabond?" to be checked by Caesar "Peace, man. Apollodorus is a famous patrician amateur." The Briton bows—"I crave the gentleman's pardon. I understood him to say he was a professional."

The introduction of this character—in spite of Shaw's own note on Britannus—has been condemned; but, as the author well knew, the excuse for his introduction lies, not in arguing that climate produces similar features in all centuries, but in the fact that he is eminently in his right dramatic place. Throughout this play, Shaw is not intent on naturalistically recreating a past period of history; over all he casts the light of his own imagination and that imagination is tinged and irradiated by his inimitable spirit of fun. It is the same with his later dramas. In *Back to Methuselah* Franklyn is introducing his brother to Burge: "I forget whether you know my brother Conrad. He is a biologist", on which Burge suddenly bursts into energetic action and words:

By reputation only, but very well, of course. How I wish I could have devoted myself to biology! I have always been interested in rocks and strata and volcanoes and so forth: they throw such a light on the age of the earth. There is nothing like biology. "The cloud-capped towers, the solemn binnacles, the gorgeous temples, the great globe itself: yea, all that it inherit shall dissolve and, like this influential pageant faded, leave not a wrack behind." That's biology, you know: good sound biology.

The words and the scene are exaggeratedly ridiculous: but again they do not clash with the serious, imaginative arguments which precede and follow because over all Shaw has thrown the mantle of his peculiarly dominating sense of fun, just as Shakespeare cast the radiance of his humour alike on Dogberry and on Claudio.

The invention and elaboration of this comedy of purposeful fun forms an important contribution to the theatre; but this is by no means all. Each one of Shaw's plays contains an element of fantastic incongruity. True, he has written some plays in the "realistic" style, but these, in my opinion, may not be compared with those in which he has allowed free rein to this imaginative fantasy. It is precisely here that Shaw's historical position becomes significant. The decade 1890–1900 presented the growing power of naturalism in the theatre; such naturalism, as we have already seen, was, owing to the outworn and useless conventions that had been encrusted on the playhouse, both necessary and desirable. This Shaw saw as clearly as any, and he aided materially in helping forward those who were intent on introducing these new aims. But even in his apprentice period, Shaw was always too big for realism. Even in 1892 he realised that realism was not enough, that the naturalistic stage was merely a step towards something beyond. He recognised that plays are definitely works of art and not merely mirrors of the life we see around us. From the beginning, then, from *Widowers' Houses*, through *Arms and the Man*, *Caesar and Cleopatra*, *Man and Superman* on to *Back to Methuselah*, *Heartbreak House* and *The Apple Cart* he has introduced this extra-realist element.

This extra-realist element is to be traced in conception of situation, and it is equally to be traced in the conception of character. Some time ago Shaw, in a private letter discussing his then new play, *Too True to be Good*, referred to "the great length to which *Too True* carries my practice of making my characters say not what in real life they could never bring themselves to say, even if they understood themselves clearly enough, but the naked soul truth, quite objectively and scientifically presented, thus combining the extreme of unnaturalness with the deepest attainable naturalness....The Shakespearean soliloquy, in so far as it was not merely an 'aside' for the information of the audience, was an attempt at this. The highest drama is nothing but a striving towards this feat of interpretation." Once more this self-judgment is a correct one; and, accepting it, we realise how far removed Shaw was in his scope from the dramatists who were his companions in the nineties.

That his work did not reach absolute perfection during his earliest efforts is, of course, obvious. *Widowers' Houses*, even though it does make a significant contribution to the theatre, clearly has not complete unity of conception, and *The Philanderer* proves unsatisfactory because in composing it Shaw has been misled by the prevailing naturalism of his day. Perhaps there is another reason for the failure of this latter play. Unquestionably autobiographical in concept, it at one and the same time approaches too near to real life and presents a picture hopelessly artificial. In Charteris we cannot fail to see Bernard Shaw himself, and the fact that this is a kind of portrait of the artist robs the character of those qualities which animate Tanner and Bluntschli. Instead of being above his characters, Shaw sits here in their midst. The essence of Shaw's comedy, moreover, demands an entire absence of emotion. Start feeling for the Elderly Gentleman and you completely misinterpret his role; stir pity in your heart for Androcles and the very spirit of the comedy vanishes. In his letter, quoted above, Shaw stated that his persons were "quite objectively and scientifically presented", and this is true of most of his work; he generally succeeds in standing above his *dramatis personae*. "I am of the true Shakespearean type," he states elsewhere,[1] "I understand everything and everyone, and am nobody and nothing." Whereas, however, Shakespeare's genius was of such a kind as to permit of an emotional approach even while this objectivity was retained intact, Shaw's power requires a complete sense of detachment

[1] Letter quoted in Frank Harris, *op. cit.* p. 224.

between the creative artist and his puppet creations. By thrusting himself into the person of Charteris he adopted a method false to his own spirit, and in the attempt to display emotion in the person of Julia he brought down his whole dramatic edifice in a mass of crumbling ruins about his head. Wilde might legitimately exploit himself; Shaw's secret strength lies in self-repression. That such is not the commonly accepted view of his work arises from the fact that there is a confusion between Shaw the man and Shaw the dramatist. The writer of the prefaces is not the writer of the plays; there may be propaganda and the enunciation of individually held opinions in the preface, say, to *Androcles and the Lion*, but in the drama itself Shaw is "nobody and nothing"; as each character speaks he gives himself to that character and of propaganda there is little or none.

Similar weaknesses are to be traced in *Mrs Warren's Profession*, which seems to have been projected for an Independent Theatre Society production of 1894 under the title of *Mrs Jarman's Profession*.[1] The construction is good, but the spirit appears at once too determined and too emotional for the free expression of his dramatic talents. *Arms and the Man*, on the other hand, and *The Devil's Disciple* are true Shaw. Technically, both of these show great theatrical progress. The element of surprise in both may thus be contrasted with the even monotony of *The Philanderer*. More important, however, is the harmonious retention of mood. All emotionalism has been banished; if Raina proposes to become passionate, she is promptly repressed by Captain Bluntschli and Dick performs the same office for Mrs Anderson. Fun rules in both; laughter holds his sides as the romantic Saranoff confronts the imperturbable Swiss officer, and any tendency to seriousness in *The Devil's Disciple* is immediately curbed by a situation of absolute merriment.

The Man of Destiny shows his progress along these lines. Again the technique is excellent; again constant surprise keeps our attention alert—no chance of boredom as we pass from the loss of the despatches and the Lieutenant's attitude

[1] See note in *The Theatre*, N.S. xxiv, Dec. 1894, 332.

to the discovery of the Strange Lady, from that to the duel between this Lady and Napoleon, to the question of Napoleon's honour, to the command concerning the despatches, to the revealing of the Lady, to the argument about the English and so to the unexpected close. The dramatist's extreme economy is evident here and his constant need of startling effect. In 1897 *The Theatre* reviewer might feel puzzled:

> *The Man of Destiny* is less a play than a simple medium for the airing of the author's well-known opinions relative to Socialism, political economy, the aggrandisement of England, and other cognate matters....Seriously to criticise a piece of the kind would be consequently a waste of time and space....That there is real cleverness to be found in the dialogue we do not deny, but it is a kind of cleverness ill-suited to the purposes of the stage—.[1]

but to-day we recognise in it those qualities which, in a more extended form, placed Shaw in the forefront of the embattled modern dramatists.

This consideration of Shaw's strength and weakness in his early work becomes of special importance when we attempt to evaluate his *Candida*. Unquestionably *Candida* relates itself to *Mrs Warren's Profession* rather than to *The Man of Destiny*. That it displays structural skill may not be denied; yet it may be questioned whether, in spite of the high critical esteem in which it is held, this play represents such a vitally effective contribution to the theatre as *Androcles* or *Arms and the Man*. There is perhaps more warmth in *Candida* than in most of Shaw's plays, but for his characteristic comedy Shaw does not need warmth—emotion is really as alien to his needs as it was to those of Etherege and his companions of the Restoration stage. *Candida* is a play which we might have imagined other dramatists writing; only Shaw could have conceived and wittily executed *The Man of Destiny* and *The Devil's Disciple*.

IV. *Naturalism and Fantasy*

During the time that Wilde and Shaw were thus writing for the stage, the naturalistic movement became more assured

[1] *The Theatre*, N.S. xxx, Aug. 1897, 101–2.

and determined. All the antiquated devices had, it is true, not been abandoned, but the aim was that of reproducing contemporary life. Two playwrights of the decade may be selected as typical. C. Haddon Chambers had begun his career with *One of Them* (Margate, Sept. 1886) and *The Open Gate* (Com. March 1887), but great success arrived to him only with *The Tyranny of Tears* (Crit. April 1899). Based on the methods and ideals of Pinero and Jones, retaining the use of such ancient instruments as the soliloquy and the aside, this drama is yet deliberately domestic in execution and concept. It presents seriously what many farces had presented amusingly in earlier years[1]—a husband, Parbury, whose wife has forced him, by means of the "tyranny of tears", to abandon all his old friends. Finding his secretary, Miss Woodward, kissing his photograph, the wife orders her to be dismissed. He succeeds in summoning up some spirit and resolutely refuses, whereupon she leaves him. The plot demands a sad or indeterminate ending, but Chambers has seen fit to bring his final curtain down sentimentally—with the return of the wife and with the arrival of Parbury's friend, Gunning, who very conveniently makes a proposal of marriage to Miss Woodward. This treatment, with its mingling of sentiment and of would-be "realism", is thoroughly characteristic of the spirit of the drama during this decade.

Even more representative are the plays of one who, in his own time, moved with the theatrical vanguard—Sydney Grundy. Like Pinero and Jones, this author had begun writing for the stage in the seventies[2]—with *A Little Change* (H. July 1872), *All at Sea* (Manchester, Aug. 1873), *Reading for the Bar* (Str. Oct. 1876) and similar farces or comediettas. The first works which give him any claim to serious attention came in the following decade—*The Silver Shield* (Str. May 1885), *A Fool's Paradise* (P.W. Greenwich, Oct. 1887, as *The Mousetrap*; Gai. Feb. 1889), *The Dean's Daughter* (St J. Oct. 1888), written in association with F. C. Philips; these were

[1] See *supra*, pp. 152–3.

[2] Sir W. Watson, *Sydney Grundy and the Critics* (*The Theatre*, N.S. xxxiii, 1894).

followed by the famous *Pair of Spectacles* (Gar. Feb. 1890)[1] and *Sowing the Wind* (Com. Sept. 1893). Grundy possessed a perfectly good comic style which he constantly vitiated by attempting serious things beyond his reach. *The Silver Shield*, for example, has some excellent scenes in which, without eccentricity, laughter is won from domestic circumstance, but there is decided weakness in the handling of a situation in which the young wife, finding among her husband's papers a section of a play he is composing, imagines it to be an amatory epistle addressed to an actress. His tragedy, *Clito* (P'cess, May 1886), written in collaboration with W. Barrett, demonstrates clearly how ill-suited he was to deal with emotional problems seriously and profoundly. In his work as a whole appears a strange contradiction, well summed up by a reviewer of *The Late Mr Castello* (Com. Dec. 1895):

> Mr Sydney Grundy presents the curious spectacle of a playwright whose method is as antiquated as his manner is distinctly modern. In the matter of construction he is half a century behind the times; in point of dialogue he is, if anything, rather in advance of them.[2]

In this he is not unrepresentative of his time. With Pinero and Jones the stage had at last reached adequate expression of realistic aims but the task of banishing the very last relics of the older conventional theatre was left to the playwrights of the first decade of our own century.

It is important to recognise that this adequate expression of realistic aims was the result of an age-long development; even at the risk of repeating what has already been emphasised, a final word must be said concerning this. One might almost treat the entirety of theatrical history from the sixteenth to the nineteenth centuries as one single movement in art, with a gradual approach being made towards an ultimate ideal. In making such a statement, one would not, of course, wish to deny the existence of a continuing tradition which linked the theatre, say, of 1750 with the theatre of 1600. Up

[1] See the biographical and critical notice in *The Theatre*, N.S. xvi, July 1890, 46–7.

[2] *The Theatre*, N.S. xxviii, Feb. 1896, 97.

to the end of the eighteenth century, actors were going about their tasks very much as Alleyn and Burbage might have done; dramatists were supplying their wares under the same conditions as had applied to Marlowe and Kyd; theatre management organised the repertoires in the same manner as Henslowe had done; and audiences still watched the performances taking place almost, if not quite, in their midst. This is true; but equally true is the fact that, with the introduction of the closed theatre and the consequent artificial lighting, with the rise of sentimental comedy and bourgeois tragedy, a definite movement was being made towards later naturalism. One great advance in this direction was being taken about 1770; another in 1810; still another in 1840; and a final one in 1870. By the end of the century little remained of the older stage save the wandering tent-playhouse. The last of these has now vanished, but even a few years ago one could find them, maintaining a precarious and doubtful vitality, in the Midland and Welsh circuits. Anyone who has been fortunate enough to have witnessed one of these shows may justifiably claim that here he has been in the presence of the last true descendants of the Elizabethan companies. A trifle melancholy is the reflection, akin to that we experience when, on some Highland roadway, we encounter a wretched group of poverty-stricken, diseased and emaciated tramps, last relics of a Stuart clan dispersed and rejected by advancing civilisation.

Realism, then, in the picture-frame stage, with the banishment of antiquated conventions, triumphed. In any art, when once virile conventions become stereotyped and hence bereft of meaning, only a return to realistic methods can produce sanity and fresh inspiration. It was Giotto's break-away from sterile, but once powerful, Byzantine models which opened up the path for the advance of Italian art during the Renaissance. Tom Robertson was the Giotto of the English theatre in the nineteenth century, and translated Ibsen was its Raphael.

Any dispassionate survey of this period convinces us that this realistic method was necessary, nay more, that it succeeded in producing a series of plays which, if not greater (as William Archer deemed) than the poetic Elizabethan dramas, are worthy of being placed alongside the masterpieces of any age. At the same time, we must recognise two things. The first is that realism can never be enough. To discuss the implications of this and show why that naturalism which was life and health and inspiration in 1900 cannot serve a later generation would take us far outside the confines of the late nineteenth century; but the second thing worthy of notice definitely belongs within these confines. It is the fact that, even in the midst of this naturalistic development, there were many attempts at escape. These must now occupy our attention.

The most obvious of the attempts is the cultivation of poetic drama, but it cannot be maintained that this age created more worthy examples of this kind than had been created in the preceding eras. During the forties Browning, encouraged by Macready, had sought to win theatrical success, but failed to secure a reasonably firm footing on the boards. He, in turn, was followed by the majestic solemnity of Tennyson. Much was hoped from Tennyson. Established as the most popular lyric writer of his day and a proven master in the realm of narrative verse, he was viewed by some as a man who might, if he desired, bring back the glories of Elizabeth's reign in the age of Victoria. Tennyson certainly desired it; of that there is no doubt, and "infinite trouble" he expended on his dramatic works. Not one of these, however, has any real theatric value. Partly the explanation for their failure may be sought in the prevailing didacticism which blunts their temper; Tennyson's patriotic orthodoxy at best is dull; but more perhaps is it to be traced to the lack of stage sense common to these poets. *Queen Mary* (Lyc. April 1876)[1] has a good theme and a wretched handling; *Harold* (printed 1877) seems to us monotonously pretentious; and *Becket* (Lyr. Feb.

[1] On the sources of Tennyson's plays see Werner Martin, *Die Quellen zu Tennysons erstem Drama "Queen Mary"* (Halle, 1912), Paul Jellinghaus, *Tennysons Drama "Harold"* (Borna-Leipzig, 1907) and Louis Grünert, *Tennysons Drama "Becket"* (Weimar, 1913).

1893) is fogged in Tennyson's most dignified gloom. True, he won a certain measure of success on the stage, but that was due, not to the inherent virtues of the plays but to a combination of the author's poetic fame and the equally popular acting of Irving and the Kendals.

After Tennyson came Stephen Phillips with his *Paolo and Francesca* (licensed 1899; St J. March 1902). *Paolo and Francesca* is a play which at once recalls the long, sorry series of its predecessors—poor ghosts revisiting the glimpses of an Elizabethan moon, and immediately differentiates itself from these. The Shakespearian plan Phillips has followed as a pattern, that is evident: Shakespeare's verse form becomes the model for his verse, and the characters are set forth in the manner of the great seventeenth-century tragedies. In so far, he shows himself a mere companion of the other poets of the time. When, however, we note that, at an early age, Phillips joined F. R. Benson's company and acted therein for a number of years, we realise that his training was not that of a lordly Byron, an eccentric Shelley or a lonely Keats. It is precisely this training on the part of the author that sets *Paolo and Francesca* apart from the other poetic plays of the nineteenth century. This drama is not a great masterpiece; there are weaknesses in it of structure, character-delineation and dialogue; but Phillips has honestly studied the technique of his craft and his tragedy is to be welcomed for its essentially dramatic qualities. Its main defect lies in its tendency towards elaborate lyricism and in its dependence upon ancient rhythmic patterns. In spite of his theatrical apprenticeship and in spite of the consequent endeavour to establish the poetic drama on a new foundation, Phillips did not succeed in breaking away from the vicious influences of the romantic style or in realising the true function of verse in the theatre. Lady Benson records that he "had a fine voice" but that he

> would insist on rolling out his lines...making his diction unnatural and stilted. I asked him his reason for this, and he replied that he put a higher value on the beauty of the words than on their dramatic effect.[1]

[1] *Mainly Players: Bensonian Memories* (1926), pp. 65–6.

This is typical. Before a new poetic drama could arise, poets had to learn to forget Shakespeare and to remember that the theatre needs more than words sonorously rolled out. The virtue of *Murder in the Cathedral* and *The Ascent of F. 6* rests in the determined effort of their authors to find an entirely fresh foundation on which to work.

With these attempts to establish poetic drama on the stage must be related a certain romantic enthusiasm which, particularly in the nineties, surprisingly manifested itself among the audiences. Already attention has been drawn to the "Boom in Shakespeare" which even contemporaries had noticed.[1] Irving's great revivals were popular, mainly of course because of the actor-manager's personality, but partly at least because the surging throb of the Elizabethan drama created a mood different from and larger than that provided by Jones and Pinero. For the same reason there came a return of interest in flamboyantly adventuresome cloak-and-sword plays. *The Prisoner of Zenda* (St J. Jan. 1896), as adapted by Edward Rose from Anthony Hope's novel, started a fashion which usurped the earlier craze for Irish comedy-dramas. *The Three Musketeers* (Manchester, Aug. 1850), as adapted by Charles Rice, had hardly been a great success in 1850, but in the last years of the century plays on the same theme swept the boards. At the Imperial W. Heron Brown brought out one version (June 1898); H. A. Saintsbury's adaptation appeared at the Parkhurst (Sept. 1898); Henry Hamilton had his produced first at the Metropole, Camberwell (Sept. 1898) and later at the Globe (Oct. 1898); another version by Brian Daly and J. M. East appeared at the Lyric, Hammersmith (Nov. 1898); while Rice's independent version (originally produced at Manchester, Aug. 1850) was revived at the Britannia (Oct. 1898). The winter of '98 was decidedly a winter of the *Musketeers*. Nor did that theme stand alone; others of a like kind proved equally successful. Martin Harvey brought out Freeman Wills's *The Only Way* at the Lyceum in February 1899; L. B. Irving's *Robespierre* (Lyc. April 1899) belongs in the same category, as do Edward

[1] See *supra*, p. 38.

Rose's *In Days of Old* (St J. April 1899) and C. B. Fernald's *The Moonlight Blossom* (P.W. Sept. 1899).

All of these tell the same tale—a tale of unconscious dissatisfaction with the prevailing tendency towards realism. It is by no means strange that Gordon Craig was reared in the Irving tradition and that his first production, that of *Dido and Aeneas*, came in the spring of 1900.[1]

Even more significant is the restless deviation from realistic method already noted in the plays of Wilde and Shaw. The eccentric wit of the former and the fantastic fun of the latter lead them far from the dull imitation of life. And by their side stands J. M. Barrie.[2] Before the turn of the century Barrie had not accomplished much in the theatre, but what he had done proved that his was not a genius likely to be content with familiar description of easily observed natural forms. In some plays he sought escape in the world of romance—*Becky Sharp* (Terry's, June 1893), *Richard Savage* (Crit. April 1891), *The Little Minister* (H. Nov. 1897); elsewhere he applied older burlesque methods to newer idols, laughing at naturalism in *Ibsen's Ghost* (Toole's, May 1891); and in one other, *Walker, London* (Toole's, Feb. 1892), he displayed an individual quality which later was to blossom into richer bloom in *The Admirable Crichton* and *Peter Pan*. Barrie's true significance for the drama lies in his effort to substitute subjectivity for objectivity, artistic form and pattern for formal recording. His elfin humour, for which the epithet "pawky" is inevitable, releases him much in the same way as Shaw is released by his impish spirit of fun.

Nor were these men wholly without companions. One example of this will suffice. Robert Marshall has a play called *Shades of Night* (Lyc. March 1896) in which Captain Trivett and Winifred Yester are brought to a haunted room and there

[1] Enid Rose, *Gordon Craig and the Theatre* (n.d.) pp. 31–2.

[2] On his career see the studies by T. Moult (1928), F. J. H. Darton (1929) and J. A. Hammerton (1929). His writings are listed in B. D. Cutler, *Sir James M. Barrie: A Bibliography* (1931). H. M. Walbrook has an essay on *J. M. Barrie and the Theatre* (1922), Walter Eschenhauer another on *Sir James Barrie als Dramatiker: Ein Beitrag zum englischen Drama des zwanzigsten Jahrhunderts* (Halle, 1929).

confronted by the ghosts of their ancestors. The dialogue is not, maybe, very brilliant, but there is evident in its fantasy a wish to break away from current domestic realism. The ghosts of Lady Mildred and Sir Ludovic have made their appearance:

LADY MILDRED (*at back*). I believe, Captain Trivett, that your mother now rules the establishment here. That being so, might I ask you, as a favour, to request her to keep this room for the future aired and dusted?

CAPTAIN. Yes, yes,—of course—by all means.

LADY MILDRED. Thanks. This, you know, is my only gown.

SIR LUDOVIC. That's one of your hardships. We can only sport the togs we died in.

CAPTAIN. Then if you die in bed?

SIR LUDOVIC. You put an awkward question. A good deal would depend on the pattern. I think we had better go on with the business, Eh, Lady Mildred?

LADY MILDRED (*with great hauteur*). I certainly think so. I have no desire to pursue the present vein of the conversation....

SIR LUDOVIC (*crosses to* CAPTAIN *and* WINIFRED, LADY MILDRED *gets to table*). Your presence here to-night is a matter of great satisfaction to me. You'll now learn the true version of our story. But you mustn't laugh. You see we've never done it to an audience before, and no doubt we shall be a little awkward at first. Are you ready, Lady Mildred?

LADY MILDRED. Quite.

SIR LUDOVIC. Very well, then, (CAPTAIN *and* WINIFRED *go to the chair*, R. *corner*. WINIFRED *sits. To the others*). We begin with the declaration of my passion. The language may seem a little stilted, but you won't mind that?

CAPTAIN. Not at all.

SIR LUDOVIC. Thanks. Now then!

Throughout the scene that follows, the action of the Phantoms takes place at the back of the stage, C. *The tone of speech is hollow, the style melodramatic, but not extravagantly so. The ordinary mode of speech is adopted when the Phantoms stop the action at intervals to discuss it with* CAPTAIN TRIVETT *and* WINIFRED. LADY MILDRED *is seated at table,* SIR LUDOVIC *bending over her. A decanter and two glasses are on the table.*

"As evening looms from out the sundown and the burnished sword of daybreak smiles the raven wings of night, still do I protest, O LADY MILDRED, that but one thought draws from my soul!"

LADY MILDRED. "Lud! Sir Ludovic. Your ideas must be vastly limited!" I should like to point out, Miss Yester, that originally this gown was of a delicate shell pink brocade, lined with pale mauve velvet, and at the time my complexion was the talk of the country. (SIR LUDOVIC *moves* R. *up to window, much annoyed.*) In the astral world, you know, we become quite colourless.

WINIFRED. Yes, yes, I understand.

SIR LUDOVIC (*comes down*). However, to continue. "There is but one passion that dominates my soul, Lady Mildred. It is the burning love I bear you!"

LADY MILDRED. "You bear my fortune! Enough, Sir Ludovic, I will have none of you!"

SIR LUDOVIC (*starting back*). "Spurned?"

LADY MILDRED. "Aye, spurned! For I too love—my fortune!"

SIR LUDOVIC. "Am I then doomed to live—alas!—alone?"

LADY MILDRED. "Lud, Sir Ludovic! 'tis I who mean to live a lass alone!" (*Laughs and turns to the others.*) You see my play upon the words "alas! alone?"

SIR LUDOVIC. Isn't it good? I remember, though, I felt it terribly at the time.

CAPTAIN. It was a little heartless.

LADY MILDRED (*sharply*). Not at all. It was said quite artlessly.

CAPTAIN. Exactly—as I say—heartlessly.

LADY MILDRED. I said a-r-t artlessly—you supplied the *h*; not being my own I dropped it. (*Crosses* L. *a little.*) Besides, I knew he cared for nothing but my money.

SIR LUDOVIC. It's quite true; she saw through me.

CAPTAIN. Ah! You admit it?

SIR LUDOVIC. Oh, dear me, yes! I felt no love at all! It was all put on, like her complexion.

Quite clearly, such work as this indicates new scope for the theatre, and, even though we may not be prepared to reckon *Shades of Night* a great masterpiece, we may acclaim Marshall as one at least among a body of playwrights who, in the nineties, were striving to open up dramatic fields the frontiers of which were being narrowed by the stricter realists.

As we leave this century, however, we still find these stricter realists in control. This was their day and they made the most of it. Their works formed the characteristic expression of the time. The seeds planted by Lytton and Boucicault in the forties had now grown to sturdy plants bearing fruit, not juicily soft and providing only a moment's enjoyment, but hard and filled with the substance of good and evil. The last years of Victoria's reign closed with almost full realisation of that promise which her early patronage of the theatre had aroused. London now was displaying a dramatic vitality of which it had been innocent since the days of Queen Anne. In spite of her prudish temper and her bourgeois-like placidity, Victoria had succeeded in bringing to life once more a theatre acknowledged and supported by all classes among her subjects—a theatre which, despite all the restrictions imposed upon it by its clinging to realism, may not find a previous rival in England unless we travel in imagination back over four centuries to the Swan and the Globe and the Fortune, theatres which sheltered a Jonson and a Shakespeare, making still more glorious the glorious reign of an earlier queen.

APPENDIX A

THE THEATRES

1850–1900

IN this list I have included (1) the theatres of London and its suburbs, (2) the London music-halls and (3) the chief provincial playhouses. Only for the first section is any attempt made to indicate precise dates. It should be noted that in the third section some of the theatres listed under varying titles were the same buildings successively renamed. Abbreviations used in the text and in Appendix B appear in square brackets immediately after the main title. Attention may be drawn to the fact that, in recording performances in the provinces, the use of T.R. for Theatre Royal has been dispensed with; thus record of a production at "Birmingham" on a certain date indicates the Theatre Royal, Birmingham. The earlier fortunes of some of the London playhouses will be found in *E.N.D.* i, 217–33. Invaluable comments regarding now vanished theatres are given by Errol Sherson in *London's Lost Theatres of the Nineteenth Century* (1925); many details regarding managements will be found in the files of *The Era*.

I. *London and Environs*

The Adelphi Theatre (Strand) [Adel.]. See *E.N.D.* i, 217. Rebuilt in 1858.

The Albert Palace (Shepherdess-walk, Britannia Fields, Hoxton) [Albert]. See *E.N.D.* i, 217.

The Albion Saloon (Poplar) [Albion]. Also known as *The Oriental Palace*.

The Alcazar Theatre [Alcazar]. See *The Connaught Theatre*.

The Alexandra Theatre (Highbury Barn, Newington) [Alex.]. Opened May 20, 1865, closed 1871. See Michael Williams, *Some London Theatres Past and Present* (1883), p. 43.

The Alexandra Theatre (Camden Town) [Alex.]. See *The Park Theatre*.

The Alexandra Theatre (Stoke Newington) [Alex.]. Opened on December 27, 1897. [It should be noted that between 1865 and 1871 the contraction "Alex." refers to the Highbury

Barn house, between 1873 and 1881 to that at Camden Town and between 1897 and 1900 to that at Stoke Newington.]

The Alexandra Palace (Muswell Hill) [Alex. Pal.]. Opened in 1889.

The Alfred Theatre [Alfred]. See *The Marylebone Theatre.*

The Alhambra Palace (Leicester-square) [Alh.]. Opened as a music-hall in 1858 and as a theatre in 1871. Destroyed by fire December 12, 1882; new building opened December 3, 1883.

The Aquarium Theatre [Aquar.]. See *The Imperial Theatre.*

Astley's Amphitheatre (Westminster Bridge-road) [Ast.]. See *E.N.D.* i, 224–5. Renamed *Sanger's Grand National Amphitheatre* in 1883. Destroyed in 1895.

The Athenaeum (Tottenham Court-road) [Athen.]. Plays were produced here between 1887 and 1889.

The Avenue Theatre (Northumberland-avenue, Charing Cross) [Aven.]. Opened March 10, 1882.

Barnard's Theatre Royal (Woolwich) [Barnard's].

The Bijou Theatre (Archer-street, Bayswater) [Bijou]. Opened in 1882 as *The Victoria Hall.* [Errol Sherson, *op. cit.* pp. 324–5, notes a Bijou Theatre in the Haymarket; my references seem to be all to the Bayswater house.]

The Borough Theatre, Stratford (Borough). Opened in 1896.

The Bower Operetta House (Stangate-street, Lambeth) [Bower]. See *E.N.D.* i, 218. Closed in 1878; sometimes known as *The Royal Stangate Theatre.*

The Britannia Theatre or *Saloon* (High-street, Hoxton) [Brit.]. See *E.N.D.* i, 218.

The Brixton Theatre (Lambeth) [Brixton]. Opened September 21, 1896.

The Broadway Theatre (New Cross) [Broadway]. Opened in 1896.

The Cabinet Theatre [Cab.]. See *The King's Cross Theatre.*

The Camborne Theatre [Camborne]. Of this house I have no record save that plays were produced there in 1889.

The Charing Cross Theatre (King William-street) [Ch. X.]. Opened in 1869, renamed *The Folly* in 1876 and *Toole's Theatre* in 1882. Demolished in 1895.

The City of London Theatre (near Bishopsgate Station, Norton Folgate) [C.L.]. See *E.N.D.* i, 225 and M. Williams, *op. cit.* pp. 47–9. Closed in 1868.

The Colosseum (Regent's Park) [Col.]. Originally opened in 1824; plays occasionally presented between 1850 and 1900.

The Comedy Theatre (Panton-street, Haymarket) [Com.]. Opened October 15, 1881.

The Connaught Theatre (Holborn) [Connaught]. Opened in November 1879; altered and renamed *The Alcazar Theatre* on December 26, 1882.

The Coronet Theatre (Notting Hill-gate). Opened on November 28, 1898.

The Court Theatre (Sloane-square, Chelsea) [Court]. Opened in 1871 as *The New Chelsea Theatre*. Demolished in 1887 and rebuilt the following year, opening on September 24, 1888. See Cecil Howard, *Dramatic Notes* (1889), p. 144.

Covent Garden Opera House (Covent Garden) [C.G.]. See *E.N.D.* i, 218–19. Burned May 6, 1856; new building opened on May 15, 1858.

Cremorne Gardens (Chelsea) [Cremorne]. Occasional plays were produced at this popular place of entertainment, which closed in April 1878.

The Criterion Theatre (Piccadilly) [Crit.]. Opened in 1874 and reconstructed in 1884.

The Crown Theatre (Camberwell) [Crown]. Opened on October 31, 1898.

The Crystal Palace (Sydenham) [C.P.]. Occasional plays and Christmas entertainments were produced here.

The Dalston Theatre (Hackney) [Dalston]. Opened September 25, 1898.

Daly's Theatre (Cranbourne-street, Leicester-square) [Daly's]. Opened in 1893.

The Theatre Royal, Drury Lane (Drury-lane) [D.L.]. See *E.N.D.* i, 219–20.

The Duchess Theatre (Balham) [Duchess]. Opened in 1899.

The Duke's Theatre [Duke's]. See *The Holborn Theatre.*

The Duke of York's Theatre (St Martin's-lane) [D.Y.]. Opened in 1892 as *The Trafalgar Square Theatre*; renamed *The Duke of York's* on September 26, 1895.

The Eastern Opera House, Pavilion Theatre. See *The Pavilion.*

The Eclectic Theatre. See *The Royalty Theatre.*

The Eden Theatre [Eden]. See *The Novelty Theatre.*

The Effingham Saloon (Whitechapel) [Eff.]. See *E.N.D.* i, 220.

The Elephant and Castle Theatre (New Kent-road, Elephant and Castle) [E.C.]. Opened in 1872; destroyed by fire in 1878; rebuilt 1879; reconstructed in 1882 and 1902.

The Empire Theatre of Varieties (Leicester-square) [Empire]. Opened as a music-hall on April 17, 1884.

The Empress Theatre (Lambeth) [Empress]. Opened in 1898.

The Folies Dramatiques [Folies Dramatiques]. See *The Novelty Theatre.*

The Folly Theatre [Folly]. See *The Charing Cross Theatre*.

The Gaiety Theatre (Strand) [Gai.]. Opened in 1868.

The Garrick Theatre (Charing Cross-road) [Gar.]. Opened in 1889.

The Globe Theatre (Newcastle-street, Strand) [Glo.]. Opened in November 1868. Destroyed in 1902.

The Grand Theatre (Islington) [Grand]. Opened in 1870 as *The Philharmonic Theatre*; burned on September 6, 1882; re-opened August 4, 1883; burned December 28, 1887; reopened August 4, 1888 as *The Grand Theatre*.

The Grand Theatre (Fulham) [Grand, Fulham]. Opened on August 23, 1897.

The Great Queen Street Theatre [Great Queen Street]. See *The Novelty Theatre*.

The Grecian Saloon (Shepherdess-walk, Britannia Fields, Hoxton) [Grec.]. See *E.N.D.* i, 220.

The Royal Opera House, Haymarket [H.]. See *E.N.D.* i, 220–1. Also called *Her Majesty's Opera House*.

The Theatre Royal, Haymarket [H.]. See *E.N.D.* i, 221. Altered in 1872 and rebuilt in 1880. See E. L. Blanchard, *History of the Haymarket Theatre* (*Era Almanac*, 1873, pp. 1–16). [It should be noted that references to "H." in Appendix B are to this theatre.]

Hengler's Amphitheatre (Argyll-street, Oxford Circus) [Hengler's]. Occasional plays were produced here from 1889 onwards.

Her Majesty's Theatre (Haymarket) [H.M.]. Opened on April 28, 1897.

The Holborn Theatre (Holborn) [Holb.]. Opened on October 6, 1866 as *The Duke's Theatre*; renamed *The Mirror* in 1875 and *The Duke's* in 1879; destroyed by fire on July 4, 1880. Rebuilt and called *The International Theatre* from December 1883 to February 1884.

The Imperial Theatre (Westminster) [Imp.]. Opened in 1876 as *The Royal Aquarium and Winter Garden*; renamed *The Imperial Theatre* in 1879, with occasional later use of the original name. Reopened after alterations on April 11, 1898.

The International Theatre [Internat.]. See *The Holborn Theatre*.

The Jodrell Theatre [Jodrell]. See *The Novelty Theatre*.

The Theatre Royal, Kilburn [Kilburn]. Opened in 1886.

The King's Cross Theatre (King's Cross, New-road) [K.X.]. See *E.N.D.* i, 225 (under *The Royal Clarence Theatre*). After being known as *The Panharmonium*, it was renamed *The King's Cross Theatre* and *The Cabinet Theatre* (1852–67).

Ladbroke Hall (Bayswater) [Ladb. H.]. Opened in 1882.

The Lyceum Theatre (Wellington-street, Strand) [Lyc.]. See *E.N.D.* i, 221–2.

The Lyric Theatre (Shaftesbury-avenue) [Lyr.]. Opened on December 17, 1888.

The Lyric Hall (Ealing) [Lyr. Ealing]. Opened in 1889.

The Lyric Opera House (Hammersmith) [Lyr. Hammersmith]. Opened in 1890.

The Manor Theatre (Hackney) [Manor]. Opened in 1896.

The Marionette Theatre [Marionette]. See *The Strand Theatre.*

The Marylebone Theatre (Church-street, Edgeware-road) [M'bone]. See *E.N.D.* i, 222. Renamed *The Royal Alfred Theatre* on October 10, 1868; reverted to *The Marylebone* in 1872; renamed *The West London Theatre* on April 1, 1893. See M. Williams, *op. cit.* p. 80.

The Matinée Theatre [Mat.]. See *St George's Hall.*

The Metropole (Camberwell) [Metro.]. Opened in 1894.

The Mirror Theatre [Mirror]. See *The Holborn Theatre.*

Morton's Theatre (Greenwich) [Morton's, Greenwich]. Opened in 1896.

The New Chelsea Theatre [New Chelsea]. See *The Court Theatre.*

The New Queen's Theatre [New Qns.]. See *The Novelty Theatre.*

The New Theatre (Ealing) [New, Ealing]. Opened in 1898.

The New Victoria Palace. See *The Victoria Theatre.*

The North London Colosseum (Hackney) [N. London Col.]. Opened about 1888; closed in 1890.

North Woolwich Gardens [N. Woolwich Gdns.].

The Novelty Theatre (Great Queen-street) [Nov.]. Opened on December 9, 1882; closed after two weeks and reopened as *The Folies Dramatiques.* Reopened in 1883 as *The Novelty.* Variously named as *The Joddrell Theatre* (1887–9), *The New Queen's Theatre* (1890), *The Eden Theatre* (1894) and *The Great Queen Street Theatre* (1900).

The Olympic Theatre (Wych-street, or Newcastle-street, Strand) [Olym.]. See *E.N.D.* i, 223.

The Opera Comique (Strand) [O.C.]. Opened in 1870; reconstructed in 1885; closed in 1899.

The Oriental Palace [Oriental]. See *The Albion Saloon.*

The Pandora Theatre [Pandora]. Of this house I have no record save that plays were being produced there in 1882–3.

The Park Theatre (Camden Town) [Park]. Opened in 1871; renamed *The Alexandra Theatre* on May 31, 1874; burned in 1881.

The Parkhurst Theatre (Camden-road, Holloway) [Parkhurst]. Opened in 1890.

The Pavilion (Whitechapel-road, Mile End) [Pav.]. See *E.N.D.* i, 226. In 1860 known as *The Eastern Opera House Pavilion Theatre.*

The Pavilion or *London Pavilion* (Piccadilly) [Pav.]. Opened in 1861; reconstructed in 1885.

The Philharmonic Theatre (Islington) [Phil.]. See *The Grand Theatre.*

Portman Rooms (Baker-street) [Portman R.]. Used for the performance of plays from 1887.

The Prince of Wales's Theatre (Tottenham Court-road) [P.W.]. Opened in 1865 [formerly *The Queen's Theatre*, for which see *E.N.D.* i, 224].

The Prince's or *The Prince of Wales's Theatre* (Coventry-street) [P's]. Opened on January 18, 1884.

The Prince's Theatre (Kew) [P's, Kew].

The Princess's Theatre (Oxford-street) [P'cess]. See *E.N.D.* i, 224. Demolished in 1880 and reopened on November 11 of the same year.

The Princess of Wales's Theatre (Kennington) [P'cess of W.]. Opened in 1897.

Punch's Playhouse. See *The Strand Theatre.*

The Queen's Theatre [Qns.]. See *The Prince of Wales's Theatre.*

The Queen's Theatre (Longacre) [Qns.]. Opened in 1867; closed in 1878.

The Queen's Theatre (Queen's-road, Battersea) [Qns. Battersea]. Opened in 1892.

The Queen's Opera House (Crouch End) [Qns. O.H.]. Opened on July 27, 1897.

The Theatre Royal, Richmond [Richmond]. For the old theatre see *E.N.D.* i, 232–3. A new *Theatre Royal* was opened on September 16, 1899.

The Royal Alfred Theatre. See *The Alfred Theatre.*

The Royal Aquarium and Winter Garden. See *The Aquarium.*

The Royal Artillery Theatre (Woolwich) [R.A. Woolwich].

The Royal City of London Theatre. See *The City of London Theatre.*

The Royal County Theatre (Kingston) [County, Kingston]. Opened on October 4, 1897.

The Royal Court Theatre. See *The Court Theatre.*

The Royal Gallery of Illustration (Regent-street) [G.I.]. Opened in 1856.

The Royal Marylebone Theatre. See *The Marylebone Theatre.*

The Royal Stangate Theatre. See *The Stangate Theatre.*

The Royalty Theatre (Dean-street, Soho) [Roy.]. Originally opened in 1840; reconstructed in 1861 and 1883. Sometimes known as *The Soho Theatre* and as *The Eclectic Theatre, Soho.*

Sadler's Wells Theatre (Rosebury-avenue, Islington) [S.W.]. See *E.N.D.* i, 226–7.

St George's Hall (Langham-place) [St G.]. Opened in 1867; renamed *The Matinée Theatre* in 1897.

St James's Theatre (King-street, St James's) [St. J.]. See *E.N.D.* i, 227.

St Martin's Hall (Longacre) [St Martin's H.]. Opened in 1850. On its site *The Queen's Theatre* was built.

Salle Erard (Regent-street) [Salle Erard]. Opened in 1895.

Sanger's Grand National Amphitheatre [Sanger's]. See *Astley's Amphitheatre.*

The Savoy Theatre (Strand) [Sav.]. Opened on October 10, 1881.

The Shaftesbury Theatre (Shaftesbury-avenue) [Shaft.]. Opened on October 20, 1888.

The Shakespeare Theatre (Clapham Junction) [Shakespeare]. Opened on November 16, 1896.

The Soho Theatre [Soho]. See *The Royalty Theatre.*

The Standard Theatre (High-street, Shoreditch) [Stand.]. See *E.N.D.* i, 226. Destroyed by fire 1866; rebuilt 1867.

The Stangate Theatre [Stangate]. See *The Bower Operetta House.*

Steinway Hall (Lower Seymour-street) [Steinway H.]. Opened in 1887.

The Strand Theatre (Strand) [Str.]. See *E.N.D.* i, 227. Mss. was called *Punch's Playhouse* and *The Marionette Theatre* from May 1851 to May 1852. Reconstructed and enlarged during November 1865. See *A History of the Strand Theatre* (*Era Almanac*, 1872, pp. 6–10).

The Theatre Royal, Stratford [Stratford]. Opened in 1894.

The Surrey Theatre (Blackfriars-road) [Sur.]. See *E.N.D.* i, 227–8. Destroyed by fire in 1865 and rebuilt, opening on December 26 of that year.

The Terriss Theatre (Rotherhithe) [Terriss]. Opened on October 16, 1899.

Terry's Theatre (Strand) [Terry's]. Opened in 1888.

Toole's Theatre [Toole's]. See *The Charing Cross Theatre.*

The Trafalgar Square Theatre [Traf.]. See *The Duke of York's Theatre.*

The Vaudeville Theatre (Strand) [Vaud.]. Opened in 1870; reconstructed in 1891.

The Victoria Hall [Vic. H.]. See *The Bijou Theatre.*

The Victoria Hall (Ealing) [Vic. Ealing]. Opened in 1891.

The Victoria Theatre (Waterloo-road) [Vic.]. See *E.N.D.* i, 226. After reconstructions, opened on December 23, 1871 as *The New Victoria Palace*. See E. L. Blanchard, *The Victoria Theatre* (*Era Almanac*, 1873, pp. 7–12).

The West London Theatre [W.L.]. See *The Marylebone Theatre.*

The West Theatre, Albert Hall [West, Albert H.].

Wyndham's Theatre (Charing Cross-road) [Wyndham's]. Opened on November 16, 1899.

II. *Music Halls*

[Only the principal houses are here listed]

Albert
Alhambra
Battersea Palace
Bedford
Camberwell Palace of Varieties
Cambridge
Canterbury
Collins's
Deacon's
Eastern Empire
Empire
Empress Palace, Brixton
Foresters'
Gatti's (Charing Cross)
Gatti's (Westminster Bridge Road)
Grand Hall, Clapham
Granville
Hammersmith
Holloway Empire
London
London Hippodrome
London Pavilion
Marylebone
Metropolitan
Middlesex
Oxford
Palace of Varieties
Paragon
Parthenon, Greenwich
People's, Peckham
Queen's, Poplar
Raglan
Royal
Sebright
South London
Standard
Star
Stratford Empire
Sun
Tivoli
Varieties, Hoxton
Victoria Palace
Washington
World's Fair

III. *The Provinces, Scotland, Wales and Ireland*

Aberdare. *The New* and *The Star.*
Aberdeen. *Her Majesty's Opera House.*
Accrington. *The Prince's.*

Aldershot.	*Theatre Royal* and *The Victory.*
Ashington.	*Miner's.*
Ashton.	*Theatre Royal, Booth's, The People's Opera House* and *The Star.*
Aston.	*Theatre Royal.*
Attercliffe.	*Theatre Royal.*
Barnsley.	*Theatre Royal* and *The Queen's.*
Barnstaple.	*The New.*
Barrow.	*The Royalty.*
Bath.	*Theatre Royal.*
Batley.	*Theatre Royal.*
Bedford.	*The County.*
Belfast.	*Theatre Royal* and *Grand Opera House.*
Bilston.	*Theatre Royal.*
Birkenhead.	*Theatre Royal* and *The Metropole.*
Birmingham.	*Theatre Royal, The Adelphi, Coutt's, The Grand, The New, The Prince of Wales's* and *The Queen's.*
Bishop Auckland.	*The Eden.*
Blackburn.	*Theatre Royal, The Lyceum* and *The Prince's.*
Blackpool.	*The Grand, Her Majesty's Opera House, The Prince of Wales's* and *The Winter Gardens.*
Blyth.	*Theatre Royal* and *The Octagon.*
Bolton.	*Theatre Royal* and *The Grand.*
Bootle.	*Muncaster.*
Bordesley.	*The Imperial.*
Boscombe.	*The Grand.*
Boston.	*The Aquarium.*
Bournemouth.	*Theatre Royal.*
Bradford.	*Theatre Royal, Pullan's Theatre of Varieties* and *The Prince's.*
Bridgend.	*The Pavilion.*
Bridlington.	*The Spa* and *Victoria Rooms.*
Brierley Hill.	*Theatre Royal.*
Brighton.	*Theatre Royal, The Alhambra, The Aquarium, The Eden* and *The Gaiety.*
Bristol.	*Theatre Royal, The Prince's* and *The Queen's.*
Bromley.	*The Grand.*
Burnley.	*The Empire, The Gaiety* and *The Victoria Opera House.*
Burton-on-Trent.	*St George's.*
Bury.	*Theatre Royal* and *The Star.*
Bury St Edmunds.	*Theatre Royal.*
Cambridge.	*The New.*

Canterbury.	*Theatre Royal.*
Cardiff.	*Theatre Royal, The Grand* and *The Philharmonic.*
Carlisle.	*Her Majesty's.*
Carmarthen.	*Warren's.*
Castleford.	*Theatre Royal.*
Chatham.	*Theatre Royal, The New* and *The Opera House.*
Chelmsford.	*Corn Exchange.*
Cheltenham.	*The Opera House.*
Chester.	*The Royalty.*
Chester-le-Street.	*The Queen's.*
Chesterfield.	*Theatre Royal.*
Chorley.	*The Grand.*
Clacton-on-Sea.	*The Operetta House.*
Coatbridge.	*Theatre Royal.*
Colchester.	*Theatre Royal.*
Consett.	*The New.*
Cork.	*The Opera House.*
Coventry.	*The Opera House.*
Crewe.	*The Albion* and *The Lyceum.*
Croydon.	*Theatre Royal* and *The Grand.*
Darlington.	*Theatre Royal.*
Darwen.	*Theatre Royal.*
Derby.	*The Grand.*
Devonport.	*The Metropole.*
Dewsbury.	*Theatre Royal.*
Doncaster.	*The Empire* and *The Royal Opera House.*
Douglas.	*The Grand.*
Dover.	*Theatre Royal* and *The Clarence.*
Dublin.	*Theatre Royal, The Gaiety* and *The Queen's.*
Dudley.	*The Opera House.*
Dundee.	*The Opera House* (*The People's*).
Durham.	*The Albany.*
Eastbourne.	*Theatre Royal, Devonshire Park* and *Floral Hall.*
Eccles.	*The Lyceum.*
Edinburgh.	*Theatre Royal, The Amphitheatre, The Grand, The Lyceum, The Operetta House, The Pavilion, The Princess's, The Southminster* and *The Waterloo Opera House.*
Evesham.	*The Victoria.*
Exeter.	*Theatre Royal, The New* and *The Victoria.*
Farnworth.	*The Queen's.*

Folkestone.	*The Pleasure Gardens.*
Gainsborough.	*The Royal Albert.*
Garston.	*Theatre Royal.*
Gateshead-on-Tyne.	*The Metropole.*
Glasgow.	*Theatre Royal, The Grand, Her Majesty's, The Lyceum, The Metropole, The Prince of Wales's, The Princess's, The Queen's* and *The Royalty.*
Gloucester.	*Theatre Royal.*
Goole.	*Theatre Royal.*
Great Yarmouth.	*Theatre Royal* and *The Aquarium.*
Greenock.	*Theatre Royal.*
Grimsby.	*Theatre Royal* and *The Prince of Wales's.*
Halifax.	*Theatre Royal* and *The Grand.*
Hanley.	*Theatre Royal* and *The Grand.*
Hartlepool, West.	*Theatre Royal, The Gaiety* and *The Grand.*
Hastings.	*The Gaiety.*
Hebburn.	*The Grand.*
Horwich.	*The New Prince's.*
Huddersfield.	*Theatre Royal* and *The Empire.*
Hull.	*Theatre Royal, The Alexandra* and *The Grand.*
Hyde.	*Theatre Royal.*
Ilkeston.	*The New.*
Inverness.	*Theatre Royal.*
Ipswich.	*The Lyceum.*
Jarrow-on-Tyne.	*Theatre Royal.*
Jersey.	*Theatre Royal.*
Keighley.	*The Queen's.*
Kidderminster.	*Theatre Royal.*
King's Lynn.	*Theatre Royal.*
Lancaster.	*The Athenaeum.*
Landport.	*The Prince's.*
Leamington.	*Theatre Royal* and *The Victoria Pavilion.*
Leeds.	*Theatre Royal, The Amphitheatre, The Grand, The Princess's* and *The Queen's.*
Leicester.	*Theatre Royal* and *The Royal Opera House.*
Leith.	*The Gaiety.*
Limerick.	*Theatre Royal.*
Lincoln.	*Theatre Royal.*
Lichfield.	*St James's Hall.*
Liverpool.	*The Adelphi, The Bijou, The Colosseum, The Court, The Empire, The Grand, The Lyric, The Prince of Wales's, The Rotunda, The Sefton, The Shakespeare* and *The Star.*

Llandudno.	*The Prince's.*
Llanelly.	*The Athenaeum Hall* and *The Royalty.*
Londonderry.	*The Opera House.*
Longton.	*The Queen's* and *The Victoria.*
Loughborough.	*The New.*
Lowestoft.	*The Marina.*
Luton.	*The Grand.*
Macclesfield.	*Theatre Royal.*
Maidenhead.	*Theatre Royal.*
Manchester.	*Theatre Royal, The Comedy, The Metropole, The Osborne, The Palace, The Prince's, The Queen's* and *The St James's.*
Margate.	*Theatre Royal* and *The Grand.*
Merthyr Tydvil.	*Theatre Royal, The Cambrian, The New, The Park* and *The Victoria.*
Mexborough.	*The Prince of Wales's.*
Middlesborough.	*Theatre Royal.*
Monmouth.	*The New.*
Morecambe.	*The Royalty.*
Neath.	*Assembly Rooms* and *The Bijou.*
New Brompton.	*The Public Hall.*
Newcastle-upon-Tyne.	*Theatre Royal, The Amphitheatre, The Empire, The Grainger, The Grand, The Palace, The Tyne* and *The Vaudeville.*
Newport.	*The Lyceum* and *The Prince of Wales's.*
Northampton.	*The Opera House.*
North Shields.	*Theatre Royal.*
Norwich.	*Theatre Royal.*
Nottingham.	*Theatre Royal* and *The Grand.*
Nuneaton.	*Theatre Royal.*
Oldham.	*Theatre Royal, The Adelphi, The Colosseum* and *The Empire.*
Openshaw.	*Harte's.*
Oxford.	*The New* and *The Victoria.*
Paignton.	*The Bijou* and *The Pier Pavilion.*
Paisley.	*The Paisley.*
Plymouth.	*Theatre Royal.*
Pontypridd.	*The Clarence.*
Portsmouth.	*Theatre Royal, The New* and *The Prince's.*
Preston.	*The Prince's.*
Radcliffe.	*The Grand.*
Ramsgate.	*The Amphitheatre* and *The Granville.*
Rawtenstall.	*The Grand.*
Reading.	*The County.*

Redditch. *The Public Hall.*

Rochdale. *Theatre Royal* and *The Prince of Wales's.*

Rochester. *Corn Exchange.*

Rotherham. *Theatre Royal.*

Runcorn. *Theatre Royal.*

St Albans. *The County.*

Salford. *The Prince of Wales's* and *The Regent.*

Salisbury. *The Queen's.*

Scarborough. *Theatre Royal, The Aquarium* and *The Londesborough.*

Seacombe. *The Irving.*

Seaham Harbour. *Theatre Royal.*

Sheffield. *Theatre Royal, The Alexandra, The City* and *The Lyceum.*

Shrewsbury. *Theatre Royal.*

Smethwick. *Theatre Royal.*

Southampton. *The Grand, The Prince of Wales's* and *The Royal Victoria Assembly Rooms.*

Southend-on-Sea. *The Empire.*

Southport. *The Bijou, The Opera House* and *The Winter Gardens.*

South Shields. *Theatre Royal* and *The Grand.*

Spennymoor. *The Cambridge.*

Stalybridge. *The Grand.*

Stanley. *The Victoria.*

Stockport. *Theatre Royal, The New* and *The People's Opera House.*

Stockton-on-Tees. *Theatre Royal.*

Stratford-on-Avon. *The Memorial.*

Sudbury. *The Victoria Hall.*

Sunderland. *Theatre Royal, The Avenue* and *The Lyceum.*

Swansea. *The Grand* and *The New.*

Swindon. *The Queen's.*

Torquay. *Theatre Royal* and *The Lyceum.*

Tunstall. *The St James's.*

Wakefield. *The Opera House.*

Wallsend. *Theatre Royal.*

Walsall. *The Alexandra Palace, The Grand, Her Majesty's, The Imperial* and *The St George's.*

Walsingham. *The New.*

Walthamstow. *The Victoria.*

Warrington. *Theatre Royal* and *The Court.*

Wednesbury. *Theatre Royal.*

West Bromwich.	*Theatre Royal.*
Wexford.	*Theatre Royal.*
Weymouth.	*The Jubilee Hall.*
Widnes.	*The Alexandra.*
Wigan.	*Theatre Royal* and *The Court.*
Wimbledon.	*The Drill Hall.*
Windsor.	*Theatre Royal.*
Wolverhampton.	*The Grand, The Prince of Wales's* and *The Star.*
Wombwell.	*The Gaiety.*
Worcester.	*Theatre Royal.*
Workington.	*The Queen's Opera House.*
Wrexham.	*The St James's.*
York.	*Theatre Royal.*

APPENDIX B

HAND-LIST OF PLAYS

1850–1900

IN presenting the following hand-list of plays for the second half of the nineteenth century, I can only repeat what was said in Volume IV of this *History*[1] concerning the difficulties involved in preparing such a catalogue. That this list is not complete I am aware, although I have used every endeavour to render it as comprehensive as I possibly could. Even those who during recent years have devoted special research to the works of individual authors of this period have found that an exact recording of production and publishing dates has proved an almost impossible task. Sometimes adequate records are unavailable; sometimes the kaleidoscopic change in titles (a favourite device of the time) renders available records uncertain or ambiguous. It is probable that several plays given here under the names of their writers reappear with a different nomenclature among the dramas by "unknown authors". I have done my best to equate the Lord Chamberlain's manuscripts to plays concerning which there is notice of production, but unquestionably some manuscript versions must have been permitted to slip in as separate entities alongside their other selves, the acted plays.

The arrangement of material here follows largely the arrangement adopted in the hand-list to my last volumes. The chief deviation is that, in order to save space, I have not indicated the precise days of the week on which the various dramas were performed or the dates of licensing marked on the Lord Chamberlain's manuscripts. Only occasionally, where the original licensing was for a theatre different from that in which a play ultimately appeared, where no dates of production have been found, or where the licensing date was considerably in advance of the date of production has such information been included. A summary of the methods employed will make the system clear.

[1] Pp. 245–6.

1. First is indicated, in abbreviated form, the nature of the play itself. The abbreviations used are the following:

Ba.	Burletta	M.Ca.	Musical Comedietta
Bal.	Ballet	M.C.D.	Musical Comic Drama
Bal.P.	Ballet Pantomime	M.D.	Melodrama or Musical Drama
Bsq.	Burlesque		
C.	Comedy	M.Ent.	Musical Entertainment
Ca.	Comedietta	M.Ext.	Musical Extravaganza
C.D.	Comic Drama	M.F.	Musical Farce
C.Ent.	Comic Entertainment	M.F.C.	Musical Farcical Comedy
C.Int.	Comic Interlude	M.Int.	Musical Interlude
C.O.	Comic Opera	M.Monol.	Musical Monologue
C.Oa.	Comic Operetta	Monol.	Monologue
C.R.	Comic Romance	M.R.	Musical Romance
C.Sk.	Comic Sketch	M.Sk.	Musical Sketch
D.	Drama	O.	Opera
D.D.	Domestic Drama	Oa.	Operetta
Div.	Divertisement	O.F.	Operatic Farce
D.O.	Dramatic Opera	P.	Pantomime
D.Poem.	Dramatic Poem	Poet.D.	Poetic Drama
D.Sk.	Dramatic Sketch	Past.	Pastoral
Duol.	Duologue	Past.O.	Pastoral Opera
Ent.	Entertainment	Prel.	Prelude
Equest.D.	Equestrian Drama	R.C.	Romantic Comedy
Equest.Spec.	Equestrian Spectacle	R.C.D.	Romantic Comic Drama
Ext.	Extravaganza	R.D.	Romantic Drama
F.	Farce	R.O.	Romantic Opera
Fa.	Farcetta	Rev.	Revue (or Review)
F.C.	Farcical Comedy	Sk.	Sketch
Hist.R.	Historical Romance	Spec.	Spectacle
Int.	Interlude	Spec.D.	Spectacular Drama
Lyr.D.	Lyric Drama	T.	Tragedy
M.	Masque	T.C.	Tragi-comedy
Milit.D.	Military Drama	T.F.	Tragic Farce
M.Bsq.	Musical Burlesque	Vaud.	Vaudeville
M.C.	Musical Comedy		

As will readily be realised, these designations are in no way final, and are often indefinite. Where possible, the designation employed in the original bills has here been followed.

2. The dates enclosed in round brackets after the title are those of production. To indicate the places of production various abbreviations have been employed; a full list of theatres appears in Appendix A, with indications of the contracted forms. Several plays during the half-century were originally produced in halls and assembly rooms; to indicate such places the contraction H. indicates Hall; P.H. is used for Public Hall, T.H. for Town Hall[1] and

[1] But O.H. stands for Opera House.

R. for Room or Rooms. It should be noted that when these abbreviations stand without the name of a town following the location is London. The name of only one provincial city has been abbreviated, L'pool standing for Liverpool. Where a city name is employed without indication of a particular theatre, The Theatre Royal is to be understood. Provincial productions are noted only when a play was presented originally outside of London. The abbreviations *mat.*, *copy.* and *amat.* refer to matinée, copyright and amateur performances respectively.

3. Immediately following comes the record of Lord Chamberlain's manuscripts, indicated by the abbreviation L.C. As stated above, licensing dates and theatres are not noted except where there are major discrepancies between these and the information regarding production. "MS. Birmingham" refers to the collection of dramatic manuscripts formerly in the possession of Mr Crompton Rhodes and now housed in the Public Library, Birmingham.

4. Then are given indications of published editions, starting with separate issues (if any) and proceeding to texts provided in the several collections of the period. Dramatic bibliography during this time is hopelessly confused owing to the fact that many authors were in the habit of bringing out printed versions of their works "not for publication". Generally, only a few copies were printed off and consequently there was no compulsion to send exemplars to the privileged libraries. To attempt the task of tracing and enumerating such issues would have been impossible; only such printed texts are noted here as came immediately to hand. Presumably a fuller bibliography must wait until individual attention has been devoted to the works of at least the more important writers of this time. The abbreviation *priv.* indicates "private" or "unpublished" texts of the kind noted above. Among the more important series of plays are:

Cumberland. [Cumberland's British Theatre: ending about 1860.]
Dicks. [Dicks's Standard Plays; 1883–1908.]
Duncombe. [Duncombe's Edition: ending about 1853.]
French. [French's Acting Edition: a continuation of *Lacy*, with several of the *Lacy* plays reissued under French's name.]
Lacy. [Lacy's Acting Edition of Plays: 1851 onwards.]

It should be noted that under *French* has been placed a number of dramas originally published by different firms (such as Lynn's Acting Edition and the plays issued by Joseph Williams) which were bought by Samuel French and reissued, mostly with new title-pages.

5. The present list includes several plays written by American authors and acted in England. In such instances a single square bracket precedes the name of the author and the plays are listed in the order of their appearance in English theatres. In view of the increased dramatic productivity of the period, all mention of foreign operas and plays has been omitted.

6. Theatrical conditions between 1850 and 1900 led towards much collaboration. In listing such collaborative pieces, an endeavour has been made to provide complete cross-references, but no effort has been made to maintain absolute consistency in the placement of the dramas themselves. Thus if two authors, A and B, wrote six plays together, the main entries for three of these may be found under A and the rest under B. In explanation of this seeming inconsistency, it should be pointed out that I have adopted the principle of placing the main entry of any particular play under the name of that author whose name appeared first in the play-bill, newspaper advertisement or review from which information regarding authorship was obtained.

ABBOTT, CHARLES HARRIE

C.O. Captain Kidd; or, The Bold Buccaneer (P.W. L'pool, 10/9/83). L.C.

[Music by E. Solomon.]

C. Fast Asleep (Crit. 1/3/92, *mat.*). L.C.

F.C. The Sleepwalker (P.W. L'pool, 5/4/93; Str. 25/7/93).

[A revised version of the above.]

M.F. The Celestials; or, The Flowery Land (O.H. Blackpool, 1/8/98). L.C.

[Lyrics by *J. W. HOUGHTON*. Music by F. O. Carr.]

ABBOTTS, or *ABBOTS, F. M.*

D. Forbidden Fruit (P.W. L'pool, 7/6/69; Lyc. 6/11/69). L.C.

À BECKETT, ARTHUR WILLIAM ["*BERTIE VYSE*"]

D. Faded Flowers (H. 6/4/72). L.C. *French.*

D. £.S.D. (Roy. 29/6/72). L.C.

C. About Town (Court, 12/5/73). L.C.

D. On Strike: A Social Problem (Court, 14/10/73).

D. Long Ago (Roy. 22/4/82). L.C.

D. From Father to Son (Bijou, L'pool, 2/10/82). L.C.

[Written in collaboration with *J. P. SIMPSON*.]

À BECKETT, GILBERT ABBOTT

[For his earlier plays see iv, 249–51.]

Bsq. O Gemini; or, Brothers of Coarse (H. 12/4/52). L.C. *Webster.*

[Written in collaboration with *M. LEMON*.]

D. Angelo; or, The Actress of Padua (New York, 5/52). *French.*

Bsq. Sardanapalus, the "Fast" King of Assyria (Adel. 20/7/53). *Webster.*

[Written in collaboration with *M. LEMON*.]

À BECKETT, GILBERT ARTHUR

F. Lending a Hand (Str. 22/1/66). L.C. *Mod. Eng. Comic Th.*

P. Ali Baba and the Forty Thieves; or, Harlequin and the Genii of the Arabian Nights (C.G. 26/12/66). L.C. 8° [1866].

Oa. Terrible Hymen (C.G. 26/12/66). L.C.

[Music by E. Jonas.]

C. Diamonds and Hearts (H. 4/3/67). L.C.

C. Not Guilty (P's. Manchester, 9/12/67).

Bsq. An Utter Perversion of the Brigand; or, Lines to an Old Ban-ditty (H. 24/12/67). L.C.

P. The Babes in the Wood; or, Harlequin Robin Hood and his Merry Men (C.G. 26/12/67). L.C. 8° [1867].

Oa. The Two Harlequins (Gai. 21/12/68). L.C.

[Music by E. Jonas.]

C. Glitter (St J. 26/12/68). L.C. *Lacy.*

D. The Red Hands (St J. 30/1/69). L.C.

D. Face to Face (P.W. L'pool, 29/3/69).

P. The Sleeping Beauty; or, Harlequin and the Spiteful Fairy (C.G. 26/12/70). L.C. 8° [1870].

[Written in collaboration with *C. H. ROSS*.]

P. Ali Baba and the Forty Thieves (C.P. 21/12/71).

Ext. Christabelle; or, The Bard Bewitched (Court, 15/5/72). L.C.

Bsq. Charles II; or, Something like History (Court, 25/11/72). L.C.
Bsq. The Happy Land (Court, 3/3/73). See *W. S. GILBERT*.
Bsq. The Last of the Legends; or, The Baron, the Bride and the Battery (Ch.X. 1/9/73). L.C. *Lacy*.
Ext. In the Clouds: A Glimpse of Utopia (Alex. 8/12/73). L.C. as *Castles in the Air; or, Up in the Clouds*. *Lacy*.
F. Three Tenants. L.C. St G. 14/12/74. *French*.
[Written in collaboration with *G. REED*.]
Ent. The Ancient Britons. L.C. St G. 7/1/75.
M.F. A Spanish Bond. L.C. St G. 22/10/75.
[Written in collaboration with *G. REED*.]
M.C. The Wicked Duke. L.C. St G. 31/5/76.
[Written in collaboration with *G. REED*.]
Ca. Once in a Century. L.C. St G. 8/11/77.
[Written in collaboration with *V. BLIGH*.]
O. L'Ombra (H.M. 12/1/78). L.C.
M.C. Grimstone Grange. L.C. St G. 7/3/79.
M.Ca. The Pirate's Home. L.C. St G. 13/10/79.
[Written in collaboration with *V. BLIGH*.]
F. A Christmas Stocking. L.C. St G. 11/12/79.
[Written in collaboration with *K. HALL*.]
M.Sk. Many Happy Returns (St G. 28/3/81). L.C.
[Written in collaboration with *C. SCOTT*. Music by L. Benson.]
M.Ca. That Dreadful Boy (St G. 26/12/82). L.C.
M.Ca. The Mountain Heiress (St G. 7/3/83). L.C.
[Music by L. Benson.]
O. The Canterbury Pilgrims (D.L. 28/4/84). L.C.
[Music by C. V. Stanford.]
O. Savonarola (C.G. 9/7/84). L.C.
[Music by C. V. Stanford.]
O. Signa (C.G. 30/6/94). L.C.
[Music by Cowen. Written in collaboration with *H. A. RUDALL* and *F. E. WEATHERLEY*.]
[Davenport Adams, *op. cit.* (p. 2) attributes to him *The Two Foster Brothers* and states that he was responsible for lyrics in *Captain Thérèse* (P.W. 25/8/90) and *La Cigale* (Lyr. 9/10/90) by *F. C. BURNAND*. He also declares that he was co-author with *C. SCOTT* of *An Indian Puzzle*. The last-mentioned play I have been unable to locate.]

ABEL, W. H.

D. Weeds and Flowers; or, The Garden of Life (E.L. 25/7/70). L.C.
D. An Angel's Visit; or, The Trials of Love (E.L. 21/9/70). L.C. as *Light of Love; or, An Angel's Visit*.
D. A Life's Devotion (E.L. 2/11/70).
D. Under Two Flags (Norwich, 14/11/70).
D. War—the Fugitives; or, Surrounded (Ipswich, 7/1/71).
D. The Last Express; or, The Station Master's Daughter (E.L. 19/6/71). L.C.
D. The Bell-Ringer of Notre Dame; or, The Hunchback's Love (E.L. 8/7/71). L.C.
D. Only a Shilling and What became of it (Pav. 22/4/72). L.C.
D. Lily's Love; or, Weary of Waiting (Pav. 17/8/72). L.C.

D. Faith under Peril (Pav. 9/8/73). L.C. as *Faithful under Peril; or, A Father's Dishonour and a Daughter's Shame.*
D. The Last Hope (E.L. 26/12/73).
D. From Beneath the Deep (Pav. 28/2/76). L.C.
D. Slow and Sure (Pav. 28/8/76). L.C.

ABRAHAMS, HENRY
F. The Alderman's Gown; or, A Trip to Paris (Str. 6/10/51). L.C. *Fairbrother.*

ACHURCH, JANET
D. Frou-Frou (Com. Manchester, 9/12/86).
[Written in collaboration with *C. CHARRINGTON.*]

ADAMS, CATHERINE
Oa. Feminine Strategy (Drill H. Basingstoke, 16/11/93). 8° [1899].
[Music by F. G. Hollis.]

ADAMS, E.
Ext. King Foo (Phil. 26/12/73). L.C.

ADAMS, Mrs EDWARD
Oa. Don Pedro (P.H. New Cross, 18/10/92).
[Music by F. Idle.]

ADAMS, FLORENCE DAVENPORT
C.D. The Three Fairy Gifts (Assembly R. Worthing, 7/4/96). *French.*

ADAMS, HENRY
Ext. Madeira; or, W[h]ines from the Wood (K.X. 25/10/75).
Bsq. Innocentinez; or, The Magic Pipe and the Fatal I.O.U. (K.X. 29/3/76).
Bsq. Squire's Maria; or, Too too far from the Madding Crowd (Hanley, 17/7/82). L.C.

ADAMS-ACTON, Mrs [JEANIE HERING]
C.D. Woman's Wit (Sunnyside, Langford-place, Abbey-road, 20/7/93).
F. Who's Married? (Bijou, 22/6/93). L.C.
F. Dulverydotty (St John's Wood, 2/3/94, *amat.*; Terry's, 15/6/94). L.C.
Ent. The Triple Bill (St John's Wood, 2/3/94, *amat.*).
D. The Darkest Hour (St John's Wood, 6/4/95, *amat.*).
F.C. The Woman in Black (St John's Wood, 21/12/95, *amat.*).

ADDERLEY, J. G.
Oa. Mummies and Marriage (Exhibition Pal. Folkestone, 6/12/88). See *A. M. MACKINNON.*

ADDERSLEY, FRED
D. Regan-na-Glenna (Cambridge, 16/9/78).

ADDISON, Captain (later Lieutenant-Colonel) HENRY ROBERT
[For his earlier plays see iv, 251.]
F. International Visits; or, The Garde Nationale. L.C. Sur. 27/8/50.
F. What? No Cab? (Adel. 8/8/53).
D. The Abbé Vaudreuil and the Court of Louis XV (Lyc. 18/3/60). L.C.
F. No. 117, Arundel Street, Strand (Lyc. 24/3/60). L.C. *Lacy.*
F. Mr Gorilla (Adel. 1/7/61). L.C.
F. Locked in with a Lady (Roy. 2/2/63). 8° [1870; New York].

Oa. Saved by a Song (P'cess, 21/12/68). L.C.
[Music by E. J. Loder.]
D. Tempted, Fallen and Saved (Cheltenham, 24/10/71).

ADDISON, JOSEPH

F. Toss up (Recreation R. Woolwich, 11/11/76).
D. The Cid; or, Love and Duty (K.X. 25/3/78). L.C.
[Written in collaboration with *J. H. HOWELL.*]
P. King Trickee; or, Harlequin the Demon Beetle, the Sporting Duchess and the Golden Casket (Brit. 26/12/87).
Oa. Our Court (R.A. Woolwich, 17/11/88). See *E. HUMPHREY.*
P. The Magic Dragon of the Demon Dell; or, The Search for the Mystic Thyme (Brit. 26/12/88). L.C.
P. The Bold Bad Baron; or, The Fairy Fountain of Enchanted Waters (Brit. 26/12/89). L.C.
P. The Spider and the Fly (Brit. 26/12/90). L.C.
P. The Old Bogie of the Sea; or, The Enchanted Well (Brit. 26/12/91). L.C.
P. The Man in the Moon (Brit. 26/12/92). L.C.
P. The King o' the Castle (Brit. 26/12/93). L.C.
P. The Giant of the Mountains (Brit. 26/12/94). L.C.
P. The Demon Oof Bird (Brit. 26/12/95). L.C.
P. The Giant and the Dwarf (Brit. 26/12/96). L.C.
P. The Will o' the Wisp (Brit. 27/12/97). L.C.
P. King Klondyke (Brit. 26/12/98). L.C.
P. Red Riding Hood (R.A. Woolwich, 26/12/98). L.C.

AIDÉ, HAMILTON

D. Philip (Lyc. 7/2/74). L.C.
C.D. A Nine Days' Wonder (Court, 12/6/75). L.C. *French.*
C.O. Die Fledermaus (Alh. 18/12/76). L.C.
Ca. All for Nothing (Queen Anne's-gate, 17/7/80).
C. Cousins (Sir Percy Shelley's house, Chelsea, 13/12/82).
C. A Great Catch (Olym. 17/3/83). L.C.
Oa. Not at Home (Grosvenor House, 1/6/86).
[Music by A. Scott-Gatty.]
D. Incognito (H. 11/1/88, *mat.*). L.C.
F.C. Dr Bill (Aven. 1/2/90). L.C.
C.D. Lord and Lady Guilderoy (Brighton, 9/4/96). L.C.

AIKIN, JAMES

F.C. New York Politics (Brentford, 28/8/90, *copy.*).

AITKEN, J. E. M.

C.Oa. St Valentine's (West, Albert H. 11/6/97). L.C.
[Written in collaboration with *H. à C. BERGNE.* Music by R. Clarke.]

AKERMAN, WILLIAM

R.O. Rip van Winkle (H.M. 4/9/97). L.C. 8° [1897]
[Music by F. Leoni.]

AKHURST, W. M.

P. This is the House that Jack built; or, Harlequin Pussycat, where have you been, the Leetle Wee Dog and the Good Child's History of England (Alfred, 23/12/71). L.C.
P. Lady Godiva; or, Harlequin St George and the Dragon and the Seven Champions (Ast. 26/12/71). L.C.

P. The Birth of Beauty; or, Harlequin William the Conqueror and the Pretty White Horse with the Golden Shoe (Sanger's, 26/12/72). L.C. 8° [1872].
Spec.D. Fair Rosamond; or, The Days of the Plantagenets (Sanger's, 3/3/73). L.C.
P. Cinderella and the Little Glass Slipper (Sanger's, 26/12/73). L.C. 8° [1874].
Ext. To the Green Isles Direct (Brit. 25/5/74). L.C.
P. Cinderella (Pav. 26/12/74). L.C.
Ext. Sarah Jane in the Harem (L'pool, 30/8/75).
P. Tom Tom the Piper's Son (E.C. 27/12/75). L.C.
Pantomimic D. Kolaf; or, The Frozen Gift (Ast. 1/4/76). L.C.
Bsq. The Grand Duke of Camberwell (E.C. 17/4/76). L.C.
D. Deadly Sampson (Pav. 16/9/76). L.C.
[Written in collaboration with *J. TWIGG.*]
D. Waterloo (Sanger's, 21/10/76). L.C.
P. Little Tom Tucker (E.C. 23/12/76). L.C.
P. Gulliver on his Travels (Sanger's, 26/12/76). L.C. as *Robinson Crusoe and Gulliver's Travels.* 8° [1876].
P. Whittington and his Cat (Sanger's, 26/12/77). 8° [1877].

ALBERG, ALBERT
D. Fifty Years After (St G. 25/2/88). L.C.

ALBERTON, J. R.
D.Sk. Foiled (Glo. 10/10/91).

ALBERY, JAMES
D. Doctor Davy (New, Greenwich, 6/2/65, as *How to Act: A Lesson taught by Garrick*; Lyc. 4/6/66).
[Written in collaboration with *H. VEZIN* and *W. G. WILLS.*]
F. The Mate of the Mountjoy (Dramatic Academy, 1867). See *J. DILLEY.*
C. Two Roses (Vaud. 4/6/70). L.C. *French.*
F. Chiselling (Vaud. 27/8/70). L.C.
[Written in collaboration with *J. DILLEY.* This play was originally produced by amateurs at the Ingoldsby Club, on 21/9/64, as *Alexander the Great.*]
C. The Two Coquettes (P.W. L'pool, 29/10/70).
C. Two Thorns (St J. 4/3/71). L.C.
[A revised version of the above.]
C.D. Tweedie's Rights (Vaud. 27/5/71). L.C.
C. Apple Blossoms (Vaud. 9/9/71). L.C. *French.*
C. Pickwick (Lyc. 23/10/71). L.C.
C. Forgiven (Glo. 9/3/72). L.C.
Fairy C. Oriana (Glo. 15/2/73). L.C.
Ext. The Will of Wise King Kino (P'cess, 13/9/73). L.C.
C. Married (Roy. 29/11/73). L.C.
C.D. Wig and Gown (Glo. 6/4/74). L.C.
C. Pride (Vaud. 22/4/74). L.C.
C. The Spendthrift; or, The Scrivener's Daughter (Olym. 24/5/75). L.C.
D. The Man in Possession (Gai. 4/12/76). L.C.
F.C. The Pink Dominos (Crit. 31/3/77). L.C. 4° [1878].
Oa. The Spectre Knight (O.C. 9/2/78). L.C.
[Music by A. Cellier.]

F.C. Jingle (Lyc. 8/7/78).
[A revised version of *Pickwick* (Lyc. 1871).]
D. No. 20; or, The Bastille of Calvados (P'cess, 30/11/78). L.C.
[Written in collaboration with *J. HATTON*.]
C. The Crisis (H. 2/12/78; Court, 21/2/85, as *The Denhams*). L.C.
C. Duty (P.W. 27/9/79). L.C. *French*.
C.D. The Old Love and the New (Court, 15/12/79). See *B. HOWARD*.
C. Jacks and Jills (Vaud. 29/5/80). L.C.
C. Where's the Cat? (Crit. 20/11/80). L.C.
F.C. The Mulberry Bush (Brighton, 19/6/82; Crit. 2/9/82, as *Little Miss Muffet*). L.C.
F.C. Featherbrain (Crit. 23/6/84). L.C.
C.D. The Vicar (Windsor, 28/1/85). See *J. HATTON*.
C. Welcome Little Stranger (Crit. 6/8/90). L.C.
[This is said to have been acted at the Shakespeare, L'pool, in 1889 under another name.]

ALDIN, CHARLES A.
D. On his Oath (Scarborough, 18/1/87).
M.C.D. Bright Days (Rotunda, L'pool, 1/4/89). See *H. WHEATLEY*.
D. The Slums of London (Grainger, Newcastle, 19/12/92; Brit. 24/4/93). L.C.
D. Our British Empire; or, The Gordon Highlanders (Muncaster, Bootle, 1/8/98; Stratford, 12/12/98). L.C. Metro. Devonport, 20/6/98.

ALDRED, A. A.
F.C. Bachelors (P.H. New Cross, 18/6/84). L.C.

ALDRICH, R.
Duol. Pauline Paulovna (T.H. Westminster, 4/2/96, *amat.*).

ALEXANDER, ARTHUR
Bsq.M.C. Laughs (Edinburgh, 30/6/94). See *A. R. MARSHALL*.

ALEXANDER, GRANT
D.Sk. My Lord Cardinal (Aven. 16/11/94, *copy.*). L.C.

ALEXANDER, W. D. S.
D. Ruy Blas. 8° 1890.

ALFRIEND, E. M.
D. The Great Diamond Robbery (Pav. 16/5/98). L.C. as *The Heart of Fire; or, The G.D.R.*
[Written in collaboration with *A. C. WHEELER*.]

ALLAN, A. W.
Bsq. Conrad Converted; or, The Corsair Reformed (St J. 19/12/73). L.C.
Bsq. Rienzi Reinstated; or, The Last of the Cobbler (Glo. 21/12/74). L.C. Dundee.

ALLAN-FISHER, C.
C.O. Cinderella (Macclesfield, 6/5/95).

ALLEN, Miss A. M.
D. The Madcap Prince (Pleasure Gdns. Folkestone, 13/4/94, *amat.*).

ALLEN, FRANCIS
F. Oh! my Head! (Alh. 24/4/71). L.C.

ALLEN, HORACE

D. The Bells of the Sledge (Leigh, 26/12/91). L.C. P.H. Wrexham, 10/12/89.

ALLEN, OSWALD

D. Fairly Foiled (Grec. 29/5/71). L.C.

Bsq. Ingomar the Idiotic; or, The Miser, the Maid and the Mangle (Alfred, 19/8/71). L.C.
[Written in collaboration with *B. HOWARD*.]

D. Strangers Yet: A Commonplace Chronicle (Grec. 20/5/72). L.C.

D. A Tangled Skein (Grec. 19/8/72). L.C.
[Written in collaboration with *D. FLECK*.]

P. A Frog he would a-wooing go (M'bone, 24/12/75). L.C.

Bsq. The Light of the Isles (Qns. Dublin, 21/8/76). L.C. Sheffield.

M.F. Jo versus Jo (Sur. 25/9/76). See *F. W. GREEN*.

P. Little Jack Horner (M'bone, 23/12/76). L.C.

P. Little Tom Tucker (Albion, 24/12/77). See *F. W. GREEN*.

F. Pity Poddlechock (Alex. L'pool, 27/6/81).

P. Little Jack Horner (E.C. 26/12/81). See *T. L. CLAY*.

P. Cinderella (Sanger's, 26/12/83). See *F. W. GREEN*.

P. Old Dame Trot; or, Harlequin Godiva and Peeping Tom, St George and the Seven Champions of Christendom (Sanger's, 26/12/84). L.C.

P. Little Red Riding Hood (Pav. 26/12/84). L.C.
[Written in collaboration with *J. TABRAR*.]

P. Sinbad the Sailor (E.C. 24/12/85). L.C.

P. Jack the Giant Killer (Pav. 26/12/85). L.C.

P. Cinderella (Pav. 27/12/86). L.C.

ALLEN-JEFFERYS, JEFFERYS

D. The Antipodes (Prince's Assembly R. Yeovil, 2/7/96).

ALLERTON, —

D. A Gay Husband (Devonshire Park, Eastbourne, 31/5/86; Crit. 15/6/86, *mat.*). L.C.

ALLEYN, ANNIE

D. Woman's Love (P.W. Manchester, 22/8/81).

ALLEYNE, Major F.

D. Mate (Ladb. H. 31/1/95). See *W. E. GROGAN*.

ALLINGHAM, WILLIAM

D. Ashby Manor. 8° [1883].

ALLISON, W.

O. The Crusader and the Craven (Glo. 7/10/90). L.C.
[Music by P. Reeve.]

ALLWOOD, —

O. Haymaking; or, The Pleasures of a Country Life (O.H. Kilmarnock, 19/3/77).

ALMAR, GEORGE

[For his earlier plays see iv, 252–3.]

D. The Castle Burners (Vic. 1/3/52).
[This may be a revision of *The Mountain King; or, The C.B.*, published by Duncombe in 1834.]

D. The Corsican Brothers; or, The Scarlet Letter (Vic. 15/3/52). L.C.

Equest.Spec. The Chinese Insurrection; or, The Wonderful Wall and the Wise Elephants of the East (Ast. 5/12/53). L.C.

[Also called *The Wise Elephants of the East.*]

ALMA-TADEMA, Miss LAURENCE

D. The Unseen Helmsman (Com. 17/6/1901). L.C. H. 28/9/97.

AMBIENT, MARK

R.D. Christina (P.W. 22/4/87). See *P. LYNWOOD.*

C. The Anonymous Letter (Lyr. 5/5/91, *mat.*). L.C.

[Written in collaboration with *F. LATIMER.*]

Ent. Froggie goes to Eaton (Lyr. Ealing, 23/4/92). L.C.

Duol. Kept In (Qns. H. 25/2/95).

F.C. Oh! Susannah! (Eden, Brighton, 6/9/97; Roy. 5/10/97). L.C. *French.*

[Written in collaboration with *A. ATWOOD* and *R. VAUN.*]

C. A Little Ray of Sunshine (Assembly R. Yeovil, 3/5/98); Roy. 31/12/98).

[Written in collaboration with *W. HERIOT.*]

AMBROSE, VINCENT

C. A Professional Beauty (Imp. 1/6/80). L.C.

AMCOTTS, VINCENT

Ext. Lurline; or, The Rhine and its Rhino (Brit. 9/4/60). L.C. *Lacy.*

D. Pentheus. 8° 1866 [Oxford].

[Written in collaboration with *Sir W. R. ANSON.*]

C. Adonis Vanquished (revised by *T. W. ROBERTSON* as *A Rapid Thaw*, St J. 2/3/67). *Lacy.*

Ext. Lalla Rookh (G.I. 19/6/68). *Lacy.*

Oa. The Statue Bride (G.I. 19/6/68).

[Music by E. Aspa.]

Ca. The Love Tests. *Lacy.*

D. Poisoned. *Lacy.*

[Amcotts is also credited with an *Ariadne* and *Fair Helen.*]

AMORY, T. S.

D. The Adventuress (Newcastle, 15/5/82). L.C. Worcester, 30/11/81.

ANDERSON, CHARLES

M.F. Just in Time (St Nicholas H. Guildford, 21/7/97). L.C.

[Music by H. M. McNey.]

C.D. Lord Dolly (Parish H. Wellington, 18/6/98; Mat. 12/11/98, as *Grandmother's Gown*). L.C. *French* [as *Grandmother's Gown*].

ANDERSON, GERALD

T. In Spite of All (Margate, 18/7/98). L.C. O.H. Chatham.

D. Outwitted (Margate, 13/7/99). L.C.

ANDERSON, JAMES R.

[See iv, 254.]

D. The Robbers (D.L. 21/4/51). L.C. D.L. 26/12/45.

D. Schamyl; or, The Circassian Chief and the Prophet's Son. L.C. Stand. 29/9/54.

D. Cloud and Sunshine; or, Love's Revenge (D.L. 22/2/58). L.C. Stand. 16/10/56. *Lacy.*

D. The Scottish Chief and the Maid of Ellerslie (Sur. 12/9/63). L.C.

D. The Soldier of Fortune; or, The Devil's Death Tower (Sur. 28/3/64). L.C.

Ext. The Three Great Worthies (Stand. 1/10/66). L.C. as *The T.G.W.; or, The King, the Hangman and the Barber.*

ANDERSON, J. T. R.

O. Victorian (Sheffield, 6/4/83; C.G. 19/1/84). L.C. Grand, Birmingham.

[Music by J. Edwards.]

ANDERTON, H. O.

D. Baldur. 8° 1893.

ANDERTON, JOHN

F. The Lunacy Commission (P.W. Birmingham, 10/3/76). L.C.

ANDRÉ, R.

C.Oa. The Mystery of a Handsome Cap [in *Beeton's Christmas Annual*, xxix, 1888].

C.Oa. Minette's Birthday [in *Beeton's Christmas Annual*, xxx, 1889].

Vaud. Red and White [in *Beeton's Christmas Annual*, xxxii, 1891].

Oa. The New Moon (Savoy Hotel, 6/2/93). L.C. 8° 1891 [Northampton].

[Music by I. de Solla.]

ANDREÆ, PERCY

Ca. Two's Company (Bradford, 20/5/95; Parkhurst, 12/12/95). L.C.

ANDREWS, E.

C.D. A Timely Moment (P.H. Harrow, 9/2/88). L.C.

ANDREWS, WALTER

Bsq. Touch and Go (P.W. L'pool, 8/3/86).

ANGUS, J. KEITH

— Children's Theatricals. 8° 1879.

— Theatrical Scenes for Children. 8° 1880.

F. Send 30 Stamps (S.W. 12/4/84). L.C. *French.*

Ca. By this Token (S.W. 6/5/84). L.C. *French.*

ANSON, G. W.

Bsq. Hamlet à la mode (P.W. L'pool, 16/10/76). See *G. L. GORDON.*

Bsq. The Babes in the Wood (P.W. L'pool, 16/4/77). See *G. L. GORDON.*

ANSON, Sir WILLIAM REYNALL, Baronet.

D. Pentheus. 8° 1866. See *V. AMCOTTS.*

ANSTRUTHER, EVA

D. A Secret of State (St Cuthbert's H. Earl's Court, 23/6/98). L.C.

ANTONINI, Mdlle

C.D. The Incognito (H.M. Richmond, 11/6/81). L.C. as *The Poverty of Gold.*

APPLETON, G. W.

C.D. A Fair Sinner (Ipswich, 23/1/85; Gai. 4/3/85). L.C.

D. Zana (Croydon, 16/3/85). L.C.

F.C. The Co-Respondent (P.W. L'pool, 20/6/96, *copy.*; Grand, Birmingham, 3/8/96; Metro. 21/9/96). L.C.

APPLEYARD, CHARLES
D. Remorse. 4° [1871].
C. A Lucky Hit (Roy. 21/11/72). L.C.

ARBUTHNOT, Captain
Bsq. L'Africaine; or, The Belle of Madagascar L.C. C.G. 21/10/65. *Lacy*.

ARCHER, Miss
D. My Life (Gai. 6/12/82). L.C.

ARCHER, CHARLES
D. Rosmersholm (Vaud. 23/2/91). L.C. 8° 1891.
D. Peer Gynt. 8° [1892].
[Translated in collaboration with *W. ARCHER*.]

ARCHER, C. J.
Bsq. Kenilworth (Croydon, 1/4/93).
[Written in collaboration with *A. E. AUBERT*. Music by J. Reille.]

ARCHER, D.
Duol. The Unexpected Visit (Mat. 21/6/98).

ARCHER, W. J.
D. Broken Pearls (C.L. 10/6/67). L.C.
D. Captain Gerald; or, The Highwayman's Revenge (Pav. 23/11/67). L.C.
D. Our Dear Old Home (C.L. 20/6/68). L.C.
D. Granna Waile and the Bridal Eve (E.L. 26/12/74). L.C.
D. Face to Face (M'bone, 19/5/77). L.C.
D. Stand and Deliver; or, The Perils of the Road (E.C. 23/11/85).

ARCHER, WILLIAM
C.D. Quicksands; or, The Pillars of Society (Gai. 15/12/80). L.C.
D. A Doll's House (Nov. 7/6/89; Crit. 2/6/91). L.C. 8° 1889.
D. Pillars of Society (O.C. 17/7/89). L.C.
[See *Quicksands*, above.]
D. An Enemy of the People (reading at H. 19/6/90; H. 14/6/93). L.C.
— Ibsen's Prose Dramas. 8° 1890 [and following years].
D. Ghosts (Indep. Theatre Soc. at Roy. 13/3/91).
D. Peer Gynt. 8° [1892]. See *C. ARCHER*.
D. A Visit (Indep. Theatre Soc. at Roy. 4/3/92). L.C.
D. The Master Builder (Traf. 20/2/93, *mat.*; Vaud. 6/3/93). 8° 1893.
[Written in collaboration with *E. GOSSE*.]
D. Hannele. 8° 1894.
D. Little Eyolf (Aven. 23/11/96). L.C. 8° 1895.
D. John Gabriel Borkman (Str. 3/5/97). L.C. 8° 1897.
D. Alladine and Palomides [and] Interior. 8° 1899.
[Several later translations and dramas.]

ARDEN, CHARLES
Ca. Ups and Downs; or, Blackley's Mistake (Athen. 25/7/88).

"*ARDEN, H. T.*" See *H. T. ARNOLD*

ARGENT-LONERGAU, Mrs E.
C.D. A Woman's Secret (Clarendon H. Watford, 9/5/94, *copy*.).
D. A Love Letter (Str. 10/5/94). L.C.
[Apparently the above play under another title.]

ARGLES, A.
F.C. Our Cousins (Torquay, 25/4/98). L.C.
[Written in collaboration with *F. STAYTON.*]

ARIA, Mrs ELIZA
F.C. The Runaways (Crit. 11/5/98). L.C. as *The Baby and the Bachelor.*

ARLISS, GEORGE
F.C. There and Back (Bath, 7/12/95, *copy.*). L.C.
F.C. The Deputy (S. Shields, 2/9/97; Grand, Wolverhampton, 23/1/99; Crit. 25/7/99, as *The Wild Rabbit*). L.C.

ARLON, FRANK
M.Ext. Nightingale's Wooing (Phil. 10/4/71). See *A. RUSHTON.*
F. A Capital Idea (Phil. 26/12/71). L.C.
[Written in collaboration with *A. RUSHTON.*]

ARMBRUSTER, CARL
Fairy D. The Children of the King (Court, 13/10/97). L.C.
[Written in collaboration with *J. DAVIDSON.* On 29/9/1902 a new act was added and the title altered to *Children of Kings.*]

ARMITAGE, ETHEL
Ca. Archibald Danvers, M.D. (Pav. Southport, 20/10/93). See *G. SOUTHAM.*

ARMSTRONG, ARCHIE
M.Sk. Dan'l's Delight (St G. 1/4/93). L.C. as *Daniel Daisytop's Delight.*
[Music by J. W. Elliott.]

ARMSTRONG, Captain W. H.
Spect.D. The Turkish Lovers; or, The Pacha's Revenge (D.L. 7/3/53). L.C.

ARNCLIFFE, HENRY
C.D. Love or Honour (Corn Exchange, Stamford, 11/5/86).

ARNOLD, CHARLES
D. Rosedale (Parkhurst, 6/2/93).
C.D. Paul of the Alps (Colchester, 15/4/98). See *D. C. MURRAY.*

ARNOLD, Sir EDWIN
T. Griselda. 8° 1856.
D. Adzuma; or, The Japanese Wife. 8° 1893.

ARNOLD, HENRY THOMAS ["*H. T. ARDEN*"]
D. The Amourer's Daughter (Cremorne, 11/8/66). L.C. 12° [1866].
Ext. Princess Charming; or, The Bard, the Baron, the Beauty, the Buffer and the Bogey (Cremorne, 29/4/67). *Lacy.*
Ba. The Belle of the Barley Mow; or, The Wooer, the Waitress and the Willain (Cremorne, 23/9/67). *Lacy.*
Bsq. Nobody's Child (Cremorne, 10/8/68). *Lacy.*
P. Harlequin Little Boy Blue and Little Bo Peep who lost her Sheep; or, The Wicked Dragon and the Enchanted Horn (C.P. 21/12/68).
[Written in collaboration with *T. L. GREENWOOD.*]
Ba. Bluebeard the Great Bashaw; or, The Loves of Selim and Fatima (C.P. 29/3/69).
P. Little Tom Tittlemouse (Ast. 26/12/70). See *T. L. GREENWOOD.*
Ba. Nell Gwynne; or, The King and the Actress (Roy. 12/6/71). L.C.

P. Harlequin Prince Happy-go-lucky; or, Princess Beauty and the Demon Dwarf (Alh. 26/12/71). L.C.
[Written in collaboration with *J. MILANO*.]
Ext. The Sylvan Statue; or, The Festival of the Fauns (Surrey Zoological Gdns. 13/5/72). L.C.
F. An Injured Female (Park, 6/11/76).
Bsq. The Right-full Heir. *Lacy*.

ARNOLD, MATTHEW
T. Merope. 8° 1858.

ART, H.
M.C. Finnegan's Fortune (Harte's, Openshaw, 12/6/97). L.C.

ARTHUR, ALFRED
Ca. Howard Howard (St G. 10/11/88). L.C. as *Reconciled*.
M.Sk. Home Chimes; or, The Home and the Love of Yore (St G. 10/11/88). L.C.
[Music by T. Normandale.]
F. A Wedding Present (St G. 10/11/88). L.C.
D.Sk. The Celebrated Case (St G. 10/11/88). L.C.

ARTHUR, BERNARD
Oa. "1990" (Myddleton, Islington, 16/10/95). L.C. Parkhurst.
[Music by A. Robey.]

[*ARTHUR, JOSEPH*
R.C.D. The Still Alarm (Fourteenth Street, New York, 30/8/87; P'cess, 2/8/88). L.C.
[Written in collaboration with *A. C. WHEELER*.]
D. Blue Jeans (Fourteenth Street, New York, 6/10/91; O.H. Northampton, 14/2/98; Shakespeare, Clapham, 28/2/98). L.C.

ARTLETT, B.
Bsq. The Babes in the Wood (Willenhall, 27/4/95). See *J. C. GRAHAME*.

ASCHER, Mrs GORDON
Ca. The Horn of Plenty (Central H. Acton, 15/12/97).

ASCHER, ISIDORE F.
Ca. Circumstances alter Cases (C.P. 23/4/88; Gai. 27/6/89, *mat.*). L.C. *French*.

ASHCROFT, T.
P. Little Red Riding Hood (Greenwich, 24/12/73)

ASHDOWN, CHARLES HENRY
D. Shrove Tuesday in St Albans in 1461 (County H. St Albans, 17/5/98).
[Music by W. H. Pell.]
D. A Day in Kingsbury Castle, A.D. 851 (County H. St Albans, 6/4/99).

ASHDOWN, W.
D. Raymond Remington (County H. St Albans, 11/12/93). L.C.

ASHLEY, J. B.
D. Aurora Floyd (Imp. 24/8/85).
[Written in collaboration with *C. MELTON*.]

ASHLEY, Mrs J. B. [EVELYN UNSWORTH]

D. For Queen and Country (Bijou, Neath, 26/12/90). L.C. St Helen's.

ASHLYN, QUENTIN

Ext. The Woman who wooed while the Wealth wobbled (Qns. H. 13/12/97).

Duol. Merely Acting (St James's H. 28/6/98).

ASHTON, J. T.

M.F. The Fire Eater (Roy. 15/4/74). L.C.

ASHWORTH, JOHN H. E.

C.O. Léonore (Pleasure Gdns. Folkestone, 10/4/94). L.C. 8° [1893]. [Music by the author. Title altered to *La Gaia*, 17/7/97.]

ASKMORE, RUSSEN

F. Up-to-date Photography (Oxford M.H. 3/8/96).

ATKINSON, THOMAS

F. Suggs in Danger (S.W. 10/10/82). L.C.

D. The Substance and the Shadow (Art Gall. Newcastle, 30/1/94). See *F. MULLEN*.

ATKYNS, SAMUEL

[For his earlier plays see iv, 257.]

D. Rookwood; or, The Tree of Fate. L.C. Albion, 13/1/50.

ATTENBOROUGH, FLORENCE GERTRUDE

Oa. Won by Wit (Myddleton H. Islington, 16/10/95). L.C. Parkhurst. [Music by A. Robey.]

ATWELL, E.

F. A Stuffed Dog (Park H. Camden Town, 2/11/89). See *J. A. KNOX*.

ATWOOD, ALBAN

F. Aunt Rebecca (O.H. Cheltenham, 19/12/95; Kilburn, 3/2/96). L.C. [Written in collaboration with *R. VAUN*.]

F. A Tale of a Tub (New, Cambridge, 22/10/96). See *R. VAUN*.

F. Caroline's Pupils (Bijou, 19/12/96). See *R. VAUN*.

Ca. Mrs H— will give Lessons in Lovemaking (Parkhurst, 12/3/97). [Written in collaboration with *R. VAUN*.]

F.C. Oh! Susannah! (Eden, Brighton, 6/9/97). See *M. AMBIENT*.

Ca. The Little Culprit (Pleasure Gdns. Folkestone, 19/11/97; Mat. 6/5/98). L.C. [Written in collaboration with *R. VAUN*.]

F.C. Naughty Rosina (Brixton, 15/8/98). See *L. A. D. MONTAGUE*.

AUBERT, A. E.

Bsq. Kenilworth (Croydon, 1/4/93). See *C. J. ARCHER*.

AUSTEN-LEE, CYRIL

D. The Shadow Hand (Alex. Widnes, 8/3/93, *copy*.; Macclesfield, 5/1/94; S. Shields, 12/7/97). L.C.

D. After the Storm (Burgh H. Dumbarton, 11/12/95). L.C.

AUSTIN, ALFRED

Poet.D. The Tower of Babel. 8° 1874.

T. Savonarola. 8° 1881.

D. Prince Lucifer. 8° 1887.

D.Poem. England's Darling. 8° 1896.

[For his later work see *C.B.E.L.* iii, 329.]

AUSTIN, H.
C.Sk. Madge (St G. 10/3/91). See *F. WADE.*

AUSTIN, W. J.
F. The Tempting Bait (O.C. 16/10/75). L.C.
M.Ca. Answer Paid (St G. 1878). See *F. C. BURNAND.*

AVELING, Dr EDWARD BIBBINS ["*ALEC NELSON*"]
D. A Test (Ladb. H. 15/12/85). L.C.
[Written in collaboration with *P. B. MARSTON.*]
D. By the Sea (Ladb. H. 28/11/87). L.C.
D. A Love Philtre (Torquay, 7/1/88). L.C.
D. The Bookworm (Athen. 18/4/88). L.C. Strand.
D. The Scarlet Letter (Olym. 5/6/88, *mat.*).
D. For Her Sake (Olym. 22/6/88). L.C.
[Evidently the above under another title.]
Ca. The Landlady (Shaft. 4/4/89, *mat.*). L.C.
D.Sk. Dregs (Vaud. 16/5/89, *mat.*). L.C. Hastings, 29/8/87.
C. The Jackal (Str. 28/11/89, *mat.*). L.C.
Ca. The Madcap (Com. 17/10/90). L.C.
Oa. A Hundred Years Ago (Roy. 16/7/92, *mat.*). L.C.
[Music by H. J. Wood.]
C. The Frog (Roy. 30/10/93). L.C.
D. Judith Shakespeare (Roy. 6/2/94, *mat.*). L.C.

AVELING, ELEANOR MARX
D. The Lady from the Sea (Terry's, 11/5/91, *mat.*). L.C.

AVERY, E. W.
D. A Little Vagrant (Alex. Cleethorpes, 8/7/97). See *F. MOULE.*

AVONDALE, J. H.
D. A Tough Yarn (Swiss Gdns. Shoreham, 24/9/77).
M.D. The Old Clay Pipe (Swiss Gdns. Shoreham, 30/9/78).
D. Oude Doullagh (Swiss Gdns. Shoreham, 7/6/79).

AVONDALE, WALTER
D. Satan's Daughter (P.W. Wolverhampton, 4/11/82). L.C. Wright's Travelling Co.
[See *Folle Farine*, below.]
D. Smouldering Fires (Alex. Walsall, 23/4/83). L.C.
D. Folle Farine (Bishop Auckland, 10/3/84; S.W. 18/10/84). L.C.
[A revised version of *Satan's Daughter* (P.W. Wolverhampton, 4/11/82).

AYLEN, H.
C.O. Gaiété (Sheffield, 26/10/74). See *J. ELDRED.*

AYLMER, BARRY
C. Outwitted (Holb. 21/1/73).
D. Shamus-na-Glanna; or, The Speidhoir (Qns. Manchester, 21/8/76).
D. Derry Driscoll (Alex. L'pool, 16/4/77). See *S. J. MACKENNA.*

AYLMER, JOHN
P. Mother Goose; or, The Fairy of the Golden Egg (Alex. 26/12/68). L.C.
C. Changes (Toole's, 25/4/90, *mat.*). L.C.

AYLMER, Mrs JOHN
C. The Charlatan (Torre Parish R. Torquay, 5/2/89). L.C.

AYRES, ARTHUR
C. His Own Guest (O.C. 19/5/83). L.C. *Lacy*.
[Written in collaboration with *P. BLAKE*.]
Ca. The Little One (Vaud. 22/1/85). L.C. St G. 29/2/84.

AYRTON, F.
M.F.C. One of the Family (Grand, Boscombe, 9/4/98). See *G. CAPEL*.

AYTOUN, WILLIAM EDMONSTOUNE ["*T. PERCY JONES*"]
Bsq. Firmilian. 8° 1854.

BADDELEY, G. C.
F. A Case of Pickles (Roy. 6/5/71). L.C.
F. The Little Blue Bottle (Bijou, 15/12/73).
D. The End of the Tether; or, A Legend of the Patent Office. *Lacy*.

BAGOT, ARTHUR GREVILLE
C. The Rubber of Life; or, The Best of Three Games (Brighton, 1/10/85; Str. 3/11/85). L.C.
[Written in collaboration with *F. R. BAGOT*.]
F. Which? (Gai. 18/2/86). L.C. Portland H. Portsmouth, 8/1/86. *French*.
F.C. The Widow (Windsor, 18/11/90, *amat.*; Com. 21/4/92).
D. A Stroke of Luck (Grand, Cardiff, 7/8/99). L.C.
[Written in collaboration with *J. K. MURRAY*.]

BAGOT, F. R.
C. The Rubber of Life (Brighton, 1/10/85). See *A. G. BAGOT*.

BAILDON, ARTHUR
C.O. Giralda (Lyc. 21/9/76). L.C.
[Music by A. Adam.]

BAILDON, HENRY BELLYSE
T. Rosamund. 8° 1875.

BAILEY, —
M.D. Both Sides of the World (E.C. 29/5/82). L.C.

BAILEY, SIDNEY F.
M.Sk. A Trip to the Isle of Man (County H. Bootle, 10/11/98).

BAILEY, WILLIAM E.
M.D. Tricky Esmeralda; or, Woman's Wit (W.L. 13/2/97). L.C.
[Written in collaboration with *E. WARD*.]
P. Dick Whittington and his Cat (W.L. 24/12/97).
P. The Babes in the Wood (W.L. 24/12/98). L.C.

BALCOUR, CHARLES
Ca. Ripplings (S.W. 24/3/83). L.C.

BALDIE, DACRE
D. Found in London; or, Playing their Game (Barrow-in-Furness, 3/3/79).

BALLANTYNE, JAMES
Oa. The Provost's Daughter (Edinburgh, 20/10/52).
D. The Gaberlunzie Man (Edinburgh, 7/6/58).

BALSILIO, D.
D.Sk. Gelert; or, Every Dog has his Day (Kilburn, 3/2/96). L.C.

BANCROFT, GEORGE PLEYDELL

C. The Birthday (Court, 8/12/94). L.C.

D. Teresa (Com. 30/7/97, *copy.* as *Angela Teresa*; Metro. 16/5/98; Gar. 8/9/98). L.C.

C. What will the World say? (Terry's, 26/1/99). L.C.

BANCROFT, LADY [MARIE EFFIE WILTON]

C.D. A Riverside Story (H. 22/5/90). L.C.

D. My Daughter (Gar. 2/1/92). L.C.

BANDMANN, DANIEL EDWARD

C. Only a Player (P'cess, 1/3/73). L.C.

D. Tom's Revenge (Edinburgh, 25/3/74).

D. The Cross and the Crescent (Huddersfield, 16/9/76).

D. Madeline Morel (Qns. 20/4/78). L.C. W. Hartlepool, 26/1/78.

D. Marie Jeanne; or, The Woman of the People (Bristol, 10/3/79). L.C.

D. Dr Jekyll and Mr Hyde (O.C. 6/8/88). L.C.

BANDMANN, MAURICE

D. The Egyptian Idol (Sunderland, 16/12/95). See *R. SAUNDERS.*

"*BANERO, J. M.*"

F. The Ar-rivals; or, A Trip to Margate (Aven. 24/6/84). L.C. [Written in collaboration with "*A. D. PINCROFT*".]

BANKS, BARNWELL

C. Turkington's Talisman (Leinster H. Dublin, 11/12/93). [Music by C. Krall.]

BANKS, WALTER

D. Dred (P.W. Wolverhampton, 19/11/72).

D. The Foundling of Notre Dame (L'pool, 7/8/76). L.C.

D. Under the Stars; or, The Stolen Heiress (Oldham, 1/9/79; M'bone, 2/8/80).

D. Del. Trem.; or, The Power of Drink (Gai. W. Hartlepool, 22/9/79).

BANNISTER, JOHN

C.O. Dolly (H.M. Carlisle, 27/10/90). L.C.

BANNISTER, T. B.

D. Geraldine's Ordeal (Greenock, 18/4/71).

D. A Theft for a Life (P.W. Wolverhampton, 23/4/77).

C. Mistaken Identity (Runcorn, 12/2/83). L.C. Gai., W. Hartlepool.

D. The Red Reef (Alex. Walsall, 8/9/84). L.C. Leeds. [Written in collaboration with — *WOODS.*]

D. False Lights (Birkenhead, 9/4/86; M'bone, 22/11/86).

D. The Wheel of Time (West Bromwich, 26/12/92; Stratford, 5/6/93). L.C.

D. The Gladiators (Cardiff, 5/6/93). L.C.

BANTOCK, Sir GRANVILLE

O. Caedmon (C.P. 18/10/92). L.C.

M.Ent. Harlequinade; or, Only a Clown (Eastbourne, 26/10/99). L.C. Ladb. H.

BARCKLAY, A. J.

F. Shorthand (Lyr. Hammersmith, 11/2/89). L.C.

BARCLAY, T. G.

D. The Gold Slave (Longton, 8/7/86).

BARCZINSKI, ARMIZER

C. His Lordship (Warlingham School, 6/8/90, *amat.*).

BARING, STEPHEN

D.Sk. Snatched from Death (Nov. 12/10/96). L.C.
[Written in collaboration with *W. BEAUMONT.*]

D. A Life for a Life (Osborne, Manchester, 10/7/99). L.C.
[Written in collaboration with *W. BEAUMONT.*]

BARING-GOULD, S.

C.O. The Red Spider (Marina, Lowestoft, 25/7/98). L.C. Wells.
[Music by L. Drysdale.]

BARKER, Miss

Ca. Lady Barbara's Birthday (Brighton, 12/2/72). L.C.

BARKER, HARLEY GRANVILLE

C. The Weather Hen (Terry's, 29/6/99). See *B. W. THOMAS.*
[For his later plays see A. E. Morgan, *Tendencies of Modern English Drama* (1924), p. 306.]

BARKER, JOHN

D. Vice versus Virtue (Grand, Nelson, 22/8/91). L.C.

BARLAS, JOHN

T. Punchinello and his Wife Judy. 8° 1886 [Chelmsford].

BARLOW, GEORGE

D. The Two Marriages. 8° 1878.

T. Jesus of Nazareth. 8° 1896.

BARLOW, R. J.

D. The Wings of the Storm (Glo. 5/10/91). L.C.
[Written in collaboration with *W. NORTH.*]

BARNARD, CECIL

Oa. Constancy; or, Two Blighted Loves (Vic.H. Sudbury, Suffolk, 7/6/92).

[*BARNES, ELLIOT*

C.D. Only a Farmer's Daughter (Birkenhead, 22/2/97). L.C. Woking.
[Written in collaboration with *F. LEVICK.*]

BARNES, F. A.

D. A Sailor's Fortune (Cambridge, Spennymoor, 22/12/88). L.C.

M.C. The New Servant (Colchester, 29/4/89). L.C.

BARNETT, BENJAMIN

F. Out on the Loose (Str. 11/3/50). See *M. BARNETT.*

D. The Pride of Poverty; or, The Real Poor of London (Str. 16/2/57). L.C.
[Written in collaboration with *J. B. JOHNSTONE.*]

BARNETT, MORRIS

[For his earlier plays see iv, 261.]

F. Out on the Loose (Str. 11/3/50). L.C. *Lacy.*
[Written in collaboration with *B. BARNETT.*]

D. Power and Principle (Str. 10/6/50). L.C. *Lacy.*

F. Serve him right (Lyc. 16/10/50). L.C. *Lacy.*
[Written in collaboration with *C. J. MATHEWS.*]

D. The Czarina; or, Ivan the Armourer (Sur. 21/4/51). L.C. *Lacy*.
[Written in collaboration with *A. B. REACH.*]
F. Love and Murder. L.C. 20/10/51.
D. Dreaming and Waking (Sur. 20/10/51). L.C.
[Written in collaboration with *A. B. REACH.*]
D. Circumstantial Evidence (Str. 27/10/51). *Lacy*.
D. Sarah Blange (Olym. 27/10/52). L.C. *Lacy* [as *Sarah the Creole*].
D. Lilian Gervais (Olym. 17/1/53). L.C. *Lacy*.
D. Salvatori; or, The Bandit's Daughter (Olym. 28/3/53). L.C.
D. The Married Unmarried (P'cess. 25/3/54). L.C. *Lacy*.
F. Capers and Coronets (Adel. 12/10/54).
F. The Perils of Crinoline (Str. 19/1/57).
Oa. Love by Lantern Light (Soho, 20/1/62). *Lacy*.
[A version of *Le mariage aux lanternes*, libretto M. Carré and L. Battu, music J. Offenbach (Paris, 10/10/57).]

BARNETT, R. W.
O. The White Cockade (Salle Erard, 7/3/95).
[Written in collaboration with *C. HARRIS.*]

BARON, JOSEPH
F. Grandfather's Clock (S.W. 17/12/83).

BARRETT, FRANK
F.C. Fast Friends (Nottingham, 17/9/84). L.C. A. Henry's Travelling Co., Grand, Douglas.

BARRETT, J. C.
Vaud. The Maid of Normandy (Str. 7/11/53). L.C.

BARRETT, OSCAR
P. The Forty Thieves (C.P. 21/12/82). L.C.
[Written in collaboration with *W. R. OSMAN.*]
P. Red Riding Hood (C.P. 23/12/86). L.C.
[Written in collaboration with *C. DALY.*]
P. Robinson Crusoe (Lyc. 12/95).

BARRETT, REDMOND
F. A Sharp Way to catch a Wife (Qns. Dublin, 13/1/69).

BARRETT, WILSON
D. Twilight (Lyc. Sunderland, 20/9/71).
O. Moro (H.M. 28/1/82).
[Music by M. W. Balfe.]
D. Hoodman Blind (P'cess. 18/8/85). See *H. A. JONES*.
R.D. The Lord Harry (P'cess. 18/2/86). See *H. A. JONES*.
D. Sister Mary (Brighton, 8/3/86; Com. 11/9/86). L.C.
[Written in collaboration with *C. SCOTT*. Title altered to *Captain Leigh, V.C.* 5/1900.]
T. Clito (P'cess. 1/5/86). See *S. GRUNDY*.
D. The Golden Ladder (Glo. 22/12/87). See *J. P. SIMPSON*.
R.D. The Ben-my-Chree (P'cess. 17/5/88). See *H. CAINE*.
D. The Good Old Times (P'cess. 12/2/89). See *H. CAINE*.
D. Nowadays: A Tale of the Turf (P'cess. 28/2/89, *mat.*). L.C.
D. The People's Idol (Olym. 4/12/90). L.C.
[Written in collaboration with *V. WIDNELL.*]
D. The Acrobat (Olym. 21/4/91). L.C.
F. Jenny the Barber (P's. Bristol, 10/12/91). L.C.

D. Pharaoh (Grand, Leeds, 29/9/92). L.C.

C.D. Our Pleasant Sins (Grand, Leeds, 13/2/93, *copy.*; Pier Pav. St Leonards, 3/8/96). L.C.
[Written in collaboration with *C. HANNAN.*]

D. The Manxman (Grand, Leeds, 22/8/94; Shaft. 18/11/95). L.C.
[Music by S. Jones.]

D. The Sign of the Cross (Grand, Leeds, 26/8/95; Lyr. 4/1/96). L.C. *Souvenir of The Sign of the Cross*, 8° [1896].

D. The Daughters of Babylon (Lyr. 6/2/97). L.C. *Souvenir of The Daughters of Babylon*, 8° [1897].

D. The Sledgehammer (Kilburn, 22/2/97). L.C.

D. Man and his Makers (Lyc. 7/10/99). L.C.
[Written in collaboration with *L. N. PARKER.*]
[For his later plays see Davenport Adams, *op. cit.* p. 115.]

BARREZ, M.

Bal. The Star of the Rhine (D.L. 24/2/52).

BARRI, HORACE

P. Robin Hood (M'bone, 26/12/90).

BARRI, ODOARDO

M.Ext. M.D. (Gar. 9/6/79). L.C.

BARRIE, Sir JAMES MATTHEW

D. Richard Savage (Crit. 16/4/91, *mat.*). L.C. 8° 1891 [*priv.*].
[Written in collaboration with *H. B. M. WATSON.*]

Bsq. Ibsen's Ghost; or, Toole up-to-date (Toole's, 30/5/91, *mat.*). L.C.

C. Walker, London (Toole's, 25/2/92). L.C. 8° 1907. *French.*

C.D. Jane Annie; or, The Good Conduct Prize (Sav. 13/5/93). L.C. 8° 1893.
[Written in collaboration with *A. C. DOYLE.* Music by E. Ford.]

C.D. Becky Sharp (Terry's, 3/6/93). L.C.

D. The Professor's Love Story (Com. 25/6/94). L.C.

C.D. The Little Minister (H. 6/11/97). L.C.

Duol. A Platonic Friendship (D.L. 17/3/98). L.C.
[For his later plays see A. E. Morgan, *op. cit.* pp. 306–307.]

BARRINGTON, ERNEST

Ext. Robinson Crusoe Junior (Qns. Battersea, 3/4/93). See *C. W. McCABE.*

BARRINGTON, RUTLAND

D. Mr Barnes of New York (Olym. 23/3/88, *mat.*; Olym. 16/5/88, *revised*, as *To the Death*). L.C. Ladb. H. 22/2/88.

O.F. A Swarry Dansong (Crit. 5/6/90, *mat.*).
[Music by E. Solomon.]

C. Bartonmere Towers (Sav. 1/2/93, *mat.*). L.C.

Oa. The Knight Errant (Lyr. 14/11/94). L.C.
[Music by Caldicott.]

Duol. The Professor (St G. 15/7/95). L.C.
[Music by E. Solomon.]

BARRON, H.

M.C. His Satanic Majesty (Empire, Southend, 13/11/99). See *F. MARLOW.*

BARRON, OSWALD
F. A Family Novelette (P.H. New Cross, 21/2/94). See *E. NESBIT*.

BARROW, PERCY JAMES
C. A Slight Headache (Portland H. Southsea, 25/1/98). L.C.
F. The Brain Reviver (P's. Portsmouth, 27/1/98). L.C.
M.C. The Wishing Oak (P's. Portsmouth, 27/1/98). L.C.
[Music by J. H. Nicholson.]
F.C. The Lunatic (Bournemouth, 30/8/98, *copy*.). L.C.
F. Captain Spent's Proposals (Southsea, 14/12/99).

BARRS, HERBERT
D. Life (Swansea, 1894; Stratford, 22/7/1901).
D. The War Cloud (Castleford, 12/1/95; Grand, Wolverhampton, 17/6/95; Stratford, 8/5/99). L.C.

BARRY, HELEN
F.C. A Night's Frolic (Str. 1/6/91). See *A. THOMAS*.

BARRY, HENRY
Ca. The Charitable Man (Nov. 15/2/87). L.C.

BARRY, J. L.
P. Little Red Riding Hood (Morton's, Greenwich, 24/12/97). L.C.
Bsq. The Little Coquette (Alex. Widnes, 31/7/99). L.C.
[Music by A. Langstaffe.]

BARRY, PAUL
Ca. French Law (Athen. 15/3/93). L.C.

BARRYMORE, MAURICE
D. Honour (Court, 24/9/81). L.C.
D. Nadjezda (H. 2/1/86). L.C.

BARTHOLEYNS, A. O'D.
F. À la Française (Aven. 8/7/93). L.C.
Oa. Military Manœuvres (Aven. 8/7/93). L.C.
C. A Lord-in-Waiting (Aven. 8/7/93). L.C.
C. Our Hostess (Kilburn, 5/4/97). L.C.

BARTLETT, HUBERT
D. A Harvest of Wild Oats (St Mary's, Henley, 8/3/97). L.C.
[Title altered later to *The Blackmailers*.]
C. No Actress (Sur. 6/6/98). L.C.
Ca. The Blue Dahlia (Metro. Devonport, 27/10/98). See *H. SUTCLIFFE*.
M.D. The Avenging Hand (P's. Blackburn, 31/7/99). L.C.

BARTON, —
Bsq. Hamlet Travestie (Str. 7/11/53). L.C.

BARWICK, EDWIN
F. A Kitchen Tragedy (Sanger's, 21/5/87).
P. Cinderella (Broadway, 27/12/97). L.C.
P. Cinderella (Coronet, 24/12/98).
P. Aladdin (Broadway, 26/12/98). L.C.

BASING, S. HERBERTE
D. Gringoire (Park T.H. Battersea, 4/2/90). See *E. BESSLE*.

BATEMAN, ALFRED

Oa. Deene Farm (St Andrew's, Stoke Newington, 23/1/94; Myddleton H. Islington, 5/4/94).
[Music by G. Richardson.]

BATEMAN, FRANK

D. A Bunch of Shamrocks (Roy. Edinburgh, 2/6/96, *copy.*; Brixton, 12/7/97, as *The Cross for Valour*). L.C.
[Written in collaboration with *J. T. DOUGLASS.*]

D. From Scotland Yard (P'cess. Accrington, 16/8/97). See *J. T. DOUGLASS.*

BATEMAN, H. L.

F. Corporal Max (St J. 15/9/51).

BATEMAN, Mrs H. L.

T. Geraldine; or, The Master Passion (Adel. 12/6/65). L.C.

D. Fanchette; or, The Will o' the Wisp (Edinburgh, 6/5/71; Lyc. 11/9/71). L.C.

BATEMAN, ISABEL

C.D. The Courtship of Morrice Buckler (Grand, 6/12/97). See *A. E. W. MASON.*

BATEMAN, RICHARD

C. Baden Baden; or, The Pretty Hunchback (Barnstaple, 12/1/72).

BATHO, R.

F. The Bogus Agent (Assembly R. Balham, 1/10/95).

BATSON, JOHN H.

D. A Deadlock (Bijou, 7/2/98). See *D. COWIS.*

BATTAMS, J. SCOTT

C. Sister Grace (Aven. 26/6/84). L.C.

F. A Mock Doctress (Lyr. Ealing, 7/5/87). L.C.

D. After (Vaud. 27/5/87, *mat.*). L.C.

C. The Parson's Play (Grand, 8/7/89). L.C.

BAYLEY, WENTWORTH V.

Ba. Alfred the Ingrate (Plymouth, 8/5/71).

BAYLIFF, C. M. A.

Ca. Our Hated Rival (Richmond, 17/12/91). See *R. L. BAYLIFF.*

BAYLIFF, Capt. R. L.

Ext. St George and the Dragon (Richmond, 16/12/91).

Ca. Our Hated Rival (Richmond, 17/12/91).
[Written in collaboration with *C. M. A. BAYLIFF.*]

BAYNE, P.

D. The Days of Jezebel. 8° 1872.

BAYNE, RONALD

D.Sk. Just Retribution (Bijou H. Bedford, 27/10/93).

BEACH, WILLIAM

M.C. Weather or No (Sav. 15/8/96). See *A. ROSS.*

C. A Comedy of Trifles (P.H. W. Norwood, 2/12/99).

"BEALE, WILLERT." See *W. MAYNARD.*

"*BEAMUL, J.*" See *J. B. MULHOLLAND*

BEAN, FRANK

D.Sk. True to his Colours (S.W. 15/8/92).

BEARNE, A.

C. Tom (Lecture H. Derby, 28/12/93). See *H. DALROY.*

BEATTY, HARCOURT

Ca. The Sins of the Fathers (Roy. Glasgow, 24/4/96). L.C.
[Written in collaboration with *S. F. HARRISON.*]

BEATTY-KINGSTON, WILLIAM

C.O. The Beggar Student (Alh. 12/4/84; Com. 13/12/86). L.C.
[Music by C. Millöcker.]

C.O. Frivoli (D.L. 29/6/86). L.C.
[Music by Hervé.]

O. The Light of Asia (C.G. 11/6/92). L.C.
[Music by I. de Lara.]

O. Irmengarda (C.G. 8/12/92). L.C.
[Music by L. E. Bach.]

O. Inez Mendo (C.G. 10/7/97). L.C.
[Music by F. D'Erlanger.]

BEAUCHAMP, EMILY

Ca. The Anti-matrimonial Society (Gai. Dublin, 9/3/76; Pav. Gravesend, 20/2/84).

C. Yes or No (Dublin, 2/5/77; K.X. 7/12/78).

C. The Matrimonial Agency (Str. 8/12/96).

BEAUMONT, FRANK

D. Called to the Front (Brit. 29/4/85). See *Sergeant TOWNER.*

BEAUMONT, WALTER

D.Sk. Snatched from Death (Nov. 12/10/96). See *S. BARING.*

D. A Life for a Life (Osborne, Manchester, 10/7/99). See *S. BARING.*

BECHER, MARTIN

F. A Domestic Hercules (D.L. 24/9/70). L.C.

F. Rule Britannia (D.L. 26/12/70). L.C. *Lacy.*

F. Number Six, Duke Street (D.L. 23/9/71). L.C. *Lacy.*

F. In Possession (D.L. 26/12/71). L.C. *Lacy.*

Ca. A Poetic Proposal (Glo. 20/3/72). L.C. *Lacy.*

F. A Crimeless Criminal (Str. 20/4/74). L.C. *Lacy.*

F. Painless Dentistry (Adel. 12/6/75). L.C. *Lacy.*

Ca. Belling the Cat (St G. 6/11/86).

BECK, P.

D. Madame Midas, the Gold Queen (Stratford, 7/7/88, *copy.*; Vic. Exeter, 5/12/88). L.C.
[Written in collaboration with *F. HUME.*]

BECKETT, Mrs HARRY

C. Jack (Roy. 14/6/86). L.C.

BECKWITH, CHARLES

D. In Mary's Cottage (Terry's, 21/12/96). L.C.

BEDDING, THOMAS

D. The Maternal Instinct (D.Y. 9/6/98). L.C.

BEDFORD, EDWARD
Ext. Suited at Last (Stavely Inst. Stavely, 25/3/95).
[Music by G. Burton.]

BEDFORD, HENRY
D. Gypsy Jack (Vic. Burnley, 5/8/99). L.C.

BEDWELL, HORACE
Duol. Anthony Jolt (Qns. Gate H. Kensington, 11/5/96).

BEERBOHM, CONSTANCE
Ca. A Secret (St G. 26/6/88). L.C.

BELAC, D.
D. The Thunderbolt; or, May Blossom (W. Bromwich, 4/4/94, *copy.*). L.C.
[Written in collaboration with *W. HAMILTON.*]

[*BELASCO, DAVID*
D. La Belle Russe (Baldwin, San Francisco, 18/7/81; Wallack's, New York, 8/5/82; P'cess. Edinburgh, 26/6/82; Pav. 17/1/86). L.C. Tyne, Newcastle.
D. The Senator's Wife (Lyc. New York, 1/11/87, as *The Wife*; Manchester, 30/9/92). L.C.
[Written in collaboration with *H. C. DE MILLE.*]
D. The Girl I left behind me; or, The Country Ball (S.W. 6/1/93, *copy.*; Adel. 13/4/95). L.C.
[Written in collaboration with *F. FYLES.*]
C.D. Man and Woman (O.C. 25/3/93). See *H. C. DE MILLE.*
D. The Heart of Maryland (E.C. 25/9/95, *copy.*; Adel. 9/4/98). L.C.
C.D. Zaza (Lafayette O.H. Washington, 25/12/98; Gar. 16/4/1900). L.C. D.Y. 24/3/99.

BELL, ALEXANDER B.
D. Fair and Square (Barnsley, 7/9/88). L.C.

BELL, CYRUS
D.Sk. Briggate; or, The Outcast (Grand, Leeds, 3/3/84).

BELL, FRANK
C. True Hearts (St G. 28/5/74). L.C.

BELL, G.
C.O. The Silver Cage (O.C. 31/7/74). L.C.

BELL, Mrs HUGH [*FLORENCE EVELEEN ELEANORE, Lady BELL*]
Ca. L'Indécis (Newcastle, 9/9/87, as *Between the Posts*; Roy. 10/11/87). *French.*
Duol. A Chance Interview (St G. 12/6/89).
D.Sk. A Lost Thread (P's. H. 20/5/90). L.C. Str. 17/2/93.
— Chamber Comedies, A Collection of Plays and Monologues for the Drawing Room. 8° 1890.
Ca. Time is Money (Newcastle, 5/9/90; Com. 21/4/92). L.C. *French.*
[Written in collaboration with *A. CECIL.*]
Ca. A Joint Household (Steinway H. 13/3/91; Grand, 2/5/92). *French.*
Ca. A Superfluous Lady (Lyr. Club, 2/6/91).
D. Karin (Vaud. 10/5/92). L.C.
— Nursery Comedies: Twelve Tiny Plays for Children. 8° 1892.
F.C. Nicholson's Niece (Terry's, 30/5/92, *mat.*). L.C.

Ca. An Underground Journey (Com. 9/2/93).
[Written in collaboration with *C. H. E. BROOKFIELD*.]
Ca. The Masterpiece (Roy. 15/4/93). L.C.
D. Alan's Wife (Indep. Theatre Soc. at Terry's, 28/4/93). L.C. 8° 1893.
Ca. In a Telegraph Office (Parish H. Sloane-square, 11/5/93).
Bsq. Jerry-Builder Solness (St G. 10/7/93).
Ca. The Great Illusion (West, Albert H. 28/6/95).
D.Sk. The Bicycle (Com. 12/3/96).
Ca. Blue or Green? (Com. 12/3/96).
Ca. A Sixpenny Telegram. *French*.

BELL, MALCOLM
Ca. The Substitute (Steinway H. 23/3/93).
Duol. Mrs Eversley—Wednesdays (Steinway H. 18/4/93).
M.C. The Merry Monk (Mat. 15/7/97). See *M. DURÉ*.

BELL, MINNIE
Ca. Is Madame at Home? (P's. H. 23/5/87).
D.Sk. The Gavotte (Steinway H. 1/4/90, *mat.*).
C. Lady Browne's Diary (Str. 28/6/92, *mat.*). L.C.

BELL, R.
D. The Court, the Prison and the Scaffold (Brit. 30/11/74).

BELL, R. S. WARREN
D. A Woman's Heart (Sur. 17/12/97). L.C.

BELL, STEWART
C.D. Mother and Son (P'cess. Manchester, 14/9/83). L.C.
O. Holyrood (P'cess. Glasgow, 5/10/96).
[Music by J. Greig.]

BELLAMY, CLAXSON
C.O. Erminie (Grand, Birmingham, 26/10/85; Com. 9/11/85). L.C. 8° [1885].
[Music by E. Jakobowski. Written in collaboration with *H. PAULTON*.]
Oa. A Raw Recruit (Star, Wolverhampton, 7/89).
[Music by P. Rowe.]

BELLAMY, G.
D. The Golden Harvest (Qns. Hull, 17/8/68).

BELLAMY, G. SOMERS
C. Flirtation (Glo. 14/7/77). See *F. ROMER*.
D. Two Wedding Rings (Brit. 27/2/82). L.C.
[Written in collaboration with *F. ROMER*.]
C. Tact (Aven. 14/3/85). L.C.
[Written in collaboration with *F. ROMER*.]
C. April Showers (Terry's, 24/1/89). See *F. ROMER*.

BELLEW, HAROLD KYRLE
D. Yvonne (H.M. Richmond, 5/3/81).
Poet. D. Hero and Leander (P's. Manchester, 9/5/92; Shaft. 2/6/92). L.C.
D. Charlotte Corday (Calcutta, 1/94; Grand, 13/12/97; Adel. 21/1/98). L.C.

BELLINGHAM, HENRY

D. The Mansion of Terrors (Sur. 26/1/52).

Bsq. Arline the Lost Child; or, The Pole, the Policeman and the Polar Bear (S.W. 23/7/64). L.C. 8° 1864.
[Written in collaboration with *W. BEST.*]

Ext. The Magic Horse and the Ice-maiden Princess (P'cess. 26/12/64). L.C.
[Written in collaboration with *W. BEST.*]

Ext. Prince Camaralzaman; or, The Fairy's Revenge (Olym. 12/8/65). L.C. *Lacy.*
[Written in collaboration with *W. BEST.*]

Bsq. Princess Primrose and the Four Pretty Princes (Olym. 13/1/66). L.C. *Lacy.*
[Written in collaboration with *W. BEST.*]

Bsq. Bluebeard Re-paired (Olym. 2/6/66). L.C. 12° 1866. *Lacy.*
[Music by J. Offenbach, arranged by J. H. Tully.]

D. Monsieur Laroche. 12° 1878.

D.Sk. Darby and Joan (Newcastle, 11/9/85; Terry's, 11/2/88, *mat.*). L.C. O.H. Perth.
[Written in collaboration with *W. BEST.*]

Ca. My Love and I (P.W. 3/5/86). L.C.
[Written in collaboration with *W. BEST.*]

D. Sol Gandy (O.H. Leicester, 1/4/87). L.C.
[Written in collaboration with *W. BEST.*]

F. A Socialist (Roy. 16/4/87). L.C.

F. Meddle and Muddle (Roy. Glasgow, 3/6/87; Terry's, 17/10/87). L.C. *French.*
[Written in collaboration with *W. BEST.*]

Duol. Keep your own Counsel (Terry's, 14/1/95).
[Written in collaboration with *W. BEST.*]

D.D. The Light of his Eyes (O.H. Bury, 22/2/95; O.H. Blackpool, 26/11/97). L.C.
[Written in collaboration with *W. BEST.*]

BELMORE, C.

D. Mad Ruth of Wilton; or, The Prophet of Stonehenge (Pav. Salisbury, 29/1/72).

BELMORE, GEORGE

Bsq. Babes in the Wood (Qns. Battersea, 3/4/93). See *C. W. McCABE.*

BELOT, ADOLPHE

D. The Governess (Olym. 21/10/86).

BELTON, FRED

D. Lucrezia Borgia (S.W. 4/11/71).

BELVERSTONE, J.

Ca. The Young Pretender; or, Quite a Mistake (Dundee, 29/6/74; Blackburn, 30/9/78).

Ca. Charley Stuart (S. Shields, 23/8/75).
[This is probably the above under another title.]

Ca. All by Chance (Leicester, 9/6/79).

BENHAM, ARTHUR

C.D. The County (Terry's, 2/6/92). See *E. BURNEY.*

C. The Awakening (Gar. 1/10/92). L.C.

Ca. Theory and Practice (Indep. Theatre Soc. at Terry's, 28/4/93). L.C. *Lacy.*

BENINGTON, W.

D. Honours Divided (St Benet's Church R. Lupton Street, N.W., 14/5/95). See *C. K. BURROW.*

BENNETT, —

Ext. A Trip to India (Crit. 25/11/75). L.C.

BENNETT, EMELIE

C. Among the Amalekites (Portsmouth, 22/6/89). L.C.

BENNETT, GEORGE JOHN

[For his earlier plays see iv, 265.]

D. Retribution (S.W. 11/2/50).

BENNETT, GEORGE WYNNE

D. Hunted Down; or, The Italian's Vengeance (Norwich, 31/1/81).

BENNETT, H. LEIGH

F. Birdcage Walk (T.H. Hove, 20/4/92). L.C.
[Written in collaboration with *A. B. TAPPING.*]

C. The Egotist (Metropole Hotel, Brighton, 20/2/95). L.C.

BENNETT, JOHN E.

D. Paul Rabaut; or, The Huguenots under Louis XV. 12° 1878.
[Written in collaboration with *C. WAKELY.*]

BENNETT, JOSEPH

O. Manon (Court, L'pool, 17/1/85; D.L. 7/5/85). L.C.
[Music by Massenet.]

O. Thorgrim (D.L. 22/4/90). L.C.
[Music by F. H. Cowen.]

O. Djamileh (P's. Manchester, 22/9/92). L.C.
[Music by G. Bizet.]

O. Jeanie Deans (Lyc. Edinburgh, 15/11/94; Daly's, 22/1/96). L.C. 8° [1894].
[Music by H. MacCunn.]

BENSON, E.

Ca. Midgelet; or, A Day up the River (Str. 11/7/93). L.C.

BENSON, LIONEL

M.Ca. The Turquoise Ring. L.C. St G. 12/10/80. See *G. W. GODFREY.*

BENTON, FRED

C. Two Old Boys. L.C. 27/11/80. See *G. CAPEL.*

D. Rogues and Vagabonds (Scarborough, 12/6/97). See *E. HILL-MITCHELSON.*

M.F.C. One of the Family (Grand, Boscombe, 9/4/98). See *G. CAPEL.*

D. Brave Hearts (Middleton, 3/11/98). See *G. COMER.*

BERESFORD, ISABEL

C.D. Until the Day break (Bijou, 17/5/98). L.C.

BERG, A. E.

C.D. Down the Slope (Grand, Stalybridge, 28/6/97). L.C.

BERGNE, H. à COURT

C.Oa. St Valentine's (West, Albert H. 11/6/97). See *J. E. M. AITKEN.*

BERINGER, Mrs OSCAR (AIMÉE DANIELL)

D. Tares (P.W. 31/1/88; O.C. 21/1/89). L.C.

C.D. The Prince and the Pauper (Gai. 12/4/90, *mat.*). L.C. Park H., Camden Town.

C. That Girl (H. 30/7/90). See *H. HAMILTON.*

C.D. The Holly Tree Inn (Terry's, 15/1/91, *mat.*; Terry's, 28/12/96). L.C. *French.*

D. Bess (Nov. 17/11/91). L.C.

D.Sk. Salve (O.C. 15/3/95). L.C.

D. A Bit of Old Chelsea (Court, 8/2/97). L.C.

C.D. My Lady's Orchard (Glasgow, 23/8/97; Aven. 2/10/97). L.C. [Written in collaboration with *G. P. HAWTREY.*]

C.D. The Plot of his Story (Gar. 15/12/99). L.C.

BERLIN, IVAN

D. The Queen of the Night (W. Bromwich, 12/7/97). See *F. T. TRACEY.*

BERLYN, ALFRED

D. The Violin Players (Shaft. 22/4/90). L.C.

BERNARD, CHARLES

F. The County Fair (Brixton, 12/4/97; P'cess. 5/6/97). L.C.

BERNARD, FRED

Bsq. The Fair Princess (Gai. Walsall, 20/12/86).

BERNARD, WILLIAM BAYLE

[For his earlier plays see iv, 265–6.]

D. The Passing Cloud (D.L. 8/4/50). L.C. *Lacy.*

F. Platonic Attachments (P'cess. 28/9/50). L.C. *Lacy*; *Mod. Eng. Comic Th.*

D. Mont St Michel; or, The Fairy of the Sands (P'cess. 9/52). L.C.

C. A Storm in a Teacup (P'cess. 20/3/54). *Lacy*; *Mod. Eng. Comic Th.*

F. The Balance of Comfort (H. 23/11/54). L.C. *Lacy.*

D. Leon of the Iron Mask (M'bone, 5/2/55). L.C.

D. Charlotte Corday (Adel. 10/10/55). *Dicks.*

C. The Evil Genius (H. 8/3/56). L.C. *Lacy.*

F. A Splendid Investment (Olym. 11/2/57). L.C. *Lacy.*

D. A Life's Trial (H. 19/3/57). L.C. *Lacy.*

C. The Tide of Time (H. 13/12/58). L.C. *Lacy.*

D. No Name. 8° 1863.

R.D. Faust; or, The Fate of Margaret (D.L. 20/10/66). L.C. *Lacy.* [Music by various composers arranged by J. H. Tully.]

R.D. The Doge of Venice (D.L. 2/11/67). L.C.

D. Love's Revenge (Greenwich, 21/11/68).

D. The Man of Two Lives (D.L. 29/3/69). L.C. *Lacy.*

BERNHARDT-FISHER, Mrs

D. Claire (P.H. New Cross, 7/5/87).

BERRIE, ERNIE

Ca. Little Fibs (Ch.X. 11/9/69). L.C.

F. Captain Smith (Ch.X. 4/4/70). L.C. *Lacy.*

D. Pure as Snow (Bradford, 2/4/73).

BERTIE, J. C.

C.D. Hearts (Bishop Auckland, 17/7/74).

D. Homeward Bound (Lyc. Sunderland, 28/8/74).

BERTON, PAUL M.

Ca. My Landlady's Daughter (Grand H. Maidenhead, 2/1/93). L. C.

D. The New Man (Ladb. H. 20/12/95). See *H. WOODGATE.*

D. The Sorrows of Satan (Shaft. 9/1/97). See *H. WOODGATE.*

BERTRAND, E. C.

Bsq. Robinson Crusoe Rewived (Dumfries, 5/2/77). L.C.

D. Grandfather's Clock (Pav. 30/8/79). L.C. P.W. Warrington, as *Old Adam's Trust; or, G.C.*

D. In Black and White; or, A Bitter Wrong (Pav. 18/9/80). L.C.

D. Hidden Gold (Portsmouth, 4/12/82). L.C.
[Written in collaboration with *F. GOULD.*]

D. Blind Justice (Wolverhampton, 23/9/86; Stand. 11/4/87). L.C.

C.D. Eve's Temptation (Cheltenham, 22/11/88). L.C.

BESANT, Sir WALTER

C. Such a Good Man (Olym. 18/12/79). L.C.
[Written in collaboration with *J. RICE.*]

C.D. The Charm (St G. 22/7/84). L.C.
[Written in collaboration with *W. H. POLLOCK.*]

R.D. The Ballad Monger (H. 15/9/87). L.C.
[Written in collaboration with *W. H. POLLOCK.*]

BESEMERES, JOHN ["JOHN DALY"]

D. Broken Toys (S.W. 4/11/50). L.C. *Lacy.*

C. Young Husbands (S.W. 30/8/52; Str. 9/7/55, as *Married Daughters and Y.H.*). L.C. *Fairbrother*; *Lacy.*

D. The Times (Olym. 18/7/53). L.C. *Lacy.*

D. The Old Salt (Str. 11/1/68). L.C.

Ca. A Roving Commission (Roy. 7/4/69). L.C.

C. Dotheboys Hall (Court, 26/12/71). L.C.

D. Marriage Lines (Court, 17/3/73). L.C.

C.D. Forget and Forgive (Ch.X. 5/1/74). L.C.

BESLEY, HENRY

M.D. Devil-may-care (Lyr. Ealing, 10/8/93). L.C.

D. Denham's Folly (Paisley, 2/2/94). L.C.

BESSLE, ELIZABETH

C. The Electric Spark (Olym. 8/5/89, *mat.*). L.C. Ladb. H.

Ca. The Tinted Venus (Bramblebury, Wandsworth Common, 12/10/89).

D. Gringoire (Park T.H. Battersea, 4/2/90). L.C. New, Oxford, 18/1/90.
[Written in collaboration with *S. H. BASING.*]

Duol. The Understudy (O.C. 30/7/92). L.C.

BEST, WILLIAM

Bsq. Arline (S.W. 23/7/64). See *H. BELLINGHAM.*

Ext. The Magic Horse (P'cess. 26/12/64). See *H. BELLINGHAM.*

Ext. Prince Camaralzaman (Olym. 12/8/65). See *H. BELLINGHAM.*

Bsq. Princess Primrose (Olym. 13/1/66). See *H. BELLINGHAM.*

Ent. Aladdin's Lamp (St G. 3/3/83).

D.Sk. Darby and Joan (Newcastle, 11/9/85). See *H. BELLINGHAM.*

Ca. My Love and I (P.W. 3/5/86). See *H. BELLINGHAM.*

D. Sol Gandy (O.H. Leicester, 1/4/87). See *H. BELLINGHAM.*

F. Meddle and Muddle (Roy. Glasgow, 3/6/87). See *H. BELLINGHAM.*

C. Law and Physic (Terry's, 20/4/88). L.C.
Duol. Keep your own Counsel (Terry's, 14/1/95). See *H. BELLINGHAM.*
D. The Light of his Eyes (O.H. Bury, 22/2/95). See *H. BELLINGHAM.*

BEVERLEY, HENRY ROXBY
Spec. The Romance of the Rose (Lyc. 9/11/50). L.C.
D. The Collier's Wife; or, The Dark Deeds of a Coal Pit (Col. L'pool, 17/5/69).
D. Rupert Dreadnought; or, The Poisoner and the Secrets of the Iron Chest (Qns. Barnsley, 13/2/71).
D. Chicago, the City of Flames (Col. L'pool, 29/1/72).

BEYRUTH, PAUL
D. Southern Climes (Birkenhead, 29/4/76).

BICKLEY, A. C.
C. The Barn at Beccles (Manor R. Hackney, 8/12/91). See *G. HUGHES.*

BIDALLES, ADELAIDE HELEN
D. Amy Lawrence, the Freemason's Daughter. L.C. 26/10/51.

BIDWELL, HAYWARD
F. How's that, Umpire? (H.M. Richmond, 19/10/80). L.C.

"*BILKINS, TAYLOR.*" See *W. A. VICARS*

BINGHAM, FREDERICK
F. A Portmanteau Predicament (H.M. Richmond, 31/10/81). L.C.
F.C. Friendly Hints (Parish H. S. Acton, 9/12/89). L.C.
Ca. Jones and Co., Matrimonial Agents (P.H. Croydon, 4/2/93). L.C. as *The Matrimonial Agents.*
D.Sk. The Gipsy Princess (Masonic H. Middlesex, 13/3/95).
D.Sk. Counsel's Opinion (Richmond, 24/3/98). L.C. *French.*

BINGHAM, GRAHAM CLIFTON
C.O. The Coquette (P.W. 11/2/99). See *H. J. W. DAM.*

BINNS, GERTRUDE
D.Sk. The School for Husbands (Mount View H. 20/12/97).
[Written in collaboration with *J. HALFORD.*]

BINYON, ROBERT LAURENCE
Lyr.Sk. The Supper. 8° 1877 [*priv.*]. [For his later plays see **C.B.E.L.** iii, 332.]

BIRCH, A.
M.C. A Village Venus (Grand, Nottingham, 5/8/95). See *V. STEPHENS.*
M.C. A Merry Madcap (Grantham, 30/7/96). See *V. STEPHENS.*

BIRCH, WILLIAM HENRY
Oa. Eveleen, the Rose of the Vale (T.H. Reading, 21/10/69). 8° [1869; Reading].
O. The Wreck of the Argosy (T.H. Reading, 3/10/71).

BIRD, FRANK
D. Eric's Good Angel (Newcastle, 23/5/94; E.C. 4/7/94). L.C.
[Written in collaboration with *C. CROFTON.*]

BIRD, FRED. W.
D. A Woman's Love (Woolwich, 10/3/90).

BIRD, HORTON
Fairy D. Change for Love. *Lacy.*

BIRD, W. W.
Bsq. Alonzo and Imogene; or, The Dad, the Lad, the Lord and the Lass (Richmond, 17/4/69).

BISGOOD, J. J.
D. Right or Wrong (Crit. 4/5/87).
D. Jess (Adel. 25/3/90). See *E. LAWRENCE.*

BISPHAM, DAVID
D. Adelaide (Mat. 20/6/98). See *G. HEIN.*

BLACKBURN, SYDNEY
F.C. The Cousin from Australia (O.C. 11/4/98). L.C. Olym.

BLACKBURN, VERNON
O. Messalina (C.G. 13/7/99).
[Music by I. de Lara.]

BLACKMORE, W. T.
Ca. An Old Flame (Gai. 16/9/82). L.C.
R.D. The Roundhead (C.P. 12/6/83). See *B. F. BUSSY.*
C. Squire Humphrey (New, Oxford, 20/6/87). L.C.
C.D. Freda (Str. 19/7/87). See *B. F. BUSSY.*

BLAIR, JAMES
C. Sixteen—not out (P.W. 25/2/92, *mat.*). L.C.
C.D. Mr Richards (Shaft. 10/3/92). See *A. BOURCHIER.*

BLAKE, CHARLES
Oa. The Electric Spark (P's. Manchester, 28/5/83). See *C. PIDGIN.*

BLAKE, P.
C. His Own Guest (O.C. 19/5/83). See *A. AYRES.*

"*BLAKE, ROBERT.*" See *R. H. THOMPSON.*

BLAKE, THOMAS G.
[For his earlier plays see iv, 267–8.]
D. The Port of London. L.C. Pav. 15/1/51.
D. Fanny Wild, the Thief-taker's Daughter. L.C. 24/9/51.
D. Life as it is; or, The Pauper's Crib and the Model Lodginghouse. L.C. Pav. 30/9/52. *Dicks.*
D. Bess of the Bell (Ast. 20/3/54). MS. Birmingham.
— Home Plays. In *Mod. Eng. Comic Th.*

BLANCHARD, CECIL
M.C. Dolly (P'cess. Leith, 9/5/96). See *A. PARRY.*

BLANCHARD, EDWARD LEMAN
[For his earlier plays see iv, 268–9.]
F. Adam Buff; or, The Man without a Shirt (Sur. 4/3/50). L.C. *Duncombe.*
F. Taking the Census (Str. 6/5/51). L.C.
P. Harlequin Blue Cap (Sur. 26/12/51). L.C.
P. Sir John Barleycorn; or, Harlequin Champagne (M'bone, 26/12/51). L.C.
Spec.D. The Three Perils of Man—Wine, Wit and Woman. L.C. Sur. 29/3/52.

P. Harlequin and the World of Flowers; or, The Fairy of the Rose and the Sprite of the Silver Star (Sur. 27/12/52). L.C.

P. Harlequin Hudibras; or, Dame Durden and the Droll Days of the Merry Monarch (D.L. 27/12/52). L.C. *Lacy.*

P. Undine, the Spirit of the Waters; or, Harlequin and the Magic Cup and the Sorcerer (M'bone, 27/12/52). L.C.

F. The Royal Menagerie (Grec. 13/6/53).

P. Harlequin Humming Top; or, The World of Toys (D.L. 26/12/53). L.C. *Davidson.*

[Written in collaboration with *N. LEE.*]

P. Jack and Jill; or, Harlequin King Mustard and the Four and Twenty Blackbirds baked in a Pie (D.L. 26/12/54). L.C.

P. Hey Diddle Diddle; or, Harlequin King Nonsense and the Seven Ages of Man (D.L. 26/12/55). L.C.

P. The Fisherman and the Genie; or, Harlequin Padmanaba and the Enchanted Fishes of the Silver Lake (S.W. 26/12/56). L.C.

P. See Saw Margery Daw; or, Harlequin Holiday and the Island of Ups and Downs (D.L. 26/12/56). L.C.

P Little Jack Horner (D.L. 26/12/57). L.C. as *J.H.; or, Harlequin A.B.C.*

D.Sk. Please Copy the Address (Edinburgh, 9/5/59).

Ext. The Children of the Wood; or, The Fairy Birds of the Forest L.C. Adel. 18/7/59.

P. Peter Wilkins; or, Harlequin and the Flying Women of the Loadstone Rock (D.L. 26/12/60). 12° [1860].

[Music by J. H. Tully.]

P. Harlequin and Tom Thumb; or, Merlin the Magician and the Good Fairies of the Court of King Arthur (H.M. 26/12/60). L.C. 12° [1861].

[Music by J. H. Tully.]

P. Harlequin Sinbad the Sailor; or, The Fairy of the Diamond Valley and the Little Man of the Sea (S.W. 26/12/60). L.C.

P. Cherry and Fair Star; or, Harlequin and the Singing Apple, the Talking Bird and the Dancing Waters (S.W. 26/12/61). L.C. 8° [1862].

P. Harlequin and the House that Jack built; or, Old Mother Hubbard and her Wonderful Dog (D.L. 26/12/61). L.C. 8° [1862].

[Music by J. H. Tully.]

P. Goody Two Shoes; or, Harlequin Cock Robin (D.L. 26/12/62). L.C. 12° [1863].

P. Riquet with the Tuft; or, Harlequin and Mother Shipton (P'cess. 26/12/62). L.C. 12° [1863].

[Music by C. Hall.]

P. Harlequin Tom Tucker (P'cess. 26/12/63).

[Written in collaboration with *T. L. GREENWOOD.*]

P. Harlequin Sinbad the Sailor (D.L. 26/12/63). L.C. 8° [1864].

P. Cinderella; or, Harlequin and the Magic Pumpkin and the Great Fairy of the Little Glass Slipper (C.G. 26/12/64). L.C.

[Written in collaboration with *T. L. GREENWOOD.* This and later collaborative productions were issued under the name of "The Brothers Grinn".]

P. Hop o' my Thumb and his Eleven Brothers; or, Harlequin and the Ogre of the Seven-League Boots (D.L. 26/12/64). L.C.

P. Little King Pippin; or, Harlequin Fortunatus and the Magic Purse and Wishing Cap (D.L. 26/12/65). L.C.
[Music by J. Bernard.]

P. Aladdin and the Wonderful Lamp; or, Harlequin and the Flying Palace (C.G. 26/12/65). L.C. 8° [1865].

P. Harlequin Number Nip; or, Harlequin and the Gnome King of the Giant Mountains (D.L. 26/12/66). L.C. 12° 1866.
[Music by J. H. Tully.]

P. Faw, Fee, Fo, Fum; or, Harlequin Jack the Giant Killer (D.L. 26/12/67). L.C. 8° 1867.

P. Grimalkin the Great; or, Harlequin Puss in Boots and the Miller's Son (D.L. 26/12/68). L.C. 8° 1868.

Ent. The Carpet Bag (Egyptian H. 29/11/69).

P. Beauty and the Beast; or, Harlequin and Old Mother Bunch (D.L. 27/12/69). L.C. 8° 1869.

P. The Dragon of Wantley; or, Old Mother Shipton (D.L. 26/12/70). L.C. 8° 1870.

Ext. The Man in the Moon; or, The Eagle's Flight: A Freak of Fancy (P'cess. 10/4/71). L.C.

P. Little Dicky Dilver with his Stick of Silver; or, Harlequin Pretty Prince Pretty boy and the Three Comical Kings (P'cess. 26/12/71). L.C.
[Written in collaboration with *T. L. GREENWOOD*.]

P. Tom Thumb the Great; or, Harlequin King Arthur and the Knights of the Round Table (D.L. 26/12/71). L.C. 8° 1871.

M. Jack and Jill (C.P. 21/12/72).

P. Little Goody Two Shoes (P'cess. 26/12/72). L.C.
[Written in collaboration with *T. L. GREENWOOD*.]

P. The Children in the Wood (D.L. 26/12/72). L.C. 8° [1872].

M.F. Nobody in London (D.L. 20/9/73). L.C.

P. Puss in Boots (C.P. 20/12/73).

P. Jack in the Box; or, Harlequin Tom Tucker and the Wise Men of Gotham (D.L. 26/12/73). L.C. 8° 1873.

P. Cinderella (C.P. 22/12/74).

P. Aladdin; or, The Wonderful Lamp (D.L. 26/12/74). L.C. 8° 1874.

P. Beauty and the Beast (P'cess. 23/12/74). L.C.
[Written in collaboration with *T. L. GREENWOOD*.]

P. The Children in the Wood (Adel. 24/12/74). L.C.
[Written in collaboration with *T. L. GREENWOOD*.]

F. The Invisible Client (P'cess. Edinburgh, 1/3/75). L.C.

Ext. The Bunch of Berries (Adel. 8/5/75). L.C.

P. Jack in Wonderland (C.P. 22/12/75).

P. The Yellow Dwarf (Alex. Pal. 24/12/75). L.C.
[Written in collaboration with *T. L. GREENWOOD*.]

P. Whittington and his Cat (D.L. 27/12/75). L.C. 8° 1875.

P. Little Goody Two Shoes (Adel. 20/12/76). L.C.

P. Sinbad the Sailor (C.P. 21/12/76). L.C.
[Written in collaboration with *T. L. GREENWOOD*.]

P. The Forty Thieves (D.L. 26/12/76). L.C.

P. Little Red Riding Hood; or, Harlequin Grandmamma (Adel. 4/7/77). L.C.

Ext. The Enchanted Barber; or, Hans Ketzler's Close Shave (Adel. 22/12/77). L.C.
[Written in collaboration with *T. L. GREENWOOD*.]

P. Robin Hood and his Merry Little Men (Adel. 22/12/77). L.C.
P. St George and the Dragon (Alex. Pal. 22/12/77). L.C.
[Written in collaboration with *T. L. GREENWOOD*.]
P. The White Cat (D.L. 26/12/77). L.C.
P. Aladdin and the Wonderful Lamp (Imp. 21/12/78).
[Written in collaboration with *T. L. GREENWOOD*.]
P. Cinderella; or, Harlequin and the Fairy Slipper (D.L. 26/12/78). L.C. 8° 1878.
P. Bluebeard (D.L. 26/12/79). L.C.
[Written in collaboration with *T. L. GREENWOOD*.]
P. Aladdin (C.P. 22/12/80). L.C.
[Written in collaboration with *T. L. GREENWOOD*.]
P. Mother Goose and the Enchanted Beauty (D.L. 27/12/80). L.C.
P. Robinson Crusoe (D.L. 26/12/81). L.C.
P. Sinbad the Sailor (D.L. 26/12/82). L.C. 16° [1882].
— Lazinetta and Other Drawing-Room Plays. 8° 1883.
P. Cinderella (D.L. 26/12/83). L.C.
P. Whittington and his Cat (D.L. 26/12/84). L.C.
P. Aladdin (D.L. 26/12/85). L.C.
P. The Forty Thieves (D.L. 27/12/86). L.C.
[Music by F. Wallerstein.]
P. Puss in Boots (D.L. 26/12/87). L.C.
C.O. Carina (O.C. 27/9/88). L.C. 8° [1888; lyrics only].
[Written in collaboration with *C. BRIDGMAN*. Music by Julia Woolf.]
P. The Babes in the Wood (D.L. 26/12/88). See *Sir A. HARRIS*.

BLANCHARD, FRED
C. Our Wives (Eastbourne, 16/9/85).

BLATCHFORD, M.
C.O. Phyllis (Halifax, 14/4/90).
[Music by A. T. McEvoy.]
R.O. Sylvia; or, The Baron's Bride (Grand, Halifax, 20/10/91).
[Music by J. H. Sykes.]

BLATCHFORD, ROBERT
C.O. In Summer Days (Bradford, 2/3/91). L.C.
[Music by C. C. Corri.]

BLAU, HEINRICH
O. San Lin (Manchester, 11/5/99; Grand, 3/8/99).
[Music by V. Holländer.]

BLEAKLEY, E. O.
C. Real Life (Qns. Manchester, 9/12/72). L.C.

BLESSLEY, W. S.
F.C. Mixed Pickles (Cardiff, 19/12/99). L.C.

BLIGH, VIVIAN
Ca. Once in a Century. L.C. St G. 8/11/77. See *G. A. À BECKETT*.
M.Ca. The Pirate's Home. L.C. St G. 13/10/79. See *G. A. À BECKETT*.

BLISS, HENRY
T. Robespierre. 8° 1854.
D. Theckla. 8° 1866.

BLOOD, JAMES J.
M.C. Faust in Three Flashes (P.W. Birmingham, 5/3/84).
[Music by W. A. Langston.]

C. Our Lodger (Brighton, 27/5/85). L.C. as *Cut Blooms.*
C.D. Her Trustee (Vaud. 2/3/87, *mat.*). L.C.
D. 'Twixt Kith and Kin (P.W. Birmingham, 25/8/87; Grand, 10/10/87). L.C.
D. Fate and Fortune; or, The Junior Partner (P'cess. 27/7/91). L.C.

BLOOMER, J. E.
C.O. The Squire's Daughter (Alex. Sheffield, 7/11/79). L.C.

BLOUET, PAUL ["MAX O'RELL"]
C. The Dear Neighbours. 8° [1885].
F.C. On the Continong (Court, L'pool, 5/4/97; Qns. Crouch End, 1/5/99). L.C.
Ca. Two in the Dark (Qns. Crouch End, 1/5/99). L.C. Bournemouth, 23/4/97.

BLUNT, RICHARD
M.Sk. What shall I sing? (Lyr. Ealing, 22/9/92).

BLYTH, HARRY
C.D. Our Great Surprise (Glasgow, 20/2/90).

BLYTH, ROBERT J.
D. Sarah, the Fair Maiden of the Rhine (St G. 10/7/79).

BLYTHE, J. S.
C.D. A Brave Coward (Str. 3/12/86, *mat.*). L.C.
D. The Blind Witness (Grand, Margate, 6/3/99; Shakespeare, Clapham, 13/3/99). L.C.
D. Kenilworth (Glasgow, 5/6/99). L.C.

BOAS, FREDERICK SAMUEL
D. The Favourite of the King (Com. 11/3/90). L.C. 8° 1888 [as *Buckingham*].
[Written in collaboration with *J. BRANDON.*]

BODE, MILTON
D. Viva (Levino's Circus, Merthyr Tydvil, 12/9/87).

BOGUE, J. RUSSELL
C.D. My Sin (Cambridge, Spennymoor, 2/1/88).
F.C. O'Hooligan's Holiday (Vic., W. Stanley, 12/2/94). L.C. Athen. Lancaster.
D. In Luck's Way (Vic. Huddersfield, 26/12/95). L.C. Alh. Barrow, 30/6/91.
M.F.C. Ballyhooley; or, A Night on the Big Wheel (O.H. Doncaster, 5/5/98, *copy.*; Workington, 14/10/1901). L.C.
[Title altered to *A Warm Member*, 2/12/1918.]

BOISSIER, F.
Play without Words. A Pierrot's Life (P.W. 8/1/97). L.C.
[Music by M. Costa.]

[BOKER, GEORGE HENRY
D. The Betrothal (D.L. 19/9/53). L.C. Birmingham, 26/8/53 as *The Betrothed.*

BOLTON, CHARLES
D.Sk. Caught in a Line; or, The Unrivalled Blondin (Str. 3/3/62). L.C. *Lacy.*

BONAWITZ, J. H.
O. Irma (St G. 17/3/85). L.C.
D. Edgar the Socialist. 8° [1892].

BOND, STEPHEN
D. Bantry Bay (Sur. 17/12/97). L.C.

BOOSEY, WILLIAM
C.O. The Royal Watchman (Exeter, 11/4/87). L.C.
[Music by F. L. Moir.]

BOOTH, GEORGE
Bsq. Hamlet, whether he will or no (Alex. Sheffield, 2/6/79). L.C.

BOOTH, J. B.
C. Papa (Tivoli, Dover, 21/3/98). L.C.

BOOTH, J. H.
Ext. Moonshine; or, The Pirate's Plunder (Athen. Hereford, 8/12/92). L.C.
[Music by F. Swift.]

BOOTH, OTTO
Oa. Prizes and Blanks (Ladb. H. 29/6/85).

BOOTH, W.
F. A Tale of a Tub (New, Cambridge, 22/10/96). See *R. VAUN.*

BOSWELL, ROBERT BRUCE
— The Dramatic Works of Jean Racine. 8° 1890.

BOSWORTH, H.
D. The Collier's Daughter (P.W. Wolverhampton, 29/9/73).

BOUCICAULT, AUBREY
C. A Court Scandal (Court, 24/1/99; Gar. 10/5/99). L.C. Aven.
[Written in collaboration with *O. SHILLINGFORD.*]

BOUCICAULT, DION [DIONYSIUS L. BOURCICAULT]
[For his earlier plays see iv, 269–70.]
F. A Radical Cure. *French* [1850].
F. La Garde Nationale L.C. Qns. 9/1/50.
D. Giralda; or, The Miller's Wife (H. 12/9/50). L.C.
[This was revived as *A Dark Night's Work* (P'cess. 7/3/70). *Giralda* has been ascribed to *B. WEBSTER*, who may have been a co-author.]
D. Sixtus V; or, The Broken Vow (Olym. 17/2/51). L.C. 12° 1851; *French* [as *The Pope of Rome*]; *Lacy* [as *A Romance in the Life of Sixtus the Fifth, entitled, The Broken Vow*].
[Written in collaboration with *J. V. BRIDGEMAN.*]
C. Love in a Maze (P'cess. 6/3/51). L.C. 12° 1851; *Lacy.*
D. The Queen of Spades; or, The Gambler's Secret (D.L. 29/3/51). L.C. *Lacy* [as *The Dame of Spades*].
C. O'Flannigan and the Fairies (Adel. 21/4/51).
D. The Corsican Brothers (P'cess. 24/2/52). L.C. 8° [1852]; *Lacy.*
D. The Vampire (P'cess. 14/6/52). L.C. *French* [as *The Phantom*].
F. The Prima Donna (P'cess, 18/9/52). *Lacy.*
O. The Sentinel (Str. 10/1/53). L.C.
D. Genevieve; or, The Reign of Terror (Adel. 20/6/53). L.C.

D. Faust and Margaret (P'cess. 19/4/54). L.C. 8° [1854]; *French.*
[This play has been attributed variously to Boucicault and *T. W. ROBERTSON.*]

D. Pierre the Foundling (Adel. 11/12/54). L.C.

D. Eugénie; or, A Sister's Vow (D.L. 1/1/55). L.C.

T. Louis XI, King of France (P'cess. 13/1/55). L.C. 8° [1855].

D. Janet Pride (Metro. Buffalo, 11/8/54; Adel. 5/2/55). L.C.

M.Int. The Young Actress (Burton's, New York, 22/10/53; D.L. 26/5/56).

D. George Darville (Adel. 3/6/57). L.C.

D. Jessie Brown; or, The Relief of Lucknow (Wallack's, New York, 22/2/58; Plymouth, 11/58; Brit. 11/4/59; D.L. 15/9/62, as *The Relief of Lucknow*). L.C. Brit. 26/1/58 and D.L. 11/9/62. *French*; *Dicks.*

D. The Colleen Bawn; or, The Brides of Garryowen (Laura Keene's, New York, 28/3/60; Adel. 10/9/60). L.C. *French*; *Dicks.*

D. The Octoroon; or, Life in Louisiana (Winter Garden, New York, 6/12/59; Adel. 18/11/61). L.C. *French*; *Dicks.*

C.D. Andy Blake; or, The Irish Diamond (Boston, 3/1/54; Adel. 10/2/62, as *The Dublin Boy*). L.C. as *The Irish Boy*. *French*; *Dicks.*

D. The Life of an Actress (National, Cincinnati, 24/9/55, as *Grimaldi; or, Scenes in the Life of an Actress*; National, Philadelphia, 2/5/56, as *Violet; or, Scenes in the Life of an Actress*; Adel. 1/3/62). L.C. *French*; *Dicks.*

O. The Lily of Killarney (C.G. 2/2/62). See *J. OXENFORD.*

D. Dot (Winter Garden, New York, 14/9/59; Adel. 14/4/62). L.C.

P. Lady Bird; or, Harlequin Lord Dundreary (Ast. 26/12/62). L.C.
[Produced also on the same day at Wallack's, New York.]

D. The Trial of Effie Deans; or, The Heart of Midlothian (Laura Keene's, New York, 9/1/60; Ast. 26/1/63). L.C.

D. Pauvrette L.C. P.W. L'pool, 22/8/63. *French*; *Dicks.*
[Originally produced at Niblo's Garden, New York, 10/4/58.]

C. How she loves him! (P.W. L'pool, 7/12/63; P.W. 21/12/67). L.C. 8° [1868]; *French.*

D. The Poor of Liverpool (Amphi. L'pool, 11/2/64). L.C.
[See *The Streets of London* (P'cess. 1/8/64).]

C. The Fox Chase (Burton's, New York, 23/11/53, as *The Fox Hunt; or, Don Quixote II*; St J. 11/5/64). L.C.

D. The Streets of London (Wallack's, New York, 8/12/57, as *The Poor of New York*; P'cess. 1/8/64). *French* [as *The Streets of New York*].

D. Omoo; or, The Sea of Ice (Amphi. L'pool, 30/10/64). L.C.

D. Arrah-na-Pogue; or, The Wicklow Wedding (Dublin, 7/11/64; P'cess. 22/3/65). L.C. Manchester, 26/9/64; P'cess. 21/3/65. 8° [1865]; *French.*

D. Rip van Winkle (Adel. 4/9/65). L.C.
[Written in collaboration with *J. JEFFERSON.*]

D. The Poor of the London Streets (Grec. 2/4/66). L.C.
[Another version of *The Streets of London.*]

D. The Two Lives of Mary Leigh (P's. Manchester, 30/7/66; St J. 5/11/66, as *Hunted Down; or, The T.L. of M.L.*). L.C.

D. The Parish Clerk (Manchester, 30/7/66). L.C. P's. Manchester.

D. The Long Strike (Lyc. 15/9/66; Nov. 24/8/96, as *The Strike*). L.C. *French.*

D. The Flying Scud; or, Four Legged Fortune (Holb. 6/10/66). L.C.

D. A Wild Goose (H. 29/4/67). L.C. as *The Scamp.*
[Written in collaboration with *J. L. WALLACK.*]

D. Foul Play (Holb. 28/5/68; Leeds, 1/6/68, *revised*). L.C. 8° [1868].
[Written in collaboration with *C. READE.*]

D. After Dark: A Tale of London Life (P'cess. 12/8/68). L.C. *French.*
[See also under *H. L. WILLIAMS.*]

D. Presumptive Evidence (P'cess. 10/5/69). L.C. as *Mercy Dodd; or, P.E.*

C. Seraphine; or, A Devotee (Qns. 1/5/69). L.C.

D. Formosa; or, The Railroad to Ruin (D.L. 5/8/69; D.L. 26/5/91, *revised*). L.C. *Dramatic Publ. Co.*

D. Lost at Sea: A London Story (Adel. 2/10/69). L.C.
[Written in collaboration with *H. J. BYRON.*]

D. Paul La Farge; or, Self Made (P'cess. 7/3/70).

D. The Rapparee; or, The Treaty of Limerick (P'cess. 9/9/70). L.C. *Dramatic Publ. Co.*

D. Jezebel; or, The Dead Reckoning (Holb. 5/12/70). L.C.

D. Elfie; or, The Cherry-tree Inn (Glasgow, 10/3/71; Gai. 4/12/71). L.C. *Dramatic Publ. Co.*

D. Night and Morning (P's. Manchester, 7/9/71; Gai. 19/11/71; Terry's, 9/1/93, revised as *Kerry; or, N. and M.*). *Dramatic Publ. Co.*

C. John Bull (Gai. 8/7/72).
[A revised version of G. Colman's play (C.G. 1803).]

Spec. Babil and Bijou; or, The Lost Regalia (C.G. 29/8/72). L.C.
[Written in collaboration with *J. R. PLANCHÉ.*]

C. Led Astray (Union Square, New York, 6/12/73; Gai. 1/7/74). L.C. *French.*

D. The Shaughraun (Wallack's, New York, 14/11/74; D.L. 4/9/75). L.C. 4° [1880]; *French*; *Dicks*; *Webster.*

C. Forbidden Fruit (Wallack's, New York, 3/10/76; St J. H. L'pool, 22/10/77; Adel. 3/7/80). L.C.

D. Norah's Vows (Brighton, 6/7/78). L.C. as *Norah.*

D. Rescued; or, A Girl's Romance (Booth's, New York, 4/9/79; K.X. 27/8/79. L.C.

C. Contempt of Court (M'bone, 1/10/79).

C. A Bridal Tour (Wallack's, New York, 1/10/77, as *Marriage*; H. 2/8/80). L.C.

C.D. The O'Dowd; or, Life in Galway (Booth's, New York, 17/3/73, as *Daddy O'Dowd*; Adel. 21/10/80). L.C. *Lacy.*

D. Mimi (Wallack's, New York, 1/7/72; Court, 7/11/81). L.C.

D. The Amadan (Richmond, 29/1/83). L.C.

D. Robert Emmett (P.W. Greenwich, 4/11/84).

C. The Jilt (E.C. 13/5/85, *copy.*; P.W. 29/7/86). L.C. *Lacy.*

D. The Spae Wife (E.C. 30/3/86). L.C.

C. Fin Maccoul (Booth's, New York, 10/8/74, as *Belle Lamar*; E.C. 2/2/87, *mat.*, *copy.*). L.C.

D. Jimmy Watt (E.C. 1/8/90, *copy.*). L.C.

D. 99 (Stand, 5/10/91).
[This play has been attributed to Boucicault, but it is by no means certain that he was the author.]

BOUCICAULT, DION GEORGE
Ca. My Little Girl (Court, 15/2/82). L.C. *French.*
D. Devotion (Court, 1/5/84). L.C.

BOULDING, JAMES WIMSETT
T. Mary Queen of Scots. 8° [1873].
Lyr.D. Satan Bound. 8° 1881.
D. The King Maker (Adel. 15/4/82). L.C.
D. The Double Rose (Adel. 17/6/82). L.C.
D. The White Queen (S.W. 12/10/83; *revised*, Birmingham, 26/6/99; Grand, 17/7/99). L.C.
D. For Wife and State (Lyc. Edinburgh, 19/10/83). See *E. LANCASTER-WALLIS.*
D. Jane Shore (Court, L'pool, 31/8/85, as *The King's Favourite*; Grand, 15/3/86). L.C.
[Written in collaboration with *R. PALGRAVE.*]
R.D. Dorothy Vernon (Ashton, 4/10/89; Sav. 6/10/92, *mat.*). L.C.
D. The Gambler (Roy. 5/12/91). L.C.
D. Harold the Saxon (O.H. Leicester, 21/10/97). L.C.

BOULT, WALTER
Bsq. The Sphinx: A Touch from the Ancients (P.W. L'pool, 6/1/72).

BOURCHIER, ARTHUR
F. The New Baby (Roy. 8/1/96, *copy.*; Gai. Hastings, 6/4/96; Roy. 28/4/96). L.C.
F. A Woman's Tears (Com. 27/6/89).
D. Good-bye (Canterbury, 6/8/89, *amat.*).
C.D. Mr Richards (Shaft. 10/3/92). L.C.
[Written in collaboration with *J. BLAIR.*]
C. The Chili Widow (Roy. 7/9/95). L.C.
[Written in collaboration with *A. SUTRO.*]
D.Sk. Mr versus Mrs (Roy. 4/12/95). L.C.
[Written in collaboration with "*MOUNTJOY*".]

BOURNE, WILLIAM
F. Very Low Spirits (Exeter, 27/11/76). L.C.
Ca. Household Words (Plymouth, 13/2/84).
D. Man to Man (Qns. Manchester, 24/3/84; Sur. 4/7/87). L.C.
D. Work and Wages; or, The Great Strike (Hanley, 27/1/90; Pav. 23/6/90). L.C.
D. A Big Fortune (Blyth, 14/5/91; Sur. 6/7/91). L.C.
D. A London Mystery (Pav. 15/7/95). L.C. Aquar. Great Yarmouth.
D. Two Men (Grand, Cardiff, 7/12/96; W.L. 14/12/96). L.C. O.H. Cheltenham.
[Title altered later to *The Three Criminals.*]
D. Voices of London (Grand, Cardiff, 30/3/99; Stratford, 26/6/99).

BOUSFIELD, FRED
D. Adrift on the World; or, Every Cloud has a Silver Lining (Oriental, 13/4/68). L.C.
F. Bachelors' Wives (Str. 15/12/86, *mat.*). L.C. Colchester.
F.C. The Jockey (Vic.H. Walthamstow, 22/10/94). L.C. as *The Double Event; or, Winning the Winner.*

BOWEN, CYRIL
D. Evening Shadows (Aquar. 17/8/78). L.C.

BOWKETT, SIDNEY

D. A Snowstorm (Gai. 1/10/92). L.C. *French.*
D. The Catspaw (L'pool, 10/4/93).
C.D. Clouds; or, A Broken Faith (Metro. Hotel, Brighton, 20/1/94).
D. The Ne'er-do-well (Str. 22/5/94).
D. What Greater Love L.C. T.H. Streatham, 12/6/94. *French.*
D. The Diamond Rush (Cambridge, 6/2/95). See *G. D. DAY.*
F.C. The Mummy (Roy. Chester, 6/9/95). See *G. D. DAY.*
CO. The Willow Pattern Plate (P.H. Lowestoft, 24/8/97, *copy.*). L.C.
[Music by E. Dean. Written in collaboration with *G. D. DAY.*]
D. The First Violin (Crown, Peckham, 27/3/99). L.C.

BOWLES, EDWARD W.

Bsq. Prince Sohobazar; or, Eighteen Carat Soup (T.H. Kilburn, 11/12/85). L.C.
Bsq. The Water Babes (Nov. 9/2/87; St G. 12/3/89; revised, Leamington, 6/8/94; Parkhurst, 2/12/95). L.C. [both versions].
Ext. Troy Again (St G. 13/3/88, *amat.*). L.C.
C.O. Simon the Smith; or, A Mediæval Strike (Vic.H. 18/4/90). L.C.
[Music by L. N. Parker and M. Clark.]
Bsq. Tawno's Bride (St G. 16/2/92, *amat.*). L.C. T.H. Kilburn, 15/12/91, as *T.B.; or, The Maiden of Myrtlewood Manor.*
[Written in collaboration with *G. R. PHILLIPS.*]
Bsq. The Baron's Daughter; or, Mine Host of the Flagon (West, Albert H. 7/2/93). L.C.
[Written in collaboration with *G. R. PHILLIPS.*]

BOWLES, T. G.

D. The Port Admiral. *French.*

BOWRING, C. C.

C. Pedigree (Lecture H. Derby, 10/12/89, *amat.*; Toole's, 28/3/90). L.C.
[Written in collaboration with *F. H. COURT.*]

BOWYER, FREDERICK

P. Quem Dodo; or, Harlequin Basilio and the Three Wonders (Brit. 26/12/83). L.C.
Bsq. Little Lohengrin; or, The Lover and the Bird (Holb. 16/8/84). L.C. Plymouth, 2/3/81.
P. King Kookoo; or, Harlequin Bon-Bon and the Golden Serpent (Brit. 26/12/84). L.C.
P. Daddy Long Legs (Brit. 26/12/85). L.C.
Oa. The Two Pros (P.W. 4/12/86). L.C. *French.*
[Music by G. Jacobi.]
P. The Goblin Bat; or, Harlequin Meloda and the Little Oof Bird (Brit. 27/12/86). L.C.
Bsq. The Other Little Lord Fondleboy (Aven. 18/6/88, *mat.*).
C. The Parting of the Ways (Terry's, 8/2/90).
[Written in collaboration with *W. EDWARDES-SPRANGE.*]
M.Monol. For Charity's Sake (Terry's, 9/1/93).
[Written in collaboration with *W. H. HEDGECOCK.*]
D. Ragged Robin (P.W. Southampton, 17/3/93).
[Written in collaboration with *W. EDWARDES-SPRANGE.*]
D.Sk. The Phunnygraph (Pleasure Gdns. Folkestone, 28/5/94).
[Written in collaboration with *H. SPARLING.*]

M.F. Claude Duval (P's. Bristol, 23/7/94; P.W. 25/9/94). L.C.
[Written in collaboration with "*PAYNE NUNN*". Music by J. Crook and L. Monckton.]

M.C. The New Barmaid (O.H. Southport, 1/7/95; Metro. 19/8/95; Aven. 12/2/96). L.C.
[Written in collaboration with *W. EDWARDES-SPRANGE*. Music by J. Crook.]

M.C. The White Blackbird (Grand, Croydon, 1/8/98; Grand, 8/8/98). L.C.
[Written in collaboration with *W. EDWARDES-SPRANGE*.]

P. The Babes in the Wood (Grand, 26/12/98). L.C.

BOYCE, WILLIAM

C.O. Hydropathy (Myddleton H. Islington, 26/1/92). L.C.
[Music by A. C. Davies.]

C.O. The Prince of Sauerkrautenberg (St G. 7/3/95). L.C.
[Music by A. C. Davies.]

BOYD, MALCOLM

D. Bonnie Dundee; or, The Last of the Cavaliers (Torquay, 24/2/81; Olym. 22/7/84, as *The Lost Cause*). L.C.

BOYD, WALTER

Ca. Dropped In (Ladb. H. 24/11/93). L.C.

BOYLE, FREDERICK

D. Old London (Qns. 5/2/73). L.C.

BOYNE, WILLIAM

D. The Ladder of Life (Borough, Stratford, 30/5/98). See *C. ROGERS*.

D. The War Correspondent (Sur. 28/11/98). See *Mrs G. CORBETT*.

D. A Soldier's Son (P'cess. of W. 7/8/99). See *C. NEWTON*.
[For his later plays see A. E. Morgan, *op. cit.* p. 307.]

BRABNER, W. A.

D. A Dead Letter (Gai. Dublin, 17/4/91; O.C. 26/9/91).

Ca. Her True Colours (Assembly R. Ruthin, 6/11/91; Aven. 10/6/92, *mat.*). L.C.

D. Kenneth Dunbar, a City Man (Athen. H. Manchester, 29/3/93, *amat.*). L.C.

D. The Queen o' Diamonds (St J. Manchester, 22/12/94). L.C.

D. A Woman's Victory (Pav. 19/8/95).

M.D. The Heiress of Daventry (Metro. Glasgow, 28/6/99, *copy.*). L.C.
[Title altered to *Two Mothers*, 16/3/1919.]

D. For the Colours (Metro. Manchester, 14/8/99; Carleton, Greenwich, 14/4/1902). L.C.

M.D. Dare Devil Max (Metro. 11/12/99). L.C.

BRACEWELL, JOSEPH

D. England, Home and Beauty (Qns. Manchester, 22/8/82). L.C.

F. F.F.F.; or, Fidget's First Floor (Qns. Manchester, 22/8/82). L.C.

F. Up for the Jubilee (Grand, 30/5/87).

BRADBERRY, CHARLES S.

D.O. The Corsican Brothers (C.P. 25/9/88). L.C.
[Music by G. Fox.]

BRADDON, MARY ELIZABETH

Ca. The Loves of Arcadia (Str. 12/3/60). L.C.
D. Griselda; or, The Patient Wife (P'cess. 13/11/73). L.C.
D. Genevieve (Alex. L'pool, 6/4/74).
D. The Missing Witness. 8° [1880].
C. Dross, or, the Root of Evil. 8° [1882].
C. Married beneath him. 8° [1882].
M.D. For Better, for Worse (Westcliff Saloon, Whitby, 6/9/90, *copy.*; Gai. Brighton, 6/4/91). L.C.

BRADFORD, HENRY

D. The Gasman; or, Fight against Fate (Oriental, 14/4/73).

BRADLEY, CHARLES

C. Rosebuds; or, The Old Soldier (Cheltenham, 22/6/85). L.C.
D. Nobly Won (Cheltenham, 22/6/85). L.C.
F. Distraction (Cheltenham, 29/6/85). L.C.

BRADLEY, W. E.

F. The Lord Mayor (Str. 1/11/95). L.C.
[Written in collaboration with *H. PAULTON* and *E. A. PAULTON*.]

BRADSHAW, Mrs ALBERT [*ANNE M. TREE*]

D. The Skyward Guide (Roy. 9/5/95). L.C.
[Written in collaboration with *M. MELFORD*.]

BRADY, E. J.

D. Home Rule (Adel. L'pool, 12/1/80; E.C. 15/3/80). L.C.
D. The Hue and Cry; or, The Kithogue (S. Shields, 16/4/83). L.C. Blyth, 7/12/82.
D. Long Live the Queen (Hednesford, 17/2/87, *copy.*).

BRADY, F.

Bsq. Willy Reilly and his Own Dear Colleen Bawn (M'bone, 5/5/61).

BRADY, WILLIAM

D. Gentleman Jack (D.L. 21/4/94). See *C. T. VINCENT*.

BRAHAM, H.

D. The Spalpeen (Bijou, Paignton, 11/10/75). L.C.

BRAHAM, Captain WARD

F. D'ye know me now? (Reading, 14/6/72).
[Written in collaboration with *N. WELLSEY*.]

BRAMWELL, E. W.

D. The Dead Secret (Lyc. 29/8/77). L.C.

BRAND, OLIVER

Oa. The Mummy (St G. 22/4/84). L.C.
[Music by Gauthier.]
Oa. The Fairy Glen (St G. 22/4/84). L.C.
[Music by P. von Tugginer.]
M.Ca. Fairly Puzzled (St G. 19/5/84). L.C.
[Music by H. Clarke.]

BRAND, OSWALD

D. Milady (Aven. 28/5/85). L.C.
D. Love and Stratagem (Gai. 15/3/86, *mat.*; S.W. 20/6/92). L.C.
[Title altered later to *Leona; or, Love and Stratagem.* Written in collaboration with *E. W. LINGING*.]

F. A Modern Hercules (Grand, 11/10/86). L.C.
C.O. The Magic Ring (Grand, 11/10/86).
[Music by I. Liebich.]
C.O. Mignonette (Roy. 4/8/89). L.C.
[Music by H. Parker.]
D. Agatha; or, The Lawful Wife (S.W. 15/8/92).
M.C. 'Endon Way (Imp. 24/10/98). L.C.
[Title altered to *The Coster's Holiday*, 1/4/1901. Written in collaboration with *C. CALVERT*; music by F. Woodward.]

BRANDON, JOCELYN
Poet.D. The Love that Kills (P.W. 27/1/88, *mat.*). L.C.
Idyll. Only a Dream (Crit. 7/12/88). L.C.
D. The Favourite of the King (Com. 11/3/90). See *F. S. BOAS*.

BRANSCOMBE, ARTHUR
M.F.C. Morocco Bound (Shaft. 13/4/93). L.C.
[Title altered later to *I've seen a Harem*. Lyrics by *A. ROSS*; music by F. O. Carr.]
Bsq. King Kodak (Terry's, 30/4/94). L.C.
M.C. The American Heiress (Birmingham, 3/4/99; Grand, Fulham, 1/5/99; Tyne, Newcastle, 7/8/99, *revised*). L.C.
[Written in collaboration with *G. D. DAY*. Music by H. Simpson, G. Jones, E. Dean and F. Lambert.]

BRANSON, W. S.
D. Dead o' Night Boys (Greenwich, 19/9/74).
D. Never too late to learn (Greenwich, 14/11/74).
P. Harlequin Little Bo Peep and Tom Tucker (Greenwich, 24/12/74).
D. Who's to win? or, The Pool of the Four Willows (M'bone, 18/6/77).
D. A Man of the People; or, The Top of the Ladder and how to get there honestly (L'pool, 17/3/79).

BRASHIER, HENRY
F. A Cure for Foolery (Vic. H. Walthamstow, 21/1/88). See *E. J. JONES*.

BREARE, W. H.
Oa. A Dark Page (T.H. Harrowgate, 19/1/85, *amat.*). L.C.

[*BREITENBACH, ROBERT*
Ent. A Trip to Midget-town (Olym. 1/9/99). L.C.
[Music by V. Holländer.]

BRENNAN, JOHN CHURCHILL
P. Beauty and the Beast; or, Harlequin Mother Gum and the Love Enchanted Roses (Greenwich, 23/12/71).
Bsq. Don Giovanni (Greenwich, 11/3/72).

BRIDGEMAN, JOHN V.
[For an earlier play see iv, 270.]
D. Jessie Gray (Adel. 18/11/50). See *R. B. BROUGH*.
D. Sixtus V (Olym. 17/2/51). See *D. BOUCICAULT*.
F. I've eaten my Friend (Olym. 8/9/51). L.C. *Lacy*.
F. Matrimonial—A Gentleman etc.: for further particulars apply at the Royal Olympic Theatre (Olym. 12/2/52). L.C. *Lacy*.
D. Love or Avarice (Olym. 28/6/53). L.C.
F. A Telegram (Str. 23/11/57). L.C.
F. A Good Run for it (S.W. 13/2/54). L.C. *Lacy*.

F. The Rifle and how to use it (H. 20/9/59). L.C. *French.*
P. Bluebeard; or, Harlequin and Freedom in her Island Home (C.G. 26/12/60). L.C.
O. The Puritan's Daughter (C.G. 30/11/61). L.C.
[Music by M. W. Balfe.]
O. The Armourer of Nantes (C.G. 12/2/63). L.C.
[Music by M. W. Balfe.]
Ca. Where's your Wife? (Str. 21/9/63). L.C. *French.*
D. Sunny Vale Farm (H. 28/11/64). L.C.

BRIDGES, ROBERT SEYMOUR
T. Nero. 8° 1885.
C. The Feast of Bacchus. 8° 1889.
D. Palicio. 8° 1890.
D. The Return of Ulysses. 8° 1890.
D. The Christian Captives. 8° 1890.
D. Achilles in Scyros. 8° 1890.
C. The Humours of the Court. 4° [1893].

BRIDGMAN, CUNNINGHAM
C. Shipmates (Lyc. Sunderland, 3/3/73). L.C. *Lacy.*
C.D. Art (Bijou, Paignton, 24/8/74).
C.D. Devotion and Prejudice (Brighton, 7/9/74). See *R. B. BROUGH.*
Oa. Lovers' Knots (St G. 5/5/80). L.C. *French.*
[Music by W. Bendall.]
Ca. Satisfaction (Bristol, 20/8/80).
Vaud. Quid pro Quo (Dilettante Circle, 10/3/81; St G. 11/12/85, revised as operetta).
[Music by W. Bendall.]
Ca. Under Cover (Gai. 9/1/86). L.C.
C. Mischief (Gai. 23/6/86, *mat.*). L.C.
C.O. Carina (O.C. 27/9/88). See *E. L. BLANCHARD.*
Oa. Love's Trickery (Lyr. 31/8/89). L.C.
[Music by I. Caryll.]
Oa. He stoops to win (Lyr. Club, 15/12/91, *mat.*).

BRIERLEY, BENJAMIN
F. Insuring his Life (Manchester, 24/3/75). L.C. Free Trade H. Manchester, 14/10/72.
D. The Lancashire Weaver Lad (Free Trade H. Manchester, 10/10/77; Com. Manchester, 13/11/85).

BRIGHT, A. ADDISON
D. Ruth (P's. Bristol, 20/3/90, *copy.*). L.C.
[Written in collaboration with *J. K. JEROME.*]
D. The Bugle Call (H. 23/11/99). See *L. N. PARKER.*

BRIGHT, Mrs AUGUSTUS [KATE PITT]
C.D. Not false but fickle (Alex. Sheffield, 22/3/78; Phil. 10/3/80). L.C. *Lacy.*
D.D. Noblesse oblige (Exeter, 4/10/78). L.C. Alex. Sheffield.
D. Bracken Hollow (Alex. Sheffield, 27/11/78).
D. Naomi's Sin; or, Where are you going to, my Pretty Maid? (Alex. Sheffield, 7/5/79). L.C.
D. Dane's Dyke (Sheffield, 22/8/81). L.C.

BRIGHT, EVA

Ca. Tabitha's Courtship (Com. 18/2/90, *mat.*). L.C.
[Written in collaboration with *F. BRIGHT.*]

C.D. Love's Young Dream (Str. 21/4/91, *mat.*). L.C.

BRIGHT, FLORENCE

Ca. Caught out (St G. 17/7/88). L.C.

Ca. Tabitha's Courtship (Com. 18/2/90). See *E. BRIGHT.*

[*BROADHURST, GEORGE H.*

F. What happened to Jones (Vaud. 24/8/97, *copy.*; Grand, Croydon, 30/5/98; Str. 12/7/98). L.C. *French.*

F. Why Smith left home (Grand, Margate, 27/4/99; Str. 1/5/99). L.C. *French.*

C.D. The Last Chapter (Garden, New York, 6/3/99; Str. 4/9/99). L.C. D.Y. 26/5/98.

Oa. The Prince of Borneo (Str. 5/10/99). See *J. W. HERBERT.*

F. The Wrong Mr Wright (Bijou, New York, 6/9/97; Devonshire Park, Eastbourne, 2/11/99; Str. 6/11/99). L.C.

BROCK, FRED

F. Troubled Waters (Bijou, 2/12/99). L.C.

BROCKBANK, JAMES, Jr.

Bsq. The Good Fairy of St Helen's; or, King Coal and his Merry Men (St Helen's, 22/4/72).

C. Life (Cambridge, 7/10/73).

C. The Brothers (Cambridge, 7/8/75).

Ca. Mutual Ground (P'cess. 7/8/75).

BRODIE-INNES, J. W.

D. Ermingarde (Vestry H. Chiswick, 15/12/91; P.W. Club, 23/2/94, as *Ermyngarde in Fairyland*). L.C.

BROKE, BASIL

D. Jealous in Honour (Gar. 27/4/93). L.C.

BROOK, B.

Oa. The Well of Wishes (Ladb. H. 10/5/89).
[Music by J. E. Barkworth.]

BROOKE, CLIVE

C.D. Uncle Thatcher (Court, 1/6/96). L.C.

F.C. The Extraordinary Behaviour of Mrs Jallowby (Nov. 19/12/96). L.C.

M.D. Wanted by the Police (O.H. Chatham, 23/5/98). L.C.

BROOKE, D.

F. The Shopwalker (Myddleton H. Islington, 5/2/92).

BROOKE, E. H. [*EDWIN JAMES MACDONALD BROOK*]

D. Little Em'ly's Trials (S.W. 4/3/71).

D. Gustave (Alex. L'pool, 26/5/73). L.C.

D. Bessie (Roy. 1/5/78). L.C.

BROOKE, H.

C.D. Mr Dick's Heir (Chatsworth, 1/1/95). See *C. CROFTON.*

BROOKFIELD, CHARLES HALLAM ELTON

Monol. Nearly Seven (H. 7/10/82). L.C. *French.*

F.C. Godpapa (Com. 22/10/91). See *F. C. PHILIPS.*

Bsq. The Poet and the Puppets (Com. 19/5/92). L.C.
[Music by J. M. Glover.]
F. The Burglar and the Judge (H. 5/11/92). See *F. C. PHILIPS.*
C. To-day (Com. 5/12/92).
Ca. An Underground Journey (Com. 9/2/93). See *Mrs H. BELL.*
M.C. Poor Jonathan (P.W. 15/6/93). L.C.
[Written in collaboration with *H. GREENBANK.*]
Bsq. A Pal o' Archies' (Pal. 11/7/93). L.C.
[Written in collaboration with *Sir A. HARRIS.* Music by G. M. Glover.]
Ext. Under the Clock (Court, 25/11/93). L.C.
[Written in collaboration with *S. HICKS.* Music by E. Jones.]
Bsq. A Model Trilby; or—A Day or Two after Du Maurier (O.C. 16/11/95). L.C.
[Written in collaboration with *W. YARDLEY.* Music by M. Lutz.]
D. A Woman's Reason (Shaft. 27/12/95). L.C.
[Written in collaboration with *F. C. PHILIPS.*]
Ext. The Mermaids (Aven. 2/10/97). See *W. G. MACKAY.*
O. The Grand Duchess (Sav. 4/12/97). L.C.
[Lyrics by *A. ROSS.* Music by Offenbach.]
C.O. The Lucky Star (Sav. 7/1/99). L.C.
[Lyrics by *A. ROSS* and *A. HOPWOOD.* Music by I. Caryll.]
C. The Cuckoo (Aven. 2/3/99). L.C.
Ca. An Old Admirer (Aven. 23/9/99). L.C.
F. One Law for Man (Crit. 12/12/99). L.C.
D.Sk. Comrades in Khaki (Gar. 15/12/99). L.C.
[For a later play see Davenport Adams, p. 213.]

BROOKLYN, HARTBURY

D. Chandos; or, The Jester who turned Traitor (Adel. 30/9/82). L.C.

BROOKS, CHARLES WILLIAM SHIRLEY

[For his earlier plays see iv, 271.]
D. The Daughter of the Stars (Str. 5/8/50). L.C. *Lacy.*
Ext. The Exposition (Str. 28/4/51). *Lacy.*
D. Number Nip and the Spirit Bride (Adel. 26/12/53). L.C.
[Written in collaboration with *M. LEMON.*]
F. The Lowther Arcade; or, Waiting for an Omnibus on a Rainy Day. L.C. Adel. 24/6/54.
Ext. Timour the Tartar (Olym. 26/12/60). See *J. OXENFORD.*
Ent. Our Card Basket (G.I. 3/4/61).
Ent. The Pyramids; or, Footprints in the Sand (G.I. 7/2/64). L.C.

BROOKS, SHERIDAN

Bsq. Telemachus and Calypso (S.W. 17/4/65). L.C. *Lacy*, as *Calypso, Queen of Ogygia.*

BROUGH, ROBERT BARNABAS

[For his earlier plays see iv, 271.]
Bsq. The Last Edition of Ivanhoe, with all the latest Improvements (H. 1/4/50). L.C.
[Written in collaboration with *W. BROUGH.*]
D. Jessie Gray (Adel. 18/11/50). L.C.
[Written in collaboration with *J. V. BRIDGEMAN.*]

Bsq. The Second Calender; or, The Queen of Beauty who had the Fight with the Genie (H. 26/12/50). L.C. *Nat. Acting Drama.*
[Written in collaboration with *W. BROUGH.*]
Bsq. Arline (H. 21/4/51). See *W. BROUGH.*
F. Kensington Gardens; or, Quite a Lady's Man (Str. 12/5/51). L.C. *Lacy.*
Ext. The Princess Radiant (H. 26/12/51). See *W. BROUGH.*
Ext. The Twelve Labours of Hercules (Str. 26/12/51). L.C. *Lacy.*
— A Cracker Bon-Bon for Christmas Parties. 8° 1852.
Ext. Mephistopheles; or, An Ambassador from Below (Adel. 14/4/52). *Lacy.*
[Written in collaboration with *H. S. EDWARDS.*]
F. The Moustache Movement (Adel. 30/3/54). L.C. *Lacy.*
Ext. The Overland Journey to Constantinople as undertaken by Lord Bateman, with interesting Particulars of the Fair Sophia (Adel. 17/4/54). L.C.
P. Ye Belle Alliance (C.G. 25/12/55). See *W. BROUGH.*
Bsq. Medea; or, The Best of Mothers with a Brute of a Husband (Olym. 14/7/56). L.C. *Lacy.*
F. Crinoline (Olym. 18/12/56). L.C. *Lacy.*
Bsq. Masaniello; or, The Fish-o'-Man of Naples (Olym. 2/7/57). L.C. *Lacy.*
Ext. The Doge of Duralto; or, The Enchanted Eyes (Olym. 26/12/57). L.C. *Lacy.*
Bsq. The Siege of Troy (Lyc. 27/12/58). L.C. as *The Iliad; or, The S. of T.* 8° 1858.
Ext. Alfred the Great; or, The Minstrel King (Olym. 26/12/59). L.C. *Lacy.*
F. Open to Correction (Adel. 10/1/70). L.C.
C.D. Devotion and Prejudice (Brighton, 7/9/74).
[Written in collaboration with *J. V. BRIDGEMAN.*]

BROUGH, WILLIAM

[For his earlier plays see iv, 271.]
Bsq. The Last Edition of Ivanhoe (H. 1/4/50). See *R. B. BROUGH.*
Bsq. The Second Calender (H. 26/12/50). See *R. B. BROUGH.*
Bsq. Arline; or, The Fortunes and Vicissitudes of a Bohemian Girl (H. 21/4/51). L.C. *Lacy.*
[Written in collaboration with *R. B. BROUGH.*]
F. Apartments—Visitors to the Exhibition may be accommodated (P'cess. 14/5/51). *Lacy.*
Ext. The Princess Radiant; or, The Story of the Mayflower (H. 26/12/51). L.C.
[Written in collaboration with *R. B. BROUGH.*]
C.D. The Chameleon; or, The Art of Pleasing (S.W. 10/7/52). L.C. *Lacy.*
D.Sk. Uncle Tom's Crib; or, Nigger Life in London (Str. 18/10/52). L.C.
F. A House out of Windows (Lyc. 18/10/52). L.C. *Lacy.*
F. Those Dear Blacks! (Lyc. 17/11/52). L.C. *Lacy.*
Ext. A Phenomenon in a Smock Frock (Lyc. 13/12/52). L.C. *Lacy.*
Bsq. King Richard Cœur de Lion; or, The Knight of the Couchant Leopard (D.L. 28/3/53). L.C.
F. Trying it on (Lyc. 3/5/53). *Lacy.*

F. How to make Home happy (Lyc. 7/11/53). *Lacy.*
F. Number One round the Corner (Lyc. 12/3/54). L.C. *Lacy.*
D.Sk. Bona Fide Travellers; or, The Romance of the New Beer Bill (Adel. 30/10/54). L.C. *Lacy.*
F. A Comical Countess (Lyc. 27/11/54). L.C. *Lacy.*
Ext. Prince Pretty-Pet and the Butterfly (Lyc. 26/12/54). L.C.
P. Ye Belle Alliance; or, Harlequin Good Humour and ye Fielde of ye Clothe of Golde (C.G. 25/12/55). L.C.
[Written in collaboration with *R. B. BROUGH.*]
Bsq. Perdita, the Royal Milkmaid; or, The Winter's Tale (Lyc. 15/9/56). L.C. *Lacy.*
Bsq.P. Conrad and Medora; or, Harlequin Little Fairy at the Bottom of the Sea (Lyc. 26/12/56). L.C. *Lacy.*
Ext. Lalla Rookh; or, The Princess, the Peri and the Troubadour (Lyc. 24/12/57). L.C. *Lacy.*
F. Seaside Studies (G.I. 20/6/59).
Ext. Dinorah under Difficulties (Adel. 7/11/59). L.C. *Lacy.*
Ext. The Sylphide (P'cess. 9/4/60). L.C. *Lacy.*
Ext. Endymion; or, The Naughty Boy who cried for the Moon (St J. 26/12/60). L.C. *French.*
F. An Illustration in Discord (G.I. 3/4/61).
F. The Census (Adel. 15/4/61). L.C. *Lacy.*
[Written in collaboration with *A. HALLIDAY.*]
F. The Pretty Horsebreaker (Adel. 15/7/61). L.C. *Lacy*; *French.*
[Written in collaboration with *A. HALLIDAY.*]
Ext. Perseus and Andromeda; or, The Maid and the Monster (St J. 26/12/61). L.C. *French.*
Ext. Prince Amabel; or, The Fairy Roses (St J. 5/5/62; St J. 2/9/65, *revised*). L.C. *French.*
Ext. A Shilling Day at the Great Exhibition (Adel. 9/6/62). L.C. *French.*
[Written in collaboration with *A. HALLIDAY.*]
F. The Colleen Bawn settled at last (Lyc. 5/7/62). L.C.
[Written in collaboration with *A. HALLIDAY.*]
Bsq. Rasselas Prince of Abyssinia; or, The Happy Valley (H. 26/12/62). L.C. *French.*
F. A Valentine; or, A Compliment of the Season (Adel. 12/2/63). L.C. *French.*
[Written in collaboration with *A. HALLIDAY.*]
D. The Wooden Spoon Maker (Adel. 13/5/63). See *A. HALLIDAY.*
F. My Heart's in the Highlands (D.L. 9/11/63). L.C. *French.*
[Written in collaboration with *A. HALLIDAY.*]
Ext. King Arthur; or, The Days and Knights of the Round Table (H. 26/12/63). L.C.
Bsq. The Great Sensation Trial; or, Circumstantial Effie Deans (St J.). L.C. St J. 6/4/63.
F. The Area Belle (Adel. 7/3/64). L.C. *French.*
[Written in collaboration with *A. HALLIDAY.*]
F. An April Fool (D.L. 11/4/64). See *A. HALLIDAY.*
Ext. A Shakespearian Reverie: The Bard and his Birthday (G.I. 20/4/64). L.C.
F. The Actor's Retreat (Adel. 11/8/64). See *A. HALLIDAY.*
F. Doing Banting (Adel. 24/10/64). L.C. *Lacy.*
[Written in collaboration with *A. HALLIDAY.*]

Bsq. Hercules and Omphale; or, The Power of Love (St J. 26/12/64). L.C. *Lacy.*

F. Going to the Dogs (D.L. 6/3/65). L.C. *Lacy.*
[Written in collaboration with *A. HALLIDAY.*]

F. Upstairs and Downstairs; or, The Great Percentage Question (Str. 15/5/65). L.C. *Lacy.*
[Written in collaboration with *A. HALLIDAY.*]

Bsq. Ernani; or, The Horns of a Dilemma (Alex. 20/5/65). L.C. *Lacy.*

F. The Mudborough Election (P.W. 13/7/65). L.C. *Lacy.*
[Written in collaboration with *A. HALLIDAY.*]

Bsq. Papillionetta; or, The Prince, the Butterfly and the Beetle (P.W. L'pool, 26/12/65). L.C. *Lacy.*

Ext. Pygmalion and the Statue Fair (Str. 20/4/67). L.C. *Lacy.*

C. Kind to a Fault (Str. 11/11/67). L.C. *Lacy.*

Ext. The Caliph of Bagdad (Str. 26/12/67). L.C. *Lacy.*

Ext. The Field of the Cloth of Gold (Str. 11/4/68). L.C. *Lacy.*

Ext. The Gnome King; or, The Fairy of the Silver Mine (Qns. 26/12/68). L.C. *Lacy.*

Ext. Turko the Terrible; or, The Fairy Roses (Holb. 26/12/68).

Bsq. Joan of Arc (Str. 29/3/69). L.C. *Lacy.*

F.C. Fox versus Goose (Str. 8/5/69). L.C. as *The Goose Chase.*
[Written in collaboration with *J. D. STOCKTON.*]

Bsq. The Flying Dutchman; or, The Demon Seaman and the Lass that loved a Sailor (Roy. 2/12/69). L.C.

BROUGHAM, JOHN

[For his earlier plays see iv, 271–2.]

D. The Irish Immigrant (Vic. 22/5/54). *Lacy*; *Dicks* (as *Temptation; or, The I.I.*)

D. The Actress of Padua (Broadway, New York, 12/5/52; H. 4/5/55). L.C.

Ca. All's Fair in Love and War (S.W. 9/4/59). L.C. *Lacy.*

D. The Gunmaker of Moscow; or, The Black Monk and the Emperor's Secret (Brit. 12/3/60). L.C. *French.*

C. Romance and Reality; or, Truth and Fiction (Grec. 18/7/60). L.C. *Lacy.*
[Apparently a revised form of *Romance and Reality* (P'cess. 1/6/47).]

Oa. Shakspeare's Dream (Academy of Music, N.Y. 2/8/58). *Lacy.*

C. Playing with Fire (Manchester, 3/6/61; P'cess. 28/9/61). L.C. *Lacy.*

D. Night and Morning; or, She's very like her Mother (Wallack's, New York, 15/1/55; Grec. 10/10/61). L.C. *Lacy.*

F. Love and Murder (P'cess. 14/10/61). L.C. *Lacy.*

Ext. Pocahontas; or, The Gentle Savage (Wallack's, New York, 24/12/55; P'cess. 19/10/61; St J. 27/11/69, as *La Belle Sauvage*). L.C. *Lacy.*

D. The Angel of Midnight (P'cess. 15/2/62). L.C.

D. The Duke's Daughter; or, The Hunchback of Paris (Lyc. 10/1/63, as *The Duke's Motto*; Grec. 18/1/64, as *The Duke's Motto*; later as *The Duke's Crest*). L.C. *Lacy.*

D. While there's Life there's Hope (Str. 2/7/63). L.C.

D. Bel Demonio: A Love Story (Lyc. 31/10/63). L.C.

D. The Game of Life; or, The Swallows of Paris (Wallack's, New York, 12/12/53; Sur. 14/11/63). L.C. *Lacy.*

D. Might of Right; or, The Soul of Honour (Ast. 30/1/64). L.C.
D. The Demon Lover (Bowery, New York, 20/10/56; Roy. 10/10/64). L.C. *Lacy*.
D. The Child of the Sun (Ast. 9/10/65). L.C.
D. Caught in the Toils (St J. 14/10/65). L.C.
D. Nellie's Trials; or, Love and Honour (Str. 8/1/66). L.C.
D. Jane Eyre (Laura Keene's, New York, 26/5/56; Sur. 16/11/67). L.C. *Lacy*.
D. Franklin. *Lacy* [1868].
F. Among the Breakers (P.W. L'Pool, 6/6/68; Str. 26/7/69). L.C.
C. Flies in the Web (Manchester, *c.* 1870). *Lacy*.
D.Sk. Captain Cuttle (Gai. 20/11/80).

BROUGHTON, FREDERICK W.

Ca. Withered Leaves (Sheffield, 5/4/75; Terry's, 31/10/92). *French*.
Ca. A Labour of Love (P.W. Birmingham, 22/10/75).
Ca. Ruth's Romance: A Summer's Evening's Sketch (Bath, 6/3/76). L.C. York. *French*.
C. Light and Shade (P.W. Birmingham, 9/11/77; Imp. 29/10/79, *mat.*). L.C. Southampton, 26/3/79.
C.D. A Debt of Honour (W. Hartlepool, 23/1/79). L.C. Halifax.
D. Christine; or, A Dutch Girl's Troubles (Tyne, Newcastle, 21/5/79). L.C. Wigan.
[Written in collaboration with *J. W. JONES*.]
C. Sunshine (Bristol, 5/1/80; Str. 2/6/84). *French*.
C. Runaways (Chester, 6/9/80). L.C.
C. A Good Turn (Chester, 6/9/80). L.C.
D.Sk. Glass Houses (P.W. L'pool, 11/4/81; Swansea, 6/3/93). L.C.
C. Dr Dora (Gar. 18/4/81).
D. Mates (Burnley, 20/6/81). L.C.
M.F. A Simple Sweep (Grand, Leeds, 1/3/82; P'cess. 26/4/82). L.C.
[Music by J. F. Downes.]
C. One Summer's Night (Worcester, 20/3/82; Com. 23/11/89).
D. The Trump Card (Grand, Leeds, 3/4/82). L.C.
[Written in collaboration with *J. W. JONES*.]
C.D. Sisters (P.W. L'pool, 31/3/83). See *H. PETTITT*.
C. Elsie (Glo. 8/9/83). L.C.
D. Before the Mast (Olym. 8/3/84). L.C.
Ca. Once Again (Alex. L'pool, 24/3/84; Lyr. Ealing, 17/2/85; Toole's, 22/8/85). L.C.
[Written in collaboration with *G. W. BROWNE*.]
Ca. Written in Sand (Olym. 29/8/84). L.C. *French*.
Ext. The Circassian (Crit. 19/11/87). L.C. *French*.
Ca. Why Women weep (Crit. 23/1/88).
C. The Poet (Vaud. 4/1/89). L.C.
C.D. A Soldier of Fortune (Jarrow, 16/3/89).
Ca. Her Own Rival (O.C. 13/4/89).
[Written in collaboration with *S. B. LAWRENCE*.]
C. The Beggar (Str. 8/7/89). L.C.
C.D. Caprice (Glo. 22/10/89). L.C.
[A revised version of a play by H. Taylor (Park, New York, 11/8/84).]
C. Fool's Mate (Toole's, 12/12/89, *mat.*; Aven. 1/2/90). L.C.

D. The Bailiff (Bath, 5/4/90; Roy. 17/5/90). L.C. Portsmouth. *French.*
R.D. A Peer of the Realm (Bolton, 4/6/90, *copy.*). L.C. Stratford.
Oa. Edelweiss (O.H. Cork, 3/4/93). L.C. Terry's.
[Music by T. Gmur.]
C.O. Lady Laura's Arcadia (Bijou, 10/7/97).
[Music by F. Pascal.]

BROWN, ALBANY
F. An Appeal to the Audience (St J. 6/12/52).

BROWN, J. R.
F. Cat and Dog (Alex. L'pool, 22/5/71; Roy. 9/3/78). L.C.
F. £100 a Side (S.W. 12/2/81).
Ca. Love's Secret (Ladb. H. 2/1/88). L.C. H. 17/2/86.
O. Adela (Mechanics' H. Nottingham, 8/2/88). L.C.
[Written in collaboration with *T. L. SELBY.*]
F.C. The Linen Draper (Com. 17/4/90). L.C.
[Written in collaboration with *J. F. THORNTHWAITE.*]
Ca. Her Guardian (Roy. 9/3/95).
F.C. The Medium (St Alban's H. Acton Green, 12/10/99). L.C. T.H. Herne Bay.

BROWN, THOMAS
T. Borgia. 8° 1874 [Edinburgh].

BROWN, W. HERON
Oa. The Nuptial Noose (Gai. 20/2/84). L.C. Imp.
[Music by C. Dubois.]
Ext. Amorel of Lyonnesse; or, The Cleverest Man in Town (O.C. 30/12/90, *copy.*).
[Written in collaboration with *S. B. LAWRENCE.*]
D. Suggestion (Lyr. Hammersmith, 21/11/91). See *M. COLLINS.*
F.C. His Other I (Worcester, 20/5/98). See *L. S. OUTRAM.*
R.D. The Three Musketeers (Imp. 25/6/98, *copy.*). L.C.

BROWN, W. M.
D. The Will and the Way; or, The Secret Vault and the Voice of Death (Stand. 16/5/53). L.C.

BROWN, WILLIAM
F. Married from School (Qns. Manchester, 10/3/76). L.C.
C. Bob Bragshawe (O.H. Stockport, 17/8/76). L.C. Qns. Manchester.
C. Mrs Jollybutt's Out; or, A Day at Blackpool (P.W. Rochdale, 15/12/76). L.C. Qns. Manchester, as *M.J.O.; or, Playing at Lovers.*
D. Christopher Tadpole (P.W. Blackpool, 28/9/77). L.C. Qns. Manchester.

BROWNE, GEORGE WALTER
C. Hearts and Homes (York, 11/2/76). L.C.
Ext. The Yellow Dwarf; or, Harlequin King of the Gold Mine, Britannia and the Demon Zulus (York, 14/4/79). L.C.
Milit.D. The Kaffir War (Sanger's, 26/4/79). L.C.
F. A Camera Obscura (Sanger's, 24/10/79). L.C.
C. Ripples (York, 19/11/80). L.C.
[Written in collaboration with *H. MOSS.*]
Ca. Once Again (Alex. L'pool, 24/3/84). See *F. W. BROUGHTON.*
F.C. A Wet Day (Vaud. 21/8/84). L.C.

M.F. Im-patience (P.W. L'pool, 25/8/84). L.C. Vaud.
[Music by F. Stanislaus.]

M.Ca. A Love Game (Lyr. Ealing, 17/2/85; Roy. 21/12/92). L.C. *French.*
[Music by A. T. McEvoy.]

F. Fits and Starts (Gai. 2/5/85). See *J. W. JONES.*

F. Helter Skelter (Alex. Sheffield, 28/6/86). L.C.

D. Clarice; or, Only a Woman (Str. 17/11/86, *mat.*). L.C.
[Written in collaboration with *F. ROBERTS.*]

F. Blue Ribbons (Gai. 11/5/87, *mat.*). L.C.
[Written in collaboration with *J. E. SODEN.*]

M.F. The Bo'sun's Mate (St G. 26/11/88). L.C.
[Music by A. J. Caldicott.]

Oa. Mates (St G. 27/3/90, *mat.*). L.C.
[Music by H. Clarke.]

D.Sk. Possession (St G. 1/12/90). L.C.
[Music by A. J. Caldicott.]

BROWNE, Rev. MARMADUKE

Oa. Christmas Eve (C.G. 13/12/65). See *C. DEFFELL.*

Oa. Five Hundred Francs (Vaud. 6/7/85). L.C.
[Music by G. de Solla.]

O. The Barber of Bagdad (Sav. 9/12/91, *amat.*).

BROWNING, ROBERT

[During this period *Colombe's Birthday* (1844) was acted at the Haymarket (25/4/53). L.C.]

BROWNSON, JOHN H.

D. A Man of No Principle (Hyde, 4/3/95). L.C.

BRUCE, EDGAR

Spect.D. The Highlanders (Portsmouth, 11/11/72).

BRUCE, HARRY P.

Bsq. Faust Reversed; or, The Bells all gone wrong (Hoxton, 2/4/88).

Ext. Sweep for a King (Hoxton, 2/4/88).

Spect.D. Duty; or, Balaclava Heroes (Sunderland, 30/12/89).
[Music by J. Tabrar.]

Spect.D. The Two Hussars (M.H. Sebright, 18/8/90).

D. Hearts (Gloucester, 20/4/91).

D. A Desperate Remedy (Str. 21/4/92, *mat.*). L.C.

D. The Two Hussars (Darwen, 4/8/94). See *W. BURNOT.*
[Apparently a revision of *The Two Hussars* (M.H. Sebright, 18/8/90.]

F.C. A (K)night in Armour (Leith, 5/8/95). See *W. BURNOT.*

D. On Distant Shores (R.A. Woolwich, 18/4/97). See *W. BURNOT.*

F.C. Shadows on the Blind (P.W. L'pool, 27/9/97). See *J. H. DARNLEY.*

F.C. On Guy Fawkes Day (P.W. L'pool, 29/11/97). See *J. H. DARNLEY.*

M.D. The Snares of London (Stratford, 16/4/1900). See *W. BURNOT.*

BRUCE, JOSEPH

D. The Wild Violet (Colne, 13/9/94). L.C.
[Title altered to *The Belle of the West* for Grand, Nelson, 12/5/98.]

BRUMELL, B.
M.F. Our Agency (Aven. 19/7/86).
[Written in collaboration with *W. G. MATCHEM.*]

BRUMMEL, HARRY
F.C. The Chaperon (Bury, 3/8/99, *copy.*). L.C.

BRUNNER, Mme
F. Our Lodgers (Lyc. Sunderland, 26/6/68).

BRUNTON, ANNIE
Ca. The Family Ghost (Hanley, 17/3/81). L.C. Standard.
C.D. The Queen of Diamonds (Coatbridge, 20/3/82).
C.D. Won by Honours (Brighton, 21/4/82; Com. 12/7/82). L.C.

BRUSH, The BROTHERS
Ext. Pallettaria (St G. 4/6/95). L.C.

BRUTON, JAMES
[For his earlier plays see iv, 272.]
F. All in Hot Water (1858).
F. What's your Game? (Sur. 27/9/58). L.C.
F. I will if you will (St J. 13/2/60). L.C.

BRYANT, E.
D. The Danger Signal (Pav. 5/10/67). L.C.

BRYANT, W.
D. Mirza (O.C. 4/11/93). L.C. O.C. 20/10/93 [withdrawn, 7/11/93].

BRYCE, LLOYD
D. Dr Palgrave (Glo. 28/2/94, *copy.*). L.C.

BUCHANAN, R. C.
C. Very, very much engaged (Athen. Glasgow, 16/10/95). See *J. HAWORTH.*

BUCHANAN, ROBERT
T. Wallace (P's. Glasgow, 3/62, *amat.*). L.C. 8° 1856.
D. Canute's Birthday in Ireland. 8° 1868.
— Tragic Dramas from Scottish History and Other Poems. 12° 1868.
[Contains: *The British Brothers, Gaston Phoebus, Edinburga* and *King James the First.*]

BUCHANAN, ROBERT
D. The Rathboys (Stand. 17/5/62).
D. The Witch Finder (S.W. 8/10/64). L.C.
C. A Madcap Prince (H. 3/8/74). L.C.
D. Corinne (Lyc. 26/6/76). L.C.
D. The Nine Days' Queen (Gai. 22/12/80). L.C.
D. The Exiles of Erin; or, St Abe and his Seven Wives (Olym. 7/5/81). L.C.
D. The Shadow of the Sword (Brighton, 9/5/81; Olym. 8/4/82). L.C.
R.D. Lucy Brandon (Imp. 8/4/82). L.C.
D. Storm Beaten (Adel. 14/3/83). L.C.
D. Lady Clare (Glo. 11/4/83). L.C.
D. A Sailor and his Lass; or, Love and Treason (D.L. 15/10/83). L.C. as *Hearts.*
[Written in collaboration with *Sir A. HARRIS.*]
C. Bachelors (H. 1/9/84). L.C. as *Bachelors' Hall.*
[Written in collaboration with *H. VEZIN.*]

C. Agnes (Com. 21/3/85). L.C.
D. Alone in London (Olym. 2/11/85). L.C.
[Written in collaboration with *H. JAY.*]
C. Sophia (Vaud. 12/4/86). L.C.
Poet.C. A Dark Night's Bridal (Vaud. 9/4/87). L.C.
D. The Queen of Connaught (P.W. Salford, 1/8/87).
C.D. The Blue-bells of Scotland (Nov. 12/9/87). L.C.
C. Fascination (Nov. 6/10/87). See *H. JAY.*
C. Partners (H. 5/1/88). L.C.
C.D. Joseph's Sweetheart (Vaud. 8/3/88, *mat.*). L.C.
D. Roger-la-Honte; or, Jean the Disgraced (E.C. 29/11/88, *copy.*; H. 12/9/89, as *A Man's Shadow*). L.C. [two versions].
C. That Doctor Cupid (Vaud. 14/1/89, *mat.*). L.C.
C.D. The Old Home (Vaud. 19/6/89, *mat.*; Vaud. 21/6/89). L.C.
D. Theodora (Brighton, 18/11/89; P'cess. 5/5/90). L.C.
D. The Man and the Woman (Crit. 19/12/89, *mat.*). L.C.
C. Miss Tomboy (Vaud. 20/3/90, *mat.*; Vaud. 26/5/91). L.C.
Poet.D. The Bride of Love (Adel. 21/5/90, *mat.*; Lyr. 9/6/90). L.C.
D. Clarissa (Vaud. 8/2/90). L.C.
C. Sweet Nancy (Lyr. 12/7/90). L.C.
D. An English Rose (Adel. 2/8/90). See *J. P. SIMPSON.*
D. The Struggle for Life (Aven. 25/9/90). L.C.
[Written in collaboration with *F. HORNER.*]
R.D. The Sixth Commandment (Shaft. 8/10/90). L.C.
D. Marmion (Glasgow, 8/4/91). L.C.
D. The Gifted Lady (Aven. 2/6/91). L.C. as *Heredity.*
D. The Trumpet Call (Adel. 1/8/91). See *J. P. SIMPSON.*
R.D. The White Rose (Adel. 23/4/92). See *J. P. SIMPSON.*
D. The Lights of Home (Adel. 30/7/92). L.C.
[Written in collaboration with *G. R. SIMS.*]
D. The Black Domino (Adel. 1/4/93). See *J. P. SIMPSON.*
O. The Piper of Hamelin (Com. 20/12/93). L.C. 8° 1893.
[Music by F. W. Allwood.]
D. The Charlatan (H. 18/1/94). L.C.
C. Dick Sheridan (Com. 3/2/94). L.C.
C.D. Lady Gladys (O.C. 7/5/94, *copy.*). L.C.
C. A Society Butterfly (O.C. 10/5/94). L.C.
[Written in collaboration with *H. MURRAY.*]
F. The Strange Adventures of Miss Brown (Vaud. 26/6/95). L.C. *French.*
[Written in collaboration with *H. JAY.*]
C.D. The New Don Quixote (Roy. 19/2/96, *copy.*). L.C.
[Written in collaboration with *H. JAY.*]
C. The Romance of the Shopwalker (Colchester, 24/2/96; Vaud. 26/2/96). L.C.
[Written in collaboration with *H. JAY.*]
C. The Wanderer from Venus (Grand, Croydon, 8/6/96). L.C.
[Written in collaboration with *H. JAY.*]
R.D. The Mariners of England (Grand, Nottingham, 1/3/97; Olym. 9/3/97). L.C.
[Written in collaboration with *H. JAY.*]
C.D. Two Little Maids from School (Metro. Camberwell, 21/11/98). See *H. JAY.*

BUCKINGHAM, LEICESTER SILK

C.D. Aggravating Sam (Lyc. 6/12/54). L.C. *Lacy.*
[This appeared under the name of C. J. Matthews; but it seems to have been from Buckingham's pen.]

F. Take that Girl away (Lyc. 5/3/55). L.C. *Lacy.*

Ext. Belphegor (Str. 29/9/56). L.C. *Lacy.*

F. Don't lend your Umbrella (Str. 26/1/57). *Lacy.*

F. Do shake Hands (Str. 16/3/57).

Bsq. William Tell: A Telling Version of an Old Tell-Tale (Str. 13/4/57; Str. 27/6/57, *revised*). L.C. *Lacy.*

Bsq. La Traviata; or, The Lady Cameleon (Str. 7/9/57). L.C.

P. Harlequin Novelty and the Princess who lost her Heart (Str. 24/12/57). L.C. *Lacy.*

F. Quixote Junior (Str. 13/7/59). L.C.

Bsq. Virginius; or, The Trials of a Fond Papa (St J. 1/10/59). L.C. *French.*

C. Cupid's Ladder (St J. 29/10/59). L.C.

Bsq. Lucrezia Borgia at Home and All Abroad (St J. 9/4/60). L.C. *Lacy.*

F. Jeannette's Wedding (P'cess. 9/10/61). *Lacy.*
[Written in collaboration with *A. G. HARRIS.*]

Ext. Little Red Riding Hood; or, The Fairies of the Rose, the Shamrock and the Thistle (Lyc. 26/12/61). L.C. *Lacy.*

Ext. Pizarro (Str. 21/4/62). L.C.

C. The Merry Widow (St J. 31/1/63). L.C. *French.*

C. Silken Fetters (H. 14/11/63). L.C. *French.*

C. A Silver Lining (St J. 30/1/64). L.C. *French.*

Ca. Love's Young Dream (Roy. 28/3/64). L.C.

C. Faces in the Fire (St J. 25/2/65). L.C. *Lacy.*

D. Love's Martyrdom (Olym. 25/4/66). L.C. *Lacy.*

F. A Fretful Porcupine (Adel. 20/4/67). L.C.

BUCKLAND, JAMES

C.D. Men and Women. L.C. (Kilburn, 3/6/99, *copy.*).

BUCKLAND, WARWICK

D. Foiled (St G. 25/10/90). L.C.

D. The Sorrow of a Secret (Ladb. H. 28/3/92). L.C.

BUCKLAW, A.

C.D. Baby's Birthday. L.C. Assembly R. Kennington, 21/3/93.

BUCKLE, GEORGE

F. Paired Off (Stratford, 4/85). L.C.

BUCKLE, H. OSBORNE

D. The Duke's Boast (Aven. 21/3/89, *mat.*). L.C. Glo. 21/12/88, as *The Duke's Wager.*

BUCKLEY, F. R.

D.D. For an Old Debt (Bijou, 26/2/95). L.C.
[Written in collaboration with *J. H. PANTING.*]

BUCKNALL, EDWARD

C. Heiress Hunting (H.M. Richmond, 27/2/82). L.C. as *Hunting an Heiress.*

BUCKSTONE, JOHN BALDWIN

[For his earlier plays see iv, 272–5.]

C. Leap Year; or, The Ladies' Privilege (H. 15/1/50). L.C. *Dicks*; *Lacy*.
C.D. Good for Nothing (H. 4/2/51). L.C. *Dicks*; *Lacy*.
C.D. Grandmother Grizzle (H. 10/9/51). L.C.
C. The Foundlings (H. 16/6/52). L.C.
P. Harlequin and the Three Bears; or, Little Silver Hair and the Fairies (H. 26/12/53). L.C.
P. Little Bo-Peep; or, Harlequin and the Girl who lost her Sheep (H. 26/12/54). L.C.
C.D. Married for Money (H. 14/8/57).
P. The Sleeping Beauty in the Wood (H. 26/12/57). L.C.
M.C. Josephine, the Child of the Regiment (Lyc. 5/8/58).
[A revision of his *Josephine* (H. 7/3/44.]
P. Little Miss Muffett and Little Boy Blue; or, Harlequin and Old Daddy Long Legs (H. 26/12/61). L.C.
C. The Little Treasure (P'cess. 31/3/62).
C. Brother Sam (H. 24/5/65). See *J. OXENFORD*.

BUENN, MICHEL
D. The Sensualist (O.H. Northampton, 18/12/91, *copy.*; same theatre, 27/6/92). L.C.
[Written in collaboration with *F. A. LAIDLAW*. The title was altered to *Her Hero*, 28/7/93, and to *It is Fate*, 30/5/94.]

BULLOCK, J. M.
O. The Earthly Twins (St J. 6/7/96). See *T. H. LEWIS*.

BUNN, ALFRED
[For his earlier plays see iv, 276.]
O. The Sicilian Bride (D.L. 6/3/52). L.C. *Chappell*.
[Music by M. W. Balfe.]
O. The Devil's in it (Sur. 26/7/52). L.C.
[Music by M. W. Balfe.]

BUNNER, H. C.
Oa. The Land of Pie (Great Meeting School, Leicester, 17/1/99).
[Music by C. R. W. Cuckson.]

BURBEY, E. J.
D. John Aylmer's Dream (Sheffield, 6/9/86).

BURFORD, U.
C.D. The Fair Bigamist (Roy. 20/9/88). L.C.

BURGESS, GILBERT
Oa. The Wooden Spoon (Traf. 26/9/92). L.C.
[Music by Hope Temple.]

BURGIN, G. B.
C. Allendale (Str. 14/2/93). See *E. PHILLPOTTS*.

BURNAND, FRANCIS COWLEY
Bsq. Guy Fawkes Day (Worthing, 8/9/52).
F. Villikins and his Dinah; or, The Cup of Cold Poison (Sur. 27/2/54). L.C. *Lacy*.
Bsq. Alonzo the Brave; or, Faust and the Fair Imogene (Str. 5/2/55). L.C. *Lacy*.
F. Romance under Difficulties (Cambridge, 1856). *Lacy*.
Ext. Lord Lovel and Lady Nancy Bell; or, The Bounding Brigade of the Bakum-boilum (A.D.C. Cambridge, 11/56). *Lacy*.

Bsq. Dido, the Celebrated Widow (St J. 11/2/60). L.C.
[Acted as *The Widow Dido* (Roy. 20/11/65).]

F. B.B.; or, The Benicia Boy (Olym. 22/3/60). L.C.
[Written in collaboration with *M. WILLIAMS.*]

F. A Volunteer's Ball (Str. 19/7/60). L.C.

D. The Isle of St Tropez (St J. 20/12/60). See *M. WILLIAMS.*

F. A Turkish Bath (Adel. 29/4/61). L.C. *French.*
[Written in collaboration with *M. WILLIAMS.*]

F. Deerfoot (Olym. 16/12/61). L.C. *French.*

Ext. The King of the Merrows; or, The Prince and the Piper (Olym. 26/12/61). L.C. *Lacy.*
[Written in collaboration with *J. P. SIMPSON.*]

Ext. Fair Rosamond; or, The Maze, the Maiden and the Monarch (Olym. 21/4/62). L.C. *French.*

Ext. Robin Hood; or, The Forester's Fate (Olym. 26/12/62). L.C. *French.*

Ca. Carte de Visite (St J. 26/12/62). See *M. WILLIAMS.*

Ext. Acis and Galatea; or, The Nimble Nymph and the Terrible Troglodyte (Olym. 6/4/63). L.C.

F. Easy Shaving (H. 11/6/63). L.C. *French.*
[Written in collaboration with *M. WILLIAMS.*]

D. The Deal Boatman (D.L. 21/9/63). L.C. as *The Boatman of Deal. French.*

Ext. Ixion; or, The Man at the Wheel (Roy. 28/9/63). L.C. *French.*

Bsq. Patient Penelope; or, The Return of Ulysses (Str. 25/11/63). L.C. *Lacy.*
[Written in collaboration with *M. WILLIAMS.*]

Ca. Madame Berliot's Ball; or, The Chalet in the Valley (Roy. 26/12/63). L.C. *Lacy.*

Ext. Rumpelstiltskin and the Maid; or, The Woman at the Wheel (Roy. 28/3/64). L.C. *French.*

Bsq. Venus and Adonis; or, The Two Rivals and the Small Boar (H. 28/3/64). L.C. *French.*

Ext. Faust and Marguerite: 'An Im-morality' (St J. 9/7/64). L.C.

Ext. Snowdrop; or, The Seven Mannikins and the Magic Mirror (Roy. 21/11/64). L.C. *Lacy.*

Bsq. Cupid and Psyche; or, Beautiful as a Butterfly (Olym. 26/12/64). L.C.

Ent. The Foster Brothers (St G. 1865).
[Written in collaboration with *K. HALL.*]

F. Too Many by One (St G. 1865).
[Written in collaboration with *F. COWAN.*]

Bsq. Pirithous, the Son of Ixion (Roy. 13/4/65). L.C. *Lacy.*

Bsq. Ulysses; or, The Ironclad Warriors and the Little Tug of War (St J. 17/4/65). L.C. *Lacy.*

Bsq. Windsor Castle (Str. 5/6/65). L.C. *Lacy.*
[Written in collaboration with *M. WILLIAMS.* Music by F. Musgrave.]

Bsq. L'Africaine; or, The Queen of the Cannibal Islands (Str. 18/11/65). L.C.
[Written in collaboration with *M. WILLIAMS.*]

Bsq. Paris; or, Vive Lemprière (Str. 2/4/66). L.C. *Lacy.*

Ent. A Yachting Cruise (G.I. 2/4/66). L.C.

Ext. Boabdil el Chico; or, The Moor the Merrier (Ast. 2/4/66). L.C.

Bsq. Helen; or, Taken from the Greek (Adel. 30/6/66). L.C. *Lacy.*
Bsq. Der Freischutz; or, A Good Cast for a Piece (Str. 8/10/66). L.C.
[Music by F. Musgrave.]
Bsq. Antony and Cleopatra; or, History and Her-story in a Modern Milo-metre (H. 21/11/66). L.C.
Bsq. The Latest Edition of Black-eyed Susan; or, The Little Bill that was taken up (Roy. 29/11/66). L.C. *Lacy.*
[Written in collaboration with *M. WILLIAMS.*]
Bsq. Guy Fawkes; or, The Ugly Mug and the Couple of Spoons (Str. 26/12/66). L.C.
[Music by F. Musgrave.]
Bsq. Olympic Games; or, The Major, the Miner and the Cock-a-doodle-do (Olym. 22/4/67). L.C. 8° 1867.
M.F. Cox and Box; or, The Long-Lost Brothers (Adel. 11/5/67 (*amat.*); G.I. 29/3/69). *Lacy.*
[Written in collaboration with *J. M. MORTON.* Music by Sir A. Sullivan.]
Bsq. Mary Turner; or, The Wicious Willin and Wictorious Wirtue (Holb. 25/10/67). L.C. *Lacy.*
C.O. The Contrabandista; or, The Lord of the Ladrones (St G. 18/12/67). L.C.
[Music by Sir A. Sullivan.]
C. Humbug (Roy. 19/12/67). L.C. *Lacy.*
Ext. The White Fawn; or, The Loves of Prince Buttercup and the Princess Daisy (Holb. 13/4/68). L.C. *Lacy.*
Ext. Hit or Miss; or, All my Eye and Betty Martin (Olym. 13/4/68). L.C.
Bsq. Fowl Play; or, A Story of Chicken Hazard (Qns. 20/6/68). L.C.
Oa. Enquire within (G.I. 20/7/68). L.C.
Bsq. The Rise and Fall of Richard III; or, A New Front to an Old Dicky (Roy. 24/9/68). L.C.
Bsq. The Frightful Hair (H. 26/12/68). L.C.
P. Fayre Rosamond; or, Harlequin Henry the Second, the Monarch, the Mazed Maid and the Maize of the Churchmen (Greenwich, 26/12/68).
[See *Fayre Rosamond* under *UNKNOWN AUTHORS.*]
Bsq. Claude Duval; or, The Highwayman for the Ladies (Roy. 22/1/69). L.C.
C.O. The Girls of the Period; or, The Island of Nowarpartickeler Folley (D.L. 25/2/69). L.C. 8° 1869.
M.Ca. The Military Billy Taylor; or, The War in Carriboo (Roy. 22/4/69). L.C.
D. The Turn of the Tide (Qns. 29/5/69). L.C.
Bsq. Very Little Faust and More Mephistopheles (Ch.X. 18/8/69). L.C.
Bsq. The Beast and the Beauty; or, No Rose without a Thorn (Roy. 4/10/69). L.C.
D. Morden Grange (Qns. 4/12/69). L.C.
Bsq. Sir George and a Dragon; or, We are seven (Str. 31/3/70). L.C.
Ext. F.M. Julius Caesar; or, The Irregular Rum'un (Roy. 7/9/70). L.C.
Bsq. E—liz—abeth; or, The Don, the Duck, the Drake and the Invisible Armada (Vaud. 17/11/70). L.C.
Bsq. The White Cat; or, Prince Lardi-Dardi and the Radiant Rosetta (Glo. 26/12/70). L.C. *Lacy.*

D. Dead Man's Point; or, The Lighthouse on the Carn Ruth (Adel. 4/2/71). L.C. *Lacy*.

Bsq. Poll and Partner Joe (St J. 6/5/71). L.C. as *My Poll and My Partner Joe*.

Ext. All about the Battle of Dorking; or, My Grandmother (Alh. 7/8/71). L.C.
[Written in collaboration with *A. SKETCHLEY*. Music by T. Hermann.]

D. Paul Zegers; or, The Dream of Retribution (Alfred, 13/11/71). L.C.

Bsq. Arion; or, The Story of a Lyre (Str. 20/12/71). L.C.

Vaud. My Aunt's Secret (St G. 3/3/72) L.C.

Bsq. King Kokatoo; or, Who is who and which is which? (Leeds, 4/3/72).

C.O. La Vie Parisienne in London (Holb. 30/3/72). L.C.

C.O. Little Chang (Tyne, Newcastle, 6/5/72).

Oa. Very Catching (G.I. 18/11/72). L.C.
[Written in collaboration with *J. L. MOLLOY*.]

M.Ca. Mildred's Well: A Romance of the Middle Ages (G.I. 5/5/73). L.C.
[Written in collaboration with *G. REED*.]

Bsq. Kissi-Kissi; or, The Pa, the Ma and the Padishah (O.C. 12/7/73).
[A revised version of *King Kokatoo* (Leeds, 4/3/72).]

Ext. La Belle Hélène (Alh. 16/8/73).
[A revised version of *Helen* (Adel. 30/6/66).]

Bsq. Our Own Anthony and Cleopatra (Gai. 8/9/73). L.C.

Ext. Little Tom Tug; or, The Freshwater Man (O.C. 12/11/73). L.C.

Ext. The Great Metropolis; or, The Wonderful Adventures of Daddy Daddles and his Son in their Journey from Stoke-in-the-Mud to Venice, via London, with Diddler's Tourist Tickets (Gai. 6/4/74). L.C. 8° [n.d.].

D. Archie Lovell (Roy. 16/5/74). L.C.

Ext. He's coming via Slumborough, Snoozleton and Shoreham. L.C. St G. 16/5/74.

Bsq. Here's Another Guy Mannering (Vaud. 23/5/74).

Oa. One too many. L.C. St G. 24/6/74. *French*.

C. Better Late than Never (Roy. 27/6/74). L.C.

Ext. Ixion Rewheeled (O.C. 21/11/74). L.C.

Ent. A Tale of Old China (St G.). L.C. St G. 6/4/75.
[Written in collaboration with *J. L. MOLLOY*.]

C. Proof Positive (O.C. 16/10/75). L.C.

Bsq. On the Rink; or, The Girl he left behind him (Duke's, 26/2/76). L.C.

M.Ca. Matched and Mated (St G.). L.C. St G. 2/11/76.
[Written in collaboration with *G. REED*.]

F. Artful Cards (Gai. 24/2/77). L.C.

Bsq. Our Babes in the Wood; or, The Orphans Released (Gai. 2/4/77). L.C.

M.Ca. Number 204 (St G.). L.C. St G. 28/4/77.

C.O. King Indigo (Alh. 24/9/77). L.C.
[Music by J. Strauss.]

F. Family Ties (Str. 29/9/77). L.C.

F. A Musical Box (Gai. 1/10/77). L.C.

Bsq. The Red Rover (Str. 26/12/77). L.C.

M.Ca. Answer Paid (St G.). L.C. St G. 23/1/78.
[Written in collaboration with *W. J. AUSTIN*.]
P. The Forty Thieves (Gai. 13/2/78). See *H. J. BYRON*.
Bsq. Dora and Diplunacy; or, A Woman of Uncommon Scents (Str. 14/2/78; Traf. 6/5/93, as *Diplunacy*). L.C.
D. Proof; or, A Celebrated Case (Adel. 20/4/78). L.C. *French.*
C. Our Club (Str. 9/5/78). L.C.
F.C. Jeames (Gai. 26/8/78). L.C.
Vaud. A Tremendous Mystery (St G. 11/78). L.C.
[Written in collaboration with *K. HALL*.]
Bsq. Over-Proof; or, What was found in a Celebrated Case (Roy. 6/11/78). L.C.
Bsq. The Hunchback back again; or, Peculiar Julia (Olym. 23/12/78). L.C. 8° (1879).
F.C. Boulogne (Gai. 30/4/79). L.C.
C. Betsy (Crit. 6/8/79). L.C. *Lacy.*
F.C. Unlimited Cash (Gai. 27/10/79). L.C.
Bsq. Robbing Roy; or, Scotched and Kilt (Gai. 11/11/79). L.C. 8° (1879).
Ext. Balloonacy; or, A Flight of Fancy (Roy. 1/12/79). L.C.
[Music by E. Solomon. Written in collaboration with *H. P. STEPHENS*.]
C. Ourselves (Vaud. 29/1/80). L.C.
Bsq. The Corsican Brothers and Co., Limited (Gai. 25/10/80). L.C.
[Written in collaboration with *H. P. STEPHENS*.]
M.Sk. Sandford and Merton's Christmas Party (St G. 27/12/80). L.C.
[Music by A. S. Gatty.]
P. Valentine and Orson; or, Harlequin and the Magic Shield (C.G. 27/12/80). L.C.
C. The Colonel (P.W. 2/2/81). L.C.
Bsq. Whittington and his Cat (Gai. 15/10/81). L.C.
C. A Lesson (H. 26/11/81). L.C.
F. The Manager (Court, 15/2/82). L.C.
Bsq. Blue Beard; or, The Hazard of the Dye (Gai. 12/3/83). L.C.
Bsq. Stage Dora; or, Who Killed Cock Robin? (Toole's, 26/5/83). L.C.
Bsq. Ariel (Gai. 8/10/83). L.C.
Bsq. Camaralzaman (Gai. 31/1/84). L.C.
Bsq. Paw Clawdian; or, The Roman Awry (Toole's, 14/2/84). L.C.
C.D. Just in Time (Aven. 12/11/84). L.C.
Bsq. Mazeppa (Gai. 12/3/85). L.C.
Bsq. The O'Dora; or, A Wrong Accent (Toole's, 13/7/85). L.C.
P. Cinderella (C.P. 22/12/85). L.C.
Bsq. Faust and Loose; or, Brocken Vows (Toole's, 4/2/86). L.C.
C. The Doctor (Glo. 9/7/87). L.C.
Bsq. Airey Annie (Str. 4/4/88). L.C.
M.F. Pickwick (Com. 7/2/89, *mat.*; Traf. 13/12/93). L.C.
[Music by E. Solomon.]
C. The Headless Man (Crit. 27/7/89). L.C.
Bsq. Tra-la-la Tosca; or, The High-toned Soprano and the Villain Base (Roy. 9/1/90). L.C.
Oa. Domestic Economy (Com. 7/4/90).
[Music by E. Solomon.]
M.F. The Tiger (St J. 3/5/90).
[Music by E. Solomon.]

C.O. Captain Thérèse (P.W. 25/8/90). L.C.
[Music by R. Planquette.]
C.O. La Cigale (Lyr. 9/10/90). L.C.
[Music by E. Audran.]
F.C. Private Enquiry (O.H. Leicester, 25/11/90; Str. 7/1/91). L.C.
C.O. Miss Decima (Crit. 23/7/91). L.C.
[Lyrics by *P. REEVE*. Music by E. Audran.]
F. The Saucy Sally (O.H. Southport, 1/7/92; Com. 10/3/97). L.C.
C.O. Incognita (Lyr. 6/10/92). L.C.
[Lyrics by *H. GREENBANK*. Music by C. Lecocq.]
C. The Orient Express (Daly's, 25/10/93). L.C.
F.C. Sandford and Merton (Com. 20/12/93). L.C.
[Music by E. Solomon.]
F.C. A Gay Widow (Court, 20/10/94). L.C.
O. The Chieftain (Sav. 12/12/94). L.C.
[Music by Sir A. Sullivan. A revised version of *The Contrabandista* (St G. 18/12/67).]
F.C. Mrs Ponderbury's Past (Aven. 2/11/95). L.C.
[Also acted as *Mrs Ponderbury*.]
M.C. The Telephone Girl (Grand, Wolverhampton, 25/5/96). See *Sir A. HARRIS*.
C.O. His Majesty; or, The Court of Vignolia (Sav. 20/2/97). L.C.
[Written in collaboration with *R. C. LEHMANN*. Music by Sir A. C. Mackenzie.]
F. The Lady of Ostend (Bournemouth, 19/6/99; Terry's, 5/7/99). L.C. Gai. 31/12/97, as *Number Nine; or, The Lady of Ostend*.
F. In for a Holiday. *Lacy*.

BURNE, ARTHUR E.
M.C. A Trip to Brighton (P's. Harwich, 7/8/99). See *T. SEYMOUR*.

BURNET, WALTER
Bsq. Damon and Pythias (Soho, 1860). L.C. Soho, 14/12/59.

[*BURNETT, Mrs FRANCES HODGSON*
C.D. Young Folks' Ways (Madison Square, New York, 29/10/81, as *Esmeralda*; St J. 20/10/83). L.C.
[Written in collaboration with *W. GILLETTE*.]
C.D. The Real Little Lord Fauntleroy (Terry's, 14/5/88, *mat.*). L.C.
C.D. Phyllis (Glo. 1/7/89, *mat.*). L.C.
D. Editha's Burglar (Bijou, Neath, 3/1/90). L.C. Stratford.
[Written in collaboration with *S. TOWNSEND*.]
D. Nixie (Terry's, 7/4/90, *mat.*).
[Written in collaboration with *S. TOWNSEND*.]
C.D. A Lady of Quality (Ladb. H. 7/3/96, *copy.*; New, Cambridge, 23/2/99; Com. 8/3/99). L.C.
[Written in collaboration with *S. TOWNSEND*.]

BURNETT, HERBERT
F. Hazard (Margate, 1/7/91). L.C.
D. The End of a Day (Roy. 5/12/91). L.C.
D.Sk. Out of the World (Vaud. 23/2/92, *mat.*). L.C.

BURNETT, J. P.
D. Bleak House (P.W. L'pool, 8/11/75; Glo. 21/2/76, as *Jo*).
C. Midge (Gai. Dublin, 23/5/79). See *R. J. MARTIN*.
C. Good Luck; or, The Chances of the Cards (Str. 13/4/85). L.C.

BURNETTE, CLARENCE

D. Mad Meg (Workington, 9/11/85).

D. A Man in a Thousand (N. Shields, 11/8/90; Sur. 7/3/92, as *Beaten at Last; or, A M. in a T.*). L.C. Grand, Douglas, Isle of Man.

M.C. Surprises; or, A Day at Coney Island (Workington, 3/10/90).

D. Our Guardian Angel (provinces, 8/95; Nov. 6/1/96). L.C. P'cess. Leith, 8/8/95.

D. The Dawn of Hope (Nov. 20/1/96). L.C. Warrington, 1/9/88. [Written in collaboration with *H. B. COOPER.*]

D. A Border Heroine (Blyth, 29/6/96).

BURNEY, ESTELLE

C.D. The County (Terry's, 2/6/92, *mat.*). L.C. [Written in collaboration with *A. BENHAM.*]

Duol. An Idyll of the Closing Century (Lyc. 2/12/96). *French.*

C.D. Settled out of Court (Glo. 3/6/97). L.C.

Duol. The Ordeal of the Honeymoon (P.W. 9/5/99). L.C.

BURNLEY, JAMES

C.D. Fetters (Bradford, 13/12/75). L.C. 8° 1876 [*priv.*; Bradford].

D. The Shadow of the Mill (Pullan's, Bradford, 24/8/85). L.C.

BURNOT, WALTER

P. Old Mother Goose and the Golden Eggs; or, Harlequin Riddle Me, Riddle Me Ree; or, Come and see what this will be (E.C. 26/12/82). L.C.

Bsq. The German Silvery King (E.C. 24/3/83). L.C.

C.D. Good Old Barnes of New York (Ladb. H. 25/9/88, *copy.*).

D. The Two Hussars (Darwen, 4/8/94; York, 17/2/96, *revised*; Sur. 8/6/96). L.C. [Written in collaboration with *H. P. BRUCE.*]

F.D. A (K)night in Armour (Leith, 5/8/95; Sur. 5/7/97). L.C. [Written in collaboration with *H. P. BRUCE.*]

D. On Distant Shores (R.A. Woolwich, 18/4/97; Aldershot, 2/5/98; Stratford, 29/4/1901). L.C. [Written in collaboration with *H. P. BRUCE.*]

M.D. The Snares of London (Stratford, 16/4/1900). L.C. P's. Llandudno, 22/12/99. [Written in collaboration with *H. P. BRUCE* and *M. TREVOSPER.*]

"*BURNS, CORRIE.*" See *E. RIGHTON*

BURNSIDE, THOMAS

F.C. Coercion (Gai. 17/11/86). See *W. H. DENNY.*

BURNSIDE, WILLIAM

C. The Duke of Swindleton (O.C. 11/6/85). L.C.

F.C. All Abroad (Parkhurst, 10/12/92). L.C.

BURROW, C. K.

D. Honours Divided (St Benet's Church R. Lupton Street, N.W. 14/5/95). [Written in collaboration with *W. BENINGTON.*]

BURSLEM, CHARLES

F. A Lover's Ruse (Dewsbury, 27/10/73).

C. Men o' Sense (Dewsbury, 5/4/76).

C. Heads and Hearts (Dewsbury, 20/8/77). L.C.

BURTON, Mrs

Oa. The Repentance of King Aethelred the Unready (Shrewsbury, 31/1/87).

[Music by W. Hay.]

BURTON, A. E.

Ext. The Wilful Beauty (St G. 14/11/85).

BURTON, E. G.

D. The Lad of the Village; or, The Sporting Boots of the Inn. L.C. Pav. 10/6/50.

D. The White Spirit; or, The Dauntless Boy of the Lake L.C. Pav. 10/11/50.

D. The Warrior Boy; or, Innate Heroism (Vic. 21/7/51). L.C.

BURTON, J. BLOUNDELLE

D. The Silent Shore (Olym. 8/5/88, *mat.*). L.C.

BURTON, JOHN

Oa. Arcadie (Margate, 17/9/88). L.C.

[Music by F. Willoughby.]

BUSCH, WILLIAM

C.D. Dr Syntax the Hypnotist (Adel. L'pool, 24/9/94). L.C.

BUSH, E. H.

Oa. Red, White and Blue (Vaudeville Club, Walworth, 3/2/75).

[Music by E. A. Stunt.]

BUSSY, BERNARD F.

R.D. The Roundhead (C.P. 12/6/83; Terry's, 20/2/91, *mat.*). L.C. *Lacy.*

[Written in collaboration with *W. T. BLACKMORE.*]

C.D. Freda (Str. 19/7/87). L.C. as *Daisy.*

[Written in collaboration with *W. T. BLACKMORE.*]

BUSSY, F. MOIR

D. Sealed to Silence (Str. 10/4/96). L.C.

[Written in collaboration with *H. M. HOLLES.*]

BUTLER, ARTHUR GRAY

T. Charles I. 8° 1874.

D. Harold. 8° 1892.

BUTLER, FRANK

P. Blue Beard (E.C. 24/12/90). L.C.

P. Aladdin; or, The Scamp, the Lamp and the Villain on the Tramp (Lyr. Hammersmith, 26/12/95). L.C.

BYAM, MARTIN

P. Sinbad the Sailor (Stand. 26/12/89). See *J. F. McARDLE.*

Bsq. Captivating Carmen (Pier, Folkestone, 4/8/90).

[Written in collaboration with *E. B. WYKE.*]

P. The Forty Thieves (Stand. 26/12/90).

[Written in collaboration with *A. MELVILLE.*]

Bsq. The Babes in the Wood (Lyr. H. Rhyl, 14/9/91).

[Written in collaboration with *E. B. WYKE.*]

P. Robinson Crusoe (Stand. 23/12/91).

[Written in collaboration with *A. MELVILLE.*]

Ext. Puss in Boots up to Scratch (Croydon, 25/7/92).

[Written in collaboration with *E. B. WYKE.*]

P. The Babes in the Wood (R.A. Woolwich, 24/12/97). L.C.
[Written in collaboration with *F. GRAHAM* and *W. T. VINCENT*.]

BYATT, HENRY

D. The Brothers (Vaud. 10/3/87). L.C. *French.*
D. The Barren Land (Olym. 11/4/88, *mat.*; Wolverhampton, 16/2/89, *revised*). L.C.
[Written in collaboration with *Sir W. MAGNAY.*]
D. True Heart (Leamington, 23/11/88; P'cess. 3/6/89). L.C.
[Written in collaboration with *Sir W. MAGNAY.*]
Oa. Pierrot's Dream (Birmingham, 17/3/93).
[Music by H. Grey.]
D. John Thurgood, Farmer (Glo. 26/6/93). L.C.
D. The Wastrel (Roy. 2/8/94, *copy.*). L.C.
[Written in collaboration with *H. MOSS.*]
D. Before the Dawn (O.C. 15/4/95). L.C.
M.R. The Golden Age; or, Pierrot's Sacrifice (Sav. 5/7/97). L.C. St G. 20/7/96.
[Music by F. Pascal.]
C.O. L'Amour mouille (Lyr. 5/4/99). See *W. YARDLEY.*

BYFORD, ROY.

F.C. Topsyturvydom (Court, L'pool, 29/3/95). L.C.

BYNG, G. W.

D.Sk. The Guilty Pair (M.H. Cambridge, 28/11/99). See *P. H. T. SYKES.*

[*BYRNE, C. A.*

D. Coward Conscience (Roy. Glasgow, 10/9/88). L.C.
[Written in collaboration with *A. WALLACK.*]
O. Gabriella (St G. 25/11/93, *copy.*).
[Revised by *M. MARRAS.*]

BYRNE, E. RAVEN

D. Restored (Qns. Dublin, 27/2/72; Dublin, 27/4/76, *revised*).

BYRON, HENRY JAMES

Bsq. Richard of the Lion Heart (Str. 23/11/57). L.C.
Bsq. The Lady of Lyons; or, Twopenny Pride and Pennytence (Str. 1/2/58). L.C.
Bsq. Fra Diavolo Travestie; or, The Beauty and the Brigands (Str. 5/4/58). L.C. *French.*
Ext. The Bride of Abydos; or, The Prince, the Pirate and the Pearl (Str. 31/5/58). L.C. *Lacy.*
Bsq. The Maid and the Magpie; or, The Fatal Spoon (Str. 11/10/58). L.C. *French.*
Bsq. The Very Latest Edition of the Lady of Lyons (Str. 11/7/59). L.C. *French.*
Ext. The Babes in the Wood and the Good Little Fairy Birds (Adel. 18/7/59). *French.*
Ext. Jack the Giant Killer; or, Harlequin King Arthur and ye Knights of ye Round Table (P'cess. 26/12/59). L.C. *Lacy.*
Bsq. Mazeppa (Olym. 26/12/59). L.C. *Lacy.*
Ext. The Nymph of the Lurleyburg; or, The Knight and the Naiads (Adel. 26/12/59). L.C. *French.*
Ext. The Pilgrim of Love (H. 9/4/60). L.C. *French.*

Ext. The Miller and his Men (Str. 9/4/60). See *F. TALFOURD.*

F. The Garibaldi Excursionists (P'cess. 8/11/60). L.C. *French.*

Ext. Blue Beard from a New Point of Hue (Adel. 26/12/60). L.C. *Lacy.*

Ext. Cinderella; or, The Lover, the Lackey and the Little Glass Slipper (Str. 26/12/60). L.C. *Lacy.*

P. Robinson Crusoe; or, Harlequin Friday and the King of the Caribbee Islands (P'cess. 26/12/60). L.C. *French.*
[Music by W. Montgomery.]

Bsq. Aladdin; or, The Wonderful Scamp! (Str. 1/4/61). L.C. *Lacy.*

C. The Old Story (Str. 29/4/61). L.C. *French.*

Ext. Esmeralda; or, The "Sensation" Goat! (Str. 28/9/61). L.C. as *E.; or, The Gipsey and the Gentle Goat. French.*

Bsq. Miss Eily O'Connor (D.L. 25/11/61). L.C. *French.*

Bsq. Puss in a New Pair of Boots (Str. 26/12/61). L.C.
[Music by F. Musgrave.]

P. Whittington and his Cat; or, Harlequin King Kollywobbol and the Genius of Good Humour (P'cess. 26/12/61). L.C.
[Music by W. H. Montgomery.]

Ext. The Rival Othellos (Str. 28/11/60). L.C. Str. 29/11/61; Str. 23/3/76 [new introduction].

Ext. Goldenhair the Good (St J. 26/12/62). L.C.

P. Harlequin Beauty and the Beast; or, The Gnome Queen and the Good Fairy (C.G. 26/12/62). L.C.

Bsq.P. George de Barnwell; or, Harlequin Folly in the Realms of Fancy (Adel. 26/12/62). L.C. *Lacy.*

Bsq. Ivanhoe in accordance with the Spirit of the Times (Str. 26/12/62). L.C. *French.*
[Music by F. Musgrave.]

Ext. Ali Baba; or, The Thirty Nine Thieves, in accordance with the Author's Habit of Taking One Off! (Str. 6/4/63). *French.*

Ext. Beautiful Haidee; or, The Sea Nymph and the Sallee Rovers (P'cess. 6/4/63). L.C. *Lacy.*

Ext. Ill-treated Il Trovatore; or, The Mother, the Maiden and the Musician (Adel. 21/5/63). L.C. *French.*

F. The Motto: 'I am all there' (Str. 16/7/63). L.C. *French.*

F. The Rosebud of Stinging-nettle Farm; or, The Villainous Squire and the Virtuous Villager (Adel. 9/9/63). *French.*

P. Harlequin St George and the Dragon; or, The Seven Champions and the Beautiful Princess (C.G. 26/12/63). L.C.

Ext. Lady Belle Belle; or, Fortunio and his Seven Magic Men (Adel. 26/12/63). L.C. *Lacy.*

Ext. Orpheus and Eurydice; or, The Young Gentleman who charmed the Rocks (Str. 26/12/63). L.C. *Lacy.*

Ext. 1863; or, The Sensations of the Past Season: with a Shameful Revelation of Lady Somebody's Secret (St J. 26/12/63). L.C. *Lacy.*

Bsq. Mazourka; or, The Stick, the Pole and the Tartar (Str. 27/4/64). L.C. *French.*

F. Timothy to the Rescue (Str. 23/5/64). L.C. *French.*

F. Lord Dundreary married and done for (H. 13/6/64). L.C.

Bsq. The "Grin" Bushes; or, Missis Brown of the "Missis"sippi (Str. 26/12/64). L.C. *Lacy.*

P. The Lion and the Unicorn were fighting for the Crown (H.M. 26/12/64). L.C.

Ext. Princess Springtime; or, The Envoy who stole the King's Daughter (H. 26/12/64). L.C.

Past. Pan; or, The Loves of Echo and Narcissus (Adel. 10/4/65). L.C. *Lacy.*

Ext. La! Somnambula!; or, The Supper, the Sleeper and the Merry Swiss Boy (P.W. 15/4/65). L.C. *French.*

C. War to the Knife (P.W. 10/6/65). *Lacy.*

Ext. Lucia di Lammermoor; or, The Laird, the Lady and the Lover (P.W. 25/9/65). L.C. *Lacy.*

Bsq. Little Don Giovanni; or, Leporello and the Stone Statue (P.W. 26/12/65). L.C. *Lacy.*

C. A Hundred Thousand Pounds (P.W. 5/5/66). L.C. *Lacy.*

Bsq. Der Freischutz; or, The Bill! the Belle!! and the Bullet!!! (P.W. 10/10/66). L.C. *Lacy.*

Bsq. Pandora's Box; or, The Young Spark and the Old Flame (P.W. 26/12/66). L.C. *Lacy.*

Bsq. Robinson Crusoe; or, The Injun Bride and the Injured Wife (H. 6/7/67). See *W. S. GILBERT*

Bsq. William Tell with a Vengeance; or, The Pet, the Patriot and the Pippin (Alex. L'pool, 4/9/67; Str. 5/10/67). L.C. *Lacy.*

D. The Lancashire Lass; or, Tempted, Tried and True (Alex. L'pool, 28/10/67; Qns. 24/7/68). L.C. *French.*

D. Dearer than Life (Alex. L'pool, 26/11/67; Qns. 8/1/68). L.C.

D. Blow for Blow (Holb. 5/9/68). L.C. *French.*

Ext. Lucrezia Borgia, M.D.; or, La Grande Doctresse (Holb. 28/10/68). L.C. *Lacy.*

C. Cyril's Success (Glo. 28/11/68). L.C. *Lacy.*

C. Not such a Fool as he looks (Manchester, 4/12/68; Glo. 23/10/69). L.C. *French.*

P. Robinson Crusoe; or, Friday and the Fairies (C.G. 26/12/68). L.C.

D. Lost at Sea (Adel. 2/10/69). See *D. BOUCICAULT.*

D. Minnie; or, Leonard's Love (Glo. 29/3/69). L.C.

Bsq. The Corsican "Bothers"; or, The Troublesome Twins (Glo. 17/5/69). L.C. *Lacy.*

D. Uncle Dick's Darling (Gai. 13/12/69). L.C. *French.*

Bsq. Lord Bateman; or, The Proud Young Porter and the Fair Sophia (Glo. 27/12/69). L.C. *Lacy.*

P. The Yellow Dwarf; or, Harlequin Cupid and the King of the Gold Mines (C.G. 27/12/69). L.C.

Ext. The Colleen Bawn (Var. Hoxton, 14/3/70).

D. The Prompter's Box: A Story of the Footlights and the Fireside (Adel. 23/3/70; Str. 9/72, as *Two Stars*). L.C. *French.*

Bsq. Robert Macaire; or, The Roadside Inn turned inside out (Glo. 16/4/70). L.C. *Lacy.*

Ext. The Enchanted Wood; or, The Three Transformed Princes (Adel. 4/5/70). L.C. *French.*

D. An English Gentleman; or, The Empty Pocket (Bristol, 8/11/70; H. 13/5/71). L.C.
[Also called *The Squire's Last Shilling.*]

D. Wait and Hope (Gai. 1/3/71). L.C.

Ext. Eurydice; or, Little Orpheus and his Lute (Str. 24/4/71). *Lacy.*
[A "second edition" of *Orpheus and Eurydice* (Str. 26/12/63).]

D. Daisy Farm (Olym. 1/5/71). L.C. *French.*

Bsq. The Orange Tree and the Humble Bee; or, The Little Princess who was lost at Sea (Vaud. 13/5/71). L.C. *Lacy*.
Ext. Not if I know it (H. 17/6/71).
Ext. Giselle; or, The Sirens of the Lotus Lake (Olym. 22/7/71). L.C. *Lacy*.
C. Partners for Life (Glo. 7/10/71). L.C. *French*.
Ext. Camaralzaman and the Fair Badoura; or, The Bad D(j)inn and the Good Spirit (Vaud. 22/11/71). L.C. *French*.
P. Blue Beard (C.G. 26/12/71). L.C.
D. Haunted Houses; or, Labyrinths of Life: A Story of London and the Bush (P'cess. 1/4/72). L.C.
F. The Spur of the Moment (Glo. 4/5/72). L.C. as *On the S. of the M. French*.
D. Time's Triumph (Gai. Dublin, 19/8/72; Ch.X. 12/5/73). L.C. Huddersfield.
C. Good News (Gai. 31/8/72). L.C.
Bsq. The Lady of the Lane (Str. 31/10/72). L.C.
D. Mabel's Life; or, A Bitter Bargain (Adel. 2/11/72). L.C.
C. Old Soldiers (Str. 25/1/73). L.C. *French*.
D. Fine Feathers (Glo. 26/4/73). L.C. *French*.
D. Chained to the Oar (P.W L'pool, 16/6/73; Gai. 31/5/83). L C.
F. A Wife for a Day (Whitehaven, 20/6/73).
O. La Fille de Mme Angot (Phil. 4/10/73).
C. Sour Grapes (Olym. 4/10/73). L.C. *French*.
Bsq. Don Juan (Alh. 22/12/73). L.C.
Bsq. Guy Fawkes (Gai. 14/1/74). L.C.
C. An American Lady (Crit. 21/3/74). L.C.
D. The Thumbscrew (Holb. 4/4/74). L.C. P'cess. Manchester, 6/11/73, as *Blackmail*.
M.F. Normandy Pippins (Crit. 18/4/74). L.C.
C.O. The Pretty Perfumeress (Alh. 18/5/74). L.C.
[Music by J. Offenbach.]
Bsq.O. The Demon's Bride (Alh. 7/9/74). L.C.
[Music by G. Jacobi.]
C. Old Sailors (Str. 19/10/74). L.C. *French*.
F. Oil and Vinegar (Gai. 4/11/74). L.C.
C. Our Boys (Vaud. 16/1/75). L.C. *French*.
C. Weak Woman (Str. 6/5/75). L.C. *French*.
C. Married in Haste (H. 2/10/75). L.C. *French*.
F. Tottles (Gai. 22/12/75). L.C.
C. Wrinkles: A Tale of Time (P.W. 13/4/76). L.C. *French*.
F. £20 a Year, all found (Folly, 17/4/76). L.C. *French*.
Ext. Little Don Caesar de Bazan (Gai. 26/8/76). L.C.
C. The Bull by the Horns (Gai. 28/8/76). L.C.
D. Widow and Wife (Bristol, 11/9/76). L.C.
C. Old Chums (O.C. 16/12/76). L.C.
F Pampered Menials. *French* (1876).
Bsq. The Bohemian G'yurl and the Unapproachable Pole (O.C. 31/1/77). L.C.
D. Guinea Gold; or, Lights and Shadows of London Life (P'cess. 10/9/77). L.C.
Bsq. Little Doctor Faust (Gai. 13/10/77). L.C.
D. A Fool and his Money (Glo. 17/1/78). L.C.

P. Ali Baba and the Forty Thieves (Gai. 13/2/78). L.C.
[Written in collaboration with *W. S. GILBERT*, *F. C. BURNAND* and *R. REECE*.]
Bsq. Il Somnambulo and Lively Little Alessio (Gai. 6/4/78). L.C.
D. The Crushed Tragedian (H. 11/5/78). L.C.
D. A Hornet's Nest (H. 17/6/78). L.C.
D. Conscience Money (H. 16/9/78). L.C.
F.C. Uncle (Gai. Dublin, 4/11/78; Gai. 1/2/79). L.C. *French.*
Bsq. Young Fra Diavolo; the Terror of Terracina (Gai. 18/11/78). L.C. as *Little Fra Diavolo.*
P. Jack the Giant Killer (Gai. 21/12/78).
Ext. Pretty Esmeralda and Captain Phœbus of Ours (Gai. 2/4/79). L.C.
Ca. Our Girls (Vaud. 19/4/79). L.C. Vaud. 20/11/75, as *Pelican Lodge. French.*
Bsq. Handsome Hernani; or, The Fatal Penny Whistle (Gai. 30/8/79). L.C.
C. Courtship; or, The Three Caskets (Court, 16/10/79). L.C. *French.*
Ext. Gulliver's Travels (Gai. 26/12/79). L.C.
C. The Upper Crust (Folly, 31/3/80). L.C.
Bsq. Il Trovatore; or, Larks with a Libretto (Olym. 26/4/80). L.C.
C. Without a Home (Cardiff, 24/5/80).
C. Bow Bells (Roy. 4/10/80). L.C. *French.*
F. The Light Fantastic (Folly, 20/11/80). L.C.
D. Michael Strogoff (Adel. 14/3/81). L.C.
C.D. Punch (Vaud. 26/5/81). L.C. *French.*
F. New Brooms (Gai. Dublin, 18/7/81).
Bsq. Pluto; or, Little Orpheus and his Lute (Roy. 26/12/81).
[A revised version of *Orpheus and Eurydice* (Str. 26/12/63).]
F.C. Fourteen Days (Crit. 4/3/82). L.C.
F.C. Auntie (Toole's, 12/3/82). L.C.
Past. The Villainous Squire and the Village Rose (Toole's, 5/6/82).
[A revised version of *The Rosebud of Stinging-nettle Farm* (Adel. 9/9/63).]
C.O. Frolique (Str. 18/11/82). See *H. B. FARNIE.*
F.C. Open House (Vaud. 16/4/85).
C. The Shuttlecock (Toole's, 16/5/85). L.C.
[Completed by *J. A. STERRY*.]

BYRON, JOSIAH
F. Slightly Suspicious (Glo. 5/10/91).

BYRTON, H.
D. A Life's Bondage (M'bone, 12/5/90). L.C.

CADOGAN, Lady
Ca. Caught at Last (Aven. 23/10/89). L.C.

CAHILL, W. B.
D. Inchavogue (E.L. 21/4/73). L.C.

CAINE, HALL
R.D. The Ben-my-Chree (P'cess. 17/5/88). L.C.
[Written in collaboration with *W. BARRETT*.]
D. The Good Old Times (P'cess. 12/2/89). L.C.
[Written in collaboration with *W. BARRETT*.]
D. The Bondsman (Bolton, 19/11/92; D.L. 20/9/1906). L.C. Birmingham, 29/10/92.

D. The Christian (Grand, Douglas, 7/8/97, *copy.*; Shakespeare, L'pool, 9/10/99; D.Y. 16/10/99). L.C.

CALHAEM, STANISLAUS

C. Caught (Com. 29/6/86, *mat.*).

CALLENDER, E. ROMAINE

D. Always Ready (Newcastle, 28/7/73; E.L. 31/10/74). L.C.
D. The Two Paths of Life (Plymouth, 9/4/75; Vic. 22/4/76).
D. The Poor Law Board (Bolton, 25/10/75).
D. D.T.; or, Lost by Drink (Bradford, 4/8/79). L.C.
D. Number Fifty One; or, Circumstantial Evidence (L'pool, 30/8/80).
C.D. Light (Sheffield, 7/8/82; Gai. 13/2/83, as *My Darling*). L.C.

CALMOUR, ALFRED C.

D. Trust and Trial (Hull, 6/9/80; Gai. 9/10/80). L.C.
C. A Woman's Heart (Richmond, 11/7/81). L.C.
D. Law, not Justice (Sur. 27/7/82). L.C. as *Justice.*
C.D. Wives (Vaud. 8/3/83). L.C.
D. Broken Bonds (Brighton, 14/11/83). L.C. Scarborough.
C.D. Cupid's Messenger (Nov. 22/7/84). L.C. 8° [1884]; *Lacy.*
C. Homespun (Nov. 11/11/84). L.C.
T. Love's Martyrdom (Crit. 3/7/86). L.C.
D. Elsa Dene (Brighton, 14/10/86; Str. 25/10/86). L.C.
C.D. The Amber Heart (Lyc. 7/6/87, *mat.*; Lyc. 23/5/88). L.C. 8° [1888].
D. Beau Blandish the Rake. 8° 1887 [*priv.*].
C.D. The Widow Winsome (Crit. 27/11/88, *mat.*). L.C.
D.Sk. Cyrene (Aven. 27/6/90, *mat.*). L.C.
C. The Gay Lothario (St J. 31/1/91). L.C. as *The Lady Killer. French.*
D. Gabriel's Trust (Vaud. 4/7/91). L.C.
D. The Bread Winner (Aven. 26/3/92). L.C.
D.Sk. The Broken String (Richmond, 14/12/96; Mat. 16/6/97). L.C.
F.C. Frolicsome Fanny (Gai. 25/11/97). L.C.
[Several later plays: see *Who's Who*, 1913.]

CALTHORPE, W. D.

F.C. The Mormon (Vaud. 10/3/87, *mat.*; Com. 28/3/87). L.C.

CALVERT, CAYLEY

M.C. 'Endon Way (Imp. 24/10/98). See *O. BRAND.*

CALVERT, CHARLES

D. Rube the Showman (Newcastle, 5/9/70).
[Written in collaboration with *J. COLEMAN.*]

CALVERT, Mrs CHARLES [*ADELAIDE HELEN BIDDLES*]

D. Trotty Veck (Gai. 26/12/72). L.C.
C.D. Can he forgive her? (Com. Manchester, 18/9/91). L.C.

CALVERT, WILLIAM

D. The Vendetta; or, The Corsican's Revenge (S.W. 7/7/88). L.C.
D. Blanche Farreau (L'pool, 6/10/90; E.C. 18/12/93, as *Life and Honour*). L.C.
D.Sk. A Surprise (Mat. 22/5/97).

CAMERON, CHARLES

C.D. Matrimony (Alh. Barrow, 6/9/86).

CAMERON, KATE

D.D. Fatality (Eden, Bishop Auckland, 26/1/98, *copy.*). L.C.

CAMPBELL, A. V.

D. Mont Blanc; or, The Ice Fiend of the Alps (Brit. 16/5/53). L.C.

D. The Swindler; or, The Captive Maid (Brit. 25/8/73). L.C.

CAMPBELL, Lady ARCHIBALD

D. Tamlin (Edinburgh, 27/11/99). L.C.

[*CAMPBELL, BARTLEY*

D. Fate (Wallack's, New York, 6/74; Gai. Glasgow, 21/2/76; Ladb. H. 6/5/82, as *F.; or, Driven from Home*; Gai. 6/8/84). L.C.

D. The Virginian (Hooley's, Chicago, 9/73; St J. 20/11/76). L.C.

D. The Galley Slave (Chestnut Street, Philadelphia, 29/9/79; Hull, 22/11/80; Grand, 8/2/86). L.C.

D. My Partner (Union Square, New York, 16/9/79; W. Hartlepool, 17/3/84; Olym. 10/4/84). L.C.

[Title altered to *Her Sin*, 10/6/1919.]

D. The White Slave (Haverley's, New York, 3/4/82; P's. Bristol, 4/8/84; Grand, 18/8/94). L.C.

[The above plays have been edited by Napier Wilt, Princeton, 1941.]

D. Paquita (E.C. 20/8/84). L.C.

D. Clio (McVicker's, Chicago, 1878; E.C. 14/8/85). L.C.

M.D. Siberia (California, San Francisco, 26/11/82; P'cess. 14/12/87). L.C.

CAMPBELL, Lady COLIN

F. Bud and Blossom (Terry's, 3/6/93). L.C.

CAMPBELL, DUNCAN

D. A Winning Defeat (Nov. 30/5/91). L.C.

[Written in collaboration with *M. QUAIRE*. Title altered to *His Word, his Bond*, 27/12/94.]

CAMPBELL, HOWARD

D. The Tollcross; or, The Murder at the Turnpike Gate 100 Years Ago (Adel. Glasgow, 19/3/77).

"*CAMPBELL, J. A.*" See *J. A. GAMBLE*

CAMPBELL, J. M.

D. Through my Heart first (Edinburgh, 17/3/84; Grand, 2/6/84). L.C.

D. By Land and Sea! (Birmingham, 8/6/86). L.C.

[Written in collaboration with *J. L. SHINE*.]

D. The Viper on the Hearth (Crit. 15/5/88). L.C.

F.C. The Deputy (Crit. 15/5/88, *mat.*). L.C.

Ca. The Refugees (Adel. 19/7/88). L.C.

CAMPBELL, N. S.

D. Held in Judgement (Brit. Garston, 11/11/91).

CAMPBELL, Mrs VERE

D. Rizpah Misery (Grand, Glasgow, 6/2/94; Gar. 19/11/96). L.C.

Duol. The Maid of Yesterday (Qns. Gate H., S. Kensington, 11/5/96; Gar. 19/11/96).

C.D. The King's Password (Shakespeare, L'pool, 21/5/1900; Metro. 28/5/1900). L.C. Rowland's, Folkestone, 11/8/94, as *Trelawney*.

CANE, BEVIS

D. The Uttermost Farthing (O.H. Coventry, 23/11/95, *copy.*; P.W. Southampton, 6/12/95). L.C.

CANE, CLAUDE
Bsq. Romeo and Juliet up-to-larks (Qns. Dublin, 21/8/93, *amat.*).
[Music by H. A. Douglas.]

CANN, R. W.
Ca. Taken for Granted (Village H. Esher, 5/5/98, *copy.*).

CANNAM, T.
D. The Queen of Fashion (Oldham, 1887; S.W. 19/3/88). L.C. Rochdale, 23/6/87.
[Written in collaboration with *J. F. PRESTON.*]

CANNINGE, GEORGE
D. Vivianne; or, The Romance of a French Marriage (Olym. 6/7/78). L.C.
Bsq. Shylock and Co. (Park, Camden Town, 5/12/90, as *I.O.U.*; New, Richmond, 17/1/91; Crit. 18/6/91). L.C.
[Written in collaboration with *A. CHEVALIER.*]

CANTWELL, R. F.
D. No Pain, no Gain; or, Life's Shadows (Brit. 8/7/72). L.C.
D. Confidence (Brit. 21/10/72). L.C.
D. Life down South; or, Up for Sale (Brit. 15/6/74). L.C.

CAPE, FREDERICK
D. Isabel. L.C. 5/10/74.

CAPEL, GEORGE
F. Woggles' Waxworks (Sur. 2/6/79). L.C.
F. Her Cousin Frank (Sur. 2/6/79).
C.O. Bears, not Beasts (Booth's, Ashton-under-Lyne, 22/11/80). L.C. P'cess. Glasgow.
[Music by H. Round.]
C. Two Old Boys. L.C. 27/11/80.
[Written in collaboration with *F. BENTON.*]
D. A Link o' Gold (Alex. Sheffield, 6/4/82). L.C. Halifax.
D. Above Suspicion (York, 19/5/82; S.W. 24/3/84). L.C.
Oa. The Nymph of the Danube (Sunderland, 31/7/82). L.C. P'cess. Edinburgh.
Ca. In the Gloaming (Bath, 17/3/84). L.C. Halifax, 7/2/83.
C. The Little Vixen (Huddersfield, 21/7/84). L.C.
Bsq. The Babes in the Wood (Gai. Douglas, 26/7/84).
D. A Fool's Fidelity (Birmingham, 14/3/87; N. London Col. 6/6/87). L.C.
[Title altered to *A Stroke of the Pen*, 1903.]
C. See-Saw (Terry's, 22/2/89, *mat.*). L.C.
[Written in collaboration with *J. R. PHILLIPS.*]
M.F.C. One of the Family (Grand, Boscombe, 9/4/98).
[A revised version of *Two Old Boys*, L.C. 27/11/80. Written in collaboration with *F. BENTON*; lyrics by *F. DIX* and *F. AYRTON*. Music by H. W. May and A. Cooke.]

CAPES, BERNARD
M.F. Bustle's Bride (Aven. 12/11/84).
[Music by J. P. Cole.]

CAPES, J. M.
O. The Druid (St G. 22/2/79).

CAPPER, H. W.

Ca. A Friend in Need, a Friend indeed (St G. 18/12/89, *amat.*).

O.Bsq. Tell Re-told; or, The Pest, the Patriot and the Pippin (St G. 17/2/94, *amat.*).
[Written in collaboration with *H. WALTHER.*]

CAPPER, MARTIN

C. Pick me up (Ipswich, 18/9/92).

CAREW, RAYMOND

C. Circumstantial Evidence (Bijou, 6/4/93). L.C.

CARL, FREDERICK

D. The Three Musketeers (Pier Pav. St Leonard's, 16/1/99; St G. 9/5/99, as *His Majesty's Musketeers*). L.C.

[*CARLETON, HENRY GUY*

D. Victor Durand (P's. 13/12/84).

CARLOS, DON [evidently a pseudonym]

D. The Captain (Mechanics' Inst. Swindon, 23/2/83).

CARLTON, ARTHUR

D. A Sailor's Honour (Lincoln, 8/6/94). L.C.
[Written in collaboration with *W. R. WALDRON.*]

D. The Prairie Flower (Jersey, 14/3/95). See *B. ELLIS.*

CARLTON, CHARLES

Bsq. The Bey of Bagdad (P.H. Whittlesea, 30/8/97).

CARLTON, SIDNEY

M.C. Monte Carlo (Str. 20/9/94, *copy.*; Aven. 27/8/96). L.C.
[Lyrics by *H. GREENBANK.* Music by H. Talbot.]

CARLYLE, GEORGE

Ca. Ruralising (Hanley, 15/4/72).

CARLYLE, RITA

D. Falsely Accused (Pav. 5/7/97). L.C. Nov. 5/3/97.

CARLYON, FRANK

M.C.D. A Game of Cards (Shrewsbury, 10/1/98). L.C.
[Music by G. Dixon.]

CARNE-ROSS, J.

D. Forgery (Ladb. H. 10/4/88). L.C.

CARNEGIE, WILLIAM

C.O. The Miller of Hazlebury (Cannon Street Hotel, 26/3/90, *amat.*; St G. 10/4/94). L.C.

CARNES, MASON

O. The Taboo (Leamington, 22/5/94; Traf. 19/1/95). L.C.

CARPENTER, EDGAR T.

C. Rest at Last (Shawbury H. Dulwich, 10/5/88).

CARPENTER, JOSEPH EDWARDS

M.D. The Sanctuary; or, England in 1450 (Sur. 8/10/55). L.C.

D. Love and Honour; or, Soldiers at Home—Heroes abroad (Sur. 5/11/55). L.C. under sub-title. *French.*

D. Adam Bede; or, The Hall, the Workshop and the Farm (Sur. 28/2/62). L.C.

Oa. Coming of Age (Ch.X. 19/6/69). L.C.
[Music by E. L. Hime.]

CARR, J. W. COMYNS

C.D. Frou Frou (P'cess. 4/6/81). L.C.

D. Far from the Madding Crowd (P.W. L'pool, 27/2/82). See *T. HARDY*.

D. Called Back (P.W. 20/5/84). See *H. CONWAY*.

T.F. A Fireside Hamlet (P's. 27/11/84). L.C.

D. Dark Days (H. 26/9/85). L.C.
[Written in collaboration with *H. CONWAY*.]

M.Ca. A United Pair (St G. 5/4/86). L C. *French*.
[Music by A. J. Caldicott.]

Past.O. The Friar (St G. 15/12/86). L.C.
[Music by A. J. Caldicott.]

M.Sk. The Naturalist (St G. 11/4/87). L.C. *French*.
[Music by K. Hall.]

F.C. Nerves (Com. 7/6/90).

C. Forgiveness (St J. 30/12/91). L.C.

D. King Arthur (Lyc. 12/1/95). L.C. 8° 1895 [*priv.*]; 8° 1895.

D. Delia Harding (Com. 17/4/95). L.C.

D. Boys Together (Adel. 26/8/96). See *C. H. CHAMBERS*.

C. Madame Sans-Gene (Lyc. 10/4/97). L.C. Lyc. 28/8/96.

D. In the Days of the Duke (Adel. 9/9/97). See *C. H. CHAMBERS*.

M.D. The Beauty Stone (Sav. 28/5/98). See *Sir A. PINERO*.
[For his later plays see *Who's Who*, 1913.]

CARR, Mrs J. COMYNS

C.D. The Butterfly (Gai. Glasgow, 12/9/79). L.C.

CARR, WILFRED

D. Cruel Destiny; or, Thrown on the World (R.A. Woolwich, 23/10/99). L.C.

CARRIDEN, WILLIAM

D. A Spin for Life (Qns. Edinburgh, 16/10/97, *copy.*; W. Bromwich, 25/7/98). L.C.
[Title altered to *The American Girl*, 14/4/99.]

CARRILL, G. B.

M.D. The Institute Abroad (Mat. 6/5/97). See *A. STALMAN*.

CARSON, LINGFORD

D. Saved from the Scaffold (M.H. Peterhead, 20/10/97; Darwen, 5/8/99, as *The Heart of a Hero*). L.C.

CARSON, S. MURRAY ["*THORNTON CLARK*"]

F. Two in the Bush (Olym. 15/8/91). L.C.

D. David (Gar. 7/11/92). See *L. N. PARKER*.

C. Gudgeons (Terry's, 10/11/93). L.C.
[Written in collaboration with *L. N. PARKER*.]

F. The Blue Boar (Court, L'pool, 31/8/94). See *L. N. PARKER*.

D. Rosemary (Crit. 16/5/96). See *L. N. PARKER*.

M. The Spell-bound Garden (Roy. Glasgow, 30/11/96). See *L. N. PARKER*.

C.D. The Termagant (H.M. 1/9/98). See *L. N. PARKER*.

D. The Jest (Crit. 10/11/98). L.C.
[Written in collaboration with *L. N. PARKER*.]

C. Change Alley (Gar. 25/4/99). See *L. N. PARKER*.
[For his later plays see *Who's Who*, 1913.]

CARTE, CHARLES
D. The Scamps of Society (Darwen, 3/2/96). L.C.
D. Temptation (Scarborough, 12/8/98). L.C. S.W. 23/3/95.

CARTE, RICHARD D'OYLY
Oa. Marie (O.C. 26/8/71). L.C.

CARTER, ALLEN
D. False Hearts (W. Bromwich, 3/12/86). L.C.

CARTER, BARRINGTON
C.O. The Maid o' the Mill (Pleasure Gdns. Folkestone, 5/1/97). L.C.
[Music by R. Forsyth.]

[*CARTER, LINCOLN J.*
D. The Fast Mail (Rochdale, 26/12/91; Grand, 27/6/92). L.C.
M.D. The Tornado (Northampton, 6/2/99; Brixton, 12/6/99). L.C.

"*CARTON, RICHARD CLAUDE*" [*RICHARD CLAUDE CRITCHETT*]
F. The Great Pink Pearl (Olym. 7/5/85, *mat.*; P's. 7/6/85). L.C.
[Written in collaboration with *C. RALEIGH.*]
D. The Pointsman (Olym. 29/8/87). L.C.
[Written in collaboration with *C. RALEIGH.*]
F. The Treasure (Str. 1/5/88, *mat.*). L.C.
[Written in collaboration with *C. RALEIGH.*]
C.D. Sunlight and Shadow (Aven. 1/11/90). L.C. as *Sunshine and Shadow. French.*
F. The Porter's Knot (C.P. 18/8/92, *mat.*).
C. Liberty Hall (St J. 3/12/92). L.C. 12° 1892 [*priv.*]; *French.*
C.D. Robin Goodfellow (Gar. 5/1/93). L.C.
Ca. Dinner for Two (Brighton, 9/3/93; Traf. 22/3/93). L.C. *French.*
D. The Fall of the Leaf (Manchester, 7/9/93). L.C.
D. The Home Secretary (Crit. 7/5/95). L.C.
C. The Squire of Dames (Crit. 5/11/95). L.C.
F. A White Elephant (Com. 19/11/96). L.C.
D. The Tree of Knowledge (St J. 25/10/97). L.C.
C. Lord and Lady Algy (Com. 21/4/98). L.C.
C. Wheels within Wheels (Court, 23/5/99). L.C.
[For his later plays see *Who's Who*, 1913.]

CARTWRIGHT, C.
D. A King of Fools (Grand, 25/9/99). See *H. J. W. DAM.*

CARTWRIGHT, G. L.
D. Ponsonby Hall (St G. Wolverhampton, 10/10/92, *amat.*).

CASSEL, H.
F. The Churchwarden (Newcastle, 17/9/86; Olym. 16/12/86). L.C.
[Written in collaboration with *C. OGDEN.*]
F. My First Patient (Technical College, Bradford, 12/2/87).
[Written in collaboration with *C. OGDEN.*]
F.C. In Charge (P's. Bradford, 29/6/88). L.C.
[Written in collaboration with *H. C. DUCKWORTH.*]
F.C. A State Secret (P's. Bradford, 20/12/89). L.C. Alh. Barrow-in-Furness, 12/12/89.
[Written in collaboration with *H. C. DUCKWORTH.*]

CASSIDY, J. R.
D. Hearts of the West (Darwen, 3/12/96). L.C.

CASSILIS, INA LEON

D. At Bay (Ladb. H. 9/4/88). See *C. LANDER.*

F.C. The Wrong Door (Com. 20/5/90, *mat.*). L.C.

Duol. Hearts or Diamonds (Steinway H. 12/5/91).

Duol. The Unfinished Story (St J. H. 22/6/91).

Duol. Cheerful and Musical (St Peter's, Jersey, 14/8/91). *French.*

D. Vida (Ladb. H. 12/10/91, *copy.*; Londesborough, Scarborough, 17/11/91; P.W. 1/3/92, *mat.*). L.C.
[Written in collaboration with *C. LANDER.*]

D. The Light of Pengarth (O.C. 17/12/91, *mat.*).

D. A Noble Atonement (O.C. 21/1/92). L.C.

M.D. A Hidden Foe (Lecture H. Greenwich, 28/5/92). L.C.

C. Cash for Coronets (N. London Inst. Dalston, 14/6/94). L.C. Parish H. S. Acton, 12/5/94, as *Claire; or C. for C.*
[Written in collaboration with *F. H. MORLAND.*]

D. Michael Dane's Grandson (Lyr. Hammersmith, 18/4/96). L.C.

M.D. Demon Darrell (Brit. 20/6/98). L.C.
[Written in collaboration with *F. H. MORLAND.*]

Ca. Those Landladies. *French.*

CASTLES, FRANK

Ext. The Big Blue Bowl (St G. 29/5/88).

CASTLETON, ROBERT

D. The Cross of Olga (Woodside H. 29/1/96; Qns. Longton, 18/7/98). L.C.
[Written in collaboration with *G. GURNEY.* Title altered to *The Slaves of Passion*, 22/4/1904.]

D. Lucifer, Son of the Morning; or, The Sorrows of Satan (Lyc. Stafford, 15/12/98). L.C.

D. The Eleventh Commandment; or, An Unwritten Law (Margate, 4/12/99). L.C.

CAVE, JOSEPH ARNOLD

D. The Casual Ward; or, Workhouse Life (M'bone, 19/2/66). L.C.

D. The Mysterious House in Chelsea (M'bone, 30/9/76). L.C.
[Written in collaboration with *G. ROBERTS.*]

P. A Frog he would a-wooing go (Aquar. 22/12/77). L.C.

CAVE, R. H.

D. Forgiven; or, The Wife's Victory. 8° 1873.

CAVENDISH, Lady CLARA

D. A Woman of the World (Qns. 13/11/58). L.C. *Lacy.*

CAVENDISH, PAUL

D. The Welsh Orphan; or, The Work Girl of Cardiff (Gai. Cardiff, 12/3/94, *copy.*).

[*CAZAURAN, AUGUSTUS R.*

D.D. The Esmonds of Virginia (Roy. 20/5/86). L.C.

"*CECIL, ARTHUR*" [*ARTHUR CECIL BLUNT*]

O. Dora's Dream (G.I. 17/6/73; O.C. 17/11/77). L.C.
[Music by A. Cellier.]

Ca. Time is Money (Newcastle, 5/9/90). See *Mrs H. BELL.*

CELLI, FRANK H.

Oa. Stirring Times (O.H. Southport, 2/8/97; Shakespeare, Clapham, 9/8/97). L.C. Regent, Salford.
[Written in collaboration with *B. DALY*.]

CHALLIS, ROSS

C.D. The Curate (P.W. Gt Grimsby, 3/5/86). L.C. Albert, Gainsborough.
M.D. Follow the Drum (O.H. Wakefield, 2/4/88). L.C.
D. Parson Thorn (O.H. Wakefield, 3/4/91). L.C.

CHAMBERLAINE, C. W.

D. Dora's Love; or, The Struggles of a Poor Engineer (P.W. Wolverhampton, 12/8/72).

CHAMBERLAINE, EDWARD

Bsq. Timour the Tartar; or, The Swell Belle of the Period (Alex. 27/12/69). L.C.

CHAMBERS, CHARLES HADDON

F.C. One of Them (Margate, 10/9/86, *copy*.). L.C.
D. The Open Gate (Com. 28/3/87). L.C. *French*.
D. Devil Caresfoot (Vaud. 12/7/87, *mat.*; Str. 6/8/87). L.C.
[Written in collaboration with *J. S. LITTLE*.]
D. Captain Swift (H. 20/6/88, *mat.*; H. 1/9/88). L.C. *French*.
D. The Idler (Lyc. New York, 11/11/90; St J. 26/2/91). L.C. Aven. 31/5/90. *French*.
D. The Pipe of Peace. L.C. St J. 15/4/91.
C.D. The Honourable Herbert (Vaud. 22/12/91). L.C. Brighton.
F. The Collaborators (Vaud. 7/1/92). L.C. *French*.
D. The Queen of Manoa (H. 15/9/92). L.C.
[Written in collaboration with *W. O. TRISTRAM*.]
C. The Old Lady (Crit. 19/11/92). L.C.
D. The Fatal Card (Adel. 6/9/94). L.C.
[Written in collaboration with *B. C. STEPHENSON*.]
D. John-a-Dreams (H. 8/11/94). L.C.
D. Boys Together (Adel. 26/8/96). L.C.
[Written in collaboration with *J. W. C. CARR*.]
D. In the Days of the Duke (Adel. 9/9/97). L.C.
[Written in collaboration with *J. W. C. CARR*.]
C. The Tyranny of Tears (Crit. 6/4/99). L.C. 8° 1900.
[For his later plays see A. E. Morgan, *op. cit.* p. 308.]

CHAMBERS, F. OWEN

D. The Silence of Dean Maitland (O.H. Kidderminster, 12/4/98). L.C.

CHANDLER, Miss B.

F. Powder and Shot (Drill H. Basingstoke, 2/1/96). L.C.

CHANDLER, W. A.

D. A Judicial Separation (Macclesfield, 10/10/85).
F.C. Ribston's Ride (Nov. 7/5/97, *copy*.). L.C.

CHANDOS, ALICE ["*A. D. LIVANDAIS*"]

Ca. Jealous of the Past (New Cross H. 17/9/85). L.C. as *Green-eyed; or, J. of the P.*
F.C. Philanthropy (P'cess. 3/9/88). L.C.

CHAPIN, ALICE

Ext. Dresden China (Vaud. 21/7/92, *mat.*). L.C.
[Written in collaboration with *E. H. C. OLIPHANT.*]

D. Shame (Vaud. 21/7/92, *mat.*). L.C.
[Written in collaboration with *E. H. C. OLIPHANT.*]

Ca. The Wrong Legs (Ilkeston, 14/9/96). L.C.

Duol. Sorrowful Satan; or, Lucifer's Match (Stanley H. Kentish Town, 27/10/97). L.C.
[Music by P. Rex.]

D. A Woman's Sacrifice (St G. 3/6/99). L.C.

CHAPMAN, ARTHUR

Ca. The Widow's Cap (Ladb. H. 7/4/88). L.C.

Ca. My Daughter (Athen. Shepherd's Bush, 9/4/88). L.C.

Oa. Head or Heart (Com. 29/5/90, *mat.*). L.C.
[Music by M. van Lennep.]

Ca. The Composer (Richmond, 29/10/91; Str. 9/1/92). L.C.
[Music by J. M. Capel.]

CHAPMAN, W.

D. A Man of Business (St G. 26/3/87). See *W. OLAF.*

CHARLES, G. F.

D. The King's Pledge; or, A Mission of Mercy (Qns. Barnsley, 3/1/70).

CHARLES, H.

D. The Last Call (Shakespeare, L'pool, 1/4/95). L.C.
[Written in collaboration with *H. J. S. GREIGG.*]

CHARLES, T. W.

M.F. Pickles (P.W. L'pool, 9/4/94). See *H. MILLS.*

CHARLESON, A. J.

D. Hard Hearts; or, Other Men's Sins (Grand, 26/4/86). L.C.
[Written in collaboration with *C. WILMOT.*]

Ca. Anthony's Legacy (Wigan, 18/4/91; Parkhurst, 11/12/93). L.C. *French.*

CHARLTON, F.

D. The Alchemist of Modena; or, The Wrongs of a Life (Brit. 10/11/68). L.C. as *Zaueri the Alchemist*

CHARRINGTON, CHARLES

D. Frou-Frou (Com. Manchester, 9/12/86). See *J. ACHURCH.*

CHATTERTON, F. B.

P. Ali Baba and the Forty Thieves (S.W. 26/12/81). L.C.
[Written in collaboration with *H. P. GRATTAN.*]

Bsq. The Sleeping Beauty (Aldershot, 3/8/85). See *C. DALY.*

CHEATHAM, F. G.

D. The Foundling of Fortune; or, Next of Kin (Vic. 22/4/67). L.C.

P. Little Red Riding Hood; or, Harlequin Prince Hopeful, Baa, Baa, Black Sheep and the Cruel Wolf (S.W. 26/12/67). L.C.

P. Ye Faire Maide of Merrie Islington; or, Harlequin the Cruel Prince of Canonbury and the Chivalrous Knights of St John (S.W. 27/12/69). L.C.

D. Devotion (S.W. 21/3/70). L.C.

CHELTNAM, CHARLES SMITH

[For an earlier play see iv, 279.]

C. More Precious than Gold (Str. 8/7/61). L.C. *Lacy.*

C.D. A Lucky Escape (Str. 9/9/61). L.C. *Lacy.*

F.Ca. Slowstop's Engagements (Olym. 13/1/62). L.C. *French.*

D. A Fairy's Father (Olym. 24/2/62). L.C. *French.*

D. Aurora Floyd; or, The Deed in the Wood (P'cess. 11/3/63). L.C.

D. Deborah; or, The Jewish Maiden's Wrong (Vic. 12/7/64). L.C. *French.*

C. A Lesson in Love (St J. 22/12/64). L.C. *Lacy.*

F. Mrs Green's Snug Little Business (Str. 16/1/65). L.C. *Lacy.*

F. A Dinner for Nothing (P.W. 16/10/65). L.C. *Lacy.*

D. Six Years After; or, The Ticket-of-Leave Man's Wife (Greenwich, 2/4/66; Olym. 4/8/66). L.C. as *May Brierley; or, The T. of L. M. W. Lacy*

D. Edendale (Ch.X. 19/6/69). L.C. *French.*

C.D. The Greenwich Pensioner (Adel. 21/7/69).

D. Grace Holden (Belfast, 23/8/69). *Lacy* [as *The Shadow of a Crime*].

F. Christmas Eve (St J. 21/11/70). *French* (as *Christmas Eve in a Watchhouse*).

F.C. The Matchmaker (Gai. 11/10/71). L.C. *Lacy.*

Ext. Leatherlungos the Great, how he stormed, reigned and mizzled (Adel. 1/7/72). L.C. *Lacy.*

C. Charming Mrs Gaythorne (Crit. 19/4/94). L.C.

CHESTER, VERE

C. A Tangled Web (Crit. 3/7/84). L.C.

CHESTERLEY, F.

R.D. The Wave of War (Terry's, 15/12/87, *mat.*). L.C.
[Written in collaboration with *H. PIFFARD.*]

CHEVALIER, ALBERT

C. Peebles (Gai. Glasgow, 14/8/82). L.C. P'cess. Glasgow, 19/7/81.
[Written in collaboration with *W. MACKINTOSH.*]

F.C. The Lady Killer (Plymouth, 13/7/85). L.C.
[Written in collaboration with *W. MACKINTOSH.*]

Bsq. Called back again (Plymouth, 13/7/85). L.C.

Ca. Cycling (Str. 11/7/88). L.C.

Bsq. Aladdin; or, The Wonderful Scamp (Str. 15/9/88).

Bsq. Shylock and Co. (Park, Camden Town, 5/12/90). See *G. CANNINGE.*

Bsq. Shattered 'Un (Vaud. 3/6/91, *mat.*).

M.C. The Land of Nod (Lincoln, 24/5/97; Roy. 24/9/98). L.C.
[Music by A. West.]

M.Sk. When Widows wooed (Ladb. H. 19/5/99). L.C.
[*Who's Who*, 1913, states that he is the author of over a hundred sketches, monologues and plays.]

CHEVERELLES, HAROLD

Duol. A Dumaur'alised Trilby (St G. 6/12/95).
[Music by J. Franklin.]

CHILD, H.

D. The Prayer (Birmingham, 1/9/98).

[*CHILDS, NAT*

M.C. A Dream; or, Binks' Photographic Gallery (Aven. 16/7/83; Str. 17/10/93, as *Binks the Downy Photographer*). L.C.

[Title altered to *Binks the Downy Photographer*, 19/9/93. Written in collaboration with *W. EDOUIN*.]

CHIPPENDALE, Mrs MARY JANE

C. Mamma (Gai. Dublin, 8/5/76).

CHORLEY, HENRY FOTHERGILL

D. Old Love and New Fortune (Sur. 18/2/50). L.C.

Oa. Son and Stranger (H. 7/7/51). L.C. 8° [1851].

[Version of *Die Heimkehr aus der Fremde*, libretto K. Klingemann, music F. Mendelssohn (Leipzig, 10/4/51).]

O. White Magic (H. 17/3/52). L.C.

C. The Love Lock (Olym. 13/2/54).

D. The Duchess Eleanour (H. 13/3/54). L.C.

O. Dinorah (C.G. 3/10/59). L.C.

O. The Black Domino (C.G. 20/2/61). L.C.

O. Faust (H.M. 23/1/64). L.C. 8° [1864].

CHRICHTON, W.

D. Eventide (Middlesborough, 5/8/95; Parkhurst, 17/2/96). L.C.

CHURCH, CARR

Ca. Fair Deceivers (T.H. Eastbourne, 23/9/93). L.C.

"*CHURCHILL, F.*" [*G. H. LEWES*]

F. Taking by Storm (Lyc. 3/6/52). L.C. *Lacy*.

CHURCHILL, M. L.

C.D. Blanchette (West, Albert H. 8/12/98). See *J. T. GREIN*.

CHUTE, JOHN

D. Connemara (P. W. Warrington, 24/5/80).

D. Moths (Croydon, 28/8/82).

D. Called back (Devonshire Park, Eastbourne, 25/8/84; Sanger's, 20/9/84). L.C.

R.D. Our Bonnie Prince (Grand, Glasgow, 24/10/87). L.C. as *Bonnie Prince Charlie*.

[Written in collaboration with *J. COLEMAN*.]

CIMINO, —

D. A Shattered Idol (Oxford, 6/1/77). L.C.

CLAIR, H. BUCKSTONE

P. Cinderella (Nov. 26/12/91). L.C.

P. Aladdin (E.C. 27/12/97). L.C.

CLARANCE, LLOYD

P. Goody Two Shoes (Stockton-on-Tees, 24/12/77). L.C.

P. Little Tom Tucker (Gt Grimsby, 24/12/77).

D. Domino; or, The Fall of the Curtain (Stockton-on-Tees, 7/3/79; Darwen, 26/2/83). L.C.

Bsq. A Tale of Tell; or, The Pole, the Patriot and the Pippin (Darwen, 26/2/83).

Bsq. Aladdin; or, The Scamp, the Tramp and the Lamp (Grand, Blackpool, 14/5/83).

Bsq. The Lass that loved a Sailor; or, The Perfidious Pirate, the Modest Maiden and the Trusty Tar (Gt Grimsby, 17/9/83).

D. At Last; or, A New Life (Gt Grimsby, 17/9/83; Barnsley, 3/3/84, as *A New Life*).
Bsq. Robert Macaire Renovated (Barnsley, 3/3/84).
F.C. Mixed; or, All in the Wrong (Raike's Hall Gdns. Blackpool, 2/6/84). L.C.
Bsq. Old Pals (S. Shields, 7/8/84).
[Music by W. Haunt.]
D. The Beacon Light; or, The Wrecker's Doom (Stockton-on-Tees, 1/6/91). L.C.

CLARE, CYRIL
D. The Duchess of Coolgardie (D.L. 19/9/96). See *E. LEIGH.*

CLARENCE, REGINALD
P.Spect. The New Year; or, Peace with Honour (Assembly R. Balham, 27/12/99).
[Music by T. Lebrunn.]

CLARIDGE, C. J., Jr.
F. The Fast Coach (Olym. 9/6/51). See *J. SOUTAR, Jr.*

CLARK, H. F.
Bsq. Ruy Blas (Grand, Birmingham, 3/9/89). See *F. LESLIE.*
Bsq. Guy Fawkes Esq. (Nottingham, 7/4/90). See *F. LESLIE.*

CLARK, MARWOOD
C.D. Our Emmie (O.C. 1/8/92, *mat.*). L.C.

CLARK, T. G.
D. London Life (Grec. 24/9/81). L.C.

"*CLARK, THORNTON.*" See *S. M. CARSON.*

CLARKE, ALBERT H.
R.D. Wings of Wealth; or, A Disputed Marriage (Willenhall, 25/10/94). L.C.
D. Roving Meg; or, A Bargeman's Secret (Coutts', Birmingham, 26/6/99). L.C.

CLARKE, ALFRED CLAUDE
Ext. Innocents all abroad (Winter Gdns. Blackpool, 9/6/86). L.C.
[Music by J. Gregory.]

CLARKE, CAMPBELL
D. Awaking (Gai. 14/12/72). L.C. *French.*
D. The Sphinx (Edinburgh, 12/8/74; H. 22/8/74). L.C.
C.O. Giroflé Girofla (Phil. 3/10/74). See *C. O'NEIL.*
D. Rose Michel (Gai. 27/3/75). L.C.
C.D. Love and Honour (Birmingham, 30/6/75; Glo. 14/8/75). L.C.

CLARKE, CHARLES A.
D. The Waxwork Man (Vic. 26/6/71). L.C.
D. Joan of Arc; or, The Maid, the Amazon and the Martyr (Vic. 7/8/71). L.C.
D. Cagliostro the Magician (Park, 12/6/75).
D. Clear ahead! (Oldham, 3/8/85; Stratford, 22/11/86). L.C.
D. Current Cash (N. Shields, 3/5/86; P.W. Greenwich, 24/5/86; Sur. 25/7/87). L.C.
D. Right's Right (W. Bromwich, 8/11/86; Dewsbury, 2/6/88, *revised*; Stratford, 1/10/88). L.C.
[Written in collaboration with *J. O. STEWART.*]
D. Won by a Head (Woolwich, 5/9/87).

R.D. Day to Day (P.H. Warrington, 1/7/89; Pav. 7/7/90, as *Men and Money*).
D. The Silver Shaft (P.H. Warrington, 21/11/89). L.C.
R.D. The Bishop of the Fleet (Londesborough, Scarborough, 26/12/89). L.C. P's. Bradford.
[Written in collaboration with *F. MOUILLOT*.]
R.D. Noble Love (Goole, 27/1/90; E.C. 20/7/91). L.C.
[Written in collaboration with *J. J. HEWSON*.]
C.D. Held in Harness (Qns. Keighley, 29/5/90). L.C.
M.D. Liberty (Morton's, Bromley, 25/8/90). L.C.
D. Men of Metal (Barnsley, 3/10/90; Pav. 20/7/91). L.C.
[Written in collaboration with *H. R. SILVA*.]
R.D. Days of Terror (Bishop Auckland, 24/3/91).
D. Trust to Luck (New, Newport, 27/4/91).
D. Joan of Arc (Star, Wolverhampton, 31/8/91).
[Evidently a revised version of *Joan of Arc* (Vic. 7/8/71).]
D. The String of Pearls (Birkenhead, 26/11/92). L.C.
[Written in collaboration with *H. R. SILVA*. This play was later acted as *Sweeney Todd*.]
D. The Downward Path (Huddersfield, 17/7/93). L.C.
[The title was later altered to *Base Coin*. Written in collaboration with *H. R. SILVA*.]
F.C. The Bounders (N. Shields, 8/3/94). L.C.
D. The Starting Price (Runcorn, 21/7/94).
D. The Prodigal Son (P.W. Salford, 24/3/98). See *F. L. CONNYNGHAME*.
D. A Queen of England (Eastbourne, 2/5/98; Kilburn, 21/11/98). L.C.
D. Honour thy Father (Imp. 12/9/98). L.C.
[Written in collaboration with *H. R. SILVA*.]
D. They all love Jack (Muncaster, Bootle, 3/10/98). L.C.

CLARKE, F.
D. The Stolen Fortune; or, The Blind Wife and the Detective (Birkenhead, 9/4/77). L.C. Hanley.

[*CLARKE, GEORGE H.*
D. Born to save (Wolverhampton, 3/12/83).
[Written in collaboration with *L. DOUGLAS*.]

CLARKE, HAMILTON
M.Ca. Castle Botherem (St G.). L.C. St G. 13/1/80. See *A. LAW*.

CLARKE, HENRY SAVILE
C. Love wins (Cambridge, 11/8/73; Croydon, 12/10/74; Sur. 26/5/77).
[Written in collaboration with *L. H. F. DU TERREAUX*.]
D. Pendarvon (Alex. L'pool, 2/3/74). See *A. E. T. WATSON*.
D. A Fight for Life (Bradford, 26/8/76; Park, 10/3/77). L.C.
[Written in collaboration with *L. H. F. DU TERREAUX*.]
F. That Beautiful Biceps (D.L. 23/9/76). L.C.
F. A Tale of a Telephone (D.L. 12/1/79). L.C.
Bsq. Another Drink (Folly, 12/7/79). L.C.
[Written in collaboration with *L. CLIFTON*.]
Bsq. Rip Van Winkle; or, A Little Game of Nap (Portsmouth, 29/3/80). L.C.

Ca. A Lyrical Lover (Imp. 24/3/81). L.C. 8° 1892; *French.*
C.O. An Adamless Eden (O.C. 13/12/82). L.C. 8° 1892.
[Music by W. Slaughter.]
C.O. Gillette (Roy. 19/11/83). L.C.
[Music by E. Audran.]
F. Inventories (Str. 8/7/85). L.C.
C.O. Alice in Wonderland (P.W. 23/12/86, *mat.*; Glo. 26/12/88). L.C. 8° 1888.
[Music by W. Slaughter.]
C.O. The Rose and the Ring (P.W. 20/12/90). L.C.
[Music by W. Slaughter.]
— A Little Flutter. 8° 1892.
[This volume contains, besides the play which gives it its title, *An Adamless Eden*, *A Lyrical Lover* and *Dolly*.]

CLARKE, J. J.
D. For Bonnie Prince Charlie (Shaft. 29/1/97, *copy*.). L.C.

CLARKE, JOHN S.
D.Sk. A Youngster's Adventure (Str. 19/8/95). L.C.

CLARKE, MARLANDE
Ext. Hearts and Hampers (Gloucester, 21/11/81).

CLARKE, RICHARD
F. A Matrimonial Advertisement (Metro. 28/10/95).

[*CLARKE, WILFRED*
F. A New York Divorce (Str. 19/8/95). L.C.

CLARKSON, HOWARD
D. Exiled; or, The Forced Marriage (P.W. Birkenhead, 12/2/77). L.C L'pool, 4/2/76, as *The Exile.*

CLAY, CECIL
Bsq. A Pantomime Rehearsal (Terry's, 6/6/91). L.C.
M.C. On the March (Sheffield, 18/5/96). See *W. YARDLEY.*

CLAY, FREDERICK
C.O. A Sensational Novel in Three Volumes (G.I. 30/1/71). L.C.
D. Defeated (Cardiff, 11/4/81). L.C.

CLAY, T. L.
P. Sinbad the Sailor (Albion, 24/12/78). L.C.
P. Little Red Riding Hood (Pav. 26/12/78). L.C.
P. Cinderella (M'bone, 24/12/79). See *F. W. GREEN.*
P. The Children in the Wood (Pav. 26/12/79). L.C.
P. Jack and the Beanstalk (Pav. 27/12/80). See *F. W. GREEN.*
P. Little Jack Horner; or, Tom, Tom the Piper's Son, stole a fat Pig and away he ran (E.C. 26/12/81). L.C.
[Written in collaboration with *O. ALLEN.*]

CLAYPOLE, CLARKE
D. The Christian's Cross (Roy. Chester, 7/4/97). See *F. OAKLEY.*

CLEARY, EDWIN
C.D. Editha's Burglar (P'cess. 28/10/87). L.C.
D. The Mirage (P'cess. 9/2/88). L.C.

CLEATON, E. R.
C.D. The Unionist (P.W. L'pool, 8/9/90). L.C.

CLEAVER, MARY

Int. The Erl King's Daughter; or, The Fairy Reformed. L.C. 30/9/51.
Int. The Ballybaggerty Bequest (Adel. Edinburgh, 14/6/52).

CLEMENS, SAMUEL LANGHORNE. See "*MARK TWAIN*"

CLEMENT, FRANK A.

C.Oa. Waiting for the Coach (Ladb. H. 7/7/91). L.C.
[Music by O. Notcutt.]
C.Oa. Bumble (Ladb. H. 7/7/91). L.C.
[Music by O. Notcutt.]

CLEMENT, WILL

F. Making it pleasant (Woolwich, 22/8/87).
D. Only a Waif; or, The Lion and the Mouse (Woolwich, 28/5/88).
Bsq. Oh! those Babes; or, The Unhappy Uncle, the Virtuous Villains and the Cheeky Children (Woolwich, 18/6/88).
M.C. Odd Man Out (Grand, Nottingham, 19/4/97). See *M. TURNER.*
P. Cinderella (Stratford, 26/12/98). See *G. THORN.*

CLEMENTS, ARTHUR

F. The Irish Footman; or, Two to One (S.W. 17/12/72). L.C. *French.*
O. The Blind Beggars of Burlington Bridge (Gai. 31/8/74). L.C.
[Written in collaboration with *J. MALONE.* This was acted also as *The Two Blinds.*]
P. Jack and Jill (Vic. 24/12/74). L.C.
[Written in collaboration with *R. SOUTAR.*]
Bsq. Cracked Heads (Str. 2/2/76). See *F. HAY.*
Bsq. Dan'l Tra-Duced, Tinker (Str. 27/11/76). L.C.
F. The Telephone (Str. 22/4/78). L.C. *Lacy.*
F. The Two Photographs (Str. 6/3/84). *Lacy.*

CLEMENTS, W. R.

M.F. Paradise up-to-date (P.H. Gravesend, 26/3/94). L.C.
[Music by G. Jones.]

CLEVE, J. B.

D. Fathoms Deep (S.W. 24/3/83). L.C. Wakefield, 13/4/81, as *Right must conquer.*

CLEVEDON, ALICE

D. The Worship of Plutus; or, Poses (Ladb. H. 6/7/88, *copy.*). L.C.

CLEVELAND, ELLIS A.

D.Sk. Miss Galatea of Oregon (Aven. 16/11/94, *copy.*; Lyc. Stafford, 4/12/95). L.C.
C.D. His Wives (Aven. 16/11/94). L.C.

CLEVELAND, H.

D. Woman's Love; or, The Gipsy's Vengeance (E.C. 8/5/75). L.C.

CLIFFE, F. H.

T. The Fatal Ring (Ladb. H. 12/9/93, *copy.*). L.C.

CLIFFORD, Mrs W. K.

D.Sk. An Interlude (Terry's, 3/6/93). L.C.
[Written in collaboration with *W. H. POLLOCK.*]
Ca. A Honeymoon Tragedy (Com. 12/3/96). *French.*
[For her later plays, see *Who's Who,* 1913.]

CLIFFORD, WALTER T.
M.D. In Old Madrid (Garston, 23/1/97). See *F. KIRKE.*

CLIFT, R.
D. Duplicity (Eclectic, Soho, 14/12/71).

CLIFTON, LEWIS
Bsq. Another Drink (Folly, 12/7/79). See *H. S. CLARKE.*
F. A Military Manœuvre (Vaud. 26/12/79). See *J. J. DILLEY.*
F. Summoned to Court (Imp. 4/3/80). See *J. J. DILLEY.*
C.D. Tom Pinch (Vaud. 10/3/81). See *J. J. DILLEY.*
C.O. Marjorie (P.W. 18/7/89, *mat.*; P.W. 18/1/90). L.C.
[Written in collaboration with *J. J. DILLEY.* Music by W. Slaughter.]

CLINCH, J. H.
D. Criminals; or, Fashion and Famine (P.W. Gt Grimsby, 29/6/85).

CLIVE, WYBERT
D. The Conscript (Workington, 25/2/89).
D. Zamet; or, Bonny Bohemia (Gateshead, 12/8/91; Stand. 21/11/92, as *The Romany's Revenge*). L.C.

CLOTHIER, R.
F. Our Tom (Leicester, 8/2/75).

CLOWES, W. LAIRD
F. The Pump (Toole's, 27/3/86). L.C.

CLYDE, CARROL
F. Mesmerism (O.C. 22/5/90). L.C.

CLYNE, HENRY
F. The Scheme (Bristol, 29/6/80).

COAPE, H. C.
D. A Conspirator in spite of himself (Olym. 24/1/52). L.C.
C.D. The Queen of the Market (Adel. 12/4/52). *Webster.*
[Written in collaboration with *B. N. WEBSTER.*]

COATES, ALFRED
D. The Snow Drift; or, The Cross on the Boot (Brit. 15/2/69). L.C.
D. The Frozen Stream; or, The Dead Witness (Brit. 4/3/72). L.C.
D. Poacher Bill; or, The Gipsy Outcast (Brit. 1/4/72). L.C.
D. Bitter Cold (Lyr. Hammersmith, 11/2/89).

COBHAM, E. MEREDITH
C.D. The Soldier's Daughter (P.H. Gravesend, 11/5/97). L.C.

COCKBURN, Mrs T.
Oa. Princess Verita (Art Gallery, Newcastle, 7/10/96).
[Music by F. J. Smith.]

CODY, S. F.
D. The Klondyke Nugget (St G. Walsall, 5/12/98; E.C. 7/8/99). L.C.

"COE, Captain"
Bsq. Orpheus and P(Eurydice) (Aquar. Gt Yarmouth, 20/7/91). See *E. ROSE.*
M.F. The Favourite (C.P. 24/4/93).
[Music by G. L. Chesterton.]

COEN, LEWIS
Ca. En Voyage (Vaud. 20/12/83). L.C.
D. The Land of Diamonds (S.W. 2/6/84). L.C.

COFFIN, EMILY
Ca. My Jack (P'cess. 6/10/87).
C. Run wild (Str. 30/6/88). L.C. as *Uncle John.*
Ca. No Credit (Str. 11/4/92). L.C.

"*COGGAN, JAN*"
D. Redeemed; or, A Life's Bondage (Vaud. 7/6/83). L.C.

COGHILL, Sir JOHN JOSCELYN, Bart.
Ca. Bric-a-Brac (Ladb. H. 20/10/88). L.C.
M.Vaud. The Burglar and the Bishop (Pier, Folkestone, 22/5/93). L.C. [Music by W. Batson.]

COGHLAN, CHARLES F.
Ca. As Good as Gold (Lyc. 18/12/69). L.C.
C. Lady Flora (Court, 13/3/75). L.C.
Ca. A Quiet Rubber (Court, 8/1/76). L.C.
C. Brothers (Court, 4/11/76). L.C.
C. The House of Darnley (Court, 6/10/77). See *Baron LYTTON.*
D. For Life (Grand, Leeds, 9/8/80; P.W. 18/12/80, as *A New Trial*). L.C.
C. Good Fortune (St J. 4/12/80). L.C.
C.D. Enemies (P.W. 28/1/86). L.C.
C. Lady Barter (P'cess. 28/2/91). L.C.
[Davenport Adams, *op. cit.* p. 309, adds *Madame, The Royal Box* and *Citizen Pierre.*]

COHEN, G. MANCHESTER
Ext. Y'lang, Y'lang, the Fair Maid of Too Bloo (Normansfield, Hampton Wick, 5/1/93, *amat.*). L.C.
[Music by J. W. Ivimey.]

COHEN, JULES
D. Estella (C.G. 3/7/80). L.C.

COLE, EDWARD F.
D. Virginia; or, The Soldier's Daughter (Glo. 28/6/89, *mat.*). L.C.

COLE, J. PARRY
M.Sk. The Golden Wedding (Wellington H. St John's Wood, 5/6/99).

COLEMAN, H.
D. Pretty Poll of Paddington (M'bone, 9/2/52). L.C.
D. Lelia the Betrothed; or, The Savoyard Assassin (M'bone, 1/3/52). L.C.

COLEMAN, JOHN
D. Wedded, not Wived (Hull, 5/4/86). L.C.
R.D. Our Bonnie Prince (Grand, Glasgow, 24/10/87). See *J. CHUTE.*
D. Marina (Gai. 4/8/88). L.C.
D. A Silent Witness (Olym. 18/5/89).
D. Soggarth Aroon (Grand, Birmingham, 29/11/97). L.C.
[Davenport Adams, *op. cit.* p. 310, lists some other plays which I have been unable to trace.]

COLERIDGE, Hon. STEPHEN
R.D. The Scarlet Letter (Roy. 9/5/88, *copy.*; Roy. 4/6/88). L.C.
[Written in collaboration with *N. FORBES.*]

COLES, CELLAS
D. Deserted (Athen. Shepherd's Bush, 13/12/94). L.C.

COLES, EDMUND
Ext. La Reine des Naiades (K.X. 30/4/70). L.C. as *The Naiad Queen.*

COLETTI, ANTONIO
Ent. Ancient and Modern Magic (Str. 2/4/60).

COLLETT, LOUIS
M.Sk. A Matrimonial Agency (Athen. 1/6/92; Bijou, 10/7/97). L.C. Vic. H. 15/11/88; L.C. Com. 21/9/91, *revised.*

COLLETTE, CHARLES
F. While it's to be had (Holb. 17/12/74). L.C. as *Bounce.*
F. Cryptoconchoidsyphonostomata (Roy. 8/12/75). L.C.
[This seems to be a revised version of the above.]

COLLETTE, MARY
D.Sk. Cousin's Courtship (Lyr. 24/9/92; Shaft. 26/9/92). L.C.

COLLIER, HAL
D. The Wheel of Fortune; or, The Hawk's Nest (Rotherham, 4/5/83).
D. The Missing Link (Workington, 22/2/86).
F.C. Is Marriage a Failure? (Woolwich, 19/11/88). L.C.
[Written in collaboration with *F. H. DUDLEY.*]
M.C. My Nadine; or, André the Mountaineer (Exhibition Pal. Folkestone, 20/5/89). L.C.
[Music by J. de Croix.]
D. Taken by Storm (Brit. 20/11/89). L.C.
D. In Deadly Peril (Aquar. Scarborough, 3/2/90). L.C. Gateshead, 3/10/89.

COLLIER, J. W.
[For his earlier plays see iv, 281.]
P. Harlequin Callandrack Callabando (Brit. 27/12/52).

COLLIER-EDWARDS, HAL
D. Barnes of New York (M'bone, 23/6/88).
D. The Phantom (Adel. L'pool, 22/10/88). L.C.

COLLINGHAM, GEORGE GERVASE
D. Oliver Twist (Olym. 21/12/91).
D. Meroflède; or, Love's Awakening (Preston, 31/12/92). L.C.
D. The Pilgrim's Progress (Olym. 10/6/96, *copy.*; Olym. 24/12/96). L.C.
D. The Idol of an Hour (Windsor, 16/1/99).

COLLINS, ARTHUR
P. Babes in the Wood (D.L. 27/12/97). See *A. STURGESS.*
P. The Forty Thieves (D.L. 26/12/99). See *A. STURGESS.*

COLLINS, CHARLES
D. Blind Hearts (Birmingham, 17/12/77). L.C.

COLLINS, C. J.
F. Take care of your Pockets (Str. 17/5/58). L.C.

COLLINS, EDWARD

C.D. Ashes (P.W. 30/11/94). L.C.
[Written in collaboration with *R. SAUNDERS*.]

COLLINS, H. BEALE

D. The Three Graces (County, Kingston, 11/2/98). L.C.

COLLINS, J. P.

D. Aileen; or, Foiled at Last (Grec. 15/4/72). L.C.

COLLINS, MABEL

D. Suggestion; or, The Hypnotist (Lyr. Hammersmith, 21/11/91, *copy*.). L.C.
[Written in collaboration with *W. H. BROWN*.]

D. A Modern Hypatia: A Drama of Today (Bijou, 22/2/94, *copy*.; Terry's, 17/6/95). L.C.

COLLINS, O. B.

D. The Waifs of New York (Albion, 18/5/78).

COLLINS, WILLIAM WILKIE

D. The Frozen Deep (Tavistock House, 6/1/57, *amat*.; Olym. 27/10/66). L.C.

D. The Lighthouse (Tavistock House, 1857, *amat*.; Olym. 10/8/57). L.C.

D. The Red Vial (Olym. 11/10/58). L.C.

D. A Message from the Sea (Brit. 7/1/61). L.C. 8° 1861.

D. Armadale. 8° 1866.

D. No Thoroughfare (Adel. 26/12/67). See *C. DICKENS*.

D. Black and White (Adel. 29/3/69; Exeter, 24/9/77). L.C. 8° 1869.

D. No Name. 8° 1870 [*priv*.].

D. The Woman in White (Olym. 9/10/71). L.C. 8° 1871 [*priv*.].

D. Man and Wife (P.W. 22/2/73). L.C.

D. The New Magdalen (Olym. 19/5/73). L.C. 8° 1873 [*priv*.].

D. Miss Gwilt (Alex. L'pool, 9/12/75; Glo. 15/4/76). L.C. 8° 1875 [*priv*.].

D. The Moonstone (Olym. 17/9/77). L.C. 8° 1877 [*priv*.].

D. Rank and Riches (Adel. 9/6/83). L.C.

D. The Evil Genius (Vaud. 30/10/85, *copy*.). L.C.

COLMAN, J.

D. Dred (Sur. 10/56). See *F. L. PHILLIPS*.

COLNAGHI, C. P.

C.O. Doctor D. (Roy. 30/5/85). L.C.
[Music by C. Dick.]

Bsq. David Garrick (Crit. 11/5/88).
[Written in collaboration with *E. PONSONBY*.]

C.D. The Up Train (H. 22/5/90, *mat*.).

Oa. The Spring Legend (O.C. 17/12/91, *mat*.).
[Music by C. Dick.]

Dual. A Debt of Honour (O.C. 17/12/91, *mat*.). L.C. *French*.

COLOMB, Captain

Ca. Davenport Done; or, An April Fool (Dublin, 4/2/67). *Lacy*.

COLONA, EDGARDO

D. Crime and its Atonement (Amphi. Leeds, 15/11/75). L.C. E.C. 29/7/76, as *Crime's Atonement*.

D. Don John of Seville (E.C. 30/9/76). L.C.

COLTHURST, NICHOLAS

F. My Astral Body (Court, 22/4/96). See *C. HUDSON.*

COLVILLE, Sir HARRY

Bsq. The Nick of Time (Chelsea Barracks, 23/3/96).

COLVILLE, W. F.

C.D. A Link of Love (Cambridge, Spennymoor, 18/7/82). L.C. Rotherham.

COMBE, JOHN

D. Master Alfred. 8° 1876 [Edinburgh].

COMER, GEORGE

D. Hard Lines (Qns. Manchester, 16/4/83). L.C.
D. Till Death do us part (Sur. 20/4/85). L.C.
D. The Main Hope (W. Bromwich, 31/8/85; Brit. 30/8/86). L.C.
D. Dead Beat (Sur. 22/10/85). See *G. CONQUEST.*
D. The Lock-Keeper's Daughter (Stratford, 4/9/86).
R.D. Never despair (Gai. Halifax, 5/5/87; S.W. 9/3/89).
M.D. The Right Man (Sanger's, 7/5/87). L.C. P.W. Salford, 23/9/86.
[Written in collaboration with *L. ELLIS.*]
D. The Lucky Star (Darlington, 1/8/87; E.C. 6/5/89). L.C. W. Bromwich.
[Written in collaboration with *E. C. MATTHEWS.*]
C.D. Life's Battle (Pav. Lytham, 3/8/91). L.C.
D. The Red Barn (Alh. Barrow-in-Furness, 10/6/92). L.C. Birkenhead, 13/4/92.
[Written in collaboration with *L. ELLIS.*]
D. The Royal Scout (Court, Wigan, 10/10/92). L.C. Amphi. Ramsgate, 16/4/92.
D. Homeless (Leicester, 19/7/93). See *J. K. MURRAY.*
D. The Tiger's Grip (Lyc. Ipswich, 23/3/98). See *M. GOLDBERG.*
D. Brave Hearts (Middleton, 3/11/98, *copy.*; Darwen, 6/3/99; Stratford, 24/6/1901). L.C.
[Written in collaboration with *F. BENTON.*]

COMERFORD, MAURICE

D. Waiting for Death (E.C. 9/2/78). See *L. ROBERTSON.*
F. An Artful Little Spouser. L.C. Alh. Barrow-in-Furness, 19/7/82. See *L. ROBERTSON.*

COMPTON, CHARLES G.

C. A Family Matter (Gar. 27/6/94). L.C.
[Written in collaboration with *A. G. HOCKLEY.*]

COMPTON, Mrs CHARLES G.

Duol. A Vacant Place (Terry's, 23/6/99). L.C.

COMPTON, EDWARD

C. A Strange Relation (P.W. L'pool, 22/5/76). L.C.
Ca. A Mutual Separation (P'cess. Edinburgh, 7/12/77; Bijou, 10/1/79). L.C.
D. Faithful unto Death (Bristol, 2/9/81). See *E. M. ROBSON.*

CONDIE, —

D. The Man in the Iron Mask (Grand, Walsall, 17/4/99). See —. *PERTH.*
D. Citizen Robespierre (Roy. Chester, 2/6/99). See —. *PERTH.*

CONNELL, E. J.

C. Caught and Caged (Cambridge H. Southport, 26/2/77).

CONNELL, W. J.

D. Perfidy (Bolton, 10/11/87). See *E. FALCONER.*

CONNOR, BARRY

D. Gra-Gal-Machree (Brit. 31/7/76). L.C.
D. The Sumachaun (Brit. 5/8/78). L.C.
D. Corney Rhill; or, The Pilgrim's Well (Brit. 4/8/79). L.C.
M.D. Ony-na-Pocas (Limerick, 27/9/79).
D. Emigration (Qns. Dublin, 13/7/80).

CONNYNGHAME, FREDERIC L.

D. The Prodigal Parson; or, For Ever and Ever (P.W. Salford, 24/3/98, *copy.*; Lincoln, 16/5/98; Stand. 19/6/99). L.C.
[Written in collaboration with *C. A. CLARKE.*]
F.C. What happened to Hooley (Star, Wolverhampton, 11/3/99, *copy.*). L.C.
D. Is he a Christian? (Rotunda, L'pool, 10/12/1900). L.C. Blyth, 18/8/98.
[Written in collaboration with *F. PRICE.*]

CONQUEST, GEORGE

D. Woman's Secret; or, Richelieu's Wager (Grec. 17/10/53). L.C.
P. Harlequin Sun and Moon; or, The Seven Sisters of the Zodiac in an Uproar. L.C. Grec. 17/12/55.
P. The Forty Thieves. L.C. Grec. 10/4/57.
D. The Angel of Death (Grec. 10/6/61). L.C. *Lacy.*
P. Number Nip (Grec. 26/12/62).
P. The Devil on Two Sticks; or, Harlequin the Golden Tree, Bird and Apple (Grec. 24/12/66). L.C.
D. The Rescue on the Raft; or, Sunlight through the Mist (Grec. 20/5/67). L.C.
F. Obliging a Friend (Grec. 11/11/67).
P. Harlequin Rik Rak, the Giant of the Mountains; or, The Goblin's Gift of the Kingdoms Three, and the Good Fairy and the Princess (Grec. 24/12/67). L.C.
[Written in collaboration with *H. SPRY.*]
P. The Flying Dutchman; or, Harlequin the Riddle of the Sphinx and the Pretty Princess who was made by a Charm (Grec. 24/12/68). L.C.
[Written in collaboration with *H. SPRY.*]
D. The Streets to the Hulks; or, The Old World and the New (Grec. 17/5/69). L.C. with titles reversed.
P. The Gnome Fly; or, Harlequin and the Nine Dwarfs and the Magic Crystal (Grec. 24/12/69). L.C.
[Written in collaboration with *H. SPRY.*]
P. Herne the Hunter; or, Harlequin the Demon Oak and the Maid, the Monarch and Young Mischief (Grec. 24/12/70). L.C.
[Written in collaboration with *H. SPRY.*]
P. Zig Zag the Crooked; or, Harlequin the King, the Cat and the Pretty Princess; or, The Frog, the Fairy and the Wishes Three (Grec. 23/12/71). L.C.
[Written in collaboration with *H. SPRY.*]
D. Genevieve; or, The Lost Wife (Grec. 22/4/72).

P. Nix, the Demon Dwarf; or, Harlequin and the Seven Charmed Bullets (Grec. 24/12/72). L.C.
[Written in collaboration with *H. SPRY.*]

D. The Elixir of Life (Grec. 29/9/73).

P. The Wood Demon (Grec. 24/12/73). L.C.
[Written in collaboration with *H. SPRY.*]

D. Velvet and Rags (Grec. 6/4/74). See *P. MERRITT.*

D. Hand and Glove (Grec. 25/5/74). See *P. MERRITT.*

D. Seven Sins (Grec. 27/8/74). See *P. MERRITT.*

D. The Blind Sister (Grec. 26/10/74). See *P. MERRITT.*

P. Snip Snap Snorum; or, Harlequin Birds, Beasts and Fishes (Grec. 24/12/74). L.C.
[Written in collaboration with *H. SPRY.*]

D. Dead to the World (Grec. 12/7/75). L.C.
[Written in collaboration with *H. PETTITT.*]

D. Sentenced to Death (Grec. 14/10/75). L.C.
[Written in collaboration with *H. PETTITT.*]

P. Spitz-Spitze, the Spider Crab (Grec. 27/12/75). L.C.
[Written in collaboration with *H. SPRY.*]

D. Snatched from the Grave (Grec. 13/3/76). L.C.
[Written in collaboration with *H. PETTITT.*]

D. Queen's Evidence (Grec. 5/6/76). L.C.
[Written in collaboration with *H. PETTITT.*]

D. Neck or Nothing (Grec. 3/8/76). L.C.
[Written in collaboration with *H. PETTITT.*]

D. The Sole Survivor; or, A Tale of the Goodwin Sands (Grec. 5/10/76). L.C.
[Written in collaboration with *H. PETTITT.*]

P. The Grim Goblin (Grec. 23/12/76). L.C.
[Written in collaboration with *H. SPRY.*]

D. Schriften, the One-eyed Pilot (Grec. 2/4/77).
[Written in collaboration with *H. PETTITT.*]

D. During Her Majesty's Pleasure (Grec. 21/5/77). L.C.
[Written in collaboration with *H. PETTITT.*]

D. Bound to Succeed; or, A Leaf from the Captain's Log Book (Grec. 29/10/77). L.C.
[Written in collaboration with *H. PETTITT.*]

P. Roley Poley; or, Harlequin Magic Umbrella (Grec. 24/12/77). L.C.
[Written in collaboration with *H. SPRY.*]

D. Notice to Quit; or, The Clutch of the Law (Grec. 20/4/78). L.C.
[Written in collaboration with *H. PETTITT.*]

D. The Green Lanes of England (Grec. 5/8/78). L.C.
[Written in collaboration with *H. PETTITT.*]

D. The Royal Pardon; or, The House on the Cliff (Grec. 28/10/78). L.C.
[Written in collaboration with *H. PETTITT.*]

P. Hokee Pokee (Grec. 24/12/78). L.C.
[Written in collaboration with *H. SPRY.*]

D. The Queen's Colours (Grec. 31/5/79). L.C.
[Written in collaboration with *H. PETTITT.*]

D. The Mesmerist (Grec. 4/10/79). L.C.
[Written in collaboration with *H. ROBINSON.*]

P. Harlequin Rokoko, the Rock Fiend (Grec. 24/12/79). L.C.
[Written in collaboration with *H. SPRY.*]

D. Mankind; or, Beggar your Neighbour (Sur. 3/10/81). L.C.
[Written in collaboration with *P. MERRITT*.]

P. Mother Bunch and the Man with the Hunch; or, The Reeds, the Weeds, the Priest, the Swell, the Gipsy Girl and the Big Dumb Bell (Sur. 24/12/81). L.C.
[Written in collaboration with *H. SPRY*.]

D. For Ever (Sur. 2/10/82). See *P. MERRITT*.

P. Puss in Boots, the Ogre, the Miller and the King of the Rats; or, The Pretty Princess and the Queen of the Cats (Sur. 23/12/82). L.C.
[Written in collaboration with *H. SPRY*.]

M.D. The Crimes of Paris (Sur. 22/10/83). See *P. MERRITT*.

P. Jack and Jill and the Well on the Hill (Sur. 24/12/83). L.C.
[Written in collaboration with *H. SPRY*.]

D. The King of Diamonds (Sur. 12/4/84). See *P. MERRITT*.

D. The Sins of the City (Sur. 29/9/84). See *P. MERRITT*.

P. Aladdin, the Lad with the Wonderful Lamp; or, The Precious Princess and the Precious Greek Scamp (Sur. 24/12/84). L.C.
[Written in collaboration with *H. SPRY*.]

D. The Devil's Luck; or, The Man she loved (Adel. L'pool, 8/85; Sur. 21/9/85). L.C.
[Written in collaboration with *L. TINSLEY*.]

D. Dead Beat (Sur. 22/10/85). L.C.
[Written in collaboration with *G. COMER*.]

P. Robinson Crusoe (Sur. 24/12/85). L.C.
[Written in collaboration with *H. SPRY*.]

D. Saved from the Streets; or, Waifs and Strays (Sur. 18/10/86). L.C.
[Written in collaboration with *R. H. EATON*.]

P. Jack and the Beanstalk (Sur. 24/12/86). L.C.
[Written in collaboration with *H. SPRY*.]

D. A Dead Man's Gold; or, The History of a Crime (Sur. 7/11/87). L.C.
[Written in collaboration with *H. SPRY*.]

P. Sinbad and the Little Old Man of the Sea (Sur. 24/12/87). L.C.
[Written in collaboration with *H. SPRY*.]

P. The Forty Thieves and their Wonderful Cave (Sur. 24/12/88). L.C.
[Written in collaboration with *H. SPRY*.]

P. Dick Whittington and his Cat; or, The Demon Rat, the Merchant's Daughter and the Charity Brat (Sur. 24/12/89). L.C.
[Written in collaboration with *H. SPRY*.]

D. The Village Forge (Sur. 15/9/90).
[Written in collaboration with *T. CRAVEN*.]

P. The Sleeping Beauty with the Golden Hair; or, Valentine and Orson and the Big Black Bear (Sur. 26/12/90). L.C.
[Written in collaboration with *H. SPRY*.]

P. The Fair One with the Golden Locks (Sur. 26/12/91). L.C.
[Written in collaboration with *H. SPRY*.]

P. Puss in Boots (Sur. 26/12/92). L.C.
[Written in collaboration with *H. SPRY*.]

P. Cinderella, the Sweet Kitchen Belle; or, The Little Glass Slipper and the Fairy Shell (Sur. 26/12/93). L.C.
[Written in collaboration with *H. SPRY*.]

D. Phantoms (Sur. 1/10/94). L.C. T.H. Luton, 23/8/92; Sur. 20/9/94.
[Written in collaboration with *A. SHIRLEY.*]
P. Red Riding Hood (Sur. 17/12/94). L.C.
[Written in collaboration with *H. SPRY.*]
D. The Work Girl (Sur. 15/4/95). L.C.
[Written in collaboration with *A. SHIRLEY.*]
D. The Winning Hand (Sur. 9/9/95). L.C.
[Written in collaboration with *St A. MILLER.*]
D. A Tale of the Thames (Sur. 28/10/95). L.C.
[Written in collaboration with *A. SHIRLEY.*]
P. Aladdin, a Lad with a Wonderful Lamp (Sur. 26/12/95). L.C.
[Written in collaboration with *H. SPRY.*]
P. Sinbad the Sailor (Sur. 26/12/96). L.C.
[Written in collaboration with *H. SPRY.*]
P. The Yellow Dwarf (Sur. 27/12/97). L.C.
[Written in collaboration with *H. SPRY.*]
P. Jack and Jill (Sur. 26/12/98). L.C.
[Written in collaboration with *H. SPRY.*]

CONQUEST, Mrs GEORGE
Bal. L'Union des Nations (Grec. 22/11/52).

CONRAD, R. T.
D. Jack Cade, the Captain of the Commons (Niblo's Garden, New York, 18/2/61; Qns. Dublin, 13/3/68). *Lacy.*

CONWAY, A. G.
C.D. Lita (New Cross H. 7/1/88). L.C.

CONWAY, HUGH [F. J. FARGUS]
D. Called back (P.W. 20/5/84). L.C.
[Written in collaboration with *J. C. CARR.*]
D. Dark Days (H. 26/9/85). See *J. C. CARR.*
C.O. Iduna (Com. Manchester, 28/10/89). L.C.
[Music by A. H. Behrend.]

CONYERS, FRANK N.
D. Wrexford (Star, Wolverhampton, 17/6/89). L.C.
[Title altered to *On Oath*, 23/12/89.]

COOK, DAVID
Oa. The White Cockade (St Andrew's H. Glasgow, 24/11/92, *amat.*).
[Music by Dr McMillan.]

COOK, KENINGALE
D. The King of Kent (H.M. Richmond, 28/10/81). L.C.

COOKE, CHARLES
D. Marian; or, The Earlier Days of Wallace (Southminster, Edinburgh, 6/6/70; Greenwich, 25/11/71, as *Marian and the Knight Templar*).
D. Madeline (Alex. Sheffield, 30/11/74).
D. Cœur de Lion; or, The Maid of Judah (Vic. 4/9/76).

COOKE, FREDERICK
D. Maureen na Laveen (Greenock, 7/2/73).
D. '98; or, Faugh a Ballagh (P.W. Rochdale, 13/7/74).
D. The Diver's Luck; or, The Crime Beneath the Waves (Jarrow, 30/5/87).
[Written in collaboration with *W. R. WALDRON.*]

D. The New Mazeppa (Croydon, 10/3/90; S.W. 22/9/90).
[Written in collaboration with *W. R. WALDRON*.]
D. Icebound; or, The Exiles of Fortune (Star, Wolverhampton, 25/7/92; Pav. 3/7/93). L.C. Hanley.
[Title altered to *The Brand of Shame*, 16/3/1904.]
D. On Shannon's Shore; or, The Blackthorn (P's. Reading, 14/2/95). L.C.

COOKE, J. F.
C.D. Our Sons and Daughters (P.W. Glasgow, 31/10/79).
C.D. Mrs Annesley (Crit. 1/7/91, *mat.*). L.C.
C.D. A Casual Acquaintance (Traf. 25/5/93). L.C.

COOKE, St CLAIR
Ca. A Dead Heat (Athen. Shepherd's Bush, 11/11/91). L.C.

COOKE, W.
Spec. The Arab of the Desert and his Faithful Steed (Ast. 18/2/56). L.C.

COOPER, F.
C.D. The Bow of Orange Ribbon (Daly's, 3/8/97, *copy.*). L.C.
[Written in collaboration with *F. JARDINE*.]

COOPER, FREDERICK FOX
[For his earlier plays see iv, 283.]
Ca. Shooting the Moon (Str. 29/10/50). *Lacy*.
D. Ovingdean Grange: A Tale of the South Downs (Sur. 29/9/51). *Dicks*.
Ca. A Race for a Wife (Adel. 19/8/76).

COOPER, G.
M.C. Billy (Tyne, Newcastle, 11/4/98). L.C.
[Written in collaboration with *A. ROSS*. Music by O. Carr.]

COOPER, HARWOOD
D. Hunted to Death (Vic. 26/10/67). L.C.

COOPER, HERBERT B.
C. 'Twixt Love and Art (Wolverhampton, 18/12/82). L.C. Concert H. Lewes, 23/10/82, as *Pauline Gordon; or, 'T. L. and A.*
C.D. Bank Holiday (P.W. L'pool, 14/7/86). L.C.
D. The Dawn of Hope (Nov. 20/1/96). See *C. BURNETTE*.

COOPER, J. B.
F. Our Geordie (Newcastle, 7/3/72; Glasgow, 1872, as *Oor Geordie; or, The Horrid Barbarian*). L.C.
C.Oa. Juanita; or, A Night in Seville (L'pool, 2/4/72).

COOPER, W.
F.C. Angelina (Vaud. 9/5/89, *mat.*). L.C.

COPPING, BERNARD
D. A Woman's Guilt (Nov. 12/10/96). L.C.

COPPING, EDWARD
F. A Real Lady Macbeth (Park H. Camden Town, 1/4/89).

CORBETT, Mrs GEORGE
D. The War Correspondent (Sur. 28/11/98). L.C.
[Written in collaboration with *W. BOYNE*.]
C.D. A Bit of Human Nature (Terry's, 27/6/99). L.C.

CORCORAN, LESLIE

C. Grandpapa's Promise (Cheltenham, 4/11/87). L.C.

CORD, D. M.

Ca. The Choice (P.H. Ealing Deane, 5/2/87).

CORDER, FREDERICK

C.O. The Noble Savage (Aquar. Brighton, 3/10/85; Stand. 30/4/87). L.C.

[Written in collaboration with *Mrs F. CORDER.*]

R.O. Nordisa (Court, L'pool, 26/1/87; D.L. 4/5/87). L.C.

C.O. The Golden Web (Court, L'pool, 15/2/93). See *B. C. STEPHENSON.*

CORDER, Mrs FREDERICK

Oa. A Storm in a Teacup (Aquar. Brighton, 18/2/82; Gai. 22/3/82).

C.O. The Noble Savage (Aquar. Brighton, 3/10/85). See *F. CORDER.*

CORDINGLEY, C.

D. The Ferryman's Daughter (Lyr. Hammersmith, 31/7/91). See *H. T. JOHNSON.*

CORDYCE, —

D. £1000 Reward (Aquar. Scarborough, 15/12/92, *copy.*; Grand, Cardiff, 6/3/93; Pav. 16/7/94). L.C.

[Written in collaboration with *G. ROBERTS.*]

CORNEY, MARK

M.C.D. The Vicar's Daughter; or, Smiles and Tears (Halifax, 20/8/96). L.C.

COSHAM, ERNEST

D. The Home Coming (Com. 4/7/92). L.C.

COSTELLO, Miss

C.D. The Plebeian (Vaud. 28/7/91, *mat.*). L.C.

Ca. A Bad Quarter of an Hour (Qns. Dublin, 31/8/96). L.C. O.H. Cheltenham, 23/9/97.

COTHER, T.

Bsq. Fayre Rosamond; or, Ye Dagger and ye Poisoned Bowl (Gloucester, 19/4/69).

COTTELL, LOUIS

C.Oa. A First Rehearsal (Athen. 1/6/92; Bijou, 2/11/95).

[Music by the author.]

COTTINGHAM, C. WILBRAHAM

M.C. The Red Marine; or, The Spectre's Compact (Preston Assembly R. Brighton, 28/5/96). L.C.

COURT, F. H.

C. Pedigree (Lecture H. Derby, 10/12/89). See *C. C. BOWRING.*

COURTE, S. X.

D. Villon: Poet and Cut-throat (Grand, Birmingham, 12/4/94; Roy. 28/6/94). L.C.

C.D. The Great Pearl Case (Birmingham, 27/8/94; O.C. 26/11/94, as *The Wife of Dives*). L.C.

C.D. An Average Man; or, How the Average became the Abnormal (Pleasure Gdns. Folkestone, 6/3/95; O.C. 13/6/95). L.C.

COURTENAY, EDITH

C.D. Sisters (Jubilee H. Addlestone, 28/12/93; Assembly R. Balham, 30/9/95).

COURTENAY, FOSTER

D. In the King's Name (Eastbourne, 18/6/88; O.H. Northampton, 25/7/92, as *The Crimson Mask*). L.C.

COURTICE, THOMAS

Duol. My First Case (O.H. Chatham, 25/3/97). L.C.
[Music by E. Ramsay.]

COURTNEIDGE, ROBERT

F. Kitchen Love (Olym. 29/9/88). L.C.
D. Upon the Waters (P's. Manchester, 13/6/98). L.C.
[Written in collaboration with *A. THOMPSON*.]

COURTNEY, G. F.

F. The Dangers of Science (Swiss Gdns. Shoreham, 22/4/96). L.C.
D. Her Secret (Swiss Gdns. Shoreham, 24/11/97). L.C.

COURTNEY, JOHN

[For his earlier plays see iv, 283–4.]
F. The Two Polts (Sur. 25/11/50). *Lacy.*
D. Belphegor the Itinerant (Sur. 20/1/51). L.C. *Lacy.*
D. The World's Games; or, High and Low (Sur. 24/2/51). L.C.
D. Living in Glass Houses (Str. 28/4/51). L.C.
D. Roland the Rider (Sur. 9/6/51). L.C.
D. The Magic of Life (Sur. 23/6/51). L.C. Sur. 24/8/50.
D. The Castle of Valenza (Olym. 15/7/51).
Ext. The Two Bloomers (Sur. 13/10/51). L.C.
Oa. The Charmed Harp (Sur. 30/8/52). L.C.
[Music by M. Lutz.]
Ext. Going to Cremorne (Sur. 4/10/52). L.C.
D. The Seasons (Sur. 4/10/52). L.C. Stand. 2/2/50.
D. Off to the Diggings (Sur. 18/10/52). L.C.
D. Uncle Tom's Cabin (Sur. 1/11/52). L.C.
D. The Life Chase (Sur. 15/11/52).
D. The Gambler's Wife (Sur. 3/10/53). L.C.
D. Old Joe and Young Joe (Sur. 31/10/53). L.C. as *The Martin Family; or, O.J. and Y.J. French.*
D. Eustache Baudin (Sur. 30/1/54). L.C. *Lacy.*
D. Deeds, not Words; or, The Drooping Flower (Sur. 8/1/55).
C. Double-faced People (H. 7/2/57). L.C. *Lacy.*
C.D. A Wicked Wife (H. 16/2/57). L.C. *Lacy.*

COURTNEY, WILLIAM LEONARD

D. Kit Marlowe (Shaft. 4/7/90, *mat.*; St J. 31/10/92).
D. Gaston Boissier (Herkomer, Bushey, 9/1/93).

COURTOIS, M. A.

D. The Queen's Tragedy (St G. 13/10/99). L.C.

COVENEY, G. H.

D. Jean; or, That Lass o' Lowrie's (Coventry, 8/7/78). L.C.
D. The Golden Calf; or, Dollars and Dimes (Stand. 18/6/83). L.C.

[*COVENEY, HOWARD*

C. Uncle Jonathan (Pier Pav. St Leonard's, 3/7/99). L.C. E.C. 28/12/99.

COWAN, F.

F. Too Many by One (St G. 1865). See *F. C. BURNAND.*

COWARD, J. M.

Bsq. Forlorn Hope (H.M. Oxford, 22/5/96). See *C. W. SCOTT.*

COWELL, A. E.

F. My Wife (Pier Pav. Eastbourne, 17/10/92).

F. Baby (Pier Pav. Eastbourne, 24/12/92).

COWEN, HENRIETTA

D.Sk. A Quiet Pipe (Folly, 17/3/80). L.C.
[Written in collaboration with *S. M. SAMUEL.*]

COWEN, L.

F. The Great Demonstration (Roy. 17/9/92). See *I. ZANGWILL.*

COWIE, R., Sen.

D. Ivanhoe (Dundee, 15/2/75). L.C.

COWIS, DAVID

D. A Deadlock (Bijou, 7/2/98). L.C.
[Written in collaboration with *J. H. BATSON.*]

COWPER, ARCHIE

D. Eva's Inheritance (Alex. L'pool, 6/4/70).

COX, ALFRED

C.D. Wolves and Waifs (Gai. Brighton, 20/7/91). L.C.
[Title altered to *The Detective*, 20/11/91.]

COX, Mrs DOUGLAS

Ca. The Pink Letter (Maidenhead, 27/1/98). L.C.

COX, R. DOUGLAS

D. The Fifth of November (Adel. 6/11/54).

COYNE, GARDINER

D. Wolves (Whitehaven, 17/11/82).

COYNE, JOSEPH STIRLING

[For his earlier plays see iv, 284–5.]

F. An Unprotected Female (Str. 4/2/50). *Lacy.*

C. My Wife's Daughter (Olym. 14/10/50). L.C. *Lacy.*

F. Presented at Court (H. 6/2/51). L.C. *Webster.*

F. A Duel in the Dark (H. 31/1/52; Sur. 18/2/56, as *Jasper Langton; or, A D. in the D.*). L.C. *Lacy.*

F. Wanted 1000 Spirited Young Milliners for the Gold Diggings (Olym. 2/10/52). L.C. *Lacy.*

F. Box and Cox married and settled (H. 14/10/52). L.C. *Lacy.*

Bsq. Leo the Terrible (H. 27/12/52). L.C. *Lacy.*
[Written in collaboration with *F. TALFOURD.*]

C. The Hope of the Family (H. 3/12/53). L.C. as *Borrowed Plumes. Lacy.*

Ba. Willikind and his Dinah (H. 16/3/54). L.C. *Lacy.*

D. The Old Chateau; or, A Night of Peril (H. 24/7/54). L.C. *Lacy.*

C. The Secret Agent (H. 10/3/55). L.C. *Lacy.*

C. The Man of Many Friends (H. 1/9/55). L.C. *Lacy.*

Ext. Catching a Mermaid (Olym. 20/10/55). L.C. *Lacy.*

F. Urgent Private Affairs (Adel. 7/1/56). L.C. *Lacy.*

M.D. Fraud and its Victims (Sur. 2/3/57). L.C. as *The Victims of Fraud. Lacy.*

D. Angel or Devil (Lyc. 2/3/57). L.C. *Lacy.*
F. The Latest from New York (Adel. 29/6/57). L.C.
F. What will they say at Brompton? (Olym. 23/11/57). L.C. *Lacy.*
C. The Love Knot (D.L. 8/3/58). L.C. *Lacy.*
F. Samuel in Search of Himself (P'cess. 5/4/58). L.C. *Lacy.*
C. Nothing Venture, nothing Win (Str. 5/4/58). L.C. *Lacy.*
C. Everybody's Friend (H. 2/4/59; St J. 16/10/67, as *The Widow Hunt*). L.C. *Lacy.*
F. The Talking Fish (Adel. 26/5/59). L.C.
Vaud. Pets of the Parterre; or, Love in a Garden (Lyc. 5/11/60). L.C. *French.*
F. The Little Rebel (Olym. 1/4/61). L.C. *French.*
C. Black Sheep (H. 22/4/61). L.C. *Lacy.*
Ca. The Particulars of that Affair at Finchley (Str. 14/10/61). L.C. *French.*
F. A Terrible Secret (D.L. 28/10/61). L.C. *French.*
F. Duck Hunting (H. 29/9/62). *French.*
Sk. Mr Buckstone at Home; or, The Manager and his Friends (H. 6/4/63). L.C. *Lacy.*
C. The Woman in Red (Vic. 28/3/64). L.C. *Lacy.*
F. Dark Doings in the Closet by the Knotting 'em Brothers (Adel. 29/12/64). L.C. as *The Knotting 'em Brothers*. *French.*
Ca. The Broken-hearted Club (H. 16/1/68). L.C.
C. The Woman of the World (Olym. 17/2/68). L.C. *Lacy.*
D. The Homewreck (Sur. 8/2/69). L.C. *Lacy.*
[Completed by *J. DENIS.*]

CRAFT, JOSEPH
C. The Sculptor (Leinster H. Dublin, 18/8/93). See *T. G. WARREN.*

CRAIGIE, Mrs P. M. T. See "*JOHN OLIVER HOBBES*"

CRAUFORD, A. L.
D. Home once more; or, A False Accusation (Brit. 6/4/85). L.C.

CRAUFORD, J. R.
Oa. I'll see you right (O.H. Leicester, 3/6/78; Gai. 30/11/82). L.C. Huddersfield.
F. Smith's Mixture (Phil. 19/4/79). L.C. Norwich, 17/2/79.
D. A Ruined Life (Grand, 15/9/84). See *A. GOODRICH.*
C. They were married (Str. 17/6/92, *mat.*). L.C.
[Written in collaboration with *F. HAWLEY.*]

CRAVEN, HENRY THORNTON [*HENRY THORNTON*]
[For his earlier plays see iv, 285.]
F. Not to be done (Str. 6/5/50). L.C. *French.*
Ba. The Village Nightingale; or, The Spider, the Fly and the Butterfly (Str. 23/6/51). *French.*
D.D. Our Nelly (Sur. 28/3/53). L.C. *Lacy.*
D. Unlucky Friday (S.W. 17/11/58). *Lacy.*
F. Bowled out; or, A Bit of Brummagem (P'cess. 9/7/60). L.C. *Lacy.*
D. The Post Boy (Str. 31/10/60). L.C. *French.*
D. The Chimney Corner (Olym. 21/2/61). L.C. *Lacy.*
F. My Preserver (Str. 2/3/63). L.C. *Lacy.*
D. Miriam's Crime (Str. 9/10/63). L.C. *French.*
Sk. Bunkum Muller (H. 24/2/64). L.C.
D. Milky White (P.W. L'pool, 20/6/64; Str. 28/9/64). L.C. *Lacy.*

D. One Tree Hill (Str. 17/4/65). L.C. *Lacy.*
C. The Needful (P.W. L'pool, 4/6/66; St J. 1/1/68). L.C.
C.D. Meg's Diversion (Roy. 17/10/66). L.C. *Lacy.*
D. Philomel (Glo. 10/2/70). L.C. *Lacy.*
[Title altered to *The Curse of Kin*, 4/5/85.]
C. Barwise's Book (Edinburgh, 13/4/70; H. 25/4/70). L.C.
D. Coals of Fire (Court, 20/11/71). L.C. *Lacy.*
D. Too True (Duke's, 22/1/76). L.C.

CRAVEN, SCOTT
F.C. The Future Mrs Skillimore (Marine, Ramsgate, 5/6/97). L.C.

CRAVEN, TOM
D. All Lost (S.W. 21/7/83). L.C. Margate, 30/11/81.
F. Mumps the Masher (Nottingham, 2/6/84; Pav. 11/8/84). L.C. Longton.
[Written in collaboration with *R. NELSON.*]
D. The Stowaway (Dewsbury, 29/9/84; S.W. 21/2/85; Middlesborough, 14/6/86, *revised*). L.C.
[Title altered to *Success*, 3/5/86.]
Ca. Grasping a Shadow (W. Hartlepool, 20/7/85).
F. The Visiting Card (Brit. 30/5/87). L.C.
D. The Fugitive (Alh. Barrow-in-Furness, 1/8/87; Sur. 4/6/88). L.C.
D. The Miser's Will (Gai. Hastings, 3/12/88; Sur. 4/11/89). L.C.
D. The Village Forge (Sur. 15/9/90). See *G. CONQUEST.*
Ca. The Workbox (Worcester, 31/10/90; Weymouth, 9/7/91). L.C. *French.*
M.D. The Ballad Singer (Gai. Hastings, 16/7/91; Morton's Greenwich, 8/8/92; E.C. 12/9/92). L.C. Winter Gdns. Blackpool, 18/6/89, as *Margery Daw.*
D. Time the Avenger (Sur. 10/10/92). L.C. Rotherham, 1/1/92.
D. Half-mast High (Pav. 1/4/93). L.C.
P. Aladdin in Luck (Parkhurst, 23/12/93). L.C.
P. The Bonnie Babies in the Wood (Parkhurst, 22/12/94). L.C.
[Music by T. P. Fish.]

CRAVEN, WALTER STOKES
C. Nowadays (Croydon, 2/3/82). L.C.
F. An Innocent Abroad (Belfast, 9/11/94; Terry's, 14/1/95). L.C. Blackpool.
C.D. The Cruel Law (Stratford, 16/12/95). L.C.
F. Four Little Girls (Crit. 17/7/97). L.C.
C.D. No Appeal (Eden, Brighton, 6/12/97).

[*CRAWFORD, F. MARION*
C. Dr Claudius (Vaud. 29/1/97). L.C.
[Written in collaboration with *H. St MAUR.*]

CRAWFORD, J.
M.D. Prince Charles Edward Stuart; or, The Rising of 1745 (R. Exchange R. Paisley, 12/10/68).

CRAWSHAW, T.
D. In the Eye of the Law (P's. Portsmouth, 24/4/93). L.C.

CREAMER, AUGUSTUS
D. False Cards (Athen. H. Bury, 11/1/73).
D. Blarney (Newcastle, 1/3/75).

D. The Informers (Leeds, 31/8/83).
D. United (Consett, 1/10/86). See *J. N. HARLEY.*
D. Irish Life (Lowestoft, 22/10/88; S.W. 17/11/90).
[Written in collaboration with *L. T. DOWNEY.*]

CRESSWELL, Mrs G.
D. The King's Banner (Dublin, 6/12/72). 8° 1873.

CRESSWELL, Rev. HENRY
D. The Conversion of England (St Peter's H. Vauxhall, 1885).
D. In Danger (Brighton, 24/10/87). See *W. LESTOCQ.*

CRICHTON, H.
M.D. Lovers (Cork, 5/5/86). See *W. E. MORTON.*

CRITCHETT, RICHARD CLAUDE. See "*R. C. CARTON*"

CROFTE, A.
D. Woman's Peril (Vic. 23/7/77). See *W. E. SUTER.*

CROFTON, CECIL
D. Eric's Good Angel (Newcastle, 23/5/94). See *F. BIRD.*
C.D. Mr Dick's Heir (Chatsworth, 1/1/95).
[Written in collaboration with *H. BROOKE.*]

CROFTON, EDWARD
C.D. The 24th Geo. II, Cap. 23 D (Roy. 2/5/66). L.C.

CROFTON, MARION
Duol. My Paying Guest (Qns. H. 25/2/95).

CROMER, WEST
M.Ca. A Night Surprise. L.C. St G. 8/2/77.
[Written in collaboration with *G. REED.*]

CROSS, A. F.
D. Keen Blades; or, The Straight Tip (Sheffield, 22/5/93). L.C. Bolton.
[Written in collaboration with *J. F. ELLISTON.*]

CROSS, FRANK
D. Penal Servitude: A Story of Manchester Life (P.W. Salford, 29/11/83). L.C.

CROSS, JULIAN
D. Heinrich; or, From Fatherland to the Far West (Bristol, 3/4/76). L.C.
C. Current Coin (Bristol, 28/2/79). L.C. Nottingham, 24/6/78.
D. The Crimson Rock (Pav. 31/5/79). L.C.
D. The Outcast Poor; or, The Byways of London (Sur. 25/8/84).
F.C. Boiling Water (Com. 22/7/85). L.C.
D. A Miser (Brighton, 16/11/87; Glo. 5/5/90). L.C. *French.*
D. The Penalty (Terry's, 2/12/90, *mat.*). L.C.
C. Sweet Cupid's Net (Str. 21/4/92, *mat.*). L.C.
C. Floating a Company (Roy. 28/6/94). L.C. *French.*

CROWE, CATHARINE
D. The Cruel Kindness (H. 6/6/53). L.C. as *The Physician's Daughter.* 8° 1853.

"*CROWQUILL, ALFRED*" [*ALFRED HENRY FORRESTER*]

CROZIER, CHARLES

D. Scarlet Sins (O.H. Wakefield, 4/10/88; P's. Bradford, 6/5/89 and Morton's, Greenwich, 3/3/90; as *Fair Play*; Athen. 27/11/89, as *Run to Earth*). L.C.
[Written in collaboration with *P. MILTON*.]

F. Blobb's Holiday (M'bone, 18/4/92). L.C.

F. An Unlucky Coincidence (Ladb. H. 26/2/97). L.C.

D. An Old Promise (Ladb. H. 13/5/98). L.C.

CUBITT, SIDNEY

C.O. The Competitors; or, The Nymph of Nozenaro (Subscription R. Stroud, 19/1/93, *amat.*).
[Music by T. Hackwood.]

O. Zanone; or, The Dey and the Knight (Subscription R. Stroud, 8/11/99).
[Music by T. Hackwood.]

CULLERNE, E. A.

F. Dreadfully Alarming (Phil. 30/9/71). See *C. T. M. EDWARDES.*

CULLUM, H. C.

Ca. Catching the Idea (Empire, Blackpool, 2/6/99). See *H. W. HATCHMAN.*

CULLUM, HERBERT H.

Sk. Wilfred's Choice (Corn Exchange, Maidstone, 14/12/94).

CULLUM, W. T.

Ca. A Welsh Heiress (Com. 21/1/93). L.C.

CUMBERLAND, STUART

D. The Wonder-worker; or, A Modern Magician (Margate, 1/6/94). L.C.

CUNNINGHAM, Major A. C.

C.Oa. Lansdown Castle; or, The Sorcerer of Tewkesbury (Corn Exchange, Cheltenham, 7/2/93, *amat.*).
[Music by G. van Holst.]

CURLING, HENRY

C.D. The Merry Wags of Warwickshire; or, The Early Days of Shakespere. 8° 1854.

CURRY, CLIVE F.

D.Sk. That Fatal Hour (Athen. Shepherd's Bush, 8/10/95).

CURTIN, J. M.

D. 'Twixt Love and Duty (P.H. Lowestoft, 26/3/94, *amat.*).

D. Under the British Flag (P.H. Lowestoft, 26/12/96, *amat.*). L.C.

CUTHBERT, ERNEST

Ca. Legacy Love (Vaud. 7/12/72). L.C.

Ca. A Happy Cruise (Vaud. 17/11/73). L.C.

Ca. Once Again (Vaud. 25/1/79). L.C.

Oa. A Gay Cavalier (Manchester, 15/9/79). L.C.
[Music by A. A. Nicholson.]

F. Families supplied (Adel. 7/8/82). L.C.

CUTHELL, EDITH E.

F. The Wrong Envelope (Str. 19/7/87; Nov. 20/6/88, *mat.*, *revised*). L.C.

CUTLER, JOHN
Monol. Her First Ball (Terry's, 29/6/99). L.C.

CYMPSON, E.
C.O. Dolly Varden; or, The Riots of '80 (Aquar. Brighton, 4/11/89). [Music by the author.]

DABBS, Dr GEORGE HENRY ROQUÉ
C.D. Blackmail (Literary Inst. Shanklin, 3/9/87; Crit. 17/10/88, *mat.*). L.C.
Ca. The Understudy (Literary Inst, Shanklin, 15/12/87, *amat.*). L.C.
C.D. The Contractor (Literary Inst. Shanklin, 15/12/87, *amat.*). L.C.
Ca. Popsy (Literary Inst. Shanklin, 13/4/88, *amat.*).
C.D. Our Pal (Literary Inst. Shanklin, 24/4/89, *amat.*).
C.D. The Village Post-office (Literary Inst. Shanklin, 24/4/89, *amat.*).
C.D. Her Own Witness (P.W. Southampton, 24/5/89, as *The Witness*; Crit. 6/11/89, *mat.*). L.C.
C.D. Punchinello (Aven. 24/6/90, *mat.*). L.C.
D.Idyll. Dante (Literary Inst. Shanklin, 31/12/90, *copy.*; Independent Theatre Soc. at St G. H. 10/7/93).
[Written in collaboration with *E. RIGHTON.*]
D. Our Angels (Vaud. 3/3/91, *mat.*). L.C.
D. The Jewels (Literary Inst. Shanklin, 31/8/93). L.C.
D. The Blind Singer (Com. 22/4/98). L.C.

DACRE, HENRY S.
D. The Sorrows of Satan (Brit. 5/7/97). L.C.

DAKIN, T. M.
D. The Lost Heir of Macclesfield (Macclesfield, 15/2/75).

DALBY, —
P. Queen Mab; or, Harlequin Romeo and Juliet (Sur. 26/12/57).

DALE, BERNARD
D. Jezebel's Husband (Middleton, 1/12/93).

DALE, C.
C. The Whip Hand (Cambridge, 21/1/85). See *H. C. MERIVALE.*

DALE, E.
F. Our Accomplished Domestic (Str. 21/8/78).

"*DALE, FELIX*" [*HERMAN CHARLES MERIVALE*]
Ca. Six Months Ago (Olym. 26/7/67). L.C. *Lacy.*
F. He's a Lunatic (Qns. 24/10/67). L.C. *Lacy.*

DALE, G.
F.C. You never Know (Gai. 28/11/99). L.C.

DALGLEISH, SCOTT
D. A Soldier's Wife; or, Not on the Strength (Grand H. Hotel Cecil, 25/2/98). L.C.
[Written in collaboration with *W. PEACOCK.* Music by M. Brook.]

DALLAS, J.
M.C. One of the Girls (Grand, Birmingham, 9/3/96). See *J. H. DARNLEY.*

DALLAS, MERVYN
D. Broken to Harness (Brighton, 30/6/83). L.C.
D. Moths (Str. 26/6/84). L.C. Hamilton H. Salisbury, 7/2/83.

D'ALMEIDA, WILLIAM BARRINGTON

Ca. A Trip to Gretna (Vaud. 3/6/91, *mat.*). L.C. as *Gretna Green.*

DALROY, HERBERT

D. Twilight (Middlesborough, 19/6/93; Parkhurst, 7/5/94). L.C.

C. Tom (Lecture H. Derby, 28/12/93). L.C.
[Written in collaboration with *A. BEARNE.*]

Ca. Sweet Olden Days (Plymouth, 15/10/94). L.C.

[*DALRYMPLE, J. S.*

Spec. The Naiad Queen; or, The Revolt of the Water Nymphs (P'cess. Manchester, 27/8/83). *French.*

DALRYMPLE, LINA

Ca. Tricked (Barracks, Athlone, 9/84).

DALTON, LIONEL

F. The Magnet (Bijou, 27/4/93). L.C.

C.D. The Light (Bijou, 27/4/93). L.C.

DALTON, MAURICE

C.O. Atlantis; or, The Lost Land (Gai. 17/3/86, *mat.*; O.C. 17/6/93). L.C.
[Written in collaboration with *E. GENET.* Music by T. M. Haddow.]

D.Sk. Worcester Fight (St G. 11/1/90). L.C.

[*DALY, AUGUSTIN*

D. Leah, the Jewish Maiden (Boston, 8/12/62, as *Leah the Forsaken*; Adel. 1/10/63). L.C. *Lacy.*

D. Under the Gaslight; or, Life and Love in These Times (New York, 12/8/67; Tyne, Newcastle, 20/4/68; Pav. 20/7/68). *Lacy.*

D. Frou Frou (Fifth Avenue, New York, 12/2/70; St J. 25/5/70). L.C. *Lacy.*

C.D. Garrick; or, Acting in Earnest (P'cess. Edinburgh, 22/8/74).

C. Come here; or, The Debutante's Test (H. 4/5/76). L.C.

D. The Penal Code (Gai. Dublin, 11/2/78).

C.D. Divorce (Fifth Avenue, New York, 9/9/71; Edinburgh, 12/12/81).

D. Only a Woman (Fifth Avenue, New York, 14/12/75, as *Pique*; Brighton, 16/10/82; Gai. 26/3/84, as *Her Own Enemy*). L.C. as *Pique.*

C. Casting the Boomerang (Daly's, New York, 24/2/83; Toole's, 19/7/84). L.C. as *Seven Twenty Eight.*

C. Dollars and Sense (Daly's, New York, 2/10/83; Toole's, 1/8/84). L.C.

F.C. Needles and Pins (Daly's, New York, 9/11/80; C.P. 12/8/84). L.C.

C. A Night Off; or, A Page from Balzac (Daly's, New York, 4/3/85; Str. 27/5/86). L.C.

F. Nancy and Company (Daly's, New York, 24/2/86; Str. 7/7/86). L.C.

C. The Railroad of Love (Daly's, New York, 1/11/87; Gai. 3/5/88). L.C.

F.C. Miss Hoyden's Husband (Daly's, New York, 26/3/90; Shaft. 4/7/90, *mat.*).

C. The Great Unknown (Daly's, New York, 22/10/89; Lyc. 5/8/90). L.C.

C. The Last Word (Daly's, New York, 28/10/90; Lyc. 19/9/91). L.C.

F.C. Love in Tandem (Daly's, New York, 9/2/92; Daly's, 18/7/93). L.C.

C. The School for Scandal (Daly's, 13/11/93).
[Rearranged by Daly.]

C. The Countess Gucki (Daly's, New York, 28/1/96; Com. 11/7/96). L.C.

C. Love on Crutches (Daly's, New York, 25/11/84; Com. 28/7/96). L.C.

DALY, BRIAN

P. The Babes in the Wood (Lyr. Hammersmith, 26/12/96). L.C.
[Written in collaboration with *J. M. EAST.*]

Oa. Stirring Times (O.H. Southport, 2/8/97). See *F. H. CELLI.*

P. Cinderella (Lyr. Hammersmith, 27/12/97). L.C.
[Written in collaboration with *J. M. EAST.*]

D. The Three Musketeers (Lyr. Hammersmith, 7/11/98). L.C.
[Written in collaboration with *J. M. EAST.*]

P. Puss in Boots (Lyr. Hammersmith, 26/12/98). L.C.
[Written in collaboration with *J. M. EAST.*]

D. Faust and Marguerite (O.H. Leicester, 30/1/99; W.L. 13/2/99).
[Written in collaboration with *C. W. SOMERSET.*]

D.Sk. Bulldogs, Ahoy! (S.W. 30/12/99). L.C.
[Written in collaboration with *A. SYMS.*]

DALY, CHARLES

D. A Flash of Lightning (Amphi. Leeds, 1/8/70). See *J. M. MURDOCH.*

D. War (Albert H. Portsmouth, 23/1/71).

D. The Woman he loved and the Woman who loved him (Grec. 8/7/72). L.C.

Bsq. Lord Bateman (Seaham Harbour, 17/4/76).

Bsq. The Sleeping Beauty; Her Seven Fairy Godmothers and a Wicked Fairy (Aldershot, 3/8/85). L.C.
[Written in collaboration with *B. CHATTERTON.*]

P. Red Riding Hood (C.P. 23/12/86). See *O. BARRETT.*

F. Sly Dogs (Torquay, 11/4/87). L.C.

Ext. The Sleeping Beauty (Lyr. Hammersmith, 28/3/91).
[A new version of his earlier burlesque (Aldershot, 3/8/85).]

D. Woman's Idol (Margate, 20/7/91). L.C.
[Written in collaboration with *C. RAPHAEL.*]

F.C. Baboo or Prince? (Neville Dramatic Studio, 5/4/97).

D. Bonnie Annie Laurie (Lyc. Edinburgh, 1/8/98). L.C. Aquar. Gt Yarmouth, 9/2/97 as *Annie Laurie.*

P. Santa Claus (C.P. 24/12/98). L.C.
[Music by H. Godfrey and I. Corsi.]

"*DALY, JOHN.*" See *JOHN BESEMERES*

DAM, HENRY J. W.

D. Diamond Deane (Vaud. 18/3/91). L.C.

D. Prince Karatoff (P.W. Birmingham, 2/12/92; Aven. 15/4/93, as *The Silver Shell*). L.C.

M.F. The Shop Girl (Gai. 24/11/94). L.C.
[Additions by *A. ROSS* and *L. MONCKTON.* Music by I. Caryll.]

M.F. The White Silk Dress (P.W. 3/10/96). L.C.
[Music by A. McLean and R. Somerville.]

C.O. The Coquette (P.W. 11/2/99). L.C.
[Written in collaboration with *G. C. BINGHAM.*]

D. A King of Fools (Grand, 25/9/99). L.C.
[Written in collaboration with *C. CARTWRIGHT* and *B. LANDECK.*]

DAMERELL, STANLEY

D.Sk. A Rose among Thorns (Myddleton H. Islington, 21/11/98). L.C.

DAMPIER, ALFRED

D. Saint or Sinner? (Sur. 26/3/81). L.C.

D. Uncle Tom's Cabin (P'cess. 24/12/87).
[Written in collaboration with *J. F. SHERIDAN.*]

D. Robbery under Arms (P'cess. 22/10/94). L.C.
[Written in collaboration with *G. WALCH.*]

DANCE, CHARLES

[For his earlier plays see iv, 288–9.]

C. A Morning Call (D.L. 17/3/51). L.C. *Lacy*; 12° [1851].
[This was apparently licensed first for the Marylebone in 1847; see iv, 289.]

Ca. The Victor Vanquished (P'cess. 25/3/56). L.C. *Lacy.*
[For this also see iv, 289.]

F. The Stock Exchange; or, The Green Business (P'cess. 5/4/58). L.C. *Lacy.*

F. Marriage a Lottery (Str. 20/5/58). L.C. *Lacy.*

DANCE, GEORGE

Bsq. Oliver Grumble; or, The Terrible Twins (P.W. L'pool, 15/3/86; Nov. 25/3/86). L.C.

C.O. The Nautch Girl; or, The Rajah of Chutneypore (Sav. 30/6/91). L.C.
[Lyrics by *F. DESPREZ.* Music by E. Solomon.]

C. The Barmaid (Com. Manchester, 31/8/91). L.C.

R.O. Ma mie Rosette (Glo. 17/11/92). L.C.
[Music by I. Caryll.]

M.F. A Modern Don Quixote (Nottingham, 17/7/93; Str. 25/9/93; Lyr. 21/5/98, *revised*). L.C.
[Music by J. Crook.]

M.C. The Lady Slavey (O.H., Northampton, 4/9/93; Aven. 20/10/94). L.C.
[Music by J. Crook.]

M.C. The Gay Parisienne (O.H. Northampton, 1/10/94; E.C. 23/3/96; D.Y. 4/4/96). L.C.
[Music by I. Caryll.]

M.C. Buttercup and Daisy (Court, L'pool, 17/6/95; Kilburn, 9/9/95). L.C. Aven. 20/6/95.
[Music by A. Richards.]

M.F. Lord Tom Noddy (Bradford, 6/4/96; Gar. 15/9/96). L.C.
[Music by F. O. Carr.]

M.C. The New Mephistopheles (Grand, Leeds, 29/3/97; Brixton, 4/10/97). L.C.
[Music by E. Vousden.]

M.C. The Gay Grisette (Bradford, 1/8/98; Metro. 5/12/98). L.C.
[Music by C. Kiefert.]

M.C. A Chinese Honeymoon (Hanley, 16/10/99; Str. 5/10/1901). L.C.
[Written in collaboration with *H. TALBOT.*]

DANCY, A. T.
Ca. A Daring Device (Bijou, 7/6/79). L.C.

DANE, MORRIS
Ca. Wide Awake (Portsmouth, 18/7/87). L.C.

DANIELL, AIMÉE. See *Mrs OSCAR BERINGER*

DANVERS, HENRY
F. A Fascinating Individual; or, Two agreeable by half (Olym. 9/6/56). L.C.
F. A Conjugal Lesson (Olym. 3/7/56). L.C. as *The Married Flirt; or, A C. L. Lacy.*

DANVILLE, ARTHUR
P. Blue Beard (Imp. 26/12/98). L.C.

"*DARÂLE, FREDERIC*"
Duol. Little Jessie (Steinway H. 2/7/91).
Monol. The Strange Adventures of a French Pianist (Steinway H. 2/7/91).

DARBEY, EDWARD
D. Lily (Greenwich, 4/2/78). L.C.
D. The Forged Cheques (H.M. Richmond, 7/12/82). L.C.
D. Ever Faithful (Hastings, 7/85; Holb. 26/12/85).
D. Tempest Tossed (M'bone, 15/11/86). L.C.
D. Hearts of Gold (Qns. Keighley, 13/2/88). L.C.
C.D. Hand-in-hand (Rotherham, 5/8/89; Sur. 24/3/90). L.C.
D. Brought to Light (Rotherham, 12/8/89; Morton's, Greenwich, 28/7/90). L.C.
D. Exiled (Qns. Keighley, 12/2/91). See *W. MANNING.*
D. The Bells of Fate (Qns. Keighley, 21/9/91; S.W. 9/11/91). L.C.
D. The Diamond Gang (Bilston, 30/7/92; Sur. 3/7/93). L.C.
D. The Heiress of Hazledene (Bilston, 4/8/93). L.C.
D. The Scarlet Brotherhood; or, The Nihilist's Doom (Grand, Stalybridge, 2/10/93). L.C.
[Written in collaboration with *W. MANNING.*]
D. The Great Bank Robbery (Qns. Keighley, 9/3/96). L.C.

DARCY, FRED
M.D. The Devil's Mine (Grand H. Maidenhead, 25/4/94; Pav. 23/7/94; W.L. 23/5/98, as *The New World*). L.C. Plymouth.
C.D. The Black Ball (Bristol, 26/10/95, *copy.*). L.C.

D'ARCY, G.
D. The Lantern Light (E.C. 15/2/73). L.C.
[Written in collaboration with *C. H. ROSS.*]
C.O. The Blush Rose (Plymouth, 22/5/76). L.C.
[Music by J. Offenbach.]
Oa. Cigarette (Glo. 9/9/76). L.C. P.W. L'pool, 12/4/76.
D. Lelio (Olym. 15/8/85).

D'ARCY, Major
C. A Capricious Beauty (Aldershot, 15/3/86). L.C.

DARLINGTON, W.
D. The Weaver's Daughter (S.W. 10/3/83). L.C.

DARNLEY, J. HERBERT
F.C. The Barrister (Grand, Leeds, 19/3/87). See *G. M. FENN.*

F.C. The Balloon (Terry's, 13/11/88, *mat.*; Str. 6/2/89). L.C. *French.*
[Written in collaboration with *G. M. FENN.*]
D. A Wife's Devotion (Shakespeare, L'pool, 6/5/89; W.L. 13/4/96). L.C.
[Written in collaboration with *G. M. FENN.*]
F.C. Wanted, a Wife (Edinburgh, 4/11/89; Terry's, 28/5/90). L.C.
F.C. The Solicitor (Court, L'pool, 5/5/90; Toole's, 3/7/90). L.C. *French.*
F.C. Mrs Dexter (Court, L'pool, 26/12/91; Str. 28/2/94). L.C.
M.C. One of the Girls (Grand, Birmingham, 9/3/96; Metro. 1/6/96). L.C.
[Written in collaboration with *J. DALLAS.* Music by J. Crook, S. Jones and M. Lutz.]
D. The Queen's Pardon (Cardiff, 19/8/97, *copy.*). L.C. P's. Bristol.
F.C. Shadows on the Blind (P.W. L'pool, 27/9/97; Terry's, 29/4/98). L.C. Lyr. Hammersmith, 3/9/97, as *The Little Intruder.*
[Written in collaboration with *H. P. BRUCE.*]
M.C.D. A Race for a Wife (Grand, Walsall, 3/11/97, *copy.*; Stratford, 11/4/98). L.C.
F.C. On Guy Fawkes Day (P.W. L'pool, 29/11/97). L.C. Ladb. H. 26/12/95, as *Ways and Means.*
[Written in collaboration with *H. P. BRUCE.*]
C.D. A New Leaf (Roy. 30/11/97). L.C.
F.C. Facing the Music (P.W. L'pool, 22/5/99; Brixton, 5/6/99). L.C. Leicester, as *The Other Mr Smith. French.*

DARRELL, CHARLES
M.D. When London sleeps (Lyc. Crewe, 19/3/96; Darlington, 18/5/96; Shakespeare, Clapham, 28/6/97). L.C.
D. The Defender of the Faith (Grand, Birmingham, 20/9/97; Stand. 9/5/98). L.C. Preston, 23/4/97.
M.D. The Power and the Glory (Leeds, 29/4/98, *copy.*; Broadway, New Cross, 20/2/99). L.C.
[Title altered to *London's Light o' Love*, 7/11/1906.]
D. A Ghost of the Past (County H. St Alban's, 1/3/99). L.C.

[*DARRELL, GEORGE*
D. The Sunny South (Grand, 27/10/84; Sur. 5/9/98). L.C.

DARWIN, PHILIP
Ca. An Italian Romance (County Asylum, Middlesex, 14/11/89).
F. The Sword of Damocles (County Asylum, Middlesex, 14/11/89; St G. 11/1/90).

"*DAUBIGNY, DELACOUR.*" See *J. R. SIMS*

"*DAUNCEY, SYLVANUS*"
C.D. A Divided Duty (Jewish Inst. Highbury, 18/10/85; County, Reading, 27/2/88, as *A Month after Date*; Glo. 25/3/91). L.C. *French.*
C. Charity's Cloak (Roy. Glasgow, 25/2/91).
F. Love at Home (W. Hartlepool, 14/5/91; Parkhurst, 16/11/91). L.C.
D. The Reckoning (Glo. 3/12/91, *mat.*; Grand, 13/5/95). L.C.
M.F. Bilbery of Tilbury (Brixton, 18/7/98; Crit. 8/8/98; Hanley, 13/3/99, as *The Lady Detective*). L.C.
[Written in collaboration with *G. D. DAY.*]

DAVENPORT, H.
D. Poor Jo (Southampton, 25/2/78).

DAVENTRY, GEORGE

D. Under Two Flags (Pav. 8/11/84). L.C. Dundee, 15/9/82.

D. The Indian Mutiny (Gai. Burnley, 26/12/92). L.C. Var. 26/5/87, as *An Idol's Eye*.

DAVEY, PETER

Bsq. The Weeping Willow (Staines, 5/5/86).
[Written in collaboration with *H. LINFORD* and *H. S. RAM*.]

O. The Red Rider (St G. 23/3/95). L.C. Assembly R. Surbiton.
[Written in collaboration with *A. P. POLEY*. Music by J. W. Ivimey.]

P. Beauty and the Beast (County, Kingston, 27/12/97). L.C.

DAVEY, RICHARD

D. Paul and Virginia (Nov. 17/11/86). L.C.

D. Marion Delorme (P'cess. 28/6/87, *mat.*). L.C.

C. Lesbia (Lyc. 17/9/88). L.C.

D. A Shadow Hunt (Ladb. H. 25/4/91, *copy.*). L.C.
[Written in collaboration with *W. H. POLLOCK*.]

D. St Ronan's Well (Traf. 12/6/93). L.C.
[Written in collaboration with *W. H. POLLOCK*.]

DAVIDSON, Mrs

F. Giralda; or, Which is my Husband? (Grec. 25/10/50). L.C.

DAVIDSON, JOHN

D. Bruce. 8° 1886 [Glasgow].

T. Smith. 8° 1888 [Glasgow].

— Plays. 8° 1889 [Greenock].
[Contains: *An Unhistorical Pastoral, A Romantic Farce* and *Scaramouch in Naxos*.]

R.D. For the Crown (Lyc. 27/2/96). L.C.

Fairy D. The Children of the King (Court, 13/10/97). See *C. ARMBRUSTER*.

DAVIDSON, W.

D. Sins of the Father (Eden, Bishop Auckland, 23/12/97). See *W. J. MACKAY*.

DAVIES, B.

C.O. The Past Master (Str. 21/12/99). See *N. PRESCOTT*.

DAVIES, DAVID

D. Farnley (St G. 27/10/94, *amat.*).

DAVIES, HILL

Ca. An Old Garden (Brighton, 14/10/95; Terry's, 12/11/95). L.C. *French*.

DAVIES, JOSEPH

C. Our Town; or, The First of November (P.H. Warrington, 16/11/71).

DAVIES, RICHARD COLEMAN

D.D. No Escape (Preston, 2/7/88). L.C.

C.D. The Pedlar; or, Friends in Need (Lowestoft, 30/12/89). L.C.

DAVIS, ALFRED

F. Lottie's Love; or, How to choose a Husband (P.W. Glasgow, 15/5/68).

D. The Power of the Heart (Lyc. Sunderland, 21/3/73). L.C.

C.D. Danger (Leeds, 19/9/73).

DAVIS, HELEN

D. A Life Policy (Terry's, 20/7/94). L.C. Ladb. H. 8/5/94, as *Lawrence Maber*.

DAVIS, MAITLAND

M.D. The Haunted Glen (R.A. Woolwich, 27/4/88). See *H. WEBBER*.

DAVIS, SIDNEY

D. Elizabeth Storey, the Brave Lass of Haltwhistle (Newcastle, 4/5/68).

D. Poor Miss Finch (Lyc. Sunderland, 13/3/73). L.C.

DAWE, W. CARLETON

F.C. A Hard Case (Terry's, 26/10/93). L.C.

DAWSON, FORBES

D. A Fight against Fate (Vic. Newport, 2/3/85). See *H. P. GRATTAN*.

M.D. The Outsider (Aquar. Gt Yarmouth, 2/3/91). L.C. Park, Camden Town, 15/10/90.

D. The Diamond King; or, Life in London (Athen. Shepherd's Bush, 14/5/92, *copy.*). L.C.

D. The New World; or, Under the Southern Cross (Bath, 21/3/93). L.C.

D. The Days to come (E.C. 29/5/93). L.C.

M.D. Reported Missing (Bristol, 4/6/94). L.C.

D. Cherry Hall (Aven. 14/6/94). L.C.

F. Scotch (Lyr. Ealing, 12/9/95). L.C.

D. The Bank Robbery (Str. 24/1/96, *copy.*). L.C.

D. Glorie Aston (Star, Wolverhampton, 7/3/98). L.C.
[Title altered to *Good Luck; or, The Hand of the Prisoner*, 28/5/1902.]

D. For the Sake of the Duchess (Grand, Fulham, 31/8/99). L.C.

DAWSON, LEONARD

D. Crooked Paths (P.W. Southampton, 19/1/88).

DAWTREY, R. AUGUSTIN

M.C. Little 18-Carat; or, A Rough Nugget (Sunderland, 16/11/85).
[Music by R. W. Manning.]

C.D. Robin Hood and ye Curtall Fryer. 4° [1892].

DAY, ERNEST

R.D. The Orchard of the King (Lincoln, 20/11/89, *amat.*). L.C.
[Written in collaboration with *M. H. FOOTMAN*.]

DAY, GEORGE D.

D.Sk. His Mother (Grand, 23/3/91). L.C. Cardiff.

C.D. Fairly Caught (Parkhurst, 23/5/92). L.C.

D. The Diamond Rush (Cambridge, 6/2/95, *copy.*). L.C.
[Written in collaboration with *S. BOWKETT*.]

M.F. A Near Shave (Court, 6/5/95). L.C.
[Music by E. Jones.]

F.C. The Mummy (Roy. Chester, 6/9/95, *copy.*; Com. 2/7/96, *mat.*; Com. 11/8/96). L.C.
[Written in collaboration with *S. BOWKETT*.]

C.O. Willow Pattern Plate (P.H. Lowestoft, 24/8/97). See *S. BOWKETT*.

M.F. Bilbery of Tilbury (Brixton, 18/7/98). See *S. DAUNCEY*.

M.C. Campano; or, The Wandering Minstrel (Grand, Leeds, 8/9/98; Com. 15/12/98, as *Milord Sir Smith*). L.C.
[Music by E. Jakobowski.]
D.Sk. The Two Dumas Skiteers (Com. 25/1/99, introduced into Act II of *Milord Sir Smith*).
M.C. The American Heiress (Birmingham, 3/4/99). See *A. BRANSCOMBE.*

DAY, JOHN T.
Ca. Love's Crosses (Wolverhampton, 28/1/81).
D. Fair Fame (Longton, 8/8/84; T.H. Kilburn, 5/2/85). L.C.
C.D. The Pharisees (Llanelly, 8/12/84).
F.C. The Purser (Portsmouth, 12/7/97; Str. 13/9/97). L.C.
D. The Fanatic (Margate, 23/7/97; Str. 21/10/97). L.C.
D. Intruders (Colchester, 9/12/98, as *The Claychester Scandal*; Worcester, 16/1/99; Brixton, 6/2/99). L.C.

[*DAZEY, CHARLES TURNER*
C.D. The Rival Candidates (Wolverhampton, 9/4/94, *copy.*). L.C. Bolton.
[Written in collaboration with *J. N. MORRIS.*]
D. The War of Wealth (Bolton, 8/2/95; Sur. 31/10/98). L.C.
[Written in collaboration with *S. VANE.*]

DEANE, CECIL
Oa. Those Mysterious Shots (St G. 28/6/94).
[Music by N. Comyn.]

DEAR, PHILLIP J.
D. Louis XVI (Bath, 7/2/95, *copy.*).

DEARLOVE, W. H.
M.C. Love's Devotion (T.H. Harrowgate, 11/1/90; T.H. Harrowgate, 20/3/90, as *Cissy*).
[Written in collaboration with *J. FRANKLIN.*]
Ca. Jealousy (Spa, Harrowgate, 17/1/91). L.C.
[Title altered to *Little Lady Loo*, 20/4/1900.]
D. Mad; or, Back to Life (Castleford, 2/1/93; Goole, 9/1/93). L.C.
C.D. Jack o' Hearts (Mechanics' Inst. Swindon, 26/3/94). See *S. VEREKER.*
M.D. The Path of Life (Halifax, 9/6/96; Grantham, 7/6/97). L.C.
O.D. In Sunny Spain (St G. Walsall, 9/11/96). L.C.
[Written in collaboration with *P. WOODROFFE.*]
C.D. Vengeance is Mine (Maidenhead, 3/4/99).

DE BANZIE, E. T.
M.F. Pim-Pom (P'cess. Glasgow, 21/2/90). L.C. O.H. Southampton, 25/9/94.
F. Strawberries and Cream (P'cess. Glasgow, 26/2/91).
[Written in collaboration with *J. GRANT.*]
C.D. The Inkslinger (Roy. Glasgow, 22/2/93). See *C. WHITLOCK.*
F. Our Burlesque Baby (Glasgow, 13/2/95).
C.D. Her Wedding Day (Roy. Glasgow, 28/3/95, *copy.*; County, Reading, 30/9/95; Sur. 8/5/99). L.C.
M.D. Honour Bright (Bilston, 22/9/97). See *R. GRAHAME.*

DE CORDOVA, R.

D. The Executioner's Daughter (Gai. Hastings, 6/4/96). See *A. RAMSAY.*

D. As a Man sows (Grand, 22/8/98). See *A. RAMSAY.*

DEFFELL, CHARLES

Oa. Christmas Eve (C.G. 13/12/65). L.C.
[Written in collaboration with *M. BROWNE.*]

O. The Corsair (C.P. 25/3/73).

DE FRECE, MAURICE

Ca. Deception (L'pool, 18/12/71).

F. Carry's Breach of Promise; or, The Two Adolphuses (L'pool, 29/1/72; Operetta H. Edinburgh, 14/10/72, as *Carry's Triumph*).

F. He's so nervous (L'pool, 4/3/72).

F. Pat's Thanksgiving (L'pool, 18/3/72).

F. The Three Hunchbacks (L'pool, 15/4/72).

F. Not so mad as he looks (L'pool, 20/5/72).

F. Uncle Starlight's Will (L'pool, 8/7/72).

F. Is Brown at Home? (L'pool, 24/2/73).

F. Tiddlediwink (L'pool, 4/5/74).

DE LA BRETESCHE, BLANCHARD

Mimo D. Jean Mayeux (P'cess. 12/5/94).
[Music by Thony.]

DELAFIELD, J. H.

D. The Quarry Dell (Col. L'pool, 6/7/68).

D. Lily Dale (Amphi. Leeds, 12/4/69). L.C.

DELANNOY, BURFORD

D. The Great Diamond Robbery (S.W. 10/10/92). L.C.
[Written in collaboration with *W. R. WALDRON.*]

D. Crime and Justice; or, The Shadow of the Scaffold (S.W. 15/12/92). L.C.
[Written in collaboration with *N. HARVEY.*]

D. A Desperate Deed (S.W. 7/2/93). L.C.

M.D. Denes Rest (Empire, Southend, 6/12/97). L.C.

DE LA PASTURE, Mrs HENRY

D. The Modern Craze (St G. 2/11/99). L.C.

C. Poverty 8° (n.d., Brighton; *priv.*).

DE LA PLUME, C. A.

C. 'Twixt Cup and Lip (Olym. 14/6/73). L.C.

DE LARA, FREDERIC

Ca. A Stage Coach (Ladb. H. 17/5/87 as *Another Matinée*; Glo. 7/5/92).

C. Another Elopement (Ladb. H. 6/12/88). L.C.

Oa. A Capital Joke (St G. 31/5/89, *mat.*). L.C.
[Music by B. Brigata and L. Ronald.]

D. The Vagrant (Aquar. Scarborough, 7/12/91; S.W. 17/10/92). L.C.

Ca. Sweet Seventeen (Aquar. Brighton, 26/11/94). L.C.

DE LARA, GEORGE

D. Gold Dust (Winter Gdns. Blackpool, 29/4/87).

DE LATOUR, Mlle

C.D. Change of Fortune is the Lot of Life (Bath, 10/11/74).

DELILLE, H. A.
D. Lily (O.H. Leicester, 27/2/88). L.C.
D. In the Queen's Name (Colchester, 5/2/90). See *H. TREVOR.*

DELLOW, H.
D. The Man-o'-War's Man (P.W. Mexborough, 10/8/94).
[Written in collaboration with *C. LIVESEY.*]

[*DE MILLE, HENRY C.*
D. The Senator's Wife (Manchester, 30/9/92). See *D. BELASCO.*
C.D. The Lost Paradise (Adel. 22/12/92). L.C. *French.*
[Version of a play by Ludwig Fulda.]
C.D. Man and Woman (O.C. 25/3/93). L.C.
[Written in collaboration with *D. BELASCO*; Act IV rewritten by *T. M. WATSON.*]

DENBIGH, LOUIS S.
D. Black Diamonds (Alex. Southend, 30/9/90). See *R. F. MACKAY.*
D. The Life we lead (P'cess. 16/4/92). See *R. F. MACKAY.*

DENING, Mrs CHRISTINA
M.D. Olympus (Somerville Club, 21/2/93, *amat.*). L.C.
Duol. Training a Husband (Somerville Club, 21/2/93, *amat.*). L.C. Assembly R. St Leonard's, 3/12/92.
Duol. An Awful Experience (Somerville Club, 21/2/93, *amat.*).
D. Justice (T. H. Westminster, 12/5/93, *amat.*).
C.D. Mistakes (Pioneer Club, 19/10/93, *amat.*).

DENIS, J.
D. The Homewreck (Sur. 8/2/69). See *J. S. COYNE.*

DENNY, J. T.
Ext. Fra Diavolo the Second (Phil. 28/8/82).
P. Beauty and the Beast (M'bone, 24/12/84). L.C.
Ext. Little Lalla Rookh (Gai. Hastings, 31/8/85; Grand, 14/9/85).
P. Sinbad the Sailor (M'bone, 24/12/85).
P. Beauty and the Beast (S.W. 22/12/88).

DENNY, W. H.
F.C. Coercion (Gai. 17/11/86, *mat.*). L.C.
[Written in collaboration with *T. BURNSIDE.*]
F.C. The First Breeze (W. Hartlepool, 6/3/91). L.C.
F. A Mutual Mistake (Court, 21/3/91).
[Probably the above under a variant title.]
Ca. A Chance Acquaintance (Richmond, 28/6/94). L.C.
F.C. Helping a Friend (Str. 19/5/99). L.C. Richmond.

DENSMORE, G. B.
D. Fates and Furies (Sur. 20/10/77). L.C.

DENT, BERT
Bsq. Lady Daisy (Temperance H. Gt Grimsby, 12/2/96).

DE PASS, E. A.
D. Under False Colours. L.C. Ch. X. 19/9/70. 8° [1870]; *French.*
Ca. Debt (Gai. 23/11/72). L.C. *French.*

DERING, CHARLES E.

C.D. Mirabel (Macclesfield, 24/1/83; Plymouth, 8/10/83, as *The Guards*). L.C.

[Written in collaboration with *J. HOLLOWAY*.]

D. The Power of England (Imp. 17/6/85). L.C.

D. The Road to Fortune (Grand, Stonehouse, Plymouth, 27/3/93; Lyr. Hammersmith, 16/7/94). L.C.

D.Sk. The Aristocratic Burglar (Roy. Glasgow, 14/6/97). L.C.

DE ROHAN, DAPHNE

M.Ca. Oh! my Wife! (Lyr. Ealing, 30/8/97). L.C.

DERRICK, JOSEPH

C.D. The American (Alex. Pal. 19/6/82). L.C.

F.C. Confusion (Vaud. 17/5/83). *French.*

C. The Twins (Olym. 2/8/84). L.C.

C. The Plebeians (Vaud. 12/1/86). L.C.

F.C. Curiosity (Vaud. 14/9/86, *mat.*). L.C.

DE SMART, Mrs A.

Duol. Purely Platonic L.C. Kilburn, 26/4/98. *French.*

DESPREZ, FRANK

C.O. Madame Angot (Roy. 4/6/75).

M.Past. Happy Hampstead (Alex. L'pool, 3/7/76; Roy. 13/1/77). L.C.

[Music by M. Lynne.]

Vaud. After All (O.C. 16/12/78).

[Music by A. Cellier.]

M.Sk. Tita in Tibet (Roy. 1/1/79). L.C.

C. 1313 (Folly, 7/5/79). L.C.

Oa. In the Sulks (O.C. 21/2/80). L.C.

[Music by A. Cellier.]

F. Brum (Leeds, 15/3/80).

F. On Business (H.M. Aberdeen, 30/8/80). L.C. P'cess. Edinburgh.

Oa. Quite an Adventure (Olym. 7/9/81). L.C.

[Music by E. Solomon.]

M.F. Mock Turtles (Sav. 17/10/81). L.C.

[Music by E. Faning.]

C.O. Lurette (Aven. 24/3/83).

[Written in collaboration with *A. MURRAY*; lyrics by *H. S. LEIGH*. Music by J. Offenbach.]

Oa. A Private Wire (Sav. 31/3/83). See *A. FELIX*.

Ext. The Carp (Sav. 11/2/86). L.C.

[Music by A. Cellier.]

Oa. Mrs Jarramie's Genie (Sav. 14/2/88).

[Music by A. Cellier.]

R.D. Matamoros; or, A Night in Spain (Lyr. Ealing, 18/12/89).

C.O. The Nautch Girl (Sav. 30/6/91). See *G. DANCE*.

C.O. Brother George (Portsmouth, 16/5/92). L.C. Ladb. H. 14/3/92.

[Music by P. Bucalossi.]

DE SVERTCHKOFF, A.

C. Bungles (Lyr. Ealing, 16/12/92). L.C.

[Written in collaboration with *H. MORPHEW*.]

DE VERE, FLORENCE

T. and C. Eugenie; or, The Spanish Bride. The Lady and the Lawyers. 8° 1857.

DE VERE, FRED

D. The Penny Hedge; or, The Murder of the Eskdale Hermit (Scarborough, 29/10/83).

DEWAR, F.

F.C. The New Housekeeper (Myddleton H. Islington, 15/2/95). L.C.

DE WITT, EMILIE

D. The Guilty Shadows (Imp. 6/2/85). L.C.

DICK, COTSFORD

Ca. Back from India. L.C. St G. 10/6/79. See *P. STEVENS.*
D. The Stroller (P'cess. 10/87; H. 11/5/92, *mat.*, as *The Waif*). L.C.
M.F. On Lease (Crit. 12/5/91, *mat.*).
C.O. The Baroness (Roy. 5/10/92). L.C.
[Music by the author.]
M.Ext. Our Toys (St J. 16/7/95). See *W. YARDLEY.*
Duol. Marriage à la mode (Qns. H. 29/11/95).
Duol. The New Husband (H. 16/12/95). L.C.
C. The Great Comet (Bournemouth, 14/12/96). L.C.

DICKENS, CHARLES, Jr.

D. No Thoroughfare (Adel. 26/12/67). L.C.
[Written in collaboration with *W. W. COLLINS.*]
D. The Battle of Life (Gai. 26/12/73). L.C.
D. The Old Curiosity Shop (O.C. 12/1/84). L.C.

DICKENS, FANNY

D. A Living Lie; or, Sowing and Reaping (Roy. Blackburn, 18/6/83). L.C.

[*DICKINSON, Miss ANNA*

D. Mary Tudor. 8° 1876.
D. Anna Boleyn. 8° 1877.

DICKINSON, CHARLES H.

D. Hard Lines (St G. 19/3/87). L.C.
D.D. The Last Straw (St G. 3/3/88). L.C.
D. Parson Jim (Terry's, 24/5/89, *mat.*). L.C.
D. Released (Com. 9/4/90, *mat.*). L.C.
D. An Unpaid Debt (St G. 19/12/93, *amat.*). L.C.
Ca. The Third Time (St G. 22/2/96). L.C. *French.*
D. A Court of Honour (Roy. 18/5/97). See *J. LART.*
D. In Spite of Society (D.Y. 10/11/98). L.C.
D. Only Three Years Ago (D.Y. 10/11/98). L.C.
D. The Rift within the Lute (D.Y. 10/11/98). L.C. *French.*
[Written in collaboration with *A. GRIFFITHS.*]

DICKSON, J. HERMAN

D. United we stand (170 Belsize Road, S. Hampstead, 28/3/92, *amat.*).

DIDCOTT, H. J.

P. Jack the Giant Killer (Imp. 26/12/82). See *F. W. GREEN.*

[*DIETRICHSTEIN, LEO*

D. Gossip (Grand, 3/6/95). See *C. FITCH.*

DIETZ, LINDA

Ca. Lessons in Harmony (St G. 26/6/75). L.C.
D. Wild Love; or, Eagle Wally (Bristol, 18/4/81). L.C.

DIGGES, WEST

D. Fair France (Qns. 18/4/74). L.C.
D. Double Dick (Halifax, 18/10/75). L.C.
D. Forbidden Love (Duke's, 21/5/77). L.C.
Ext. A China Wedding (Duke's, 21/5/77). L.C.
D. The Stage (Duke's, 21/5/77). L.C.
C.D. On Service; or, A Soldier's Life (Lecture H. Derby, 26/12/78).
D. Robert Emmet (Leicester, 2/5/81). L.C.
D. The Poor Player (Plymouth, 22/9/84). L.C.

DILLEY, JOSEPH J.

F. The Mate of the Mountjoy (Dramatic Academy, 1867).
[Written in collaboration with *J. ALBERY.*]
C. The Sleeping Hare (Cavendish R. 6/4/68, *amat.*). *Lacy.*
C. Illusions (Ch.X. 21/5/70). L.C.
F. Chiselling (Vaud. 27/8/70). See *J. ALBERY.*
C.D. Auld Acquaintance (St G. 23/3/78). L.C. *Lacy.*
F. A Highland Fling (Vaud. 4/1/79). L.C. *Lacy.*
F. A Military Manœuvre (Vaud. 26/12/79). L.C.
[Written in collaboration with *L. CLIFTON.*]
F. Summoned to Court (Imp. 4/3/80). L.C. *Lacy.*
[Written in collaboration with *L. CLIFTON.*]
C.D. Tom Pinch (Vaud. 10/3/81). L.C. *French.*
[Written in collaboration with *L. CLIFTON.*]
F.C. A Glimpse of Paradise (Lyr. Ealing, 1/1/87). L.C. *Lacy.*
C.D. Whips of Steel (St G. 7/5/89). L.C.
[Written in collaboration with *M. C. ROWSELL.*]
C.O. Marjorie (P.W. 18/7/89). See *L. CLIFTON.*
Ca. Richard's Play (Ladb. H. 14/1/91). See *M. C. ROWSELL.*
D. At the Cross Roads (P's. H. Kew, 20/10/94). L.C.

DILLON, ARTHUR

D. The Maid of Artemis (Albany Club, Kingston, 13/7/95). L.C.
[Music by C. Baughan.]

DILLON, CHARLES

D. Stricken Down (Glasgow, 13/6/70).

DILLON, CLARA

M.D. His Own Enemy (Aldershot, 13/12/98, *copy.*).

DIRCKS, RUDOLPH

D. The Haunted Man (Adel. 20/6/63). L.C.
Ca. A Mean Advantage (Newcastle, 29/6/88, *amat.*; P.W. Blackpool, 6/9/89). L.C.
Ca. In the Corridor (Court, 25/5/89). L.C.
Ca. Retaliation (Pav. Whitby, 6/8/90; Grand, 27/7/91). L.C. *French.*

DIX, FRANK

D. True till Death; or, The Cradle of Crime (Bristol, 13/7/96). L.C.
M.C. Odd Man Out (Grand, Nottingham, 19/4/97). See *M. TURNER.*
D. Held in Terror (Bristol, 21/6/97; Imp. 29/8/98). L.C.
M.F.C. One of the Family (Grand, Boscombe, 9/4/98). See *G. CAPEL.*
D. Delivered from Evil (Bristol, 27/3/99). L.C.

DIXEY, HENRY A.

Bsq. Adonis (Gai. 31/5/86). See *W. GILL.*

DIXEY, KATE
F.C. A Girl's Freak (St G. 6/2/99). See *L. FELTHEIMER.*

DIXON, BERNARD HOMER
C. Behind a Mask (Roy. 8/3/71). L.C.
[Written in collaboration with *A. WOOD.*]
C. A Friend of the Family (Bijou, 27/9/94).

DIXON, GERALD
C. A Doctor in spite of himself (Glo. 23/6/77). L.C.
Ca. Married another (O.C. 1/9/77). L.C.

DIXON, H. J.
Ca. Electrophobia (P's. Manchester, 26/3/98, *mat.*).

DIZANCE, FRANK
D. Davey Crockett (Southminster, Edinburgh, 29/9/73).

D'LANOR, GUY
M.C. The Principal Boy (Lyr. L'pool, 5/6/99). L.C.

DOBB, THOMAS
D. The Battle of Life (Adel. L'pool, 6/8/94). See *A. W. PARRY.*

DOBELL, FRED
C.D. On the Verge (Wolverhampton, 10/3/88). See *E. S. FRANCE.*

DOBELL, SYDNEY THOMPSON
D.Poem. The Roman. 8° 1850.

DOBSON, MARTIN S.
C.D. A Secret Crime (Qns. Birmingham, 12/12/92). L.C.
[Title altered to *A Man's Ambition*, 11/12/93.]

DODSON, ERNEST
D.Sk. Better than Gold (Lyr. Hammersmith, 28/5/94). See *J. M. EAST.*

DODSON, H.
D. The Regicide; or, The Days of Cromwell and the Civil Wars of England (Vic. 28/3/53). L.C. as *Old Christmas Eve; or, The Halls of my Fathers.*

DODSON, ROBERT
D. Stanfield Hall; or, The Protector's Oath. L.C. Bower, 20/2/51.
D. Two Hundred Years Ago; or, Two Loves and Two Lives (Vic. 13/4/72). L.C.
D. Anne Boleyn; or, The Jester's Oath (Vic. 22/3/73). L.C.
D. The King Maker; or, The Last of his Race (Vic. 4/10/73). L.C. as *The K. M.; or, The Wars of the Roses and the Last of the Barons.*
P. The King of Trumps; or, Little Jack and the Farrier of the Enchanted Isle (Vic. 24/12/73). L.C.
D. Stolen Away (Brit. 15/3/75). L.C.
D. Glashen Glora; or, The Lovers' Well (Pav. 25/9/75). L.C.
F. A School for Muffs (Sur. 21/2/76). L.C.
D. The Armourer (Brit. 27/3/76). L.C.
D. Leonard; or, The Secret of Twenty Years (L'pool, 21/8/76). L.C.
D. The Queen's Jewels; or, The Puritan's Bride (E.L. 25/11/76). L.C.
D. Deoch and Durass; or, Oonah of the Hills (Brit. 3/10/77). L.C.
D. A True Woman (Brighton, 13/4/78). L.C.
D. Twig Folly (Pav. 22/4/78). L.C.
D. The Penal Law (Brit. 24/3/79). L.C.

D. The Thames; or, Adrift on the Tide (Sur. 29/9/79). L.C.
D. Real Life (Sur. 21/8/82).
D. The Wreckers; or, Martial Law (H.M. Carlisle, 4/12/84). L.C. Dundee.
C.D. A Woman's Victory (Com. 8/7/85). L.C.

DODSWORTH, CHARLES
D.Sk. Fleeting Clouds (Ladb. H. 25/1/89). See *P. F. MARSHALL.*

"*DOE, JOHN.*" See *CLEMENT SCOTT*

DOLARO, SELINA
C.D. In the Fashion (Ladb. H. 28/12/87, *copy.*). L.C.

DON, LOFTUS
C.D. A Life's Victory (Oxford, 16/7/85).
D. The Hawk's Grip (P.W. Southampton, 14/2/87). L.C.
M.Sk. A Streak o' Sunshine (Aquar. Gt Yarmouth, 12/3/88; S.W. 7/5/88).

DOONE, NEVILLE
D. A Daughter's Sacrifice (Glo. 17/5/88, *mat.*). L.C.
D.Sk. During the Dance (St Andrew's H. Newman Street, 22/2/89).
C.D. A Modern Marriage (Com. 8/5/90, *mat.*). L.C.
D. The Two Suicides (R. Society of British Artists, 24/1/91).
C.D. Summer Clouds (Toole's, 16/2/91). L.C.
Ca. My Awful Luck (Lyr. Club, 24/1/92).
Oa. The Lass that loved a Sailor (Pier, Folkestone, 22/5/93). L.C.
[Music by Bond Andrews.]
Ca. Sparkle's Little System (Pier, Folkestone, 1/6/93; Metro. 2/3/1903). L.C.
C.D. A Ministering Angel (Bijou, 8/6/93). L.C.
[Written in collaboration with *H. C. W. NEWTE.*]
C.D. Snowdrop (Bijou, 1/2/94). L.C.
[Written in collaboration with *H. C. W. NEWTE.*]
F. A Woman Tamer; or, How to be happy though married (Brompton Hospital, 10/3/96).
C.D. A Sweet Deception (Brompton Hospital, 24/11/96).
Duol. Breaking it off (Empire, Southend, 21/3/98). L.C.
[Music by J. Crook.]

DORISI, LISA
C.D. Preciosita (St G. 4/7/93). L.C.
M.C. A Japanese Lamp (Drill H. Tiverton, 25/2/97). L.C.

DORRELL, ALEXANDER
D. The House in Thames Street (Ipswich, 7/5/85). L.C. Lyr. Ealing.

DOUGLAS, DULCIE
C. The Librarian (Athen. Limerick, 22/5/85).

DOUGLAS, G. R.
C. Stage Land (Vaud. 2/1/75). L.C.
C. The Rival Candidates (Folly, 17/3/80). L.C.

DOUGLAS, Sir GEORGE
Ca. Irish Eyes (Corn Exchange, Kelso, 4/1/89).

DOUGLAS, LIONEL
D. Born to save (Wolverhampton, 3/12/83). See *G. H. CLARKE.*

DOUGLAS, Miss JOHNSTONE

C.D. Pamela (Falkirk, 7/11/98). L.C.

DOUGLASS, JOHN

P. Harlequin and the Golden Alphabet (Stand. 27/12/52).

P. Harlequin Roast Beef and Plum Pudding (Stand. 26/12/53). L.C.

P. Georgey Porgey Pudding and Pie, Kissed the Girls and made them Cry (Stand. 26/12/57). L.C.

DOUGLASS, JOHN THOMAS

D. The Market Cross (Stand. 24/9/64). L.C.

Ext. The Cockney Caliph. L.C. Stand. 30/4/66.

Bsq. Der Freischutz; or, The Bride, the Bullet and the Bobby. L.C. Stand. 16/10/66.

F. A Royal Marriage (Stand. 20/4/68). L.C.

D. A Dead Calm; or, The Fisher's Story (Stand. 4/8/68).

D. For Sale (Stand. 3/2/69). L.C.

F. The Young Man of the Period (Stand. 5/7/69). L.C.

F. In and out of Service (Stand. 25/10/69). L.C.

Bsq.O. Guy Fawkes; or, A New Way to blow up a King (Stand. 16/4/70). L.C.

Ca. Venus versus Mars (Stand. 5/9/70). L.C.

F. A Chapter of Accidents (Stand. 26/9/70). L.C. *Lacy.*

D. The Vicar of Wakefield (Stand. 31/10/70). L.C. as *Vicar Primrose.*

P. Ride-a-cock-horse to Banbury Cross; or, Harlequin and the Silver Amazons (Stand. 26/12/70). L.C.

D. Germans and French; or, Incidents of the War of 1871 (Stand. 8/3/71). L.C.

C. Warranted Sound and Quiet in Harness (Greenwich, 10/11/71). L.C. Stand. 2/5/65, as *In Jest or in Earnest; or, W. S. and Q. in H.*

P. Harlequin Aladdin and the Wonderful Lamp (Stand. 26/12/71). L.C.

F. Brave as a Lion (Stand. 11/3/72). L.C.

F. Thompson's Visit (Stand. 23/9/72). L.C.

P. Harlequin Cinderella and the Little Glass Slipper (Stand. 26/12/72). L.C.

F. What will the Neighbours say? (Stand. 1/9/73). L.C.

P. Whittington and his Cat (Stand. 26/12/73). L.C.

P. Robinson Crusoe and his Man Friday (Stand. 26/12/74). L.C.

P. The Children in the Wood (Stand. 27/12/75). L.C.

P. Open Sesame; or, The Forty Thieves (Stand. 26/12/76). L.C.

D. The Queen of an Hour (Stand. 1/10/77). L.C.
[Written in collaboration with *F. STAINFORTH.*]

P. The Enchanted Prince; or, The Beauty and the Bears (Stand. 24/12/77). L.C.

P. Ali Baba and the Forty Thieves (Park, 24/12/78). L.C.

P. Robin Hood (Stand. 26/12/78). L.C.

P. Blue Beard Re-wived (Stand. 26/12/79). L.C.

P. Harlequin and the Wide-awake Sleeping Beauty (Stand. 27/12/80). L.C.

P. Harlequin and Sinbad the Sailor; or, The Genii of the Diamond Valley (Stand. 26/12/81). L.C.

P. Little Red Riding Hood; or, Harlequin Boy Blue, Miss Muffit, the Wolf and the Bears (Stand. 26/12/82). L.C.

P. Harlequin Puss in Boots (Stand. 26/12/83). L.C.
D. A Bitter Wrong (Stand. 14/4/84). See *G. LANDER.*
P. Cinderella; or, The Fairy of the Little Glass Slipper (Stand. 24/12/84). L.C.
F.C. A Bubble Reputation (Stand. 6/4/85). See *J. WILLING.*
P. Harlequin Whittington and his Cat (Stand. 26/12/85). L.C.
M.D. A Dark Secret (Stand. 28/10/86). See *J. WILLING.*
P. Aladdin (Stand. 27/12/86). L.C.
D. The Royal Mail (Stand. 18/8/87). L.C.
D. The Tongue of Slander (Stand. 17/10/87). See *T. G. WARREN.*
P. Fee-fi-fo-fum; or, Harlequin Jack the Giant Killer (Stand. 24/12/87). L.C.
[Written in collaboration with *F. MARSHALL.*]
D. The Lucky Shilling (Stand. 20/2/88). See *J. WILLING.*
D. Her Father (Vaud. 16/5/89). See *E. ROSE.*
D. No Man's Land (Leicester, 21/11/90; Grand, 3/4/93). L.C.
M.D. Winifred's Vow (Nov. 19/3/92). L.C.
D. Nance; or, Reclaimed (Pav. 13/11/93). L.C.
D. The Birthright; or, The Brigand's Ransom (Huddersfield, 1/6/94; Lyr. Hammersmith, 31/5/97). L.C.
F. Down on his Luck (Oxford, 4/10/94). L.C.
D. A Bunch of Shamrocks (Roy. Edinburgh, 2/6/96). See *F. BATEMAN.*
D. From Scotland Yard (P'cess. Accrington, 16/8/97; Parkhurst, 27/9/97). L.C.
[Written in collaboration with *F. BATEMAN.*]
C.D. The Burglar's Baby (Lyr. Ealing, 27/10/97). L.C.
[Written in collaboration with *C. WILLIAMS.*]
D. Known to the Police (P's. Portsmouth, 10/12/97, *copy.*; Sur. 6/3/99). L.C.
C.D. Joy of the House (Central, Northwich, 24/10/98). L.C.
D. The Mistress of the Seas (W.L. 27/2/99). L.C.

DOVE, AYLMER H.
F. Out at Elbows (Toole's, 3/82). L.C.

DOVE, OWEN [GUSTAVE DE MEIRELLES SOARES]
F. The Three Hats (Bath, 22/6/83; Roy. 20/12/83). L.C. *French.*
[Written in collaboration with *A. MALTBY.*]
F.C. Not a Word (Aven. 28/4/84). L.C.
C. Knight against Rook (Gai. 23/7/86, *mat.*; Ladb. H. 18/4/93). L.C.
[Written in collaboration with *J. G. LEFEBRE.*]

DOWIE, W. J. S.
C. A Self Made Man (Middlesborough, 8/3/78). L.C.

DOWLING, MILDRED T.
D. Dangerfield '95 (Gar. 26/5/98). L.C.

DOWLING, RICHARD
D. Below London Bridge (Nov. 6/4/96). L.C.

DOWNES, JOSEF F.
D. Mutines, the Traitor (St G. H. L'pool, 14/11/98). L.C.
D.Sk. The American Singer Downstairs (Qns. Gate H. 18/12/99). See *T. LOCKE.*

DOWNEY, LYNCH T.

D. The Lover's Leap (P.W. Glasgow, 16/2/74; Vic. 1/10/77, as *The Wearing of the Green; or, The L. L.*). L.C.

D. Irish Life (Lowestoft, 22/10/88). See *A. CREAMER.*

DOWNSHIRE, Dowager Marchioness of

Oa. The Ferry Girl (Sav. 13/5/90, *mat.*).
[Music by Lady Arthur Hill.]

DOWSE, G. D.

D. A Secret Sorrow (Manor R. Hackney, 11/12/90). L.C.

DOWSETT, EDWARD

F. Altogether (T.H. Edmonton, 17/2/94).

Bsq. On the Road (T.H. Edmonton, 15/5/94).
[Music by Amy Davis.]

DOWTY, A. A.

D.D. After Darkness, Dawn (Toole's, 27/5/82). L.C.

DOYLE, Sir ARTHUR CONAN

C.D. Jane Annie (Sav. 13/5/93). See *Sir J. M. BARRIE.*

D. Foreign Policy (Terry's, 3/6/93). L.C.

D. A Story of Waterloo (P's. Bristol, 21/9/94; Lyc. 4/5/95). L.C. *French.*

C.D. Halves (H.M. Aberdeen, 10/4/99; Gar. 10/6/99). L.C.

DOYLE, T. F.

F. Quakers and Shakers (L'pool, 14/7/73).

F. An Irish Intrigue (Var. Sunderland, 29/9/73).

DRAGNIL, W. H.

Ba. Brother Pelican (Belfast, 8/2/94). See *A. RAE.*

DRAKE, FRANCIS

F. Squaring the Circle (Glo. 8/5/76). L.C.

DRAPER, E.

Ext. Guy Fawkes (Olym. 31/3/55). See *T. TAYLOR.*

DRAPER, J. F.

Bsq. The Goose and the Golden Eggs (Royal H. Jersey, 19/11/69, *amat.*).

Bsq. Antony and Cleopatra (Royal H. Jersey, 16/12/70, *amat.*).

Bsq. The Dragon of Hogue Bie; or, The Little Prince's Tour (Royal H. Jersey, 8/12/71, *amat.*).

Bsq. Norma (Royal H. Jersey, 5/3/75, *amat.*).

DRAYTON, E.

D. A Struggle for Life; or, A Burglar's Fate (S.W. 22/9/84). L.C.

DRAYTON, HENRI

M.Sk. Pierre (St J. 5/11/53). L.C.

Oa. Nanette; or, Better Late than Never (Stand. 24/8/68).

DREW, EDWIN

D. A Woman Outwitted (Nov. 16/11/86). L.C. as *Outwitted.*
[Written in collaboration with *D. M. HENRY.*]

D. The New Actress (Athen. 24/7/88). L.C. Ladb. H.

D. The Vicar's Daughter (Athen. 28/1/89). L.C.

Ca. The Play's the Thing (Athen. 28/1/89). L.C.

F. Tricking a 'Tec (St G. 21/7/91).
[Music by S. Howard.]

D.Sk. Cynthia's Sacrifice (St G. 11/4/93).
D. A Noble Falsehood (St G. 2/6/94). L.C.

DRINKWATER, ALBERT E.
— Plays and Poems. 8° 1885.
C.D. A Fair Conquest (P.W. Gt Grimsby, 18/7/87). L.C.
D.D. Two Christmas Eves (Shakespeare, L'pool, 1/12/88; Vic. H. Ealing, 5/2/91). L.C. as *Thou Shalt not Kill.*
Ca. A Legend of Vandale (Grand, 1/9/90). L.C. 8° 1892.
D.D. A Golden Sorrow (Vic. H. Ealing, 2/2/91; Glo. 16/6/91). L.C.
D. True as Truth (Roy. Glasgow, 4/12/91). L.C. Pier, Folkestone, 22/6/91. 8° 1892.
D. The Red Knave. L.C. T.H. Chorley, Lancs. 22/12/92.
Oa. Nice Boy, Jim! (Bijou, 16/11/93, *amat.*). L.C. 8° [1893]. [Music by W. S. Vining.]
Ca. The Lords of Creation (New, Oxford, 4/2/95; Kilburn, 17/2/96). L.C.
C. The Talk of the Town (O.H. Cork, 4/12/96). L.C. Bath, as *The T. of the T.; or, Agnes Bramber.*
D.Sk. Afterthoughts (Bijou, 12/6/99). L.C.

DRURY, Captain W. P.
C.O. H.M.S. Missfire; or, The Honest Tar and the Wicked First Luff (Plymouth, 11/3/95). L.C. O.H. Chatham, 30/10/94. [Music by G. Nifosi and S. Blythe.]

DRYDEN, CHARLES
Bsq. Damon the Dauntless and Phyllis the Fair (St G. 28/12/69).

DRYDEN, J. POPE
D. The Dean of Hazeldene (Grand, Nelson, 20/4/89). L.C.

DUBOURG, AUGUSTUS W.
D. A Sister's Penance (Adel. 26/11/66). See *T. TAYLOR.*
C. New Men and Old Acres (Manchester, 20/8/69). See *T. TAYLOR.*
C. Women and Men (Manchester, 22/5/71). L.C.
Ca. Sympathy (Manchester, 29/4/72).
D. Without Love (Olym. 16/12/72). See *E. YATES.*
Int. Twenty Minutes' Conversation under an Umbrella (H. 4/7/73).
D. Bitter Fruit (Alex. L'pool, 6/10/73).
C.D. Art and Love (O.C. 17/2/77). L.C.
C. Just like a Woman (Gai. 22/11/79, *mat.*).
C. Land and Love (Glo. 26/5/84). L.C.
R.D. Vittoria Contarini (P'cess. 11/5/87, *mat.*). L.C. Star, Swansea, 24/9/86. 8° 1875.

DUCKWORTH, H. C.
F.C. In Charge (P's. Bradford, 29/6/88). See *H. CASSEL.*
F.C. A State Secret (Barrow, 13/12/89). See *H. CASSEL.*
F.C. All the Comforts of Home (Glo. 24/1/91). See *W. GILLETTE.*

DUCKWORTH, WILLIAM
D. Cromwell. 8° 1870.
D. Under a Ban (Alex. L'pool, 7/3/70). L.C.
C. After All (P.W. L'pool, 13/10/73).

DUDLEY, F. H.
F.C. Is Marriage a Failure? (Woolwich, 19/11/88). See *H. COLLIER.*

DUFFEY, HENRY A.
M.C. Cupid (Southampton, 14/4/82).

DU MAURIER, GUY
Bsq. Morgiana (Royal Fuselier Barracks, Woolwich, 8/1/92).

DUNBAR, E. C.
Oa. The Merry Blacksmith (Vaud. 25/9/93).

DUNCAN, GEORGE
T. The Marston Brothers. 8° 1867 [Glasgow].
D. The Pretender (P'cess. 27/5/76).
D. The Bairn (H.M. Aberdeen, 17/6/78). L.C.

DUNDAS, H.
D.Sk. A Daughter of England (Grand, Halifax, 27/8/96, *copy.*). L.C. Leamington.
[Written in collaboration with *H. SHELLEY.*]

DUNN, SINCLAIR
C.O. The Three Beggars; or, A Night at an Inn (R. Academy of Music, 28/7/83).
[Music by E. Belville.]

DUNSTAN, H. MAINWARING
Ca. Houp La! Tra, la, la! (Roy. 20/5/86). L.C.

DURANT, HELOISE
Ca. Our Family Motto; or, Noblesse Oblige (Qns. Gate H. 27/2/89). L.C

DURÉ, MICHAEL
M.C. The Merry Monk (Mat. 15/7/97). L.C.
[Written in collaboration with *M. BELL.* Music by A. Llewellyn.]

DUREZ, H.
F.C. The Spiritualist (Ladb. H. 1/8/91, *copy.*). L.C.
[Title altered to *Whose Wife?*, 11/5/92.]

[*DU SOUCHET, H. A.*
F.C. My Wife's Step Husband (Assembly R. Tenby, 14/9/97, *copy.*). L.C.

DUTCH, J. S.
C. Grace (Sale, 5/3/80; P's. Manchester, 24/4/84).

DU TERREAUX, LOUIS HENRY
Bsq. The Last of the Barons (Str. 18/4/72). L.C.
C.O. Vokin's Vengeance; or, The Poisoned Picalilly; or, The Greengrocer and the Ungovernable Governess (St G. 19/6/72). L.C.
[Music by J. P. Cole.]
C. A Cabinet Secret (Phil. 19/10/72). L.C.
C. Love wins (Cambridge, 11/8/73). See *H. S. CLARKE.*
C.O. La Fille de Madame Angot (P.W. L'pool, 16/2/74; Glo. 5/74).
C.O. The Broken Branch (O.C. 22/8/74). L.C.
D. A Fight for Life (Bradford, 26/8/76). See *H. S. CLARKE.*

DUTNALL, MARTIN
Bsq. The Cooleen Drawn (Sur. 14/10/61). L.C.
[Written in collaboration with *J. B. JOHNSTONE.*]
P. Harlequin Old Mother Goose; or, The Queen of Hearts and the Wonderful Tarts (Sur. 26/12/62). L.C.

DUVAL, C.

D. The Seven Poor Travellers (Blackburn, 11/1/69).

DWYER, JAMES

D. The Fireman of Glasgow (Adel. Glasgow, 5/4/75).

DYALL, CHARLES

C.O. The Fox Glove; or, The Quaker's Will (P.W. L'pool, 2/5/83). L.C.
[Music by G. W. Rohner.]

DYCE-SCOTT, ROBERT

D. The Play-actress (Grand, 28/1/96, *copy*.). L.C.

EARLE, ARTHUR W.

Ext. Architopia, Unlimited: A Lyrical Lay of Ladye Land (T.H. Holborn, 4/5/94).
[Written in collaboration with *E. H. SIM*.]

Bsq. King Arthur (James Street, Buckingham Gate, S.W. 16/5/95).
[Written in collaboration with *E. H. SIM*.]

EARLESMERE, HENRY

D. Shattered Fetters (Cambridge H., Sheffield, 10/7/94).

EAST, JAMES M.

C. The Double Event (T.H. Kilburn, 6/5/91, *copy*.). L.C.

F. The Typewriter (Park T.H. Battersea, 13/2/92, *copy*.). L.C.

D.Sk. Better than Gold (Lyr. Hammersmith, 28/5/94).
[Written in collaboration with *E. DODSON*.]

P. The Babes in the Wood (Lyr. Hammersmith, 26/12/96). See *B. DALY*.

P. Cinderella (Lyr. Hammersmith, 27/12/97). See *B. DALY*.

D. The Three Musketeers (Lyr. Hammersmith, 7/11/98). See *B. DALY*.

P. Puss in Boots (Lyr. Hammersmith, 26/12/98). See *B. DALY*.

F. The Kitchen Girl (Parade Assembly R. Taunton, 26/10/99).

EASTWOOD, FRED

D. Hertford (Bradford, 29/8/79; Roy. 22/3/80). L.C. Leeds.

D. The Decoy (Gai. 18/4/83). L.C.

EASTWOOD, L. B.

C.D. Tennis (Swansea, 6/3/93). L.C.

EATON, R. H.

D. Saved from the Streets (Sur. 18/10/86). See *G. CONQUEST*.

EBSWORTH, JOSEPH

[For his earlier plays see iv, 308–9.]

D. The Advocate and his Daughter (Olym. 26/2/52). L.C.

C. £150,000 (Edinburgh, 1/9/54).

EDEN, GUY

C.O. The 'Prentice Pillar (Colchester, 13/2/95, *copy*.; H.M. 24/9/97). L.C.
[Music by R. Somerville.]

Oa. The Mysterious Musician (Terry's, 27/6/99). L.C.
[Music by G. W. Byng.]

EDGAR, D. W.

Bsq. Moths Quitoes; or, Ouida's Moths (Middlesborough, 21/4/82). L.C.

EDGAR, H. TRIPP

Ca. A Happy Thought (Bijou, 2/3/94; Str. 2/1/95). L.C.

EDGAR, RICHARD HARTLEY

Bsq. Crichton (Ch.X. 30/8/71). L.C. as *The Admirable Crichton; or, The Scottish Gentleman who was good all round. Lacy.*

D. Ivanhoe; or, The Maid of York (Amphi. L'pool, 27/11/71).

EDGAR, WHYTE

Bsq. Van der Decken; or, The Flying Anglo-Dutchman's Phantom Penny Steamer (Nov. 9/12/85). L.C.

[Music by M. Lutz.]

EDISON, JOHN SIBBALD

D. Henry of Richmond. 8° 1857 [Part I], 8° 1860 [Part II].

D.Poem. Jephtha. 8° 1863.

EDLIN, HENRY

C.D. Her Release (Pier Pav. Folkestone, 1/6/92). L.C. as *Sister Grace.*

Oa. Giddy Galatea (D.Y. 15/11/95). L.C.

[Music by E. Jones.]

P. Robinson Crusoe (Richmond, 27/12/97). L.C.

EDMONDS, E. VIVIAN

D. A Brother's Crime (Warrington, 27/3/93). L.C.

D. A Hidden Past (Grand, Walsall, 18/5/96). L.C.

EDMUND, CHARLES

M.D. The Maid of Athens (O.C. 3/6/97). L.C.

[Written in collaboration with *H. C. NEWTON.*]

EDWARDES, CONWAY THEODORE MARRIOTT

Bsq. Linda di Chamouni; or, The Blighted Flower (Bath, 20/2/69). *Lacy.*

Bsq. Don Carlos; or, The Infante in Arms (S. Shields, 6/8/69; Vaud. 16/4/70). L.C.

F. Board and Residence (Glo. 8/10/70). L.C. *Lacy.*

F. Dreadfully Alarming (Phil. 30/9/71). L.C. *Lacy.*

[Written in collaboration with *E. A. CULLERNE.*]

Bsq. The Rows of Castille (Brighton, 4/3/72).

Oa. The Love Bird (Vaud. 19/6/72). L.C.

[Music by A. Nicholson.]

Ext. Anne Boleyn (Roy. 7/9/72). L.C. *French.*

C. Our Pet (Ch.X. 12/11/73). *French.*

C. Heroes (P.W. L'pool, 20/11/76; Aquar. 10/1/77). L.C. *French.*

C. Long Odds (Bath, 10/2/83; O.C. 1/2/87). L.C. Exeter. *French.*

EDWARDES, GEORGE

D. One of the Best (Adel. 21/12/95). See *Sir S. HICKS.*

EDWARDES-SPRANGE, W.

D. Wrecked (Margate, 4/12/84). L.C. Grimsby, 20/10/84.

Duol. The Requital (Exeter, 1/4/87).

C. The Parting of the Ways (Terry's, 8/2/90). See *F. BOWYER.*

C.D. Time's Revenges (Toole's, 20/5/90, *mat.*).

D. Ragged Robin (P.W. Southampton, 17/3/93). See *F. BOWYER.*

Oa. Sport (P's. Portsmouth, 6/6/95). See *M. TURNER.*

M.C. The New Barmaid (O.H. Southport, 1/7/95). See *F. BOWYER.*

M.C. The White Blackbird (Grand, Croydon, 1/8/98). See *F. BOWYER.*

EDWARDS, ALBERT

F.C. The Diamond Queen (St G. 6/8/89). L.C.

EDWARDS, FRANK

D. A Miner's Luck; or, Sons of Toil (Clarence, Pontypridd, 4/6/94). L.C.

EDWARDS, H. SUTHERLAND

C.D. The Poor Relation (Str. 29/5/51). See *A. MAYHEW.*
F. My Wife's Future Husband (Str. 21/7/51). See *A. MAYHEW.*
F. A Squib for the Fifth of November (Str. 10/11/51). See *A. MAYHEW.*
Ext. Mephistopheles (Adel. 14/4/52). See *R. B. BROUGH.*
F. The Goose with the Golden Eggs (Str. 1/9/59). See *A. MAYHEW.*
F. Christmas Boxes (Str. 16/1/60). See *A. MAYHEW.*
O. Rose; or, Love's Ransom (C.G. 26/11/64). L.C.
[Music by J. L. Hatton.]
D. Frou Frou (Olym. 16/4/70). L.C.
D. Fernande (St J. 15/10/70). L.C.
C.D. The Four Cousins (Glo. 5/71). See *A. MAYHEW.*
C. The Late Ralph Johnson (Roy. 26/2/72). L.C.
C.O. La Marjolaine (Roy. 11/10/77). L.C.
[Music by Lecocq.]
Ca. Simpson and Delilah (Aven. 3/6/82). L.C.
D. A Wife's Sacrifice (St J. 25/5/86). See *S. GRUNDY.*
C. Nellie's Flight (C.P. 20/7/86, *mat.*). L.C.
[Written in collaboration with *B. THOMAS.*]
Oa. Minna; or, The Fall from the Cliff (C.P. 20/7/86). L.C.
[Music by I. de Lara.]
C.O. Madame Cartouche (O.H. Leicester, 21/9/91). L.C.
Ext. The Fiend at Fault (Vaud. 4/4/94). L.C.
[Written in collaboration with *W. TAYLOR.*]

EDWARDS, JAMES CARTER

D. Life's Mistakes; or, The House of McOuld (P'cess. Glasgow, 27/7/85). L.C.
[Title altered to *By the Hand of Woman*, 15/9/86.]

EDWARDS, JOHN

C.D. No. 22A Curzon Street (Gar. 2/3/98). See *B. THOMAS.*

EDWARDS, JULIAN

Oa. Cornarino's Mistake (Corn Exchange, Hereford, 30/9/72).
Oa. Love's Test (Vic. H. Norwich, 4/9/74).
C.O. Le Marquis de St Valéry (T.H. Reading, 20/1/76). L.C.
Oa. Dorothy (Leeds, 2/4/77; Ladb. H. 24/9/77). L.C.
C.Oa. Buckingham (T.H. Northampton, 28/12/77). L.C.

EDWARDS, MORRIS

Ca. At Last (P's. Bristol, 19/3/86). See *H. GOUGH.*
Ca. Hope's Answer (S. Shields, 19/11/86). L.C.
[Written in collaboration with *H. GOUGH.*]
C. Dan and Dick (Ladb. H. 14/5/87). See *H. GOUGH.*
C.D. Constance Frere (Vaud. 27/6/87). See *H. GOUGH.*

EDWARDS, OSMAN

C.D. A Gauntlet (Roy. 20/1/94). L.C.
[Version revised by *G. P. HAWTREY.*]

EDWARDS, PIERPONT

D. Honour before Wealth; or, The Romance of a Poor Young Man (Qns. 23/3/61; H. 3/68). *Lacy.*

EDWIN, PERCY

D. From Shore to Shore (Star, Wolverhampton, 30/4/91).

EGAN, F. B.

D. The Scottish Chiefs (Leith, 12/3/68).

EGLINGTON, HENRY

D. Harvest of Hate (Castleford, 1/2/99). See *F. WITHERS.*

ELDRED, JOSEPH

F. Private and Confidential (P.W. L'pool, 1/4/70).
[Written in collaboration with *H. PAULTON.*]

Bsq. The Gay Musketeers; or, All for Number One (P.W. L'pool, 18/4/70).
[Written in collaboration with *H. PAULTON.*]

C.O. Gaiété (Sheffield, 26/10/74).
[Written in collaboration with *H. AYLEN.*]

D. Follies of the Day (Bristol, 16/10/82). See *H. P. GRATTAN.*

D. The Echoes of the Night (Pullan's, Bradford, 7/1/84). See *H. P. GRATTAN.*

D. The Outcasts of the City (Jarrow, 3/11/84). L.C. H.M. Aberdeen.
[Written in collaboration with *H. P. GRATTAN.*]

ELDRIDGE, H. W.

C. Rogue and Vagabond (P.H. Tottenham, 15/4/95). L.C.

ELIOT, ARTHUR

C.O. The Money Spider (Mat. 19/4/97). L.C.
[Music by C. Lucas.]

M.F. The Belle of the Bath; or, His Hydropathic Highness (Bijou, 17/6/98). L.C. as *Miss Letty.*
[Music by F. S. Ward.]

"ELIOT, GEORGE" [MARY ANN CROSS]

D.Poem. The Spanish Gipsy. 8° 1868 [Edinburgh].

D.Poem. Armgart. 8° 1874.

ELKINGTON, CARR

D. The Guiding Star (P.W. Gt Grimsby, 17/7/99; Stratford, 17/6/1901). L.C.

ELLIOT, S.

C.O. The Maypole (Limerick, 6/10/87). See *C. B. WADE.*

ELLIOTT, CHARLOTTE

C.D. One Fault (Wigan, 9/10/85). See *E. WARREN.*

ELLIOTT, GILBERT

D. A Sinless Shame (Cheltenham, 28/2/87).

D. The Love King (County, Reading, 9/3/93; Eden, Brighton, 7/9/96, as *A Crown of Thorns*; Olym. 10/10/96). L.C.

ELLIOTT, J. C.

D. A Double Life (Dundee, 21/10/72).

ELLIS, BRANDON

D. The Poisoned Cup (Weymouth, 13/1/69).

D. Poor Em'ly (Southampton, 10/10/70). L.C. as *Little Emily.*

D. The Poison Doctor of Paris (Southampton, 31/10/70).
C.D. Without Money or Friends (P's. Portsmouth, 7/9/74).
C. Those Volunteers (Bath, 20/9/75).
D. My Heart's Darling (Bath, 14/2/76).
C. Three Blind Mice; or, The Right Maria (Gt Grimsby, 5/3/83). L.C.
D. The Thugs of Paris (Goole, 11/4/87). L.C.
[This was also called *Behind a Mask; or, The Perils of Life.*]
C. Pets (St G. 31/5/89, *mat.*).
D. The Irish Priest (Grand, Glasgow, 12/5/90).
D. The City Outcast (Gateshead, 18/4/92; Stratford, 4/1/97). L.C.
D. Fair Rosamond; or, A Queen's Vengeance and a Fool's Fidelity (Alex. Widnes, 7/8/93; Brit. 18/7/98, as *A Queen's Vengeance*). L.C.
D. The Prairie Flower (Jersey, 14/3/95). L.C.
[Written in collaboration with *A. CARLTON.*]
D. Beneath the Stars (Pal. Newcastle, 21/4/99; Sur. 8/10/1900). L.C.

ELLIS, F. R.
D. The Song of the River (Bath, 4/7/98). See *M. LOADER.*

ELLIS, GEORGE
P. Harlequin Billy Taylor (P'cess. 26/12/51). See —. *SALA.*
P. Harlequin Cherry and Fair Star; or, The Queen Bird, the Dancing Waters and the Singing Trees (P'cess. 27/12/52). L.C. *Lacy.*

ELLIS, HAROLD
M.F. The New Dean (New, Cambridge, 11/6/97, *amat.*). L.C.
[Music by J. W. Ivimey.]
F.C. Young Mr Yarde (Pav. Buxton, 15/8/98; Richmond, 22/8/98; Roy. 2/11/98). L.C.
[Written in collaboration with *P. RUBENS.*]

ELLIS, JOSEPH
D. Excelsior (Brentford, 8/12/87). L.C.
Bsq. Valentine and Orson (Brentford, 1/11/88).

ELLIS, LIONEL
M.D. The Right Man (Sanger's, 7/5/87). See *G. COMER.*
D. The Red Barn (Alh. Barrow-in-Furness, 10/6/92). See *G. COMER.*
D. Baby (P's. Preston, 23/3/96). See *W. R. WALDRON.*

ELLIS, Mrs R.
C.D. The Last of the Latouches (Croydon, 3/12/77). L.C.
[Written in collaboration with *C. R. RENNELL.*]

ELLIS, R. CASTLETON
D. Shall we remember? (Surrey Masonic H. Camberwell, 13/12/93). See *W. TURNBULL.*

ELLIS, WALTER
Ca. Our Relatives (Olym. 11/12/80). L.C. *French.*
C. Major and Miner (Glo. 6/8/81). L.C. *French.*
Ca. Vol. III (Ladb. H. 12/1/91). L.C. Glo. 11/12/77, as *A Long Engagement. French.*
C.D. Marion (Roy. 6/12/98). L.C.
[Written in collaboration with *P. GREENWOOD.*]
F. The Sleepwalker (Roy. 6/12/98). L.C.
F. The Pasha (T.H. Hounslow, 11/12/99). L.C.
[Written in collaboration with *P. GREENWOOD.*]

ELLISTON, J. F.
D. Keen Blades (Sheffield, 22/5/93). See *A. F. CROSS.*

ELMER, GEORGE
M.C. A Military Manœuvre; or, The Lady Lady's Maid (Manor, Hackney, 15/9/99). L.C.

ELPHINSTONE, JAMES
D. Bleak House (C.L. 6/6/53). L.C.
[Written in collaboration with *F. NEALE.*]
D. The Grand National; or, Sporting Youth from the Counting House to the Hulks (Col. L'pool, 29/3/69).
D. How Time flies; or, Things that happen every Hour (Vic. 24/4/69).
Spec. The Franco-Prussian War (Hanley, 12/8/72).
Spec. King Coffee; or, The Ashantee War (Hanley, 16/3/74).
D. 1874; or, High and Low, Rich and Poor (Hanley, 17/8/74).

ELTON, A. E.
D. In Life or Death (Olym. 24/3/85).

ELTON, E.
Bsq. King Lear and his Daughters Queer (Brit. 20/3/71).

ELTON, ERNEST
F.C. A Country Dance (O.H. Northampton, 18/3/96, *copy.*). L.C.

ELWOOD, ARTHUR
Ca. After Many Days (Glo. 14/3/87). L.C.

EMDEN, W. S.
[For his earlier plays see *E.N.D.* ii, 299–300.]
Ca. The Head of the Family (Olym. 14/11/59). L.C. *French.*

EMERY, C. P.
Bsq. Romeo the Radical and Juliet the Jingo; or, Obstruction and Effect (Alex. Walsall, 14/8/82). L.C.
D. Balaclava Joe; or, Saved from the Jaws of Death L.C. Var. 27/6/92.
D. The Little Stowaway. L.C. Ashton, Birmingham, 12/6/94.

EMERY, S.
D. The Polish Jew (Bradford, 18/3/72).

EMSON, FRANK E.
C.Int. Bumble's Courtship. *French.*

ENGLAND, ALFRED
D. From Shore to Shore (O.H. Northampton, 6/6/92). L.C.
[Written in collaboration with *C. R. NOBLE.*]
P. Cinderella (Brixton, 26/12/96). L.C.
[Written in collaboration with *C. R. NOBLE.*]
P. Robinson Crusoe (Brixton, 27/12/97). L.C.
[Written in collaboration with *C. R. NOBLE.*]
P. Aladdin (Brixton, 26/12/98). L.C.
[Written in collaboration with *C. R. NOBLE.*]

ERSKINE, WALLACE
M.C. In Search of a Father (Grand, Derby, 1/8/98; County, Kingston, 8/8/98). L.C. Alh. W. Hartlepool, 7/6/98.
[Written in collaboration with *A. STUART.*]

ERWIN, H.
C.O. Pat (R.A. Woolwich, 16/11/91). See *G. ROBERTS.*

"*ESMOND, HENRY V.*" [*HENRY VERNON JACK*]
C.D. Rest (Aven. 10/6/92, *mat.*). L.C.
D. The Bogey (St J. 10/9/95). L.C.
C.D. The Divided Way (Manchester, 31/10/95; St J. 23/11/95). L.C.
Duol. In and out of a Punt (St J. 9/3/96). L.C. *French.*
C.D. One Summer's Day (Com. 16/9/97). L.C. 8° [1901, New York]; *French.*
F. Cupboard Love (Court, 3/12/98). L.C.
C.D. Grierson's Way (H. 7/2/99). L.C. 8° 1899 [*priv.*].
[For his later plays see A. E. Morgan, *op. cit.* p. 309.]

EVANS, FRANK
C. Culture (Bournemouth, 5/12/84). See *S. EVANS.*

EVANS, ROSE
D. Quite Alone (Gt Yarmouth, 25/5/74).
D. Disinherited; or, Left to her Fate (Gt Yarmouth, 1/6/74).

EVANS, SEBASTIEN
C. Culture (Bournemouth, 5/12/84; Gai. 5/5/85). L.C.
[Written in collaboration with *F. EVANS.*]

EVANSON, FRED
M.C.D. My Playmate (Seaham Harbour, 8/11/88).
[Music by H. W. May.]
M.D. Fond Hearts; or, A Brother's Love (P.W. Southampton, 7/10/89). L.C. Vic. Stalybridge.

EVELYN, Miss J.
D. A Life Race (Alfred, 19/2/72). L.C.
C. A Crown for Love (P'cess. Edinburgh, 17/6/74; Gai. 16/10/75). L.C.

EVERARD, WALTER
F.C. Uncles and Aunts (Com. 22/8/88). See *W. LESTOCQ.*

EVERITT, Lieutenant-Colonel H.
C.D. On the Ranch (St G. 1/2/96, *amat.*). L.C.

EXLEY, CHARLES
Spec. Bonnie Prince Charlie (Hengler's, 21/12/78).

EYLES, FRED
Bsq. Pietro Wilkini; or, The Castaways, the Wild Men and the Winged Beauty (Swiss Gdns. Shoreham, 18/8/70).
Bsq. Villekyns and his Dinah (Swiss Gdns. Shoreham, 7/7/73).

EYRES, A. R.
C. After Many Years (St G. 5/2/80). L.C.

FAGAN, JAMES B.
D. The Rebels (Metro. 4/9/99). L.C.

FAIRBAIRN, Mrs R. [*MAY HOLT*]
Ca. Waiting Consent (Folly, 11/6/81). L.C.
D. Dark Deeds (Oldham, 7/6/81, as *Jabez North*; Phil. 11/3/82).
Ca. Sweetheart, Good-bye (Scarborough, 10/10/81; Str. 22/12/84). L.C.
D. Men and Women (Sur. 17/7/82). L.C.
C.D. False Pride (Norwich, 24/9/83; Vaud. 22/5/84). L.C.
D. Every Man for Himself (Aquar. Gt Yarmouth, 22/6/85; Pav. 24/10/85). L.C.

FAIRFAX, MAX

D. Never to Know (County, Reading, 15/5/99). L.C.

FAIRFAX, Mrs

C. The Best People (Glo. 14/7/90). L.C. West, Albert H. 14/4/90.

FALCONER, EDMUND

D. The Cagot; or, Heart for Heart (Lyc. 6/12/56). L.C.
F. The Husband of an Hour (H. 1/6/57). L.C. *Lacy*.
O. The Rose of Castile (Lyc. 29/10/57). See *A. G. HARRIS*.
C. Extremes; or, Men of the Day (Lyc. 26/8/58). L.C. *French*.
F. Too much for Good Nature (Lyc. 11/9/58). L.C. *French*.
O. Satanella (C.G. 20/12/58). See *A. G. HARRIS*.
T. Francesca; or, A Dream of Venice (Lyc. 31/3/59). L.C. as *Francesca da Rimini*.
F. Husbands, Beware! (Lyc. 31/3/59). L.C.
D. The Master Passion; or, The Outlaws of the Adriatic (P'cess. 2/11/59). L.C. *Lacy* [as *Outlaws of the Adriatic; or, The Female Spy and the Chief of the Ten*].
O. Victorine (C.G. 19/12/59). 8° [1859].
[Music by A. Mellon.]
Ca. Next of Kin (Lyc. 9/4/60). L.C. *French*.
C. The Family Secret (H. 9/5/60). L.C. *French*.
C. Does he love me? (H. 23/6/60). L.C. *French*.
D. Ruy Blas (P'cess. 27/10/60). L.C.
Ext. Chrystabelle; or, The Rose without a Thorn (Lyc. 26/12/60). L.C. *Lacy*.
D. Woman; or, Love against the World (Lyc. 19/8/61). L.C.
F. The Fetches (Lyc. 24/8/61). L.C.
D. Peep o' Day; or, Savourneen Deelish (Lyc. 9/11/61). L.C. *Lacy*.
C.D. Killarney (Lyc. 21/4/62).
D. Bonnie Dundee; or, The Gathering of the Clans (D.L. 23/2/63). L.C.
C. Nature's above Art: A Romance of the Nursery (D.L. 12/9/63). L.C.
D. Night and Morn (D.L. 9/1/64).
M. The Fairies' Festival on Shakespeare's Birthday (D.L. 23/4/64). L.C. *Lacy*.
F. The O'Flahertys; or, The Difficulties of identifying an Irishman (D.L. 17/10/64). L.C.
C.D. Love's Ordeal; or, The Old and New Regime (D.L. 3/5/65). L.C.
D. Galway Go Bragh; or, Love, Fun and Fighting (D.L. 25/11/65; Amphi. L'pool, 22/4/71, as *Charles O'Malley; or, L. F. and F.*). L.C.
D. Oonagh; or, The Lovers of Lisnamora (H.M. 19/11/66). L.C.
C.D. A Wife well won; or, My Grandfather's Legacy (H. 30/12/67; Str. 6/11/68, as *The Widow Hunt*). L.C.
D. Innisfallen; or, The Men in the Gap (Lyc. 17/9/70). L.C.
D. Eileen Oge; or, Dark's the Hour before the Dawn (P'cess. 29/6/71). L.C. *French*.
[A revised version of *Innisfallen*.]
D. Agra-ma-chree (Manchester, 8/3/75). L.C. Newcastle, 21/5/67, as *A.-m.-c.; or, Gems of Ould Ireland*.

D. The O'Donoghue's Warning (Dublin, 28/10/78).
D. Perfidy; or, What Money can do (Bolton, 10/11/87). L.C. Oldham.
[Revised by *W. J. CONNELL.*]

FALCONER, HENRY
D. The Captain of the Vulture (Swindon, 6/11/88). See *J. LEWIS.*

FANE, FAWNEY
F.C. The Grass Widow (Worthing, 9/5/98). L.C.

FANSHAW, FRED
F.C. Red and Blue (Wolverhampton, 19/12/92). L.C.

FARADAY, P. M.
M.C. The Ogre and the Witch (Myddleton H. Islington, 21/12/97).

FARGUS, F. J. See *H. CONWAY*

FARJEON, B. L.
D. Home Sweet Home (Olym. 19/6/76). L.C. *French.*

FARJEON, ELEANOR
O. Floretta (St G. 17/7/99).
[Music by H. Farjeon.]

FARNIE, HENRY BROUGHAM
Oa. The Bride of Song (C.G. 3/12/64). L.C.
[Music by J. Benedict.]
Oa. Punchinello (H.M. 28/12/64). L.C.
[Music by W. C. Levy.]
D. The Golden Dustman (S.W. 16/6/66). L.C.
D. Reverses (Str. 13/7/67). L.C.
Bsq.O. Le Petit Faust (Lyc. 18/4/70). L.C. 8° [n.d.].
C.Oa. Breaking the Spell (Lyc. 2/5/70). L.C.
[Music by J. Offenbach.]
Bsq. The Idle 'Prentice, A Tyburnian Idyll of High, Low, Jack and his Little Game (Str. 10/9/70). L.C.
P. Gulliver; or, Harlequin Brobdignag (C.P. 21/12/70).
Ext. Little Gil Blas and how he played the Spanish Deuce (P'cess. 24/12/70). L.C.
Bsq. The Mistletoe Bough, a Merrie Jest of an Old Oak Chest (Adel. 26/12/70). L.C.
Bsq. Vesta (St J. 9/2/71). L.C.
F. The Rival Romeos (St J. 8/4/71). L.C.
C.O. The Crimson Scarf (Alh. 24/4/71; H. 24/11/73). L.C.
[Music by J. E. Legouix].
Bsq.O. L'Oeil crevé (O.C. 21/10/72). L.C.
Bsq.O. Geneviève de Brabant (Phil. 11/11/71). L.C.
[Music by J. Offenbach.]
Oa. Forty Winks (H. 2/11/72).
Bsq.O. The Bohemians (O.C. 24/2/73). L.C.
[Music by J. Offenbach.]
Bsq.O. Fleur de Lys (Phil. 5/4/73). L.C.
Ext. Nemesis; or, Not wisely but too well (Str. 17/4/73). L.C.
C.O. La Fille de Mme Angot (Gai. 10/11/73).
C. The Main Chance (P.W. L'pool, 6/12/73; Roy. 15/4/74). L.C.
Bsq.O. Eldorado (Str. 19/2/74). L.C.
Bsq.O. Loo and the Party who took Miss (Str. 28/9/74). L.C.

Bsq.O. The Black Prince (St J. 24/10/74). L.C.
[Music by C. Lecocq.]
Bsq.O. Whittington (Alh. 26/12/74). L.C.
[Music by J. Offenbach.]
Ext. Intimidad; or, The Lost Regalia (Str. 8/4/75). L.C.
M.F. The Antarctic (Str. 27/12/75). L.C.
Bsq.O. Madame l'Archiduc (O.C. 13/1/76). L.C.
[Music by J. Offenbach.]
Ext. Piff Paff; or, The Magic Armoury (Crit. 31/1/76). L.C.
Ext. Robinson Crusoe (P's. Manchester, 7/10/76; Folly, 11/11/76). L.C.
C.O. Nell Gwynne (P's. Manchester, 16/10/76). L.C.
[Music by A. Cellier.]
F.C. Hot Water (Crit. 13/11/76). L.C.
Bsq. Oxygen (Folly, 31/3/77). See *R. REECE.*
C.O. The Creole (Brighton, 3/9/77; Folly, 15/9/77). L.C.
[Written in collaboration with *R. REECE.* Music by J. Offenbach.]
C.O. The Sea Nymphs (Brighton, 3/9/77; Folly, 15/9/77). L.C.
[Written in collaboration with *R. REECE.* Music by C. Lecocq.]
Oa. Up the River (Folly, 15/9/77). L.C.
[Written in collaboration with *R. REECE.* Music by Hervé.]
Bsq. Champagne; A Question of Phiz (Str. 29/9/77). L.C.
[Written in collaboration with *R. REECE.*]
D. Hester Gray (P's. Manchester, 27/10/77). See *R. REECE.*
D. Russia; or, The Exiles of Siberia (Qns. 27/10/77). L.C.
[Written in collaboration with *R. REECE.*]
Ext. Wildfire (Alh. 24/12/77). L.C.
[Written in collaboration with *R. REECE.*]
M.F. Madcap (Roy. 7/2/78). See *R. REECE.*
C.O. Les Cloches de Corneville (Folly, 23/2/78). L.C.
[Written in collaboration with *R. REECE.* Music by R. Planquette.]
Bsq. Stars and Garters (Folly, 21/9/78). See *R. REECE.*
C.O. Madame Favart (Str. 12/4/79). L.C.
[Music by J. Offenbach.]
Oa. The Barber of Bath (Olym. 18/12/79). L.C.
[Music by J. Offenbach.]
M.Ext. Rothomago; or, The Magic Witch (Alh. 22/12/79). L.C.
O. Irene (Manchester, 10/3/80). L.C.
[Music by C. Gounod.]
C.O. La Fille du tambour major (Alh. 19/4/80). L.C.
[Music by J. Offenbach.]
C.O. Olivette (Str. 18/9/80). L.C.
[Music by E. Audran.]
C.O. Les Mousquetaires au Couvent (Glo. 31/10/80). L.C.
[Music by Varney.]
C.O. La Boulangère (Glo. 16/4/81). L.C.
[Music by J. Offenbach.]
C.O. La Mascotte (Brighton, 19/9/81; Com. 15/10/81). L.C.
[Written in collaboration with *R. REECE.* Music by E. Audran.]
C.O. Manola (Str. 11/2/82). L.C.
[Music by C. Lecocq.]

C.O. Boccaccio (Com. 22/4/82). L.C.
[Written in collaboration with *R. REECE*. Music by F. von Suppé.]
R.O. Rip van Winkle (Com. 14/10/82). L.C.
[Music by R. Planquette.]
C.O. Frolique (Str. 18/11/82). L.C.
[Written in collaboration with *H. J. BYRON*.]
C.O. La Vie (Brighton, 17/9/83; Aven. 3/10/83). L.C.
[Music by J. Offenbach.]
C.O. Falka (Com. 29/10/83). L.C.
[Music by F. Chassaigne.]
C.O. Nell Gwynne (Aven. 7/2/84). L.C.
[Music by R. Planquette.]
C.O. The Grand Mogul (Com. 17/11/84). L.C.
[Music by E. Audran.]
Ext. Kenilworth (Aven. 19/12/85). See *R. REECE*.
Bsq. Lurline (Aven. 24/4/86). See *R. REECE*.
Bsq.O. The Commodore (Aven. 10/5/86, *mat.*). L.C.
[Written in collaboration with *R. REECE*. Music by J. Offenbach.]
C.O. Glamour (Edinburgh, 30/8/86). L.C.
[Written in collaboration with *A. MURRAY*. Music by W. M. Hutchinson.]
C.O. Indiana (Com. Manchester, 4/10/86; Aven. 11/10/86). L.C.
[Music by E. Audran.]
Bsq. Robinson Crusoe (Aven. 23/12/86). L.C.
[Written in collaboration with *R. REECE*. Music by J. Crook.]
C.O. The Old Guard (Grand, Birmingham, 10/10/87; Aven. 26/10/87). L.C.
[Music by R. Planquette.]
C.O. Paul Jones (Bolton, 20/12/88; P.W. 12/1/89). L.C.
C.O. La Prima Donna (Aven. 16/10/89). L.C. as *The Grand Duke*.
[Written in collaboration with *A. MURRAY*. Music by T. Mattei.]
O. Romeo and Juliet (Court, L'pool, 15/1/90). L.C.
[Music by C. Gounod.]
D. The Soul of Honour. *French*.

FARREN, FRANK
Duol. For Better, for Worse (Working Men's Club, Aldgate, 8/2/91).

FARREN, WILLIAM
D.D. The Vicar of Wakefield (Ladb. H. 2/1/88). L.C.
Ca. The Player Queen (Bath, 21/11/92). L.C.

FAUCIT, HENRY SAVILLE
D. The Amber Witch (C.L. 3/51). L.C.
[Possibly by John Saville Faucit, although a play of this name (Vic. 1862) is attributed to Henry Saville.]
D. My Lady Hilda; or, The Buried Secret (Nottingham, 21/3/70).
D. The Bond of Life (Assembly R. Reading, 14/5/70).
D. Spell-bound (Dundee, 3/2/71).
D. Life's Battle: A Story of the River Thames (Vic. 3/8/78). L.C.

FAUCQUEZ, ADOLPHE
D. The Clouds and Sunshine in a Life (S.W. 27/10/62).

D. The Orphan's Legacy; or, A Mother's Dying Words (Grec. 10/6/67). L.C.
D. Sons of Freedom (C.L. 27/6/68). L.C.
D. Passion's Peril; or, The Broken Marriage (Brit. 23/3/74). L.C.
D. Is she guilty? (Brit. 23/6/77). L.C.
D. Eugene Aram (Stand. 21/7/79).

FAWCETT, Mrs
C.D. At the Ferry (Kilburn, 26/4/97). L.C. Bijou.

FAWCETT, CHARLES S.
F. Jolliboy's Woes (Olym. 26/12/78). *Lacy.*
C. Bubbles (Gai. 8/10/81). L.C. *French.*
Ca. Bearding the Lion (P's. Manchester, 25/2/84). *French.*
Oa. Polly's Birthday (Gai. 3/3/84). L.C.
F.C. A Tragedy (Roy. 28/4/87). L.C. *French.*
F. Katti, the Family Help (P'cess. Glasgow, 30/9/87; Str. 25/2/88). L.C.
C. Madcap Midge (O.C. 5/12/89). L.C.
C.D. For Charity's Sake (Com. 29/1/91). L.C. *French* [as *Our Lottie*].
D. For Valour (York, 16/10/91). L.C.
C.O. Trooper Clairette (P.W. L'pool, 31/10/92; O.C. 22/12/92). L.C. [Music by V. Roger.]
F. The Lady Killer (P.W. L'pool, 25/9/93; Str. 17/10/93). L.C.
F.C. Beauty's Trials (Str. 21/12/93). L.C.

FEATHERSTONE, J. L.
D. The Fatal Triumph (P.H. New Cross, 11/12/86; Ipswich, 13/10/87). L.C.
[Written in collaboration with *J. C. HURD.*]

FELIX, ARNOLD
Oa. A Private Wire (Sav. 31/3/83). L.C.
[Written in collaboration with *F. DESPREZ.* Music by P. Reeve.]
M.Ca. A Water Cure (St G. 22/10/83). L.C.
[Music by G. Gear.]

FELL, TALBOT
C.D. In One Day (Assembly R. Durham, 17/2/96). L.C.
[Written in collaboration with *G. TOMPKINS.*]

FELTHEIMER, LILLIAN
F.C. A Girl's Freak (St G. 6/2/99). L.C.
[Written in collaboration with *K. DIXEY.*]

FENDALL, PERCY
F.C. Ascot (Adel. Oldham, 13/10/79; Folies Dram. 29/3/83). L.C.
F.C. Husband and Wife (Crit. 30/4/91). See *F. C. PHILIPS.*
C.D. Margaret Byng (Crit. 8/12/91). See *F. C. PHILIPS.*
F.C. Fireworks (Vaud. 29/6/93). See *F. C. PHILIPS.*
Duol. Fashionable Intelligence (Court, 5/3/94). L.C. *French.*

FENIBOND, PAUL
C. Too Kind (Coventry, 3/7/76).

FENN, FREDERICK
D.Sk. Two Confessions (St G. 11/4/99). L.C.
[Several later plays.]

FENN, GEORGE MANVILLE

D. Land Ahead (Hull, 4/3/78; Sanger's, 30/9/78). L.C.

D.D. The Foreman of the Works (Stand. 8/3/86). L.C.

C. Jewels and Dust; or, The Romance of a Court (C.P. 18/5/86). L.C.

F.C. The Barrister (Grand, Leeds, 19/3/87; Com. 6/9/87). L.C. *French.* [Written in collaboration with *J. H. DARNLEY.*]

F.C. The Balloon (Terry's, 13/11/88). See *J. H. DARNLEY.*

C.D. Her Ladyship (Str. 27/3/89, *mat.*). L.C.

D. A Wife's Devotion (Shakespeare, L'pool, 6/5/89). See *J. H. DARNLEY.*

C. The Tin Box (Glo. 16/4/92). L.C.

FENTON, C.

D. Edward the Black Prince (Vic. 3/4/54). [The same as the play in *UA*, p. 672.]

FENTON, CHARLES

Ca. An Artistic Dilemma (Surrey Masonic H. Camberwell, 13/12/93). L.C.

Ca. Saved on the Post (Surrey Masonic H. Camberwell, 13/12/93). L.C.

FENTON, FRED

D. Link by Link (Sur. 8/10/70). See *F. HAY.*

FERNALD, CHESTER BAILEY

C.D. The Cat and the Cherub (Lyr. 30/10/97). L.C.

C.D. The Moonlight Blossom (P.W. 21/9/99). L.C.

FERNEYHAUGH, G. F.

C.D. Mabel's Secret (Drill H. Derby, 1/3/70, *amat.*).

F. The Fight at Dame Europa's School (Lecture H. Derby, 17/3/71, *amat.*).

FERNIE, LORING

F.C. The Almshouse (Parkhurst, 6/12/92). See *W. LOCKHART.*

FERRERS, ERNEST

Ca. A Private View (St G. 6/6/93). L.C. *French.*

FERRIS, EDWARD

C.D. A White Stocking (Com. 3/10/96). L.C. [Written in collaboration with *A. STEWART.*]

C.D. Nicolete (Crit. 3/1/99). L.C. *French.* [Written in collaboration with *A. STEWART.*]

FIDDES, JOSEPHINE

D. Deadly Foes (Belfast, 20/11/68).

FIELD, H. J.

C. The Rightful Heiress (Guildhall School of Music, 17/7/95).

FIELD, H. K. HAMILTON

M.Ca. Artless Cinderella (St Andrew's Inst. Carlisle Place, 9/5/95).

FIELD, JULIAN

C. Too Happy by Half (St J. 5/1/95). L.C. *French.*

FIELD, KATE

Ca. Extremes Meet (St J. 12/3/77). L.C.

FIELD, MARTYN

D. How London lives (P'cess. 27/12/97). L.C. [Written in collaboration with *A. SHIRLEY.*]

"FIELD, MICHAEL" [*KATHARINE HARRIS BRADLEY* and *EDITH EMMA COOPER*]

Poet.D. Callirrhoe. 8° [1884].
D. Fair Rosamond. 8° [1884]; 8° 1897.
— The Father's Tragedy; William Rufus; Loyalty or Love. 8° 1885.
T. Brutus Ultor. 8° [1886].
— Canute the Great [and] The Cup of Water. 8° [1887].
T. The Tragic Mary. 8° 1890.
Trialogue. Stephania. 4° 1892.
D. A Question of Memory (Indep. Theatre Soc. at O.C. 27/10/93). L.C. 8° 1893.
D. Attila, my Attila. 8° 1896.
D. The World at Auction. 4° 1898.
D. Anna Ruina. 8° 1899.
D. Noontide Branches. 4° [1899, Oxford].
[For their later plays see *C.B.E.L.* iii. 340.]

FIELD, WILFORD F.

C.D. A Merrie Family (Var. Brentford, 3/3/86).
F.C. The Chicks (Var. Brentford, 15/4/86).
F. The Captain (T.H. Maidenhead, 27/12/86).
M.C. On Tour; or, A Trip to Heidelberg (Drill H. Ealing, 5/1/87).
C. Our Flossie (New, Addlestone, 2/4/88).
Duol. Mistaken (P.R. Southall, 9/4/88).
D. The Ebb and Flow (Brentford, 19/11/88). L.C.
D.Sk. Cupid's Frolic (Vestry H. Ealing, 30/3/89).
F.C. Tricks (Barnsley, 9/5/89). L.C.
[A revised version of *The Captain*.]
D.Sk. Grapeshot (P.R. Southall, 27/11/89).
F. Hymen wins (P.R. Southall, 17/11/90).
Ca. Sweet Simplicity (P.R. Southall, 23/2/91).
C. The Modern Tutor (P.R. Southall, 8/2/92).
Bsq. Little Claude and the Big Lady of Lyons (Var. Southampton, 22/8/92).
F.C. The Bishop (Tottenham, 25/10/94; St G. 24/11/94, as *Martha*).

FIELDING, HENRY

D. The Klondyke Rush (Brit. 30/5/98). L.C.

FIELDING, MARY

D. John Wharton; or, The Wife of a Liverpool Mechanic (Qns. Manchester, 5/10/68).

FILIPPI, ROSINA

P. Little Goody Two Shoes (Court, 26/12/88).
[Music by A. Levey.]
D.Sk. An Idyll of New Year's Eve (T.H. Chelsea, 31/1/90; P.W. 30/5/99, as *An Idyll of Seven Dials*).
[Music by Amy E. Horrocks.]
C.D. In the Italian Quarter (Vaud. 30/11/99). L.C.

FILMORE, LEWIS

D. The Winning Suit (P'cess. 16/2/63). L.C.

FINDON, B. W.

C. Troubles (St G. 22/11/88, *amat.*).
C.D. Stella (St G. 21/11/89). L.C.
D. The Primrose Path (Vaud. 11/5/92). L.C.
C.D. Fancourt's Folly (Pleasure Gdns. Folkestone, 14/5/94).

FINEMAN, SIGMUND H.

D. The Hero of Jerusalem (Stand. 13/6/96). L.C.

FINNAMORE, JOHN

R.D. Carpio (P's. Bradford, 24/5/86).

FISHER, C. ALLEN

C. Pa's Pills (Bijou, Aberystwyth, 1/6/94).

D. The Atonement (Bijou, Aberystwyth, 11/6/94).

FISHER, DAVID

F. Music hath Charms (P'cess. 7/7/56). L.C. *Lacy.*

F. Heart Strings and Fiddle Strings (P'cess. 27/2/65). L.C.

D. St Ronan's Well (Belfast, 31/1/76). L.C.

C.D. A Bill of Exchange (Brighton, 18/9/79). L.C.

FISHER, JOHN M.

D. A Burnt Offering (St Alban's Mission H. 17/7/94). See *A. FRYERS.*

M.C. The President; or, The Republic of Teentan (Grand, Maidenhead, 19/10/96). L.C.

[Written in collaboration with *E. TURNER.* Music by H. Vernon.]

FISHER, W. J.

F. Lot 49 (Gai. 17/1/88). L.C. *French.*

FISKE, STEPHEN

D. Robert Rabagas (St J. 25/2/73). L.C.

[FITCH, CLYDE

C. Pamela's Prodigy (Court, 21/10/91). L.C.

C.D. Marriage, 1892 (Union Square, New York, 14/3/92, as *A Modern Match*; Roy. Glasgow, 28/10/92). L.C.

D. Gossip (Palmer's, New York, 11/3/95; Grand, 3/6/95; Com. 22/2/96). L.C.

[Written in collaboration with *L. DIETRICHSTEIN.*]

M.C. The Merry-Go-Round (Gai. 13/1/98). L.C.

[Written in collaboration with *K. PEILE.*]

C. The Cowboy and the Lady (Broad Street, Philadelphia, 13/3/99; D.Y. 5/6/99). L.C.

F.C. The Masked Ball (Palmer's, New York, 3/10/92; Crit. 6/1/1900). L.C. Crit. 28/12/99.

FITZBALL, EDWARD

[For his earlier plays see iv, 312–17.]

Spec. The Four Sons of Aymon; or, The Days of Charlemagne (Ast. 1/4/50). L.C.

P. Alonzo the Brave and the Fair Imogene; or, Harlequin and the Baron all covered with Spangles and Gold (P'cess. 26/12/50). L.C.

Oa. The Cadi's Daughter (D.L. 27/1/51). L.C.

[Music by S. Nelson.]

Spec. Azael the Prodigal (D.L. 19/2/51).

M.D. Hans von Stein; or, The Robber Knight (M'bone, 11/8/51). L.C. *French.*

D. Vin Willoughby; or, The Mutiny of the Isis (M'bone, 25/8/51). L.C.

Spec. Azael; or, The Prodigal of Memphis (Ast. 3/11/51). L.C. Qns. 11/3/51.

M.D. The Greek Slave; or, The Spectre Gambler (M'bone, 20/11/51). L.C. *Lacy*.
D. The Last of the Fairies (Olym. 4/3/52). L.C. *Duncombe*.
M.D. The Secret Pass; or, The Khan's Daughter (Sur. 31/5/52). L.C.
D.D. Alice May; or, The Last Appeal (Sur. 23/6/52). L.C. *Lacy*; *Duncombe*.
M.D. Peter the Great (Ast. 26/7/52). L.C. *Lacy*; *Duncombe*; *Dicks*.
D. The Field of Terror; or, The Devil's Diggings (Olym. 11/8/52). L.C. as *The F. of T.; or, The Gnome Lamp*.
D. Uncle Tom's Cabin; or, The Horrors of Slavery (Olym. 20/9/52). L.C. *Duncombe*.
M.D. Uncle Tom's Cabin (Grec. 25/10/52). L.C.
M.D. Uncle Tom's Cabin (D.L. 27/12/52). L.C.
[These were all separate versions; see his *Thirty-Five Years of a Dramatic Author's Life*, ii, p. 261.]
M.D. The Rising of the Tide (M'bone, 24/1/53). L.C.
Spec. Amakosa; or, Kaffir Warfare (Ast. 28/3/53). L.C.
D. The Miller of Derwent Water (Olym. 2/5/53). L.C. *Lacy*.
R.O. Raymond and Agnes (Manchester, 1855; St J. 11/6/59).
D. Nitocris; or, The Ethiop's Revenge (D.L. 8/10/55). L.C.
D. The Children of the Castle (M'bone, 23/11/57). *Lacy*.
D. The Husband's Vengeance; or, The Knight of Wharley (M'bone, 28/11/57). L.C.
C.O. Pierette; or, The Village Rivals (Hull, 6/3/58). L.C. *Lacy*.
Ba. Auld Robin Gray (Sur. 19/4/58). L.C.
[Music by A. Lee.]
Ext. The Lancashire Witches; or, The Knight, the Giant and the Castle of Manchester (Lyc. 17/7/58). L.C.
C. The Widow's Wedding (St J. 3/10/59). L.C.
O. Lurline (C.G. 23/2/60). L.C.
[Music by W. V. Wallace.]
D. Christmas Eve; or, A Duel in the Snow (D.L. 12/3/60; S.W. 4/6/62, as *The Duel in the Snow*). L.C.
D. Robin Hood; or, The Merry Outlaws of Sherwood (Ast. 8/10/60). L.C. *French*.
O. She Stoops to Conquer (C.G. 10/2/64). L.C.
[Music by Macfarren.]
O. The Magic Pearl (Alex. 29/9/73). L.C.
[Music by T. Pede.]

FITZGEORGE, Captain
Bsq. Round the World in W'Eighty Days (Brighton, 13/3/77).

FITZGERALD, AUBREY
F. The Agony Column (Kilburn, 10/7/94). L.C. Bijou.

FITZGERALD, DAN
D. The Rose of Rathboy (P'cess. of W. 14/8/99). L.C.

FITZGERALD, EDWARD
— Six Dramas of Calderon freely translated. 8° 1853.
T. Agamemnon. 8° [1876; *priv*.].
T. The Downfall and Death of King Œdipus. 8° 1880 [*priv*.].
D. Such Stuff as Dreams are made of (St G. 15/5/99). L.C. as *Life's a Dream*. 8° 1865 [*The Mighty Magician* and *Such Stuff as Dreams are made of*].

FITZGERALD, PERCY

Ca. The William Simpson (Olym. 16/12/72). L.C.
D. Vanderdicken (Lyc. 8/6/78). See *W. G. WILLS.*
F.C. The Henwitchers (H. 2/12/78). L.C.
F. Room 70 (H. 4/1/86).

FITZGERALD, S. J. ADAIR

D. The Barringtons (Nov. 6/3/84). L.C.
[Written in collaboration with *J. H. MERRIFIELD.*]
M.D. A Lucky Girl (L'pool, 18/11/89). L.C. County H. Bootle.
F.C. The Parson (Glo. 10/10/91). L.C.
C.D. Two Hearts (Roy. 6/2/94, *mat.*). L.C.
C.O. The Bric-a-brac Will (Lyr. 28/10/95). L.C.
[Written in collaboration with *H. MOSS.* Music by E. Pizzi.]
D.Sk. A Jealous Mistake (Glo. 27/4/99). L.C.
Ca. The Parting (Hotel Cecil, 15/5/99). L.C.
Duol. Waiting for the Train (Salle Erard, 3/6/99). L.C.
D. Rip van Winkle (P'cess. of W. 27/11/99).

FITZHAMON, LEWIN

C.D. The Tipster (Corn Exchange, Dunstable, 22/1/98).

FITZROY, CECIL N. T.

D. The Coiner's Dream (Lecture H. Derby, 12/5/90; Stand. 17/7/99). L.C. Ipswich.
D. Catherine (Nov. 22/3/97). L.C.

FITZSIMON, JUSTIN F.

C.O. Bazilette (Phil. 21/2/81). L.C.

FITZWILLIAM, EDWARD FRANCIS

O. Love's Alarms (H. 17/11/53). L.C.

FLAXMAN, ARTHUR J.

D. Light (Gai. 3/11/77).
D. True Grit (Wigan, 29/3/94). See *H. PETTITT.*
M.F.C. Playing the Game (Str. 12/6/96). See *W. YOUNGE.*
F. Mr Sympkyn (Glo. 1/5/97).
[Written in collaboration with *W. YOUNGE.*]

FLECK, DUDLEY

D. A Tangled Skein (Grec. 19/8/72). See *O. ALLEN.*

"*FLEMING, GEORGE*" [*CONSTANCE FLETCHER*]

C.D. Mrs Lessingham (Gar. 7/4/94). L.C.
F. The Canary (P.W. 13/11/99). L.C.

FLEXMORE, F.

Bsq. Faust up too Late (Ladb. H. 22/10/89).
P. Aladdin (County, Kingston, 26/12/98). L.C.

FLOCKTON, C.

D. Charles the First; or, The King and the Protector (Bath, 4/8/79).

FLOYD, W. R.

D. Handy Andy; or, The Lost Heir Stand. L.C. 21/6/60. *French.*

FOGERTY, ELSIE

Duol. Love laughs at Locksmiths (West, Albert H. 13/5/99). L.C. as *The Portrait.*

FOLKARD, Dr H.

Oa. Romance and Reality; or, The Poet's Home (Roy. 30/6/70). L.C.
[Music by J. W. Elliott.]

D. The Dyke House (Assembly R. Sandgate, 12/2/77).

FOMM, LESLIE

C. Ambition (Glo. 27/4/99; Wyndham's, 26/6/1900, as *An Offer of Marriage*). L.C.

FONBLANQUE, ALBANY

F. The Metempsychosis (M'bone, 22/11/53). L.C.

FOOTE, JOHN

D. L'Assommoir; or, The Curse of Drink (Dewsbury, 27/9/79).

FOOTMAN, MAURICE H.

R.D. The Orchard of the King (Lincoln, 20/11/89). See *E. DAY.*

FORBES, NORMAN

R.D. The Scarlet Letter (Roy. 9/5/88). See *S. COLERIDGE.*

FORBES, Hon. Mrs

C.D. All Hallows' Eve (Qns. Dublin, 20/4/91).
[Written in collaboration with *J. W. WHITBREAD.*

FORD, DOUGLASS M.

F.C. The Doctor's Dilemma (Aquar. Scarborough, 13/4/99). L.C.

D. Strong as Death (Gloucester, 19/6/99). L.C.

D. The Queen's Necklace (Stockport, 5/8/99). L.C.

FORD, F.

D. Sybil the Hunchback (Huddersfield, 14/4/73; M'bone, 22/6/74). L.C.

FORD, HERBERT

D. The Mask of Death (Wedgwood, Burslem, 19/7/97). L.C.

FORD, T. MURRAY

C.O. The Punch Bowl; or, The Royal Brew (Nov. 18/6/87, *mat.*). L.C.
[Music by J. Storer.]

M.D. The Money Lender (P.H. Warrington, 6/8/88; Stratford, 29/10/88). L.C.

C.O. Commodore Bouilli (Bow and Bromley Inst. 31/10/88; Lyr. Ealing, 3/11/88).
[Music by J. Storer.]

C.O. Gretna Green (Com. 4/12/89). L.C.
[Music by J. Storer.]

C.D. True Nobility (Holcombe H. Tottenham, 16/4/92, *amat.*). L.C.

FORD, T. W.

D. Pish O'Pogue (Amphi. S. Shields, 22/5/76).

FORDE, ARTHUR C.

C.D. Only a Dream (Ipswich, 13/4/85). L.C.

FORREST, AMY

D. Trick for Trick (Stratford, 16/12/89). L.C. P.H. Torquay.

D. Out of Evil (Qns. Battersea, 4/12/93). L.C.

FORREST, HERBERT

D. North and South (Tyne, Newcastle, 24/9/77).

FORRESTER, ALFRED HENRY ["*ALFRED CROWQUILL*"]

P. Harlequin King Muffin (Sur. 26/12/53).
[Written in collaboration with *T. SHEPHERD*.]

P. The King of the Peacocks; or, Harlequin Tom Tiddler's Ground and Queen Barley Sugar (Sur. 26/12/71). L.C.

FORRESTER, STEPHANIE

C.D. Black but comely (Gai. 16/9/82). L.C.

C. My General (Ryde, 13/11/90).

FORSHAW, FRED

D. The Son of a Sinner (Parkhurst, 13/7/96). L.C.

F.C. The Last Train (Richmond, 7/5/98). L.C.

FORSTER, JOSEPH

T. Chatterton (Ladb. H. 23/1/88).

FORTESCUE, WILLIAM S.

D. Vengeance is Mine (Somerville's, Beverley, 28/1/97).

FORWARD, C. W.

M.F. The Dude and the Dancing Girl (T.H. Brixton, 4/11/93). See *C. D. STEELE*.

FOSTER, H.

C.O. The Belles of the Village (Aven. 18/11/89). L.C.
[Music by J. Fitzgerald.]

FOSTER, LEIGHTON

D. John Lester, Parson (Lyr. 20/1/92). See *R. KNIGHT*.

C.D. A Jonathan without a David (T.H. Clacton-on-Sea, 19/7/94). L.C.

FOSTER, W. C.

D. The Banker's Daughter (N. Shields, 24/5/76). L.C.

FOULTON, W.

F. A Triumph of Arms (Olym. 16/12/72). L.C.

FOX, FRANKLIN

M.F. The Two Q.C.'s (Alex. Pal. 25/7/81). L.C.
[Music by H. C. Banks.]

FOX, GEORGE D.

D. St Leger; or, Sporting Life, its Tricksters and its Trials (L'pool, 12/3/77). L.C.

Oa. Per Parcel's Post (P's. Accrington, 26/11/83).
[Written in collaboration with *W. E. MORTON*.]

C. Stepping Stones (Nov. 7/5/87, *amat.*).

R.D. Macaire (C.P. 20/9/87; Stand. 11/2/88). L.C.

C.D. Mabel (St G. 9/5/91). L.C.

O. Nydia, the Blind Girl of Pompeii (C.P. 10/5/92). L.C.

FOX, JOSEPH

D. The Union Wheel (Sheffield, 16/4/70). L.C.

D. Sweet Revenge; or, All in Honour (L'pool, 17/4/76; Pav. 22/6/78).
[Written in collaboration with *J. F. McARDLE*.]

D. Ambition's Slave; or, A Game of Chess (O.H. Leicester, 15/1/83; Stand. 24/3/83). L.C.

FRANÇAIS, J.

C.D. Number Twelve (Nov. 31/7/86). L.C.

FRANCE, C. V.

C.O. The Magician's Daughter (Bradford, 16/12/89). L.C.
[Music by W. Wadham.]

FRANCE, EDWIN SIDAWAY

D. The Pentlands (Wakefield, 23/4/72).
D. Born of Hilda (Windsor, 13/5/78). L.C.
D. The New World (Windsor, 27/9/80).
D. The Whipping Post; or, Life in the Ranks (Norwich, 10/3/84; Stand. 18/8/84). L.C. Aquar. Gt Yarmouth.
D. The Schoolmates (Norwich, 12/9/84).
D. The Ruby (S.W. 31/1/85). L.C.
C.D. On the Verge (Wolverhampton, 10/3/88, *mat.*; S.W. 21/7/88, as *A Woman's Sin; or, On the V.*). L.C.
[Written in collaboration with *F. DOBELL*. This play seems also to have been known as *The Shadow of Crime*.]

FRANCES, B.

F.C. The Medical Student (Str. 4/7/93). L.C.
[Written in collaboration with *H. J. LAELAND*.]

FRANCIS, FRANCIS

D. A Blind Marriage (Crit. 20/8/96). L.C.

FRANCKS, F. HAWLEY

F. Chizzle's Choice (Ladb. H. 28/7/88). L.C.
[Written in collaboration with *M. WOOD*.]
F. North and South (Ladb. H. 28/7/88). T.H. Richmond, Yorks. 25/5/88.
F. The Mystery of a Gladstone Bag (Pav. 24/6/89). L.C.
F. Our Bairn (Kilburn, 4/12/89).
F. His Future Wife (Aquar. Brighton, 3/2/90). L.C.
C. The Chalk Mark (Aven. 26/4/99). L.C.
[Written in collaboration with *A. TASSIN*.]

FRANKLIN, JENNY

M.C. Cissy (T.H. Harrowgate, 20/3/90). See *W. H. DEARLOVE*.

FRASER, JULIA AGNES

C. Hubert's Pride (Vic. Strathaven, 8/7/72).
D. Dermot O'Donoghue; or, The Stranger from Belfast (Vic. Strathaven, 24/7/72; Whitehaven, 21/3/77; Belfast, 25/11/78). L.C. Portsmouth, 13/4/76.
F. A Slight Mistake (Vic. Strathaven, 6/5/73).
D. Patrick's Vow (Vic. Strathaven, 23/5/73).
Ca. Barrington's Busby; or, Weathering the Admiral (Devonport, 4/10/83). L.C. Plymouth, 10/3/90.
D. Idle Words; or, Death and Glory (O.H. Edinburgh, 21/12/96, *amat.*).

FRAYNE, F. J.

D. Mardo; or, The Nihilists of St Petersburg (Qns. Manchester, 7/7/83). L.C.

FREAKE, Mrs

C. Deeds (Cromwell House, S. Kensington, 25/2/79, *amat.*).

FREEMAN, CHARLES

Ext. The Enchanted Beans (Gai., W. Hartlepool, 22/3/75).

D. Fifty Fafty, the Tyneside Mystery (N. Shields, 13/2/82; Qns. R. Berwick, 13/12/95). L.C.
D. A White Devil; or, A Morphia Maniac (P's. Blackburn, 23/6/93, *copy.*; Willenhall, 1/2/94). L.C.
M.C.D. Dr Syntax (Concert H. St Leonard's, 3/6/95). L.C.

FREETH, F.
F.C. The Banquet (T.H. Kilburn, 26/5/88). L.C.

FRENCH, HENRI P.
M.F. Collars and Cuffs (Birkenhead, 30/11/83). L.C.
P. Jack the Giant Killer and the Butterfly Queen (E.C. 24/12/87). L.C.
P. Cinderella; or, Three Jolly Butcher Boys all in a Row (E.C. 26/12/89).
P. Cinderella (E.C. 24/12/95). L.C.
P. Three Blind Mice (E.C. 24/12/96). L.C.

FRENCH, SYDNEY
C. A Friend in Need (St J. 23/4/60). L.C.
[Written in collaboration with *W. J. SORRELL.*]
Bsq. Rob Roy (M'bone, 29/6/67). L.C.
Bsq. Lucrezia Borgia (M'bone, 20/7/67).
Ext. Lord Bateman (Alh. 24/12/75). L.C.

FRENCH, W. PERCY
C.O. The Knight of the Road (Qns. Dublin, 27/4/91).
[Music by W. H. Collison.]
C.O. Strongbow; or, The Bride of the Battlefield (Qns. Dublin, 2/5/92).
[Music by W. H. Collison.]
M.Ca. Midsummer's Madness (Leinster H. Dublin, 7/11/92).
[Music by W. H. Collison.]

FRERE, CHARLES
D. Mary's Devotion (Sur. 29/4/98). L.C.

FREUND, J. C.
D. The Undergraduate (Qns. 22/6/72). L.C.

FREUND-LLOYD, MABEL
Ca. A Breach of Promise (O.C. 1/12/91, *mat.*). L.C. Str. 30/5/91. *French.*

FRIEL, C. D.
D. Our Luck (Doncaster, 22/9/76).

FRIEND, T. H.
O. The Damnation of Faust (Court, L'pool, 3/2/94). L.C.
[Music by H. Berlioz.]

FRIPP, F.
F.C. The Mysterious Widow (Neville Dramatic Studio, 26/7/97).

FRITH, WALTER
D. Ensnared (Gai. 8/3/83). L.C.
D. In the Old Time (St J. 31/5/88, *mat.*). L.C.
Oa. Brittany Folk (St G. 20/3/89). L.C.
[Music by A. J. Caldicott.]
M.C. Locked in (Sav. 28/5/89, *mat.*). L.C.

Oa. The Verger (St G. 9/12/89). L.C. *French.*
[Music by K. Hall.]
D. The Home Feud (Com. 14/2/90, *mat.*). L.C.
C.D. Molière (St J. 17/7/91). L.C.
C.D. Midsummer Day (St J. 30/3/92). L.C. *French.*
D.Sk. The Barley Mow (St G. 16/4/92). L.C.
[Music by C. Grain.]
C.D. Flight (Terry's, 16/2/93). L.C.
D. Her Advocate (D.Y. 26/9/95). L.C.
D. Not wisely but too well (Roy. Glasgow, 1/4/98; Grand, Fulham, 25/4/98). L.C.
D. The Man of Forty (Manchester, 27/10/98; St J. 28/3/1900). L.C.

"*FROST, FRANCISCO*" [*E. L. BLANCHARD*]
P. Tit, Tat, Toe—My First Go; or, Harlequin N.E.W.S. and the Fairy Elves of the Fourth Estate (M'bone, 26/12/56).

FRY, ARTHUR
C.D. A Rescued Honour (Aven. 4/6/96). L.C.

"*FRYERS, AUSTIN*" [Said to be a pseudonym for *CLEARY* or *CLERY*: possibly *E. CLEARY*, see p. 313.]
Ca. A Lesson in Acting (S.W. 9/6/83). L.C.
C.D. An Old Scapegoat (Imp. 22/11/84).
Oa. Eulalie (Foresters' H. Clerkenwell, 3/6/90; Grand, 26/3/95). L.C.
[Music by A. C. Lecocq.]
D. Beata (Glo. 19/4/92, *mat.*). L.C.
Ca. Who is Sylvia? (O.C. 12/11/92). L.C. Winter Gdns. Southport, 15/12/87.
C.D. Gentle Ivy (Str. 10/5/94). L.C.
D. A Burnt Offering (St Alban's Mission H. 17/7/94).
[Written in collaboration with *J. M. FISHER*.]
D. A Human Sport (Glo. 1/5/95). L.C. *French.*
D. The Dead Past (Parkhurst, 24/6/95). L.C.
M.C. The Japanese Girl (Plymouth, 26/6/97). L.C.
[Music by C. Lecocq.]
C.D. A Radical Candidate (C.P. 30/10/99). L.C.
D.Sk. Oh, Liza! (C.P. 22/11/99). L.C.

FULLER, CHARLES F.
M.D. Aretoeus; or, The Romance of a Patent (H.M.S. Rainbow, 7/4/81).
Vaud. The Fifteenth Century (H.M.S. Rainbow, 10/4/83).
[Music by C. Williams.]
Bsq. Fancy Land; or, The Ideal King (H.M.S. Rainbow, 9/4/84).
Bsq. Sir Marigold the Dottie; or, The Moonlight Knight (H.M.S. Rainbow, 16/4/85).
Ext. Diddlecombe Farm (H.M.S. Rainbow, 1/4/86).

FULLER, FRANK
D. Alone in the World; or, Without a Home (Dewsbury, 14/4/71).
D. The False Accusation; or, While there's Life there's Hope (M'bone, 3/5/75). L.C. E.L. 16/10/74, as *False Accusations.*
D. The Wild Flower of the Prairie; or, A Father's Legacy (E.C. 8/9/77). L.C.
[Written in collaboration with *H. RICHARDSON*.]
D. Raised from the Ashes (E.C. 31/5/79). L.C.

FULLER, HUBERT

D. The Passion of Life (Merthyr Tydvil, 31/7/99; Edmonton, 6/8/1900; W.L. 4/3/1901). L.C.

FULLERTON, Lady GEORGIANA

C.D. The Fire of London; or, Which is which? 8° 1882.

FURNESS, J. R.

D. The Massacre of Abergavenny (St G. Llandudno, 18/9/97, *copy.*). L.C.

FURNIVAL, HENRY

Ca. Once upon a Time (Brighton, 12/7/89). See *E. H. RUSSELL.*

FURRELL, JAMES W.

R.D. Midnight; or, The Wood Carver of Bruges (P'cess. 24/5/88, *mat.*). L.C.

[Written in collaboration with *E. C. STAFFORD.*]

D. The Witches' Boon (Ladb. H. 11/9/88, *copy.*). L.C.

FURTADO, CHARLES

D. Gabriel Grub the Sexton (Masonic H. Lincoln, 15/3/80). L.C.

[*FYLES, FRANKLYN*

D. The Girl I left behind me (S.W. 6/1/93). See *D. BELASCO.*

FYSHER, GYLBERT

D. The Fatal Beauty (S.W. 2/4/92).

GALER, ELLIOT JOHN NORMAN

D. Spiders and Flies; or, Caught in the Web (Grec. 8/10/68). L.C.

D. Alone in the World (Reading, 13/11/71; Leicester, 4/10/75, as *Cast on the World*). L.C.

C.O. Celia, the Gipsy Girl (O.H. Leicester, 20/10/79). L.C.

[Music by E. Mallandaine.]

D. For Gold (O.H. Leicester, 10/4/82).

D. A True Story told in Two Cities (O.H. Leicester, 7/2/84; D.L. 15/6/85). L.C.

D. With the Colours; or, A Black Seal (O.H. Leicester, 14/8/86; Grand, 23/8/86). L.C.

[Written in collaboration with *J. MEW.*]

D. Found in Exile; or, News from Home (O.H. Leicester, 11/6/88). L.C.

C.D. The Beechborough Mystery (Grand, Birmingham, 17/6/89). L.C.

[Written in collaboration with *J. MEW.*]

GALLON, TOM

D. Tatterley (Grand, Southampton, 12/12/98). See *A. SHIRLEY.*

GALLY, MAURICE

D. False Witness (P.H. New Cross, 28/10/90). See *A. SHIRLEY.*

GAMMON, R. T.

F. The Three Doctors (Hatfield, 6/2/96).

GANNON, JOHN

D. The Burglar Alarm and the Detective Camera (Adel. L'pool, 30/1/93). L.C.

D. The Torture of Shame; or, A Mother's Sin (Adel. L'pool, 25/5/96). L.C.

GANTHONY, ALFRED

Ca. Lela's Love Letters (St G. 31/5/88). See *J. E. SODEN.*

GANTHONY, NELLIE

M.Sk. In Want of an Engagement (Vaud. 3/6/91, *mat.*; Terry's, 13/4/92, as *In Search of an Engagement*).

M.Sk. Last on the Programme (Lyr. Ealing, 24/9/92).

M.Sk. Outward Bound (Terry's, 21/3/96).

GANTHONY, RICHARD

C. A Brace of Partridges (County, Kingston, 15/11/97; Str. 10/2/98). L.C. *French.*

Ca. The Muff of the Regiment (Str. 10/2/98).

M.D. Chartreuse (Richmond, 7/7/99, *copy.*). L.C.
[Music by J. W. Ivimey.]

D. A Message from Mars (Aven. 22/11/99). L.C.

GARDNER, C.

D. The Trying Scenes of Life (Lyc. Sunderland, 19/7/76).

GARDNER, HERBERT

C. Time will tell (Bridgewater House, 8/5/82; Windsor, 30/11/82; Traf. 8/5/93). L.C.

Ca. Cousin Zach (Canterbury, 8/83; Windsor, 28/11/83). *French.*

Vaud. A Night in Wales (St G. 1/6/85).
[Music by C. Grain.]

GARNETT, CONSTANCE

D. The Convert (Aven. 14/6/98). L.C.

GARRICK, C.

C. The Loyal Lovers (Vaud. 2/12/85). L.C. as *Who wins?*

GARROWAY, A. J.

Ca. The Marble Arch (P.W. L'pool, 12/12/81). See *E. ROSE.*

GARSTON, LEONARD

P. Ye Fair One with ye Golden Locks (Sur. 26/12/72). *See H. P. GRATTAN.*

P. Mother Redcap; or, Harlequin Queen Fancy (Alex. 26/12/73). L.C.

GARTON, CRESWICK

F. A Dark Horse (St G. 13/3/68, *amat.*). L.C.

GARTON, W. R.

Ca. He would be a Bohemian (G.I. 12/3/70, *amat.*). L.C.

GARVICE, CHARLES

C.D. The Fisherman's Daughter (Roy. 26/12/81). L.C.

GASCOIGNE, HENRY

D. Denounced; or, Faithful to the End (E.C. 11/8/83). L.C.
[Written in collaboration with *F. JEFFERSON.*]

D. Courage; or, The Story of a Big Diamond (M'bone, 25/10/86). L.C.

GASKELL, Mrs PENN

Ca. Run in (Constitutional H. Harlesden, 12/1/99). L.C.

GATHERCOLE, Mrs

D. Trick for Trick (Dewsbury, 16/2/77).

GATTIE, A. W.

F. Inoculation (Ladb. H. 18/2/92, *amat.*). L.C.
C.D. The Transgressor (Court, 27/1/94). L.C.
C.D. The Honourable Member (Court, 14/7/96). L.C.

GATTIE, W. M.

F. The School for Cookery (Belvedere H. Belvedere, Kent, 10/6/79). L.C.

GATWARD, HAL

Bsq. Darry the Dauntless (County, Reading, 31/7/90). L.C.
[Written in collaboration with *W. T. THOMPSON*.]

GEARY, WILLIAM

M.C. The Twilight (Gas Band R. Brentford, 24/3/87).

GEE, LOUIS

F. Brewing a Bruin (Brit. 2/6/73). L.C.

GEM, T. H.

Oa. Bardwell versus Pickwick. 8° 1881.
[Music by F. Spinney.]

GEMMELL, ROBERT

D. Montagu. 12° 1868.

GENÉE, RICHARD

C.O. Nanon (Grand, Birmingham, 16/9/89). L.C.

GENET, ERNEST

C.O. Atlantis (Gai. 17/3/86). See *M. DALTON*.
C.D. The Radical; or, The Honour of the House (Beaufort House, Walham Green, 6/11/88). L.C.
D.Sk. Worcester Fight (St G. 11/1/90). See *M. DALTON*.
C.D. The Reckoning (T.H. Chelsea, 4/5/91). L.C.

GEORGE, BEVERLEY

D. Diamond Steve and the Redemption of Sin (Runcorn, 22/7/1905). Albert, Brighouse, Yorks. 30/11/99.

GEORGE, G. H.

M.Int. Honeymoon Hints (Str. 20/9/52). L.C.
P. Harlequin Tom the Piper's Son who stole the Pig and away he run; or, Goody Two Shoes and her Ps and Qs (Oriental, 24/12/69). L.C.
P. Dame Trot; or, Harlequin Babes in the Wood and Lost Little Red Riding Hood (Oriental, 24/12/70). L.C.
P. Billy Taylor; or, Harlequin Old Father Thames and Britannia Queen of the Sea (Oriental, 26/12/71). L.C.
P. Killarney; or, The Maiden's Wish and the Fairy of the Lake (Oriental, 29/8/72).
P. Robinson Crusoe; or, The Man, the Maid and the Monkey (Oriental, 24/12/72). L.C.
P. Aladdin and the Lamp (Albion, 24/12/73). L.C.
P. The Sleeping Beauty (Albion, 24/12/74). L.C.

GERALD, FRANK

D. Rookwood (Shakespeare, L'pool, 15/4/95). See *G. ROBERTS*.

GERANT, JOHN

D. At Duty's Call (Pleasure Gdns. Folkestone, 31/1/98).

GERMAIN, J. EDWARD
Oa. The Two Poets (St G. 21/12/86). L.C.

GIBNEY, SOMERVILLE
M.C. Peggy's Plot (St G. 20/12/93). L.C.
[Music by W. Slaughter.]
C.D. Missing (St G. 9/7/94). L.C.
C.D. A Jack of All Trades (Bradford, 30/3/96). L.C. Glo. 8/4/96.

GIBSON, Miss C.
Bal. The Chamois Hunter (Qns. 13/9/52).

GIBSON, HENRY
Duol. An Ibsen Christmas (Birkbeck Inst. 20/10/97).

GIEVE, EDWARD
D. The Anarchist (Alex. Widnes, 3/9/94).

GIFFARD, ARETON
Fairy D. Sir Gorger the Giant and Little Boy Blue (Parkhurst, 19/6/97). L.C.
C.D. The Beverley Bogey (Bijou, 11/12/97). See *M. HINGESTON-RANDOLPH.*

GIFFORD, Countess of
C. Finesse; or, Spy and Counter Spy (H. 6/5/63). L.C.

GIFFORD, J. WEAR
F. Supper for Two; or, The Wolf and the Lamb (P'cess. Glasgow, 23/11/83). *French.*

GILBERT, ALFRED
D.Sk. The Rival Roses (St G. 14/7/87).

GILBERT, ARTHUR H.
D. The Swiss Express (P'cess. 26/12/91, *mat.*). L.C.
[Written in collaboration with *C. READ.*]

GILBERT, EDMUND
D. Misjudged (Qns. Manchester, 4/4/84).

GILBERT, EDWIN
D. The White Roses (Ladb. H. 20/8/91, *copy.*; Parkhurst, 14/12/91). L.C.
R.C. In the Golden Days (Mat. 17/6/97). L.C.

GILBERT, FRANCIS
D. A London Arab (Pleasure Gdns. Folkestone, 20/3/99). See *M. WALLERTON.*

GILBERT, H. P.
Bsq. The Court of Lions; or, Granada taken and done for. *Lacy.*

GILBERT, LEWIS
D. The Penalty of Crime (Metro. Devonport, 2/11/96). L.C. Muncaster, Bootle, 28/8/96.
D. The Sons of Toil (Morton's, Greenwich, 31/7/99). L.C.
[Title altered to *Partners in Crime*, 13/5/1903.]

GILBERT, WILLIAM SCHWENK ["*F. LATOUR TOMLINE*"]
F. Uncle's Baby (Lyc. 31/10/63). L.C.
[Attributed to Gilbert, doubtfully.]

Bsq. Ruy Blas [in *Warne's Christmas Annual*, 1866, pp. 50–6].
Ext. Dulcamara; or, The Little Duck and the Great Quack (St J. 29/12/66). L.C. 8° 1866.
P. Hush-a-Bye Baby (Ast. 26/12/66). See *C. MILLWARD.*
Ext. La Vivandière; or, True to the Corps (St J.H. L'pool, 15/6/67; Qns. 22/1/68). L.C. 8° 1868 [Liverpool].
Bsq. Robinson Crusoe; or, The Injun Bride and the Injured Wife (H. 6/7/67). L.C.
[Written in collaboration with *H. J. BYRON, T. HOOD, H.S. LEIGH* and *A. SKETCHLEY.*]
F. Allow me to explain (P.W. 4/11/67). L.C.
F. Highly Improbable (Roy. 5/12/67). L.C.
P. Harlequin Cock Robin and Jenny Wren; or, Fortunatus and the Water of Life, the Three Bears, the Three Gifts, the Three Wishes, and the Little Man who woo'd the Little Maid (Lyc. 26/12/67). L.C. 8° 1867.
Bsq. The Merry Zingara; or, The Tipsy Gipsy and the Pipsy Wipsy (Roy. 21/3/68). L.C. 8° 1868.
Ext. Robert the Devil; or, The Nun, the Dun and the Son of a Gun (Gai, 21/12/68). L.C. as *R. le Diable.* 8° 1868.
M.Ca. No Cards (G.I. 29/3/69). L.C. 8° [1901].
[Music by L. Elliott.]
Bsq. The Pretty Druidess; or, The Mother, the Maid and the Mistletoe Bough (Ch. X. 19/6/69). L.C. 8° 1869.
C.D. An Old Score (Gai. 19/7/69). L.C. as *Quits. Lacy.*
Oa. Ages Ago: A Ghost Story (G.I. 22/11/69). L.C. 8° 1869; 8° 1895.
[Music by F. Clay.]
Bsq. The Princess (Olym. 8/1/70). L.C. *Lacy.*
M.Ca. The Gentleman in Black (Ch. X. 26/5/70). L.C. *Lacy.*
[Music by F. Clay.]
M.Ent. Our Island Home (G.I. 20/6/70). L.C.
Fairy C. The Palace of Truth (H. 19/11/70). L.C. *Lacy.*
C.D. Randall's Thumb (Court, 25/1/71). L.C. as *Under his Thumb. Lacy.*
Oa. A Sensation Novel (G.I. 30/1/71). 8° [1912].
D. Creatures of Impulse (Court, 15/4/71). L.C. *Lacy.*
[Music by A. Randegger.]
D. Great Expectations (Court, 29/5/71). L.C.
C. On Guard (Court, 28/10/71). L.C. *French.*
C.D. Pygmalion and Galatea (H. 9/12/71). L.C. *French.*
Oa. Thespis; or, The Gods grown old (Gai. 26/12/71). L.C. 8° 1871.
[Music by Sir A. Sullivan.]
F. A Medical Man (St G. 24/10/72). Printed in C. W. Scott's *Drawing-Room Plays*, 1870.
Oa. Happy Arcadia (G.I. 28/10/72). L.C. 8° 1872; 8° 1896.
[Music by F. Clay.]
Fairy C. The Wicked World (H. 4/1/73). L.C. 8° [1873]; *French.*
Bsq. The Happy Land (Court, 3/3/73). L.C. 8° 1873.
[Written in collaboration with *G. A. À. BECKETT.*
Bsq. The Realm of Joy (Roy. 18/10/73). L.C.
C. The Wedding March (Court, 15/11/73). L.C. *French.*
D. Charity (H. 3/1/74). L.C. *French.*
C. Ought we to visit her? (Roy. 17/1/74). L.C.

Ca. Committed for Trial (Glo. 24/1/74). L.C.
Ext. Topsey Turveydom (Crit. 21/3/74). L.C. 8° [Oxford, 1931].
C.D. Sweethearts (P.W. 7/11/74). L.C. *French.*
M.F. Trial by Jury (Roy. 25/3/75). L.C. 8° 1875.
[Music by Sir A. Sullivan.]
C. Tom Cobb; or, Fortune's Toy (St J. 24/4/75). L.C. as *Buried Alive. French.*
Ca. Eyes and No Eyes; or, The Art of Seeing (St G. 5/7/75). L.C. 8° 1896.
[Music by F. Pascal.]
Fairy D. Broken Hearts (Court, 9/12/75). L.C. *French.*
C.O. Princess Toto (Nottingham, 1/7/76; Str. 2/10/76). L.C. 8° [1876].
[Music by F. Clay.]
D. Dan'l Bruce, Blacksmith (H. 11/9/76). L.C. *French.*
F.C. On Bail (Crit. 3/2/77). L.C. *French.*
[Rewritten version of *Committed for Trial.*]
F.C. Engaged (H. 3/10/77). L.C. *French.*
C.O. The Sorcerer (O.C. 17/11/77). L.C. 8° [1877].
[Music by Sir A. Sullivan.]
P. Ali Baba and the Forty Thieves (Gai. 13/2/78). See *H. J. BYRON.*
C. The Ne'er-do-Weel (Olym. 25/2/78; Olym. 25/3/78, as *The Vagabond*). L.C. Hull, 20/6/77. 8° [1878].
C.O. H.M.S. Pinafore; or, The Lass that loved a Sailor (O.C. 25/5/78). L.C. 8° [1878].
[Music by Sir A. Sullivan.]
D. Gretchen (Olym. 24/3/79). L.C. 8° 1879; *French.*
C.O. The Pirates of Penzance; or, The Slave of Duty (Bijou, Paignton, 30/12/79; Fifth Avenue, New York, 31/12/79; O.C. 3/4/80). L.C. 8° [1887].
[Music by Sir A. Sullivan.]
C.O. Patience; or, Bunthorne's Bride! (O.C. 23/4/81). L.C. 8° [1881].
[Music by Sir A. Sullivan.]
Fairy C. Foggerty's Fairy (Crit. 15/12/81). L.C. 8° [1881]; 8° 1890.
C.O. Iolanthe; or, The Peer and the Peri (Sav. 25/11/82). L.C. 8° [1885].
[Music by Sir A. Sullivan.]
C.O. Princess Ida; or, Castle Adamant (Sav. 5/1/84). L.C. 8° [1884].
[Music by Sir A. Sullivan.]
D. Comedy and Tragedy (Lyc. 26/1/84). L.C. *French.*
C.O. The Mikado; or, The Town of Titipu (Sav. 14/3/85). L.C. 8° [1885].
[Music by Sir A. Sullivan.]
C.O. Ruddygore; or, The Witch's Curse! (Sav. 22/1/87; title altered to *Ruddigore*, 27/1/87). L.C. 8° [1887].
[Music by Sir A. Sullivan.]
C.O. The Yeomen of the Guard; or, The Merryman and his Maid (Sav. 3/10/88). L.C. 8° [1888].
[Music by Sir A. Sullivan.]
D. Brantinghame Hall (St J. 29/11/88). L.C. 8° 1888.
Bsq.O. The Brigands (Plymouth, 2/9/89; Aven. 16/9/89). 8° 1871.
[Music by J. Offenbach.]
C.O. The Gondoliers; or, The King of Barataria (Sav. 7/12/89). L.C. 8° [1889].
[Music by Sir A. Sullivan.]

Bsq. Rosencrantz and Guildenstern (Vaud. 3/6/91, *mat.*; Court, 27/4/92). L.C. *French.*

C.O. The Mountebanks (Lyr. 4/1/92). L.C. 8° 1892.
[Music by A. Cellier.]

C.O. Haste to the Wedding (Crit. 27/7/92). L.C. as *The Wedding March.*
[Music by G. Grossmith.]

C.O. Utopia (Limited); or, The Flowers of Progress (Sav. 7/10/93). L.C. 8° 1893.
[Music by Sir A. Sullivan.]

C.O. His Excellency (Lyr. 27/10/94). L.C. 8° [1894].
[Music by O. Carr.]

C.O. The Grand Duke; or, The Statutory Duel (Sav. 7/3/96). L.C. 8° [1896].
[Music by Sir A. Sullivan.]

F. The Fortune Hunter (Birmingham, 27/9/97; Qns. O.H. Crouch End, 18/10/97). L.C. 8° [1897; *priv.*].
[For his later plays see Townley Searle, *Sir William Schwenck Gilbert* (n.d.).]

GILBERT-GILMER, JULIA

D. Life's Parting Ways (Parkhurst, 9/9/93, *copy.*; Manor R. Hackney, 31/5/94). L.C.

[*GILL, WILLIAM*

C. My Sweetheart (P'cess. Glasgow, 4/6/83). See *F. MAEDER.*

Bsq. Adonis (Gai. 31/5/86). L.C.
[Written in collaboration with *H. A. DIXEY.*]

M.C. Mam'zelle; or, The Little Milliner (P.W. L'pool, 22/10/94). L.C. under sub-title.

GILLETT, FRED. J.

D.Sk. Little Chap, Curly and Brown (T.H. Kilburn, 29/1/95). See *J. W. RIX.*

Bsq. Boadicea Unearthed (T.H. Kilburn, 29/1/95). See *J. W. RIX.*

[*GILLETTE, WILLIAM*

C.D. Young Folks' Ways (St J. 20/10/83). See *Mrs F. H. BURNETT.*

D. Held by the Enemy (Ladb. H. 20/2/86, *copy.*; P'cess. 2/4/87). L.C.

C. The Professor's Wooing (Madison Square, New York, 1/6/81; Roy. 15/2/87, *mat.*). L.C.

C.D. A Legal Wreck (Madison Square, New York, 14/8/88; Ladb. H. 13/8/88, *copy.*). L.C.

F.C. All the Comforts of Home (Boston Museum, 3/3/90; Glo. 24/1/91). L.C.
[Written in collaboration with *H. C. DUCKWORTH.*]

D. Secret Service (Terry's, 10/5/95, *copy.*; Adel. 15/5/97). L.C.

D. Sherlock Holmes (Star, Buffalo, 24/10/99; L'pool, 2/9/1901). L.C. D.Y. 30/8/99.

GILLINGTON, C.

Ext. Cock Robin and Jenny Wren (Roy. 12/12/91, *mat.*). L.C.
[Music by F. Pascal.]

O. The Jewel Maiden (St G. Parish H. Forest Hill, 13/12/99).
[Music by F. Pascal.]

GILMORE, JOHN FARQUHAR

F.C. Proposals (Vaud. 15/12/87, *mat.*). L.C.

GIOVANELLI, ALFRED

P. The Jolly Miller of Stratford; or, Harlequin Old Dame Goodness (Oriental, 5/7/69).

GIRAUD, Mrs

D.Sk. Dear Jack (Colchester, 30/5/92, *amat.*).

GIRNOT, H.

F. The Tale of a Tubb (Duke's, 16/3/76). L.C.
[Written in collaboration with *P. MERRITT*.]

C.D. A Pair o' Wings (Gai. Dublin, 13/12/78). See *P. MERRITT*.

GIVEEN, ROBERT F.

F.C. His Son-in-Law (County, Reading, 4/11/96). L.C.

GLEN, IDA

M.D. A Woman's Error; or, The Stolen Diamonds (Shrewsbury, 1/5/76). L.C.

GLENDINNING, JOHN

Ca. A Pantomine Prince (Belfast, 15/3/97). L.C. Huddersfield.
D. Rough and Ready (Shakespeare, Clapham, 4/10/97).
D. The Hand of Time (Darlington, 20/12/97). L.C.

GLENNEY, CHARLES

C. Matches (Com. 17/1/99). L.C.

GLENNIE, G.

Oa. Beau Lavender; or, The Butterfly of Fashion (Bijou, 21/7/96). L.C.
[Music by R. Clarke.]

GLENNY, G. W.

M.D. The Strollers; or, On the Road (Athen. Llanelly, 27/8/88).

GLOVER, EDMUND

P. The Great Bed of Ware (Glasgow, 27/12/52).
P. Whittington and his Cat (Glasgow, 26/12/53).
P. Little Bo Peep (Glasgow, 3/12/54).
D. The Indian Revolt; or, The Relief of Lucknow (Glasgow, 1860).

GLOVER, J. M.

Oa. The Fashionable Beauty (Aven. 7/4/85). See *G. MOORE*.

GLOVER, R.

D. By Command of the Czar (Vic. 5/11/77). L.C.
[Written in collaboration with *C. HERMANN*.]

GLYN, H. A.

D. Man (Gloucester, 5/1/74).

GLYNN, GORDON

D. Adam Winter, the Fiend of Private Life; or, Dark Deeds of Old London. L.C. Brit. 23/4/50.

GODBOLD, ERNEST HILDER

C.D. A Political Pair (O.H. Llandudno, 15/5/99). L.C.

GODFREY, GEORGE WILLIAM

C. Queen Mab (H. 21/3/74). L.C.
C. The Queen's Shilling (P's. Manchester, 12/10/77; Court, 19/4/79). L.C. Bristol.
M.Ca. The Turquoise Ring. L.C. St G. 12/10/80.
[Written in collaboration with *L. BENSON*.]

C.D. Coralie (St J. 28/5/81). L.C.
C. The Parvenu (Court, 8/4/82). L.C. *French.*
C. The Millionaire (Court, 27/9/83). L.C.
Ca. My Milliner's Bill (Court, 6/3/84). L.C. *French.*
C. The Opal Ring (Court, 28/1/85). L.C.
C. The Man that hesitates (Newcastle, 9/9/87; St G. 28/2/88). L.C.
C. Vanity Fair (Court, 27/4/95). L.C.
D. The Woman Hater (Manchester, 25/10/95; St J. 23/11/95, as *The Misogynist*). L.C.

GODFREY, GERALD
R.D. Bela (Belfast, 8/1/86).
Ca. After Long Years (Dewsbury, 22/12/88; Pav. 16/12/89).

GODFREY, W. P.
C.O. The Legacy (Grammar School, Bedford, 18/12/79).

GODWIN, E. W.
T. Helena in Troas (Hengler's, 17/5/86). See *J. TODHUNTER.*
D. Fair Rosamond (Wimbledon, 20/7/86).

GOLDBERG, MARCUS
F.C. Sold Up (Grand, Nottingham, 22/12/90, *amat.*).

GOLDBERG, MAX
C.D. Through Fire and Snow (Scarborough, 15/2/86). L.C. Albany, Durham, 12/3/86.
D. The Hand of Justice (S.W. 7/9/91). L.C.
D. Westward Ho! (Dewsbury, 18/7/92). L.C.
D. The Three Musketeers (St J. Manchester, 8/8/92; Osborne, Manchester, 21/11/98). L.C.
D. Kenilworth (Lyr. Hammersmith, 25/11/95). L.C.
D. The Secrets of the Harem (City, Sheffield, 24/12/96). L.C. Grand, Cardiff.
D. The Tiger's Grip (Lyc. Ipswich, 23/3/98, *copy.*). L.C.
[Written in collaboration with *G. COMER.*]
D. The Soldiers of the Queen; or, Briton and Boer (Leeds, 9/5/98). L.C. Yarrow, 30/3/98.
D. The Man in the Iron Mask (Huddersfield, 7/3/99, *copy.*; Adel. 11/3/99). L.C.

GOLDBERG, W. F.
Bsq. Dick Turpin the Second (Gai. 6/5/89, *mat.*). L.C.

GOLDMAN, LOUIS B.
D. An Act of Folly (Drill H. Basingstoke, 7/6/87).
D. A Man of the World (P.H. Treharris, 7/3/94; Leamington, 18/3/95, as *The Owner of the Works*). L.C.

GOLDSCHMIDT, ANNA
Oa. On Strike (Mechanics H. Nottingham, 15/11/94, *amat.*).
[Music by Julia Goldschmidt.]

GOLDSMITH, W. H.
F. A Female Iago (Jersey, 6/7/72; Roy. 24/7/73). L.C.
Ca. The Shelter (Stockton-on-Tees, 21/7/90). L.C. *French.*
C.D. Sure to Win (Nov. 16/11/96). L.C.

GOLDSWORTHY, ARNOLD

C.D. My Friend Jarlet (Old Stagers, Canterbury, 2/8/87; Terry's, 5/11/90). L.C. *French.*

Ca. An Old Maid's Wooing (St G. 28/1/88). L.C. Windsor, 2/11/87. [Written in collaboration with *E. B. NORMAN.*]

C. The Blacksmith's Daughter (O.C. 16/10/88). L.C.

F.C. The Picture Dealer (Ladb. H. 30/6/92). See *H. REICHARDT.*

GOLLMICK, ADOLF

C.O. Dona Constanza; or, The Forced Marriage (Crit. 20/11/75). L.C.

GOMERSALL, W.

D. Boccagh; or, Friend and Foe (Worcester, 4/8/84). L.C.

GOMM, E. H.

Oa. The Miser (P's. 17/7/84). [Music by W. Fullerton.]

GOODMAN, E. J.

C. Seeing the World (Leeds, 5/12/73).

C.D. Love in Idleness (Brighton, 13/3/96). See *L. N. PARKER.*

GOODMAN, J. C.

Ca. Don Quixote Junior (Glo. 21/4/79). L.C. [Written in collaboration with *J. HOWSON.*]

GOODMAN, W.

D.Sk. Fifteen Minutes Grace (P.W. Club, 18/2/94).

GOODRICH, ARTHUR

D. A Ruined Life (Grand, 15/9/84). L.C. [Written in collaboration with *J. R. CRAUFORD.*]

C.D. True Love (Brighton, 9/10/85). L.C.

D. The Calthorpe Case (Vaud. 14/12/87, *mat.*). L.C.

GOODWIN, —

D. Mercy (Norwich, 17/11/79).

[*GOODWIN, J. CHEEVER*

M.F. Lost, Stolen or Strayed (D.Y. 27/4/97). L.C. as *A Day in Paris.* [Music by Woolson Morse.]

GOODYER, F. R.

Ext. Once upon a Time; or, A Midsummer Night's Dream in Merrie Sherwood (Nottingham, 13/4/68).

Ext. The Fair Maid of Clifton (Nottingham, 30/3/72).

Bsq. Nottingham Castle (Nottingham, 22/9/73).

F. Goose Fair (Nottingham, 2/10/74).

GORDON, GEORGE LASH

Ca. Wedded Bliss (Cork, 3/10/71; Dublin, 2/4/73). L.C. Hamilton and Pitt Co. 5/5/76.

D. The Brand of Cain (Birkenhead, 16/7/75). L.C. Hanley.

F. Backing the Favourite (O.C. 7/8/75). L.C.

Ca. A Hornet's Nest (O.C. 13/1/76). L.C.

D. Uncle Joe (P.W. L'pool, 18/2/76). L.C.

Bsq. Hamlet à la mode (P.W. L'pool, 16/10/76; O.C. 21/4/77). L.C. [Written in collaboration with *G. W. ANSON.*]

F. Bachelors' Hall (P.W. L'pool, 13/1/77; O.C. 21/4/77). L.C.

Bsq. The Babes in the Wood (P.W. L'pool, 16/4/77). L.C. [Written in collaboration with *G. W. ANSON.*]

C.D. Millions in it (P.W. L'pool, 16/4/77). L.C.
F. Salviniana (O.C. 2/6/77).
C.D. Auld Lang Syne (P'cess. Edinburgh, 9/11/77; Park, 27/5/78). L.C.
D. The Broken Bail (P'cess. Edinburgh, 14/6/78). L.C.
D. The Treaty of Peace (Park, 3/8/78). L.C.
D. The Night Birds (Northampton, 24/2/81; Phil. 8/4/82). L.C.
[Written in collaboration with *J. MACKAY*.]
D. The Rustic Maiden (Olym, 2/1/82). L.C.
D. London Pride (Phil. 28/1/82). L.C.
[Written in collaboration with *J. MACKAY*.]
Bsq. Delights o' London (Phil. 8/4/82). See *W. MACKAY*.
D. The Conspiracy (P.W. L'pool, 16/6/82). L.C.
P. Dick Whittington and his Cat (M'bone, 23/12/82). See *F. W. GREEN*.
Ext. Tit-Bits (Winter Gdns. Blackpool, 25/5/83). L.C.
M.F. A Bunch of Keys (Aven. 25/8/83). See *C. H. HOYT*.
F.C. Oughts and Crosses (Jersey, 28/7/84). L.C.
D. The Streets; or, A Tale of Wicked London (S.W. 6/9/84). L.C.
D. No Evidence (Belfast, 15/1/86). L.C. Longton.
Bsq. Faust and Co. (Greenock, 27/2/86). L.C.
Ext. The Grand Duke; or, Change for a Sovereign (H.M. Dundee, 7/8/86). L.C. Greenock, 17/2/86.
[Music by J. Gregory.]
F.C. The Silly Season (Athen. Shepherd's Bush, 30/12/92, *copy*.). L.C.
[Written in collaboration with *B. NASH*.]

GORDON, HECTOR C.
D. Highland Hearts (Grand, Glasgow, 28/10/89). L.C.

GORDON, J.
F.C. Moses and Son, an Up-to-date Mosaic (Roy. 11/6/92). L.C.

GORDON, STUART
D. True Blue (Olym. 19/3/96). See *L. S. OUTRAM*.

GORDON, SYDNEY
D. A Drifting Spar (Edmonton, 5/8/93). L.C. Athen. Shepherd's Bush, 5/7/92.
D. True Blue (Olym. 19/3/96). See *L. S. OUTRAM*.

"*GORDON, WALTER*" [*WILLIAM AYLMER GOWING*: see p. 386]
Ca. Dearest Mama, my Mother-in-Law (Olym. 14/5/60). L.C. *French*.
Ca. Duchess or Nothing (Olym. 9/7/60). L.C. *French*.
Ca. Home for a Holiday (Olym. 12/11/60). L.C.
C.D. Old Trusty (Olym. 28/1/61). L.C. *French*.
Ca. My Wife's Relations (Olym. 1/12/62). L.C. *French*.
F. An Odd Lot (Roy. 28/3/64). L.C. *French*.
D. Through Fire and Water (Adel. 29/6/65). L.C. *Lacy*.
Ca. Pay to the Bearer—a Kiss (H. 16/7/68). L.C.
D. Eileen Dhu (Sefton, L'pool, 26/6/82).

GORDON-CLIFFORD, E. and H.
F. The Amber Girl (P's. H. Kew, 12/9/94). L.C. Lyr.
D.Sk. A Black Dove (P's. H. Kew, 12/9/94).

GOSNAY, W. A.
C.D. Struggling for Wealth (Sur. 21/12/80). L.C.

GOSSE, Sir EDMUND
D. Hedda Gabler (Vaud. 20/4/91, *mat.*). L.C.
D. The Master Builder (Traf. 20/2/93). See *W. ARCHER.*

GOTT, HENRY
D. The Wizard of the Moor (W.L.). *Lacy.*

GOUGH, HERBERT
D. The Marriage Bells (Vaud. 28/11/81). L.C. Park, 9/9/81.
Ca. At Last (P's. Bristol, 19/3/86).
[Written in collaboration with *M. EDWARDS.*]
Ca. Hope's Answer (S. Shields, 19/11/86). See *M. EDWARDS.*
[Probably the same play as the above.]
C. Dan and Dick (Ladb. H. 14/5/87, *copy.*, *amat.*). L.C.
[Written in collaboration with *M. EDWARDS.*]
C.D. Constance Frere (Vaud. 27/6/87, *mat.*). L.C.
[Written in collaboration with *M. EDWARDS.*]

GOULD, FRED
D. Hidden Gold (Portsmouth, 4/12/82). See *E. C. BERTRAND.*
D. The Father's Oath (P'cess. Glasgow, 24/10/92; Sur. 29/5/93).

GOVER, FRED
D. Cast Adrift (Bristol, 27/2/82). See *R. PALGRAVE.*
Ca. Conquered Pride (P's. Bristol, 19/3/86). See *R. MACKENZIE.*
D. God Save the Queen (P's. Bristol, 24/4/86). See *R. PALGRAVE.*

GOWER, JAMES
D. The Little Red Cross (Alh. Wigan, 16/7/85).
D. Simon Moneypenny (T.H. Linlithgow, 3/5/88).
D. Marjory Gilzean; or, The Life and Adventures of General Anderson (T.H. Elgin, 16/11/88).

GOWING, WILLIAM AYLMER [" *WALTER GORDON*": see p. 385]
D. The State Prisoner (18/2/51). *French.*

GRAFTON, STAFFORD
D. England and Glory (Gai. Walsall, 11/10/88). L.C. Var. 17/12/88, as *Death and Glory.*

GRAHAM, DAVID
D. Rizzio. 8° 1898.
D. Darnley. 8° 1900.

GRAHAM, F.
P. The Babes in the Wood (R.A. Woolwich, 24/12/97). See *M. BYAM.*

GRAHAM, H.
F.C. The Kidnapper (Lecture H. Derby, 29/5/88).
C.D. Daisy Land (Lecture H. Derby, 11/3/90).
C. The County Councillor (Ladb. H. 7/10/91, *copy.*; Str. 18/11/92, *mat.*; C.P. 17/11/92; Traf. 4/2/93). L.C.
M.C. Little Miss Nobody (O.H. Cheltenham, 5/3/98; Lyr. 14/9/98). L.C.
[Music by Godfrey and Roberts.]
Ca. Pets (St G. 18/12/99). L.C.

GRAHAM, JAMES
D. Mariana (Court, 22/2/97).

GRAHAM, J. F.
D. A Life's Debt (Roy. Chester, 17/11/87, *copy*.; Vic. O.H. Burnley, 27/8/88). L.C.

GRAHAM, J. H.
F. The Baby and the Regimentals. L.C. Grec. 17/11/50.

GRAHAM, R. G.
F. The Fire Alarm (T.H. Teddington, 1/2/93). L.C.
Ca. Our Play (T.H. Teddington, 1/2/93; Vaud. 13/3/93). L.C.

GRAHAME, ARTHUR
D. Edgar Harissue (Ladb. H. 19/7/98). See *C. H. MALCOLM*.

GRAHAME, J. C.
Bsq. The Babes in the Wood (Willenhall, 27/4/95).
[Written in collaboration with *B. ARTLETT*.]

GRAHAME, RONALD
M.D. Honour Bright (Bilston, 22/9/97, *copy*.; Nuneaton, 14/3/98; W.L. 28/3/98). L.C.
[Written in collaboration with *E. T. DE BANZIE*.]

GRAIN, RICHARD CORNEY
M.Ca. A Flying Visit. L.C. St G. 14/5/80.
[Written in collaboration with *A. LAW*.]
M.Sk. A Musical Family (St G. 27/12/80).
M.Sk. Ye Fancy Fayre (St G. 30/5/81).
M.Sk. Master Tommy's Theatricals (St G. 26/12/81).
M.Sk. A Day in Boulogne. L.C. St G. 27/5/82.
M.Sk. Small and Early (St G. 5/6/82).
M.Sk. En Route (St G. 23/10/82).
M.Sk. Our Mess (St G. 1883).
M.Sk. On the Thames (St G. 22/10/83).
M.Sk. Master Tommy's School (St G. 22/12/83).
M.Sk. Spring's Delights (St G. 18/2/84).
Vaud. A Little Dinner (St G. 14/4/84).
M.Sk. Shows of the Season (St G. 18/6/84).
M.Sk. The Troubles of a Tourist (St G. 6/10/84).
M.Sk. Backsheesh (St G. 26/12/84).
M.Sk. A Vocal Recital (St G. 6/4/85).
M.Sk. Eton versus Harrow (St G. 29/6/85).
M.Sk. Election Notes (St G. 9/11/85).
M.Sk. Henley Regatta (St G. 14/6/86).
M.Sk. Jubilee Notes (St G. 11/4/87).
M.Sk. Our Servants' Hall (St G. 26/12/87).
Sk. Mossoo in London (St G. 2/4/88).
Sk. Cards of Invitation (St G. 25/6/88).
Sk. John Bull Abroad (St G. 15/10/88).
M.Sk. A Day's Sport (St G. 28/1/89).
Monol. I've taken a House (St G. 4/11/89).
Sk. My Aunt's in Town (St G. 10/6/89).
M.Sk. A Family Party (St G. 26/12/89).
M.Sk. Tommy at College (St G. 7/4/90).

Sk. The Society Peepshow (St G. 14/6/90).
M.Sk. Seaside Mania (St G. 29/9/90).
Sk. At the Pantomime (St G. 18/12/90).
M.Sk. Then and Now! (St G. 30/3/91).
M.Sk. Dinners and Diners (St G. 25/5/91).
Monol. The Diary of a Tramp (St G. 19/10/91).
Sk. A Fancy Dress Ball (St G. 6/2/92).
M.Sk. My Wife's Party (St G. 23/5/92).
Sk. Boys and Girls (St G. 24/12/92).
M.Sk. Poor Piano (St G. 1/4/93).
M.Sk. Box B (St G. 22/5/93). L.C.
M.Sk. Echoes of the Opera (St G. 15/6/93).
M.Sk. By Road and Rail (St G. 20/11/93).
M.Ca. The Ugly Duckling (St G. 20/11/93). L.C.
M.Sk. A Musical Interview with the Parish Pump (St G. 16/1/94).
M.Sk. A Funny World (St G. 26/3/94).
M.Ca. Walls have Ears (St G. 26/3/94). L.C.
M.Sk. Bond Street, 4 p.m. (St G. 4/6/94).
M.Ca. That Fatal Menu (St G. 29/10/94). L.C.
M.Sk. Back in Town (St G. 29/10/94).
M.Sk. Uncle Dick (St G. 20/12/94).
M.Sk. Music à la mode (St G. 11/2/95).

GRAND, SARAH
C.D. The Fear of Robert Clive (Lyc. 14/7/96). L.C.
[Written in collaboration with *H. McFALL.*]

GRANGE, A. DEMAIN
C.D. For Old Sake's Sake (Pav. Edinburgh, 7/5/98).

GRANT, GEORGE
D. The Kiss of Delilah (D.L. 27/11/96). L.C.
[Written in collaboration with *J. LISLE.*]

GRANT, JAMES
F. Strawberries and Cream (P'cess. Glasgow, 26/2/91). See *E. T. DE BANZIE.*

GRANT, NOEL
C.D. Lady Jemima (Assembly R. Whitstable, 29/8/88). L.C.

GRANT, ROLAND
F. The Doctor's Boy (Sur. 8/1/77). L.C.

GRANTHAM, JOHN
Bsq.O. Les Cent Vierges (Brighton, 17/10/74).
[Music by A. C. Lecocq.]

GRANVILLE, H. SUCH
Bsq. Æneas; or, Dido Done (Cork, 2/3/68).
Bsq. Sardanapalus (Limerick, 15/5/68; St G. 23/12/68). L.C.
D. Saved (St G. 23/12/68). L.C.
C.D. That's why she loved him (Preston, 8/5/76). L.C.
C. 'Twas all for Love (K. X. 12/11/77). L.C.
D. Falsely Judged (Connaught, 7/8/80). L.C.

GRATIENNE, Mlle.
C. Only an Actress (Mont Dore H. Bournemouth, 12/1/98). L.C.

GRATTAN, H. P. [*HENRY WILLOUGHBY GRATTAN PLUNKETT*]

F. Glory (Halifax, 2/1/71; Ch. X. 16/6/73). L.C.
D. A Line of Life (P.W. Glasgow, 28/10/71). See *W. SIDNEY*.
D. Nobody's Fortune (Sur. 5/2/72). L.C.
D. The Claimant; or, The Lost One Found (Sur. 1/4/72). L.C. Gar. 13/10/71.
D. The White Boys of Kerry (Bradford, 14/10/72).
P. Ye Fair One with ye Golden Locks (Sur. 26/12/72). L.C.
[Written in collaboration with *L. GARSTON*.]
P. Sinbad the Sailor (Holb. 26/12/74). L.C.
P. Sinbad the Sailor (Park, 27/12/75). L.C.
D.Sk. Orson (Adel. 12/8/76). L.C.
D. The Omadhaun (Qns. 24/11/77). L.C.
D. Seven Years Ago (Grec. 18/3/79). L.C.
D. The Death Warrant; or, A Race for Life (Grec. 25/10/79).
P. Ali Baba and the Forty Thieves (S.W. 26/12/81). See *F. B. CHATTERTON*.
D. Follies of the Day; or, Fast Life (Bristol, 16/10/82; Pav. 9/7/83; St. 22/9/90). L.C. Cardiff.
[Written in collaboration with *J. ELDRED*.]
D. Ye Legende; or, The Four Phantoms (Imp. 22/9/83). L.C.
D. The Echoes of the Night (Pullan's, Bradford, 7/1/84; Pav. 7/7/84). L.C.
[Written in collaboration with *J. ELDRED*.]
D. The Outcasts of the City (Jarrow, 3/11/84). See *J. ELDRED*.
D. A Fight against Fate (Vic. Newport, 2/3/85). L.C. Bristol, 22/1/85.
[Written in collaboration with *F. DAWSON*.]
D. Lady Godiva; or, For the People (Greenwich, 2/10/85). L.C.
F. Wanted, an Enemy (Tyne, Newcastle, 10/12/86). L.C.
D. The Rake's Will (Terry's, 16/7/89, *mat.*). L.C.

GRATTAN, HENRY

Ext. Merry Mr Merlin (E.C. 11/2/95). See *E. H. PATTERSON*.
D.Sk. Satan (M.H. Bedford, 23/10/99).
[Written in collaboration with *E. JONES*.]

GRAVES, A. P.

Ca. Out of the Frying Pan (Holborn, 4/5/72). L.C. *French*.
[Written in collaboration with *P. TOFT*.]
Ca. Clever Sir Jacob (Gai. 15/12/73).
[Written in collaboration with *P. TOFT*.]

GRAVES, CLOTILDE

F. The Skeleton (Vaud. 27/5/87). See *Y. STEPHENS*.
Poet.D. Nitocris (D.L. 2/11/87, *mat.*). L.C.
D. She (Nov. 10/5/88). See *E. ROSE*.
D.Sk. Rachel (H. 7/5/90, *mat.*).
D. Dr and Mrs Neill (Manchester, 28/9/94; Grand, 9/9/95). L.C. Lyc. 23/6/93 as *The Physician*.
F. A Mother of Three (Com. 8/4/96). L.C. *French*.
C. A Matchmaker (Shaft. 9/5/96). L.C.
[Written in collaboration with *G. KINGSTON*.]
D. Princess Tarakanoff; or, The Northern Night (P.W. 29/7/97, *copy*.). L.C.
C. A Florentine Wooing (Aven. 6/7/98, *copy*.). L.C. as *The Wooing*.
[Several later plays.]

GRAY, —

C. An Unsanctified Garment (St G. 20/12/95). L.C.
[Written in collaboration with — *MARTIN*.]

GRAY, ALFRED

D. A Hidden Enemy (Woolwich, 13/6/87). L.C.

GRAY, GEORGE

D. The Football King (E.C. 13/7/96). L.C. Stratford, 24/7/95.
M.Bsq. Turpin à la mode (Roy. Chester, 29/3/97). See *G. P. HUNTLEY*

GRAY, JOHN

C.D. The Kiss (Independent Theatre Soc. at Roy. 4/3/92).
M. Sour Grapes (West, Albert H. 17/4/94).
[Music by F. Gilbert and C. Dick.]
D. The Blackmailers (P.W. 7/6/94), *mat.*).
[Written in collaboration with *A. RAFFALOVITCH*.]

GRAY, LOUISA

C.Oa. Between Two Stools (Glendower Mansions, S. Kensington, 30/7/86).
Oa. Tricks and Honours (West, Albert H. 7/5/97; Mat. 11/11/97). L.C.

GRAYLE, PERCIVAL

C.D. Out of the Past (St G. 6/6/93, *amat.*). L.C.

GREEN, FRANK W.

Bsq. Cinderella in quite another Pair of Shoes (Royal Gardens, N. Woolwich, 20/5/71). L.C.
Ext. Carrot and Pa-snip; or, The King, the Tailor and the Mischievous F (Royal Gardens, N. Woolwich, 11/5/72).
P. Aladdin; or, Harlequin Shoeblack (M'bone, 23/12/72).
P. Gulliver and the Fair Persian; or, Harlequin Lilliput and the Magic Balm (Vic. 24/12/72). L.C.
Bsq. Lothair, Batti, Batti and Shah Dee Doo (L'pool, 13/10/73). L.C.
[Written in collaboration with *R. SOUTAR*.]
P. Jack and the Beanstalk (Sur. 24/12/73). L.C.
Bsq. Cherry and Fair Star; or, The Pretty Green Bird and the Fairies of the Dancing Waters (Sur. 4/4/74). L.C. *Lacy*.
Bsq.O. Mullibaloo (Brighton, 21/9/74).
Bsq. Aladdin; or, The Wonderful Lamp (Ch. X. 23/12/74).
Bsq.O. Dagobert (Ch. X. 28/8/75). See *R. SELLMAN*.
F. Flamingo (Str. 18/9/75). See *F. HAY*.
M.F. Slaviana (Brighton, 11/10/75). See *F. HAY*.
P. The Forty Thieves and the Court Barber (Sur. 24/12/75).
P. Jack and the Beanstalk (Albion, 24/12/75). L.C.
P. Jack the Giant Killer (Sur. 27/12/75). L.C.
F. The Dress Coat (Str. 29/6/76). L.C.
M.F. Jo versus Jo (Sur. 25/9/76). L.C.
[Written in collaboration with *O. ALLEN*.]
Bsq. The Lying Dutchman (Str. 21/12/76). L.C.
[Written in collaboration with *W. H. SWANBOROUGH*.]
P. Hop o' my Thumb (Albion, 23/12/76). L.C.
P. Jack and Jill (Sur. 23/12/76). L.C.
Bsq. Blue Beard and Fat Emma; or, The Old Man who cried Heads (Royal Gardens, N. Woolwich, 25/9/77).

P. Harlequin Jack in the Box; or, Little Bo Peep (M'bone, 24/12/77). L.C.

P. Dick Whittington and his Cat (Sur. 24/12/77). L.C.

P. Little Tom Tucker, who sang for his Supper (Albion, 24/12/77). L.C.

[Written in collaboration with *O. ALLEN.*]

P. Beauty and the Beast (Pav. 26/12/77). L.C.

P. Jack and the Beanstalk (C.G. 26/12/78). L.C.

Bsq. Sinbad the Sailor; or, The "Tar" that was "pitched" into (P'cess. Edinburgh, 31/3/79). L.C.

Bsq. Conn; or, Out of Sight, out of 'Erin (Alex. L'pool, 28/4/79).

P. Jack and Jill (Albion, 24/12/79). L.C.

P. Cinderella (M'bone, 24/12/79). L.C.

[Written in collaboration with *T. L. CLAY.*]

P. Sinbad the Sailor (C.G. 26/12/79). L.C.

P. Sinbad the Sailor; or, Harlequin the Old Man of the Sea (M'bone, 24/12/80). L.C.

[Written in collaboration with *J. F. McARDLE.*]

P. Hop o' my Thumb; or, Harlequin Nobody, Somebody, Busybody and the Wicked Ogre with the Seven-League Boots (Sur. 24/12/80). L.C.

P. Jack and the Beanstalk; or, Harlequin King Blushrose, the Fairy Flowers and the Wicked Weeds of the Nightshade Dell (Pav. 27/12/80). L.C.

[Written in collaboration with *T. L. CLAY.*]

P. Dick Whittington and his Good Cat; or, The Demon Rat of Bow Bells (Pav. 24/12/81). L.C.

P. Aladdin and his Wonderful Lamp; or, Harlequin and Cheeky Lad, the Wizard Bad, and the Beautiful Fairy who made Folks Glad (M'bone, 26/12/81). L.C.

P. Hop o' my Thumb; or, Harlequin Nobody, Busybody and the Wicked Ogre with the Seven-League Boots (Alex. Pal. 26/12/81). L.C.

P. Dick Whittington and his Cat; or, Harlequin and the Demon Rat (M'bone, 23/12/82). L.C.

[Written in collaboration with *G. L. GORDON.*]

P. Jack the Giant Killer; or, Harlequin and the Magic Sword, and the Brave Young Boy who kept his Word (Imp. 26/12/82). L.C.

[Written in collaboration with *H. J. DIDCOT.*]

P. Cinderella and the Little Glass Slipper (Pav. 26/12/82). L.C.

P. Dick Whittington and his King of Pussy Cats (E.C. 24/12/83).

P. Little Red Riding Hood; or, The Wizard and the Wolf (H.M. 26/12/83). L.C.

P. Sinbad the Sailor and the Old Man of the Sea (Pav. 26/12/83). L.C.

P. Cinderella; or, Humpty Dumpty sat on a Wall (Sanger's, 26/12/83). L.C.

[Written in collaboration with *O. ALLEN.*]

P. Jack and the Beanstalk (Grand, 26/12/84). L.C.

Bsq. Charibel (P's. Manchester, 4/5/85).

[A revision of *Cherry and Fair Star* (Sur. 4/4/74).]

P. Jack in the Box (E.C. 24/12/86).

[Written in collaboration with *F. HALL.*]

GREEN, HERBERT

D. English Hearts (Lincoln, 10/6/92). See *M. HALL.*

GREEN, J.

C.O. The Baron of Corvelle (Grand, Halifax, 3/10/92).
[Written in collaboration with *E. HANSON.*]

GREEN, JOHN

D. Under the Line; or, The Life of a Slaver, from her fitting out to her destruction (Wear M.H. Sunderland, 17/12/81).

GREEN, KATHERINE

Duol. What's in a Name? (Qns. H. 9/2/95).

GREENBANK, HARRY

F. The Director (Terry's, 7/5/91, *mat.*). L.C.
Oa. Captain Billy (Sav. 24/9/91). L.C.
[Music by F. Cellier.]
C.O. Incognita (Lyr. 6/10/92). See *F. C. BURNAND.*
Oa. Beef Tea (Lyr. 27/10/92). L.C.
[Music by W. Bendall.]
Oa. Mr Jericho (Sav. 24/3/93). L.C.
[Music by E. Ford.]
M.C. Poor Jonathan (P.W. 15/6/93). See *C. H. E. BROOKFIELD.*
M.C. A Gaiety Girl (P.W. 14/10/93). See *O. HALL.*
O. Mirette (Sav. 3/7/94; 6/10/94, *revised*). L.C.
[Lyrics by *F. E. WEATHERLEY.* Music by A. Messager.]
Oa. The House of Lords (Lyr. 5/7/94). L.C.
[Music by G. W. Byng and E. Ford.]
M.C. Monte Carlo (Str. 20/9/94). See *S. CARLTON.*
M.C. The Artist's Model (Daly's, 2/2/95). See *O. HALL.*
M.C. The Geisha (Daly's, 25/4/96). See *O. HALL.*
M.C. In the Ring (Gai. 27/5/96). See *J. T. TANNER.*
Oa. Old Sarah (Sav. 17/6/97). L.C.
[Music by F. Cellier.]
C.O. The Scarlet Feather (Shaft. 17/11/97). L.C.
[Music by C. Lecocq and L. Monckton.]
M.C. A Greek Slave (Daly's, 8/6/98). See *O. HALL.*
M.C. San Toy (Daly's, 21/10/99). See *E. MORTON.*
[For his later plays see Davenport Adams, *op. cit.* p. 609.]

GREENE, A. E.

D. Lord Darcy; or, True till Death (Corn Exchange, Cheltenham, 1/12/96). L.C.

[*GREENE, CLAY M.*

M.C. Hans the Boatman (Sheffield, 7/3/87; Grand, 4/7/87; Str. 21/12/91). L.C.
R.D. Chispa (Shakespeare, L'pool, 18/3/89).
C.D. Carl's Folly (Hull, 26/3/91). L.C.
D.Sk. A Musical Discord (Grand, Hull, 14/5/97; Borough, Stratford, 9/7/97).

GREENLAND, ALFRED

Bsq. The Rival Rascals; or, Virtue Rewarded and Vice Versa (St G. 3/5/77). L.C.

GREENWOOD, P.

C.D. Marion (Roy. 6/12/98). See *W. ELLIS.*
F. The Pasha (T.H. Hounslow, 11/12/99). See *W. ELLIS.*

GREENWOOD, THOMAS LONGDON

P. The House that Jack built in 1851 (S.W. 26/12/50).
P. Harlequin and the Yellow Dwarf (S.W. 26/12/51). L.C.
P. Dick Whittington and his Cat; or, Old Dame Fortune and Harlequin Lord Mayor of London (S.W. 27/12/52). L.C.
P. Harlequin and Tom Thumb; or, Gog and Magog and Mother Goose's Golden Goslings (S.W. 26/12/53). L.C.
P. Harlequin and Beauty and the Beast (S.W. 26/12/57).
P. Harlequin and the Wonderful Horse; or, Percinet and Graciosa, the Ugly Duchess and the Greedy King (Ast. 26/12/60). L.C.
P. Harlequin Tom Tucker (P'cess. 26/12/63). See *E. L. BLANCHARD.*
P. Cinderella (C.G. 26/12/64). See *E. L. BLANCHARD.*
[This, and subsequent collaborations of Greenwood and Blanchard, were issued under the *nom de plume* of "The Brothers Grinn".]
P. Harlequin Nobody and Little Jack Horner, Goody Two Shoes, Oranges and Lemons, and the Three Men in a Tub (Ast. 26/12/67). L.C.
P. Harlequin Little Boy Blue (C.P. 21/12/68). See *H. T. ARNOLD.*
P. Harlequin Humpty Dumpty and Dame Trot and her Cat; or, The Old Woman from Babyland and the Little Bachelor who lived by himself (Lyc. 26/12/68).
[Written in collaboration with *H. T. ARNOLD.*]
P. Little Tom Tittlemouse and the Eleven Dancing Princesses (Ast. 26/12/70). L.C.
[Written in collaboration with *H. T. ARNOLD.*]
D. Fadette, the Golden Gadfly (P.W. Rochdale, 9/10/71).
P. Little Dicky Dilver (P'cess. 26/12/71). See *E. L. BLANCHARD.*
P. Little Goody Two Shoes (P'cess. 26/12/72). See *E. L. BLANCHARD.*
P. Beauty and the Beast (P'cess. 23/12/74). See *E. L. BLANCHARD.*
P. The Children in the Wood (Adel. 24/12/74). See *E. L. BLANCHARD.*
P. The Yellow Dwarf (Alex. Pal. 24/12/75). See *E. L. BLANCHARD.*
P. Sinbad the Sailor (C.P. 21/12/76). See *E. L. BLANCHARD.*
Ext. The Enchanted Barber (Adel. 22/12/77). See *E. L. BLANCHARD.*
P. St George and the Dragon (Alex. Pal. 22/12/77). See *E. L. BLANCHARD.*
P. Aladdin and the Wonderful Lamp (Imp. 21/12/78). See *E. L. BLANCHARD.*
P. Bluebeard (D.L. 26/12/79). See *E. L. BLANCHARD.*
P. Aladdin (C.P. 22/12/80). See *E. L. BLANCHARD.*

GREET, DORA V. [*Mrs WILLIAM GREET*]

Ca. Elsie's Rival (Str. 9/5/88, *mat.*). L.C. *French.*
Ca. To the Rescue (P.W. 13/6/89). L.C.
Ca. A Flying Visit (Crit. 6/11/89). L.C.
M.D. Jackson's Boy (H.M. Carlisle, 28/3/91). L.C.
Monol. A Folded Page (Steinway H. 12/5/91).
C.D. A Real Prince (Bijou, 27/1/94). L.C.
C. The Little Squire (Lyr. 5/4/94, *mat.*). L.C.
[Written in collaboration with *H. SEDGER.*]
Ca. Thrown Together. *French.*

GREGG, TRESHAM D.
D. King Edward the Sixth. 8° 1857.
D. Mary Tudor. 8° 1858.

GREGORY, EDMUND
C.D. A Secret Agreement (Nov. 31/7/86). L.C. P.H. Leatherhead, 9/2/86.

GREGORY, Miss H. G.
D. Fate (Middlesborough, 9/3/74).

GREIGG, H. J. S.
D. The Last Call (Shakespeare, L'pool, 1/4/95). See *H. CHARLES*.

GREIN, J. T.
D. A Man's Love (P.W. 25/6/89, *mat.*; O.C. 15/3/95). L.C
[Written in collaboration with *C. W. JARVIS*.]
Idyl. In the Garden of Citrons. 8° 1891.
Ca. Spring Leaves (Court, 14/3/91). L.C.
[Written in collaboration with *C. W. JARVIS*.]
D. Reparation (Vaud. 12/5/92). L.C.
[Written in collaboration with *C. W. JARVIS*.]
Duol. Makebeliefs (Roy. 27/5/92). L.C.
Ca. The Compromising Coat (Glo. 27/6/92). L.C.
[Written in collaboration with *C. W. JARVIS*.]
C.D. Blanchette (West, Albert H. 8/12/98; Court, 24/5/1901).
[Written in collaboration with *M. L. CHURCHILL*.]

GREVILLE, EDEN E.
C. Shakespeare (Grand H. Maidenhead, 27/5/91; Glo. 27/6/92). L.C.
Ca. The Author (Grand H. Maidenhead, 6/8/91). L.C.
D. "He loves me, he loves me not" (Grand H. Maidenhead, 16/12/91).
F.C. The Prophet (Grand H. Maidenhead, 2/1/93). L.C.

GREVILLE, Lady VIOLET
C.D. Old Friends (St J. 26/6/90). L.C. *French*.
C.D. Baby; or, A Warning to Mesmerists (Brighton, 31/10/90; Terry's, 9/4/91).
D. Nadia (Lyr. 3/5/92).
C. An Aristocratic Alliance (Crit. 31/3/94). L.C.

GREY, ALLEN
D. Peg the Rake (Bijou, 25/10/97). L.C.
C. The Pasha (Kilburn, 28/2/98). L.C.

GREY, CRESWICK
C. A New Apollo (Everton, L'pool, 10/6/89). L.C.

GRIFFITH, GEORGE
D. Charles the Second. 8° 1867.

GRIFFITHS, ARTHUR
D. The Rift within the Lute (D.Y. 10/11/98). See *C. H. DICKINSON*.

GRIFFITHS, J. CHERRY
D. Banished from Home (Brit. 3/5/75). L.C.
D. Falsely Accused (Brit. 7/8/76). L.C.
D. All for Gold (Brit. 9/9/78). L.C.

GRIST, WILLIAM

C.O. The Impresario (C.P. 13/9/77). L.C. as *The Manager*.

O. Fadette (Court, L'pool, 18/1/86). L.C.
[Music by Maillart.]

O. Ruy Blas (Court, L'pool, 4/2/86). L.C.

O. At Santa Lucia (Manchester, 1/10/94).
[Music by P. Tasca.]

GROGAN, WALTER E.

C.D. Not wholly bad (P.H. Torquay, 13/4/93; Bijou, 2/3/94). L.C.

C.D. A Vain Sacrifice (Str. 14/11/93). L.C.

D. The Cardinal (Torquay, 8/9/94, *copy*.). L.C.

D. Mate (Ladb. H. 31/1/95). L.C. as *Foiled*.
[Written in collaboration with *F. ALLEYNE*.]

D. The Night Cometh (Ladb. H. 31/1/95). L.C.

D. Lord Alingford (Torquay, 16/5/95). L.C.

C.D. His Success (Bijou, 3/12/95). L.C.

D. Noel Ainslie, V.C. (Ladb. H. 26/2/97). L.C.
[Written in collaboration with *N. V. NORMAN*.]

D. The Daughter of the Tumbrils (West, Albert H. 17/5/97). L.C.

O. Lorraine (Torquay, 10/1/98; St G. 31/10/99). L.C.
[Music by J. Clerice.]

D. As the Night Cometh (Grand, Wolverhampton, 23/1/99).
[A revised version of *The Night Cometh*.]

D. The Scarlet Coat (New, Oxford, 22/11/99). L.C.
[Several later plays.]

GROSSMITH, GEORGE

Bsq. No Thoroughfare (Vic. 22/3/69).

Bsq. "Two" Much Alike (G.I. 12/2/70). See *A. R. ROGERS*.

M.Sk. Cups and Saucers (O.C. 5/8/78).

M.T. Mr Guffin's Elopement (Alex. L'pool, 29/9/82). See *A. LAW*.

M.F. The Real Case of Hide and Seekyl (Roy. 3/9/88).

GROSSMITH, GEORGE, Jr.

Bsq. Great Cæsar (Com. 29/4/99). L.C.
[Written in collaboration with *P. RUBENS*.]
[Several later plays.]

GROSSMITH, WEEDON

Ca. A Commission (Terry's 6/6/91). L.C. *French*.

Ca. What an Escape! L.C. Brighton, 28/12/99.
[For his later plays see Davenport Adams, *op. cit.* p. 916.]

GROVE, F. CRAWFORD

C.D. Forget-me-not (Lyc. 21/8/79). See *H. C. MERIVALE*.

C.D. As in a Looking Glass (O.C. 16/5/87).

D. La Tosca (Gar. 28/11/89). L.C.
[Written in collaboration with *H. HAMILTON*.]

D. The Bigot (Lyr. Ealing, 19/11/90, *copy*.). L.C.

GROVER, JOHN HOLMES

D. The Way of the Wicked; or, The Knights of the Green Baize (Col. L'pool, 11/2/71).

D. Cluricanne's Tower; or, The White Maiden of Tiernaboul (Col. L'pool, 24/2/71).

D. The Postheen Phewn (Cardiff, 19/2/72).

D. I.O.U. (Sunderland, 20/2/79; E.C. 28/6/79, as *I.O.U.; or, The Way of the Wicked.*)
D. The Exile (E.C. 9/8/79).
D. Bombo the Dwarf (Qns. Dublin, 10/5/80).
F. That Rascal Pat. *French.*

GROVER, LEONARD
C. Nadine (Alex. L'pool, 22/10/87, *copy.*; P's. Manchester, 3/9/88, as *My Brother's Sister*; Gai. 15/2/90). L.C.
C.D. Lost in New York (Olym. 3/8/96). L.C.

GRUNDY, SYDNEY
F. A Little Change (H. 13/7/72). L.C. *Lacy.*
Ca. All at Sea (Manchester, 8/8/73). L.C.
F. Reading for the Bar (Str. 2/10/76). L.C.
C. Mammon (Str. 7/4/77). L.C.
Ca. Man Proposes (Duke's, 18/3/78). L.C. as *A Will and a Way. French.*
C. The Snowball (Str. 2/2/79). L.C. *French.*
Ca. A Bad Bargain. L.C. Str. 21/3/79.
[Apparently this was acted only in the provinces.]
D. After Long Years (Folly, 6/12/79). L.C.
C. In Honour Bound (P.W. 25/9/80). L.C. *French.*
M.F. Popsey Wopsey (Roy. 4/10/80). L.C.
[Music by E. Solomon.]
F. Over the Garden Wall (Folly, 20/7/81). L.C. as *The Highgate Mystery.*
C. Dust (Roy. 12/11/81). L.C.
C.O. The Vicar of Bray (Glo. 22/7/82; Sav. 28/1/92, *revised*). L.C. 8° [1882].
[Music by E. Solomon.]
F.C. May and December (Glo. 28/9/82, *priv.*; Crit. 25/4/87, *mat.*; Com. 15/11/90). [Originally called *The Novel Reader*, this fell foul of the censor in 1877, but was eventually passed as *M. and D.* 7/10/82.]
[Written in collaboration with *J. MACKAY.*]
C. The Glass of Fashion (Grand, Glasgow, 26/3/83; Glo. 8/9/83). L.C. *French.*
[Written in collaboration with *G. R. SIMS.*]
D. Rachel (Olym. 14/4/83). L.C.
D. The Queen's Favourite (Olym. 2/6/83). L.C.
F. Hare and Hounds (P'cess. Edinburgh, 13/8/83). L.C.
C.O. La Cosaque (Gai. Hastings, 7/4/84; Roy. 12/4/84). L.C.
C.O. Pocahontas, the Great White Pearl (Empire, 26/12/84). L.C.
[Music by E. Solomon.]
C. The Silver Shield (Str. 19/5/85, *mat.*; Com. 20/6/85). L.C. *French.*
T. Clito (P'cess. 1/5/86). L.C. *Lacy.*
[Written in collaboration with *W. BARRETT.*]
D. A Wife's Sacrifice (St J. 25/5/86). L.C.
[Written in collaboration with *H. S. EDWARDS.*]
D. The Bells of Haslemere (Adel. 28/7/87). See *H. PETTITT.*
C.D. A Fool's Paradise (P.W. Greenwich, 7/10/87, as *The Mousetrap*, *copy.*; Gai. 12/2/89, *mat.*; Gar. 2/1/92). L.C. Adel. *French.*
C. The Arabian Nights (Glo. 5/11/87). L.C. *French.*
D. The Pompadour (H. 31/3/88). See *W. G. WILLS.*

D. The Union Jack (Adel. 19/7/88). See *H. PETTITT.*
F.C. Mamma (Court, 24/9/88). L.C.
C.D. The Dean's Daughter (St J. 13/10/88). L.C.
[Written in collaboration with *F. C. PHILIPS.*]
C.D. A White Lie (Nottingham, 8/2/89; Court, 25/5/89; Aven. 7/1/93, *revised*). L.C.
F. Merry Margate (Com. 27/3/89). L.C.
C.D. Esther Sandrez (P.W. 11/6/89, *mat.*; St J. 3/5/90). L.C.
D. Deep Waters (Manchester, 19/9/89). L.C. Shakespeare, L'pool.
C. A Pair of Spectacles (Gar. 22/2/90). L.C. *French.*
C.D. A Village Priest (H. 3/4/90). L.C.
C.D. A House of Cards (Brighton, 13/11/91). L.C.
O. Haddon Hall (Wolverhampton, 29/12/92; Sav. 24/9/92). L.C. 8° 1892.
[Music by Sir A. Sullivan.]
D. Sowing the Wind (Com. 30/9/93). L.C. 8° 1893 [*priv.*]; *French.*
C. An Old Jew (Gar. 6/1/94). L.C. 8° 1894 [New York].
[Title altered to *Julius Sterne*, 20/9/1905.]
C.D. A Bunch of Violets (H. 25/4/94). L.C. *French.*
C. The New Woman (Com. 1/9/94). L.C.
C.D. Slaves of the Ring (Gar. 29/12/94). L.C. 8° 1894 [*priv.*].
D. "The Greatest of These—" (Grand, Hull, 13/9/95; Gar. 10/6/96). L.C. 8° 1896 [*priv.*].
F. The Late Mr Castello (Com. 28/12/95). L.C. *French.*
D. A Marriage of Convenience (H. 5/6/97). L.C. *French.*
C. The Silver Key (H.M. 10/7/97). L.C.
M.D. The Musketeers (H.M. 3/11/98). L.C.
C. The Degenerates (H. 31/8/99). L.C
C.D. The Black Tulip (H. 28/10/99). L.C.
[Several later plays.]

GRUNFELD, P.
C. The Road to Fame (Vaud. 7/5/85). See *A. WHITE.*

GUION, NETTIE CORTELYON
D. A Modern Judas (Vaud. 25/2/92, *mat.*). L.C.

GUIVER, JAMES
D. The Last Stroke of Midnight (Grec. 18/3/79). L.C.

[*GUNTER, ARCHIBALD C.*
C. Prince Karl (Lyc. 19/10/88). L.C.
C. My Official Wife (Lyr. 10/11/92). L.C.

GUNTON, R. T.
O. The Lancashire Witches (Manchester, 20/10/79). L.C.
[Music by F. Stanislaus.]
Oa. His Last Cruise (P.H. Hatfield, 8/2/93, *amat.*; County, St Albans, 11/12/93).
[Music by W. Williams.]
Oa. Seagull Rock (P.H. Hatfield, 21/2/95, *amat.*).
[Music by W. Williams.]

GURNEY, ARCHER THOMPSON
D. Turandot, Princess of China. 8° 1836.
T. Faust...Part the Second. 8° 1842.
D.Poem. King Charles the First. 8° 1846.
T. Iphigenia at Delphi. 8° 1855; 8° 1860.

GURNEY, EDMUND

R.D. Glendelough (Qns. Manchester, 14/12/91). L.C.

D. Verdict—Suicidal Murder? (W.L. 13/5/95). L.C.

D. The New East Lynne (Metro. Birkenhead, 6/6/98; Stand. 18/7/98). L.C.

D. The King of Steel; or, The Building of the Ship (Preston, 12/12/98). L.C.

D. Grandad's Darling. *French.*

GURNEY, GERALD

D. Prince Otto (Spa Concert R. Harrogate, 24/3/88). See *T. B. THALBERG.*

D. The Cross of Olga (Woodside H. 29/1/96). See *R. CASTLETON.*

GWINDON, HAROLD

Ca. The Ladies' Champion (H. 18/5/68). L.C. as *Defend the Sex.*

GWYNNE, PERCY

F.C The Spinster (New Cross H. 30/4/87). L.C.
[Written in collaboration with *C. HARRISON.*]

D.D. Reconciled; or, Good for Evil (Lincoln, 3/11/88). L.C.
[Written in collaboration with *C. HARRISON.*]

HADEN, THOMAS

D. The Blacksmith's Daughter and the Red Hand; or, The Deserted Mine (Bilston, 8/9/93). L.C.
[Also called *John Grant's Daughter and the Flaming Hand.*]

HALE, Mrs CHALLOW

D. For the King's Sake (Albany Club, Kingston, 9/1/97, *amat.*; County, Kingston, 6/10/98). L.C.

HALE, WILLIAM PALMER

Ba. Godiva; or, Ye Ladye of Coventry and the Exiled Fairy (Str. 7/7/51). L.C. *Lacy.*
[Written in collaboration with *F. TALFOURD.*]

Bsq. Thetis and Peleus; or, A Chain of Roses (Str. 27/10/51). L.C. *Lacy.*
[Written in collaboration with *F. TALFOURD.*]

Ext. The Willow-Pattern Plate (Str. 26/12/51). L.C. as *The Mandarin's Daughter: Being the Simple Story of the Willow Pattern Plate. Lacy.*
[Written in collaboration with *F. TALFOURD.*]

Bsq. The Bottle Imp; or, Spirits in Bond (Grec. 12/4/52). L.C.
[Written in collaboration with *F. TALFOURD.*]

Ext. Guy Fawkes (Olym. 31/3/55). See *T. TAYLOR.*

Ext. William Tell (Lyc. 2/6/56). See *T. TAYLOR.*

HALFORD, J.

P. Harlequin King Nutcracker (Str. 26/12/53).
[Written in collaboration with *J. R. PLANCHÉ.*]

Bsq. Faust and Marguerite (Str. 17/7/54). L.C. *Lacy.*

M.Sk. Marguerite: A Legend of Love (D.L. 24/3/56).
[Music by J. H. Tully.]

Bsq. Faust and Marguerite; or, The Devil's Draught (Olym. 24/11/66). L.C. *Lacy.*
[Revised version of the play given at the Strand, 17/7/54.]

HALFORD, J.

D.Sk. The School for Husbands (Mount View H. 20/12/97). See *G. BINNS.*

HALL, MRS CAROLINE

D. The Will and the Way (C.L. 16/5/53). L.C.

HALL, CHARLES IRVING

D. The Life of a Shingler; or, A Pedlar's Revenge (Adel. Coatbridge, 2/12/70).

D. Face to Face; or, At Home and Abroad (Macclesfield, 24/10/72).

HALL, FRANK

P. Twinkle, Twinkle, Little Star (Aquar. 26/12/76). L.C.

Ext. La Poule aux Oeufs d'or (Alh. 23/12/78). L.C.

P. Tom Tiddler (Vic. 24/12/78). L.C.

P. Jack the Giant Killer (M'bone, 24/12/78). L.C.

P. Harlequin and Bluff King Hal (Vic. 24/12/79). L.C.

Ext. Lalla Rookh (Phil. 26/12/79). L.C.

Ext. The Yellow Dwarf; or, The Good Sovereign and the Bad Yellow Boy (Phil. 29/3/80). L.C.

Bsq. Robin Hood; or, Sherwood Forest, that's where the Foresters lodge (Phil. 7/7/80). L.C.

Bsq. O'Jupiter; or, The Fiddler's Wife (Phil. 2/10/80). L.C.

Bsq. The Coster Twin Brothers (Phil. 20/11/80). L.C.

P. The Babes in the Wood; or, Harlequin the Wicked Uncle and the Good Fairy of the Forest (Phil. 27/12/80). L.C.

P. Cinderella and the Little Glass Slipper; or, Harlequin Prince Peerless and his Pretty Sisters and the Three Young Knights of Sicily (Alcazar, 26/12/82). L.C.

P. The Frog he would a-wooing go; or, Harlequin Sleeping Beauty and the Demon of the Mystic Pool (E.C. 24/12/84). L.C.

P. Jack in the Box (E.C. 24/12/86). See *F. W. GREEN*

HALL, HOLLAND

Bsq. Villiam the Vicious (P's. Blackburn, 25/2/95). L.C.
[Music by E. Jonghmanns.]

HALL, K. E.

D. The Brave Scottish Hearts (P's. Coatbridge, 9/6/73).

D. Nightshade (P's. Coatbridge, 12/7/73).

F. The Shah; or, The Peepshowman's Visit (P's. Coatbridge, 12/7/73).

D. Never Again (P's. Coatbridge, 1/12/73).

HALL, KING

Ent. The Foster Brothers (St G. 1865). See *F. C. BURNAND.*

Ca. An Artful Automaton (St G.). L.C. St G. 27/6/78. See *A. LAW.*

Vaud. A Tremendous Mystery (St G. 11/78). See *F. C. BURNAND.*

F. A Christmas Stocking. L.C. St G. 11/12/79. See *G. A. À BECKETT.*

HALL, MATTHEW

D. English Hearts (Lincoln, 10/6/92). L.C.
[Music by C. Harrison. Written in collaboration with *H. GREEN.*]

"*HALL, OWEN*" [*JAMES DAVIES*]

M.C. A Gaiety Girl (P.W. 14/10/93). L.C.
[Lyrics by *H. GREENBANK.* Music by S. Jones.]

M.C. An Artist's Model (Daly's, 2/2/95). L.C.
[Lyrics by *H. GREENBANK*. Music by S. Jones.]
M.F. All Abroad (Portsmouth, 1/4/95; Crit. 8/8/95). L.C.
[Written in collaboration with *J. T. TANNER*; lyrics by *W. H. RISQUE*. Music by F. Rosse.]
M.C. The Geisha (Daly's, 25/4/96). L.C.
[Lyrics by *H. GREENBANK*. Music by S. Jones.]
M.C. A Greek Slave (Daly's, 8/6/98). L.C.
[Lyrics by *H. GREENBANK* and *A. ROSS*. Music by S. Jones.]
M.C. Florodora (Lyr. 11/11/99). L.C.
[Music by L. Stuart.]

HALL, ROBERT W.
D. Alive or Dead (St G. 25/5/76). L.C.
C. There's many a Slip 'twixt the Cup and the Lip (St G. 4/1/77). L.C.
D. A Cruel Test (Margate, 19/4/81). L.C.

HALL, W. J. COLLING
D.D. The Landlord (Sunderland, 8/2/86). L.C.

HALLATT, W. H.
D. The Iron Maiden (Hanley, 3/6/96). See *M. WILKINSON*.

HALLEY, W. F.
C.O. The Rustic (P.W. H. Swansea, 3/4/88; Assembly R. Neath, 31/5/88).
[Music by A. E. Siedle.]

HALLIDAY, ANDREW [ANDREW HALLIDAY DUFF]
Bsq. Kenilworth; or, Ye Queene, ye Earle and ye Maydenne (Str. 27/12/58). L.C. *Lacy*.
[Written in collaboration with *F. LAWRANCE*.]
Ext. Romeo and Juliet; or, The Cup of Cold Poison (Str. 3/11/59). L.C. *Lacy*.
F. The Census (Adel. 15/4/61). See *W. BROUGH*.
F. The Pretty Housebreaker (Adel. 15/7/61). See *W. BROUGH*.
Ext. A Shilling Day at the Great Exhibition (Adel. 9/6/62). See *W. BROUGH*.
F. The Colleen Bawn settled at last (Lyc. 5/7/62). See *W. BROUGH*.
F. A Valentine (Adel. 12/2/63). See *W. BROUGH*.
D. The Wooden Spoon Maker (Adel. 13/5/63). L.C.
[Written in collaboration with *W. BROUGH*.]
F. My Heart's in the Highlands (D.L. 9/11/63). See *W. BROUGH*.
F. The Area Belle (Adel. 7/3/64). See *W. BROUGH*.
F. An April Fool (D.L. 11/4/64). L.C.
[Written in collaboration with *W. BROUGH*.]
F. The Actor's Retreat (Adel. 11/8/64). L.C.
[Written in collaboration with *W. BROUGH*.]
F. Doing Banting (Adel. 24/10/64). See *W. BROUGH*.
F. Going to the Dogs (D.L. 6/3/65). See *W. BROUGH*.
F. Upstairs and Downstairs (Str. 15/5/65). See *W. BROUGH*.
F. The Mudborough Election (P.W. 13/7/65). See *W. BROUGH*.
Ext. The Mountain Dhu; or, The Knight, the Lady and the Lake (Adel. 26/12/66). L.C.
C.D. The Great City (D.L. 22/4/67). L.C.

D. Daddy Grey (Roy. 1/2/68). L.C. *Lacy.*
D. The King of Scots (D.L. 26/9/68). L.C.
D. The Loving Cup (Roy. 26/11/68). L.C. *Lacy.*
F. A Teetotal Family (Alex. L'pool, 7/4/69). L.C. as *The Teetotalers; or, The Maine Liquor Law.*
C. Checkmate (Roy. 15/7/69). L.C. *Lacy.*
D. Little Emily (Olym. 9/10/69). L.C.
Ca. Love's Doctor (Roy. 27/1/70). L.C.
C. For Love or Money (Vaud. 16/4/70). L.C.
D. Amy Robsart (D.L. 24/9/70). L.C.
D. Nell; or, The Old Curiosity Shop (Olym. 19/11/70). L.C. as *Little Nell.*
D. Notre Dame; or, The Gipsy Girl of Paris (Adel. 10/4/71). L.C.
D. Rebecca (D.L. 23/9/71). L.C.
D. Hilda; or, The Miser's Daughter (Adel. 1/4/72). L.C.
D. The Lady of the Lake (D.L. 21/9/72). L.C.
D. Fritz, Our German Cousin (Adel. 30/11/72). L.C.
C. Heart's Delight (Glo. 17/12/73). L.C.
D. Richard Cœur de Lion (D.L. 26/9/74). L.C.
D. Nicholas Nickleby (Adel. 20/3/75). L.C.

HALLIDAY, GEORGE B.
Ca. The Wager (Southampton, 13/10/79). L.C.
F.Ca. An Eye to Business (P.W. Southampton, 31/8/83). L.C.
[Written in collaboration with *P. TARDREW.*]

HALLWARD, CYRIL
D.Sk. The Guinea Stamp (Com. 8/4/96). *French.*
Duol. Constancy (Com. 21/4/98). L.C.
Duol. The Lady Bookie (Terry's, 9/11/98). L.C.

HAMILTON, COSMO
C.D. Jerry and a Sunbeam (Str. 26/9/98). L.C. *French.*
C.D. Because of Billy Rudd (Str. 19/12/98). L.C.
D.Sk. Patricia in a Quandary (Str. 19/12/99). L.C.
C.D. Before the Sun goes Down (Terry's, 26/12/99). L.C.
[Several later plays.]

HAMILTON, E.
C.O. Rhampsinitus (Dublin, 6/5/76).
[Music by A. Cellini.]

HAMILTON, GEORGE
D. Emily (Albion, 30/4/77). L.C. as *Little Emily.*
D. Effie and Jeanie Deans; or, The Sisters of St Leonard (Albion, 29/10/77). L.C.

HAMILTON, HENRY
D. Moths (Glo. 25/3/82). L.C. as *The Star and the Flame.*
D. The Shadow Sceptre (P's. Manchester, 15/4/82). L.C.
C. Our Regiment (Vaud. 13/2/83, *mat.*; Glo. 21/1/84). L.C. *French.*
C. No Coronet (Sheffield, 5/9/83). L.C.
C.O. The Lady of the Locket (Empire, 11/3/85). L.C.
[Music by W. Fullerton.]
C.D. The Harvest (P'cess. 18/9/86). L.C. *French.*
F.C. A Mare's Nest (Glo. 17/11/87, *mat.*). L.C.
C.D. Handfast (P.W. 13/12/87, *mat.*; Shaft. 16/5/91). L.C.
[Written in collaboration with *M. QUINTON.*]

D. The Armada; A Romance of 1588 (D.L. 22/10/88). L.C.
[Written in collaboration with *Sir A. HARRIS.*]
R.D. The Royal Oak (D.L. 23/9/89). L.C.
[Written in collaboration with *Sir A. HARRIS.*]
D. La Tosca (Gar. 28/11/89). See *F. C. GROVE.*
C. That Girl (H. 30/7/90, *mat.*). L.C.
[Written in collaboration with *Mrs O. BERINGER.*]
C.D. Lord Anerley (St J. 7/11/91). See *M. QUINTON.*
C. The Lady's Maid (P.W. L'pool, 17/4/93) L.C.
D. The Derby Winner (D.L. 15/9/94). See *Sir A. HARRIS.*
P. Dick Whittington (D.L. 26/12/94). See *Sir A. HARRIS.*
D.Sk. Fortune's Fool (H. 28/3/95).
D. Cheer, Boys, Cheer! (D.L. 19/9/95). See *Sir A. HARRIS.*
D. Carmen (Gai. 6/6/96). L.C.
M.C. Captain Fritz (Lyr. Hammersmith, 5/4/97).
D. The White Heather (D.L. 16/9/97). See *C. RALEIGH.*
P. Dick Whittington (Alex. Stoke Newington, 27/12/97). See *Sir A. HARRIS.*
D. The Three Musketeers (Metro. 12/9/98; Glo. 22/10/98). L.C.
D. The Great Ruby (D.L. 15/9/98). See *C. RALEIGH.*

HAMILTON, W.
D. The Thunderbolt (W. Bromwich, 4/4/94). See *D. BELAC.*

HAMLYN, CLARENCE
F. Poor Mr Potton (Vaud. 11/10/95). L.C.
[Written in collaboration with *H. M. PAULL.*]

HANCOCK, E. LA TOUCHE
Oa. Female Barbarism (T. H. Kilburn, 17/12/90).
[Music by C. Locknane.]

HANCOCK, WILLIAM
F. John Smith (Str. 13/1/62). L.C. *French.*
F. Stolen; or, £20 Reward (Roy. 26/12/63). L.C. *Lacy.*
F. Margate Sands (Str. 10/1/64). L.C. *Lacy.*

HANKIN, ST JOHN E. C.
D. Andrew Paterson (Bijou, 22/6/93). See *N. VYNNE.*
[For his later plays see A. E. Morgan, *op. cit.* 310.]

HANNAN, CHARLES
D. The Fisher Girl (Ladb. H. 16/1/90, *copy.*; Shaft. 28/10/90, as *Mons. Moulan; or, The Shadow of Death*). L.C.
Ca. The Setting of the Sun (Court, L'pool, 12/10/92; Aven. 27/4/98, as *Love Wisely; or, The S. of the S.*). L.C. *French.*
C.D. A House of Lies (Rugby, 24/11/92, *copy.*; Lyr. Hammersmith, 20/7/95). L.C.
C.D. Our Pleasant Sins (Grand, Leeds, 13/2/93). See *W. BARRETT.*
C.D. The Vicar (Torquay, 22/4/93). L.C.
C.D. A Fragment (Roy. Glasgow, 11/12/94). L.C. *French.*
D. The Opium Eater (Ayr, 31/12/94, *copy.*; Richmond, 31/7/95). L.C.
C.D. Honour among Thieves (Pier, Hastings, 6/5/95; Mat. 15/11/98). L.C. as *Stephen Arncliffe.*
D. The Secret Society (Caledonian, Girvan, 6/7/95, *copy.*). L.C.
[Title altered to *The Iron Hand and Velvet Glove*, 10/6/1909; so acted at Gaiety, Douglas, 24/6/1909.]

C. The Lily of the Field (Ayr, 6/11/96, *copy.*). L.C.
C. The Master of the Situation (Pier Pav. St Leonard's, 24/7/99). L.C.
C. The New Groom (Roy. Chester, 13/10/99). L.C. Empress, Brixton, 16/2/99, as *Our New Man. French.*
[Several later plays.]

HANNON, G. W.
Ca. White Stockings (Stratford, 31/8/88). L.C.

HANRAY, LAWRENCE
M.F. Betsy Baker (Bijou, 26/2/95).
Bsq.Oa. Il Jacobi; or, The Fatal Peanut (Bijou, 26/2/95). L.C.

HANSON, E.
C.O. The Baron of Corvelle (Grand, Halifax, 3/10/92). See *J. GREEN.*

HARBON, W. J.
F. Little Billie Carlyle; or, The Bell and the Hare (P.W. Wolverhampton, 18/4/81). L.C.

HARBOURN, ARTHUR
C. Face to Face; or, My Aunt's Luggage (Var. Chiswick, 6/9/69).

HARBURY, CHARLES
D. Fortune's Fool (Stratford, 28/7/90).

HARCOURT, F. C.
D. The Chain Gang; or, The Convict's Vengeance (Siddall's, S. Shields, 8/7/81; Star, Wolverhampton, 2/6/90, as *Enlisted*; S.W. 9/2/91, *revised*).
D. Clear the Way (Stacey's, Sheffield, 18/7/92).

HARCOURT, J. A.
Oa. The Science of Love (Noverre's R. Norwich, 16/10/74).

HARDACRE, J. P.
D. East Lynne (Olym. 26/12/98).

HARDIE, FRANK
D.Sk. Oh, Woman! (Assembly R. Balham, 20/3/95).

HARDING, CHARLES
D. The Bride of Albi (Grec. 18/7/53).
F. Coal and Coke (Str. 27/1/68). L.C.
[Written in collaboration with *W. H. SWANBOROUGH.*]
Ca. A Bone of Contention (St G. 23/11/70, *amat.*). L.C.

HARDMAN, T. H.
Ca. Coal-ition (Alex. L'pool, 21/2/81). L.C.
[Written in collaboration with *H. NORTH.*]

HARDWICKE, PELHAM
C.D. A Bachelor of Arts (Lyc. 23/11/53). L.C. *Lacy.*

HARDY, EVELYN
Ca. Thanks to Jack (Devonshire Park, Eastbourne, 11/4/91). L.C.

HARDY, H.
D. The Working Man (Col. Oldham, 10/7/90). L.C.

HARDY, THOMAS

D. Far from the madding Crowd (P.W. L'pool, 27/2/82; Glo. 29/4/82). L.C.
[Written in collaboration with *J. W. C. CARR*.]

D. The Three Wayfarers (Terry's, 3/6/93). L.C.
[Several later plays.]

HARE, F. LUMSDEN

Ca. The New Housekeeper (Lyr. Ealing, 11/6/96).
[Music by D. Barone.]

HARKINS, T.

D. The Red Squadron (Bijou, 9/8/94, *copy.*; Pav. 18/2/95). L.C.
[Written in collaboration with *J. MACMAHON*.]

HARLEIGH, L. W.

D. Thirty Thousand Pounds; or, The Dread Secret (E.C. 11/10/75). L.C.

HARLEY, G.

F.C. A Fair Bargain (Mechanics' Inst. Whaley Bridge, 7/9/94).

HARLEY, J. N.

D. United (Consett, 1/10/86).
[Written in collaboration with *A. CREAMER*.]

HARLOWE, FRANCIS

C.D. Parts and Players (St Andrew's R. Stoke Newington, 11/4/87).

HARRADEN, HERBERT

Ca. His Last Chance (Gai. 13/10/90). L.C.
[Music by Ethel Harraden.].

M.Ca. That Woman in Pink (Terry's, 30/4/91, *mat.*). L.C.

M.Ca. Charlie (Terry's, 30/4/91, *mat.*). L.C.

M.Ca. All about a Bonnet (Terry's, 30/4/91, *mat.*). L.C.

M.Ca. Aunt Agatha's Doctor (Terry's, 30/4/91, *mat.*). L.C.

[*HARRIGAN, EDWARD*

D. Mordecai Lyons (New Comique, New York, 26/10/82; H.M. Richmond, 26/10/82). L.C.

HARRINGTON, N. H.

F. A Night at Notting Hill (Adel. 5/1/57). L.C. *Lacy.*
[Written in collaboration with *E. YATES*.]

F. My Friend from Leatherhead (Lyc. 23/2/57). L.C. *Lacy.*
[Written in collaboration with *E. YATES*.]

F. Double Dummy (Lyc. 3/3/58). See *E. YATES.*

F. Your Likeness, One Shilling (Str. 22/4/58). L.C. *Lacy.*
[Written in collaboration with *E. YATES*.]

F. Good for Nothing (Adel. 27/12/58). See *E. YATES.*

F. If the Cap fits (P'cess. 13/6/59). L.C. *Lacy.*
[Written in collaboration with *E. YATES*.]

F. Hit him, he has no friends (Str. 17/9/60). See *E. YATES.*

HARRINGTON, RICHARD

D. The Pedlar Boy; or, The Old Mill Race (S.W. 22/1/66). *Lacy.*

HARRIS, AUGUSTUS GLOSSOP

R.D. The Avalanche; or, The Trials of the Heart (Sur. 3/10/54). L.C. *Lacy.*

F. Too much of a good thing (Lyc. 22/2/55). L.C. *Lacy.*

C. The Little Treasure (H. 11/10/55). L.C. *Lacy.*
F. Doing the "Hansome" (Lyc. 3/11/56). L.C. *Lacy.*
D. Ruth Oakley (M'bone, 15/1/57). L.C. *Lacy.*
[Written in collaboration with *T. J. WILLIAMS.*]
F. My Son, Diana (H. 25/5/57). L.C. *Lacy.*
F. A Very Serious Affair (Lyc. 10/10/57). L.C. *Lacy.*
O. The Rose of Castile (Lyc. 29/10/57). L.C.
[Written in collaboration with *E. FALCONER.* Music by M. W. Balfe.]
O. Satanella; or, The Power of Love (C.G. 20/12/58). L.C. 8° [1858].
[Written in collaboration with *E. FALCONER.* Music by M. W. Balfe.]
D. Ruthven (Grec. 25/4/59). L.C. *French.*
C. The Gossip (P'cess. 23/11/59). L.C. *Lacy.*
[Written in collaboration with *T. J. WILLIAMS.*]
F. Cruel to be Kind (P'cess. 6/3/60). See *T. J. WILLIAMS.*
F. Susan Smith (P'cess. 29/10/60).
F. Jeannette's Wedding (P'cess. 9/10/61). See *S. L. BUCKINGHAM.*
O. The Desert Flower (C.G. 12/10/63).
[Written in collaboration with *T. J. WILLIAMS.* Music by W. V. Wallace.]
Ca. Human Nature (Olym. 22/7/67). L.C.
[Written in collaboration with *T. J. WILLIAMS.*]
F. Tom Thrasher (Adel. 6/7/68). L.C. *Lacy.*

HARRIS, Sir AUGUSTUS HENRY GLOSSOP
P. The Sleeping Beauty (C.P. 22/12/77). L.C.
[Written in collaboration with *W. R. OSMAN.*]
P. Robinson Crusoe (C.P. 23/12/78). L.C.
Bsq. Venus (Roy. 27/6/79). L.C.
[Written in collaboration with *E. ROSE.*]
M.D. The World (D.L. 31/7/80). See *P. MERRITT.*
F. The Stores (D.L. 14/3/81). See *E. ROSE.*
D. Youth (D.L. 6/8/81). See *P. MERRITT.*
D. Pluck (D.L. 5/8/82). See *H. PETTITT.*
D. Freedom (D.L. 4/8/83). See *G. F. ROWE.*
Ca. The Opera Cloak (D.L. 8/9/83). See *L. D. POWLES.*
D. A Sailor and his Lass (D.L. 15/10/83). See *R. BUCHANAN.*
D. Human Nature (D.L. 12/9/85). See *H. PETTITT.*
D. A Run of Luck (D.L. 28/8/86). See *H. PETTITT.*
C.D. Pleasure (D.L. 3/9/87). See *P. MERRITT.*
D. The Armada (D.L. 22/10/88). See *H. HAMILTON.*
P. The Babes in the Wood, Robin Hood and his Merry Men, and Harlequin who killed Cock Robin (D.L. 26/12/88). L.C.
[Written in collaboration with *E. L. BLANCHARD* and *H. NICHOLS.*]
R.D. The Royal Oak (D.L. 23/9/89). See *H. HAMILTON.*
P. Jack and the Beanstalk (D.L. 26/12/89). See *H. NICHOLS.*
Bsq. Venus; or, The Gods as they were and not as they ought to have been (P.W. L'pool, 26/3/90; Grand, 22/9/90). L.C.
[Rewritten version of *Venus* (Roy. 27/6/79), mainly by *W. YARDLEY.*]

D. A Million of Money (D.L. 6/9/90). See *H. PETTITT.*

P. Beauty and the Beast (D.L. 26/12/90). See *W. YARDLEY.*

C.O. Basoche (R.E. O.H. 3/11/91). L.C.
[Music by A. Messager.]

P. Humpty Dumpty (D.L. 26/12/91). L.C.
[Written in collaboration with *H. NICHOLS.*]

Bsq. The Young Recruit (Tyne, Newcastle, 14/3/92). See *B. C. STEPHENSON.*

C.Oa. The Serenaders; or, The Lovers of Venice (Lyric Club, 30/6/92). L.C. St G.
[Written in collaboration with *W. PARKER.* Music by B. Andrews.]

D. The Prodigal Daughter (D.L. 17/9/92). See *H. PETTITT.*

P.Bal. From London to Paris (Pal. 10/12/92). See *C. RALEIGH.*

Bal. The Sleeper Awakened (Pal. 10/12/92). L.C.
[Written in collaboration with *R. HENRY.*]

P. Little Bo-Peep, Little Red Riding Hood and Hop o' my Thumb (D.L. 26/12/92). L.C.
[Written in collaboration with *J. W. JONES.* Music by J. Crook.]

D. Frailty (Tyne, Newcastle, 3/7/93). L.C.
[Written in collaboration with *P. MERRITT.*]

Bsq. A Pal o' Archie's (Pal. 11/7/93). See *C. H. E. BROOKFIELD.*

R.O. Amy Robsart (C.G. 20/7/93). See *F. E. WEATHERLEY.*

D. A Life of Pleasure (D.L. 21/9/93). L.C.
[Written in collaboration with *H. PETTITT.*]

P. Robinson Crusoe (D.L. 26/12/93). See *H. NICHOLS.*

O. The Lady of Longford (C.G. 21/7/94). L.C.
[Written in collaboration with *F. E. WEATHERLEY.* Music by L. E. Bach.]

D. The Derby Winner (D.L. 15/9/94). L.C.
[Written in collaboration with *C. RALEIGH* and *H. HAMILTON.*]

P. Dick Whittington (D.L. 26/12/94). L.C. 8° 1894.
[Written in collaboration with *C. RALEIGH* and *H. HAMILTON.*]

D. Denise (P.W. Birmingham, 28/8/95). See *C. W. SCOTT.*

D. Cheer, Boys, Cheer! (D.L. 19/9/95). L.C.
[Written in collaboration with *C. RALEIGH* and *H. HAMILTON.*]

P. Cinderella (D.L. 26/12/95). L.C.
[Written in collaboration with *C. RALEIGH* and *A. STURGESS.*]

M.C. The Telephone Girl (Grand, Wolverhampton, 25/5/96; Metro. 27/7/96). L.C.
[Written in collaboration with *F. C. BURNAND* and *A. STURGESS.* Music by G. Serpette and J. M. Glover.]

C.O. The Little Genius (Shaft. 9/7/96). L.C.
[Written in collaboration with *A. STURGESS.* Music by E. von Taund, J. M. Glover and L. Ronald.]

P. Dick Whittington (Alex. Stoke Newington, 27/12/97). L.C.
[Written in collaboration with *C. RALEIGH* and *H. HAMILTON.*]

HARRIS, CHARLES

Bsq. Cupid (Roy. 26/4/80). See *H. P. STEPHENS.*

O. The White Cockade (Salle Erard, 7/3/95). See *R. W. BARNETT.*

HARRIS, RICHARD

C. Young Wives and Old Husbands (O.C. 16/12/76). L.C.

HARRIS-BURLAND, J. R.

D. A Bitter Lesson (Lyr. 15/5/96). L.C.
[Written in collaboration with *A. WEATHERLEY.*]

F. Wanted, a Typewriter (Assembly R. Portishead, 16/7/96). L.C. P's. Bristol, 28/8/96.
[Written in collaboration with *A. WEATHERLEY.*]

HARRISON, —

F. Once a Week (Rochester, 5/5/81). See *A. A. WILMOT.*

HARRISON, CYRIL

F.C. The Spinster (New Cross H. 30/4/87). See *P. GWYNNE.*

R.D. The Coroner (Bath, 4/8/88). See *J. W. HEMMING.*

D. Reconciled (Lincoln, 3/11/88). See *P. GWYNNE.*

D. The Tramp; or, Bygone Days (Public H. Warrington, 4/10/89). L.C.

F.C. The Sub-Editor (Brixton, 5/11/96). See *E. PAYNE.*

C.O. Bygone Days (Pier Pav. St Leonards, 23/1/99).
[Apparently a revised version of *The Tramp*, above.]

HARRISON, EVA

Ca. Chaperoned (Assembly R. Cheltenham, 3/6/87).

HARRISON, KABER

Ca. Mrs Mackenzie No. 2 (Qns. Gate H. 11/5/96). L.C.

HARRISON, SAM M.

Bsq. Alonzo ye Brave and ye fayre Imogene (Alex. L'pool, 2/4/76). L.C.

HARRISON, S. FORTESCUE

Ca. The Sins of the Fathers (Roy. Glasgow, 24/4/96). See *H. BEATTY.*

HARRISON, WILMOT

Oa. The Marriage of Georgette (C.G. 27/12/60). L.C.
[Music by F. M. V. Massé.]

F. Special Performances (Holborn, 13/4/68). L.C. *Lacy.*

F. New Brighton Sands (Rotunda, L'pool, 27/6/81). *French* [as *Margate Sands*].

HARRISON, W. B.

Duol. Account Rendered (Collard's R. 6/7/94).

Ca. The Letter Box (Steinway H. 27/5/95). L.C.

HART, FRITZ

C.D. A Mean Advantage (Roy. Chester, 11/6/97). L.C.
[Written in collaboration with *G. HERBERT.* Title changed to *In Harbour*, 24/9/97.]

[*HARTE, BRET*

D. Sue (Hoyt's, New York, 15/9/96; Gar. 10/6/98). L.C. 8° 1902.
[Written in collaboration with *T. E. PEMBERTON.*]

HARTLEY, CHARLES

D. True Colours (Vaud. 4/6/89, *mat.*).

HARTOPP, W. W.

F. Eclipsing the Son (P'cess. 14/12/61, *amat.*). L.C. Brighton, 3/12/60. *Lacy.*

HARVEY, FRANK

Ca. The Old Bachelor's Birthday (Preston, 7/3/73). L.C.

F. Flirtation (Edinburgh, 11/8/73).

C.D. Bought (Sunderland, 18/12/73). L.C. as *B.; or, Oakland's Mists.*

F. An Hour at Ipswich Station (Ipswich, 19/1/74).

F. Flighty's Flirtation (Amphi. L'pool, 25/2/74).

D. Jacqueline (Amphi. Leeds, 8/5/74). L.C.

C. False Glitter; or, The Manchester Girl (Huddersfield, 22/4/75). L.C.

C.D. John Jasper's Wife (Ipswich, 12/1/76; Stand. 8/5/76). L.C.

D. Married, not Mated (Brighton, 31/8/77; Olym. 26/4/79). L.C.

D. The Mother (Olym. 31/5/79). L.C.

D. The Workman; or, The Shadow on the Hearth (Sunderland, 10/5/80; Olym. 18/7/81). L.C.

D. The Love that lasts (Northampton, 10/1/81). L.C.

D. Madeline Martel; or, Woman wronged by Woman (Northampton, 9/2/82). L.C.

D. The Wages of Sin (Coventry, 3/8/82; Stand. 21/8/82). L.C.

D. Woman against Woman (Portsmouth, 9/3/83; Grand, 22/3/86). L.C.

D. Right and Wrong (Star, Swansea, 22/10/83).

D. A Mad Marriage (Northampton, 16/1/84; Grand, 21/8/85). L.C.

D. A Ring of Iron (Portsmouth, 15/9/84; Grand, 3/8/85). L.C.

D. Primrose Farm (Ipswich, 14/1/85). L.C.

F.C. The Naughty Men (Gai. Dublin, 1/6/85).

D. Built on Sand (Alex. Sheffield, 3/5/86). L.C.

D. Life or Death (Grand, 16/8/86). L.C.

D. Lord Marple's Daughter; or, A House Divided (Grand, 29/11/86). L.C.

D. The World against her (Preston, 11/1/87; Grand, 1/8/87; Surrey, 2/7/88). L.C.

D. Cruel London (Oldham, 22/3/88). L C.
[Title altered to *Wicked London*, 12/4/88.]

D. A Woman's Vengeance (Stand. 28/5/88).

D. Judge Not (Pav. 13/8/88). L.C. Alex. Barrow-in-Furness, 20/6/88, as *A Woman's Glory*.

D. The Land of the Living (P.W. Gt Grimsby, 16/3/89; Grand, 29/7/89; Sur. 8/6/91). L.C.

M.D. Acting the Law (Brentford, 29/9/90). L.C.

D. Fallen among Thieves (Grand, 29/9/90). L.C. County, Reading, 4/9/90.

D. A Daughter of the People (S. Shields, 16/2/91; Grand, 29/6/91). L.C.

M.D. A Fight for Honour (S. Shields, 23/3/92; Sur. 13/6/92). L.C.

D. Sins of the Night (Barnsley, 30/3/93; Grand, 22/5/93). L.C.

D. Shall he forgive her? (Alex. Sheffield, 2/4/94; Adel. 20/6/94). L.C. P's. Bradford, 23/2/94, as *The Woman he married*.

D. Brother against Brother (Lyc. Ipswich, 10/8/95; Lyr. Hammersmith, 23/3/96). L.C.
D. The Shebeen (Harvey Inst. Folkestone, 5/5/96). L.C.
D. A Musician's Romance (Grand, Halifax, 21/3/98; Metro. 13/6/98). L.C.
D. The House of Mystery (P's. Portsmouth, 2/5/98; Imp. 2/5/98). L.C.

HARVEY, Sir JOHN MARTIN
C.D. 'Twixt Love and Duty (P.W. Southampton, 11/7/89). L.C. Stand. 17/11/85.

HARVEY, NORMAN
D. Crime and Justice (S.W. 15/12/92). See *B. DELANNOY.*

HARVEY, W.
D. Guilty at Last (Pelton Fell, 12/9/98).

HARWOOD, ISABELLA. See "*ROSS NEIL*"

HARWOOD, R.
C.D. Justice Nell (Lyc. 2/5/99). See *J. F. SOUTAR.*

HASTINGS, GILBERT
C. Sweet Bells Jangled (Olym. 28/6/79). L.C.
D. Through the Fire (Leeds, 8/9/79). L.C.

HATCH, P. H.
F. Dearest Anna Maria (Str. 7/7/51).

HATCHMAN, HENRY W.
D. On Her Majesty's Service (Aven. Sunderland, 20/11/91, *copy.*). L.C.
[Written in collaboration with *H. G. MAY.*]
Ca. Catching the Idea (Empire, Blackpool, 2/6/99).
[Written in collaboration with *H. C. CULLUM.*]

HATTON, BESSIE
D. The Village of Youth (Rectory Grounds, Radstock, 12/7/99, *amat.*).

HATTON, JOSEPH
C. Romantic Caroline. 8° [1874].
F. Much too clever (Gai. 23/2/74). See *J. OXENFORD.*
D. Clytie (Amphi. L'pool, 29/11/75; Olym. 10/1/76). L.C.
D. Hester Prynne; or, The Scarlet Letter (Tyne, Newcastle, 27/3/76). L.C.
D. Liz (Amphi. L'pool, 9/7/77). See *A. MATTHISON.*
D. No. 20 (P'cess. 30/11/78). See *J. ALBERY.*
D. Loved and Lost (Qns. Manchester, 3/11/79). L.C.
[Written in collaboration with *A. MATTHISON.*]
C.D. The Vicar (Windsor, 28/1/85). L.C.
[Written in collaboration with *J. ALBERY.*]
C.D. The Prince and the Pauper (Vaud. 12/10/91).
D.Sk. Homburg (Toole's, 3/5/93). L.C.
D. The Roll of the Drum (St Helen's, 23/3/96; Sur. 29/6/96, as *When Greek meets Greek*). L.C.
D. Jack Sheppard (Pav. 9/4/98). L.C. Glo. 30/11/97, as *J.S.; or, The Idle Apprentice.*

HAVARD, PHILIP

Ca. Well Matched (Public H. Ealing, 26/3/87; Com. Manchester, 24/9/88; St J. 14/5/89). L.C. *French.*

F. Fanny's Flirtations (Pav. 11/7/87). See *W. F. MILLER.*

M.C.D. The Silver Fortune (Sanger's, Ramsgate, 15/10/88). See *W. F. MILLER.*

C.D. Myrtle (Birmingham, 8/4/89). L.C. as *My Dad.*

D. Major Raymond (Terry's, 25/6/96). L.C.

HAWKINS, LANWARNE

D. The Oxford Agreement (Barnsley, 29/10/97). L.C.

D. The Master of Hope (Grand, Stalybridge, 2/12/98, *copy.*). L.C. as *Mills of the Eternal.*

[Title altered to *When George was King*, 11/9/99.]

HAWKINS, Mrs P. L.

C.D. Ciceley's Secret (Bijou, 15/1/95).

HAWKINS, W. T.

C.O. The Vigilant Detectives (Fine Arts Exhibition, Huddersfield, 13/9/83).

[Music by W. H. Cross.]

Oa. Birds of Prey (Vic. Huddersfield, 8/4/84).

[Music by W. H. Cross.]

HAWLEY, FREDERICK

D. Agnes of Bavaria (Manchester, 2/3/74; Gai. 31/10/83).

C. They were married (Str. 17/6/92). See *J. R. CRAUFORD.*

HAWORTH, J.

C. Very, very much engaged (Athen. Glasgow, 16/10/95, *copy.*). L.C.

[Written in collaboration with *R. C. BUCHANAN.*]

HAWTHORN, MAY

D.Sk. Day Dreams (Park H. Camden Town, 23/5/88).

HAWTREY, CHARLES

F. The Private Secretary (Cambridge, 14/11/83; P's. 29/3/84). L.C. *French.*

D. Mr Martin (Com. 3/10/96). L.C.

HAWTREY, GEORGE P.

Ca. Good Gracious! (Court, 21/1/85). L.C.

F.C. The Pickpocket (Glo. 24/4/86). L.C.

F. In the Clouds (Lyr. Ealing, 20/10/87). L.C.

C. I.O.U. (Hove, 20/12/87). L.C.

Bsq. Atalanta (Str. 17/11/88). L.C.

[Music by A. E. Dyer.]

M.F. Penelope (Com. 9/5/89, *mat.*; Com. 24/9/89).

C.D. A Gauntlet (Roy. 20/1/94). See *O. EDWARDS.*

F. Behind the Scenes (Com. 4/7/96). See *F. MORRIS.*

C.D. My Lady's Orchard (Glasgow, 23/8/97). See *Mrs OSCAR BERINGER.*

HAXELL, EDWARD NELSON

C.D. Sybil; or, Love rules (Terry's, 25/9/89, *mat.*). L.C.

HAY, FREDERICK

Vaud. Furnished Apartments (St J. 12/6/60). L.C. *Lacy.*
F. Caught by the Cuff (Vic. 23/9/65). L.C. *Lacy.*
F. A Photographic Fix (Vic. 4/11/65). L.C. *Lacy.*
F. A Suit of Tweeds (Str. 14/1/67). L.C. as *First in the Field. Lacy.*
F. The French Exhibition (Str. 1/4/67). L.C. *Lacy.*
F.C. Our Domestics (Str. 15/6/67). L.C. *Lacy.*
F. Beautiful for Ever (P.W. L'pool, 14/9/68). L.C. *Lacy.*
F. Hue and Dye (Str. 11/1/69).
F. A Lame Excuse (P.W. 19/4/69). L.C. *Lacy.*
F. The Chops of the Channel (Str. 8/7/69). L.C. *Lacy.*
F. Cupboard Love (Vaud. 18/4/70). L.C. *Lacy.*
D. Jim Drags, the Drayman (P.W. L'pool, 26/5/70).
F. A Striking Similarity (P.W. L'pool, 30/5/70; Sur. 8/10/70).
D. Link by Link (Sur. 8/10/70). L.C. *Lacy.*
[Written in collaboration with *F. FENTON.*]
F. A Fearful Fog (P.W. Glasgow, 11/2/71; Vaud. 22/4/71). L.C.
F. Bubble and Squeak (Vaud. 12/5/71). L.C.
F. Lodgers and Dodgers (Str. 13/5/71). L.C. *Lacy.*
F. A Restless Night (Holb. 3/3/73). L.C.
F. An Earnest Appeal (Str. 6/5/75).
Ca. Brought to Book (Ch. X. 28/8/75). L.C.
F. Another Pair of Shoes (Glo. 13/9/75). L.C.
F. Flamingo; or, The Rook and the Cause (Str. 18/9/75). L.C.
[Written in collaboration with *F. W. GREEN.*]
M.F. Slaviana (Brighton, 11/10/75). L.C.
Bsq. Cracked Heads (Str. 2/2/76). L.C.
[Written in collaboration with *A. CLEMENTS.*]
D. From Stem to Stern (Sur. 15/4/76). L.C.
Ent. Crotchets (Str. 10/6/76). L.C.
F. Slate Pencillings; or, Out of Spirits (Glo. 24/10/76). L.C.
M.F. A Will with a Vengeance (Glo. 27/11/76). L.C.
[Music by E. Solomon.]
F. Linnet's Lark (Park, 14/9/78). L.C.
F. An Awkward Affair (Duke's, 19/10/78). L.C.
F. Corporal Shako (Sur. 13/9/79). L.C.
D. Mabel (Olym. 16/10/80). L.C.
Ca. Wet Paint (Vaud. 19/2/94). L.C. Nov. 15/4/86.

HAYDON, M.

D. Held in Slavery (Cambridge, Spennymoor, 3/9/94).

HAYES, FRED. W.

Ca. Medusa (St J. 3/82). L.C. St J. 3/3/82.

HAYMAN, H.

F. The White Elephant (E.C. 27/11/75). L.C.
D. The Privateer's Venture (Vic. 5/6/76). L.C.
F. A Sewing Machine on Easy Terms (E.C. 30/9/76). L.C.
D. Silas Bruton; or, The Murder at the Old Crook Farm (Vic. 12/4/77). L.C.

HAYMAN, PHILIP

Ca. That Idiot Carlo (Blackburn, 12/2/91). L.C.
Oa. The Scribe; or, Love and Letters (Glo. 5/10/91).
Bsq. All My Eye-Vanhoe (Traf. 31/10/94). L.C.
[Music by J. Crook, H. Talbot, P. Hayman and E. Solomon.]

HAYWARD, ARTHUR

D. Shandy the Spalpeen (Gai. Barnsley, 24/6/79).

"*HAYWELL, FREDERICK*" [*FRED HAWLEY*]

D. Agnes of Bavaria; or, Love and Love's Vision (Nottingham, 9/11/68). L.C.

D. Found (Nottingham, 9/4/69; Gai. 14/11/83). L.C.

C. Jerry's Wagers (Manchester, 3/8/74).

F. Phil's Folly (Roy. 30/4/77). L.C.

HAZLETON, FREDERICK

M.D. Sweeney Todd, the Barber of Fleet Street; or, The String of Pearls (Bower, 7/65). L.C. as *The String of Pearls; or, The Barber of Fleet Street. Lacy.*

D. Happy-go-lucky (Bower, 6/73; M'bone, 10/7/75). L.C.

D. Tot (Grec. 14/4/79). L.C.

D. Intemperance; or, A Drunkard's Sin (E.C. 19/7/79). L.C.

HAZLEWOOD, COLIN HENRY

F. Going to Chobham; or, The Petticoat Captains (C.L. 30/7/53). L.C. *Lacy.*

F. The Bonnet Builder's Tea Party (Str. 22/5/54).

D. Jenny Foster, the Sailor's Child; or, The Winter Robin (Brit. 10/55). L.C. *Lacy.*

D. Jessy Vere; or, The Return of the Wanderer (Brit. 2/56). L.C. *Lacy.*

D. The Marble Bride; or, The Nymphs of the Forest (Brit. 3/57). L.C. *Lacy.*

P. Goody Goose; or, Harlequin Greenhead and the Good Boy who helped the Poor Old Woman Home from Market (M'bone, 26/12/58). L.C.

D. Waiting for the Verdict; or, Falsely Accused (C.L. 29/1/59). *French.*

D. Capitola; or, The Masked Mother and the Hidden Hand (Sur. 4/7/59). L.C. *Lacy.*

R.D. The Chevalier of the Moulin Rouge; or, The Days of Terror (Acton, 1/8/59).

D. The Life of a Weaver (Brit. 28/11/59).

D. A Life for a Life; or, The Burden of Guilt (Brit. 20/8/60). L.C.

D. The Bridal Wreath (C.L. 1861).

D. The Staff of Diamonds (Sur. 14/1/61). L.C.

D. The House on the Bridge of Notre Dame (M'bone, 1/4/61). L.C. *French.*

D. The Rescue of the Orpheus; or, The Father's Grave (Brit. 30/9/61). L.C.

D. The Clock on the Stairs (Brit. 3/2/62). *Lacy.*

D. Our Lot in Life; or, Brighter Days in Store (Brit. 22/4/62). L.C.

D. Cast on the Mercy of the World; or, Deserted and Deceived (Brit. 13/10/62). L.C.

D. Charity (S.W. 7/11/62). L.C.

D. Mary Edmonstone (Brit. 22/12/62). L.C. as *The Fate of M.E.*

D. Aurora Floyd; or, The First and Second Marriage (Brit. 21/4/63). L.C.

[This play has a variant sub-title, *The Dark Duel in the Wood.*]

D. Ashore and Afloat (Sur. 15/2/64). L.C.

D. The Downfall of Pride (Brit. 27/6/64). L.C. as *The Fall of Pride; or, The Mechanic's Wife.*

D. The Detective; or, The Ticket-of-Leave's Career (Vic. 9/7/64). L.C.

D. The Mother's Dying Child; or, Woman's Fate (Brit. 10/64). L.C. *Lacy.*

D. The False Mother; or, The Parent Guardian (Brit. 3/4/65).

D. Poul a Dhoil; or, The Fairy Man (Brit. 10/65). L.C. *Lacy.*

D. The Castaway; or, Life's Thorny Path and the Orphan's Highborn Husband (Brit. 12/3/66). L.C.

D. The Last Link of Love (Brit. 25/2/67). L.C.

Bsq. Faust; or, Marguerite's Mangle (Brit. 25/3/67). L.C.

D. The Life Signal (Brit. 25/4/67). L.C.

Bsq. Cherry and Fair Star (Brit. 25/4/67).

D. The Marriage Certificate (Brit. 10/6/67). L.C. with sub-title, *or, A Mother's Honour.*

D. The Ballanasloe Boy; or, The Fortunes of an Irish Peasant (Brit. 24/6/67). L.C.

D. Jack o' Lantern; or, The Blue Ribbon of the Turf (Brit. 8/7/67).

D. Pale Janet (Pav. 31/8/67). L.C.

D. The Gray Lady of Fernlea (Brit. 9/9/67). L.C.

D. Alone in the Pirate's Lair (Brit. 23/9/67). L.C. with sub-title, *or, Danger and Fatality.*

D. Break but not bend; or, Phantom Honour (Brit. 2/10/67). L.C.

D. Wild Charley, the Link Boy (Brit. 28/10/67). L.C.

D. The King's Death Trap (Brit. 25/11/67). L.C.

P. Robin Hood and his Merry Men; or, Harlequin Ivanhoe, the Knight Templar and the Jewess (Pav. 24/12/67). L.C.

P. Don Quixote; or, Sancho Panza and his Wife Teresa (Brit. 26/12/67). L.C.

D. The Young Apprentice; or, The Watchwords of Old London (Brit. 9/3/68). L.C.

D. He would be a Sailor; or, Breakers Ahead (Brit. 23/3/68). L.C.

D. Wait till I'm a Man; or, The Play Ground and the Battle Field (Brit. 13/4/68). L.C.

D. Hearts, Hearts, Hearts; or, Good and Bad (Col. L'pool, 25/5/68).

D. The Bride's Death Sleep (C.L. 4/7/68).

D. The Dead Reckoning; or, Pressed for the Navy (Brit. 10/8/68). L.C.

D. The Scarlet Mark; or, The Witch, the Rover and the Mystery (Brit. 18/11/68). L.C.

D. Jolly Joe (Alex. 21/11/68). L.C.

D. The Headless Horseman; or The Ride of Death (Brit. 11/68). L.C.

D. When the Clock strikes Nine (Brit. 8/3/69). L.C. with sub-title, *or, Ruth the Mountain Rose.*

D. Hop Pickers and Gipsies; or, The Lost Daughter (Brit. 17/5/69). L.C. *Lacy.*

D. The Blue-eyed Witch; or, Not a Friend in the World (Brit. 16/6/69). L.C.

D. The Demon Bracelets; or, The Mystic Cypress Tree (Brit. 16/8/69). L.C.

D. Good as Gold; or, A Friend in need when others fail (Brit. 13/9/69). L.C.

D. Far away where Angels dwell (Brit. 6/10/69). L.C.
D. Flower Makers and Heart Breakers; or, A Tale of Trials and Temptations (Grec. 7/10/69). L.C. *Lacy* [as *Lizzie Lyle; or, The Flower Makers of Finsbury*].
D. Pure as Driven Snow; or, Tempted in Vain (Brit. 17/11/69). L.C.
D. True as Steel; or, The Regent's Daughter (Brit. 6/12/69). L.C.
D. The Hedge Carpenter (Brit. 7/2/70). L.C. with sub-title, *or, The Hidden Treasure.*
D. The Pace that Kills; or, Fast Life and Noble Life (Brit. 7/3/70). L.C.
D. One Black Spot; or, The Law of the Plantation (Brit. 4/4/70). L.C.
D. Erin-go-Brach; or, The Wren Boys of Kerry (Brit. 18/4/70). L.C.
D. Taking the Veil; or, The Harsh Step-Father (Brit. 30/7/70). L.C.
D. The Sons of the Forge; or, The Blacksmith and the Baron (Brit. 29/8/70). L.C.
D. A Seven Years' Secret; or, The Noble Foundling (Brit. 31/10/70). L.C.
D. Joe Sterling; or, A Ragged Fortune (Vic. 7/11/70). L.C.
D. The Magic Whisper (Brit. 14/11/70). L.C.
D. Wealth Got and Lost (Brit. 5/12/70). L.C.
F. Leave it to me (Sur. 26/12/70). L.C. *French.*
[Written in collaboration with *A. WILLIAMS.*]
D. Aileen Asthore; or, Irish Fidelity (Albert, Portsmouth, 20/2/71).
D. The Forlorn Hope (Brit. 8/5/71). L.C.
D. Happiness at Home (Brit. 29/5/71). L.C.
D. The Lightning's Flash; or, The Wild Steed of the Prairies (P'cess. Edinburgh, 5/6/71). L.C. Pav. 24/9/73.
D. The Bitter Reckoning; or, A Rover from Many Lands (Brit. 19/6/71). L.C.
D. The Lost Wife; or, A Husband's Confession (Brit. 7/8/71). L.C. *Lacy.*
D. Cast Aside; or, Loving not wisely but too well (Brit. 4/10/71). L.C.
D. The Artificial Flower Maker; or, The Last New Year's Gift (Brit. 18/12/71). L.C.
D. A French Girl's Love (Brit. 12/2/72). L.C.
D. The Stolen Jewess; or, The Two Israelites (Brit. 1/4/72). L.C.
D. The Wife's Evidence (Brit. 1/5/72). L.C.
D. The Unlawful Present (Brit. 3/6/72). L.C.
D. Parted and Reunited (Brit. 24/6/72). L.C.
D. Naomi, the Gipsy Girl (Brit. 19/8/72). L.C.
D. The Imperial Guard; or, The Priceless Jewels (Brit. 2/9/72). L.C.
D. Life, its Morn and Sunset (Brit. 2/10/72). L.C.
D. The Fair Circassian; or, The Cavalier, the Count and the Italian (Brit. 25/10/72). L.C.
D. The Price of Existence (Brit. 18/12/72). L.C.
D. Mabel Lake (Brit. 10/2/73). L.C.
D. Napoleon; or, The Story of a Flag (Brit. 14/4/73). L.C.
Bsq. The Four Kings; or, Paddy in the Moon (Brit. 14/4/73). L.C.
D. Phillis Mayburn (Brit. 28/7/73). L.C.
D. Blackbirding (Brit. 8/9/73).
D. For Honour's Sake (Brit. 1/10/73). L.C. *Lacy.*
D. First Favourite (Brit. 25/10/73). L.C.
D. Briars and Blossoms (Brit. 3/12/73). L.C.
P. Cocorico; or, The Hen with the Golden Eggs (Brit. 26/12/73). L.C.

D. The Bells in the Storm (S.W. 14/2/74).
D. The Russian Bride (Brit. 9/3/74). L.C.
D. Lady Jane Grey (Brit. 25/5/74). L.C.
D. The Shadow on the Heart (Brit. 8/6/74). L.C.
D. The Devil at the Elbow; or, Two Mothers to One Child (Brit. 3/8/74). L.C.
D. The Red Man's Rifle (Brit. 26/12/74). L.C.
D. The Basket Girls of Liverpool (Col. L'pool, 11/1/75).
D. The Mortgage Deeds (Brit. 22/2/75). L.C.
F. Jessamy's Courtship (Phil. 12/4/75). L.C.
D. The Old Mill Stream (Brit. 14/6/75). L.C.
D. Honest John (Brit. 19/7/75). L.C. Brit. 10/8/74.
D. The Old Fox Inn (Brit. 2/8/75). L.C.
D. Simon; or, More Ways than One (Phil. 17/1/76). L.C.
C. The Fighting Forty-First (Brit. 11/9/76). L.C.
D. Lady Audley's Secret. L.C. Olym. 25/6/77.
D. Only for Life; or, A Convict's Career (Brit. 6/8/77).
Bsq. A New King Richard III (Brit. 1/4/78). L.C.
D. The Sisters (Brit. 10/6/78). L.C. Brit. 3/11/73.
D. The King's Secret; or, Dudley Castle in the Olden Time (Bilston, 20/6/78).
D. Against the Tide (Brit. 2/6/79). L.C.
D. The Man and the Spirit (Brit. 28/2/81). L.C.

HAZLEWOOD, HENRY C. Jr.
P. Little Giselle, the Dancing Belle; or, Harlequin the Demon-hunter and the Fairies of the Willie Lake (Alex. 26/12/67). L.C.
Bsq. No Thoroughfare beyond Highbury; or, The Maid, the Mother and the Malicious Mountaineer (Alex. 13/4/68).
P. Harlequin Prince Pippo (Alfred, 24/12/70).
D. Our Daily Bread (Wolverhampton, 5/10/85). L.C.

HAZLEWOOD, Miss
M.D. Kevin's Choice (St G.H. 2/12/67; Adel. 25/3/82). L.C.
[Music by T. A. Wallworth. Title altered to *The Maid of Glendalough* (P.W. 13/6/99).]
D. London by Gaslight (S.W. 19/9/68). L.C.

HEAD, F. D.
F. Old Moss (Bijou, 24/5/94). L.C. *French.*

HEATH, STEBBINGS
D. The Mermaid (Ladb. H. 15/2/87, *amat.*).

HEATHCOTE, ARTHUR M.
Ca. Woman's Wrongs (Toole's, 12/9/87). *French.*
Ca. The Duchess of Bayswater and Co. (H. 8/12/88). L.C.
Ca. His Toast (Court, 13/7/89). L.C. *French.*
D.Sk. Till the Half Hour (Ladb. H. 31/1/91). *French.*
Ca. The Tailor makes a Man (West, Albert H. 5/5/92).
D.Sk. Open Sesame; or, Love in a Mist (West, Albert H. 6/5/92).
Ca. The Ghost of an Idea (Brompton Hospital, 20/12/92).
Ca. Breaking the News (Brompton Hospital, 14/3/93).
C. Echo (Traf. 25/4/93). L.C.
Ca. A White Elephant (Brompton Hospital, 6/2/94).
D. The Super (Crit. 24/5/94). L.C.
Ca. In Two Minds (Gar. 27/6/94). L.C. *French.*

HEAVYSEGE, CHARLES

D. Saul. 8° 1859.

HEDGECOCK, W. H.

M. Monol. For Charity's Sake (Terry's, 9/1/93). See *F. BOWYER*.

HEDMONDT, E. C.

M.C. The Highwayman Knight (Court, L'pool, 14/3/98). L.C. Gai. 10/11/97.
[Written in collaboration with *F. NEILSON*. Music by G. Meyer.]

HEIGHT, R.

F. Cremation (St J.H. L'pool, 14/7/79).

HEIN, GUSTAVE

D. Beethoven (H.M. Aberdeen, 17/10/79). L.C. *French.*
D. Adelaide (Mat. 20/6/98).
[Written in collaboration with *D. BISPHAM*.]
D. Wreckage. *French.*

HEINEMANN, WILLIAM

D. The First Step. 8° 1895.
D. Summer Moths. L.C. 8° 1898.

HELMORE, WALTER

M.F. The Casting Vote (P's. 7/10/85). L.C.
[Music by W. Slaughter.]
F. The Policeman (Lyric H. Ealing, 12/1/87; Terry's, 1/11/88, *mat.*). L.C.
[Written in collaboration with *E. PHILLPOTTS*.]
Ca. The Cuckoo (Crit. 5/10/87). L.C.

HEMMING, J. W.

R.D. The Coroner (Bath, 4/8/88; E.C. 26/8/89). L.C.
[Written in collaboration with *C. HARRISON*.]
P. The Forty Thieves (Shakespeare, Clapham, 26/12/96). See *F. LOCKE*.

HENDER, DAVIDGE

M.D. The Silver Cross (Birkenhead, 25/4/98). L.C.

HENDERSON, EDITH

F.C. The Mischief Maker (Glo. 12/6/91, *mat.*; Vaud. 4/7/91). L.C.

HENDERSON, ETTIE

D. Almost a Life (Court, L'pool, 6/11/82). L.C.

HENDERSON, ISAAC

D. Agatha (Crit. 24/5/92, *mat.*; Crit. 8/12/92, as *The Silent Battle*). L.C.

HENDERSON, JOHN

D. Iron Gates (Todmorden, 29/10/83).
M.D. The Old Clay Pipe (Todmorden, 19/11/83). L.C.
O.D. 'Twas in Trafalgar's Bay (Cardiff, 2/2/89; M'bone, 21/11/91). L.C.
P. Little Bo-Peep (E.C. 24/12/92). L.C.
M.F. A Modern Wizard (Torquay, 26/12/95). L.C.
D. The Tower (Bijou, 22/4/96, *copy.*). L.C.
D. Joan of Arc (Bijou, 24/7/96, *copy.*). L.C.

HENDERSON, T. B.
D. The Lost Heir (Kendal, 7/12/68).

HENDRICKS, HERMAN
C. The Hurly Burly; or, No. 728 (New Cross H. 24/5/84; Glo. 21/6/84). L.C.

HENDRIE, ERNEST
Ca. The Genii of the Ring (Limerick, 1/82).
C. The Elder Miss Blossom (Grand, Blackpool, 10/9/97; St J. 22/9/98). L.C.
[Written in collaboration with *M. WOOD.*]
D. The Poverty of Riches (Grand, Blackpool, 7/4/99). L.C.
[Written in collaboration with *M. WOOD.*]

HENLEY, WILLIAM ERNEST [*"BYRON McGUINNESS"*]
C.D. Deacon Brodie (Pullan's, Bradford, 28/12/82). See *R. L. STEVENSON.*
D. Macaire. 8° 1885.
[Written in collaboration with *R. L. STEVENSON.*]
Bsq. Mephisto (Roy. 14/6/86). L.C. 8° 1887.
C.D. Beau Austin (H. 3/11/90, *mat.*). L.C. 8° 1884.
[Written in collaboration with *R. L. STEVENSON.*]
— Collected Plays. 8° 1892.
D. Admiral Guinea (Aven. 29/11/97). L.C. 8° 1884.
[Written in collaboration with *R. L. STEVENSON.*]

HENNING, ALBERT
C. His Wife's Little Bill (Bijou, Strand, 17/5/94).

HENRY, A.
P. Whittington and his Cat (Aven. 23/12/82). L.C.
P. St George and the Dragon; or, The Seven Champions of Christendom (C.G. 26/12/84). L.C.

HENRY, B.
D. Twenty Straws (Octagon, Blythe, 27/1/73).
D. The Spider's Web (L'pool, 17/7/76).

HENRY, D.M.
D. A Woman Outwitted (Nov. 16/11/86). See *E. DREW.*

HENRY, RE
F. The Waiter (Ladb. H. 7/7/87). L.C.
C.D. A Laughing Philosopher (Ladb. H. 11/4/89).
C.D. Norah (Grand, 30/8/97). L.C. *French.*

HENRY, Mrs RE
M.C. Going on the Stage (Corn Exchange, Blandford, 18/2/95).
[Music by E. Crook.]

"*HENRY, RICHARD*" [*RICHARD BUTLER and H. CHANCE NEWTON*]
C. Fast Friends (Steinway H. 14/6/78). *French.*
D. Madame de Raimont (Gai. 8/5/83). L.C.
F. A Happy Day (Gai. 6/10/86). L.C. *French.*
Bsq. Monte Cristo, Jr. (Gai. 23/12/86). L.C.
M.Sk. Jubilation (P.W. 14/5/87). L.C.
[Music by I. Caryll and H. J. Leslie.]
Bsq. Frankenstein (Gai. 24/12/87). L.C.
D. Game (Roy. Glasgow, 9/3/88). L.C. Hull, 28/2/88.

D. The First Mate (Gai. 31/12/88). L.C. *Lacy*.
Bsq. Lancelot the Lovely; or, The Idol of the King (Aven. 22/4/89). L.C.
[Music by J. Crook.]
P. Cinderella, Ladybird, Ladybird, fly away home (H.M. 26/12/89). L.C.
[Written in collaboration with *C. W. SCOTT*. Music by E. Solomon.]
D.Sk. Adoption (Toole's, 26/5/90). L.C. *French*.
F. Crime and Christening (O.C. 10/3/91). L.C.
D. Queer Street (Gai. 21/3/92). L.C. *French*.
Duol. Opposition (Lyr. 28/6/92). L.C.
Bal. The Sleeper Awakened (Pal. 10/12/92). See *Sir A. HARRIS*.
Bsq. Jaunty Jane Shore (Str. 2/4/94). L.C.
[Music by J. Crook.]
C. A Silver Honeymoon (Traf. 8/5/94).
C.D. Not in Society (Bijou, 2/12/99).

HENRY, S. CREAGH
Bsq. Romeo and Juliet Up-to-date (Bijou, 20/5/93). L.C.
D. A Knave of Diamonds (County, Kingston, 8/4/1901). L.C. S.W. 7/8/96, as *The Napoleon of Crime*.
D. The Prince of Darkness (Plymouth, 14/12/96; Lyr. Hammersmith, 3/5/97, as *The Sorrows of Satan*). L.C.
D. The Voice of Conscience (Ladb. H. 1/2/98, *copy*.). L.C.
D. Time's Revenge (P.H. Tonbridge, 20/6/98; Eastbourne, 4/5/99).

HERAUD, J. A.
D. Videna; or, The Mother's Tragedy (M'bone, 23/10/54). L.C.
D. A Wife and No Wife (H. 23/7/55). L.C.
T. Medea in Corinth (S.W. 12/8/57). L.C.

HERBERT, Miss
C. Up the Ladder (Limerick, 1/12/76).

HERBERT, FRANK H.
F. A Criminal Couple (P'cess. 29/6/71). L.C. *Lacy*.
F. A Fast Friend (Olym. 2/7/77). L.C.
Bsq. Moths à la Mode (P'cess. Edinburgh, 5/3/83). L.C.
M.D. Lovers (Cork, 5/5/86). See *W. E. MORTON*.
F.C. Baby (Alex. Southend, 17/7/90). See *R. SOUTAR*.
F. All through a Wire (St Albans H. 12/6/94).
D. A Wasted Life (St Alban's H. 12/6/94). See *L. OSMOND*.
Bsq. For a Woman's Honour (Holb. Restaurant, 15/11/99).

HERBERT, GALWAY
C.D. A Mean Advantage (Roy. Chester, 11/6/97). See *F. HART*.

HERBERT, G. C.
D. Our Bitterest Foe (Glo. 4/74). L.C. *French*.
Ca. Second Thoughts (Court, 6/4/74). L.C.

HERBERT, J. W.
Oa. The Prince of Borneo (Str. 5/10/99).
[Lyrics by *G. H. BROADHURST*. Music by E. Jones.]

HERBERT, LESTER
D. The Strike (Northampton, 23/6/73).

HERBOLD, A. F.

D. Narcisse (Lyc. 17/2/68). L.C. M.S. Birmingham.

HEREFORD, C. H.

[Scene.] Brand (O.C. 2/6/93). L.C.

HERIOT, PAUL

Ca. A Remarkable Cure (Vaud. 8/3/83).
C.D. Sidonie (Nov. 14/12/87). See *F. LYSTER.*
C.D. Sally in our Alley (S.W. 31/8/88). See *F. LYSTER.*
Ca. In Strict Confidence (Com. 9/10/93).
C. Parson Wynne's Trust (Com. 22/4/98). L.C.

HERIOT, WILTON

C. A Little Ray of Sunshine (Ass. R. Yeovil, 3/5/98). See *M. AMBIENT.*

HERMAN, HENRY

D. Jeanne Dubarry (Ch. X. 15/5/75). L.C.
F. Slight Mistakes (Ch. X. 31/1/76). L.C. *French.*
Bsq. My Niece and my Monkey (Ch. X. 10/6/76). L.C.
D. Caryswold: A Story of Modern Life (P.W. L'pool, 21/9/77). L.C. Ch. X. 9/6/76.
[Written in collaboration with *J. MACKAY.*]
D. Adrienne Lecouvreur (Court, 11/12/80). L.C. *French.*
D. The Silver King (P'cess. 16/11/82). See *H. A. JONES.*
D. Claudian (P'cess. 6/12/83). L.C.
[Written in collaboration with *W. G. WILLS.*]
D. Breaking a Butterfly (P's. 3/3/84). See *H. A. JONES.*
D. Chatterton (P'cess. 22/5/84). L.C.
[Written in collaboration with *H. A. JONES.*]
C.O. The Fay o' Fire (O.C. 14/11/85). L.C.
[Music by E. Jones.]
D. The Golden Band (Olym. 14/6/87). L.C.
[Written in collaboration with *F. WILLS.*]
D. For Old Virginia (Shakespeare, L'pool, 25/3/91; Grand, 4/6/91). L.C.
D. Eagle Joe (P'cess. 26/12/92). L.C. Drill H. Kingston-on-Thames, 20/5/91.
D. For a Child's Sake (New, Cambridge, 2/1/99; Morton's, Greenwich, 4/9/99). L.C. Vic. Kettering, 30/12/98.
[Written in collaboration with *M. TURNER.* Title altered to *The Gambler's Wife*, 20/4/1900.]

HERMANN, CHARLES

D. Uncle Tom's Cabin (Manchester, 1/2/53; P'cess. 31/10/92). *Lacy.*
D. By Command of the Czar (Vic. 5/11/77). See *R. GLOVER.*
D. Ordsall Hall (P.W. Salford, 27/8/83).
D. Buffalo Bill (Sanger's, 28/5/87). See *H. J. STANLEY.*

[*HERON, MATILDA*

T. Medea (D.L. 5/11/61). L.C. *Lacy*; *French.*

HERSEE, HENRY

O. Pauline (Lyc. 22/11/76). L.C.
[Music by F. H. Cowen.]
O. Carmen (H.M. 5/2/79). L.C.
C.O. The Dragoons (Folly, 14/4/79). L.C.

O. Aida (H.M. 19/2/80). L.C.
O. The Piper of Hamelin (Qns. Manchester, 16/11/82; C.G. 7/1/84). L.C.
C.O. The Royal Ward (Gai. 17/4/83). L.C.
P. Jack and the Beanstalk; or, The Seven Champions (C.G. 26/12/87). L.C.
[Written in collaboration with *H. LENNARD*]

HERVEY, R. K.
F. Good Business (Nov. 14/12/87, *mat.*). L.C.
Ca. In the Express (Aven. 24/12/89).

HESTER, EDWARD
F. Where's Prodgers? (Grand, Maidenhead, 27/8/96). L.C.

HEWSON, JAMES J.
F. A Great Success (Birkenhead, 19/9/84). L.C.
D. Recalled to Life (W. Bromwich, 10/10/85; Bijou Swiss Gardens, Shoreham, 28/7/88). L.C. Scarborough, 7/10/85.
F. My Cousin (Belfast, 16/10/85; Olym. 21/3/87). L.C. *French.*
F.C. Found Out (St G.H. L'pool, 20/1/88). L.C.
M.F. A Pair of Kids (Com. Manchester, 2/7/88).
D. Manhood (Gai. Burnley, 20/9/88; M'bone, 29/7/89). L.C.
R.D. Noble Love (Goole, 27/1/90). See *C. A. CLARKE.*
F. Flashes (L'pool, 7/4/90; M'bone, 20/7/91). L.C.
[Written in collaboration with *E. L. WEST.*]
M.F. Nipped in the Bud (Aquar. Brighton, 28/11/92). L.C.
D. A Marked Man (Colchester, 2/1/93). L.C.
D. The Line of Fate (Macclesfield, 26/3/94). L.C.
M.C. Cherry (Shakespeare, L'pool, 18/7/95). L.C.
Ca. My Sister and I (P.W. L'pool, 29/11/97).
P. Robinson Crusoe (Pav. 26/12/98). L.C.

HEYNE, MARY
C.O. The Rose and the Ring (Dublin, 23/3/78).
[Music by Elena Norton.]

HICHENS, R. S.
D. The Medicine Man (Lyc. 4/5/98). See *H. D. TRAILL.*

HICKMAN, C. B.
Ca. Obliging his Landlady (Grand, Birmingham). *French.*

HICKS, Sir SEYMOUR
D. This World of Ours (Brighton, 20/7/91; Pav. 1/8/92). L.C.
D. The New Sub (Court, 27/4/92). L.C. *French.*
D. Uncle Silas (Shaft. 13/2/93, *mat.*). L.C.
[Written in collaboration with *L. IRVING.*]
Ext. Under the Clock (Court, 25/11/93). See *C. H. E. BROOKFIELD.*
D. Good-bye (Court, 25/11/93). L.C.
Duol. Papa's Wife (Lyr. 26/1/95).
[Written in collaboration with *F. C. PHILLIPS.* Music by Ellaline Terriss.]
D. One of the Best (Adel. 21/12/95). L.C.
[Written in collaboration with *G. EDWARDES.*]
M.D. The Yashmak (Shaft. 31/3/97). See *C. RALEIGH.*

D. Sporting Life (Shakespeare, Clapham, 18/10/97). See *C. RALEIGH.*

M.Ca. The Lady Wrangler (D.Y. 4/3/98). L.C.
[Music by Ellaline Terriss.]

M.C. The Runaway Girl (Gai. 21/5/98). L.C.
[Written in collaboration with *H. NICHOLS.* Music by I. Caryll and J. Moncton.]

M.C. The Merry-go-round (Coronet, 24/4/99). L.C.
[Music by M. Lutz.]

D. With Flying Colours (Adel. 19/8/99). L.C.
[Written in collaboration with *F. LATHAM.*]

HIGGIE, THOMAS H.

[For his earlier plays see iv, 325.]

D. Belphegor the Buffoon; or, The Murderer of the Pyrenees (Vic. 27/1/51). L.C.

F. The Bloomer's Bride (Vic. 13/10/51).

P. The Lion and the Unicorn; or, Harlequin Britannia, True Blue and Merry England (Vic. 26/12/51). L.C.

F. A Frightful Accident (Str. 5/3/60). L.C.

Spec. The Trap of Gold (Ast. 28/3/64). L.C.
[Music by J. H. Tully.]

D. Watch and Wait (Sur. 23/9/71). L.C. *Lacy.*
[Written in collaboration with *R. SHEPHERD.*]

HIGGINS, D. H.

M.D. The Plunger (O.H. Burnley, 5/8/93; E.C. 2/10/93). L.C.

HILDER, CHARLES F.

D. Guilty or Not Guilty (Grec. 24/7/82). L.C.

HILL, BROWNLOW

D. The Dagger and the Cross; or, The Gibbet of Mont Faucon (Grec. 10/10/67). L.C.

HILL, HILTON

Ca. Ma's Old Bean (Leigh, 16/10/88). L.C.

F.C. The Muddler (Grand, Nottingham, 18/7/90). L.C.

C.D. The Sceptic (Metro. 22/6/96). L.C.

HILL, W. J.

Ca. The Blue-legged Lady (Court, 4/3/74). L.C.

HILLER, HARRY CROFT

D. The Contract (Margate, 6/6/87). L.C.

D. The Three Keys (St J. Manchester, 7/6/88). L.C.

F.C. Number Two (Vaud. 24/3/90, *mat.*). L.C. Gai. Preston, 14/9/89.

HILLES, M. W.

D. A Queen's Love. 4° 1879.

HILLIARD, H. L.

Ent. Our Amateur Theatricals (Croydon, 23/7/94).
[Music by O. Barri.]

HILLIARD, ROBERT

C.D. The Littlest Girl (Court, 15/7/96). L.C.

HILLIER, ALFRED

D. Camilla, the Wild Flower of the Wilderness (Middlesborough, 30/3/74).

HILL-MITCHELSON, E.

D. The Terror of Paris (Vic. O.H. Burnley, 2/7/94; Pav. 24/6/95). L.C.
[Written in collaboration with *C. H. LONGDEN.*]

D. Victims of Power (Qns. Keighley, 15/3/95; W. Hartlepool, 23/12/95, as *The Serpent's Coil*; Sur. 15/6/96). L.C.
[Written in collaboration with *C. H. LONGDEN.*]

D. Rogues and Vagabonds (Scarborough, 12/6/97, *copy.*; Sur. 17/7/99). L.C.
[Written in collaboration with *F. BENTON.*]

D. The French Spy (Morton's, Greenwich, 5/3/1900). L.C. Gai. Brighton, 17/5/99).

D. The Assassin (Wigan, 23/12/1901). L.C. Col. Oldham, 19/7/90.

HILLS, Miss HAMMOND

D. A Lost Eden (Nov. 1/6/97). L.C.

HILLYARD, J.

D. Pride; or, The Curse (Sur. 3/11/51). L.C.

D. The Bag of Gold (Olym. 28/6/52). L.C.

HILTON, B.H.

C. Lady D'Arcy (Bristol, 25/5/70).

C.D. The Adventuress (Alex. L'pool, 28/2/71). L.C.

F. Heavy Fathers (Folly, 14/4/79). L.C.

D. Tristan (Court, L'pool, 7/9/82).

HILTON, HILDA

C.D. Princess Carlo's Plot (Nov. 31/1/87).

HINGESTON-RANDOLPH, MARY

C.D. The Beverley Bogey (Bijou, 11/12/97).
[Written in collaboration with *A. GIFFARD.*]

HIPKINS, T. H.

D. Grimaldi; or, The Street Juggler (M'bone, 25/11/61). See *GASTON MURRAY.*

F. A Nice Quiet Day (Roy. 26/12/61). L.C. *Lacy.*
[Written in collaboration with *GASTON MURRAY.*]

HOARE, FLORENCE

Fairy O. Snow White (St G. 3/5/99). L.C.
[Music by Mme Mely.]

"*HOBBES, JOHN OLIVER*" [*Mrs P. M. T. CRAIGIE*]

Proverb. "Journeys End in Lovers Meeting" (Daly's, 5/6/94).
[Written in collaboration with *G. MOORE.*]

C. The School for Saints (Lyc. 30/3/96, *copy.*). L.C.

C. The Ambassador (St J. 2/6/98). L.C.

D. A Repentance (St J. 28/2/99). L.C. 8° 1899 [*priv.*].

D. Osbern and Ursyne. 8° 1899 [*priv.*].

HOBDAY, E. A. P.

Bsq. Dr Faust and Miss Marguerite (Qns. Dublin, 24/8/85). See *R. J. MARTIN.*

HOCKLEY, A. G.

C. A Family Matter (Gar. 27/6/94). See *C. G. COMPTON.*

HODGES, F. SYDNEY

F. A Gunpowder Plot (Olym. 12/5/73).
D. Gabrielle (Gai. 5/3/84). L.C.
D. Petrovna; or, The Price of Freedom (Colchester, 6/4/85). L.C.

HODGSON, AGATHA H.

C.D. Doomed (Philharmonic H. Southampton, 8/2/90). L.C.
[Written in collaboration with *A. C. HODGSON.*]
Ca. In Olden Days (Philharmonic H. Southampton, 8/2/90; Vaud. 5/6/90, *mat.*). L.C.
[Written in collaboration with *A. C. HODGSON.*]
C.D. The Gamekeeper's Wife (P.W. Southampton, 22/9/90). L.C. Derby, 25/4/90.
[Written in collaboration with *A. C. HODGSON.*]
C. The Captain's Daughter (Drill H. Southampton, 3/12/90, *copy.*).
[Written in collaboration with *A. C. HODGSON.*]
C. Watching and Waiting (P.W. Southampton, 15/1/91, *amat.*; Terry's, 28/6/91, *mat.*). L.C.
[Written in collaboration with *A. C. HODGSON.*]
C.D. On Zephyr's Wings (T.H. Teddington, 30/7/91).
[Written in collaboration with *A. C. HODGSON.*]
C. The Clerk of the Weather (O.H. Torquay, 11/6/92). See *K. OSBORNE.*

HODGSON, ARCHIBALD C.

C.D. Doomed (Philharmonic H. Southampton, 8/2/90). See *A. H. HODGSON.*
Ca. In Olden Days (Philharmonic H. Southampton, 8/2/90). See *A. H. HODGSON.*
C.D. The Gamekeeper's Wife P.W. Southampton, 22/9/90). See *A. H. HODGSON.*
C. The Captain's Daughter (Drill H. Southampton, 3/12/90). See *A. H. HODGSON.*
C. Watching and Waiting (P.W. Southampton, 15/1/91). See *A. H. HODGSON.*
C.D. On Zephyr's Wings (T.H. Teddington, 30/7/91). See *A. H. HODGSON.*

HODGSON, G. S.

F. Peggy's Little Game (Greenwich, 18/5/68). L.C. *Lacy.*
F. Beautiful for Ever (Sur. 5/10/68). L.C.
F. Master's Lodge Night (Sur. 24/2/72). L.C.
D. Bobby No. 1; or, A Warm Reception (Sur. 7/10/72). L.C. *French.*

HODSON, EMILY

F.C. Another (Vaud. 14/12/85). L.C.

HODSON, G.

Bsq. Macbeth according to Act of Parliament (Str. 18/4/53). L.C.

HOFFMAN, A. A.

D. The Rockleys (T. H. Kilburn, 10/12/87). L.C.

HOFFMAN, MAURICE H.

D. Midocean (Alex. Southend, 26/6/89). L.C. Warrington, 28/2/88.
D. After Twenty Years (Mechanics' Inst. Stockport, 23/1/96).
Bsq. The Southdown A.D. Society's Dress Rehearsal of East Lynne (Mechanics' Inst. Stockport, 23/1/96).
C.D. The Little Baronet (Pav. Edinburgh, 14/10/97). L.C.

HOGARTH, WILLIAM
C.O. Gipsy Gabriel (Bradford, 3/11/87). See *W. PARKE.*

HOLCROFT, GERALD
D. The Broad Arrow (Stand. 7/9/85). L.C.
D. The Extreme Penalty (Doncaster, 6/12/86). L.C.
D. A Stranger to Himself (Qns. Birmingham, 17/6/89). L.C.
D. The Night Express (Edmonton, 10/10/90). L.C.

HOLDERNESS, CHARLES T.
D. The Honour of the House (Corn Exchange, Driffield, 25/7/93). L.C.
[Written in collaboration with *H. S. WARWICK.*]
D. Fetters of Passion (Eden, Bishops Auckland, 12/1/94). See *H. S. WARWICK.*

HOLFORD, Mrs
D. Marie de Courcelles; or, A Republican Marriage (Olym. 9/11/78). L.C.

HOLL, HENRY
[For his earlier plays see iv, 326.]
C. Caught in a Trap (P'cess. 8/2/60). L.C.
D. The Forest Keeper (D.L. 15/2/60). L.C. *French.*

HOLLAND, JOHN
D. For the Sake of a Name (Swiss Gdns. Shoreham, 1/6/88). See *F. PILMORE.*

HOLLES, H. M.
D. Sealed to Silence (Str. 10/4/96). See *F. M. BUSSY.*

HOLLES, W.
F. Mrs Slimmer's Lodgers (Bolton, 17/7/93).

HOLLINGSHEAD, JOHN
F. The Birthplace of Podgers (Lyc. 10/3/58). L.C. *Lacy.*
C. The Man of Quality (Gai. 7/5/70).
D.Sk. Bardwell v. Pickwick (Gai. 24/1/71). L.C.
F. Seeing Toole (Gai. 3/9/73). L.C.
[Written in collaboration with *R. REECE.*]
C. Grasshopper (Gai. 9/12/77). L.C.
O. Miami (P'cess. 16/10/93).
[Lyrics by *W. ST LEDGER.* Music by H. Parry.]

HOLLOWAY, JOHN
C.D. Mirabel (Macclesfield, 24/1/83). See *C. E. DERING.*

HOLMES, HENRY
C.D. Broken Links (Richmond, 20/3/82; Stratford, 6/2/88). L.C.

HOLT, CLARENCE
D. The Barricade (Croydon, 11/10/69; Duke's, 7/9/78).

HOLT, MAY. See *Mrs R. FAIRBAIRN*

HOLT, N.
F. Wanted A Husband (Olym. 28/1/50). L.C.

HOLTON, FLORENCE
D His Hidden Revenge (P.H. Upton Park, 10/10/87).
D. From the Vanished Past (P.H. Upton Park, 30/4/88).

HOMRIGH, ALEC VON

F. Jumping at Conclusions (T.H. Wandsworth, 23/11/92, *amat.*). L.C.

HONEYMAN, W. C.

Ca. Loaded with a Legacy (Aven. Sunderland, 10/2/90).

HONIG, LOUIS

F.C. The Quack; or, The Nervous Family (Roy. 11/8/87). L.C.

HOOD, BASIL

Oa. The Gipsies (P.W. 25/10/90).
[Music by W. Bendall.]

C.O. Donna Luiza (P.W. 23/3/92). L.C.
[Music by W. Slaughter.]

Ca. Auld Lang Syne (P.W. 5/11/92).

M.Sk. The Crossing Sweeper (Gai. 8/4/93).
[Music by W. Slaughter.]

M.F. Gentleman Joe, the Hansom Cabby (P.W. 2/3/95). L.C.
[Music by W. Slaughter.]

M.C. The French Maid (Bath, 4/4/96; Metro. 4/5/96; Terry's, 24/4/97; Portsmouth, 20/9/97, as *The Duchess of Dijon*). L.C.
[Music by W. Slaughter.]

M.C. Belinda (P's. Manchester, 5/10/96). See *B. C. STEPHENSON*.

Duol. Her Apron Strings (Terry's, 9/6/97). L.C.

M.C. Dandy Dan, the Lifeguardsman (Belfast, 23/8/97; Lyr. 4/12/97). L.C. Court, L'pool, 28/9/97.
[Music by W. Slaughter.]

Fairy D. The Soldier and the Tinder Box (Terry's, 23/12/97). L.C.
[Music by W. Slaughter.]

Fairy D. Little Claus and Big Claus (Terry's, 23/12/97). L.C.
[Music by W. Slaughter.]

Fairy D. The Emperor's New Clothes (Terry's, 23/12/97).
[Music by W. Slaughter.]

Fairy D. The Princess and the Swineherd (Terry's, 23/12/97). L.C.
[Music by W. Slaughter.]

M.C. Orlando Dando (Grand, Fulham, 1/8/98). L.C.
[Music by W. Slaughter.]

Ext. Her Royal Highness (Bournemouth, 22/8/98; Vaud. 3/9/98). L.C.
[Music by W. Slaughter.]

M.D. Robin Hood and Maid Marion (P.H. Hastings, 18/9/99). L.C.
[Music by W. W. Hedgcock.]

C.O. The Rose of Persia; or, The Storyteller and the Slave (Sav. 29/11/99). L.C.
[Music by Sir A. Sullivan.]

HOOD, THOMAS

Bsq. Robinson Crusoe (H. 26/7/67). See *W. S. GILBERT*.

HOOK, WALTON

F.C. Baby; or, A Slight Mistake (Ipswich, 4/6/88; Vaud. 7/6/88, *mat.*). L.C.

HOPE, ANTHONY

D. The Price of Empire (St J. 18/2/96, *copy.*). L.C.

C. The Adventure of Lady Ursula (D.Y. 11/10/98). L.C. *French.*

C. When a Man's in Love (Court, 19/10/98). L.C.
[Written in collaboration with *E. ROSE*.]

D. Rupert of Hentzau (Glasgow, 5/10/99). L.C. Court, L'pool, 27/12/98.

HOPE, NAOMI
D. The Armourer (Whitehaven, 20/9/94). L.C.
M.D. Forgive us our Trespasses (Gai. Brighton, 1/6/96). L.C.

HOPE, PRESTON
Ca. A Bit of Drapery (Metro. 30/8/97).
C.O. The Scribe (P.H. Sydenham, 3/11/99).

HOPE, VIVIAN
C.D. His Second Wife (Aven. 29/6/92, *mat.*). L.C.

HOPKINS, CLEMENT
C.D. Self (De Grey R. York, 10/4/96, *amat.*).

HOPKINS, FRANCIS
D. All for Gold; or, Fifty Millions of Money (Birmingham, 15/7/78; Sur. 21/2/81). L.C.

HOPKINS, J. B.
D. The Yogi's Daughter. 8° 1854.

HOPKINS, M.
M.D. Love on Wheels (Qns. Gate H. 30/5/1901). L.C. P.W. 20/6/98.

HOPKINSON, A. F.
D.Sk. Boadicea. 12° 1888 [*priv.*].
D.Sk. Dramatic Sketches: Lorenzo...Death of King Edmund... Boadicea. 12° 1889.

HOPPIN, WILLIAM J.
Ca. Circumstances alter Cases. *French.*

HOPWOOD, A.
C.O. The Lucky Star (Sav. 7/1/99). See *C. H. E. BROOKFIELD.*

HORN, JAMES
D. Twice Wedded (Exchange H. Banbury, 9/8/82).

HORNCASTLE, —
D. Danger (Sur. 23/10/79). L.C.

HORNE, F. LENNOX
[For an earlier play see iv, 328.]
F. Two Heads are better than one (Lyc. 14/12/54). L.C. *Lacy.*
F. A Chinese Romance. L.C. Roy. 27/1/62.
M.F. The Baronet Abroad and the Rustic Prima Donna (St J. 9/11/64). L.C. *Lacy.*
F. A Tale of a Comet (D.L. 13/1/73). L.C.

HORNE, RICHARD HENGIST
[For his earlier plays see iv, 328.]
T. The Duchess of Malfi (S.W. 20/11/50). L.C.
D. Prometheus the Fire Bringer. 8° 1864 [Edinburgh].
T. Laura Dibalzo; or, the Patriot Martyrs. 8° 1880.

HORNER, ARTHUR
D. The Sins of New York (Birkenhead, 10/2/90). L.C. P's. Blackburn, 25/1/90.

HORNER, BURNHAM
D. Cantata. Penelope (Colchester, 30/5/92, *amat.*).

HORNER, FRED.

F.C. The Two Johnnies (Northampton, 27/4/88; Com. 6/6/89, *mat.*; Traf. 5/10/93). L.C.

C. On Toast (Aven. 16/7/88, *mat.*; Toole's, 7/10/89). L.C.

F.C. The Bungalow (P.W. 21/1/89, *mat.*, *copy.*, as *Bachelor Quarters*; Toole's, 7/10/89). L.C.

[Written in collaboration with *F. WYATT.*]

D. Isalda (Toole's, 14/2/90). L.C.

D. The Struggle for Life (Aven. 25/9/90). See *R. BUCHANAN.*

F. The Late Lamented (Court, 6/5/91). L.C.

F.C. Happy Returns (Vaud. 1/3/92). L.C.

F.C. The Great Unpaid (Com. 9/5/93). L.C.

F. The Other Fellow (Court, 9/9/93). L.C.

F.C. The Sunbury Scandal (Terry's, 11/6/96). L.C.

F. On Leave (Aven. 17/4/97). L.C.

C. The Other Lady (Lyc. Edinburgh, 20/6/98). L.C.

HORNER, JAMES

D. Lost to Life (Leicester, 3/3/84). L.C.

Bsq. Dick Whittington and his Cat-astrophe (Alex. Walsall, 16/6/84).

Bsq. Sinbad; or, The Dry Land Sailor (Coventry, 7/7/84).

HORNIMAN, ROBERT

D. A Reprieve (County, Kingston, 18/5/98). L.C.

HORNIMAN, ROY

D. Judy (P.W. 15/5/99). L.C.

HORRIDGE, FRANK

F.C. Whose Wife? or, A Coroner's Honeymoon (Bournemouth, 30/8/98, *copy.*). L.C.

HORSMAN, CHARLES

D. The Free Lance; or, Who wins? (Alfred, 2/8/69).

Bsq. Charmian and Badoura (Edinburgh, 19/5/73).

D. Won by a Neck (Exeter, 16/8/79).

D. My Comrade; or, The Last Command (Stratford, 18/5/85).

HORTON, Lieut. S. G.

F.C. Robert and Bertram; or, The Volatile Vagrants (R.A. Woolwich, 2/4/88). L.C. 14/2/87.

HOSKINS, FRANCIS RADCLIFFE

F. Goldfinch (Olym. 26/12/51).

D. The Life Buoy (Swansea, 12/5/69).

Bsq. The Blossom of Churnington Green; or, Love, Rivalry and Revenge. *Lacy.*

HOSKINS, W. H.

C. Weighed in the Balance (Margate, 9/8/81). L.C.

HOUGHTON, J. W.

M.F. Did you ring? (P.W. 27/6/92). L.C.

[Written in collaboration with *J. W. MABSON.* Music by Landon Ronald.]

M.F. The Celestials (P.W. L'pool. 5/4/93). See *C. H. ABBOTT.*

C.O. His Highness (O.C. 13/6/93, *mat.*). L.C.

[Written in collaboration with *A. TATE.*]

[*HOWARD, BRONSON*

Bsq. Ingomar the Idiotic (Alfred, 19/8/71). See *O. ALLEN*.

C. Brighton (Fifth Avenue, New York, 21/12/70, as *Saratoga*; Court, 25/5/74). *L.C. French*.
[Written in collaboration with *F. MARSHALL*.]

C.D. Ivers Dean (Hanley, 12/11/77). See *Sir C. L. YOUNG*.

C. Truth (Hooley's, Chicago, 27/5/78, as *Hurricanes*; Crit. 8/2/79). L.C.

C.D. The Old Love and the New (Court, 15/12/79). L.C.
[Adapted by *J. ALBERY* from *The Banker's Daughter* (Union Square, New York, 30/11/78.]

D. Baron Rudolph (Hull, 1/8/81). L.C.

C.D. Young Mrs Winthrop (M'bone, 21/9/82, *copy*. Court, 6/11/84). *French*.

C. One of Our Girls (E.C. 4/11/85; Newcastle, 26/8/89, as *Cousin Kate*). L.C. 8° 1897 [*priv.*].

C.D. Camping Out (E.C. 13/12/86, *copy*.). L.C.

C.D. The Henrietta (E.C. 28/9/87, *copy*.; Aven. 28/3/91). L.C. 8° 1901 [*priv.*].

HOWARD, FLAVELL

Oa. The Music Master (Exchange H. Wolverhampton, 19/11/87). L.C.

HOWARD, Dr JOHN

D. The Forester King (Macclesfield, 19/9/92). L.C. as *Huntingdon the Disinherited; or, the F.K.*

HOWARD, WALTER

Oa. The Wearin' o' the Green (Workington, 1/8/96; Morton's, Greenwich, 10/4/99). L.C.

R.D. A Life's Revenge (Shaft. 16/7/97, *copy*.; Metro. Manchester, 16/1/99; Morton's, Greenwich, 5/6/99). L.C.

R.D. For the King (Windsor, 21/1/99, *copy*.; Grand, Croydon, 27/3/99). L.C.
[Written in collaboration with *S. PEASE*. Title altered to *Brothers in Heart*, 17/10/1901.]

D. The Two Little Drummer Boys (Grand, Glasgow, 1/6/99, *copy*.; New, Loughborough, 23/10/99). L.C.

M.D. Midst Shot and Shell (Manchester Junction, 1/4/1907; W.L. 19/8/1907). L.C. Qns. O.H. Workington, 26/10/99.

HOWE, J. B.

D. Handsome Jack. L.C. Pav. 4/4/61.

D. The Wedding Eve (Brit. 8/4/67). L.C. as *The Bridal Eve*.

D. The Shamrock of Ireland; or, The Flower of Erin (Brit. 20/5/67). L.C.

D. Scarlet Dick; or, The Road and the Riders (Brit. 24/7/67). L.C.

D. Captain Gerald; or, False and Fair (Brit. 27/11/67). L.C.

D. The Poor Parisheen; or, The Fugitives of Derrinane (Brit. 27/9/69). L.C. as *The P.P.; or, The Outcast's Return*.

D. The Huguenots; or, The Mask and the Surgeon (Sur. 16/6/73).

D. Haunted for Ever (Brit. 23/2/80). L.C.

D.Sk. The Cur (Woolwich, 5/9/91).

D. The British Slave. *French*.

HOWELL, J. H.

D. The Cid (K.X. 25/3/78). See *J. ADDISON*.

HOWELL-POOLE, W.

D. The Miracle (Sur. 24/3/83). L.C.

D. Through the Furnace (Olym. 29/7/85). L.C.
[This was later played as *Wronged* in the provinces.]

Ca. Holding the Mirror (Tyne, Newcastle, 26/10/85). L.C.

F.C. Boys Together (P.W. L'pool. 28/3/87).

M.D. The Game of Life (Court, L'pool. 15/8/87; Grand, 12/12/87). L.C.

M.D. The Wheel of Fortune (Workington, 2/8/90; S.W. 12/1/91). L.C.

HOWELLS, C. E.

C. Etiquette (Alex. Walsall, 1/3/80). L.C.

Ext. Golden Plume; or, The Magic Crystal (Alex. Walsall, 14/5/83). L.C. Alex. Walsall, 23/3/80.

[*HOWELLS, WILLIAM DEAN*

T. Yorick's Love (Euclid Avenue O.H. Chicago, 25/10/78; Lyc. 12/4/84). L.C.

C. A Dangerous Ruffian (Aven. 30/11/95).

HOWLETT, SHIRLEY

F.C. Safe and Sound (County H. Bootle, 19/11/91, *copy.*; Grand O.H. L'pool, 8/6/96). L.C.

D. A False Friend (Gordon Working Lads' Inst. L'pool, 8/4/93). L.C.

C. The Gay Chaperon (Muncaster, Bootle, 22/11/94). L.C.

D. A Glimpse of the World (Gordon Working Lads' Inst. L'pool. 23/11/95). L.C.

HOWSON, J.

Ca. Don Quixote Junior (Glo. 21/4/79). See *J. C. GOODMAN.*

[*HOYT, CHARLES HALE*

M.F. A Bunch of Keys (Newark, New Jersey, 12/82; Aven. 25/8/83). L.C.
[Written in collaboration with *G. L. GORDON.*]

M.C. A Trip to Chinatown (Hoyt's, New York, 9/11/91; Toole's, 29/9/94). L.C.

M.C. A Stranger in New York (Gai. 11/2/97, *copy.*; D.Y. 21/6/98). L.C.

HUDSON, CHARLES

C.D. Father Buonaparte (Olym. 19/3/91, *mat.*).

F. My Astral Body (Court, 22/4/96). L.C.
[Written in collaboration with *N. COLTHURST.*]

HUDSON, ERIC V.

D. The Handcuffs (Nottingham, 11/5/93). See *R. STOCKTON.*

D. Man's Enemy (P's. Blackburn, 14/1/97). See *C. H. LONGDEN.*

HUEFFER, FRANCIS

Lyrical D. Colomba (D.L. 9/4/83). L.C.
[Music by Sir A. C. Mackenzie.]

O. The Troubadour (D.L. 8/6/86). L.C.
[Music by Sir A. C. Mackenzie.]

HUGH, EDWIN
M.C. Dotty (P'cess. Leith, 9/5/96). See *A. PARRY.*

HUGHES, ANNIE
Ca. A Husband's Humiliation (Crit. 25/6/96). L.C.

HUGHES, BEAUMONT
D. The Widow's Son; or, The Twin Brothers (Paisley, 1/5/68).

HUGHES, FRED
F. My Wife's Baby (Roy. 7/9/72). L.C. *French.*

HUGHES, GEORGE
C. The Barn at Beccles (Manor R. Hackney, 8/12/91). L.C.
[Written in collaboration with *A. C. BICKLEY.*]

HUGHES, H.
M.C. The Lady Philosopher (Conservative H. Heaton Moor, 4/3/98; Dalston, 17/10/98). L.C.
[Music by A. A. Bancroft.]

HUGHES, JULIAN
D. Bail Up (Kidderminster, 19/5/93, *copy.*). L.C.

HUGHES, TALBOT
M.Rom. At Zero (County, Reading, 4/7/98). See *L. TEALE.*

HUGHES, T. B.
Oa. Six-and-Six (Hull, 9/8/80). L.C.
[Music by P. W. Halton.]
C. Daisy (Roy. Glasgow, 23/7/83). L.C.
Oa. Quits (St J. Manchester, 10/11/84; Aven. 1/10/88). L.C.
[Music by J. Crook.]

HUME, C. L.
Ca. A Practical Joker (Com. 15/6/95). L.C.

HUME, FERGUS
D. The Mystery of a Hansom Cab (P'cess. 23/2/88). See *A. LAW.*
D. Madame Midas (Stratford, 7/7/88). See *P. BECK.*
F.C. Indiscretion (Exhibition Pal. Folkestone, 13/11/88).
C. The Fool of the Family (D.Y. 30/1/96). L.C.
F.C. Teddy's Wives (Eastbourne, 4/4/96; Kilburn, 1/8/96; Str. 24/9/96).

HUME, HAMILTON
D. The Tangled Path. 8° 1863 [*priv.*; Calcutta].

HUMPHREY, EDWARD
Oa. Our Court (R.A. Woolwich, 17/11/88). L.C.
[Written in collaboration with *J. ADDISON.*]

HUNGERFORD, Mrs
D. Donna (Ladb. H. 11/3/92, *copy.*). L.C.
[Written in collaboration with *Mrs N. PHILLIPS.*]

HUNT, G. W.
Ext. The Very Latest Edition of the Gathering of the Clans (E.L. 18/10/73).

HUNT, HENRY
D. Seventeen Hundred and Ninety (Bath Saloon, Sheffield, 30/10/94). L.C.

HUNT, LEIGH
[For his earlier plays see iv, 329.]

HUNTER, Mrs TALBOT
D. Lost to the World (Lyc. Crewe, 15/2/92; M'bone, 4/7/92). L.C.

HUNTLEY, FREDERICK
Oa. Daphne (Kyrle Social H. Birmingham, 16/11/95, *amat.*).
[Music by J. Granville.]

HUNTLEY, G. P.
M.Bsq. Turpin à la mode (Roy. Chester, 29/3/97). L.C.
[Written in collaboration with *G. GRAY*; lyrics by *J. J. WOOD*. Music by H. C. Barry.]

HURD, J. C.
D. The Fatal Triumph (P.H. New Cross, 11/12/86). See *J. L. FEATHERSTONE.*

HURST, BRANDON
D.Sk. A Losing Hazard (Parkhurst, 11/4/92). L.C.
F.C. His Highness (O.C. 5/2/94, *copy.*). L.C.

HURST, CYRIL
C.Oa. Royal Vagrants; A Story of Conscientious Objection (Earlham H. Forest Gate, 27/10/99). L.C.
[Music by H. Waldo-Warner.]
M.Ca. The Lady Clerk (Earlham H. Forest Gate, 27/10/99).
[Music by A. Cleveland.]

HURST, JAMES P.
Ca. Sugar and Cream (Windsor, 13/1/83; Glo. 3/84). L.C. *French.*
F.C. Double Zero (Str. 10/10/83). L.C.
C. Loose Tiles (Vaud. 28/1/85). L.C.
Ca. April Folly (Olym. 6/4/85). L.C. *French.*
Ca. Nearly Severed (Com. Manchester, 31/8/85; Vaud. 12/9/85). L.C. *French.*
D. In Fetters (Str. 30/11/85). L.C.
C. True Colours (Glo. 11/6/88). *French.*
C.D. The Begum's Diamonds (Aven. 22/1/89, *mat.*). L.C.
F.C. Æsop's Fables (Str. 19/6/89). L.C.
C. Woman's World (Court, 8/12/96). L.C.

HYDE, H. F.
C.D. Snow Flakes (P's. Portsmouth, 14/3/78).
C. Success; or, The Modern Cinderella (Gt Grimsby, 30/4/79).

"*IGNIS, ALTON.*" See *E. STUART-SMITH*

ILLINGWORTH, J. H.
D. Lost for Gold; or, Oakmere Hold (Guildhall, Westminster, 26/12/85).

INGRAM, A.
C. A Folly of Age (O.C. 26/11/94). L.C. Shakespeare, L'pool, 11/9/94.

INGRAM, PRENTISS
M.D. Alone in the World (P'cess. 23/4/92, *mat.*). L.C.

INMAN, J. W.
D. Orioma, the Reclaimed. 8° 1858.

INNES, G. W.
D. Joan of Arc (S.W. 15/9/90). L.C. Warrington, 7/8/90.

INNES, Lieut.-Col. P. R.
D. Donellan (Str. 13/6/89, *mat.*). L.C.

IRISH, ANNIE
C.D. Across her Path (Terry's, 21/1/90, *mat.*). L.C.

IRVINE, Mrs MARY CATHARINE
D.Poem. Heart Repose. 12° 1867.

IRVING, LAWRENCE B.
D. Uncle Silas (Shaft. 13/2/93). See *Sir SEYMOUR HICKS.*
D. Time, Hunger and the Law (Crit. 24/5/94). L.C.
Duol. A State Trial (Gar. 19/11/96).
D. Peter the Great (Lyc 1/1/98). L.C.
D. Richard Lovelace (Bath, 11/7/98). L.C.
D. Robespierre (Lyc. 15/4/99). L.C.
[Several later plays.]

IRWIN, EDWARD
D. King O'Toole's Goose; or, The Legend of Glendalough (Qns. Dublin, 24/3/56). *Lacy.*

ISAACSON, WILLIAM PARR
D. Newmarket: A Tale of the Turf (Holb. 17/10/74). L.C.

ISLA, Count DE LA
C.D. The Glow-worm (H.M. Aberdeen, 10/3/84). L.C.

IVIE, FRITZ
Bsq.O. The Belle of Madrid (Pier Pav. Rhyl, 19/9/98). L.C.
[Music by W. C. Pike.]

JACKSON, J. P.
O. The Flying Dutchman (Lyc. 3/10/76). L.C.
O. The Golden Cross (Adel. 2/3/78). L.C.
O. Rienzi (H.M. 27/1/79). L.C.
O. Lohengrin (H.M. 7/2/80). L.C.

JACKSON, WALTER H.
D. Zilpha (Theatre of Varieties, Brentford, 24/2/87). L.C.
F. Runaway Husbands (P's. Kew Bridge, 14/2/93). L.C.

JACOBS, W. W.
D. The Grey Parrot (Str. 6/11/99). L.C. *French.*
[Several later plays.]

JACQUES, FREDERICK
F. Anonymous Letters (Park H. Camden Town, 17/10/88, *amat.*).

JAMES, ADA
C.D. Arts and Crafts (Ladb. H. 9/3/97). L.C.
[Written in collaboration with *D. JAMES.*]

JAMES, C. STANFIELD
[For his earlier plays see iv, 330.]
D. The Bronze Statue; or, The Virgin's Kiss. L.C. Qns. 14/2/50.
D. The Dogs of the Grange. L.C. Qns. 26/3/50.
D. The Cornfield. L.C. Qns. 15/5/50.

P. Cinderella and the Fairy Glass Slipper; or, Harlequin and the Silver Lily, the Naiads of the Golden Grot and the Fay of the Magic Fountain. L.C. Qns. 20/12/50.
D. Azael the Arab; or, The Profligate of Memphis (D.L. 19/2/51). L.C.
D Plunder Creek; or, The Leopard Pirate and the Brothers of the Coast (Qns 21/4/51) L.C.
D. The Kaffir War (Qns. 25/8/51). L.C.
Ext. The Bloomer Costume (Qns. 6/10/51). L.C.
D.Spec. The Marble King (Qns. 27/10/51). L.C.
P. Beauty and the Beast; or, Harlequin Azor, the Queen of the Roses and the King of the Thorns (Qns. 26/12/51). L.C.
D. The Betting Boy's Career (Qns. 13/9/52). L.C.
[Written in collaboration with *J. B. JOHNSTONE.*]
Ext. The Silver Tower; or, The Prince of the Orange Islands (Qns. 11/10/52). L.C.
D. The Rats of the Seine (Qns. 22/11/52). L.C.
P. Harlequin King of Carbuncles (Qns. 27/12/52).
P. Harlequin King Richard III; or, The Magic Arrow and the Battle of Bosworth Field (Qns. 26/12/53) L.C.

JAMES, CHARLES
Ca. The Lady Burglar (Kilburn, 3/5/97). See *E. J. MALYON.*
C. A Mere Question of Time (Kilburn, 14/7/97). See *E. J. MALYON.*
C. A Lesson in Manners (Portsmouth, 25/10/97). See *E. J. MALYON.*
C. At the Kirk Arms (Aquar. Brighton, 29/11/97). See *E. J. MALYON.*
C. The Honourable John (Qns. Crouch End, 12/12/98). See *F. MOUILLOT.*

JAMES, DAVID S.
D. Wife or No Wife (Torquay, 21/5/83). L.C.
D. My Uncle (Torquay, 28/5/83).
[Written in collaboration with *W. Y. STEWART.*]
C.D. Blotted Out (Wigan, 11/8/84). L.C. Bolton, 17/7/84.
Bsq. Little Robinson Crusoe (Oxford, 13/4/85).
D. Man and Wife; or, A Scotch Marriage (Margate, 29/6/85).
P. Whittington and his Cat (Lyr. Hammersmith, 26/12/92).

JAMES, DUDLEY
C.D. Arts and Crafts (Ladb. H. 9/3/97). See *A. JAMES.*

JAMES, FRED
Ca. Parallel Attacks (Str. 11/7/93). L.C.
D. A Princess of Orange (Lyc. 2/12/96). L.C.
Ca. An Attic Drama (Gar. 18/4/98). L.C.

[*JAMES, HENRY*
C.D. The American (Winter Gdns. Southport, 3/1/91; O.C. 26/9/91). L.C.
— Theatricals. Two Comedies: Tenants. Disengaged. 8° 1894.
— Theatricals (Second Series). The Album, The Reprobate. 8° 1895.
D. Guy Domville (St J. 5/1/95). L.C.

JAMES, RAYMOND
O. Grace Darrell (Leinster, Dublin, 12/9/96).
[Music by F. C. Collinge.]

JAMES, SAM

C.D. Clare Cottage (Margate, 16/4/88). L.C.

JAMES, S. THEODORE

D. The Squire of Undercliff (P's. Accrington, 10/7/95). L.C.

JAMES, WALTER

F. A Return Ticket to the International Exhibition (St J. 11/8/62). See *G. SPENCER*.

F. To be continued in our next (M'bone, 17/6/67).

D. Never despair (Grec. 7/12/71). L.C.

D. The Terror of London (Grec. 23/10/79). L.C.
[Written in collaboration with *H. WHYTE*.]

F.C. George (County H. St Albans, 11/3/95).

JAMESON, Mrs

C. The Odds are Even (Northampton, 22/6/93).

JARDINE, F.

C.D. The Bow of Orange Ribbon (Daly's, 3/8/97). See *F. COOPER*.

JARMAN, FRED

D. The Cat's Paw (Albany, Durham, 3/11/85).

M.D. The Mark of Cain (P.W. Greenwich, 25/7/87). L.C.

M.D. The Squire's Wife (Huddersfield, 15/7/89).

C.D. Pansy (Preston, 28/2/90). L.C.

F.C. The Mesmerist (Bath, 5/5/90). L.C.

D. A Golden Harvest (L'pool, 26/5/90). L.C.

R.D. A Noble Lie (Jersey, 23/7/90).

F.C. The Little Widow (L'pool, 2/2/91; Lyr. Hammersmith, 20/4/91).

D. The Man Hunter (Vic. Newport, 11/5/91). L.C.

D. Wedded to Crime (S.W. 25/5/91).
[Written in collaboration with *W. SELWYN*.]

F.C. Our Relations (Aquar. Brighton, 5/10/91). L.C.

D. The Miners' Queen (Lincoln, 25/1/92).

D. Lota; or, A Mother's Love (S.W. 8/8/92). L.C.

C. The Dayes of Olde (Leamington, 8/11/92). L.C. Lincoln, 7/11/92.

F.C. Sarah (Waterford, 27/12/92).

D. The Shadow of Sin (Hanley, 20/2/93). L.C. Aquar. Gt Yarmouth, 23/8/92.

C. The Marriage Knot (Amphi. Ramsgate, 8/6/94). L.C.

D. Under the Czar (Colosseum, Oldham, 9/7/94; E.C. 13/4/96). L.C.

D. Right or Wrong (P's. Blackburn, 9/11/96; Brit. 25/7/98). L.C.

D. At the Foot of the Altar (O.H. Londonderry, 20/9/97; Stratford, 25/10/97; W.L. 1/11/97). L.C.

M.C. The Varsity Belle (Dover, 20/2/1905). L.C. Vic. Bayswater, 9/8/98, as *The V. Girl*.
[Lyrics by *G. PORRINGTON*. Music by E. Jones.]

D. The Rebel's Wife (Consett, 8/12/98; Brit. 5/6/99). L.C.

JARVIS, C. W.

D. A Man's Love (P.W. 25/6/89). See *J. T. GREIN*.

Ca. Spring Leaves (Court, 14/3/91). See *J. T. GREIN*.

D. Reparation (Vaud. 12/5/92). See *J. T. GREIN*.

Ca. The Compromising Coat (Glo. 27/6/92). See *J. T. GREIN*.

JARVIS, J. H.

O.Bsq. Fleur de Thé (Tyne, Newcastle, 15/3/75; Crit. 9/10/75). L.C.

JAY, HARRIET (*pseud.* "*CHARLES MARLOWE*")
D. Alone in London (Olym. 2/11/85). See *R. BUCHANAN*.
C. Fascination (Nov. 6/10/87, *mat.*; Vaud. 19/1/88). L.C.
[Written in collaboration with *R. BUCHANAN*.]
F. The Strange Adventure of Miss Brown (Vaud. 26/6/95). See *R. BUCHANAN*.
C.D. The New Don Quixote (Roy. 19/2/96). See *R. BUCHANAN*.
C. The Romance of the Shopwalker (Colchester, 24/2/96). See *R. BUCHANAN*.
C. The Wanderer from Venus (Grand, Croydon, 8/6/96). See *R. BUCHANAN*.
R.D. The Mariners of England (Grand, Nottingham, 1/3/97). See *R. BUCHANAN*.
C.D. Two Little Maids from School (Metro. Camberwell, 21/11/98). L.C.
[Written in collaboration with *R. BUCHANAN*.]

JAYE, HAROLD
D. Love's Loyalty (Greenwich, 2/9/76). L.C.

JECKS, ALBERT E.
M.Sk. The Captain of the Night Hawk (Assembly R. Balham, 23/9/97). L.C.
[Music by Arthur Workman.]
M.Sk. A Military Tournament (W. Hartlepool, 7/2/98).

JEFFERS, CHARLES
O. Thérèse; or, The Orphan of Geneva (P'cess. 26/4/50). L.C.

JEFFERSON, ARTHUR
D. The World's Verdict (Empire, Merthyr Tydvil, 10/7/90, *copy.*; N. Shields, 4/12/90; Sur. 5/8/95). L.C.
D. The Orphan Heiress (Eden, Bishop Auckland, 23/12/95; Sur. 25/9/99). L.C. O.H. Bury, 24/7/95.
D. The Bootblack (N. Shields, 11/1/97, *copy.*; Alex. Sheffield, 26/7/97; W.L. 18/7/98). L.C. Blyth, 21/12/96.
[Title altered to *London by Day and Night*, 4/10/98.]

JEFFERSON, FRANK
D. Denounced (E.C. 11/8/83). See *H. GASCOIGNE*.
D. Pilgrims; or, The World between them (Scarborough, 18/8/84; P.W. Gt Grimsby, 26/1/85, as *Severed*). L.C.

[*JEFFERSON, JOSEPH*
D. Rip van Winkle (Adel. 4/9/65). See *D. BOUCICAULT*.
D. Shadows of a Great City (P'cess. Glasgow, 28/2/87; P'cess. 14/7/87). L.C.
[Written in collaboration with *L. R. SHEWELL*.]

JEFFERYS, CHARLES
D.O. The Gipsy's Vengeance (D.L. 24/3/56). L.C.
O. Esmerelda; or, The Hunchback of Notre Dame (D.L. 30/6/56). L.C.
[Music by Battista.]

JEFFERYS, C. ALLEN
D. The Haunted House at Lodore (Guilford, 11/2/95).

JEFFREY, G. E.
Bsq. Ingomar (Douglas, Isle of Man, 2/9/68).

JEFFREY, P. SHAW

Oa. The Golden Days (Village H. Chislehurst, 17/10/93; P.H. Sidcup, 10/2/97).
[Written in collaboration with *W. T. SHORE*. Music by H. S. Moore.]

JENKINS, Dr T. J. PRICE

D. The Sands of Time (Assembly R. Neath, 24/5/94). L.C.

JENNER, ANNABEL

M.Past. My Lady Fanciful (Tivoli Gdns. Margate, 15/8/99).

JENNINGS, H. J.

C.D. Summer Storms (Birmingham, 18/12/76). L.C.

JEPHSON, R. M.

C.D. Under the Mistletoe (Imp. 5/12/81). See *S. MOLYNEUX*.

JEROME, JEROME K.

C.D. Barbara (Glo. 19/6/86). L.C. *French.*
C.D. Sunset (Com. 13/2/88). L.C. *French.*
R.D. Fennel (Nov. 31/3/88). L.C. *French.*
C. Woodbarrow Farm (Com. 18/6/88, *mat.*; Vaud. 13/1/91). L.C.
D.Sk. Pity is akin to Love (Olym. 8/9/88).
F. New Lamps for Old (Terry's, 8/2/90). L.C.
D. Ruth (P's. Bristol, 20/3/90). See *A. A. BRIGHT*.
C.D. What Women will do (Birmingham, 17/9/90).
C. Birth and Breeding (Edinburgh, 18/9/90, *copy.*). L.C. 8° 1895.
C. The Prude's Progress (Cambridge, 16/5/95; Com. 22/5/95). L.C. *French.*
[Written in collaboration with *E. PHILLPOTTS*.]
D. The Rise of Dick Halward (Gar. 19/10/95). L.C.
M.F. Biarritz (P.W. 11/4/96). L.C.
[Written in collaboration with *A. ROSS*. Music by F. O. Carr.]
F. The MacHaggis (Peterborough, 22/2/97; Glo. 25/2/97). L.C.
[Written in collaboration with *E. PHILLPOTTS*.]
C. Miss Hobbs (D.Y. 18/12/99). L.C.

JERROLD, DOUGLAS WILLIAM

[For his earlier plays see iv, 331–2.]
C. The Spendthrift (Olym. 5/3/50).
D. The Mother's Dream; or, The Gipsy's Revenge (Adel. 18/3/50).
C. The Catspaw (H. 9/5/50). L.C. 8° 1850.
F. Retired from Business (H. 3/5/51). L.C.
C. St Cupid; or, Dorothy's Fortune (Windsor Castle, 21/1/53; P'cess. 22/1/53). L.C. 8° 1853; *French.*

JERROLD, M. W. BLANCHARD

F. Cool as a Cucumber (Lyc. 24/3/51). L.C. *Lacy.*
F. The Rifle Club; or, A Shot at a Passing Bubble (Str. 16/2/52). L.C.
D. Beau Brummel (Lyc. 11/4/59). L.C.
Ca. The Chatterbox (St J. 30/11/59). L.C.
C. Cupid in Waiting (Roy. 22/7/71). L.C. *Lacy.*

JERROLD, TOM

O. All in the Downs; or, Black-eyed Susan (Gai. 5/11/81). L.C.
[Music by M. Lutz.]

[*JESSOP, GEORGE H.*

C. On Probation (E.C. 5/9/89). See *B. MATTHEWS.*

C. A Gold Mine (Gai. 21/7/90). See *B. MATTHEWS.*

C.D. Sam'l of Posen (Gai. 4/7/95).

R.C.O. Shamus O'Brien (O.C. 2/3/96). L.C.
[Music by C. V. Stanford.]

D. The Power of the Press (P'cess. Glasgow, 3/8/96). See *A. PITOU.*

JESSUP, —

F.C. Muddles (Imp. 2/3/85). L.C.

JOCELYN, Major J. K. J.

Ca. Love at First Sight (R.A. Woolwich, 3/5/89). L.C.

Oa. Love's Magic (R.A. Woolwich, 18/2/90). L.C.
[Music by L. Zavertal.]

JOHN, GODFREY

C. Auntie's Motor (Manor, Hackney, 26/2/99). L.C.
[Written in collaboration with *C. WAR.*]

JOHNSON, EDWARD COCKBURN

D. A Double Life (Metro. Birkenhead, 11/4/92). L.C.

Bsq. The Mystic Ring (Pav. Birkenhead, 17/3/93).

JOHNSON, ELLEN

Ca. My Aunt Grumble (Brighton, 21/4/77). L.C.

JOHNSON, G. D.

F. Our Gal (Adel. 26/7/56). L.C. *Lacy.*

JOHNSON, HENRY T.

Ca. Love and Politics (O.C. 9/2/88).

F. Back in Five Minutes (Parkhurst, 16/2/91; Str. 22/4/91). L.C.

D. The Ferryman's Daughter (Lyr. Hammersmith, 31/7/91). L.C.
[Written in collaboration with *C. CORDINGLEY.*]

D. Loyal (Vaud. 9/8/94). L.C.

C. Q.Q. (P's. Bristol, 12/12/95; Terry's, 28/3/98). L.C.

C.D. Goodbye (Str. 21/5/96; Glo. 21/12/96, as *The Muff of the Regiment*). L.C.

C. That Couple from Cuba (Lyc. Edinburgh, 27/5/98). L.C.

P. Dick Whittington (Grand, Fulham, 24/12/98). See *E. C. MATTHEWS.*

JOHNSON, Miss S. A.

C.D. Caleb; or, The Curse (Terry's, 6/6/93, *mat.*). L.C.

JOHNSTON, J. R. H.

O. The Magic Fountain (St G. H. 1/2/94). L.C.
[Music by H. S. Moore.]

JOHNSTON, MAURICE

Oa. The Musical Village (Co-operative H. Morley, 28/12/93).

Oa. Agatha; or, The Lost Child of the Manor (Co-operative H. Morley, 30/4/94).

O. The Magic Cup (T.H. Morley, 21/10/95).

JOHNSTON, ROBERT

C.D. 'Twixt Love and Duty (Preston, 9/12/89). See *J. WORDEN.*

JOHNSTON, THOMAS P.

T. Patrick Hamilton. 12° 1882.

[*JOHNSTONE, ANNIE LEWIS*

M.D. On the Frontier (Shakespeare, L'pool. 30/3/91; Morton's, Greenwich, 27/7/91; Pav. 10/8/91). L.C.

JOHNSTONE, A. S.

O. The Spanish Bridal (Harborne and Edgbaston Inst. Birmingham, 14/12/83).
[Music by F. Robinson.]

JOHNSTONE, HORACE

D. The Black Boarder (Kilburn, 17/5/97). L.C.

JOHNSTONE, JOHN BEER

[For his earlier plays see iv, 333.]

D. Minnie Grey (Stand. 12/4/52). L.C.
D. The Betting Boy's Career (Qns. 13/9/52). See *C. S. JAMES*.
D. The House on the Bridge; or, The Storm, the Fire and the Ball (Stand. 1/11/52). L.C.
D. The Gipsey's Romance (Vic. 29/11/52).
D. The Gold Regions of Australia (Vic. 31/1/53).
D. Pop goes the Weasel (M'bone, 9/5/53).
D. Brother Bob (Sur. 31/10/53).
D. The Sailor of France; or, The Republicans of Brest (Sur. 28/11/53). L.C. *Lacy*.
D. Ben Bolt (Sur. 28/3/54). L.C. *Lacy*.
D. Jack and Jack's Brother (Edinburgh, 25/4/55).
D. Tufelhausen; or, The Legend of a Lawyer (Sur. 24/3/56). L.C.
D. The Pride of Poverty (Str. 16/2/57). See *B. BARNETT*.
D. Pedrillo; or, A Search for Two Fathers (M'bone, 16/11/57). L.C. *Lacy*.
Bsq. The Cooleen Drawn (Sur. 14/10/61). See *M. DUTNALL*.
D. Rat of Rat's Castle (Grec. 11/1/64).
D. The Coal Mine (Pav. 11/3/67).
D. Paved with Gold (C.L. 16/5/68). L.C. Vic. 11/9/58.
D. Oliver Twist (Sur. 18/5/68). L.C.
D. Bonnie Prince Charlie (E.L. 18/7/68).
D. Fannette; or, Up in the Dark (Pav. 24/10/68). L.C.
P. Jump a Little Wagtail; or, Harlequin 1, 2, 3 and the Magic Arrow (Bower, 26/12/68). L.C.
Ca. Seaweed Hall; or, Jack and Jill (Var. Hoxton, 14/3/70). L.C. as *S. H.; or, Patrician and Pensioners*.
M.D. A Romantic Tale (Alh. 7/8/71).
D. The Pearl of Paris (Alb. Portsmouth, 18/12/71).
D. The Old Mint (Grec. 1873). L.C. Grec. 26/2/73.
D. Balaclava (Stand. 10/6/78). L.C.
P. Shepherd's Star; or, Capricorne and the Plant Sprite (Brit. 26/12/79). L.C.
D. The Tiger of Mexico; or, A Rough Road to a Golden Land (Brit. 18/4/81). L.C.

JOHNSTONE, J. H.

Ca. Young Couples (Gai. 20/2/84). L.C.

JONES, Major —

O. Virginia (Swansea, 12/7/83).
[Music by J. Parry.]

JONES, A. C.

D. Elmine; or, Mother and Son (W. Hartlepool, 9/4/83). L.C.

JONES, C. FOSTER

F.C. Tom's Mother-in-Law (Corn Exchange, Swindon, 14/5/94). L.C.

JONES, E.

D.Sk. Satan (M.H. Bedford, 23/10/99). See *H. GRATTAN*.

JONES, E. B.

C. Newmarket (P's. Manchester, 22/6/96; O.C. 22/8/96). L.C. [Written in collaboration with *Mrs F. TAYLOR*.]

Oa. Toto and Sata (Grand, Leeds, 23/8/97). See *A. M. THOMPSON*.

JONES, E. J.

F. A Cure for Foolery (Vic. H. Walthamstow, 21/1/88). [Written in collaboration with *H. BRASHIER*.]

JONES, FRED

P. Cinderella (Qns. Crouch End, 24/12/98).

JONES, HENRY ARTHUR

D. Hearts of Oak; or, A Chip of the Old Block (Exeter, 29/5/79). L.C. *French*.

C.D. Harmony Restored (Grand, Leeds, 13/8/79; Str. 14/1/84, as *Harmony*; Lyc. New York, 5/92, as *The Organist*; Roy. 25/9/95). L.C. *Lacy*.

C. Elopement (Oxford, 19/8/79; Belfast, 16/8/80). L.C. *Lacy*.

D. A Drive in June. 8° 1879 [Ilfracombe; *priv.*].

F. A Clerical Error (Court, 13/10/79). L.C. *Lacy*.

C.D. It's Only Round the Corner (Exeter, 11/12/79).

Ca. A Garden Party. 8° 1880 [Ilfracombe; *priv.*].

C. Lady Caprice. 8° 1880 [Ilfracombe; *priv.*].

Ca. An Old Master (P'cess. 6/11/80). L.C. *Lacy*.

Ca. Humbug. 8° 1881 [Ilfracombe; *priv.*].

D. His Wife (S.W. 16/4/81). L.C.

C. Home Again (Oxford, 7/9/81). L.C.

Ca. A Bed of Roses (Glo. 26/1/82). L.C. *Lacy*.

Ca. The Wedding Guest. 8° 1882 [Ilfracombe; *priv.*].

D. The Silver King (P'cess. 16/11/82). L.C. *Lacy*. [Written in collaboration with *H. HERMAN*.]

D. Breaking a Butterfly (P's. 3/3/84). L.C. 8° [1884, *priv.*]. [Written in collaboration with *H. HERMAN*.]

D. Chatterton (P'cess. 22/5/84). See *H. HERMAN*.

D. Saints and Sinners (P.W. Greenwich, 17/9/84; Margate, 22/9/84; Vaud. 25/9/84). L.C. 8° 1891.

D. Hoodman Blind (P'cess. 18/8/85). L.C. *Lacy*. [Written in collaboration with *W. BARRETT*.]

R.D. The Lord Harry (P'cess. 18/2/86). L.C. [Written in collaboration with *W. BARRETT*.]

R.D. The Noble Vagabond (P'cess. 22/12/86). L.C.

D. Hard Hit (H. 17/1/87). L.C.

D. Heart of Hearts (Vaud. 3/11/87, *mat.*; Vaud. 10/11/87). L.C. Vaud. 6/4/87, as *Fair Play's a Jewel*.

D. Wealth (H. 27/4/89). L.C.

D. The Middleman (Shaft. 27/8/89). L.C. 8° [1907].

D. Judah (Shaft. 21/5/90). L.C. 8° 1894 [New York].

C. Sweet Will (New Club, C.G. 5/3/87; Shaft. 25/7/90, *mat.*). L.C. *Lacy*.
C.Sk. The Deacon (Shaft. 27/8/90, *mat.*). L.C. *Lacy*.
D. The Dancing Girl (H. 15/1/91). L.C. 8° [1907].
C. The Crusaders (Aven. 2/11/91). L.C. 8° 1893.
C.D. The Bauble Shop (Crit. 26/1/93). L.C. 8° [1893].
T. The Tempter (H. 20/9/93). L.C. 8° 1898.
C. The Masqueraders (St J. 28/4/94). L.C. 8° [1894, *priv.*]; 8° 1899.
C. The Case of Rebellious Susan (Crit. 3/10/94). L.C. 8° 1897.
D. Grace Mary. 8° [1895]; 8° 1915 [in *The Theatre of Ideas*].
C. The Triumph of the Philistines, and how Mr Jorgan preserved the morals of Market Pewbury under very trying circumstances (St J. 11/5/95). L.C. 8° 1899.
D. Michael and his Lost Angel (Lyc. 15/1/96). L.C. 8° 1896.
D. The Rogue's Comedy (Gar. 21/4/96). L.C. 8° 1898.
D. The Physician (Crit. 25/3/97). L.C. 8° 1899.
C. The Liars (Crit. 6/10/97). L.C. 8° 1901 [New York].
Ca. The Manœuvres of Jane (H. 29/10/98). L.C. 8° 1904.
D. Carnac Sahib (H.M. 12/4/99). L.C. 8° 1899.
[For his later plays see A. E. Morgan, *op. cit.* pp. 310–11.]

JONES, J. McLENNAN
C.Oa. The Major (Assembly H. Holywell, 8/4/90).

JONES, JOSEPH STEVENS
D. The Carpenter of Rouen; or, The Massacre of St Bartholomew (D.L. 3/3/53). *Lacy*.
D. The People's Lawyer. L.C. Str. 19/5/56. *Lacy*.

JONES, J. WILTON
Ext. The Little Wonder (Gravesend, 14/3/74).
Ca. After Marriage (Leeds, 30/4/75).
M.F. In Advance of the Times (Amphi. Leeds, 23/9/75). L.C.
Bsq. Jack Robinson Crusoe; or, The Good Friday that came on Saturday (Windsor, 14/10/76).
Ext. Cinderella; A Story of the Slip and the Slipper (Leicester, 3/10/78).
Ca. On an Island (Bradford, 8/3/79; Vaud. 4/2/82). *French*.
D. Christine (Tyne, Newcastle, 21/5/79). See *F. W. BROUGHTON*.
Ext. Cruel Carmen; or, The Demented Dragoon and the Terrible Toreador (P's. Manchester, 29/3/80). L.C. Grand, Leeds, 9/3/80.
Bsq. Jane Shore; or, The Fearful Penance and the Fatal Penny Roll (P'cess. L'pool, 16/8/80). L.C.
C.O. The King's Dragoons (Manchester, 1/11/80). L.C.
[Music by J. Crook.]
Ext. Young Dick Whittington (Leicester, 18/4/81). L.C. Manchester, 2/3/81.
D. The Trump Card (Grand, Leeds, 3/4/82). See *F. W. BROUGHTON*.
C.O. Merry Mignon; or, The Beauty and the Bard (Court, L'pool, 26/4/82). L.C.
[Music by J. Crook.]
F.C. What's the Odds? (Bolton, 1/5/82). L.C.
D. Recommended to Mercy (Harrowgate, 6/5/82; Dewsbury, 9/10/82; Pav. 2/7/83). L.C.

Ca. A First Experiment (Dewsbury, 10/10/82; Grand, Leeds, 14/3/83). L.C.

C. Fixed (Wigan, 12/3/83). L.C.

D. Haunted Lives (Hull, 7/4/84; Olym. 10/5/84; Stand. 2/12/95, as *The Woman in Black; or, H. L.*). L.C.

F. Fits and Starts (Gai. 2/5/85). L.C.
[Written in collaboration with *G. W. BROWNE.*]

Ext. Larks (Pav. Southport, 22/2/86; Grand, 29/3/86; Lyr. Hammersmith, 17/7/99, as *Larks in London*). L.C.
[Music by H. Emm.]

Bsq. Little Cinderella (Tyne, Newcastle, 25/6/87).

D. Kismet (Hull, 20/2/88). L.C.

D. Princess Diana (Hull, 4/2/89). L.C.

C.O. Belphegor (S. Shields, 26/10/89).
[Music by A. Christensen.]

D. A Yorkshire Lass (Olym. 18/2/91, *mat.*). L.C.

D. The Scapegoat (Glo. 7/7/91). L.C.

P. Little Boy Blue (D.L. 26/12/92). See *Sir A. HARRIS.*

M.F. Helen of Troy up-to-date; or, The Statue Shop (Pier, Folkestone, 22/5/93). L.C. as *The Statue Shop; or, Beautiful Helen of Troy.*
[Music by J. Crook.]

P. Dick Whittington and his Cat (Stand. 26/12/93). See *A. MELVILLE.*

O.Bsq. Crusoe the Cruiser (Parkhurst, 23/7/94). L.C.
[Music by A. Christensen.]

P. Aladdin and the Wonderful Lamp (Stand. 24/12/94).

P. Robinson Crusoe (Lyr. Hammersmith, 26/12/94). L.C.

P. The Babes in the Wood (Pav. 26/12/94). L.C.

Ca. In an Attic (St J. 25/3/95). L.C. *French.*

Duol. Woman's Proper Place (St J. 29/6/96). L.C. *French.*
[Written in collaboration with *G. WARDEN.*]

D. A Cruel City (Sur. 5/10/96). See *G. WARDEN.*

P. Aladdin (Metro. Camberwell, 26/12/96). L.C.
[Written in collaboration with *L. TOWNROW* and *J. B. MULHOLLAND.*]

P. Mother Goose (Stand. 26/12/96). L.C.

P. Sinbad (Stand. 27/12/97).
[Written in collaboration with *W. MELVILLE.*]

P. The Babes in the Wood (E.C. 24/12/98). L.C.

JONES, KENNEDY

F. My Collaborator (P.W. Birmingham, 8/3/92). L.C.

JONES, R. St CLAIR

Spec. The Bride of Golconda; or, The Genius of the Ring (Ast. 1/11/52). L.C.

JOPLING, Mrs

D. Affinities. 8° 1885. See *Mrs C. PRAED.*

JORDAN, LEOPOLD

D. A Woman's Revenge (Ladb. H. 18/3/82).

JOURDAIN, JOHN

D. Khartoum (Sanger's, 14/3/85). See *W. MUSKERRY.*

D. The Threatening Eye (P.W. Greenwich, 2/5/85). See *E. F. KNIGHT.*

F.Oa. Soft Soap (E.C. 29/9/88).
[Music by H. G. French.]

P. The Babes in the Wood; or, Baron the Knave, the Two Ruffians and a Fairy Hand at Nap (E.C. 24/12/88). L.C.
[Music by H. G. French.]

D. The Rose of Devon; or, The Spanish Armada (E.C. 18/2/89). L.C.

KAPPEY, J. A.
Oa. The Wager (Marine, Chatham, 20/6/71; Gai. 23/11/72). L.C.

KAY, C. B.
Ext. An Altogether Moral Trilby (Alex. H. Newton Abbot, 11/2/96).

KAYE, ARTHUR
O. Midsummer Eve (Albemarle College, Beckenham, 7/4/93).
[Music by W. Boyd.]

KEAN, LESLIE
D. Sons of France (P.W. Wolverhampton, 8/12/73).

KEAN, L. G.
D. Crime; or, The Black Heart (Vic. 6/8/77).

KEAST, G. V.
Bsq. The Forty Thieves up-to-date (Grand, Stonehouse, Plymouth, 16/6/90).

KEATING, Miss
P. Little Bo Peep (Brighton, 24/10/60).

KEEBLE, Mrs
Ca. The Baronet's Wager (Drill H. Peterborough, 25/6/69).

KEELING, HENRY
C.D. Marriage (Court, 7/6/92). See *B. THOMAS*.

KEEN, HERBERT
C.D. The Broken Melody (P.W. 28/7/92). L.C.
[Written in collaboration with *J. LEADER*.]

KEENE, EDWIN
Bsq. Little Ben Bolt; or, The Meritorious Maiden and the Millicious Milliner (Subscription Ground, Gravesend, 24/6/79; Colchester, 2/8/80).

KEITH, HERBERT
D. The Note of Hand (Vaud. 13/1/91). L.C.
D. Hush Money (Terry's, 23/6/92, *mat.*). L.C.

KEITH, ROYSTON
D. Elaine (Kilburn, 26/6/90; Str. 5/5/98). L.C. Terry's, 23/6/92.
Ca. All Change Here (Eastbourne, 8/8/98). L.C.

KEMBLE, FRANCES ANNE [*Mrs BUTLER*]
[For her earlier plays see iv, 335.]
D. Mademoiselle de Belle Isle (H. 3/10/64). L.C. 8° 1863.

KEMPE, ALFRED
D. Lady Isabel (Holborn, 16/1/73).

KENNE, MILNER
D. Fettered Freedom (Vaud. 28/9/87, *mat.*). L.C.
[Written in collaboration with *C. H. STEPHENSON*.]

KENNEDY, CHARLES RANN

[For an earlier play see iv, 336.]

T. Francis Beaumont. 8° 1860 [Birmingham].

KENNEDY, H. ARTHUR

F.C. The New Wing (Str. 27/5/90, *mat.*; Str. 9/1/92). L.C.

C.D. A Throw of the Dice (Str. 27/5/90, *mat.*). L.C.

Ca. Scholar's Mate (T.H. Chelsea, 25/4/93).

F.C. The Wrong Girl (Str. 21/11/94). L.C.

KENNEDY, JOHN

Ca. Good for Both (O.H. Londonderry, 11/2/87; P.W. Southampton, 5/5/88, *mat.*).

F.C. In for a Penny (P.W. Southampton, 5/5/88, *mat.*). L.C.

KENNEDY, J. P.

M.C. Pa's Odd Trick; or, Hero and Error Win (Nottingham, 4/2/97, *copy.*).

[Music by John Armstrong.]

KENNERLEY, JUBA

C.O. Melita, the Parsee's Daughter (Nov. 9/12/82). L.C.

[Music by H. Pontet.]

KENNEY, C. H.

D.Sk. College Chums (Bijou, 27/3/95).

KENNEY, CHARLES LAMB

C.O. The Mock Doctor (C.G. 27/2/65). L.C. 8° 1865.

C.O. L'Africaine (C.G. 21/10/65). 8° [1865].

[Music by G. Meyerbeer.]

F. Wanted, Husbands for Six (D.L. 11/3/67). L.C.

Ext. The Grand Duchess of Gerolstein (C.G. 18/11/67). L.C. 8° [1867].

Ext. Valentine and Orson; or, Harlequin the Big Bear and the Little Fairy (Holborn, 24/12/67).

C.O. The Princess of Trebizonde (Gai. 16/4/70). L.C.

F. Our Autumn Manœuvres (Adel. 21/10/71). L.C.

C.O. La Belle Hélène (Gai. 23/10/71). L.C.

C.O. The Wonderful Duck (O.C. 31/5/73). L.C.

Ca. Maids of Honour (Mirror, 24/4/75). L.C.

C.O. The Mock Doctor (Grand, 24/11/90). See *R. TEMPLE.*

KENNEY, JAMES

[For his earlier plays see iv, 336–8.]

C. London Pride; or, Living for Appearances (St J. 9/11/59). L.C.

KENNION, Mrs

D. Nina; or, The Story of a Heart (Wigan, 13/4/85; Str. 13/7/87, *mat.*). L.C.

KENYON, J. REDFERN

C. A Leap Year's Comedy (Muncaster, Bootle, 23/10/99).

KERR, FREDERICK

Duol. Leap Year (Ladb. H. 8/92; Terry's, 10/11/93). L.C. *French.*

KERR, JOHN

[For his earlier plays see iv, 338.]

D. Rip Van Winkle; or, A Legend of Sleepy Hollow (W.L.). *Lacy.*

KILLICK, J. MORTON

D. A Cruel Wrong (Cabinet, 28/10/69, *amat.*).
Bsq. Don Quixote (Cabinet, 28/10/69, *amat.*).
F. In the Stationery Line (Cabinet, 19/2/70, *amat.*).
C. At Stake (St G. 26/10/70, *amat.*). L.C.
Bsq. The Norman Invasion (St G. 26/10/70, *amat.*). L.C.
D. Mistaken (St G. 15/11/72). L.C.
D. Polyphonus; or, Experientia docet (St G. 15/11/72, *amat.*). L.C.
D. Right (St G. 10/2/81).

KILMARNOCK, Lord

C.D. The Collaborators (Mat. 6/7/97). L.C.

KILMOREY, The Earl of

F. The Recruiting Party (Shrewsbury, 14/1/95). L.C.

KILPATRICK, JAMES A.

D.Sk. An Erring Sister (Gai. Hastings, 5/11/92). L.C.

KIMM, H.

C.D. For the Old Love's Sake (Gai. Hastings, 17/3/84). See *T. S. ROGERS.*

KING, A. FITZ

D. An Old Song (Great H. Tunbridge Wells, 2/8/94). See *F. WILLS.*

KING, H. N.

D. The Angel's Whisper; or, The Spirit of Peace (Bath, 20/2/69).

KINGDOM, J. M.

D. The Old Ferry House; or, The Midnight Crime. L.C. C.L. 25/2/50.
Bsq. The Three Princes (Sur. 1/4/50). L.C. *Lacy.*
Spec. Tancred; or, The Triumph of the Crusaders (Ast. 1/3/52). L.C. *Lacy.*
D. Marcoretti (Grec. 30/5/53). *Lacy.*
Ext. The Fountain of Beauty; or, The King, the Princess and the Genie (D.L. 5/9/53). L.C. *Lacy.*
D. The Old House on Thames Street (Brit. 15/9/61). *Lacy.*
D. Madeline. *Lacy.*
D. Giralda. *Lacy.*

KINGSLEY, CHARLES

M.Play. Two Rubies (Adel. L'pool, 12/1/94). L.C.

KINGSLEY, ELLIS

Duol. Accepted by Proxy (Steinway H. 8/6/93). *French.*
C.D. His Treasures (Brompton Hospital, 9/3/97, *amat.*). L.C.
F. Lizer's New Lodger (Brompton Hospital, 9/3/97, *amat.*).
Duol. The Other Woman (H.M. 11/11/97). *French.*

KINGSTON, GERTRUDE

C. A Matchmaker (Shaft. 9/5/96). See *C. GRAVES.*

KINGSTON, HOLMES

C. For Himself Alone (Ladb. H. 7/4/88).

KINGSTON, W. BEATTY

C.O. The Poet's Dream (Roy. Glasgow, 18/2/98). L.C.
[Music by A. Thomas.]

KINGTHORNE, MARK

Ext. Rival Artistes; or, Shakers and Quakers (Sur. 14/5/73). L.C.

Bsq. Amy Robsart (Norwich, 10/5/80).

KIRKE, F. J.

M.C. Our Sailor Lad (Muncaster, Bootle, 6/5/95; Nov. 13/1/96). L.C. [Music by G. Dixon.]

KIRKE, FRED

M.D. In Old Madrid (Garston, 23/1/97, *copy.*; Alb. Gainsborough, 17/2/98; Stratford, 13/11/99). L.C.

[Written in collaboration with *W. T. CLIFFORD.*]

KITTS, C. S.

R.D. Bitter Sweet (Bristol, 29/10/95, *copy.*). L.C. *French.*

[*KLEIN, CHARLES H.*

C. Truthful James (Gt Yarmouth, 24/9/94). See *J. MORTIMER.*

C. A Night in Paris (Newcastle, 13/4/96; Vaud. 29/4/96, as *A Night Out*). L.C.

C.D. Dr Belgraff (Vaud. 31/10/96, *copy.*). L.C.

C.O. El Capitan (Lyr. 10/7/99).

[Music by J. P. Sousa.]

C.O. The Mystical Miss (Com. 13/12/99). L.C.

[Music by J. P. Sousa.]

KNIGHT, A.

Ca. Love Limited; or, A Provoking Predicament (T.H. Reading, 10/11/94). L.C.

[Music by E. W. Brown.]

KNIGHT, A. F.

F. Well Played; or, The Mayor's Dilemma (T.H. Uxbridge, 28/1/88). L.C. *French.*

KNIGHT, C. J.

Oa. A Bath Roll (Deal, Kent, 26/4/94, *amat.*).

KNIGHT, E. F.

D. The Threatening Eye (P.W. Greenwich, 12/5/85). L.C.

[Written in collaboration with *J. JOURDAIN.*]

KNIGHT, F. HAMILTON

Ca. The Postscript (P.W. 14/2/88, *mat.*; Vaud. 24/8/89). L.C. *French.*

C.D. Success (O.H. Cheltenham, 29/2/92; E.C. 11/4/92). L.C.

KNIGHT, GEORGE

C.D. A Tangle (Shakespeare, L'pool, 26/7/94). L.C.

KNIGHT, RIDER

D. John Lester, Parson (Lyr. 20/1/92).

[Written in collaboration with *L. FOSTER.*]

[*KNOBLAUCH, EDWARD* [*EDWARD KNOBLOCK*]

F.C. The Club Baby (Lyr. Ealing, 19/9/95). See *L. STERNER.*

[Several later plays.]

KNOWLES, EUSTON

D. Condemned; or, £1000 Reward (Castleford, 25/8/87).

KNOWLES, JAMES SHERIDAN

[For his earlier plays see iv, 338–9.]

D. Alexina (Str. 21/5/66). L.C.

KNOWLES, JOHN

D. The Enchanter's Slave; or, The Magic Rose. L.C. Manchester, 7/5/50.

D. The Jewess. L.C. Manchester, 7/5/50.

KNOX, J. ARMORY

C.D. Shane-na-Lawn (Alex. L'pool, 22/4/89). See *J. C. ROCHE.*

F. A Stuffed Dog (Park H. Camden Town, 2/11/89, *copy.*). L.C.
[Written in collaboration with *E. ATWELL.*]

KORRELL, PAUL

D. Deadwood Dick (Pav. 12/3/94). L.C.

KRUSARD, EDWARD

C.O. Lelamine (Gai. Hastings, 14/2/89). L.C.
[Music by A. R. Moulton.]

KUMMER, CLARE

C.O. Captain Kidd; or, The Buccaneers (D.Y. 11/7/98, *copy.*). L.C.

LABOUCHERE, HENRY

D. Fatherland (Qns. 3/1/78). L.C.

LACY, J. W.

D. Destroyed by Drink (Qns. Dublin, 25/8/79).

LACY, MICHAEL ROPHINO

[For his earlier plays see iv, 340.]

D. Doing for the Best (S.W. 13/11/61). L.C. *Lacy.*

D. Alice Wingold; or, The Pearl of London City (Ast. 5/5/62). L.C.

D. Primrose Hall (Sur. 6/4/63). L.C.
[A revised version of the above.]

F. Doing my Uncle (Sur. 8/9/66). *Lacy.*

C.D. Wealth (Roy. 8/10/70). L.C.

LADISLAW, WILL

C. Peterkin (Roy. 4/9/93). L.C.
[Music by L. Camerana.]

LAELAND, H. J.

F.C. The Medical Student (Str. 4/7/93). See *B. FRANCES.*

LAIDLAW, CHARLES W.

Bsq. Seraphina the Fair (P.H. Southend, 26/12/74).

LAIDLAW, F. ALLAN

D. The Sensualist (O.H. Northampton, 18/12/91). See *M. BUENN.*

LAKE, ERNEST

M.C. Sweepstakes (Terry's, 21/5/91, *mat.*). L.C.

LALLEN, J. P.

D. Judge Lynch (Brierly Hill, 10/6/97). L.C.

LAMB, THOMAS

T. The Life and Death of Sir William Wallace. 12° 1866 [Carluke].

LAMPARD, EDWARD J.

D. A Mad Passion (Castleford, 23/1/88). L.C.

D. The Wealth of the World (Blyth, 29/6/91).

M.D. The Red Signal (Clarence, Pontypridd, 17/6/92, *copy.*; Birkenhead, 17/10/92). L.C.

D. Between the Lights (Muncaster, Bootle, 17/12/94). L.C.

LANCASTER-WALLIS, ELLEN

D. For Wife and State (Lyc. Edinburgh, 19/10/83; Belfast, 21/10/84, as *A Bitter Love*). L.C.
[Written in collaboration with *J. W. BOULDING*.]
D. The Pharisee (Shaft. 17/11/90). See *T. M. WATSON*.
D. My Son and I (Steinway H. 25/5/94).
Duol. Cissy's Engagement (Steinway H. 19/11/95).
D. The Wand of Wedlock (Grand, Cardiff, 13/4/96). L.C.
[Written in collaboration with *H. MACPHERSON*.]
F.C. An Amateur Wife (Crit. 27/4/97).
Ca. Cupid in Ermine (P'cess. of W. Kennington, 27/3/99). L.C.
D.Sk. Summer Clouds (Grand, Wolverhampton, 15/4/99; Grand, 17/4/99). L.C.

LANDECK, BENJAMIN

Ca. At Mammon's Shrine (O.H. Leicester, 30/5/87). L.C.
D. Vultures (Star, Wolverhampton, 20/2/88). L.C.
C. With Heart and Hand (Pastoral Players, Highgate, 21/7/88).
[Written in collaboration with *E. E. NORRIS*.]
M.D. My Jack (Sur. 9/9/89). L.C.
F.C. Jones (Bury, 16/10/91). See *A. SHIRLEY*.
D. A Lion's Heart (Parkhurst, 25/7/92). See *A. SHIRLEY*.
D. Midnight (Sur. 19/12/92). See *A. SHIRLEY*.
Bsq. Cavalearyer Costercana; or, Never Introduce your Dinah to a Pal (Edmonton, 14/6/93). L.C.
[Written in collaboration with *E. TURNER*.]
D. To Call her Mine (Sur. 18/12/93). L.C.
D. A Guilty Mother (Hull, 8/1/94; Pav. 9/4/94). L.C.
D. The River of Life (Grand, Hull, 24/2/94). See *A. SHIRLEY*.
M.D. A Fight for Freedom (Aquar. Brighton, 28/5/94).
[Written in collaboration with *A. SHIRLEY*. Music by C. Vernon and E. Ward.]
D. A British Hero (Assembly R. Worthing, 12/7/94; O.H. Coventry, 29/8/98, as *A Soldier and a Man*; Shakespeare, Clapham, 5/9/98). L.C.
D. A Daughter's Honour (Sur. 17/12/94). L.C.
[Written in collaboration with *A. SHIRLEY*.]
D. Tommy Atkins (Pav. 16/9/95). See *A. SHIRLEY*.
D. Jack Tar (Pav. 12/10/96). See *A. SHIRLEY*.
D. A Hue and Cry (Pav. 26/4/97). See *A. SHIRLEY*.
D. Women and Wine (Pav. 11/10/97; P'cess. 8/3/99). L.C.
[Written in collaboration with *A. SHIRLEY*.]
D. Going the Pace (Star, Wolverhampton, 24/8/98). See *A. SHIRLEY*.
D. A King of Fools (Grand, 25/9/99). See *H. J. W. DAM*.

LANDER, CHARLES

C.D. The Advocate (T.H. Kilburn, 3/12/86). L.C.
D. At Bay (Ladb. H. 9/4/88; Nov. 20/4/96). L.C.
[Written in collaboration with *I. L. CASSILIS*.]
D. Vida (Ladb. H. 12/10/91). See *I. L. CASSILIS*.

LANDER, GEORGE

D. The Verdict of the World (Brit. 5/8/72; Albion, 22/2/75, as *Inch Verra*). L.C.

P. The Babes in the Wood; or, The Little Old Woman who lived in a Shoe (S.W. 26/12/73). L.C.
D. Bleak House (Pav. 25/3/76). L.C.
D. The Trail of the Serpent (E.C. 4/8/79). L.C.
D. A Bitter Wrong; or, A Wife in England, No Wife in France (Stand. 14/4/84). L.C.
[Written in collaboration with *J. T. DOUGLASS.*]
D. Not Alone (Grand, Birmingham, 12/10/85; Grand, 19/10/85). L.C.
[Written in collaboration with *Mrs WELDON.*]
D. The Land of Gold; or, Life in England and California (E.C. 25/2/88). L.C.
M.D. The Great World of London (Stand. 31/10/98). L.C.
[Written in collaboration with *W. MELVILLE.*]

LANE, FRED
F. The Medico (Ladb. H. 7/5/94).

LANE, Mrs S.
D. Taken from Memory (Brit. 10/11/73). L.C.
D. Dolores (Brit. 6/4/74). L.C.
D. Albert de Rosen (Brit. 30/8/75). L.C.
D. The Faithless Wife (Brit. 15/4/76). L.C.
D. St Bartholomew; or, A Queen's Love (Brit. 21/5/77). L.C.
D. The Cobbler's Daughter (Brit. 23/3/78).
D. Red Josephine; or, Woman's Vengeance (Brit. 5/11/80). L.C.
D. Devotion; or, The Priceless Wife (Brit. 14/3/81). L.C.

LANE, W.
D. Oakwood Hall; or, A Curious Will (Worcester, 1/4/71).

LANE-FOX, FLORENCE
D. The Jew's Eye (Vic. H. Bayswater, 4/6/89).

LANG, JOHN
D. Plot and Passion (Olym. 17/10/53). See *T. TAYLOR.*

LANGBRIDGE, Rev. FREDERICK
Bsq. Fair Rosamond's Bower; or, The Monarch, the Maiden, the Maze and the Mixture. *Lacy.*

LANGE, FRANK
Ca. A Strange Guest (Glo. 16/4/92). L.C.

LANGFORD, —
D. Like and Unlike (Adel. 9/4/56). L.C.
[Written in collaboration with *W. J. SORRELL.*]

LANGFORD, JOHN ALFRED
D. The King and the Commoner. 8° 1870 [Birmingham; *priv.*].

LANGLOIS, H. A.
D. Spottie, the Terror of Wearside (Lyc. Sunderland, 20/8/77). L.C.
C.D. Love's Retribution (Middlesborough, 4/12/82). L.C. Dundee, 15/11/82.

"*LANKESTER, E. G.*" See *ROBERT REECE*

LANNER, KATTI
Bal. Red Riding Hood (C.P. 16/6/92).
[Music by O. Barrett.]

LART, JOHN
C.D. Faith; or, Eddication and Rights (Gai. 27/8/84).
R.D. The Monk's Room (P.W. 20/12/87, *mat.*; Olym. 18/4/88, *mat.*; Glo. 2/10/88). L.C.
D. A Court of Honour (Roy. 18/5/97). L.C.
[Written in collaboration with *C. H. DICKINSON.*]

LASHBROOKE, H.
D. At the Sword Point (Norwich, 9/6/84). L.C.
[Written in collaboration with *R. D. PERRY.*]

LATHAIR, HENRY
Oa. John and Angelina (T.H. Kilburn, 16/4/90).
[Music by L. Elliot.]

LATHAM, FRANK
D. With Flying Colours (Adel. 19/8/99). See *Sir S. HICKS.*

LATHAM, GRACE
O. Florian (Nov. 14/7/86). L.C.
[Music by I. Walter.]
Monol. Beside a Cradle (Willis R. 18/4/88).

LATIMER, FRANK
Oa. Love and Law (Lyr. 4/3/91). L.C.
[Music by I. Caryll.]
C. The Anonymous Letter (Lyr. 5/5/91). See *M. AMBIENT.*

LATIMER, Miss K. M.
Ca. Cousin Charlie (Devonshire Park, Eastbourne, 9/2/89). L.C.

LAUN, H. T. VAN
D. The Royal Berkshire Regiment (Com. 29/6/86, *mat.*). L.C.
[Written in collaboration with *F. REMO.*]

LAURI, CHARLES, Jr.
F.C. As in a Glass (O.C. 17/10/87). See *G. H. RODWELL.*

LAURI, EDWARD
F.C. His Lordship's Birthday (Parkhurst, 19/3/94). See *F. RAPHAEL.*

LAVINGTON, W. F.
D. The Puritan's Daughter (Bijou, 8/3/75).

LAW, ARTHUR
M.Ca. The Happy Bungalow (St G.). L.C. St G. 5/6/77. *French.*
Ca. An Artful Automaton (St G.). L.C. St G. 27/6/78. *French.*
[Written in collaboration with *K. HALL.*]
Fairy Play. Enchantment. L.C. St G. 6/12/78. *French.*
M.Ca. Castle Botherem (St G.). L.C. St G. 13/1/80. *French.*
[Written in collaboration with *H. CLARKE.*]
M.Ca. A Flying Visit (St G.). L.C. St G. 14/5/80. See *R. C. GRAIN.*
M.Ca. A Merry Christmas (St G. 27/12/80). *French.*
[Music by K. Hall.]
M.Sk. All at Sea (St G. 28/2/81). L.C. *French.*
[Music by C. Grain.]
M.Ca. A Bright Idea (St G. 30/5/81). L.C. *French.*
[Music by A. Cecil.]
M.Ca. Cherry Tree Farm (St G. 30/5/81). L.C. *French.*
[Music by H. Clarke.]

M.Ca. The Head of the Pole (St G. 28/2/82). L.C. *French.*
[Music by E. Fanning.]

M.Ca. Nobody's Fault (St G. 5/6/82). L.C.
[Music by H. Clarke.]

M.F. Mr Guffin's Elopement (Alex. L'pool, 29/9/82; Toole's, 7/10/82). L.C.
[Written in collaboration with *G. GROSSMITH.*]

C.D. Hope (Stand. 2/10/82; P.W. L'pool, 25/9/91, as *Major Hope*; Vaud. 11/2/92). L.C.

Vaud. A Strange Host; or, A Happy New Year (St G. 26/12/82). *French.*
[Music by K. Hall.]

Ca. The Happy Return (Court, 9/1/83). L.C. *French.*

M.Ca. Treasure Trove (St G. 6/6/83). L.C. *French.*
[Music by A. J. Caldicott.]

M.Ca. A Moss Rose Rent (St G. 17/12/83). L.C. *French.*
[Music by A. J. Caldicott.]

F.C. A Mint of Money (Toole's, 10/1/84). L.C.

Vaud. A Double Event (St G. 18/2/84).
[Written in collaboration with *A. REED*. Music by C. Grain.]

M.Ca. A Terrible Fright (St G. 18/6/84). L.C. *French.*
[Music by C. Grain.]

M.Ca. Old Knockles (St G. 24/11/84). L.C. *French.*
[Music by A. J. Caldicott.]

Oa. A Peculiar Case (St Leonards, 2/12/84; St G. 8/12/84). L.C. *French.*
[Music by G. Grossmith.]

Ext. The Great Taykin (Toole's, 30/4/85).
[Music by G. Grossmith.]

M.Ca. Chirruper's Fortune (Portsmouth, 31/8/85). L.C.

C.D. After Long Years (Torquay, 20/10/86). See *Mrs H. PURVIS.*

C. Gladys; or, The Golden Key (Str. 1/12/86, *mat.*; O.H. Leicester, 2/4/88, as *The Golden Key*; Aven. 25/8/88). L.C.

D. The Mystery of a Hansom Cab (P'cess. 23/2/88). L.C.
[Written in collaboration with *F. HUME.*]

Oa. John Smith (P.W. 28/1/89). L.C.
[Music by A. J. Caldicott.]

Oa. All Abroad (P.W. 21/2/90). L.C.
[Music by A. J. Caldicott.]

D. Dick Venables (Shaft. 5/4/90). L.C.

F. The Judge (Terry's, 24/7/90). L.C.

F. Culprits (P.W. L'pool, 29/8/90; Terry's, 5/3/91). L.C.

Ca. In Three Volumes (P.W. 6/1/93).

Oa. The Magic Opal (Lyr. 19/1/93; P.W. 11/4/93, as *The Magic Ring*). L.C.
[Music by Señor Albeniz.]

F.C. The Boy (Devonshire Park, Eastbourne, 1/2/94; Terry's, 21/2/94, as *The New Boy*). L.C.

F.C. The Ladies' Idol (Bournemouth, 28/3/95; Vaud. 18/4/95). L.C.

D. The Sea Flower (Com. 5/3/98). L.C.

C.D. A Showman's Sweetheart (Qns. Crouch End, 29/8/98). L.C.
[Music by G. Byng.]

D. A Night Surprise. *French.*

Ca. A Day in Boulogne. *French.*

LAWRANCE, F.

Bsq. Kenilworth (Str. 27/12/58). See ***A. HALLIDAY.***

LAWRENCE, EWERETTA

C. On 'Change; or, The Professor's Venture (Str. 1/7/85; Toole's, 22/8/85). L.C. *French.*

D. Isofel (Ipswich, 2/2/87). L.C.

D. Jess (Adel. 25/3/90, *mat.*). L.C.

[Written in collaboration with *J. J. BISGOOD.*]

LAWRENCE, F.

M.C. Our Servant Girl (Edmonton, 15/6/96). L.C.

[Written in collaboration with *C. A. VANE.* Music by J. L. S. Moss and J. S. Baker. Title altered to *Matilda, Our Servant Girl,* 25/7/1913.]

LAWRENCE, S. BOYLE

Ca. Her Own Rival (O.C. 13/4/89). See *F. W. BROUGHTON.*

C.D. A Promise (Glo. 29/10/89). L.C.

Ext. Amorel of Lyonnesse (O.C. 30/12/90). See *W. H. BROWN.*

C.D. Pretence (St G. 7/5/91, *amat.*).

Ext. Cinderella the Second (Bijou, 18/2/93). L.C.

"*LAWRENCE, SLINGSBY.*" See *G. H. LEWES*

LAWRENCE, WOODS

C.D. Rushford's Last Ruse (Greenwich, 21/10/78). L.C.

C.D. Hearts are Trumps (Huddersfield, 27/3/79). L.C.

F. Perfidious Robinson (Stand. 31/3/82). L.C.

D. Deadly Weapons (Gt Yarmouth, 9/7/84).

D. The Scapegoat (Huddersfield, 27/1/90).

C.D. An Honest Living (O.H. Wakefield, 13/3/91).

LAWSON, ENNIS

D. Peel Castle in the Olden Time (Barrow-in-Furness, 19/9/73).

LAYTON, G. M.

Bsq. Chrystaline (K.X. 6/3/71). L.C.

Ext. The Marble Maiden; or, Zampa in Miniature (Roy. 24/7/73). L.C.

Ext. Melusine the Enchantress (Holborn, 17/10/74). L.C.

M.F. Eighteen Years in One Hour (Alex. 15/2/75). L.C.

Oa. Liline and Valentin (Gai. 13/9/75).

C.O. The Duke's Daughter (Roy. 10/1/76). L.C.

Bsq. The Gwilty Governess and the Downey Doctor (Ch.X. 8/5/76). L.C.

LEACH, RICHARD

Ca. In the Wrong Box (Lowestoft, 4/1/89).

"*LEADER, JAMES*" [*J. T. TANNER*]

C.D. The Broken Melody (P.W. 28/7/92). See *H. KEEN.*

LEATHES, EDMUND

D. For King and Country (Gai. 1/5/83). L.C.

D. The Actor's Wife (St J. Manchester, 24/10/84). L.C.

LE BLONDE, H. M.

D. The Ocean Waif (St J. Wrexham, 16/5/93). See *G. TEMPLE.*

LE CLERCQ, PIERRE

C. Croquet (Cavenish Square Assembly R. 19/11/68, *amat.*).

C.D. The Love Story (Str. 23/5/88, *mat.*). L.C.

D. Illusion (Str. 3/7/90, *mat.*). L.C.

D. This Woman and That (Glo. 2/8/90, *mat.*). L.C.

D. The Rule of Three (Shaft. 30/6/91, *mat.*). L.C.

LEE, HAROLD

Ca. A Mutual Misunderstanding (P.W. L'pool, 31/1/76). L.C.

Ca. On the Indian Ocean (Alex. L'pool, 11/3/78). L.C.

C.O. The Happy Valley (P.H. Warrington, 10/2/80). [Music by T. M. Pattison.]

LEE, KENNETH

D. Whiter than Snow (O.C. 25/6/85). L.C.

LEE, NELSON

[For his earlier plays see iv, 342–3.]

P. Knife, Fork and Spoon; or, Harlequin Breakfast, Dinner, Tea and Supper. L.C. C.L. 10/12/50.

P. Harlequin Alfred the Great; or, The Magic Banjo and the Mystic Raven (M'bone, 26/12/50). L.C. *Lacy*.

P. Harlequin and O'Donoghue; or, The White Horse of Killarney (Ast. 26/12/50). L.C. *Lacy*.

P. Industry and Idleness; or, Harlequin Little Tom Tucker. L.C. Eff. 18/12/51.

P. Harlequin Hogarth (D.L. 26/12/51). See *J. M. MORTON*.

P. Red Rufus; or, Harlequin Fact, Fiction and Fancy (Olym. 26/12/51). L.C.

F. Mr and Mrs Briggs (Ast. 26/12/51). See *G. H. RODWELL*.

P. Harlequin Fortunio and his Horse Comrade (Ast. 27/12/52). L.C.

P. King Emerald; or, Harlequin's Crystal Palace in Fairy Land (C.L. 27/12/52). L.C.

P. Nell Gwynne; or, Harlequin Merry Monarch (Adel. 27/12/52). L.C.

P. Romeo and Juliet; or, Harlequin Queen Mab and the World of Dreams (Olym. 27/12/52). L.C.

P. Billy Button's Journey to Brentford; or, Harlequin and the Ladies' Favourite (Ast. 26/12/53). L.C.

P. Harlequin Humming Top (D.L. 26/12/53). See *E. L. BLANCHARD*.

P. Harlequin King Ugly Mug; or, My Lady Lee of Old London Bridge (M'bone, 26/12/53). L.C.

P. The Ocean Queen and the Sleeping Beauty of the Deep; or, Harlequin and the Magic Branch (C.L. 26/12/53). L.C.

Spec. A Tale of the Spanish War (Ast. 17/4/54). L.C.

P. Young Norval of the Grampian Hills; or, Harlequin Lord Ullin's Daughter (M'bone, 26/12/54). L.C.

P. William II and ye Fayre Maid of Harrow (C.L. 26/12/57).

LEE, NELSON, Jr.

D. A Woman of the World. L.C. C.L. 25/9/58.

M.D. The Star of the Woodlands (C.L. 11/3/61). L.C.

D. Caught at Last (C.L. 3/63). L.C.

P. King Flame and Queen Pearly-drop; or, Harlequin Simple Simon and the Pretty Little Mermaid at the Bottom of the Sea (C.L. 26/12/65). L.C.

P. Ding Dong Bell, Pussy's in the Well (C.L. 26/12/66). L.C.
Ent. Derby Day (Pav. 9/2/67).
D. The Sin of a Life (Vic. 28/9/67).
P. Wat Tyler; or, Harlequin Love, War and Peace (C.L. 24/12/67). L.C.
P. Bluff King Hal; or, Harlequin Anne Boleyn and the Jolly Miller of the River Dee (Pav. 26/12/68).
P. Sinbad the Sailor; or, Harlequin Navigator and the Great Roc of the Diamond Valley (S.W. 24/12/70). L.C.
C.O. La Fille de Mme Angot (L'pool, 23/2/74).
F. M.D.; or, Sweets and Bitters (L'pool, 7/3/74).
D. Lot No. 1; or, The Man in Possession (L'pool, 5/10/74).
Ext. The Blighted Bachelors (L'pool, 29/3/75).

LEE, RICHARD
C. Ordeal by Touch (Qns. 4/5/72). L.C.
D. Chivalry (Glo. 13/9/73). L.C.
Ca. Home for Home (Vaud. 16/8/79). L.C.
D. Branded (P'cess. 2/4/81). L.C.
C.D. Ariadne (O.C. 8/2/88). See *Mrs C. PRAED.*
D. The Accuser (Margate, 29/9/90). L.C.

LEE-BENNETT, HERBERT
Ca. Boodles (Richmond, 5/5/94). L.C.

LEEDS, A.
C.O. The Minkalay (Metro. Devonport, 10/12/96, *copy.*).
[Written in collaboration with *G. READE.*]

LEES, SYDNEY
M.C. The Magic Love Philtre (St Matthews Parish R. Upper Clapton, 20/11/96).
[Music by R. Brown.]

LEFEBRE, J. G.
C. Knight against Rook (Gai. 23/7/86). See *O. DOVE.*

LEGG, F. W.
O. Queen of the May (Argyle, Birkenhead, 28/7/96). L.C.
[Music by Sir Sterndale Bennett.]

LEGGE, ROBERT GEORGE
F. The Fay o' the Fern (New, Oxford, 4/2/93; Com. 6/3/93, *mat.*). L.C.

LEHMANN, R. C.
C.O. His Majesty (Sav. 20/2/97). See *F. C. BURNAND.*

LEIFCHILD, FRANK
D. The Buried Titan. 8° 1859.

LEIGH, AGNES
F. No. 17. *French.*
Ca. Contradictions. *French.*
Ca. A Lady in Search of an Heiress. *French.*

LEIGH, CHANDOS
Ext. The Musical Clock (Stoneleigh Abbey, 22/1/83, *amat.*).

LEIGH, E. M.
Monol. Last Act (T.H. St Andrews, 2/11/99). L.C.

LEIGH, EUSTON

D. The Duchess of Coolgardie (D.L. 19/9/96). L.C.
[Written in collaboration with *C. CLARE*.]

LEIGH, HENRY S.

C.O. Falsacappa; or, The Brigands (Glo. 22/4/71). L.C.
[Music by J. Offenbach.]

C.O. Le Roi Carotte (Alh. 3/6/72). L.C. 8° [1872].
[Music by J. Offenbach.]

C.O. The Bridge of Sighs (St J. 18/11/72). L.C.
[Music by J. Offenbach.]

Ext. The White Cat (Qns. 2/12/75). L.C.

C.O. Le Voyage dans la Lune (Alh. 15/4/76). L.C.
[Music by J. Offenbach.]

C.O. Fatinitza (Alh. 20/6/78). L.C. 8° 1878.
[Music by F. Von Suppé.]

C.O. The Great Casimir (Gai. 27/9/79). L.C.

C.O. La Petite Mademoiselle (Alh. 6/10/79). See *R. REECE*.

C.O. Lurette (Aven. 24/3/83). See *F. DESPREZ*.

C.O. Prince Methuselem (Nov. 19/5/83). L.C.
[Music by J. Strauss.]

Oa. Cinderella; A Little Opera for Big Children, or, A Big Opera for Little Children (Harrow, 12/83; St J. H. 2/5/84).
[Music by J. Farmer.]

O. Suzanne (Portsmouth, 1/3/84). L.C.

D. The Brigands. 8° 1884.

LEIGH, NORMA

D. Auld Lang Syne (Ladb. H. 19/6/91). L.C.

LEIGH, S.

Ca. A Private Detective (St J. 1/4/86). L.C.
[Written in collaboration with *M. PEMBERTON*.]

LEIGHTON, Sir BALDWYN

C. Day Dreams (Loton Park, Salop, 5/11/75).

LEIGHTON, DOROTHY

D. Thyrza Fleming (Indep. Theatre Soc. at Terry's, 4/1/95). L.C.

LEMAIN, BARRY

D. The Hand of Elmsley (Tyne, Newcastle, 27/8/77).

D. The Twin Sisters (Tunstall, 8/10/77). L.C.

LEMON, HARRY

F. Up for the Cattle Show (Adel. 7/12/67). L.C. *Lacy*.

F. A Co-operative Movement (H. 6/4/68). L.C.

F. Go to Putney; or, The Story of the Boat Race (Adel. 6/4/68). L.C. *Lacy*.

C. Gertrude's Money Box (S.W. 9/1/69). L.C. *Lacy*.

F. Wait for an Answer (Holborn, 25/9/69). L.C. *Lacy*.

P. Dick Whittington and his Wonderful Cat; or, The Butterflies' Ball and Grasshoppers' Feast and the Troublesome Cat of Morocco (C.P. 22/12/69).

P. Jack the Giant Killer, Jack and the Beanstalk, Merry Jill, and the Gnome Fairies of Number Nip (Ast. 27/12/69). L.C.

Ext. Cinderella (C.P. 18/4/70).

D.Sk. The Turf (Wigan, 29/2/84).

D. Sin and its Shadows (Oxford, 21/9/85). L.C.

LEMON, MARK

[For his earlier plays see iv, 343–5.]

F. Jack in the Green; or, Hints on Etiquette (Adel. 23/5/50). L.C. *Lacy.*

F. The School for Tigers; or, The Shilling Hop (Adel. 28/10/50). L.C.

F. A London Fog (Adel. 10/4/51). L.C.

F. Mr Nightingale's Diary (Hanover Square R. 18/6/51). L.C.

Bsq. O Gemini; or, Brothers of Coarse (H. 12/4/52). See *G. A. À BECKETT.*

D. Mind Your Own Business; or, The Man of Tact (H. 24/4/52). L.C. *Lacy.*

D. Sea and Land (Adel. 17/5/52). L.C. *Webster.*

F. Keeley Worried by Buckstone (H. 5/6/52). L.C. *Webster.*
[Written in collaboration with *B. N. WEBSTER.*]

D. Slave Life (Adel. 29/11/52). See *T. TAYLOR.*

F. Webster at Home (Adel. 28/3/53).

F. The Camp at Chobham (Adel. 30/6/53). L.C. *Webster*; *Lacy.*

Bsq. Sardanapalus (Adel. 20/7/53). See *G. A. À BECKETT.*

D. Number Nip and the Spirit Bride (Adel. 26/12/53). See *C. W. S. BROOKS.*

M.D. The Begging Letter (D.L. 31/12/53). L.C.

D. Paula Lazaro; or, The Ladrone's Daughter (D.L. 9/1/54). L.C.

F. A Moving Tale (Adel. 7/6/54). L.C. *Lacy.*

F. The Railway Belle (Adel. 20/11/54). L.C. *Lacy.*

F. The Slow Man (Adel. 20/11/54). *Lacy.*

Ext. Petticoat Parliament; or, A Woman's Suffrage (Olym. 26/12/67). L.C.

LEMORE, CLARA

C.D. A Crooked Mile (Com. Manchester, 23/1/85; Vaud. 26/4/88, *mat.*). L.C.

LENNARD, HORACE

Bsq. Delights o' London (Phil. 8/4/82). See *W. MACKAY.*

F. Namesakes (Toole's, 24/2/83). L.C.

P. Blue Beard (C.P. 22/12/83). L.C.

Ca. Reaping the Whirlwind (Nov. 26/4/84; Richmond, 5/90, as *The Lord Burleigh*). L.C.

Ext. Lalla Rookh (Nov. 1/5/84). L.C.

P. Jack and the Beanstalk (C.P. 22/12/84). L.C.

P. Robinson Crusoe (C.P. 24/12/87).

P. Jack and the Beanstalk (C.G. 26/12/87). See *H. HERSEE.*

M.Bsq. Too Lovely Black-Eyed Susan (C.P. 2/4/88; Str. 11/4/88). L.C.
[Music by O. Barrett.]

P. Cinderella (C.P. 24/12/88). L.C.
[Music by O. Barrett.]

P. Aladdin and the Wonderful Lamp; or, The Willow Pattern Plate and the Flying Crystal Palace (C.P. 24/12/89). L.C.

P. Whittington and his Cat (C.P. 24/12/90). L.C.
[Music by O. Barrett.]

P. The Forty Thieves (C.P. 24/12/91). L.C.

P. The Babes in the Wood and Bold Robin Hood (C.P. 24/12/92). L.C.
[Music by O. Barrett.]

P. Dick Whittington (Olym. 26/12/92).
[Music by O. Barrett.]

F. A Laggard in Love (Traf. 27/4/93). L.C.
P. Jack and the Beanstalk (C.P. 23/12/93). L.C.
[Music by O. Barrett.]
P. Cinderella (Lyc. 26/12/93). L.C.
Bsq. Cupid and Co. (City, Sheffield, 6/8/94). L.C.
[Title altered to *The School of Love*, 4/10/98.]
P. Blue Beard (C.P. 22/12/94). L.C.
P. Santa Claus (Lyc. 26/12/94). L.C.
P. Robinson Crusoe (Lyc. 26/12/95). L.C.
P. Aladdin (D.L. 26/12/96). See *A. STURGESS.*
P. Robinson Crusoe (Lyc. 26/12/96).
P. Dick Whittington (Adel. 26/12/98). L.C.
[Music by O. Barrett.]

LEONARD, HERBERT
D. Light Ahead (Sur. 23/11/91; Lyr. Hammersmith, 12/10/96, altered as *A Merciless World*). L.C.
D. The Enemy's Camp (Pav. 26/3/94). L.C.
D. The Daredevil (P's. Portsmouth, 19/10/94). See *A. SHIRLEY.*
D. The Girl o' my Heart; or, Jack Ashore (Sur. 21/12/96). L.C.
D. Serving the Queen (Sur. 17/10/98). L.C.
D. On Active Service (Sur. 23/10/99). L.C.

LEOPOLDS, —
Ext. Frivolity (T.H. Kilburn, 12/8/95).

LE QUEUX, W. T.
Bsq. Tootsie's Lovers (Var. Brentford, 19/4/86).
Ca. A Gem of a Girl (Beach's H. Brentford, 24/6/86).

LE ROSS, CHRISTIAN
F. The Great Gun Trick; or, Half an Hour with the Original Lyceum Wizard (D.L. 31/12/55). L.C.

LESLIE, ALFRED
F. The Cricket Match (Norwich, 12/5/70).
Bsq. Little Mr Faust (Parkhurst, 18/8/94, *copy.*). L.C.
[Music by the author and F. Foster.]

LESLIE, BERNARD
F. Marmaduke Snooks (O.H. Leicester, 10/2/79). L.C.

LESLIE, FRED ["*A. C. TORR*"]
Bsq. Miss Esmeralda; or, The Maid and the Monkey (Gai. 8/10/87) L.C.
[Written in collaboration with *H. MILLS.*]
Bsq. Ruy Blas; or, The Blasé Roué (Grand, Birmingham, 3/9/89; Gai. 21/9/89). L.C.
[Written in collaboration with *H. F. CLARK.* Music by M. Lutz.]
Bsq. Guy Fawkes Esq. (Nottingham, 7/4/90; Gai. 26/7/90). L.C.
[Written in collaboration with *H. F. CLARK*; lyrics by *P. F. MARSHALL.* Music by G. W. Byng.]
Bsq. Cinder-Ellen, up too late (Gai. 24/12/91). L.C.
[Written in collaboration with *W. T. VINCENT.* Music by M. Lutz.]
F. Mrs Othello (Toole's, 11/11/93). L.C.
[Written in collaboration with *A. SHIRLEY.*]

LESLIE, HENRY T.

D. Adrienne; or, The Secret of a Life (Lyc. 12/11/60). L.C. *Lacy.*
D. The Family Secret (Manchester, 3/61).
D. A Trail of Sin (Vic. 9/63). L.C. Vic. 5/9/63.
D. The Orange Girl (Sur. 24/10/64). L.C. *Lacy.*
[Written in collaboration with *N. ROWE.*]
D. The Mariner's Compass (Ast. 4/3/65). L.C. *Lacy.*
D. The Sin and the Sorrow (Grec. 17/9/66). L.C. *Lacy.*
D. Tide and Time; or, Mildred's Vow (Sur. 9/3/67). L.C. *Lacy* [as *Time and Tide: A Tale of the Thames*].
D. The Black Country; or, Little Jim, the Collier's Son (Birmingham, 1867).
D. The Village Blacksmith; a Story of Two Christmas Eves (Greenwich, 10/2/68).
D. Friendship, Love and Truth (Sur. 14/3/68). L.C.
D.Sk. A Pearl among Women (Amphi. L'pool, 11/3/70).
D. Muriel; or, The Warning Voices (Amphi. L'pool, 16/4/70).
D. Meg Merrilies (Glasgow, 10/11/73).

LESTER, GEORGE

C. Love (Gloucester, 11/12/76).

LESTER, SIDNEY

M.Bsq. The Giddy Miss Carmen (Aquar. Brighton, 27/8/94).

LESTOCQ, W.

C.O. The Sultan of Mocha (P's. Manchester, 16/10/74; St J. 17/4/76; Str. 21/9/77, *revised*). L.C.
[Music by A. Cellier.]
C.D. A Bad Penny (Vaud. 13/7/82). L.C.
D. The Sins of the Fathers (Glo. 30/1/86). L.C. *Lacy.*
F. A Merry Meeting (O.C. 26/2/87). L.C. *French.*
D. In Danger (Brighton, 24/10/87; Vaud. 1/11/87, *mat.*; Vaud. 29/7/89). L.C. *Lacy.*
[Written in collaboration with *H. CRESSWELL.*]
Ca. Through the Fire (Str. 25/2/88). L.C. *Lacy.*
[Written in collaboration with *Y. STEPHENS.*]
F.C. Uncles and Aunts (Com. 22/8/88). L.C. *French.*
[Written in collaboration with *W. EVERARD.*]
C.O. The Brazilian (Newcastle, 19/4/90). See *M. PEMBERTON.*
F. Jane (Com. 18/12/90). See *H. NICHOLS.*
D. Grif (Sur. 5/10/91). L.C.
F.C. The Sportsman (Com. 3/10/92, *copy.*; Com. 21/1/93). L.C.
F. The Foundling (Terry's, 30/8/94). L.C.
[Written in collaboration with *E. M. ROBSON.*]

L'ESTRANGE, L.

D. The Oculist (Progressive Club, N. Camberwell, 25/8/94).

LETERRIER, E.

F.Oa. The Fifteenth of October (Alh. 22/3/75; P.W. 8/8/91). L.C.
[Written in collaboration with *A. VANLOO.* Music by G. Capel.]

LETERRIER, JENNIE

F.C. My Courier (Com. Manchester, 23/8/86).

"*LEUBERTS, HORTHUR*"
M.Sk. A Star Turn (Traf. 27/4/93).
[Music by M. A. Maurice.]

LEVEY, JOHN C.
D. Life in the Coal Pits; or, Self Doomed (Vic. 26/2/67). L.C.
D. Gold is Nothing—Happiness is All (Amphi. Leeds, 5/10/68; E.L. 29/11/69). L.C.
D. Luck; or, The Yorkshire Lass (Amphi. Leeds, 8/3/69; Brit. 19/7/69, as *Luck; or, A Story of a Pastoral Life*). L.C.
D. Marriage not Divorce; or, The Love that blooms for ever (Brit. 2/5/70). L.C.
D. The Lighthouse (E.L. 29/4/71). L.C.
D. Honour; or, The Redeeming Spark (Grec. 4/9/71). L.C.
D. Cushla-ma-Cree (Adel. L'pool, 1/9/73; M'bone, 18/10/73). L.C.
D. Sons of Toil; or, English Hearts and Homes (M'bone, 8/11/73).
D. Moyna a-Roon; or, The Rapparee's Bride (Chester, 25/10/75; E.C. 8/11/75). L.C.
D. The Banshee; or, The Spirit of the Boreen (E.C. 28/2/76). L.C.
D. The Leprechaun; or, The Lovers of Tara's Vale (L'pool, 19/2/77).
D. Garry Owen; or, The Belles of the Shannon (Vic. 21/5/77). L.C. Qns. Manchester, 14/5/77.
D. The Nimble Shilling (E.C. 11/6/77). L.C.
F. An Irishman's Heart; or, A Kiss o' the Blarney (Brit. 29/9/79). L.C.
D. Daniel O'Connell; or, Kerry's Pride and Munster's Glory (Worcester, 21/6/80). L.C.

LEVEY, R. M.
F. I Dine with my Mother (Dublin, 23/1/71).
F. Wanted, a Companion (Dublin, 10/2/73).

[*LEVICK, FRANCIS*
C.D. Only a Farmer's Daughter (Birkenhead, 22/2/97). See *E. BARNES*.

LEVY, E. LAWRENCE
Ca. Love's Eyes (P.W. Birmingham, 5/3/91). L.C.
M.Ca. Wooing and Waiting (Institute, Birmingham, 18/10/95). L.C.
[Music by F. W. Beard.]

LEVY, J.
D. The Charm of Iamblichus (Institute, L'pool, 18/12/96).

LEWES, GEORGE HENRY ["*SLINGSBY LAWRENCE*"]
T. The Noble Heart (Manchester, 16/4/49; Olym. 19/2/1850). L.C. *Lacy*.
C. The Game of Speculation (Lyc. 2/10/51). L.C. *Lacy*.
D. A Chain of Events (Lyc. 12/4/52). L.C. *Lacy*.
[Written in collaboration with *C. J. MATHEWS*.]
D.Sk. Taking by Storm (Lyc. 3/6/52).
D. A Strange History in Nine Chapters (Lyc. 29/3/53). L.C. *Lacy*.
[Written in collaboration with *C. J. MATHEWS*.]
C. The Lawyers (Lyc. 19/5/53). L.C. *Lacy*.
F. "Wanted, a She Wolf" (Lyc. 23/3/54). L.C.
F. A Cozy Couple (Lyc. 4/54). L.C. *Lacy*.
F. Give a Dog a Bad Name (Lyc. 18/4/54). *Lacy*.
D. Sunshine through the Clouds (Lyc. 15/6/54). L.C.

F. Buckstone's Adventure with a Polish Princess (H. 4/7/55). L.C. *Lacy*.
F. Stay at Home (Olym. 12/2/56).

LEWIN, WALPOLE
Bsq. Good Old Queen Bess; or, The Pearl, the Peer and the Page (Vaud. 3/6/91, *mat.*).
[Music by W. Robins.]

LEWIS, CATHARINE
D. My Missis (O.C. 8/10/86, *copy.*).
[Written in collaboration with *D. ROBERTSON*.]
C. Cupid's Odds and Ends (Parkhurst, 1/6/95, *copy.*). L.C.

LEWIS, G.
D. It's never too late to repent (Brit. 18/8/75). L.C.

LEWIS, H. H.
D. The Honour of the House (Nottingham, 15/7/95; Pav. 29/7/95).

LEWIS, H. M.
C. The Old Boys and the New (T.H. Twickenham, 14/5/88).
Ca. Woman's Caprice and Man's Obstinacy (P.W. 13/4/95). L.C.

LEWIS, JOSEPH
D. The Captain of the Vulture (Swindon, 6/11/88, *copy.*; Warrington, 20/3/89). L.C.
[Written in collaboration with *H. FALCONER*.]
D. The Pit's Mouth; or, Life in the Mine (Corn Exchange, Dunstable, 24/8/95).

LEWIS, LEOPOLD DAVID
D. The Bells (Lyc. 25/11/71). L.C. *Lacy*.
D. The Wandering Jew (Adel. 14/4/73). L.C.
D. Give a Dog a Bad Name (Adel. 18/11/76). L.C.
D. Foundlings; or, The Ocean of Life (S.W. 8/10/81). L.C.

LEWIS, T. HANSON
O. The Earthly Twins (St J. 6/7/96). L.C.
[Lyrics by *J. M. BULLOCK*. Music by A. Bingham.]

LEWIS-CLIFTON, ALFRED
Bsq. Ye Ladye of Lyons (Aquar. Gt Yarmouth, 10/4/82).

LIBBY, LAURA JEAN
D. Parted on the Bridal Hour (S.W. 8/2/88, *copy.*). L.C.

LIGHTFOOT, —
F. What will he do with it? (Assembly R. Vauxhall Bridge Road, 11/7/71).

LILLE, HUBERT
F. As Like as Two Peas (H. 30/6/54). L.C. *Lacy*.

LINCOLN, W. J.
D. The Bush King (Sur. 6/11/93). L.C.

LINDEN, HENRY
D. Wool (L'pool, 9/9/78).

LINDLEY, HENRIETTA
D. The Power of Love (P.W. 6/3/88, *mat.*). L.C.
D. For England's Sake (H. 10/7/89, *copy.*). L.C.
C.D. Her Dearest Foe (Crit. 2/5/94). L.C.

LINDO, FRANK

D. An Old Man's Dream (Ladb. H. 27/9/89).

R.D. The Mechanic (Ladb. H. 28/9/89).

R.D. A Sinless Secret (Com. 7/1/90, *mat.*). L.C.

C. Men and Women (Ladb. H. 17/6/90).

Bsq. The Bab-Ballad Monger; or, The Mysterious Musician and the Duke of Dis-Guisebury (O.C. 30/7/92). L.C.

C. The Legacy (Roy. 6/2/94, *mat.*; Parkhurst, 17/6/95). L.C.

Duol. New Year's Eve (Grosvenor Club, New Bond Street, 12/7/94).

Bsq. The Minx and the Man (H.M. Carlisle, 15/4/95; Parkhurst, 17/6/95). L.C.

[Lyrics by *W. SKELTON* and *R. H. LINDO.* Music by T. Prentis.

C.D. Garrick's Sacrifice (Spa, Harrowgate, 9/9/97; Stratford, 14/10/98). L.C.

[Written in collaboration with *Sir C. L. YOUNG.*]

C.D. The Bird's Nest (Grand, Fulham, 11/7/98). L.C.

F. My "Soldier" Boy (Grand, Fulham, 11/7/98). See *A. MALTBY.*

LINDO, R. H.

Bsq. The Minx and the Man (H.M. Carlisle, 15/4/95). See *F. LINDO.*

D.Sk. The New Agent (Nov. 6/4/96). L.C.

LINDON, ERNEST

Ca. Our Social Parlour (Roy. Whitehaven, 7/5/92). L.C.

LINDSAY, ALFRED

Ca. Sixes (Vaud. 5/8/93).

LINFORD, H.

Bsq. The Weeping Willow (Staines, 5/5/86). See *P. DAVEY.*

LINGARD, H.

C.O. The Wreck of the Pinafore (O.C. 27/5/82). L.C.

[Music by L. Searelle.]

LINGHAM, F. TEALE

D. Bred in the Bone: A Story of Circus Life (Edmonton, 24/5/90, *mat.*, *copy.*). L.C.

LINGING, E. W.

D. Love and Stratagem (Gai. 15/3/86). See *O. BRAND.*

LINLEY, GEORGE

[For his earlier plays see *E.N.D.* ii, 336.]

O. Linda di Chamouni (Sur. 22/9/51).

Ca. Law versus Love (P'cess. 6/12/62). L.C. *Lacy.*

O. The River Sprite (C.G. 9/2/65). L.C. 8° [1865].

[Music by F. Mori.]

LIPTHWAITE, A. O.

D. Brothers; or, A Plunge in the Dark (M'bone, 25/11/85). L.C.

LISLE, J.

D. The Kiss of Delilah (D.L. 27/11/96). See *G. GRANT.*

LISLE, MALCOLM

P. Aladdin (W.L. 24/12/96). L.C.

LISLE, WALTER

Ca. The Love Test (Gai. 22/6/72). L.C. *French.*

Ca. Mem. 7 (Roy. 20/10/79). L.C. *French.*

C. The Upper Hand (Terry's, 29/5/99). See *C. WINTHORP.*

LITTLE, ARCHIBALD
Ent. Borrowing Boots (St G. 21/2/99).

LITTLE, J. STANLEY
D. Devil Caresfoot (Vaud. 12/7/87). See *C. H. CHAMBERS*.
D. Doubt (Str. 4/6/89, *mat.*). L.C.

LITTON, EDWARD
D. Conscience (Vaud. 17/7/88, *mat.*). L.C.

"*LIVANDAIS, A. D.*" See *A. CHANDOS*

LIVESEY, CARTER
D. The Man-o'-War's Man (P.W. Mexborough, 10/8/94). See *H. DELLOW*.
D. The Days of Cromwell (Aven. Sunderland, 9/7/96). See *C. ROGERS*.

LLEWELLYN, FEWLASS
D. Only a Quaker Maid (Grand, Fulham, 19/7/98, *copy.*). L.C.

LLOYD, ARTHUR
C. Major Baggs (Barrow-in-Furness, 2/9/78; Phil. 5/6/82). L.C.
C. Our Party (Croydon, 4/8/84). L.C.
C.D. Ballyvogan (Tyne, Newcastle, 25/7/87; P.W. Greenwich, 1/10/88). L.C.
P. Little Jack and the Big Beanstalk (Greenwich, 24/12/87). L.C.
F. An Amateur Detective (Pier Pav. Hastings, 23/5/98). L.C.

LLOYD, DAVID DEMAREST
F. The Woman Hater (Denver, Colorado, 31/7/86; Newcastle, 2/9/87; Terry's, 1/12/87). L.C. *French.*
[Written in collaboration with *E. TERRY*.]
C. The Senator (O.H. Chicago, 16/9/89; E.C. 22/10/89, *copy.*). L.C.
[Written in collaboration with *S. ROSENFELD*.]

LLOYD, FRED
P. Harlequin Prince Agib; or, Little Blossom and the Seven Dwarf Hunchbacks of the Sunny Valley (Edinburgh, 26/12/51).

LLOYD, HENRY
D. Mabel the Forsaken (Longton, 27/9/69).

LLOYD, H. H.
C. The Central Figure (Drill H. Wolverhampton, 27/10/97, *amat.*). L.C.
Ca. Judge's Eye (Grand, Wolverhampton, 19/12/98, *copy.*). L.C.

LLOYD, MABEL FREUND
D. Sacrificed (Vaud. 2/7/91, *mat.*). L.C.
C.D. For Claudia's Sake (Vaud. 2/7/91, *mat.*). L.C.

LOADER, McLEOD
D. The Song of the River (Bath, 4/7/98). L.C.
[Written in collaboration with *F. R. ELLIS*.]

LOBB, HARRY
R.O. Sappho (O.C. 10/2/86, *mat.*). L.C.
[Music by W. Slaughter.]
C.D. Wyllard's Weird (Crit. 29/12/87, *mat.*). L.C.

[*LOCK, E. A.*
D. Nobody's Claim (Greenock, 31/7/86). L.C.

LOCKE, FRED

Bsq. Faust in Forty Minutes (Gai. Glasgow, 17/8/85).
F. Hunt the Slipper (O.H. Cork, 18/4/87). L.C.
P. Aladdin; or, The Wonderful Lamp (M'bone, 26/12/89). L.C.
P. Cinderella (Pav. 26/12/92). L.C.
[Music by C. S. Parker and J. Tabrar.]
P. The Forty Thieves (Shakespeare, Clapham, 26/12/96). L.C.
[Written in collaboration with *J. W. HEMMING*.]
P. Ali Baba (Metro. 26/12/98). L.C.

LOCKE, TEESDALE

D.Sk. The American Singer Downstairs (Qns. Gate H. 18/12/99).
[Written in collaboration with *J. F. DOWNES*.]

LOCKE, W. J.

Ca. Mr Cynic (Traf. 2/5/93). L.C.
[Written in collaboration with *G. ROPER*.]
D. The Lost Legion (Shakespeare, L'pool, 7/11/98; Brixton, 14/11/98). L.C.

LOCKHART, WILLIAM

F.C. The Almshouse (Parkhurst, 6/12/92). L.C. Grand, Cardiff, 28/10/92.
[Written in collaboration with *L. FERNIE*.]

LOCKSLEY, CHARLES

D. Humanity; or, Life for Life (Sanger's, 15/10/81). L.C.

LODGE, ADAM

D. Won, not Wooed (Bijou, 16/4/77).

LOGAN, —

C.D. For Ever Mine (Darlington, 21/6/89). See — *STEVENS*.

LOGAN, GUY

M.C. An Actor's Frolic (O.H. Clacton-on-Sea, 30/9/95). L.C.
[Music by Storer.]
M.C. A Society Scandal (S. Shields, 31/8/96). L.C.
[Music by A. Cooke.]

[*LOGAN, Mrs OLIVE* [*OLIVE SYKES*]

C. The Stroller (Park, New York, 6/10/78, as *La Cigale*; P'cess. 22/10/87, *mat.*). L.C.

LOGUE, J. D.

F. Blarney (Norwich, 12/3/75).
D. The Colleen Glas (Norwich, 1/12/75). L.C.

LOMAX, FAWCETT

Bsq. Done-to-a-Cinderella; or, The Drudge, the Prince and the Plated Glass Slipper (Exeter, 12/9/81). L.C.

LONERGAN, Mrs E. ARGENT

Duol. To Be or Not to Be (National H. Hornsey, 24/11/94).
D.Sk. Love versus Science (S.W. London Polytechnic, 9/5/96).
Ca. Betwixt the Cup and the Lip (Mortley H. Hackney, 28/11/96).

LONGDEN, CHARLES H.

D. The Kimberley Mail; or, The Robbery of the Cape Diamonds (P's. Blackburn, 8/4/92). L.C.
D. The Terror of Paris (Vic. O.H. Burnley, 2/7/94). See *E. HILL-MITCHELSON*.

D. Victims of Power (Qns. Keighley, 15/3/95). See *E. HILL-MITCHELSON.*

D. Man's Enemy; or, The Downward Path (P's. Blackburn, 14/1/97; Wigan, 25/2/97; W.L. 25/4/98). L.C.
[Written in collaboration with *E. V. HUDSON.*]

D. The Organ Grinder (Leicester, 24/6/98). See *A. SHIRLEY.*

D. The Orphans (Pav. 8/7/98). See *A. SHIRLEY.*

[*LONGFELLOW, HENRY WADSWORTH*

T. The Spanish Student (Bijou, 13/11/95, *amat.*). 8° 1843.

LONGLAND, J.

C.D. King Charles II. 8° 1872.

LONGMUIR, ANDREW

Ca. Cleverly Managed (Steinway H. 28/6/87). L.C. Albert H. Edinburgh, 25/3/87.

Ca. A Handsome Apology (Edinburgh, 2/3/88; P.W. 3/7/88). L.C.

F.C. Deception (Edinburgh, 27/5/89).

LONGRIDGE, A.

C. Wool-gathering (St G. 26/6/88). L.C.

LONSDALE, W. H.

F. Flagger's Telegram (Gt Grimsby, 24/2/71).

LONSDELL, H. A.

D.Sk. The Vagabond; or, Parted in Crime (Qns. Poplar, 23/9/95).

LORD, FRANCES

D. Nora (School of Dramatic Art, 25/3/85).

LORENZO, C. H.

D. Simple Hearts (P.H. Wrexham, 24/12/88).

LORNE, The Marquis of

O. Diarmid (C.G. 23/10/97). L.C.
[Music by H. McCunn.]

LOUNDE, SUTTON

Duol. Love in a Flat (Grand, Fulham, 13/2/99). L.C.

LOUTHER, H.

F. The New Lodger (Dumbarton, 22/11/94).

LOVEGROVE, W.

D. The War Balloon; or, The Nightly Courier of the Air (Qns. Barnsley, 3/4/71; Vic. 6/5/71, as *The W. B.; or, The Crime in the Clouds*). L.C.

LOVELL, Mrs G. W. [*Miss MARIA LACY*]

D. Ingomar the Barbarian (D.L. 9/6/51). L.C. *Lacy.*

D. The Beginning and the End (H. 27/10/55). L.C. *Lacy.*

LOVELL, GEORGE WILLIAM

[For his earlier plays see iv, 347.]

D. The Trial of Love; or, Self Devotion (P'cess. 7/6/52). L.C.

LOVER, SAMUEL

[For his earlier plays see iv, 347.]

F. The Sentinel of the Alma (H. 18/11/54). L.C.

F. Barney the Baron; or, The Haunted Chamber (Adel. 16/2/57). L.C.

C.D. MacCarthy More; or, Possession Nine Points of the Law (Lyc. 1/4/61). L.C. *Lacy.*

LOWE, WILLIAM

D. The Miller of Fife; or, Cromwell in Scotland (Col. Glasgow, 24/3/69).

Bsq. Wattie and Meg (O.H. Dundee, 20/1/73).

Bsq. Tam o' Shanter (O.H. Dundee, 10/2/73).

D. The Ashantee War (Greenock, 27/2/74).

D. Bonnie Prince Charlie (Dumfries, 13/3/76). L.C. Greenwich, 8/1/75.

P. Mr Robert Roy, Hielan Helen, his Wife and Dougald the Dodger (P.W. Pav. Glasgow, 11/12/80). L.C.

F.C. Spoons (Gai., W. Hartlepool, 9/5/81). L.C.

D. The Crocodile; or, Accused of Murder (Cardiff, 4/3/82). L.C.

C. The Enthusiast (Blackburn, 7/5/84). L.C. Alh. Barrow-in-Furness, 25/7/81.

LOWRY, J. M.

F. Peculiar Proposals (Gai. Dublin, 9/3/76). *Lacy.*

LOWTHER, AIMÉE

Ext. The Dream Flower (Com. 30/6/98). L.C.

LUBIMOFF, A.

C. The Young Wife (Vaud. 1/7/84). L.C.

D. Roma; or, The Deputy (Eastbourne, 16/11/85; Adel. 28/11/85). L.C.

C. My Boy (Bournemouth, 12/11/86; Vaud. 5/1/88). L.C. Ryde, 9/11/86.

F.C. You mustn't laugh (O.C. 5/11/92). L.C.
[Title altered to *A Close Shave.*]

LUCAS, J. TEMPLETON

D. Blanche Westgarth; or, The Nemesis of Crime (Grec. 6/3/71). L.C.

F. Browne the Martyr (Court, 22/1/72; Vaud. 3/11/92, as *The Martyr*). L.C. *French.*

LUCAS, WILLIAM JAMES

[For his earlier plays see iv, 347–8.]

D. The White Farm; or, The Widow's Vision (Qns. 1856). *Lacy.*

LUCAS, Sergeant

D. Manola; or, The Gitana's Love (Plymouth, 21/10/72).

LUDOVICI, LOUIS

D. The Jewess (Shaft. 27/6/99).

LUMLEY, RALPH R.

Duol. Palmistry (P.W. 13/4/88, *mat.*). L.C.

F.C. The Deputy Registrar (Crit. 7/12/88, *mat.*). L.C.

F. Aunt Jack (Court, 13/7/89). L.C.

F. The Volcano (Court, 14/3/91). L.C.

Ca. Fancy Fair (Lyric H. Ealing, 22/9/92). L.C. *French.*

C.D. The New Boy (Margate, 29/5/93). L.C. Margate, 22/4/93, as *Under Suspicion.*

F. The Best Man (Toole's, 6/3/94). L.C.
C. Thorough-bred (Toole's, 13/2/95).
D. Belle Belair (Aven. 19/5/97). L.C.

LUNDIN, COLIN
D. In Another Man's Castle (T.H. Neston, 13/7/98, *amat.*).

LUNN, H. C.
C. The Golden Bait (T.H. Kilburn, 6/4/91, *amat.*). L.C.

LUTZ, MEYER
C.Oa. The Miller of Milberg (Gai. 13/4/72). L.C.
[Apparently Lutz was responsible for both words and music of this operetta.]

LYLE, KENYON
D. Catharine Howard; or, Under a Crimson Crown (Qns. Glasgow, 15/8/98).
D. The Human Spider (Gai. Burnley, 14/11/98). L.C.
[Title altered to *Crime and the Criminal*, 23/7/92.]

LYNCH, G. D.
O.Ba. Quite the Don Quixote (Ladb. H. 12/6/93). L.C.
[Music by C. Young.]
Oa. My Lady, M.D. (Baths, Wimbledon, 29/1/95). L.C.
[Music by W. M. George.]
F.Bsq. Dick; or, The Beau of the Belles (Baths, Wimbledon, 29/1/95). L.C.
[Music by W. M. George and H. Verrinder.]
Oa. The Lady Lawyer (Gar. 8/3/97). L.C.

LYNE, LEWIS C.
C.O. Frilled Petticoats (Gai. 28/10/71). L.C.

LYNN, NEVILLE
F. The Artist's Model (Park T.H. Battersea, 5/3/92). L.C. *French.*
Oa. The Transferred Ghost (Gar. 19/11/96). L.C. Pier Pav. Llandudno, 17/3/94.
[Music by J. Crook.]

LYNWOOD, PERCY
R.D. Christina (P.W. 22/4/87, *mat.*; Olym. 8/3/88). L.C.
[Written in collaboration with *M. AMBIENT.*]

LYON, W. F.
D. The Outlawed Son (H.M. Richmond, 30/7/81). L.C.
D. Bob the Outcast (H.M. Richmond, 19/9/81). L.C. Sefton, L'pool, 8/2/81.
D. Destiny (H.M. Richmond, 14/11/81; Glo. 16/2/82). L.C.
D. Moths (Peterborough, 12/2/83). L.C.
D. The Veiled Picture (P'cess. Edinburgh, 11/6/83). L.C.
Poet.Play. Nadel (Coventry, 11/3/86). L.C.

LYSTE, HENRY P.
C. Loyalty (Crit. 13/3/76). L.C.
Ca. All for Them (Folly, 17/4/76). L.C.

LYSTER, FRED

C. Three Millions of Money (St J. 14/10/76). L.C.
[Written in collaboration with *J. MACKAY*.]

M.C. Kittens (Brighton, 4/4/87). L.C.
[Music by J. M. Glover. Title altered to *The Girl of Today*, 8/4/1903.]

F.C. Bridget O'Brien, Esq. (O.C. 29/10/87). L.C.
[Written in collaboration with *J. F. SHERIDAN*.]

C.D. Sidonie (Nov. 14/12/87, *mat.*). L.C.
[Written in collaboration with *P. HERIOT*.]

C.D. Sally in Our Alley (S.W. 31/8/88, *copy.*). L.C.
[Written in collaboration with *P. HERIOT*.]

LYTTLETON, GEORGE

M.D. The Terrors of a Gay City (Cradley Heath, 21/1/97). L.C.

LYTTON, Baron [EDWARD GEORGE EARLE LYTTON BULWER-LYTTON]

[For his earlier plays see iv, 349.]

C. Not so bad as we seem; or, Many Sides to a Character (Picture Gallery, Devonshire House, 14/5/51; Hanover Square R. 18/5/51; H. 12/2/53). L.C. H. 13/5/51. 8° 1851.

D. The Rightful Heir (Lyc. 3/10/68). L.C. 8° 1868.

D. Walpole. 8° 1869.

C. The House of Darnley (Court, 6/10/77). L.C.
[Revised by *C. F. COGHLAN*.]

D. Junius Brutus; or, The Household Gods (P'cess. 26/2/85). L.C.

MABSON, J. W.

M.F. Did you ring? (P.W. 27/6/92). See *J. W. HOUGHTON*.

McARDLE, J. F.

F. Taffy's Triumph (L'pool, 10/8/74).

Bsq. The Talisman (L'pool, 10/8/74; Phil. 29/3/75). L.C.

Spec. Round the Globe (Alex. L'pool, 29/3/75).

F. Ye Wyn-Wyn-Wyn (Olym. 17/11/75).

D. Sweet Revenge (L'pool, 17/4/76). See *J. FOX*.

C. The Musical Marionettes (P.W. L'pool, 6/10/76).

Bsq. Zampa; or, The Cruel Corsair and the Marble Maid (P.W. L'pool, 9/10/76). L.C.

P. Robinson Crusoe (C.G. 26/12/76). L.C.

Ext. Round the Clock (Alex. L'pool, 25/3/78; Sur. 2/6/79). L.C. Manchester, 28/2/78.

D. Olivia's Love (L'pool, 6/5/78). L.C.
[Written in collaboration with *R. MANSELL*.]

M.F. Marionettes (H. 16/6/79). See *R. REECE*.

P. Aladdin and the Wonderful Lamp (Sur. 24/12/79). L.C.

P. Sinbad the Sailor (M'bone, 24/12/80). See *F. W. GREEN*.

C. Flint and Steel (Alex. Sheffield, 5/81). L.C.

Bsq. Fluff; or, A Clean Sweep (O.H. Leicester, 1/8/81). L.C. Seaham Harbour, Durham, 15/7/81.

Oa. The Innocents Abroad; or, Going Over to Rome (Bijou, L'pool, 15/5/82). L.C.
[Music by W. H. Jude.]

Ent. Sugar and Spice; or, A Gorilla Warfare (Gai., W. Hartlepool, 11/9/82). L.C.

D. Fif; or, Lost for Love (Pullan's, Bradford, 12/82).
P. Sinbad the Sailor (Stand. 26/12/89).
[Written in collaboration with *M. BYAM* and *A. MELVILLE.*]
D.Sk. Puppets (Crit. 20/7/93, *mat.*).

McARTHUR, JAMES

C.D. Beside the Bonny Briar Bush (Shakespeare, L'pool, 3/4/1905; St J. 27/12/1905). L.C. D.Y. 26/4/98.

McCABE, CHARLES W.

F. Who is Sarah? L.C. St Luke's H. Nightingale Lane, Wandsworth Common, 12/4/89.
[Title altered to *Compromising Letters*, 23/4/89.]
Oa. St Valentine's Day (T.H. Battersea Park, 16/5/91). L.C.
[Music by W. J. Jennings.]
Ext. Robinson Crusoe Junior (Qns. Battersea, 26/12/93).
[Written in collaboration with *E. BARRINGTON.*]
Bsq. Babes in the Wood (Qns. Battersea, 3/4/93).
[Written in collaboration with *G. BELMORE.* Music by W. C. Vernon.]
P. Cinderella (Qns. Battersea, 23/12/93).
Bsq. Dick Whittington and his Cat (Qns. Battersea, 26/12/94). See *J. T. VIRGO.*
C.D. A Baffled Crime (Nov. 23/11/96). L.C.
M.F. The Merry Marchioness (Assembly R. Balham, 21/6/97).
[Music by S. Dickinson.]
C. Wanted, an Heiress (Lecture H. Greenwich, 23/11/97; Assembly R. Balham, 11/6/98). L.C.

MACCABE, FRED

P. Little Bo-Peep who lost her Sheep; or, Harlequin Jack and the Ogre of the Brazen Castle (M'bone, 24/12/67). L.C.

McCARTHY, JUSTIN HUNTLY

C. The Candidate (Crit. 22/11/84). L.C.
C.O. Francois the Radical (Roy. 4/4/85). L.C.
F.C. The Excursion Train (O.C. 6/4/85). L.C.
[Written in collaboration with *W. YARDLEY.*]
D. Vanity (Plymouth, 11/8/86). L.C.
Ca. A Red Rag (Toole's, 18/2/88). L.C.
R.D. The Binbian Mine (Margate, 6/10/88). See *Mrs C. PRAED.*
Duol. The Will and the Way (Aven. 21/5/90, *mat.*). L.C.
F.C. Your Wife (St J. 26/6/90). L.C.
Duol. Vanity of Vanities (Shaft. 4/7/90, *mat.*). L.C.
Duol. The Highwayman (O.C. 5/6/91). L.C.
D.Sk. A Caprice (Vaud. 10/5/92, *mat.*; Gar. 7/11/92). L.C.
D.Sk. By the Midland Sea (Crit. 21/6/92, *mat.*). L.C.
D.Sk. The Ring of Polycrates (Str. 24/6/92, *mat.*). L.C.
D.Sk. The Round Tower (Palace, 10/12/92). L.C.
D. The Cavalier (Belfast, 19/4/94).
D. Terpsichore (Lyr. 12/7/94).
C. His Little Dodge (Roy. 24/10/96). L.C.
C. My Friend the Prince (Gar. 13/2/97). L.C. as *My Friend from India.*

McCLELLAN, W. T.

F.C. What! More Trouble! (P.W. 20/7/99). L.C. Grand H. Bromley, 9/2/97, as *Auntie's Young Man.*

McCLELLAND, HARRY F.

Bsq. A China Tale from a Delph Point of View (Belfast, 11/11/78).
Ext. Beauty and the Beast (Lyr. Hammersmith, 26/12/92).
P. Jack and the Beanstalk; or, The Man in the Moon, the Merry Tune and the Giant who owned a War Balloon (E.C. 26/12/93). L.C.
P. Dick Whittington and his Cat (E.C. 26/12/94). L.C.
P. Cinderella (Pav. 26/12/96). L.C.
P. Jack and the Beanstalk (Pav. 27/12/97). L.C.

[*McCLOSKEY, JAMES*

D. Across the Continent (Alfred, 8/7/71). L.C.
D. For a Life (Qns. Manchester, 19/7/86; Sur. 6/5/89).

McCORD, T. D.

F. Fools (Park Lecture H. Camden Town, 14/2/85).
F. Tonight at 8 (Park Lecture H. Camden Town, 18/4/87).
[Written in collaboration with *G. A. TOPLIS.*]

McCULLOUGH, BRIAN

F. My Little William (P.W. Wolverhampton, 17/4/76).
C.D. Self; or, Man's Inhumanity (Bolton, 6/83; Brit. 26/7/86).
C.D. Light o' Day (Gai. Burnley, 18/6/88; Nov. 30/8/90). L.C. Warrington, 17/12/87.
C.D. The Hypnotist (Qns. Poplar, 30/12/95).
D. The Tramps (W.L. 19/2/96). See *W. STEPHENS.*

MACDERMOTT, G. H.

D. The Weeds and Flowers of Erin (Col. L'pool, 14/3/70; Grec. 1/8/70). L.C.
D. The Headsman's Axe; or, Queen, Crown and Country (Grec. 24/10/70). L.C.
F. Playing at Loo Loo (Grec. 8/5/71). L.C.
D. Driven from Home (Grec. 31/7/71). L.C.
D. The Mystery of Edwin Drood (Brit. 22/7/72). L.C.
D. A Bright Beam at Last; or, True Life in the Brickfields (Brit. 9/9/72). L.C.
D. The Ku-Klux-Klan; or, The Secret Death Union of South America (Brit. 12/5/73). L.C.
[Written in collaboration with *H. A. MAJOR.*]
D. Brought to Book (Brit. 8/5/76). L.C.
[Written in collaboration with *H. PETTITT.*]
D. Racing (Star, Wolverhampton, 5/4/86; Grand, Islington, 5/9/87). L.C.

McDONALD, BERNARD P.

C. For Family Fame; or, The Sea and its Dead (Roy. 25/3/95). L.C.
Ca. A Complete Change (St G. 9/1/96). L.C.
F. The Conscientious Constable (Kilburn, 7/6/97). L.C.
C.D. Not All Smoke (Bijou, 12/5/98). L.C.
C.D. Rights and Privileges (Bijou, 12/5/98). L.C.

McDONALD, RONALD

D. All the Difference (St G. 9/1/96). L.C.
D. The Eleventh Hour (Olym. 18/7/96). See *H. A. SAINTSBURY.*

MACDONNELL, Mrs A. J. [*CICELY*]

D. For Good or Evil (Roy. 18/6/94).
Duol. Life's Sarcasm (Mat. 6/5/98). L.C.

MACDONNELL-GREEN, A.
D. Peer or Pauper (Olym. 21/9/85). L.C.

MACDONOUGH, G. F.
D. Run to Earth (Alex. Sheffield, 2/3/74).

McDONOUGH, GLEN
O.Vaud. The Algerian (Parkhurst, 25/9/93, *copy*.). L.C.
[Music by R. de Koven.]
F. The Prodigal Father (New, Oxford, 25/1/97; Str. 1/2/97). L.C.
[Title altered to *Jones's Aunt*, 7/9/1902.]

McEWAN, NICOL
D. The Choice (Hartlepool, 1893, *amat*.).

McFALL, HALDANE
C.D. The Fear of Robert Clive (Lyc. 14/7/96). See *S. GRAND*.

MACFARREN, G. A.
D. The Soldier's Legacy. L.C. M'bone, 10/7/63. See *J. OXENFORD*.
Ent. Jessy Lea (G.I. 2/11/63). L.C. G.I. 29/10/63.

McGILCHRIST, JOHN
T. Roseallan's Daughter. 8° 1861 [*Edinburgh*].

MAGGOWAN, Dr W. S.
O. The Lady of Bayonne (O.H. Cheltenham, 9/2/97). L.C.
[Music by Dr Dryer.]

"*McGUINNESS, BYRON*" [pseudonym of *W. E. HENLEY*]

McGUIRE, T. C.
Bsq. Robin the Rover (Aquar. Brighton, 19/7/97).
D. Perils of Life (Empress, E. Hartlepool, 11/9/99). L.C.

MACHALE, LUKE
Oa. The High Street Mystery (T.H. Cheetham, 23/9/85). L.C.
Oa. John and Jeannette (T.H. Cheetham, 23/9/85).
[Music by J. Batchelder.]
C.O. La Serenata (P's. Manchester, 18/6/88). L.C.
[Music by J. Batchelder and O. Gaggs.]

MACINTYRE, W. T.
F.C. Squire Crossmate's Vow (Glasgow, 29/9/92, *copy*.). L.C.
D. 92; or, A Fatal Love (Glasgow, 29/9/92). L.C.

MACIVAY, —
Oa. The Flower Girl (P.W. Rooms, Jersey, 10/5/70).

MACKAIL, J. W.
T. Pelléas and Mélisande (P.W. 21/6/98). L.C.

MACKAY, COLIN
D. Old Clo' (Metro. Birkenhead, 7/12/94). L.C. Shrewsbury 15/11/94.

MACKAY, DOUGLASS
Bsq. Monmouth Up-to-date (Shepton Mallet, 23/4/95).

MACKAY, J. LINDSAY
O. Natalie (Burgh H. Glasgow, 28/4/92).

MACKAY, J. W.
M.D. Sons of the Empire (Brit. 20/11/99). L.C.

MACKAY, JOSEPH

C. Three Millions of Money (St J. 14/10/76). See *F. LYSTER.*
D. Caryswold (P.W. L'pool, 21/9/77). See *H. HERMAN.*
D. Hawkes Nest (Park, 3/6/78). L.C.
D. Mayfair and Ragfair (Glo. 31/8/78). L.C.
P. The House that Jack built (Sur. 24/12/78). L.C.
D. Peggy (Roy. 14/2/81). L.C.
D. The Night Birds (Northampton, 24/2/81). See *G. L. GORDON.*
Ext. Macfarlane's Will (Imp. 26/12/81). L.C.
D. London Pride (Phil. 28/1/82). See *G. L. GORDON.*
F.C. May and December (Glo. 28/9/82). See *S. GRUNDY.*
[For *The Novel Reader*, which was the original title of this play, see *S. GRUNDY.*]
Ca. Boys will be Boys (O.C. 29/7/89). L.C. S.W. 16/5/88.
F.C. Our Doctors (Terry's, 24/3/91). See *Sir R. ROBERTS.*

MACKAY, R. FENTON

D. Black Diamonds; or, Lights and Shadows of Pit Life (Alex. Southend, 30/9/90, *copy.*; Gai., W. Hartlepool, 15/1/91; Sur. 11/7/92). L.C.
[Written in collaboration with *L. S. DENBIGH.*]
D. The Life we Lead (P'cess. 16/4/92). L.C.
[Written in collaboration with *L. S. DENBIGH.*]
D. Spellbound (Stacey's, Sheffield, 28/11/92). L.C.
D. Westminster; or, The House of Commons (H.M. Dundee, 18/2/93, *copy.*). L.C.
C.D. Another Man's Wife (P's. Blackburn, 7/8/93). See *W. J. VAUGHAN.*
Ca. The Queen's Prize (Str. 21/11/94). L.C.
F. Qwong-Hi (P's. Bristol, 1/4/95; Terry's, 27/6/95). L.C.
F.C. The J.P.; or, Gay Boulogne (O.C. 16/3/97, *copy.*; Bury St Edmunds, 22/3/97; Shakespeare, Clapham, 14/3/98; Str. 9/4/98). L.C.
M.C. The Skirt Dancer (R.A. Woolwich, 28/3/98). See *G. RIDGWELL.*

MACKAY, WALLACE

F. The Way of the Wind; or, Love's Weathercock (Brighton, 28/8/76; Glo. 11/9/76). L.C.
Bsq. Delights o' London (Phil. 8/4/82). L.C.
[Written in collaboration with *H. LENNARD* and *G. L. GORDON.*]

MACKAY, W. GAYER

M.Fantasy. In the Depths of the Sea (Aven. 5/7/94). L.C.
[Music by Angela Goetze.]
D. The New Life (Aven. 5/7/94).
M.Fantasy. The Mermaids (Aven. 2/10/97). L.C.
[Altered version of *In the Depths of the Sea*. Lyrics by *C. BROOKFIELD*. Music by C. Nugent.]
D. The King's Outcast (Metro. Camberwell, 24/4/99). L.C.

MACKAY, W. J.

D. A Day will come (P.H. Chatham, 7/3/92; S.W. 12/1/93). L.C. [as *The Shadow of the Rope.*]
D. One False Step (S.W. 9/2/93).

D. Sins of the Father (Eden, Bishop Auckland, 23/12/97; Stratford, 17/10/98). L.C.
[Written in collaboration with *W. DAVIDSON*.]

D.Sk. Captain Starlight; or, The Lost Earl (S.W. 22/5/99).

MACKAY, WILLIAM

F. The Great Tichborne Case (Leicester, 20/5/72).

[*MACKAYE, JAMES STEELE*

D. Hazel Kirke (Madison Square, New York, 4/2/80; Vaud. 30/6/86, *mat.*). L.C. Gai., W. Hartlepool, 28/3/81. *French.*

D. Anarchy; or, Paul Kauvar (Stand. New York, 24/12/87; E.C. 27/4/87, *copy.*; D.L. 12/5/90, as *Paul Kauvar*). L.C.

D. Sir Alan's Wife (T.H. Herne Bay, 17/8/88). L.C.

C. An Arrant Knave (O.H. Chicago, 30/9/89). L.C. E.C. 19/8/89.

D. Money Mad (Stand. New York, 7/4/90; Sur. 3/4/93). L.C. St J. 3/4/90.

MACKENNA, S. J.

D. Derry Driscoll; or, The Sportsman Pearl (Alex. L'pool, 16/4/77). L.C.
[Written in collaboration with *B. AYLMER*.]

MACKENZIE, ROSS

Ca. Conquered Pride (P's. Bristol, 19/3/86).
[Written in collaboration with *F. GOVER*.]

MACKERSY, W. A.

Ca. Old Pals. *French.*

MACKINNON, A. M.

Oa. Mummies and Marriage (Exhibition Palace, Folkestone, 6/12/88).
[Written in collaboration with *J. G. ADDERLEY*.]

MACKINTOSH, W.

C. Peebles (Gai. Glasgow, 14/8/82). See *A. CHEVALIER*.

F.C. The Lady Killer (Plymouth, 13/7/85). See *A. CHEVALIER*.

MACKLIN, ARTHUR

Ca. My Lady Help (Shaft. 24/11/90). L.C. *French.*

McLACHLAN, C.

Ca. I Dine with my Mother (Str. 1/12/86). *French.*

MACLAREN, J. BRANDON

Ca. A Preference Bond (Nottingham, 15/8/87).

MACLEAN, WILLIAM

T. Brennus; or, The Downfall of Tyranny [and] Alexander; or, Love and Friendship. 8° 1871 [Glasgow].

MACMAHON, J.

D. The Red Squadron (Bijou, 9/8/94). See *T. HARKINS*.

McNAB, JAMES

D. London Bridge a Hundred and Fifty Years Ago; or, The Old Mint (Qns. 5/2/73).

MACNAIR, ANDREW

T. The Painter of Athens. 8° 1862 [Glasgow].

McNAMARA, ANNIE

Oa. Our Garden (Parkhurst, 15/12/94). L.C.
[Music by C. Shäfer.]

McNEILL, A. D.

D. St Ronan's Well (P'cess. Edinburgh, 16/9/71).

MACPHERSON, HERBERT

D. The Wand of Wedlock (Grand, Cardiff, 13/4/96). See *E. LANCASTER-WALLIS.*

D. The Gamekeeper (Aquar. Brighton, 16/5/98; Kilburn, 13/3/99). L.C.

[Written in collaboration with *F. MARRYAT.*]

M.D. Buried Alive (Amphi. Newcastle, 1/5/99). L.C.

[Title altered to *Brought to Bay*, 1/8/99 and to *King's Pardon*, 27/2/1902.]

MACRAE, F.

F.C. Charlotte Maria (Ladb. H. 25/5/92). L.C.

[Written in collaboration with *Mrs N. PHILLIPS.*]

McSWINEY, PAUL

O. Amergau (O.H. Cork, 23/2/81).

MADDOX, J. M.

F. A.S.S. (Lyc. 23/4/53). L.C.

F. A Fast Train! High Pressure!! Express!!! (Lyc. 25/4/53). L.C. *Lacy.*

F. Chesterfield Thinskin (P'cess. 20/7/53). *Lacy.*

F. The First Night (P'cess. 1/10/53). *Lacy.*

MAEDER, FRED

C. My Sweetheart (P'cess. Glasgow, 4/6/83; Grand, 17/9/83). L.C.

[Written in collaboration with *W. GILL.*]

D. The Blacksmith (H.M. Carlisle, 30/1/92).

D. Shamus O'Brien, the Bould Boy of Glengall (W.L. 26/4/97).

[Written in collaboration with *C. VERNON.*]

MAGNAY, Sir WILLIAM

D. The Barren Land (Olym. 11/4/88). See *H. BYATT.*

D. True Heart (Leamington, 23/11/88). See *H. BYATT.*

"*MAIA*"

Oa. For Lack of Gold (Assembly R. Cheltenham, 2/12/80).

[Music by F. von Lesen.]

MAINPRICE, W. T.

Ca. Comin' thro' the Rye (Halifax, 11/10/86). See *J. A. ROSIER.*

MAJOR, ALBANY F.

C.D. Marjorie's Cousin (Temperance H. Westminster, 10/5/86).

MAJOR, H. A.

D. Primrose Farm (Grec. 12/7/71). L.C.

D. The Ku-Klux-Klan (Brit. 12/5/73). See *G. H. MACDERMOTT.*

MATCHEM, W. G.

M.F. Our Agency (Aven. 19/7/86). See *B. BRUMELL.*

MALCOLM, C. H.

D. Edgar Harissue (Ladb. H. 19/7/98). L.C.

[Written in collaboration with *A. GRAHAME.*]

MALET, Sir EDWARD

O. Harold (C.G. 8/6/95). L.C.

[Music by F. H. Cowen.]

MALONE, J.

O. The Blind Beggars of Burlington Bridge (Gai. 31/8/74). See *A. CLEMENTS.*

MALTBY, ALFRED

F. Just my Luck. L.C. Olym. 1/5/52.
F. Borrowed Plumes (S.W. 3/66). L.C. *Lacy.*
F. Sea Gulls (Roy. 10/8/69). L.C. *Lacy.*
[Written in collaboration with *F. STAINFORTH.*]
F. I'm not myself at all (D.L. 27/12/69). L.C. *Lacy.*
F. For Better for Worse (Croydon, 18/9/70).
F. Should this meet the Eye (Lyc. 10/6/72). L.C. *French.*
F. Two Flats and One Sharp (Glo. 17/12/73). L.C. *French* [as *An Original Domestic Trio, entitled*

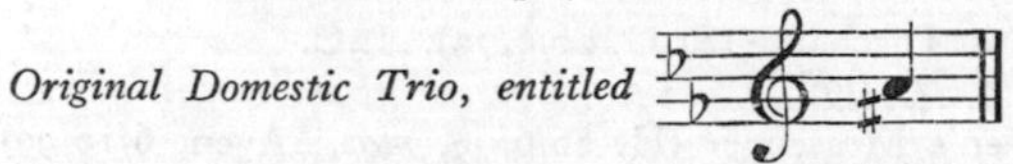

F. Your Vote and Interest (Court, 4/2/74). L.C. *French.*
Ext. Cleon; or, Clean out of Sight, out of Mind (Alex. L'pool, 23/3/74).
F. Found Brummy (P'cess. 21/9/74). L.C.
F. Make yourself at home (Mirror, 24/4/75). L.C. *French.*
F. Bounce (P.W. L'pool, 7/8/76; O.C. 30/10/76). L.C.
C.O. Don Quixote (Alh. 25/9/76). See *H. PAULTON.*
C. Jilted; or, An Old Coat with a New Lining (P.W. L'pool, 18/6/77; Crit. 28/7/79). L.C.
F. Just my Luck (Lyc. 29/10/77). L.C.
C. A Fool's Paradise (W. Hartlepool, 20/1/79). See *P. MERRITT.*
Ca. Verbum Sap (Crit. 20/3/80). L.C.
Oa. Sage and Onions (Manchester, 12/4/80).
[Music by J. Crook.]
C.O. Mefistofele II (Alh. 20/12/80). L.C.
[Music by Hervé.]
C.O. La Belle Normande (Glo. 26/1/81). L.C.
[Written in collaboration with *R. MANSELL.* Music by Vasseur and Grevé.]
F. The Three Hats (Bath, 22/6/83). See *O. DOVE.*
F. Old Flames (O.C. 26/2/84).
F. Taken by Storm (Aven. 11/84). *French.*
F. My "Soldier" Boy (Grand, Fulham, 11/7/98; Crit. 3/1/99). L.C.
[Written in collaboration with *F. LINDO.*]
R.D. The Tender Chord (Terry's, 27/6/99).

MALYON, E. J.

Ca. The Lady Burglar (Kilburn, 3/5/97; Aven. 16/10/97). *French.*
[Written in collaboration with *C. JAMES.*]
C. A Mere Question of Time (Kilburn, 14/7/97, *copy.*). L.C.
[Written in collaboration with *C. JAMES.*]
C. A Lesson in Manners (Portsmouth, 25/10/97). L.C.
[Written in collaboration with *C. JAMES.*]
C. At the Kirk Arms (Aquar. Brighton, 29/11/97). L.C.
[Written in collaboration with *C. JAMES.*]
C. The Honourable John (Qns. Crouch End, 12/12/98). See *F. MOUILLOT.*

MANBY, FRANCIS H.

F. Sly and Shy (Southampton, 4/11/70, *amat.*).

C.D. Love's Error (Southampton, 20/12/70, *amat.*).

MANCHESTER, G.

C.O. The School Girl (Grand, Cardiff, 2/9/95; Stand. 14/10/95). L.C. [Music by A. Maurice.]

MANDEVILLE, HENRY

D. Red Snow (Qns. Londonderry, 13/1/73).

MANLEY, HERBERT

Oa. The Beauty Show (Pier Pav. St Leonards, 26/6/99). L.C. [Music by G. Morgans.]

MANN, C. P.

Ca. The Lost Discharge (St G. 20/6/73). L.C.

MANNERS, J. HARTLEY

D. A Queen's Messenger (H. 26/6/99, *mat.*; Aven. 6/10/99). L.C. *French.*

MANNING, EDGAR

Oa. Change of Air (Assembly R. Cheltenham, 24/10/78).

MANNING, J. C.

C.O. The Coastguard; or, The Last Cruise of the Vampire (Robinson's Assembly R. Neath, 27/11/84). [Music by W. F. Hulley.]

MANNING, M. A.

D. Rent (O.H. Waterford, 19/9/81).

MANNING, WILLIAM

C.D. Condemned (P.W. Warrington, 3/9/78).

D. Kindred Souls (Sturton T.H. Cambridge, 4/2/84). L.C. [Title altered to *A Hot Night*, 25/9/1901.]

D. Proclaimed (Stockton-on-Tees, 29/10/86). L.C. [Title altered to *In Fear of the Law*, 8/87.]

D. Exiled (Qns. Keighley, 12/2/91). L.C. [Written in collaboration with *E. DARBEY*. Title altered to *The Red Hand*, 9/6/1903.]

D. My Native Land (Coatbridge, 29/10/91; Lyr. Hammersmith, 5/12/92). L.C.

D. The Scarlet Brotherhood (Grand, Stalybridge, 2/10/93). See *E. DARBEY.*

MANNON, C. H.

F. Uncle Yank's Mishaps (Shakespeare, L'pool, 27/6/92). See *C. WILMOT.*

MANSELL, E.

M.C. The Skirt Dancer (R.A. Woolwich, 28/3/98). See *G. RIDGWELL.*

MANSELL, HERMAN

C.O. Vert Vert (St J. 2/5/74). L.C. [Written in collaboration with *R. MANSELL.*]

MANSELL, RICHARD

C.O. Vert Vert (St J. 2/5/74). See *H. MANSELL.*

D. Olivia's Love (L'pool, 6/5/78). See *J. F. McARDLE.*

C.O. La Belle Normande (Glo. 26/1/81). See *A. MALTBY.*

D. Betrayed; or, The Vicar's Daughter (Qns. Manchester, 28/6/86). L.C.

MANSFIELD, FELIX

R.D. Castle Sombras (Bijou, 27/10/96). See *R. G. SMITH.*

MANSFIELD, J. G.

D. Sally Cavanagh; or, A Tale of Tipperary (Dewsbury, 18/11/71).

MANSFIELD, R.

M.F. Ten Minutes for Refreshments (Olym. 14/1/82). L.C.
[Music by J. M. Glover.]

MANUEL, E.

F. One for his Nob; or, 39 Honeysuckle Villas, N.W. (Brit. 16/2/74). L.C.
F. The Man in the Ulster (Brit. 16/11/74). L.C.
D. Margot (Brit. 29/3/75). L.C.
D. Bras de Fer (Brit. 17/5/75). L.C.
D. The Detective (Mirror, 29/5/75). See *C. W. SCOTT.*
F. The Doctor's Brougham (Str. 9/10/75). L.C.
D. Perla; or, The Court Belle (Brit. 1/11/75). L.C.
D. Expiation (Brit. 5/6/76). L.C.
D. Jewess and Christian; or, The Love that kills (Brit. 2/4/77). L.C.
D. Two Sons (Brit. 12/11/77). L.C.
D. Rachel's Penance; or, A Daughter of Israel (Brit. 22/4/78). L.C.
D. Daisy (Brit. 28/10/78). L.C.
D. The Crimson Cross (Adel. 27/2/79). See *C. W. SCOTT.*
D. The Rabbi's Son; or, The Last Link in the Chain (Brit. 14/4/79). L.C.

MARCH, CHARLES

D. The Gamester of Metz (Gai., W. Hartlepool, 31/7/97). L.C.

MARCH, or MARSH, M. GEORGE

Oa. Who's the Heir? (G.I. 5/3/69). *Lacy.*
[Music by V. Gabriel.]
Oa. Lost and Found (G.I. 5/2/70; Alex. L'pool, 27/6/70). L.C. *Lacy.*
[Music by V. Gabriel.]
C.D. Our Friends (Olym. 6/5/72). L.C. Brighton, 30/3/72.
Oa. The Shepherd of Cournouailles (St G. L'pool, 28/4/79). *Lacy.*
[Music by V. Gabriel.]
D. The Life and Death of Chatterton (Rotunda, L'pool, 31/7/85).

MARCHANT, FREDERICK

D. Lost in the Snow (Pav. 18/1/64).
D. Ellen Porter: A Secret of the Sewers of London (C.L. 16/5/64).
P. The Wood Demon; or, Harlequin One O'Clock, and ye Knyghte, ye Minstrelle and ye Maydenne (Oriental, 24/12/67). L.C.
D. The Village Blacksmith: A Christmas Story of Joy and Sorrow (Oriental, 13/1/68). L.C.
D. The Old Old Story; or, The Fall of a Shattered Flower (Brit. 7/10/68). L.C.
P. Bluff King Hal; or, Herne the Hunter and the Miller's Daughter of the River Dee (Vic. 24/12/68). L.C.
P. Blutzherranbhothrum; or, The Dwarf of the Diamond Dell (Brit. 26/12/68). L.C.
D. Forsaken: an Every Day Story (Vic. 27/3/69). L.C.
D. The Old Ragshop (Vic. 23/10/69). L.C.

P. Chi Chow Chi Chan, the Naughty Man who kills all he can; or, Harlequin the Princess, the Peri and the Palace of Pearls (Vic. 24/12/69). L.C.
P. The Giant of the Mountains; or, The Savage, the Shipwreck and the Girl of the Period (Brit. 27/12/69). L.C.
D. The Man in the Cloak; or, The Assassin (Vic. 7/2/70). L.C.
D. Honest Labour; or, The Shifting Scenes of a Workman's Life (Brit. 3/8/70). L.C.
D. Sharps and Flats; or, The Race Course of Life (Brit. 15/8/70). L.C.
D. The Three Perils; or, Wine, Women and Gambling (Brit. 5/10/70). L.C.
D. A Rolling Stone sometimes gathers Moss (Vic. 15/10/70). L.C.
P. The Man loaded with Mischief; or, King Cricket and Polly put the Kettle on (Brit. 26/12/70). L.C.
P. Rip Van Winkle; or, Cease Rude Boreas, and the Demon Slumber of Twenty Years (Pav. 23/12/71). L.C.
P. Little Bo Peep, who lost her Sheep, and Humpty Dumpty; or, Harlequin Boy Blue and the Little Woman who lived in a Wood (E.L. 23/12/71). L.C.
P. Harlequin Nimble Nip; or, The Pig who went to Market and the Pig who stayed at Home (Vic. 24/12/71). L.C.
D. What will become of him? or, Life in London as it was and is (Brit. 20/5/72). L.C.
D. Under the Shadow of Old St Paul's (E.L. 12/10/72). L.C.
P. Harlequin Hop o' my Thumb; or, The Sleeping Beauty and the Beast, and the Ogre and his Seven-leagued Boots (Pav. 26/12/72). L.C.
D. Windsor Castle (E.L. 15/2/73). L.C.
P. Puss in Boots (Pav. 26/12/73). L.C.
D. The Sea is England's Glory (Brit. 20/9/75). L.C.
P. Little Bo-Peep who lost her Sheep (Stangate, 27/12/75). L.C.
P. Flambo (Brit. 27/12/75). L.C.
M.F. Woman's Rights (Brit. 3/4/76). L.C.
P. Turlututu (Brit. 26/12/76). L.C.
P. Jack the Valiant (E.C. 24/12/77). L.C.
P. Rominagrobis; or, The Tail of a Cat (Brit. 26/12/77). L.C.
D. The Wrecker (Brit. 1/7/78). L.C.
[Written in collaboration with *C. I. PITT.*]
P. The Magic Mule (Brit. 26/12/78). L.C.

MARCHANT, PRESTON
D. Her Mother's Ransom (Rugby, 7/5/91).

"*MARCUS*"
Ca. Jack and Jill (Brit. 8/5/82). L.C.

MARIUS, C. D.
Play without words. The Silver Line (Gai. 25/5/91).

MARK, Mrs
D. Half Seas Over (St G. Kendal, 24/6/82).

MARKWELL, H.
Bal. The Spirit of the Valley (D.L. 6/6/53). L.C.
[Music by M. St Leon.]

MARKWELL, W. R.

D. Louis XI (D.L. 14/2/35). L.C. *Lacy.*

D. The Spirits of the Night; or, The Legend of the Lake (Sur. 28/3/53). L.C. *Lacy.*

D. Amy Robsart. *Lacy.*

D. Faust and Margaret. *Lacy.*

D. 'Tis an Ill Wind that blows nobody Good. *Lacy.*

D. York Roses. *Lacy.*

D. The Prophet's Curse. 8° 1862.

MARLOW, F.

M.C. His Satanic Majesty; or, A Society Devil (Empire, Southend, 13/11/99). L.C.
[Written in collaboration with *H. BARRON.*]

"*MARLOWE, CHARLES.*" See *HARRIET JAY*

MARRAS, MOWBRAY

O. Gabriella (St G. 25/11/93). See *C. A. BYRNE.*

MARRIOTT, FANNY

F.C. Capers (Vestry H. Hampstead, 18/3/99, *amat.*). L.C.
[Written in collaboration with *A. K. MATTHEWS.*]

MARRIOTT, G. M.

D. A Weird Experience (S.W. 9/12/95). L.C.

MARRIS, EDWARD

M.C. Somebody's Sweetheart (W. Hartlepool, 17/7/99).

MARRIS, HILDYARD

M.C. Sunny Florida (Court, Warrington, 2/11/96).

M.C. An Armenian Girl (Com. Manchester, 2/8/97).

MARRYAT, FLORENCE

D. Miss Chester (Holborn, 5/10/72). See *Sir C. L. YOUNG.*

D. Her World against a Lie (Alh. Barrow-in-Furness, 24/5/80; Adel. 12/2/81). L.C.
[Written in collaboration with *G. F. NEVILLE.*]

D. The Gamekeeper (Aquar. Brighton, 16/5/98). See *H. MACPHERSON.*

MARRYAT, FRANK

D. By Special Licence (Longton, 16/5/87).

D. The Golden Goblin (Croydon, 5/3/88; M'bone, 23/7/88). L.C.

MARSDEN, FRED

D. Otto, a German (P.W. Birmingham, 28/7/79; S.W. 12/7/80). L.C.

D. Musette; or, The Secret of the Guilde Court (O.C. 22/12/83). L.C.

C.D. Bob (Alex. L'pool, 3/9/88; Jodrell, 26/12/88).

MARSH, C. H.

D. The Heroine of Glencoe (Grand, L'pool, 11/12/99). L.C.

MARSH, M. GEORGE. See *M. GEORGE MARCH*

MARSHALL, A. R.

Bsq.M.C. Laughs (Edinburgh, 30/6/94; Parkhurst, 8/4/95). L.C.
[Written in collaboration with *A. ALEXANDER.* Music by C. E. Howells.]

MARSHALL, E.

P. Harlequin; or, The Good Fairy of the Invisible Grotto (C.P. 26/12/62).

MARSHALL, EDWIN
Bsq. Noodledom (Lecture H. Walworth, 10/1/77).

MARSHALL, F.
P. Fee-fi-fo-fum (Stand. 24/12/87). See *J. T. DOUGLASS.*

MARSHALL, F. W.
C.O. The Little Duchess (Stockton-on-Tees, 9/9/97; Borough, Stratford, 8/8/98). L.C.
[Written in collaboration with *F. MOUILLOT.* Music by F. Congden.]

MARSHALL, FRANK
F. Mad as a Hatter (Roy. 7/12/63). L.C. *Lacy.*
T.C. Corrupt Practices (Lyc. 22/1/70). L.C.
Ca. Q.E.D.; or, It's all a Mistake (Court, 25/1/71). L.C.
D. False Shame (Glo. 4/11/72). L.C. *French.*
C. Brighton (Court, 25/5/74). See *B. HOWARD.*
D. No. 50; or, A Tale of the Commune (Gai. Glasgow, 21/9/76). L.C.
O. Biorn (Qns. 17/1/77). L.C.
[Music by Rossi.]
D. Cora (Glo. 28/2/77). See *W. G. WILLS.*
D. Family Honour (Aquar. 18/5/78). L.C.
C.O. Lola, the Belle of Baccarato (Olym. 15/1/81). L.C.
[Music by Orsini.]

MARSHALL, PERCY F.
M.Sk. On the Sands (P.H. Harwich, 14/7/87).
D.Sk. Fleeting Clouds (Ladb. H. 25/1/89). L.C.
[Written in collaboration with *C. DODSWORTH.*]
Bsq. Guy Fawkes Esq. (Nottingham, 7/4/90). See *F. LESLIE.*
C.D. Best Intentions (O.H. Northampton, 11/12/90). L.C.
[Written in collaboration with *R. PURDON.*]
M.C. Shipped by the Light of the Moon (County, Reading, 24/8/96). See *J. P. SIMPSON.*

MARSHALL, ROBERT
Fantasy. Shades of Night (Lyc. 14/3/96). L.C. *French.*
C. His Excellency the Governor (Court, 11/6/98). L.C.
C.D. The Broad Road (Terry's, 5/11/98). L.C.
C. A Royal Family (Court, 14/10/99). L.C. *French.*
[For his later plays see A. E. Morgan, *op. cit.* p. 311.]

MARSHALL, W. F.
Bsq. The Right Fellow; or, The Wrong Fellow and the Felo d'ye see (Royal Naval School, New Cross, 22/12/68, *amat.*).

MARSTON, HUGH
D. True till Death (Stand. 23/10/76). L.C.
D. Home Again (Stand. 24/3/77).
D. The Courier of the Czar (Stand. 21/5/77). L.C.
D. Humanity; or, A Passage in the Life of Grace Darling (Leicester, 27/3/82; Stand. 10/4/82). L.C.
[Written in collaboration with *L. RAE.*]

MARSTON, JOHN WESTLAND
[For his earlier plays see iv, 353.]
T. Philip of France and Marie de Meranie (Olym. 4/11/50). L.C. 8° 1850.

D. Anne Blake (P'cess. 28/10/52). L.C. *Lacy.*
D. A Life's Ransom (Lyc. 16/2/57). L.C. *Lacy.*
D. A Hard Struggle (Lyc. 1/2/58). L.C. *Lacy.*
D. The Wife's Portrait; or, A Household Picture under Two Lights (H. 10/3/62). L.C.
D. Pure Gold (S.W. 9/11/63). L.C. *Lacy.*
C. Donna Diana (P'cess. 2/1/64). L.C.
C. The Favourite of Fortune (H. 2/4/66). L.C. 8° 1866.
Ca. A Mere Child (H. 26/12/66). L.C.
D. A Hero of Romance (H. 14/3/68). L.C.
D. Life for Life (Lyc. 6/3/69). L.C. 8° 1869.
D. Lamed for Life (Roy. 12/6/71). L.C.
D. Broken Spells (Court, 27/3/72). L.C.
[Written in collaboration with *W. G. WILLS.*]
D. Put to the Test (Olym. 24/2/73). L.C.
C. Under Fire (Vaud. 1/4/85). L.C. *French.*

MARSTON, PHILIP BOURKE
D. A Test (Ladb. H. 15/12/85). See *E. B. AVELING.*

MARSTON, W.
C. Relations; or, Put to the Test (Olym. 24/2/73). L.C. Olym. 14/6/69.

MARTELL, EVELYN
F. Opera Mad (Dumfries, 14/5/77).

MARTIN, —
C. An Unsanctified Garment (St G. 20/12/95). See — *GRAY.*

MARTIN, J. R.
Oa. The Rose of Romford (P.W. Birmingham, 16/2/85).
[Music by F. Robinson.]

MARTIN, ROBERT J.
C. Midge (Gai. Dublin, 23/5/79; Roy. 12/1/80). L.C. P.W. L'pool, 27/1/79.
[Written in collaboration with *J. P. BURNETT.*]
Bsq. Dr Faust and Miss Marguerite; or, The Young Duck with the Old Quack (Qns. Dublin, 24/8/85, *amat.*).
[Written in collaboration with *E. A. P. HOBDAY.*]
C.O. Joan; or, The Brigands of Bluegoria (O.C. 9/6/90, *amat.*). L.C.
[Music by E. Ford.]

MARTIN, Sir THEODORE
D. Adrienne Lecouvreur (Manchester, 10/4/52). L.C.
D. King René's Daughter (H. 6/7/55). 8° 1850.
T. Madonna Pia. 8° 1855 [*priv.*].

MARTIN, WILLIAM
Bsq. Chang Ching Fow, Cream of Tartar; or, The Prince, the Princess and the Mandarin (Luton, 11/4/64). *Lacy.*

MARTYN, EDWARD
D. The Heather Field (Antient Concert R. Dublin, 9/5/99; Terry's, 6/6/99). L.C.
[For his later plays see A. E. Morgan, *op. cit.* p. 311.]

MASON, A. E. W.
D. Blanche de Maletroit (Ladb. H. 30/6/94). L.C.
C.D. The Courtship of Morrice Buckler (Grand, 6/12/97). L.C.
[Written in collaboration with *I. BATEMAN*.]

MASON, J. A.
C. Cupid from Jewry; or, Love beyond Price (Kilburn, 3/5/97). L.C.

MASON, W. H.
Bsq. Macbeth Mystified (Brighton, 3/5/69).
[Written in collaboration with *J. E. RAE*.]
Bsq. A New Edition of the Corsican Brothers; or, The Kompact, the Kick and the Kombat (Brighton, 18/7/70).

MASSINGER, G.
C.D. The Sergeant's Daughter (Cheltenham, 13/2/88). L.C.

MASSON, ARTHUR
C.D. The Express; or, A Brother's Sacrifice (St G. 14/2/68, *amat.*). L.C.

MASTERS, JULIA C.
C.D. The Scarlet Dye (Brighton, 15/2/87; St G. 25/5/88). L.C.
C. Les Scellés (St G. 25/5/88).

MASTERS, W. C.
Oa. The Forester's Daughter (St G. 13/11/67). L.C.

MATHEWS, CHARLES JAMES
[For his earlier plays see iv, 353–4.]
F. Serve him right (Lyc. 16/10/50). See *M. BARNETT*.
D. A Chain of Events (Lyc. 12/4/52). See *G. H. LEWES*.
F. Little Toddlekins (Lyc. 15/12/52). L.C. *Lacy*.
D. A Strange History in Nine Chapters (Lyc. 29/3/53). See *G. H. LEWES*.
F. Married for Money (D.L. 10/10/55). *French*.
F. His Excellency (H. 11/7/60). L.C. *Lacy*.
C. The Adventures of a Love Letter (D.L. 19/11/60). L.C. *Lacy*.
C. The Soft Sex (H. 31/8/61). L.C.
F. Paul Pry married and settled (H. 3/10/61). L.C. *Lacy*.
Ca. A Bull in a China Shop (Boston, 1864). L.C. H. 7/11/63.
C. Who killed Cock Robin? (H. 13/11/65). L.C. *Lacy*.
C. The Liar (Olym. 9/3/67). *Lacy*.
F.C. My Awful Dad (Gai. 13/9/75). L.C. *Lacy*.

MATTHEWS, A. KENWARD
M.C. When the Cat's Away (Gar. 19/11/96). L.C.
[Music by B. Andrews.]
F.C. Capers (Vestry H. Hampstead, 18/3/99). See *F. MARRIOTT*.

[*MATTHEWS, BRANDER*
C. Margery's Lovers (Court, 18/2/84). L.C.
C. On Probation (E.C. 5/9/89, *copy.*). L.C.
[Written in collaboration with *G. H. JESSOP*.]
C. A Gold Mine (Fifth Avenue, New York, 4/3/89; Gai. 21/7/90). L.C. *French*.
[Written in collaboration with *G. H. JESSOP*.]

MATTHEWS, E. C.

D. The Lucky Star (Darlington, 1/8/87). See *G. COMER.*

D. Rogue Riley; or, The Four-leaved Shamrock (H.M. Aberdeen, 26/2/94). L.C.

D. The Wearin' o' the Green (Qns. Dublin, 22/6/96).

P. Dick Whittington (Grand, Fulham, 24/12/98). L.C.
[Written in collaboration with *H. T. JOHNSON.*]

P. Cinderella (Alex. Stoke Newington, 26/12/98). See *A. STURGESS.*

D. The Boys of Wexford (Metro. Glasgow, 26/6/99; Grand, L'pool, 22/9/99). L.C.

MATTHEWS, M. J.

P. Valentine and Orson; or, The Queen of Lilies and Gems, and the Knight so Green of the Horrible Dell (C.L. 24/12/68).

MATTHISON, ARTHUR

Bsq.O. Ten of 'em (D.L. 2/12/74). L.C.
[Music by F. von Suppé.]

F. The Wall of China (Crit. 15/4/76).

C. The Great Divorce Case (Crit. 15/4/76). See *C. SCOTT.*

D. Mary's Secret (Crit. 15/5/76). L.C.

D. Enoch Arden (C.P. 14/12/76). L.C. *Lacy.*

Oa. Contempt of Court (Folly, 5/5/77). L.C.
[Music by E. Solomon.]

D. Liz; or, That Lass o' Lowrie's (Amphi. L'pool, 9/7/77; O.C. 1/9/77). L.C.
[Written in collaboration with *J. HATTON.*]

Oa. Barbazon; or, The Fatal Peas (D.L. 22/9/77). L.C.
[Music by F. Wallerstein.]

M.F. A Night of Terror (Folly, 22/12/77). See *Sir C. WYNDHAM.*

C.D. Scandal (Roy. 1/6/78). L.C.

C. Engineering (Park, 22/6/78). L.C.

M.D. A Black Business (Huddersfield, 19/8/78). L.C.

F. Tantalus; or, Many a Slip 'twixt Cup and Lip (Folly, 14/10/78).
[Written in collaboration with *Sir C. WYNDHAM.*]

C. A Battle Royal (Alex. L'pool, 25/11/78).

D. A False Step. L.C. 1878 [banned]. 8° [1878].

C.O. Marigold (Olym. 29/10/79). L.C.
[Music by L. Vasseur.]

D. Loved and Lost (Qns. Manchester, 3/11/79). See *J. HATTON.*

C.O. The Cadi (P's. Manchester, 8/12/80). L.C.

D. Brave Hearts (Crit. 24/1/81).

C. A Thread of Silk (C.P. 3/11/81).

D. Not Registered (Roy. 10/4/82). L.C.

Bsq. More than ever (Gai. 1/11/82). L.C. *French.*

MATTOS, A. TEXEIRA DE

D. Thérèse Raquin (Indep. Theatre Soc. at Roy. 9/10/91; Roy. 14/10/91). L.C.
[Revised by *G. MOORE.*]

D. The Goldfish (Indep. Theatre Soc. at O.C. 8/7/92). L.C.

D. Leida (Com. 2/6/93). L.C.

D. The Cradle (Indep. Theatre Soc. at St G. 10/7/93).

C. The Heirs of Rabourdin (Indep. Theatre Soc. at O.C. 24/2/94). L.C.
[Several later translations.]

MAUDE, ALWYNE
D. Cinq-Mars (Olym. 12/6/83). L.C.
[Written in collaboration with *M. MINTON.*]

MAUDE, CYRIL
C.D. A Golden Wedding (H. 23/6/98). See *S. VALENTINE.*

MAUNDY-GREGORY, A. J.
D. Self Condemned (Phil. Southampton, 1/8/98). L.C.

MAURICE, WALTER
D. Ready Money Mortiboy (Court, 12/3/74). L.C. as *My Son Dick.*
[Written in collaboration with *J. RICE.*]

MAXWELL, C.
M.C. Bombay to Henley (Ladb. H. 14/3/95). See *W. PARKE.*

MAXWELL, FRED
D. Our Volunteers (Eden, Brighton, 19/7/97). L.C.

MAXWELL, G.
F. The Professor (Cambridge, 31/5/94). L.C.

MAXWELL, HENRY B.
D.Sk. Settled in Full (Pier Pav. St Leonards, 24/11/98).
Duol. Follow my Leader (Pier Pav. St Leonards, 22/11/99).

MAXWELL, P. DOVETON
D.Sk. My Own Familiar Friend (Dumfries, 24/11/98). L.C.

MAXWELL, W. B.
D. Wild Violets (Parkhurst, 1/9/91). L.C.

MAY, H. GOMER
D. On Her Majesty's Service (Aven. Sunderland, 20/11/91). See *H. W. HATCHMAN.*

MAY, VICTOR
Bsq. Elsa's Hand; or, The Squire and Someone Elsa (Swansea, 6/3/93). L.C.
[Music by G. Bryer.]

MAYER ,—
D. The Two Mothers (Duke's, 31/3/77). L.C.

MAYER, HENRI
Bsq. Ace Soir (Roy. 17/5/97).
[Music by A. Bert.]

MAYER, SILVAIN
C. Papa's Honeymoon (Crit. 28/6/90, *mat.*). L.C.
[Written in collaboration with *W. B. TARPEY.*]
C. A Gay Widower (Vaud. 11/3/92, *mat.*). L.C.

MAYHEW, AUGUSTUS
C.D. The Poor Relation (Str. 29/5/51). L.C. *French.*
[Written in collaboration with *H. S. EDWARDS.*]
F. My Wife's Future Husband (Str. 21/7/51). L.C.
[Written in collaboration with *H. S. EDWARDS.*]
F. A Squib for the Fifth of November (Str. 10/11/51). L.C.
[Written in collaboration with *H. S. EDWARDS.*]
F. The Goose with the Golden Eggs (Str. 1/9/59). L.C.
[Written in collaboration with *H. S. EDWARDS.*]

F. Christmas Boxes (Str. 16/1/60). L.C. as *The Christmas Box System.*
[Written in collaboration with *H. S. EDWARDS.*]
C.D. The Four Cousins (Glo. 5/71).
[Written in collaboration with *H. S. EDWARDS.*]
C. Mont Blanc (H. 25/5/74). L.C.

MAYNARD, WALTER ["*WILLERT BEALE*"]
D. A Shadow on the Hearth (C.P. 21/2/87). L.C.
F. The Three Years' System (C.P. 21/2/87). L.C.
Oa. An Easter Egg (Terry's, 7/12/93, *mat.*). L.C.
[Music by S. Ward.]

MAYNE, ALBERT
F. A Runaway Match (Sunderland, 2/2/72).
D. The Mysteries of Prince's Tower (Jersey, 9/6/79).

MAYNE, W.
F.C. The Earl of Mulligatawny (Lecture H. Greenwich, 22/10/98). See *M. B. SPURR.*

[*MAYO, F.*
C. Puddinhead Wilson (E.C. 5/4/95). L.C.

MEAD, MABEL S.
Duol. Imogen's New Cook (Ladb. H. 26/4/98, *amat.*). L.C. *French.*

MEAD, T.
D. The Convict Brother (M'bone, 6/6/53). L.C.
C.D. The Coquette (H. 8/7/67). L.C.
D. Rudolpho the Hungarian; or, The Throne, the Tomb and the Cottage (Vic. 1/4/71).
D. Shadow of Wrong (Cardiff, 2/7/72).
D. Passing through the Fire (E.C. 1/9/73). L.C. as *Passion's Battle-ground; or, P. through the F.*
D. The Order of the Night; or, Twenty Years of a Soldier's Life (E.C. 22/9/73). L.C.
D. Under the Screw; or, A Young Wife's Trials (E.C. 6/10/73).
P. Babes in the Wood (E.C. 26/12/73). L.C.

MEADE, JAMES A.
M.D. The Oath (Qns. Manchester, 4/4/87; Str. 14/6/87, *mat.*). L.C.

MEADOW, A.
Ca. His Own Enemy (H. 8/3/73). L.C.
C. My Daughter the Duchess (Vaud. 30/10/84). L.C.

MEADOWS, ALICE MAUD
M.Sk. A Run down to Brighton (St Martin's T.H. 24/7/93).

MEADOWS, LAWRENCE
D. The Greek Brigands; or, The Massacre of English Tourists by the Aravaniteakai (Col. L'pool, 18/7/70).

MEDINA, Miss ROSE
D. Ernest Maltravers (Brit. 28/9/74).

"*MEE, HUAN*"
M.C. A Man about Town (Aven. 2/1/97). L.C.
[Music by A. Carpenter.]

MEIGHAN, JOHN
F.Sk. Maria (T.H. Rutherglen, 5/12/90). *French.*

MELFORD, MARK

D. Midnight Mail; or, Ella's Love (Dumfries, 30/4/77).

C. The Flower of the Flock (Exeter, 8/11/80; Jersey, 18/10/86, as *Ups and Downs*). L.C.

C. The Family Fool (P's. Edinburgh, 6/3/82; Vaud. 23/6/85). L.C. St J. Tunstall, 26/9/81.

F.C. The Major (P.W. Wolverhampton, 20/10/82).

F.C. A Willing Slave (Bristol, 13/7/83). L.C.

F.C. Frivolity (Alex. L'pool, 6/8/83). L.C.

D. No Mercy (Dundee, 31/8/83; E.C. 18/5/85). L.C.

D. One of Us (St J. H. L'pool, 20/6/84).

D. The Nightingale (Lyc. Edinburgh, 10/7/84; Stand. 25/8/84). L.C.

F. A Man in the House (Huddersfield, 4/8/84). L.C.

F.C. Burglars (Brighton, 2/3/85; Aven. 9/4/85, as *A Reign of Terror*). L.C.

D. The Sins of the Fathers; or, The Unnatural Brothers (Pav. 4/5/85). L.C.

F. Too much married (Grand, Glasgow, 19/4/86; Vaud. 27/5/86, *mat.*, as *Turned up*; Str. 14/2/91). *French.*

C.D. Blackberries (P.W. L'pool, 14/6/86; Com. 31/7/86).

M.C. No Rose without a Thorn (Nottingham, 2/8/86). L.C.

D. Secrets of the Police (Sur. 27/11/86). L.C.

F. The Coming Clown (Roy. 21/12/86). L.C.

C.D. Ivy (Manchester, 4/4/87; Roy. 16/4/87).

F. Kleptomania (Portland H. Southsea, 30/4/88; Str. 12/6/88, *mat.*; Str. 15/9/88). L.C. *French.*

Ca. Venus and Adonis (Wolverhampton, 13/8/88). L.C.

F. Stop Thief! (Halifax, 24/5/89; Str. 14/11/89). L.C.

D. A Brace of Gaol Birds (Sheffield, 14/9/89).

F. The Best Man Wins (Nov. 27/1/90). L.C.

Ca. A Clever Capture (York, 7/3/90). L.C.

F. The Rope Merchant (York, 8/3/90). L.C.

M.D. Flying from Justice (P.W. Southampton, 26/5/90; S.W. 15/6/91). L.C.

M.D. Missing (Huddersfield, 2/6/90).

C.O. Jackeydora; or, The Last Witch (Leamington, 26/12/90). L.C.
[Music by P. Rowe.]

D. Hidden Terror (P.W. Southampton, 16/3/91; Shaft. 9/4/92, as *The Maelström*). L.C.

F.C. The Jerry Builder (P.W. Southampton, 13/6/92; Grand, 11/6/94).

D. In the Moonlight (Sur. 16/10/93).
[Revised version of *The Nightingale.*]

F.C. A Screw Loose (Vaud. 4/11/93). L.C.

C.D. Her Level Best (Eden, Brighton, 9/11/94). L.C.

D. The Skyward Guide (Roy. 9/5/95). See *Mrs A. BRADSHAW*.

C.D. Sleeping Dogs (New, Cambridge, 18/1/97; Imp. 2/5/98). L.C.

F.C. The New Adam (Empire, Southend, 27/5/97). L.C.

M.D. Black and White (P.W. Southampton, 27/12/97; Shakespeare, Clapham, 1/8/98). L.C.
[Lyrics by *W. SAPTE*. Music by J. Crook. Title altered to *Eastern Treasure*, 8/4/1902.]

F. That Beastly Child (Middlesex M.H. 9/1/99).

D.Sk. The Hampshire Hog; or, Never say die (Bedford M.H. 13/3/99).

MELLER, ROSE

D.Sk. The Light of Other Days (Middlesex County Asylum, 14/11/89).
D.Sk. A Summer's Dream (Aven. 14/7/91). L.C.

MELTON, CYRIL

D. Aurora Floyd (Imp. 24/8/85). See *J. B. ASHLEY.*

MELVILLE, A.

D. Millions of Money; or, The Soldier's Trust (Sanger's, 1/3/86).
P. Sinbad the Sailor (Stand. 26/12/89). See *J. F. McARDLE.*
P. The Forty Thieves (Stand. 26/12/90). See *M. BYAM.*
P. Robinson Crusoe (Stand. 23/12/91). See *M. BYAM.*
P. Dick Whittington and his Cat (Stand. 26/12/93).
[Written in collaboration with *J. W. JONES.*]

MELVILLE, WALTER

P. Sinbad (Stand. 27/12/97). See *J. W. JONES.*
M.D. The Great World of London (Stand. 31/10/98). See *G. LANDER.*
P. Dick Whittington (Stand. 26/12/98).
M.D. The Worst Woman in London (Stand. 23/10/99). L.C.

MERCER, J. A.

D. Del Ombra; or, The Son of Night (L'pool, 12/4/79).

MEREDITH, JAMES CREED

Ext. Zimmeradski (Coffee Pal. Concert H. Dublin, 21/10/96).

MERION, CHARLES

P. Valentine and Orson; or, Harlequin Progress and the Peri of the Period (Pav. 27/12/69). L.C.
P. The Bronze Horse (Vic. 23/12/71). See *R. SOUTAR.*
P. Tommy and Harry; or, The Spelling-Book, the Lion and the Mouse (Brit. 26/12/72). L.C.
P. Fairy Land; or, Harlequin Valentine and Orson, the Wonderful Wood, the Benevolent Bear and the Knight that fought and gained the day (E.C. 26/12/72). L.C.
P. The Man in the Moon; or, Harlequin Wonderland and all among the Little Stars up in a Balloon (M'bone, 24/12/73). L.C.
P. Little Boy Blue, come blow your Horn (M'bone, 24/12/74). L.C.
P. The Babes in the Wood (Greenwich, 27/12/75). L.C.
P. Valentine and Orson (Gai. 22/12/77). L.C.

MERITT or MERRITT, PAUL

C.D. Sid; or, Good out of Evil (Grec. 12/6/71). L.C.
D. Against the Stream. L.C. Grec. 17/8/71.
D. Not in Vain. (Grec. 5/10/71). L.C.
D. Glin Gath; or, The Man in the Cleft (Grec. 1/4/72). L.C. *Lacy.*
C. Thad; or, Linked by Love (Grec. 29/7/72). L.C. *French.*
D. British Born (Grec. 17/10/72). L.C. *Lacy.*
[Written in collaboration with *H. PETTITT.*]
D. The Snae Fell: A Manx Legend (Gai. 30/6/73). L.C.
[Written in collaboration with *H. SPRY.*]
F. Chopsticks and Spikins (Grec. 25/9/73). L.C. *French.*
D. Rough and Ready (Brighton, 21/11/73; Adel. 31/1/74). L.C.
D. Velvet and Rags (Grec. 6/4/74). L.C. *French.*
[Written in collaboration with *G. CONQUEST.*]

D. Hand and Glove; or, Page 13 of the Black Book (Grec. 25/5/74). L.C. *Lacy.*
[Written in collaboration with *G. CONQUEST.*]

D. Seven Sins; or, Passion's Paradise (Grec. 27/8/74). L.C. *French.*
[Written in collaboration with *G. CONQUEST.*]

D. The Word of Honour: A Jersey Love Story (Grec. 22/10/74). L.C. *Lacy.*

D. The Blind Sister (Grec. 26/10/74). L.C.
[Written in collaboration with *G. CONQUEST.*]

D. The Olive Branch (Leicester, 15/3/75). L.C.

F. The Tale of a Tubb (Duke's, 16/3/76). See *H. GIRNOT.*

D. Grace Royal (P'cess. Edinburgh, 31/5/76). L.C.

D. The Seigneur's Daughter; or, The Word of Honour (Jersey, 24/7/76).
[A revised version of *The Word of Honour.*]

C. Stolen Kisses; or, The Lion and the Mouse (Amphi. L'pool, 6/11/76; Glo. 2/7/77). L.C. *Lacy.*

Ca. It never rains but it pours (Alex. L'pool, 16/4/77).

D. A Daughter of Eve (P.W. Birmingham, 30/7/77). L.C.

D. The Golden Plough (Adel. 11/8/77). *French.*
[A revised version of *Grace Royal.*]

Ca. Over the Way (Str. 14/2/78). L.C.

D. Such is the Law (St J. 20/4/78). See *T. TAYLOR.*

D. The New Babylon (Qns. Manchester, 10/6/78; Duke's, 13/2/79). L.C.
[Written in collaboration with *G. F. ROWE.*]

D. Love and Life (Olym. 10/6/78). See *T. TAYLOR.*

C.D. A Pair o' Wings (Gai. Dublin, 13/12/78; Portsmouth, 27/5/81). L.C.
[Written in collaboration with "*H. GIRNOT*".]

C. A Fool's Paradise (W. Hartlepool, 20/1/79). L.C.
[Written in collaboration with *A. MALTBY.*]

C. Pickles (Preston, 15/3/79).

D. The Worship of Bacchus (Olym. 21/7/79). L.C.
[Written in collaboration with *H. PETTITT.*]

F. Flip, Flap, Flop (Norwich, 10/11/79; Sur. 9/9/82). L.C.

D. Brought to Justice (Sur. 27/3/80). See *H. PETTITT.*

D. The Lost Witness (Grec. 22/5/80). See *H. PETTITT.*

M.D. The World (D.L. 31/7/80). L.C.
[Written in collaboration with *H. PETTITT* and *Sir AUGUSTUS HARRIS.*]

D. The White Cliffs (Hull, 13/12/80). L.C. as *The W. C. of Albion.*
[Written in collaboration with *H. PETTITT.*]

D. Mankind (Sur. 22/5/81). See *G. CONQUEST.*

D. Youth (D.L. 6/8/81). L.C.
[Written in collaboration with *Sir AUGUSTUS HARRIS.*]

D. For Ever (Sur. 2/10/82). L.C.
[Written in collaboration with *G. CONQUEST.*]

M.D. The Crimes of Paris (Sur. 22/10/83). L.C.
[Written in collaboration with *G. CONQUEST.*]

D. The King of Diamonds; or, The History of a Rough Gem (Sur. 12/4/84; Sur. 2/3/96, revised as *The Raid in the Transvaal*). L.C.
[Written in collaboration with *G. CONQUEST.*]

D. The Sins of the City (Sur. 29/9/84). L.C.
[Written in collaboration with *G. CONQUEST.*]
C.D. Pleasure (D.L. 3/9/87). L.C.
[Written in collaboration with *Sir AUGUSTUS HARRIS.*]
D. Round the Ring (Hull, 14/7/90; Sur. 2/11/91). L.C.
D. Frailty (Tyne, Newcastle, 3/7/93). See *Sir AUGUSTUS HARRIS.*

MERIVALE, HERMAN CHARLES ["*FELIX DALE*"]
D. A Son of the Soil (Court, 4/9/72). L.C. *French.*
C.D. Alone (Court, 25/10/73). See *J. P. SIMPSON.*
Ca. A Husband in Clover (Lyc. 26/12/73). L.C. *French.*
D. The White Pilgrim; or, Earl Olaf's Vow (Court, 14/2/74). L.C. 8° 1874 [*priv.*]; *French*; 8° 1883.
M.D. Peacock's Holiday (Court, 16/4/74). L.C. *French.*
D. All for her (Mirror, 18/10/75). See *J. P. SIMPSON.*
Bsq. The Lady of Lyons married and settled (Gai. 5/10/78). L.C. *French.*
C.D. Forget-me-not (Lyc. 21/8/79). L.C.
[Written in collaboration with *F. C. GROVE.*]
D. The Lord of the Manor (Imp. 3/1/80). L.C.
C. The Modern Faust (Manchester, 19/11/81; Glo. 14/1/82, as *The Cynic*). L.C.
D. Fédora (H. 5/5/83). L.C.
T. Florien. 8° 1884.
Bsq. Called there and back (Gai. 15/10/84). L.C.
C. The Whip Hand (Cambridge, 21/1/85). L.C.
[Written in association with *C. DALE.*]
C. The Butler (Manchester, 24/11/86; Toole's, 6/12/86). L.C.
[Written in collaboration with *Mrs H. MERIVALE.*]
D. Civil War (Gai. 27/6/87).
D. Our Joan (P.W. Birmingham, 22/8/87; Grand, 3/10/87). L.C.
[Written in collaboration with *Mrs H. MERIVALE.*]
O. The Magic Glass (Hove T.H. Brighton, 8/11/87).
[Music by Harriet Young.]
C. The Don (Toole's, 7/3/88). L.C.
[Written in collaboration with *Mrs H. MERIVALE.*]
M.D. Ravenswood (Lyc. 20/9/90). L.C.
[Music by A. C. Mackenzie.]
C. The Queen's Proctor; or, Decree Nisi (Roy. 28/2/96, *copy.*; Roy. 2/6/96). L.C.

MERIVALE, Mrs HERMAN CHARLES
C. The Butler (Manchester, 24/11/86). See *H. C. MERIVALE.*
D. Our Joan (P.W. Birmingham, 22/8/87). See *H. C. MERIVALE.*
C. The Don (Toole's, 7/3/88). See *H. C. MERIVALE.*

MERRICK, LEO
D. The Free Pardon (Olym. 28/1/97). See *F. C. PHILIPS.*
M.D. When the Lamps are lighted (Regent, Salford, 11/10/97). See *G. R. SIMS.*
F.C. My Innocent Boy (Roy. 11/5/98). See *G. R. SIMS.*
F.C. The Elixir of Youth (Vaud. 9/9/99). See *G. R. SIMS.*

MERRIFIELD, J. H.
D. The Barringtons (Nov. 6/3/84). See *S. J. A. FITZGERALD.*

MERTON, CLIFFORD
D. The Unmasked (Pav. 13/11/75). L.C.
D. Wedding Bells (Brit. 2/10/76). L.C.

MERVYN, E.
M.D. The Village Madcap (Alh. Stourbridge, 5/12/98). L.C.

MERYON, EDWARD
D. The Hugenot. 8° 1876.

METCALFE, C.
Bsq. Hecuba à la mode (Vestry H. Anerley, 1/5/93).

MEW, JAMES
D. With the Colours (O.H. Leicester, 14/8/86). See *E. J. N. GALER.*
C.D. The Beechborough Mystery (Grand, Birmingham, 17/6/89). See *E. J. N. GALER.*

MICKLETHWAITE, T. D. F.
C. Vanity (Grand Assembly R. Leeds, 27/3/82). L.C.

MILANO, J.
P. Harlequin Prince Happy-go-lucky (Alh. 26/12/71). See *H. T. ARNOLD.*

MILES, R.
Oa. 'Twixt Love and War (T.H. Wells, 18/1/92).

MILL, JOHN
D. Vengeance is Thine (Brit. 29/7/95). L.C.
D. Death or Glory (Brit. 7/10/96). L.C.
D. Death or Victory (Attercliffe, 22/9/98).
[Written in collaboration with *H. MOUNTFORD.* This may be a revision of the above.]

MILLAIS, W. H.
O. The Princess of Parmesan (Mat. 21/2/98).
[Music by M. Lathom.]

MILLARD, ALFRED
T. Moncrieff (Court, Wigan, 22/4/96, *copy.*). L.C.

MILLARS, HADYN
Oa. Mariette's Wedding (Adel. 30/9/82). See *W. E. MORTON.*

MILLER, ARTHUR
Bsq. Antony and Cleopatra (P.H. Sutton, 2/12/96, *amat.*). L.C.
[Music by A. D. Adamson and W. R. Cazenove.]

MILLER, E. T. W.
Bsq. Competition; or, Much Ado about Nothing (as usual) (T.H. Westminster, 30/4/89, *amat.*).

[*MILLER, JOAQUIN*
D. The Danites (Broadway, New York, 22/8/77; S.W. 26/4/80). L.C.

MILLER, ST AUBYN
D. Paid in Full (Ladb. H. 14/11/87).
D. The Golden Chance (Gateshead, 23/11/91; Stand. 1/8/92).
D. An Englishwoman (O.H. Chatham, 1/1/94; Stand. 1/10/94).
D. The Silver Horseshoe (Aquar. Brighton, 4/2/95; Nov. 3/2/96). L.C.
D. The Winning Hand (Sur. 9/9/95). See *G. CONQUEST.*
M.C. The Lady Cyclist; or, A Bicycle Belle (T.H. Luton, 24/4/97). L.C.
[Music by G. D. Fox.]

MILLER, WYNN F.

F. Fanny's Flirtations (Pav. 11/7/87).
[Written in collaboration with *P. HAVARD.*]

M.C.D. The Silver Fortune (Sanger's, Ramsgate, 15/10/88). L.C.
[Written in collaboration with *P. HAVARD*. Music by E. Lawson.]

C.D. Dream Faces (Sanger's, Ramsgate, 18/10/88; Terry's, 1/11/88, *mat.*; Gar. 22/2/90). L.C. *French.*

C.D. May and December (Sanger's, Ramsgate, 2/10/90). L.C.

F. That Awful Boy (P.W. Southampton, 15/1/91). L.C.

C.D. Jasper's Revenge (Shaft. 25/6/91, *mat.*). L.C.

D. False Evidence (Pav. 14/9/91). L.C.

D. The Mouth of the Pit (Middlesborough, 8/2/92). L.C. Sanger's, Ramsgate, 1/1/92.
[Title altered later to *Birds of Prey.*]

D. A Cowardly Foe (Crit. 12/7/92, *mat.*). L.C.

D. The Scapegrace (Sanger's, Ramsgate, 19/1/93).

MILLETT, Major

Bsq. All at C; or, The Captive, the Coffer and the Cocoatina (on board H.M.S. Tamar, 29/12/73).
[Written in collaboration with *Lieut. WILCOX.*]

MILLS, ALTON

D. The Doctor's Story (Ladb. H. 26/12/94). L.C.

C.D. A Friendly Foe (Ladb. H. 15/4/95). L.C.

MILLS, HORACE

Bsq. Pimple the Pirate; or, The Baronet and the Bandit (Bijou, Woolwich, 10/12/85). L.C.
[Music by A. Mills and J. G. Wingrove.]

Bsq. The Royal Riddle (Woolwich, 16/2/87). L.C.
[Music by A. Mills.]

Bsq. Miss Esmeralda (Gai. 8/10/87). See *F. LESLIE.*

P. Robin Hood; or The Bold Highwayman and his Mary-Ann (R.A. Woolwich, 26/12/88). 8° 1888 (Woolwich).

M.F. Pickles (P.W. L'pool, 9/4/94). L.C.
[Written in collaboration with *T. W. CHARLES.*]

MILLWARD, CHARLES

F. Bloomerism (Adel. 2/10/51). See *J. H. NIGHTINGALE.*

P. Sir Hugh Middleton and the Fairy of the Crystal Stream; or, Harlequin and the Bailiff's Daughter of Islington (S.W. 24/12/64). L.C.

P. Cock-a-doodle-doo; or, Harlequin Prince Chanticleer and the Princess of the Golden Valley (S.W. 26/12/65).

P. Hush-a-bye Baby on the Tree-top (Ast. 26/12/66). L.C.
[Written in collaboration with *W. S. GILBERT.*]

Ext. Little Snow White (Adel. 26/12/71). L.C.

Bsq. Jack and the Beanstalk (Adel. 26/12/72). L.C.

P. Jack and the Beanstalk (Park, 26/12/77). L.C.

D. Rose Michel; or, Sinning to Save (Blyth, 13/9/86).

MILLWARD, HENRY

Oa. Love and the Law (Exchange H. Wolverhampton, 26/2/86). L.C.
[Music by C. F. Hayward.]

M.F. Dolly's Dilemma (Wolverhampton, 22/4/87).
[Music by C. F. Hayward.]

MILNER, H. T.
Ca. The Major Proposes (Rotherham, 17/3/84).

MILTON, ARTHUR
Bsq. Hit or Miss; or, The Last of the Barons (Middlesborough, 19/2/83).
Bsq. Don Quixote (Darlington, 24/7/93; Alex. Stoke Newington, 28/8/99). L.C.
[Written in collaboration with *P. MILTON*.]

MILTON, MEYRICK
C. His Romance (Olym. 16/2/88, *mat.*). L.C.
C. Out of the Beaten Track (Str. 11/7/89, *mat.*). L.C.
C. The Adventures of a Night (Lyc. Edinburgh, 19/6/93; Str. 21/7/93, *mat.*).

MILTON, PERCY
D. Scarlet Sins (O.H. Wakefield, 4/10/88).
Bsq. Don Quixote (Darlington, 24/7/93). See *A. MILTON.*

MINTO, W.
F. The Colorado Beetle (P'cess. 13/10/77). L.C.

MINTON, M.
D. Cinq-Mars (Olym. 12/6/83). See *A. MAUDE.*

[*MITCHELL, LANGDON ELWYN*
D.Sk. George Cameron (Steinway H. 13/3/91).
D. Deborah (Aven. 22/2/92, *mat.*; P'cess. Bristol, 26/9/93, as *The Slave Girl*). L.C.
D. Don Pedro (Str. 26/5/92, *mat.*). L.C.
C.D. In the Season (Str. 26/5/92, *mat.*). L.C. *French.*
D. Ruth Underwood (Str. 26/5/92, *mat.*). L.C.

MITCHELL, Dr S. WEIR
Fantasy. The Miser (Olym. 9/5/91).

MITCHELL, W. H.
C.D. The Battle through Life (Barnsley, 25/2/90). L.C.

MOHAMED & MARLEN
M.D. Andrew (Bournemouth, 25/2/95). L.C.
[The authors' names are here given according to '*The Stage*' *Cyclopaedia* (1909), p. 23. I do not know the authority for this ascription.]

MOLLOY, J. L.
Oa. Very Catching (G.I. 18/11/72). See *F. C. BURNAND.*
Ent. A Tale of Old China (St G. 1875). See *F. C. BURNAND.*

MOLYNEUX, ST JOHN
C.D. Under the Mistletoe (Imp. 5/12/81). L.C.
[Written in collaboration with *R. M. JEPHSON*.]

MOMERIE, Dr A. W.
T. Phèdre (P'cess. 16/4/88, *mat.*). L.C.

MONCKTON, Lady
D. The Countess (Sir Percy Shelley's Theatre, 2/6/82, *amat.*).
Oa. Tobacco Jars (St G. 12/6/89).
[Music by H. Young.]

MONCKTON, L.
M.F. The Shop Girl (Gai. 24/11/94). See *H. J. W. DAM.*

MONCRIEFFE, E.
F. Clementina (Sur. 5/9/92).

MOND, ALFRED M.
C. Such is Love (Aven. 5/7/94).

MONK, F.
D. Uncle Jack (T.H. Sutton Coldfield, 4/4/93, *amat.*).
[Written in collaboration with *A. C. F. WOOD.*]

MONK, MATTHEWS
Ca. Good as Gold (Imp. 13/8/83).
D.Sk. London Streets (M.H. Canterbury, 22/5/99).

MONKHOUSE, HARRY
C.O. Pat (R.A. Woolwich, 16/11/91). See *G. ROBERTS.*
C.O. La Rosière (Shaft. 14/1/93). L.C. Ladb. H. 14/3/92.
[Music by E. Jakobowski.]

MONTAGUE, LEOPOLD A. D.
F.C. The Custom House (Vaud. 24/3/92, *mat.*), L.C.
F. Browne with an E. L.C. Pav. Woodhall Spa, 15/8/93. *French.*
C. The Mahatma (St James's H. Lichfield, 15/2/94). L.C.
C. The Spare Room (Roy. 18/6/94). L.C. T.H. Crediton, 6/10/93.
C.D. A Bogus Bandit (T.H. Crediton, 5/2/96). L.C.
D.Sk. The Crystal Gazer (Qns. H. 5/6/96; Coronet, 26/6/99). L.C. *French.*
F.C. Naughty Rosina (Brixton, 15/8/98). L.C.
[Written in collaboration with *A. ATWOOD.*]
C. An Act of Piracy. *French.*
C. Castles in Spain. *French.*
Ca. The Strange Relation. *French.*

MONTAGUE, VERE
Ext. Myfisto (Colchester, 24/1/87).
[Written in collaboration with *F. St CLARE.*]

MONTEFIORI, EADE
D. Temptations of the Great City (Bath, 3/10/98). L.C.

MONTGOMERY, B. S.
D. The Bartons of Barton Wold [see under *UA*].

MONTGOMERY, HUGH
D. Rescued from Death (Alh. Barrow-in-Furness, 25/4/90). L.C.

MOONEY, HERBERT
C.Oa. The Pet of Newmarket (S.W. 12/11/81). L.C.
D. Karl; or, The Love that wins (Stand. 23/6/84). L.C.

MOONIE, J. A.
M.F. The Broken Coupling (Waterloo R. Edinburgh, 21/2/90).

MOORE, ADA
F. A Sneaking Regard (Sur. 16/4/70). L.C.

MOORE, A. M.
Bsq. Posterity: An Operatic Andissipation (Newcastle, 10/3/84). L.C.
[Music by M. Lutz.]

MOORE, ARTHUR
F. Change of Name (S.W. 14/9/67). L.C.

MOORE, F. (or J. G.)
F. That Blessed Baby (Adel. 11/2/56). L.C. *Lacy*.

MOORE, F. FRANKFORT
Ca. A March Hare Hunt (Lyc. 29/8/77).
C.D. Moth and Flame (Hull, 20/5/78). L.C.
C.D. Forgotten (Grand, Islington, 5/7/89; Peterborough, 10/10/89, *revised*). L.C.
Poet.D. The Queen's Room (O.C. 20/10/91). L.C.
C. The Mayflower (O.C. 9/1/92). L.C.
C. Oliver Goldsmith (Limerick, 24/6/92). L.C. Spa, Scarborough, 20/8/92.
C. Kitty Clive, Actress (Roy. 11/12/95). L.C. *French*.

MOORE, FRANCIS W.
D.Sk. Confusion (Roy. 23/2/76).
D. When George IV was King (Birmingham, 17/9/96; Grand, 12/10/96). L.C.

MOORE, GEORGE
C. Worldliness. 8° [1874].
T. Martin Luther. 8° 1879.
Oa. The Fashionable Beauty (Aven. 7/4/85). L.C.
[Written in collaboration with *J. M. GLOVER*.]
D.Sk. The Honeymoon in Eclipse (St G. 12/4/88).
D. Thérèse Raquin (Roy. 9/10/91). See *A. T. DE MATTOS*.
D. The Strike at Arlingford (Indep. Theatre Soc. at O.C. 21/2/93). L.C. 8° 1893.
D.Sk. "Journeys End in Lovers Meeting" (Daly's, 5/6/94). See *J. O. HOBBES*.
[For his later plays see *C.B.E.L.* iii, 327.]

MOORE, H. T.
Oa. In Chrysanthemum Land (David's H. Redruth, 17/1/99, *amat.*).

MOORE, H. W.
O. Love's Trial (Bijou, L'pool, 5/5/82).
[Music by S. Shaw.]

MOORE, REGINALD
D. A Merchant's Venture (Nottingham, 3/2/68).
D. Wind and Wave; or, The Forgotten Trust (Nottingham, 30/3/68).
D. Ruth (P'cess. 7/7/68). L.C. as *Ruth the Jewess*.
D. Guido and Imilda (Nottingham, 24/2/69).
C.D. Better Luck Next Time (York, 20/5/70).
D. Waiting for the Dawn (Sheffield, 6/6/70).
F. Unblushing Impudence (Gai. Dublin, 10/5/75).
D. Struck in the Dark (Granville H. Ramsgate, 5/10/75).

MOORE, THEODORE
Bsq. The Princess's Idea (T.H. Westminster, 6/5/92, *amat.*).
Bsq. Mythology Run Mad; or, Les Chumps de Mars (T.H. Westminster, 17/5/93, *amat.*).
[Written in collaboration with *E. RUNTZ*.]

MORDAUNT, JOHN
D. Oliver Twist (M'bone, 9/6/56; Alex. 10/4/69).

MORELL, H. H.

D. The Dark Continent (Barnsley, 11/6/91). See *F. MOUILLOT.*
Ext. The Nineteenth Century (Roy. Chester, 12/5/94, *copy.*). L.C.
[Written in collaboration with *F. MOUILLOT.*]

MORETON, F. LESLIE

O. Massaroni (Leinster H. Dublin, 23/1/94).
O. La Gitana (S. Shields, 22/11/95; Parkhurst, 10/3/96). L.C.
P. Dick Whittington (Parkhurst, 24/12/95).
[Music by T. P. Fish.]
P. Ali Baba (Qns. O.H. Crouch End, 27/12/97).
[Written in collaboration with *H. MOUNTFORD.*]

MORETON, RICHARD

P. Little Red Riding Hood (Metro. Camberwell, 27/12/97). L.C.

MORICE, HUBERT JAY

Ext. The Beggars' Uproar (Sur. 7/5/70). L.C.

MORLAND, CHARLOTTE E.

F.C. The Matrimonial Agency (Vic. H. Bayswater, 15/11/88).
C.D. Quicksands (Com. 18/2/90, *mat.*). L.C.
C.D. A Shower of Kisses (Lyr. Hammersmith, 27/6/93).

MORLAND, F. H.

C. Cash for Coronets (N. London Inst. Dalston, 14/6/94). See *I. L. CASSILIS.*
F. Aunt Tabitha (P.H. Lowestoft, 3/9/94). L.C.
M.D. Demon Darrell (Brit. 20/6/98). See *I. L. CASSILIS.*

MORLEY, F. G.

C. Well Paired (Bijou, 7/6/79). L.C.

MORPHEW, HARRY

C. Bungles (Lyr. H. Ealing, 16/12/92). See *A. DE SVERTCHKOFF.*

MORRIS, ARTHUR

Ca. Pepper's Diary (Roy. 6/10/90). L.C.

MORRIS, FELIX

F. Behind the Scenes (Com. 4/7/96). L.C.
[Written in collaboration with *G. P. HAWTREY.*]

MORRIS, FRANK

C. Our Summer Holiday (Alex. H. Clifton, 25/11/86, *amat.*; Ladb. H. 25/11/89). L.C. Assembly R. Leamington, 15/1/87.
Ca. Cupid's Blunders (Alex. H. Clifton, 7/1/92, *amat.*).
Ca. An Old Man's Darling (Park H. 4/5/93).

MORRIS, J. N.

C.D. The Rival Candidates (Wolverhampton, 9/4/94). See *C. T. DAZEY.*

MORRIS, Sir LEWIS

T. Gycia. 8° 1886.

MORRIS, PAUL

C.D. Dick Drayton's Wife (Ladb. H. 24/7/88). L.C.

[*MORRIS, RAMSEY*

C.D. The Tigress (Com. 29/6/89). L.C.

MORRIS, ROBERT GRIFFIN

Monol. Maids and Matrons; or, The Seven Ages of Woman (Crit. 29/6/92, *mat.*).

MORRISON, —

C.O. The Uhlans (Gai. Dublin, 10/3/84). L.C. Court, L'pool, 22/1/85.

MORTIMER, JAMES

C. Joy is Dangerous (D.L. 9/2/71). L.C.
Ca. A Warning to Bachelors (Vaud. 9/12/71).
C.D. Madeleine (Vaud. 1/2/73). L.C.
F.C. The Tender Chord (Ch. X. 19/4/73). L.C.
C. The School for Intrigue (Olym. 1/12/73). L.C.
D. Sundown till Dawn (Brighton, 1/3/75; Brit. 15/7/76). L.C.
D. Heartsease (P'cess. 5/6/75; Court, 1/5/80, *mat.* revised; Olym. 9/1/92). L.C.
F. The Bridal Trip (Brighton, 6/3/76). L.C.
D. Charlotte Corday (Dublin, 14/12/76). 8° 1876 [*priv.*]
C.D. Dorothy's Stratagem (Crit. 23/12/76). L.C.
C. The Little Cricket (Brighton, 11/3/78; Duke's, 8/6/78). L.C.
D. The Miser's Treasure (Olym. 29/4/78). L.C.
C. A Gay Deceiver (Roy. 3/2/79). L.C.
F.C. Butterfly Fever (Crit. 17/5/81). L.C.
C. Reclaimed (H. 14/9/81). L.C.
C. Gammon (Vaud. 13/7/82). L.C.
C.D. Diane (Toole's, 9/9/82). L.C.
D. Move on; or, The Crossing Sweeper (Grand, 1/9/83).
C.O. Polly (Nov. 4/10/84). L.C.
[Music by E. Solomon.]
Ca. Wifey (Str. 10/11/85). L.C.
Ca. On Tour (Str. 30/3/86).
C. Old Sinners (Gai. 16/6/86, *mat.*).
C. The Alderman (Crit. 29/4/87, *mat.*; Jodrell, 24/11/88). L.C.
C. A White Lie (Jodrell, 24/11/88). L.C.
F.C. Oh! These Widows! (Terry's, 1/5/89, *mat.*). L.C.
F. Queen's Counsel (Com. 24/5/90). L.C.
C. Gloriana (Glo. 10/11/91; Terry's, 22/8/96, as *My Artful Valet*). L.C.
C. Truthful James (Gt Yarmouth, 24/9/94; Roy. 2/10/94). L.C.
[Written in collaboration with *C. H. KLEIN.*]

MORTIMER, JOHN

D. The Orphan and the Outcast; or, The Perils of a Steam Forge Hammer (Blackburn, 20/10/71).

MORTIMER, L.

D. The World of Silence (S.W. 13/6/98). L.C.
[Written in collaboration with *P. WILSON.*]
D. Christian's Crime (S.W. 14/8/99). L.C. Bernard's, Woolwich, 24/3/99.
[Written in collaboration with *P. WILSON*. Title altered to *The Land of Promise*, 30/5/1907.]

MORTON, C. H.

D. Three Years in a Man Trap (Amphi. L'pool, 20/1/79).

MORTON, EDWARD A.

D.Sk. Miss Impudence (Terry's, 2/6/92, *mat.*). *French.*

M.C. San Toy; or, The Emperor's Own (Daly's, 21/10/99). L.C.
[Lyrics by *H. GREENBANK* and *A. ROSS*. Music by S. Jones.]

[*MORTON, HUGH*
C.O. The Belle of New York (Shaft. 12/4/98). L.C.
[Music by G. Kerker.]

MORTON, JOHN MADDISON
[For his earlier plays see iv, 361–3.]
F. My Precious Betsy (Adel. 18/2/50). L.C. *Lacy*.
F. The Three Cuckoos; or, Ticklish Times (H. 13/3/50). L.C. *Lacy*.
F. Friend Waggles (Str. 15/4/50). L.C. *Lacy*.
F. Sent to the Tower (P'cess. 24/10/50). L.C. *Lacy*.
F. Betsey Baker; or, Too attentive by half (P'cess. 13/11/50). L.C. *Lacy*.
C. All that glitters is not gold (Olym. 13/1/51). *Lacy*.
[Written in collaboration with *T. MORTON*.]
F. Grimshaw, Bagshaw and Bradshaw (H. 1/7/51). L.C. *Lacy*.
F. A Hopeless Passion (Str. 15/9/51). L.C. *Lacy*.
F. The Two Bonnycastles (H. 25/11/51). L.C. *Lacy*.
[Originally advertised as *A Highway Robbery*; the Licenser of Plays objected to the title.]
P. Harlequin Hogarth (D.L. 26/12/51). L.C.
[Written in collaboration with *N. LEE*.]
F. Too late for the Train (D.L. 17/2/52). L.C. as *My Husband's Widow*.
F. Who stole the Pocketbook? or, A Dinner for Six (Adel. 29/3/52). L.C. H. 23/6/51, as *Dinner for Six*. *Lacy*.
D. The Writing on the Wall (H. 9/8/52). L.C. *Lacy*.
[Written in collaboration with *T. MORTON*.]
F. The Woman I adore (H. 9/10/52). L.C. *Lacy*.
F. A Capital Match (H. 4/11/52). L.C. *Lacy*.
F. To Paris and back for Five Pounds (H. 5/2/53). L.C. *Lacy*.
F. A Desperate Game (Adel. 9/4/53). L.C. as *Honour among Thieves; or, A.D.G. Lacy*.
F. Whitebait at Greenwich (Adel. 14/11/53). L.C. *Lacy*.
P. Harlequin and the Miller and his Men; or, King Salamander and the Fairy of the Azure Lake (P'cess. 26/12/53). L.C.
F. Away with Melancholy (P'cess. 13/3/54). L.C. *Lacy*.
Ca. From Village to Court (P'cess. 5/6/54). L.C. *Lacy*.
F. Waiting for an Omnibus in Lowther Arcade on a Rainy Day (Adel. 26/6/54). *Lacy*.
P. Harlequin Bluebeard, A Great Bashaw; or, The Good Fairy Triumphant over the Demon Discord (P'cess. 26/12/54). L.C. *Lacy*.
F. A Game of Romps (P'cess. 12/3/55). L.C. *Lacy*.
D. The Muleteer of Toledo; or, King, Queen and Maid (P'cess. 9/4/55). L.C. *Lacy*.
F. How stout you're getting (P'cess. 16/7/55). L.C. *Lacy*.
F. Don't judge by appearances (P'cess. 22/10/55). L.C.
F. A Prince for an Hour (P'cess. 24/3/56). L.C. *Lacy*.
F. The Rights and Wrongs of Woman (H. 24/5/56). L.C. *Lacy*.
C.D. Our Wife; or, The Rose of Amiens (P'cess. 18/11/56). L.C. *Lacy*.

P. Aladdin and the Wonderful Lamp (P'cess. 25/12/56). L.C. *Lacy.*
F. An Englishman's House is his Castle (P'cess. 11/5/57). L.C. *Lacy.*
F. Take care of Dowb (H. 23/11/57). L.C. *Lacy.*
P. Harlequin White Cat; or, The Princess Blanche and the Fairy Godmother (P'cess. 26/12/57). L.C.
F. Aunt Charlotte's Maid (Adel. 1858). *Lacy.*
F. Ticklish Times (Olym. 8/3/58). L.C.
F. Our French Lady's Maid (Adel. 22/5/58). L.C. Adel. 6/10/53.
F. Dying for Love (P'cess. 28/6/58). L.C.
F. The Little Savage (Str. 22/11/58). L.C.
F. Thirty Three Next Birthday (P'cess. 22/11/58). L.C. *Lacy.*
F. Which of the Two? (Str. 25/4/59). L.C. *Lacy.*
F. Love and Hunger (Adel. 26/9/59). L.C. *Lacy.*
F. A Husband to Order (Olym. 17/10/59). L.C. *Lacy.*
F. FitzSmythe of FitzSmythe Hall (H. 26/5/60). L.C. *Lacy.*
F. A Regular Fix (Olym. 11/10/60). *Lacy.*
Ext. The Pascha of Pimlico (St J. 15/4/61). L.C. as *The Pasha of Paradise Place, Pimlico; or, Turkish Life in London.*
Ca. Wooing One's Wife (Olym. 21/10/61). L.C. *Lacy.*
F. Margery Daw; or, The Two Bumpkins. L.C. Adel. 16/12/61. *Lacy.*
P. Harlequin Gulliver; or, Giants and Dwarfs (C.G. 26/12/61). L.C.
Ca. Catch a Weazel (Str. 17/3/62). L.C.
C. She Would and He Wouldn't (St J. 6/9/62). L.C. *Lacy.*
F. One Good Turn deserves another (P'cess. 10/11/62). L.C.
Ca. Killing Time (P'cess. 6/4/63). L.C.
F. A Lad from the Country (Olym. 4/6/63).
Ca. The Alabama (D.L. 7/3/64). L.C.
F. Drawing Room, Second Floor and Attics (P'cess. 28/3/64). L.C. *Lacy.*
C.F. Woodcock's Little Game (St J. 6/10/64). L.C. *Lacy.*
F. On the Sly (H. 24/10/64). L.C.
F. My Wife's Bonnet (Olym. 2/11/64). L.C. *Lacy.*
F. You know who (H.M. 7/11/64). L.C.
F. The Steeple Chase; or, In the Pigskin (Adel. 22/3/65). L.C. *Lacy.*
F. Pouter's Wedding (St J. 19/6/65). L.C. as *Simeon Pouter's W. Lacy.*
F. Newington Butts (St J. 2/11/66). L.C. *Lacy.*
M.F. Cox and Box (Adel. 5/67). See *F. C. BURNAND.*
F. A Slice of Luck (Adel. 17/6/67). L.C. *Lacy.*
F. The Two Puddifoots (Olym. 14/10/67). L.C.
C. If I had a Thousand a Year (Olym. 21/10/67). L.C. *Lacy.*
F. Master Jones's Birthday (P'cess. 24/8/68). L.C. *Lacy.*
C. Atchi— (P.W. 21/9/68). L.C.
F. A Day's Fishing (Adel. 8/3/69). L.C. *Lacy.*
Ca. Little Mother (Roy. 21/4/70). L.C. *Lacy.*
C. A Threepenny Bit (Brighton, 18/8/70). L.C.
[Written in collaboration with *A. W. YOUNG.*]
F. The Wrong Man in the Right Place (P'cess. 10/4/71). L.C.
Ca. Maggie's Situation (Court, 27/1/75). L.C. *Lacy.*
Ca. The Garden Party (H. 13/8/77).

D. Mother and Child (P'cess. Edinburgh, 17/11/79).
F.C. Going it (Roy. Glasgow, 13/11/85; Toole's, 7/12/85). L.C. Alex. L'pool, 23/10/85, as *Old Gossett*.
[Written in collaboration with *W. A. VICARS*.]
C. The Auctioneer (Bournemouth, 30/5/98).
[Written in collaboration with *R. REECE*.]

MORTON, MARTHA
C.D. A Bachelor's Romance (Gai. 11/9/96). L.C.
C.D. The Sleeping Partner (Crit. 17/8/97). L.C.

MORTON, MICHAEL
F.C. The Leading Lady (Gai. 15/5/96, *copy*.; O.H. St Leonard's, 18/8/97, as *Miss Francis of Yale*; Glo. 7/9/97). L.C.

MORTON, THOMAS, Jr.
[For his earlier plays see iv, 364.]
C. All that glitters is not gold (Olym. 13/1/51). See *J. M. MORTON*.
D. Sink or Swim (Olym. 2/8/52). L.C. *Lacy*.
D. The Writing on the Wall (H. 9/8/52). See *J. M. MORTON*.
F. Go-to-Bed Tom (Olym. 25/11/52). L.C. *Lacy*.
F. A Pretty Piece of Business (H. 12/11/53). L.C. *Lacy*.
F. The Great Russian Bear; or, Another Retreat from Moscow (Str. 3/10/59). L.C. *Cumberland*.
D. Plain English (Holborn, 25/9/69). L.C.

MORTON, W. E.
D. Love's Revenge (Portsmouth, 13/2/82). L.C.
Oa. Mariette's Wedding (Adel. 30/9/82). L.C. Reading, 25/2/82, as *Marietta*.
[Written in collaboration with *H. MILLARS*.]
Oa. Per Parcels' Post (P's. Accrington, 26/11/83). See *G. D. FOX*.
D. The Tinsel Queen (S.W. 10/12/83). L.C.
M.D. Lovers (Cork, 5/5/86). L.C. Court, 29/4/86.
[Written in collaboration with *F. H. HERBERT* and *H. CRICHTON*. Music by G. D. Fox.]
F. Out for the Day (New, Oxford, 2/8/86). L.C.
D. Fallen among Thieves (E.C. 10/3/88). L.C.
C.D. Our Babies (Eastbourne, 26/11/88). L.C.
[Music by G. D. Fox.]
D. A Foundered Fortune; or, The Secrets of an Old Iron Safe (E.C. 15/12/90). L.C.

MOSENTHAL, J. G.
C.O. Babette (Str. 26/1/88). See *A. MURRAY*.

MOSS, ARTHUR B.
C.D. The Organist (P.H. New Cross, 14/11/87). See *H. WILTON*.
D. Lured to London (Lyc. Crewe, 14/2/89). See *W. J. PATMORE*.
D. Capital and Labour (Vic. O.H. Burnley, 18/8/90). See *W. J. PATMORE*.
D. The Land and the People (P.H. New Cross, 16/10/93, *amat*.). L.C.
[Written in collaboration with *W. J. PATMORE*.]

MOSS, HUGH
C. Ripples (York, 19/12/80). See *G. W. BROWNE*.
Ca. A Metaphysical Muddle. L.C. Margate, 18/4/82.
F. P.U.P.; or, The Dog in the Manger (Grand, Leeds, 6/8/83.).

C. The Love Trap (Bristol, 9/83). L.C.
C.D. A Mad Match (Assembly R. Malvern, 28/10/87, *copy.*). L.C.
C.D. Bootle's Baby (Stratford, 16/2/88, *copy.*; Glo. 8/5/88).
D. Strathlogan (P'cess. 9/6/92). See *C. OVERTON.*
D. Sea Fruit (Swansea, 29/5/93).
D. Sin's Angel (Lyc. Ipswich, 16/11/93).
D. The Wastrel (Roy. 2/8/94). See *H. BYATT.*
C.O. The Bric-a-brac Will (Lyr. 28/10/95). See *S. J. A. FITZGERALD.*

MOUILLOT, FREDERICK
D. Gentleman Jack (Stratford, 19/10/88). L.C.
Ca. A Mare's Nest (Norwich, 2/10/89).
R.D. The Bishop of the Fleet (Londesborough, Scarborough, 26/12/89). See *C. A. CLARKE.*
D. The Cloven Foot (Blackburn, 27/1/90; Pav. 30/6/90). L.C.
[Written in collaboration with *J. STEER.*]
D. The Dark Continent; or, The Story of a Great Diamond (Barnsley, 11/6/91; Grand, Stonehouse, Plymouth, 29/2/92, *revised*; Grand, 10/10/92). L.C.
[Written in collaboration with *H. H. MORELL.*]
Ext. The Nineteenth Century (Roy. Chester, 12/5/94). See *H. H. MORELL.*
C. Brought together (E.C. 29/10/94). L.C.
C.O. The Little Duchess (Stockton-on-Tees, 9/9/97). See *F. W. MARSHALL.*
C. The Honourable John (Qns. Crouch End, 12/12/98). L.C.

MOULE, FRED
D. A Little Vagrant (Alex. Cleethorpes, 8/7/97). L.C.
[Written in collaboration with *E. W. AVERY.*]
M.D. The Avenger; or, Slaves of Passion (Qns. Leeds, 29/9/99). L.C.

MOUNTFORD, HARRY
P. Ali Baba (Qns. O.H. Crouch End, 27/12/97). See *F. L. MORETON.*
D. Death or Victory (Attercliffe, 22/9/98). See *J. MILL.*

[*MOWATT, ANNA C. O.* [*Mrs RITCHIE*]
C. Fashion; or, Life in New York (Olym. 9/1/50). L.C.

MOWBRAY, LILLIAN
D. King and Artist. L.C. Str. 30/6/97. 8° 1897.
[Written in collaboration with *W. H. POLLOCK.*]
R.D. The Were Wolf (Aven. 15/2/98, *copy.*). L.C.
[Written in collaboration with *W. H. POLLOCK.*]

MOWBRAY, THOMAS
F. This Little Back Parlour (Soho, 28/9/57).
P. Harlequin King Aboulifar (Soho, 26/12/57). L.C.
Ext. Raymond in Agonies (Soho, 24/12/60). L.C.

MUDIE, GEORGE
Duol. Mr Greenlea's Courtship (Park H. Camden Town, 3/2/91). L.C.
[Music by M. Dwyer.]
M.C. The Duke's Diversion (Park H. W. Norwood, 21/5/92; Parkhurst, 13/6/92).
[A revision of J. R. Planché's *Follies of a Night* (D.L. 1842). Music by M. Dwyer.]
F. His Landlady (Parkhurst, 13/6/92). L.C.

MULHOLLAND, J. B. ["*J. BEAMUL*"]

C.D. Mizpah (Arcade, Stirling, 12/85; Gt Grimsby, 25/1/86; Brit. 18/5/91). L.C.

D. Conspiracy (P'cess. Glasgow, 5/3/88). L.C. Gai. Halifax, 13/2/88. [Title altered to *Disowned*, 22/1/89.]

P. Aladdin (Metro. Camberwell, 26/12/96). See *J. W. JONES*.

MULLEN, FRANK

D. The Substance and the Shadow (Art Gall. Newcastle, 30/1/94). L.C.

[Written in collaboration with *T. ATKINSON*.]

MÜLLER, H.

O. The Bride of Messina (Portman R. 23/4/87).

[Music by J. H. Bonawitz.]

MUNNS, H. T.

D. Ulvene, the Syren Queen (Birmingham, 31/3/74). L.C.

D. Face to Face (P.W. Birmingham, 27/11/77). L.C.

[*MURDOCH, FRANK HITCHCOCK*

D. Davy Crockett (Rochester, New York, 11/72; Alex. L'pool, 9/6/79; Olym. 9/8/79).

MURDOCH, J. MORTIMER

D. Waifs; or, Working in the Dark (Edinburgh, 1/11/69).

D. A Flash of Lightning (Amphi. Leeds, 1/8/70; Grec. 21/11/70). L.C.

[Written in collaboration with *C. DALY*.]

D. Old Grimey; or, Life in the Black Country (Grec. 23/12/72). L.C.

D. Beneath the Surface; or, The Loss of the Eurydice (Grec. 2/6/73). L.C.

D. Cead Mille Failthe (E.L. 29/12/77). L.C. as *C.M.F.; or, The Old House in the West*.

D. The Hoop of Gold (Pav. 2/3/78). L.C.

D. Strayed from the Fold; or, The Vicar's Fireside (Pav. 8/6/78). L.C.

D. In Duty Bound (Pav. 3/8/78). L.C.

D. Yours till Death (Pav. 2/11/78). L.C.

D. Lost Love; or, A Woman's Sacrifice (Pav. 8/3/79). L.C.

D. Transported for Life (E.C. 30/10/80). L.C.

D. Old Steady (Pav. 3/9/81). L.C.

D. Proved True (S.W. 7/5/83).

D. Innocence; or, A Lightning's Flash (Scarborough, 4/8/84).

[Apparently a revised version of *A Flash of Lightning*.]

D. Honour's Price (Whitehaven, 25/8/84; M'bone, 27/6/85). L.C.

D. Dora Ingram (Pav. 23/2/85). L.C.

MURRAY, ALFRED

F. Seeing Frou Frou (Glo. 16/4/81). L.C.

Bsq.O. Gibraltar (H. 6/8/81). L.C.

[Music by L. Varney. Revised as *Madame Rose*, L.C. 14/9/81.]

C.O. Lurette (Aven. 24/3/83). See *F. DESPREZ*.

Bsq. Little Carmen (Glo. 7/2/84). L.C.

C.O. Dick (Glo. 17/4/84). L.C.

[Music by E. Jakobowski.]

F. Mistaken Identity (Gai. 4/2/86, *mat.*). L.C.

C.D. Round the World (Empire, 3/3/86). L.C.

C.O. The Lily of Léoville (Grand, Birmingham, 3/5/86). See *F. REMO*.

Ext. The Palace of Pearl (Empire, 12/6/86). See *W. YOUNGE.*
C.O. Glamour (Edinburgh, 30/8/86). See *H. B. FARNIE.*
C.O. La Béarnaise (Grand, Birmingham, 27/9/86; P.W. 4/10/86). L.C.
[Music by A. Messager.]
C.O. Nadgy (P.W. Greenwich, 19/10/87, *copy.*; Aven. 7/11/88). L.C.
[Music by F. Chassaigne.]
C.O. Babette (Str. 26/1/88). L.C.
[Written in collaboration with *J. G. MOSENTHAL.* Music by G. Michiels.]
C.O. La Prima Donna (Aven. 16/10/89). See *H. B. FARNIE.*
C.O. La Périchole (Gar. 14/9/97). L.C.
[Music by J. Offenbach.]

MURRAY, DAVID CHRISTIE
C.D. Ned's Chum (O.H. Auckland, New Zealand, 4/4/90, as *Chums*; Glo. 27/8/91).
C.D. The Puritan (Traf. 26/7/94). L.C.
[Written in collaboration with *J. L. SHINE.*]
C.D. An Irish Gentleman (Glo. 9/6/97). L.C.
[Written in collaboration with *J. L. SHINE.*]
C.D. Paul of the Alps (Colchester, 15/4/98). L.C. P'cess. Portsmouth, 30/11/97, as *An Alpine Romance.*
[Written in collaboration with *C. ARNOLD.*]

MURRAY, DOMINICK
Ca. Worryburry's Whims (Alex. 20/5/65). See *C. H. ROSS.*

MURRAY, GASTON
C. Family Pride (S.W. 5/62). L.C.
D. Lost Emily (P.W. Birmingham, 30/6/70).

MURRAY, Sir GILBERT
D. Carlyon Sahib (O.H. Southport, 6/4/99, *copy.*; P'cess. of W. Kennington, 19/6/99). L.C.

MURRAY, HENRY
D.Sk. Absolution (Glasgow, 8/4/92).
C. A Society Butterfly (O.C. 10/5/94). See *R. BUCHANAN.*

MURRAY, J. K.
D. Homeless (Leicester, 19/7/93). L.C.
[Written in collaboration with *G. COMER.*]
D. A Woman's Error (St J. Manchester, 28/2/98). L.C.
D. The Luck of Life (Osborne, Manchester, 30/5/98; Stand. 15/8/98). L.C.
D. A Stroke of Luck (Grand, Cardiff, 7/8/99). See *A. G. BAGOT.*

MURRAY, PERCY
C.D. Our John (Gar. 10/6/99). L.C.

MUSGRAVE, Mrs H.
C. Our Flat (Winter Gdns. Southport, 10/4/89; P.W. 13/6/89, *mat.*). L.C.
F.C. Cerise and Co. (P.W. 17/4/90, *mat.*). L.C.
C.D. Dick Wilder (Vaud. 20/6/91). L.C. as *The Weeping Cross.*

MUSKERRY, WILLIAM
D. A Secret of the Sea (Cheltenham, 17/1/70).
D. Hilda's Inheritance; or, Livingstone's Son (Pav. 21/10/71). L.C.
D. Atonement (Vic. 31/8/72; S.W. 14/9/72). L.C.

D. For Dear Life (Vic. 2/6/73). L.C.
D. The Gascons; or, Love and Loyalty (Olym. 21/2/76). L.C.
D. Khartoum (Sanger's, 14/3/85). L.C. *Lacy*.
[Written in collaboration with *J. JOURDAIN*.]
D. Garrick; or, Only an Actor (Str. 9/8/86). L.C. *Lacy*.
P. Cinderella (Sanger's, 27/12/86). L.C.
P. The Frog who would a-wooing go (M'bone, 24/12/87). L.C.
P. Blue Beard the Grand Bashaw (Sanger's, 26/12/87). L.C.
P. Whittington and his Cat (M'bone, 24/12/88).
P. Robinson Crusoe; or, Harlequin Man Friday and the King of the Cannibal Islands (Sanger's, 26/12/88). L.C.
P. Lady Godiva; or, St George and the Dragon, and the Seven Champions of Christendom (Sanger's, 26/12/89). L.C.
P. Robinson Crusoe (M'bone, 24/12/91). L.C
P. Little Red Riding Hood (M'bone, 24/12/92). L.C.
C. An Odd Trick (Bradford, 27/5/95). L.C. *French*.
D.Sk. Dollusions (Wonderland, Whitechapel, 11/5/96).
Bsq. Thrillby (Richmond, 11/5/96). L.C. *Lacy*.
[Music by F. O. Carr.]

NADEN, ANGELO THOMAS
F.C. Limited Liability (Stratford, 4/5/88). L.C.
F.C. The Junior Partner (Windsor, 22/9/90). L.C.
D. A Noble Coward (Gt Grimsby, 23/2/91). L.C. Windsor, 11/9/90.
D. Clarice de Clermont; or, The Count's Treasure (St J. H. Wrexham, 16/3/92). L.C.

NANCE, A.
Oa. The Mountain King (Portsmouth, 25/1/75).
[Written in collaboration with *J. WINTERBOTTOM*.]
D. Harold (P's. Portsmouth, 29/3/75). L.C.

NANTON, LEWIS
D. Wait and Hope; or, The Stain upon the Hand (E.L. 14/6/69).

NASH, BRANSTON
F.C. The Silly Season (Athen. Shepherd's Bush, 30/12/92). See *G. L. GORDON*.

NAUCAZE, ANNA DE
C.D. The Peruvian (O.C. 12/11/91). L.C.

NEALE, FREDERIC
[For his earlier plays see iv, 365–6.]
D. Constantia (M'bone, 1/3/52).
P. Harlequin Uncle Tom; or, Britannia, the Pride of the Ocean and Guardian Genius of the Slave (Pav. 27/12/52). L.C.
D. Bleak House (C.L. 6/6/53). See *J. ELPHINSTONE*.
P. Ladye-Bird, fly away home; or, Harlequin and the Fiend of the Golden Stone (Pav. 26/12/53). L.C.

"*NEIL, ROSS*" [*ISABELLA HARWOOD*]
— Lady Jane Grey [and] Inez; or, The Bride of Portugal. 8° 1871.
— Plays: King and the Angel: The Cid: Duke for a Day; or, The Taylor of Brussels. 8° 1874.
D. Elfinella; or, Home from Fairyland (P'cess. Edinburgh, 15/10/75; P'cess. 6/6/78). L.C. 8° 1876.
O. The Heir of Lynne. L.C. St G. 11/6/77.

— Arabella Stuart...The Heir of Lynne...Tasso. 8° 1879.
C.D. Paul and Virginia (Gai. Dublin, 23/9/81). L.C. Edinburgh, 30/11/81, as *The Lovers of Palma*.
— Andrea the Painter; Claudia's Choice; Orestes; Pandora. 8° 1883.
D. The Angel King (Westwood House, Sydenham, 17/7/84).
R.D. Loyal Love (Gai. 13/8/87). L.C.
[A stage version of *Inez*.]

NEILSON, F.
M.C. The Highway Knight (Court, L'pool, 14/3/98). See *E. C. HEDMONDT*.
D. Philip Strong; or, In his Steps (Gar. 16/11/99, *copy*.).

"*NELSON, ALEC.*" *See E. B. AVELING*

NELSON, R.
F. Mumps the Masher (Nottingham, 2/6/84). See *T. CRAVEN*.

NESBIT, E.
F. A Family Novelette (P.H. New Cross, 21/2/94).
[Written in collaboration with *O. BARRON*.]

NETMORE, F.
F. After Dinner (Uxbridge, 18/5/71).

NEVILLE, GEORGE F.
C. Loving Hearts and Buried Diamonds (Str. 21/5/70). L.C.
Ca. Reconciliation (Olym. 21/2/76). L.C.
F. Little Vixens (Olym. 2/2/78). L.C.
D. Her World against a Lie (Alh. Barrow-in-Furness, 24/5/80). See *FLORENCE MARRYAT*.
C. Trapped at Last (Roy. 25/3/82). L.C.

NEVILLE, HENRY
D. The Convict (Amphi. L'pool, 3/8/68). L.C.
D. The Yellow Passport (Olym. 7/11/68). 8° 1872 [*priv*.].
D. The Violin Maker of Cremona (Olym. 2/7/77). L.C.
D. The Enemy. L.C. 10/11/79. MS. Birmingham.

NEWBIGGING, THOMAS
Poet.D. Old Gamul. 12° 1892.

NEWBOUND, EDGAR
D. Zelma; or, An Indian's Love (Brit. 13/12/75). L.C.
D. Faithful unto Death (Brit. 13/3/76). L.C.
T. Chloris (Brit. 18/12/76). L.C.
D. Saved by a Word (Brit. 26/2/77). L.C.
D. Man's Talisman—Gold; or, The Forget-me-not (Brit. 17/12/77). L.C.
D. Dora Mayfield; or, Love the Leveller (Brit. 25/2/78). L.C.
D. Lasting Love (Brit. 15/7/78). L.C.
D. Castruccio; or, The Deformed (Brit. 24/7/78).
D. The Legend of Wehrendorf (Brit. 16/12/78). L.C.
D. Eversleigh House (Brit. 17/3/79). L.C.
D. Ingulph (Brit. 15/12/79). L.C.
D. Gemea (Brit. 29/3/80). L.C.
C. Only My Cousin; or, The Blessing of Education (Brit. 19/4/80). L.C.
C. Major Marie Annie (Brit. 17/5/80). L.C.
D. The Reign of Blood (Brit. 17/5/80). L.C.
D. Entrapped (Brit. 24/7/80). L.C.

D. Only a Head; or, The Hempen Cravat (Brit. 20/11/80). L.C.
D. On Ruin's Brink (Leicester, 28/2/81). L.C.
D. Missing; or, Saved from the Scaffold (Brit. 6/6/81). L.C.

NEWLAND, H. C.
M.C. Juanita; or, Love's Strategy (Empire, Southend, 15/11/94). [Music by A. Wellnone.]

NEWNHAM, FRANCIS
D.Poem. The Pleasures of Anarchy. 8° 1852.

NEWRY, Lord
D. Écarté (Glo. 3/12/70). L.C.
D. The Danischeffs; or, Married by Force (St J. 6/1/77). L.C.

NEWTE, HORACE C. W.
Ca. Taking the Bull by the Horns (Iffley H. Hammersmith, 6/6/89).
C.D. Trust (Ladb. H. 30/4/91).
D. The Journey's End (Ladb. H. 11/6/91; Glo. 30/1/95). L.C.
D. Leonore (Ladb. H. 11/5/92). L.C.
C.D. A Ministering Angel (Bijou, 8/6/93). See *N. DOONE.*
C.D. Snowdrop (Bijou, 1/2/94). See *N. DOONE.*
F.Oa. Mr Fitz W—? (Bijou, 1/2/94). [Lyrics by *W. PARKE.* Music by B. Andrews.]
T. Semiramis (Bijou, 13/10/94, *copy.*). L.C.
D. A Ray of Sunlight (Bijou, 27/4/96). L.C.
C.D. A Labour of Love (Com. 26/7/97). L.C.
Duol. The Eternal Masculine (Terry's, 8/3/98).
D.Sk. The Ugly Lover; or, The Plainest Man in France (Ladb. H. 11/3/98).

NEWTON, CECIL
D. The Adopted Son (Athen. H. Tottenham Court Road, 9/5/94).
D. A Soldier's Son; or, The Gallant Twenty First (P'cess. of W. Kennington, 7/8/99). L.C. [Written in collaboration with *W. BOYNE.*]

NEWTON, E.
D. Wealth and Want (Pullan's, Bradford, 3/3/84). L.C.

NEWTON, GEORGE
C.D. Obed Snow's Philanthropy (P.W. 11/7/87, *mat.*). L.C.

NEWTON, H. CHANCE ["*RICHARD HENRY*"]
Bsq. Giddy Godiva; or, The Girl that was sent to Coventry (Sanger's, 13/10/83). L.C.
O.Bsq. Cartouche and Co. Ltd.; or, The Ticket-of (French)-Leave Man (Birmingham, 22/8/92). L.C. [Music by G. Le Brunn.]
F. Letters addressed here (Shaft. 14/2/93).
Ext. Weatherwise (Lyr. 27/12/93). L.C. [Music by E. Ford.]
P. The House that Jack built (O.C. 24/12/94). L.C.
M.F. The Newest Woman (Aven. 4/4/95). L.C. [Music by G. Jacobi.]
M.D. The Maid of Athens (O.C. 3/6/97). See *C. EDMUND.*
D. Honour or Love (Empire, Oldham, 3/2/98; Metro. Camberwell, 21/2/98). L.C.
M.Bsq. The A.B.C.; or, Flossie the Frivolous (Grand, Wolverhampton, 21/3/98; Borough, Stratford, 2/5/98). L.C.

"*NIBB, JAY.*" See *H. A. SAINTSBURY*

NICHOL, JOHN
D. Hannibal. 8° 1873 [Glasgow].

NICHOL, J. SCRYMOUR
D. In the Days of Trafalgar (Church R. Ampthill, 12/9/99).

NICHOLS, G. B.
R.O. In the Days of the Siege (Plymouth, 4/7/98). L.C.
[Music by H. A. Jeboult. Title altered to *The Puritan Girl.*]
C. A Country Cricket Match (London Assembly R. Taunton, 5/8/98). L.C.

NICHOLS, HARRY
F. Simpson's Little Holiday (D.L. 13/9/84).
P. The Babes in the Wood (D.L. 26/12/88). See *Sir A. HARRIS.*
P. Jack and the Beanstalk; or, Harlequin and the Midwinter Night's Dream (D.L. 26/12/89). L.C.
[Written in collaboration with *Sir A. HARRIS.*]
F. Jane (Com. 18/12/90). L.C.
[Written in collaboration with *W. LESTOCQ.*]
P. Humpty Dumpty (D.L. 26/12/91). See *Sir A. HARRIS.*
P. Robinson Crusoe (D.L. 26/12/93). L.C.
[Written in collaboration with *Sir A. HARRIS.*]
M.C. The Runaway Girl (Gai. 21/5/98). See *Sir S. HICKS.*

NICHOLSON, G. A.
D. Lost for Ever; or, Milly, the Collier's Wife (Qns. Barnsley, 11/1/69).
F. Sport (Park, 5/2/76). L.C.

NICHOLSON, S.
D. Jane Seton; or, The Witch of Edinbro' (Leith, 28/3/70).

NIE, JOHN
P. Robinson Crusoe (E.C. 24/12/92). L.C.

NIEL, COLA
C. Cross Strokes (Richmond, 7/4/94, *amat.*). L.C.

NIGHTINGALE, J. H.
F. Bloomerism; or, The Follies of the Day (Adel. 2/10/51). L.C. *Webster.*
[Written in collaboration with *C. MILLWARD.*]

NISBET, J. F.
C. Cousin Johnny (Str. 11/7/85). L.C. *Lacy.*
[Written in collaboration with *C. M. RAE.* Title altered later to *Hot Potatoes.*]
D. Dorothy Gray (P'cess. 10/4/88, *mat.*). L.C.

NOBLE, CECIL
D. Shame (Huddersfield, 12/10/83). L.C.

NOBLE, CHARLES RIDER
D. From Shore to Shore (O.H. Northampton, 6/6/92). See *A. ENGLAND.*
P. Cinderella (Brixton, 26/12/96). See *A. ENGLAND.*
P. Robinson Crusoe (Brixton, 27/12/97). See *A. ENGLAND.*
P. Aladdin (Brixton, 26/12/98). See *A. ENGLAND.*

NOEL, MAURICE

F. Tea (Bath Saloon, Torquay, 11/1/87; Crit. 4/5/87). L.C.

C.D. An American Bride (Lyr. 5/5/92). See *Sir W. L. YOUNG*.

NOLAN, HUGH

D.Sk. Out of the Past (Roy. Barrow-in-Furness, 4/2/98). L.C.

NORDON, JULIA B.

Duol. Misunderstood (Steinway H. 6/5/99).

NORMAN, E. B.

Ca. The Old Maid's Wooing (St G. 28/1/88). See *A. GOLDSWORTHY*.

C. The Blacksmith's Daughter (O.C. 16/10/88). See *A. GOLDSWORTHY*.

NORMAN, G. PARSONS

C.O. Matrimony (Ladb. H. 22/6/93). L.C.
[Music by F. S. Lacy.]

NORMAN, G. TEMPLEMAN

D.Sk. Dolls (Ladb. H. 11/7/92, *mat.*).

D.Sk. One Half Hour (Ladb. H. 11/7/92, *mat.*).

Duol. A May Morning (Bijou, 3/12/95). L.C.

Ca. Frank Charington's Return (Ladb. H. 26/2/97). L.C.

Duol. Between the Acts (Com. 22/3/98). L.C.

D.Sk. In an Afternoon (Ladb. H. 13/5/98).

NORMAN, NORMAN V.

D. Noel Ainslie, V.C. (Ladb. H. 26/2/97). See *W. E. GROGAN*.

NORRIS, ERNEST E.

C. With Heart and Hand (Pastoral Players, Highgate, 21/7/88). See *B. LANDECK*.

NORTH, H.

Ca. Coal-ition (Alex. L'pool, 21/2/81). See *T. H. HARDMAN*.

NORTH, WILLIAM

D. The Wings of the Storm (Glo. 5/10/91). See *R. J. BARLOW*.

NORTH, W. S.

Oa. Blue Beard (National Childrens' Hospital, Dublin, 13/1/94, *amat.*).
[Music by J. McCullum.]

Oa. Robinson Crusoe (Mansion H. Dublin, 16/2/95).
[Music by J. McCullum.]

NORTON, SMEDLEY

D. Sealed to Silence (Nov. 28/9/96). See *H. V. REES*.

NORWOOD, EILLE

Ca. Hook and Eye (Grand, Leeds, 22/3/87; O.C. 14/11/91). L.C.

D.Sk. A Welcome Visit (P.H. Harwich, 14/7/87). L.C. *French* [as *Assault and Battery*].
[Title altered to *Assault and Battery*, 27/12/92.]

Ca. Chalk and Cheese (Village H. Esher, 6/1/88; Vaud. 10/11/99). L.C. Winter Gdns. Southport, 31/12/87. *French*.

F. The Noble Art (York, 11/4/92; Terry's, 25/5/92, *mat.*; Terry's, 22/6/92). L.C.

C. The Silver Keepsake (York, 19/12/94). L.C.

F.C. Newspaper Nuptials (Str. 10/8/1901). L.C. Central H. Exhibition Buildings, 17/5/99. *French*.

NOWELL, HARRY
Oa. May Meetings (T.H. Reading, 6/10/94).
[Written in collaboration with *H. WYNNE.*]

NUGENT, E. C.
Bsq. The Real Truth about Ivanhoe; or, Scott Scotched (Chelsea Barracks, 1/2/89).
[Music by E. Solomon.]

NUGENT, Lieut. G.
O.Bsq. Miss Maritana; or, Not for Jo (Qns. Dublin, 21/4/90).
[Written in collaboration with *J. W. WHITBREAD.*]

NUGENT, JAMES FITZGERALD
F. Dhrame; or, Barney's Mistake (Birkenhead, 10/7/76). L.C.

O'BRYAN, CHARLES
D. Lugarto the Mulatto (Sur. 20/5/50).

O'BYRNE, —
D. Banks and Breaks (Amphi. L'pool, 17/5/69).

O'CONNELL ALICE
F. All Jackson's Fault (Athen. H. Tottenham Court Road, 27/11/89).

O'CONNOR, T.
D. The Rent Warner (Limerick, 1/12/82).

O'DOWD, J. C.
D. The Maid of Cefn Ydfa (Model, Aberdare, 21/4/70).

OGDEN, C.
F. The Churchwarden (Newcastle, 17/9/86). See *H. CASSEL.*
F. My First Patient (Technical College, Bradford, 12/2/87). See *H. CASSEL.*

OGILVIE, G. STUART
D. Hypatia (H. 2/1/93). L.C.
R.D. The Sin of St Hulda (Shaft. 9/4/96). L.C.
C. The White Knight (Terry's, 26/2/98). L.C.
C. The Master (Glo. 23/4/98). L.C.

O'GRADY, HUBERT
F. A Shindy in a Shanty (Gai. W. Hartlepool, 7/8/76).
D. The Gommoch (Stockton-on-Tees, 16/3/77). L.C.
D. The Eviction (P'cess. Glasgow, 24/1/80; Stand. 9/8/80). L.C. Gai. Barnsley, 27/11/79.
D. Emigration (P'cess. Glasgow, 14/5/83). L.C.
D. The Famine (Qns. Dublin, 26/4/86; Grand, 28/6/86). L.C.
R.D. The Fenian (P'cess. Glasgow, 1/4/89; Stand. 2/9/89). L.C. Philharmonic, Tewkesbury, 23/11/88.
D. The Priest Hunter (Qns. Manchester, 3/4/93; Grand, 17/4/93). L.C. Clarence, Pont-y-Pridd, 3/12/92.
D. A Fast Life (Operetta H. Rhyl, 26/10/96; Imp. 24/10/98). L.C.

O'HALLORAN, G. B.
P. Dick Whittington and his Cat (Alex. Pal. 21/12/78). L.C.

O'HARE, J. F.
F.C. The Bachelor's Widow (Roy. Glasgow, 14/6/97; Terry's, 14/6/98). L.C.
[Lyrics by *M. T. PIGGOTT.* Music by E. Boggetti.]

OLAF, W.
D. A Man of Business (St G. 26/3/87). L.C.
[Written in collaboration with *W. CHAPMAN*.]

OLDE, BASIL
C.O. Love and War (Portsmouth, 17/6/95; E.C. 15/7/95). L.C.
[Written in collaboration with *Sir W. L. YOUNG*.]

"*OLDE, LAWRENCE*." See *Sir W. L. YOUNG*

OLIPHANT, E. H. C.
Ext. Dresden China (Vaud. 21/7/92). See *A. CHAPIN*.
D. Shame (Vaud. 21/7/92). See *A. CHAPIN*.

OLIVER, EDWIN
Ca. A Widow's Wooing (County H. St Alban's, 23/10/93). L.C.
D. An Old Man's Darling (Ladb. H. 19/3/95). L.C.

O'NEIL, ARTHUR
Ext. The Golden Cask, the Princess, the Page and the Pageant; or, Harlequin and Queen Grumble (S.W. 26/12/66). L.C.
Bsq. William Tell (S.W. 19/10/67). L.C. as *W.T.; or, The Arrow, the Apple and the Agony*.
Bsq. Abon Hassan; or, An Arabian Knight's Entertainment (Ch. X. 11/12/69). L.C.
C. Bohemia and Belgravia (Roy. 8/6/72). L.C.

O'NEIL, CLEMENT
C.O. Giroflé Girofla (Phil. 3/10/74). L.C.
[Version of the opera, libretto A. Vanloo and E. Leterrier, music C. Lecocq (Brussels, 21/3/54). Written in collaboration with *C. CLARKE*.]
Bsq.O. Bluff King Hal (Cheltenham, 10/4/77).
D. Veva; or, The Beggars of the Sea (Str. 26/4/83). L.C.
C.D. Twice Married (Gai. 25/4/87, *mat.*). L.C.
[Written in collaboration with *H. SILVESTER*.]

O'NEIL, J. R. ["*HUGO VAMP*"]
Ext. The United Services (Marionette, 9/2/52).
Ext. Who's Wife is she? (Marionette, 22/3/52).
Ext. The Happy Manager (Marionette, 26/4/52).
Ext. The Arcadian Brothers; or, The Spirit of Punch (Marionette, 3/5/52).
Ext. Roscius in Spirits (Marionette, 21/6/52).
F. Mrs Johnson (D.L. 26/7/52). L.C.
D. Don Roderic; or, The Outlaws of Braganza (M'bone, 23/10/52). L.C.
P. Harlequin Ali Baba (St J. 27/12/52).
D. The Guardian Spirit (M'bone, 14/2/53). L.C.
F. The Barber of Paris (M'bone, 14/2/53).
Ext. In for a Dig; or, Life at the Diggings (Ast. 25/4/53). L.C.

ORCHARD, J. ROBERTSON
D. The Ladder of Wealth (County H. Guildford, 23/10/99). L.C.

"*O'RELL, MAX*." See *P. BLOUET*

O'ROURKE, —
D. The Husband of an Hour (H. 1/6/57). L.C.

ORRES, F.
C.D. The Second Volume (St G. 2/3/95). L.C.

OSBORN, S.
Ca. The Regiment (E.C. 12/5/88). L.C.

OSBORNE, CHARLES
D. Hernani; or, The Double Wrong (Belfast, 5/10/68). L.C.
D. Chance (Belfast, 4/10/69).
D. The Face in the Moonlight (Amphi. Leeds, 30/10/71).
D. Iron before Gold (Belfast, 12/2/72).
D. The Old Forge (Gai. 22/6/72). L.C.
C.D. Dangerous (Lyc. Sunderland, 22/9/73). L.C.
D. A Slave's Ransom (Newcastle, 4/6/74).
D. The Courier of the Czar (L'pool, 14/5/77). L.C.
D. The Mask of Love (Plymouth, 23/5/77). L.C.
D. Death's Bridal (O.H. Bolton, 10/6/78).
D. A Midnight Marriage (Margate, 30/8/83). L.C.
Ca. After the Rehearsal (Wolverhampton, 9/9/88). L.C.
M.C. The Bicycle Girl (Grand, Nottingham, 29/3/97). L.C. Brixton, 18/11/96.
[Written in collaboration with *E. M. STUART*; lyrics by *H. SETON*. Music by O. Powell.]

OSBORNE, KATE
C. The Clerk of the Weather (O.H. Torquay, 11/6/92, *copy.*; Aquar. Brighton, 26/2/94). L.C.
[Written in collaboration with *A. H. HODGSON.*]

OSMAN, W. R.
D. Islington; or, Life in the Streets (S.W. 11/5/67).
F. A Mesmeric Mystery (Vic. 17/8/67).
P. St George and the Dragon; or, Old Father Time and the Seven Champions of Christendom (Sur. 27/12/69). L.C.
D. The Power of Gold; or, Honesty is the Best Policy (Sur. 19/2/70).
Bsq. The Seven Champions of Christendom; or, Good Little St George and the Naughty Snapdragon (Alex. 22/8/70).
P. The Children in the Wood; or, Harlequin Cock Robin (Regent, Manchester, 23/12/71). L.C.
Bsq. Greenleaf the Graceful; or, The Palace of Vengeance (Roy. 26/2/72). L.C.
Ext. The Daughter of the Danube (Holb. 3/3/73).
P. Ye Faust and Marguerite (E.L. 26/12/73). L.C.
P. The Sleeping Beauty (C.P. 22/12/77). See *Sir A. HARRIS.*
P. Harlequin Cock Robin (C.P. 22/12/81). L.C.
P. The Forty Thieves (C.P. 21/12/82). See *O. BARRETT.*

OSMOND, L.
D. A Wasted Life (St Alban's H. 12/6/94).
[Written in collaboration with *F. H. HERBERT.*]

OSWALD, FRANK
D. Dawn (Vaud. 30/6/87). See *G. THOMAS.*

OTLEY, —
F. How to win a Wager (Bristol, 30/11/74).

OUSELEY, MULREY
D. Tristernagh (Walsall, 23/7/83).
D. Not yet (Croydon, 19/3/86). L.C. Coventry, 19/1/86.

OUTRAM, LEONARD S.

C.Oa. Uncle Joe at Oxbridge (Cambridge, 12/6/85). L.C.
C.D. Late Love (Reading, 7/1/86). L.C.
C. April Rain (Reading, 10/5/86). L.C.
R.D. A Mighty Error (Aven. 14/7/91). L.C.
D. The Fiat of the Gods (Aven. 25/8/91). L.C.
D. Go straight; or, Honest Hearts (Glo. 2/8/94, *copy*.). L.C.
D. True Blue; or, Afloat and Ashore (Olym. 19/3/96). L.C.
[Written in collaboration with *S. GORDON*.]
F.C. His other I (Worcester, 20/5/98, *copy*.). L.C.
[Written in collaboration with *W. H. BROWN*.]

OVERBECK, Miss E.

D.Sk. Round the Links (West, Albert H. 9/5/95). L.C.
[Title altered to *The Tipster*, 22/4/96.]
D.Sk. Sonia (West, Albert H. 9/5/95). L.C.

OVERTON, CHARLES

D. Strathlogan (P'cess. 9/6/92). L.C.
[Written in collaboration with *H. MOSS*.]

OVERTON, RICHARD

Ca. The Man in Possession (Assembly R. Leytonstone, 10/12/92). L.C.

OVERTON, ROBERT

D. The Two Common Sailors (Colchester, 9/4/83).
M.D. The Next of Kin (Sanger's, 28/2/87). L.C. Cheltenham, 25/1/87.
[Title altered later to *Better Days; or, N. of K.*]
D. The Mills of God (Lecture H. Greenwich, 6/2/92, *copy*.; Bijou, 25/5/93). L.C.

OXENFORD, EDWARD

C.O. The Great Mogul (Roy. 22/6/81). L.C.
[Music by W. Meadows.]
C.O. This House to let (Aquar. Brighton, 21/6/84).
[Music by J. Greekes.]

OXENFORD, JOHN

[For his earlier plays see iv, 367.]
O. The Sleeper Awakened (H.M. 15/11/50).
[Music by G. H. Macfarren.]
D. Pauline (P'cess. 17/3/51). L.C.
C. Tartuffe (H. 25/3/51). L.C. *Webster*.
C. Make the best of it (H. 27/3/51). L.C.
C.O. Aminta; or, A Match for a Magistrate (H. 26/1/52). L.C. *Webster*.
Ext. The Leghorn Bonnet (Adel. 16/2/52). L.C.
F. The Charming Widow (Lyc. 8/3/54). L.C.
F. Only a Half-penny (H. 30/5/55). L.C.
F. £5 Reward (Olym. 3/12/55). L.C. *Lacy*.
F. A Family Failing (H. 17/11/56). L.C.
Ca. A Doubtful Victory (Olym. 26/4/58). L.C. *Lacy*.
D. The Porter's Knot (Olym. 2/12/58). L.C.
D. The Last Hope (Lyc. 16/2/59). L.C.
F. Retained for the Defence (Olym. 23/5/59). L.C.
D. Ivy Hall (P'cess. 24/9/59). L.C.
Bal.F. The Magic Toys (St J. 24/10/59).
Bal. My Name is Norval (St J. 18/1/60).

D. Uncle Zachary (Olym. 8/3/60). L.C.
O. Robin Hood (H.M. 11/11/60). L.C.
Ext. Timour the Tartar; or, The Iron Master of Samarkand by Oxus (Olym. 26/12/60). L.C. *Lacy.*
[Written in collaboration with *C. W. S. BROOKS*.]
F. A Legal Impediment (Olym. 28/10/61). L.C.
O. The Lily of Killarney (C.G. 10/2/62). L.C. 12° 1863.
[Written in collaboration with *D. BOUCICAULT*.]
Ca. The World of Fashion (Olym. 17/3/62). L.C. as *Fashionable Intelligence.*
F. I couldn't help it (Lyc. 19/4/62). L.C.
F. Bristol Diamonds (St J. 11/8/62). L.C.
F. Sam's Arrival (Str. 8/9/62). L.C. *Lacy.*
D. The Triple Alliance (P'cess. 24/11/62). L.C.
Bal. Freya's Gift (C.G. 10/3/63).
D. The Soldier's Legacy; or, The Old Corporal's Story. L.C. M'bone, 10/7/63.
[Written in collaboration with — *McFARREN*.]
F. Beauty or the Beast (D.L. 2/11/63). L.C.
D. The Monastery of St Juste (P'cess. 27/6/64). L.C. *French.*
D. Stephen Digges (Adel. 14/9/64). L.C.
O. Helvellyn (C.G. 3/11/64). L.C.
[Music by G. A. Macfarren.]
F. A Young Lad from the Country (D.L. 21/11/64). L.C. *Lacy.*
Ca. Billing and Cooing (Roy. 16/1/65). L.C. *Lacy.*
C. Brother Sam (H. 24/5/65). L.C.
[Written in collaboration with *E. A. SOTHERN* and *J. B. BUCKSTONE*.]
D. Eleanor's Victory (St J. 29/5/65). L.C.
O. Felix; or, The Festival of Roses (Roy. 23/10/65). L.C.
[Music by M. Lutz.]
C. A Cleft Stick (Olym. 8/11/65). L.C.
F. Please to remember the Grotto; or, The Manageress in a Fix (St J. 26/12/65). L.C. *French.*
D. East Lynne (Sur. 5/2/66). L.C.
C. A Dangerous Friend (H. 31/10/66). L.C.
C. Neighbours (Str. 10/11/66). L.C. as *My Neighbour and Myself.*
P. The Grim Griffin Hotel; or, The Best Room in the House (Holb. Amphi. 25/5/67). L.C.
D. Oliver Twist (Qns. 11/4/68). L.C.
T. Pietra (H. 7/12/68). L.C.
D. A Life Chase (Gai. 11/10/69). L.C. *Lacy.*
[Written in collaboration with *H. WIGAN*.]
Ca. Widow's Weeds (Str. 19/3/70). L.C.
F. Down in a Balloon (Adel. 10/4/71). L.C. *Lacy.*
D. Hidden Treasure (Adel. 25/11/71). See *T. PARRY.*
D. The Last Days of Pompeii (Qns. 8/1/72). L.C.
C. A Dream of Love (O.C. 21/10/72). L.C.
Ca. No Cards (Adel. 30/11/72). L.C.
F. Much too clever; or, A Friend indeed (Gai. 23/2/74). L.C. as *Too Clever by Half.* 8° [1874].
[Written in collaboration with *J. HATTON*.]
F. A Waltz by Arditi (Adel. 7/3/74). L.C. *Lacy.*
D. The Two Orphans (Olym. 14/9/74). L.C.

O. The Porter of Havre (P'cess. 15/9/75). L.C.
[Music by Cagnoni.]
D. Self (Mirror, 27/9/75). L.C.
[Written in collaboration with *H. WIGAN*.]

[*PACHECO, Mrs R.*
F.C. Tom, Dick and Harry (originally produced in America as *Incog.*; Manchester, 24/8/93; Traf. 2/11/73). L.C.

PAGET, —
D. Fair Sinners; or, Desperate Women (Wolverhampton, 2/5/81). L.C. S. Shields, 16/12/80.

PALEY, G. B.
D. Saul of Tarsus. 8° 1885.

PALGRAVE, R.
D. The Faithful Heart (Bristol, 18/10/75). L.C.
D. Cast Adrift (Bristol, 27/2/82; S.W. 8/4/82). L.C.
[Written in collaboration with *F. GOVER*.]
D. Shadow and Sunshine (Edinburgh, 31/3/83). L.C.
D. Jane Shore (Court, L'pool, 31/8/85). See *J. W. BOULDING*.
D. God save the Queen (P's. Bristol, 24/4/86; Sanger's, 13/9/86). L.C.
[Written in collaboration with *F. GOVER*.]

PALINGS, W.
M.C. In the Ring (Gai. 27/5/96). See *J. T. TANNER*.

PALMER, Mrs BANDMANN
D. Catherine Howard; or, The Tomb, the Throne and the Scaffold (Weymouth, 2/1/92).

PALMER, EDWIN
D. Better late than never (Middlesborough, 5/9/70). L.C. Adel. L'pool, 7/10/65, as *It's better late than never; or, Sunshine through the Mist*.

PALMER, F. GROVE
C. Change (Cavendish R. 30/12/70). See *F. H. PRIDE*.
P. Robinson Crusoe and Billie Taylor (S.W. 23/12/82). See *G. PALMER*.
P. Jack and the Beanstalk (S.W. 27/12/86). See *G. THORNE*.
C.O. Daisy (T.H. Kilburn, 1/5/90). L.C.
[Music by H. T. Wood.]
Oa. Returning the Compliment (Park H. Camden Town, 5/11/90). See *O. WALDEN*.
P. Ye Miller and hys Men (Corn Exchange, Maidstone, 26/12/93). See *G. THORNE*.

PALMER, GEORGE
P. Robinson Crusoe and Billie Taylor; or, Harlequin Man Friday and the King of the Cannibal Islands (S.W. 23/12/82).
[Written in collaboration with *F. G. PALMER*.]

PALMER, L. S.
D. Nero's Niece (Worthing, 26/6/99). L.C.

PALMER, T. A.
D. Too late to save; or, Doomed to die (Exeter, 1861). 8° 1878; *Lacy*.
D. Brought to Light; or, Watching and Winning (Plymouth, 7/12/68).
C.D. Among the Relics (Plymouth, 22/11/69). *Lacy*.

C.D. Hard Hands and Happy Hearts (Plymouth, 22/11/69).
Ca. Rely on my Discretion (Roy. 17/1/70). L.C. *French.*
D. Insured at Lloyd's (Qns. Manchester, 5/11/70; Plymouth, 4/10/75). L.C. *Lacy.*
D. Florence (Plymouth, 20/11/72).
F. A Dodge for a Dinner (Str. 28/12/72). L.C. *Lacy.*
D. The Last Life (Greenwich, 9/2/74). *Lacy.*
D. East Lynne (Nottingham, 19/11/74). *French.*
C. Moral Suasion (Nottingham, 4/1/75).
F. An Appeal to the Feelings (Nottingham, 15/3/75). *Lacy.*
F. Fascinating Fellows (Olym. 18/3/76). L.C. as *My Medical Man.*
F.C. Cremorne (Str. 27/11/76). L.C.
[This was played in the provinces as *Seeing Life.*]
C. Memories (Court, 12/10/78). L.C.
F. Roasting a Rogue. L.C. Toole's, 19/7/82.
C. Woman's Rights (Grand, Douglas, I. of M. 8/82). *French.*

PALMER, W. H. G.
R.D. Mehalah (Gai. 11/6/86). See *W. POEL.*

PANTING, J. HARWOOD
D. Hector's Retribution (Walworth Inst. 9/2/81).
D. For an Old Debt (Bijou, 26/2/95). See *F. R. BUCKLEY.*

PARK, TOM
F. Mashing Mamma; or, A Domestic Mash (Cheltenham, 22/11/88). L.C.

PARKE, WALTER
C.O. Manteaux Noirs (Aven. 3/6/82). L.C.
[Music by Bucalossi.]
C.O. Estrella (P's. Manchester, 14/5/83; Gai. 24/5/83). L.C.
[Music by L. Searelle.]
F.C. Veracity (Gai. 20/4/86, *mat.*). L.C.
C.O. Rhoda (Croydon, 27/9/86; Grand, 1/11/86). L.C.
[Music by A. L. Mora.]
F. Ferdinando (Grand, 1/11/86). L.C.
C.O. Herne's Oak; or, The Rose of Windsor (P.W. L'pool, 24/10/87). L.C.
[Music by J. C. B. Andrews.]
C.O. Gipsy Gabriel (Bradford, 3/11/87). L.C.
[Written in collaboration with *W. HOGARTH.* Music by F. Pascal.]
C.O. The Rose of Windsor; or, King Hal and Herne the Hunter (P's. Accrington, 16/8/89). L.C.
[A revision of *Herne's Oak.*]
Oa. The Dear Departed (Com. 29/5/90, *mat.*). L.C.
F.Oa. Mr Fitz W—? (Bijou, 1/2/94). See *H. C. W. NEWTE.*
M.C. Bombay to Henley: A Yachting Trip (Ladb. H. 14/3/95, *copy.*; Parkhurst, 21/9/96, revised, as *En Route*). L.C.
[Music by P. and E. Bucalossi. Written in collaboration with *C. MAXWELL.*]
M.F. Daye and Knight (St G. 4/11/95). L.C.
[Music by L. Barone.]
C.O. Kitty (O.H. Cheltenham, 30/8/97; Kilburn, 11/10/97, as *The Convent Maid*). L.C.
[Written in collaboration with *H. PARKER.*]

PARKER, ALFRED D.

C. Friends (St J. Lichfield, 17/2/87).

PARKER, CHARLES S.

Ext. The Rose of the Alhambra (Stratford, 6/6/91; Parkhurst, 27/3/93). L.C.

P. Little Red Riding Hood (Pav. 26/12/91). L.C.

[*PARKER, GILBERT*

D. The Seats of the Mighty (H.M. 28/4/97). L.C. P.W. Birmingham, 21/10/96.

PARKER, HENRY

C.O. Kitty (O.H. Cheltenham, 30/8/97). See *W. PARKE.*

[*PARKER, LOTTIE BLAIR*

D.Sk. Red Roses (D.Y. 12/11/98).

PARKER, LOUIS N.

C.D. A Buried Talent (Digby Hotel, Sherborne, 3/12/86; Roy. Glasgow, 23/5/90; Vaud. 5/6/90, *mat.*; Com. 19/5/92). L.C.

D. Taunton Vale (Manchester, 12/6/90). L.C. as *In Taunton Vale.*

M.Sk. Love in a Mist (C.P. 9/7/91; Devonshire Park, Eastbourne, 2/1/93). L.C. Woodland Players Co. 2/7/90.

D. The Sequel (Vaud. 15/7/91). L.C.

D. A Bohemian (Glo. 18/2/92). L.C.

D. Chris (Vaud. 28/3/92, *mat.*; Grand, 2/5/92, as *A Broken Life*; Terry's, 30/10/99, revised, as *Captain Birchell's Luck*). L.C.

D. William (Parkhurst, 12/5/92). L.C.

D. The Love Knot (York, 7/10/92). L.C.

D. David (Gar. 7/11/92). L.C. as *The Bar Sinister.*
[Written in collaboration with *S. M. CARSON.*]

C. Gudgeons (Terry's, 10/11/93). See *S. M. CARSON.*

D. Once upon a Time (H. 27/2/94, *copy.*; H. 28/3/94). L.C.
[Written in collaboration with *Sir H. B. TREE.*]

D. The Man in the Street (Aven. 14/5/94). L.C.

Duol. Reply Paid (Ladb. H. 22/6/94). L.C. Vic. R. Savoy Hotel, 9/12/92.

F. The Blue Boar (Court, L'pool, 31/8/94; Terry's, 23/3/95). L.C.
[Written in collaboration with *S. M. CARSON.*]

D. A Sorceress of Love (Shakespeare, L'pool, 1/10/94).

C. The Peruvians (Bijou, 7/5/95, *copy.*; Metro. 18/10/97, as *The Vagabond King*; Court, 4/11/97). L.C.

F. A Bold Advertisement (Steinway H. 19/11/95, *mat.*). L.C. as *The Agony Column.*

C.D Love in Idleness (Brighton, 13/3/96; Terry's, 21/10/96). L.C.
[Written in collaboration with *E. J. GOODMAN.*]

D. Rosemary (Crit. 16/5/96). L.C.
[Written in collaboration with *S. M. CARSON.*]

D. Magda (Lyc. 3/6/96). L.C.

Masque. The Spell-bound Garden (Roy. Glasgow, 30/11/96; Brixton, 7/12/96). L.C.
[Written in collaboration with *S. M. CARSON.*]

C. The Happy Life (D.Y. 6/12/97; Terry's, 13/11/99). L.C. 4° [1897; *priv.*].

Ca. A Tame Cat (Mat. 21/6/98).

C.D. Ragged Robin (H.M. 23/6/98). L.C.

C.D. The Termagant (H.M. 1/9/98). L.C. 4° 1899 [*priv.*].
[Written in collaboration with *S. M. CARSON.*]
D. The Jest (Crit. 10/11/98). See *S. M. CARSON*.
D. The Mayflower (Metro. 6/3/99). L.C. Vic. H. Bayswater, 30/3/97.
C. Change Alley (Gar. 25/4/99). L.C.
[Written in collaboration with *S. M. CARSON.*]
D. Man and his Makers (Lyc. 7/10/99). See *W. BARRETT*.
D. The Sacrament of Judas (P.W. 9/10/99). L.C.
D. Captain Birchell's Luck (Terry's, 30/10/99). L.C.
[See *Chris* (Vaud. 28/3/92).]
D. The Bugle Call (H. 23/11/99). L.C.
[Written in collaboration with *A. A. BRIGHT.*]

PARKER, NELLA
Ca. Tom's Wife (Assembly R. Worthing, 7/4/96). L.C.

PARKER, WALTER
F.C. A Lost Sheep (Bradford, 13/7/91; O.C. 30/7/92, *mat.*). L.C.
[Written in collaboration with *A. SHIRLEY.*]
C.Oa. The Serenaders (Lyr. Club, 30/6/92). See *Sir A. HARRIS*.

PARKER, WILLIAM
F.C. Ma's Mistake (Qns. Dublin, 26/8/95).
Ca. A Capital Match (Richmond, 26/4/97).

PARKER, W. S.
C.Oa. Dora (Doblane School, Manchester, 22/4/93, *amat.*).

PARLEY, PETER
F. Pop goes the Weasel (Living Marionettes, 11/4/53).

PARR, F. C. W.
D. Jack White's Trial (Alex. Sheffield, 16/3/83). L.C. *Lacy*.

PARRY, ALFRED
D. Bitter Sweets; A Story of the Footlights (Cambridge, 8/8/78; Oxford, 13/1/80).
D. The Pride of the Family (Cambridge, 9/9/78).
M.C. Dotty (P'cess. Leith, 9/5/96). L.C.
[Written in collaboration with *E. HUGH*. Lyrics and music by *C. BLANCHARD* and *E. HUGH.*]

PARRY, A. W.
D. Shattered Lives (Granby H. L'pool, 12/12/90).
D. The Crystal Queen (Adel. L'pool, 7/8/93). L.C.
D. The Battle of Life (Adel. L'pool, 6/8/94). L.C.
[Written in collaboration with *T. DOBB.*]

PARRY, JOHN
F. The Wedding Breakfast (G.I. 23/6/66).

PARRY, JOSEPH
O. Blodwin (M.H. Swansea, 20/6/78).
O. Arianween (Cardiff, 5/6/90). L.C.

PARRY, MENDELSSOHN
O. Sylvia (Cardiff, 12/8/95). L.C.
[Music by Joseph Parry.]

PARRY, PERCY F.
D. 'Twixt Crime and Prison (P.H. Woolwich, 11/11/97).

PARRY, SEFTON

D. The Odds—What they were; who won; and who lost them (Holb. 1/10/70). L.C.

C.D. A Bright Future (Grand, 4/8/83). L.C.

PARRY, THOMAS

[For his earlier plays see iv, 368.]

D. The Disowned; or, Helen of the Hurst (Adel. 24/3/51). L.C.

D. The Summer Storm (Adel. 19/10/54). L.C.

PARRY, TOM

D. Hidden Treasure (Adel. 25/11/71). L.C.
[Written in collaboration with *J. OXENFORD*.]

PARSELLE, J.

D. The Orphan of Glencoe (Sur. 28/7/51). L.C.

Ca. My Son's a Daughter (Str. 15/9/62). L.C. *Lacy*.

Ca. Cross Purposes (Str. 27/3/65). L.C.

PASS, G. F.

Ca. False Colours (Roy. 8/10/81).

PATMORE, W. J.

D. Lured to London (Lyc. Crewe, 14/2/89). L.C.
[Written in collaboration with *A. B. MOSS*.]

C.D. Light at Last (Manchester, 28/7/90). L.C.

D. Capital and Labour (Vic. O.H. Burnley, 18/8/90; Brit. 14/9/91; Lyr. Hammersmith, 28/11/92). L.C.
[Written in collaboration with *A. B. MOSS*.]

D. The Star-Spangled Banner (Parkhurst, 11/2/92, *copy*.). L.C.

D. Sons of Erin (Sur. 11/9/93).

D. The Land and the People (P.H. New Cross, 16/10/93). See *A. B. MOSS*.

D.Sk. From the Jaws of Death (Pav. 7/12/93). L.C.

Ca. No. 72 (Bath, 11/12/93). L.C.

D. The Brine Oge (Dewsbury, 6/5/96, *copy*.). L.C.

D. Miriam Gray; or, The Living Dead (St J. Manchester, 20/7/96; Lyr. Hammersmith, 31/8/96; Sur. 8/3/97, as *A Daughter of Ishmael*). L.C.

PATTERSON, E. H.

Ext. Merry Mr Merlin; or, Good King Arthur (E.C. 11/2/95). L.C. Art Gallery, Newcastle, 16/12/93).
[Written in collaboration with *H. GRATTAN*.]

PATTERSON, G.

D. Fearless Fred, the Fireman (Alex. Sheffield, 13/7/74).

PATTINSON, R. E.

C.O. Coquette (5 Queen's Gate Place, W. 17/12/92; West, Albert H. 5/6/93; Bijou, 2/11/95).
[Music by D. Sopwith and A. Rawlinson.]

[*PAUL, HOWARD M.*

D. Blanche of Chillon. *Lacy*.

C. The Mob Cap; or, Love's Disguises (D.L. 13/4/53). L.C. *Lacy*.

F. Rappings and Table Movings (H. 16/6/53). L.C. *Lacy*.

F. Thrice Married (D.L. 12/3/54; P'cess. 16/5/60, revised). L.C. *Lacy*.

D. The Queen of Aragon (S.W. 12/5/54).

C. Opposite Neighbours (Str. 10/7/54). *Lacy.*
F. The Man that follows the Ladies (Str. 19/7/56). *Lacy.*
F. Patchwork (St J. 27/6/59).
Ca. A Change of System (St J. 9/4/60). L.C. *Lacy.*
F. A Lucky Hit (P'cess. 9/5/66). *Lacy.*
[The Lacy edition states that this was presented at S.W. in 1854.]
Ca. The Old Folks (Str. 16/9/67). L.C.
F. Locked out (H. 12/7/75). L.C. *Lacy.*
C.O. The Bronze Horse (Alh. 4/7/81). L.C.

PAUL, T. H.
D. Jane Eyre (Adel. Oldham, 13/10/79). L.C.

PAUL, W.
D. The Twin Brothers; or, The Warning Vision (M'bone, 16/2/74).

PAULL, H. M.
C. The Great Felicidad (Gai. 24/3/87, *mat.*).
F.C. Tenterhooks (Com. 1/5/89). L.C.
D.Sk. The Old Bureau (St G. 18/11/91). L.C.
[Music by A. J. Caldicott.]
Ca. At a Health Resort (Com. 2/6/93). L.C.
C.D. The Gentleman Whip (Devonshire Park, Eastbourne, 1/2/94; Terry's, 21/2/94). L.C.
C.D. Hal, the Highwayman (Vaud. 15/12/94).
F. Poor Mr Potton (Vaud. 10/10/95). See *C. HAMLYN.*
C. Merrifield's Ghost (Vaud. 13/11/95). L.C. *French.*
D. The Spy (Lyr. Ealing, 23/4/96). L.C. *French* [as *In Nelson's Days.*]

PAULTON, E. A.
F. The Lord Mayor (Str. 1/11/95). See *W. E. BRADLEY.*

PAULTON, EDWARD
Ext. Niobe (All Smiles) (P.W. L'pool, 1/9/90). See *H. PAULTON.*
C.D. A World of Trouble in a Locket (Grand, Birmingham, 3/12/94). See *H. PAULTON.*
C.O. Dorcas (Kilburn, 21/2/98). See *H. PAULTON.*

PAULTON, HARRY
F. Private and Confidential (P.W. L'pool, 1/4/70). See *J. ELDRED.*
Bsq. The Gay Musketeers (P.W. L'pool, 18/4/70). See *J. ELDRED.*
Bsq. The Three Musket Dears (Str. 5/10/71). See *J. PAULTON.*
C.O. The Black Crook (Alh. 23/12/72). See *J. PAULTON.*
P. Little Bo-Peep (Pav. 27/12/75). L.C.
[Written in collaboration with *J. PAULTON.*]
C.O. Don Quixote (Alh. 25/9/76). L.C.
[Written in collaboration with *A. MALTBY.* Music by F. Clay.]
C. Pecksniff (Folly, 23/10/76). L.C.
P. Gulliver's Travels (Pav. 26/12/76). L.C.
Ca. Wedded Bliss (Aven. 16/10/82). L.C.
C.O. Cymbra; or, The Magic Thimble (Str. 24/3/83). L.C.
[Music by F. Pascal.]
Bsq. The Babes; or, Whines from the Wood (Birmingham, 9/6/84; Toole's, 9/9/84; rewritten by *A. C. SHELLEY*, Str. 4/2/95). L.C.
[Music by W. C. Levey.]

F.C. Lilies; or, Hearts and Actresses (P.W. L'pool, 10/11/84; Gai. 22/11/84; Regent, Salford, 11/9/99, as *The Dear Girls*, revised). L.C.
[Music by K. Pierce, C. Locknane, T. Fitzgerald and E. Paulton.]

C. Noah's Ark (Bath, 30/5/85; Roy. 27/10/86, *mat.*). L.C.
[Title altered later to *The Trustee*.]

Bsq. Japs; or, The Doomed Daimio (P's. Bristol, 31/8/85; Nov. 19/9/85). L.C.
[Written in collaboration with *M. TEDDE*.]

O. Erminie (Grand, Birmingham, 26/10/85). See *C. BELLAMY*.

Bsq. Masse-en-yell-oh (Com. 23/3/86).
[Written in collaboration with *M. TEDDE*. Music by E. Jakobowski.]

C.O. Mynheer Jan (Grand, Birmingham, 7/2/87; Com. 14/2/87). L.C.
[Written in collaboration with *M. TEDDE*. Music by E. Jakobowski.]

F.C. A Bad Lot (O.H. Northampton, 24/6/87; Metro. 23/5/98). L.C. Str. 13/11/95.
[Written in collaboration with *M. TEDDE*.]

M.D. M.D. (Doncaster, 2/4/88).
[Written in collaboration with *M. TEDDE*.]

C.O. Paola (Lyc. Edinburgh, 16/12/89).
[Written in collaboration with *M. TEDDE*. Music by E. Jakobowski.]

Ext. Niobe (All Smiles) (P.W. L'pool, 1/9/90; Str. 11/4/92). L.C.
[Written in collaboration with *E. PAULTON*.]

C.D. A World of Trouble in a Locket (Grand, Birmingham, 3/12/94; Str. 16/9/95, as *In a Locket*). L.C.
[Written in collaboration with *E. PAULTON*.]

F. The Lord Mayor (Str. 1/11/95). See *W. E. BRADLEY*.

C.O. Dorcas (Kilburn, 21/2/98).
[Written in collaboration with *E. PAULTON*.]

PAULTON, JOSEPH

Bsq. The Three Musket Dears, and a Little One In (Str. 5/10/71). L.C. *Lacy*.
[Written in collaboration with *H. PAULTON*.]

C.O. The Black Crook (Alh. 23/12/72).
[Written in collaboration with *H. PAULTON*.]

P. Little Bo Peep (Pav. 27/12/75). See *H. PAULTON*.

D. East Lynne (M'bone, 9/9/89).

PAULTON, T. G.

D. Quilp; or, The Wanderings of Little Nell (P.W. Wolverhampton, 10/4/71).

D. The Wandering Jew (M'bone, 7/7/73). L.C.

PAULTON, TOM

Ext. Princess Amaswazee (Pier, Eastbourne, 15/4/95).

PAXTON, —

Ca. A Point of Law (Park, 26/3/81). L.C.
[Written in collaboration with *WOODVILLE*.]

PAYN, DOROTHEA

Bsq. A Midnight Shriek (Gai. Dublin, 5/1/96).

PAYN, JAMES
F. A Substitute (Court, 9/9/76). L.C.

PAYNE, EDMUND
Bsq. Richard Whittington, Esq. (Bury, 9/9/92). L.C.
F.C. The Sub-Editor (Brixton, 5/11/96). L.C.
[Written in collaboration with *C. HARRISON*.]

PAYNE, GEORGE S.
C. Byeways (Com. 10/3/97). L.C.

PAYNE, WILTON B.
D. The Way of the World (Dewsbury, 12/2/83; Brit. 13/9/86).
D. Another Man's Money (Dewsbury, 4/9/84). L.C.

PEACOCK, W.
D. A Soldier's Wife (Grand H. Hotel Cecil, 25/2/98). See *S. DALGLEISH*.

PEARCE, GEORGE
D. A Soldier's Fortune (Hanley, 11/2/78). L.C.

PEARCE, JOSEPH E.
Ca. An Artful Girl (Birkbeck Inst. 29/6/92). See *W. P. RIDGE*.

PEARL, E. M.
D. Martin Guerre; or, The Guilty Claim (Woolwich, 13/9/73).

PEASE, SYDNEY
F.C. Aunt Margaret (Croydon, 11/6/97). L.C.
R.D. For the King (Windsor, 21/1/99). See *W. HOWARD*.

PEDE, THORPE
Oa. Marguerite (Alex. Camden Town, 31/5/73).

PEEL, GEORGE
D. Firm as Oak; or, England's Pride (Brit. 2/6/73). L.C.
D. The Southern Cross (Vic. 9/8/73). L.C.
D. A Daughter's Secret (Brit. 26/2/74). L.C.
D Fairleigh's Birthright (Brit. 26/8/78). L.C.

PEILE, F. KINSEY
Ca. The Dancing Dervish (Gai. 6/94). L.C.
Ca. After the Ball (St J. 16/7/95). L.C.
M.D. The Belle of Cairo (Court. 10/10/96). See *C. RALEIGH*.
F.C. Solomon's Twins (Vaud. 11/5/97). L.C.
M.C. The Merry-go-round (Gai. 13/1/98). See *C. FITCH*.
D. The Other Man's Wife (Worcester, 16/5/98). L.C.
C. An Interrupted Honeymoon (Aven. 23/9/99). L.C. Worcester, 20/6/98.

PELZER, JOSEF
M.C. Donnybrook (Coatbridge, 5/8/99).

PEMBERTON, M.
Ca. A Private Detective (St J. 1/4/86). See *S. LEIGH*.
Ca. The Dancing Master (O.C. 2/10/89). L.C.
[Written in collaboration with *M. WELLINGS*.]
C.O. The Brazilian (Newcastle, 19/4/90, *copy*.). L.C.
[Written in collaboration with *W. LESTOCQ*. Music by F. Chassaigne.]

PEMBERTON, T. EDGAR

Ca. Weeds (P.W. Birmingham, 20/11/74). *Lacy.*
Ca. The Happy Medium (H. 8/11/75). L.C. *Lacy.*
F. A Grateful Father (P.W. Birmingham, 15/4/78). *Lacy.*
Ca. My Wife's Father's Sister (Brighton, 21/10/78). *Lacy.*
F. Davenport Brothers and Co. (Birmingham, 24/4/79). *Lacy.*
F. Freezing a Mother-in-Law (Birmingham, 17/12/79; Leeds, 6/9/80; Arlington Manor, 27/12/96).
M.D. Gentle Gertrude; or, Doomed, Drugged and Drowned at Datchet (Alex. L'pool, 21/2/81; Gai. 14/5/84). L.C. *Lacy.*
[Music by T. Anderton.]
C.O. The Chiltern Hundreds (Alex. L'pool, 17/4/82). L.C.
[Music by T. Anderton.]
C.D. On the Bench; or, Distant Cousins (Alex. L'pool, 22/2/83). L.C. *Lacy.*
Ca. Melting Moments (P.W. Birmingham, 18/2/84). *Lacy.*
C.O. Thorough Base (Bijou, Birmingham, 7/4/84). *Lacy.*
[Music by T. Anderton.]
C.D. Happy-go-lucky (Glo. 11/6/84). L.C. Alex. L'pool, 10/4/84. *Lacy.*
C. Off Duty (Toole's, 9/9/84). L.C. *Lacy.*
F.C. Double and Quits (Aven. Sunderland, 4/3/85). L.C. Carlisle, 9/2/85.
C. Title (Alex. L'pool, 8/6/85). L.C.
C. Yeoman's Service (Nov. 19/9/85). L.C.
C. Money Bags (Nov. 5/11/85). L.C.
[Written in collaboration with — *SHANNON.*]
C. The Actor (P.W. Birmingham, 14/5/86; H.M. Dundee, 6/2/91, revised, as *Step Brothers*). L.C.
C. The Steeple Jack (P.W. L'pool, 23/3/88). L.C. *Lacy.*
D. The Loadstone (Lyc. 7/4/88, *mat.*). L.C.
[Written in collaboration with *W. H. VERNON.*]
Ca. The Postman (Str. 26/7/92, *mat.*). L.C.
D. Sydney Carton (Norwich, 2/1/93). L.C.
D. Edmund Kean, Tragedian (W. Hartlepool, 4/1/95; Metro. 23/10/96). L.C.
D. Loyal to the Last (Birmingham, 16/6/96). L.C.
D. Henry Esmond (Lyc. Edinburgh, 5/3/97; Qns. Crouch End, 26/11/97). L.C.
D. Sue (Gar. 10/6/98). See *B. HARTE.*

PENDRED, LOUGHNAN ST L.

C.O. The Buccaneers (T.H. Streatham, 9/4/94).
[Music by B. F. Pendred and E. Glazier.]

PENLEY, W. S.

F. Tickle and Scrubbs (Traf. 31/5/93). L.C.

PENN, RACHEL. See *Mrs E. S. WILLARD*

PENTREATH, F. G.

O. No (Horn's Concert R. Kennington, 25/1/81).
[Music by — McLean.]

PERCIVAL, ARTHUR

C.D. Clouds (Exeter, 1/4/72).

PERCIVAL, J.

D. Brought to Light (Aberdeen, 27/3/72).

C.O. Les Amourettes (Ancient Concert R. Dublin, 14/4/85).
[Music by D. F. R. G. Josè.]

PERCIVAL, WALTER

D. Under Two Reigns (Park, 3/5/79). L.C.
[Written in collaboration with *J. WILLING.*]

PERCY, H.

C. The Society Tailor (T.H. Guildford, 12/2/95).

PERRY, Mrs

M.C. Our Last Rehearsal (Pleasure Gdns. Folkestone, 25/4/93). L.C.
[Music by A. Oake.]

PERRY, J.

Ent. Merrymaking; or, Birthday Festivities (G.I. 13/5/67).

PERRY, RICHARD DAVIS

D. At the Sword Point (Norwich, 9/6/84). See *H. LASHBROOKE.*

F.C. My Husband's Wife; or, T.T.T.—Tom Trimmer's Trials (P.W. Greenwich, 19/3/85). L.C.

PERRY, T. GILBERT

M.C. The Indian Prince (Grand, Walsall, 26/7/97). L.C.
[Music by H. Richardson. Title altered to *The Rajah of Ram Jain Poore*, 5/1/1919.]

PERTENCE, ERNEST

Oa. Thyra (Bijou, 17/12/96, *amat.*).
[Music by A. Lindo.]

PERTH, —

D. The Man in the Iron Mask (Grand, Walsall, 17/4/99).
[Written in collaboration with — *CONDIE.*]

D. Citizen Robespierre (Roy. Chester, 2/6/99). L.C. as *C.R. the Incorruptible.*
[Written in collaboration with — *CONDIE.*]

PETTITT, HENRY

D. British Born (Grec. 17/10/72). See *P. MERRITT.*

D. Golden Fruit; or, Englishmen Abroad (E.L. 14/7/73). L.C.

D. Man; or, Golden Fetters (Amphi. Leeds, 10/11/73).

C. True Lovers' Knots (Gloucester, 8/1/74).

D. Lynch Law (W. Hartlepool, 19/9/74).

D. Dead to the World (Grec. 12/7/75). See *G. CONQUEST.*

D. The Promised Land; or, The Search for the Southern Star (Grec. 13/9/75). L.C.

D. Sentenced to Death (Grec. 14/10/75). See *G. CONQUEST.*

D. Snatched from the Grave (Grec. 13/3/76). See *G. CONQUEST.*

D. Brought to Book (Brit. 8/5/76). See *G. H. MACDERMOTT.*

D. Queen's Evidence (Grec. 5/6/76). See *G. CONQUEST.*

D. Neck or Nothing (Grec. 3/8/76). See *G. CONQUEST.*

D. The Sole Survivor (Grec. 5/10/76). See *G. CONQUEST.*

D. Schriften (Grec. 2/4/77). See *G. CONQUEST.*

D. During Her Majesty's Pleasure (Grec. 21/5/77). See *G. CONQUEST.*

D. Bound to Succeed (Grec. 29/10/77). See *G. CONQUEST.*

D. Notice to Quit (Grec. 20/4/78). See *G. CONQUEST.*

D. The Green Lanes of England (Grec. 5/8/78). See *G. CONQUEST.*

D. The Royal Pardon (Grec. 28/10/78). See *G. CONQUEST*.
D. An Honest Man (Sur. 16/11/78). L.C.
D. The Queen's Colours (Grec. 31/5/79). See *G. CONQUEST*.
D. The Worship of Bacchus (Olym. 21/7/79). See *P. MERRITT*.
D. The Black Flag; or, Escaped from Portland (Grec. 9/8/79). L.C.
C. An Old Man's Darling (Grec. 12/11/79). L.C. as *An O.M.D.; or, May and December*.
C.D. Not Proven (Leeds, 15/3/80).
D. Brought to Justice (Sur. 27/3/80). L.C.
[Written in collaboration with *P. MERRITT*.]
D. The Lost Witness (Grec. 22/5/80).
[Written in collaboration with *P. MERRITT*.]
F. Sock and Buckskin; or, Muddled and Mixed (Sur. 19/6/80).
M.D. The World (D.L. 31/7/80). See *P. MERRITT*.
D. The White Cliffs (Hull, 13/12/80). See *P. MERRITT*.
P. Harlequin King Frolic; or, The Coral Tree, the Golden Key and the Naughty Boy who was wrecked at Sea (Grec. 24/12/80). L.C.
D. The Nabob's Fortune; or, The Adventures of a Sealed Packet (Plymouth, 16/7/81). L.C.
D. Taken from Life (Adel. 31/12/81). L.C.
D. Pluck: A Story of £50,000 (D.L. 5/8/82). L.C.
[Written in collaboration with *Sir A. HARRIS*.]
M.D. Love and Money (Adel. 18/11/82). See *C. READE*.
C.D. Sisters (P.W. L'pool, 31/3/83). L.C.
[Written in collaboration with *F. W. BROUGHTON*.]
D. In the Spider's Web; or, The Cockney Farmer (Grand, Glasgow, 28/5/83; Olym. 1/12/83, as *The Spider's Web*). L.C.
D. In the Ranks (Adel. 6/10/83). See *J. P. SIMPSON*.
D. Human Nature (D.L. 12/9/85). L.C.
[Written in collaboration with *Sir A. HARRIS*.]
D. The Harbour Lights (Adel. 23/12/85). See *G. R. SIMS*.
D. A Run of Luck (D.L. 28/8/86). L.C.
[Written in collaboration with *Sir A. HARRIS*.]
D. The Bells of Haslemere (Adel. 28/7/87). L.C.
[Written in collaboration with *S. GRUNDY*.]
D. The Union Jack (Adel. 19/7/88). L.C.
[Written in collaboration with *S. GRUNDY*.]
D. Hands across the Sea (Manchester, 30/7/88; P'cess. 10/11/88). L.C.
Bsq. Faust up-to-date (Gai. 30/10/88). See *G. R. SIMS*.
D. The Silver Falls (Adel. 29/12/88). See *G. R. SIMS*.
D. Master and Man (P.W. Birmingham, 25/3/89). See *G. R. SIMS*.
D. London Day by Day (Adel. 14/9/89). See *G. R. SIMS*.
D. A Million of Money (D.L. 6/9/90). L.C.
[Written in collaboration with *Sir A. HARRIS*.]
Bsq. Carmen up-to-date (Shakespeare, L'pool, 22/9/90). See *G. R. SIMS*..
D. A Sailor's Knot (D.L. 5/9/91). L.C.
C.O. Blue-eyed Susan (P.W. 6/2/92). See *G. R. SIMS*.
D. The Prodigal Daughter (D.L. 17/9/92). L.C.
[Written in collaboration with *Sir A. HARRIS*.]
D. A Woman's Revenge (Adel. 1/7/93). L.C.
D. A Life of Pleasure (D.L. 21/9/93). See *Sir A. HARRIS*.
D. True Grit (Wigan, 29/3/94). L.C.
[Written in collaboration with *A. J. FLAXMAN*.]

PHELPS, C. H.

D. A Blind Foundling (Birkenhead, 18/12/99; Carlton, Greenwich, 15/4/1901). L.C.

PHELPS, S., Jr.

F. The Obstinate Family (S.W. 21/2/53). L.C.

PHELPS, Miss SYDNEY

Ca. The Lady Volunteers (Parkhurst, 13/7/96). L.C. Garrison, Shoeburyness, 18/9/94.

PHILIPS, F. C.

C.D. The Dean's Daughter (St J. 13/10/88). See *S. GRUNDY*.

F.C. Husband and Wife (Crit. 30/4/91, *mat.*; Com. 7/7/91, revised). L.C. as *Tiger Lilies*.
[Written in collaboration with *P. FENDALL*.]

F.C. Godpapa (Com. 22/10/91). L.C.
[Written in collaboration with *C. H. E. BROOKFIELD*.]

C.D. Margaret Byng (Crit. 8/12/91, *mat.*). L.C.
[Written in collaboration with *P. FENDALL*.]

F. The Burglar and the Judge (H. 5/11/92). L.C.
[Written in collaboration with *C. H. E. BROOKFIELD*.]

F.C. Fireworks (Vaud. 29/6/93). L.C.
[Written in collaboration with *P. FENDALL*.]

Duol. Papa's Wife (Lyr. 26/1/95). See *Sir S. HICKS*.

D. A Woman's Reason (Shaft. 27/12/95). See *C. H. E. BROOKFIELD*.

D. Dr Chetwynd (O. H. Cheltenham, 20/1/96). L.C.
[Title altered to *John Chetwynd's Wife*, 24/3/96.]

D.Sk. The Fortune of War (Crit. 19/5/96).

D. The Free Pardon (Olym. 28/1/97). L.C.
[Written in collaboration with *L. MERRICK*.]

PHILLIPS, A. R.

Oa. Sly and Shy (P'cess. Edinburgh, 21/5/83).
[Music by W. Slaughter.]

D.Sk. Crazed (Assembly R. Wood Green, 1/10/92).

PHILLIPS, ALFRED

F. The Original Bloomers (Olym. 10/11/51). L.C.

PHILLIPS, Mrs ALFRED

F. Caught in his Own Trap (Olym. 13/10/51). L.C. *Lacy*.

F. An Organic Affection (Olym. 15/1/52). L.C. as *An Affection of the Heart*. *Lacy*.

C. The Master Passion (Olym. 1/9/52). L.C. *Lacy*.

D. Life in Australia, from Our Own Correspondent (Olym. 21/2/53). L.C.

F. Uncle Crotchet (Olym. 18/4/53). L.C. *Lacy*.

Ca. My Husband's Will (Olym. 19/9/53). L.C.

PHILLIPS, FREDERIC LAURENCE

[For his earlier plays see iv, 372.]

D. Dred (Sur. 10/56). L.C.
[Written in collaboration with *J. COLMAN*.]

C. A Bird in the Hand worth Two in the Bush (Sur. 19/1/57). L.C.

D. Cromwell; or, The Conspiracy (Sur. 2/59). L.C.

D. The Tramp's Adventure; or, True to the Last (Sur. 17/11/60).

PHILLIPS, G. R.

Bsq. Tawno's Bride (St G. 16/2/92). See *E. W. BOWLES.*

Bsq. The Baron's Daughter (West, Albert H. 7/2/93). See *E. W. BOWLES.*

PHILLIPS, J. RAGLAND

C. See-Saw (Terry's, 22/2/89). See *G. CAPEL.*

PHILLIPS, L.

D. Marianne Duval the Vivandière; or, The Brand of Time and the Mystery of 20 Years (Stand. 3/3/51). L.C.

PHILLIPS, Mrs NEWTON

Ca. Alpine Tourists (Ladb. H. 24/1/88). L.C.

C.D. Some Day (St G. 13/5/89, *mat.*). L.C.
[Written in collaboration with *J. TRESAHAR.*]

Ca. All a Mistake (Ladb. H. 28/1/90). L.C.
[Title altered to *Polly Plumtree*, 1893.]

D. Donna (Ladb. H. 11/3/92). See *Mrs HUNGERFORD.*

Ca. Broken Off (Ladb. H. 24/5/92). L.C.

F.C. Charlotte Maria (Ladb. H. 24/5/92). See *F. MACRAE.*

PHILLIPS, STEPHEN

T. Paolo and Francesca (St J. 6/3/1902). L.C. St J. 15/11/99.
[Several later plays.]

PHILLIPS, WATTS

D. Joseph Chavigny; or, Under the Thumb (Adel. 11/5/56). L.C.

D. The Poor Strollers (Adel. 18/1/58). L.C.

D. The Dead Heart (Adel. 10/11/59). L.C. *Lacy.*

C. Paper Wings (Adel. 27/2/60). L.C.

D. A Story of the '45 (D.L. 12/11/60). L.C.

D. His Last Victory (St J. 21/6/62). L.C. *Lacy.*

D Camilla's Husband; or, Married in Haste (Olym. 22/11/62). L.C. *Lacy.*

F. Ticket of Leave (Adel. 1/12/62). L.C. *Lacy.*

C. Paul's Return (P'cess. 15/2/64). L.C. *Lacy.*

D. The Woman in Mauve (P.W. L'pool, 12/64; H. 18/3/65). L.C. *Lacy.*

T. Theodora, Actress and Empress (Sur. 9/4/66). L.C. *Lacy.*

D. The Hugenot Captain (P'cess. 2/7/66). L.C. *Lacy.*

D. Barnaby Rudge (P'cess. 12/11/66). L.C.
[Written in collaboration with — *VINING.* Music by C. Hall.]

D. Lost in London (Adel. 16/3/67). L.C. *Lacy.*

D. Nobody's Child (Sur. 14/9/67). L.C.

D. Maud's Peril (Adel. 23/10/67). L.C. as *Maud. Lacy.*

D. Land Rats and Water Rats (Sur. 5/9/68). L.C.

D. A Lion at Bay. *Lacy* [1869].

D. Not Guilty (Qns. 13/2/69). L.C. *Lacy.*
[Title altered later to *Back from the Land of Yesterday.*]

D. Fettered (Holborn, 17/2/69). L.C. *Lacy* [as *A Golden Fetter*].

D. The White Cockade. *Lacy* [1871].

D. On the Jury (P'cess. 16/12/71). L.C.

D. Amos Clark (Qns. 19/10/72). L.C.

D. Marlborough; or, Three Phases of a Life (Brighton, 21/10/72). L.C. Manchester, 23/11/70.

D. Blackmail (Grec. 16/10/80).

PHILLIPSON, G.

C.D. So runs the World away (St G. 22/1/89).

PHILLPOTTS, EDEN

F. The Policeman (Lyr. H. Ealing, 12/1/87). See *W. HELMORE.*

C. A Platonic Attachment (Lyr. H. Ealing, 20/2/89). L.C.

Ca. A Breezy Morning (Grand, Leeds, 27/4/91; Com. 8/12/91). L.C. *French.*

C. Allendale (Str. 14/2/93, *mat.*). L.C.
[Written in collaboration with *G. B. BURGIN.*]

C. The Prude's Progress (Cambridge, 16/5/95). See *J. K. JEROME.*

F. The MacHaggis (Peterborough, 22/2/97). See *J. K. JEROME.*

C. For Love of Prim (Court, 24/1/99). L.C.

Ca. A Pair of Knickerbockers (St G. 26/12/99). L.C.
[Several later plays.]

PHILPOTT, STEPHEN R.

O. Zelica (Gresham H. Brixton, 17/12/90; P's H. 8/12/91).

PHIPPS, A. J.

F. My Very Last Proposal (Belfast, 30/3/74). *Lacy.*

F. Pretty Predicaments (Belfast, 27/11/76).

[*PIDGIN, CHARLES*

Oa. The Electric Spark (P's. Manchester, 28/5/83). L.C.
[Written in collaboration with *C. BLAKE.*]

PIFFARD, HAMILTON

R.D. The Wave of War (Terry's, 15/12/87). See *F. CHESTERLEY.*

PIGGOTT, MOSTYN T.

F.C. The Bachelor's Widow (Roy. Glasgow, 14/6/97). See *J. F. O'HARE.*

PIGOTT, J. W.

C. The Bookmaker (Terry's, 19/3/89, *mat.*; Gai. 9/8/90). L.C.

C.D. Which wins? (Terry's, 12/6/89, *mat.*). L.C.

PIKE, A. E.

Ext. Aladdin; or, The Magic Lamp (St Catherine's Inst. Birkenhead, 30/1/96).

PILGRIM, JAMES

D. The Wild Irish Girl. L.C. C.L. 1/9/50. *French.*

Ca. The Limerick Boy (Roy. 12/8/65). *Lacy.*

PILMORE, F.

D. For the Sake of a Name (Swiss Gdns. Shoreham, 1/6/88). L.C.
[Written in collaboration with *J. HOLLAND.*]

"*PINCROFT, A. D.*" See *J. M. BANERO*

PINEO, MABEL. See "*MAX PIREAU*"

PINERO, Sir ARTHUR WING

F. Two Hundred a Year (Glo. 6/10/77). L.C.

D. La Comète; or, Two Hearts (Croydon, 22/4/78). L.C.

Ca. Two can play at that Game. L.C. Lyc. 20/5/78.

Ca. Daisy's Escape (Lyc. 20/9/79). L.C.

Ca. Hester's Mystery (Folly, 5/6/80). L.C. *Lacy.*

D. Bygones (Lyc. 18/9/80). L.C.

C. The Money Spinner (P's. Manchester, 5/11/80; St J. 8/1/81). L.C. *Lacy.*

C. Imprudence (Folly, 27/7/81). L.C.
D. The Squire (St J. 29/12/81). L.C. 8° [1905].
C. Girls and Boys: A Nursery Tale (Toole's, 1/11/82). L.C.
D. The Rector: The Story of Four Friends (Court, 24/3/83). L.C.
C. The Rocket (P.W. L'pool, 30/7/83; Gai. 10/12/83). L.C. 8° [1905].
C. Lords and Commons (H. 24/11/83). L.C.
C. Low Water (Glo. 12/1/84). L.C.
D. The Iron Master (St J. 17/4/84). L.C.
C. In Chancery (Lyc. Edinburgh, 19/9/84; Gai. 24/12/84). L.C. 8° [1905].
F. The Magistrate (Court, 21/3/85). L.C. 8° 1892.
C.D. Mayfair (St J. 31/10/85). L.C.
F. The Schoolmistress (Court, 27/3/86). L.C. 8° 1894.
C. The Hobby-horse (St J. 25/10/86). L.C. 8° 1892.
F. Dandy Dick (Court, 27/1/87). L.C. 8° 1893.
C.D. Sweet Lavender (Terry's, 21/3/88). L.C. 8° 1893.
C.D. The Weaker Sex (Manchester, 28/9/88; Court, 16/3/89, revised). L.C. 8° 1894.
D. The Profligate (Gar. 24/4/89). L.C. 8° 1892.
F. The Cabinet Minister (Court, 23/4/90). L.C. 8° 1892.
D. Lady Bountiful (Gar. 7/3/91). L.C. 8° 1892.
C. The Times (Terry's, 24/10/91). L.C. 8° 1891.
F. The Amazons (Court, 7/3/93). L.C. 8° 1895.
D. The Second Mrs Tanqueray (St J. 27/5/93). L.C. 8° 1895.
D. The Notorious Mrs Ebbsmith (Gar. 13/3/95). L.C. 8° 1895.
C. The Benefit of the Doubt (Com. 16/10/95). L.C. 8° 1896.
C. The Princess and the Butterfly; or, The Fantastics (St J. 29/3/97). L.C. 8° 1898.
Ca. Trelawny of the "Wells" (Court, 20/1/98). L.C. 8° 1898 [New York]; 8° 1899.
M.D. The Beauty Stone (Sav. 28/5/98). L.C. 8° 1898.
[Written in collaboration with *J. W. C. CARR*. Music by Sir A. Sullivan.]
C. The Gay Lord Quex (Glo. 8/4/99). L.C. 8° 1900.
[For his later plays see *C.B.E.L.*, iii, 616.]

PINKERTON, PERCY
C. At the Harbour Side (Brighton, 17/3/1900).

"*PIREAU, MAX*"
C. The Double Deception (Bijou, 25/10/97, *copy.*; Bijou, 17/6/99, as *Phyllis*). L.C.
[Written in collaboration with *L. ROYD.*]

PIRKIS, C.
Oa. Tempests in Teacups (St G. Parish H. Forest Hill, 13/12/99). L.C.
[Written in collaboration with *A. ROSS.*]

[*PITOU, AUGUST*
D. The Power of the Press (P'cess. Glasgow, 3/8/96). L.C. as *Lights of Liberty*.
[Written in collaboration with *G. H. JESSOP.*]

PITT, CECIL
D. Lion Limb; or, The King of the South Sea Islands (Brit. 25/9/67). L.C.
D. The White Phantom (M'bone, 19/10/67).

D. Fred Frolic, his Life and Adventures; or, The Dark Deeds of the Devil's Grip (Brit. 17/6/68). L.C.
D. The Night Guard; or, The Secret of the Five Masks (Brit. 23/9/68).
D. Jack Stedfast; or, Wreck and Rescue (Brit. 30/8/69). L.C.
D. The Black Tower of Linden; or, A Foster Brother's Revenge (Brit. 22/9/69).
D. Bob Lumley's Secret; or, The Dark Deeds of Bluegate Fields (Brit. 20/12/69). L.C.

PITT, C. I.
D. Manhood (St Helen's, 27/3/76).
D. The Wrecker (Brit. 1/7/78). See *F. MARCHANT*.

PITT, GEORGE DIBDIN
[For his earlier plays see iv, 372–6.]
D. Little Bidette; or, Good for Evil L.C. Brit. 24/1/50.
D. Black Adder; or, The Devil of the Dardanelles. L.C. Pav. 23/2/50.
D. Napoleon, the Star of France. L.C. Brit. 5/3/50.
D. Old Father Thames; or, The Ferryman's Daughter. L.C. Qns. 2/5/50.
D. Borachio the Bandit; or, The Hunter and his Dogs. L.C. Brit. 12/6/50.
D. The Golden Witness; or, The Witch of Highbury. L.C. Brit. 30/6/50.
D. The Fatal Brand; or, The Fall of the Inquisition (Brit. 7/50). L.C. 21/7/50.
D. Dora O'Donovan; or, The Lily of Limerick. L.C. Brit. 31/7/50.
D. Love and Duty; or, My Mother, my Wife and my Child. L.C. Brit. 21/8/50.
D. Pride and Patience; or, A Daughter's Error. L.C. Stand. 16/12/50.
D. Love and Error; or, Emmeline the Female Parricide. L.C. 1851 [licence refused].
D. The Welsh Wolf; or The Lily of Snowdon (Qns. 20/1/51). L.C.
D. The Warning Dream; or, Constancy unto Death. L.C. Brit. 6/2/51.
D. The Trials and Triumphs of Temperance (Stand. 21/7/51). L.C.
F. Bravo Rouse!!! or, Catch 'em alive! L.C. 4/9/51.
D. The Three Weavers; or, The Vaults of Mount St Bernard (Stand. 27/12/51). L.C.
D. The Will and the Way; or, The Khan and the Country Man (Pav. 23/4/53). L.C.
Ba. Pop goes the Weasel; or, The Devil's Dance (Pav. 7/5/53). L.C.
D. Spirit Rappers (Pav. 25/6/53).
D. The Spanish Girl; or, The Spy of Naples (C.L. 13/4/57). L.C.

PITT, HARRY M.
Bsq. Julius See-Saw; or, Dauntless Decius, the Doubtful Decemvir (Sheffield, 29/3/69). L.C.
Ca. Returned (Sheffield, 7/5/69).
Bsq. Louis XI; or, The Tricksey Monarch and the Wicksey Warrior (W. Hartlepool, 9/7/69).
D. How we spent Christmas Day in '69 (Sur. 31/1/70). L.C.
D. Paul Clifford; or, The Highwayman of Life (Vic. 2/7/70).
D. Iron Hands (P'cess. Edinburgh, 29/9/73; Grec. 12/10/74). L.C.

PITT, KATE. See *Mrs AUGUSTUS BRIGHT*

PITT, W. H.

D. Striking the Hour; or, Firematch the Trooper (C.L. 20/5/67). L.C.
D. Biddy O'Neal; or, The Daughter of Erin (Brit. 29/3/69). L.C.
D. Gratitude; or, Life's Battle for Gold (Brit. 12/6/69). L.C.
D. The Deer Slayers; or, The Free Archers of the New Forest (Brit. 19/12/70). L.C.
Spec. Truth; or, The Spells of Love (Brit. 10/4/71). L.C. as *The Daughter of Truth; or, The S. of L.*
D. Woman—her Rise and Fall in Life (Brit. 13/11/71). L.C.
D. Man's Mercy (Darlington, 5/5/74).
D. A Kind Heart with a Rough Covering (Pav. 3/7/75). L.C.
D. Rough Honesty (Alex. Walsall, 25/6/77).

PLANCHÉ, JAMES ROBINSON

[For his earlier plays see iv, 376–83.]
D. Fiesco; or, The Revolt of Genoa (D.L. 4/2/50).
Ext. Cymon and Iphigenia (Lyc. 1/4/50). L.C. 8° 1879 [in *Extravaganzas*, iv].
C. My Heart's Idol; or, A Desperate Remedy (Lyc. 16/10/50).
D. The White Hood (Lyc. 11/11/50). L.C.
M.D. A Day of Reckoning (Lyc. 4/12/50). L.C.
Ext. King Charming; or, The Blue Bird of Paradise (Lyc. 26/12/50). L.C. 8° 1879 [in *Extravaganzas*, iv].
Ext. The Queen of the Frogs (Lyc. 21/4/51). L.C. *Fairbrother*; 8° 1879 [in *Extravaganzas*, iv].
Ext. The Prince of Happy Land; or, The Fawn in the Forest (Lyc. 26/12/51). L.C. *Fairbrother*; 8° 1879 [in *Extravaganzas*, iv].
C. The Mysterious Lady (Lyc. 18/10/52). L.C. *Lacy*.
Ext. The Good Woman in the Wood (Lyc. 27/12/52). L.C. *Lacy*; 8° 1879 [in *Extravaganzas*, iv].
D.Rev. Mr Buckstone's Ascent of Mount Parnassus (H. 28/3/53). L.C. *Lacy*; 8° 1879 [in *Extravaganzas*, iv].
D.Rev. The Camp at the Olympic (Olym. 17/10/53). L.C. *Lacy*; 8° 1879 [in *Extravaganzas*, iv].
P. Harlequin King Nutcracker (Str. 26/12/53). See *J. HALFORD*.
Ext. Once upon a time there were two kings (Lyc. 26/12/53). L.C. *Lacy*; 8° 1879 [in *Extravaganzas*, iv].
D.Rev. Mr Buckstone's Voyage round the Globe (in Leicester Square) (H. 12/4/54). L.C. 8° 1879 [in *Extravaganzas*, v].
C. The Knights of the Round Table (H. 20/5/54). L.C.
Ext. The Yellow Dwarf and the King of the Gold Mines (Olym. 26/12/54). L.C. 8° 1879 [in *Extravaganzas*, v].
D.Rev. The New Haymarket Spring Meeting (H. 9/4/55). L.C. 8° 1879 [in *Extravaganzas*, v]; *French*.
Ext. The Discreet Princess; or, The Three Glass Distaffs (Olym. 26/12/55). L.C. 8° 1879 [in *Extravaganzas*, v].
Ext. Young and Handsome (Olym. 26/12/56). L.C. 8° 1879 [in *Extravaganzas*, v]. *Lacy*.
C.D. An Old Offender (Adel. 22/7/59). L.C.
C. Love and Fortune (P'cess. 24/9/59). L.C. 8° 1879 [in *Extravaganzas*, v].
C. My Lord and my Lady; or, It might have been worse (H. 12/7/61). L.C.
F. All in the Dark (Roy. 21/11/61). L.C.

O. Love's Triumph (C.G. 3/11/62). L.C. 8° [1862].
[Music by W. V. Wallace.]

Bsq. Orpheus in the Haymarket (H. 26/12/65). L.C. 8° 1879 [in *Extravaganzas*, v].

P. Queen Lucidora, the Fair One with the Golden Locks, and Harlequin Prince Graceful; or, The Carp, the Crow and the Owl (S.W. 24/12/68).

Masque. King Christmas (G.I. 26/12/71). L.C. 8° 1879 [in *Extravaganzas*, v]; *Lacy*.

Spec. Babil and Bijou (C.G. 29/8/72). See *D. BOUCICAULT*.

PLANCHÉ, S.

P. Androcles and the Lion (Bristol, 26/12/93). L.C.

D. A Voice from the Grave (Maidenhead, 19/4/97; Grand, Walsall, 21/7/1902). L.C.
[Written in collaboration with *F. D. WOOD*.]

PLANT, FREDERIC W.

D. A Morning Drive (Mechanics' Inst. Stockport, 2/12/96). L.C.

PLATT, WILLIAM

D. Youth's Love-lore. 8° 1896 [*priv.*].

PLAYFAIR, G. M. H.

M.Ca. The Best Man (St Bartholomew's H. Brighton, 21/2/98). L.C.
[Music by W. F. Winckworth.]

[*PLEON, HARRY*

F. Muldoon's Picnic (M'bone, 8/11/86). L.C. *Dicks*.

Ext. On the Brain (Gt Grimsby, 23/7/88). *Dicks*.

Ext. Dutch Justice; or, Up before the Magistrate (Gai. Birmingham, 30/7/88). *Dicks*.

D.Sk. Farmer Hayseed (Clarence, Dover, 15/4/89). *Dicks*.

Ext. Been had (Clarence, Dover, 25/4/89). *Dicks*.

F. The Waiter; or, All comes to he who waits (Brit. 23/3/91). *Dicks*.

C. Peck's Bad Boy (Brit. 1/6/91). *Dicks*.

Ext. A Vision of Venus; or, A Midsummer-Night's Nightmare (Brit. 20/3/93). *Dicks*.

Ext. The Shop Boy (Alh., W. Hartlepool, 10/10/95).
[A revised version of *Peck's Bad Boy* (Brit. 1/6/91).]

Bsq. A Terrible Trilby (Lyc. Crewe, 9/11/95; Eden, Brighton, 12/3/96). L.C.

M.C. The Coster Baron (Col. Leeds, 12/3/97, *copy*.). L.C.

PLETTS, M.

D. Mike; or, The Miller's Trials (Alb. 12/5/76). L.C.

PLOWMAN, THOMAS F.

Ext. Acis and Galatea; or, The Beau! the Belle!! and the Blacksmith!!! (Vic. Oxford, 12/69, *amat*.). 8° 1869 [Oxford].

Bsq. Isaac of York; or, The Saxons and Normans in England (Court, 29/11/71). L.C.

Bsq. Zampa; or, The Buckaneer and the Little Dear (Court, 2/10/72). L.C.

Bsq. Isaac Abroad; or, Ivanhoe settled and Rebecca righted (Oxford, 15/1/78).
[See *Isaac of York* (Court, 29/11/71).]

POEL, WILLIAM

F. The Man of Forty (K.X. 29/6/80).
Ca. Absence of Mind; or, Wanted £5 (Olym. 11/7/84). L.C.
D. Priest or Painter (Olym. 11/7/84). L.C.
D. Lady Jane Grey (St G. 12/6/85).
R.D. Mehalah; or, The Power of Will (Gai. 11/6/86, *mat.*). L.C.
[Written in collaboration with *W. H. G. PALMER.*]
D.Sk. Adelaide (Vaud. 5/7/87). L.C.
Ca. Mrs Weakly's Difficulty (Vaud. 5/7/87). L.C.
C.D. Love and Halfpence (St G. 31/1/88). L.C.
Oa. Equality Jack (Ladb. H. 28/2/91). L.C.
[Music by W. S. Vining.]
Ca. The Coquette (Portman R. 12/5/92).
Ca. The Wayside Cottage. *French.*

POLEY, A. P.

O. The Red Rider (St G. 23/3/95). See *P. DAVEY.*

POLLOCK, Mrs JULIUS

D. Judael (Olym. 14/5/85). L.C.

POLLOCK, WALTER H.

C.D. The Charm (St G. 22/7/84). See *Sir W. BESANT.*
C. Evergreen (H. 9/8/84). L.C.
R.D. The Ballad Monger (H. 15/9/87). See *Sir W. BESANT.*
D. The Dead Heart (Lyc. 28/9/89).
[A revision of *The Dead Heart* (Adel. 10/11/59) by *WATTS PHILLIPS.*]
D. A Shadow Hunt (Ladb. H. 25/4/91). See *R. DAVEY.*
D.Sk. An Interlude (Terry's, 3/6/93). See *Mrs W. K. CLIFFORD.*
D. St Ronan's Well (Traf. 12/6/93). See *R. DAVEY.*
D. King and Artist. 8° 1897. See *L. MOWBRAY.*
R.D. The Were Wolf (Aven. 15/2/98). See *L. MOWBRAY.*

POND, ANSON PHELPS

D. The Desperate Man; or, At any cost (Str. 15/5/91, *copy.*). L.C.

PONSONBY, E.

Bsq. David Garrick (Crit. 11/5/88). See *C. P. COLNAGHI.*

POOLE, W. HOWELL

D. My Queen (Gai. 20/3/84). L.C.
D. Adam Bede (Holb. 2/6/84). L.C.
D. A Child of Chance (Court, L'pool, 6/8/86). L.C.
D. A People's Hero (Grand, Glasgow, 21/2/89; Vaud. 12/6/90).

POOLE, WILLIAM

D. Richard Armstrong (Assembly R. Stoke Newington, 19/12/76).

PORRINGTON, GEORGE

M.C. The Varsity Belle (Dover, 20/2/1905). L.C. 9/8/98. See *F. JARMAN.*

PORTER, J. HEWELSON

D. Victory (Warrington, 28/4/90). L.C.

POST, W. H.

Bsq. The Regenerates (Com. 30/10/99). L.C.

POTTER, MARY

Duol. A Bag of Tricks (Brighton, 18/5/96).

POTTER, PAUL M.
D. Trilby (Manchester, 7/9/95; H. 30/10/95). L.C.
D. The Conquerors (St J. 14/4/98). L.C.

POWER, TYRONE
M.D. The Texan (P'cess. 21/6/94). L.C.

[*POWERS, FRANCIS*
D. The First Born (Glo. 1/11/97). L.C.

POWLES, L. D.
Ca. The Opera Cloak (D.L. 8/9/83). L.C.
[Written in collaboration with *Sir A. HARRIS*.]

PRAED, Mrs CAMPBELL [*ROSA CAROLINE MURRAY*]
D. Affinities. 8° 1885.
[Written in collaboration with *Mrs JOPLING*.]
C.D. Ariane (O.C. 8/2/88). L.C. as *Wedlock*.
[Written in collaboration with *R. LEE*.]
R.D. The Binbian Mine (Margate, 6/10/88, *copy*.; P's. Bristol, 23/11/88, as *Two Friends*). L.C.
[Written in collaboration with *J. McCARTHY*.]

PRAEGÈR, NITA
Ca. Outwitted (Meistersingers' Club, 20/6/90).

PRATESI, GIOVANNI
P. La Figlia di Boby (C.P. 4/8/98). L.C.
[Music by R. Marenco.]

PRATT, F. W.
D. The Star of the North (Court, 1/2/89).

PRATT, W.
D. Ten Nights in a Bar-room. L.C. Vic. 26/11/67.
[Title altered to "*Father, come home!*"; *or, The Curse of Drunkenness*.]

PRESCOTT, N.
C.O. The Past Master (Str. 21/12/99). L.C.
[Lyrics by *B. DAVIES*.]

PREST, T. P.
D. The Miser of Shoreditch (Stand. 2/11/54). L.C.

PRESTON, JOHN F.
D. The Queen of Fashion (Oldham, 1887). See *T. CANNAM*.
D. Wilful Murder (Woolwich, 2/4/88). L.C.
D. She; or, The Fire of Life (Woolwich, 24/9/88). L.C.

PREVOST, Miss CONSTANCE M. ["*TERRA COTTA*"]
C. Meadow Sweet (Vaud. 5/3/90). L.C.
C. The Silence of a Chatterbox (Terry's, 30/10/99). L.C.

PRICE, EDWARD
D. The Lost Heir (Aberdeen, 20/3/72).
D. Poor Nell (Aberdeen, 18/11/72; L'pool, 1/5/75).
D. Rich and Poor (Huddersfield, 21/7/73).
C. The Life and Death of Jo (Coventry, 15/5/76). L.C.

PRICE, FRANK
M.D. The Dark Past (Barnsley, 23/10/90). L.C.
D. Is he a Christian? (Rotunda, L'pool, 10/12/1900). See *F. L. CONNYNGHAME*.

PRICE, JOHN
D. Belle Vue; or, Hard Times in Manchester (P.W. Salford, 17/9/83).

"*PRICE, MORTON*" [*Capt. HORTON RYHS*]
D. Ellie Brandon; or, Revenge and Love (C.L. 13/4/68). L.C.
D. Viola (Halifax, 9/8/70).

PRIDE, F. H.
C. Change (Cavendish R. 30/12/70). L.C.
[Written in collaboration with *F. G. PALMER*.]

PRIEST, —
D. Lucy Wentworth, the Village-born Beauty (C.L. 10/57). L.C.

PRIESTLY-GREENWOOD, H. P.
C.D. The Rescue of Oliver Goldsmith (D.Y. 12/2/98). L.C.

PRINGLE, WALLACE
C.O. Inez, the Dancing Girl (Lyc. Stafford, 3/8/96). L.C.
D. A Woman scorned (Workington, 10/10/98). L.C.

PRINSEP, VAL
Ca. Cousin Dick (Court, 1/3/79). L.C.
C. Monsieur le Duc (P's. Manchester, 28/8/79; St J. 4/10/79). L.C.

PRIOR, HERBERT
F. Marry yourselves (Edinburgh, 4/3/73).

PRITCHARD, JOHANNA
D. Auromania; or, The Diamond's Daughter (Alfred, 4/9/71). L.C.

PRITT, STEPHEN
C. A Lover of Two (Preston, 27/7/96). L.C.
C.D. Under the Old Name (Preston, 27/7/96). L.C.
D. The Reapers (Preston, 21/6/97). L.C.

PROCTOR, H.
D. Changes (St G. 12/10/76).

PRYCE, RICHARD
Ca. The Partition War. L.C. Drill H. Wimbledon, 11/1/89.
C.D. Miss Rutland (Gai. 3/4/94, *mat.*). L.C.

PRYCE-CLAIREMONT, J.
C.D. The Old Sport (Pier, Folkestone, 27/11/93). See *C. RIMINGTON*.

PRYCE-JENKINS, T. J.
C.D. Give and Take (Robinson's Assembly R. Neath, 1/11/94). L.C.

PURCHASE, F. H.
D. Two Men and a Maid (Com. 20/6/93). L.C.
[Written in collaboration with *J. WEBSTER*.]

PURDON, RICHARD
C.D. Best Intentions (O.H. Northampton, 11/12/90). See *P. F. MARSHALL*.

PURVIS, Mrs HERBERT
C.D. After Long Years (Torquay, 20/10/86; Crit. 2/2/87, *mat.*). L.C.
[Written in collaboration with *A. LAW*.]

PYAT, FELIX
D. The Waif; or, Sprung from the Streets (Holb. 3/73). L.C.

QUAIRE, MARCUS

D. A Winning Defeat (Nov. 30/5/91). See *D. CAMPBELL.*

QUAYLE, CHARLES

F. The Seven Charmed Spuds (Qns. Barnsley, 29/4/72).
F. The Rival Flunkies (Qns. Barnsley, 14/3/73).
D. Too Late; or, The Hands of Destiny (Circus of Var. Barnsley, 2/4/76; Albion, 14/8/76; Imp. 21/9/85). L.C.

QUINTON, MARK

D. In his Power (Com. Club, 1893, *amat.*; Alex. L'pool, 20/9/84; Olym. 21/1/85). L.C.
C.D. Handfast (P.W. 13/12/87). See *H. HAMILTON.*
C.D. Lord Anerley (St J. 7/11/91). L.C.
[Written in collaboration with *H. HAMILTON.*]

QUITTENDEN, R.

D. Belle Vue (Vic. 2/4/77). L.C.

RACER, P.

M.C. Anything Else (Ladb. H. 8/4/92, *mat.*). L.C.
C.D. A Work of Mercy (Ladb. H. 8/4/92, *mat.*). L.C.

RACKOW, NAHUM

D. Captain Dreyfuss (Stand. 18/6/98). L.C.
D. Faigale; or, Love conquers all (Stand. 13/8/98). L.C.

RADFORD, ERNEST

Ca. In the Train (Athen. Tottenham Court Road, 18/4/88).

RAE, ALFRED

C.O. Fauvette (Lyc. Edinburgh, 18/5/91; Roy. 16/11/91). L.C.
[Music by A. Messager.]
Ba. Brother Pelican; or, Falka's Baby (Belfast, 8/2/94). L.C. Ashton-under-Lyne, 13/2/94.
[Written in collaboration with *W. H. DRAGNIL.* Music by G. Operti, E. Allen and W. C. Levey.]

RAE, CHARLES MARSHAM

F. Poppleton's Predicaments (Roy. 21/7/70). L.C.
F. My Villa in Italy (Ch.X. 14/8/71). L.C. *Lacy.*
C. Follow the Leader (Ch.X. 12/4/73). L.C. *French.*
F. Billy Doo (Glo. 20/4/74). L.C. *Lacy.*
C. A Fair Encounter (H. 30/1/75). L.C. *Lacy.*
F. Birds in their little nest agree (H. 13/11/76). L.C.
C. Fame (H. 7/4/77). L.C. *Lacy.*
Ca. Love's Alarms (Roy. 1/1/78). L.C. *Lacy.*
M.F. Rummin's Reputation (Newark, 8/2/79). L.C.
Ca. Castles in the Air (Vaud. 26/12/79). L.C.
C. First in the Field (Brighton, 21/5/81; Glo. 20/5/82). L.C. *Lacy.*
Ca. The Sunny Side (Str. 18/5/85). L.C. *Lacy.*
C. Cousin Johnny (Str. 11/7/85). See *J. F. NISBET.*
F. The Man with Three Wives! (Crit. 23/1/86). L.C.
F. Doo, Brown and Co. (Vaud. 11/3/86). L.C.
C.O. Our Diva (O.C. 29/10/86). L.C.
D. The Witch (P'cess. 26/4/87, *mat.*; P'cess. 13/10/87).

RAE, J. E.

Bsq. Macbeth Mystified (Brighton, 3/5/69). See *W. H. MASON.*

RAE, JOSEPHINE

D.Sk. Bars of Gold (St Leonards, 6/6/92).
[Written in collaboration with *T. SIDNEY.*]

C.D. Pretty Mollie Barrington (St Leonards, 6/6/92).
[Written in collaboration with *T. SIDNEY.*]

D.Sk. The Ruby Heart (St Leonards, 6/6/92).
[Written in collaboration with *T. SIDNEY.*]

C.D. Love the Magician (Shaft. 7/7/92, *mat.*). L.C.
[Written in collaboration with *T. SIDNEY.*]

C.D. My Little Red Riding Hood (Pav. St Leonards, 16/10/95). L.C.
[Written in collaboration with *T. SIDNEY.*]

D.Sk. Interviewed (W. Pier, Brighton, 1/9/96). L.C.
[Written in collaboration with *T. SIDNEY.*]

RAE, LEONARD

D. Hal o' the Wynd (Stand. 14/9/74). L.C.

D. Rank and Fame (Stand. 29/3/75). L.C.
[Written in collaboration with *F. STAINFORTH.*]

C. Quiet in Harness (Stand. 30/10/76).

D. Uncle Tom (Stand. 30/9/78). L.C. as *Eliza and U.T.*

P. Harlequin Little Red Riding Hood; or, Little Boy Blue and the Fairies of the Coral Reef (Park, 24/12/80). L.C.
[Written in collaboration with *W. WALDEN.*]

D. Humanity (Leicester, 27/3/82). See *H. MARSTON.*

RAE-BROWN, CAMPBELL

F. A Sixpenny Wire (St Andrew's H. Kensington, 18/1/87).

D. Clara Vere de Vere (P.W. 8/6/88, *mat.*). L.C.

D. Kissing Cup Race (Ladb. H. 4/4/91, *copy.*; Lyr. Ealing, 20/4/91). L.C.

Bsq. The Prancing Girl (P.W. 26/11/91). L.C.
[Music by B. Brigata.]

RAFFALOVICH, ANDRÉ

D.Sk. Roses of Shadow (Athen. Tottenham Court Road, 26/1/93, *mat.*).

Past.D. Black Sheep (West, Albert H. 17/4/94).
[Music by C. Dick.]

D. The Blackmailers (P.W. 7/6/94). See *J. GRAY.*

RAINBOW, J. G.

D. California Joe (Rotherham, 21/1/78).

RALEIGH, CECIL

F. The Great Pink Pearl (Olym. 7/5/85). See *R. C. CARTON.*

D. The Pointsman (Olym. 29/8/87). See *R. C. CARTON.*

F. The Treasure (Str. 1/5/88). See *R. C. CARTON.*

D. The Spy (Com. 21/9/88). L.C.

F. The Inheritance (Com. 16/5/89, *mat.*). L.C.

Bsq. The New Corsican Brothers (P.W. L'pool, 11/11/89; Roy. 20/11/89). L.C.
[Written in collaboration with *W. SLAUGHTER.*]

D. Unreal Riches (County, Reading, 22/9/90). L.C.

F.C. The Grey Mare (Com. 23/1/92). See *G. R. SIMS.*

F.C. The Guardsman (Court, 20/10/92). See *G. R. SIMS.*

P.Bal. From London to Paris (Pal. 10/12/92).
[Written in collaboration with *Sir A. HARRIS.* Music by J. M. Glover and G. Serpette.]

D. Uncle John (Vaud. 3/4/93). See *G. R. SIMS.*
C.O. Little Christopher Columbus (Lyr. 10/10/93). See *G. R. SIMS.*
D. The Derby Winner (D.L. 15/9/94). See *Sir A. HARRIS.*
P. Dick Whittington (D.L. 26/12/94). See *Sir A. HARRIS.*
F. Fanny (P.W. L'pool, 8/4/95). See *G. R. SIMS.*
D. Cheer, Boys, Cheer! (D.L. 19/9/95). See *Sir A. HARRIS.*
P. Cinderella (D.L. 26/12/95). See *Sir A. HARRIS.*
M.D. The Belle of Cairo (Court, 10/10/96). L.C.
[Written in collaboration with *F. K. PEILE.*]
M.D. The Yashmak (Shaft. 31/3/97). L.C.
[Written in collaboration with *Sir S. HICKS.* Music by N. Lambelet.]
D. The White Heather (D.L. 16/9/97). L.C.
[Written in collaboration with *H. HAMILTON.*]
D. Sporting Life (Shakespeare, Clapham, 18/10/97; Shaft. 22/1/98). L.C.
[Written in collaboration with *Sir S. HICKS.*]
P. Dick Whittington (Alex. Stoke Newington, 27/12/97). See *Sir A. HARRIS.*
D. The Secret of the Keep (Gar. 8/9/98). L.C.
D. The Great Ruby (D.L. 15/9/98). L.C.
[Written in collaboration with *H. HAMILTON.*]
P. Cinderella (Alex. Stoke Newington, 26/12/98). See *A. STURGESS.*
D. Hearts are Trumps (D.L. 16/9/99). L.C.

RALEIGH, WALTER S.
D. Queen and Cardinal (H. 26/10/81). L.C.

RAM, H. S.
Bsq. The Weeping Willow (Staines, 5/5/86). See *P. DAVEY.*

RAMSAY, ALICIA
C. Gaffer Jarge (Com. 11/1/96). L.C.
D. The Executioner's Daughter (Gai. Hastings, 6/4/96; Roy. 16/4/96 as *Monsieur de Paris*). L.C.
[Written in collaboration with *R. DE CORDOVA.*]
D. As a Man sows (Grand, 22/8/98). L.C.
[Written in collaboration with *R. DE CORDOVA.*]

RAMSDALE, TERENCE
P. Aladdin (P.H. Addlestone, 26/8/89).
Bsq. Babes in the Wood (Aldershot, 3/8/91).
Bsq. Aladdin (Aldershot, 1/8/92).

RANDFORD, MAUD
C. Streaks of Gold (Sunderland, 14/3/78).
D. A Harvest of Crime (Brierly Hill, 27/5/97). L.C.

RANGE, IVAN
C.O. The Two Rings (P.H. Hastings, 6/4/85). L.C.

RANGER, —
C. Vanity cured; or, The School for Old Gentlemen (Str. 31/10/53). L.C.

RANSOM, H. A. V.
Ca. The Man who wasn't (Bijou, 22/2/95). L.C. *French.*

RAPHAEL, C.
D. Woman's Idol (Margate, 20/7/91).

RAPHAEL, FRANCIS

F. The Agent (Parkhurst, 21/3/92). L.C.

F. A Breeze from New York (P's. H. Kew Bridge, 20/11/93). L.C.

F.C. His Lordship's Birthday (Parkhurst, 19/3/94).
[Written in collaboration with *E. LAURI.*]

RAPHAEL, S. A.

C.D. Beethoven's Romance (Roy. 1/12/94). L.C.

RASSINDYLL, E.

C. A Man in Love (New, Wimbledon, 1/11/95). L.C.
[Title altered to *When a Man's in Love*, 28/10/98.]

RATTON, E. R.

Bsq. Aladdin; or, The Lamp and the Scamp (Bijou, 4/12/97). L.C.

RAVANI, E. C.

D. The Parasite (Athen. Tottenham Court Road, 15/1/94).

D. The Colonists (Ideal Club, Tottenham Court Road, 28/3/95).

RAY, EILEEN

D. Caroona (Torquay, 20/1/99, *copy.*; St G. 11/4/99). L.C.

RAY, LESLIE

Oa. Sir Reginald (St G. 6/1/94). See *J. M. TAYLOR.*

RAYMOND, EDGAR

Vaud. Ye Good Old Days (Masonic H. Surrey, 28/4/97).
[Music by J. Ansell.]

RAYMOND, KATE

D. The Waifs of New York (L'pool, 13/9/75). L.C.

RAYMOND, W.

D. Hunger (Gt Grimsby, 10/3/69).

RAYNER, ALFRED

D. The Scarlet Letter; or, Lost in the Snow (Grec. 5/10/63).

D. Danger (Stand. 7/11/68).

D. The Three Warnings (Pav. 30/3/72). L.C.

RAYNER, EDGAR

Ext. The Happy Village (Drill H. Flodden Road, Camberwell, 17/2/94. *amat.*).

RAYNER, JOSEPH

F. Pretty Alice of Portsmouth (Stand. 20/4/52).

REACH, ANGUS BETHUNE

[For his earlier plays see iv, 389.]

D. The Czarina (Sur. 21/4/51). See *M. BARNETT.*

F. The Shot Tower (Str. 4/8/51). L.C.

D. Dreaming and Waking (Sur. 20/10/51). See *M. BARNETT.*

READ, CHARLES

Ca. The Swiss Express (P'cess. 26/12/91). See *A. H. GILBERT.*

READE, CHARLES

C.D. The Ladies' Battle (Olym. 7/5/51). 8° [1851]; *Lacy.*

D. Angelo (Olym. 11/8/51). L.C. *Lacy.*

D. A Village Tale (Str. 12/4/52).

D. The Lost Husband (Str. 26/4/52). L.C. *Lacy.*

C. Masks and Faces (H. 20/11/52). See *T. TAYLOR.*

D. Gold (D.L. 10/1/53). L.C. 8° [1853]; *Lacy*; *Dicks.*

D. Two Loves and a Life (Adel. 20/3/54). See *T. TAYLOR.*
D. The Courier of Lyons (P'cess. 26/6/54; Lyc. 19/5/77, as *The Lyons Mail*). L.C. *Lacy* [as *The C. of L.; or, The Attack upon the Mail*].
D. The King's Rival (St J. 2/10/54). See *T. TAYLOR.*
F. Honour before Titles; or, Nobs and Snobs (St J. 3/10/54). L.C. Str. 30/4/52.
D. Peregrine Pickle (St J. 11/54). 8° 1851 [Oxford].
C. Art (St J. 17/2/55). L.C.
D. The First Printer (P'cess. 3/3/56). See *T. TAYLOR.*
D. Poverty and Pride. 8° 1856.
D. The Libertine's Bet (St J. 23/1/57, *amat.*).
— Le Faubourg St Germain. 8° 1859 [Paris].
D. It's never too late to mend (Leeds, 1864; P'cess. 4/10/65). L.C. Manchester, 25/7/65. 8° [1865]; 8° [1873]; 8° 1890 [*priv.*].
Past.D. Dora (Adel. 1/6/67). L.C. 8° [1867]; *Lacy.*
D. The Double Marriage (Qns. 24/10/67; Worcester, 2/1/88, *revised*; P.W. 26/6/88). L.C. 8° [1867].
D. Foul Play (Holborn, 28/5/68). See *D. BOUCICAULT.*
D. Put Yourself in his Place (Leeds, 11/3/70; Adel. 28/5/70, as *Free Labour; or, P.Y. in his P.*). L.C.
C. The Robust Invalid (Adel. 15/6/70). L.C. 8° 1857 [as *The Hypochondriac*].
D. An Actress by Daylight (St J. 8/4/71).
D. Griffith Gaunt (Leicester, 9/10/71; Qns. 1874).
C. Shilly Shally (Gai. 1/4/72). L.C.
D. The Wandering Heir (Amphi. L'pool, 10/9/73; Qns. 15/11/73). L.C.
D. Kate Peyton's Lovers (Qns. 20/12/73).
D. Rachel the Reaper (Qns. 9/3/74). L.C.
[A revision of *A Village Tale* (Str. 12/4/52).]
D. The Scuttled Ship (Olym. 2/4/77).
D. The Well-born Workman; or, A Man of the Day. 8° 1878.
D. Jealousy (Olym. 22/4/78). L.C. 8° [1872; as *Kate Peyton; or, Jealousy*]; 8° 1883.
[A revised version of *Kate Peyton's Lovers* (Qns. 20/12/73).]
D. Joan (Amphi. L'pool, 31/8/78). L.C.
D. Drink (P'cess. 2/6/79). L.C.
[Written in collaboration with *C. WARNER.*]
D. Single Heart and Double Face (P'cess. Edinburgh, 1/6/82).
M.D. Love and Money (Adel. 18/11/82). L.C. 8° 1883.
[Written in collaboration with *H. PETTITT.*]
C.D. The Countess and the Dancer (Olym. 27/2/86). L.C. 8° 1883.
[An altered version of *Jealousy* (Olym. 22/4/78).]
D. Nance Oldfield (Olym. 24/2/83). 8° [1883: *priv.*].

READE, GERTRUDE
C.O. The Minkalay (Metro. Devonport, 10/12/96). See *A. LEEDS.*

READING, EDWIN
D. A Cruel Father; or, A Terrible Revenge (Assembly R. Coventry, 29/10/85). L.C.

REDCLIFFE, STRATFORD DE
T. Alfred the Great at Athelney. 8° 1876.

REDE, WILLIAM LEMAN
[For his earlier plays see iv, 389–91.]

REDGRAVE, ROY

M.C. Lord Dunnohoo (Aldershot, 5/7/97). L.C.
[Lyrics by *M. TURNER*. Music by G. O. Walker.]

C.D. Black Ey'd Susan (Tivoli, Dover, 7/5/98). L.C.

REDMOND, JAMES

Ca. Domestic Diplomacy (Gai. Dublin, 1/4/72).

Ba. A Mechanical Partner (Gai. Dublin, 10/5/73).

REECE, ROBERT ["*E. G. LANKESTER*"]

O. Castle Grim (Roy. 2/9/65). L.C. Vic. H. 21/5/65.
[Music by G. B. Allen.]

Ext. Prometheus; or, The Man on the Rock (Roy. 23/12/65). L.C. *Lacy.*

C.O. Love's Limit (Roy. 6/1/66). L.C.

Ext. Ulf the Minstrel (Roy. 31/3/66). L.C.

Bsq. The Lady of the Lake—Plaid in a Tartan (Roy. 8/9/66). L.C. *Lacy.*

Bsq. Guy Mannering (Edinburgh, 12/66).

C. A Game of Dominoes (Ryde, I. of W. 8/67).

Ext. A Wild Cherry (Reigate, 2/9/67).

F. Honeydove's Troubles (D.L. 26/12/67). L.C.

M.Ca. Our Quiet Chateau (G.I. 26/12/67). L.C.

Bsq. Agamemnon and Cassandra; or, The Prophet and Loss of Troy (P.W. L'pool, 13/4/68). L.C.

D.Sk. A Public Dinner in aid of a Philanthropic Object (G.I. 13/4/68).

Ext. The Stranger—stranger than ever (Qns. 4/11/68). L.C. *Lacy.*

Ext. The Last of the Paladins (G.I. 23/12/68). L.C.

C.O. The Ambassadress (St G. 12/68).

Bsq. Brown and the Brahmins; or, Captain Pop and the Princess Pretty-Eyes! (Glo. 23/1/69). L.C. *Lacy.*

O. Chilperic (Lyc. 22/1/70). L.C.

R.D. Undine (Olym. 2/7/70).

Bsq. Whittington Junior and his Sensation Cat (Roy. 23/11/70). L.C. *Lacy.*

Bsq. Faust in a Fog L.C. K.X. 7/12/70.

C. Dora's Device (Roy. 11/1/71). L.C. *Lacy.*

Fairy D. Perfect Love; or, The Triumph of Oberon (Olym. 25/2/71). L.C. *Lacy.*

Bsq. Little Robin Hood; or, Quite a New Beau (Roy. 19/4/71). L.C.

Oa. In Possession (G.I. 22/6/71). L.C.
[Music by F. Clay.]

C.O. Paquita; or, Love in a Frame (Roy. 21/10/71). L.C. *Lacy.*
[Music by Mallandaine.]

Bsq. The Very Last Days of Pompeii; or, A Complete Bulwer-sement of the Classical Drama (Vaud. 13/2/72). L.C. *Lacy.*

Bsq. The Vampire (Str. 15/8/72). L.C.

Ext. Ali Baba à la mode (Gai. 14/9/72). L.C.

Bsq. Romulus and Remus; or, The Two Rum'uns (Vaud. 23/12/72). L.C. *Lacy.*

Bsq. Don Giovanni in Venice (Gai. 17/2/73). L.C.

C.Sk. The Wizard of the Wilderness (Gai. 8/3/73). L.C.

Bsq. Martha; or, A Fair Take-in (Gai. 14/4/73). L.C.

D. Friendship; or, Golding's Debt (Alex. Camden Town, 31/5/73). L.C.

F. Seeing Toole (Gai. 3/9/73). See *J. HOLLINGSHEAD.*

Bsq. Richelieu Redressed (Olym. 27/10/73). L.C.
Oa. Moonstruck (Alex. 10/11/73).
[Music by T. Pede.]
P. Little Puss in Boots; or, Harlequin and the Ogre, and the Miller's Son (P'cess. 26/12/73). L.C.
Bsq. Ruy Blas Righted; or, The Lover, the Lugger and the Lacquey (Vaud. 3/1/74). L.C. *Lacy*.
Bsq. Plucky Parthenia (Portsmouth, 26/2/74).
D. May; or, Dolly's Delusion (Str. 4/4/74). L.C. *French*.
Oa. Cattarina; or, Friends at Court (P's. Manchester, 17/8/74; Ch.X. 15/5/75). L.C.
[Music by F. Clay.]
O.Bsq. The Island of Bachelors (Gai. 14/9/74). L.C. 8° 1874.
[Music by C. Lecocq.]
D.Sk. Green Old Age (Vaud. 31/10/74). L.C. *Lacy*.
C.O. Les Près St Gervais (Crit. 28/11/74).
[Music by C. Lecocq.]
Ext. Spectresheim (Alh. 14/8/75). L.C.
Bsq. The Half-crown Diamonds (Mirror, 27/9/75; Imp. 2/10/80, *revised*). L.C.
F. Toole at Sea (Gai. 3/12/75). L.C.
Ca. Pretty Poll (St J. 8/1/76). L.C.
F. A Spelling Bee (Gai. 16/2/76). L.C.
D. An Old Man (Duke's, 25/3/76). L.C. *Lacy*.
Bsq. Young Rip Van Winkle (Ch.X. 17/4/76). L.C.
M.F. Coming Events (Roy. 22/4/76). L.C.
[Music by Bucalossi.]
M.F. Over Heads and Ears (Park, 10/6/76). L.C.
Bsq. William Tell Told Over Again (Gai. 21/12/76). L.C. 8° (1876).
Ba. Clockwork (Olym. 7/2/77). L.C.
Bsq. Oxygen; or, Gas in Burlesque Meter (Folly, 31/3/77). L.C.
[Written in collaboration with *H. B. FARNIE*.]
Ba. The Lion's Tail and the Naughty Boy who wagged it (Glo. 16/6/77). L.C.
C.O. The Creole (Brighton, 3/9/77). See *H. B. FARNIE*.
C.O. The Sea Nymphs (Brighton, 3/9/77). See *H. B. FARNIE*.
Oa. Up the River (Folly, 15/9/77). See *H. B. FARNIE*.
Bsq. Champagne (Str. 29/9/77). See *H. B. FARNIE*.
D. Russia (Qns. 27/10/77). See *H. B. FARNIE*.
D. Hester Gray; or, Blind Love (P's. Manchester, 27/10/77). L.C.
[Written in collaboration with *H. B. FARNIE*.]
Ext. Wildfire (Alh. 24/12/77). See *H. B. FARNIE*.
M.F. Madcap (Roy. 7/2/78). L.C.
[Written in collaboration with *H. B. FARNIE*.]
P. Ali Baba and the Forty Thieves (Gai. 13/2/78). See *A. J. BYRON*.
C.O. Les Cloches de Corneville (Folly, 23/2/78). See *H. B. FARNIE*.
F. A National Question (Glo. 16/3/78). L.C.
C. Mind the Shop (Glo. 22/4/78). L.C.
[Written in collaboration with *E. RIGHTON*.]
Bsq. Stars and Garters (Folly, 21/9/78). L.C.
[Written in collaboration with *H. B. FARNIE*.]
Bsq. Carmen; or, Sold for a Song (Folly, 25/1/79). L.C.
C.O. Babiole (P's. Manchester, 10/3/79). L.C.
[Music by L. de Rille.]

M.F. Marionettes (H. 16/6/79). L.C.
[Written in collaboration with *J. F. McARDLE.*]
C.O. La Petite Mademoiselle (Alh. 6/10/79). L.C.
[Written in collaboration with *H. S. LEIGH.*]
F.C. My Enemy (Olym. 15/1/80). L.C.
Ent. Voyage en Suisse (Gai. 27/3/80). L.C.
[Music by C. Meyder.]
F.C. The Guv'nor (Vaud. 23/6/80). L.C.
F.C. Parlours (Roy. 24/7/80). L.C.
Ext. Don Juan Junior (Roy. 3/11/80; Aven. 27/8/88, *revised*). L.C.
[Written in collaboration with *E. RIGHTON.*]
Bsq. The Forty Thieves (Gai. 23/12/80). L.C.
F. Divorce (Vaud. 29/1/81). L.C.
C.O. Jeanne, Jeannette and Jeanneton (Alh. 28/3/81). L.C.
[Music by P. Lacome.]
F. Welsh Rabbits (Folly, 21/5/81). See *K. SUMMERS.*
Bsq. Herne the Hunter (Gai. 24/5/81). L.C.
[Written in collaboration with *W. YARDLEY.*]
C.O. La Mascotte (Brighton, 19/9/81). See *H. B. FARNIE.*
F. Out of the Hunt (Roy. 8/10/81). L.C.
[Written in collaboration with *T. THORPE.*]
Bsq. Aladdin (Gai. 24/12/81). L.C.
C.O. Boccaccio (Com. 22/4/82). See *H. B. FARNIE.*
C.O. Wicklow Rose (P's. Manchester, 3/5/82). L.C.
[Music by G. B. Allen.]
Bsq. Little Robin Hood (Gai. 15/9/82). L.C.
Oa. On Condition (O.C. 9/10/82). L.C.
[Music by M. Lutz.]
C.O. The Merry War (Alh. 16/10/82). L.C.
[Music by J. Strauss.]
Bsq. Valentine and Orson (Gai. 23/12/82). L.C. 8° 1882.
Bsq.Ext. The Yellow Dwarf (H.M. 30/12/82).
[Written in collaboration with *A. THOMPSON.*]
Bsq. The Flying Dutchman (P.W. L'pool, 3/83). L.C.
Ext. Our Cinderella (Gai. 8/9/83). L.C.
Bsq. Our Helen (Gai. 8/4/84). L.C.
Bsq. Out of the Ranks (Str. 3/6/84). L.C.
Bsq. The Lady of Lyons Married and Claude Unsettled (Roy. Glasgow, 27/9/84). L.C.
Ext. Kenilworth (Aven. 19/12/85). L.C.
[Written in collaboration with *H. B. FARNIE.*]
P. Aladdin and the Forty Thieves (Sanger's, 26/12/85). L.C.
Oa. Keep your Places (St G. 15/2/86, *mat.*).
[Music by G. B. Allen.]
Bsq. Lurline (Aven. 24/4/86). L.C.
[Written in collaboration with *H. B. FARNIE.*]
Bsq. The Commodore (Aven. 10/5/86). See *H. B. FARNIE.*
Bsq. Robinson Crusoe (Aven. 23/12/86). See *H. B. FARNIE.*
C.O. Girouette (Portsmouth, 25/3/89; Aven. 24/6/89). L.C.
C. The Auctioneer (Bournemouth, 30/5/98). See *J. M. MORTON.*

REED, ARTHUR

Vaud. A Double Event (St G. 18/2/84). See *A. LAW.*
C.O. Faddimir; or, The Triumph of Orthodoxy (Vaud. 29/4/89, *mat.*). L.C. Vic. H. Bayswater, 3/1/89.
[Music by O. Neville.]

REED, GERMAN

Ent. A Peculiar Family (G.I. 15/3/65). L.C.
M.Ca. Mildred's Well (G.I. 5/5/73). See *F. C. BURNAND.*
F. Three Tenants. L.C. St G. 14/12/74. See *G. A. À BECKETT.*
M.F. A Spanish Bond. L.C. St G. 22/10/75. See *G. A. À BECKETT.*
M.Ca. Matched and Mated (St G. 1876). See *F. C. BURNAND.*
M.C. The Wicked Duke. L.C. St G. 31/5/76. See *G. A. À BECKETT.*
M.Ca. Number 204 (St G. 1877). See *F. C. BURNAND.*
M.Ca. A Night Surprise. L.C. St G. 8/2/77. See *W. CROMER.*

REED, R. L.

C. Honour (Tyne, Newcastle, 1/12/76). L.C.

REES, H. VICKERS

D. Sealed to Silence (Nov. 28/9/96). L.C.
[Written in collaboration with *S. NORTON.*]

REEVE, PERCY

C.O. Miss Decima (Crit. 23/7/91). See *F. C. BURNAND.*
Oa. Poor Mignonette (Crit. 2/8/92). L.C.
[Music by J. Offenbach.]

REEVE, WYBERT

Ca. A Match for a Mother-in-Law (Manchester, 20/6/59). *Lacy.*
D. The Dead Witness; or, Sin and its Shadow (Sheffield, 11/63). L.C.
D. Pike O'Callaghan; or, The Irish Patriot (Swansea, 5/4/66; Scarborough, 29/9/68; Sur. 7/2/70). *Lacy.*
D. The Better Angel; or, The Legacy of Wrong (S. Shields, 24/2/68; Tyne, Newcastle, 5/12/70). L.C.
D. Anna of Norway (Sheffield, 8/3/69).
C.D. Won at Last! (Scarborough, 13/9/69; Ch.X. 30/10/69). L.C. *Lacy.*
C. Not so bad after all (Ch.X. 8/1/70). L.C. Swansea, 5/4/66. *Lacy.*
Ca. Too Agreeable to be True (Tyne, Newcastle, 9/12/70).
C. True as Steel (Scarborough, 8/71). L.C. *Lacy.*
F. A Supper Gratis; or, An Impudent Intruder. L.C. Scarborough, 26/8/71. *Lacy.*
F. Never Reckon your Chickens before they are Hatched (Olym. 26/12/71). L.C. *Lacy.*
F. Obliging a Friend (Newcastle, 9/9/72). L.C. *Lacy.*
Ca. I Love You! (Newcastle, 13/9/72). L.C. *Lacy.*
C.D. Parted (Scarborough, 2/9/74). L.C.
D. George Geith; or, A Romance of City Life (Scarborough, 6/8/77; C.P. 30/10/83). L.C.
D. No Name (Newcastle, 26/10/77). L.C.

REEVES, GEORGE

D.Sk. The Mountain Devil (Sur. 26/3/79).
Bsq. The King, the Ring and the Giddy Young Thing; or, Herne the Hunter, Anne Boleyn and the Fair Maid of the River Dee (E.C. 18/4/82). L.C.

REICHARDT, HENRY

F.C. The Picture Dealer (Ladb. H. 30/6/92, *copy.*; Str. 4/7/92). L.C.
[Written in collaboration with *A. GOLDSWORTHY.*]

REID, BESSIE

D. Desperation (W. Bromwich, 10/6/87). See *G. ROY.*

D. The Colonel's Wife (Coventry, 6/2/88). L.C.
[Written in collaboration with *L. SMITH.*]

REISS, F. R.

F. A Tale in a Tub (Ladb. H. 23/1/93, *amat.*). L.C.

RÉMO, FELIX

C.O. The Lily of Léoville (Grand, Birmingham, 3/5/86; Com. 10/5/86).
[Written in collaboration with *A. MURRAY*; lyrics by *C. SCOTT.* Music by I. Caryll.]

D. The Royal Berkshire Regiment (Com. 29/6/86). See *H. T. VAN LAUN.*

M.Vaud. The Sentry (Lyr. 5/4/90). L.C.
[Written in collaboration with *T. M. WATSON.* Music by I. Caryll.]

RENDALL, WALTER

D. A Sailor's Devotion (Star, Swansea, 19/6/74).

RENDELL, H. W.

Oa. The Lost Prince (C.P. 18/5/95, *amat.*).

RENNELL, CHARLES R.

D. The Ark on the Sands (Brighton, 19/10/70).

D. Dick Swiveller (Brighton, 5/12/70).

C.D. Did she mean it? (Portsmouth, 17/4/71).

D. The Glittering Gem (Oldham, 21/9/74).

C.D. The Last of the Latouches (Croydon, 3/12/77). See *Mrs R. ELLIS.*

D. Help in Time (Crit. 14/6/79).

REVOLTI, FELIX

P. Valentine and Orson (Hengler's, 27/12/75). L.C.

REYNOLDS, CLARY FRANCES

D.Sk. Ups and Downs (Pier Pav. St Leonards, 4/6/97).

REYNOLDS, EDWARD

D. Tempted (Longton, 2/12/72).

REYNOLDS, EDWIN

D. Chance the Idiot (Longton, 5/12/72).

REYNOLDS, ELLIS

F. An Anxious Time (St G. 29/1/89). L.C. P.H. New Cross, Lewisham, 15/2/87, as *On the Wrong Tack.*

REYNOLDS, WALTER

D. A Mother's Sin (E.C. 25/7/85, *copy.*; Grand, 26/7/86). L.C.

D. Sweet Innisfail (Qns. Manchester, 16/8/86; Sur. 18/7/92). L.C.

D. A Woman's Truth (Grand, Nottingham, 24/12/86; Stand. 4/7/87). L.C.

D. Church and Stage (Wolverhampton, 16/1/88; Aven. 30/4/88, *mat.*). L.C.
[Title altered to *Back from the Grave*, 12/12/89.]

D. Vanity Fair (Bristol, 10/10/88, *copy.*). L.C.

D. The Slave of Drink (Qns. O.H. Workington, 4/8/90).

D. The Shamrock and the Rose (Huddersfield, 7/10/91; Grand, 26/9/92). L.C.

D. Knaves and Fools (Leeds, 9/6/99). L.C.

D. Keep to the Right (Leeds, 7/8/99). L.C.

REYNOLDSON, THOMAS H.

[For his earlier plays see iv, 393.]

O. Gustavus III; or, The Masked Ball. L.C. P'cess. 9/4/50.

D. The Barrister (Sur. 1/3/52). L.C.

Bal.O. William and Susan; or, All in the Downs (D.L. 28/2/59). L.C. [Music by J. H. Tully.]

RHOADES, JAMES

Poet.D. Dux Redux; or, A Forest Tangle (Nov. 18/1/87, *amat.*). L.C.

RHOADES, WALTER C.

C.D. The Butterfly (Drill H. Bloomsbury, 4/5/87, *amat.*).

Ca. The Widow (Park T.H. Battersea, 4/2/89). L.C. P.W. 23/4/87.

F. Non-suited (Vestry H. Tooting, 7/4/91). L.C. P.H. Addlestone, 19/3/91.

RHODES, A.

F. The Tallow-chandler Bewitched; or, Love's Disguises (Greenwich, 28/11/68).

RHOYDS, HERBERT

D. Joe, the Waif (Greenwich, 24/4/76).

RHYS, Captain HORTON ["MORTON PRICE"]

Ent. Punch and Fun (S.W. 9/6/62).

P. The Rose of Blarney; or, Harlequin Dannymanoranyotherman (S.W. 26/12/62). L.C.

RIBTON-TURNER, C. J.

C. Handsome is that handsome does (Vaud. 6/6/88, *mat.*). L.C.

RICE, CHARLES

D. The Three Musketeers; or, The Queen, the Cardinal and the Adventurer (Manchester, 2/8/50; Grec. 20/10/51). *French.*

P. The Fairy and the Fawn; or, Life in the Dog Star and the Voyage of Taste (Grec. 26/12/52). L.C.

F. Enchanted Wives (Grec. 28/3/53). L.C.

D. Eola (Grec. 28/3/53).

D. Quatre Bras (Grec. 10/53). L.C.

D. The Merchant and the Mendicant (Sur. 22/10/60).

P. Red Riding Hood (C.G. 26/12/73).

P. The Babes in the Wood; or, The Big Bed of Ware (C.G. 26/12/74). L.C.

P. Cinderella (C.G. 27/12/75). L.C.

P. Puss in Boots (C.G. 26/12/77). L.C.

RICE, JAMES

D. Ready Money Mortiboy (Court, 12/3/74). See *W. MAURICE.*

C. Such a Good Man (Olym. 18/12/79). See *W. BESANT.*

RICHARDS, ALFRED BATES

[For his earlier plays see iv, 394.]

D. Vandyck: A Play of Genoa. 8° 1850.

D. The Prisoner of Toulon; or, The Peasant's Revenge (D.L. 2/3/68). L.C. [as *The Convict of Toulon*].

T. Norma (Belfast, 5/2/75).

RICHARDS, J.

P. Dick Whittington and his Cat; or, The Demon of Discord and the Fairy (Gar. 24/12/70). L.C.

RICHARDS, P.

D. Ruth (Sur. 18/2/71). See *C. H. ROSS.*

RICHARDSON, E.

M.C. The Specialist; or, An Initial Blunder (Myddleton H. Islington, 21/4/96). L.C. Manor, Hackney, 1/6/97.
[Music by G. Richardson.]

RICHARDSON, F.

M.C. The Royal Star (P.W. 16/9/98). L.C.
[Music by J. Clerice.]

RICHARDSON, HARRY

F. An Irishman's Policy (Mechanics' H. Barnsley, 9/9/75).
F. The Little Pest (Halifax, 11/10/75).
D. Liberty; or, The Dhu Colleen of Ballyfoyle (Vic. 16/9/76). L.C.
D. The Wild Flower of the Prairie (E.C. 8/9/77). See *F. FULLER.*

RICHLEY, R.

D. The Maid of Croxdale (Cambridge, Spennymoor, 8/1/77).

RIDGE, W. PETT

Ca. An Artful Girl (Birkbeck Inst. 29/6/92, *amat.*).
[Written in collaboration with *J. E. PEARCE.*]

RIDGEWAY, T.

Ent. Les Trois Fêtes de Bois; or, The Pretty Milliners (Grec. 1/12/51).

RIDGWELL, G.

M.C. The Skirt Dancer (R.A. Woolwich, 28/3/98; Grand, Fulham, 27/6/98). L.C.
[Written in collaboration with *E. MANSELL* and *R. F. MACKAY.* Music by H. Trotère.]

RIGHTON, EDWARD ["*CORRIE BURNS*"]

C. Mind the Shop (Glo. 22/4/78). See *R. REECE.*
Ext. Don Juan Junior (Roy. 3/11/80). See *R. REECE.*
C.D. Hard Up (Reading, 26/3/83; Str. 20/10/83). L.C.
C. Gone Away (Com. Manchester, 9/8/86). L.C. as *Revolution; or, G.A.*
[Written in collaboration with *D. STOW.*]
D.Idyll. Dante (Literary Inst. Shanklin, 31/12/90). See *G. H. R. DABBS.*
D. Our Angels (Vaud. 3/3/91). See *G. H. R. DABBS.*
D. Insurance Money; or, The Story of a Coffin Ship (Lyr. Hammersmith, 4/6/94). L.C.

RIGHTON, MARY

Ca. Our Friends (Ladb. H. 16/3/88; Vaud. 24/7/90, *mat.*).
C. Little Nobody (Vaud. 24/7/90, *mat.*). L.C.
M.Sk. Cupid and Psyche (Bijou, 20/4/95, *amat.*).

RIGNOLD, HARRY H.

D. Such is Life (Qns. Longton, 2/12/93, *copy.*). L.C.
[Title altered to *The Waif*, 25/7/97.]

RIMINGTON, CHARLES

C.O. The Eagle's Wing (Pier, Folkestone, 26/12/92). L.C.
[Music by R. Forsyth.]
C.D. The Old Sport (Pier, Folkestone, 27/11/93). L.C.
[Written in collaboration with *J. PRYCE-CLAIREMONT*
C.O. When George III was King (Pier, Folkestone, 26/12/93).
[Music by R. Forsyth.]

RIPLEBY, R.
M.D. Schneider (Alex. Widnes, 16/4/92). See *A. SHIRLEY.*

RISQUE, W. H.
M.F. All Abroad (Portsmouth, 1/4/95). See *O. HALL.*
F. Round a Tree (Vaud. 11/11/96). L.C.
Rev. Potpourri (Coronet, 3/4/99). See *J. T. TANNER.*

RIST, R. ERNEST
C.D. The Brothers of Eden (St Helens, 1/5/85).

RIX, WILTON J.
P. Pip's Patron (T.H. Beccles, 26/1/92).
D.Sk. Little Chap, Curly and Brown (T.H. Kilburn, 29/1/95). L.C.
[Written in collaboration with *F. J. GILLETT.*]
Bsq. Boadicea Unearthed (T.H. Kilburn, 29/1/95).
[Written in collaboration with *F. J. GILLETT.*]

"*ROAKES, JOHN.*" See *T. TAYLOR*

ROBBINS, ALFRED F.
F. A Pleasant Hour (Pullan's, Bradford, 6/9/78).
Ca. Helps (Lincoln, 13/12/78). L.C. Bradford, 13/10/77.
D. Over the Cliff; or, By Accident or Design (Gt Grimsby, 11/2/84). L.C.
D. Notes and Gold (Pullan's, Bradford, 31/8/85). L.C.
F.C. Mixed Marriages (Pier Pav. Hastings, 3/6/95). L.C.

ROBE, —
D. Wallace and Bruce (Adel. Coatbridge, 27/11/69).

ROBERTS, FRANK
D. Clarice (Str. 17/11/86). See *G. W. BROWNE.*

ROBERTS, GEORGE ["*ROBERT WALTERS*"]
F. Under the Rose (St J. 24/3/62).
F. Forty Winks (St J. 2/6/62). L.C. *Lacy.*
D. Lady Audley's Secret (St J. 28/2/63). L.C.
Ca. Cousin Tom (P'cess. 8/6/63). L.C.
F. An Ample Apology (P'cess. 13/3/65). L.C.
C. The Three Furies (St J. 13/3/65). L.C. *Lacy.*
D. Idalia (St J. 22/4/67). L.C.
D. Behind the Curtain (Holb. 18/4/70). L.C.
Ca. The Absent Man (Holb. 18/6/70). *Lacy.*
D. Passion (Tyne, Newcastle, 3/12/73). L.C.
D. Ship Ahoy (Sur. 3/10/74). L.C.
D. The Mysterious House in Chelsea (M'bone, 30/9/76). See *J. A. CAVE.*
F. A Warning to Parents (Albion, 5/3/77). L.C.
D. Gin (Vic. 27/3/80). L.C.
D. Birthdays (Newcastle, 20/2/83). L.C.
D. My Wife; or, Sunshine through the Mist (Gai. Burnley, 6/4/85). L.C. Cheltenham, 10/6/84.
D. Minnie Grey (E.C. 14/6/86). See *H. YOUNG.*
D. Outcast London (E.C. 2/10/86). See *H. YOUNG.*
D. The Forger; or, Good and Evil (E.C. 13/11/86).
D. The Secret of a Life (Grand, 18/11/86). See *A. WILLIAMS.*
D. Run to Earth; or, A Golden Fortune (E.C. 11/4/87). L.C.

D. Buffalo Bill (E.C. 1/8/87). L.C.
D. Wrecked in London (E.C. 1/8/87). L.C.
[Title altered to *At the Mercy of the World*, 24/3/96.]
D. A Plunge in the Dark (S.W. 26/3/88). L.C.
D. The Trapper (S.W. 2/4/88).
C.O. Pat (R.A. Woolwich, 16/11/91; Aquar. Gt Yarmouth, 1/8/92; Parkhurst, 12/9/92). L.C.
[Written in collaboration with *H. MONKHOUSE* and *H. ERWIN*.]
D. £1000 Reward (Aquar. Scarborough, 15/12/92). See — *CORDYCE*.
D. Justice at Last (N. Camp, Farnborough, 24/11/94).
D. Rookwood (Shakespeare, L'pool, 15/4/95; W.L. 24/8/96, as *The King's Highway*). L.C.
[Written in collaboration with *F. GERALD*.]

ROBERTS, Sir RANDAL
Ca. Under a Veil (Richmond, 7/1/76; Olym. 15/5/76). L.C.
D. A Dangerous Game; or, Chicotte (Grand, 6/4/85). L.C.
D. Separation (Lyr. Ealing, 2/10/86).
F. Apollo M.D. (Jodrell, 26/12/88). L.C.
F.C. Our Doctors (Terry's, 24/3/91, *mat*.). L.C.
[Written in collaboration with *J. MACKAY*.]

ROBERTS, TOM
C. Friends and Foes (Rochester, 24/6/58; Vic. H. 22/5/89). L.C.

ROBERTS, WALTER
D. The Dead Letter; or, Second Sight (M'bone, 11/12/73). L.C.

ROBERTSON, DONALD
D. My Missis (O.C. 8/10/86). See *C. LEWIS*.

ROBERTSON, IAN
C. A Play in Little (Shaft. 2/6/92). L.C.
D. The Pity of it (Lyr. Ealing, 15/4/96; Sav. 29/6/96). L.C.
D. The Plague (Lyc. Edinburgh, 16/10/96). L.C.
[Music by L. Drysdale.]
D. The Storm (Roy. 24/10/96). L.C.

ROBERTSON, J.
D. Daniel O'Connell (Qns. Dublin, 14/8/82).

ROBERTSON, JESSIE
D. Dan the Outlaw (T.H. Kilburn, 29/12/88; Nov. 14/5/92, *mat*.).
F.Sk. Venus (Nov. 11/5/96). L.C.

ROBERTSON, LIONEL
D. Waiting for Death; or, The Iron Grave (E.C. 9/2/78). L.C. Croydon, 15/10/77.
[Written in collaboration with *M. COMERFORD*.]
F. An Artful Little Spouser. L.C. Alh. Barrow-in-Furness, 19/7/82.
[Written in collaboration with *M. COMERFORD*.]

ROBERTSON, STUART
C.O. Wapping Old Stairs (King's Lynn, 4/1/94; Vaud. 17/2/94). L.C.
[Music by H. Talbot.]

ROBERTSON, THOMAS WILLIAM

D. The Chevalier de St George (P'cess. 20/5/45). 8° [n.d.]; *Lacy.*
D. Ernestine (P'cess. 14/4/46). *Lacy* [*as Noemi*].
D. The Battle of Life. L.C. Norwich, 23/1/47.
F. The Haunted Man (Qns. 1/1/49). L.C.
C.D. A Night's Adventure; or, Highways and Byways (Olym. 25/8/51). L.C.
D. The Ladies' Battle (H. 18/11/51). *Lacy.*
D. Faust and Marguerite (P'cess. 19/4/54). *Lacy.*
[See note under *D. BOUCICAULT.*]
D. Castles in the Air (C.L. 29/4/54). L.C.
Ca. A Wife's Journal (Olym. 18/12/54). L.C. *Lacy* [as *My Wife's Diary*].
D. The Star of the North (S.W. 5/3/55, as *The Northern Star*). *Lacy.*
F. The Clockmaker's Hat (Adel. 8/3/55, as *Betty Martin*; St J. 3/7/65). L.C.
F. Peace at any Price (Str. 13/2/56). L.C. *Lacy.*
Ca. The Muleteer of Toledo. L.C. Grec. 6/5/56.
D. The Half Caste; or, The Poisoned Pearl (Sur. 8/9/56). L.C. *Lacy.*
F. The Cantab (Str. 14/2/61). L.C. *Lacy.*
D. Jocrisse the Juggler (Adel. 1/4/61). L.C. as *Magloire; or, The Prestigitator*. *Lacy.*
C.D. David Garrick (P.W. Birmingham, 4/64; H. 30/4/64). L.C. *French.*
Oa. Constance (C.G. 23/1/65). L.C.
[Music by F. Clay.]
C. Society (P.W. L'pool, 8/5/65; P.W. 11/11/65). L.C. *French.*
C. Ours (P.W. L'pool, 23/8/66; P.W. 15/9/66). L.C. 8° [1879, New York]; *French.*
D. Shadow-tree Shaft (P'cess. 6/2/67). L.C.
Ca. A Rapid Thaw (St J. 2/3/67). L.C.
Oa. A Dream in Venice (G.I. 18/3/67). L.C.
C. Caste (P.W. 6/4/67). L.C. 8° [1879, New York]; *French.*
D. For Love (Holb. 5/10/67). L.C.
D. The Sea of Ice; or, The Prayer of the Wrecked (Col. Glasgow, 28/11/67).
C. Play (P.W. 15/2/68). L.C. *French.*
D. Passion Flowers (Hull, 28/10/68).
C. Home (H. 14/1/69). L.C. 8° [1879, New York]; *French.*
C. School (P.W. 16/1/69). L.C. *French.*
C. My Lady Clara (Alex. L'pool, 22/2/69; Gai. 27/3/69, as *Dreams*). L.C. *French* [as *Dreams*].
C.D. A Breach of Promise (Glo. 10/4/69). L.C. *Lacy.*
Ca. Dublin Bay (Manchester, 18/5/69; Folly, 18/12/75). L.C.
C. Progress (Glo. 18/9/69). L.C. *Lacy.*
D. The Nightingale (Adel. 15/1/70). L.C. *French.*
C. The M.P. (P.W. 23/4/70). L.C. *French.*
C. Birth (Bristol, 5/10/70). *Lacy.*
C.D. War (St J. 16/1/71). L.C. *Lacy.*
C. Policy (Glasgow, 13/2/71).
F. Not at all Jealous (Court, 29/5/71). L.C. *Lacy.*
Ca. Which is it? L.C. D.L. 27/7/81.
C.D. Other Days (Hull, 12/4/83). L.C.

F. A Row in the House (Toole's, 30/8/83). L.C. *French.*
C.O. Cinderella (Newcastle, 15/8/92; Grand, 3/10/92).
C. Over the Way (Court, 20/1/93). L.C.
[In addition to these plays Robertson wrote: *Photographs and Ices, Up in a Balloon, Down in Our Village, Post Haste, Birds of Prey, The Duke's Daughter* and *Two Gay Deceivers.*]

ROBERTSON, W. GRAHAM
Bsq. Fickle Fatima (T. H. Streatham, 6/2/92, *mat.*).

ROBINSON, DAVID
C.D. On Thorns (H.M. Richmond, 8/11/80).

ROBINSON, Mrs C. See *MARIE ZECH*

ROBINSON, EMMA
D. Richelieu in Love (H. 30/10/52). 8° 1844; 8° 1852.

ROBINSON, H.
D. The Mesmerist (Grec. 4/10/79). See *G. CONQUEST.*

ROBINSON, MAURICE
D. Remembrance (Terry's, 8/6/99). L.C. Dumfries, 16/2/99.

ROBINSON, NUGENT
D. Poor Humanity (Sur. 11/4/68). L.C.
F. Looey Napoleong (Dublin, 12/9/68).
D. Janet O'Brien (Dublin, 27/2/69).
F. Miss Tibbett's Back Hair (Dublin, 5/12/70).
F. Anna Maria's Piano (Dublin, 13/5/72).
F. Doing the Shah (Glo. 5/7/73). L.C. as *Mrs Smiffin's Carte de Visite; or, D. the S.*
F. Mr Joffin's Latchkey (Ch.X. 25/1/75). L.C.

ROBSON, E. M.
D. Faithful unto Death (Bristol, 2/9/81). L.C.
[Written in collaboration with *E. COMPTON.*]
F. The Foundling (Terry's, 30/8/94). See *W. LESTOCQ.*

ROBSON, FRED
F. The Varsity Boat Race (Lyc. 6/4/70). See *C. H. STEPHENSON.*
Oa. Popocatapetl (Holb. 18/12/72). L.C. Greenwich, 19/8/71. *Lacy.*
[Music by G. Richardson.]
Bsq. Lady Godiva (Middlesborough, 5/5/73; S.W. 6/12/73). L.C. Exeter, 1/5/73.
F. How to kill him (Stockton-on-Tees, 14/7/73).

ROBSON, WILLIAM JAMES
[For his earlier plays see *E.N.D.* ii, 385.]
T. Waltheof (Sur. 17/3/51).
D. Love and Loyalty (M'bone, 13/11/54). L.C.
D. Bianca. 8° 1856.

[*ROCHE, JAMES C.*
C.D. Shane-na-Lawn (Chicago, 1885; Alex. L'pool, 22/4/89). L.C.
[Written in collaboration with *J. A. KNOX.*]

RODGERS, ARTHUR
D. The Brewer of Tadcaster (Empire, Tadcaster, 5/8/97).

RODGERS, WILFRED
D. Taken by Force (Nov. 8/3/97). L.C.

RODMAN, ALFRED

F.Sk. His Son-in-law (Herne Bay, 12/9/90). See *W. G. WATSON.*

RODNEY, C. M.

Bsq. The Black Cat (St G. Walsall, 31/7/93; E.C. 14/8/93; O.C. 24/12/94, as *Eastward Ho*). L.C.
[Music by C. E. Howells.]

RODNEY, STRATTON

Oa. Constable Jack; or, The Bobby's Bride (Bath, 16/5/89). L.C.
[Music by C. F. Drummond.]

RODWAY, JAMES

D. Faith and Hope (P.H. New Cross, 12/4/86).

RODWELL, GEORGE HERBERT

[For his earlier plays see iv, 395.]

Spec. The Devil's Ring; or, Fire, Water, Earth and Air (D.L. 1/4/50). L.C. *Lacy.*

Spec. Eleanor the Amazon; or, Queen of France and England (Ast. 21/4/51). L.C.

D. Azael; or, The Prodigal in London (Olym. 13/10/51).

F. Mr and Mrs Briggs; or, Harlequin Punch's Festival (Ast. 26/12/51). L.C.
[Written in collaboration with *N. LEE.*]

F.C. As in a Glass; or, His Double (O.C. 17/10/87).
[Written in collaboration with *C. LAURI.*]

ROE, J. E.

Ba. La Ba Kan; or, The Prince's Nap and the Snip's Snap (Swiss Gdns. Shoreham, 7/6/60)

"*ROE, RICHARD.*" See *F. G. B. PONSONBY*

ROGERS, A. R.

Bsq. "Two" Much Alike (G.I. 12/2/70, *amat.*).
[Written in collaboration with *G. GROSSMITH.*]

ROGERS, CHARLES

D. Reality (Barnsley, 30/12/89). L.C.

D. The Democrat (Grand, Nottingham, 22/3/93, *copy.*). L.C.

D. Sherlock Holmes (Glasgow, 28/5/94).

F.C. Josiah's Dream; or, The Woman of the Future (Str. 21/5/96). L.C.

D. The Days of Cromwell (Aven. Sunderland, 9/7/96, *copy.*; Borough, Stratford, 19/10/96; W.L. 2/11/96). L.C.
[Written in collaboration with *C. LIVESEY.*]

P. The Forty Thieves (Borough, Stratford, 26/12/96). L.C.

D. The Ladder of Life; or, The Gordons to the Front (Borough, Stratford, 30/5/98). L.C.
[Written in collaboration with *W. BOYNE.*]

ROGERS, FRANK

F.C. Our Boarding School (International, 1/2/84). L.C.

D. Nadine (Vaud. 5/3/85). L.C.

D. Madge (Middlesborough, 24/3/88). L.C.

D. The Angels of Paris (Scarborough, 17/5/94). L.C.
[Written in collaboration with *M. WILKINSON.*]

ROGERS, MAUD M.

D. When the Wheels run down (St G. 29/4/99, *amat.*). L.C.

ROGERS, ROBERT

Ca. Baby's Engagement (Wolverhampton, 19/12/92). L.C.

ROGERS, T. STANLEY

Ext. The Enchanted Orange Tree (Qns. H. L'pool, 10/5/80). L.C.
C. Squabbles (Bijou, L'pool, 17/12/81). L.C.
C.D. For the Old Love's Sake (Gai. Hastings, 17/3/84; Roy. 25/5/86). L.C.
[Written in collaboration with *H. KIMM.*]
Bsq. Nap; or, A Midsummer Night's Scream (Blyth, 5/4/90; E.C. 21/7/90).
[Music by G. Salmon and M. Adeson.]
F.C. The Housebreaker (Stockton-on-Tees, 25/3/92; E.C. 31/7/93). L.C.
M.F. Naughty Titania (New, Aston, 7/8/93; Leamington, 6/4/96). L.C.
[Written in collaboration with *J. RUSHWORTH.* Music by J. H. Yorke.]
Bsq. Robin Hood Esq. (Roy. Chester, 6/8/94).
[Music by H. May.]
P. Jack the Giant Killer (York, 5/4/97).
P. Cinderella (Parkhurst, 24/12/97). L.C.
P. Aladdin (Grand, Fulham, 27/12/97). L.C.
P. Robinson Crusoe (Morton's, Greenwich, 24/12/98).
P. Aladdin (Dalston, 26/12/98). L.C.
P. Cinderella (Shakespeare, Clapham, 26/12/98). L.C.

ROGERS, WILLIAM

D. Marrying for Money; or, The Scheming Dog Fancier. L.C. Brit. 24/7/50.

ROGERSON, HARRY

M.Ext. Jacko (Grand, Stalybridge, 11/4/98; Stratford, 29/7/1901, as *Jacko; or, Comical Complications*). L.C.

ROLFE, V. C.

F. That Ring (St G. 4/5/93).
F. Winkhopper's Plot (Nov. 7/6/97).

ROMAINE, EDWARD

D. True as Steel (Darlington, 21/8/71; Alf. 25/9/71). L.C.

ROMER, ARTHUR

D. Our Cousins (Bijou, 14/6/69, *amat.*). L.C.

ROMER, F.

C. Flirtation (Glo. 14/7/77). L.C.
[Written in collaboration with *G. S. BELLAMY.*]
D. Two Wedding Rings (Brit. 27/2/82). See *G. S. BELLAMY.*
C. Tact (Aven. 14/3/85). See *G. S. BELLAMY.*
C. April Showers (Terry's, 24/1/89, *mat.*). L.C.
[Written in collaboration with *G. S. BELLAMY.*]

ROPER, GARNHAM

Ca. Mr Cynic (Traf. 2/5/93). See *W. J. LOCKE.*

ROSE, EDWARD

Ca. Our Farm (Qns. 29/6/72). L.C.
C. Misconception; or, Love me, love my dog (Portsmouth, 27/8/73). L.C.
F. A Congress at Paris (Olym. 15/7/78). L.C.

D. Incognita (Ipswich, 17/2/79). L.C.

Bsq. Under Proof; or, Very much above Pa (P'cess. Edinburgh, 1/5/79). L.C.

Oa. Nicette (Roy. 2/6/79). L.C.
[Music by R. Labrocetta.]

Bsq. Venus (Roy. 27/6/79). See *Sir A. HARRIS.*

Ca. Mad (Olym. 12/6/80). L.C.

Ca. Wild Flowers (Roy. 4/10/80). L.C.

F. The Stores (D.L. 14/3/81). L.C.
[Written in collaboration with *Sir A. HARRIS.* Music by Bucalossi.]

Ca. The Marble Arch (P.W. L'pool, 12/12/81; P.W. 2/2/82). L.C. *French.*
[Written in collaboration with *A. J. GARROWAY.*]

D.Sk. Vice Versa; A Lesson for Fathers (Gai. 9/4/83). L.C.

C. Equals (P's. Manchester, 28/6/83; Alex. L'pool, 2/7/83; Iffley H. Hammersmith, 6/6/89). L.C. *French.*

Ca. Bella's Intended (Alex. L'pool, 15/10/83). L.C.

F. My Benefactor (Str. 21/11/83). L.C.

F.C. Our Square (Winter Gdns. Southport, 11/2/84; Gai. 30/4/84). L.C. 8° 1882 [Ipswich].

C. The Scorpion: A Journal of Society and Satire (T.H. Oxford, 1/12/84; Vaud. 23/12/84). L.C.

D. Two Women (Stand. 6/4/85). L.C.

Ca. A Girl Graduate: An Idyll of Commem. (New, Oxford, 28/6/86). L.C.

F.C. Odd! to say the least of it (New, Oxford, 6/11/86; Nov. 6/11/86). L.C.

D. She (Nov. 10/5/88, *copy.*; Gai. 6/9/88). L.C.
[Written in collaboration with *W. SIDNEY* and *C. GRAVES.*]

D. Her Father (Vaud. 16/5/89, *mat.*).
[Written in collaboration with *J. T. DOUGLASS.*]

Ca. Clever People (County, Reading, 23/9/89). L.C. Ipswich, 11/12/79.

Bsq. Orpheus and P(Eurydice) (Aquar. Gt Yarmouth, 20/7/91). L.C.
[Written in collaboration with "*Captain COE*".]

C. The Plowdens (P.W. 8/3/92). L.C.

C. The Adventurers (Str. 24/6/92, *mat.*). L.C.

D. Agatha Tylden, Merchant and Shipowner (H. 17/10/92). L.C.

Bsq. The Babble Shop; or, Lord Wyndhamere's Fan (Traf. Sq. 30/3/93). L.C.

F.C. The Cat's Eye (New, Oxford, 22/5/93).

Ca. The Young Folks (Baths, Wimbledon, 21/10/95). L.C.

R.D. The Prisoner of Zenda (St J. 7/1/96). L.C.

R.D. Under the Red Robe (H. 17/10/96). L.C.

C. When a Man's in Love (Court, 19/10/98). See *A. HOPE.*

D. In Days of Old (St J. 26/4/99). L.C.

ROSENFELD, SIDNEY

C.O. The Lady or the Tiger (E.C. 7/5/88, *mat.*, *copy.*). L.C.

C. The Senator (E.C. 22/10/89). See *D. D. LLOYD.*

C. The Whirlwind (E.C. 27/9/90, *copy.*). L.C.

ROSIER, J. A.

Ca. Comin' thro' the Rye (Halifax, 11/10/86). L.C.
[Written in collaboration with *W. T. MAINPRICE.*]

"*ROSS, ADRIAN*" [*A. R. ROPES*]

Bsq. Joan of Arc (O.C. 17/1/91). See *J. L. SHINE.*

M.F. In Town (P.W. 15/10/92). L.C.
[Music by O. Carr.]

M.F.C. Morocco Bound (Shaft. 13/4/93). See *A. BRANSCOMBE.*

Bsq. Don Juan (Gai. 28/10/93). See *J. T. TANNER.*

M.F.C. Go bang (Traf. Sq. 10/3/94). L.C.
[Music by O. Carr.]

M.F. The Shop Girl (Gai. 24/11/94). See *H. J. W. DAM.*

Oa. Bobbo (P's. Manchester, 12/9/95). See *J. T. TANNER.*

M.F. Biarritz (P.W. 11/4/96). See *J. K. JEROME.*

M.C. The Clergyman's Daughter (Birmingham, 13/4/96). See *J. T. TANNER.*

M.C. In the Ring (Gai. 27/5/96). See *J. T. TANNER.*

M.C. Weather or No (Sav. 15/8/96). L.C.
[Written in collaboration with *W. BEACH.* Music by B. L. Selby.]

M.C. The Ballet Girl (Grand, Wolverhampton, 15/3/97). See *J. T. TANNER.*

O. The Grand Duchess (Sav. 4/12/97). See *C. H. E. BROOKFIELD.*

M.C. The Transit of Venus (Dublin, 9/4/98). See *J. T. TANNER.*

M.C. Billy (Tyne, Newcastle, 11/4/98). See *G. COOPER.*

M.C. A Greek Slave (Daly's, 8/6/98). See *O. HALL.*

C.O. The Lucky Star (Sav. 7/1/99). See *C. H. E. BROOKFIELD*

M.C. San Toy (Daly's, 21/10/99). See *E. MORTON.*

Oa. Tempests in Teacups (St G. Parish H. Forest Hill, 13/12/99). See *C. PIRKIS.*

ROSS, CHARLES H.

Ca. Worryburry's Whims (Alex. 20/5/65). L.C.
[Written in collaboration with *D. MURRAY.*]

D. Charm (Sur. 16/4/70). L.C.

P. The Sleeping Beauty (C.G. 26/12/70). See *G. A. À BECKETT.*

D. Ruth; or, A Poor Girl's Life in London (Sur. 18/2/71).
[Written in collaboration with *P. RICHARDS.*]

D. Silence (Holb. 6/5/71). L.C.

D. The Lantern Light (E.C. 15/2/73). See *C. D'ARCY.*

Oa. The Prisoners at the Bar (Alex. L'pool, 17/6/78). L.C.
[Music by F. Musgrave.]

Bsq. The Desperate Adventures of the Baby; or, The Wandering Heir (Str. 14/12/78).

M.Ca. Lodgings to Let. L.C. Albert H. Reading, 6/5/79.

ROSS, ERIC

D. Grelley's Money; or, A Manchester Man's Million (P.W. Salford, 30/10/82; M'bone, 8/8/87). L.C.

ROSS, RONALD

D. The Deformed Transformed. 8° 1891.

ROSS, RUSSELL

Ca. The Dawn of Love (Exeter, 26/1/85).

ROTHERY, W. G.

Oa. The Judgment of Paris (Lyr. 30/10/97). L.C.

ROUSBY, ALFRED

D. Not Dead; or, Saved from the Sea (Bolton, 16/3/74).

ROUTLEDGE, W.

Bsq. Leah: A Hearty Joke in a Cab Age (G.I. 23/1/69, *amat.*). L.C.
F. Mrs Beflat's Blunder (G.I. 23/1/69, *amat.*). L.C.
Bsq. What's it on? or, Shakespeare-ience Teaches (G.I. 29/1/70, *amat.*). L.C.

"ROWE, BEDFORD"

D. Aliens (Lyr. 3/6/89, *mat.*, *copy.*). L.C.

"ROWE, BOLTON." See *B. C. STEPHENSON*

ROWE, C. J.

M.Duol. A Puff of Smoke. L.C. St G. 23/10/76.

ROWE, GEORGE FAWCETT

F. Sampson's Wedding (Croydon, 19/11/69; Lyc. 30/3/70). L.C.
D. Found Drowned; or, Our Mutual Friend (O.C. 26/12/70). L.C.
D. Sleigh Bells (P.W. L'pool, 11/3/72). L.C.
M.Sk. The Geneva Cross (Adel. 17/10/74). L.C.
C.D. Brass (Alex. L'pool, 11/5/77; H. 13/8/77).
D. The New Babylon (Qns. Manchester, 10/6/78). See *P. MERRITT*.
D. Uncle Tom's Cabin (Manchester, 19/8/78; P'cess. 31/8/78). L.C.
D. Freedom (D.L. 4/8/83). L.C.
[Written in collaboration with *Sir A. HARRIS*.]
D. The Donagh; or, Sinlish Macree (Grand, 12/4/84). L.C.
D. Forward to the Front (Norwich, 1/10/88). L.C.

ROWE, NICHOLAS

D. The Orange Girl (Sur. 24/10/64). See *H. T. LESLIE*.

ROWE, R.

M.F. Zoo (St J. 5/6/75). L.C.
[Music by Sir A. Sullivan.]

"ROWE, SAVILLE." See *C. W. SCOTT*

ROWSELL, MARY C.

C.D. Whips of Steel (St G. 7/5/89). See *J. J. DILLEY*.
Ca. Richard's Play (Ladb. H. 14/1/91, *copy.*; Terry's, 20/2/91, *mat.*) L.C. *French*.
[Written in collaboration with *J. J. DILLEY*.]
D. The Friend of the People (H. 17/2/93, *copy.*). L.C.
[Written in collaboration with *H. A. SAINTSBURY*.]

ROY, GEORGE

D. Miscarriage of Justice (S.W. 27/5/82). L.C.
D. Auld Robin Gray (Imp. 22/9/83). L.C.
D. A Dash for Freedom (Olym. 29/11/84). L.C.
D. Desperation (W. Bromwich, 10/6/87). L.C.
[Written in collaboration with *B. REID*.]
C.D. Golden Hearts (Athen. Shepherd's Bush, 22/9/92, *copy.*).

ROYD, LOIS

C. The Double Deception (Bijou, 25/10/97). See *M. PINEO*.

ROYD, LYNN

C.O. Hawkwood Hall (Myddleton H. Islington, 31/1/95). L.C.
[Music by G. C. Richardson.]

RUBENS, PAUL

F.C. Young Mr Yarde (Pav. Buxton, 15/8/98). See *H. ELLIS.*

Bsq. Great Caesar (Com. 29/4/99). See *G. GROSSMITH, Jr.*

RUBENSTEIN, ANTON

O. The Demon (Jodrell, 22/10/88). L.C.

RUDALL, H. A.

O. Signa (C.G. 30/6/94). See *G. A. À BECKETT.*

R.D. Her Father's Friend (Sav. 29/6/96). L.C.

RUMSEY, MARY C.

Ca. The Midsummer Night; or, Shakespeare and the Fairies. 8° 1854. [Translated from L. Tieck, *Die Sommernacht.*]

RUNCIMAN, FRANK

Ca. A Friend in Need (Nov. 19/4/97). L.C.

RUNTZ, ERNEST

Bsq. Mythology Run Mad (T.H. Westminster, 17/5/93). See *T. MOORE.*

"*RUSHTON, ARTHUR*" [*JOHN PLUMMER*]

M.Ext. Nightingale's Wooing (Phil. 10/4/71). L.C. [Written in collaboration with *F. ARLON.*]

F. A Capital Idea (Phil. 26/12/71). See *F. ARLON.*

RUSHWORTH, J.

M.F. Naughty Titania (New, Aston, 7/8/93). See *T. S. ROGERS.*

RUSS, SIDNEY

F.C. The Junior Partner (Berry Wood Asylum, Northampton, 21/4/87).

RUSSELL, C.

D. Nell Snooks; or, No Room to Live (W.L. 3/4/99). L.C. [Title altered to *Wasted Lives*, 2/5/99.]

RUSSELL, E. HASLINGDEN

D.Sk. Only To-night (P.W. L'pool, 26/11/88). L.C.

Ca. Once upon a Time (Brighton, 12/7/89). [Written in collaboration with *H. FURNIVAL.*]

M.Ca. A Fair Equestrienne; or, The Circus Rider (P's. Bristol, 14/3/90; Traf. 8/3/93). L.C. Norwich, 12/2/90, under sub-title.

C.D. The Earl's Daughter (Croydon, 21/7/90; Parkhurst, 4/8/90). L.C.

Monol. Her First Appearance (Court, L'pool, 7/11/90). L.C.

Ca. Moonbeams (Shakespeare, L'pool, 30/7/91). L.C.

M.Ca. A Knight of the Road (Wolverhampton, 9/12/92).

D.Sk. The Squire's Will (P.W. L'pool, 6/12/97). L.C.

RUSSELL, FRANK

F. Caught Courting (H.M. Richmond, 12/7/80). L.C.

P. Puss in Boots (H.M. Richmond, 24/12/80). L.C.

M.Sk. Bat and Ball (H.M. Richmond, 15/9/81).

F. Luggage per Rail (H.M. Richmond, 12/7/82).

RUSSELL, W. C.

D. Fra Angelo (H. 30/8/65). L.C.

RUTTER, REGINALD P.

D. The Power of Conscience (Grand, Stalybridge, 23/7/91). L.C.

D. Divorced (Imp. 19/5/98). L.C.

RYLEY, J. H.
F. Congenial Souls (P'cess. Edinburgh, 3/10/78).

[*RYLEY, MADELEINE LUCETTE*
C. Jedbury Junior (Empire, N.Y. 23/9/95, as *Christopher Junior*, Terry's, 14/2/96). L.C.
F. The Vanishing Husband (Stockton-on-Tees, 29/1/97, *copy.*; Str. 29/5/1900, as *The Mysterious Mr Bugle*). L.C.
C. A Coat of Many Colours (W.L. 22/7/97). L.C.
C. An American Citizen (D.Y. 19/6/99). L.C.

RYMER, JAMES
D. Gold Dust (Montague H. Worthing, 23/7/78).

SAGER, R. F.
D. Modern Ireland (P.H. Bacup, 13/9/90).
D. Brothers (Mechanics' Inst. Barnoldswick, 17/7/97).

ST AUBYN, DAISY
D. The Dark Hour (St G. 1/4/85). L.C. Ladb. H. 13/3/77.

ST CLARE, FRANK
Ext. Myfisto (Colchester, 24/1/87). See *V. MONTAGUE.*

ST CLARE, GEORGE
Ext. The Isle of Utopia (Devonshire Park, Eastbourne, 26/12/92; Com. 6/3/93). L.C.
[Music by C. Nugent.]

ST JOHN, ARTHUR
D. Dishonoured (Macclesfield, 3/8/96). L.C.
C.D. Vengeance (Macclesfield, 11/9/97). L.C.

ST LEGER, E. WARHAM
C.O. Cigarette (Cardiff, 15/8/92; Lyr. 7/9/92). L.C.
[Music by J. H. Parry.]
O. Miami (P'cess. 16/10/93). See *J. HOLLINGSHEAD.*

ST MAUR, HARRY
F. My Life by Myself (P.W. L'pool, 8/7/76).
C. Dr Claudius (Vaud. 29/1/97). See *F. M. CRAWFORD.*

ST RUTH, Miss ABBEY
Bsq. The Key to King Solomon's Riches, Limited (O.C. 24/12/96) L.C.

SAINTSBURY, H. A. ["*JAY NIBB*"]
C. Betrayed by a Kiss (O.C. 5/5/91). L.C.
D. The Friend of the People (H. 17/2/93). See *M. C. ROWSELL.*
D. The Doctor's Shadow (P's. Accrington, 2/1/96, *copy.*). L.C.
F.C. His Relations (Aven. 28/5/96). L.C.
D. The Eleventh Hour (Olym. 18/7/96, *copy.*; P.W. Birmingham, 14/9/96). L.C.
[Written in collaboration with *R. MACDONALD.*]
D. The Three Musketeers (Parkhurst, 5/9/98). L.C.
D. Chicot the Jester (Gai. Hastings, 15/12/98, *copy.*). L.C.
D. The First Night (P'cess. of W. Kennington, 21/8/99).
D. Don Caesar de Bazan (P'cess. of W. Kennington, 21/8/99).

SAKER, MARIE EDWARD
C. Duplicity (Birkenhead, 28/5/83).
D. A Sinless Sinner (Lyr. Ealing, 15/4/96). L.C.
D. Till we meet again (County, Kingston, 21/11/98). L.C.

SALA, — [Brothers SALA]
P. Harlequin Billy Taylor (P'cess. 26/12/51). L.C.
[Written in collaboration with *G. ELLIS.*]
D. The Corsicans; or, The Brothers Salacarro (Sur. 15/3/53). L.C.

SALA, GEORGE AUGUSTUS
Bsq. Wat Tyler, M.P. (Gai. 20/12/69). L.C.

SALAMAN, MALCOLM CHARLES
F.C. Deceivers Ever (Str. 26/11/83). L.C.
M.Ca. Boycotted (St G. 5/7/84). L.C.
[Music by E. Barnett.]
F. Dimity's Dilemma (Gai. 19/2/87). L.C.
Duol. Both Sides of the Question (Steinway H. 14/7/91).
C. A Modern Eve (H. 2/7/94, *mat.*). L.C.

SALLENGER, W.
Oa. A Merry Sell (R.A. Woolwich, 21/5/88).
[Music by B. H. Hancock.]
O.Bsq. The Spectre of Shooter's Hill; or, The Broken Hot Cross Bun (R.A. Woolwich, 20/10/88). L.C.
[Music by B. J. Hancock.]

SALSBURY, N.
Ext. The Brook (Alex. L'pool, 12/7/80; Alex. 13/9/80). L.C.

SAMUEL, S. M.
D.Sk. A Quiet Pipe (Folly, 17/3/80). See *H. COWEN.*

SAMUELS, WILLIAM R.
D. A Bitter Repentance (Sneinton Inst. Nottingham, 19/12/89, *amat.*).

SANDERSON, W WAITE
D. The Age of Love (Art Gallery, Newcastle, 8/9/95). L.C.

SANDFORD, EDITH
D. The Firefly (Sur. 17/5/69).

SANDFORD, JAMES
Bsq. The Ashantee War (Alex. O.H. Sheffield, 25/5/74).

[*SANFORD, WALTER*
D. The Power of Gold (Grand, Birmingham, 29/3/97; Stratford, 20/2/99). L.C. Metro. Gateshead, 20/7/97.
[Title altered to *A Social Outcast*, 24/3/97; apparently original title restored.]

SANGER, GEORGE
Spec. The Last of the Race; or, The Warrior Women (Ast. 21/10/71). L.C.
Spec. The Jockey Club (Sanger's, 26/12/92).

SANTLEY, KATE
C.O. Vetah (Portsmouth, 30/8/86).

SANTLEY, —
C.O. Joconde (Lyc. 25/10/76). L.C.
[Music by N. Isonard.]

SAPTE, WALTER, Jr.
C. Speculation (P.W. 23/1/86, *mat.*). L.C.
Ca. Tottie's Telegram (Cheltenham, 29/4/86).

Duol. Sample versus Pattern (Alex. L'pool, 11/4/87; P.W. 15/6/87). L.C.
C. The Step-Sister (Com. 4/6/87). L.C.
F. Uncle's Ghost (P.W. 15/6/87, *mat.*; O.C. 17/1/94). L.C.
Ca. The Portrait (Olym. 15/5/88, *mat.*). L.C.
Ext. The Abduction of Bianca; or, The Brigand's Doom (Silver Fête, Kensington, 11/7/88).
[Written in collaboration with *C. M. YORKE.*]
C. The Spotted Lion (Gai. 8/10/88). L.C.
F.C. The Plunger (Ladb. H. 24/10/88, *copy.*). L.C.
[Written in collaboration with *E. SPENCER.*]
F. That Telegram (Glo. 12/11/88).
C.D. 'Twixt Cup and Lip (Lyr. Ealing, 18/4/89; Str. 18/11/93). L.C.
C.D. Marah (P.W. 31/5/89, *mat.*; Grand, 19/5/90, as *A Convict's Wife; or, The Romance of Marriage*). L.C.
Bsq. Mlle. Cleopatra (Aven. 2/3/91).
[Music by J. M. Glover.]
F.C. A Lucky Dog (Str. 4/7/92, *mat.*; Terry's, 3/10/92). L.C.
C.O. Marigold Farm; or, The Simple Squire and the Evil Eye (O.C. 7/2/93, *copy.*).
[Music by H. Parry.]
C. There she goes (P'cess. 25/1/96). L.C.
M.D. Black and White (P.W. Southampton, 27/12/97). See *M. MELFORD.*
F. A Perfect Crime (O.H. Cheltenham, 1/8/98). L.C.

SARGENT, HENRY
D. Gain (E.C. 14/6/80). L.C.

SARGENT, JOHN
D. The Cross Roads; or, Dove Nest Farm (Clarence, Dover, 13/7/85).
D. Our Native Home (Sur. 19/9/92). See *C. WHITLOCK.*

SAULL, Miss J. A.
M.Ext. Prince Pedrillo; or, Who's the Heir? (Central H. Nottingham, 21/11/93). L.C.

SAUNDERS, CHARLES
D. Run to Earth (Qns. Dublin, 27/9/73).

SAUNDERS, JOHN.
D. Love's Martyrdom (H. 13/6/55). L.C.
D. Arkwright's Wife (Leeds, 7/7/73). See *T. TAYLOR.*
D. Abel Drake (Leeds 9/10/74). See *T. TAYLOR.*

SAUNDERS, JOHN D.
D. The Silence of the Night (Shakespeare, Clapham, 19/7/97). L.C.
D. The Battle of the Sexes (Shakespeare, Clapham, 18/7/98). L.C.

SAUNDERS, RICHARD
C.D. Ashes (P.W. 30/11/94). See *E. COLLINS.*
Duol. Hope (Brompton Hospital, 8/1/95).
D. The Egyptian Idol (Sunderland, 16/12/95). L.C. Lincoln, 18/10/95.
[Written in collaboration with *M. BANDMANN.*]

SAUNDERS, TOM
O.Ext. Prince Cherrystar (Hereford, 25/10/93).
[Music by H. Richardson.]

SAVILE-CLARK, CLARA

Duol. A Woman's Vengeance (St G. 19/12/92, *mat.*). L.C.
[Title altered to *A Cruel Alternative*, 7/93.]

SAVILLE, HENRY FAUCIT. See *HENRY SAVILLE FAUCIT*

SAWYER, WILLIAM

[For an earlier play see *E.N.D.* ii, 387.]
F. Eight Hours at the Seaside. L.C. Brighton, 18/11/57.
D. Jessie Ashton; or, London by Day and Night (Sur. 6/4/63). L.C.
M.D. Garibaldi in Sicily (Adel. 22/4/67). L.C.

SAXBY, ARGYLE

D.Sk. A Bit of Fun (Finsbury Park H. 14/3/98).

[*SAYRE, Dr*

C. Our Strategists (O.C. 29/5/86). L.C.

SCARLETT, WYNNE

F. Ali Baba, M.P. (H.M. Aberdeen, 3/4/93; Empire, Southend, 4/6/94, *revised*).
F. An Awkward Dilemma (Consett, 24/4/93).
Spect. On Parade; or, A Sailor's Sweetheart (Star, Wolverhampton, 8/4/95).
M.F. The Cookettish Cook; or, The Area Bell rung too many times (Aquar. Brighton, 11/11/95).

SCHIFF, EMMA

D. The Countess; or, A Sister's Love (Alfred, 21/2/70). L.C.
C. The Twin Sisters (Ch.X. 18/4/70). L.C.
Ca. The Rights of Women (Glo. 9/1/71). L.C.
C.D. On the Brink (Amphi. L'pool, 23/10/75). L.C.

SCHON, OSCAR H.

D. Love's Anguish (Adel. 3/5/82, *mat.*). L.C.

[*SCHONBERG, JAMES*

F.C. Washington Watts (Margate, 15/8/79). L.C.
D. Let not your angry passions rise (Roy. 22/6/81). L.C.
T. Narcisse, the Vagrant (Vaud. 3/7/83).

SCOTT, CLEMENT WILLIAM ["*JOHN DOE*"; "*SAVILLE ROWE*" in association with "*BOLTON ROWE*"=*B. C. STEPHENSON*]

D. Off the Line (Gai. 1/4/71). L.C.
D. Tears, idle Tears (Glo. 4/12/72). L.C.
D. The Detective (Mirror, 29/5/75). L.C.
[Written in collaboration with *E. MANUEL*.]
D. The Dogs of St Bernard (Mirror, 21/8/75). L.C.
C. The Great Divorce Case (Crit. 15/4/76). L.C.
C. Peril (P.W. 30/9/76). L.C.
[Written in collaboration with *B. C. STEPHENSON*.]
Ca Tears (O.C. 17/2/77). L.C. Canterbury, 28/7/74.
[Written in collaboration with *B. C. STEPHENSON*.]
C. The Vicarage: A Fireside Story (P.W. 31/3/77). L.C.
D. Diplomacy (P.W. 12/1/78) L.C.
[Written in collaboration with *B. C. STEPHENSON*.]
C.O. The Little Duke (Phil. 27/4/78). L.C.
[Written in collaboration with *B. C. STEPHENSON*.]

D. The Crimson Cross (Adel. 27/2/79).
[Written in collaboration with *E. MANUEL*.]
D. Anne Mie (P.W. 1/11/80). L.C.
M.Sk. Many Happy Returns (St G. 28/3/81). See *G. A. À BECKETT*.
D. The Cape Mail (P.W. L'pool, 23/9/81; St J. 27/10/81). L.C. *French*.
F.C. Bad Boys (Com. 29/4/85). L.C.
Ext. Jack-in-the-Box (Brighton, 24/8/85). See *J. P. SIMPSON*.
Ca. The Last Lily (T.H. Kilburn, 23/2/86).
D. Sister Mary (Brighton, 8/3/86). See *W. BARRETT*.
C.O. The Lily of Léoville (Grand, Birmingham, 3/5/86). See *F. REMO*.
P. Cinderella (H.M. 26/12/89). See *R. HENRY*.
C.D. Odette (P'cess. 29/9/94).
D. Denise (P.W. Birmingham, 28/8/95). L.C.
[Written in collaboration with *Sir A. HARRIS*.]
D. The Swordsman's Daughter (Adel. 31/8/95). See *B. THOMAS*.
Bsq. Forlorn Hope (H.M. Oxford, 22/5/96).
[Written in collaboration with *J. M. COWARD*.]
Ca. A Merry Christmas (Str. 1/2/97). L.C.
M.C. Oh! What a Night! (O.H. Wakefield, 15/1/98). See *W. TERRISS*.

SCOTT, DAVID
C.O. The Golden Bough (Broughty Ferry, 27/1/87, *amat.*).
[Music by J. Pelzer.]

SCOTT, FREDERIC
D. Her Talisman (Masonic H. Camberwell, 16/1/96). L.C.

SCOTT, JAMES
D. Daniel (Ryde, 30/1/73).
D. Dead; or, The Living Will (T.H. Brierley Hill, 25/11/91, *copy*.).

SCOTT, MARY AFFLECK
F. The Tarantula (H. 4/9/97). L.C.

SCOTT, PHILIP
Bsq.O. Corinne (Qns. Dublin, 26/8/95).
[Music by W. Parker.]

SCOTT, SHAFTO
D. The Field of the Cloth of Gold; or, Henry the Eighth and Francis the First (Ast. 24/4/69).

SCOTT, W. S.
D. On the Clyde (Dundee, 27/8/75). L.C.

SCOTTI, SOPHIE
D. Resemblance (Vaud. 10/12/85). L.C.
C.D. Happier Days (Ladb. H. 17/6/86).
F. Peaceful War (P.W. 24/5/87, *mat.*). L.C.
[Written in collaboration with *L. WAGNER*.]

SCUDAMORE, F. A.
D. Fighting Fortune (Bolton, 9/5/81; M'bone, 24/7/82). L.C.
D. Presence of Mind (P'cess. Edinburgh, 19/8/81; Belfast, 22/11/82, as *Dad*).
D. Might and Right (Bolton, 23/11/81). L.C.
D. Rags and Bones (Cardiff, 23/7/83; Sur. 30/7/83). L.C.

D. The Oakdell Mystery (Eastbourne, 25/8/84). L.C.
[The same as *Keep to the Right* in *UA*: see p. 702.]
D. First Class (P.W. Greenwich, 14/9/85). L.C.
D. Is Life worth living? (P's. Bristol, 1/9/87; Sur. 9/7/88). L.C.
D. Dangers of London (Cardiff, 9/6/90; Sur. 23/6/90). L.C.
D The Mystery of the Seven Sisters (Sur. 27/10/90).
D. The Ups and Downs of Life (O.H. Northampton, 1/8/92; Pav. 8/8/92). L.C.
D. Settling Day (O.H. Northampton, 14/9/93; Sur. 3/6/95). L.C.
D. Our Eldorado (O.H. Northampton, 6/8/94; Pav. 13/8/94; Sur. 8/7/95, as *Flight for Life*). L.C.
D. Against the Tide (Sur. 3/8/96). L.C.
D. The Destroying Angel (Barnsley, 8/12/96, *copy.*; Brixton, 1/3/97). L.C.
D. Dangerous Women (Brixton, 1/8/98). L.C.
D. Thou shalt not kill (Shakespeare, Clapham, 31/7/99). L.C.

SCUDAMORE, J. F.
D. Nature's Nobleman (Gai. Dublin, 7/82).

SEAMAN, WILLIAM
D. The Will and the Way (Brit. 16/5/53). L.C.
D. The Student's Grave (Brit. 4/7/53).
D. Woman and her Master (C.L. 26/11/53). L.C.
D. The Earl's Housekeeper (Brit. 22/4/72). L.C.
D. The Drowned Man's Legacy (Brit. 23/9/72). L.C.
D. The Silver Bullet (Brit. 16/8/75). L.C.
D. The Storm Deed; or, Black Gang Chine (E.C. 2/4/77). L.C.

SEARELLE, LUSCOMBE
M.D. The Black Rover (Glo. 23/9/90). L.C.

SEARLE, CHARLES
C.O. Venice (Alh. 5/5/79). L.C.
Ca. Marleyvale (Devonshire Park, Eastbourne, 31/5/86). L.C.
R.O. The Castle of Como (O.C. 2/10/89). L.C.
[Music by G. Cockle.]

SEARLE, CYRIL
D. Nancy Sykes (Olym. 9/7/78). L.C.

SEATON, A. M.
Ca. My Brave Little Wife (Toole's, 24/7/82). L.C.
D. Moths (Rotunda, L'pool, 19/3/83).

SEATON, PRYCE
Ca. Daggers Drawn (Str. 9/1/91). L.C. Str. 26/6/90.
F. A Warm Member (Terry's, 9/4/98). L.C.

SEATON, ROSE
T. Andromeda (Vaud. 24/3/90, *mat.*). L.C.
Ca. Mr Donnithorpe's Rent (O.H. Chatham, 9/6/90). L.C.
C. Music at Home (O.H. Chatham, 9/6/90; O.C. 30/7/92). L.C.

[*SEAWELL, Miss ELLIOT*
D.Sk. The Sprightly Romance of Marsac (Ladb. H. 2/2/98). L.C.

SEDDON, FREDERICK H.
O. The Squire of Burleigh (Hudson's Works, Bootle, 30/11/92, *amat.*).

SEDGER, HORACE

D. Hidden Worth (P.W. 3/11/86, *mat.*). L.C.
C. The Little Squire (Lyr. 5/4/94). See *DORA V. GREET.*

SEEBOHM, E. V.

C. Little Lord Fauntleroy (P.W. 23/2/88, *mat.*). L.C.

SEED, HARRY

F. The Literary Nephew (Sussex H. Bouverie Street, 6/2/68, *amat.*).
F. Old Husbands and Young Wives (Cavendish R. 7/7/68, *amat.*).

SELBY, CHARLES

[For his earlier plays see iv, 397–9.]
F. The White Serjeants; or, The Buttermilk Volunteers (Adel. 6/5/50). L.C.
C.D. The Husband of my Heart (H. 23/10/50). L.C. *Lacy.*
F. The Fire Eater (Olym. 30/6/51)· L.C. *Lacy.*
F. My Sister from India (Str. 5/1/52). L.C. *Lacy.*
Prel. The Camberwell Brothers; or, The Mystical Milkman (Olym. 12/4/52). L.C.
F. Hotel Charges; or, How to Cook a Biffin (Adel. 13/10/53). L.C.
D. The Marble Heart; or, The Sculptor's Dream: A Romance of Real Life (Adel. 22/5/54). L.C. *Lacy.*
F. My Friend the Major (St J. 2/10/54). L C. *Lacy.*
Ba. The Spanish Dancers; or, Fans and Fandangoes (St J. 18/10/54). L.C. *Lacy.*
Ext. The Elves; or, The Statue Bride (Adel. 18/11/56). L.C.
F. A Fearful Tragedy in the Seven Dials (Adel. 4/5/57). L.C. *Lacy.*
F. The Drapery Question; or, Who's for India? (Adel. 28/10/57). L.C.
F. An Hour in Seville (Adel. 10/3/58). L.C. *Lacy.*
Ca. The Last of the Pigtails (Str. 6/9/58). L.C. *Lacy.*
F. The Bonnie Fish Wife (Str. 20/9/58). L.C. *Lacy.*
D. Harold Hawk; or, The Convict's Vengeance (Sur. 27/9/58). L.C. *Lacy.*
F. My Aunt's Husband (Str. 27/9/58). L.C. *Lacy.*
D. The Young Mother (H. 28/2/59). L.C. *Lacy.*
F. Caught by the Ears (Str. 30/5/59). L.C. *Lacy.*
D. Gis, the Armourer of Tyre (Stand. 26/11/59). L.C.
D. Paris and Pleasure; or, Home and Happiness (Lyc. 28/11/59). L.C.
Ca. The Pet Lamb (Str. 10/9/60). L.C. *Lacy.*
D. The Poor Nobleman (St J. 14/11/61). L.C. *Lacy.*
C. Court Gallants (Roy. 31/8/63). L.C. as *The Court Page.*
Ext. The Pirates of Putney (Roy. 31/8/63). L.C. *Lacy.*
D. London by Night; or, The Dark Side of our Great City. L.C. Brit. 7/3/68. *Dicks.*

SELBY, HENRY C.

D. Chosen for Life (Temperance H. Merthyr Tydfil, 20/1/82).
D. Saved from Sin; or, A Soldier's Honour (Star, Neath, 26/2/84).

SELBY, T. L.

O. Adela (Mechanics' H. Nottingham, 8/2/88). See *J. R. BROWN.*

SELDEN, EDGAR

F. McKenna's Flirtation (O.H. Coventry, 1/8/92). L.C.

SELF, C. STANLEY

D.Sk. Forgery; or, Another Man's Crime (S.W. 18/9/99). L.C.

SELLMAN, RICHARD

Bsq.O. Dagobert (Ch.X. 28/8/75). L.C.
[Lyrics by *F. GREEN.*]

SELWYN, ALFRED

C.D. United (Vic. H. Ealing, 18/12/90).

SELWYN, WILFORD

D. Wedded to Crime (S.W. 25/5/91). See *F. JARMAN.*

SENNETT, THOMAS

Ca. Caught (Sunderland, 21/9/83). L.C.

D. Iron True; or, Convicted (Stratford, 3/5/86). L.C.

SERLE, THOMAS JAMES

[For his earlier plays see iv, 399–400.]

C. Tender Precautions; or, The Romance of Marriage (P'cess. 24/11/51). L.C. *Lacy.*

D. Annie Tyrell; or, The Tempter and the Tempted (Sur. 26/1/52). L.C.

D. A Village Story; or, The Shadows and Sunshine of Life. L.C. Brit. 8/7/59.

SERLE, Mrs WALTER

Ca. Outwitted (Aquar. Scarborough, 26/4/89).

SETON, HUGH

M.Ca. A Royal Roundhead (Blackburn, 11/9/93; Mat. 17/4/97). L.C.
[Music by D. Harrison.]

M.C. The Bicycle Girl (Grand, Nottingham, 29/3/97). See *C. OSBORNE.*

M.C. An American Belle (O.H. Cheltenham, 19/4/97; Metro. 17/5/97). L.C. Grand, Croydon, 18/12/96.

SEYMOUR, EDWARD MARTIN

D. Through a Glass, darkly (Olym. 28/4/96, *copy.*). L.C.
[Title altered to *In Letters of Fire*, 23/7/1902.]

D.Sk. 'Twixt Night and Morn (Aven. 28/5/96). L.C.

SEYMOUR, FRANK

F. The Proscribed Royalist; or, Who stole the Ducks? (O.H. Leicester, 1/8/81). L.C.

SEYMOUR, TOM

M.C. A Trip to Brighton (P's. Harwich, 7/8/99). L.C.
[Lyrics by *A. E. BOURNE.* Music by Perrini.]

SHAEL, V.

Oa. Cloris (Wolverhampton, 17/4/85). See *M. WYCOMBE.*

SHANDS, G. W.

F. Whisky and Water (Edinburgh, 25/2/54).

SHANNON, —

C. Money Bags (Nov. 5/11/85). See *T. E. PEMBERTON.*

SHARP, EVELYN

Fairy D. The Green Enchantress (Residence of E. J. Griffiths, Regent's Park, 21/7/98).

SHARP, THEODORE

Ca. The Lady and the Magistrate (Bexhill-on-Sea, 20/7/97). L.C.

SHARPE G. F.

C.O. St Valentine (Halifax, 14/3/92).
[Music by H. H. Boman.]

SHAW, GEORGE BERNARD

D. Widowers' Houses (Independent Theatre Soc. at Roy. 9/12/92). L.C. 8° 1893.

R.C. Arms and the Man (Aven. 21/4/94). L.C. 8° 1898 [in *Plays, Pleasant and Unpleasant*].

C.D. Candida (S. Shields, 30/3/95, *copy.*; H.M. Aberdeen, 30/7/97; Str. 1/7/1900). L.C. 8° 1898 [in *Plays, Pleasant and Unpleasant*].

D. The Devil's Disciple (Bijou, 17/4/97, *copy.*; P'cess. of W. Kennington, 26/9/99). L.C. 8° 1901 [in *Three Plays for Puritans*].

D. The Man of Destiny (Grand, Croydon, 1/7/97; Com. 29/3/1901). L.C. 8° 1898 [in *Plays, Pleasant and Unpleasant*].

C. The Gadfly; or, The Son of the Cardinal (Vic. H. Bayswater, 31/3/98).

D. Caesar and Cleopatra (Newcastle, 15/3/99, *copy.*; Leeds, 16/9/1907; Sav. 25/11/1907). L.C. 8° 1901 [in *Three Plays for Puritans*].

C. You Never Can Tell (Stage Soc. at Roy. 26/11/99). L.C. Vic. H. 30/3/98. 8° 1898 [in *Plays, Pleasant and Unpleasant*].

D. Mrs Warren's Profession (New Year Club at Lyr. 6/1/1902). L.C. Vic. H. 30/3/98. 8° 1898 [in *Plays, Pleasant and Unpleasant*].

C. Captain Brassbound's Conversion (Stage Soc. at Str. 16/12/1900; Qns. Manchester, 12/5/1902; Court, 20/3/1906). L.C. Court, L'pool, 15/11/99. 8° 1901 [in *Three Plays for Puritans*].

C. The Philanderer (Cripplegate Inst. 20/2/1905; Court, 5/2/1907). L.C. Vic. H. 30/3/98. 8° 1898 [in *Plays, Pleasant and Unpleasant*].
[For his later plays see A. E. Morgan, *op. cit.* 313–14.]

SHEEN, WILLIAM P.

D. Braving the Storm (Rugby, 24/3/90). L.C.
[Title altered to *In the Jaws of Death*, 13/5/1903.]

D. Lady Satan; or, A Female Judas (P'cess. Leith, 26/11/96, as *A Female Judas*; Harte's, Oppenshaw, 28/6/97). L.C.

D. O'er Land and Sea (Leeds, 30/9/99, *copy.*; Wigan, 10/5/1900, as *Why Woman Sins*; Terriss, 28/1/1901). L.C.

SHELLEY, A. C.

Bsq. The Babes (Str. 4/2/95). See *H. PAULTON*.

SHELLEY, HERBERT

D.Sk. A Daughter of England (Grand, Halifax, 27/8/96). See *H. DUNDAS*.

F.C. A Family Fix (O.H. Northampton, 8/3/97). L.C.

M.D. Sweet Brier (Bath, 6/6/98; Lyr. Hammersmith, 4/7/98). L.C. Ladb. H. 26/4/98.
[Music by Graban.]

D. East Lynne (Grand, Fulham, 20/2/99).

D. The Mighty Hand (County, Reading, 12/6/99). L.C.
[Title altered to *An English Violet*, 30/10/99 and to *The Echo of a Crime*, 3/6/1903.]

SHENTON, J.

C.D. Footlights (Doncaster, 25/9/72).

C. Croquet (Cheltenham, 20/6/77).

SHEPHERD, EDWIN

F.C. A Scotch Mist (Vaud. 10/11/86, *mat.*). L.C.

SHEPHERD, R.

D. The Tradesman's Son (Sur. 22/11/62). L.C. *Lacy.*

D. Watch and Wait (Sur. 23/9/71). See *T. H. HIGGIE.*

SHEPHERD, T.

P. Harlequin King Muffin (Sur. 26/12/53). See — *FORESTER.*

P. Harlequin and Little One Eye, Little Two Eyes, Little Three Eyes; or Beasts and Beauties (Sur. 26/12/54). L.C.

SHERBURN, H. A.

F.C. Hubby (Lyr. H. Ealing, 22/4/84; Shaft. 25/5/91). L.C.

F.C. A Night in Town (Str. 21/4/91, *mat.*; Roy. 28/6/94). L.C.

SHERIDAN, BRINSLEY

D. The Mill Girl (Coventry, 23/6/84).

SHERIDAN, JOHN F.

F.C. Bridget O'Brien, Esq. (O.C. 29/10/87). See *F. LYSTER.*

D. Uncle Tom's Cabin (P'cess. 24/12/87). See *A. DAMPIER.*

SHEWELL, L. R.

D. Shadows of a Great City (P'cess. Glasgow, 28/2/87). See *J. JEFFERSON.*

SHIELD, HENRY

F. The Russian Ambassador (Newcastle, 25/4/71).

C. Katie's Birthday (Newcastle, 21/2/73).

SHILLINGFORD, OSMOND

Duol. The Backslider (Str. 15/4/95). L.C.

D. The Alchemist (Birmingham, 25/3/97). L.C.

F.C. Tommy Dodd (Cardiff, 13/12/97; Glo. 30/8/98). L.C.

C. A Court Scandal (Court, 24/1/99). See *A. BOUCICAULT.*

SHINE, J. L.

D. By Land and Sea! (Birmingham, 8/6/86). See *J. M. CAMPBELL.*

Bsq. Joan of Arc (O.C. 17/1/91). L.C.
[Written in collaboration with *A. ROSS.* Music by F. O. Carr.]

C.D. The Puritan (Traf. 26/7/94). See *D. C. MURRAY.*

C.D. An Irish Gentleman (Glo. 9/6/97). See *D. C. MURRAY.*

SHIRLEY, ARTHUR

D. Reparation; or, Loyal Love (P.H. New Cross, 6/5/82). L.C.

C. A Lazy Life (P.H. New Cross, 12/10/82; St J. Ramsgate, 6/8/83). L.C.

D. Pity; or, Gringoire the Ballad Monger (P.H. New Cross, 18/11/82; C.P. 27/2/83). L.C. 8° 1882 [*priv.*]; *Lacy.*

D. The Danicheffs; or, Married by Force (P.H. New Cross, 7/83). L.C. *Lacy.*

D. Saved; or, A Wife's Peril (Leicester, 8/10/83; Holb. 26/12/85). L.C. *Lacy.*

F.C. The Parcels Post (Belfast, 4/2/84). L.C.

D. The Hand of Fate (Alh. Barrow-in-Furness, 3/3/84; E.C. 10/9/87, as *Shadows of Life; or, The Hand of Fate*; Stand. 26/11/94, as *The Queen of Diamonds; or, The Shadows of Life*). L.C.

D. Passion's Power (P.H. New Cross, 25/3/86; P.W. Birmingham, 13/6/87, as *Her Second Love*; Parkhurst, 3/4/93).

D. Guiltless (P.H. New Cross, 8/1/87). L.C.
[Title altered to *Madame de Moray's Secret*, 4/11/1913.]

D. The Stranglers of Paris (Sur. 17/10/87; Lyr. Hammersmith, 14/11/92, as *The Grip of Iron*; P'cess. 29/6/96). L.C.

F.C. A Lost Sheep (Bradford, 13/7/91). See *W. PARKER.*

C.O. A Shower of Blacks (Terry's, 26/12/87). L.C.
[Music by E. Bucalossi.]

D. The Ace of Clubs (Darlington, 22/3/89).

F. A Double Dose (Sur. 10/3/90).

F. As Large as Life (Terry's, 13/5/90, *mat.*).

D. False Witness (P.H. New Cross, 28/10/90; O.H. Wakefield, 14/3/92, as *The Cross of Honour*; Roy. 29/7/92). L.C.
[Written in collaboration with *M. GALLY.*]

M.D. New Year's Chimes (Bradford, 30/1/91). L.C. Park H. Camden Town, 13/11/90.

F.C. Cleopatra (Shaft. 25/6/91, *mat.*). L.C. Athen. H. Shepherd's Bush, 14/9/89.

D. Old London (Qns. Manchester, 25/7/91; M'bone, 29/8/92). L.C.

F.C. Jones (Bury, 16/10/91). L.C.
[Written in collaboration with *B. LANDECK.*]

D. A Lightning Flash (Sur. 17/12/91). L.C.

M.D. Schneider (Alex. Widnes, 16/4/92; Aquar. Brighton, 28/5/94, as *A Fight for Freedom*). L.C.
[Written in collaboration with *R. RIPLEBY* and revised with *B. LANDECK.*]

D. A Lion's Heart (Parkhurst, 25/7/92; P'cess. 14/10/95). L.C.
[Written in collaboration with *B. LANDECK.*]

D. Midnight; or, The Bells of Notre Dame (Sur. 19/12/92). L.C.
[Written in collaboration with *B. LANDECK.* Title altered to *The King of Crime.*]

F. Mrs Othello (Toole's, 11/11/93). See *F. LESLIE.*

D. In Old Kentucky (Hull, 10/2/94, *copy.*; Bury, 7/5/94; Pav. 6/6/98; P'cess. 6/11/99). L.C.

D. The River of Life (Grand, Hull, 24/2/94, *copy.*; Pav. 12/10/96, as *Jack Tar*). L.C.
[Written in collaboration with *B. LANDECK.*]

F. The Missing Link (Sur. 24/3/94). L.C.

D. Phantoms (Sur. 1/10/94). See *G. CONQUEST.*

D. The Daredevil (P's. Portsmouth, 19/10/94, *copy.*). L.C.
[Written in collaboration with *H. LEONARD.*]

D. A Daughter's Honour (Sur. 17/12/94). See *B. LANDECK.*

D. Saved from the Sea (Pav. 4/3/95; P'cess. 3/8/95). L.C.

D. The Work Girl (Sur. 15/4/95). See *G. CONQUEST.*

D. Tommy Atkins (Pav. 16/9/95; D.Y. 23/12/95). L.C.
[Written in collaboration with *B. LANDECK.*]

D. A Tale of the Thames (Sur. 28/10/95). See *G. CONQUEST.*

D. The Star of India (P'cess. 4/4/96). See *G. R. SIMS.*

M.D. Two Little Vagabonds (P'cess. 21/5/96). See *G. R. SIMS.*

D. Straight from the Heart (Pav. 3/8/96). See *S. VANE.*

D. A Hue and Cry (Pav. 26/4/97). L.C.
[Written in collaboratlon with *B. LANDECK.* Title altered to *Nick Carter*, 1/11/1909.]

D. The Bell Ringer; or, The Spirit of the Chimes (Plymouth, 27/5/97, *copy.*; Qns. Manchester, 21/3/98; Grand, 25/7/98). L.C.
[Written in collaboration with *S. VANE.*]

D. The Perils of Paris (Lyr. Hammersmith, 20/9/97). L.C.

D. Women and Wine (Pav. 11/10/97). See *B. LANDECK.*

D. How London lives (P'cess. 27/12/97). See *M. FIELD.*

D. The Organ Grinder (Leicester, 24/6/98, *copy.*). L.C.
[Written in collaboration with *C. H. LONGDEN.*]

D. The Orphans; or, The Bridge of Notre Dame (Pav. 8/7/98, *copy.*). L.C.

D. None but the Brave (Brighton, 12/8/98). See *S. VANE.*

D. Going the Pace (Star, Wolverhampton, 24/8/98, *copy.*; Pav. 24/10/98). L.C.
[Written in collaboration with *B. LANDECK.*]

D. Tatterley (Grand, Southampton, 12/12/98). L.C. St Helen's, 12/2/98.
[Written in collaboration with *T. GALLON.*]

D. A Great Temptation (Lyr. Hammersmith, 20/2/99; E.C. 31/7/99, as *The Eve of Marriage*). L.C. 10/10/98 [Grand, Stalybridge; as *Great Temptations*].
[This seems to be the same play as *The River of Life* (Grand, Hull, 24/2/94) and *Jack Tar* (Pav. 12/10/96).]

D. Brother for Brother; or, A Duel to the Death (Pav. 7/8/99). L.C.

D. In London Town (Crown, Peckham, 7/8/99). See *G. R. SIMS.*

M.D. The Absent-minded Beggar; or, For Queen and Country (P'cess. 25/11/99). L.C.

SHORE, LOUISA

D. Hannibal. 8° 1898.

SHORE, W. TEIGNMOUTH

Oa. The Golden Days (Village H. Chislehurst, 17/10/93). See *P. S. JEFFREY.*

SHUTE, EDWARD ARNOLD

D. Old Father Time; or, The Clockmaker of Mardyk (Drill H. Nuneaton, 7/11/89). L.C.

M.D. Life's Harvest (Drill H. Nuneaton, 25/2/91, *amat.*). L.C. as *Reaping the Harvest.*

Ca. Betsy's Bailiff (Drill H. Nuneaton, 10/10/93, *amat.*). L.C.

SIDDONS, HARRY

F. An Aristocratic Assassin (Dumfries, 10/8/75).

SIDNEY, FRED. W.

C. American Assurance (Devonshire Park, Eastbourne, 6/9/94). L.C.

F.C. A Loving Legacy (Devonshire Park, Eastbourne, 28/1/95; Str. 12/3/95). L.C.

M.C. That Terrible Turk and his Loving Legacy (Shakespeare, Clapham, 4/4/98). L.C.
[Lyrics by *E. TURNER.* Music by O. Barri.]

C. Hogmanay; or, New Year's Eve (Mat. 21/6/98; Glo. 30/8/98). L.C. H.M. Dundee, 26/12/96.

F.C. Brixton Burglary (Terry's, 6/12/98). L.C.

SIDNEY, THOMAS

D.Sk. Bars of Gold (St Leonard's, 6/6/92). See *J. RAE.*

C.D. Pretty Mollie Barrington (St Leonard's, 6/6/92). See *J. RAE.*

D.Sk. The Ruby Heart (St Leonard's, 6/6/92). See *J. RAE.*

C.D. Love the Magician (Shaft. 7/7/92). See *J. RAE.*

C.D. My Little Red Riding Hood (Pav. St Leonard's, 16/10/95). See *J. RAE.*

D.Sk. Interviewed (W. Pier, Brighton, 1/9/96). See *J. RAE.*

SIDNEY, W.

D. Light in the Dark; or, Life Underground (Greenwich, 11/3/67). L.C.

D. Edith; or, The Fall of Pride (H.M. Richmond, 22/8/70).

D. The Old Curiosity Shop; or, The Life and Death of Little Nell (Norwich, 6/2/71). L.C.

D. A Line of Life; or, Mind your Points (P.W. Glasgow, 28/10/71; Norwich, 8/10/77).
[Written in collaboration with *H. P. GRATTAN*.]

C. Neale O'Neale; or, The Jacket of Green (P.W. L'pool, 20/7/74). L.C.

D. L'Assommoir; or, The Curse of Drink (P.W. Glasgow, 16/8/79). L.C.

D. She (Nov. 10/5/88). See *E. ROSE.*

SIEDLE, A. E.

C.O. Rustic (P.W. Drill H. Swansea, 3/4/88).
[Music by W. F. Hulley.]

SIEVIER, R. STANDISH

Ca. Stone-broke (Blackburn, 23/3/92; Grand, 28/3/92). L.C.

C. The Younger Son (Gai. 9/6/93). L.C.

SIKES, FRANK

Bsq. Hypermnestra, the Girl of the Period (Lyc. 27/3/69). L.C. as *H.; or, The Danaides.*

SILVA, HUGH R.

D. Men of Metal (Barnsley, 3/10/90). See *C. A. CLARKE.*

D. The String of Pearls (Birkenhead, 26/12/92). See *C. A. CLARKE.*

D. The Downward Path (Huddersfield, 17/7/93). See *C. A. CLARKE.*

D. Greed of Gold (Sur. 6/7/96). L.C. Barnsley, 19/12/94.

D. Honour thy Father (Imp. 12/9/98). See *C. A. CLARKE.*

SILVESTER, FRANK

O. The Golden Apple (P.H. Godalming, 11/4/91). L.C.

F. The Coming Member (Country Club, St Alban's, 13/2/93, *amat.*). L.C.

M.Sk. Uncle's Blunder (T.H. St Alban's, 18/12/93).
[Written in collaboration with *M. WELLINGS*.]

Oa. Who stole the Tarts? (Polytechnic, Regent Street, 2/6/94).

M.Bsq. Arthur's Bakery Co.; or, the Original A.B.C. (St G. 22/11/98). L.C.
[Music by Ellen G. Elwes.]

SILVESTER, HARVEY

C.D. Twice Married (Gai. 25/4/87). See *C. O'NEIL.*

SIM, E. HOWLEY

Ext. Architopia, Unlimited (T.H. Holborn, 4/5/94). See *A. W. EARLE.*

Bsq. King Arthur (James Street, 16/5/95). See *A. W EARLE.*

Bsq. The Celestial Institute (T.H. St Martin's, 15/5/96).
[Music by L. Butler.]

SIMONTON, H. W.

C.O. The White Cuirassier; or, The Bivouac of Life (Jersey, 9/10/95). L.C.
[Music by J. Arscott.]

SIMPSON, ELLA G.

Oa. The Demon Spider (Art Gallery, Newcastle, 29/10/95).
[Music by W. E. Lawson.]

SIMPSON, FISHER

M.C. Little Tom Bowling (Albert, Gainsborough, 5/8/89). L.C.

SIMPSON, JOHN PALGRAVE

D. Poor Cousin Walter (Str. 8/4/50). L.C.
F. Without Incumbrances (Str. 12/8/50). L.C. *Lacy.*
F. That Odious Captain Cutter (Olym. 24/2/51). L.C. Olym. 1/9/50. *Lacy.*
F. Only a Clod (Lyc. 20/5/51). L.C. *Fairbrother.*
F. Matrimonial Prospectuses (Str. 4/3/52). *Lacy.*
F. Very Suspicious (Lyc. 12/6/52). *Lacy.*
D. Marco Spada (P'cess. 28/3/53). L.C. *Lacy.*
C.D. Ranelagh (H. 11/2/54). L.C.
[Written in collaboration with *C. WRAY.*]
Ca. Heads or Tails (Olym. 29/6/54). L.C. *Lacy.*
Spec. Schamyl, the Warrior Prophet (P'cess. 6/11/54). L.C.
C. Second Love (H. 23/7/56). L.C. *Lacy.*
D. The Black Book (D.L. 2/2/57). L.C.
D. Daddy Hardacre (Olym. 26/3/57). L.C. *French.*
Ca. A Case for Reflection. L.C. Plymouth, 15/5/57.
F. Deadly Reports (Olym. 26/10/57). L.C.
Oa. Caught and Caged. L.C. Durham, 31/12/58. *French.*
C. World and Stage (H. 12/3/59). L.C. *Lacy.*
Ca. The School for Coquettes (Str. 4/7/59). L.C. *Lacy.*
C.D. Prison and Palace. L.C. Canterbury, 5/8/59.
Oa. Romance (C.G. 2/2/60). L.C.
C. First Affections (St J. 13/2/60). L.C. *Lacy.*
C. Appearances (Str. 28/5/60). L.C. *Lacy.*
Interlude. A Smack for a Smack (St J. 26/11/60). L.C.
O. Bianca, the Bravo's Bride (C.G. 6/12/60). L.C.
[Music by Balfe.]
C. A Scrap of Paper (St J. 22/4/61). L.C. as *Only a Scrap of Paper. Lacy.*
Ca. Court Cards (Olym. 25/11/61). L.C. *Lacy.*
Ext. The King of the Merrows (Olym. 26/12/61). See *F. C. BURNAND.*
D. Dreams of Delusion (Sur. 11/4/62). L.C. Plymouth, 7/10/57.
Ca. Sybilla; or, Step by Step (St J. 29/10/64). L.C. under sub-title. *Lacy.*
D. The Road-side Inn (Lyc. 21/1/65). L.C.
D. A Fair Pretender (P.W. 10/5/65). L.C. *Lacy.*
D. The Watch Cry (Lyc. 6/11/65). L.C.
O. Ida; or, The Guardian Storks (C.G. 15/11/65). L.C.
[Music by H. Leslie.]
D. The Master of Ravenswood (Lyc. 23/12/65). L.C.
[Music by W. H. Montgomery.]
Ca. Jack in a Box (St J. 11/6/66). L.C. *Lacy.*
F. An Atrocious Criminal (Olym. 18/2/67). L.C. *Lacy.*
D. Shadows of the Past (Brighton, 1/11/67; P.W. Birmingham, 7/5/69). L.C. Manchester, 11/5/67. *French.*
D. Black Sheep (Olym 25/4/68). L.C.
[Written in collaboration with *E. YATES.*]

D. Time and the Hour (Qns. 29/6/68). L.C. *Lacy.*
D. Stage and State (Edinburgh, 2/10/68).
D. Marie Antoinette (Dublin, 12/10/68; P'cess. 15/2/69). L.C. Brighton, 2/11/68.
D. The Serpent on the Hearth (Adel. 2/8/69). L.C. *Lacy.*
R.D. The Watchdog of the Walsinghams (Amphi. L'pool, 28/8/69; Sur. 16/10/69). L.C. *Lacy.*
D. The Siren (Lyc. 27/11/69). L.C.
O. Who is she? (G.I. 29/4/71).
[Music by W. Plumpton.]
C.O. Letty, the Basket Maker. L.C. Gai. 8/7/71.
D. Broken Ties (Olym. 8/6/72). L.C. L'pool, 26/2/66. *Lacy.*
C.D. Alone (Court, 25/10/73). L.C. *French.*
[Written in collaboration with *H. C. MERIVALE.*]
D. Lady Deadlock's Secret (H.M. Aberdeen, 3/4/74; Windsor, 28/11/83; O.C. 26/3/84). L.C. Amphi. L'pool, 18/3/74.
D. All for her (Mir. 18/10/75; Grand, 17/5/97). L.C.
D. The Scar on the Wrist (St J. 9/3/78). L.C.
[Written in collaboration with *C. TEMPLAR.*]
Oa. Bold Dick Turpin (St J. 17/5/78).
[Music by H. Leslie.]
C. The New Cinderella (Roy. 1/1/79). L.C.
D. Zillah (Lyc. 2/8/79). L.C.
[Written in collaboration with *C. TEMPLAR.*]
D. From Father to Son (Bijou, L'pool, 2/10/82). See *A. W. À BECKETT.*
D. Reputation (Bournemouth, 13/8/83). L.C.
C.O. The Fairy's Post Box (Court, 21/5/85). L.C.
[Music by A. Hervey.]

SIMPSON, KATE
Oa. Elfiana; or, The Witch of the Woodlands (Olympia, Newcastle, 30/9/95). L.C.
[Music by W. M. Wood.]
Oa. Nanette (Assembly R. Newcastle, 12/11/95). L.C.
[Music by E. Lorence.]

SIMS, GEORGE R.
C. Crutch and Toothpick (Roy. 14/4/79). L.C.
Ext. The Corsican Brother-babes-in-the-wood (Hull, 19/3/81). L.C.
F. Mother-in-Law (P.W. L'pool, 23/4/81; O.C. 31/12/84). L.C.
C. The Member for Slocum (Roy. 4/5/81). L.C.
F.C. Flats (Crit. 23/7/81). L.C.
F.C. The Gay City (Nottingham, 8/9/81). L.C.
D. The Lights o' London (P'cess. 10/9/81). L.C.
C. The Halfway House (Vaud. 1/10/81). L.C.
M.Ca. The Girl he left behind him (Vaud. 28/11/81). L.C.
D. Romany Rye (P'cess. 10/6/82). L.C.
F.C. A Wise Child (P.W. L'pool, 31/7/82). L.C.
C. The Glass of Fashion (Grand, Glasgow, 26/3/83). See *S. GRUNDY.*
C.O. The Merry Duchess (Roy. 23/4/83). L.C. 8° [1883].
[Music by F. Clay.]
D. In the Ranks (Adel. 6/10/83). L.C.
[Written in collaboration with *H. PETTITT.*]

O. The Golden Ring (Alh. 3/12/83). L.C.
[Music by F. Clay.]

D. The Last Chance (Adel. 4/4/85). L.C.

Ext. Jack-in-the-Box (Brighton, 24/8/85; Str. 7/2/87). L.C.
[Written in collaboration with *C. W. SCOTT*.]

D. The Harbour Lights (Adel. 23/12/85). L.C.
[Written in collaboration with *H. PETTITT*.]

D. The Golden Ladder (Glo. 22/12/87). L.C.
[Written in collaboration with *W. BARRETT*.]

Bsq. Faust up-to-date (Gai. 30/10/88). L.C.
[Written in collaboration with *H. PETTITT*. Music by M. Lutz.]

D. The Silver Falls (Adel. 29/12/88). L.C.
[Written in collaboration with *H. PETTITT*.]

D. Master and Man (P.W. Birmingham, 25/3/89; Pav. 16/9/89. Grand, 25/11/89; P'cess. 18/12/89). L.C.
[Written in collaboration with *H. PETTITT*.]

D. London Day by Day (Adel. 14/9/89). L.C.
[Written in collaboration with *H. PETTITT*.]

D. An English Rose (Adel. 2/8/90). L.C.
[Written in collaboration with *R. BUCHANAN*.]

Bsq. Carmen up-to-date (Shakespeare, L'pool, 22/9/90; Gai. 4/10/90). L.C.
[Written in collaboration with *H. PETTITT*. Music by M. Lutz.]

D. The Trumpet Call (Adel. 1/8/91). L.C.
[Written in collaboration with *R. BUCHANAN*.]

F.C. The Grey Mare (Com. 23/1/92). L.C.
[Written in collaboration with *C. RALEIGH*.]

C.O. Blue-eyed Susan (P.W. 6/2/92). L.C.
[Written in collaboration with *H. PETTITT*. Music by F. O. Carr.]

R.D. The White Rose (Adel. 23/4/92). L.C.
[Written in collaboration with *R. BUCHANAN*.]

D. The Lights of Home (Adel. 30/7/92). See *R. BUCHANAN*.

F.C. The Guardsman (Court, 20/10/92). L.C.
[Written in collaboration with *C. RALEIGH*.]

D. The Black Domino (Adel. 1/4/93). L.C.
[Written in collaboration with *R. BUCHANAN*.]

D. Uncle John (Vaud. 3/4/93). L.C.
[Written in collaboration with *C. RALEIGH*.]

C.O. Little Christopher Columbus (Lyr. 10/10/93). L.C. 8° 1893.
[Written in collaboration with *C. RALEIGH*. Music by I. Caryll.]

Bsq. Dandy Dick Whittington (Aven. 2/3/95). L.C. 8° 1895.
[Music by I. Caryll.]

F. Fanny (P.W. L'pool, 8/4/95; Str. 15/4/95). L.C.
[Written in collaboration with *C. RALEIGH*.]

D. The City of Pleasure (P.W. Birmingham, 22/4/95; Grand, Islington, 31/8/1903). L.C.

D. The Star of India (P'cess. 4/4/96). L.C.
[Written in collaboration with *A. SHIRLEY*.]

M.D. Two Little Vagabonds (P'cess. 21/5/96, *copy*.; P'cess. 23/9/96). L.C.
[Written in collaboration with *A. SHIRLEY*.]

M.C. Shipped by the Light of the Moon (County, Reading, 24/8/96; Metro. 5/4/97; O.C. 27/4/99, as *A Good Time; or, S. by the L. of the M.*). L.C.
[Lyrics by *P. MARSHALL*. Music by G. Pack and H. May.]
M.D. When the Lamps are lighted (Regent, Salford, 11/10/97; Grand, 22/11/97). L.C.
[Written in collaboration with *L. MERRICK*.]
C.O. The Dandy Fifth (P.W. Birmingham, 11/4/98; D.Y. 16/8/98). L.C.
[Music by C. Corri.]
F.C. My Innocent Boy (Roy. 11/5/98). L.C.
[Written in collaboration with *L. MERRICK*.]
D. The Gipsy Earl (Adel. 31/8/98). L.C.
M.C. Miss Chiquita (P.W. Birmingham, 7/8/99; Coronet, 14/8/99). L.C.
[Music by C. Corri.]
D. In London Town (Crown, Peckham, 7/8/99). L.C.
[Written in collaboration with *A. SHIRLEY*.]
F.C. The Elixir of Youth (Vaud. 9/9/99). L.C.
[Written in collaboration with *L. MERRICK*.]
M.C. In Gay Piccadilly (Glasgow, 9/10/99; Alex. Stoke Newington, 27/11/99). L.C.
[Written in collaboration with C. Corri.]

SINCLAIR, HENRY
C.D. The Baronet (St G. 6/6/93, *amat.*). L.C.

SINCLAIR, KATE
C.D. Plucky Nancy (T.H. Kilburn, 16/3/89). See *Mrs G. THOMPSON*.
C.D. A Broken Sixpence (Ladb. H. 11/4/89). See *Mrs G. THOMPSON*.
Ca. Mademoiselle de Lira (Com. 7/1/90). See *Mrs G. THOMPSON*.
C. Duskie (Ladb. H. 17/6/90). See *Mrs G. THOMPSON*.
D.Sk. Pounds, Shillings and Pence (T.H. Kilburn, 18/1/92). See *Mrs G. THOMPSON*.
D. Saint Angela (T.H. Kilburn, 18/1/92). See *Mrs G. THOMPSON*.

SINCLAIR, LEWIS
D. A Double Life; or, The Shadow of Crime (Swansea, 4/12/71).

SKEA, JAMES
D. The Maid of St Aubin's; or, Love against Money (Royal H. Jersey, 15/3/70; Barrow-in-Furness, 9/9/72, as *The Maid of Biggar*).

SKELTON, ARTHUR
M.D. Napoleon Bonaparte (Colosseum, Dudley, 19/6/99; Stratford, 16/10/99). L.C.

SKELTON, W.
• Bsq. The Minx and the Man (H.M. Carlisle, 15/4/95). See *F. LINDO*.

"*SKETCHLEY, ARTHUR*" [*GEORGE ROSE*]
D. The Dark Cloud (St J. 6/1/63).
F. Mrs Brown at the Play (D.L. 8/5/63).
Monol. Paris (Egyptian H. 2/64).

C. How will they get out of it? (St J. 12/8/64). L.C.
Bsq. Robinson Crusoe (H. 26/7/67). See *W. S. GILBERT*.
C. Blanche (Alex, L'pool, 14/3/70). L.C. as *Light of Love; or, Paying for the Post*.
C. Living at Ease (Str. 5/10/70). L.C.
C. Up in the World (Str. 9/2/71). L.C.
Ext. All about the Battle of Dorking (Alh. 7/8/71). See *F. C. BURNAND*.
F. Near Relations (G.I. 14/8/71). L.C.
Ca. Only a Governess (Holb. 30/3/72). L.C.
Oa. The Romance of the Harem (St G. 19/6/72). L.C.
[Music by J. P. Cole.]
Oa. The Stepmother (St G. 5/5/80). L.C.
[Music by W. Austin.]
D. Craft (Leicester, 19/8/82). L.C.

SKUSE, E.
D.Sk. The Victoria Stakes (Nov. 1/6/96). L.C.

SLATER, ALBERT
C.O. Mona, the Bride of Glen Maye (Hyde, 11/12/93). L.C.
[Music by J. Broadbent.]

SLAUGHTER, WALTER
Bsq. The New Corsican Brothers (P.W. L'pool, 11/11/89). See *C. RALEIGH*.

SLOMAN, C.
Bsq. The Conquest of the Eagle; or, The Triumph of the Grecian (Grec. 16/5/53). L.C.

SLOUS, ANGELO R.
D. The Templar (P'cess. 9/11/50). L.C.
D. The Duke's Wager (P'cess. 4/6/51). L.C.
T. Hamilton of Bothwell Haugh (S.W. 24/10/55). L.C.
D. The Borgia Ring (Adel. 24/1/59). L.C.
D. Light and Shadow (P'cess. 6/6/64). L.C.
D. True to the Core; A Story of the Armada (Sur. 8/9/66). L.C. 8° 1866.
D. Æsop; or, The Golden Bubble (P.W. Birmingham, 3/3/79).

SMALE, Mrs T. E.
Ca. A Compromising Case (H. 26/5/88). L.C. *French*.
F. Bravado (Str. 3/7/89, *mat.*). L.C.
Ca. Old Spoons (Vestry H. Turnham Green, 2/2/99).

SMART, HAWLEY
C.O. Berta; or, The Gnome of the Hartsberg (H. 29/5/55). L.C.
C. The Coquette (Assembly R. Cheltenham, 10/4/85).

SMELT, THOMAS
Ca. Magpie and Thimble (Glo. 17/3/77). L.C.

SMITH, Miss A.
Oa. A Rainy Day (Gallery of Music, 23/5/68, *amat.*).
[Music by Virginia Gabriel.]

SMITH, A. IVOR
D. A Silver Veil (Park T.H. Lavender Hill, 6/2/88).

SMITH, ALBERT RICHARD
[For his earlier plays see *E.N.D.* ii, 392.]
Rev. Novelty Fair (Lyc. 21/5/50). See *T. TAYLOR.*
Bsq. Esmeralda (Adel. 3/6/50). L.C.
Ext. The Alhambra; or, The Three Moorish Princesses (P'cess. 21/4/51). L.C. *Lacy.*
Ent. Mr Albert Smith's Ascent of Mont Blanc. L.C. Egyptian H. 15/2/54.
Ent. Mr Albert Smith's Ascent of Mont Blanc; Holland and up the Rhine. L.C. Egyptian H. 23/12/54.
Ext. Guy Fawkes (Olym. 31/3/55). See *T. TAYLOR.*
Bsq. Valentine and Orson (Adel. 7/11/55).
P. William Tell (Lyc. 2/6/56). See *T. TAYLOR.*

SMITH, ARTHUR
Ext. Guy Fawkes (Olym. 31/3/55). See *T. TAYLOR.*

SMITH, BRUCE
Bsq. A-lad-in and well out of it (T.H. Folkestone, 15/1/89; Albert H. 22/3/1909).
Bsq. Forte Thieves, played piano (T.H. Folkestone, 29/10/89).

SMITH, E. T.
Ext. Friar Bacon (Ast. 26/12/63). L.C.

SMITH, ELLIS
D. Vera (Glo. 1/7/90, *mat.*). L.C.

SMITH, FRANK STANLEY
Bal. La Reine de la Glace (Brighton, 18/11/97).

SMITH, HARRY BURROWS
D. A Father's Sin (Woolwich, 5/4/86).
C.O. Don Quixote (Park H. Camden Town, 8/11/89, *copy.*). L.C.
[Music by R. de Koven.]
C.O. Maid Marian and Robin Hood (Park H. Camden Town, 20/9/90, *copy.*; P.W. 5/2/91). L.C.
[Music by R. de Koven.]
C.O. The Fencing Master (S.W. 26/9/92, *copy.*). L.C.
[Music by R. de Koven.]
C.O. Rob Roy (Morton's, Greenwich, 29/9/94). L.C.
[Music by R. de Koven.]
C.O. The Tzigane (Assembly R. Balham, 16/5/95, *copy.*). L.C.
[Music by R. de Koven.]
C.O. The Wizard of the Nile; or, The Egyptian Beauty (Shaft. 6/9/97). L.C.
[Music by R. de Koven.]

SMITH, H. GUTHRIE
D. Crispus. 8° 1891.

SMITH, HENRY JOHN
D. From Gulf to Gulf (Aven. 29/11/92, *mat.*). L.C.
D. The Adventures of the Count de Monte Cristo (Lyr. Hammersmith, 6/3/99).

SMITH, J. C.
D. The Legend of Notre Dame (Birmingham, 25/9/71; Sur. 9/11/72).

SMITH, LITA

Ca. Domestic Medicine (Grantham, 2/6/87). L.C. York, 20/5/87.

D. The Colonel's Wife (Coventry, 6/2/88). See *B. REID*.

D.Sk. Mistress Peg (Vaud. 23/2/92, *mat.*). L.C.

Ca. Mr and Mrs Muffett; or, Domestic Experiment (Gai. Hastings, 6/6/92).

F. Bridget's Blunders (Devonshire Park, Eastbourne, 5/8/92). L.C.

Oa. My Friend Gomez (Assembly R. Preston, 28/5/96). L.C. Traf. 20/4/93.
[Music by E. Stanley.]

SMITH, R. GREENHOUGH

R.D. Castle Sombras (Bijou, 27/10/96, *copy.*). L.C.
[Written in collaboration with *F. MANSFIELD*.]

SMITH, S. THEYRE

Ca. A Happy Pair; or, A Fly in the Honey (St J. 2/3/68). L.C. *French.*

Ca. Uncle's Will (H. 24/10/70). L.C.

Ca. Cut off with a Shilling (P.W. 10/4/71). L.C. *French.*

Ca. Which is which? (Court, 10/7/71). L.C. *French.*

Ca. Old Cronies; or, A Narrow Escape (St J. 6/3/80). L.C.

Ca. A Case for Eviction (Court, L'pool, 22/9/82; St J. 20/12/83). L.C.

Ca. Castaways (St J. 10/6/85). L.C.

F. My Lord in Livery (P'cess. 9/10/86). L.C.

Ca. Mrs Hilary Regrets (Crit. 21/6/92. *mat.*). L.C. *French.*

SMITH, VALENTINE

R.O. A King for a Day (Art Gallery, Newcastle, 20/2/93; Parkhurst, 23/5/93). L.C.

SMYTHE, ALFRED

R.C.O. The Warlock (Qns. Dublin, 1/2/92).
[Music by E. Little.]

M.C.D. Victoire (Leinster H. Dublin, 17/4/93).
[Music by E. Little.]

SMYTHIES, W. GORDON

Ca. Outwitted (May Street H., W. Kensington, 16/12/91). *Lacy.*

Ca. A Lady by Birth (Cardiff, 9/1/93). L.C.

SNOW, ROBERT

Bal. Vert Vert (D.L. 6/2/52).

SNOW, W. R.

Ca. Weather Permitting (Glo. 27/11/72). L.C.

SOANE-ROBY, BERNARD

F. A Deserter in a Fix (O.H. Leicester, 10/2/79; Grand, 23/3/85).

SOARES, GUSTAVE DE MEIRELLES. See *O. DOVE*

SODEN, JOHN EDWARD

F. Wanted, a Wife and Child (Alfred, 16/10/71).

F. A Trip to Scarborough (St G. H. Scarborough, 24/8/74).

F. A Trip to Brighton (Glo. 9/11/74).

F. The Tailor makes the Man (Glo. 21/2/76). L.C.

F. Blue Ribbons (Gai. 11/5/87). See *G. W. BROWNE*.

Ca. Lela's Love Letters (St G. 31/5/88). L.C.
[Written in collaboration with *A. GANTHONY*.]

D. For the Cross; or, The Dawn of Christianity (Catholic H. Navan, 16/7/98).
[Music by T. C. L. White.]

SOLLY, Rev. HENRY

T. Gonzaga: A Tale of Florence (St G. 28/4/77). L.C.

SOMERSET, CHARLES A.

[For his earlier plays see iv, 404–5. The plays of more than one Somerset may be listed here; initials vary, C. A., C. Z., C. E. and W. all appearing.]

F. The Bloomers (Grec. 13/10/51). L.C. as *Bloomer Wives; or, The Birds of Bloomsbury Bower.*

D. The Life and Death of Guy Fawkes; or, Gunpowder Treason. L.C. Bower, 30/10/51.

Ent. Queen Mab (Grec. 26/12/51). L.C.

C.O. Good Night, Signor Pantalon (Grec. 15/3/52). L.C.

Spec. Bonaparte in Egypt (Ast. 12/4/52). L.C.

Bsq. Venus with a Tippet on (Grec. 5/7/52). L.C.

D. The School for Kings (D.L. 7/3/53). L.C.

Vaud. The Tender Chord; or, How to touch the Ladies' Hearts (Grec. 17/4/53). L.C.

F. The Electric Telegraph (Grec. 13/6/53). L.C.

D. The Chevalier de St George (Grec. 22/8/53). L.C.

P. Sinbad the Sailor, Harlequin King Mammon and the Island of Jewels (Brighton, 26/12/54).

P. Ladye Bird Bower; or, Harlequin Prince Peacock and the Fair Brillanta (L'pool, 1858).

SOMERSET, C. W.

D. Foul Weather (Roy. Glasgow, 30/5/81). L.C. Shrewsbury, 13/1/81.

D. Faust and Marguerite (O.H. Leicester, 30/1/99). See *B. DALY.*

SORRELL, HENRY

D. No Cross, no Crown (People's, Attercliffe, Sheffield, 26/7/97). See *B. WILLIAMS.*

SORRELL, W. J.

D. Like and Unlike (Adel. 9/4/56). See — *LANGFORD.*

C.D. A Border Marriage (Adel. 3/11/56). L.C. *Lacy.*

C. A Friend in Need (St J. 23/4/60). See *S. FRENCH.*

F. Harvey's Portrait—Twelve for One Shilling (W. Hartlepool, 22/6/69).

F. Always sit up for your Husband (M.H. Hastings, 24/11/73).

F. That Naughty Can-Can (P'cess. Edinburgh, 24/11/73).

F. Haste to the Wedding (P'cess. Edinburgh, 1/12/73).

SOTHERN, EDWARD ASKEW

Ca. Aunt's Advice (H. 2/12/61). L.C.

C. Brother Sam (H. 24/5/65). See *J. OXENFORD.*

SOTHERN, E. H.

F. Gertie's Garter (Newcastle, 12/4/83). L.C.

"*SOULBIEN, F.*"

R.C.O. Delia (P's. Bristol, 11/3/89).
[Music by P. Bucalossi.]

SOUTAR, J. Jr.

F. The Fast Coach (Olym. 9/6/51). L.C. *Lacy.*
[Written in collaboration with *C. J. CLARIDGE, Jr.*]

SOUTAR, J. FARREN

D.Sk. Justice Nell (Lyc. 2/5/99). L.C.
[Written in collaboration with *R. HARWOOD.*]

SOUTAR, ROBERT

D. A Deed without a Name (Olym. 14/2/53). L.C.
F. Never taste Wine at the Docks (Str. 4/9/54).
P. Ding, Dong, Bell, Pussy's in the Well; or, Harlequin, who killed Cock Robin? (M'bone, 26/12/66). L.C.
P. Charles the Second and Pretty Nell Gwynne; or, Harlequin Oliver Cromwell and the Little Fairies in the Enchanted Oak (Vic. 26/12/67). L.C.
D. Quicksands and Whirlpools (Vic. 21/3/68). L.C. Brighton, 18/1/60.
P. Aladdin; or, Harlequin and the Bronze Horse (E.L. 24/12/68).
P. Whittington and his Cat; or, Zakkolums and the King of the Cannibal Islands (Alfred, 24/12/68). L.C.
P. Jack and Jill and the Sleeping Beauty; or, Harlequin Humpty-Dumpty (Sur. 26/12/68). L.C.
P. Harlequin Jack and the Beanstalk; or, Little Red Riding Hood and the Wicked Wolf (E.L. 24/12/69). L.C.
P. Gulliver's Travels; or, Harlequin Lilliput, the King of Laputa, the Pretty Princess and the Merry Elf of the Stalactite Caves (Alfred, 27/12/69). L.C.
P. Harlequin and the White Cat; or, The Magic Sapphire (E.L. 24/12/70). L.C.
P. My Son Jack; or, Harlequin Mother Goose and the Gaping, Wide-mouthed, Waddling Frog (Sur. 26/12/70). L.C.
P. The Bronze Horse; or, Harlequin the Sly Sultan, the Pert Princess, and the Fascinating Fays of Fairy Land (Vic. 23/12/71). L.C.
[Written in collaboration with *C. MERION.*]
F. The Fast Coach (Gai. 29/9/73).
Bsq. Lothair (L'pool, 13/10/73). See *F. W. GREEN.*
P. Jack and Jill (Vic. 24/12/74). See *A. CLEMENTS.*
F. Sold again (Brighton, 31/7/76; Gai. 26/8/76). L.C. *Lacy.*
F. A Regular Turk (Gai. 3/2/77).
F. Cut and come again (Olym. 9/8/79). L.C.
P. Jack the Giant Killer (C.P. 23/12/79). L.C.
M.F. Oh! those Girls! (Gai. 4/3/82). L.C.
[Music by M. Lutz.]
Ca. Blindfold (Gai. 4/5/82). L.C.
F.C. Baby (Alex. Southend, 17/7/90).
[Written in collaboration with *F. H. HERBERT.*]

SOUTHAM, GERTRUDE

Ca. Archibald Danvers, M.D. (Pav. Southport, 20/10/93). L.C.
[Written in collaboration with *E. ARMITAGE.*]

SPACKMAN, J. S.

D. Simon; or, The Lost Heir Restored (Greenock, 10/5/75).

SPARLING, H.

D.Sk. The Phunnygraph (Pleasure Gdns. Folkestone, 28/5/94). See *F. BOWYER.*

SPEDDING, B. J.

Bsq. Ino; or, The Theban Twins (P.W. L'pool, 30/8/69; Str. 30/10/69). L.C. 8° (1869).

SPEIGHT, T. W.

D. The Ebony Casket; or, Mabel's Two Birthdays (Gai. 9/11/72). L.C.

C.D. Salt Tears (Roy. 24/7/73). L.C.

F. A Close Shave (H. 9/8/84). L.C.

SPENCER, E.

Oa. Wanted, a Wife (M. H. Leamington, 15/11/71).
[Music by R. Aspe.]

F.C. The Plunger (Ladb. H. 24/10/88). See *W. SAPTE, Jr.*

SPENCER, GEORGE

F. A Return Ticket to the International Exhibition (St J. 11/8/62). L.C. *Lacy.*
[Written in collaboration with *W. JAMES.*]

D. Entrances and Exits (E.L. 27/4/68). L.C.

D. The Road, the River and the Rail (E.L. 7/9/68).

D. Truth against the World (E.L. 27/4/70). L.C.

SPENCER, SYDNEY

D. A Stolen Birthright; or, The Father's Revenge (Colne, 28/9/96). L.C.

SPICER, HENRY

[For his earlier plays see iv, 405.]

D. Alcestis (St J. 15/1/55).

D. Haska (D.L. 10/3/77). L.C.

F. His Novice (D.L. 26/12/78). L.C.

SPIER, MONTAGUE H.

C. The Matrimonial Noose (P's. 1/5/85). L.C.

D. Tecalco (Terry's, 24/5/89, *mat.*). L.C.

D. Griffith Murdoch (St G. 4/3/93, *amat.*, *copy.*). L.C.

SPIERS, H. F.

D. Father Satan (Ilkestone, 27/2/96, *copy.*; Brit. 22/6/96). L.C.

SPRANGE, W. E. See *W. EDWARDES-SPRANGE*

SPRINGATE, H. S.

D. The Pitman's Daughter (P.W. Wolverhampton, 12/5/79).

D. Robespierre (P.W. Wolverhampton, 25/8/79).

D. Boscabel; or, The Royal Oak (P.W. Wolverhampton, 8/3/80). L.C.

SPRY, HENRY

P. Harlequin Rik Rak (Grec. 24/12/67). See *G. CONQUEST.*

P. The Flying Dutchman (Grec. 24/12/68). See *G. CONQUEST.*

P. The Gnome Fly (Grec. 24/12/69). See *G. CONQUEST.*

Bsq. Quasimodo, the Deformed; or, The Man with the Hump, and the Belle of Notre Dame (Grec. 18/4/70). L.C.

Bsq. Don Juan, the Little Gay Deceiver (Grec. 20/6/70). L.C.

P. Herne the Hunter (Grec. 24/12/70). See *G. CONQUEST.*

P. Zig Zag the Crooked (Grec. 23/12/71). See *G. CONQUEST.*

P. Nix, the Demon Dwarf (Grec. 24/12/72). See *G. CONQUEST.*

D. The Snae Fell (Gai. 30/6/73). See *P. MERRITT.*

P. The Wood Demon (Grec. 24/12/73). See *G. CONQUEST.*

P. Snip Snap Snorum (Grec. 24/12/74). See *G. CONQUEST.*

P. Aladdin and the Wonderful Lamp; or, Harlequin and the Forty Thieves (Sanger's, 26/12/74). L.C.

P. Lady Godiva and Peeping Tom (Sanger's, 27/12/75). L.C.

P. Spitz-Spitze (Grec. 27/12/75). See *G. CONQUEST*.
P. The Grim Goblin (Grec. 23/12/76). See *G. CONQUEST*.
P. Roley Poley (Grec. 24/12/77). See *G. CONQUEST*.
P. Hokee-Pokee; or, The Fiend of Fungus Forest (Grec. 24/12/78). See *G. CONQUEST*.
P. Cinderella and the Glass Slipper (Sanger's, 26/12/78). L.C.
P. Harlequin Rokoko (Grec. 24/12/79). See *G. CONQUEST*.
P. Aladdin; or, The Wonderful Lamp (Sanger's, 26/12/79). L.C.
P. Love's Dream; or, The Daughter of a King without a Kingdom (Brit. 27/12/80). L.C.
P. Harlequin St George and the Dragon, and the Seven Champions (Sanger's, 27/12/80). L.C.
P. Mother Bunch and the Man with the Hunch (Sur. 24/12/81). See *G. CONQUEST*.
P. Blue Beard done Brown; or, Fatima the Sweetest of Girls, and Selim's Voyage to the Island of Pearls (Sanger's, 26/12/81). L.C.
P. Puss in Boots (Sur. 23/12/82). See *G. CONQUEST*.
P. Happy-go-lucky, True-love and Forget-me-not; or, The Jewel Elves of the Magic Dell, and the Good Little Fairy Pastorelle (Grec. 24/12/82). L.C.
P. Bluff King Hal; or, The Field of the Cloth of Gold (Sanger's, 26/12/82). L.C.
P. The Diamond Statue; or, The King of the Genii (Brit. 26/12/82). L.C. as *The King of the Genii; or, Prince Quyn and the Statue of Diamonds*.
P. Jack and Jill (Sur. 24/12/83). See *G. CONQUEST*.
P. Aladdin (Sur. 24/12/84). See *G. CONQUEST*.
P. Robinson Crusoe (Sur. 24/12/85). See *G. CONQUEST*.
P. Jack and the Beanstalk (Sur. 24/12/86). See *G. CONQUEST*.
D. A Dead Man's Gold (Sur. 7/11/87). See *G. CONQUEST*.
P. Sinbad and the Little Old Man of the Sea (Sur. 24/12/87). See *G. CONQUEST*.
P. The Forty Thieves (Sur. 24/12/88). See *G. CONQUEST*.
P. Dick Whittington (Sur. 24/12/89). See *G. CONQUEST*.
P. The Sleeping Beauty (Sur. 26/12/90). See *G. CONQUEST*.
P. The Fair One with the Golden Locks (Sur. 26/12/91). See *G. CONQUEST*.
P. Puss in Boots (Sur. 26/12/92). See *G. CONQUEST*.
P. Cinderella (Sur. 26/12/93). See *G. CONQUEST*.
P. Red Riding Hood (Sur. 17/12/94). See *G. CONQUEST*.
P. Aladdin (Sur. 26/12/95). See *G. CONQUEST*.
P. Sinbad the Sailor (Sur. 26/12/96). See *G. CONQUEST*.
P. The Yellow Dwarf (Sur. 27/12/97). See *G. CONQUEST*.
P. Jack and Jill (Sur. 26/12/98). See *G. CONQUEST*.

SPURR, M. B.

Ca. For Papa's Sake. L.C. Winter Gdns. Stockport, 18/11/96. *French*.
F.C. The Earl of Mulligatawny (Lecture H. Greenwich, 22/10/98). L.C.
[Written in collaboration with *W. MAYNE*.]

SQUIER, CHARLES

F. A Cloud of Smoke (H.M. Richmond, 15/9/81). L.C.
F. Bottles (H.M. Richmond, 17/10/81). L.C.
D. A Prince of Egypt (Richmond, 21/8/82). L.C.

SQUIRE, BARCLAY

R.O. The Veiled Prophet (C.G. 26/7/93). L.C.
[Music by C. V. Stanford.]

STACK, T. A.

F. My Beaux; or, The First of April (M'bone, 1/4/68). L.C.

STACQUELER, M.

D. The Conquest of Magdala; or, The Fall of Theodore (Ast. 12/9/68). L.C.

STAFFORD, ALFRED

D. The Wild West (Woolwich, 6/6/87). L.C.
D. True Grit; or, Reaping the Harvest (Woolwich, 27/6/87; E.C. 3/12/87, as *Reaping the Harvest*). L.C.

STAFFORD, EUGENE C.

R.D. Midnight (P'cess. 24/5/88). See *J. W. FURRELL.*

STAHL, RICHARD

F. Capers; or, All about a Lost Will (Stand. 23/11/85). L.C.

STAINFORTH, FRANK

F. Sea Gulls (Roy. 10/8/69). See *A. MALTBY.*
D. Rank and Fame (Stand. 29/3/75). See *L. RAE.*
D. The Queen of an Hour (Stand. 1/10/77). See *J. T. DOUGLASS.*
P. Little Jack Horner (Alex. Pal. 20/12/79).
P. Puss in Boots (Alex. Pal. 24/12/80). L.C.
P. Little Bo-Peep! Boy Blue! or, The Grim Gold Goblin and the Great Gorilla (E.C. 27/12/80). L.C.
Ca. If I were rich (Park, 16/4/81). L.C.
D. Glad Tidings (Stand. 29/8/83). See *J. WILLING.*

STALMAN, ALFRED

M.D. The Institute Abroad (Mat. 6/5/97).
[Written in collaboration with *G. B. CARGILL.* Music by L. Butler. A revised version of *The Celestial Institute* (T.H. St Martin's, 15/5/96) by *E. H. SIM.*]

STANFORD, C. VILLIERS

R.C.O. Shamus O'Brien (O.C. 2/3/96). See *G. H. JESSOP.*

[*STANFORD, FREDERICK*

C.D. Naughtology; or, Nothing (St G. 5/11/89). L.C.

STANFORD, GILBERT

C.Oa. Proscribed (Vic. H. Bayswater, 22/4/89). L.C.
[Music by C. Hardie.]

STANGE, STANISLAUS

Sk. A Man about Town (Str. 1/5/99). L.C.

STANHOPE, BUTLER

D. The Black Knight of Ashton (People's H. Stalybridge, 30/3/74).
D. O'Donnell Abou (St Helen's, 3/2/75).
D. Crime and Virtue (Adel. L'pool, 30/6/79).
D. The Zulu War; or, The Fight for the Queen's Colours (Birkenhead, 6/6/81).
D. The Egyptian War; or, The Fall of Arabi (Birkenhead, 10/82).
C.O. The Great Tom-Tom (Birkenhead, 14/6/86).
[Music by J. R. Reid.]
D. The Blackleg (Birkenhead, 18/10/86).

D. Creeping Shadows (Birkenhead, 18/4/87). L.C.
D. Mexican Bill; or, Life in the Far Wild West (Birkenhead, 29/8/87).
D. Darkest London (Birkenhead, 4/4/91).
D. Dashing Dick Turpin (Birkenhead, 6/6/92).

STANHOPE, WALTER
D. The Schemer (Margate, 14/12/87, *copy.*). L.C.
D. A Sister's Vow (P.W. L'pool, 19/5/88). L.C.
D. A Weird Destiny (Margate, 13/8/88). L.C.
D. Faustine's Love (Str. 25/6/89, *mat.*). L.C.

STANLEY, A.
D. The Officer of Fortune (Tyne, Newcastle, 19/4/75).

STANLEY, A. G.
D. Australia; or, The Bushrangers (Grec. 16/4/81). L.C.
[Written in collaboration with *W. ARCHER.*]

STANLEY, HERBERT JOHN
D. Sentenced to Death (Longton, 18/8/73).
D. A Life's Peril (Qns. Barnsley, 19/1/74).
D. Trick for Trick (Qns. Barnsley, 2/3/74).
D. Brave Harry Thorn (Vic. Longton, 31/8/74).
D. The Red Light; or, The Signal of Danger (Longton, 28/9/74; Adel. L'pool, 29/3/97). L.C.
D. Face to Face (Dewsbury, 5/4/75).
D. The Strike; or, Heads, Hands and Hearts (Albion, 3/5/75). L.C. as *The Miners' Strike.*
D. Ragged Jack (Rotunda, L'pool, 24/5/80).
D. The Shirtmaker of Toxteth Park (Sefton, L'pool, 28/6/80).
Spect. The Fall of Khartoum (P.W. Salford, 6/4/85). L.C.
D. Guarded by Honour (Sefton, L'pool, 20/4/85).
D. Buffalo Bill; or, Life in the Wild West (Sanger's, 28/5/87). L.C.
[Written in collaboration with *C. HERMANN.* I am not certain whether the former author is H. J. Stanley: he is recorded as "Col. Stanley" in the newspapers.]
C.O. The Famous Beauty (Paragon, Hoyland, 15/3/92, *copy.*). L.C.
[Music by C. R. Engel.]
D. Blackmail (Adel. L'pool, 27/4/96). L.C.
D. Fadorougha and the Black Prophet (Adel. L'pool, 4/7/98). L.C.

STANLEY, HORACE
D. The 10.30 Down Express (Muncaster, Bootle, 19/6/99). L.C.

STANNARD Mrs ["*JOHN STRANGE WINTER*"]
D. Rumour (Vaud. 2/4/89, *mat.*). L.C.
Ca. A Ring Fence (Portsmouth, 27/11/93). L.C.

STAPLES, EDITH BLAIR
Ca. Was it a Dream? (Mechanics' Inst. Stockport, 23/1/96).

STARR, HARRY
M.D. Carl the Clockmaker (Swansea, 16/7/94; Stratford, 15/4/95). L.C. Constitutional Club, Leyton, 28/6/94.
M.C. Fritz's Folly (Barnsley, 4/5/96). L.C.
C.D. Otto the Outcast; or, The Birdseller of Paris (Grand, Nelson, 4/4/98). L.C.

STAYTON, F.
F.C. Our Cousins (Torquay, 25/4/98). See *A. ARGLES.*

STEAD, G.
F. The Antiquarian (R.A. Woolwich, 15/11/89). L.C.

STEELE, Mrs
D. Under False Colours (St G. 9/2/69). L.C.

STEELE, CHARLES D.
C.D. Fickle Fortune (Park T.H. Battersea, 14/4/90, *amat.*). L.C.
M.F. The Dude and the Dancing Girl (T.H. Brixton, 4/11/93).
[Written in collaboration with *C. W. FORWARD*. Music by E. W. Eyre.]
Ca. For Mildred's Sake (P.H. W. Norwood, 8/5/95).

STEER, JANET
D. The Cloven Foot (Blackburn, 27/1/90). See *F. MOUILLOT*.
C.D. Idols of the Heart (Shakespeare, L'pool, 21/2/90; Grand, 8/6/91; Crit. 12/7/92). L.C.

STEIN, FRED JULES
C.D. Quiet Lodgings (Octagon, Blyth, 30/10/72).
D. Found (Gateshead, 16/1/88). L.C.

STEINBERG, AMY [Mrs JOHN DOUGLASS]
F.C. My Uncle (Terry's, 16/7/89, *mat.*). L.C.
F. My Mother (Toole's, 20/5/90, *mat.*). L.C.

STEPHENS, HENRY P.
Ext. Balloonacy (Roy. 1/12/79). See *F. C. BURNAND*.
F.C. Themis (Roy. 29/3/80). L.C. with sub-title, *or, Shuttlecock's Flutter*.
Bsq. Cupid; or, Two Strings to a Beau (Roy. 26/4/80). L.C.
[Written in collaboration with *C. HARRIS*.]
Bsq. The Corsican Brothers and Co. Ltd. (Gai. 25/10/80). See *F. C. BURNAND*.
C.O. Billee Taylor (Imp. 30/10/80). L.C.
[Music by E. Solomon.]
C.O. Claude Duval; or, Love and Larceny (Olym. 24/8/81). L.C.
[Music by E. Solomon.]
C.O. Lord Bateman; or, Picotee's Pledge (Gai. 29/4/82). L.C.
[Music by E. Solomon.]
M.F. Through the Looking Glass (Gai. 17/7/82).
[Music by E. Solomon.]
C.O. Virginia and Paul (Gai. 16/7/83). L.C.
[Music by E. Solomon.]
Bsq. Galatea; or, Pygmalion Reversed (Gai. 26/12/83). L.C.
M.Ca. Hobbies (St G. 6/4/85). L.C.
[Written in collaboration with *W. YARDLEY*. Music by G. Gear.]
Bsq. The Vicar of Wideawakefield; or, The Miss-Terry-ous Uncle (Gai. 8/8/85). L.C.
[Written in collaboration with *W. YARDLEY*.]
Bsq. Little Jack Shepherd (Gai. 26/12/85). L.C.
[Written in collaboration with *W. YARDLEY*.]
C.D. Hand and Heart (Gai. 21/5/86). See *W. YARDLEY*.
C.O. The Red Hussar (Lyr. 23/11/89). L.C.
[Music by E. Solomon.]
C.O. The Black Squire (O.H. Torquay, 5/11/96). L.C. St G. 7/8/96, as *The B.S.; or, Where there's a Will there's a Way*.
[Music by F. Pascal.]

STEPHENS, J.
M.F.C. That Terrible Girl (Roy. 9/3/95). L.C.

STEPHENS, L. E. B.
Ca. Perichon (H.M. Richmond, 19/6/82). L.C.
D. For Love's Sake (H.M. Richmond, 11/12/82). L.C.
D. London; or, The Life of a Street Boy (Barnstaple, 11/1/85). L.C.
D. Madcap Madge (Edmonton, 22/6/95; Imp. 5/10/98).

STEPHENS, or *STEVENS, VICTOR*
Ext. Randolph the Reckless (P.W. Salford, 6/8/88; E.C. 9/9/89; O.H. Cork, 1/6/94, *revised*). L.C.
Bsq. Bonnie Boy Blue (O.H. Chatham, 18/4/92; Parkhurst, 20/5/92). L.C.
Ext. The Saucy Sultana (Cambridge, 26/12/94). L.C.
[Music by the author and J. C. Shepherd.]
M.C. A Village Venus (Grand, Nottingham, 5/8/95). L.C.
[Written in collaboration with *A. BIRCH*. Title altered later to *Merry Major Muddle*.]
M.C. A Merry Madcap (Grantham, 30/7/96, *copy*.; Lyr. Ealing, 3/8/96). L.C.
[Lyrics by *A. BIRCH*. Title altered to *The Golden Goddess*, 25/1/98.]
P. Red Riding Hood (Nov. 24/12/96).
P. Richard Whittington and his Cat (Kilburn, 25/1/97).
M.C. The Last Man on Earth (P's. Bradford, 26/2/97, *copy*.). L.C.
[Music by G. Burton.]

STEPHENS, or *STEVENS, WALTER*
D. A Woman's Whim (St G. 3/12/67, *amat*.).
D. The Vendetta; or, The Pursuit of Vengeance (St G. 17/4/68, *amat*.). L.C.
D. Fashion (Olym. 21/6/69). L.C.
D. Poor Lost Emily; or, The Wreck of the Rosa (Uxbridge, 5/12/70).
D. Little Paul (Lyc. Rochester, 6/3/71).
D. The Mystery of Edwin Drood (Sur. 4/11/71).
D. Passion (Vaud. 8/2/73). L.C.
D. Mystery; or, Greed for Gold (Olym. 5/4/73). L.C.
D. Three Years in a Man Trap (Birkenhead, 29/4/74).
D. Dalham Forge (P.W. Warrington, 19/10/74).
D. Captain Tom Drake (Macclesfield 6/11/74).
D. Arthur Orton (P.W. Warrington, 11/12/74).
D. Ethel's Revenge (Court. 9/9/76). L.C.
D. The Softy of Merrington (Seaham Harbour, 11/2/78).
D. Renforth, the Pride of the Tyne (Darlington, 17/6/78).

STEPHENS, WILFORD or *WILFRED*
D. Wicked Paris; or, Under the Red Flag (Gloucester, 28/4/84). L.C.
D. Our Lass (P.W. Salford, 30/4/86; S.W. 28/7/88). L.C.
D. Living or Dead (S.W. 9/10/86). L.C.
C.D. Mr Potter of Texas (Adel. L'pool, 20/8/88). L.C.
D. The Tramps (W.L. 19/12/96). L.C.
[Written in collaboration with *B. McCULLOUGH*.]

STEPHENS, YORKE
F. The Skeleton (Vaud. 27/5/87). L.C.
[Written in collaboration with *C. GRAVES*.]
Ca. Through the Fire (Str. 25/2/88). See *W. LESTOCQ*.

STEPHENSON, B. C. ["BOLTON ROWE", in association with "SAVILLE ROWE" = *C. W. SCOTT*]

Oa. The Bold Recruit (Canterbury, 4/8/68; G.I. 19/7/70). L.C.

M.Sk. Charity begins at home (G.I. 7/2/72; Gai. 7/2/77; St G. 22/6/92, *revised*). L.C.
[Music by A. Cellier.]

C. Peril (P.W. 30/9/76). See *C. W. SCOTT.*

Ca. Tears (O.C. 17/2/77). See *C. W. SCOTT.*

D. Diplomacy (P.W. 12/1/78). See *C. W. SCOTT.*

C.O. The Little Duke (Phil. 27/4/78). See *C. W. SCOTT.*

Oa. Out of Sight (Cromwell House, 8/7/81). L.C.
[Music by F. Clay.]

D. Impulse (St J. 9/12/82). L.C.

C. Comrades (Court, 16/12/82). See *B. THOMAS.*

C. A Woman of the World (H. 4/2/86, *mat.*). L.C.

C.O. Dorothy (Gai. 25/9/86). L.C.
[Music by A. Cellier.]

M.F. Warranted Burglar Proof (P.W. 31/3/88). L.C. as *Sarah.*
[Music by I. Caryll and H. J. Leslie.]

C.O. Doris (Lyr. 20/4/89). L.C.
[Music by A. Cellier.]

C. Faithful James (Vestry H. Turnham Green, 24/10/89; Lyr. Ealing, 16/11/89; Court, 16/7/92). L.C.

Duol. An Engagement (Newcastle, 29/8/90).

Bsq. The Young Recruit (Tyne, Newcastle, 14/3/92; Grand, 13/6/92).
[Written in collaboration with *Sir A. HARRIS.* Music by L. Wenzel and J. Crook.]

C.O. The Golden Web (Court, L'pool, 15/2/93; Lyr. 11/3/93). L.C.
[Written in collaboration with *F. CORDER.* Music by A. G. Thomas.]

C.O. A Venetian Singer (Court, 25/11/93). L.C.
[Music by E. Jakobowski.]

D. The Fatal Card (Adel. 6/9/94). See *C. H. CHAMBERS.*

D. The Passport (Glo. 15/10/94, *copy.*; Terry's, 25/4/95). L.C.
[Written in collaboration with *W. YARDLEY.*]

M.C. On the March (Sheffield, 18/5/96). See *W. YARDLEY.*

M.C. Belinda (P's. Manchester, 5/10/96). L.C.
[Written in collaboration with *B. HOOD.* Music by W. Slaughter.]

C.D. Carthusiana (H. 26/6/99). L.C.

D. Gringoire (H. 26/6/99).

STEPHENSON, CHARLES H.

D. Wrecked but not Lost (C.L. 9/11/67). L.C.

D. The Convict; or, Hunted to Death (Pav. 1/2/68). L.C.

D. Pindee Singh (Alfred, 10/10/68). L.C.

D. Never Despair, for out of Evil cometh Good (Vic. 30/8/69). L.C.

F. The Varsity Boat Race (Lyc. 6/4/70).
[Written in collaboration with *F. ROBSON.*]

Ext. Tromb-al-ca-zar (Gai. 22/8/70). L.C.
[Music by J. Offenbach.]

D. Quits; or, The Lucky Bag of Life (Belfast, 29/8/70).

C. Man and Wife (Belfast, 2/9/70).

F. Ample Security (Southampton, 5/9/72).

M.F. Bella's Birthday (P'cess. 9/1/73). L.C.
F. Pyramus and Thisbe; or, The Margate Milkmaid (P's. Manchester, 12/10/77).
D. Wrath; or, A Message from the Dead (Huddersfield, 6/10/82; Stand. 18/12/82).
D. Fettered Freedom (Vaud. 28/9/87). See *M. KENNE.*

STERNER, LAWRENCE
F.C. The Club Baby (Lyr. Ealing, 19/9/95; Parkhurst, 14/10/95; Aven. 27/4/98). L.C.
[Written in collaboration with *E. KNOBLAUCH.*]

STERRY, J. ASHBY
C. The Shuttlecock (Toole's, 16/5/85). See *H. J. BYRON.*

STEVEN, ALEXANDER
C.D. A Romance of Love (Qns. R. Berwick, 13/10/91). L.C.

STEVENS, —
C.D. For Ever Mine (Darlington, 21/6/89).
[Written in collaboration with — *LOGAN.*]

STEVENS, ERNEST
D. Scots wha ha'e wi' Wallace bled (Grand, Glasgow, 15/10/95). L.C.
D. Ivanhoe (Grand, Glasgow, 14/3/96). L.C.
R.D. For Bonnie Scotland (Grand, Glasgow, 12/10/97). L.C.

STEVENS, JOHN A.
D. Unknown, a River Mystery (Sur. 31/7/82). L.C.
M.D. Passion's Slave (Bradford, 1/11/86; Stand. 1/8/87). L.C.
D. A Secret Foe (Brighton, 25/8/87; O.C. 27/8/87). L.C.
C.D. A Narrow Escape (Ladb. H. 20/3/88, *copy.*). L.C.

STEVENS, POTTINGER
Ca. Back from India. L.C. St G. 10/6/79.
[Written in collaboration with *C. DICK.*]

STEVENS, STANLEY
C.O. Guinevere; or, Love Laughs at Law (T.H. Kilburn, 19/3/90). L.C.
[Music by H. T. Pringer.]

STEVENS, VICTOR. See *VICTOR STEPHENS*

STEVENS, WALTER. See *WALTER STEPHENS*

STEVENSON, —
D. Revelations of London (Grec. 6/7/68).

STEVENSON, ROBERT LOUIS
C.D. Deacon Brodie; or, The Double Life (Pullan's, Bradford, 28/12/82; P's. 2/7/84). L.C. 8° 1880 [*priv.*]; 8° 1888.
[Written in collaboration with *W. E. HENLEY.*]
C.D. Beau Austin (H. 3/11/90). See *W. E. HENLEY.*
D. Admiral Guinea (Aven. 29/11/97). See *W. E. HENLEY.*

STEWART, ARTHUR
C.D. A White Stocking (Com. 3/10/96). See *E. FERRIS.*
C.D. Nicolete (Crit. 3/1/99). See *E. FERRIS.*

STEWART, DOUGLAS
D. The Female Pirate; or, The Lioness of the Sea (Vic. 31/10/70).
D. Hubert, the Bowyer's Son (Vic. 28/2/74). L.C.
D. Tom Truant (M'bone, 7/3/74). L.C.

STEWART, J. O.

D. Right's Right (W. Bromwich, 8/11/86). See *C. A. CLARKE.*
D. The Great Globe (Vic. Stalybridge, 23/8/89). L.C.

STEWART, KATHERINE

Ca. An Episode (Pleasure Gdns. Folkestone, 17/5/95, *copy.*). L.C.

STEWART, W. Y.

D. My Uncle (Torquay, 28/5/83). See *D. S. JAMES.*

STIRLING, EDWARD

[For his earlier plays see iv, 406–9.]
F. Wild Ducks (M'bone, 7/1/50). L.C.
D. The Woodman's Spell; or, Temperance and Intemperance (M'bone, 20/7/50). L.C. *Lacy.*
F. The Teacher Taught (S.W. 18/10/50). L.C. *Lacy.*
F. A Cheap Excursion (Str. 19/5/51). L.C. *Lacy.*
F. Left in a Cab (Sur. 11/8/51). L.C. *Lacy.*
D. Passion's Slave (Vic. 11/8/51).
F. A Figure of Fun (Str. 15/9/51). L.C. *Fairbrother.*
F. The Bloomer Costume; or, The Figure of Fun (Str. 26/12/51). L.C.
[Evidently a revision of the above.]
F. A Plain Cook in the Strand (Str. 23/2/52). *Duncombe.*
D. The Ragged School (Str. 15/3/52). L.C. *Duncombe.*
F. A Pet of the Public (Str. 7/11/53). L.C. *Lacy.*
D. A Legacy of Honour (D.L. 13/4/53). *Lacy.*
D. The Thieves of Paris (Sur. 1853). *Dicks.*
D. The Gold Mine; or, The Miller of Grenoble (D.L. 1854). *Dicks.*
D. A Struggle for Gold; or, A Mother's Prayer (C.L. 1/54). L.C.
D. The Reapers; or, Forget and Forgive (Str. 4/8/56).
D. The Orphan of the Frozen Sea (Adel. 1856). *Dicks.*
D. The Jew's Daughter (Str. 5/1/57).
[This is probably *The Miser's Daughter* (Adel. 24/10/42).]
F. A Pair of Pigeons (Lyc. 5/11/57). L.C.
C.D. A Lucky Hit (D.L. 1/2/58). L.C.
[Stirling has an earlier play of this title: see iv, 406.]
F. The Rifle Volunteers; or Riflemen! Riflemen! Riflemen! Form! (Adel. 13/6/59). L.C. *Lacy.*
D. The Pawnbroker's Shop (M'bone, 18/6/60).
D. War with the Waves; or, Eric of the Hills (Pav. 15/2/64). [Revised version of *The Sea King's Vow* (Sur. 16/2/46).]
D. The Three Black Seals (Ast. 25/4/64). L.C. *Dicks.*
D. The Spy of the Republic (Ast. 16/5/64). L.C. as *The Police Spy.*
C.D. Trapping a Tartar (Ast. 6/6/64). *Lacy.*
D. Madge Wildfire (Str. 18/10/68).
D. A Slight Mistake (Folkestone, 4/8/69).
D. The Dark Glen of Bally Foihl (Ipswich, 28/10/71).
D. The Patriot's Daughter; or, Tried and True (Albert, Portsmouth, 15/1/72).
D. The Shingawn; or, Old Ireland's Shamrock has not withered yet (Albert, Portsmouth, 5/2/72).
D. King George's Shilling (Grec. 28/4/79). L.C.

STOCKTON, ELLA

C.D. Madcap Violet (S.W. 18/3/82). L.C.

STOCKTON, J. D.

F.C. Fox versus Goose (Str. 8/5/69). See *W. BROUGH.*

STOCKTON, REGINALD

Ca. Uncle Robert (Terry's, 24/7/89, *mat.*). L.C. Londesborough, Scarborough, 2/8/88.

Oa. Our Family Legend (Aquar. Brighton, 8/10/92). L.C. [Music by J. S. Jones, Jr.]

D. The Handcuffs (Nottingham, 11/5/93, *copy.*; Bolton, 23/7/94, as *Under Remand*; Sur. 1/6/96). L.C. [Written in collaboration with *E. V. HUDSON.*]

F. Bagging a Barrister (W.L. 10/8/96). L.C.

STOCQUELER, JOACHIM HAYWARD

[For his earlier plays see iv, 409.]

F. Any Port in a Storm; or, The Bal Masqué (H. 5/12/53). L.C.

Spec. England and France in the Days of Chivalry (Ast. 28/5/55). L.C.

STODDARD, LORIMER

D. Tess of the D'Urbervilles (St J. 2/3/97, *copy.*). L.C.

STONES-DAVIDSON, T. W.

F. Taradiddles; or, White Lies (Swiss Gdns. Shoreham, 31/7/96, *copy.*).

STOW, DALTON

C. Gone Away (Com. Manchester, 9/8/86). See *E. RIGHTON.*

STOW, W. R.

F. Autumn Manœuvres (Vaud. 14/10/71). L.C.

STRACHAN, JOHN S.

Bsq. Cœur de Lion Revised, and his Enemies Corrected (Str. 22/12/70). L.C.

F. Our Own Correspondent (Ch.X. 14/8/71).

P. Goody Two Shoes and her Queen Anne's Farthing; or, Harlequin Old King Counterfeit and the World of Toys (S.W. 26/12/72). L.C.

P. Twinkle, Twinkle, Little Star (Greenwich, 23/12/76). L.C.

STRACHAN, W, Jr.

Bsq. Such a Guy Mannering (Tyne, Newcastle, 27/4/68).

STRATFORD, WALTER

Bsq. Beauty and the Beast (T.H. Buckingham, 25/1/94). [Music by the Rev. L. E. Goddard.]

STRAUSS, S. Z. M.

F. A Model Uncle (D.L. 26/10/68). L.C.

STRETTELL, J. D. C.

D. The Rector's Daughter (Mat. 20/5/98). L.C.

STUART, ADELINE

M.C. In Search of a Father (Grand, Derby, 1/8/98). See *W. ERSKINE.*

STUART, BARRY

D. Fred Walters, a Grimsby Fishing Apprentice (Gt Grimsby, 13/4/77).

STUART, E. M.

M.C. The Bicycle Girl (Grand, Nottingham, 29/3/97). See *C. OSBORNE.*

STUART, MARY
D. Out of the Shadow-land (Bijou, 17/6/99). L.C.

STUART-SMITH, E. [" *ALTON IGNIS*"]
C.D. A Slender Thread (Parish Church, New School, Rochdale, 18/4/96).
Ca. A Lively Honeymoon (Drill H. Merthyr Tydvil, 14/7/97).

STUCKEY, HARRY DYMOND
Bsq. Camilla of Camden Town (Park H. Camden Town, 3/4/93).
F. Local Veto Villa (Assembly R. Weston-super-Mare, 30/10/95). L.C.

STURGESS, ARTHUR
P. Cinderella (D.L. 26/12/95). See *Sir A. HARRIS.*
M.C. The Telephone Girl (Grand, Wolverhampton, 25/5/96). See *Sir A. HARRIS.*
C.O. The Little Genius (Shaft. 9/7/96). See *Sir A. HARRIS.*
P. Aladdin (D.L. 26/12/96). L.C.
[Written in collaboration with *H. LENNARD.*]
C.O. La Poupée (P.W. 24/2/97). L.C.
[Music by E. Audran.]
C.O. Regina B.A.; or, The King's Sweetheart (Grand, Birmingham, 2/8/97; Metro, Camberwell, 7/3/98). L.C.
[Music by J. M. Glover.]
P. Babes in the Wood (D.L. 27/12/97). L.C.
[Written in collaboration with *A. COLLINS.*]
C.D. Julia (Com. Manchester, 28/3/98; Roy. 7/4/98). L.C.
M.C. The Topsy Turvey Hotel (Com. 21/9/98). L.C.
[Music by V. Roger and L. Monckton.]
P. Cinderella (Alex. Stoke Newington, 26/12/98).
[Written in collaboration with *C. RALEIGH* and *E. C. MATTHEWS.*]
Bsq. The Rightful Heir; or, The Usual Thing (P.H. Hastings, 18/9/99). L.C.
[Music by J. W. Glover.]
C.O. The Snow Man (Lyc. 21/12/99). L.C.
[Music by A. Banès and W. Slaughter.]
P. The Forty Thieves (D.L. 26/12/98). L.C.
[Written in collaboration with *A. COLLINS.*]

STURGIS, JULIAN
Ca. Picking up the Pieces (Court, 14/11/82). L.C.
O. Nadeshda (D.L. 16/4/85). L.C.
[Music by G. Thomas.]
C. Apples (Ladb. H. 28/11/87).
O. Ivanhoe (R.E.O.H. 13/1/91). L.C.
[Music by Sir A. Sullivan.]

SULLIVAN, J. P.
D. Leaves of Shamrock (S.W. 22/6/91). L.C.

SULLIVAN, ROBERT
[For his earlier plays see iv, 409.]
C.D. The Old Love and the New (D.L. 16/1/51). L.C. 8° 1851.
C. Elopements in High Life (H. 7/4/53). L.C. *Lacy.*

[*SULLIVAN, THOMAS RUSSELL*
D. Dr Jekyll and Mr Hyde (Boston Museum, 9/5/87; Lyc. 4/8/88). L.C.

SULLIVAN, W. C.

F. Nipped in the Bud (P.W. Birmingham, 15/3/83). L.C.

SUMMERS, KNIGHT

F. M.P. for Puddlepool; or, The Borough Election (S.W. 23/11/68). L.C.

F. A Hero of an Hour (Ch.X. 29/9/69). L.C.

F. Welsh Rabbits (Folly, 21/5/81).
[Written in collaboration with *R. REECE*.]

Oa. What an Idea! (Aquar. Brighton, 25/6/83). L.C.
[Music by H. M. H. Terry.]

Oa. The King's Command (Pier Concert R. Lowestoft, 7/9/93; Salle Erard, 19/5/98).
[Music by L. Honig.]

F.Ca. Out of Sight, out of Mind (Sneinton Inst. Nottingham, 29/5/94). L.C.

Ca. Hobson's Choice (Central H. Nottingham, 24/4/95). L.C.

Ext. Katawompas (W. Pier, Brighton, 24/11/96). L.C.

Oa. That Rascal Rudolph (Bijou, 29/3/97). L.C.
[Music by D. Harrison.]

[*SUMMERS, W. J.*

M.C. A Noble Brother (Shakespeare, L'pool, 28/10/89; O.C. 3/2/90). L.C.

SUMMERS, WALTER

D. One of the Boys (Grand, Stonehouse, Plymouth, 20/7/96). L.C.

P. Cinderella (P'cess. of W. 26/12/98).

SUTCLIFFE, HALLWELL

Ca. The Blue Dahlia (Metro. Devonport, 27/10/98).
[Written in collaboration with *H. BARTLETT*.]

SUTER, WILLIAM E.

D. Poison in Jest (Grec. 24/11/51).

D. Noemie (Grec. 26/4/52).

Spec. The Chase; or, Life on the Turf (Ast. 16/5/53). L.C.

Spec. Jupiter's Decree and the Fall of Phaethon; or, The Fiery Coursers of the Sun (Ast. 10/9/53). L.C.

D. The Ladies of the Convent (Grec. 15/9/53). L.C.

F. A Husband on Trial (Grec. 24/10/53). L.C.

D. The Life of an Actress (Grec. 14/11/53).

D. The Waiter at Cremorne (Sur. 26/3/55; Grec. 25/7/66, as *The Waiter at the Eagle*). L.C. Grec. 12/11/63. *Lacy* [as *Our New Man*].

D. Il Trovatore (C.G. 10/5/55). *French.*
[Written in collaboration with *W. TRAVERS*.]

F. Sarah's Young Man (Sur. 21/4/56). L.C. *Lacy.*

D. Dred; or, The Great Dismal Swamp (Qns. 10/56). L.C.

D. A Life's Revenge; or, Two Loves for One Heart (Grec. 11/10/58).

D. Catherine Howard; or, Woman's Ambition (Grec. 24/1/59). L.C. *Lacy.*

D. The Felon's Bond! (Grec. 30/5/59). L.C. *Lacy.*

F. Give me my Wife (Grec. 13/6/59). L.C. *Lacy.*

F. The Woman that was a Cat (P'cess. 10/59).

D. Holly Bush Hall; or, The Track in the Snow (Qns. 25/2/60). L.C. *Lacy.*

D. The Accusing Spirit; or, The Three Travellers of the Tyrol (Grec. 5/3/60). L.C. *French.*

F. John Wopps; or, From Information Received (Sur. 15/10/60). L.C. *Lacy.*

D. The Syren of Paris (Qns. 1/4/61). L.C. *Lacy.*

D. The Pirates of the Savannah; or, Tiger Hunters of the Prairies (Eff. 29/4/61).

D. The Angel of Midnight (Grec. 20/5/61).

D. Dick Turpin (Brit. 22/7/61).

D. The Idiot of the Mountain (Sur. 7/9/61). L.C. *Lacy.*

Ca. The Jeweller of St James's (O.C. 17/2/62). *Lacy.*

D. The Robbers of the Pyrenees (Eff. 22/9/62). L.C. *Lacy.*

D. Jack o' the Hedge (Qns. 19/11/62). L.C. *Lacy.*

D. Lady Audley's Secret (Qns. 21/2/63). L.C.

C.D. A Glass of Water; or, Causes and Effects (Qns. 2/5/63). L.C.

D. Fan-Fan, the Tulip; or, A Soldier's Fortune (P'cess. 27/5/63, as *Court and Camp*; Brit. 18/10/63, as *The Days of Louis XV*; Lyc. 22/10/64, as *The King's Butterfly*). L.C. *Lacy.*

D. First Love; or, The Widowed Bride (Grec. 15/6/63). L.C.

F. Whom shall I marry? (Grec. 10/7/63).

F. The Highwayman's Holiday (Qns. 14/9/63). L.C. *French.*

F. The Lost Child; or, A Father in search of his Child (Lyc. 26/12/63). L.C. *Lacy.*

F. We all have our little Faults (Grec. 6/10/64). L.C. *Lacy.*

F. A Quiet Family (Sur. 19/11/64). *Lacy.*

D. Baccarat; or, The Knave of Hearts (S.W. 4/3/65). L.C.

D. The Brigands of Calabria (Grec. 12/2/66). *Lacy.*

D. Rocambole; or, The Knave of Hearts and the Companions of Crime (Grec. 26/2/66). L.C.

[A revised version of *Baccarat*. Also played as *The Mysteries of Crime.*]

D. The Child Stealer (Birmingham, 16/4/66; Grec. 11/6/66).

D. The Woman of the World (Grec. 21/6/66).

F. Brother Bill and Me (Grec. 26/9/66). *Lacy.*

D. The Guiding Star; or, The Adventurer's Bride (E.L. 1/2/68). L.C.

D. The Fatal Letter; or, The Midnight Revelation (E.L. 9/5/68). L.C.

C. The Test of Truth; or, It's a Long Lane that has no Turning (*c.* 1869). *French.*

D. Old Mortality; or, The Heir of Milnwood (S.W. 13/9/69).

D. The Bavarian Girl; or, The Black Helmet (S.W. 13/11/69). L.C. *Lacy* [as *Isoline of Bavaria*].

D. Woman's Peril; or, Saved from Death (Vic. 23/7/77). L.C.

[Written in collaboration with *A. CROFTE.*]

[In addition to these Suter is credited with the authorship of the following plays: *Wanted, a Young Lady!*; *A Very Pleasant Evening*; *Two Gentlemen in a Fix; or, How to lose the Train; More Free than Welcome* (acted also as *Lending a Hand*); and *Incompatibility of Temper.*]

SUTRO, ALFRED

C. The Chili Widow (Roy. 7/9/95). See *A. BOURCHIER.*

[For his later plays see A. E. Morgan, *op. cit.* 314.]

SWAN, MYRA

Ca. Her First Engagement (Middlesborough, 5/3/94). L.C.

SWANBOROUGH, W. H.

F. Coal and Coke (Str. 27/1/68). See *C. HARDING*.

Bsq. The Lying Dutchman (Str. 21/12/76). See *F. W. ALLEN*.

SWARBRECK, J. W.

M.D. The Queen (Duke's, 15/3/79). L.C.

D.Sk. Monica (P.H. Hatfield, 8/2/93, *amat.*).

SWEARS, HERBERT

Duol. Love and Dentistry (Lecture H. Greenwich 5/12/93; O.C. 8/5/95). L.C. *French*.

C.D. Day Dreams (Eden, Brighton, 5/12/94; O.C. 6/7/95). L.C.

F.C. Home Sweet Home (St G. 2/3/95, *amat.*). L.C.

C.D. Twilight (Lyr. Hammersmith, 31/8/96). L.C. *Lacy*.

D.Sk. The Lady Interviewer (Richmond, 14/12/96).

C.D. Wayfarers (Mat. 20/5/98). L.C. *French*.

[Several later plays.]

SWIFT, J.

C.D. A Pot of Money (H.M. Richmond, 15/3/81). L.C. K.X. 24/1/79.

SWINBURNE, ALGERNON CHARLES

T. The Queen-Mother [and] Rosamund. 8° 1860.

T. Chastelard. 8° 1865.

T. Atalanta in Calydon. 8° 1865.

T. Bothwell. 8° 1874.

T. Mary Stuart. 8° 1881.

T. Marino Faliero. 8° 1885.

T. Locrine (St G. 20/3/99). L.C. 8° 1887.

T. The Sisters. 8° 1892.

T. Rosamund, Queen of the Lombards. 8° 1899.

SWINERD, H.

D. Woman's Vengeance (R.A. Woolwich, 15/11/89). L.C.

SYKES, BEN

D. Mizpah (International, 22/12/83). L.C.

SYKES, PERCIVAL H. T.

D. For the Czar (Str. 3/11/96). L.C.

F.C. Poor Old Perkins (Str. 3/11/96). L.C.

D.Sk. The Last Temptation (Nov. 5/4/97).

D.Sk. The Guilty Pair (M.H. Cambridge, 28/11/99).

[Written in collaboration with *G. W. BYNG*.]

SYLVESTER, FRANK. See *FRANK SILVESTER*

SYMONS, ARTHUR

D. The Minister's Call (Independent Theatre Soc. at Roy. 4/3/92. L.C.

SYMS, ALGERNON

D.Sk. Bulldogs, Ahoy! (S.W. 30/12/99). See *B. DALY*.

TABRAR, JOSEPH

M.F. The Sham Solicitor (Imp. 1/10/83). L.C.

P. Puss in Boots (Grand, 24/12/84). L.C.

P. Little Red Riding Hood (Pav. 26/12/84). See *O. ALLEN*.

Bsq. Abon; or, The Sleeper Awakened (Coventry, 3/8/85). L.C.

F.C. My Friend (Vaud. 17/11/85). L.C.

F.C. The Jones's Notes (Bournemouth, 14/6/86; Gai. 12/7/86). L.C.

P. Sinbad the Sailor (Pav. 26/12/93). L.C.

TADDEI, E.

C.O. Ali Baba; or, The Forty Thieves (Lyc. 17/1/71). L.C.
[Music by Bottesini.]

TALBOT, H.

M.C. A Chinese Honeymoon (Hanley, 16/10/99). See *G. DANCE.*

TALFOURD, FRANCIS

[For his earlier plays see iv, 410.]

Bsq. Alcestis, the Original Strong-minded Woman (Str. 4/7/50). L.C. *Lacy.*

Bsq. The Princess in the Tower; or, A Match for Lucifer (Olym. 2/9/50). L.C.

Bsq. La Tarantula; or, The Spider King (Adel. 26/12/50). L.C.

Ba. Godiva: or, Ye Ladye of Coventry (Str. 7/7/51). See *W. P. HALE.*

Bsq. Thetis and Peleus (Str. 27/10/51). See *W. P. HALE.*

Ext. The Willow-Pattern Plate (Str. 26/12/51). See *W. P. HALE.*

Bsq. The Bottle Imp (Grec. 12/4/52). See *W. P. HALE.*

Bsq. Ganem, the Slave of Love (Olym. 31/5/52). L.C. *Lacy.*

F. Butcher versus Baker (Olym. 28/6/52). L.C.

Bsq. Leo the Terrible (H. 27/12/52). See *J. S. COYNE.*

T. The Castilian. 8° 1853.

Bsq. Shylock; or, The Merchant of Venice Preserved (Olym. 4/7/53). L.C. *Lacy.*

F. "Wanted, a Situation" (Olym. 29/8/53). L.C.

Ext. Abou Hassan; or, The Hunt after Happiness (St J. 26/12/54). L.C.

F. Tit for Tat (Olym. 22/1/55). L.C. *Lacy.*
[Written in collaboration with *A. S. WIGAN.*]

P. William Tell (Lyc. 2/6/56). See *T. TAYLOR.*

Ba. Atalanta; or, The Three Golden Apples (H. 13/4/57). L.C. *Lacy.*

Bsq. Pluto and Proserpine; or, The Belle and the Pomegranate (H. 5/4/58).

F. The Rule of Three (Str. 20/12/58). L.C. *Lacy.*

Ext. Electra, in a New Electric Light (H. 25/4/59). L.C.

D.Sk. The Household Fairy (St J. 24/12/59). L.C. *Lacy.*

Bsq. King Thrushbeard; or, The Little Pet and the Great Passion (Lyc. 26/12/59). L.C. *Lacy.*

P. Tell and the Strike of the Cantons; or, The Pair, the Meddler and the Apple (Str. 26/12/59). L.C. *Lacy.*

Ext. The Miller and his Men (Str. 9/4/60). L.C. *Lacy.*
[Written in collaboration with *H. J. BYRON.*]

TAMPLIN, AUGUSTUS L.

Oa. Fleurette (Gai. 1/3/73). L.C.

TAMPLIN, HADDINGTON

D. Edmund Kean (Assembly R. Chichester, 20/11/93). L.C.

TANNER, JAMES T. ["*J. LEADER*"]

Bsq. Don Juan (Gai. 28/10/93; Gai. 12/4/94, *revised*). L.C.
[Lyrics by *A. ROSS.* Music by M. Lutz.]

M.F. All Abroad (Portsmouth, 1/4/95). See *O. HALL.*

Oa. Bobbo (P's. Manchester, 12/9/95). L.C.
[Written in collaboration with *A. ROSS.* Music by F. O. Carr.]

F. Madame (O.C. 7/12/95). L.C.

M.C. The Clergyman's Daughter (Birmingham, 13/4/96; Gai. 13/7/96, as *My Girl*). L.C.
[Lyrics by *A. ROSS*. Music by F. O. Carr.]

M.C. In the Ring (Gai. 27/5/96, *copy*.; Gai. 5/12/96, as *The Circus Girl*). L.C.
[Written in collaboration with *W. PALINGS*; lyrics by *H. GREENBANK* and *A. ROSS*. Music by I. Caryll and L. Monckton.]

M.C. The Ballet Girl (Grand, Wolverhampton, 15/3/97; Brixton, 2/8/97). L.C.
[Lyrics by *A. ROSS*. Music by C. Kiefert.]

M.C. The Transit of Venus (Dublin, 9/4/98; Qns. Crouch End, 26/9/98). L.C.
[Lyrics by *A. ROSS*. Music by N. Lambelet.]

Rev. Potpourri (Coronet, 3/4/99; Aven. 9/6/99). L.C.
[Lyrics by *W. H. RISQUE*. Music by N. Lambelet.]

C. On the Move (Vic. O.H. Burnley, 9/10/99). L.C. as *One of the Boys*.

TAPPING, A. B.

F. Birdcage Walk (T.H. Hove, 20/4/92). See *H. L. BENNETT*.

TARDREW, P.

F.Ca. An Eye to Business (P.W. Southampton, 31/8/83). See *G. B. HALLIDAY*.

TARPEY, W. B.

C. Papa's Honeymoon (Crit. 28/6/90). See *S. MAYER*.

Ca. His Evening Out (Ladb. H. 28/2/99, *copy*.).

TASSIN, ALGERNON

C. The Chalk Mark (Aven. 26/4/99). See *F. H. FRANCKS*.

TATE, ANSCAL

C.O. His Highness (O.C. 13/6/93, *amat*.). See *J. W. HOUGHTON*.

[*TAYLEURE, CLIFTON W.*

D. Si Slocum; or, Life on the Western Border (Amphi. L'pool, 8/6/76; Olym. 18/12/76). L.C.

D. Wife or Widow (Grand, 15/2/86).

TAYLOR, F. C.

C. Under False Colours (Cavendish R. 15/6/70, *amat*.).

TAYLOR, H. G. F.

Bsq. Ruddy George; or, Robin Redbreast (Toole's, 19/3/87, *mat*.). L.C.
[Music by P. Reeve.]

TAYLOR, J. G.

D. For Life through Thick and Thin (Alex. 7/3/68). L.C.

D. Home Rule: A Fireside Story (P.W. L'pool, 19/3/77).

TAYLOR, MARION

Vaud. The Mechanical Toy (Brit. 21/3/70).

TAYLOR, T. M.

C.O. The Mystic Mahatma; or, The Reincarnated Robber (St G. 5/1/92). L.C.
[Music by V. Phillips.]

Oa. Sir Reginald; or, An Ancestral Incubus (St G. 6/1/94, *amat*.). L.C.
[Written in collaboration with *L. RAY*. Music by V. Phillips.]

TAYLOR, T. R.

D. The Anchor's Weighed (Stand. 14/5/83).

TAYLOR, TOM ["JOHN ROAKES"]

[For his earlier plays see iv, 411 and 614. These earlier works are also given below.]

F. A Trip to Kissingen (Lyc. 14/11/44). L.C. *Dicks.*

Ext. Valentine and Orson (Lyc. 23/12/44).
[Written in collaboration with *A. SMITH* and *C. KENNEY.*]

Bsq. Cinderella (Lyc. 12/5/45).
[Written in collaboration with *A. SMITH* and *C. KENNEY.*]

D. To Parents and Guardians (Lyc. 14/9/46). L.C. *Dicks.*

Ext. Diogenes and his Lantern; or, The Hue and Cry after Honesty (Str. 26/12/49).

D. The Vicar of Wakefield; or, The Pastor's Fireside (Str. 4/3/50). L.C. *Dicks*; *Lacy.*

Ext. The Philosopher's Stone (Str. 20/5/50). L.C. *Lacy.*

Rev. Novelty Fair; or, Hints for 1851 (Lyc. 21/5/50). L.C.
[Written in collaboration with *A. R. SMITH.*]

Ext. Prince Dorus; or, The Romance of the Nose (Olym. 26/12/50). L.C. *Lacy.*

C.D. Sir Roger de Coverley; or, The Widow and her Wooers (Olym. 21/4/51). L.C. *Lacy.*

Bsq. Little Red Riding Hood (Adel. 26/12/51). L.C.

F. Our Clerks; or, No. 3, Fig Tree Court, Temple (P'cess. 6/3/52). L.C. *Lacy.*

Ext. Wittikind and his Brothers; or, The Seven Swan Princes and the Fair Melusine (P'cess. 12/4/52). L.C. *Lacy.*

C. Masks and Faces; or, Before and Behind the Curtain (H. 20/11/52). L.C. 8° 1854; *Dicks*; *Lacy.*
[Written in collaboration with *C. READE.*]

D. Slave Life; or, Uncle Tom's Cabin (Adel. 29/11/52). L.C. *Webster.*
[Written in collaboration with *M. LEMON.*]

D. Plot and Passion (Olym. 17/10/53). L.C. as *Mine and Countermine.* 8° 1877; *Dicks*; *Lacy.*
[Written in collaboration with *J. LANG.*]

C.D. A Nice Firm (Lyc. 16/11/53). L.C. *Lacy.*

P. Harlequin Columbus; or, The Old World and the New (Olym. 26/12/53). L.C.

Ca. To Oblige Benson (Olym. 6/3/54). L.C. *Lacy.*

D. Two Loves and a Life (Adel. 20/3/54). L.C. 8° 1854; *Dicks*; *Lacy.*
[Written in collaboration with *C. READE.*]

F. Barefaced Imposters (Canterbury, 15/8/54; Richmond, 21/5/60). *Lacy.*

D. The King's Rival (St J. 2/10/54). L.C. 8° 1854; *Lacy.*
[Written in collaboration with *C. READE.*]

F. A Blighted Being (Olym. 16/10/54). L.C. *Lacy.*

Ext. Guy Fawkes; or, A Match for a King (Olym. 31/3/55). 12° [1855; *priv.*].
[Written in collaboration with *ALBERT R. SMITH, W. P. HALE, E. DRAPER* and *ARTHUR SMITH.*]

C. Still Waters run deep (Olym. 14/5/55). L.C. *Lacy*; *Dicks.*

D. Helping Hands (Adel. 20/6/55). L.C. *Lacy.*

D. The First Printer (P'cess. 3/3/56). L.C.
[Written in collaboration with *C. READE.*]

D. Retribution (Olym. 12/5/56). L.C. *Lacy.*
P. William Tell (Lyc. 2/6/56, *amat.*; Lyc. 14/7/56).
[Written in collaboration with *A. R. SMITH, F. TALFOURD* and *W. P. HALE.*]
D. A Sheep in Wolf's Clothing (Olym. 19/2/57). L.C. *Dicks*; *Lacy.*
C. Victims (H. 8/7/57). L.C. *Lacy.*
C. An Unequal Match (H. 7/11/57). L.C. *Lacy.*
C. Going to the Bad (Olym. 5/6/58). L.C. *Lacy.*
Ca. Nine Points of the Law (Olym. 11/4/59). L.C. *Lacy.*
C. The House or the Home? (Adel. 16/5/59). L.C. as *The Member's Wife; or, The House versus the Home. Lacy.*
C. The Contested Election (H. 29/6/59). L.C. 8° 1868 [*Manchester*].
D. Payable on Demand (Olym. 11/7/59). L.C. *Lacy.*
D. Garibaldi (Ast. 17/10/59). L.C.
D. The Fool's Revenge (S.W. 18/10/59). L.C. 8° 1877; *Lacy.*
Ca. The Late Lamented (H. 17/11/59). L.C.
D. A Tale of Two Cities (Lyc. 30/1/60). L.C. *French.*
C. The Overland Route (Manchester, 1860; H. 23/2/60). L.C. 8° 1866 [*Manchester*].
D. The Seasons (Stand. 17/3/60).
F. A Christmas Dinner (Olym. 23/4/60). L.C.
C. A Lesson for Life (Lyc. 18/7/60, *amat.*; H. 26/12/66). L.C. 8° [1867].
D. The Brigand and his Banker (Lyc. 1/10/60). L.C.
C. Up at the Hills (St J. 29/10/60). L.C. *Lacy.*
C. The Babes in the Wood (H. 10/11/60). L.C. *Lacy.*
[This was later acted as *Eloped; or, Babes and Beetles.*]
C. A Duke in Difficulties (H. 6/3/61). L.C.
C.D. Our American Cousin (Laura Keene's, New York, 18/10/58; H. 11/11/61). L.C. Adel. 9/10/52; re-entered H. 7/11/60. 8° 1869 [*priv.*]. *Lacy.*
Oa. Court and Cottage (C.G. 11/11/61). L.C.
[Music by F. Clay.]
D. The Ticket-of-Leave Man (Olym. 27/5/63). *Lacy.*
Ext. An Awful Rise in Spirits (Olym. 7/9/63). L.C. as *The Ghost! The Ghost!*
Ext. Sense and Sensation; or, The Seven Saints of Thule (Olym. 16/5/64). L.C. *Lacy.*
D. The Hidden Hand (Olym. 2/11/64). L.C. *Lacy*; *French.*
D. Settling Day (Olym. 4/3/65). L.C. *Lacy.*
D. Hearts and Hands (Manchester, 2/5/65). L.C.
D. The Serf; or, Love levels all (Olym. 30/6/65). L.C. *Lacy.*
D. Henry Dunbar; or, A Daughter's Trial (Olym. 9/12/65). *Lacy*
D. The White Boy (Olym. 27/9/66). L.C.
D. A Sister's Penance (Adel. 26/11/66). L.C. *Lacy.*
[Written in collaboration with *A. W. DUBOURG.*]
D. The Antipodes; or, The Ups and Downs of Life (Holb. 8/6/67). L.C.
C. Won by a Head; or, Forewarned is Forearmed (Qns. 29/3/69). L.C.
D. Mary Warner; or, Tried in the Fire (H. 21/6/69). L.C.
C. New Men and Old Acres; or, A Managing Mama (Manchester, 20/8/69; H. 25/10/69). L.C. as *Love or Money. Lacy.*
[Written in collaboration with *A. W. DUBOURG.*]

D. 'Twixt Axe and Crown; or, The Lady Elizabeth (Qns. 22/1/70). L.C.; revised version, Manchester, 12/10/89. 8° 1877; *French.*

C.D. Handsome is that Handsome does: A Story of the Lake Country (P's. Manchester, 15/8/70; Olym. 3/9/70). L.C.

T. Joan of Arc (Qns. 10/4/71). L.C. 8° 1877.

D. Dead or Alive (Qns. 22/7/72). L.C.

D. Arkwright's Wife (Leeds, 7/7/73; Glo. 6/10/73). L.C. 8° 1877.
[Written in collaboration with *J. SAUNDERS.*]

D. Lady Clancarty; or, Wedded and Wooed (Olym. 9/3/74). L.C. *Lacy.*

D. The White Cockade (Croydon, 26/9/74). L.C.

D. Abel Drake (Leeds, 9/10/74; P'cess. 20/5/76). L.C.
[Written in collaboration with *J. SAUNDERS.*]

D. Anne Boleyn (H. 5/2/76). L.C. 8° 1877.

D. Such is the Law (St J. 20/4/78). L.C.
[Written in collaboration with *P. MERRITT.*]

D. Love and Life (Olym. 10/6/78). L.C.
[Written in collaboration with *P. MERRITT.*]

TAYLOR, WILLIAM

Ext. The Fiend at Fault (Vaud. 4/4/94). See *H. S. EDWARDS.*

TEALE, LESTER

M.Rom. At Zero (County, Reading, 4/7/98). L.C.
[Lyrics by *T. HUGHES.* Music by F. Rosse.]

"*TEDDE, MOSTYN*"

Bsq. Japs (P's. Bristol, 31/8/85). See *H. PAULTON.*

Bsq. Masse-en-yell-oh (Com. 23/3/86). See *H. PAULTON.*

C.O. Pepita (Court, L'pool, 30/12/86; P.W. Greenwich, 15/8/87; Toole's, 30/8/88). L.C.
[Music by C. Lecocq.]

C.O. Mynheer Jan (Grand, Birmingham, 7/2/87). See *H. PAULTON.*

F.C. A Bad Lot (O.H. Northampton, 24/6/87). See *H. PAULTON.*

M.D. M.D. (Doncaster, 2/4/88). See *H. PAULTON.*

C.O. Paola (Lyc. Edinburgh, 16/12/89). See *H. PAULTON.*

TEMPLAR, CLAUDE

D. The Scar on the Wrist (St J. 9/3/78). See *J. P. SIMPSON.*

D. Zillah (Lyc. 2/8/79). See *J. P. SIMPSON.*

Ca. Luck (Imp. 15/11/79). L.C.

TEMPLE, GRACE

D. The Ocean Waif (St J. Wrexham, 16/5/93).
[Written in collaboration with *H. M. LE BLONDE.*]

TEMPLE, RICHARD

C.O. The Mock Doctor (Grand, 24/11/90).
[Lyrics by *C. L. KENNEY.* Music by Gounod.]

TENNYSON, ALFRED Lord

D. Queen Mary (Lyc. 18/4/76). L.C. 8° 1875.

D. Harold. 8° 1877.

D. The Falcon (St J. 18/12/79). L.C. 8° 1882 [in *The Cup and the Falcon*].

D. The Cup (Lyc. 3/1/81). L.C. 8° 1881 [*priv.*]; 8° 1882 [in *The Cup and The Falcon*].

D. The Promise of May (Glo. 11/11/82). L.C. 8° 1883.

D. The Foresters, Robin Hood and Maid Marian (Lyc. 17/3/92, *copy.*; Daly's, 3/10/93). L.C. 8° 1892.
[Music by Sir A. Sullivan.]

T. Becket (Lyc. 6/2/93). L.C. 8° 1879 [*priv.*]; 8° 1884; 8° 1893 [arranged by Henry Irving].

TENNYSON, M. HOWARD

F.C. The Joker (Aven. 13/11/94). L.C. Margate, 29/8/94, as *The Bombay Brothers.*

"*TERRA COTTA.*" See *Miss C. M. PREVOST.*

TERRISS, T. H.

D. Bonnie Prince Charlie (Bedford Park Club, Chiswick, 8/6/89).

TERRISS, WILLIAM

M.D. The Great Metropolis (P'cess. 11/2/92). L.C.
[Revised version of an American play by G. H. Jessop and B. Teal (N.Y. 8/89).]

M.C. Oh! What a Night! (O.H. Wakefield, 15/1/98, *copy.*). L.C.
[Lyrics by *C. SCOTT.* Music by J. Crook.]

TERRY, E.

P. Bo Peep (Woolwich, 26/12/63).

TERRY, EDWARD

F. The Woman Hater (Newcastle, 2/9/87). See *D. D. LLOYD.*

THALBERG, T. B.

D. Prince Otto (Spa Concert R. Harrowgate, 24/3/88). L.C.
[Written in collaboration with *G. GURNEY.*]

F.C. A Close Shave (Stockton-on-Tees, 16/2/95).

THARP, THEODORE A.

D. Talbot's Trust (Glo. 13/9/75). L.C.

D. Fair Women and Brave Men (New, Barnstaple, 23/9/97; Parkhurst, 7/11/98). L.C.

THIBOUST, LAMBERT

D. Lost (Stand. 16/10/71).

THIERRE, GUILLON LE

C. All for Money (H. 12/7/69). L.C.

THOM, ROBERT W.

D. Cleon. 12° 1855.

[*THOMAS, AUGUSTUS*

F.C. A Night's Frolic (Str. 1/6/91). L.C. E.C. 20/6/90, as *Tit for Tat.*
[Written in collaboration with *HELEN BARRY.*]

D. Alabama (Madison Square, New York, 1/4/91; Gar. 2/9/95). L.C.

THOMAS, BERTE W.

D. Joe the Miner (Margate, 12/6/93). L.C.

C. The Weather Hen (Terry's, 29/6/99).
[Written in collaboration with *H. G. BARKER.*]

THOMAS, BRANDON

C. Comrades (Court, 16/12/82). L.C.
[Written in collaboration with *B. C. STEPHENSON.*]

C.D. The Colour Sergeant (P'cess. 26/2/85). L.C.

C. Nellie's Flight (C.P. 20/7/86). See *H. S. EDWARDS.*
F. The Lodgers (Glo. 18/1/87). L.C.
[Written in collaboration with *M. DE VERNEY.*]
F. A Highland Legacy (Str. 17/11/88). L.C.
D. The Gold Craze (P'cess. 30/11/89). L.C.
C.D. The Lancashire Sailor (Terry's, 6/6/91). L.C.
F. Charley's Aunt (Bury St Edmund's, 29/2/92; Roy. 21/12/92). L.C.
C.D. Marriage (Court, 7/6/92, *mat.*; Court, 17/5/94). L.C.
[Written in collaboration with *H. KEELING.*]
C. Clever Alice (Roy. 6/4/93). L.C.
C.O. The Queen of Brilliants (Lyc. 8/9/94). L.C.
[Music by E. Jakobowski.]
D. The Swordsman's Daughter (Adel. 31/8/95). L.C.
[Written in collaboration with *C. W. SCOTT.*]
C.D. No 22A Curzon Street (Gar. 2/3/98). L.C.
[Written in collaboration with *J. EDWARDS.*]

THOMAS, CHARLES
Oa. The Queen of Hearts (Pav. Brighton, 7/11/77). L.C. Rochdale, 29/12/76.
[Music by Harriet Young.]
Oa. Breaking the Ice (Pav. Brighton, 25/11/78; Aquar. Brighton, 13/3/80; Court, 9/11/85). L.C.
[Music by Harriet Young.]
M.Sk. When one Door shuts another opens (T.H. Hove, 29/10/85; Qns. Gate H. 14/5/96).
[Music by Harriet Young.]
D. Lady Fortune (Glo. 17/9/87). L.C.
Ca. Trespassers Beware! (Aven. 26/4/88).
C. The Paper Chase (St G. 1/5/88, *copy.*; Str. 9/6/88, *mat.*; Toole's, 9/7/88). L.C.
D. Hermine (Court, 24/9/88). L.C.
C. A Patron Saint (St J. 17/10/88). L.C. *French.*
C. The Scarecrow (Str. 29/5/89, *mat.*). L.C.
Oa. The Holly Branch (Lyr. Ealing, 11/12/91).
[A revised version of *Breaking the Ice* (Pav. Brighton, 25/11/78).]

THOMAS, Mrs EDWARD
D. The Merchant's Daughter of Toulon (Stand. 10/3/56). L.C. Stand. 11/12/55.
D. The Wife's Tragedy (Stand. 10/12/70). L.C.

THOMAS, EVELYN L.
Oa. Thomas the Rhymer (T.H. Marlborough, 30/3/94).
[Music by J. Farmer.]

THOMAS, GEORGE
D. Dawn (Vaud. 30/6/87, *mat.*). L.C.
[Written in collaboration with *F. OSWALD.*]

THOMAS, LEIGH
Ext. The Pirate; or, The Wicked Father who sold his Daughter and the Don who bought her (S. London Assembly R. 8/12/71, *amat.*).
Bsq. Domenico the Vile 'un (Assembly R. Camberwell, 26/4/72, *amat.*).

THOMAS, WALTER
Bsq. Merrie Prince Hal (S.W. 31/8/91). L.C.
[Music by C. C. Corri.]

THOMPSON, Miss A.

C.D. A Woman's Freak (M.H. Chester, 15/12/82). L.C.

"*THOMPSON, ALFRED*"

Bsq.O. The Lion's Mouth (Lady Collier's house, Eaton Place, 2/5/67, *amat.*).
[Music by V. Gabriel.]

C. On the Cards (Gai. 21/12/68). L.C.

Ext. Columbus; or, A New Pitch in A-Merry-Key (Gai. 17/5/69). L.C.

F. The Bird of Paradise (Gai. 26/6/69). L.C.

Bsq. Linda of Chamouni; or Not a Formosa (Gai. 13/9/69). L.C.

D. The King's Pleasure (Gai. 12/4/70, *amat.*). L.C.

Ext. Aladdin the Second (Gai. 24/12/70).

Bsq. Cinderella the Younger (Gai. 23/9/71). L.C.

Bsq. How I found Crusoe; or, The Flight of Imagination (Olym. 28/12/72). L.C.

Ext. Calypso; or, The Art of Love (Court, 6/5/74). L.C.

M.F. The Three Conspirators (Belfast, 16/10/74). L.C. Ch.X. 12/7/75.

C.O. Bella Donna; or, The Little Beauty and the Great Beast (P's. Manchester, 27/4/78). L.C.
[Music by A. Cellier.]

Ca. The Cynic's Defeat; or, All is Vanity (P.W. L'pool, 19/8/78; H. 9/4/79). L.C.

Bal. Hawaia; or, The Burning Gulf (Alh. 27/12/80).

Bsq.Ext. The Yellow Dwarf (H.M. 30/12/82). See *R. REECE.*

D. Upon the Waters (P's. Manchester, 13/6/98). See *R. COURTNEIDGE.*

THOMPSON, A. M.

Oa. Toto and Sata (Grand, Leeds, 23/8/97; Metro. Camberwell, 20/9/97). L.C.
[Lyrics by *E. B. JONES* and *J. J. WOOD.* Music by A. Banès. Title altered to *Jack and Jill*, 7/11/1906.]

THOMPSON, C. T.

P. Mother Shipton: Her Wager; or, Harlequin Knight of Love and the Magic Whistle (Adel. 1/1/57). L.C.

THOMPSON, F.

F. A Double Mistake (Pier, Hastings, 23/6/84).

THOMPSON, Mrs G.

C.D. Plucky Nancy (T.H. Kilburn, 16/3/89).
[Written in collaboration with *K. SINCLAIR.*]

C.D. A Broken Sixpence (Ladb. H. 11/4/89; Toole's, 15/6/89). L.C.
[Written in collaboration with *K. SINCLAIR.*]

Ca. Mademoiselle de Lira (Com. 7/1/90, *mat.*).
[Written in collaboration with *K. SINCLAIR.*]

C. Duskie (Ladb. H. 17/6/90; St G. 13/5/93).
[Written in collaboration with *K. SINCLAIR.*]

D.Sk. Pounds, Shillings and Pence (T.H. Kilburn, 18/1/92).
[Written in collaboration with *K. SINCLAIR.*]

D. Saint Angela (T.H. Kilburn, 18/1/92).
[Written in collaboration with *K. SINCLAIR.*]

THOMPSON, GEORGE F.

D. Too Late (Glo. 29/6/81). L.C.

THOMPSON, HELEN

D. Rex Cann, the Whipper-in (Sefton, L'pool, 20/10/84). L.C.

D. The Shades (Sefton, L'pool, 21/10/84). L.C.

D. My Maggie (Sefton, L'pool, 22/10/84). L.C.
[Title altered to *Darkest London*, 29/11/93.]

THOMPSON, LIONEL

D. The Man of Two Lives (L'pool, 16/6/79).

THOMPSON, MARY ANNE

D. O'Shaughan; or, The Fatal Secret. L.C. Birmingham, 23/10/50.

THOMPSON Mrs NOEL

D. Myra (H.M. Richmond, 27/9/80). L.C.

THOMPSON, ROBERT HELY ["*ROBERT BLAKE*"]

D. The Nuns of Minsk. 8° 1878.

T. Mary Queen of Scots (Richmond, 10/12/94). L.C. 8° 1894 [2 editions].

F.C. Skittles Limited (Richmond, 17/1/95; Lyr. Hammersmith, 18/4/96, as *Limited*). L.C.

T. Kirk-o-Field. 24° [1895; Omagh].

THOMPSON W. J.

D. Signal Lights (Metro. Birkenhead, 30/7/94; Pav. 10/9/94). L.C.

THOMPSON, W. T.

Bsq. Darry the Dauntless (County, Reading, 31/7/90). See *H. GATWARD.*

THOMSON, AUGUSTA

M.D. Sunshine and Shadow (M'bone, 25/3/67). L.C.

M.F. Violet's Playthings (M'bone, 1/4/67).

THOMSON, J. E.

F. My Love the Captain (Str. 8/3/52). L.C.

THORNE, ELIZA

D. Bleak House; or, Poor Jo the Crossing Sweeper (Alex. O.H. Sheffield, 28/4/76). L.C.

"*THORNE*, or *THORN, GEOFFREY*" [*CHARLES TOWNLEY*]

Bsq. Blue-eyed Blue Beard, the Masher Pasha (Grand, 24/12/85). L.C.

P. Robinson Crusoe; or, A Christmas Story of a Good Friday (Grand, 27/12/86). L.C.

P. Whittington and his Cat (Grand, 26/12/87). L.C.

P. Robinson Crusoe (Pav. 26/12/87). L.C.

P. The Babes in the Wood; or, Harlequin Robin Hood and Little John (Pav. 26/12/88). L.C.

P. Sweet Cinderella; or, Harlequin the Prince and the Lass, and the Slipper of Glass (Grand, 26/12/88). L.C.

Bsq. Dandy Dick Turpin; or, The Mashing Highwayman (Grand, 27/4/89, *mat.*, *copy.*; Grand, 6/10/89). L.C.

P. Dick Whittington and his Cat (Pav. 26/12/89). L.C.

P. Aladdin; or, The Saucy Young Scamp that collared the Lamp (Grand, 26/12/89). L.C.

P. Aladdin (Pav. 26/12/90). L.C.

P. Babes in the Wood; or, Bold Robin Hood and his Foresters Good (Grand, 26/12/90). L.C.
[Music by W. H. Brinkworth.]

P. Whittington and his Cat (Grand, 26/12/91). L.C.
P. The Naughty Forty Thieves (Grand, 26/12/92). L.C.
[Music by W. H. Brinkworth.]
P. Jack and the Beanstalk; or, Harlequin, Old Mother Hubbard, Little Bo-Peep, and the Old Woman who lived in her Shoe (Grand, 26/12/93). L.C.
P. Robinson Crusoe (Grand, 26/12/94). L.C.
P. Aladdin up-to-date (Grand, 26/12/95). L.C.
P. Cinderella (Grand, 26/12/96). L.C.
P. Cinderella (Gar. 27/12/97). L.C.
P. Dick Whittington (Grand, 27/12/97). L.C.
P. Dick Whittington (Crown, Peckham, 24/12/98). L.C.
P. Aladdin (Parkhurst, 24/12/98). L.C.
P. Cinderella (Borough, Stratford, 26/12/98).
[Written in collaboration with *W. CLEMENT*.]

THORNE, GEORGE
Bsq. Le Raw Carotte (Margate, 19/9/73).
P. Jack and the Beanstalk (S.W. 27/12/86). L.C.
[Written in collaboration with *F. G. PALMER*.]
P. Ye Miller and hys Man (Corn Exchange, Maidstone, 26/12/93). L.C.

THORNE, RICHARD L.
[For an earlier play see iv, 413.]
D. Rough Rob, the Gipsy Thief of Hangman's Hollow; or, The Brothers. L.C. Pav. 24/1/50.
P. Sugar and Spice and all that's nice; or, Harlequin March of Intellect. L.C. (Qns. 20/12/50).
P. Cowardy Cowardy Custard ate his Father's Mustard; or, Harlequin the Demon Vice and the Fairy Queen Virtue (Pav. 26/12/51). L.C.

THORNEYCROFT, Lieut.-Col.
O. The Thorneycroft Cousins (Tettenhall Towers, Wolverhampton, 17/4/88).
[Music by Andrani.]

THORNTHWAITE, J. F.
F.C. The Linen Draper (Com. 17/4/90). See *J. R. BROWN*.

THORNTON, HENRY. See *H. T. CRAVEN*

THORNTON, L. M.
F. The Postman's Knock (H. 10/4/56). L.C.

THORP, A. C.
F. Mad as a Hatter (Alex. Dublin, 12/3/72, *amat.*).

THORP, J. H.
D. Serge Panine (Aven. 4/6/91). L.C.

THORPE, COURTENAY
D. The Story of a Sin (Richmond, 1/8/95). L.C.
D. The Light that failed (Roy. 7/4/98). L.C. 2/7/91.

THORPE, T.
F. Out of the Hunt (Roy. 8/10/81). See *R. REECE*.

THORRINGTON, JAMES E.
D. Travers' Secret (Pier Pav. Southend, 21/2/99). L.C.
[Title altered to *Forced to Crime*, 14/12/99, and to *Secrets of the Past*, 30/6/1911.]

THURGOOD, A. V.
C.O. Claudio (Portsmouth, 1/12/88, *copy.*; Grand, Nottingham, 5/8/89). L.C.
[Music by T. Hunter.]

THURSBY, CHARLES
Duol. Lady Di's Visit (O.H. Chatham, 26/4/97). L.C.
D. Broken Fetters (Mat. 22/7/97). L.C.

TILBURY, WILLIAM HARRIES
F. Counter Attraction (Str. 25/11/51). *Lacy.*
[Also acted as *Counter Attraction; or, Strolling and Stratagem.*]

TINSLEY, LILY
D. The Devil's Luck (Adel. L'pool, 8/85). See *G. CONQUEST.*

TODHUNTER, JOHN
D. Poem. Alcestis. 8° 1879.
T. Helena in Troas (Hengler's, 17/5/86, *mat.*). 8° 1886
[Prepared in collaboration with *E. W. GODWIN.*]
Past. A Sicilian Idyll (Club Theatre, Bedford Park, 5/5/90; St G. 1/7/90; Vaud. 15/6/91). L.C. 8° 1890.
D.Sk. How Dreams come true (Grosvenor Gallery, 17/7/90).
D.Sk. The Poison Flower (Vaud. 15/6/91, *mat.*). L.C.
D. The Black Cat (Independent Theatre Soc. at O.C. 8/12/93). L.C.
C. The Comedy of Sighs (Aven. 29/3/94).

TOFT, P.
Ca. Out of the Frying Pan (Holb. 4/5/72). See *A. P. GRAVES.*

TOLKIEN, FREDERICK
O. Adela (Court, Wigan, 14/4/97). L.C.

"*TOMLINE, F. LATOUR.*" See *W. S. GILBERT*

TOMPKINS, GORDON
C.D. In One Day (Assembly R. Durham, 17/2/96). See *T. FELL.*

TOOLE, J. L.
F. Trying a Magistrate (Glo. 17/12/77).

TOPLIS, G. A.
F. In Want of a Wife (Park Lecture H. Camden Town, 14/2/85).
F. Tonight at 8 (Park Lecture H. Camden Town, 18/4/87). See *T. D. McCORD.*

"*TORR, A. C.*" See *F. LESLIE*

TOTTEN, R. C.
D. Death's Head Dick, the Skeleton Pirate; or, The Tigers of the Sea (Cambria, Merthyr Tydvil, 31/3/70).

TOWERS, EDWARD
Bsq. King, Queen and Knave; or, The Flower of Castille (Vic. 24/2/62).
D. The Demon Doctor (Eff. 21/1/67). L.C.
D. Carynthia (Eff. 13/3/67). L.C.
D. False Hands and Faithful Hearts (C.L. 22/4/67). L.C.
D. Ready and Willing (Eff. 13/5/67). L.C.
D. A Mine of Wealth (C.L. 1/7/67). L.C.
D. The Gray Ladye of Fernlea (C.L. 31/8/67). L.C.
D. Footmarks in the Snow (C.L. 14/10/67). L.C.

D. Brighter Days in Store (C.L. 23/11/67). L.C. as *The Gaoler's Daughter; or, B.D. in S.*
D. A Quarter of a Million of Money (E.L. 17/2/68). L.C. as *The Heiress and the Orphan; or, A. Q. of a M. of M.*
D. Black Hearts; or, The King of Darkness (E.L. 30/5/68). L.C.
D. Destiny; or, A Fight with Fate (E.L. 24/2/69). L.C.
D. This House to Let (E.L. 11/9/69). L.C.
D. The Twelve Angels (E.L. 6/11/69). L.C.
D. Not Found (E.L. 7/2/70). L.C.
D. The Fatal Marriage (E.L. 10/9/70). L.C.
D. The Bouquet; or, The Language of the Flowers (E.L. 24/10/70). L.C.
D. Honor Bright; A Story of the Stage (E.L. 18/4/70). L.C. with sub-title, *or, The Prompter's Story.*
D. Broken Vows; or, Love's Conflict (E.L. 18/2/71). L.C.
D. The Double Event (E.L. 10/4/71). L.C.
D. Twenty Thousand Pounds a Year (Pav. 18/9/71). L.C.
D. By Command of the King (Pav. 25/11/71). L.C. as *By the King's Command.*
D. Pride; or, The Usurer's Daughter (Pav. 20/5/72). L.C.
D. Woman's Trust; or, The Flower of Lucerne (Pav. 2/9/72). L.C.
D. Angling in Troubled Waters (Pav. 14/10/72). L.C.
D. Married for Money (Pav. 12/3/73). L.C. as *Mine; or, M. for M.*
D. The Divorce (Southminster, Edinburgh, 24/11/73).
C.D. Cheap Jack; or, Loved and Deceived (Pav. 6/4/74). L.C.
D. The Millionaire (Pav. 25/5/74). L.C.
D. Lancashire Life; or, Poor Joe the Factory Lad (Pav. 15/5/75). L.C.
D. La Gitana; or, Orphans of the Iron Chain (Pav. 15/4/76). L.C.
D. Death by the Law; or, The Iron Collar (Pav. 5/8/76). L.C.
D. Shamus-na-Lena; or, The Speidhair (L'pool, 6/3/76; Pav. 7/10/76).
D. Pomona (E.L. 13/1/77). L.C.
D. Boatmen of the Shannon (Pav. 24/2/77). L.C.
D. Honour among Thieves (Pav. 4/8/77). L.C.
D. On the Track; or, The Convict's Wife (E.L. 24/11/77). L.C.
D. The Thief Maker; or, Toiling up the Hill (E.L. 1/2/78). L.C.
D. Common Sense; or, The Slaves of Mammon (Pav. 11/5/78). L.C.
D. Trained to Crime (Pav. 28/9/78). L.C.
D. Committed for Trial (E.L. 30/11/78). L.C.
D. A Broken Lily (E.L. 24/12/78). L.C.
D. Love wins the Day (Pav. 12/7/79). L.C.
D. Bellamonde; or, The King's Avenger (Pav. 15/11/79). L.C.
D. Lady Lillian; or, Flowers of Joy and Flowers of Sorrow (Pav. 29/3/80). L.C. as *Lost Lady Lillian.*
D. The Workman (Pav. 9/10/80). L.C. as *Lily Lyle.*
D. Bella-go-faugh; or, The Foster Sisters (Pav. 13/11/80). L.C.
D. Our Polly (Pav. 16/4/81). L.C. as *Pretty Polly, the Farmer's Daughter.*
D. Cinderella (Pav. 4/6/81). L.C.
D. Jack in the Box (Pav. 5/11/81) L.C.
D. Eunice; or, Love and Duty (Pav. 6/11/82). L.C.

TOWERS, E. J.
D. The Nihilist (Castle Abertillery, 25/2/97). L.C.

TOWERS, FRANK
D. Grif (S. Shields, 9/4/77). L.C.
C.D. Grateful (Exeter, 23/4/77). L.C. S. Shields, 28/3/77.

TOWNE, LEONARD
D. Percy (Glo. 29/4/77). L.C.

TOWNER, Sergeant
D. Called to the Front (Brit. 29/4/85). L.C.
[Written in collaboration with *F. BEAUMONT*.]

TOWNLEY, A. HOUGHTON
F. Tootsie (Park H. Camden Town, 16/5/88).
C.D. Love Conquers; or, No Spy (Park H. Camden Town, 21/2/89).

TOWNROW, L.
P. Aladdin (Metro. Camberwell, 26/12/96). See *J. W. JONES*.

TOWNSEND, STEPHEN
D. Editha's Burglar (Bijou, Neath, 3/1/90). See *Mrs F. H. BURNETT*.
D. Nixie (Terry's, 7/4/90). See *Mrs F. H. BURNETT*.
C.D. A Lady of Quality (Ladb. H. 7/3/96). See *Mrs F. H. BURNETT*.

TOWNSEND, W. THOMPSON
[For his earlier plays see iv, 414.]
D. The Gold Fiend; or, The Demon Gamester (Qns. 5/50).
[This seems to be the same as, or an earlier version of, *The Gold Fiend of Australia*, L.C. Vic. 5/7/52.]
D. The Fatal Wedding Day (M'bone, 23/9/52).
D. The Cardinal's Daughter (M'bone, 27/9/52). L.C.
D. Old Adam; or, A Father's Dream (C.L. 6/8/53). L.C. *New British Theatre*.
D. The Flower Girl and the Convict Marquis (Sur. 1/11/55).
F. A Blow in the Dark (Sur. 3/12/55). L.C. *Lacy*.

TRACEY, F. THORPE
D. At Break of Day (Swiss Gdns. Shoreham, 12/12/94). L.C.
D. The Queen of the Night (W. Bromwich, 12/7/97; Stratford, 26/5/1902). L.C.
[Written in collaboration with *I. BERLIN*.]

TRAILL, F. T.
Bsq. Glaucus: A Fish Tale (Olym. 5/7/65). L.C.

TRAILL, H. D.
D. The Medicine Man (Lyc. 4/5/98). L.C. 8° 1891 [*priv.*]
[Written in collaboration with *R. S. HICHENS*.]

TRAVERS, WILLIAM
D. Il Trovatore (C.G. 10/5/55). See *W. E. SUTER*.
D. A Poor Girl's Temptations; or, A Voice from the Streets (C.L. 2/58). L.C.
D. Kathleen Mavourneen; or, St Patrick's Eve (Pav. 2/62). L.C.
D. The Boy Detective (Eff. 10/6/67). L.C.
D. Nearly Lost; or, Lights and Shadows in a Young Girl's Path (C.L. 5/8/67). L.C.
D. The Bride of the Wave (E.L. 12/10/67). L.C.
D. The Last Moment (E.L. 26/10/67). L.C.
D. All but One (Brit. 15/2/68). L.C.
D. The Tempest of the Heart (E.L. 18/3/68).

D. The Infanticide; or, A Trial for Life (Col. L'pool, 16/3/68).
D. The Knights of the Road; or, The Gipsy's Prophecy (M'bone, 13/4/68). L.C.
D. The Wolf of the Pyrenees (Brit. 13/4/68). L.C.
D. The Dark Side of the Great Metropolis (Brit. 11/5/68).
D. The Abyssinian War and the Death of King Theodore (Brit. 1/6/68). L.C.
D. Spring-heeled Jack (M'bone, 1/6/68). L.C. as *The Terror of London.*
D. Fair Words and Foul Deeds; or, The Children of the Abbey (E.L. 6/7/68). L.C.
D. Lady Anne's Well; or, The Warning Spirit (Brit. 20/7/68). L.C.
D. Wedded and Lost; or, The Perils of a Bride (Brit. 5/9/68).
D. Admiral Tom, King of the Buccaneers (Brit. 21/9/68).
D. St Valentine's Day; or, The Fatal Choice (E.L. 17/7/69). L.C. with titles reversed.
D. The Wanderer; or, A Gleam of Sunshine (Grec. 4/10/69). L.C.
D. At the Foot of the Ladder (E.L. 16/10/69). L.C.
D. Escaped; or, Thrice Married (E.L. 6/6/70). L.C.
D. The Emerald Queen (Brit. 18/7/70). L.C.
D. Strayed Away (E.L. 15/8/70). L.C.
D. One False Step; or, The Perils of a Beauty (Pav. 13/7/74). L.C.
D. Norah O'Neille (E.L. 22/12/76). L.C.

TRAVIS, W. J.
D. Erin-go-Bragh; or, The Milesian's Trust in Luck (Vic. 3/5/73). L.C.

TREE, Sir HERBERT BEERBOHM
D. Once upon a Time (H. 27/2/94). See *L. N. PARKER.*

TRESAHAR, JOHN
Ca. Favette (Vaud. 29/1/85). L.C.
C.D. Some Day (St G. 13/5/89). See *Mrs N. PHILLIPS.*
C.D. The Catspaw (Terry's, 24/7/89, *mat.*). L.C.
C. The Chinaman (City, Sheffield, 16/7/94; Traf. 13/9/94, as *Naughty Boys*). L.C.

TREVELYAN, CLAUDE
M.Ca. Fairy Madge; or, The Slavery of Drink (Park T.H. Battersea, 28/11/91). L.C.
M.C. The Twentieth-Century Girl; or, The Weaker Vessel (Norwich, 26/12/95). L.C.
C.D. My Guardie (P's. Kew Bridge, 19/12/96). L.C.
C.D. Those...put asunder (Central H. Acton, 15/12/97). L.C.

TREVOR, HARRY
D. In the Queen's Name (Colchester, 5/2/90; S.W. 15/12/90). L.C.
[Written in collaboration with *H. A. DELILLE.* Title altered to *In the King's Name*, 18/2/1901.]
C.O. The Lass of Richmond Hill (Richmond, 12/4/93)
[Music by B. Horner.]
C.O. The Commandant (Richmond, 26/4/94).
[Written in collaboration with *L. TREVOR.* Music by B. Horner.]
C.O. Good Queen Bess (Richmond, 1/5/95). L.C.
[Written in collaboration with *L. TREVOR.* Music by B. Horner.]

TREVOR, LEO

C.O. The Commandant (Richmond, 26/4/94). See *H. TREVOR.*

C.O. Good Queen Bess (Richmond, 1/5/95). See *H. TREVOR.*

D.Sk. Doctor Johnson (Richmond, 11/5/96; Str. 23/4/97). L.C.

C. Brother Officers (Gar. 20/10/98). L.C. Com. 12/2/98.

TREVOSPER, M.

M.D. The Snares of London (Stratford, 16/4/1900). See *W. BURNOT.*

TRIEVNOR, J. W.

Ca. Hunting a Fox (Portsmouth, 5/4/78).

TRISTRAM, W. OUTRAM

F.C. The Undergraduates (O.C. 6/10/86, *mat.*; Vaud. 21/12/86, as *The Referee*). L.C.

R.D. The Red Lamp (Com. 20/4/87). L.C.

D. The Panel Picture (O.C. 28/3/89). L.C.

D. The Queen of Manoa (H. 15/9/92). See *C. H. CHAMBERS.*

D. A Packet from England (Vic. H. Bayswater, 24/4/95). L.C.

TROLLOPE, ANTHONY

Ca. Did He Steal It? 8° 1869 [*priv.*].

TROUGHTON, ADOLPHUS C.

F. Living too fast; or, A Twelve Month's Honeymoon (P'cess. 9/10/54). L.C. *Lacy.*

C. Leading Strings (Olym. 19/10/57). L.C. *Lacy.*

F. Wooing in Jest and Loving in Earnest (Str. 1/11/58). L.C. *Lacy.*

F. Vandyke Brown (Str. 24/3/59). L.C. *Lacy.*

Ca. Shameful Behaviour (Str. 28/11/59). L.C. *Lacy.*

F. Short and Sweet (Str. 10/10/61). L.C. *Lacy.*

Ca. Unlimited Confidence (Str. 21/1/64). L.C. *Lacy.*

C. The Fly and the Web (Str. 5/2/66). *Lacy.*

TRYON, —

O. Ostrolenka (St G. 2/4/84). See — *WETHERILL.*

TULLOCK, AUGUSTA

D. The Web of Fate (Lecture H. Braintree, 9/10/99; E.C. 9/7/1900). L.C.

TULLY, JOHN HOWARD

[For his earlier plays see iv, 414.]

Bsq. Sambodampalus (Str. 11/7/53). L.C.

Bsq. The Very Earliest Edition of Il Trovatore; or, Who killed the —? (Roy. 26/12/61). L.C.

Oa. Which is it? (S.W. 12/7/62). L.C. with sub-title, *or, A Page's Escapade.*

TURNBULL, W.

D. Shall we remember? (Surrey Masonic H. Camberwell, 13/12/93; St G. 13/10/99). L.C. as *Too Late.*

[Written in collaboration with *R. C. ELLIS.*]

TURNER, EARDLY

Monol. The Chopper's Wedding Morn (St G. 4/4/89).

Bsq. Cavalearyer Costercana (Edmonton, 14/6/93). See *B. LANDECK.*

F. My Good Name (R.A. Woolwich, 24/2/96; Lyr. Hammersmith, 27/7/96). L.C.

M.C. That Terrible Turk and his Loving Legacy (Shakespeare, Clapham, 4/4/98). See *F. W. SIDNEY.*

TURNER, EDGAR

M.C. The President (Grand, Maidenhead, 19/10/96). See *J. M. FISHER.*

TURNER, GEORGE

D. The Spy: A Story of the American Rebellion (Nov. 30/11/89). L.C.

TURNER, H. C.

D. Founded on Facts (Qns. Keighley, 14/2/90).

TURNER, Rev. J. H.

C.O. The King's Cure (Warrington, 19/12/92).

TURNER, L. C.

D. Arling Lodge (Bath, 5/72).

TURNER, MONTAGUE

O.Bsq. Shylock; or, The Venus of Venice (Gateshead, 1/2/92). L.C. [Music by H. C. Barry.]

Oa. Sport; or, The Queen's Bounty (P's. Portsmouth, 6/6/95, *copy.*; Plymouth, 30/3/96; Parkhurst, 19/5/96). L.C. [Written in collaboration with *W. EDWARDES-SPRANGE.* Music by T. Hunter. Title altered to *The Seaside Girl*, 23/7/1902.]

M.C. The Tourist; or, Here, There and Everywhere (P's. Portsmouth, 5/11/95). L.C. [Music by T. Hunter.]

M.C. Odd Man Out (Grand, Nottingham, 19/4/97). L.C. [Written in collaboration with *F. DIX*; lyrics by *W. L. CLEMENT.* Music by S. Shaw and T. Hunter.]

M.C. Lord Dunnohoo (Aldershot, 5/7/97). See *R. REDGRAVE.*

D. For a Child's Sake (New, Cambridge, 2/1/99). See *H. HERMAN.*

["*TWAIN, MARK*" [*SAMUEL LANGHORNE CLEMENS*]

C.D. Colonel Sellers (California, San Francisco, 23/4/74, as *The Gilded Age*; Gai. 19/7/80). L.C. as *Gilded Age.*

TWEDDELL, EDWARD WASHINGTON

D. Napoleon's Barber. 8° 1857.

TWIGG, Lieut. JAMES

D. The Ruined Merchant. L.C. Sheffield, 27/1/51.

D. Deadly Sampson (Pav. 16/9/76). See *W. M. AKHURST.*

TWIST, J. C.

D. Adrift on the World (Pier Pav. Southend, 23/1/94).

TYLAR, WILLIAM

C. Fibs (Toole's, 14/6/82). L.C.

UNIACKE, JOHN

D. The Marquesa (O.C. 11/7/89, *mat.*). L.C.

UNSWORTH, EVELYN. See *Mrs J. B. ASHLEY*

UNWIN, W. E.

Oa. Zoriada (P.H. Sidcup, 9/1/91). [Music by R. Pickel.]

UPWARD, ALLEN

C. A Flash in the Pan (Gai. Dublin, 23/10/96; Shakespeare, Clapham, 9/5/98, as *A Cruel Heritage*). L.C. Court, L'pool, 18/11/96.

VAILE, —
D. Michaelmas Day; or, Eveline of the Hall (Sur. 12/5/51).

VALLINGS, HAROLD
D. Alexis (C.P. 26/11/85). L.C.

"*VAMP, HUGO.*" See *J. R. O'NEIL.*

VANCE, L.
O. Genoveva (D.L. 6/12/93).
[Version of the opera, libretto O. R. Reinick, music R. Schumann (Leipzig, 25/6/50).]

VANDENHOFF, Miss
D. Woman's Heart (H. 14/2/52). L.C.

VANDENHOFF, HENRY
D. Only a Woman's Hair (Warrington, 21/10/73).
D. Conscience (Alex. Sheffield, 13/11/77).

VANDERBILT, CORNELIUS
Oa. Cupid Incog. (St G. 12/6/88). L.C.
[Music by M. van Lennep.]

VANDERVELL, W. F.
Bsq. Prince Love; or, The Fays of the Forest (Phil. 26/12/70). L.C.
F. Mary's Holiday (Sur. 29/9/79). L.C.

VAN DE VELDE, Mme
D. Lena (Lyc. 9/7/89).
Ca. A Bijou Residence to Let (Nottingham, 18/9/89).

VANE, C. A.
M.C. Our Servant Girl (Edmonton, 15/6/96). See *F. LAWRENCE.*

VANE, FAWNEY
D. Honours (Grec. 4/10/79). L.C.

VANE, SUTTON
D. V.C. (Parkhurst, 13/4/91).
D. Terry; or, True to his Trust (Parkhurst, 27/4/91). L.C.
R.D. Vengeance is Mine (Assembly R. Cheltenham, 29/4/91, *copy.*; Pav. 22/2/92). L.C.
D. The Span of Life (Alex. Sheffield, 6/11/91, *copy.*; Grand, 6/6/92; P'cess. 18/5/96). L.C.
D. Then Flowers grew fairer (Lyr. H. Ealing, 18/2/92; Terry's, 30/8/94). L.C.
D. For England (Qns. Manchester, 27/2/93; Pav. 15/5/93). L.C.
D. Beyond the Breakers (Grand, 9/10/93). L.C.
D. The Cotton King (Adel. 10/3/94). L.C. as *The Scales of Justice.*
D. The Mask of Guilt (Sur. 21/6/94, *copy.*; Eden, Brighton, 29/10/94, as *Under the Mask of Truth*; Metro. Camberwell, 19/11/94). L.C. as *Under a Mask.*
D. Under Compulsion (P's. Accrington, 17/1/95, *copy.*). L.C.
D. The War of Wealth (Bolton, 8/2/95). See *C. F. DAZEY.*
M.D. John Martin's Secret (R.A. Woolwich, 30/9/95). L.C.
D. In Sight of St Paul's (P'cess. 1/8/96; P'cess. 26/6/97, *revised*).
D. Straight from the Heart (Pav. 3/8/96). L.C.
[Written in collaboration with *A. SHIRLEY.*]
D. The Bell Ringer (Plymouth, 27/5/97). See *A. SHIRLEY.*
M.Sk. His Masterpiece (Mat. 18/3/98). L.C.
[Music by E. Jones.]

M.D. The Leap for Life (Grand, Hebburn, 2/4/98, *copy.*; Imp. 13/6/98). L.C.
[Music by C. Callahan.]

D. None but the Brave (Brighton, 12/8/98, *copy.*). L.C.
[Written in collaboration with *A. SHIRLEY*. Title altered to *The Woman Pays*, 23/7/1902.]

D. The Crystal Globe (P'cess. 24/12/98). L.C.

D. Send Her Victorious (Pav. 13/11/99). L.C.
[A revised version of *For England* (Qns. Manchester, 27/2/93).]

VANLOO, A.

F.Oa. The Fifteenth of October (P.W. 8/8/91). See *E. LETERRIER*.

VANNECK, FREDERICK

D. False Steps (Bristol, 19/9/87). L.C. T.H. Newbury, 9/4/86.

D. Stormcoast (Glo. 11/12/88, *mat.*). L.C. Olym. 11/6/88.

D. A Social Pest (Nov. 3/1/91).

VARTY, W. R.

D. A Father's Sacrifice (School of Dramatic Art, 16/2/87).

VAUGHAN, A.

D. Weal or Woe (Rotherham, 10/4/78).

VAUGHAN, Mrs

C. Outwitted (St G. 14/7/71). L.C.

C.D. Monsieur Alphonse. L.C. Amphi. L'pool, 16/6/75.

C. Mated (Crit. 28/6/79). L.C.

VAUGHAN, W. J.

C.D. Another Man's Wife (P's. Blackburn, 7/8/93; Grand, Croydon, 28/5/1900; Shakespeare, Clapham, 4/6/1900). L.C.
[Written in collaboration with *R. F. MACKAY*.]

VAUN, RUSSELL

D.Sk. The Polka (Ladb. H. 19/3/95; Grand, 3/6/95). L.C.

F. Aunt Rebecca (O.H. Cheltenham, 19/12/95). See *A. ATWOOD*.

D. What might have been (Rivière's O.H. Llandudno, 14/5/96; Bijou, 19/12/96; Wyndham's, 13/12/1900). L.C.

F. A Tale of a Tub (New, Cambridge, 22/10/96). L.C.
[Written in collaboration with *A. ATWOOD* and *W. BOOTH*.]

F. Caroline's Pupils; or, Mrs Hardup's Advertisement (Bijou, 19/12/96). L.C.
[Written in collaboration with *A. ATWOOD*.]

Ca. Mrs H— will give Lessons in Lovemaking (Parkhurst, 12/3/97). See *A. ATWOOD*.

F.C. Oh! Susannah! (Eden, Brighton, 6/9/97). See *M. AMBIENT*.

Ca. The Little Culprit (Pleasure Gdns. Folkestone, 19/11/97). See *A. ATWOOD*.

C. C'est la vie (Mat. 6/5/98). L.C.

C. Nicandra (New, Cambridge, 2/6/98; Parkhurst, 3/10/98). L.C.
[Also acted as *A Classical Trip*.]

VELLÈRE, Dr —

D. Meted Out! *French* [1873].

D. King and Rebel. *French* [*c.* 1873].

VERE, CHARLES C.

D. In the Dead of Night (Hanley, 13/8/77).

D. Diana an Adventuress (Scarborough, 29/3/80). L.C.

VEREKER, S.
C.D. Jack o' Hearts (Mechanics' Inst. Swindon, 26/3/94). L.C. [Written in collaboration with *W. H. DEARLOVE.*]

VERICOUR, — DE
D. The Gladiator of Ravenna. 8° 1859.

VERNEY, MAURICE DE
F. The Lodgers (Glo. 18/1/87). See *B. THOMAS.*

VERNON, C.
D.Sk. Sowing and Reaping (Crit. 5/6/90, *mat.*; Crit. 5/7/90). L.C.
D. Shamus O'Brien (W.L. 26/4/97). See *F. MAEDER.*

VERNON, G. C.
C.D. Cupid in Camp (Crit. 22/5/82). L.C. as *Love's Device.*

VERNON, Capt. LEICESTER
D. The Lancers; or, The Gentleman's Son (P'cess. 1/11/53). L.C. *Lacy.*

VERNON, PERCY H.
D. After Ten Years (Metro. Birkenhead, 21/10/92). L.C.

VERNON, W. H.
D. The Loadstone (Lyc. 7/4/88). See *T. E. PEMBERTON.*
Ca. The Letter (Gateshead, 6/5/91).

VEZIN, HERMANN
D. Doctor Davy (Greenwich, 6/2/65; Lyc. 4/6/66). See *J. ALBERY.*
C. The Little Viscount (Gai. 2/8/84).
C. Bachelors (H. 1/9/84). See *R. BUCHANAN.*
C. Claimants (Assembly R. Worthing, 28/9/91; Mat. 15/11/98). L.C.
C. Mrs M.P. (Assembly R. Worthing, 28/9/91; O.C. 1/12/91, *mat.*). L.C.
C. Cousin Jack (Assembly R. Worthing, 30/9/91; O.C. 12/11/91). L.C.

VICARS, W. A. ["*TAYLOR BILKINS*"]
F. In Three Volumes (Str. 27/2/71). L.C.
F. A Christmas Pantomime (Court, 26/12/71). L.C. *Lacy.*
F. Down among the Coals (Court, 15/11/73). L.C.
F. Shank's Mare (Duke's, 9/2/78). L.C. Str. 28/2/77.
F.C. Going it (Roy. Glasgow, 13/11/85). See *J. M. MORTON.*

"*VICARSON, A.*"
C. The Vicar's Dilemma (Clarendon, Watford, 31/1/98; Terry's, 11/7/98). L.C.

VICTOR, HOWELL
D. Carolan (T.H. Bootle, L'pool, 13/1/92, *amat.*). L.C.

VIESON, CHARLES
C.D. Today (Aven. 7/8/95, *copy.*; Grand, Hull, 26/8/95). L.C.

VILLARS, GEORGE
C. Lady Lovington; or, A Soirée Dramatique (Athen. Tottenham Court Road, 28/6/88; Ladb. H. 24/3/90; St G. 28/6/94).

VILLIERS, E.
D. Joan of Arc (E.L. 26/8/71). L.C.

[*VINCENT, C. T.*
D. Gentleman Jack (D.L. 21/4/94). L.C.
[Written in collaboration with *W. BRADY.*]
C. Little Miss Cute (Roy. 14/9/94). L.C.

VINCENT, E. HOWARD
C.D. The Baronet (Bury, 3/7/85).

VINCENT, GEORGE F.
Oa. Romany Lore (St G. 2/4/89). L.C. Winter Gdns. Morecambe, as *Romany Revels; or, The Bo Girl up-to-date.*

VINCENT, W. T.
Bsq. Cinder-Ellen, up too late (Gai. 24/12/91). See *F. LESLIE.*
P. The Babes in the Wood (R.A. Woolwich, 24/12/97). See *M. BYAM.*

VINING, —
D. Barnaby Rudge (P'cess. 12/11/66). See *W. PHILLIPS.*

VIRGO, J. T.
Bsq. Dick Whittington and his Cat (Qns. Battersea, 26/12/94).
[Written in collaboration with *C. W. McCABE.*]

VOKES, VICTORIA
D. In Camp (P.W. L'pool, 24/9/83). L.C.

VOLLAIRE, H.
D. Who did it? or, The Mystery of Rosedale Hollow (Scarborough, 11/5/75).

VORZANZER, CHARLES
D. Her Retaliation (S. Hackney Club, Homerton, 18/11/89).

VOTIERI, ADELINE
Ca. A Fool's Trick (St G. 20/6/91). L.C.
F.C. Prudes and Pro's (St G. 20/6/91). L.C.
Duol. An Unknown Quantity (Bijou, 29/2/97). L.C.
[Music by D. Harrison.]
C.D. The Syndicate (Mat. 16/6/97). L.C.
C. That Charming Mrs Spencer (Lyc. Ipswich, 18/11/97). L.C.

VROOM, EDWARD
C. Marsac of Gascony (P.W. Birmingham, 11/11/99). L.C.

VYE, BIRCH
D. "1870" (W. Hartlepool, 22/8/96, *copy.*; Grand, Birmingham, 11/9/96). L.C.

VYNNE, CHARLES
D. Annie of Edenside; or, The Coquette Cured (Bijou, Carlisle, 27/2/68).
C. Vincent Veriphleet; or, He couldn't say No (Bijou, Carlisle, 5/8/69).

VYNNE, NORA
D. Aftermath (Bijou, 22/6/93). L.C.
D. Andrew Paterson (Bijou, 22/6/93). L.C.
[Written in collaboration with *ST J. E. C. HANKIN.*]

"*VYSE, BERTIE.*" See *ARTHUR W. À BECKETT*

VYSE, BURDETT
R.O. The Last Crusade. L.C. Soho, 28/10/50.
[Music by A. Mitchell.]

WADDIE, CHARLES

D. Wallace; or, The Battle of Stirling Bridge (T.H. Stirling, 10/9/98). L.C.

T. Dunbar; or, The King's Advocate (Athen. Glasgow, 2/10/99). L.C.

T.C. The Heir of Linn (Athen. Glasgow, 9/10/99). L.C.

C. The Unmasked (Athen. Glasgow, 23/10/99). L.C.

WADE, C. B.

C.O. The Maypole; or, Mad for Love (Limerick, 6/10/87).
[Written in collaboration with *S. ELLIOT.*]

WADE, FLORENCE

C.Sk. Madge (St G. 10/3/91; Roy. 3/9/92). L.C. Alex. Southend, 14/7/90.
[Written in collaboration with *H. AUSTIN.*]

WADE, FRANK E.

R.D. The Golden Leek (Assembly R. Tenby, 5/3/91). L.C.

WAGNER, LEOPOLD

D. Passion and Principle (S.W. 9/6/83). L.C.

P. Cinderella (M'bone, 27/12/86). L.C.

F. Peaceful War (P.W. 24/5/87). See *S. SCOTTI.*

WAKELY, CHARLES

D. Paul Rabant. 12° 1878. See *J. E. BENNETT.*

WALBY, —

O. Benvenuto Cellini (C.G. 25/6/53). L.C.
[Music by Berlioz.]

WALCH, GARNET

F. Helen's Babies (Gai. 15/9/78). L.C. Birmingham, 5/8/78.

D. Robbery under Arms (P'cess. 22/10/94). See *A. DAMPIER.*

[*WALCOT, C. M.*

F. Nothing to Nurse (Str. 13/9/58).

WALCOT, MARIA GRACE

D. The Cup and the Lip (Olym. 21/10/86). *French.*

WALDAN, OTTO

Oa. Returning the Compliment (Park H. Camden Town, 5/11/90). L.C.
[Written in collaboration with *F. G. PALMER.* Music by H. T. Wood.]

WALDEN, R.

P. Beauty and the Beast (Park, 24/12/79). L.C.

WALDEN, W.

P. Harlequin Little Red Riding Hood (Park, 24/12/80). See *L. RAE.*

WALDRON, W. RICHARD

D. Woman and her Master; or, The Lost Children. L.C. Pav. 2/6/54.

D. The Will and the Way; or, The Mysteries of Carrow Alley (Leeds, 19/4/60).

D. Lizzie Leigh; or, The Murder near the Old Mill: A Story of Three Christmas Nights (C.L. 14/9/63). L.C.

D. Right and Might; or, The Call of Fate. L.C. Grec. 29/9/64.

D. The Toilers of the Thames; or, The Dark Side of London Life (Grec. 1/3/69). L.C.
D. Ruth Lee (Amphi. Leeds, 1/5/69).
D. Found Dead in the Streets (Cheltenham, 30/8/69; Grec. 14/4/73, as *Dead in the Streets; or, All for Gold*). L.C.
D. Outcast Joe; or, The Street Arab (Bolton, 28/3/70). L.C. Gar. 19/9/71, as *The Street Arab; or, Adrift on the World.*
C.D. Worth a Struggle (K.X. 18/2/71). L.C. *Lacy.*
D. The Diver's Luck (Jarrow, 30/5/87). See *F. COOKE.*
D. A Terrible Secret (Free Trade H. Colne, 30/9/89).
D. The New Mazeppa (Morton's, Greenwich, 24/3/90). See *F. COOKE.*
D. The Great Diamond Robbery (S.W. 10/10/92). See *B. DELANNOY.*
D. A Sailor's Honour (Lincoln, 8/6/94). See *A. CARLTON.*
D. The Scales of Justice (Stand. 10/12/94). L.C.
D. Baby; or, The Midnight Trust (P's. Preston, 23/3/96; Brit. 1/5/99, as *A Midnight Trust*). L.C.
[Written in collaboration with *L. ELLIS.*]

WALFORD, Miss H. L.
D. A Lost Life (G.I. 24/11/70, *amat.*). L.C. as *A Life Lost.*
Bsq. The Veiled Prophet of Korassan; or, The Maniac, the Mystery and the Malediction (G.I. 24/11/70, *amat.*). L.C.
D. Ambition (G.I. 14/12/70).
Bsq. Edwin and Angelina; or, The Children of Mystery (G.I. 6/5/71, *amat.*). L.C.
C. Weeds (G.I. 6/5/71, *amat.*). L.C.
D. Impeached (G.I. 24/5/73). L.C.
Ca. Lord Fitzharris (G.I. 24/5/73). L.C.

WALKER, GEORGE RALPH
D. Sithors to Grind (Edinburgh, 7/4/73). L.C.
D. Coming Home (Glo. 5/7/73).
C. Loving and Scheming (Brighton, 16/3/74). L.C.
D. Twine the Plaidon; or, The Improvisatore (Plymouth, 10/8/77; Glo. 22/5/78). L.C.
C.D. A Mad Revenge (Scarborough 2/2/80; Stand. 4/6/83, as *Uncle Zac; or, A M.R.*). L.C.
Ca. In the Orchard (Folly, 14/2/80). L.C.
Oa. School of (He)Arts; or, The Maids of Merrie England (Park, 27/3/80). L.C.
D. The Madman (Gloucester, 6/5/81). L.C.

WALKER, MILLER
D. The Haven of Rest; or, A Mother's Love (Worksop, 14/3/68).

WALKER, WILLIAM
D. The Trail of the Serpent (Armoury, Huddersfield, 18/1/81).

WALKES, W. R.
F. A Pair of Lunatics (D.L. 1889).
F. A Show of Hands (Grosvenor House, Park Lane, 6/3/90).
Ca. Miss Cinderella (Aven. 15/3/90). L.C.
D.Sk. Her New Dressmaker (Newcastle, 18/12/91; St G. 13/5/95). *French.*
D.Sk. Gentleman Jim (Shakespeare, L'pool, 1/11/93). L.C.

D.Sk. Rain Clouds (Qns. H. Langham Place, 21/5/94).
Duol. Villain and Victim (H. 11/12/94).
C. Mary Pennington, Spinster (St J. 24/4/96). L.C.

WALLACE, J. R.
D. A Society Saint (St G. 16/1/92). L.C.

WALLACE, MARGARET
D. Tiger Lily (St G. 16/1/92). L.C.

WALLACK, A.
D. Coward Conscience (Roy. Glasgow, 10/9/88). See *C. A. BYRNE.*

[*WALLACK, LESTER*
C.D. The Romance of a Poor Young Man (Wallack's, New York, 24/1/60). L.C. Qns. 23/11/60. *Lacy.*
C.D. Rosedale (Wallack's, New York, 30/9/63; P.W. Wolverhampton, 1/5/76).
D. A Wild Goose (H. 29/4/67). See *D. BOUCICAULT.*

WALLER, F.
Ca. Queen Stork (P.W. 17/9/70). L.C.

WALLERSTEIN FERDINAND
C.O. Quick March (Qns. 5/2/70). L.C.

WALLERTON, MYLES
D. A London Arab (Pleasure Gdns. Folkestone, 20/3/99; Sur. 10/4/99). L.C. Stratford, 30/12/98.
[Written in collaboration with *F. GILBERT*. Title altered to *A French Jezebel*, 8/4/1903.]

WALROND, J. R.
D. The Shadow of Death (Vic. 25/9/76). L.C.

WALTER, T. NORMAN
Ca. A Clear Conscience (Lincoln, 14/10/89). L.C.
D. The Golden Serpent (Stratford, 15/11/97). L.C.
M.D. The Mermaid (Alex. Sheffield, 31/5/98; Grand, Chorley, 26/12/98. L.C.
[Music by R. W. Manning.]

WALTERS, F.
D. The Life of a Pottery Lass (Pottery, Hanley, 9/3/69).
F. Quite by Accident (P.W. 11/9/69). L.C.

"*WALTERS, ROBERT.*" See *GEORGE ROBERTS.*

WALTHER, H.
O.Bsq. Tell Re-told (St G. 17/2/94). See *H. W. CAPPER.*

WALTON, GEORGE
M.C. Living Models (Maidenhead, 5/5/98).

WALTON, HENRY
D. Fooled by Fortune (L'pool, 28/9/74).

WALTON, KATE A.
D. Drop by Drop; or, Old England's Curse (Adel. L'pool, 24/3/84). L.C.

WALTON, T.

M.C. Lady Dorothy's Scheme (Art Gallery, Newcastle, 24/6/95). L.C. [Music by W. Bendall.]

WALTON, WALTER

P. The Sleeping Beauty and the Mystic Yellow Dwarf (Parkhurst, 26/12/95). L.C. [Music by T. P. Fish.]

WALTON, WILLIAM

P. Robinson Crusoe (Parkhurst, 26/12/91). L.C.

P. Cinderella (W.L. 24/12/95). L.C.

WAR, CARLO

C. Auntie's Motor (Manor, Hackney, 26/2/99). See *G. JOHN*.

WARBURTON, H.

D.Sk. Playmates (Stratford, 13/8/88, *copy*.). L.C.

[*WARD, ARTEMUS*

Monol. Among the Mormons (Egyptian H. 13/11/66).

WARD, ARTHUR H.

C.O. Cinderella the First (Bijou, Neath, 29/8/92). [Music by H. Vernon.]

C.O. Sir Jack o' Lantern, the Knight of (K)nights; or, A Curious Curse Curiously Cured (Bijou, Neath, 31/8/92). L.C. [Music by H. Vernon.]

D. The Heiress of Maes-y-Felin; or, The Flower of Llandovery (Vic. Merthyr Tydvil, 2/2/93, *copy*.). L.C.

C.O. Le Bal Masqué (Parkhurst, 16/5/98). [Music by H. Vernon.]

D. The Shadow of the Cross; or, Anno Domini 670 (Stratford, 26/9/1904). L.C. Pav. Redditch, 10/10/98.

WARD, CHARLES E. D.

C. A Leader of Men (Com. 9/2/95).

"*WARD, E. V.*" [*WILLIAM ARCHER* and *E. R. V. DIBDIN*]

Oa. Blue and Buff; or, The Great Muddleborough Election (Bijou, L'pool, 24/1/80; H. 5/9/81). L.C. [Music by W. L. Frost.]

WARD, EDGAR

D. The Shadow of a Crime (Qns. Manchester, 19/12/87). L.C.

M.D. Tricky Esmeralda (W.L. 13/2/97). See *W. E. BAILEY*.

WARD, MONTGOMERY A.

C.O. The Fisherman's Daughter (Qns. Dublin, 15/2/92). [Music by Mrs G. A. Curran.]

WARDEN, FLORENCE

D. The House on the Marsh (Nottingham, 2/3/85; Stand. 1/6/85). L.C.

D. In the Lion's Mouth (Bath, 25/9/85). L.C.

D. Uncle Mike (Terry's, 8/12/92). L.C.

D. The Guinea Pigs (P'cess. of W. Kennington, 24/7/99). L.C.

WARDEN, GERTRUDE

Duol. Woman's Proper Place (St J. 29/6/96). See *J. W. JONES*.

D. A Cruel City; or, London by Night (Sur. 5/10/96). L.C. [Written in collaboration with *J. W. JONES*.]

WARDHAUGH, MATTHEW

D. The Dead Man's Hollow (Longton, 4/10/69).

D. Found Dying in the Streets; or, A Will made in a Snowdrift on the Flyleaf of a Rake's Diary (Qns. Barnsley, 21/3/70).

D. Angela; or, Faithful and True (Qns. Barnsley, 23/1/71).

D. Light and Dark; or, The Wreck of the Ship Silver Star (Longton, 30/10/71; Qns. Barnsley, 29/1/72).

D. Herod the Tetrarch (Qns. Barnsley, 16/2/74).

D. Found Dying; or, The Watchman's Secret (E.C. 21/5/77). L.C.

D. The Indian Queen; or, A Home in the Mountains (Vic. 24/12/77). L.C.

D. Dormea, the Lawyer's Daughter (Vic. Longton, 2/9/78). L.C.

D. Lord Halifax (Longton, 14/10/78). L.C.

WARDROPER, HENRY

O.F. The Fancy Ball; or, Nubby the Q.C. (O.H. Ipswich, 11/2/89). [Music by W. T. Meadows.]

WARDROPER, WALTER

C.O. The Miraculous Doll (Sheffield, 12/7/86). [Music by A. Adam.]

WARE, J. REDDING

D. The Death Trap; or, A Catspaw (Grec. 6/6/70). L.C.

D. The Polish Jew; or, The Sledge Bells (Grec. 4/3/72). L.C.

D. Bothwell. *Dicks.*

D. The Juggler; or, Father and Daughter. *Dicks.*

WARHAM, W.

Bsq. Silver Gilt; or, Ado about Nothing (Str. 9/6/83). L.C.

WARLOW, PERCY

D. A Devil's Device (Grand, Stalybridge, 19/8/95). L.C.

F. That Awful Legacy (Grand, Stalybridge, 27/9/98). L.C.

WARMAN, J. I.

C.D. A Silver Wedding (Co-operative Assembly R. Coventry, 2/2/85). L.C.

WARNER, A.

D. The Three Warnings; or, Ruin, Degradation and Death (Hanley, 20/10/73).

WARNER, CHARLES

D. Drink (P'cess. 2/6/79). See *C. READE.*

WARR, —

T. The Story of Orestes (P's. H. 13/5/86).

T. The Story of Troy (P's. H. 14/5/86).

WARREN, ERNEST

C. Borrowed (New X. H. 17/9/85). L.C.

C.D. One Fault: A Home Story (Wigan, 9/10/85). [Written in collaboration with *C. ELLIOTT.*]

C. Antoinette Rigaud (St J. 13/2/86). L.C.

Ca. The Nettle (Court, 13/10/86). L.C. *French.*

F. Modern Wives (Roy. 20/1/87). L.C.

WARREN, F. BROOKE

D. The Face at the Window (P's. Blackburn, 17/6/97, *copy.*; Regent, Salford, 26/7/97; W.L. 1/5/99). L.C.

D. An Evil Life (Smethwick, 19/9/98).

D. The Poisoner of Milan (Darwen, 7/11/98; Stratford, 10/7/99). L.C.

D. How Money's Made (Regent, Salford, 31/7/99). L.C.

WARREN, J. L.

Poet.D. Orestes. 8° 1871.

Poet.D. Philoctetes. 8° 1871.

WARREN, T. GIDEON

F.C. Nita's First (Oxford, 14/12/83; Nov. 4/3/84).

F.C. Chums (Pav. Southport, 8/5/85). L.C.

F.C. Our Tuner (Shrewsbury, 15/10/85; Crit. 2/12/86, *mat.* as *My Bonny Boy*). L.C.

Ca. Ned Knowles (O.C. 5/2/87). L.C. Athen. Lancaster, 12/8/85.

D. The Tongue of Slander (Stand. 17/10/87). L.C.
[Written in collaboration with *J. T. DOUGLASS.*]

F.C. His Wives (Str. 23/5/88). L.C. as *Bigamy*.

C. Daughters (Portsmouth, 30/6/90; Str. 15/4/91, *mat.* as *Our Daughters*; Str. 22/4/91). L.C.
[Written in collaboration with *W. EDOUIN.*]

Ca. Houp-la! (Com. 18/8/91). L.C.
[Title altered to *Rosabelle*, 24/10/91.]

C. The Sculptor (Leinster H. Dublin, 18/8/93). L.C. Roy. Chester, 19/7/93.
[Written in collaboration with *J. CRAFT.*]

Ca. The Interview (Gar. 11/11/95). L.C.

D. Nannie (O.C. 16/11/95). L.C.

D. The Hand of Providence (Sur. 2/8/97). L.C.

WARRINER, G. A.

D. Coraline; or, Snares and Pitfalls (K.X. 27/2/73).

WARRINGTON, F.

D. All but lost; or, The Totem of the Tortoise (Dundee, 11/10/69).

D. A March on Magdala (Qns. Dublin, 21/2/70).

WARWICK, HUBERT S.

D. The Honour of the House (Corn Exchange, Driffield, 25/7/93). See *C. T. HOLDERNESS.*

D. Fetters of Passion (Eden, Bishops Auckland, 12/1/94). L.C.
[Written in collaboration with *C. T. HOLDERNESS.*]

C.D. The House of Sleep (Assembly R. Balham, 6/12/97). L.C.

WATERS, J.

D. Maid of Honour (Dublin, 25/2/99). L.C. New, Cambridge, 13/4/99.

WATNEY, REX

D. The Tidal Hour (Vic. H. Bayswater, 1/2/90, *amat.*).

WATSON, A. E. T.

D. Pendarvon (Alex. L'pool, 2/3/74).
[Written in collaboration with *W. S. CLARKE.*]

[*WATSON, F.*

Ca. A Bachelor's Wife (N.Y. 11/1/58; D.L. 29/10/60). L.C.

WATSON, F. MARRIOT

D. The Wide World (P's. Blackburn, 8/7/95). L.C.
[Title altered to *An Evil Life*, 26/7/98.]

D. The Trail of the Serpent (Gai. Burnley, 6/7/96). L.C.

D. The Black Mask (St J. Manchester, 31/7/99; Stratford, 29/12/1902). L.C.

WATSON, H. B. MARRIOTT

D. Richard Savage (Crit. 16/4/91). See *Sir J. M. BARRIE.*

WATSON, J. S. W.

Ca. The Banshee's Spell (Torquay, 22/5/82). L.C. as *The Blush Rose; or, The Fairy Tempter.*

WATSON, T. MALCOLM

Oa. A Lesson in Magic (R.A. Woolwich, 27/4/83). L.C.

Vaud. A Pretty Bequest (St G. 29/6/85).
[Music by H. Clarke.]

M.Ca. In Cupid's Court (St G. 30/11/85).
[Music by A. J. Caldicott.]

Ca. By Special Request (Str. 7/2/87). L.C.

M.Ent. Tally-Ho! (St G. 9/11/87). L.C.
[Music by A. J. Caldicott.]

M.C. "Wanted, an Heir" (St G. 2/4/88). L.C.
[Music by A. J. Caldicott.]

D. Held Asunder (P.W. 3/4/88, *mat.*). L.C.

C. Polly's Venture (Gai. 9/8/88). L.C.

C.D. Calumny (Shaft. 4/4/89, *mat.*). L.C.

Bsq. Tuppins and Co. (St G. 24/6/89). L.C.

F. Christopher's Honeymoon (Str. 3/7/89, *mat.*). L.C.

M.Vaud. The Sentry (Lyr. 5/4/90). See *F. RÉMO.*

M.Sk. Carnival Time (St G. 7/4/90).
[Music by C. Grain.]

D. The Pharisee (Shaft. 17/11/90). L.C.
[Written in collaboration with *E. LANCASTER-WALLIS.*]

C.D. Rachel's Messenger (P'cess. 28/2/91). L.C.

D.Sk. Killiecrumper (St G. 30/3/91). L.C.
[Music by E. Solomon.]

C.D. Man and Woman (O.C. 25/3/93). See *H. C. DE MILLE.*

Duol. A Drawn Battle (O.C. 17/4/93). L.C.

D.Sk. An Odd Pair (St G. 10/7/93). L.C.
[Music by A. J. Caldicott.]

M.F. A Big Bandit (St G. 30/4/94). L.C. as *The Biter Bit.*
[Music by W. Slaughter.]

M.C.D. Melodramania (St G. 20/12/94). L.C.
[Music by W. Slaughter.]

C.D. The Haven of Content (P's. Bristol, 22/10/96; Gar. 17/11/96). L.C.

WATSON, W. G.

F.Sk. His Son-in-law (Herne Bay, 12/9/90).
[Written in collaboration with *A. RODMAN.*]

WATSON, W. R.

D. A Sailor's Honour (Lincoln, 8/6/94). See *A. CARLTON.*

WATTS, F. J.

Bsq. Little Boy Blue (Swiss Gdns. Shoreham, 17/5/75).

WAUGH, ARTHUR

Oa. Corney Courted (Com. 6/3/93, *mat.*). L.C.
[Music by C. Nugent.]

WEATHERLEY, A.

D. A Bitter Lesson (Lyr. 15/5/96). See *J. R. HARRIS-BURNLAND.*

F. "Wanted, a Typewriter" (Assembly R. Portishead, 16/7/96). See *J. R. HARRIS-BURNLAND.*

WEATHERLEY, FREDERICK EDWARD

T. King René's Daughter (Edinburgh, 2/10/73). 8° 1872 [Bristol].

O. Rustic Chivalry (Court, L'pool, 14/1/92).
[Music by Mascagni.]

R.O. Amy Robsart (C.G. 20/7/93).
[Written in collaboration with *Sir A. HARRIS.* Music by I. de Lara.]

O. Signa (C.G. 30/6/94). See *G. A. À BECKETT.*

O. Mirette (Sav. 3/7/94). See *H. GREENBANK.*

O. The Lady of Longford (C.G. 21/7/94). See *Sir A. HARRIS.*

WEBB, CHARLES

[For his earlier plays see iv, 417.]

Ent. The Great Exhibition of 1851 (Sur. 5/5/51).

F. Your Head's in Peril (S.W. 17/2/51).

D. Woman (Grec. 5/7/52).

F. Webb worried by Wyndham (Adel. Edinburgh, 17/8/52).

D. The Betting Boy (Adel. Edinburgh, 13/9/52).

D. The Bohemian Gipsy and the Duel at the Willows; or, The Lone House on the Bridge (Vic. 28/3/62).

D. Thc Garret Angel (M'bone, 11/8/67).

D. The Lady of the Lake (Glasgow, 14/8/71).

D. 1679 (Glasgow, 23/9/72).

WEBB, GEORGE

D. Ye Merrie England; or, The Days of the Second Charles (L'pool, 12/11/77).

WEBB, MARION GRACE

D. Puck; or, The Lass o' Moorside (Bournemouth, 13/8/83; Athen. Shepherd's Bush, 31/7/84; Olym. 18/4/85, as *Heartless*). L.C.

WEBB, THOMAS H.

P. Harlequin and the World of Flowers (Vic. 27/12/52).

F. New Tontine (Qns. 27/6/53).

P. Harlequin Charity Brat; or, The Christmas Piece (Grec. 26/12/53). L.C.

D. Turned out to starve; or, The Hand that governs all (Brit. 21/2/70). L.C.

WEBBER, HARRY

M.D. The Haunted Glen (R.A. Woolwich, 27/4/88). L.C.
[Written in collaboration with *M. DAVIS.* Music by A. Mills.]

WEBSTER, AUGUSTA

T. The Prometheus Bound of Æschylus. 8° 1866.

T. The Medea of Euripides. 8° 1867.

D. The Sentence. 8° 1887.

Poet.D. In a Day (Terry's, 30/5/90, *mat.*). L.C. 8° 1882.

WEBSTER, BENJAMIN, the Younger

[For his earlier plays see *E.N.D.* ii, 407.]

Ca. A Gray Mare (Adel. 11/2/63). L.C.

D. Aurora Floyd (Adel. 11/3/63). L.C.

D. The Trumpeter's Daughter (D.L. 22/4/63).

Ca. A Woman of Business (Adel. 29/8/64). L.C.

C.D. The Hen and Chickens (Adel. 1/9/64). L.C. *Lacy.*

F. Behind Time (Adel. 26/12/65). L.C.

C.D. The Fast Family (Adel. 5/5/66).

D. Ethel; or, Only a Life (Adel. 13/10/66). L.C.

D. The Grasshopper (Olym. 14/8/67).

D. Man is not perfect, nor Woman neither (Adel. 14/10/67). L.C.

F. The Laughing Hyena (Col. Glasgow, 28/11/67). *Lacy.*

C. From Grave to Gay (Olym. 4/12/67). L.C.

D. Eve (Adel. 31/5/69). L.C.

D. Frou-Frou; or, A School for Levity (Brighton, 14/3/70; St J. 14/4/70, as *F.F.; or, Fashion and Passion*). L.C.

Ca. Smoke (Adel. 26/12/70). L.C.

F. Just like Roger (Adel. 15/4/72). L.C. *Lacy.*

F. A Yule Log (Adel. 17/2/73). L.C. *Lacy*

[Evidently a revised version of *The Yule Log* (Olym. 22/2/47).]

D. The Woman of the People (Amphi. L'pool, 17/2/77; Olym. 5/8/78). L.C.

D. The Drunkard (Holte, Birmingham, 29/9/79). M.S. Birmingham.

WEBSTER, BENJAMIN NOTTINGHAM

[For his earlier plays see iv, 417–18.]

D. None but the Brave deserve the Fair (H. 8/6/50). L.C.

C.D. Giralda; or, The Miller's Wife (H. 12/9/50). L.C. *Lacy.*

[See note under *D. BOUCICAULT.*]

D. Belphegor the Mountebank; or, The Pride of Birth (Adel. 13/1/51). L.C. *Webster.*

D. The Courier of Lyons (Adel. 10/3/51). L.C. *Dicks.*

D. The Queen's Secret; or, The Iron Mask (Adel. 8/9/51). L.C.

C. The Man of Law (H. 9/12/51). L.C. *Webster.*

C.D. The Queen of the Market (Adel. 12/4/52). See *H. C. COAPE.*

F. Keeley worried by Webster (H. 5/6/52). See *M. LEMON.*

F. A Novel Expedient (H. 30/6/52; Court, 12/6/75, as *Book the Third, Chapter the First*). L.C. *Webster.*

D. The Discarded Son (Adel. 10/10/53). L.C. *Webster.*

D. The Thirst of Gold; or, The Lost Ship and the Wild Flower of Mexico (Adel. 5/12/53). L.C. *Lacy.*

[Title altered to *The Prayer in the Storm*, 25/4/74.]

F. Boots at the Holly Tree Inn; or, The Infant Elopement to Gretna Green (Adel. 4/2/56). L.C.

D. One Touch of Nature (Adel. 6/8/59). L.C. *Lacy.*

WEBSTER, Miss DAVIES

C. Mine Hostess (Bijou, 12/6/99). L.C.

WEBSTER, JAMES

D. Two Men and a Maid (Com. 20/6/93). See *F. H. PURCHASE.*

WEBSTER, J. PROVAND

F. A Voice from the Bottle (P'cess. 17/3/88). L.C.

D. His Last Stake (P'cess. 24/4/88). L.C.

WEBSTER, N. S.

F. I'll tell your Wife; or, Highly improper (Adel. 10/3/55). L.C.

WEDMORE, FREDERICK

D. The Farm by the Sea (Vaud. 29/5/89, *mat.*). L.C.

WEEMORE, —

P. The Forty Thieves; or, Abdalla's Arrys (S.W. 24/12/79). L.C.

WEIL, OSCAR

C.O. The Daughter of the Regiment (P's. Bristol, 13/10/90).
[Music by Donizetti.]

C.O. Fanchette (Court, L'pool, 13/1/94). L.C.
[Music by Bernicot and Messager.]

WELDON, Mrs

D. Not Alone (Grand, Birmingham, 12/10/85). See *G. LANDER.*

WELLINGS, MILTON

Ca. The Dancing Master (O.C. 2/10/89). See *M. PEMBERTON.*

M.Sk. Uncle's Blunder (T.H. St Alban's, 18/12/93). See *F. SILVESTER.*

WELLS, H. S.

C.D. A Wonderful Visit (Gai. Hastings, 8/4/96, *copy.*). L.C.

WELLSEY, NITRAM

D. D'ye know me now? (Reading, 14/6/72). See *Capt. W. BRAHAM.*

WELSTEAD, HENRY

D. Giralda; or, The Invisible Husband (Olym. 12/9/50). L.C. *Lacy.*

WERNER, CHARLES J.

C. Phadrig the Bocaun (Athen. Kilkenny, 9/5/79).

WEST, ALBERT

D. Outcast London (W.L. 14/2/98). See *H. YOUNG.*

WEST, E. LEWIS

F. Flashes (L'pool, 7/4/90). See *J. J. HEWSON.*

WESTON, —

P. Cinderella (Bolton, 26/12/64).

WESTON, JAMES PITNEY

D. The State Courier (Wigan, 20/11/71).

WETHERILL, —

O. Ostrolenka (St G. 2/4/84). L.C.
[Translated in collaboration with — *TRYON.* Music by Bonawitz.]

WHARTON, C. H. M.

C.O. Bachelors (P's. Manchester, 8/6/85). L.C.
[Music by A. Taylor.]

WHEATCROFT, NELSON

Ca. Raven's Oak (P.H. Warrington, 9/82).

D. Gwynne's Oath (Stratford, 2/4/88). L.C.

WHEATLEY, HORACE

M.C.D. Bright Days; or, The Bride of Two Isles (Rotunda, L'pool, 1/4/89; E.C. 1/7/89). L.C.
[Written in collaboration with *C. A. ALDIN.*]

WHEATLEY, J. A.
— Dramatic Sketches. 8° 1890.

[*WHEELER, A. C.*
R.C.D. The Still Alarm (P'cess. 2/8/88). See *J. ARTHUR*.
D. The Great Diamond Robbery (Pav. 16/5/98). See *E. M. ALFRIEND*.

WHISHAW, Mrs BERNARD. [See also under *WISHAW*.]
F.C. The Statute of Albemarle (Traf. 16/11/92, *mat.*). L.C.
[Music by F. Whishaw.]

WHITAKER, JOHN, Jr.
C.D. Love brooks no jesting (Glow-worms' Amateur Dramatic Soc. 2/12/82).

WHITBREAD, J. W.
D. The Victoria Cross (Var. Brentford, 22/3/86; Qns. Dublin, 7/9/96; Stratford, 19/10/96; Pav. 26/7/97). L.C. St G. Walsall, 21/10/96.
D. Shoulder to Shoulder (Limerick, 8/11/86; Qns. Dublin, 15/11/86). L.C. Burnley, 14/12/86.
D. The Race of Life (Qns. Dublin, 21/11/87). L.C. Swansea, 14/4/88.
M.D. True to the Last (E.C. 16/7/88). L.C.
D. A Hero of Heroes (Qns. Dublin, 12/8/89; P'cess. Glasgow, 30/6/90; Brit. 4/7/92, as *Lured to Ruin*). L.C.
O.Bsq. Miss Maritana (Qns. Dublin, 21/4/90). See *Lieut. G. NUGENT*.
D. The Irishman (E.C. 4/11/89).
C.D. All Hallows' Eve (Qns. Dublin, 20/4/91). See *Hon. Mrs FORBES*.
D. The Nationalist (Qns. Dublin, 21/12/91). L.C. Grand, Plymouth, 26/7/92.
D. Spectres of the Past (Qns. Dublin, 30/1/93).
D. Lord Edward; or, '98 (Qns. Dublin, 26/3/94; Pav. 6/8/94). L.C. Preston, 4/5/94.
D. Wolfe Tone (Qns. Dublin, 26/12/98). L.C. Coatbridge, 13/4/99.

WHITE, A.
C. The Road to Fame (Vaud. 7/5/85, *mat.*). L.C.
[Written in collaboration with *P. GRUNFELD*.]

WHITE, BARTON
F.C. A Young Pretender (Sanger's, Ramsgate, 3/7/90; O.C. 10/12/91). L.C.
F.C. Margate (Terry's, 5/2/95). L.C.
C.D. Social Debts (County, Kingston, 2/12/97). L.C.
F.C. The Tourist (Aquar. Brighton, 12/6/99).

WHITE, Miss E.
D. Ambitious Mrs Moresby (Com. 22/4/98). L.C.

WHITE, Rev. JAMES
[For his earlier plays see iv, 419.]
T. James the Sixth; or, The Gowrie Plot (S.W. 6/3/52). L.C. 8° 1845, as *The Earl of Gowrie*.
C. The Mouse Trap (H. 14/5/53). L.C.

WHITE, JOHN W.
P. Aladdin (Bijou, 26/12/93).

WHITE, M.
C.D. Right against Might (Nov. 27/7/91).

WHITEHOUSE, S.
M.Sk. Fly-away's Race (T.H. Kilburn, 9/3/92).
[Music by H. E. Pether.]

WHITELAW, ROBERT
T. Antigone (C.P. 6/11/90).

WHITING, G. LANDER
D. The Wandering Jew (Brit. 18/6/73). L.C.
D. Remorse; or, The Perils of a Night (Vic. 1/11/73).

WHITLOCK, CHARLES
C.O. The Hermit (Wolverhampton, 20/6/92). L.C. Aven. Sunderland, 23/5/92.
[Music by T. G. W. Goddard.]
D. Our Native Home (Sur. 19/9/92). L.C.
[Written in collaboration with *J. SARGENT.*]
C.D. The Inkslinger (Roy. Glasgow, 22/2/93). L.C.
[Written in collaboration with *E. T. DE BANZIE.*]
D. The God of War (Wigan, 18/4/98; Stratford, 27/2/99). L.C. Hanley, 31/12/97.

WHITMORE, H. E.
Duol. Sixes and Sevens (Crit. 14/6/94). L.C. *French.*
C.D. A Soldier's Wife (Grand, Margate, 29/5/99). L.C.

WHITNEY, HERBERT
O. The Three Musketeers (Court, L'pool, 24/3/99). L.C.
[Music by R. Somerville.]

WHITTAKER, JOEL H. G.
F. My Name is Jones (Amphi. Leeds, 28/10/72). L.C. Bradford, 21/12/70.
D. A Charmed Life (Barrow-in-Furness, 10/5/75).
C. Grass Widows (Qns. Dublin, 19/9/79).

WHITTY, W. D.
F. My Husband's Secret (Vaud. 22/4/74). L.C.

WHYTE, GEORGE
O. The Vivandière (Court, L'pool, 10/3/96; Gar. 20/1/97). L.C.
[Music by B. Godard.]

WHYTE, HAROLD
D. The Terror of London (Grec. 23/10/79). See *W. JAMES.*
D. Fettered Lives (Brit. 31/7/93). L.C.
D. England's Flag (P.W. Salford, 15/4/95). L.C.
D. At Dead of Night (Nov. 26/4/97).

WIBROW, G. V.
Ca. The Artist (Eastbourne, 6/8/94).

WIDNELL, VICTOR
D. The People's Idol (Olym. 4/12/90). See *W. BARRETT.*

WIGAN, ALFRED SYDNEY
[For his earlier plays see iv, 419.]
F. A Dead Take In (Olym. 28/1/50).
C.D. Lucky Friday (P'cess. 7/5/52). L.C.
F. Tit for Tat (Olym. 22/1/55). See *F. TALFOURD.*

WIGAN, HORACE

C.O. The Daughter of the Regiment (Adel. 18/8/59).
[Music G. Donizetti.]

Ca. A Base Impostor (Olym. 28/11/59). L.C.

Ca. Observation and Flirtation (Str. 26/7/60). L.C. *Lacy.*

F. Savage as a Bear (Olym. 17/9/60).

Ca. Change for a Sovereign (Str. 14/3/61). L.C.

Ca. Charming Woman (Olym. 20/6/61). *Lacy.*

C. Friends or Foes (St J. 8/3/62). L.C. *Lacy.*

C. Real and Ideal (Olym. 8/9/62). L.C.

F. A Southerner just arrived (Olym. 3/11/62). L.C. *Lacy.*

C. Taming the Truant (Olym. 19/3/63). L.C.

F. Goggin's Gingham (Str. 4/5/63). L.C.

Ca. Always Intended (Olym. 3/4/65). L.C.

Ca. The Best Way (Olym. 27/9/66). L.C. *Lacy.*

D. Martin Chuzzlewit (Olym. 2/3/68). L.C.

D. Love and Hate (Olym. 23/6/69). L.C.

D. A Life Chase (Gai. 11/10/69). See *J. OXENFORD.*

Ca. Widow's Weeds (Str. 19/3/70). See *J. OXENFORD.*

C. Bosom Friends (Bradford, 1/9/71).

D. Rag Fair (Vic. 20/5/72). L.C.

C. Business is Business; or, Satisfactory Settlement (Brighton, 22/6/74). L.C.

D. Self (Mirror, 27/9/75). See *J. OXENFORD.*
[Other titles attributed to him in *Lacy* are: *The Absent One* and *Pyramus and Thisbe.*]

WILCOX, Lieut. —

Bsq. All at C (on board H.M.S. Tamar, 29/12/73). See *Major MILLETT.*

WILD, G.

F. Catch 'em alive, oh! (M'bone, 17/11/51). L.C.

WILD, W. J.

D. A Diamond Ring (Qns. Manchester, 6/3/85). L.C.

D. Love or Hate (P.W. Salford, 19/4/86). L.C.
[Written in collaboration with *F. WILLIAMS.*]

D. Played and Lost (N. Shields, 1/8/87).

D. A True Woman (Mechanics' Inst. Stockport, 3/2/97, *amat.*). L.C.

WILDE, LILLA

D. East Lynne (Cradley Heath, 19/12/98).

WILDE, OSCAR FINGALL O'FLAHERTIE WILLS

D. Vera; or, The Nihilists (Union Square, New York, 20/8/83). 8° 1880 [*priv.*]; 8° 1882 [*priv.*]; 8° 1902 [*priv.*].

D. The Duchess of Padua (Broadway, New York, 26/1/91, as *Guido Ferrandi*). 8° 1883 [New York, *priv.*]; 8° 1907.

C. Lady Windermere's Fan (St J. 20/2/92). L.C. 8° 1892; 8° 1903.

C.D. A Woman of No Importance (H. 19/4/93). L.C. 8° 1894.

C. An Ideal Husband (H. 3/1/95). L.C. 8° 1899.

C. The Importance of Being Earnest (St J. 14/2/95). L.C. 4° 1899.

D. Salomé (Théâtre de l'Œuvre, Paris, 11/2/96; New Stage Club at Bijou, 10/5/1905). 8° 1893 [Paris]; English trans. by Lord Alfred Douglas, 4° 1894.

WILDE, W. C. K.

Ext. The Dumb Princess (Boscombe House, W. Kensington, 17/1/94).
Ca. French Polish. 8° (?1895, Dublin).

WILKINS, JOHN H.

[For his earlier plays see iv, 419–20.]
D. Zenobia, Queen of Palmyra (C.L. 5/51). L.C.
D. The Man with the Red Beard; or, Friends and their Shadows (C.L. 19/7/52). L.C.
D. Civilization (C.L. 10/11/52). L.C. *Lacy.*
D. The Egyptian (C.L. 4/4/53). L.C. *Lacy.*
[A revised version of *Zenobia* (C.L. 5/51).]
D. St Marc; or, A Husband's Sacrifice (D.L. 6/6/53). L.C.
D. St James's and St Giles's (C.L. 3/10/53). L.C.
D. Charity's Love (C.L. 3/54). L.C.
D. Money and Misery; or, High Crime and Low Crime (C.L. 10/55). L.C.
D. The Frost of Life; or, Hearts against Diamonds and the Struggle of Life (C.L. 9/56). L.C.
D. Twenty Years in a Debtor's Prison (C.L. 20/9/58).

WILKINSON, ALFRED

D.Sk. Trooper Hugh (York, 8/5/91). L.C.
Ca. A Double Event (York, 7/8/91). L.C.

WILKINSON, MATT.

D. The Angels of Paris (Scarborough, 17/5/94). See *F. ROGERS.*
D. Sons of the Sea (Qns. Birmingham, 8/4/95; W.L. 9/5/98). L.C.
D. The Iron Maiden; or Hunted by the Law (Hanley 3/6/96; P.W. Southampton, 31/12/96; Stratford, 17/1/98). L.C.
[Written in collaboration with *W. H. HALLATT.* Title altered to *Is Law Justice?*, 31/12/1903.]
D. Saturday Night in London (Bristol, 12/6/99). L.C.

WILKS, THOMAS EGERTON

[For his earlier plays see iv, 420–1.]
D. Mont Blanc; or, The Witch of the Alps (Qns. 5/9/53). L.C.
F. How's your Uncle; or, The Ladies of the Court (Adel. 27/8/55). L.C.
D. The Miller of Whetstone; or, The Cross-bow Letter (Stand. 1/8/57).
D. Eily O'Connor (Brit. 22/10/60). L.C.

WILLARD, Mrs E. S. [RACHEL PENN]

Ca. Tommy (Olym. 9/2/91).
Ent. The Merry Piper of Nuremberg (Sav. 8/6/93). L.C. Traf. 15/3/93).
C. Punch and Judy (Sav. 8/6/93). L.C. Traf. 15/3/93.
[Music by E. Jones.]
C.O. The Lucky Bag (Sav. 8/6/93). L.C.
[Music by L. N. Parker.]

WILLARD, JAMES

D. In the Shadow of Night (Brit. 5/12/98). L.C. Grand, Stalybridge, 18/8/98, as *In the Shadow of Death.*

WILLETT, E. N.

O. A Prodigal Son (Domestic Mission, L'pool, 18/3/96). L.C.
[Music by F. C. Nicholls.]

WILLIAMS, Capt.

D. The Woman of Colour; or, Slavery and Freedom (Sur. 14/11/53). L.C.

WILLIAMS, —

D. Millicent; or, The Pirate's Life (P.W. Birmingham, 2/11/68). L.C.

WILLIAMS, ARTHUR

F. Leave it to me (Sur. 26/12/70). See *C. H. HAZLEWOOD.*
D. The Christmas Chimes; or, Trotty Veck's Dream (Pav. 3/2/73).
F. Funnibone's Fix (Sur. 27/3/80). L.C.
D. The Secret of a Life (Grand, 18/11/86, *mat.*). L.C.
[Written in collaboration with *G. ROBERTS.*]

[*WILLIAMS, Mrs B.*

F. Irish Assurance and Yankee Modesty (Adel. 12/8/56). L.C. *Lacy.*

WILLIAMS, BARRY

D. No Cross, no Crown (People's, Attercliffe, Sheffield, 26/7/97). L.C. Guildhall, Winchester, 28/9/96.
[Written in collaboration with *H. SORRELL.*]
D. The Black Bishop (Kidderminster, 14/4/98; Bilston, 7/10/98; Stratford, 18/6/1900). L.C.
D. The Mighty Motive (Lyc. Stafford, 11/8/99).
D. The Red Coat (W.L. 21/6/1900). L.C. Stafford, 29/7/99.
[Probably this is the same play as the above.]

WILLIAMS, C.

C.D. The Burglar's Baby (Lyr. Ealing, 27/10/97). See *J. T. DOUGLASS.*

WILLIAMS, E. A.

Oa. A Cruise in the Bay of Biscay (P.H. New X. 30/8/84). L.C.
[Music by A. G. Pritchard.]

WILLIAMS, F.

D. Love or Hate (P.W. Salford, 19/4/86). See *W. J. WILD.*

WILLIAMS, H. ESPEY

R.D. The Man in Black (Vaud. 3/9/97, *copy.*). L.C.

WILLIAMS, HENRY LLEWELLYN

D. After Dark. 4° [1880].
[Based on the drama by *D. BOUCICAULT.*]
F.C. Blighted Bachelors (Corn Exchange, Derby, 29/8/81). L.C.

WILLIAMS, MONTAGU

F. B.B. (Olym. 22/3/60). See *F. C. BURNAND.*
F. A Fair Exchange (Olym. 27/8/60). L.C.
D. The Isle of St Tropez (St J. 20/12/60). L.C.
[Written in collaboration with *F. C. BURNAND.*]
F. A Turkish Bath (Adel. 29/4/61). See *F. C. BURNAND.*
Ca. Carte de Visite (St J. 26/12/62). L.C.
[Written in collaboration with *F. C. BURNAND.*]
F. Easy Shaving (H. 11/6/63). See *F. C. BURNAND.*
Bsq. Patient Penelope (Str. 25/11/63). See *F. C. BURNAND.*
Bsq. Windsor Castle (Str. 5/6/65). See *F. C. BURNAND.*

Bsq. L'Africaine (Str. 18/11/65). See *F. C. BURNAND.*
Bsq. The Latest Edition of Black-eyed Susan (Roy. 29/11/66). See *F. C. BURNAND.*

WILLIAMS, MORTON
Bsq. Bluebeard in a Black Skin (Norwich, 7/6/75).

WILLIAMS, ROBERT A. P.
M.F. Aunt Chimpanzee (St J. Wrexham, 30/10/97, *copy.*; Albert, Gainsborough, 9/3/99, as *The Joking Girl*). L.C.
[Music by J. C. Woodruffe.]

WILLIAMS, THOMAS
D. Elizabeth, Queen of England (D.L. 14/7/82). L.C.

WILLIAMS, THOMAS J.
Bsq. Medea; or, A Libel on the Lady of Colchis (Adel. 10/7/56).
D. Ruth Oakley (M'bone, 15/1/57). See *A. G. HARRIS.*
Ca. I've written to Browne; or, A Needless Stratagem (Olym. 7/2/59). L.C. *Lacy.*
F. Ici on parle français (Adel. 9/5/59). L.C. *Lacy.*
F. Nursey Chickweed (P'cess. 12/11/59). L.C. *Lacy.*
C. The Gossip (P'cess. 23/11/59). See *A. G. HARRIS.*
F. Cruel to be kind (P'cess. 6/3/60). L.C. *Lacy.*
[Written in collaboration with *A. G. HARRIS.*]
Ca. A Race for a Widow (Str. 23/4/60). L.C.
F. The Lion Slayer; or, Out for a Prowl (H. 22/11/60). L.C. *Lacy.*
F. An Ugly Customer (Adel. 6/12/60). L.C. *Lacy.*
D. Truth and Fiction (P'cess. 21/5/61). L.C.
F. On and off (Str. 6/6/61). L.C. *Lacy.*
F. Peace and Quiet (Str. 29/6/61). L.C. *Lacy.*
F. The Silent System (Str. 3/7/62). L.C.
F. Jack's Delight (Str. 3/11/62). L.C.
F. The Trials of Tomkins (Adel. 6/4/63). L.C. *Lacy.*
Ca. The Little Sentinel (St J. 4/5/63). L.C. *Lacy.*
F. A Charming Pair (P'cess. 27/5/63). L.C. as *A Capital Pair. Lacy.*
F. Turn him out (Str. 17/8/63). L.C. *Lacy.*
O. The Desert Flower (C.G. 12/10/63). See *A. G. HARRIS.*
Ca. Little Daisy (H. 9/11/63). L.C. *Lacy.*
F. My Wife's Maid (Adel. 8/8/64). L.C.
F. My Dress Boots (Roy. 5/9/64). L.C. *Lacy.*
Ca. The Better Half (Str. 26/6/65). L.C. *Lacy.*
F. Pipkin's Rustic Retreat (Adel. 18/1/66). L.C. *Lacy.*
F. Found in a Four-wheeler (Roy. 24/4/66). L.C.
F. Larkin's Love Letters (Holb. 6/10/66). L.C. *Lacy.*
F. Tweedleton's Tail Coat (Lyc. 8/10/66). L.C. *Lacy.*
F. My Turn Next (Holb. 17/12/66). L.C. *Lacy.*
Ca. Human Nature (Olym. 22/7/67). See *A. G. HARRIS.*
F. A Cure for the Fidgets (Sur. 14/9/67). L.C.
F. Dandelion's Dodges (Holb. 5/10/67). L.C. *Lacy.*
F. Cabman No. 93 (Lyc. 26/12/67).
Ca. Who's to win him? (Lyc. 20/1/68). L.C. *Lacy.*
F. One too many for him (Sur. 10/2/68). L.C.
D. The Peep-show Man (Sur. 10/2/68). L.C. *Lacy.*

Ca. A Silent Protector (P.W. 7/3/68). L.C. *Lacy.*
F. Flo's First Frolic (P'cess. 23/5/68). L.C.
F. The Young Man in Green; or, The Volunteer Review (Lyc. 1/2/69). L.C. *Lacy* [as *The Volunteer Review; or, The Little Man in Green*].
F. Old Gooseberry (Olym. 9/10/69). L.C. *Lacy.*
F. All in a Fog (Sur. 16/10/69). *Lacy* [as *Who is who? or, All in a Fog*].
F. A Terrible Tinker (Ast. 27/12/69). *Lacy.*
F. A Tourist's Ticket (Glo. 1/4/72). L.C. *Lacy.*
F. Up a Tree (Adel. 10/3/73). L.C. *French.*
F. Keep your Eye on her (Olym. 30/9/76). L.C.

WILLIAMSON, H. W.
D. Shadragh the Hunchback (S. Shields, 8/4/78; E.C. 26/7/80).
D. Retiring (Glo. 1/5/78). L.C.
Ca. The Genius (Glo. 26/1/81). L.C.
C.D. Estranged (Glo. 3/8/81). L.C.
D. Foiled (Portsmouth, 4/5/82). L.C.
C. Ethel's Test (Str. 26/3/83). L.C.
D. Fate's Decree (Sanger's, 17/9/83). L.C.
F. Wanted (Gai. 1/4/84). L.C.
Ca. The House Boat (P.W. 24/11/86). L.C.
C.D. My Queenie (Vaud. 9/4/89, *mat.*).

"*WILLING, JAMES*" [*J. T. DOUGLASS*]
D. Under Two Reigns (Park, 3/5/79). See *W. PERCIVAL.*
D. Poor Relations; or, Jane Eyre (Park, 27/8/79). L.C.
D. Delilah; or, Married for Hate (Park, 7/10/80). L.C.
D. The Ruling Passion (Stand. 6/11/82). L.C.
D. Glad Tidings (Stand. 29/8/83). L.C.
[Written in collaboration with *F. STAINFORTH.*]
D. Daybreak (Stand. 1/9/84). L.C.
F.C. A Bubble Reputation (Stand. 6/4/85). L.C. Shrewsbury, 25/1/84.
[Written in collaboration with *J. DOUGLASS.*]
D. Judgment (Stand. 19/9/85). L.C.
[Title altered to *Day by Day*, Adel. L'pool, 10/4/89.]
D. Our Silver Wedding (Stand. 22/3/86). L.C.
M.D. A Dark Secret; or, A Tale of the Thames Valley (Stand. 28/10/86). L.C.
[Written in collaboration with *J. DOUGLASS.*]
D. The Lucky Shilling (Stand. 20/2/88). L.C.
[Written in collaboration with *J. DOUGLASS.*]

WILLOUGHBY, ALGERNON
D. Valjean; or, A Life's Sacrifice (P.W. Glasgow, 5/8/78). L.C.
D. The Lost Lady of Lynne (Coventry, 24/1/83).
F. Out for a Holiday (P.W. Wolverhampton, 9/6/84).

WILLOUGHBY, HUGH
D. The House on the Marsh (Margate, 28/9/85).

WILLS, CHARLES
C.D. All for himself (Alex. L'pool, 5/6/74).
C. Cobwebs (Vaud. 27/3/80). L.C.

WILLS, Rev. FREEMAN

D. Sedgemoor (S.W. 20/8/81). See *W. G. WILLS*.
C.D. Put Asunder (Gai. 28/5/83). L.C.
D. Faith. L.C. 30/7/84.
D. The Golden Band (Olym. 14/6/87). See *H. HERMAN*.
D. An Old Song (Great H. Tunbridge Wells, 2/8/94; Crit. 10/12/96).
[Written in collaboration with *A. F. KING*.]
D. The Only Way (Lyc. 16/2/99). L.C. Brixton, 17/5/98, as *The Jackal*.

WILLS, WILLIAM GORMAN

D. Doctor Davy (Greenwich, 6/2/65; Lyc. 4/6/66). See *J. ALBERY*.
D. The Man o' Airlie (P'cess. 20/7/67).
R.D. Hinko; or, The Headsman's Bond (Qns. 9/9/71). L.C.
D. Broken Spells (Court, 27/3/72). See *J. W. MARSTON*.
T. Medea in Corinth (Lyc. 8/7/72). L.C.
T. Charles the First (Lyc. 28/9/72). L.C. 8° 1873.
— Drawing Room Dramas. By W. G. Wills and the Hon. Mrs Greene. 8° 1873 [Edinburgh].
D. Eugene Aram (Lyc. 19/4/73). L.C.
D. Mary Queen of Scots; or, the Catholic Queen and the Protestant Reformer (P'cess. 23/2/74). L.C.
D. Cora; or, Love and Passion (Leeds, 2/3/74). L.C.
D. Jane Shore (Amphi. Leeds, 8/3/75; P'cess. 30/9/76). L.C.
T. Sappho (Gai. Dublin, 7/6/75).
D. Buckingham (Olym. 29/11/75). L.C.
D. Cora (Glo. 28/2/77).
[Written in collaboration with *F. MARSHALL*. Evidently a revision of *Cora*, above.]
D. Camille; or, An Autumnal Dream (Cambridge, 20/8/77). L.C.
D. England in the Days of Charles II (D.L. 22/9/77). L.C.
C.D. Olivia (Court, 30/3/78). L.C.
C.D. Nell Gwynn (Roy. 1/5/78). L.C.
D. Vanderdicken (Lyc. 8/6/78). L.C.
[Written in collaboration with *P. FITZGERALD*.]
C.D. Ellen; or, Love's Cunning (H. 14/4/79). L.C.
C.D. Brag (H. 12/6/79). L.C.
[A revised version of the above.]
D. Bolivar; or, Life for Love (Dublin, 3/11/79). L.C. Gai. Glasgow, 8/12/79.
D. Forced from Home (Duke's, 2/2/80). L.C. as *The Stepmother*.
M.D. Ninon (Adel. 7/2/80). L.C.
[Music by W. C. Levey.]
D. Iolanthe (Lyc. 20/5/80). L.C.
D. William and Susan (St J. 9/10/80). L.C.
T. Juana (Court, 7/5/81). L.C.
D. Sedgemoor (S.W. 20/8/81). L.C.
D. Jane Eyre (Glo. 23/12/82). L.C.
D. Claudian (P'cess. 6/12/83). See *H. HERMAN*.
C. Gringoire (P.W. 22/6/85, *mat.*; Glo. 24/1/91). L.C.
C.D. A Young Tramp (P's. Bristol, 12/9/85). L.C.
D. Faust (Lyc. 19/12/85). L.C.
D. The Little Pilgrim (Crit. 3/7/86, *mat.*). L.C.
D. The Pompadour (H. 31/3/88). L.C.
[Written in collaboration with *S. GRUNDY*.]

D. Clarissa Harlowe (Birmingham, 16/12/89). L.C.
T. Juana (O.C. 16/4/90).
[A revised version of *Juana* (Court, 7/5/81).]
R.D. A Royal Divorce (Aven. Sunderland, 1/5/91; Olym. 10/9/91; P'cess. 25/7/92). L.C.
C.D. Esmond (St G. 21/6/93, *amat.*).
C.D. A Chapter from Don Quixote (Lyc. 4/5/95). L.C.

WILMER, FREDERICK
C. The Upper Classes (P.W. L'pool, 2/10/76). L.C. Alh. 28/9/76.
Ca. Uncle Johnson (P.W. L'pool, 11/6/77). L.C.

WILMOT, ALFRED A.
F. Once a Week (Rochester, 5/5/81).
[Written in collaboration with — *HARRISON*.]
C.D. Lady Deane (St G. 26/5/87). L.C.
F. Misled (St G. 26/5/87). L.C.
Ca. Love and Art; or, The Artist's Ghost (Lyr. Hammersmith, 28/3/89; Nov. 9/3/91). L.C.
F. Queer Lodgers (Park T.H. Battersea, 1/3/90). L.C.
Ca. Waiting for the Train (Nov. 6/2/91, *copy*.). L.C.
F. Nunkey (Athen. Shepherds Bush, 4/4/92). L.C.

WILMOT, CHARLES
D. Hard Hearts (Grand, 26/4/86). See *A. J. CHARLESON*.
F. Uncle Yank's Mishaps (Shakespeare, L'pool, 27/6/92).
[Written in collaboration with *C. H. MANNON*.]

WILSON, A. JOSEPH
F. Aunt or Uncle (Church Inst. H. Wandsworth, 21/5/85).
O. Donna Theresa (Church Inst. H. Wandsworth, 21/5/85).

WILSON, C. J. S.
C.O. The Georgians (Phil. 2/10/75). L.C.
[Music by Offenbach.]

WILSON, F.
Ca. Whist (St J. H. Brighton, 20/8/79).

WILSON, JOHN CRAWFORD
D. The Gitanilla; or, The Children of the Zincali (Sur. 22/10/60). L.C. *French*.
F. My Knuckleduster (Str. 2/2/63).
D. Lost and Found; or, The Two Wild Flowers (Holb. 21/12/72). L.C.

WILSON, MOZART
M.Sk. War versus Art (Free Library, Walworth Road, 26/4/98).

WILSON, PETER
D. The World of Silence (S.W. 13/6/98). See *L. MORTIMER*.
D. Christian's Crime (S.W. 14/8/99). See *L. MORTIMER*.

WILSON, R. KNIGHT
M.C. The Dominicans (Art Gallery, Newcastle, 13/12/94). L.C.
[Music by C. S. Terry.]

WILSON, SHELDON
Oa. The Knight of the Garter (Gai. 7/12/82). L.C.
[Music by M. Lutz.]

M.F. The Laundry Belle (Gai. 5/12/83). L.C.
[Music by M. Lutz.]
C.O. Carl (Gai. 3/5/86). L.C.
[Music by M. Lutz.]
F.C. The Confidential Clerk (Gai. 18/6/86, *mat.*). L.C.
[Written in collaboration with *S. WITTMAN.*]

WILSON, W. R.
M.D. In the Heart of the Storm (P.H. Tottenham, 29/2/96). See *H. H. WINSLOW.*

WILSTACH, PAUL
C. Don't deceive your Wife (Aquar. Gt Yarmouth, 15/1/97). L.C.

WILTON, Mrs
D.Sk. A Study of Two Women (Brompton Hospital, 15/2/98).

WILTON, HENRY
C.D. The Organist (P.H. New Cross, 14/11/87).
[Written in collaboration with *A. B. MOSS.*]

WILTON, HORACE
F.Oa. The Doctor's Ward (Assembly R. Teignmouth, 7/2/99).
[Music by A. Schmidt.]

WILTON, Miss J. H.
Ca. Mrs Brown (Brit. 11/5/74). L.C.

WILTON, KATE
D. Pearl Darrell (Sefton, L'pool, 17/9/83).

WILTON, MARIE EFFIE. See *Lady BANCROFT*

WINDERMERE, C.
F.C. The New Housemaid (Margate, 19/10/93).

WINGFIELD, Hon. LEWIS
D. Voltaire's Wager; or, Despite the World (Dundee, 17/5/75). L.C.
T. Mary Stuart (Court, 9/10/80). L.C.

WINSLOW, H. H.
M.D. In the Heart of the Storm (P.H. Tottenham, 29/2/96, *copy.*).
[Written in collaboration with *W. R. WILSON.*]

"*WINTER, JOHN STRANGE.*" See *Mrs STANNARD*

WINTERBOTTOM, J.
Oa. The Mountain King (Portsmouth, 25/1/75). See *A. NANCE.*

WINTHORP, CHARLES
C. The Upper Hand (Terry's, 29/5/99). L.C.
[Written in collaboration with *W. LISLE.*]

WISE, A. B.
D. Found at Last (Leamington, 27/2/99; Morton's, Greenwich, 6/3/99). L.C.

WISE, JOHN
Ca. A Slight Mistake (Matlock H. Matlock, 7/6/97).

WISHAW, Mrs BERNARD. [See also under *WHISHAW.*]
Ca. Two or one (Aven. 3/3/91 *mat.*; P'cess. 28/5/92, *mat.*, as *Will he come home again?*).
C. Zephyr (Aven. 3/3/91, *mat.*). L.C.

WITHERS, FRANK

D.Sk. Sad Memories (Blackburn, 22/2/95). L.C. *French.*

D. Harvest of Hate (Castleford, 1/2/99, *copy.*). L.C.
[Written in collaboration with *H. EGLINGTON.*]

WITTMAN, S.

F.C. The Confidential Clerk (Gai. 18/6/86). See *S. WILSON.*

WOLFF, JOSEPH

D. Sixteen Years Ago (E.L. 11/3/71). L.C.

WOOD, ABBEY

F. Our Tutor (Assembly R. Leytonstone, 25/10/90).

WOOD, A. C. FRASER

Ca. The Phonograph (St G. Walsall, 20/11/89).

D. Uncle Jack (T.H. Sutton Coldfield, 4/4/93). See *F. MONK.*

F.C. The Milliner (Grand, Walsall, 11/8/93). L.C.

D. In the Eyes of the World (Glo. 29/3/94). L.C.

WOOD, ARTHUR

[For his play *The Artisan's Triumph* see under *UA.*]

F. My New Place (Str. 23/11/63). L.C.

F. A Romantic Attachment (H. 15/2/66). L.C. *Lacy.*

Ca. The Winning Card (H. 14/10/67). L.C.

F. The Chamber of Horrors (Holb. 18/4/70; S.W. 1/4/72, as *A Bilious Attack*). L.C. *French.*

Bsq. Paul and Virginia (Olym. 15/10/70). L.C.

C. Behind a Mask (Roy. 8/3/71). See *B. H. DIXON.*

C.D. Shoddy (Bristol, 6/11/76). L.C.

WOOD, CHARLES

C. Haste (St G. 23/1/79).

WOOD, F.D.

D. A Voice from the Grave (Maidenhead, 19/4/97). See *S. PLANCHÉ.*

WOOD, FREDERICK

C.O. The Captain of the Guard (New, Margate, 24/7/82). L.C.
[Music by G. Fox.]

Oa. Contrary Winds (New, Margate, 24/7/82). L.C.
[Music by G. Fox.]

O. Mercedes (Leinster, Dublin, 11/1/96; Grand, 24/3/96). L.C.
[Music by D. Pellegrini.]

WOOD, GEORGE MURRAY

C.D. The American (Gai. Glasgow, 16/4/83).

D. The Forge Master (Lynn, 23/10/84).

D. The House on the Marsh (Lecture H. Derby, 28/3/85).

WOOD, JOHN J.

C.O. Utopia; or, The Finger of Fate (T.H. Birkenhead, 4/5/91; Richmond, 16/12/91). L.C.
[Music by W. H. Hunt.]

M.Bsq. Turpin à-la-mode (Roy. Chester, 29/3/97). See *G. P. HUNTLEY.*

Oa. Toto and Sata (Grand, Leeds, 23/8/97). See *A. M. THOMPSON.*

P. Dick Whittington (Shakespeare, Clapham, 27/12/97). L.C.

WOOD, MARK

F. Chizzle's Choice (Ladb. H. 28/7/88). See ***F. H. FRANCKS.***

WOOD, METCALFE

C. The Elder Miss Blossom (Grand, Blackpool, 10/9/97). See *E. HENDRIE.*

D. The Poverty of Riches (Grand, Blackpool, 7/4/99). See *E. HENDRIE.*

WOOD, MURRAY

D. Dolly Varden (Bradford, 29/4/72; Sur. 5/10/72). L.C.

D. Little Nelly (Sur. 23/11/72). L.C.

D. Lost Em'ly (Sur. 8/3/73). L.C.

D. Innocent; or, Life in Death (Sur. 14/4/73). L.C.

WOOD, W.

M.D. The Almighty Dollar (Barnsley, 13/12/88). L.C.

WOODGATE, HERBERT

D. The New Man (Ladb. H. 20/12/95, *copy.*). L.C.
[Written in collaboration with *P. M. BERTON.*]

D. The Sorrows of Satan (Shaft. 9/1/97). L.C.
[Written in collaboration with *P. M. BERTON.*]

WOODHOUSE, W. ARCHER

D. The Grandsire (Terry's, 15/5/89, *mat.*). L.C.

WOODROFFE, PERCY

O.D. In Sunny Spain (St G. Walsall, 9/11/96). See *W. H. DEARLOVE.*

WOODROW, H. CORY

F.C. The Three Hats (Lyr. Ealing, 11/6/96). L.C.

WOODRUFFE, ADELAIDE

F. Braving the Storm (D.L. 24/2/71). L.C. *Lacy.*

WOODS, —

D. The Red Reef (Alex. Walsall, 8/9/84). See *T. B. BANNISTER.*

WOODVILLE, —

Ca. A Point of Law (Park, 26/3/81). See — *PAXTON.*

WOODVILLE, HENRY

C.O. Catalina; or, A Legend of Castile (T.H. Kilburn, 23/2/92, *amat.*). L.C.
[Music by C. Locknane.]

D. Confederates (Glo. 25/2/97). L.C.

D. A Woman's Love (Vaud. 16/3/99). L.C.

WOODWARD, F. W.

Oa. The Lady Aurora (O.H. Chatham, 19/11/94). L.C.
[Written in collaboration with *J. W. WOODWARD.*]

WOODWARD, J. W.

Oa. The Lady Aurora (O.H. Chatham, 19/11/94). See *F. W. WOODWARD.*

[*WOODWORTH, SAMUEL*

C. The Forest Rose and the Yankee Ploughboy (Adel. 23/9/51). L.C. *Lacy.*

WOOLER, JOHN PRATT

[For his earlier plays see iv, 422.]

F. Allow me to apologise (28/10/50). L.C.

F. The Law of the Lips (S.W. 4/8/51). L.C.

Esq. Jason et Medea (Grec. 25/8/51). L.C.

Bsq. Eulalie and Vermilion; or, The Charmed Lesson (Grec. 31/5/52). L.C.

F. A Model Husband (S.W. 9/9/53). L.C.

F. Sold to Advantage (S.W. 7/11/53). L.C.

F. I'll write to the Times (S.W. 17/10/56). L.C. *Lacy.*

T. The Branded Race (Sur. 27/9/58). L.C. as *The Fatal Secret; or, The B.R.*

Ca. A Twice Told Tale (Olym. 27/9/58). L.C. *Lacy.*

Ca. Sisterly Service (Str. 9/2/60). L.C. *Lacy.*

F. Did I dream it? (Str. 19/11/60). L.C. as *Charming Dreams.*

D. The Silver Wedding (Str. 24/1/61). L.C.

D. Old Phil's Birthday (Str. 20/1/62). L.C.

Ca. Orange Blossoms (Str. 20/2/62). L.C.

Oa. Blonde or Brunette (Roy. 19/5/62). L.C.

Oa. The Ring and the Keeper (Roy. 9/6/62). L.C. *Lacy.*

F. Keep your Temper (Str. 5/7/62). L.C. *Lacy.*

F.Ca. Marriage at any Price (Str. 28/7/62). L.C.

F. A Faint Heart which did win Fair Lady (Str. 9/2/63). L.C. *Lacy.*

F. The Minister of Spain (Stand. 28/2/63).

F. A Hunt for a Husband (Str. 28/3/64). L.C.

Ca. The Maid of Honour (Str. 16/5/64). L.C. *Lacy.*

Ca. The Wilful Ward (Str. 14/11/64). L.C. *Lacy.*

Ca. Laurence's Love Suit (Str. 9/1/65). L.C. *Lacy.*

F. Cousin Adonis; or, Too Handsome for Anything (Roy. 13/2/65). L.C.

Ca. A Winning Hazard (P.W. 15/4/65). L.C. *Lacy.*

Ca. The Squire of Ringwood Chace (Roy. 1/5/65). L.C.

F. The Haunted Mill (Roy. 12/8/65). L.C.

Ca. Room for the Ladies (Ch. X. 11/9/69). L.C.

F. Locked In (P.W. 17/9/70).

[*WOOLF, BENJAMIN E.*

D. The Mighty Dollar (Park, New York, 26/9/75; Gai. 30/8/80). L.C.

C.O. Alcantara (Connaught, 1/11/79). L.C.
[Music by J. Eichberg.]

WORDEN, JOSEPH

C.D. 'Twixt Love and Duty (Preston, 9/12/89). L.C.
[Written in collaboration with *R. JOHNSTON.*]

D. Our Coastguards (St J. Manchester, 14/11/92). L.C. P.W. Blackpool, 22/2/92.

WORTHINGTON, J.

F. Up in the World (Sur. 4/4/59). L.C. Sur. 1/10/57. *Lacy.*

WOTTON, TOM S.

Duol. A Quarrel (Brompton Hospital, 14/3/93; Parkhurst, 14/5/94). L.C.

D. The Ordeal (Com. 20/6/93). L.C.

F. The Eider-down Quilt (Terry's, 21/12/96). L.C.

WRAY, CECIL

C.D. Ranelagh (H. 11/2/54). See *J. P. SIMPSON.*

D. Through the World (Brighton, 20/8/74).

WRAY, PEYTON

Oa. The Elfin Tree (Alex. Pal. 12/5/75).
[Music by L. Diehl.]

M.Sk. A Pair of them (Gai. 1/3/79). L.C.
[Music by M. Lutz.]

WRIGHT, BRITTAIN

F. Out of the Frying Pan into the Fire (C.L. 8/7/67). L.C.

WRIGHT, E.

Duol. Sharps or Flats? (T.H. Westminster, 11/2/95).

WRIGHT, FREDERICK

D. Wealth; or, A Pitman's Secret (Bradford, 16/4/77). L.C.

D. Friend or Foe (Tyne, Newcastle, 23/3/91).

D. An Empty Stocking (Str. 5/12/98). L.C.

D.Sk. The Wicked Uncle (Gai. 6/12/1900). L.C. Portsmouth, 30/8/99.

WRIGHT, J. MACER

D. Love's Sacrifice; A Story of the Commune (Pier Pav. Hastings, 25/11/96, *copy.*). L.C.

WRIGHT, MAY

D. The Sceptre and the Cross (T.H. Oswaldtwistle, 12/10/98).

WRIGHT-MATRON, G. E.

F.C. Martha's Double (Bijou, 24/7/96, *copy.*). L.C.

WURM, JOSEPHINE

Oa. Princess Liza's Fairy (P.W. Southampton, 3/6/93).
[Music by Marie Wurm.]

WYATT, EDGAR

C.O. Count Tremolio (Nottingham, 5/9/87; Gloucester, 18/9/93, as *Fair Geraldine; or, A Very Wilful Maid of Venice*). L.C.
[Music by A. R. Watson.]

WYATT, FRANK

F.C. The Two Johnnies (Northampton, 27/4/88). See *F. HORNER.*

F.C. The Two Recruits (Roy. 6/6/90, *copy.*; Toole's, 8/11/90). L.C.

WYCOMBE, MAGDELINE

Oa. Cloris; or, Plots and Plans (Wolverhampton, 17/4/85).
[Written in collaboration with *V. SHAEL.* Music by C. F. Hayward.]

WYKE, E. BYAM

Ca. Our Awful Lads (Gai. W. Hartlepool, 15/3/78). L.C.

Ca. Loves and Gloves (Tyne, Newcastle, 23/3/78).

D. Tricks (Huddersfield, 11/5/78).

D. Slander (York, 16/9/78).

Ca. A Perilous Picnic (Dundee, 16/6/79).

C.O. Ford Frivolous (Weymouth, 11/10/80).
[Music by A. M. Edwards.]

F. Tommy's Tutors (Bijou, Rhyl, 24/6/81).

Oa. The Cruise of the Crusoes (Qns. Manchester, 8/8/81). L.C.
[Music by E. Williams.]

Oa. The Enchanted Maid (Sunderland, 31/3/82).
[Music by H. Liston.]
Oa. Lucette's Legacy (Brighton, 18/2/84). L.C.
M.F.C. Upside down (P.H. Thirsk, 1/11/86).
C.D. Hidden (Mechanics' Inst. Stockport, 21/1/88).
Bsq. Captivating Carmen (Pier, Folkestone, 4/8/90). See *M. BYAM.*
Bsq. The Babes in the Wood (Lyr. H. Rhyl, 14/9/91). See *M. BYAM.*
Ext. Puss in Boots up to Scratch (Croydon, 25/7/92). See *M. BYAM.*

WYLDE, Mrs HENRY
D. Her Oath (P'cess. 26/11/91, *mat.*). L.C.
C.D. Little Sunbeam (Lyr. 30/6/92, *mat.*). L.C.

WYNDHAM, Sir CHARLES
C.D. Lost (Bristol, 2/2/74).
M.F. A Night of Terror: A Musical Madness in Three Fyttes (Folly, 22/12/77). L.C.
[Written in collaboration with *A. MATTHISON.*]
C. The Idol (Folly, 21/9/78). L.C. as *Weeds.*
F. Tantalus (Folly, 14/10/78). See *A. MATTHISON.*

WYNNE, HUGO
Oa. May Meetings (T.H. Reading, 6/10/94). See *H. NOWELL.*

WYNNE, JOHN
D. The Advocate of Durango. 8° 1853.

WYNTER, H. J.
Ca. Mary (Aven. 16/2/97).

WYON, F. W.
D. Edwin and Ethelburga. 8° 1860.

YABSLEY, ADA G.
C.O. Lively Hal (District H. Plympton, 11/4/93). L.C.
[Music by Mrs Brooks.]

YARDLEY, W.
Bsq. Herne the Hunter (Gai. 24/5/81). See *R. REECE.*
Bsq. The Scalded Back; or, Comin' Scars (Nov. 12/7/84). L.C.
Bsq. Very Little Hamlet (Gai. 29/11/84). L.C.
F.C. The Excursion Train (O.C. 6/4/85). See *J. H. McCARTHY.*
M.Ca. Hobbies (St G. 6/4/85). See *H. P. STEPHENS.*
Bsq. The Vicar of Wideawakefield (Gai. 8/8/85). See *H. P. STEPHENS.*
Bsq. Little Jack Shepherd (Gai. 26/12/85). See *H. P. STEPHENS.*
C.D. Hand and Heart (Gai. 21/5/86, *mat.*). L.C.
[Written in collaboration with *H. P. STEPHENS.*]
Bsq. Venus (P.W. L'pool, 26/4/90). See *Sir A. HARRIS.*
P. Beauty and the Beast (D.L. 26/12/90). L.C.
[Written in collaboration with *Sir A. HARRIS.*]
F.C. The Planter (P.W. 31/10/91). L.C.
C.O. The Wedding Eve (Traf. 10/9/92). L.C.
[Music by F. Toulmouche, E. Ford and "Yvolde".]
D. The Passport (Glo. 15/10/94). See *B. C. STEPHENSON.*
M.Ext. Our Toys (St J. 16/7/95). L.C. St G. 16/12/76, as *Our Doll's House.*
[Written in collaboration with *C. DICK.*]
Bsq. A Model Trilby (O.C. 16/11/95). See *C. H. E. BROOKFIELD.*

M.C. On the March (Sheffield, 18/5/96; P.W. 22/6/96). L.C.
[Written in collaboration with *B. C. STEPHENSON* and *C. CLAY.* Music by J. Crook, E. Solomon and F. Clay.]

C.O. L'Amour mouille; or, Cupid and the Princess (Lyr. 5/4/99). L.C.
[Written in collaboration with *H. BYATT.*]

YATES, EDMUND.

F. A Night at Notting Hill (Adel. 5/1/57). See *N. H. HARRINGTON.*

F. My Friend from Leatherhead (Lyc. 23/2/57). See *N. H. HARRINGTON.*

F. Double Dummy (Lyc. 3/3/58).
[Written in collaboration with *N. H. HARRINGTON.*]

F. Your Likeness, One Shilling (Str. 22/4/58). See *N. H. HARRINGTON.*

C. After the Ball (G.I. 28/4/58).

F. Good for Nothing (Adel. 27/12/58).
[Written in collaboration with *N. H. HARRINGTON.*]

F. If the Cap fits (P'cess. 13/6/59). See *N. H. HARRINGTON.*

F. Hit him, he has no friends (Str. 17/9/60). L.C. *Lacy.*
[Written in collaboration with *N. H. HARRINGTON.*]

D. The Golden Daggers (P'cess. 19/4/62). L.C. *French.*

D. Black Sheep (Olym. 25/4/68). See *J. P. SIMPSON.*

C. Tame Cats (P.W. 12/12/68). L.C.

D. Without Love (Olym. 16/12/72). L.C.
[Written in collaboration with *A. W. DUBOURG.*]

YEATS, WILLIAM BUTLER.

Poet.D. The Land of Heart's Desire (Aven. 29/3/94). L.C.

T. The Countess Cathleen (Antient Concert R. Dublin, 8/5/99). L.C. 12° 1892.
[For his later plays see A. E. Morgan, *op. cit.* 314.]

YELDHAM, Major.

C. Sang Bleu (Ryde, 10/4/88).

Ext. Gilded Love (Ryde, 8/10/88).

YORKE, CECIL M.

Ext. The Abduction of Bianca (Silver Fête, Kensington, 11/7/88). See *W. SAPTE, Jr.*

YOULE, H. F.

D. A Sister's Love (Holb. 24/7/67, *amat.*) L.C.

YOUNG, ALFRED W.

C. A Threepenny Bit (Brighton, 18/8/70). See *J. M. MORTON.*

F. A False Alarm (Holb. 5/10/72). L.C.

YOUNG, Sir CHARLES L., Baronet.

D. Shadows (P'cess. 27/5/71). L.C. *Lacy.*

C.D. Charms (Qns. 26/7/71). L.C. *Lacy.*

T. Montcalm (Qns. 28/9/72). L.C. *French.*

D. Gilded Youth (Brighton, 30/9/72). *Lacy.*

D. Miss Chester (Holb. 5/10/72). L.C. *Lacy.*
[Written in collaboration with *F. MARRYAT.*]

C.D. Ivers Dean (Hanley, 12/11/77).
[Written in collaboration with *B. HOWARD.*]

D.Sk. Yellow Roses (High Wycombe, 14/1/78; Royal Hotel, Scarborough, 16/12/78). *French.*

D. The Regent Orleans (Hull, 2/79). L.C.
D. Infatuation (Bristol, 25/4/79; H. 1/5/79, *amat.*) L.C. *Lacy.*
D. Faustine (Bristol, 9/4/80; Olym. 24/6/80). L.C.
D. For Her Child's Sake (Windsor, 24/11/80, *amat.*; Terry's, 29/3/90). L.C. *Lacy.*
C. Childhood's Dreams. L.C. H. 14/1/81. *French.*
Ca. That Dreadful Doctor. L.C. H. 14/1/81. *French.*
Ca. Plot for Plot. L.C. H. 14/1/81. *Lacy.*
Ca. The Baron's Wager (Londesborough, Scarborough, 7/2/81; Aven. 10/2/97). *French.*
Ca. The Late Sir Benjamin (Bath Saloon, Torquay, 16/1/82). L.C. *French.*
D.Sk. Drifted Apart (Bath Saloon, Torquay, 16/1/82). *French.*
D.Sk. Her Birthday (Concert H. Lewes, 13/8/84).
Ca. Petticoat Perfidy (Court, 21/5/85). *French.*
C.D. Linda Grey (Margate, 9/6/85; P'cess. 8/4/91). L.C.
D. Jim, the Penman (H. 25/3/86, *mat.*; H. 3/4/86). L.C.
C.D. Garrick's Sacrifice (Spa, Harrowgate, 9/9/97). See *F. LINDO.*

YOUNG, GERALD.
D.Sk. Her Birthday (P.H. Hastings, 18/1/99). L.C. Ladb. H. 24/3/99.

YOUNG, H.
[For an earlier play see iv, 423.]
D. The Mysteries of Old Father Thames; or, The Lion Queen and the Lawyer's Clerk. L.C. Bower, 14/11/50.
D. Uncle Tom's Cabin (Ast. 22/11/52). L.C.
D. The Slave Hunt; or, St Clare and the Happy Days of Uncle Tom (Vic. 21/1/53). L.C.
D. Montaleoni, the Italian Brigand; or, The Outlaw's Daughter (Vic. 11/4/53). L.C.
D. The Mystery of the Abbey; or, the Murder Vision and the Wilt and the Way (Vic. 16/5/53). L.C.
P. Harlequin Seven Champions (Vic. 26/12/53).

YOUNG, HENRY.
D. Minnie Grey (E.C. 14/6/86).
[Written in collaboration with *G. ROBERTS.*]
D. Outcast London (E.C. 2/10/86). L.C. Sur. 10/3/84.
[Written in collaboration with *G. ROBERTS*: later revised by *A. WEST* and so acted at W.L. 14/2/98.]
D. Joanthan Wild (E.C. 27/11/86).

YOUNG, Mrs HENRY
D. The Light of Love; or, The Diamond and the Snowdrop (Eff. 25/2/67). L.C.
D. Jonathan Wild; or, The Storm on the Thames (E.L. 13/7/68). L.C.

YOUNG, JAMES
P. Sinbad the Sailor (Parkhurst, 24/12/96).
[Music by T. Fish.]

YOUNG, JESMOND
D. Joshua Haggard (Cheltenham, 19/5/79). L.C.

YOUNG, MARGARET
D. Trooper Blake (Gai. Dublin, 12/8/96).
C.D. Honesty—a Cottage Flower (Aven. 29/11/97). L.C.
Duol. Variations (Gar. 18/5/99).

[*YOUNG, W. H.*
D. The Cattle King (Muncaster, Bootle, 2/1/96). L.C.

YOUNG, Sir WILLIAM L. Baronet ["*LAWRENCE OLDE*"]
Duol. The Supper Dances (Steinway H. 19/5/91).
C.D. An American Bride (Lyr. 5/5/92). L.C.
[Written in collaboration with *M. NOEL.*]
C.O. Love and War (Portsmouth, 17/6/95). See *B. OLDE.*
Ca. Sylvia's Romance (Canterbury, 8/8/99).

YOUNGE, A.
[For an earlier play see *E.N.D.* ii, 413.]
C.D. A Village Tale (S.W. 1/4/50). L.C.
F. Beware of Man Traps (S.W. 1/51). L.C.

YOUNGE, WILLIAM
Bsq. The Lady of Lyons (Imp. 23/4/79). L.C.
P. Red Riding Hood; or, Little Boy Blue (Imp. 6/12/79). L.C.
P. Little Bo-Peep, Little Boy Blue and the Little Old Woman that lived in a Shoe (C.G. 26/12/81). L.C.
Ext. The Palace of Pearl (Empire, 12/6/86). L.C.
[Written in collaboration with *A. MURRAY.* Music by E. Jakobowski.]
Ext. Old King Cole and Good Queen Cole (Roy. 12/12/91, *mat.*). L.C.
[Music by F. Pascal.]
M.F.C. Playing the Game (Str. 12/6/96). L.C.
[Written in collaboration with *A. J. FLAXMAN.* Music by F. Eplett.]
F. Mr Sympkyn (Glo. 1/5/97). See *A. J. FLAXMAN.*

YUILL, A. W.
F. Married by Proxy (Greenock, 19/1/94; Toole's, 18/10/94). L.C.

ZALENSKA, WANDA
D. Marishka (Gt Grimsby, 4/8/90; S.W. 4/5/91). L.C.

ZANGWILL, ISRAEL
F. The Great Demonstration (Roy. 17/9/92). L.C.
[Written in collaboration with *L. COWEN.*]
Ext. Aladdin at Sea (P.R. Camborne, 25/1/93). L.C. T.H. Barnstaple, 9/1/93.
Duol. The Lady Journalist (Steinway H. 4/7/93). L.C. Ladb. H. 3/3/91.
Duol. Six Persons (H. 22/12/93). L.C.
F. Threepenny Bits (O.H. Chatham, 25/4/95; Gar. 6/5/95). L.C.
D. Children of the Ghetto (Oddfellows' H. Deal, 25/7/99, *copy.*; Adel. 11/12/99). L.C.

ZECH, MARIE [*Mrs C. ROBINSON*]
D. It is Justice (Bury St Edmunds, 26/12/90).

ZIMMERMAN, H.
Oa. The Eccentric Guardian (P.H. New Cross, 25/4/85).
[Music by W. R. Quinn.]
F.C. Putting things right (P.H. New Cross, 25/4/85).

ZOBLINSKY, Mme.
O. Annie of Tharau (P'cess. Edinburgh, 12/4/80). L.C.
[Music by H. Hofman.]

UNKNOWN AUTHORS

P. A Apple-Pie; or, Harlequin Jack in the Box and the Little Boy Blue (Sur. 26/12/66). L.C.
D. The Abbé Buonaparte. L.C. Olym. 17/3/91.
D. L'Abbé Laffarge. L.C. Grec. 19/7/76.
P. Abdallah; or, The Forty Thieves. L.C. Newcastle, 23/12/91.
D. Abel Drake's Wife (H.M. Richmond, 25/1/72).
Bsq. Abou Hassan; or, The Sleeper wide awake. L.C. Norwich, 22/3/50.
P. Abou Hassan, the Sleeper of Bagdad and the Fairy Elves of the Enchanted Mosque (Brit. 26/12/62). L.C.
F. The Absent-minded Man. L.C. Internat. 22/12/84.
Oa. Abu Hassan (D.L. 12/5/70). L.C.
D.Sk. The Academy. L.C. S.W. 14/9/97.
D. The Academy. L.C. Empress, 30/12/98.
C.O. The Accidental Son; or, Bruschino. L.C. D.L. 17/3/59.
M.D. Across the Atlantic; or, The Pirates' Black Flag. L.C. Gar. 18/8/71.
C. An Act in the Life of David Garrick. L.C. L'pool, 5/1/56.
D. Adam Strong, the Shipwright. L.C. Col. L'pool, 25/7/64.
D. An Adder in the Path (P.W. Glasgow, 3/7/71).
D. Adèle d'Escars, the Picklock of Paris. L.C. Eff. 26/10/66.
Bal. Adelina (H.M. 1/6/60).
Bsq. Adelphi Fare: Three Removes and a Dessert. L.C. Adel. 23/3/53.
O. Adina; or, The Elixir of Love (Court, L'pool, 24/2/92).
Sk. The Admiral (Coronet, 10/2/99).
Bsq. Admiral Jack. L.C. T.H. Maidenhead, 31/7/93.
Oa. The Admiral's Daughter. L.C. Maidstone, 24/5/69.
Ca. The Admiral's Ghost. L.C. Qns. R. Glasgow, 8/11/89.
F.C. A.D. 1; or, The Year One. L.C. O.C. 18/10/95.
D. Adrienne Lecouvreur (St. J. 2/8/55).
D. Adrienne Lecouvreur (Adel. 25/8/62).
D. Adrienne Lecouvreur. L.C. Margate, 13/9/82.
D. Adrift (Aldershot, 24/1/87).
D. Adrift on the World (M'bone, 28/11/74).
D. The Adventurer; or, The Fiend's Mountain (D.L. 13/10/56).
R.D. The Adventurer; or, Plots in Spain (Sur. 1/4/50). L.C.
D. The Adventures of a Guinea. L.C. Stand. 17/10/50.
D. The Adventures of Becky Sharp. L.C. Brighton, 29/9/99.
D. Adversity; or, The Rough Road tests the Mettle. L.C. Grec. 17/3/61.
F. An Advertisement—Wanted, Wives and Husbands (Str. 17/4/54).
F. Advertisements. L.C. Stand. 12/12/68.
D. The Advocate (Sur. 1/1/59).
D. The Advocate's Daughter (Edinburgh, 1856).
C.D. After Many Days. L.C. Pav. Southport, 25/2/82.
D.Sk. After Many Years. L.C. S.W. 8/4/96.
D. The Aftermath. L.C. Parkhurst, 9/8/95.
D. After Midnight. L.C. Gar. 25/9/68.
D. After the Ball. L.C. S.W. 30/11/94.
[See *F. K. PEILE*, 1895.]
F. After the Fancy Dress Ball. L.C. Rotunda, L'pool, 5/5/90.
F. After the Show. L.C. Empire, Leicester, 22/6/94.

D. Against her Will. L.C. N. Shields, 4/8/83.
D. The Age we live in (Grand, Birmingham, 22/5/93).
D. The Agitator. L.C. W.L. 30/11/93.
D. Agnolo Diora (Grec. 7/11/59). L.C.
F. A. H., My Daughter's Intended. L.C. Grec. 18/10/52.
C.D. L'Aide (Croydon, 19/6/76).
D. The Alabama, Privateer; or, The Scourge of the North (Col. L'pool, 23/9/72).
P. Aladdin. L.C. Alfred, 11/1/73.
P. Aladdin. L.C. Alex. Sheffield, 14/12/75.
P. Aladdin. L.C. Rotunda, L'pool, 26/12/76.
P. Aladdin. L.C. Hanley, 29/12/76.
P. Aladdin. L.C. Glasgow, 5/1/77.
P. Aladdin. L.C. Bradford, 6/12/77.
P. Aladdin. L.C. P.W. Newport, 21/12/77.
P. Aladdin. L.C. Aquar. 14/12/78.
P. Aladdin. L.C. Sheffield, 21/12/78.
P. Aladdin. L.C. Edinburgh, 30/12/78.
P. Aladdin. L.C. Park, 2/7/79.
P. Aladdin. L.C. P.W. Birmingham, 8/12/79.
P. Aladdin. L.C. Worcester, 17/12/79.
P. Aladdin. L.C. Brighton, 14/12/80.
P. Aladdin. L.C. Grand, Leeds, 18/12/80.
P. Aladdin. L.C. P'cess. Glasgow, 17/12/81.
P. Aladdin. L.C. Bristol, 20/12/81.
P. Aladdin. L.C. Qns. Manchester, 22/12/81.
P. Aladdin. L.C. P.W. L'pool, 23/12/81.
P. Aladdin. L.C. Oldham, 11/1/82.
P. Aladdin. L.C. Roy. Chester, 15/12/82.
P. Aladdin. L.C. Aven. Sunderland, 27/12/82.
P. Aladdin. L.C. Stockton-on-Tees, 24/1/83.
P. Aladdin. L.C. Croydon, 24/12/83.
P. Aladdin. L.C. Glasgow, 10/12/84.
P. Aladdin. L.C. Alex. Sheffield, 10/12/84.
P. Aladdin. L.C. Manchester, 10/12/84.
P. Aladdin. L.C. Grand, Birmingham, 20/12/84.
P. Aladdin. L.C. Pier Pav. Hastings, 26/12/84.
P. Aladdin. L.C. Alex. L'pool, 12/1/85.
P. Aladdin. L.C. York, 30/3/85.
P. Aladdin. L.C. O.H. Leeds, 17/12/85.
P. Aladdin. L.C. Newcastle, 29/12/85.
P. Aladdin. L.C. P.W. Birmingham, 13/12/86.
P. Aladdin. L.C. St J. Manchester, 21/12/86.
P. Aladdin. L.C. Nottingham, 28/12/86.
P. Aladdin. L.C. Edinburgh, 14/12/87.
P. Aladdin. L.C. Rotunda, L'pool, 21/12/87.
P. Aladdin. L.C. Cardiff, 17/12/88.
P. Aladdin. L.C. P.W. L'pool, 16/12/89.
P. Aladdin. L.C. Stockport, 17/12/89.
P. Aladdin. L.C. Brighton, 20/12/89.
P. Aladdin. L.C. Birmingham, 24/12/89.
P. Aladdin. L.C. Portsmouth, 13/11/90.
P. Aladdin. L.C. Sheffield, 24/11/90.
P. Aladdin. L.C. Bury, 5/12/90.

P. Aladdin. L.C. Stratford, 11/12/90.
P. Aladdin. L.C. P's. Bristol, 22/12/90.
P. Aladdin. L.C. Hanley, 7/12/91.
P. Aladdin. L.C. Middlesborough, 12/12/91.
P. Aladdin. L.C. R.A. Woolwich, 18/12/91.
P. Aladdin. L.C. Shakespeare, L'pool, 23/12/91.
P. Aladdin. L.C. Morton's, Greenwich, 23/12/91.
P. Aladdin. L.C. P.W. Birmingham, 6/12/92.
P. Aladdin. L.C. Edinburgh, 19/12/92.
P. Aladdin. L.C. Bradford, 19/12/92.
P. Aladdin. L.C. P's. Manchester, 22/12/92.
P. Aladdin. L.C. Alex. Sheffield, 30/11/93.
P. Aladdin. L.C. Plymouth, 30/11/93.
P. Aladdin. L.C. Bournemouth, 7/12/93.
P. Aladdin. L.C. County, Reading, 16/12/93.
P. Aladdin. L.C. Brighton, 16/12/93.
P. Aladdin. L.C. Grand, Leeds, 7/1/95.
P. Aladdin. L.C. Nottingham, 10/1/96.
P. Aladdin. L.C. Great Grimsby, 10/1/96.
P. Aladdin. L.C. Manchester, 18/12/96.
P. Aladdin. L.C. St J. Manchester, 21/12/96.
P. Aladdin. L.C. Grand, Glasgow, 21/12/96.
P. Aladdin. L.C. P.W. L'pool, 26/12/96.
P. Aladdin. L.C. S. Shields, 26/12/96.
P. Aladdin. L.C. Aquar. Great Yarmouth, 26/12/96.
P. Aladdin. L.C. Ass. Rooms, Balham, 8/1/97.
P. Aladdin. L.C. Manchester, 31/12/97.
P. Aladdin. L.C. Grand, Birmingham, 31/12/97.
P. Aladdin. L.C. Grand, Leeds, 31/12/97.
P. Aladdin. L.C. Col. Dudley, 31/12/97.
P. Aladdin. L.C. Edinburgh, 30/12/98.
Ext. Aladdin. L.C. Vic. H. Ealing, 30/12/98.
P. Aladdin. L.C. Plymouth, 30/12/98.
P. Aladdin. L.C. Paisley, 30/12/98.
P. Aladdin. L.C. Court, L'pool, 30/12/98.
P. Aladdin. (Bijou, 7/1/99, *amat.*).
P. Aladdin. L.C. R.A. Woolwich, 28/12/99.
P. Aladdin. L.C. Grand, Hull, 28/12/99.
P. Aladdin. L.C. P's. Bristol, 28/12/99.
P. Aladdin; or, Harlequin Ching-Amy-Chow. L.C. O.H. Dundee, 14/12/75.
P. Aladdin; or, The Wonderful Lamp, and the Fairies of the Silver Bells. L.C. Qns. 24/12/61.
Ext. Aladdin and the Flying Genius (Phil. 26/12/81).
P. Aladdin and the Wonderful Lamp. L.C. Manchester, 9/12/56.
P. Aladdin the First; or, The Scamp, the Lamp and the Emperor. L.C. Amphi. Leeds, 22/12/71.
P. Aladdin the Great. L.C. P's. Manchester, 14/12/75.
P. Aladdin the Second. L.C. Grand, Leeds, 11/12/88.
[See *ALFRED THOMPSON*, 1870.]
C.O. Aladdin the Third; or, An Oil Lamp in a New Light. L.C. Gai. 22/12/70.
D. Alanna, the Child of Clare. L.C. Norwich, 15/1/94.
D. Albert's Mystery. L.C. Village H. Chislehurst, 16/2/99.

M.F. The Album of Beauties. L.C. Var. 12/6/84.
Ext. The Album of Beauty. L.C. Phil. 29/9/79.
D. Alexandra (Roy. 4/3/93). L.C.
D. Alfonso and Claudina, the Faithful Spouse; or, The Hated Race (C.P. 1862).
D. Alfred. L.C. Qns. Manchester, 10/6/61.
C.O. Al Fresco. L.C. T.H. Hulme, 24/3/99.
P. Ali Baba (Vic. 20/6/65).
P. Ali Baba (Var. 26/12/73).
P. Ali Baba. L.C. H.M. Glasgow, 10/1/79.
P. Ali Baba. L.C. Plymouth, 26/12/83.
P. Ali Baba. L.C. P.W. L'pool, 25/11/92.
Ba. Ali Baba; or, The Forty Naughty Thieves (Birkenhead, 14/5/83).
P. Ali Baba; or, The Forty Thieves. L.C. Pal. Manchester, 26/12/95.
P. Ali Baba and the Forty Thieves. L.C. Gai. Hartlepool, 14/1/78.
P. Ali Baba and the Forty Thieves. L.C. Edinburgh, 14/1/78.
P. Ali Baba and the Forty Thieves. L.C. Cardiff, 27/12/79.
P. Ali Baba and the Forty Thieves. L.C. Victory, Aldershot, 13/1/80.
P. Ali Baba and the Forty Thieves. L.C. P's. Manchester, 20/11/84.
P. Ali Baba and the Forty Thieves. L.C. Morton's, Greenwich, 18/12/96.
P. Alice in Wonderland. L.C. R.A. Woolwich, 20/12/86.
D. Alice Lowrie, the Forger's Victim; or, The Jolly Young Waterman. L.C. Vic. 7/11/61.
D. Alina; or, The Daughter of Fire (Grec. 20/10/51).
F. All Alive, Oh! (Str. 16/6/97). L.C.
F. All for the Best. L.C. Alh. 27/5/80.
Bal. All Hallows' Eve (H. 11/7/59).
Oa. All Hallows' Eve. L.C. Assembly R. Cheltenham, 19/7/82.
Ca. All in a Good Humour. L.C. Windsor, 25/11/72.
D. All the Year Round. L.C. Qns. 4/6/62.
Bsq. Alma Mater. L.C. Cambridge, 18/2/92.
D. Alone in the World; or, Home and the Homeless (Grec. 14/9/63). L.C.
P. Alonzo and Imogen. L.C. P'cess. Glasgow, 26/12/95.
P. Alonzo the Artless. L.C. Grand, Halifax, 10/9/92.
Bsq. Alonzo the Brave; or, Faust and the Fair Imogene. L.C. Greenwich, 20/5/64.
Bsq. Alonzo the Brave and the Fair Imogene (Str. 30/1/55).
[By *H. T. CRAVEN*.]
F.C. The Alps (Cambridge, 2/6/86).
D. Alta; or, Right against Might (New Cross H. 4/9/84). L.C.
D. The Amazon's Oath; or, The Hour of One. L.C. Qns. 25/10/58.
D. Ambition; or, Poverty, Competence and Riches. L.C. Brit. 7/4/54.
D. Ambition; or, The Throne and the Tomb (Sur. 30/9/57). L.C. as *Catherine Howard*.
D. An Ambuscade at Inkerman (P'cess. 23/7/60).
C. The American in England. L.C. Manchester, 14/3/55.
D. American Slavery (Brit. 30/6/62).
D. Amos Tyrrell. L.C. T.H. Kilburn, 21/6/92.
C. Amphitryon. L.C. Court, 31/10/72.
D. Amy Arlington; or, The Murder in the Oak Coppice (Grec. 4/5/63). L.C.

D. Amy the Golden; or, The Drooping Lily. L.C. Sur. 12/7/60.
D. Anarchy. L.C. Empress, 13/4/99.
D. Anato (C.L. 1850). L.C.
D. Anchora Machree (Lyc. Sunderland, 13/3/71). L.C. Newcastle, 21/5/67.
D. And One Suffered. L.C. Str. 22/7/89.
D. Andrea the Painter. L.C. Memorial, Stratford-on-Avon, 10/4/88.
D. André the Miner, the Son of Toil; or, Power and Principle. L.C. Vic. 27/6/61.
D. Andrew Mills (Cambridge, Spennymoor, 16/10/76). L.C.
Duol. Andromeda. L.C. Parkhurst, 31/12/97.
Oa. Angela; or, A Woman's Wit (D.L. 28/9/78). L.C.
D. Angeline (Str. 13/11/54).
D. The Angel of Darkness (Grec. 26/9/59). L.C.
D. The Angel of Islington; or, The Merrie Days of Shakespeare and Queen Bess. L.C. Brit. 5/6/55.
D. The Angel of Peace and Pardon; or, Elodie, the Virgin of the Monastery. L.C. Brit. 31/7/63.
D. The Animated Statue. L.C. Manchester, 25/1/69.
P. Anne Boleyn; or, Harlequin King Harry and the Miller of the River Dee. L.C. C.L. 19/12/56.
D. Annie Monksworth; or, The Inheritress of a Sister's Shame (Brit. 18/7/59). L.C.
F. The Anonymous Letter (Str. 6/3/54). L.C.
D. Another Cup. L.C. Imp. 16/4/81.
F. Another Mistake. L.C. H.M. Richmond, 10/2/83.
Bsq. Anthony and Cleopatra. L.C. Aven. 26/2/91.
C.D. Anthropos. L.C. D.Y. 15/8/98.
F. The Anti-garotte (Str. 31/1/57; Str. 2/2/63, as *My Knuckle-duster*). L.C.
D. The Ape of the Prairies (Sur. 21/5/61).
Bsq. Apollo and the Flying Pegasus; or, The Defeat of the Amazons (Ast. 19/4/58). L.C.
F. An April Fool. L.C. S.W. 4/7/95.
F. April Fools. L.C. Brighton, 24/5/83.
Sk. An April Jest (Terry's, 26/7/93, *mat.*).
Oa. An Apt Pupil. L.C. P.H. Ledbury, 28/9/96.
M.F. An Arabian Eve. L.C. Pal. 5/6/94.
Ent. Arcadia (Brit. 13/8/60).
D. Archy Moore; or, The Rat of the Hold. L.C. Vic. 2/5/59.
T. Ariadne (Olym. 28/1/50). L.C.
Bal. Ariadne (D.L. 25/4/59).
Ent. The Army, the Navy and the Volunteers (Metro. M.H. 18/7/70).
D. Arrah-ma-Beg; or, Robbing the Mail (C.L. 15/10/66). L.C.
D. Arrah Niel; or, The Vale of Knockfierna (Adel. L'pool, 1/4/72).
Bsq. Arrah-No-Brogue; or, The Girl of the Lips (S.W. 25/10/65). L.C.
F. Arrested on Suspicion. L.C. Phil. 24/9/77.
C. Art. L.C. Southampton, 8/11/81.
[See *C. READE*, 1855.]
F.C. Artful Plans. L.C. Empire, Devonport, 16/9/95.
D. The Artisan's Daughter (Soho, 9/2/61).
D. The Artisan's Triumph (Brit. 15/7/61).
D. The Artist and his Family (Sur. 28/2/59). L.C.

Bal. L'Artiste de Terracina (D.L. 28/3/53).
D. An Artist's Model. L.C. W.L. 12/6/94.
[See *O. HALL*, 1895.]
D. An Artist's Wife. L.C. St J. 20/10/54.
D. As Gold through Fire (P'cess, Edinburgh, 23/6/73).
C.D. As Gold through Fire. L.C. Olym. 7/4/79.
D. Ashlynn. L.C. Croydon, 15/11/70.
C.O. Asmodeus; or, The Devil's Share. L.C. Greenwich, 23/4/85.
C.O. Asmodeus, the Devil on Two Sticks (Adel. 27/4/59).
FairyD. As Pretty as Seven. L.C. St G. 3/6/87.
D. The Assassins of the Roadside (Stand. 13/3/65). L.C. as *The Assassins of the Roadside Inn.*
D. L'Assommoir; or, The Demon of Drink. L.C. Plymouth, 21/10/79.
D. L.'Assommoir; or, The Effects of Drink. L.C. M.H. Hastings, 24/7/82.
D. The Assyrian Spy. L.C. Pav. 8/9/52.
D. Aston Hall; or, Birmingham in 1643. L.C. Birmingham, 11/4/54.
D. Astray from the Flock. L.C. Pav. 9/9/81.
D. Athelstane; or, The Blackmailed Warrior (C.L. 12/6/54). L.C.
F. At Sea. L.C. Margate, 18/4/82.
Sk. At the Races (Lincoln, 24/3/84).
P. Au Japon (St G. 20/5/96). L.C. People's Palace.
D. Auld Robin Gray; or, The Hand and the Heart. L.C. Brit. 22/8/56.
F. Aunt Dorothy (D.L. 25/1/55).
F. Aunt Hannah. L.C. Str. 29/9/99.
C. Aunt Jemima. L.C. T.H. Fulham, 28/5/94.
Ca. Aunt Madge. L.C. T.H. Hulme, 29/11/98.
R.D. Aurelian; or, Scion of the Sun. L.C. Ladb. H. 1/6/97.
C. Au Revoir. L.C. P.H. Urmston, 30/3/96.
F.C. Aurora. L.C. Toole's, 20/12/93.
Bal. Aurora; or, The Goddess of Morni. L.C. Grec. 9/6/65.
D. Aurora Floyd. L.C. Qns. 30/3/63.
D. Aurora Floyd. L.C. Eff. 20/4/63.
D. Australia Felix (Brit. 14/5/62).
D. The Author's Box. L.C. Shaft. 30/3/96.
Ext. Autumn Sheaves; or, The Harvest Home. L.C. C.P. 14/10/72.
D. Avarice (Sur. 26/10/57). L.C.
Ca. Awkward (Com. Manchester, 28/9/85).
F. An Awkward Mistake. L.C. Imp. 20/12/81.
D. Aylma's Dream. L.C. Sheffield, 2/9/86.
Bal. Azurine (Grec. 22/10/60).
D. Bab; or, Saved by a Child (Burnley, 11/9/82).
F. Babbage's Puppets (Bolton, 22/9/84).
P. The Babes in the Wood (Stand. 9/4/55).
P. The Babes in the Wood. L.C. Bradford, 11/12/69.
P. The Babes in the Wood. L.C. Hanley, 13/1/75.
P. The Babes in the Wood. L.C. Amphi. Leeds, 14/12/75.
P. The Babes in the Wood. L.C. Exeter, 6/1/76.
P. The Babes in the Wood. L.C. P'cess. Edinburgh, 14/12/76.
P. The Babes in the Wood. L.C. Bristol, 16/12/76.
P. The Babes in the Wood. L.C. Wakefield, 22/12/76.
P. The Babes in the Wood. L.C. Dundee, 26/12/76.

P. The Babes in the Wood. L.C. Oldham, 28/12/76.
P. The Babes in the Wood. L.C. Plymouth, 6/12/77.
P. The Babes in the Wood. L.C. Gai. Glasgow, 11/12/77.
P. The Babes in the Wood. L.C. P's. Manchester, 18/12/77.
P. The Babes in the Wood. L.C. Leicester, 21/12/77.
P. The Babes in the Wood. L.C. P.W. Birmingham, 6/12/78.
P. The Babes in the Wood. L.C. Blackburn, 14/12/78.
P. The Babes in the Wood. L.C. Nottingham, 27/12/78.
P. The Babes in the Wood. L.C. Dumfries, 31/12/78.
P. The Babes in the Wood. (E.C. 26/12/79). L.C.
P. The Babes in the Wood. L.C. P'cess. Glasgow, 14/12/80.
P. The Babes in the Wood. L.C. Preston, 23/12/80.
P. The Babes in the Wood. L.C. Court, L'pool, 17/12/81.
P. The Babes in the Wood. L.C. Leicester, 22/12/81.
P. The Babes in the Wood. L.C. Bradford, 12/12/83.
P. The Babes in the Wood. L.C. York, 10/4/84.
P. The Babes in the Wood. L.C. Portsmouth, 10/12/84.
P. The Babes in the Wood. L.C. Sefton, L'pool, 18/12/84.
P. The Babes in the Wood. L.C. Rotunda, L'pool, 23/12/84.
P. The Babes in the Wood. L.C. Cardiff, 7/12/85.
P. The Babes in the Wood. L.C. Grand, Birmingham, 21/12/85.
P. The Babes in the Wood. L.C. Sheffield, 21/12/85.
P. The Babes in the Wood. L.C. Stockport, 21/12/85.
P. The Babes in the Wood. L.C. Edinburgh, 23/12/85.
P. The Babes in the Wood. L.C. Grand, Glasgow, 13/12/86.
P. The Babes in the Wood. L.C. Qns. Manchester, 23/12/86.
P. The Babes in the Wood. L.C. Nottingham, 20/12/87.
P. The Babes in the Wood. L.C. P's. Bristol, 24/12/87.
P. The Babes in the Wood. L.C. Alex. Sheffield, 6/12/89.
P. The Babes in the Wood. L.C. P's. Manchester, 20/12/89.
P. The Babes in the Wood. L.C. Grand, Leeds, 1/12/90.
P. The Babes in the Wood. L.C. Pier Pav. Hastings, 15/12/90.
P. The Babes in the Wood. L.C. Rotunda, L'pool, 17/12/90.
P. The Babes in the Wood. L.C. P.W. Birmingham, 18/12/90.
P. The Babes in the Wood. L.C. Stratford, 12/12/92.
P. The Babes in the Wood. L.C. New, Exeter, 19/12/92.
P. The Babes in the Wood. L.C. Roy. Chester, 19/12/92.
P. The Babes in the Wood. L.C. Dewsbury, 19/12/92.
P. The Babes in the Wood. L.C. P's. Bristol, 24/12/92.
P. The Babes in the Wood (Stand. 24/12/92).
P. The Babes in the Wood. L.C. Alex. Widnes, 9/12/93.
P. The Babes in the Wood. L.C. Col. Oldham, 16/12/93.
P. The Babes in the Wood. L.C. Leeds, 26/11/94.
P. The Babes in the Wood. L.C. Northampton, 10/12/94.
P. The Babes in the Wood. L.C. P'cess. Glasgow, 15/12/94.
P. The Babes in the Wood. L.C. Edinburgh, 18/12/94.
P. The Babes in the Wood. L.C. Croydon, 18/12/94.
P. The Babes in the Wood. L.C. Cardiff, 19/12/94.
P. The Babes in the Wood. L.C. Shakespeare, L'pool, 26/12/96.
P. The Babes in the Wood. L.C. Richmond, 26/12/96.
P. The Babes in the Wood. L.C. Brighton, 26/12/96.
P. The Babes in the Wood. L.C. Hull, 26/12/96.
P. The Babes in the Wood. L.C. P's. Manchester, 8/1/97.
P. The Babes in the Wood. L.C. Lyr. Ealing, 8/1/97.

P. The Babes in the Wood. L.C. P's. Bradford, 8/1/97.
P. The Babes in the Wood. L.C. P.H. Barnsley, 8/1/97.
P. The Babes in the Wood. L.C. Church House, Cheddar, 31/12/97.
P. The Babes in the Wood. L.C. Tyne, Newcastle, 31/12/97.
P. The Babes in the Wood. L.C. St J. Manchester, 27/12/98.
P. The Babes in the Wood. L.C. Rotunda, L'pool, 30/12/98.
P. The Babes in the Wood. L.C. Manor, 30/12/98.
P. The Babes in the Wood. L.C. Manchester, 30/12/98.
P. The Babes in the Wood. L.C. New, Portsmouth, 22/12/99.
P. The Babes in the Wood. L.C. County, Kingston, 28/12/99.
P. The Babes in the Wood. L.C. Lyc. Eccles, 28/12/99.
P. The Babes in the Wood. L.C. New, Chatham, 28/12/99.
P. The Babes in the Wood. L.C. Eden, Brighton, 28/12/99.
P. The Babes in the Wood. L.C. Birmingham, 28/12/99.
P. The Babes in the Wood. L.C. O.H. Cheltenham, 28/12/99.
P. The Babes in the Wood. L.C. Court, L'pool, 28/12/99.
P. The Babes in the Wood. L.C. Coronet, 28/12/99.
P. The Babes in the Wood. L.C. Alex. Sheffield, 28/12/99.
P. The Babes in the Wood. L.C. O.H. Leicester, 28/12/99.
P. The Babes in the Wood; or, Harlequin and the Cruel Uncle (H. 24/12/56). L.C.
P. The Babes in the Wood; or, Harlequin Cock Robin and the Good Little Fairy Birds (Greenwich, 24/12/67).
P. The Babes in the Wood and Bold Robin Hood. L.C. Bradford, 18/12/94.
Ca. Baby. L.C. Oxford, 30/11/83.
[See *R. SOUTAR*, 1890, and *A. E. COWELL*, 1892.]
Ca. Baby Bunting. L.C. Vaud. 30/11/97.
F.C. The Baby's Hat. L.C. T.H. Kilburn, 31/1/91.
Ent. Bacchus (Stand. 30/4/55).
Bal. Bacchus and Ariadne (H. 12/7/61).
Ca. A Bachelor's Box. L.C. H. 17/1/82.
D. Baffled. L.C. Newport, 29/4/78.
D. Baffled. L.C. Var. 5/2/84.
D. Baffled; or, Parma Violets (Stand. 19/9/81). L.C.
F. The Bagpipes. L.C. S.W. 9/8/95.
D. Balaclava Day (D.L. 17/3/56).
D. The Ballad Girl; or, The Orphan of the Streets (Pav. 3/12/66). L.C.
D. The Baltic Fleet. L.C. Stand. 5/6/54.
F. Bamboozle (Grec. 12/7/60).
P. Bambuzleum; or, The Captive and the Fairy of the Magic Ring. L.C. Var. 19/11/72.
D. The Bandit King (Qns. Manchester, 16/9/95; Pav. 2/12/95).
D. The Bandit Queen (Brit. 25/11/61).
D. The Banker's Son. L.C. Portsmouth, 5/10/83.
D. The Banks of the Boyne Water (Bishop Auckland, 3/3/84). L.C. Whitehaven, 20/12/82.
M.F. The Barber. L.C. Pleasure Gdns. Folkestone, 17/3/92.
P. Barber, Barber, Shave the Cat; or, Harlequin Monopoly Humbug, Free Trade and the Magic Pins. L.C. Eff. 16/12/59.
Ext. Barber Blue. St. G. 20/5/69.
Ext. The Barber of Cadiz (D.L. 3/4/54).
Bsq. The Barber's Trip to Paris (P.W. Wolverhampton, 28/2/76).

F. Barely Possible. L.C. Alex. L'pool, 8/4/69.
D. The Bargeman of the Thames (Grec. 13/8/66). L.C.
Ext. The Bargemaster's Daughter; or, The Fog-Fiend and the Fairy Fanakin. L.C. M'bone, 21/5/63.
D. Barnaby Rudge (M'bone, 4/11/76).
F. Barney's Mistake. L.C. M'bone, 16/11/81.
D. The Baronets; or, How will it end. L.C. Birmingham, 14/5/70.
C.O. Baron Golosh (Star, Swansea, 15/4/95; Traf. 25/4/95). L.C.
P. Baron Munchausen; or, Harlequin and the Mountains of the Moon. (Vic. 24/12/64). L.C.
D. Baron Trenck. L.C. Brixton, 29/9/99.
D. Barrington, the Gentleman Pickpocket (Brit. 19/8/62). L.C. as *Barrington Geo; or, A Hundred Years Ago.*
D. The Bartons of Barton Wold. L.C. Oxford, 20/9/65.
C. The Bashful Lovers (Str. 19/8/61).
D. Basiliska (Jarrow Street R. Hull, 22/7/70).
C. Basil's Faith (Hull, 6/6/74).
D. The Battle of Austerlitz (Soho, 22/9/59).
D. The Battle of Bothwell Brig (Ast. 11/10/58). L.C. as *The Covenanters*; or, *The B. of B. B.*
D. The Battle of Chevy Chase (Tyne, Newcastle, 29/3/75).
D. The Battle of Inkerman. L.C. Pav. 2/12/54.
D. The Battle of Jersey (Jersey, 6/1/81).
D. The Battle of Life (Stand. 22/5/93).
Spec. The Battle of the Alma (Ast. 23/10/54). L.C.
[An "Additional Act, illustrating the Battles of Balaclava and Inkerman", performed at Ast. 26/2/55. This version was by *J. H. STOCQUELER.*]
D. The Battle of the Alma (Sur. 20/11/54).
D. The Battle of the Alma. L.C. Stand. 22/7/56.
D. The Battle of the Heart; or, The Pirate Merchant. L.C. C.L. 12/1/65.
D. The Battle of Waterloo. L.C. Vic. 5/4/54.
Ca. The Battle of Woman; or, Un duel d'amour. L.C. Olym. 30/4/51.
F. The Beard and Moustache Movement. L.C. Grec. 25/4/54.
D. Beaten by a Shadow. L.C. Gai. W. Hartlepool, 25/2/82.
D. Beatrice Maxwell. L.C. Olym. 4/6/96.
Spec. Beauties of the Harem (St J. 13/11/54).
Ext. The Beautiful Bride and the Bouncing Bachelor; or, The Bragging Bravos of the Brigand Band. L.C. Beaufort House, Walham Green, 3/3/66.
Ca. The Beautiful Duchess. L.C. T.H. Kilburn, 22/10/86.
Oa. The Beautiful Galatea. L.C. Bath, 28/9/82.
P. Beauty and the Beast (Sur. 12/6/54).
P. Beauty and the Beast. L.C. Manchester, 22/12/75.
P. Beauty and the Beast. L.C. L'pool, 24/12/75.
P. Beauty and the Beast. L.C. St Helen's, Lancs. 24/12/75.
P. Beauty and the Beast. L.C. Cheltenham, 30/12/75.
P. Beauty and the Beast. L.C. Worcester, 12/12/76.
P. Beauty and the Beast. L.C. Leicester, 6/1/77.
P. Beauty and the Beast. L.C. Greenock, 6/2/77.
P. Beauty and the Beast. L.C. Bristol, 19/12/77.
P. Beauty and the Beast. L.C. Blackburn, 22/12/79.
P. Beauty and the Beast. L.C. Birmingham, 24/12/81.

P. Beauty and the Beast. L.C. Qns. Manchester, 15/12/82.
P. Beauty and the Beast. L.C. P.W. L'pool, 26/12/83.
P. Beauty and the Beast. L.C. Sheffield, 10/1/84.
P. Beauty and the Beast. L.C. Blackburn, 15/12/84.
P. Beauty and the Beast. L.C. P's. Manchester, 9/12/87.
Ca. Beauty and the Beast. L.C. Swansea, 18/2/89.
P. Beauty and the Beast. L.C. Preston, 20/12/89.
Bsq. Beauty and the Beast (S.W. 12/10/91).
Bsq. Beauty and the Beast. L.C. Grand H. Maidenhead, 10/7/93.
P. Beauty and the Beast. L.C. Grand, Glasgow, 10/12/94.
P. Beauty and the Beast. L.C. Alex. Sheffield, 26/12/95.
P. Beauty and the Beast. L.C. Com. Manchester, 28/12/99.
F. Beeswing in Port. L.C. D.L. 16/10/55.
Oa. Beggar my Neighbour—a Blind Man's Bouffe. L.C. G.I. 24/3/70.
D. The Beggar of Brussels (Sur. 6/2/60).
D. The Beggar's Banquet; or, Beneath the Lamps of London. L.C. Eff. 15/10/62.
Oa. Begging the Question. L.C. Athenaeum Inst. Shepherds Bush, 11/3/82.
D. The Beginning and End of the South Wales Strike (Cardiff, 24/5/75).
D. The Beguiled One (Brit. 18/12/61). L.C. 22/11/58.
M.C. Behind the Scenes: The Prima Donna of a Night. L.C. Birmingham, 1/11/89.
[See *F. MORRIS*, 1896.]
F. Belgravia; or, North and South (Vic. Pav. Leamington, 28/8/82).
Bsq. Belinda. L.C. Birmingham, 12/5/82.
D. Belinda Seagrave; or, The Tempter and the Betrayer. L.C. 1/9/51.
D. Belinda the Blind (Brit. 1/1/59).
D. Bella Demonia. L.C. Crit. 6/4/91.
Ca. The Belle and the Boor (St J. 23/3/57). L.C.
D. La Belle Clarisse (Ladb. H. 9/3/91). L.C.
C.O. La Belle Lurette (Gai. 6/7/81). L.C.
C.O. La Belle Lurette. L.C. Aven. 22/3/83.
D. The Belle of the Season (Eff. 16/4/66). L.C.
F. The Belles of the Kitchen (Niblo's, New York, 1/74; D.L. 5/8/69).
D. Bell of Belle-Hawke (Exeter, 2/4/73). L.C.
Bsq. The Bells Bellesqued and the Polish Jew Polished Off; or, Mathias, the Muffin, the Mystery, the Maiden, and the Master (Norwich, 13/3/83).
D. The Bells of Shandon; or, The Banks of the Lee. L.C. Stand. 9/9/63.
D. The Bells of Shandon; or, The Lady of Munster: A Tale of the River Lee (Dundee, 21/9/68).
R.D. The Bells of Varnavale. L.C. Var. Hoxton, 31/5/95.
D. The Bells that Rung an Old Year Out and a New Year In. L.C. Brit. 8/12/62.
D. Belphegor; or, The Trials of a Merry-Andrew. L.C. Manchester, 8/3/51.
D. Belphegor the Mountebank (S.W. 21/4/56).
Ext. Belphegor, the Mountebank to any Amount of Property. L.C. Brit. 12/5/66.
D. Ben Bolt (Stand. 21/5/54). L.C.

D. Ben Child; or, The Swallow's Nest. L.C. M'bone. 9/5/63.
D. Beneath the Three Spires. L.C. Coventry, 13/1/76.
Sk. Beneath the Waters; or, The Sunken Treasure. L.C. Empress, 26/10/99.
D. Ben Hur. L.C. D.Y. 22/12/99.
D. Benliel (C.L. 4/5/57).
D. Benliel, the Son of the Night (People's, Dundee, 12/84).
D. Ben Lighterware; or, The Foundling of the Sea. L.C. Vic. 12/1/59.
D. The Bereaved Wife and Mother; or, The Lost Child. L.C. C.L. 22/5/57.
D. Bertha Gray. L.C. Stand. 27/8/59.
D. Bertha Gray, the Pauper's Child; or, The Death Fetch. L.C. Bower, 15/7/51.
D. Bertrand de Courcy. L.C. Pav. 29/10/63.
F. Be Sure You've Got on Your Own. L.C. Sheffield, 30/10/80.
M.F. Betha the Betrayer. L.C. Crit. 13/4/81.
D. Betrayed (Edinburgh, 18/8/73). L.C.
O. Betrothed Lovers. L.C. Carl Rosa Co. 13/4/81.
F. Betsy's Found. L.C. Grec. 1/11/56.
F.C. The Better Half. L.C. New, Merthyr Tydvil, 28/8/96.
R.D. The Better Self; or, Three Temptations (Lincoln, 13/4/82). L.C.
D. The Betting Boy's Career (Vic. 16/8/52).
D. The Betting Boy's Career, from his Home to the Hulks (C.L. 9/8/52). L.C.
D. The Betting Boy's Career, from the Counting House to the Hulks; or, 50 to 1 against him. L.C. Pav. 12/8/52.
D. The Betting Boys, from the Counting House to the Hulks (Stand. 25/7/52). L.C. MS. Birmingham.
F. Beware of Jealousy. L.C. Margate, 6/8/91.
F. Beware of the Centenier (Jersey, 25/2/77).
D. Beyond; A Study of a Woman by a Woman (Crit. 1/2/94, *mat.*).
C. Bibb and Tucker (Gai. 14/8/73). L.C.
F. Bibbins and Figgins (Sur. 26/11/60).
P. Big-bodied Bill, Big Belzebub's Boy; or, Harlequin and the Golden Goblin. L.C. Brit. 20/12/50.
D. Bill and Me; or, Only Two Common Sailors. L.C. Norwich, 31/3/83.
C. The Billet Doux. (D.L. 19/11/60). L.C.
F. Bill Stickers Beware (P.W. Birmingham, 20/9/75). L.C. Blackburn, 16/9/75.
P. Billy Button's Ride to Brentford (Vic. 8/4/54).
FairyC. Binke's Blues. L.C. O.C. 24/1/84.
D. The Birdcatchers of Whitechapel (Brit. 31/10/59).
C. Birdie's Nest. L.C. Reading, 10/12/84.
P. Birds, Beasts and Fishes; or, Harlequin and Natural History (C.L. 26/12/54). L.C.
F. A Bit of the Breast (Brit. 9/12/61).
D. Bitter Cold (M'bone, 25/1/68).
D. Bitter Cold; or, The Secret of the Holly Bough. L.C. Brit. 9/12/65.
D. The Bittern Swamp (Grec. 22/10/80).
Sk. A Bitter Wrong. L.C. S.W. 21/10/96.

F.C. Black and Blue. L.C. Star, Wolverhampton, 18/10/98.
[Title altered later to *O'Sahara.*]

D. The Black and Red Galleys; or, The Doomed Son. L.C. Pav. 22/7/54.

Ent. Black and White (Grec. 10/11/51).

Ca. Black and White. L.C. Gai. 13/4/81.

D. The Black Band; or, Companions of Midnight. L.C. Bolton, 8/3/62.

D. The Black Band; or, The Mysteries of Midnight. L.C. Pav. 25/9/61.

O.Bsq. Blackeyed Susan. L.C. Alh. 30/7/84.

D. The Black Gondola. L.C. Brit. 29/2/56.

D. The Black Hawks; or, The Wild Cauliflower of the Sansomme (Qns. Birmingham, 30/10/93). L.C.

D.Sk. Black Justice. L.C. S.W. 28/9/97.

D. The Black Kitten. L.C. Cardiff, 18/10/94.

D. Blackmail. L.C. Adel. 10/7/73.

D. The Black Rainbow. L.C. Qns. 27/1/55 [extra scenes].

P. The Black Statue; or, The Enchanted Pills and the Magic Apple-tree (Brit. 26/12/74). L.C.

F. The Black Swan at Liverpool (Str. 9/5/53). L.C.

D. Black Tom of Tyburn; or, The Saddler of Bantry. L.C. Pav. 27/3/50.

D.Sk. The Blackville Derby. L.C. Regent, Salford, 1/6/97.

D.Sk. Blanche. L.C. T.H. Shipley, 10/11/97.

D. Blanche and Brunette; or, Friends, Lovers, and Enemies. L.C. Brit. 15/5/62.

D. Blanche Dhu, the Spectre Dog (Vic. 5/6/54). L.C. as *Dhu Blanche.*

D.Sk. The Blarney Stone. L.C. S.W. 13/11/95.

D.Sk. The Blarney Stone. L.C. Workington, 12/2/98.

D. Bleak House (Str. 29/5/54). L.C.

D. Bleak House. L.C. Grand, Walsall, 24/9/92.

D. Bleak House; or, The Spectre of the Ghost Walk. L.C. Pav. 10/6/53.

D. Blight and Bloom (Sur. 5/1/55).

D. The Blighted Flower (Stand. 20/10/51).

D. A Blighted Home. L.C. Pav. 2/4/64.
[By *J. B. HOWE.*]

D. Blighted Hopes. L.C. Vic. 20/5/71.

D. Blighted Joys; or, The Nabob, the Farmer and the Miser. L.C. Pav. 6/2/52.

D. Blind. L.C. P'cess. Edinburgh, 26/6/77.

D. Blind among Enemies. L.C. Brit. 18/11/85.

D. The Blind Boy. L.C. S.W. 16/2/99.

D. The Blind Child of Africa; or, The Last Prince of Abyssinia and The True British Seaman. L.C. Pav. 15/4/51.

F. The Blind Fiddler. L.C. Grec. 11/10/72.

D. A Blind Girl's Fortune (E.L. 21/11/74).
[A version of *The Two Orphans.*]

D. Blindness among Enemies (Paisley, 25/2/78).

D. The Blind Sister (Vic. 9/3/63).

D. The Blind Wife. L.C. C.L. 16/4/50.

D. The Blind Witness of Aberdare (Cambrian, Merthyr Tydvil, 5/2/72).

F. Blondin. L.C. Grec. 17/6/61.
Oa. The Blondinette Melodists. L.C. St G. 27/3/73.
F. Blondin on the Tight Rope (H.M.O.H. Aberdeen, 5/2/73).
D. Blood of the Faithful. L.C. Grantham, 26/4/98.
F.C. Blood will tell. L.C. Glo. 20/6/95.
F. The Bloomer Costume (Stand. 13/10/51). L.C.
F. Blower Jones (S.W. 28/2/81). L.C.
C.Ext. Blown Up. L.C. Corn Exchange, Kilmarnock, 26/12/95.
P. Bluebeard. L.C. Adel. Birmingham, 22/12/63.
P. Bluebeard (Stand. 28/5/64).
P. Bluebeard. L.C. Pav. 21/12/65.
Bsq. Bluebeard. L.C. Ch.X. 14/9/74.
P. Bluebeard. L.C. Bradford, 27/11/74.
P. Bluebeard. L.C. Glo. 28/12/75.
P. Bluebeard. L.C. People's O.H. Stockport, 4/1/76.
P. Bluebeard. L.C. Edinburgh, 6/1/76.
P. Bluebeard. L.C. Stockton-on-Tees, 10/1/76.
P. Bluebeard. L.C. Sunderland, 13/1/76.
P. Bluebeard. L.C. Nottingham, 28/12/77.
P. Bluebeard. L.C. Victory, Aldershot, 14/1/78.
P. Bluebeard. L.C. O.H. Leeds, 17/12/78.
P. Bluebeard. L.C. Alex. Sheffield, 17/12/78.
P. Bluebeard. L.C. H.M.O.H. Aberdeen, 19/12/78.
P. Bluebeard. L.C. Grand, Leeds, 27/12/78.
P. Bluebeard. L.C. P.W. Glasgow, 20/1/79.
P. Bluebeard. L.C. Greenock, 2/12/80.
P. Bluebeard. L.C. Manchester, 15/12/80.
P. Bluebeard. L.C. P.W. Birmingham, 29/12/81.
P. Bluebeard. L.C. Croydon, 10/1/82.
P. Bluebeard. L.C. Alex. L'pool, 15/12/82.
P. Bluebeard. L.C. Tyne, Newcastle, 8/1/83.
P. Bluebeard. L.C. Leeds, 21/12/83.
P. Bluebeard. L.C. Edinburgh, 28/1/84.
P. Bluebeard. L.C. P.H. Hastings, 18/12/84.
P. Bluebeard. L.C. Brighton, 17/12/85.
P. Bluebeard. L.C. Rotherham, 17/12/86.
P. Bluebeard. L.C. Manchester, 29/12/86.
P. Bluebeard. L.C. P'cess. Glasgow, 10/12/87.
P. Bluebeard. L.C. Bolton, 15/12/87.
P. Bluebeard. L.C. P.W. L'pool, 16/12/87.
P. Bluebeard. L.C. R.A. Woolwich, 23/12/87.
P. Bluebeard. L.C. Bradford, 19/12/88.
P. Bluebeard. L.C. P.W. L'pool, 17/12/88.
P. Bluebeard. L.C. Sheffield, 11/12/88.
P. Bluebeard. L.C. Newcastle, 26/12/89.
P. Bluebeard. L.C. Glasgow, 15/12/90.
Ext. Bluebeard. L.C. Grand H. Maidenhead, 9/4/92.
P. Bluebeard. L.C. Corn Exchange, Maidstone, 21/12/92.
P. Bluebeard. L.C. Shakespeare, L'pool, 22/12/92.
P. Bluebeard. L.C. Morton's, Greenwich, 10/12/94.
P. Bluebeard. L.C. Qns. Manchester, 10/12/94.
P. Bluebeard. L.C. Hull, 19/12/94.
P. Bluebeard. L.C. Stockport, 31/12/95.
P. Bluebeard. L.C. Var. Manchester, 21/12/96.

P. Bluebeard. L.C. Jarrow, 30/12/98.
P. Bluebeard. L.C. Middlesborough, 30/12/98.
P. Bluebeard. L.C. Leeds, 16/2/99.
P. Bluebeard. L.C. Bury, 28/12/99.
P. Bluebeard; or, Harlequin, the Red Rover, the Fairy of the Golden Locks and the Genii of the Magic Ring. L.C. Alex. 16/12/65.
Bsq. Bluebeard and Son (Bath, 3/83).
P. Bluebeard, Cinderella and Prince Pretty-step; or, Harlequin Sister Ann and the Fairies of the Choral Cave (Gar. 26/12/72). L.C.
Bsq. Bluebeard Re-trimmed (Park, 9/7/77).
P. Bluebeard the Great. L.C. Leeds, 14/12/78.
D.Sk. Bluebeard Trimmed (S.W. 5/11/95).
P. The Blue Bird of Paradise; or, Harlequin King Charming and Prince Pigmy (Grec. 26/12/60). L.C.
Ext. The Blue Devils (Lyc. 19/4/62).
D. The Blue Dwarf; or, Mystery, Love and Crime (Brit. 23/7/62). L.C.
D. Blue Jackets. L.C. Barnsley, 21/5/96.
F. The Blue Monkey. L.C. Com. 9/4/91.
D. Blue Skin. L.C. Pav. 27/10/63.
F. Bluff (County H., St Albans, 6/4/88). L.C.
P. Bluff King Hal (Greenwich, 24/12/72).
P. Bluff King Hal. L.C. Norwich, 4/1/76.
Bsq. Bluff King Hal. L.C. Barrow, 31/8/78.
Bsq. Bluff King Hal; or The Maiden, the Masher and the Monarch (Alex. Sheffield, 12/3/83).
Ca. Blunders (O.C. 11/4/98). L.C.
Ent. The Boarding House for 1862. L.C. P'cess. 31/5/62.
F. The Boarding School Ball (H. 27/5/53). L.C.
D. The Boatswain's Whistle; or, The Storm Sails Set. L.C. Vic. 24/6/59.
C.D. Bob Bradshaw's Dream (Str. 29/5/99). L.C.
D. Bob Bretton, the Dead Shot of the Woods (Vic. 16/7/77). L.C. [with *Bush* for *Woods*].
F. Bob Cherry, Rough and Ready (Sur. 23/4/60). L.C.
Ext. Bogie. L.C. N. Woolwich Gdns. 9/6/76.
Ba. The Bohemian Girl. L.C. Bijou, 24/5/61.
O. The Bohemians (Manchester, 22/4/97). L.C. Court, L'pool, 30/3/97.
P. Bold Robin Hood. L.C. Hengler's, 30/11/82.
Oa. A Bold Stroke for a Husband. L.C. Roy. 17/4/62.
D. The Bomb. L.C. W.L. 12/6/94.
Spec. The Bombardment and Capture of Canton (Ast. 12/4/58). L.C.
Ba. Bombastio Furioso. L.C. Lyr. Ealing, 10/12/89.
D. Bondage (O.C. 31/3/83). L.C.
D. The Bond of Love. L.C. Sur. 21/10/54.
D. The Boneshaker. L.C. New, Swansea, 25/4/94.
F. The Boot on the Right Leg (S.W. 24/1/63). L.C.
P. Bo-Peep. L.C. Amphi. Edinburgh, 29/12/74.
P. Bo-Peep. L.C. Middlesborough, 18/1/76.
P. Bo-Peep. L.C. P's. Bristol, 19/12/94.
P. Bo-Peep. L.C. P's. Bradford, 31/12/97.
P. Bo-Peep. L.C. P'cess. Glasgow, 30/12/98.
P. Bo-Peep. L.C. Roy. Morecambe, 28/12/99.

P. Bo-Peep and Boy Blue. L.C. Blackburn, 12/12/76.
D. The Borderer's Son; or, The Oath of Vengeance. L.C. Brit. 10/8/74.
[By *A. COATES*.]
D. Born with a Caul (Str. 29/10/50). L.C.
Oa. A Boro' Bench. L.C. T.H. Harrowgate, 23/3/87.
F. The Bos'en and the Middy (Sur. 22/5/54).
D. The Bosjesman; or, Bushrangers and the Last of the African Settlers (M'bone, 13/10/51). L.C.
D. Le Bossu (C.L. 7/7/66).
D. Le Bossu. L.C. Sur. 10/7/63.
Ca. Both of Them (Roy. Glasgow, 18/5/89). L.C.
P. The Bottle Imp; or, Harlequin the Witch of the Woods, the Beautiful Princess and the Fine Good Little Fairies of the Magic Ring (Grec. 23/12/65). L.C.
F. A Bottle of Smoke (Adel. 22/5/56). L.C.
F. Bounce. L.C. Holb. 8/12/74.
D. Bound Apprentice to a Waterman (Grec. 4/9/61).
C.D. Bound for Life; or, The Way of the World. L.C. Dewsbury, 7/2/83.
D. Bound or Free. L.C. Vic. 14/5/73.
Ent. Bounds of the Tiger (D.L. 8/11/62).
M.Ext. Bound to Arcadia. L.C. St G. H. Walsall, 3/3/88.
D. Bound to the Wheel (Pav. 2/4/66). L.C.
Bal. Le Bouquet (H.M. 8/5/65).
Bal. La Bouquetière (H.M. 24/7/52).
D. Bow Bells; or, The Alderman's Last Wish (C.L. 25/5/63). L.C.
F. Box and Cox in Caffre Land (Str. 15/5/54).
D. Boy Bob (Metro. 25/9/99). L.C.
P. The Boy in Blue. L.C. Gar. 22/12/62.
D. The Boy Pirate; or, Life on the Ocean and the Land. L.C. Eff. 8/7/64.
D. The Boy Smuggler (Grec. 2/8/66).
F. A Brace of Uncles. L.C. Str. 9/3/76.
F. Bracewell's Adventures with a Russian Princess (Qns. Manchester, 15/2/78).
D. The Brave Gordons. L.C. S.W. 12/2/98.
D. Bravin's Brow (M'bone, 20/6/63). L.C. P'cess. Leeds, 23/1/63.
D. The Bravoes of London; or, The Blood Stain on the Grass. L.C. Eff. 8/10/63.
Ext. The Bravo Ix. L.C. Bower, 28/7/54.
F.C. A Breach of Promise (Walsall, 7/4/84). L.C.
C.O. Breach of Promise. L.C. Inverness, 5/8/92.
F. A Breakfast Appointment. L.C. Qns. 8/4/62.
F. Breakfast for Two (Str. 8/12/51). L.C.
F. Breaking it off. L.C. Aven. 31/7/99.
[See *N. DOONE*, 1898.]
D. Break of Morn; or, The Dark Hour (Brit. 23/7/62). L.C. New, Birmingham, 25/3/62.
Ca. Bred in the Bone. L.C. Winter Gdns. Stockport, 18/11/96.
[See *F. T. LINGHAM*, 1890.]
Oa. Brenda's Choice. L.C. Alex. H. Leeds, 21/10/96.
D. Bressac. L.C. P.H. W. Norwood, 17/2/86.
C.O. The Brewer of Preston (Preston, 24/1/76). L.C.

T. Brian Born. 8° 1879.
[Written by J. T. B.]
D. Briarly Farm. L.C. Grec. 7/8/58.
D. The Bridal of Beatrix (Sur. 1/10/59). L.C.
Msq. The Bridal of Beauty; or, The Marriage of Love. L.C. Cremorne, 21/5/63.
D. The Bridal Phantom; or, The Secret of Life (Grec. 24/5/63). L.C.
C. The Bridal Tour. L.C. K.X. 21/9/77.
[See *D. BOUCICAULT*, 1880; this is probably his drama.]
D. The Bride of Aldgate (Brit. 21/11/59).
D. The Bride of Garryowen; or, The Colleen Bawn. L.C. Wolverhampton, 27/3/61.
[See *D. BOUCICAULT*, 1860.]
D. The Bride of Lammermoor (S.W. 7/1/63).
D. The Bride of Poland; or, The Scout Leader. L.C. Bower, 14/2/56.
Ba. The Brigand (Vic. 2/12/65). L.C. Stand. 15/4/65.
C. The Brigand of Barcelona (Vic. 29/11/52).
D. The Brigand of London; or, A Tale of the City and the Mountain. L.C. Eff. 26/3/64.
D. The Brigand's Secret (Brit. 8/10/58). L.C.
D. A Brighter Future. L.C. Pier Pav. St Leonards, 31/12/97.
Sk. Britannia, Mistress of the Seas. L.C. W.L. 9/8/95.
Ent. British Tars (Pav. 30/3/59).
D. The British Workman. L.C. Qns. Theatre of Var. Poplar, 5/6/94.
D. Britomarte; or, The Man-hater. L.C. M'bone, 9/6/66.
D. Britomart, the Man-hater; or, Will he win her? (Eff. 2/7/66). L.C.
D. Briton and Boer. L.C. Qns. Glasgow, 22/12/99.
D. The Broad Path and the Narrow Way (Mechanics' Inst. Eccleshill, 18/3/99). L.C.
D. The Broken Branch. L.C. Stratford, 16/3/88.
D. The Broken Chain; or, Ronald the Reaper (Grec. 14/3/59). L.C.
D. Broken Faith. L.C. Grec. 26/7/55.
D. A Broken Home (C.L. 20/6/59).
D. A Broken Idol. L.C. St G. 16/1/74.
F. Broken Off. L.C. Shaft. 22/6/91.
[See *Mrs N. PHILLIPS*, 1892.]
D.Sk. A Broken String. L.C. P.H. W. Didsbury, 17/5/98.
[See *A. C. CALMOUR*, 1896.]
D. Broken Ties. L.C. Grec. 5/4/74.
[See *J. P. SIMPSON*, 1872.]
P. The Bronze Horse; or, Harlequin Assaid and Duhl Duhl the Enchanted Rose and the Mysterious Magician. L.C. Vic. 18/12/71.
P. The Bronze Horse; or, Harlequin and the Demon Gnome of the Silver Mine. L.C. M'bone, 17/12/64.
D. The Bronze Medal; or, The Flower Girl of the Innocents (Sur. 4/10/62). L.C.
F. Brother and Sister (Living Marionettes, 12/7/52).
F. Brother Bruin and Brother Sneak (Brit. 2/7/60).
Ent. Brother Sailors (Vic. 26/12/55).
D. Brothers in Arms (Sur. 30/10/54).
D. Brothers in Arms (Grand, Stalybridge, 3/9/94). L.C.
D. A Brother's Life (Bijou, Paignton, 16/7/74).
D. A Brother's Revenge. L.C. Derby, 26/3/77.

D. A Brother's Revenge; or, The Rose of Ireland and the Fairies of O'Donoghue's Lakes (Vic. 6/3/54). L.C.
D. Brought to Bay. L.C. E.C. 18/5/85.
D. Brought to Light. L.C. Greenwich, 28/9/76.
D. Brought to the Test. L.C. Windsor, 28/4/84.
F. Brown, Jones and Robinson. L.C. Alex. 19/4/66.
F. Brown, Jones and Robinson; or, The Schoolfellows' Pleasure Trips. L.C. C.L. 25/9/50.
Ba. Brown, Jones and Robinson; or, The Three Naughty Boys. L.C. Vic. 10/9/50.
Ext. The Brownies. L.C. Terry's, 8/10/94.
F.C. Brown's Boarders. L.C. Warrington, 15/11/88.
D. Bruin the Brave; or, The Woodman and his Dog. L.C. Pav. 31/8/54.
F. Brumley's Wife; or, The Sensation Scene. L.C. P.W. Glasgow, 17/2/63.
D. Brutus (D.L. 31/1/54).
D. Brutus and Caesar (Lyc. 8/10/66).
Vaud. Bubbles in the Sudds; or, The Village Washerwoman. L.C. E.C. 11/4/87.
D. The Buccaneer's Wife (Grec. 15/8/59). L.C.
F. Buffooning. L.C. Aquar. Brighton, 21/5/87.
D. The Bugle Call. L.C. Castle, Mountain Ash, S. Wales, 22/12/99.
[See *L. N. PARKER*, 1899.]
Vaud. The Bugler of the Twentieth. L.C. Birmingham, 19/11/56.
D. A Bunch of Roses. L.C. Aquar. Brighton, 5/3/97.
F. Burch and his Detractors (Preston, 3/2/75).
D. The Burgomaster's Daughter (M'bone, 25/5/63).
C. Buried Alive. L.C. Court, 12/8/74.
F. Burning his Fingers. L.C. P.W. Blackpool, 3/9/80.
D. The Burning Ship. L.C. Pav. 27/9/50.
P. Butcher Butcher Killed the Ox, Ran away with the Money Box. L.C. Gar. 26/12/59.
P. The Butterflies' Ball (Grec. 10/9/60).
P. The Butterflies' Ball and the Grasshoppers' Feast. (H. 24/12/55). L.C.
F. The Buttermilk Volunteers (Adel. 6/5/50).
Ext. Buz buz; or, The Court of the Googoos. L.C. Albert H. Edin. 14/1/91.
Oa. By Advertisement. L.C. Royal H. Ledbury, 28/9/96.
C.R. By and By (St G. 3/2/96). L.C.
Ca. By Hat and Trap. L.C. Ladb. H. 20/6/98.
C. By Special Licence. L.C. St G. 10/5/95.
[See *F. MARRYAT*, 1887.]
D. By the Deeps Nine. L.C. Pav. 19/4/50.
Ca. By the Sea (Str. 1/4/72). L.C.
F. The Cabinet Secret. L.C. Grec. 16/10/56.
D. A Cabman's Career (Pav. 7/3/59).
C.O. The Cadi; or, Amours among Moors (H. 18/6/51). L.C. *Fairbrother.*
Ca. Caesar's Wife. L.C. Park, 28/4/80.
D. Cagliostro (Grec. 27/8/60). L.C. as *C. the Magician; or, Oppression and Reprisal.*
[See *C. A. CLARKE*, 1875.]

D. Cain; or, A Year and a Day (Stockton-on-Tees, 26/8/78).
D. Cain and Abel. L.C. Blackburn, 31/12/90.
T. Caius Silius, the Warrior Captive; or, The Roman Slave. L.C. Stand. 16/11/59.
D. Calderon, the King's Favourite; or, The Jesuit's Fate. L.C. Qns. 3/3/62.
C.O. The Caliph of Bagdad (Adel. 5/4/58). L.C.
D. Called Back (Lecture H. Derby, 1/9/84). L.C. La Comédie Anglaise, Public Rooms, Bideford, 19/6/84.
D. Called Back. L.C. Lathone H. Seaforth, L'pool, 23/2/85.
D. Called Back. L.C. Fairfield Dramatic Club Theatre, L'pool, 12/1/85.
F. Called to the Bar (Portman R. Baker Street, 16/5/92).
P. Callendrack Callebrando, the Giant Zugic; or, Doctor Vulloreureoh. L.C. Brit. 21/12/52.
Bsq. Calypso and Telemachus. L.C. S.W. 12/4/65.
F. Camelia. L.C. Roy. 15/10/61.
D. The Cameronians; or, The Heir of Milnwood (Stand. 7/11/63). L.C.
D. Camille. L.C. D.L. 23/3/53 [license refused].
D. Camille. L.C. Gai. 7/2/83.
D. Camille; or, The Fate of a Coquette (P.W. 23/3/88, *mat.*).
C. Campaigning (Crit. 24/5/79). L.C.
D. The Canal Boat (Swansea, 20/9/71).
D. The Cannie Soogah; or, The Wearing of the Green (Dublin, 12/5/73).
D. Canonbury Tower. L.C. Vic. 5/9/57.
Bsq. The Can't-Sing Girl. L.C. P'cess. 2/11/91.
C. The Capers of Cupid. L.C. Athenaeum, Glasgow, 28/12/99.
D.Sk. Capital and Labour. L.C. S.W. 18/10/95.
F.C. Capriciosa. L.C. Olym. 20/5/80.
F.C. Captain Blarney. L.C. Grand H. Maidenhead, 30/3/98.
D. Captain Cartouche. L.C. Adel. 27/8/64.
D. Captain Firebrand; or, The Oath of the Twelve. L.C. Brit. 7/5/72.
D. Captain Jack. L.C. Bower, 6/10/70.
Ba. Captain Jack, the Little Sheppard, and the Black Sheep, Jonathan Wild. L.C. Alh. Brighton, 3/9/94.
D. Captain John Hall, the First Highwayman (Col L'pool, 12/2/72).
D. Captain John Luck; or, Fair Winds for Foul Ways. L.C. Vic. 4/9/50.
D. Captain Macheath. L.C. C.L. 15/4/65.
D.Sk. Captain J. D. Pitman; or, That's How He Told the Tale. L.C. S.W. 11/9/99.
D. The Captain of the Vulture (Vic. 12/9/64). L.C.
D. The Captain of the Vulture. L.C. Grec. 30/10/63.
D. The Captain's Watch (St J. 28/7/62).
F. Captured. L.C. W.L. 5/6/94.
D. Card Drawing (Grec. 4/11/61).
D. The Carib Chief (C.L. 29/9/51).
Spec. Carlo Brunari; or, The Mounted Brigands of the Abruzzi. L.C. Ast. 8/5/56.
D. Carlo Foscari, the Italian Boy (Brit. 21/10/61). L.C.
D. Carlo Leoni; or, The Irish Boy and the Gipsy Girl (Brit. 7/3/59). L.C.

D. Carlyle's Wife. L.C. Ladb. H. 5/11/83.
F. Carnation of Carnation Cottage (Roy. 8/2/62). L.C.
D. The Carnival of Venice (Grec. 15/8/59).
D. The Carrier and his Dog (Vic. 22/5/54).
Bsq. The Carrier of London (Str. 26/12/54). L.C.
D. The Carter of Liverpool (Adel. L'pool, 28/4/79).
D. Cartouche. L.C. Soho, 31/10/60.
D. Cartouche; or, The Six Escapes of a Robber (C.L. 8/8/59). L.C.
D. Cartouche, the French Robber (Stand. 16/10/60).
F. A Case of Conscience (P'cess. 16/11/57). L.C.
F. Cash versus Cupid (P'cess. 3/3/62). L.C.
D. The Casket of Jewels (D.L. 28/2/53).
M.D. Caspar Duverade, the Terror of Spain; or, The Traitor, the Jew and the Gypsey. L.C. Pav. 8/9/52.
D. Cassilda (Sur. 21/7/62). L.C.
Ext. Cassiope (Alex. 20/8/66). L.C.
D. Cast Adrift. L.C. Vic. 22/11/66.
D. The Castaways. L.C. 30/12/76.
Bsq. The Castle of Otranto. L.C. St J. 26/3/59.
D. The Cast of the Lead. L.C. St G. 16/2/99.
Bal. La Catarina (D.L. 18/11/61).
M.D. La Catarina; or, The Diamonds of the Crown. L.C. Qns. 10/11/62.
F. Catching a Gander (Sur. 6/11/54).
Oa. Catching a Husband (Roy. 21/4/62).
M.Ext. Catchwork; or, During Supper. L.C. Bath, 26/8/80.
T. Catesby, A Tragedy of the Gunpowder Plot. 4° 1897 [Guildford].
D. Catherine Hayes. L.C. Eff. 29/7/64.
D. Catherine Howard. L.C. Bolton, 16/7/58.
D. Catherine Howard. L.C. Tonypandy, 18/10/98.
D. Catherine of Russia; or, The Child of the Storm (Vic. 9/50). L.C.
Duol. Caught Card; or, The Sharper and the Conjurer. L.C. T.H. Darlington, 23/12/95.
Ca. Caught in a Shower. L.C. P.W. L'pool, 12/5/71.
F. Caught in His Own Trap; or, The Trapper Trapped. L.C. Sur. 7/4/68.
D. The Cauld Lad o' Hylton (Lyc. Sunderland, 10/9/77).
D. The Cause (Portsmouth, 29/11/76). L.C.
D. Cause and Effect (Sur. 20/2/60). L.C.
D. A Celebrated Case. L.C. Nov. 6/1/90.
C. A Certain Age. L.C. Lyc. 21/5/51.
F. Cetewayo at Last. L.C. Pav. 19/7/82.
F. Cetewayo in South Shields (South Shields, 28/8/82).
F. Chaff. L.C. Str. 8/2/77.
D. Chained to Sin and Brought up to Beg. L.C. Pav. 17/2/81.
D.Sk. The Chain of Evidence. L.C. S.W. 31/12/97.
D. The Champion Belt; or, The Ring and its Moral. L.C. C.L. 3/5/60.
F. The Champion of England; or, Tom and the Boy (Brit. 30/4/60). L.C.
F. The Champion of the World; or, The English Hero and the American Boy. L.C. M'bone, 30/4/60.
Oa. Change. L.C. Lyr. Ealing, 31/10/88.
D. The Changed Heart (Sur. 23/1/60).

D. Change for a Sovereign. L.C. Grec. 13/7/55.
[See *H. WIGAN*, 1861.]
F. A Change for the Better (Olym. 21/1/61).
D. Changes and Chances (Aven. 2/3/91). L.C.
Ent. The Changing Years. L.C. Bijou, 21/12/96.
C.D. The Chaplain of the Fleet. L.C. O.C. 31/12/90.
F. The Charade. L.C. Adel. 28/1/52.
D. Charles I and Charles II. L.C. St G. 22/12/99.
D. Charley Wag. L.C. Vic. 15/2/61.
D. Charley Wag, the Outcast of the Thames (Brit. 19/12/60). L.C.
F. Charlie's Uncle. L.C. Richmond, 9/4/94.
Ent. A Charming Cottage (G.I. 6/4/63). L.C.
D. The Chateau of Valenza (Olym. 15/7/51). L.C.
R.O. The Chatelaine; or, The Siege of Nancy. L.C. St G. 20/7/96.
D. Check and Checkmate. L.C. Grec. 23/9/68.
D. Checkmated; or, Wait and Hope (Portsmouth, 19/3/69).
C. Checkmate to Mr King. L.C. Olym. 6/5/86.
Bsq. Cheek and Plant (Vic. 16/5/64). L.C. as *C. and P.*; *or*, *The Sauce of Old Nile.*
D. The Chequer Board. L.C. P.H. West Kirby, 22/12/99.
Ca. Cherries (Gai. Dublin, 22/2/75).
F. Cherry and Blue; or, Appearances are Deceitful (D.L. 22/10/60). L.C.
P. Cherry and Fairstar; or, Harlequin the Dancing Waters, the Singing Apple and the Little Green Talking Bird. L.C. Stand. 17/12/62.
[By *F. G. CHEATHAM.*]
Ca. Cherry Blossom (Vic. H. Archer Street, 19/2/89). L.C.
M.C. Cherry Garden Stairs. L.C. C.P. 23/3/95.
D. The Chess Board. L.C. St Paul's H. Thornton Heath, 30/11/99.
D. The Chevalier de St George (Pav. 29/10/53).
D. The Chevalier de St Georges (Vic. 2/11/53). L.C.
[A MS. version of *Chevalier St George* is at Birmingham.]
C. Chez l'avocat. L.C. Gai. 11/6/77.
Ent. Chi Chu Ali (Stand. 22/9/51).
Bsq.Ent. Chickabiddies (O.H. Darwen, 1/4/89). L.C.
Ext. Chickabiddy. L.C. Rotunda, L'pool, 25/2/82.
F. Chickweed and Groundsel. L.C. Var. 4/9/84.
D. The Child of Nature. L.C. S.W. 18/11/96.
F. The Child of Science. L.C. Alex. L'pool, 15/7/81.
D. The Child of the Foundling Hospital. L.C. Grec. 6/5/56.
D. The Children in the Wood (D.L. 8/2/50).
P. The Children in the Wood. L.C. Exeter, 1/76.
P. The Children in the Wood. L.C. Alex. L'pool, 11/12/77.
P. The Children in the Wood. L.C. Corn Exchange, Cirencester, 19/12/78.
P. The Children in the Wood; or, The Cruel Uncle and the Fairies of the Golden Vines. L.C. Qns. 24/12/60.
Bsq. The Children in the Wood; or, The Vengeance Dyer and a Pair of Dirty Kids (Bijou, 1/3/75).
D. The Children of the Mist (R. Exchange R. Paisley, 26/10/68).
C.O. Chilperic. L.C. Empire, 14/4/84.
C.O. Chilperic. L.C. Alh. 4/5/75.
D. The Chimes; or, The Broken Heart. L.C. Eff. 30/10/63.

D. The Chimes; or, The Broken Heart. L.C. Vic. 19/11/63.
D. The Chimes of Big Ben. L.C. Empress, 13/4/99.
Ba. The Chinese Invasion of 1960. L.C. P'cess. 23/3/63.
Ext. Ching-a-Maree. L.C. Aquar. Brighton, 18/12/84.
Oa. Ching-Li-Wang; or, Britons in China. L.C. Birmingham, 28/3/79.
F. Ching's Bull Pup. L.C. Ladb. H. 7/2/83.
Oa. Ching-Chow-Hi; or, A Cracked Piece of China (G.I. 14/8/65). L.C.
D. The Chink of Gold. L.C. Woolwich, 12/6/94.
Ca. Chiromancy (Willis R. 18/4/88).
[By *W. POEL.*]
F. Choknosoff; or, The Two Generals. L.C. Greenwich, 9/5/71.
M.C. The Chorus Girl. L.C. O.H. Doncaster, 1/6/97.
[See *A Theatrical Duchess.*]
D. The Christening (H. 11/8/60).
D. The Christian Slave; or, The Life and Death of Uncle Tom. L.C. Brit. 22/2/56.
Oa. Christine. L.C. Roy. 25/3/62.
Ext. The Christmas Carol (Adel. 24/12/59).
F. A Christmas Party. L.C. Phil. 18/12/79.
D. A Christmas Story (Pav. 27/12/52).
D. A Christmas Story; or, Home Again. L.C. Var. 3/9/93.
Ba. Chuck and Ruck a Roo; or, Chanticleer Sleepers and Wakers and the Union of Coal and Iron. L.C. Birkenhead, 26/3/66.
D. Chums (D.Y. 6/3/99). L.C.
P. Cinderella (Sur. 9/6/51).
P. Cinderella (Grec. 31/5/52).
O. Cinderella (Ast. 29/5/65).
Bal. Cinderella (Grec. 15/10/66).
P. Cinderella. L.C. Rotunda, L'pool, 3/12/75.
P. Cinderella. L.C. Bristol, 17/12/75.
P. Cinderella. L.C. Bradford, 22/12/75.
P. Cinderella. L.C. Coventry, 19/12/76.
P. Cinderella. L.C. Plymouth, 20/12/76.
P. Cinderella. L.C. L'pool, 30/12/76.
P. Cinderella. L.C. P.W. Birmingham, 6/12/77.
P. Cinderella. L.C. Blackburn, 17/12/77.
P. Cinderella. L.C. Gai. Glasgow, 4/1/79.
P. Cinderella. L.C. P.W. L'pool, 13/1/80.
P. Cinderella. L.C. Edinburgh, 14/12/80.
P. Cinderella. L.C. P's. Manchester, 21/12/80.
P. Cinderella. L.C. Sunderland, 23/12/80.
P. Cinderella. L.C. Wakefield, 23/12/80.
P. Cinderella. L.C. Worcester, 29/12/80.
P. Cinderella. L.C. Ast. 17/12/81.
P. Cinderella. L.C. O.H. Bolton, 17/12/81.
P. Cinderella. L.C. Richmond, 5/4/82.
P. Cinderella. L.C. Nottingham, 27/12/82.
P. Cinderella. L.C. Rotunda, L'pool 30/12/82.
P. Cinderella. L.C. Birmingham, 18/12/83.
P. Cinderella. L.C. Grand, Glasgow, 21/12/83.
P. Cinderella. L.C. Bristol, 26/12/83.
P. Cinderella. L.C. West Hartlepool, 9/1/84.
P. Cinderella. L.C. Hanley, 9/1/84.
P. Cinderella. L.C. Carlisle, 23/12/84.

P. Cinderella. L.C. P's. Manchester, 17/12/85.
P. Cinderella. L.C. Tyne, Newcastle, 17/12/85.
P. Cinderella. L.C. Alex. L'pool, 21/12/85.
P. Cinderella (S.W. 26/12/85).
P. Cinderella. L.C. Birmingham, 6/1/87.
P. Cinderella. L.C. Cardiff, 9/12/87.
P. Cinderella. L.C. Grand, Leeds, 21/12/87.
P. Cinderella. L.C. Alex. Sheffield, 7/12/88.
P. Cinderella. L.C. Rotunda, L'pool, 21/12/88.
P. Cinderella. L.C. County, Reading, 26/12/88.
P. Cinderella. L.C. Edinburgh, 16/12/89.
P. Cinderella. L.C. Bradford, 17/12/89.
P. Cinderella. L.C. P's. Bristol, 21/12/89.
P. Cinderella. L.C. Birmingham, 21/12/89.
P. Cinderella. L.C. Grand, Plymouth, 11/1/90.
P. Cinderella. L.C. Brighton, 11/12/90.
P. Cinderella. L.C. R.A. Woolwich, 22/12/90.
P. Cinderella. L.C. Col. Oldham, 12/12/91.
P. Cinderella. L.C. Manchester, 17/12/91.
P. Cinderella. L.C. Nottingham, 24/12/92.
P. Cinderella. L.C. Birmingham, 19/12/92.
P. Cinderella. L.C. Blackburn, 9/1/93.
P. Cinderella. L.C. P.W. L'pool, 8/12/93.
P. Cinderella. L.C. Morton's, Greenwich, 16/12/93.
P. Cinderella. L.C. P's. Manchester, 22/12/93.
P. Cinderella. L.C. Shakespeare, L'pool, 22/12/93.
P. Cinderella. L.C. Glasgow, 10/12/94.
P. Cinderella. L.C. Stratford, 18/12/94.
P. Cinderella. L.C. Brighton, 21/12/94.
P. Cinderella. L.C. St J. Manchester, 26/12/95.
P. Cinderella. L.C. Rotunda, L'pool, 31/12/95.
P. Cinderella. L.C. City, Sheffield, 10/1/96.
P. Cinderella. L.C. P's. Bristol, 10/1/96.
P. Cinderella. L.C. Grand, Hull, 21/12/96.
P. Cinderella. L.C. P.W. Birmingham, 21/12/96.
P. Cinderella. L.C. R.A. Woolwich, 21/12/96.
P. Cinderella. L.C. Grand, Leeds, 26/12/96.
P. Cinderella. L.C. St John's H. Penzance, 8/1/97.
P. Cinderella. L.C. Manchester, 8/1/97.
P. Cinderella. L.C. Croydon, 8/1/97.
Bsq. Cinderella (Bijou, 9/1/97, *amat.*).
Ext. Cinderella. L.C. Church House, Cheddar, 5/3/97.
P. Cinderella. L.C. Grand, Croydon, 31/12/97.
P. Cinderella. L.C. Paisley, 31/12/97.
P. Cinderella. L.C. Greenock, 31/12/97.
P. Cinderella. L.C. Assembly Rooms, Balham, 31/12/97.
P. Cinderella. L.C. O.H. Southport, 31/12/97.
P. Cinderella. L.C. Lyc. Sheffield, 30/12/98.
P. Cinderella. L.C. Regent, Salford, 30/12/98.
P. Cinderella. L.C. Alex. Sheffield, 30/12/98.
P. Cinderella. L.C. Glasgow, 30/12/98.
P. Cinderella. L.C. Birmingham, 30/12/98.
P. Cinderella. L.C. Bournemouth, 30/12/98.
P. Cinderella. L.C. Vic. Walthamstow, 30/12/98.

P. Cinderella. L.C. Pier Pav. Hastings, 28/12/99.
P. Cinderella. L.C. P.W. L'pool, 28/12/99.
P. Cinderella. L.C. Shakespeare, L'pool, 28/12/99.
P. Cinderella. L.C. Crown, Camberwell, 28/12/99.
P. Cinderella. L.C. P's. Manchester, 28/12/99.
P. Cinderella. L.C. Bradford, 28/12/99.
P. Cinderella. L.C. Grand, Newcastle, 29/9/99.
P. Cinderella; or, The Fairy of the Little Glass Slipper (Sur. 26/12/60). L.C.
P. Cinderella; or, The Little Glass Slipper. L.C. Gar. 21/12/57.
P. Cinderella and the Little Glass Slipper (Metro. 26/12/94).
Ba. Cinderella up-to-date (Bijou, 9/1/97, *amat.*). L.C.
[Written by "E. S. R."]
D. The Circlet of Gold (Brit. 9/2/63).
Ca. City Friends; or, His Directions (Str. 26/2/55). L.C.
M.Ext. The City Guard (Grand, Birmingham, 26/11/83).
C.D. Clairval (Cambridge, 1/10/77).
F. Claperton Chisel. L.C. Str. 6/3/50.
D. Claribel's Mystery. L.C. Eff. 3/11/65.
D. Clarisse (S.W. 17/2/55).
D. Clarisse; or, The Foster Sister. L.C. St J. 14/2/55.
Sk. Clash of Steel. L.C. S.W. 21/12/94.
D. Clavigo (Gentlemen's Concert H. Manchester, 23/2/95).
F. Clean Your Boots (Sur. 10/5/58). L.C.
F. Clench and Wrench (Bijou, 7/6/79).
D. Clergy; or, Unequally Sentenced. L.C. Ipswich, 20/3/76.
F.C. Cliquot (Recreation H. Brentwood, 29/9/92).
D. Clinton; or, The Man of Stratagems. L.C. C.L. 7/4/58.
D. Clip. L.C. Empress, 24/3/99.
D. The Clock Maker. L.C. T.H. Luton, 23/8/92.
D. The Clockmaker of Bishopsgate. L.C. Eff. 18/8/60.
D. The Clockmaker of Clerkenwell (Grec. 19/12/60).
D. The Clockmaker's Daughter. L.C. Brit. 10/8/74.
Ba. Clodhopper's Fortune. L.C. Alh. 26/3/72.
D. The Cloud of Life; or, The Blind Man of the Pyrenees (Grec. 9/5/59). L.C.
F. Clouds. L.C. Vaud. 9/3/85.
F. The Club; or, My Wife and First Baby. L.C. S.W. 7/12/91.
F. The Cobbler Conjurer (Str. 6/7/54).
C. Cocard et Bicoquet (Leeds, 10/3/88, *copy*.).
F. Cocum; or, Purely Platonic. L.C. M'bone, 19/7/82.
D. The College Friends. L.C. Sur. 30/8/56.
D. The Collier Boy. L.C. S.W. 5/4/95.
F. The Colonel. L.C. S.W. 13/9/94.
Oa. Colonel Bombomb. L.C. Leamington Spa, 15/4/93.
D. Colonel Jack. L.C. Vic. 14/11/60.
F.C. The Colonel's Tactics. L.C. Camborne, 18/12/89.
Ext. A Coloured Commotion. L.C. Str. 14/9/52.
C. A Comedy Farce. L.C. St J. 29/9/64.
F. The Comic Tragedians. L.C. Phil. 29/9/79.
F. Coming of Age (S.W. 14/5/55).
C.D. The Coming Woman (Ladb. H. 30/4/87).
F. The Commencement of a Bad Farce but which however it is hoped will prove to be Wright-at-last (Lyc. 31/10/53). L.C.

F. The Commercial Room. L.C. Gai. W. Hartlepool, 7/9/87.
D. The Compact. L.C. Vic. 31/8/59.
D. Comrades in Arms. L.C. Woolwich, 22/6/94.
D. The Condemned Duke. L.C. Pav. 2/5/61.
D. The Confederate's Daughter; or, The Tyrant of New Orleans. L.C. Brit. 26/7/65.
D. The Confession (Sur. 5/4/58).
F.C. Confession. L.C. Vaud. 20/4/83.
Ca. Confidence. L.C. Com. 5/10/93.
D. The Confidential. L.C. Dumfries, 21/5/94.
Bsq. The Congress; or, The Czar and the Minister (Dover, 8/7/78).
C.D. Conrad and Lizette; or, Life on the Mississippi (Duke's, 29/3/80). L.C.
P. Conrad the Corsair; or, Harlequin and the Good Little Fairy at the Bottom of the Sea (Preston, 26/12/58).
D. Conrad the Invincible. L.C. Eff. 16/2/65.
Monol. Conscience. L.C. Preston, 3/9/97.
D. Conscience; or, The Voices of the Village Bells. L.C. C.L. 6/4/63.
D. The Conscript Mother (Brit. 4/3/61).
F. A Constant Follower. L.C. Str. 11/4/66.
T. Constantine. L.C. Ladb. H. 26/4/98.
Duol. The Contract. L.C. Lyc. 12/7/99.
F. A Convenient Son-in-Law (Portsmouth, 4/6/77).
D. Convict 33. L.C. Woolwich, 7/9/94.
D. The Convict's Daughter; or, Broken Fetters. L.C. Londesborough, Scarborough, 21/6/81.
D. Convicts 48 and 49. L.C. S.W. 5/4/95.
D. The Convict's Return (Sur. 14/5/59).
F. Copper and Brass. L.C. Sur. 30/10/50.
D. Cora; or, The Octoroon Slave of Louisiana. L.C. Pav. 26/10/61. [By *J. T. DOUGLASS.*]
D. Cora; or, The Slaves of the South (Grec. 26/6/65). L.C.
Bsq. Corin; or, The King of the Peaceful Isles (Qns. Dublin, 6/3/71).
D. Corinne (Stand. 23/5/85, *copy.*). L.C.
Bsq. The Corkonian Brothers (Str. 27/2/54). L.C.
D. The Cornish Brothers (Brit. 26/11/60).
D. The Corporal's Daughter; or, The Garnet King. L.C. Brit. 7/10/54.
Spec. Corse de Leon; or, The Brigand of Savoy (Ast. 11/2/50). L.C.
D. The Corsican Brothers (M'bone, 8/3/52). L.C.
D. The Corsican Brothers. L.C. Grec. 18/3/52.
D. The Corsican Brothers (C.L. 22/3/52).
D. The Corsican Brothers. L.C. Qns. Dublin, 2/4/52.
D. The Corsican Vendetta. L.C. S.W. 14/9/97.
Spec. The Cossacks; or, Vive la France (Ast. 5/6/54). L.C.
D. The Coster's Christmas Eve. L.C. Gai. Burnley, 9/2/97.
D.Sk. The Coster's Son. L.C. S.W. 18/10/95.
D. The Cottage in the Holly (Stalybridge, 22/1/72).
D. The Cotton Famine; or, Preston in the Olden Time (Blackburn, 10/3/69).
D. Counsel for the Defense (O.C. 9/9/95). L.C.
D. The Counterfeit; or, A Tale of the Times. L.C. Brighton, 30/9/65.

C. Countess d'Argentine; or, The Page's Revenge. L.C. S.W. 11/10/62.
C.O. The Countess of Castille. L.C. P.H. Clacton, 20/7/86.
D. The Countess of Fergon; or, The Wife of Two Husbands. L.C. Sur. 23/12/50.
Ca. The Count of Marolles (Var. Chiswick, 8/9/69).
D. The Count of Monte Christo. L.C. Bradford, 9/11/61.
D.Sk. The Country House. L.C. S.W. 5/3/97.
F. The Country Squire (S.W. 24/2/59).
D. Coup de combat. L.C. Terry's, 10/5/89.
F. A Couple of Thieves; or, A Night's Frolic. L.C. Cab. 26/10/65.
D. The Courier; or, The Assassins of Paris. L.C. Stand. 5/3/51.
D. The Courier of Lyons. L.C. Alex. Widnes, 13/11/91.
[Also called *The Robbery of the Mail.*]
D. The Courier of Lyons; or, The Fatal Resemblance. L.C. Brit. 3/7/54.
D. The Courier of Lyons; or, The Robbers of the Mail Post. L.C. C.L. 12/7/54.
D. The Courier of Strasbourg (Brit. 17/6/61).
D. The Courts and Alleys of London. L.C. Eff. 27/8/64.
Ca. Cousin Grace. L.C. Gai. 10/12/84.
Ent. Cousin Kate. L.C. Roy. 28/11/63.
C. Cousins. L.C. O.H. Aberdeen, 20/8/78.
D. Cousins. L.C. Art Galleries, Newcastle, 11/4/93.
F. The Covent Garden Ball. L.C. Aldershot, 10/12/94.
F. Covers for Three (Sur. 30/10/54).
F. The Cozened Cousins. L.C. Birmingham, 23/10/50.
D. The Creole of St Louis (Brit. 23/6/62).
M.F. The Cricket Match (D.L. 15/4/50). L.C.
D. The Cricket on the Hearth (Str. 19/3/55). L.C.
D. The Cricket on the Hearth (Ast. 13/2/65).
D. The Cricket on the Hearth. L.C. Alex. 19/11/67.
D. The Cries of London; or, Treasure Trove. L.C. Grec. 31/5/65.
D. Crime and Remorse; or, Shadows of the Dead. L.C. Brit. 25/5/55.
[Acted later as *The Crime and the Vision* (Brit. 2/7/60).]
D. The Criminal (Clarence, Dover, 15/12/84).
D. A Crimson Cloud. L.C. S.W. 28/9/97.
D. The Cripple of the Clink; or, London in 1840. L.C. Stand. 7/11/50.
Oa. A Critical Day (Dilettante Club, 26/10/80).
F. A Critical Position. L.C. Manchester, 5/5/52.
Masque. Crocodile's Tears (Gordon Institute, Hampstead, 17/1/89, *amat. copy.*).
D. Crooked Ways (Worcester, 18/12/75).
D. Crooked Ways; or, Base Metal and Sterling Coin (Croydon, 11/9/82).
D. Crooked Ways; or, The Straight and the Narrow Paths of Life. L.C. C.L. 28/9/66.
D. Crosby Ravensworth (Brit. 16/10/61).
F. The Cross-bow Letter (Vic. 21/6/54).
Ca. Crossed in Love. L.C. Tyne, Newcastle, 15/4/80.
D. Cross Purposes. L.C. Olym. 21/11/78.
Ca. Cross Purposes. L.C. Court, 19/3/91.
C. Crotchet Hall (St J. 23/1/52).

F. The Crowded House. L.C. Alh. 20/9/77.
D. The Cruel Brother; or, Buried Alive. L.C. C.L. 20/4/64.
C.O. A Cruise to China (Gar. 5/6/79). L.C.
F. Crushed (Ladb. H. 24/4/90). L.C.
M.F. Crusoe the Second. L.C. Sur. 3/3/75.
M.F. Crying Jenny and Laughing Johnny (Adel. 16/4/66). L.C.
D. The Cry in the Darkness; or, The Collision in the Mersey (Col. L'pool, 11/12/71).
D.Sk. A Cuban Spy. L.C. Empire, 13/4/99.
F. The Cuckoo. L.C. D.Y. 18/10/98.
[See *C. H. BROOKFIELD*, 1899.]
F. The Cupboard Skeleton (Ladb. H. 14/5/87). L.C.
F. Cupid Astray. L.C. St G. 7/11/92.
M.C. Cupid in Camp. L.C. Edmonton, 3/9/97.
F. Cupid in Plush. L.C. G.I. 7/5/69.
Ca. Cupid's Coach. L.C. Assembly R. Putney, 22/12/99.
Poet.D. Cupid's Mistake. L.C. Com. 9/8/98.
[Title changed to *La chasse* on 2/7/1920.]
C. A Cup of Tea (P'cess, 15/2/69). L.C. Birmingham, 4/9/66.
D. The Curate. L.C. Var. 16/10/88.
[See *R. CHALLIS*, 1886.]
D. The Curate's Daughter (Brit. 2/3/59).
F. A Cure for a Mother-in-Law. L.C. Ipswich, 5/1/85.
F. A Cure for the Gout. L.C. Soho, 20/10/59.
D. The Curio (Pleasure Gdns. Folkestone, 8/12/92). L.C.
M.F. A Curious Coincidence. L.C. Brighton, 30/9/87.
F. A Curious Cure. L.C. P.W. 11/10/97.
F. Curling Irons and Capers. L.C. Grec. 14/11/68.
D. The Curse of Disobedience; or, A Lesson of Life (Brit. 11/11/61). L.C.
F. The Customs of the Country (Adel. 30/6/56). L.C.
F. The Cyclist. L.C. S.W. 11/9/99.
Bsq. Cymon and Iphigenia. L.C. Bower, 9/8/64.
D. The Czar. L.C. Str. 6/6/56.
D. Dadds. L.C. T.H. Buckingham, 16/3/88.
D. Daddy the Outlaw. L.C. T.H. Kilburn, 30/11/88.
D. Daft Dora; or, The Sorrows of Susan, the Child of the Wreck. L.C. Brit. 1/9/52.
Oa. Daisy; or, The Knights of the Last. L.C. Canterbury, 17/10/87.
D. Dalila. L.C. St J. 9/2/72.
F. Dalrymple versus Tubbs (Ast. 3/4/54). L.C.
P. Dame Durden; or, Robert and Richard were Two Pretty Men (Stand. 26/12/64). L.C. as *D. D. and her Five Servant Maids*; *or, Harlequin Robert and Richard were Two Pretty Men.*
[By *J. T. DOUGLASS*.]
F. The Dancing-Master's Lesson (Stand. 24/7/55).
F. The Dancing Scotchman (St J. 5/3/55).
C.D. Danger Ahead (Grand, Nottingham, 9/9/89). L.C. Ladb. H. 16/10/88.
D. Danger on the Line. L.C. Var. 17/1/84.
D. Dangerous Playthings. L.C. Roy. 8/4/62.
D. Dangers of the Express; or, The Lost Heir. L.C. Var. 31/5/76.
D. Daniel Bartlett. L.C. Pav. Gravesend, 28/11/81.

D. The Danites; or, Life in the Golden Gulch. L.C. Sefton, L'pool, 29/7/80.
D. Daphnis. L.C. West, Albert H. 29/6/92.
D. Darby and Joan; or, The True Way to be Happy. L.C. 27/9/51.
D. Dare-Devil Dick (Grec. 25/4/61).
D. Dark before Dawn. L.C. Pav. 25/5/75.
D. Dark before Dawn; or, Murder will out. L.C. Gar. 5/10/71.
D. Dark Blue Waters (Brit. 22/4/62).
D. Dark Days. L.C. P's. 20/10/84.
[See *J. W. C. CARR*, 1885.]
D. The Dark Deeds of London. L.C. Pav. 25/2/82.
D. The Darkest Hour. L.C. S.W. 23/4/97.
[Title altered to *The Better Man* on 21/11/1906.]
D. The Dark House (Brit. 23/3/59.)
Ext. The Dark King of the Black Mountains; or, The Adventures of Florio the Foundling Prince (Brit. 2/4/66). L.C.
D. A Dark Night's Work; or, The Murder at the Dead Man's Pool. L.C. C.L. 10/3/65.
D. The Dark Shadows and Sunshine of Life (Vic. 13/4/57).
D. The Dark Woman. L.C. Eff. 17/5/61.
D. The Daughter of Midnight; or, The Mysteries of London. L.C. Pav. 17/10/63.
D. The Daughter of Night; or, A Poor Girl's Fortune (Brit. 15/6/63). L.C. 31/7/56.
Ext. The Daughter of the Danube; or, The Belle, the Baron and the Bear Hunter. L.C. Cremorne, 22/5/68.
D. A Daughter of the Million. L.C. Hyde, 29/9/99.
D. A Daughter of the People (Stand. 1/10/60). L.C.
D. A Daughter of the People. L.C. S.W. 18/10/98.
C.O. The Daughter of the Regiment (D.L. 26/9/55).
Bal. The Daughters of the Guadalquiver (H. 6/9/58).
D.Sk. David and his Wives. L.C. Aven. 15/11/94.
D. David Copperfield (Grec. 3/10/70). L.C.
D. David Copperfield. L.C. Grand, Walsall, 24/9/92.
D. David Copperfield the Younger of Blunderstone Rookery. L.C. Sur. 7/11/50.
D. David Morgan, the Jacobite (Star, Aberdare, 15/2/72).
D. Davy Crockett. L.C. S. Shields, 1/10/75.
D. Davy Garrick (Dalston, 25/7/98).
F. A Day at Boulogne; or, Run to Earth. L.C. Brighton, 4/2/60.
F. A Day at Donnybrook (Vic. 4/4/65).
D.Sk. Daybreak. L.C. Ladb. H. 25/7/95.
M.C. A Day in Boulogne. L.C. Manor, 17/5/99.
F. A Day in High Life. L.C. Marines Barrack Theatre, Chatham, 3/4/60.
D. The Day of Atonement. L.C. Pav. 26/10/99.
F. A Day of Disasters; or, Next of Kin. L.C. Birmingham. 28/2/60.
D. The Day of Reckoning. L.C. Var. 22/12/91.
[Title altered to *The Master Passion* on 28/2/1919.]
D. The Day of Reckoning (Qns. 17/2/94, *copy*.). L.C.
D. The Days of Hogarth; or, Marriage à la mode. L.C. Brit. 11/4/57.

D. The Days of Louis XV; or, Fairfair the Tulip and the Camp at Coen, the Mill at Lowfield and the Royal Gardens. L.C. Brit. 30/9/63.
D. The Days of Terror. L.C. Gai. Wombwell, 8/4/96.
D. The Dead and the Living; or, A Little of Everything. L.C. Edinburgh, 8/9/55.
D. The Dead Boxer (Albion, 20/9/75).
D. The Dead Duchess; or, The Muffled Bells of Paris (Brit. 24/3/56). L.C.
D. The Dead Guest; or, The Old Bridge of the Isle of Luis. L.C. Brighton, 5/9/63. MS. Birmingham.
D. The Dead Hand; or, The Secret of the Iron Cabinet. L.C. M'bone, 28/8/61.
C. The Dead Letter. L.C. Manchester, 12/5/62.
D. Dead Man's Cliff; or, The Blind Girl's Inheritance (Vic. Evesham, 23/9/96).
D. Dead Men's Shoes. L.C. Woolwich, 12/6/94.
D. Dead Men Tell No Tales (Grec. 9/5/66). L.C. Brit. 18/9/63.
D. A Dead Past. L.C. S.W. 1/5/84.
D. The Dead Witness. L.C. Olym. 6/5/89.
D. The Dead Woman's Secret (Grec. 25/11/61).
D.Sk. The Dear Old Flag. L.C. S.W. 28/4/96.
D. Death and Rachel. L.C. Devonshire Park Theatre, Eastbourne, 13/1/90.
[=*C. GRAVES*, *Rachel*.]
D. Death and the Lady; or, The Visions of a Night (M'bone, 21/7/51). L.C.
D. Death in the Streets. L.C. Qns. 31/8/64.
D. The Death of Eva (Str. 23/2/57).
D. The Death of White Surrey (Ast. 1/3/58).
D. Death or Glory Boys. L.C. Darlington, 14/9/97.
D. The Death Token (Soho, 26/2/58).
Bsq. Debo-Lear. L.C. Brit. 16/4/64.
D. Deborah; or, The Jewish Outcast (Grec. 15/2/64). L.C.
C. Debt (Northampton, 25/8/73).
C. Debts of Honour (Bijou, 1893, *amat.*).
Duol. A Debutante. L.C. O.C. 25/11/93.
D. The Debutante. L.C. Birmingham, 27/4/67.
D. Deceived; or, Through Life (P's. Accrington, 9/82).
C. Deception. L.C. Edinburgh, 18/5/89.
F. A Decided Fix. L.C. Olym. 17/9/60.
C. Decision of the Court. L.C. Com. 20/3/93.
D. The Decoy Bird (T.H. Luton, 5/9/92). L.C.
C. The Decoy Duck. L.C. Masonic H. N. Pagnell, 30/12/98.
F.C. Decree Nisi. L.C. Grand. Stalybridge, 22/7/92.
Ca. A Deed of Separation. L.C. P'cess. 3/4/83.
D. Deeds of Darkness. L.C. Qns. 8/5/60.
D. Deeming; or, Doomed at Last (Adel. L'pool, 6/6/92).
D. Deep Shadows. L.C. W.L. 13/9/94.
D. Deep Waters. L.C. Adel. L'pool, 10/11/97.
D. The Deformed; or, The Love of a Life. L.C. Eff. 5/8/65.
F.C. The Demon. L.C. Lyr. Ealing, 4/5/87.
D. The Demon Jockey; or, Archer rides to win (Rotherham, 16/10/82).
D. The Demon of Darkness (Vic. 17/4/65). L.C.

D.Sk. The Demon of the Cellar. L.C. S.W. 10/5/95.
Ext. The Demon of the Drachenfels; or, The Spirit of Water. L.C. Grec. 30/9/63.
D. The Denouncer (Stand. 3/12/60).
D. The Deputy Sheriff; or, Daniel Bartlett (Muncaster, Bootle, 8/8/92; E.C. 17/10/92).
D. Deserted. L.C. St G. 24/4/79.
D. The Deserted Mill (Stand. 16/4/55).
D. The Deserted Wife; or, The Heart's Secret. L.C. Brit. 12/6/73.
D. Desmore; or, The Red Hand. L.C. Eff. 21/9/66.
D. Desmore; or, The Red Hand (Pav. 24/9/66). L.C.
D. Desolation. L.C. Eff. 16/4/65.
D. Destiny. L.C. Var. Hoxton, 5/6/94.
D. Destiny; or, The Broken Heart. L.C. Vic. 30/1/60.
D. Destiny, or, The Traitor's Doom (Grec. 26/11/60). L.C.
D. The Destroyer; or, Fate's Victim (Col. L'pool, 15/6/68).
D. The Devil in Six; or, A Lucifer Match (Brit. 30/10/61). L.C. Brit. 15/10/53.
D. The Devil in Town (Sur. 18/4/63). L.C.
D. The Devil of Paris (Sur. 4/3/61). L.C.
Ext. The Devil on Two Sticks (Adel. 25/4/59). L.C.
D. The Devil's Compact (Brit. 1/4/61). L.C.
D. The Devil's Gap; or, Time Tells Tales. L.C. Grec. 25/9/62.
D. Devil's Luck. L.C. St J. Manchester, 7/12/88.
D. The Devil's Pool. L.C. Brit. 15/8/71.
D. The Devil's Three-decker; or, The Pirates' Bride. L.C. Vic. 26/5/53.
D. Devotion. L.C. Var. 7/2/84.
[See *D. G. BOUCICAULT*, 1884.]
D. Diabolus amans. 12° 1885 [Glasgow].
D. The Dial of Death. L.C. Craigland's Hydro, Ilkley, 29/9/99.
D. Diamond and Granle. L.C. Ladb. H. 5/7/94.
D. The Diamond Cavern. L.C. Pav. 16/9/50.
Oa. Diamond cut Diamond (Adel. 14/7/59). L.C.
D.Sk. A Diamond in the Rough. L.C. Grand, Bolton, 31/12/95.
D. The Diamond Necklace. L.C. Great Hall, Bishops Stortford, 31/3/91.
Bsq. Diana; or, The Goddess of the Moon (Masonic H. Lincoln, 10/82).
D. Diana's Chase; or, The Runaway Goddess and the Enchanted Daffodil. L.C. Brit. 23/3/55.
D. Dickens Jo. L.C. Vic. 12/8/76.
D. Dick Fly-by-night and Dare-Devil Dan; or, The Leap for Life (Vic. 4/10/52). L.C.
Ca. Dick's Repentance. L.C. Bijou, 18/4/93.
[Title altered to *A Broken Link* on 4/4/94.]
D. Dick's Sister. L.C. Terry's, 16/6/92.
D. Dick Tarleton; or, The Heir of Crowshall. L.C. Vic. 11/6/56.
P. Dick Whittington. L.C. Gai. Glasgow, 21/12/75.
P. Dick Whittington. L.C. Rochdale, 4/1/76.
P. Dick Whittington. L.C. Darlington, 4/1/79.
P. Dick Whittington. L.C. O.H. Leeds, 20/12/79.
P. Dick Whittington. L.C. Rotunda, L'pool, 27/12/79.
P. Dick Whittington. L.C. Manchester, 13/1/80.
P. Dick Whittington. L.C. O.H. Leicester, 23/12/80.

P. Dick Whittington. L.C. Nottingham, 23/12/80.
P. Dick Whittington. L.C. Birmingham, 24/12/80.
P. Dick Whittington. L.C. Brighton, 17/12/81.
P. Dick Whittington. L.C. Plymouth, 22/12/81.
P. Dick Whittington. L.C. Glasgow, 29/12/81.
P. Dick Whittington. L.C. Wakefield, 4/12/82.
P. Dick Whittington. L.C. Cardiff, 20/12/82.
P. Dick Whittington. L.C. New, Bristol, 20/12/82.
P. Dick Whittington. L.C. Dewsbury, 30/12/82.
P. Dick Whittington. L.C. York, 22/3/83.
P. Dick Whittington. L.C. Greenwich, 8/12/83.
P. Dick Whittington. L.C. Leicester, 8/12/83.
P. Dick Whittington. L.C. Preston, 18/12/83.
P. Dick Whittington. L.C. Winter Gdns. Southport, 18/12/83.
P. Dick Whittington. L.C. Gai. Oldham, 9/1/84.
P. Dick Whittington. L.C. Var. Burton-on-Trent, 26/12/84.
P. Dick Whittington. L.C. Leeds, 26/12/84.
P. Dick Whittington. L.C. Alex. Sheffield, 26/11/85.
P. Dick Whittington. L.C. Manchester, 11/12/85.
P. Dick Whittington. L.C. Portsmouth, 12/12/85.
P. Dick Whittington. L.C. P'cess. Glasgow, 17/12/86.
P. Dick Whittington. L.C. Court, Wigan, 9/12/87.
P. Dick Whittington. L.C. Bradford, 16/12/87.
P. Dick Whittington. L.C. Greenock, 19/12/87.
P. Dick Whittington. L.C. Edinburgh, 11/12/88.
P. Dick Whittington. L.C. Birmingham, 11/1/89.
P. Dick Whittington. L.C. Grand, Nottingham, 13/12/89.
P. Dick Whittington. L.C. Manchester, 16/12/89.
P. Dick Whittington. L.C. Leeds, 20/12/89.
P. Dick Whittington. L.C. Northampton, 23/12/89.
P. Dick Whittington. L.C. New, Stockport, 11/12/90.
P. Dick Whittington. L.C. Col. Oldham, 13/12/90.
P. Dick Whittington. L.C. Newcastle, 31/12/90.
P. Dick Whittington. L.C. New, Exeter, 9/12/91.
P. Dick Whittington. L.C. Stratford, 11/12/91.
P. Dick Whittington. L.C. P's. Manchester, 15/12/91.
P. Dick Whittington. L.C. P.W. Birmingham, 23/12/91.
P. Dick Whittington. L.C. Cardiff, 23/12/91.
P. Dick Whittington. L.C. P's. Bristol, 23/12/91.
P. Dick Whittington. L.C. Glasgow, 7/12/92.
P. Dick Whittington. L.C. Grand, Leeds, 19/12/92.
P. Dick Whittington. L.C. Birmingham, 1/12/94.
P. Dick Whittington. L.C. Hanley, 31/12/95.
P. Dick Whittington. L.C. Brighton, 31/12/95.
P. Dick Whittington. L.C. Shakespeare, L'pool, 10/1/96.
P. Dick Whittington. L.C. Osborne, Manchester, 18/12/96.
P. Dick Whittington. L.C. Birmingham, 8/1/97.
P. Dick Whittington. L.C. Leeds, 8/1/97.
P. Dick Whittington. L.C. Nottingham, 8/1/97.
P. Dick Whittington. L.C. Roy. Chester, 9/2/97.
P. Dick Whittington. L.C. Grand, Glasgow, 31/12/97
P. Dick Whittington. L.C. W.L. 31/12/97.
P. Dick Whittington. L.C. Bilston, 31/12/97.
P. Dick Whittington. L.C. Aquar. Gt Yarmouth, 31/12/97.

P. Dick Whittington. L.C. Bradford, 31/12/97.
P. Dick Whittington. L.C. Grand, Hull, 31/12/97.
P. Dick Whittington. L.C. Alex. Hull, 31/12/97.
P. Dick Whittington. L.C. Margate, 31/12/97.
P. Dick Whittington. L.C. Shakespeare, L'pool, 30/12/98.
P. Dick Whittington. L.C. Newcastle, 30/12/98.
P. Dick Whittington. L.C. P.W. L'pool, 30/12/98.
P. Dick Whittington. L.C. Greenock, 30/12/98.
P. Dick Whittington. L.C. Nuneaton, 30/12/98.
P. Dick Whittington. L.C. Dalston, 22/12/99.
P. Dick Whittington. L.C. Eastbourne, 28/12/99.
P. Dick Whittington. L.C. Paisley, 28/12/99.
P. Dick Whittington. L.C. Pav. 28/12/99.
P. Dick Whittington. L.C. E.C. 28/12/99.
P. Dick Whittington. L.C. Edinburgh, 28/12/99.
P. Dick Whittington and his Cat. L.C. Greenock, 29/12/74.
P. Dick Whittington and his Cat. L.C. Sheffield, 30/12/75.
P. Dick Whittington and his Cat. L.C. P.W. Birkenhead, 8/1/77.
P. Dick Whittington and his Cat. L.C. Lyc. Torquay, 27/12/78.
P. Dick Whittington and his Cat. L.C. Grand, Glasgow, 8/12/81.
P. Dick Whittington and his Cat. L.C. Birmingham, 23/12/84.
P. Dick Whittington and his Cat. L.C. P.W. L'pool, 21/12/85.
P. Dick Whittington and his Cat. L.C. Sheffield, 30/11/91.
P. Dick Whittington and his Cat. L.C. Rotunda, L'pool, 11/12/91.
P. Dick Whittington and his Cat. L.C. Edinburgh, 20/12/93.
P. Dick Whittington and his Wonderful Cat; or, Harlequin Humpty Dumpty and the Home of Content in the Realms of Happiness. L.C. Pav. 24/12/63.
P. Dick Whittington Returned. L.C. H.M. Richmond, 22/12/81.
P. Dick Whittington the Second. L.C. Grand, Leeds, 26/12/85.
Bsq. Dido and Æneas (Str. 26/10/93). L.C.
D. A Difference of Opinion. L.C. Aquar. Boston, 20/6/98.
F. The Diggings (Jersey, 14/5/77).
D. Ding Dong Will; or, The Ashbrooke Blacksmith (Brit. 11/6/60). L.C. 10/2/57.
M.F. Dinky Doo; or, Over the Wall. L.C. W.L. 31/10/94.
D. Diogenes in Search of a Contented Man. L.C. Brit. 9/10/57.
[By *G. D. PITT*.]
D. Dione. L.C. St G. 9/2/97.
F.C. Dione; or, The Canon's Daughter (P.H. Gravesend, 2/10/95). L.C.
D. Dirty Dick (Brit. 10/9/60). L.C.
C.O. The Disguised. L.C. St G. 14/7/79.
F. Disestablishment. L.C. Cambridge, 2/6/86.
D. Dishonoured. L.C. Brit. 13/11/95.
D. The Disputed Title; or, The False and True Heir and the Brigand of Palermo. L.C. C.L. 8/6/60.
F. Distinguished Connections. L.C. Brighton, 9/9/97.
D. The Diver's Luck (Lyr. Hammersmith, 11/7/92).
[See *F. COOKE*, 1887.]
D. The Divorce; or, Better than Gold. L.C. Eff. 27/1/66.
D. The Divorce; or, The Old Love and the New. L.C. C.L. 20/7/59.
D. The Divorced. L.C. Sur. 21/9/52.
D. Dobbin's House; or, The Lucky Horseshoe. L.C. Londesborough, Scarborough, 26/10/83.

D.Sk. The Doctor. L.C. S.W. 5/3/97.
C. The Doctor. L.C. Ladb. H. 7/11/91.
C.O. Doctor Ambrosias—his Secret (St G. 8/8/68). L.C.
[By "H. B."; music by D'Oyley Carte.]
D. Dr Clyde (Alex. Sheffield, 19/7/80). L.C. Bury, 26/8/80.
C. The Doctor in Spite of Himself. L.C. O.C. 24/8/71.
D. Dr Jeykyll and Mr Hyde (Park, Merthyr Tydvil, 26/7/88).
Ca. Doctor Miracle. L.C. Aquar. Gt Yarmouth, 13/9/82.
F. The Doctor of Music. L.C. P.H. Gravesend, 10/4/93.
C.D. Doctor Paddy (Lincoln, 14/4/84).
Oa. Doctor Porter. L.C. Cambridge, 17/10/87.
M.Ca. Dr Quisby. L.C. Ladb. H. 10/5/88.
Oa. The Doctor's Dilemma. L.C. Bradford, 10/4/93.
D. The Doctor's Secret. L.C. Masonic Theatre, Lincoln, 25/4/88.
D. Doctors Beware. L.C. Morton's, Greenwich, 31/12/97.
F. The Dodges of Cupid (S.W. 4/2/63).
D. The Dog Detectives. L.C. Sur. 23/10/79.
D. The Dogs of Australia (Grec. 29/4/63).
D. The Dogs of the Revenue Cutter (Brit. 30/4/62).
M.Ca. The Doll's House. L.C. St G. 9/12/92.
Oa. Dolly (Cork, 26/12/60; Gai. 22/8/70). L.C. *Lacy*.
Ca. Dolly's Follies. L.C. P.H. Southend-on-Sea, 21/5/84.
F. Domestic Bliss. L.C. St G. 10/7/69.
F. Domestic Discipline. L.C. Str. 24/12/55.
D. Dominique the Deserter (M'bone, 4/3/57). L.C. as *Dred; or, The Dismal Swamp*.
D. Dominique the Deserter (Ast. 11/1/65).
D. Don (M'bone, 6/2/54).
D. Donagh's Romance (Lincoln, 8/10/83).
Bsq. Don Giovanni. L.C. S.W. 17/11/64.
Bsq. Don Giovanni Jr.; or, The Shakey Page, more Funkey than Flunkey (Greenwich, 17/5/75).
Bsq. Don Giovanni, M.P. (P'cess. Edinburgh, 17/4/71).
D. Don Juan (M'bone, 12/2/55).
D. Don Juan (Soho, 26/2/58).
Bsq. Don Juan. L.C. Alh. 9/2/76.
[See *H. J. BYRON*, 1873.]
Bsq. Don Juan considerably aided (Bradford, 22/11/70). L.C.
C.O. Donna Juanita (Ladb. H. 24/2/80). L.C.
D. Donnybrook. L.C. Lyr. Hammersmith, 5/5/90.
[See *J. PELZER*, 1899.]
P. Don Quixote and the Steed Rosinante; or, Sancho Panza Harlequin (Ast. 25/12/57). L.C.
P. Don Quixote de la Mancha and the Sleep of a Hundred Years; or, Harlequin the Omened Bird and the Fairy of the Golden Waters. L.C. Birmingham, 15/11/52.
Ca. Don't Jump at Conclusions. L.C. P.H. Urmston, 18/3/95.
F. Don't Mind Me (Plymouth, 16/12/72).
Ext. "Don't Swear"; or, 1, 2, 3, 4, 5, 6, 7. L.C. Manchester, 30/3/53.
C. Don't Tell Her Husband. L.C. Glo. 14/1/95.
Bsq. Don't you wish you may get it; or, Three Wishes. L.C. Soho, 27/12/56.
D. Donzella's Oath (Vic. 19/6/54).
D. The Doomed Bridge; or, The Parricide's Curse (Vic. 24/3/56).

D. Doomed to Darkness. L.C. Brit. 11/8/76.
D. Doomed to Siberia. L.C. P's. Harwich, 30/11/97.
D. Dora's Love. L.C. Alex. 14/2/73.
[See *C. W. CHAMBERLAINE*, 1872.]
C. Dorothy's Birthday. L.C. Sav. 23/6/84.
F. Do Shake Hands. L.C. Lyc. 6/2/55.
D. The Double Conquest (Cardiff, 27/10/73).
Ca. Doubleday's Will. L.C. St G. 8/3/78.
F. The Double Dutchman. L.C. Gai. Burnley, 30/3/85.
M.Sk. A Double Engagement. L.C. S.W. 10/1/96.
Ca. The Double Event. L.C. P.H. Addestone, 19/3/91.
[See *J. EAST*, 1891.]
D. Double-Handed Dick (Brit. 14/4/62).
D. A Double Life (M'bone, 2/12/76).
D. A Double Life. L.C. Albion Assembly R. 8/1/97.
C. A Double Lover. L.C. Dundee, 29/11/83.
D. The Double Marriage. L.C. St J. 8/1/55.
D. A Double Marriage (Adel. 8/3/73). L.C.
Oa. Double or Quits. L.C. T.H. Hulme, Manchester, 17/5/98.
F. A Doubtful Advertisement. L.C. Shepley Hall, Marple, 27/2/96.
F. Doubtful Hospitality. L.C. Norwood Institute, 2/12/80.
C. Doubts and Fears. L.C. Olym. 18/1/64.
D. Dougal the Piper (Edinburgh, 2/1/52).
D. The Dove and the Serpent (C.L. 21/3/59). L.C.
D. The Dove Cote (D.Y. 12/2/98). L.C.
F. Down at Ramsgate; or, What I Think I Say. L.C. Vic. 6/9/56.
F. Down at Rosherville (Soho, 4/10/58).
F. Down South; or, Life in the Cotton Fields (Vic. 19/6/65). L.C.
D. Down the River; or, Steamboating on the Mississippi. L.C. Phil. 24/9/77.
D. Dracula; or, The Un-dead. L.C. Lyc. 1/6/97.
D. A Dramatic Legend. L.C. Olym. 26/1/54.
F. Drat that Comet. L.C. Str. 16/8/57.
F. A Dreadful Tragedy. L.C. Var. 31/10/87.
Fairy Play. A Dream. L.C. Drill Hall, Brentwood, 14/12/87.
D. The Dream. L.C. Gai. Hastings, 28/2/93.
D. The Dream. L.C. T.H. Ashford, 20/6/90.
D. A Dream and a Reality; or, The Jewel Casket. L.C. Newcastle, 29/1/59.
D. A Dream of Life (Grec. 14/3/61).
D. The Dream of the Irish Emigrant (Str. 16/5/53). L.C. as *The D. of the I. E.; or, The "Lady May"*.
D. The Dream of the White Boy (Cheltenham, 28/9/68).
Rev. A Dream of Whitaker's Almanack (C.P. 5/6/99). L.C.
D. Dred. L.C. Brit. 26/9/56.
Bsq. Dred. L.C. Bower, 16/10/56.
D. Dred (Grec. 21/4/64).
D. Dred, a Tale of the Great Dismal Swamp. L.C. Vic. 24/9/56.
[Two MS. versions of *Dred* are at Birmingham.]
D. Drifting Clouds (Bow and Bromley Institute, 31/10/94).
D. Drip, drop, Drip drop; or, The Vulture's Nest. L.C. Eff. 6/4/63.
D. Driven from Home (Grand, Birmingham, 10/10/84; Pav. 14/6/86).
F.C. Drowned for Love. L.C. P.H. Woking, 23/4/97.
Bsq. The Druids Elect (St G. 19/4/99).

D. The Druid's Oak; or, The Phantom King (Vic. 23/6/51). L.C.
D. Drumclog; or, The Covenanters (P's. Edinburgh, 5/9/71).
D. Drummed Out. L.C. Empire, L'pool, 23/4/97.
D. The Drunkard; or, The Slaves of Drink. L.C. Blackburn, 14/7/90.
D. The Drunkard's Children (Brit. 26/9/59). MS. Birmingham.
D. The Drunkard's Doom; or, The Devil's Chain (Plymouth, 8/9/79).
D. The Drunkard's Glass (Soho, 15/5/60).
D. The Drunkard's List (Col. L'pool, 1/4/72).
Ext. Drury Lane and Park Lane. L.C. Phil. 29/9/79.
D. The Dryad. L.C. Steinway Hall, 27/5/92.
D. The Duke's Device. L.C. Olym. 28/9/76.
F. The Duke's Double (Ast. 30/11/57). L.C.
D. The Duke's Double. L.C. Qns. Farnworth, Bolton, 30/11/99.
D. The Dumb Sailor (Vic. 6/6/54).
F. Dundreary a Father. L.C. H. 19/6/66.
F. Dundreary by Special Train. L.C. Newcastle, 21/11/62.
C. Duplicity. L.C. Assembly R. Surbiton, 30/1/93.
D. During Temporary Sanity. L.C. Institute, Burgess Hill, 11/9/99.
Ca. Dust in the Eyes. L.C. H. 19/2/79.
D. The Dustman's Treasure; or, Wig and the Boffins (Brit. 16/7/66). L.C.
D. Dutch Anna; or, A Tale of the French Police (Vic. 23/4/64). L.C.
D. Dutch the Diver; or, The Cuban's Treasure (L'pool, 30/9/78; Birkenhead, 11/9/82, as *D. the D.; or, Beneath the Surface*). L.C.
D. The Dying Gift; or, The Tramp's Adventure (Sur. 12/11/60). L.C.
D. Dying to Live (Ast. 21/3/59).
D. The Eagle and Child; or, A Mother's Courage (Brit. 10/10/59). L.C. 24/9/56.
Oa. The Early Bird; or, Better Late than Never. L.C. P.H. Kilmacolm, 19/11/92.
Oa. The Ear-ring. L.C. St G. 21/5/72.
D. East Lynne. L.C. Grec. 18/4/66.
Bsq. East Lynne (Birmingham, 16/9/69).
D. East Lynne. L.C. Alfred, 30/11/70.
D. East Lynne. L.C. Windsor, 21/10/75.
D. East Lynne (Stand. 28/5/83).
D. East Lynne. L.C. Barnard's, Woolwich, 16/12/93.
D. East Lynne (P'cess. 7/3/96).
D. East Lynne. L.C. Leamington, 24/3/99.
Bsq. East Lynne; or, Isabel that was a Belle (Coventry, 10/11/84).
D.Sk. An Eccentric Will. L.C. Empire, 13/4/99.
D. The Edict of Spain (Ast. 24/1/59).
D. Edith's Flight (Dundee, 15/3/75). L.C.
D. Edith the Captive; or, The Lost Heir of Maningdale Manor (Brit. 1/5/61). L.C. Vic. 22/3/61.
[By *E. TOWERS*.]
C.D. Edith West (Sheffield, 26/4/75).
D. Edmund Atherton; or, The Miser of Coventry. L.C. Bower, 10/9/53.
D. Edmund Kean (Hol. 25/9/71). L.C.
D. Edmund Kean; or, Principle and Genius. L.C. Adel. L'pool, 1/9/64.

D. Edward the Black Prince. L.C. Qns. 27/10/54 [additional act and speeches].
P. Edward the Black Prince; or, Harlequin and the Magic Feathers. L.C. Vic. 16/12/60.
D. Effie Deans (Vic. 27/5/65).
D. Effie Deans; or, The Lily of St Leonards (Sur. 7/2/63). L.C.
C.D. Effie's Angel (Sheffield, 4/9/71; L'pool, 1/5/76, as *Silas Marner's Treasure*). L.C.
F. The Egyptian Babies. L.C. Greenwich, 8/4/81.
Ext. Egyptorica. L.C. Phil. 2/12/79.
P. Egypt Three Thousand Years Ago; or, Queen Cleopatra: A Dream in the Crystal Palace. L.C. Brit. 14/12/54.
C. The Eiderdown Quilt. L.C. Roy. 12/6/94.
[See *T. S. WOTTON*, 1896.]
D. 1870. L.C. Middlesborough, 17/7/84.
D. 1870; or, The Battle of Life (Qns. Dublin, 31/10/70).
D. The Eighth Wonder of the World (Str. 3/7/55).
F. The Eight Pages (Grec. 3/10/59).
D. Eleanor's Victory. L.C. Vic. 4/3/64.
F. An Election under Difficulties. L.C. Sheffield, 22/5/65.
C.O. El Escribano. L.C. Grand, Leeds, 30/3/97.
D. Elie and Elode; or, The Gipsies of Castile. L.C. Brit. 31/10/54.
Bal.P. El Gambusino; or, The Mexican Gold Seeker (H. 24/3/56).
[Music by F. Fitzwilliam.]
Spec. El Heyder: the Chief of the Mountains (Ast. 10/8/57).
Ca. An Eligible Bachelor (Str. 9/12/71). L.C.
Oa. An Eligible Villa (Gai. 19/4/69). L.C.
D. Elise; or, Life in Santa Lucia. L.C. Sheffield, 3/3/62.
Ba. The Elixir of Life. L.C. O.C. 1/12/70.
D. Elizabeth, Queen of England (Amphi. L'pool, 14/6/69; Lyc. 18/12/69). L.C.
D. Eliza Fenning (Stand. 31/8/57).
D. Eliza Fenning, the Victim of Circumstances. L.C. Brit. 8/9/55.
D. Eliza Holmes (Grec. 19/3/62).
Duol. Ellaline (Foresters' H. Clerkenwell, 3/6/90).
D. Ellen and Susan (Brit. 9/3/63).
D. Ellie Forester. L.C. Vic. 8/2/57.
D. El Mahdi; or, The False Prophet of the Sudan (Gt Grimsby, 7/3/85).
D. Elmira, the Female Pirate; or, The Black Flag and the Vow of Vengeance. L.C. Bower, 7/10/65.
D. The Eloquence of Silence. L.C. Gar. 28/12/99.
D. Elsa's Lover: an Idyll of Rheingau. L.C. Ladb. H. 29/10/92.
D. El Toreador (Str. 13/8/55).
F. The Embarrassed Man; or, Uncle's Come. L.C. St J. 27/7/63.
D. The Emerald Isle. L.C. Stand. 2/10/61.
D The Emigrant Family; or, A Tale of New Zealand. L.C. M'bone, 20/6/64.
D. The Emigrant's Progress (C.L. 2/10/52). L.C.
D. Emigration (Sur. 1/10/55).
D. The Emigré's Daughter (Adel. 18/7/50). L.C.
D. Em'ly; or, The Ark on the Sands (Qns. Manchester, 10/3/84).
F.C. Emma (Aquar. Brighton, 17/7/93, *mat.*). L.C.
D. Emma Hardy; or, The Murder of Leyburn Mill. L.C. 19/9/51.

D. Emmeline; or, The Child of Fortune. L.C. Eff. 26/1/61.
D. The Emperor and the Exiles (Sur. 6/7/57).
D. The Emperor's Decree (Ast. 16/1/60). L.C. as *The Warrior's Career*; *or, The E. D.*
F. An Empty Wigwam. L.C. Windsor, 18/10/94.
P. The Enchanted Dove; or, The Princess, the Poodle and the Sorceress (Brit. 26/12/81). L.C.
Ba. The Enchanted Fawn. L.C. G.I. 24/6/72.
Oa. The Enchanted Fife. L.C. Gai. 20/11/72.
D. Enchanted Forth; or, Corney O'Connor and the Leprahauns. L.C. M'bone, 12/4/61.
Ent. The Enchanted Garden (D.L. 9/4/56).
P. The Enchanted Horn; or, Harlequin Fire King and the Fairy of the Frozen Dell. L.C. Vic. 17/12/60.
Ent. The Enchanted Lake (Str. 17/4/54).
Ba. The Enchanted Lake; or, The Fisherman and the Genie. L.C. Newcastle, 14/4/56.
P. The Enchanted Mountain. L.C. St J. Manchester, 31/12/97.
Spec. The Enchanted Palfrey; or, The Warrior and the Crescent. L.C. Ast. 9/7/50.
D. The Encounter and Carousal of the Wild Indian (Ast. 20/11/54).
Bsq. Endora; or, A Prime Minister a prim-in-a-stir. L.C. St G. 4/10/71.
Bsq. Endymion. L.C. Torquay, 8/4/81.
D. The Enemy Note Book. L.C. Glasgow, 17/1/57.
D.Sk. The Enemy of Man. L.C. S.W. 12/7/99.
Ca. Engaged to Appear (Crit. H. Trowbridge, 21/3/79).
D. The Engineer (Vic. 23/3/63). L.C.
D. England Ho! or, The Buccaneers of the Arctic Regions (M'bone, 6/7/78).
D.Sk. England's Defenders. L.C. W.L. 5/11/95.
D. England's Glory (Parkhurst, 20/8/94). L.C.
Spec. England's Harvest Home and National Steeplechase (Ast. 21/4/56).
D. English Born and Scottish Bred. L.C. Inverness, 26/7/89.
D. English Hawks and Irish Pigeons (Brit. 7/2/60).
D. An English Nihilist. L.C. P'cess. 11/6/83.
D. An English Nihilist L.C. Var. 23/4/87.
Ca. Enlisted (Windsor, 7/4/85). L.C.
D. Enlisted. L.C. Gai. Hastings, 14/7/92.
D.Sk. An Enthusiast (Vaud. 11/3/92, *mat.*). L.C.
Ca. L'Envoi. L.C. Vaud. 28/7/90.
D. The Episode of Eva (S.W. 13/4/57).
Ca. An Episodic Sketch. L.C. Str. 10/9/85.
Ca. An Equal Match. L.C. Olym. 16/1/61.
D. Erin Go Bragh. L.C. Gar. 23/9/71.
D. Ernani (Sur. 3/11/51).
C.O. The Erotometer. L.C. Alex. Leeds, 28/9/96.
Bsq. Erratic Evangeline (P.W. Birmingham, 10/3/84). L.C.
D. Escaped from Portland (P'cess. 9/10/69). L.C.
D. Escarte (Glo. 3/12/70).
Bsq. Esmeralda (Gai. 4/79).
C. Esmeralda. L.C. St J. 5/10/83.
D. Esperance; or, The Heart of Hours. L.C. Sur. 7/3/59.

D. Esperanza; or, The Stranger in Black. L.C. Grec. 11/5/64.
Bal. Estelle. L.C. Stand. 7/11/70.
D. Etelka. L.C. Brighton, 29/9/99.
C. L'Etrangère (H. 3/6/76). L.C.
D. Eugene Aram (M'bone, 30/3/55).
M.F. Eugénie; or, An Artist's Muddle. L.C. Londesborough, Scarborough, 1/7/85.
D. Eva (C.G. 18/4/55).
D. Eva's Home (Brit. 30/7/60).
D. Eva's Home. L.C. Var. 25/2/80.
Bsq. Evangeline (Court, L'pool, 11/6/83).
D. The Eve of St John; or, The Water Spirit and the Magic Axe. L.C. Brit. 9/6/59.
Oa. The Eve of the Wedding. L.C. T.H. Ruthlin, 4/5/89.
Oa. Everel. L.C. P.H. S. Norwood, 14/3/84.
C. Every-Day Occurrences (S.W. 5/5/62). L.C. S.W. 26/4/62.
D. Evicted. L.C. Adel. Oldham, 29/1/80.
C.O. The Evil Eye (Leicester, 21/4/76).
D. Evil Hands and Honest Hearts (Brit. 7/3/64). L.C.
Bal. Excelsior (H.M. 22/5/85).
F. The Excursion. L.C. Str. 7/11/53.
Oa. The Excursion Train (Polytechnic, 5/4/58).
D. The Exile of Siberia (Sur. 28/3/54).
D. Exiles. L.C. W.L. 16/1/94.
F. The Expected General. L.C. Grec. 4/10/70.
F. The Extra Hand. L.C. Empress, 29/9/99.
Bsq. An Extraordinary Version of the Lady of Lyons; or, The Trials and Troubles of Claude and Pauline. L.C. Brit. 10/5/60.
F. An Extra Turn. L.C. T.H. Herne Bay, 17/5/99.
Int. Extremely Peculiar (Sur. 6/7/57). L.C.
D. Eyes in the Dark; or, The Grave on the Sands (Eff. 3/12/66). L.C.
Ca. Eyes Right. L.C. Gai. 13/5/78.
D. Fabian; or, The Misalliance (Lyc. 14/11/56). L.C.
Oa. Fact and Fancy; or, Bunker's Clothes Philosophy. L.C. Ch.X. 11/5/72.
D. The Factory Girl. L.C. Bower, 25/2/52.
C. Faint Heart Never Won Fair Lady (Bijou, 9/3/93).
Oa. A Fair Exchange. L.C. G.I. 2/5/65.
Ext. The Fairies' Haunt (D.L. 2/7/56).
D. Fair Lilias; or, The Three Lives. L.C. Eff. 22/5/65.
D. Fairly Won. L.C. Blackpool, 6/9/73.
P. The Fair One with the Golden Locks. L.C. P.W. L'pool, 19/12/77.
P. The Fair One with the Golden Locks. L.C. Glasgow, 20/12/79.
P. The Fair One with the Golden Locks. L.C. Birmingham, 27/12/79. MS. Birmingham.
P. The Fair One with the Golden Locks. L.C. Tyne, Newcastle, 9/12/87.
P. The Fair One with the Golden Locks. L.C. Sheffield, 14/12/87.
P. The Fair One with the Golden Locks. L.C. Alex. L'pool, 18/12/94.
P. The Fair One with the Golden Locks; or, Harlequin and Davy Jones's Locker (Sur. 26/12/67). L.C.
P. The Fair One with the Locks of Gold; or, Harlequin Gorilla, the King, the Giant and the Gloomy Grotto (Grec. 24/12/61). L.C.

D. Fair Rosamond (Ast. 11/6/60).
D. The Fair Sylvia (Glo. 27/12/69). *Lacy*.
D. The Fairy. L.C. Newcastle, 13/2/61.
Ext. The Fairy Circle; or, Con O'Carrolin's Dream (Adel. 6/7/57). L.C.
Ext. The Fairy Elves of the Fourth Estate (M'bone, 10/1/57).
Spec. The Fairy Fern Flower; or, The Goblin Mine (M'bone, 24/3/56). L.C.
Ext. Fairy Genesta. L.C. Assembly R. Surbiton, 13/1/92.
P. The Fairy of the Coral Grot; or, Harlequin Beauty and the Beast (Adel. L'pool, 26/12/57).
D. The Fairy Page; or, The Demon's Compact. L.C. Manchester, 8/4/52.
P. The Fairy Queen of the Golden Starlight. L.C. Vic. Longton, Staffs. 18/12/77.
Bsq. The Fairy Ring (Bristol, 29/3/69).
C.O. The Fairy Ring. L.C. Grand, 21/9/86.
C.D. A Fairy Tale. L.C. Olym. 19/10/60.
Spec. The Fairy Tales of Mother Goose (Adel. 6/4/55). L.C.
D. Faith. L.C. H.M. Carlisle, 26/2/87.
D. Faith; or, Wife and Mother (Manchester, 21/8/79).
D. Faith, Hope and Charity (Brit. 6/4/63). L.C.
D. Faith in Love. L.C. Sheffield, 14/3/62.
D. Faith's Reward. L.C. Aquar. Gt Yarmouth, 26/11/85.
D. The Fallen Star. L.C. C.L. 9/11/59.
D. The Fallen Star; or, The Wide Wide World. L.C. Eff. 19/2/64.
D. The Falling Star; or, Poor Andrew of the Tyrol. L.C. C.L. 13/4/55.
D. The Fall of Clyde (Stand. 18/5/58).
D. The Fall of Delhi (M'bone, 9/11/57). L.C.
D. The Fall of Khartoum; or, The Death of General Gordon (Albany, Durham, 11/4/85).
Spec. The Fall of Sebastopol (Ast. 24/9/55). L.C.
D. The Fall of the Avalanche; or, The Mountain Home (Grec. 27/2/65). L.C.
D. The Fall of the Leaf. L.C. C.L. 31/1/52.
D. False Accusations. L.C. E.L. 16/10/74.
F. A False Alarm. L.C. Alh. 22/4/71.
D. False and True; or, Marriage a Lottery (Grec. 24/3/64). L.C. 15/8/63.
D. The False Earl; or, The Rover of the North Sea. L.C. Pav. 17/6/63.
D. False Evidence (St J. Manchester, 19/8/89).
D. A False Step; or, The Castle and the Cottage. L.C. Vic. 16/11/59.
C. A Family Failing. L.C. Shaft. 30/3/96.
C. The Family Fast. L.C. Adel. 30/4/66.
C. Family Friends. L.C. G.I. 20/12/72.
F. Family Relations. L.C. S.W. 27/11/50.
F. Family Secrets; or, How to make Home Happy. L.C. Lyc. 2/11/53.
D. Family Treason; or, Truth may be blamed but cannot be shamed. L.C. Grec. 23/9/61.
D. The Family Will. L.C. Olym. 26/4/88.
M.F. Fanchette (C.G. 4/1/64). L.C.

D. Fanchonette the Cricket; or, The Will o' the Wisp (Stand. 30/9/71). L.C.
[This seems to have been an American play.]
D. Fanchon the Cricket. L.C. Adel. L'pool, 13/9/62.
D. Fanchon the Grasshopper. L.C. Olym. 11/8/67.
C. Fanny Lear (Roy. 26/10/85).
D. Fanny Wyndham; or, Modern Life in London. L.C. Brit. 15/5/62.
Bal. Fans and Fandangas (H. 12/10/65). L.C.
C.Bal. Fantisticuff; or, The Storm Fiend. L.C. Adel. 29/5/71.
Ext. Les Farfadets. L.C. Booth's, Ashton, 23/9/81.
Bal. La Farfaletta (H.M. 30/6/66).
D. The Farmer of Inglefield Forest. L.C. Brit. 30/6/59.
Oa. The Farmer of Lyons (Sur. 5/4/58). L.C.
Bsq. Farrago (People's O.H. Ashton, 14/5/83). L.C. Vic. H. Newport, 13/3/82.
C. Fashion. L.C. M'bone, 9/10/84.
D. Fashionable Fallacy; or, The Peasant's Wife. L.C. Stand. 24/4/65.
D. Fashion and Famine. L.C. Brit. 27/1/55.
F. Fashion and Famine; or, The Strawberry Girl (Str. 2/3/57). L.C.
C. Fast Friends up a Tree (Sur. 1/10/64). L.C. as *F. F.; or, How to Shave the Governor.*
F. Fast Married Men. L.C. Eff. 17/10/63.
D. The Fatal Gift. L.C. E.C. 21/8/76.
D. Fatality (Sur. 21/6/59).
D. Fatality; or, Father and Sons. L.C. P's. Accrington, 11/6/87.
D. The Fatal Likeness. L.C. Vic. 25/8/63.
D. The Fatal Shadow; or, The Man with the Iron Heart. L.C. Eff. 16/2/61.
D. The Fatal Snowdrift (Stand. 29/5/60).
D. The Fatal Vision (Stand. 9/5/59).
D. The Fatal Wager (S.W. 27/4/59). L.C.
D. Fate (Ast. 20/4/65). L.C.
D. Fate and its Wonders; or, The Idiot and the Twin Brother. L.C. Vic. 6/9/56.
D. The Fate of a Coquette (S.W. 19/6/63).
D. A Father's Sin; or, Time will tell. L.C. W.L. 18/11/96.
D. Faust (Brit. 20/3/61).
D. Faust. L.C. Vic. 30/9/63.
D. Faust (part 1, S.W. 20/2/86).
Bsq. Faust. L.C. Grand, Birmingham, 31/3/91.
Bsq. Faust (Stand. 20/7/91).
D. Faust (Roy. 30/11/94).
Bsq. Faust and Marguerite (Olym. 24/11/66).
D. Faust and Marguerite. L.C. Grec. 11/8/54.
O. Faust and Marguerite. L.C. Sur. 16/5/55.
Ba. Faust and Marguerite. L.C. D.L. 16/8/55.
D. Faust and Marguerite. L.C. W. Hartlepool, 20/1/81.
D. Faust and Mephistopheles (Vic. 4/5/54).
C. Faustine. L.C. Gai. 23/6/87.
C. The Favourite (Sur. 4/8/51).
M.C. The Favourite. L.C. Ryde, 20/4/89.
D. The Favourite (E.C. 13/3/99). L.C. as *The F.; or, The Sport of Kings.*

P. Fayre Rosamond. L.C. Bradford, 11/12/85.
P. Fayre Rosamond, Henry II, Robin Hood and the Merry Men of Sherwood (M'bone, 26/12/65). L.C.
[By *R. SOUTAR.*]
D. The Feast of Saragossa (St J. 11/6/59).
D. La Felicidad. L.C. Gai. 4/3/87.
D. Felix Heron; or, London in the Reign of George II. L.C. Bower, 17/8/65.
C. Felix Porter. L.C. Glo. 25/5/91.
D. The Felon of Bruges (Vic. 23/3/54).
Ext. The Female Bluebeard (Brit. 10/11/62).
D. The Female Detective; or, The Foundling of the Streets. L.C. Brit. 6/6/65.
Ext. The Female Volunteers (Ast. 20/6/59).
D. Ferdinand Lassalle. L.C. Bijou, 21/11/93.
Bal. La Festa di Ballo (H.M. 7/6/64).
Spec. The Festival of Peace; or, Honour to the Brave (Ast. 29/5/56, *mat.*).
Bal. A Fête at Seville. L.C. Grec. 31/5/65.
Ent. A Fête in Andalusia (S.W. 15/5/55).
Bal. Une Fête Napolitaine (D.L. 12/4/52).
Ent. The Fête of Nations (Adel. 16/3/55).
D. Fettered at Last. L.C. Sefton, L'pool, 7/6/81.
D. Fettered Lives. L.C. W.L. 22/5/93.
[See *H. WHYTE*, 1893.]
D. Fiammina. L.C. St J. 29/1/72.
D. Fidelity. L.C. P'cess. Lancaster, 29/12/84.
D. The Field against the Favourite (Ast. 2/4/55). L.C.
D. The Field of Forty Footsteps (Sur. 27/2/58).
Bal. The Fiend of the Drachenfels (Olym. 26/4/52).
D. The Fiend's Mountain; or, The Gascon Adventurer. L.C. D.L. 8/9/55.
D. A Fiery Ordeal (Brit. 27/1/62; also called *The Fiery Furnace*, 3/2/62).
D.Sk. A Fiery Ordeal. L.C. S.W. 21/12/94.
C. The Fiery Parisienne. L.C. Kilburn, 27/12/98.
D. Fifteen Years of a British Seaman's Life (Pav. 19/2/59).
R.D. A Fight for Life. L.C. Whittenhall, 29/3/95.
D. A Fight with Fate (Sur. 17/9/64). L.C.
C.O. La Fille de Mme. Angot (Crit. 22/7/93).
D. La Fille de Roland. L.C. D.L. 12/6/93.
C.O. La Fille du Prefet. L.C. Cardiff, 31/8/78.
O. La Fille du Regiment; or, The Daughter of the Regiment. L.C. Standard, 20/5/58.
Oa. Filumbonum; or, The Dentist's Identity. L.C. P.H. Hastings, 22/12/99.
Ca. Finesse. L.C. O.H. Torquay, 31/10/81.
Ext. Fingal. L.C. Leicester, 6/5/81.
P. Fire, Fire, burn Stick; or, Harlequin Old Dame Cramp and the Silver Penny. L.C. Stand. 21/12/54.
Ext. The Fire King; or, The Yellow Boy (P.W. L'pool, 3/8/85).
F. The Fireman and the Volunteer; or, An Artful Trick and Love in the Dark. L.C. Pav. 11/5/61.
F. The First and Second Floor (H. 29/6/57). L.C.

Ca. The First Breeze. L.C. Pav. Greenwich, 31/3/82.
Ca. First Cousins. L.C. Halliday Dram. Club, L'pool, 17/4/79.
D. The First Crime (C.L. 20/10/56).
F. The First Day after the Trial. L.C. Stand. 16/3/58.
F. First Floor, Second Floor and Attics. L.C. P'cess. 23/1/63.
F. A First Floor to Let; or, Strange Arrivals in 1851. L.C. Brit. 18/5/51.
F. First Impression's Everything; or, The Young Lover and the Remembrance of Childhood (Stand. 14/3/61). L.C.
D. First Love; or, The Slave Brother (Sur. 26/12/66).
D. First Love and False Hearts; or, Sunbeams and Shadows. L.C. C.L. 14/8/56.
C. The First Night (H. 9/5/88, *mat.*).
D. The First of October. L.C. T.H. Hulme, 24/3/99.
D.Sk. Fists; or, The Rival Maidens. L.C. S.W. 22/4/95.
F. A Fit of Heroics. L.C. Phil. 4/8/80.
Oa. A Fit of the Blues. L.C. Str. 29/10/73.
F. Fizy. L.C. Ladb. H. 2/7/82.
D. The Flag; or, The Battle Field (Sur. 12/11/70).
D. The Flashing Light of Pengarth. L.C. O.C. 30/11/91.
D. A Flash in the Pan. L.C. Lecture H. Greenwich, 3/3/93.
D. A Flaw in the Diamond. L.C. Bower, 18/7/50.
Bal. La Fleur d'Amour (D.L. 6/10/58).
D.Sk. Fleur-de-Lys. L.C. S.W. 21/12/94.
C.O. Fleur de Thé. L.C. Lyc. 10/6/71.
Bal. Fleurette (C.G. 18/6/53).
Ent. Fleurette (St J. 19/6/55).
F. Fleurette and Fadette (Phil. Cardiff, 24/2/79).
P. Flighty Faust. L.C. R.A. Woolwich, 10/1/96.
F. The Flirt (Brit. 16/3/59).
M.C. Flirting (Sanger's Amphi. Ramsgate, 14/7/84).
Ca. The Flirt's Dream. L.C. Margate, 16/11/81.
F. The Flitch of Bacon; or, The Custom of Dunmow (Str. 23/7/55). L.C.
Ent. Flora and Zephyr (Grec. 21/4/62).
Bal. La Flor de la Marcarena (H. 4/9/54).
Bal. La Flor de Sevilla (Adel. 11/6/66).
D. Florence; or, The Fatal Error (Sur. 21/4/57).
M.D. Florence Montaubon; or, The Robbers of Normandy. L.C. Sur. 20/9/55.
O. Florinda; or, The Moors in Spain (H.M. 3/7/51). L.C.
Ent. The Flower Girl (Sur. 1/10/55).
Ent. The Flower Girl of Ghent (D.L. 18/7/56).
D. The Flower of the Farm (Sur. 7/7/62).
D. The Flower of the Farm (Ayr, 6/11/96, *copy.*). L.C.
D. The Flower of the Flock. L.C. Vic. 12/6/58.
Ent. The Flower of the Port (H. 24/10/54).
F. Flutters. L.C. Grand, Leeds, 9/2/86.
F. Flying Colours (Adel. 22/9/51).
D. The Flying Dutchman. L.C. P.W. Rochdale, 30/11/69.
D. The Flying Dutchman. L.C. Grec. 7/3/77.
D. The Flying Jib by Snapdragon; or, The Derby Lost and the Ledger Won. L.C. Adel. L'pool, 7/6/67.
D. Foam of the Sea. L.C. Ladb. H. 22/12/99.

F. Fogged. L.C. Sur. 21/6/82.
D. The Folds of the Flag. L.C. P's. Preston, 30/3/96.
F. Following the Ladies (D.L. 21/3/55).
C. Follow the Leader; or, Mr Neville's Sheep. L.C. Brighton, 21/11/68.
Ca. Folly (S.W. 21/4/62). L.C.
Ent. Folly Fête; or, The May Queen (Grec. 12/10/65). L.C.
M.D. Folly's Fortunes (Court, Bacup, 21/8/99). L.C.
C. Food for Gossip. L.C. Soho, 23/4/55.
F. The Fool of the Family (Adel. 12/7/60). L.C.
F. The Fool of the Family. L.C. Sur. 18/2/76.
D. Football; or, Life as it is. L.C. Cardiff, 29/5/86.
D. The Footlights; or, All the World's a Stage. L.C. Qns. Manchester, 7/10/80.
Ca. Forbidden Fruit; or, What will my Aunt say. L.C. P'cess. 9/5/50.
D. Forced from Home. L.C. Holt and Wilmot's company, 17/3/82. [The L.C. script notes that this is based on *The Step Mother*.]
D. The Forced Marriage; or, The Willow Marsh (Vic. 24/11/61). L.C.
D. For Country's Sake. L.C. Shakespeare, L'pool, 25/9/94.
D. For Cuba's Freedom. L.C. S.W. 18/10/98.
D.Sk. For England's Glory. L.C. Empire, Southend, 26/4/98.
D. The Forest Bride. L.C. T.H. Port Glasgow, 7/3/90.
D. The Forger; or, The Waif. L.C. Var. 2/1/84.
D. The Forger and his Victim. L.C. Brit. 12/11/56.
D. Forget and Forgive (Grec. 1/4/61). L.C.
D. Forget-me-not. L.C. St J. 3/2/76.
Ca. Forgiven. L.C. O.C. 14/12/78.
D. Forgiven. L.C. Assembly R. Weston-super-Mare, 29/9/99.
D. For Hearts and Home. L.C. Var. 16/1/88.
D. For Her Sake. L.C. Ladb. H. 19/4/86.
D. For Life (Bath, 6/5/71).
D. For Life; or, A Danger Signal. L.C. Var. 1/10/78.
D. For Love and Liberty. L.C. Wolverhampton, 7/11/88.
Ext. For the Benefit of the Playful Crocodile (Str. 10/7/54).
D. For the Cause. L.C. Tyndall's Park, Clifton, Bristol, 20/6/95.
D. For the Honour of the Family (Com. 10/6/97).
D. For the Honour of the House. L.C. Athen. Hammersmith, 11/9/94.
D. For the Honour of the House. L.C. Nottingham, 20/6/95.
D. For the Queen. L.C. S.W. 4/8/83.
M.D. For the Sake of a Woman. L.C. New, Swansea, 16/9/95.
D. The Fortune-teller; or, The Abduction of the Jew's Daughter. L.C. C.L. 28/9/60.
Oa. Forty Robbers (Assembly R. Wood Green, 1/10/92).
Ba. The Forty Thieves. L.C. Grec. 15/4/56.
Ext. The Forty Thieves (Stand. 7/3/59). L.C.
Ba. The Forty Thieves (Lyc. 7/3/60). L.C.
Ba. The Forty Thieves. L.C. Stand. 14/10/64.
P. The Forty Thieves. L.C. Sur. 18/12/74.
P. The Forty Thieves. L.C. Plymouth, 30/12/75.
P. The Forty Thieves. L.C. Bury, 3/1/77.
P. The Forty Thieves. L.C. Alex. Sheffield, 6/12/77.
P. The Forty Thieves. L.C. Birmingham, 26/12/77.

P. The Forty Thieves. L.C. O.H. Leeds, 27/12/79.
P. The Forty Thieves. L.C. Gai. Glasgow, 27/12/79.
P. The Forty Thieves. L.C. Alex. L'pool, 13/1/80.
P. The Forty Thieves. L.C. P's. Manchester, 13/1/80.
P. The Forty Thieves. L.C. Bradford, 22/12/81.
P. The Forty Thieves. L.C. Newcastle, 13/2/84.
P. The Forty Thieves. L.C. P.W. Birmingham, 10/12/84.
P. The Forty Thieves. L.C. P's. Bristol, 20/12/84.
P. The Forty Thieves. L.C. Nottingham, 26/12/84.
P. The Forty Thieves. L.C. Grand, Glasgow, 12/12/85.
P. The Forty Thieves. L.C. Lyc. Edinburgh, 21/12/85.
P. The Forty Thieves. L.C. Rotunda, L'pool, 23/12/85.
P. The Forty Thieves. L.C. Alex. Sheffield, 3/12/87.
P. The Forty Thieves. L.C. Aven. Sunderland, 7/12/88.
P. The Forty Thieves. L.C. Glasgow, 14/12/88.
P. The Forty Thieves. L.C. Brighton, 14/12/88.
P. The Forty Thieves. L.C. Birmingham, 24/12/90.
P. The Forty Thieves. L.C. Nottingham, 30/12/93.
P. The Forty Thieves. L.C. O.H. Cheltenham, 10/12/94.
P. The Forty Thieves. L.C. Rotunda, L'pool, 18/12/94.
P. The Forty Thieves. L.C. Exeter, 26/12/94.
P. The Forty Thieves (Standard, 3/6/95).
P. The Forty Thieves. L.C. Hull, 10/1/96.
P. The Forty Thieves. L.C. Sheffield, 26/11/96.
P. The Forty Thieves. L.C. Brighton, 31/12/97.
P. The Forty Thieves. L.C. Birmingham, 31/12/97.
P. The Forty Thieves. L.C. Grand, Plymouth, 30/12/98.
P. The Forty Thieves. L.C. Huddersfield, 30/12/98.
P. The Forty Thieves. L.C. Grand, Islington, 28/12/99.
P. The Forty Thieves; or, Harlequin Ali Baba and the Magic Cave (Bower, 29/12/69). L.C.
P. The Forty Thieves Limited. L.C. Grand, Leeds, 7/12/91.
D. The Foster Sisters of Wicklow; or, Teddy the Rollicker (Birkenhead, 31/7/82).
D. The Foster Son. L.C. Sur. 8/1/55.
D. Found at Sea (Vic. 19/4/63). L.C. [as *Picked up at Sea; or, The Fisherman's Daughter*].
D. Found Drowned; or, Marry in Haste and Repent at Leisure. L.C. Eff. 27/11/65.
D. The Foundling. L.C. Greenwich, 26/9/81.
D. The Fountain of Life. L.C. R.A. Woolwich, 5/6/86.
Ext. Four by Honours (Huddersfield, 27/10/79).
F. £452. 12*s*. 6*d*. L.C. Adel. 17/11/74.
D. The Four Knaves and the Pack; or, A Game of Life for the Odd Trick. L.C. Eff. 2/6/65. MS. Birmingham.
D. Four-leaved Shamrock; or, A Legend of the Fairy Dell. L.C. Eff. 12/9/63.
D. The Four Mowbrays (St J. 6/10/51).
F. Four O'Clock Tea. L.C. O.H. Nottingham, 6/1/87.
M.Ent. The Four Quarters of the Globe. L.C. Birmingham, 19/11/50.
Bal. The Four Seasons (D.L. 28/7/59).
D. Four Stages of Life; or, The Youth, the Lover, the Husband and the Father (Sur. 4/62). L.C.

P. The Fox and the Grapes; or, Harlequin and Old Æsop's Fables (C.L. 26/12/55). L.C.
F. Fox and Wolf (Gai. 5/10/98).
O. Fra Diavolo. L.C. Lyc. 12/7/57.
Spect. France and Austria (Ast. 2/6/59).
C. Francillon (D.Y. 18/9/97). L.C.
D. Frank Heartwell (Vic. 16/5/54).
D. Frankly Feminine. L.C. St J. 30/11/97.
D. Frank the Ploughman (Brit. 26/9/59).
D. Frank Wildeye (Brit. 13/3/61).
C.O. Frasquita (Gai. 29/5/93). L.C.
F. Fraternization (Adel. 16/7/55).
Ca. Freddie's Client. L.C. Athen. Manchester, 15/4/96.
F. The Freemason (Vic. 23/3/54).
D.Sk. A Free Pardon (Qns. Poplar, 30/1/93).
[See *F. C. PHILIPS*, 1897.]
F. Freezing a Mother-in-Law. L.C. Olym. 9/6/87.
[See *T. E. PEMBERTON*, 1879.]
O. Der Freischutz. L.C. Ast. 29/3/66.
Spec. The French in Algiers; or, Love and Honour (Ast. 13/4/57). L.C.
M.C. The Freshman. L.C. New, Cambridge, 31/7/99.
D.Sk. A Fresh Start. L.C. Corn Exchange, Wakefield, 27/2/96.
Ca. Friend Felix (Norwich, 1/12/75).
C. A Friend in Need. L.C. Bijou, 3/9/94.
C. Friends. L.C. Lichfield, 2/12/72.
Ca. Friends. L.C. Darwen, 10/4/84.
D. Friends or Foes. L.C. Grand, 27/1/86.
F. A Frightful Frost. L.C. Birmingham, 1/11/79.
F. A Frightful Murder in Hoxton. L.C. Grec. 15/6/57.
F. A Frightful Tragedy in Willow Walk. L.C. C.L. 16/5/59.
C. The Fringe of Society (Crit. 30/4/92). L.C.
D. Fritz's Wager. L.C. Buckley Hall, Chatham, 21/8/88.
P. Froggy would a-wooing go; or, Harlequin Lily White Duck, the Pretty Princess and the Fairies of the Dancing Water. L.C. Brighton, 14/12/74.
P. A Frog he would a-wooing go. L.C. Cardiff, 22/1/76.
P. A Frog he would a-wooing go. L.C. Gai. Barnsley, 13/1/80.
P. The Frog that would a-wooing go. L.C. P.W. Birmingham, 21/12/76.
Int. Frolics in France. L.C. Str. 19/11/56.
D. From Life to Death (St G. 22/5/75). L.C.
D.Sk. From Scotland Yard. L.C. County, Reading, 9/2/97.
[See *J. T. DOUGLASS*, 1897.]
D. Frontier Life. L.C. Edmonton, 23/12/95.
D. Frou-Frou (P'cess. 2/5/70.)
D. Frou-Frou (Crit. 9/7/87, *mat.*).
D. Frou-Frou (Com. 17/3/94, *mat.*).
D. The Fugitive; or, Duty and Honour. L.C. Sur. 16/4/50.
D. Fugitives; or, A Tale of India (Grec. 8/11/58). L.C.
D. The Fugitive Tree. L.C. Margate, 15/6/57.
D. A Full Moon. L.C. Bijou, Albert H. 6/4/91.
F. Full Particulars of that Affair at Finchley (Str. 14/10/61).
F. Fun in a Fog (D.L. 5/10/72). L.C.

M.F. Fun in a Japanese Tea House. L.C. Mechanics' Inst. Stockport, 18/10/98.
Bsq. Fun on an Island; or, Crusoe and Co. Ltd. L.C. S.W. 31/5/95.
F.C. Fun on the Bristol; or, A Night at Sea (Manchester, 15/5/82; Olym. 7/8/82; Gai. 5/9/87, *revised*). L.C.
P. Furioso the Terrible; or, Harlequin King Noodle and the Princess of Laburnam Grove. L.C. Qns. Manchester, 3/12/62.
Int. A Fuss about Nothing. L.C. T.H. Hounslow, 14/3/62.
Ca. The Future Mrs Ransome. L.C. Aven. 3/11/94.
D. Gabrielle the Girondist; or, The Terror of France. (C.L. 14/8/54). L.C.
D. Gabriel's Plot (H.M. Richmond, 17/4/71).
D. Gain (Leeds, 29/6/85).
O. Galatea (P.W. Bristol, 8/10/87). L.C.
D. The Galatea of Oregon (Stafford, 4/12/95).
Bal. A Galician Fête (H. 27/2/55).
D. The Galley Slaves (Sur. 28/11/59).
D. The Gambler's Dupe; or, The Unknown Friend. L.C. Qns. 27/5/63.
D. The Gambler's Wife. L.C. W. Bromwich, 9/7/83.
D. The Gambler's Wife; or, Woman's Devotion. L.C. Brit. 13/2/58.
F. Game for Anything. L.C. Imp. 25/2/86.
D. The Gamekeeper of Quarry Dell. L.C. Sunderland, 25/4/66.
Ca. A Game of Cards. L.C. Qns. Manchester, 18/4/82.
C. A Game of Chess. L.C. Edinburgh, 27/2/58.
D. The Game of Life and Death (C.L. 1/12/56).
Ent. The Gardener of Versailles (Str. 15/5/54).
O. Garibaldi. L.C. Sur. 7/7/60.
F. Garibaldi's Englishmen (St J. 24/12/59). L.C.
D. The Garret Angel (Grec. 9/4/60).
[See *C. WEBB*, 1867.]
D. Garrick the Actor. L.C. Gai. W. Hartlepool, 24/10/90.
Bal. The Gathering of the Clans (Alh. 7/10/95).
F. The Gay City; or, A Scene at the Siege (Roy. 12/6/71).
M.C. The Gay Photographer. L.C. Guildhall, Abingdon, 21/12/96.
Poet.D. Gemma of the Isles. 12° 1859.
[By "A. and L."]
F. The General Election. L.C. Lyc. 19/9/68.
D. Geneviève (St J. 27/5/61).
Oa. Geneviève. L.C. Cab. 28/10/65.
D.Sk. A Genius. L.C. Empire, 24/3/99.
Ca. The Gentleman in White (Roy. 29/11/66). L.C.
D. Gentleman Jack; or, Life on the Board. L.C. Bower, 19/9/50.
F. The Gentleman Opposite (Lyc. 3/7/54). L.C.
D. Gentle Nelly (Bradford, 8/4/71).
Ca. Gentle Thieves. L.C. P.W. L'pool, 22/2/77.
Int. Georgette (St J. 22/6/54).
D. George Vernet; or, The Life of a Cabman. L.C. Grec. 2/4/55.
[By *G. CONQUEST*. An alternative sub-title was *The Vicissitudes of Life*.]
C.O. Geraldine; or, Count Fremolio's Wedding. L.C. Nottingham, 13/8/87.
C. German Silver; or, 6000 a Year. L.C. P.H. Urmston, 7/3/95.

D. Gerty (Park, 26/3/81). L.C.
D. The Ghetto (Com. 9/9/99). L.C.
F. Ghillie Callum (Roy. Glasgow, 26/6/95). L.C.
D.Sk. A Ghost (Crit. 28/6/92, *mat.*).
D. The Ghost Hunter; or, The Body in the Boskeen. L.C. Brit. 13/12/56.
D. The Ghost Hunter; or, The Colleen Dhas. L.C. Grec. 14/3/62.
F. A Ghost in Spite of Himself (P'cess. 15/3/66).
D. The Ghost of Cock Lane. L.C. C.L. 6/8/62.
Oa. Ghosts. L.C. P's. Manchester, 18/5/86.
D. The Giant's Tomb; or, Eleanor the Accursed; or, The Sins and Sorrows of Twenty Years. L.C. Qns. 31/3/58.
D. The Giaour. L.C. Athen. Manchester, 30/11/97.
F.C. The Giddy Girl. L.C. Grand, Boscombe, 22/12/99.
M.C. The Giddy Major General. L.C. Assembly R. Surbiton, 15/8/98.
[Title altered to *The Officers' Mess* on 23/7/1901.]
F. Gideon's Ghost (Stand. 20/11/60). L.C.
O. The Gift of Venus. L.C. Athen. H. Brighton, 26/12/95.
D. Gilbert the Idiot (Soho, 6/9/59).
D. Gilded Crime. L.C. Grand, 4/3/84.
D. Gin and Water. L.C. Stand. 17/2/54.
D. Gin and Water; or, The Times we live in (Vic. 23/1/54). L.C.
D. Gin versus Water. L.C. Pav. 21/2/54.
D. The Gipsy and the Showman: A Devonshire Tale. L.C. Brit. 21/4/55.
D. The Gipsy Boy; or, The Serpent and the Doves. L.C. Brit. 12/10/55.
Oa. The Gipsy Girl; or, The Cottage of Roses. L.C. O.H. Edinburgh, 7/9/63.
D. The Gipsy Girl of Granada. L.C. Stand. 15/10/61.
D. The Gipsy Girl of Madrid (Ast. 7/2/59).
D. The Gipsy King (Grec. 6/3/61).
D.Sk. The Gipsy Princess. L.C. Brixton, 22/12/99.
Bal. The Gipsy Queen (H. 21/8/54).
D. The Gipsy Queen (W.L. 23/6/93).
D. The Gipsy Showman (Brit. 14/10/61).
D. The Gipsy Twins (Brit. 17/4/61). L.C. as *The Gipsy of Paris; or, The House on the Bridge of Notre Dame.*
Ca. The Girl I left behind me (Olym. 2/11/64). L.C.
[By *J. OXENFORD.*]
P. Giselle and the Phantom Night Dancers; or, Harlequin and the Genius of Discord. L.C. Vic. 18/12/63.
D. Gismonda (Daly's, 27/5/95).
D. The Gitano Boy; or, True at Last; or, Two Roads of Life (M'bone, 31/3/66). L.C.
Bal. Gitta la ballerina (C.G. 25/10/65).
D. Give a Dog a Bad Name; or, England and Australia. L.C. Col. L'pool, 14/9/66.
D. Glasgow in 1300. L.C. Qns. 11/9/55.
D. A Gleam in the Darkness. L.C. H. 22/12/99.
D. A Gleam of Hope (Grec. 6/8/66).
D. The Gleaners (H. 8/7/57).
D. The Glider. L.C. Runcorn, 18/10/95.

D. The Gloaming and the Mirk (P'cess, Edinburgh, 1/2/69).
D. The Globe. L.C. St. J. Tunstall, 9/9/81.
F. A Glorious Bit of Fun (Soho, 6/5/57).
D. The Glove and Fan; or, A Signal Engagement. L.C. Manchester, 1/4/57.
R.D. Godefroi and Yolande. L.C. Court, L'pool, 11/10/94.
D. Godfrida. L.C. Swiss Gdns. Shoreham, 26/4/98.
C. The Godolphins (Sur. 9/4/60).
F. Going to see the Fireworks. L.C. Grec. 11/6/56.
D. Gold. L.C. C.L. 29/1/51.
D. Gold. L.C. Var. 30/10/80.
D. Gold and Silver. L.C. Leigh, 12/3/86.
D. The Gold Diggings of Australia; or, The Life of an Emigrant. L.C. Vic. 25/1/53.
Ca. A Golden Barrier. L.C. Aquar. Brighton, 21/5/87.
D. The Golden Bond. L.C. Var. 20/12/93.
D. Golden Daggers. L.C. Grec. 5/6/77.
Bal. A Golden Dream (C.P. 29/6/89).
D. The Golden Dream; or, The Wizard of Venice (Manchester, 11/7/64). L.C.
F. The Golden Gulch (Dover, 14/4/79).
M.Ca. The Golden Hatch. L.C. St G. 30/10/85.
D. The Golden Heart. L.C. P'cess. 21/1/52.
D. Golden Hearts; or, The City of Small Trades. L.C. C.L. 2/8/62.
D. The Golden King. L.C. N. Shields, 29/9/99.
C.O. The Golden Lining. L.C. Norwich, 20/2/83.
D. The Golden Nugget; or, The Fatal Treasure. L.C. Qns. 2/11/53.
Bsq. The Golden Ring. L.C. Bijou, L'pool, 5/10/83.
Ca. The Golden Test. L.C. O.H. Nottingham, 6/1/87.
Oa. A Golden Wedding. L.C. Aven. 13/3/85.
Bal. The Golden Wreath. L.C. Alh. 20/5/78.
D. The Gold Fields of Australia; or, Off to the Diggings. L.C. Bower, 22/1/53.
D. The Gold Fiend of the Black Forest; or, The Shadowless Man and the Poor Student of Hildeburgh. L.C. Gar. 23/4/59.
D. The Gold Finders of Australia; or, Greenleaf and Redburg, the Forest Twins. L.C. Stand. 10/2/53.
D. The Goldsmith's Wife: A Chronicle of the Life and Death of Jane Shore. L.C. St J. Manchester, 23/9/89.
D. The Gombeen's Gold (S.W. 16/3/91).
Ca. Good as Gold. L.C. K.X. 3/2/77.
D. Goodbye, Sweetheart. L.C. Gymnasium Theatre, Henley, 8/2/94.
D. Good Hearts; or, Honesty is the Best Policy (Sur. 6/11/58). L.C.
D. Good Luck. L.C. Windsor, 11/7/78.
C.Oa. Good Morning, Mr Smith. L.C. Soho, 20/11/61.
O.F. Good Night, Signor Pantalon (Adel. 29/5/51). *Lacy.*
[Operatic version of *Twice Killed* by John Oxenford. See *C. A. SOMERSET*, 1852.]
Oa. Good Night, Signor Pantalon, Good Night, Sir, and Pleasant Dreams (H. 7/6/51). L.C.
D. Good or Evil (O.H. Ashton, 24/8/85).
Bsq. Good Queen Bess; or, Ye Merrie Days of Olde Englande (Str. 24/3/56). L.C.
Bsq. Good Queen Bess. L.C. C.L. 4/4/61.

D. The Good Samaritan. L.C. O.H. Southport, 19/12/92.
D. The Good Shepherd. L.C. P's. Manchester, 7/6/98.
Ext. A Good Time Coming; or, London in Exhibition Time. L.C. P'cess. 30/4/51.
P. Goody Two Shoes. L.C. Qns. Manchester, 19/12/78.
P. Goody Two Shoes. L.C. Bristol, 21/12/78.
P. Goody Two Shoes. L.C. Alex. 17/12/79.
P. Goody Two Shoes. L.C. Worcester, 9/1/84.
P. Goody Two Shoes. L.C. Sunderland, 9/1/84.
P. Goody Two Shoes. L.C. Birmingham, 24/12/87.
P. Goody Two Shoes. L.C. Court, 3/1/89.
P. Goody Two Shoes. L.C. P'cess. Glasgow, 11/12/90.
P. Goody Two Shoes. L.C. Brighton, 15/12/91.
P. Goody Two Shoes. L.C. Birmingham, 23/12/95.
P. Goody Two Shoes. L.C. Grand, Leeds, 29/12/99.
P. Goosey Goosey Gander; or, Froggy would-a-wooing go and the Fairy of the Golden Lilies (Pav. 27/12/60). L.C.
Bsq. Gore; or, The Yaller Seal (Aven. 1/7/89).
D. The Gorilla Hunt in the Forest of Gabon; or, A Tale of Africa. L.C. Brit. 11/12/63.
P. Gosling the Great; or, Harlequin Prince Bluebell; or, Baa Baa Black Sheep and the Fairy of the Spring. L.C. Birmingham, 10/12/60.
[By *Miss KEATING.*]
D. The Governor of Kentucky. L.C. H. 30/3/96.
D. Grace Mary. L.C. H.M. 30/8/99.
F. A Grand Baby Show; or, Simms in Long Clothes Again. L.C. Qns. 16/7/56.
Oa. The Grand Duchess of Gerolstein. L.C. Phil. 27/2/71.
D. Grandfather's Little Nell (Bristol, 3/12/70).
D. Grandfather's Secret (Sur. 6/6/85). L.C.
C.Sk. Grandpa's Birthday. L.C. S.W. 31/5/95.
D. The Grape Girl of Madrid; or, The Man, the Spirit and the Moral. L.C. C.L. 28/5/50.
D. Gratitude; or, The Orphan Girl's Marriage. L.C. C.L. 30/6/59.
D.Sk. Grau-a-Aille (Nov. 25/3/91).
D.Sk. A Grave Charge. L.C. County, Reading, 16/11/96.
D. The Graven Image; or, The Artist of Rome (Grec. 3/3/62). L.C.
D. The Greatest Puritan; or, Cromwell's Own. L.C. Vic. Walthamstow, 26/10/99.
D. Great Expectations. L.C. T.H. Beccles, 21/1/92.
Ent. A Great Night (S.W. 8/8/60).
D. The Great Secret (Workington, 19/10/85).
F. A Great Sensation (S.W. 3/5/62). L.C. as *Rolla in a Sensation Rôle.*
C. The Great Separation Suit. L.C. P's. Manchester, 17/7/76.
D. The Great Strike (Pav. 8/10/66). L.C.
F. The Great Temptation (E.L. 25/5/74).
D. The Great Tyrant (Brit. 17/6/61).
F. The Great Wall of China. L.C. Crit. 8/4/76.
D. Great Wealth; or, What Men will do for Money. L.C. Warrington, 15/6/85.

D. The Great World of London; or, London as it is. L.C. Stand. 29/3/93.
[See *G. LANDER*, 1898.]

C.O. Gredel. L.C. Olym. 18/6/84.

Ent. The Greek Girl (Brit. 28/4/62).

C. The Greek Soprano (Portsmouth, 12/7/97; Str. 13/9/97). L.C.

C.O. The Green Isle of the Sea (P'cess. Edinburgh, 21/9/74). L.C.

Ent. Green Lanes and Blue Waters (Brit. 11/3/61).

F. A Grim Look Out. L.C. Alh. 19/12/77.

D. The Grimthorpe Case. L.C. Woolwich, 21/5/94.

C. Gringoire. L.C. Gai. 29/5/79.

D. Gringoire. L.C. Lyc. Ipswich, 3/9/92.

D. Grip (Tyne, Newcastle, 3/4/71).

M.C. Griselides. L.C. D.L. 12/6/93.

Sk. Grump's Menage. L.C. St G. 4/4/76.

F. Gubbins stands for the Council (P.H. Peckham, 14/1/89, *amat.*).

D. A Guilty Man. L.C. Worthing, 21/10/96.

D. The Guilty Mother; or, The One False Step (Brit. 8/5/61). L.C.

D. Guilty or Not Guilty; or, Justice at Fault. L.C. P.W. Glasgow, 19/2/68.

D. The Guinea Stamp (Glo. 27/3/75). L.C.

P. Gulliver. L.C. Sefton, L'pool, 13/1/80.

P. Gulliver's Travels. L.C. P.W. Birmingham, 23/12/75.

P. Gulliver's Travels. L.C. Sunderland, 20/12/76.

P. Gulliver's Travels. L.C. Glasgow, 31/12/77.

P. Gulliver's Travels. L.C. P.W. Birmingham, 29/12/85.

P. Gulliver's Travels in the Giant and Dwarf Kingdoms; or, Harlequin Fairy Queen of the Regions of Imagination (Stand. 26/12/60). L.C.
[By *F. G. CHEATHAM*.]

P. Gulliver's Travels through Lilliput, the Horse Island and Brobdingnag; or, Harlequin and Britannia (Ast. 26/12/54). L.C.

Bsq. Gumbo at a Rehearsal of the Bohemian Girl. L.C. Str. 29/9/52.

F. Gunner Flynn. L.C. Garrison, Woolwich, 15/12/82.

D. The Gutter. L.C. Var. 23/5/79.

D. Hagar, the Outcast Jewess (Brit. 5/7/69).

D. The Halfpenny Club; or, The Archives of the Poor. L.C. Vic. 18/9/57.
[Title altered to *The Token; or, Lenza the Child of the Wanderer*.]

Bal. Hallow-'een (H. 16/7/59).

Bsq. Hallowe'en. L.C. Kilmarnock, 4/1/77.

Bal. The Halt of the Ballet; or, Dancing for Life (P'cess. 26/6/54). L.C.

O. Hamet and Zelina; or, Stratagem for Stratagem. L.C. Dublin, 26/1/54.

P. Hamilton's Excursion to America and Panstereoragma of Passing Events. L.C. Holb. Amphi. 21/12/78.

Bsq. Hamlet the Hysterical: A Delusion in Five Spasms (P'cess. 30/11/74). L.C.

M.Ca. The Hammock. L.C. Vic. H. 11/12/88.

D. The Hand of Cards (Stand. 2/3/57).

P. Handy Pandy Sugar and Candy, Which hand will you have; or, Harlequin Orpheus and the Magic Lute (Pav. 23/21/58). L.C.

D. The Hanged Man (Grec. 5/9/62). L.C.
D. Hannibal. 8° 1861.
C. Hans, an Alsatian (Qns. L'pool, 9/8/80).
FairyO. Hansel and Gretel (Daly's, 26/12/94). L.C.
D. A Hansom Cab. L.C. S.W. 20/6/88.
Ext. Hap. L.C. C.P. 18/4/82.
C. Happiness. L.C. Var. 27/11/80.
F. A Happy Family. L.C. Gai. 19/11/73.
Vaud. Happy Hours; or, Sunshine in Season. L.C. Adel. L'pool, 29/3/62.
M.Ca. A Happy New Year. L.C. St G. 28/11/82.
O. A Happy Result; or, An Alsatian Dialogue. L.C. G.I. 3/11/65.
D. The Habour Master's Secret; or, The Wreck of the Golden Eagle (Brit. 21/12/68). L.C.
D. Hard as Iron; or, Eternal Justice. L.C. Brit. 21/6/81.
D. Hard Times (Grec. 20/9/66).
D. Hard Times. L.C. Str. 10/8/54.
[By *F. F. COOPER*.]
D. Hard Times; or, Wait a Little Longer. L.C. Pav. 4/9/54.
Bal. Le Harem (H.M. 8/6/65).
P. Harlequin Aladdin; or, The Wonderful Lamp. L.C. Qns. Manchester, 27/11/60.
P. Harlequin and Buttercups and Daisies; or, Great A, Little a, Bouncing B; or, The Cat's in the Cupboard and she can't see. L.C. Stand. 20/12/50.
P. Harlequin and Cinderella (Sur. 26/12/60).
P. Harlequin and Humpty Dumpty; or, Robbin de Bobbin and the First Lord Mayor of London (D.L. 26/12/50). L.C.
P. Harlequin and Old Æsop; or, Dr Syntax and the Animated Alphabet (Vic. 23/12/65). L.C.
P. Harlequin and Old Izaak Walton (S.W. 27/12/58).
P. Harlequin and Puss in Boots; or, The Ogre of Rat Castle and all the World and his Wife (S.W. 25/12/55). L.C.
P. Harlequin and Robin Redbreast; or, Prince Cock Sparrow. L.C. Qns. Manchester, 26/11/59.
P. Harlequin and St George and the Dragon; or, The Seven Champions of Christendom (Ast. 25/12/55). L.C.
P. Harlequin and the Crystal Palace of 1851. L.C. Grec. 28/12/50.
P. Harlequin and the Five Senses; or, Happy Land and Evil Land, and the Union of the Allied Powers in the Realms of Truth and Light (Vic. 26/12/55). L.C.
P. Harlequin and the Forty Thieves; or, Ali Baba and the Fairy Ardinella. L.C. Qns. 23/12/58.
P. Harlequin and the House that Jack Built in 1851. S.W. 23/12/50.
P. Harlequin and the Kohinoor. L.C. Brit. 12/12/51.
P. Harlequin and the Little Mouse who built his House in a Christmas Cake. L.C. M'bone, 14/12/59.
P. Harlequin and the Loves of Cupid and Psyche (Adel. 26/12/57).
P. Harlequin and the Maid and the Magpie; or, The Fairy Paradisa and Hanky Panky the Enchanter (P'cess. 26/12/55). L.C.
P. Harlequin and the One-eyed King; or, The Charmed Milkmaid and the Fairy Queen of the Golden Alphabet. L.C. Stand. 21/12/52.

P. Harlequin and the Rat-catcher's Daughter; or, Old Father Thames and Tiddy Bells Alley and the Fairy of the Ruby and Emerald Cave. L.C. Bower, 17/12/55.

P. Harlequin and the Summer Queen; or, King Winter and the Fairies of the Silver Willows. L.C. Sur. 22/12/56.

P. Harlequin and the Wild Boar of Bradford; or, Roger of Mannyngham and the Fairies. L.C. Alex. Bradford, 22/12/65.

P. Harlequin and the Willow Pattern Plate; or, The Four Quarters of the Globe out on the Spree. L.C. Qns. 5/10/60.

P. Harlequin and the Yellow Dwarf; or, The King of the Gold Mines (N. Shields, 2/60).

P. Harlequin Baron Munchausen and his Comical Cream Cob; or, The Queen of the Fairy Steeds' Haunt (Ast. 27/12/58). L.C.

P. Harlequin Beauty and the Beast; or, Little Goody Two Shoes and Mother Bunch's Bookcase in Baby Land (S.W. 26/12/57). L.C.

P. Harlequin Billy Taylor; or, Britannia rules the Waves. L.C. Eff. 21/12/57.

P. Harlequin Billy Taylor; or, The Fairies of the Elfin Grove. L.C. Soho, 23/12/59.

P. Harlequin Black-eyed Sue; or, All in the Downs and Davy Jones' Locker (Str. 24/12/55). L.C.

P. Harlequin Blue Beard. L.C. Sunderland, 12/1/76.

P. Harlequin Blue Beard; or, Dame Trot and her Comical Cat (C.L. 26/12/63). L.C.

P. Harlequin Blue Beard, the Great Bashaw; or, The Enchanted Chamber and the Fairy of the Silver Palace of the Sea. L.C. Qns. 20/12/59.

P. Harlequin Christoval and the Demon Ogre of the Plains; or, The Good Fairy at the Bottom of the Sea. L.C. Vic. 12/12/61.
[By *E. TOWERS* and *H. SAVILLE*.]

P. Harlequin Cock Robin and the Children in the Wood (Vic. 26/12/66). L.C.

P. Harlequin Cock Robin and the Children in the Wood (C.P. 22/12/81).

P. Harlequin Dick Whittington and his Cat. L.C. Brighton, 19/12/63.

P. Harlequin Don Juan (R. Living Marionettes, 27/12/52).

P. Harlequin Earth Air Fire and Water; or, Mistress Mary Quite Contrary and the Black Buccaneer; or, Mary Mary Quite Contrary how does your Garden grow? L.C. Stand. 22/12/59.

P. Harlequin Eyes Nose and Mouth; or, Jump High, Jump Low and a-jumping we will go. L.C. Eff. 18/10/56.

P. Harlequin Father Thames; or, The River Queen and the Great Lord Mayor of London (Surrey, 27/12/58). L.C.

P. Harlequin Fun; or, The Judgments of Fancy and the Nursery Rhymes of Olden Time (Eff. 26/12/66). L.C.

P. Harlequin Genius; or, The Progress of Trade, the Spirit of Improvement and the Great Exhibition of 1851. L.C. Sheffield, 10/12/50.

P. Harlequin Goody Two Shoes; or, Robin the Ploughboy and the Castle of the Seven Passions. L.C. Eff. 20/12/64.

P. Harlequin Graceful. L.C. Nottingham, 3/1/77.

P. Harlequin Green Beetle; or, The Three Princesses of Pumpkin. L.C. Qns. Manchester, 30/11/58.

P. Harlequin Gulliver (Str. 27/12/52).
P. Harlequin Gulliver and his Wife; or, The Kings, the Seven Cyclops and the Fairy Faune of the Living Waters. L.C. Adel. L'pool, 26/12/64.
P. Harlequin Guy Faux (Grec. 27/12/58). L.C.
P. Harlequin Guy Fawkes; or, The Fairy of the Golden Grotto. L.C. Qns. Manchester, 17/12/67.
P. Harlequin Hans and the Golden Goose; or, The Old Mother Earth, the Little Red Man and the Princess whom Nobody could make laugh (S.W. 24/12/59). L.C.
P. Harlequin Happy-go-lucky and the Babes in the Wood. L.C. Manchester, 14/12/83.
P Harlequin Hey Diddle Diddle the Cat and the Fiddle; or, The Clock and the Spoon and the Nice Old Cow that jumped over the Moon. L.C. Eff. 21/12/61.
P. Harlequin Hey-diddle-diddle the Cat and the Fiddle and the Cow that jumped over the Moon; or, Oranges and Lemons and the 12 Dancing Princesses (Sur. 26/12/61). L.C.
P. Harlequin Humbug and the Shams of London (Str. 3/1/57).
P. Harlequin Humpty Dumpty; or, Simple Simon and the Maiden Blaeize, and the Fairies of the Silver Dell (Roy. 19/12/62). L.C.
P. Harlequin Jack in the Box. L.C. E.C. 14/12/86.
P. Harlequin Jack Sprat; or, Three Blind Mice (Ast. 26/12/64).
P. Harlequin Jack the Giant Killer (Cab. 26/12/53).
P. Harlequin Kafoozalum; or, The Bean, the Beauty and the Babah. L.C. Qns. Manchester, 21/12/66.
P. Harlequin King Candle and the Empress Rushlight; or, The Fairy Queen of the Regions of Light (Stand. 3/3/56). L.C.
P. Harlequin King Crystal; or, The Princess of the Silver Maze and the Good Little Fairy at the Bottom of the Well. L.C. Eff. 22/12/63.
P. Harlequin King Holliday; or, The Fairies of the Enchanted Valley and the King that once killed a Cat (Surrey, 29/12/59). L.C.
P. Harlequin King Humpty Dumpty; or, The Princess, the Peri and the Pearl Diver. L.C. Qns. 1/12/64.
P. Harlequin King One Eye and Davy Jones's Locker. L.C. Qns. 22/12/56.
P. Harlequin King Peewit and his Merry Little Men; or, Red Beard the Terrible and the Enchanted Fairies of the Silvery Lakes. L.C. Eff. 22/12/65.
P. Harlequin King Pumpkin; or, Richard ye Lion Hearte (Sur. 26/12/64). L.C.
P. Harlequin Little Bo Peep. L.C. Hull, 7/1/78.
P. Harlequin Little Jack Horner; or, Mother Hubbard and her Dog. L.C. Brighton, 17/12/64.
P. Harlequin Little Tom Tucker and the Fine Lady of Banbury Cross and the Old Lady who lived in a Shoe and had so many Children she didn't know what to do. L.C. P'cess. 22/12/63.
P. Harlequin Master Walter; or, The Hunchback Nunky and the Little Fairies (Soho, 27/12/58). L.C.
P. Harlequin Molly Coddle, King of Gaby Lands; or, The Giant Butcher of Lambeth Marsh and the Fairy of the Laughing Waters. L.C. Bower, 13/12/62.

P. Harlequin Noddy Toddy. L.C. Stand. 19/12/51.
P. Harlequin Ogre; or, The Invisible Princess and the Four Charmed Fish. L.C. Qns. Manchester, 12/11/56.
P. Harlequin Old King Cole; or, Ride a Cock Horse to Banbury Cross and the Frog that would-a-wooing go. L.C. Sur. 24/12/63.
P. Harlequin Prince Beaming. L.C. P.W. Glasgow, 30/12/76.
P. Harlequin Prince Fortune and Princess Fatal; or, King Stoney Batter and Queen Silvering of the Butterfly Bowers of Brilliance (Vic. 26/12/54).
P. Harlequin Prince Juless. L.C. Vic. Longton, 20/12/76.
P. Harlequin Prince Love the Day and Queen Busy Bee, Little Red Riding Hood and the Kind Wolf (Vic. 26/12/57). L.C.
P. Harlequin Punch and Judy (Brit. 26/12/53).
P. Harlequin Robinson Crusoe and his Man Friday; or, The Magic Pearl and the Deep Sea Diver (Grec. 28/12/63). L.C.
P. Harlequin Rose in Bloom and the Fairies of the Enchanted Shield; or, The Whimsical Princess and the Three Brothers of Bagdad. L.C. Eff. 15/11/62.
P. Harlequin Sinbad the Sailor; or, The Old Man of the Sea and Davy Jones' Locker. L.C. Qns. Manchester, 28/11/63.
P. Harlequin Tam o' Shanter. L.C. York H. Edinburgh, 24/11/51.
P. Harlequin the Knight of the Silver Shield; or, The Giant Ginguelphus and the Fairy of the Fuchsia Dell. L.C. Bower, 11/12/63.
P. Harlequin the Queen of Spades, and the Fairy the Fawn (Grec. 27/12/52).
P. Harlequin Tit, Tat, Toe (M'bone, 1/1/57).
P. Harlequin Tom Moody; or, Old Towler the Huntsman and the Goddess Diana (Ast. 26/12/59). L.C.
P. Harlequin Tom, Tom, the Piper's Son, Pope Joan and Little Bo-Peep; or, Old Daddy Longlegs and the Pig that went to Market and the Pig that stayed at Home (Ast. 23/12/65). L.C.
P. Harlequin Toy Horse (Lyc. 27/12/58).
P. Harlequin True Blue and Queen Britannia; or, The Demon Labulus and the Fairy of the Silver Waters. L.C. Vic. 22/12/58.
P. Harlequin Valentine and Orson (Grec. 26/12/59).
P. Harlequin Valentine and Orson. L.C. Qns. Manchester, 26/11/61.
P. Harlequin Valentine and Orson; or, The Queen of Lilies and Jewels and the Green Knight of the Horse-Shoe Dell. L.C. Bower, 7/12/66.
P. Harlequin William the Conqueror and King Vice of the Silent City; or, War, Wine and Love and Queen Virtue in the Vistas of Light and Glitter. L.C. Vic. 27/12/56.
Ca. Harmonious Discords (O.C. 31/3/73). L.C.
D. Harry Carley; or, The Oak and the Bramble. L.C. C.L. 18/10/62.
D. Harry Hawser; or, The Rocks and Shoals in the Voyage of Life. L.C. C.L. 26/1/58.
F. Harry's Disguise. L.C. Greenwich, 28/11/68.
D.Sk. The Harvest of Crime. L.C. S.W. 5/3/97.
[See *M. RANDFORD*, 1897.]
D. The Harvest of Sin. L.C. Var. 22/12/91.
F. Has anybody seen Mr Brown? L.C. Brighton, 18/1/60.
Ca. Hasty Conclusions. L.C. Egremont Inst. Egremont, 25/4/91.
D. Hatred (Oldham, 1/3/80). L.C.
D. Hawthorne; or, Far Away. L.C. Durham, 10/7/82.

D. The Headless Man (Adel. 16/11/57).
F. The Head of a Clan. L.C. P'cess. 21/10/75.
F. The Head Professor. L.C. St G. 18/12/71.
F. The Head's in Peril. L.C. S.W. 14/2/51.
R.D. The Heart and the World. L.C. Grec. 24/7/58.
D. The Heart of a Brother (Brit. 1/5/71). L.C.
D. The Heart of an Irishman (Str. 6/3/54).
D. The Heart of a Sailor (Brit. 22/4/61).
D. The Heart of Fire. L.C. Pav. 28/9/97.
D. The Heart of Midlothian. L.C. Grec. 17/11/62.
Bsq. The Heart of Midlothian; or, A New Trial of Effie Deans. L.C. Vic. 30/3/63.
D. The Heart of Old Ireland and the Lepreghaun; or, The Gold Goblin. L.C. C.L. 25/4/59.
C.D. Hearts and Homes. L.C. Assembly R. Malvern, 20/4/86.
D. Hearts are Trumps (Soho, 20/5/57).
Ca. Hearts are Trumps. L.C. St G. 28/1/89.
D. Hearts of Gold. L.C. Athen. H. Shepherds Bush, 10/9/92.
D. The Heart's Ordeal (C.L. 3/8/63).
[By *J. COURTNEY.*]
D. Hearts that Love us; or, Wild Deeds in Wild Scenes. L.C. Eff. 17/5/62.
D. The Heart's Victory (Grec. 1/10/58).
D. The Heart that can feel for another; or, The Creole's Daughter. L.C. C.L. 20/9/50.
F. A Heathen Goddess. L.C. W.L. 11/10/94.
D. The Hebrew (C.L. 9/2/52). L.C.
D. The Hebrew Diamond; or, The Eye of Light (Brit. 10/7/65). L.C.
P. The Hebrew Maiden; or, Harlequin Prince Leoline and the Fairy of the Chain of Brilliants. L.C. C.L. 20/12/69.
D. The Hebrew's Sacrifice. L.C. C.L. 24/1/52 (licence refused).
D. The Hebrew Son; or, The Child of Babylon. L.C. Olym. 7/3/52 (licence refused).
D. The Hebrew Tribe of Rome; or, The Greek Hero and the Jewish Maid (Stand. 2/2/52). L.C.
D. The Heiress of Arragon (Grec. 26/3/63).
D. The Heiress of Munster (Lyc. 28/4/55).
D. An Heir from the Ocean; or, Golden Evidence (Qns. Dublin, 25/9/71).
D. The Heir of Ellangowan. L.C. Vic. 1/8/63.
D. The Heir of Melford Castle (Brit. 1/4/61).
D. Held at Bay; or, The Exiled Mother (M'bone, 1/9/79).
D. Helen Douglas (H. 18/7/70). L.C. as *Helen's Love.*
D. Helen Porter, a Secret of the Sewers of London. L.C. C.L. 14/5/64.
Ba. Helen's Babies. L.C. N. Shields, 26/12/95.
Oa. The Help. L.C. Cambridge, 5/5/91.
D. A Helping Hand; or, Every Coat has a Hole in it (Sur. 10/1/59). L.C.
D. Helvard Solness. L.C. H. 7/12/92.
D. Her Atonement; or, Miss Multon (Windsor, 31/8/85).
D. Her Father's Sin (Str. 23/7/89, *mat.*). L.C.
C. Her Ladyship's Guardian (Amphi. L'pool, 24/7/65).
Ca. Her Living Image. L.C. Aven. 3/1/84.

Bsq. Hermesianax (Lecture H. Derby, 9/7/69).
T. Hernani. L.C. Gai. 29/5/79.
P. Herne the Hunter (Stand. 5/8/57).
P. Herne the Hunter. L.C. O.H. Leicester, 28/12/81.
Bsq. Herne the Hunter and his Demon Band; or, Bluff King Hal and the Forest Maid. L.C. Pav. 28/3/66.
P. Herne the Hunter; or, Harlequin Bluff King Hal and Anne Boleyn. L.C. M'bone, 3/12/62.
D. Hero and Leander. L.C. Gai. Hastings, 17/1/91.
[See *H. K. BELLEW*, 1892.]
D. Heroes. L.C. Leigh, 10/8/87.
[Title altered to *A Noble Hero*, 29/1/90.]
D. Heroes of the Fleet. L.C. Var. 30/8/94.
D. The Hero of the Drama (Stand. 3/11/60).
Ca. Her Only Failing. L.C. Bower, 9/8/64.
F. Her Royal Highness. L.C. Bath and Bristol, 6/2/52.
F.C. Her Uncle. L.C. Nov. 12/5/86.
D. Her Vengeance. L.C. W.L. 12/9/95.
D. Hester. L.C. Str. 15/4/93.
D. Hester's Legacy (Ladb. H. 17/6/92, *amat.*).
D. Hewie the Witless; or, Life's Cloud and Sunshine. L.C. Grec. 2/6/54.
P. Hickedy Pickedy my Black Hen; or, King Winter and Queen Spring (Stand. 19/1/57). L.C.
P. Hickory Dickory Dock; or, The Mouse ran up the Clock. L.C. Brit. 11/12/63.
D. Hidden Crime; or, The Orphans of Fleet Street. L.C. Brit. 26/7/71.
D. Hidden Light (Grec. 18/2/61). L.C.
D. High- and Low-Water Bell; or, The Ebb and Flow of Fortune. L.C. Vic. 14/9/55.
F. High Art. L.C. Pav. 5/11/83.
C. The Highest Bidder. L.C. Bournemouth, 20/6/98.
F.C. High Jinks. L.C. Aquar. Gt Yarmouth, 6/12/86.
D. Highland Jessie Brown; or, Lucknow Rescued. L.C. Qns. 4/3/58.
D. The High-mettled Racer; or, The Road to Ruin. L.C. Var. 31/10/72.
M.Ca. The Highwayman. L.C. Wolverhampton, 17/11/92.
D. High Ways and By Ways of Life (Grec. 22/4/61). L.C.
D. Hilda (P'cess. 28/5/92, *mat.*). L.C.
Ext. The Hippopotamus (H. 12/8/50). L.C.
F. His Club Friend. L.C. Traf. 29/3/93.
D. His Hidden Revenge. L.C. S.W. 18/3/90.
[See *F. HOLTON*, 1887.]
F. His Holiday. L.C. S.W. 27/9/94.
D.Sk. His Last Chance. L.C. S.W. 21/12/96.
[See *H. HARRADEN*, 1890.]
F. His Little Mania (Athen. 12/7/90).
D. His Mother's Ransom. L.C. Star, Wolverhampton, 17/3/91.
D. His Natural Life. L.C. Leicester, 7/8/96.
[The L.C. manuscript records that this was later played as *For His Life*.]
D. His Natural Life. L.C. Qns. Manchester, 9/7/86.

D.Sk. His Nephew. L.C. S.W. 26/12/96.
Ca. His New French Cook (St G. 6/2/99).
M.F. His Only Coat. L.C. Gai. 16/5/82.
F. His Own Wife (Pleasure Gdns. Folkestone, 3/11/94).
D. The History of a Flag (Ast. 3/4/60). L.C.
D. The Hive of Life: Its Drones and Workers. L.C. Glasgow, 7/6/62.
Ext. Hoddy Toddy, all Head and no Body (Stand. 26/12/51).
D. Hold Fast (Leeds, 21/9/85).
D. Holly Bush Hall. L.C. Stand. 6/2/60.
D. Holly Bush Hall. L.C. Eff. 8/2/60.
D. Holly Bush Hall (Grec. 9/7/66).
D. Holly Lodge (St Martin's H. 2/4/55).
D. The Holly Tree Inn; or, A Christmas Story (Str. 7/1/56). L.C.
Ext. Homage to Flora (Roy. 23/2/60).
D. Home; or, A Father's Love (Vic. 7/2/80).
F. Home Affairs. L.C. Alh. 15/10/79.
D. The Home Circle. L.C. C.L. 15/2/50.
C. Home Diplomacy. L.C. Sheffield, 6/2/67.
Ba. Home from War (Str. 22/1/55).
D. The Home in the Heart; or, Life's Pilot (Grec. 15/7/61). L.C.
D. The Home in the West (Sur. 2/5/53).
D. The Home of our Adoption (Ladb. H. 17/6/92, *amat.*).
F. Home Phantasies. L.C. Phil. 17/11/79.
F. The Home Rule Bill. L.C. Ladb. H. 5/4/93.
D.Sk. A Homestead Story (P'cess. 22/6/61). L.C.
F. Home Truths. L.C. Brighton, 26/11/58.
D. Home Truths (Sur. 1/3/52, as *The Barrister*; P'cess. 30/11/59). L.C. *French* [as *Good for Evil*].
D. Homeward Bound. L.C. Vic. Pav. Leamington, 21/9/82.
D. Homeward Bound (P.H. Warrington, 6/4/85).
D. The Home Wreck (Vic. 24/3/51).
D. An Honest Attorney; or, The Mathematician. L.C. Str. 9/6/55.
D. Honesty; or, Merit is its own Reward. L.C. Var. 23/12/72.
Ca. Honesty's the Best Policy. L.C. T.H. Hulme, 29/11/98.
D. Honesty the Best Policy (Sur. 26/12/65).
D. Honesty the Best Policy. L.C. Var. 26/3/79.
D. Honi Soit. L.C. Oldham, 3/7/86.
[Title changed from *The Modern Godiva.*]
C. Honour; or, The Count d'Alren. L.C. Bristol, 14/5/70.
D. Honour and Arms. L.C. Sheffield, 19/3/63.
D. Honour before Wealth (H.M. Carlisle, 7/9/85).
D. The Honour of the House; or, Pride and Passion. L.C. Brit. 18/8/57.
D. Honour Thy Father. L.C. Birmingham, 18/12/96.
[See *C. A. CLARKE*, 1898.]
F. Hooker and Snooker; or, Life in the Rail (Sur. 2/4/51). L.C.
F. Hook or Crook. L.C. Alh. 4/11/78.
D. Hope Deferred. L.C. Str. 18/11/85.
[Licence cancelled 11/3/86; relicensed as *Unmasked.*]
D. Hopes and Fears. L.C. Adel. 4/7/54.
D. Hopes and Fears. L.C. Qns. 18/2/64.
P. Hop o' my Thumb. L.C. Newcastle, 5/1/77.
P. Hop o' my Thumb; or, The Giant Ogre and his Seven-League Boots. L.C. Qns. 21/12/54.

P. Hop o' my Thumb and the Giant Ogre of the Seven Leagued Boots; or, Harlequin Prince A 1 and the Water Lilies of the Silver Lake. L.C. Adel. L'pool, 2/1/63.
D. The Hop Pickers (Adel. 28/8/61).
F. Horrors. L.C. P's. Accrington, 11/12/85.
D. The Horse Dealer of Vienna (Brit. 20/2/60).
M.F. The Horseman. L.C. C.P. 18/4/93.
D. The Horse of the Cavern; or, The Mounted Brigands of Abruzzi (Ast. 12/5/56).
F. The Horseshoe (Grec. 24/4/60).
C.O. Horseshoe; or, The Silver Farrier. L.C. Str. 30/12/98.
F. A Horse to be Sold (Brit. 5/8/61).
D. Horton Towers. L.C. Gai. Brighton, 18/3/95.
F. Hot and Cold; or, The Bath Waters. L.C. P'cess. 18/2/50.
C. Hot Potatoe. L.C. Str. 9/7/85.
C. Houp-la! L.C. Beaufort House, Walham Green, 4/6/85.
[See *T. G. WARREN*, 1891.]
Ca. An Hour at Rugby Junction. L.C. Southampton, 16/5/73.
F. An Hour in Venice (Grec. 20/4/59).
[Also called (25/4/59) *An Hour at the Carnival.*]
D. The Hour of Triumph. L.C. S.W. 28/8/96.
Oa. The Housebreaker. L.C. Church Lane H. Tooting Graveney, 31/12/97.
Fairy Pl. A Housefull of Rebels. L.C. Vestry H. Mitcham, 19/3/95.
F. Household Words (Stand. 11/10/58).
F. Household Words, All the Year Round (Lyc. 11/4/59). L.C.
F. The House in the Valley (Grec. 28/5/60). L.C.
D. The House of Dives. L.C. Lecture H. Greenwich, 3/3/93.
D. The House on the Bridge of Notre Dame (Lyc. 11/2/61). L.C.
D. The House on the Bridge of Notre Dame. L.C. Stand. 27/3/61.
D. The House on the Heath (Stand. 2/4/57).
P. The House that Jack built. L.C. Birmingham, 20/12/59.
P. The House that Jack built. L.C. Dewsbury, 31/12/77.
P. The House that Jack built. L.C. Vic. Longton, 21/12/78.
P. The House that Jack built. L.C. Wakefield, 23/1/80.
P. The House that Jack built. L.C. North Camp, Aldershot, 15/12/80.
P. The House that Jack built. L.C. H.M. Aberdeen, 4/1/81.
P. The House that Jack built. L.C. New, Portsmouth, 17/12/89.
P. The House that Jack built. L.C. Stockton-on-Tees, 18/12/90.
P. The House that Jack built. L.C. Empire Pal. Edinburgh, 30/12/98.
P. The House that Jack built; or, Harlequin the Three Witches, and the Fairy King of the Bower of Bouquets. L.C. Adel. L'pool, 2/1/64.
D. A House to Let (Stand. 7/2/59). L.C.
Ca. How does he love me? L.C. Swansea, 6/1/76.
F. How it's to be done (Str. 17/8/57).
F. How I tamed Mrs Cruiser (Soho, 26/10/58).
F.C. Howse the Informer. L.C. Mission Rooms, Fulham Palace Road, 5/3/97.
D. How Silver was tricked. L.C. Grand, Blackpool, 12/6/99.
F. How's your poor Feet? (Sur. 25/8/62). L.C.
F. How the Duchess convinced the Princess. L.C. Ladb. H. 12/7/99.
D. How to Act; or, A Lesson taught by Garrick. L.C. New, Greenwich, 13/2/65.

Ca. How Tom proposed. L.C. Kilburn, 5/3/97.
D. How we live in the World of London (Sur. 24/3/56). L.C.
D. The Huguenots (Lyc. 22/9/57).
D. The Huguenots; or, The Massacre of St Bartholomew (C.G. 22/4/51). L.C.
Ca. Hugh Weston's Mill (Hull, 17/12/80). L.C.
C. Humbug. L.C. Vaud. 23/10/85.
P. Humpty Dumpty. L.C. P.W. Glasgow, 23/12/75.
P. Humpty Dumpty. L.C. L'pool, 20/12/76.
P. Humpty Dumpty. L.C. Margate, 23/12/82.
P. Humpty Dumpty. L.C. Grand, Leeds, 8/12/83.
P. Humpty Dumpty. L.C. O.H. Crouch End, 30/12/98.
D. The Hunchback Doctor (Sur. 17/3/66).
D. Hunger. L.C. Vic. 12/10/58.
D. Hunger; or, Life in London (Grec. 26/7/60).
D. Hunted Down. L.C. Var. 8/12/83.
D. Hunted Down by Fate (Birkenhead, 11/12/83).
M.Ca. Hunting a Fox. L.C. Margate, 26/9/81.
[See *J. W. TRIEVNOR*, 1878.]
F. Hunting a Widow. L.C. Surrey, 5/12/60.
P. Hurly-Burly (Empire, 21/12/85).
F. Hush. L.C. Ch.X. 20/5/72.
P. Hush-a-by Baby on the Tree Top; or, The Comet of 1856 without his Tail. L.C. Brit. 13/12/56.
Duol. Hydropathics. L.C. Colchester, 26/5/98.
Ext. Hymen's Muster Roll (Grec. 5/9/60).
D. Hyram Balthazar; or, The Maniac Jew. L.C. Brit. 3/11/56.
F. I beg you wouldn't mention it (Str. 22/4/57).
F. Içi on (ne) parle (pas) français (Toole's, 13/6/91, *mat.*).
D. Ida Lee; or, The Child of the Wreck. L.C. Eff. 28/8/63.
D. Ida May; or, The Slave's Triangle. L.C. Vic. 25/4/55.
D. Ida May, the Kidnapped Child (M'bone, 9/2/57). L.C. as *I.M.; or, The Child of Fortune.*
C. I'd be a Butterfly; or, A Dangerous Complaint. L.C. Nottingham, 19/2/68.
D. The Idealist. L.C. Vic. H. Bayswater, 31/12/97.
D. The Idiot of the Mountain (C.L. 1/62). L.C.
D. The Idle Apprentice; or, The Two Roads of Life. L.C. C.L. 31/5/65.
D. Idle Jack (W. Bromwich, 5/11/83).
D. The Idolaters; or, The Hindoo Prince (Brit. 12/6/62). L.C.
Bsq. Iky le Noir. L.C. Axminster Literary Society, 17/12/77.
D. Ill-gotten Gains. L.C. W.L. 26/4/98.
F. I'll Tell your Wife (D.L. 10/2/55).
D. Imprisoned. L.C. St G. 9/8/98.
F. Impudence versus the World (Sur. 28/7/62).
Ca. An Impudent Puppy (D.L. 7/11/55). L.C.
D. In a Fit of Abstraction; or, The Lady Burglar. L.C. Kilburn, 1/6/97.
F. In and out of Place (Adel. 23/2/57).
D.Sk. In a Terrible Storm. L.C. Alex. Sheffield, 31/12/97.
C. In Carnival Time. L.C. St G. 25/3/90.
D. The Incendiaries; or, The Haunted Manor (Brit. 29/8/59). L.C.
F. In Charge. L.C. Alex. L'pool, 1/4/85.

D. The Incorrigibles; or, Life in 1796 (Londesborough, Scarborough, 29/5/82).
D. In Darker London. L.C. W.L. 9/10/94.
Spec. India in 1857 (Sur. 9/11/57).
D. The Indian Maid; or, A Settler's Struggles. L.C. 1850.
D.Sk. The Indian Rising. L.C. S.W. 30/1/95.
Sk. An Indian Sketch (Soho, 11/11/57).
D. Industry and Idleness. L.C. Vic. 28/1/59.
D. Inez Danton the Repentant. L.C. Brit. 30/3/58.
Bsq. Inez the Brigand Queen. L.C. Ladb. H. 23/4/85.
D. In Face of the Foe (M'bone, 25/7/92).
D. Infidelity (Grec. 4/4/59).
D.Sk. In Full Settlement. L.C. Pier Pav. Hastings, 27/12/98.
F. Injured Innocence (Grec. 3/9/60). L.C.
F. In Ladbroke Square. L.C. Brighton, 15/5/84.
D. In London's Heart (P's. Llandudno, 9/11/99, *copy.*).
Ca. In Love (Terry's, 13/5/90, *mat.*). L.C.
C. Innocence (Gloucester, 22/10/74).
D. In One Short Year. L.C. Jeffrey's H. Simbury, 4/2/89.
F. In Place or Out of Place; or, Acting Mad. L.C. Adel. 8/4/57.
D.Sk. In Slavery's Days. L.C. S.W. 30/12/98.
D. Intemperance; or, The Curse of Drink. L.C. Cullan's, Bradford, 21/10/79.
D. An Interesting Case. L.C. Vic. H. 12/7/99.
F. The International Dog Show. L.C. Vic. 27/3/63.
Spec. The International of 1862 (Sur. 30/6/62).
F. An Interrupted Wedding. L.C. Queen's Assembly R. Oxford, 7/8/85.
D. In the Afternoon. L.C. Ladb. H. 20/6/98.
Duol. In the Cause of Mrs Grundy. L.C. Town H. Herne Bay, 11/9/99.
D. In the Clutch of the Enemy (Greenwich, 4/10/73).
D. In the Coils. L.C. C.P. 17/3/84.
D. In the Future. L.C. Alh. Barrow-in-Furness, 1/1/92.
D.Sk. In the Hands of the Redskins; or, Saved by an Irishman's Pluck. L.C. S.W. 15/4/96.
D. In the Holly; or, Man's Mercy (Brit. 28/11/70). L.C.
D. In the King's Name. L.C. Stratford, 7/8/96.
D. In the Name of the Czar. L.C. Nov. 27/2/96.
D. In the Toils (Vic. Oxford, 13/1/69).
D. In the Wolf's Den: A Story of the Welsh Coast (Swansea, 30/4/69).
Ca. In the Wrong Box (Str. 15/10/66). L.C.
F. In to Win; or, The Jockey's Stratagem. L.C. Qns. 8/8/61.
D. The Intrigue (Str. 5/1/57).
C. Intrigue; or, The Lost Jewels. 8° 1876 [by "An Old Author"].
D. The Intruder (H. 27/1/92).
P. The Invisible Prince. L.C. O.H. Leicester, 7/1/78.
Bsq. Ion. L.C. Cambridge, 27/11/90.
F. I.O.U. (Gai. Dublin, 5/7/73).
D. Iran Safferi (Sur. 17/4/54). L.C.
D. Ireland as it is (Adel. 18/8/56). L.C.
D. Irene, the Greek Girl of Janina; or, The Vow of the Three Avengers. L.C. Brit. 21/6/59.

C. Irish Aristocracy (St Helen's, 2/6/84).
F.Ext. Irish Aristocracy (Stratford, 22/2/86). L.C.
F. The Irish Belle (Ch.X. 1873).
F. The Irish Diamond (H. 29/10/50). L.C.
F.C. An Irish Elopement (Qns. Manchester, 11/4/87). L.C.
D. The Irish Emigrant; or, Temptation (Stand. 13/6/60). L.C.
F. An Irish Engagement (Str. 24/8/57).
D. An Irishman's Home (Scarborough, 12/4/75).
D. The Irish Minstrel (Cheltenham, 31/1/67).
D. The Irish Minstrel. L.C. Alex. L'pool, 25/3/89.
D. The Iron Arm; or, The Stolen Marriage (Sur. 13/4/57).
D. The Iron Casket; or, The Burning Mountain (Col. L'pool, 10/2/68).
D. The Iron Chain. L.C. Warrington, 23/3/95.
D. Iron Clasp, the Gitana's Dream. L.C. Pav. 25/9/62.
D. Iron Latch Farm. L.C. Pav. 27/2/65.
D. The Iron Road. L.C. Woolwich, 30/8/99.
D. The Iron Statue (Vic. 1868).
F. The Irresistibles (H. 3/3/57).
F. Irvingmania; or, Tragedy in Trousers (Glasgow, 12/7/77).
D. Isabel D'Arville. L.C. Northern Empire, Tottenham, 9/8/95.
D. The Ishnabrogue. L.C. New, Monmouth, 25/4/91.
D. Is it the King? (Str. 14/11/61). L.C.
D. The Island Home. L.C. Manchester, 30/3/61.
D. The Island of Silver Store; or, The Pirate of the Caribbees (Stand. 6/2/58). L.C.
D. The Island of Silver Store; or, The Prisoners' Perils. L.C. Brighton, 30/1/58.
P. The Island of Trances and the Land of Flowers; or, Harlequin King Nosey and the Old Woman from Babylon. L.C. Vic. 20/12/52.
D. The Italian Bravo (Grec. 23/1/61).
D. The Italian Wife (Stand. 24/5/55).
D. The Italian Wife (Pav. 14/12/58).
[This seems to be the same play as the above.]
D. It is never to late to learn. L.C. Adel. L'pool, 17/3/64.
Ca. It must be true, 'twas in the papers (Lyc. 20/10/62). L.C.
F. It never rains but it pours. L.C. Grec. 17/11/62.
F. It runs in the Family (M'bone, 5/2/55). L.C.
F. It's all through the Lad. L.C. Var. 12/12/85.
D. It's an Ill Wind that blows Nobody Good (Adel. 14/5/60). L.C.
C.D. It was a Dream (P.W. Birmingham, 18/9/90). L.C.
Spec. Ivanhoe (Ast. 25/4/59). L.C.
D. Ivanhoe. L.C. Qns. 4/6/59.
D. Ivanhoe; or, The Fair Maid of York. L.C. Qns. 21/12/63.
D. Ivanhoe; or, The Knights of Merry England. L.C. Gar. 2/10/72.
D. Ivan the Terrible; or, Dark Deeds of Night. L.C. Brit. 18/9/66.
F. I've beat all three (Stand. 1/4/61). L.C.
D. The Ivory Tablets (Margate, 7/7/98). L.C.
D. Ivy. L.C. Athenaeum, Hammersmith, 18/9/94.
Ca. Jack. L.C. Gai. 15/11/82.
Bsq. Jack. L.C. Sanger's Amphi. Ramsgate, 7/10/84.
Bsq. Jack; or, The Magic Key (Qns. Dublin, 14/4/79).
P. Jack and Jill. L.C. Swansea, 21/12/76.
P. Jack and Jill. L.C. Tyne, Newcastle, 10/1/78.

P. Jack and Jill. L.C. Bradford, 5/12/78.
P. Jack and Jill. L.C. Plymouth, 27/12/79.
P. Jack and Jill. L.C. Brighton, 15/12/84.
P. Jack and Jill. L.C. Corn Exchange, Maidstone, 26/12/89.
P. Jack and Jill. L.C. Rotunda, L'pool, 16/12/93.
P. Jack and Jill. L.C. Pal. of Var. Manchester, 31/12/97.
P. Jack and Jill; or, Harlequin and the Four-leaved Shamrock. L.C. Pav. 21/12/54.
P. Jack and Jill, and the Sleeping Beauty. L.C. P's. 14/12/83.
Oa. Jack and Jill Up-to-date; or, The Waterpail Rebellion. L.C. P.H. Tottenham, 11/9/99.
P. Jack and the Bean Stalk (D.L. 26/12/59). L.C.
P. Jack and the Bean Stalk. L.C. Edinburgh, 1/12/74.
P. Jack and the Bean Stalk. L.C. Alex. L'pool, 22/12/74.
P. Jack and the Bean Stalk. L.C. Dundee, 23/12/75.
P. Jack and the Bean Stalk. L.C. Glasgow, 6/1/76.
P. Jack and the Bean Stalk. L.C. Tyne, Newcastle, 14/1/76.
P. Jack and the Bean Stalk. L.C. Sheffield, 20/12/76.
P. Jack and the Bean Stalk. L.C. O.H. Stockport, 23/12/76.
P. Jack and the Bean Stalk (Stangate, 26/12/76).
P. Jack and the Bean Stalk. L.C. Qns. Manchester, 20/12/77.
P. Jack and the Bean Stalk. L.C. Leeds, 23/1/78.
P. Jack and the Bean Stalk. L.C. Plymouth, 21/12/78.
P. Jack and the Bean Stalk. L.C. Margate, 20/12/79.
P. Jack and the Bean Stalk. L.C. Hull, 20/12/79.
P. Jack and the Bean Stalk. L.C. Nottingham, 22/12/79.
P. Jack and the Bean Stalk. L.C. Bradford, 14/12/80.
P. Jack and the Bean Stalk. L.C. Bristol, 18/12/80.
P. Jack and the Bean Stalk. L.C. Alex. Sheffield, 20/12/82.
P. Jack and the Bean Stalk. L.C. Pav. Hastings, 21/12/83.
P. Jack and the Bean Stalk. L.C. Lyc. Edinburgh, 15/12/84.
P. Jack and the Bean Stalk. L.C. Com. Manchester, 7/12/85.
P. Jack and the Bean Stalk. L.C. Brighton, 17/12/86.
P. Jack and the Bean Stalk. L.C. P.W. L'pool, 17/12/88.
P. Jack and the Bean Stalk. L.C. Stratford, 13/12/89.
P. Jack and the Bean Stalk. L.C. St J. Manchester, 1/1/92.
P. Jack and the Bean Stalk. L.C. Grand, Cardiff, 24/12/92.
P. Jack and the Bean Stalk. L.C. Qns. Birmingham, 20/12/93.
P. Jack and the Bean Stalk. L.C. New, Stockport, 26/11/94.
P. Jack and the Bean Stalk. L.C. R.A. Woolwich, 24/12/94.
P. Jack and the Bean Stalk. L.C. Manchester, 23/12/95.
P. Jack and the Bean Stalk. L.C. Bath, 10/1/96.
P. Jack and the Bean Stalk. L.C. Alex. Sheffield, 26/12/96.
P. Jack and the Bean Stalk. L.C. O.H. Chatham, 26/12/96.
P. Jack and the Bean Stalk. L.C. Portsmouth, 27/12/98.
P. Jack and the Bean Stalk; or, Harlequin and Mother Goose at Home Again (Adel. 24/12/55). L.C.
D. Jack Crawford (Lyc. Sunderland, 1/10/77). L.C. Lyc. L'pool, as *J. C., the Hero of Camperdown.*
P. Jack Horner. L.C. Adel. Oldham, 28/12/76.
P. Jack in the Box. L.C. Brighton, 12/12/76.
D. Jack Long of Texas (Brit. 23/12/58).
D. Jack Mingo, the London Street-Boy; or, Try Again (Brit. 11/8/66). L.C.

D. Jack of All Trades (Olym. 26/12/61). L.C.
P.Bal. Jacko, the Brazilian Ape (Ast. 12/6/61).
F. Jack on the Green; or, Hints on Etiquette (Adel. 23/5/50).
D. Jack Royal; or, Father, Mother and Son. L.C. Sur. 10/6/50.
Sk. Jack's Arrival from Canton (P'cess. 27/2/64).
D. Jack Sheppard. L.C. Pav. 13/7/55.
D. Jack Sheppard. L.C. C.L. 16/8/55.
D. Jack Sheppard. L.C. Stand. 16/8/55.
P. Jack Sprat, the Three Blind Mice, Big A Little a, Bouncer's B, The Cat's in the Cupboard and She can't See (Ast. 26/12/64). L.C.
D.Sk. Jack's Return. L.C. Empire, Doncaster, 22/4/95.
Bal. Jack's Return from Canton (H. 15/3/58).
D. Jack's the Boy. L.C. Pav. 31/12/97.
P. Jack Straw King Munkey Punkey; or, Harlequin Cock-a-doodle-do and the Funny Old Woman of Lambeth Walk. L.C. Bower, 21/12/65.
P. Jack the Giant Killer. L.C. Bek's Circus, Newcastle, 23/12/58.
P. Jack the Giant Killer. L.C. Circus, Manchester, 30/12/59.
P. Jack the Giant Killer (Glasgow, 17/12/61).
P. Jack the Giant Killer. L.C. Hengler's, 2/12/72.
P. Jack the Giant Killer. L.C. P's. Manchester, 23/12/74.
P. Jack the Giant Killer. L.C. Alex. Walsall, 23/12/75.
P. Jack the Giant Killer. L.C. Worcester, 6/12/76.
P. Jack the Giant Killer. L.C. Qns. Edinburgh, 14/1/76.
P. Jack the Giant Killer. L.C. Dumfries, 25/12/76.
P. Jack the Giant Killer. L.C. M.H. Hastings, 19/12/78.
P. Jack the Giant Killer (Greenwich, 26/12/79).
P. Jack the Giant Killer. L.C. Qns. Manchester, 23/12/80.
Ca. Jack the Giant Killer. L.C. Rotunda, L'pool, 22/12/81.
Ext. Jack the Giant Killer. L.C. North Shields, 25/2/82.
P. Jack the Giant Killer. L.C. Paisley, 30/12/82.
P. Jack the Giant Killer. L.C. Alex. L'pool, 12/12/83.
P. Jack the Giant Killer. L.C. Greenock, 10/12/84.
P. Jack the Giant Killer. L.C. P'cess. Glasgow, 10/12/84.
P. Jack the Giant Killer. L.C. Rotherham, 26/12/84.
P. Jack the Giant Killer. L.C. O.H. Southport, 31/12/95.
P. Jack the Giant Killer; or, Harlequin and Robin Goodfellow. L.C. Birmingham, 12/12/53.
P. Jack the Giant Killer; or, The Seven Champions (Stand. 27/12/69). L.C.
Ext. Jack, the Pretty Princess, the Wicked Ogre, and the Seven Champions of Christendom. L.C. Winter Gardens, Blackpool, 10/7/93.
D. Jack, the Tale of a Tramp (Blackpool, 12/11/77).
D. Jack Union and his Dog Quid (Vic. 23/2/54).
D. Jacqueline Doucette (D.L. 5/5/55).
D.Sk. Jagger's Trust. L.C. S.W. 11/9/99.
D. James Stuart, King of the Commons (Sur. 10/9/64).
C. The Janderkins. L.C. Ch.X. 14/9/74.
D. Jane Eyre. L.C. Coventry, 2/3/77.
D. Jane of the Hatchet. L.C. Vic. Longton, 23/1/77.
D. Jane Seton (Amphi. L'pool, 25/5/78). L.C.
Bsq. Jane Shore (Parkhurst, 22/6/94).

D.Sk. Jane Shore. L.C. S.W. 30/1/95.
D. Jane Shore. L.C. Hereford, 9/8/95.
C. Janet's Ruse (Roy. 1872). L.C. 11/5/72.
M.C. A Japanese Idyll. L.C. Manor, 30/11/97.
D. Jarvis, the Honest Man (Vic. 26/6/54).
Bsq. Jason and Medea. L.C. R.A. Woolwich, 6/6/78.
D. Jasper Roseblade; or, The Dark Deed in the Woods. L.C. C.L. 24/1/59.
F.C. Jasper's Uncle. L.C. Glo. 23/12/95.
D. Jealousy; or, The Confederates. L.C. Sur. 3/5/51.
D. Jean; or, La République (S.W. 28/10/82). L.C.
C.Oa. Jeannette. L.C. New, Barnstaple, 26/4/98.
D. Jeannie Deans; or, The Lily of St Leonards. L.C. Stand. 9/9/62.
Ext. Jeannie Deans; or, Any Other Gal. L.C. Brit. 9/3/63.
D. Jeannie of Midlothian; or, The Loves of Effie and Madge Wildfire. L.C. Pav. 14/2/63.
D. Jenny l'ouvrière. L.C. Soho, 18/12/54.
D. Jenny Wren. L.C. Brit. 15/12/80.
D. Jericho Jack, the Foremast Man. L.C. Eff. 22/11/61.
D. Jerry Abershaw; or, The Mother's Curse. L.C. Pav. 30/10/55.
D. Jerry Builder. L.C. St J. 15/11/99.
D. Jesmond Dene (Ipswich, 9/10/90; Athen. Shepherd's Bush, 5/3/92).
Ca. Jess. L.C. P.H. Walton-on-Thames, 13/8/87.
D. Jesse James, the Bandit King. L.C. Qns. Manchester, 18/10/95.
D. Jessie Ashton; or, The Adventures of a Barmaid. L.C. Eff. 18/4/62.
D. Jessie Farleigh (C.L. 9/2/63).
D. Jessie, the Machine Girl (Northampton, 17/2/68).
D. Jessie, the Mormon's Daughter. L.C. Brit. 9/12/65.
D. Jessie Tyrell (Vic. 3/3/66). L.C.
M.D. The Jewel Hunters; or, Countess Joan. L.C. Aven. 12/9/95.
M.D. Jewish Emigration. L.C. Stand. 15/11/99.
M.D. The Jewish Soldier in the Prussian Army. L.C. Gar. 25/2/80.
D. The Jew of Constantine (Vic. 10/6/51). L.C.
Equest.D. Jibbenainosay; or, The White Horse of Nick of the Woods (Ast. 15/2/58). L.C.
Sk. Jim Crow's Visit to Chobham (Stand. 6/7/53).
F. J.O. (S.W. 14/7/62). L.C.
D. Joan Lowrie (Blackburn, 11/2/78).
C. Joe and Nolly Stubbs; or, Trust Each Other. L.C. 6/9/76.
P. Joe Miller; or, Harlequin Wit, Mirth, Jollity and Satire. L.C. M'bone, 23/12/57.
M.F. John Bull's Dilemma. L.C. W. Bromwich, 9/11/85.
D. John Cade of Asliford. L.C. Brit. 11/7/50.
D. John Felton; or, The Maid of Erin and the Griffin of the Thames. L.C. Vic. 24/3/50.
D. John Gabriel Borkman. L.C. Aven. 26/12/96.
[See *W. ARCHER*, 1897.]
D. John Heriot, Yeoman. L.C. T.H. Uxbridge, 31/12/87.
D. John Marchmont's Legacy. L.C. P.W. Birmingham, 23/4/66.
Sk. Johnny Gilpin's Ride (Ast. 26/12/61).
D. John of the Forge; or, The Honest Man. L.C. C.L. 13/1/50.
D. John Wilson; or, The Proscribed. L.C. Adel. L'pool, 2/5/65.

P. Jolly Boy Blue. L.C. R.A. Woolwich, 22/12/93.
D. The Jolly Dogs of London; or, The Two Roads of Life. L.C. Brit. 26/7/66.
D. Jolly Jack; or, The Roscius of the Fleet. L.C. Stand. 17/11/50.
P. Jolly King Christmas; or, Harlequin Jack Frost and the Giant and the Beanstalk. L.C. M'bone, 22/12/63.
F. The Jolly Miller (P'cess. 4/3/61).
F. Jones the Avenger (Olym. 24/11/56). L.C.
Bsq. Jo; or, Love in a Fog (S.W. 16/4/64). L.C.
D. Joseph Gombert. L.C. Sur. 20/1/60.
D. Joseph's Luck. L.C. Vic. 1/6/97.
D. Jo, the Waif; or, The Mystery of Chesney Wold (Rotunda, L'pool, 7/81).
Ca. The Journey to Paris; or, The Rendez-vous. L.C. Swansea, 26/3/60.
C.D. Joy. L.C. Com. Manchester, 1/4/87.
D. Joy, Life's Great Physician. L.C. Ladb. H. 29/10/92.
C. Juanita the Devoted; or, The Midnight Journey. L.C. Brit. 18/11/56.
F. Jubilee Jimmie. L.C. P.H. Sidcup, 9/2/97.
M.F. The Jubilee T Pot. L.C. Var. 30/6/87.
F. Judge and Doctor. L.C. Durham, 5/10/94.
F. The Judge's Wooing (Tivoli, 7/5/98).
D. Judgment. L.C. Adel. L'pool, 10/4/89.
Oa. The Judgment of Solomon. L.C. P.H. Croydon, 31/10/94.
F.C. Judy. L.C. Empress, 13/4/94.
[See *R. HORNIMAN*, 1899.]
D. The Juggler of Paris (Pav. 10/9/66).
D. Julia Ackland; or, The Child of Sorrow. L.C. Gravesend, 12/4/54.
D. Julie (Lyr. 30/6/98). L.C.
D. Julie de Launay; or, The Foundlings of Notre Dame (Brit. 3/9/60). L.C.
D. A Juliet by Proxy. L.C. St J. 21/8/99.
Ca. Juliette. L.C. Swansea, 26/3/60.
M.F.C. Juno. L.C. Aquar. Brighton, 7/9/96.
[Title changed to *The Gay Goddess*, 27/8/1908.]
F. Jupiter Chuff. L.C. Grec. 3/10/65.
Bsq. Jupiter L.L.D. L.C. A.D.C. Cambridge, 28/5/94.
D. Jura; or, The Wild Flower of Mexico (Leeds, 30/10/68). L.C.
D. Just as Well. L.C. T.H. Kensington, 16/2/99.
D. Justice. L.C. Lyr. 28/3/92.
D. Justice. L.C. T.H. Westminster, 15/5/93.
D. Justice; or, The Gipsey and the Stolen Child. L.C. Manchester, 25/10/53.
D. Justice at Last. L.C. M'bone, 27/10/84.
D. Justifiable Homicide. L.C. Brighton, 10/6/84.
[With an alternative title, *Retribution; or, Serge Panine*. See *J. H. THORP*, 1891.]
D. Just in Time; or, The Gibbet and the Rampart. L.C. M'bone, 14/3/62.
F. Just One Word (O.C. 31/5/73). L.C.
F. The Juvenile Party; or, Extremes are Bad (Str. 19/1/52). L.C.
D. Kafrali Karabush, Chief of the Eagle Tribe; or, A Chieftain's Vengeance (Vic. 9/8/52). L.C.

M.C. The Kangaroo Girl (Pleasure Gdns. Folkestone, 12/7/97; Metro. 19/7/97). L.C.
[Music by Oscar Barrett.]
D. Kate Kearney (Grec. 4/4/64). L.C.
D. Kate Kearney; or, A Story of Love and Trial. L.C. Brit. 22/4/64.
D. Kate of Dover; or, The Old Spanish Guinea. L.C. Vic. 11/1/58.
D. Kate of Killarney (Grec. 11/4/64).
D. Kate's Assignation; or, The Double Ambuscade. L.C. Grec. 28/9/63.
D. Kate Wynsley: A Woman's Love (Str. 28/1/56).
D. Katharine Kavanagh. L.C. Nov. 30/9/91.
D. Kathleen (Brit. 4/3/61).
D. Kathleen; or, A True Irish Girl. L.C. W.L. 10/4/93.
Bal. Katrina (Empire, 20/2/93).
[Music by Leopold Wenzel.]
D. Keep to the Right; or, The Oakdell Mystery. L.C. Eastbourne, 15/8/84.
F. Keep your Door Locked (Adel. 29/8/66). L.C.
D. Keereda and Nana Sahib (Vic. 18/11/57).
D. Kenilworth (Ast. 17/6/58).
Bsq. Kenilworth (Str. 21/7/66).
D. Kenilworth (Manchester, 8/4/71; Edinburgh, 17/7/71).
D. Kenilworth; or, The Gentle Amy Robsart (Alfred, 12/11/70).
P. Kenilworth; or, The Golden Days of Good Queen Bess. L.C. Qns. 23/12/62.
D. Kerim (Brit. 10/10/59).
F. The Kettle-drum of the Surrey (Sur. 19/4/58). L.C.
D. The Key of the Streets (Sur. 31/3/66). L.C. with sub-title, *or, Life in London.*
C.Oa. The Keys of the Castle. L.C. Lyr. Hammersmith, 10/7/94.
F. The Key under the Doormat (Lyc. 5/12/59). L.C.
F. Kicks and Halfpence (Lyc. 1/9/58). L.C.
D. Kiddie. L.C. Brighton, 30/3/98.
D. Kiddle-a-wink (Vic. 30/1/64). L.C.
D. Kiddle-a-wink; or, The Last of the Doomed Race. L.C. C.L. 18/1/64.
D. The Kidnappers; or, London at Night (Vic. 13/11/65). L.C.
D. Kildare; or, From Start to Finish. L.C. Ringwood, Hants. 28/1/90.
Episode. The King and the Countess (St G. 9/7/97).
P. King Bluster-Bubble and the Demon Ogre; or, Harlequin Prince Honour Bright and the Dwarf King of the Ruby Mines. L.C. Birmingham, 14/12/57. MS. Birmingham.
[By *C. A. SOMERSET*.]
P. King Capital. L.C. Oldham, 28/12/66.
C. King Charles. L.C. Olym. 11/3/51.
P. King Chess; or, Tom the Piper's Son and See-Saw Margery Daw (Sur. 26/12/65). L.C.
Bsq. King Coffee; or, The Princess of Ashantee (Bijou, Southport, 8/12/73).
P. King Comet and Prince Quicksilver; or, Harlequin all the World and his Wife (C.L. 26/12/58). L.C.
P. King Crib; or, A Game of Speculation. L.C. Grec. 19/12/56.
D. The King Dreams. L.C. Queen's Gate H. 27/3/94.

D. King Galistan. L.C. Parish School, Wolverhampton, 12/2/98.
D. King Jamie; or, The Fortunes of Nigel (Qns. Manchester, 15/9/79).
Bsq. King Jupiter and the Freaks of the Graces. L.C. Eff. 19/12/56.
Ext. King Koffee; or, The Rumpus in Ashan—T. L.C. Brighton, 20/4/74.
P. King Kokolorum. L.C. Adel. 22/1/76.
D. King Liberty; or, The Devil in the Heart (C.L. 29/9/51). L.C.
P. King Muffin; or, Harlequin Heartcake and the Fairy of the Glow-worm Glade. L.C. Sur. 13/12/52.
D. The King of Clubs (Sur. 15/10/60).
D. The King of Persia; or, The Triumph of the Jewish Queen. L.C. C.L. 31/8/55 [licence refused].
D. King of Rags. L.C. S.W. 23/1/86.
D. The King of Terrors (Dover, 24/7/99).
D. The King of the Assassins; or, Love, War and Victory (Brit. 1/7/61). L.C.
P. The King of the Carbuncles; or, Harlequin Prince Peerless and the Enchanted Beauty of the Diamond Castle. L.C. Qns. 22/12/52.
P. The King of the Castle; or, Harlequin Prince Brilliant and the Princess Brighteyes (P'cess. 1/1/59). L.C.
P. The King of the Cures; or, The Triumph of Plenty over Monopoly (Brit. 26/12/61). L.C.
D. The King of the Golden Sands. L.C. Vic. 8/4/70.
P. The King of the Golden Valley; or, Harlequin Tom Tiddler, Little Boy Blue and the Old Woman who lived under a Hill (C.L. 26/12/64). L.C.
D. The King of the Mint; or, Old London Bridge by Night (Vic. 17/2/73). L.C.
P. The King of the Peacocks. L.C. Torquay, 20/1/81.
Ext. King Pluto; or, The Belle and the Pomegranate. L.C. H. 31/3/58.
Ext. King Queer and his Daughters Three (Str. 9/4/55). L.C.
D. The King's Advocate; or, Love and Hate. L.C. Cambridge, 22/9/66.
D. The King's Beggar (P'cess. Edinburgh, 15/3/73).
D. The King's Butterfly (Lyc. 22/10/64). L.C.
D. The King's Captive. L.C. Qns. 16/10/61.
D. The King's Favourite; or, The Fool of Fortune (Manchester, 29/5/73).
Ca. The King's Guardsmen (P'cess. Edinburgh, 31/1/76).
P. King Sillyninny who sold his Wife for Half-a-Guinea; or, Harlequin and the Enchanted Princess (Pav. 26/12/62). L.C.
D. The King's Mail; or, The Devil's Punch Bowl (Brit. 18/6/66). L.C.
D. The King's Musketeers (Lyc. 16/10/56). L.C.
D. The King's Musketeers. L.C. 14/9/55.
P. King Solomon; or, Harlequin Paragon and the Queen of the Valley of Perpetual Spring. L.C. L'pool, 22/12/65.
P. King Teapot the Great. L.C. Qns. 21/12/57.
D. A Kiss for a Kingdom. L.C. Educational H. Haslemere, 30/11/99.
Ext. Kiss Me Quick. L.C. Constitutional H. Harlesden, 15/4/96.
[Title altered to *A Trip to Klondyke*, 9/11/97.]
C. Kissing Kissing (Apollonian H. Dover, 13/11/73).

Bsq. The Kitchen Belles (Stand. 27/2/69).
M.F. A Kitchen Rehearsal. L.C. Margate, 14/7/80.
F. A Kitchen Rehearsal. L.C. Var. 23/10/80.
Ca. Kith and Kin. L.C. Birmingham, 17/4/79.
F.C. Kitty (New, Richmond, 25/2/91). L.C.
D. Kitty. L.C. Athen. Hammersmith, 18/9/94.
D. Klondyke the Golden. L.C. Lyr. 31/12/97.
D. The Knapsack (E.C. 14/4/84). L.C.
D. The Knave of Spades. L.C. St G. 10/5/95.
M.D. The Knight and the Water-Lily; or, Love among the Mermaids (Ast. 1/8/54). L.C.
Ca. A Knight's Lodging. L.C. New, Oxford, 20/6/98.
D. The Knights of Knavery. L.C. Woolwich, 31/12/95.
[Title altered to *The Bitter End*, 4/3/1901.]
D. Knowledge (Gai. 8/5/83). L.C.
D.Sk. Koffee Kan Brothers. L.C. S.W. 11/10/97.
Bsq. Kynge Lear and Hys Faythefull Foole (Brit. 18/6/60). L.C.
D.Sk. The Labour Leader. L.C. W.L. 19/10/95.
D. The Labour Question; or, Honour and Industry (Grec. 1/7/61). L.C.
D. The Ladder of Life (Croydon, 3/3/84). L.C.
C. The Ladies' Battle. L.C. Pier Pav. Hastings, 26/2/91.
C. Ladies Beware! (Olym. 11/10/58).
Oa. The Ladies' Chance. L.C. T.H. Harrowgate, 30/10/94.
C. The Ladies of St Cyr; or, The Runaway Husbands. *Lacy* (c. 1869).
F. The Ladies' Temperance Club (Stand. 11/10/69).
Sk. Lady Clara Vere de Vere (P.W. 8/6/88).
D. Lady Delmar. L.C. Ladb. H. 9/4/91.
Bsq. Lady Godiva (Str. 7/51).
P. Lady Godiva. L.C. Middlesborough, 20/1/77.
P. Lady Godiva. L.C. N. Shields, 18/12/94.
D.Sk. Lady Godiva, the Bare-back Rider. L.C. S.W. 18/12/96.
C. The Lady Guide; or, Breaking the Bank (Terry's, 15/4/91, *mat.*).
D. Lady Hatton (St Helen's, 3/9/83).
D. Lady Hatton; or, The Legend of Bleeding Heart Yard (Brit. 10/10/59). L.C. 4/1/50.
D. The Lady in Black; or, The Mysteries of a Private Madhouse (M'bone, 10/10/59).
D. Lady Jane Grey (P.W. Warrington, 12/2/75).
D. The Lady Judge. L.C. Alex. Association R. Blindell Sands, near Liverpool, 9/4/94.
D. Lady Lillian (Huddersfield, 15/6/85).
D. The Lady of Kildare; or, Married in Mistake (Qns. Salisbury, 4/3/72).
D. The Lady of Munster (Str. 13/7/60).
D. The Lady of St Tropez (S.W. 4/5/57).
D. The Lady of the Camelias (Vaud. 2/2/52).
D. The Lady of the Camelias (Lyc. 17/7/58).
D. The Lady of the Haystack. L.C. Qns. 22/9/62.
Bsq. The Lady of the Lake (Roy. 21/4/62). L.C.
D. The Lady of the Mill (Ast. 5/5/62).
F. Lady Tartuffe (St J. 20/6/53).
Oa. The Lady Volunteers. L.C. Waterloo O.H. Edinburgh, 2/12/67.

D. The Lakes of Killarney (Ast. 30/4/55).
O. Lakmé (Gai. 6/6/85). L.C.
[Music by Delibes.]
D. The Lambton Worm. L.C. Lyc. Sunderland, 17/3/77.
D. The Lamplighter. L.C. Stand. 30/6/54.
D. The Lamplighter; or, The Blind Girl's Protégée. L.C. Brit. 17/6/54.
F. The Landlady. L.C. Str. 31/5/88.
F. The Landlord's Dilemma. L.C. Gedney Hill Schools, Wisbech, 10/5/95.
F. The Language of Flowers (Olym. 24/5/52). L.C.
[By *J. P. WOOLER.*]
O. Lara (H.M. 31/1/65). L.C.
F. Large as Life. L.C. Terry's, 8/5/90.
F. A Lark in the Temple (Alex. 5/11/66). L.C.
D. Larks in a Cage (Roy. 31/8/63). L.C.
D. Lashed to the Helm; or, The Strike at the Mill and the Mutineers. L.C. Brit. 14/5/64.
Bal. The Lass of Gowrie (Olym. 4/4/53).
F. The Lass that Loved a Carpenter. L.C. Margate, 20/5/79.
D. The Last Appeal (Brit. 4/7/59). L.C.
D. The Last Cause; or, The Advocate (Amphi. L'pool, 25/3/68). L.C.
D. The Last Chord. L.C. Crit. 21/6/79.
D. The Last Dread Penalty. L.C. S.W. 9/2/97.
D. The Last Glass; or, Lilian Locke, the Widow of the Mill. L.C. C.L. 29/4/51.
D. The Last Moment (P's. Portsmouth, 11/10/75).
D. The Last Night and the Last Morning: A Christmas Dream (Brit. 15/10/60). L.C.
D. The Last of the Welsh Bards (Pav. Bridgend, 21/4/73).
Ca. The Last Overture. L.C. S. Shields, 25/2/92.
F. A Last Resource. L.C. R.A. Woolwich, 2/4/86.
D. The Last Sacrifice (Gt Yarmouth, 12/10/74).
D. The Last Slave. L.C. Adel. L'pool [at first banned and then, on 18/7/67, passed "in consequence of the change in American affairs"].
F.C. The Last Straw. L.C. Vaud. 22/2/92.
F. The Latch Key (Str. 13/8/55).
Bsq. The Latest Yarn of the Crusoe Crew (People's O.H. Ashton, 16/7/83).
C. Laura; or, Love's Enchantment (Nov. 20/6/88, *mat.*). L.C.
D. Laurette's Bridal; or, More than meets the Eye (Brit. 26/11/66). L.C.
Sk. The Lauri Family (Lyc. 11/10/58).
Ca. Law for Ladies; or, 'Tis so reported (Lyc. 14/3/59). L.C.
D. The Lawless Witness; or, The Convict's Vow (Lyc. Sunderland, 7/3/71).
D. The Law of the Land. L.C. P.W. Warrington, 20/1/88.
D.Sk. The Law of the Land. L.C. S.W. 28/12/99.
Ca. A Law Suit. L.C. Com. 26/11/85.
D. The Laycock of Langleyside. L.C. Qns. Manchester, 9/6/66.
Ca. The Lay Figure; or, A Serious Mistake. L.C. Pier Pav. Folkestone, 16/6/94.

D. The Lay of a Lady. L.C. O.H. Cheltenham, 28/12/99.
C. Leading Strings; or, Two Ways to Bring up a Son. L.C. H. 5/9/54.
C.Sk. A Leaf in the Life of our American Cousin (Reading, 22/11/71).
Bsq. Leah (Southminster, Edinburgh, 15/6/68).
D. Leah. L.C. Norwich, 25/2/64.
D. A Leap for Liberty. L.C. Qns. 17/4/62.
D. A Leap for Life; or, The Banker's Son and the Felon's Daughter. L.C. Eff. 15/6/61.
D. A Leap in the Dark (Buxton, 1850).
M.Ca. The Leathern Bottle. L.C. St. G. 30/1/84.
F. Leave it to me (Rotunda, L'pool, 23/4/77).
D. The Leavenworth Case (Halifax, 9/2/85). L.C. Gai. W. Hartlepool, 5/1/85.
D. Left Alone. L.C. Eff. 30/11/64.
D. Left-handed Marriages. L.C. Brit. 17/3/64.
F. Left to Himself. L.C. Lyc. 2/11/68.
F. Leg Bail. L.C. Empress, 24/3/99.
D. The Legend of a Soul. L.C. Com. 10/11/97.
D. The Legend of Mab's Cross (Wigan, 20/4/83).
Masque. The Legend of Spring; or, The Victory of the Sunbeam (C.P. 4/72). L.C.
M.D. The Legend of the Headless Man; or, The Spirit of Evil (Adel. 16/11/57). L.C.
F. The Leghorn Bonnet. L.C. Manchester, 5/3/52.
D. Lelio. L.C. King's Lynn, 3/11/75.
D. Lena Despard. L.C. O.C. 27/4/87.
M.D. Leon de Val; or, The Boy of Barcelona. L.C. Pav. 14/5/50.
M.D. Leonie, the Sutler Girl; or, A Countess in Difficulties (S.W. 9/2/63). L.C.
[By *H. RHYS*.]
D. Leon of Arragon (Stand. 22/5/57).
D. Leontine; or, Clorinde's Revenge (Bath, 7/11/70).
C.D. The Leprechaun; or, Bad Luck's Good Luck with Good looking after (Lyc. 28/2/59). L.C.
C.D. Lesbia, the Vestal Virgin (Torquay, 13/6/81). L.C.
D. A Lesser George. L.C. Aven. 20/6/98.
F. A Lesson for Husbands. L.C. D.L. 8/5/56.
D. The Lesson of Life; or, The Woodman's Dream (M'bone, 5/12/77).
C.D. A Lesson to Landlords (Str. 10/7/88). L.C.
D. A Lesson to Thieves (Soho, 22/9/59).
F. A Lesson to Wives (Soho, 8/11/58).
F. The Letter. L.C. P'cess. 1/3/54.
D. The Libertine's Ship (Vic. 22/5/54).
C.D. Lidiana. L.C. Aldershot, 5/8/85.
D. The Life and Adventures of George Barrington; or, A Hundred Years Ago. L.C. Eff. 2/8/62.
D. The Life and Adventures of Will Shakespeare, the Poacher, the Player and the Poet; or, The Golden Days of Good Queen Bess. L.C. M'bone, 7/4/64.
D. The Life and Death of a Drunkard. L.C. 13/3/58.
D. The Life and Death of Jack Sheppard (Grec. 20/9/60).
D. The Life and Struggles of a Working Man. L.C. Pav. 7/11/53.

D. The Life Boat; or, Foul Weather Jack. L.C. Pav. 2/1/50.
D.Sk. The Life Boat; or, Saved by the Sword. L.C. Var. 7/1/87.
D. A Life for a Life; or, The Reprieve (Grec. 25/3/63). L.C. Grec. 31/7/60.
D. A Life for the Czar (Com. Manchester, 9/7/88).
[Music by M. Glinka.]
C.D. Life in All Shapes (Soho, 3/3/57).
D. Life in Lambeth (Vic. 15/10/64). L.C.
D. Life in the Sunny South (Sur. 26/8/57).
D. Life in the Trenches. L.C. C.L. 31/8/55.
D. The Life of a Beggar. L.C. C.L. 14/8/57.
D. The Life of a Betting Boy; or, The Widow's Hope and the Lover's Fear. L.C. Bower, 25/8/52.
D. The Life of a Mill Girl. L.C. P.W. Warrington, 28/2/84.
D. The Life of a Miner (Grec. 25/4/66).
D. The Life of a Soldier (Brit. 14/2/61).
D. A Life of Guilt; or, The Avenging Hand of Fate and the Shilling Legacy. L.C. Brit. 7/5/51.
D. The Life of Ned Cantor; or, The Mysteries of Bordercleugh. L.C. Vic. 8/1/55.
D. Life on the Ocean (Barrow, 12/9/68).
F. The Life Preserver (Qns. Manchester, 22/5/76). L.C.
D. The Life Raft (Stand. 18/8/51).
D. Life's Highway (Stand. 4/5/57).
D. Life's Ladder (Stand. 14/5/55).
D. Life's Magic (Sur. 13/10/54).
D. Life's Mysteries and Woman's Devotion. L.C. Brit. 18/10/56.
D. Life's Seasons; or, Hearts and Homes. L.C. Sur. 2/9/52.
D. Life's Trials by Sea and Land; or, The Child of the Waves. L.C. C.L. 22/7/56.
D. Life's Troubles (Eff. 13/8/66).
D. The Life Task (P'cess. 22/2/62). L.C.
D. The Light. L.C. Str. 29/11/98.
Ca. Light as Air (Alb. Crewe, 1/9/70).
C.D. Light at Last (Oldham, 7/9/74).
D. A Light behind the Cloud. L.C. Hanley, 11/3/61.
D. The Lighthouse on the Crimson Rock (Birkenhead, 14/5/83).
D. Light in the Dark (Qns. Manchester, 16/7/83).
F. Lights of the Age. L.C. Ladb. H. 24/3/99.
Ca. Like Father like Son. L.C. Malton, 9/6/76.
Oa. Lilia. L.C. Granville, Ramsgate, 10/3/86.
D. Lillian Trafford; or, The Old World and the New. L.C. Col. L'pool, 3/6/64.
D. The Lily of Pontsarn; or, Morlais Castle in the Olden Time. L.C. Vic. Merthyr Tydvil, 22/7/93.
F. Limbs of the Law (Edin. 12/8/79). L.C.
D. The Lime Tree Chateau. L.C. M'bone, 24/10/57.
D. Lindlove's Abbey (Dundee, 27/3/77). L.C.
Spec. The Lion Conqueror (Ast. 3/12/60). L.C.
D. The Lion King (Vic. 4/8/51).
D. The Lion of England and the Eagle of France (D.L. 17/1/55). L.C.
D. The Lion Queen (Vic. 6/9/52).

D. The Lion's Den (Vic. 22/7/71). L.C.
D. The Lion's Den. L.C. Hanley, 25/2/82.
D. Lion's Love (Grec. 16/7/66). L.C. as *L.L.; or, Still in the Toils.*
O. Lisette (O.C. 26/4/73). L.C.
Bsq. Little Amy Robsart. L.C. Com. Manchester, 1/9/87.
Bsq. Little Amy Robsart from a Comic Point of View (P.W. L'pool, 22/2/72).
Bsq. Little Ben Bolt. L.C. Bijou, Nashville Gardens, 25/7/76.
C.D. The Little Blind Earl. L.C. Bow H. Guildford, 27/12/98.
P. Little Bo Peep. L.C. Bradford, 8/12/71.
P. Little Bo Peep. L.C. P'cess. Edinburgh, 17/12/75.
P. Little Bo Peep. L.C. Aberdeen, 28/12/75.
P. Little Bo Peep. L.C. Southampton, 22/12/76.
P. Little Bo Peep. L.C. Cheltenham, 31/10/77.
P. Little Bo Peep. L.C. Bath, 16/1/78.
P. Little Bo Peep. L.C. Greenock, 5/12/78.
P. Little Bo Peep. L.C. Leicester, 2/1/79.
P. Little Bo Peep. L.C. Burnley, 31/12/80.
P. Little Bo Peep. L.C. Manchester, 17/12/81.
P. Little Bo Peep. L.C. Leeds, 15/12/82.
P. Little Bo Peep. L.C. Nottingham, 21/12/83.
P. Little Bo Peep. L.C. Grand, Leeds, 10/12/84.
P. Little Bo Peep. L.C. Grand, Glasgow, 26/12/84.
P. Little Bo Peep. L.C. Worcester, 29/12/84.
P. Little Bo Peep. L.C. Portsmouth, 14/12/87.
P. Little Bo Peep. L.C. Leeds, 17/11/90.
P. Little Bo Peep. L.C. Manchester, 12/1/91.
P. Little Bo Peep. L.C. Glasgow, 9/12/91.
P. Little Bo Peep. L.C. Rotunda, L'pool, 19/12/92.
P. Little Bo Peep. L.C. Oldham, 15/1/94.
P. Little Bo Peep. L.C. Shakespeare, L'pool, 18/12/94.
P. Little Bo Peep. L.C. Roy. Chester, 10/1/96.
P. Little Bo Peep. L.C. Winter Gdns. Blackpool, 26/12/96.
P. Little Bo Peep. L.C. Oldham, 30/12/98.
P. Little Bo Peep; or, Harlequin Jack and Jill. L.C. Gai. W. Hartlepool, 22/12/76.
P. Little Bo Peep; or, Queen Butterfly's Ball and King Grasshopper's Feast in Birmingham in the Olden Time. L.C. P.W. Birmingham, 26/12/65.
P. Little Boy Blue. L.C. Sheffield, 6/12/77.
P. Little Boy Blue. L.C. Glasgow, 2/12/80.
P. Little Boy Blue and Red Riding Hood. L.C. W.L. 18/12/94.
P. Little Bright Eyes; or, Harlequin Blue-bottle Fly, the Spider and the Fairy. L.C. Worcester, 23/11/60.
P. Little Busy Bee; or, The Old Lady of Threadneedle Street (Brit. 26/12/64). L.C.
D. The Little Captive King; or, A Mother's Sorrows. L.C. Pav. 10/3/52.
D. The Little Demon (Str. 21/5/55). L.C.
D. The Little Devil's Share (Stand. 21/5/60). L.C. as *Dinorah; or, The Demon's Treasure.*
P. Little Dick Whittington. L.C. Alex. Widnes, 18/12/94.
Bsq. Little Don Quixote (Cheltenham, 9/4/83). L.C. Vic. H. Newport, 25/2/82.

D. Little Dorothy; or, Affection, Love and Gratitude, and the Fortuneteller of Briarly (C.L. 8/6/63). L.C.
D. Little Dorrit (Str. 10/11/56). L.C.
D. The Little Duchess. L.C. Hanley, 11/3/61.
M.Ca. The Little Foster Brother. L.C. St G. 5/3/77.
Bsq. Little Fra Diavolo. L.C. Grimsby, 30/6/81.
Ca. The Little Gentleman. L.C. P.W. L'pool, 2/10/67.
D. The Little Gipsy. L.C. Var. 17/8/88.
P. Little Goody Two-shoes. L.C. Greenock, 23/12/75.
P. Little Goody Two-shoes. L.C. Star, Ashton-under-Tyne, 17/12/77.
P. Little Goody Two-shoes. L.C. P.W. L'pool, 27/12/78.
P. Little Goody Two-shoes. L.C. Sur. 28/12/99.
P. Little Gulliver's Travels to the North Pole. L.C. N. Shields, 14/12/76.
D. Little Hand and Muckle Gold. L.C. Vic H. 24/6/89.
Ext. Little Jack Carpenter (L'pool, 15/5/75).
P. Little Jack Frost. L.C. R.A. Woolwich, 23/11/83.
P. Little Jack Horner. L.C. Alex. Sheffield, 14/12/80.
P. Little Jack Horner. L.C. Blackburn, 9/1/93.
P. Little Jack Horner; or, Harlequin Babes in the Wood and the Cruel Uncle. L.C. Bower, 21/12/70.
P. Little Jack the Giant Killer. L.C. Alex. L'pool, 16/12/71.
P. Little Jack the Giant Killer. L.C. Wakefield, 28/12/75.
D. Little Jessie. L.C. New, Richmond, 23/8/92.
[See *F. DARÂLE*, 1891.]
P. Little Johnny Horner. L.C. P'cess. Glasgow, 26/12/96.
D. The Little King. L.C. Hanley, 11/3/61.
Bsq. Little King Charles. L.C. Roy. Glasgow, 23/7/83.
Ca. The Little Laundress; or, False Colours. L.C. Plymouth, 12/11/56.
Bsq. The Little Madcap. L.C. Alex. L'pool, 10/4/84.
D. Little Mary Plowden. L.C. Lincoln, 18/11/96.
P. Little Miss Beauty. L.C. P.W. L'pool, 28/2/84.
Ca. Little Miss Wallflower. L.C. P.H. Gravesend, 20/6/95.
D. A Little Mistake. L.C. British Workman H. New Heddington, Oxford, 18/12/94.
P. The Little Mouse who built a House in a Christmas Cake (M'bone, 2/1/60).
C. The Little Old Man (Eden, Brighton, 6/8/1901). L.C. Globe, 28/9/97.
Ext. Little Prince Poppet; or, Old King Twiddle Twaddle, the Princess and the Naughty Boy and the Pump. L.C. Bower, 14/8/71.
D. The Little Ragamuffin; or, The World's Waif (Pav. 27/6/68).
P. Little Red Riding Hood (C.H. 27/12/58). L.C. as *Harlequin and Little Red Riding Hood.*
P. Little Red Riding Hood (Belfast, 26/12/58).
P. Little Red Riding Hood (Bristol, 26/12/59).
Spec. Little Red Riding Hood. L.C. Hengler's, 1/12/74.
P. Little Red Riding Hood. L.C. Gai. Glasgow, 16/1/75.
P. Little Red Riding Hood. L.C. Great Grimsby, 5/1/76.
P. Little Red Riding Hood. L.C. Gloucester, 5/1/77.
P. Little Red Riding Hood. L.C. Vic. Aldershot, 15/1/77.

P. Little Red Riding Hood. L.C. Dewsbury, 18/12/79.
P. Little Red Riding Hood. L.C. P.W. Birmingham, 14/12/80.
P. Little Red Riding Hood. L.C. Hull, 18/12/80.
P. Little Red Riding Hood. L.C. P.W. L'pool, 29/12/80.
P. Little Red Riding Hood. L.C. Bury, 14/1/81.
P. Little Red Riding Hood. L.C. Brighton, 15/12/82.
P. Little Red Riding Hood. L.C. Winter Gdns. Southport, 27/12/82.
P. Little Red Riding Hood. L.C. Roy. Glasgow, 18/12/83.
P. Little Red Riding Hood. L.C. Qns. Manchester, 18/12/83.
P. Little Red Riding Hood. L.C. Lyc. Edinburgh, 19/12/83.
P. Little Red Riding Hood. L.C. Rotunda, L'pool, 21/12/83.
P. Little Red Riding Hood. L.C. Newcastle, 23/12/84.
P. Little Red Riding Hood. L.C. P's. Bristol, 19/12/85.
P. Little Red Riding Hood. L.C. Nottingham, 4/1/86.
P. Little Red Riding Hood. L.C. Leeds, 15/12/87.
P. Little Red Riding Hood. L.C. Cardiff, 20/12/89.
P. Little Red Riding Hood. L.C. Edinburgh, 7/12/91.
P. Little Red Riding Hood. L.C. P.W. L'pool, 7/12/91.
P. Little Red Riding Hood. L.C. Bradford, 22/12/91.
P. Little Red Riding Hood. L.C. Sheffield, 5/12/92.
P. Little Red Riding Hood. L.C. Manchester, 21/12/92.
P. Little Red Riding Hood. L.C. Brighton, 22/12/92.
P. Little Red Riding Hood. L.C. Birmingham, 16/12/93.
P. Little Red Riding Hood. L.C. Richmond, 18/12/94.
P. Little Red Riding Hood. L.C. P's. Manchester, 20/12/94.
P. Little Red Riding Hood. L.C. Grand, Plymouth, 26/12/94.
P. Little Red Riding Hood. L.C. Col. Dudley, 30/12/94.
P. Little Red Riding Hood. L.C. Art Galleries, Newcastle, 31/12/95.
P. Little Red Riding Hood. L.C. Qns. Manchester, 26/12/96.
P. Little Red Riding Hood. L.C. P.W. L'pool, 31/12/97.
P. Little Red Riding Hood. L.C. Newcastle, 31/12/97.
P. Little Red Riding Hood and Little Bo-Peep. L.C. Cardiff, 21/12/81.
P. Little Red Riding Hood and Little Miss Muffet. L.C. Torquay, 22/12/81.
P. Little Red Riding Hood, Harlequin Boy Blue, the Fiend Wolf and the Butterfly Fairies of the Fuchsia Grove. L.C. Sheffield, 20/12/62.
Bsq. Little Red Riding Hood; or, Harlequin Prince Invisible and the Three Wolves of Wolfden. L.C. Var. 8/4/71.
P. Little Red Riding Hood; or, The Fiend of the Forest, the Ferocious Wolf and the Fairy of the Harvest Festival. L.C. Grec. 24/12/54.
F. The Little Stranger. L.C. Alex. L'pool, 13/4/81.
F. The Little Straw Bonnet Maker (Stand. 7/12/57).
F. The Little Sutler (Stand. 1/12/58). L.C.
P. Little Tom Tucker. L.C. Dewsbury, 17/12/78.
P. Little Tom Tucker sang for his Supper; or, Harlequin Hot Boiled Beans and Very Good Butter (Pav. 26/12/59). L.C.
Ext. Littletop's Christmas Party (H. 26/12/66). L.C.
Bsq. The Little Youth. L.C. Phil. 15/9/81.
F. The Lively Boy. L.C. W.L. 20/6/95.
D. A Living Death; or, Life in Russia. L.C. St J. H. Lichfield, 12/12/91.

D. Lizzie Shrie, the Brave Lass o' Haltwistle. L.C. Newcastle, 13/4/68.
D. Lizzie Stone. L.C. 13/4/68.
D. Llewelyn, the Last King of Wales (Warren's, Carmarthen, 25/11/72).
F. A Lobster Salad for Two (Stand. 4/6/59).
C. La Locandiera (Lyc. 11/7/56). L.C.
F. The Locket. L.C. Var. 18/6/91.
D. The Lock-Out (Adel. Glasgow, 6/7/74).
D. The Lock-Out. L.C. Croydon, 19/9/79.
F. Lodgers for One Lodging (Grec. 28/10/61).
F. Lodgings at Cleethorpes (Grimsby, 30/8/78).
D. The London Arab. L.C. Vic. 29/3/66.
D. The London Arab (Grec. 10/6/78).
M.F. The London Barber; or, A Cheap Excursion. L.C. Var. 4/11/75.
D. London by Night. L.C. S.W. 22/12/99.
D. London Chimes. L.C. St G. Walsall, 23/4/97.
[Title altered to *The Pleasures of London*, 6/11/1901.]
D. London Highways and Byways. L.C. Pav. 14/5/64.
D. London Labour and London Poor; or, Want and Vice. L.C. Pav. 16/3/54.
D. London's Poor. L.C. Empress, 30/8/99.
D. London Vice and London Virtue; or, Life, Love and Fortune. L.C. Vic. 11/1/61.
D. The Lone Chateau (M'bone, 23/6/51). L.C. as *The L.C.; or, The Count and his Companions.*
D. The Lone Star; or, The Seaman's Destiny. L.C. Vic. 22/7/56.
D. Long Age. L.C. Nov. 5/12/82.
Oa. A Long Engagement. L.C. Torquay, 21/12/92.
[See *W. ELLIS*, 1891.]
Dial. A Long Interview. L.C. Torquay, 28/9/96.
D.Sk. The Long Lost Brother. L.C. S.W. 17/5/99.
D. The Long Pack (Lyc. Sunderland, 17/3/79).
D. Look on the Bright Side; or, Better Late than Never (C.L. 28/7/66). L.C.
D· The Lookout and the Rescue (Brit. 14/4/62). L.C. as *The Ocean Child.*
Ca. The Loose Fish. L.C. M'bone, 2/12/52.
D. The Lord and the Lout (Vic. 31/1/59). L.C.
D. The Lord and the Peasant (Stand. 10/9/60).
F. Lord Bateman's Overland Journey (Adel. 17/4/54).
F. Lord Macninney (Vaud. 21/12/86). L.C.
F. Lord Mayor's Day (Folly, 30/6/79). L.C.
D. Lord Peebles' Secret. L.C. Bijou, 21/10/96.
D. Lorna Doone. L.C. Ladb. H. 31/12/97.
D. Lorris and Fedora. L.C. Whitehaven, 16/1/83.
D. Lost and Found; or, The Story of a Pocket-book. L.C. Pav. 9/10/62.
D. The Lost Bride of Garryowen; or, St Patrick's Eve. L.C. Qns. 29/10/62.
D. Lost by a Head. L.C. P.W. Birmingham, 16/3/76.
D. The Lost Fortune; or, The Story of a Pocket-book. L.C. Brit. 30/9/65.

F. The Lost Husband. L.C. H. 2/9/62.

Oa. The Lost Husband (Devonshire House, Belgrave Square, 21/11/84; Brighton, 16/2/85; Crit. 28/2/85). L.C. O.C. 6/5/86.
[Music by Lady Arthur Hill.]

D. The Lost Inheritance; or, The Idiot, the Roué and the Miser. L.C. Grec. 27/7/64.

D. Lost in the Snow, a Tale of Christmas Joys and Christmas Sorrows (M'bone, 8/2/64). L.C.

F. The Lost Letter (P'cess. 25/5/60).

M.Ca. The Lost Overture (Middlesborough, 25/3/92).

D. The Lost Ship (M'bone, 18/3/57).

F. The Lost Son Found; or, The Nigger's New Place. L.C. Lyme Regis, 14/3/55.

D. Lost £30,000 (M'bone, 24/3/56). L.C.

D. The Lost Will. L.C. Amphi. L'pool, 2/4/64.

D.Sk. The Lottery of Life. L.C. S.W. 26/10/99.

C.D. Lottie (Nov. 20/11/84). L.C.

O.Bal. Lotus Land. L.C. Connaught, 15/10/79.

D. Louisa; or, Love's Fidelity. L.C. Amphi. L'pool, 13/5/67.

D. Louisa Meller, the Musician's Daughter. L.C. Brit. 14/11/53.

D. Louis XIV; or, The Orphan Boy of Savoy. L.C. Brit. 3/4/55.

D. The Louisiana Creole; or, Article 47 (Preston, 30/5/91).

C.D. Love; or, False and True. L.C. Gloucester, 5/1/77.

C.D. Love à la mode. L.C. P'cess. Edinburgh, 8/2/75.

D. A Love and a Fate (Brit. 7/5/60).

D. Love and Chastity (St J. 9/12/54).

D. Love and Crime; or, The Fatal Passion (Grec. 24/5/58). L.C.
[By *J. M. KINGDOM*.]

Ca. Love and Dentistry. L.C. New, Richmond, 17/3/91.
[See *H. SWEARS*, 1893.]

D.Sk. Love and Duty. L.C. S.W. 16/9/95.

Bal. Love and Folly (Ast. 26/6/65).

D. Love and Hate (Brit. 12/4/75).

F. Love and Laudanum (Vic. 2/9/65).

D. Love and Lucre. L.C. Manchester, 23/11/60.

Oa. Love and War. L.C. Market H. Appleby, 23/4/97.

M.F. The Love Apple (Gai. 24/9/74). L.C.

F. Love Birds. L.C. Var. 16/7/83.

Sk. The Love Gift (Stand. 27/6/59).

Int. Love, Honour and Obey. L.C. Qns. 23/10/60.

Ca. Love in a China Cupboard. L.C. St G. 8/2/81.

F. Love in all Corners (Str. 19/7/58).

D. Love in a Mist. L.C. Richmond, 16/11/81.

F. Love in a Tub (Grec. 29/3/66).

D. Love in Humble Life (S.W. 16/10/62).

F. Love in Livery (Str. 6/7/57).

F.C. Love Letters; or, The Naughty Man. L.C. Oldham, 11/5/85.

Oa. Love me, love my dog. L.C. P.H. Croydon, 31/10/94.

C. Love on Crutches. L.C. Str. 20/5/86.

C. Love or Duty—which wins? L.C. Margate, 29/7/64.

F. Lovers at Play; or, Double Dummy and Hearts for Trumps (Str. 5/5/56).

F. Lovers, Friends and Enemies (Brit. 28/5/62).

D. The Lover's Leap. L.C. Grec. 30/9/63.

D. Love's Compact (Vic. 18/10/52).
D. Love's Devotion (M'bone, 30/1/54).
Ca. Love's Dilemma. L.C. E.C. 28/7/81.
Bal. Love's Labyrinth; or, The Duke and the Demon. L.C. Cremorne, 25/7/65.
D. Love's Legacy. L.C. Richmond, 28/11/82.
Ba. The Loves of Cupid and Psyche. L.C. Adel. 22/12/57.
Ca. The Loves of Venus. L.C. Caste Travelling Co. 23/3/80.
Bsq. The Loves of Willikind and his Dinah; or, The Cup of Cowld Poison (Edin. 18/5/54).
[See *J. S. COYNE*, 1854.]
Ext. Love's Paradise. L.C. H. 1/4/74.
Ca. Love's Politics. L.C. O.C. 8/2/88.
D. Love's Trial; or, The Game of Hearts. L.C. Brit. 3/12/57.
D. Love's Triumph. L.C. Manchester, 29/9/66.
D. The Love Test. L.C. Eff. 28/5/59.
D. The Love that Kills. L.C. S.W. 21/12/68.
Oa. Love wins the Day. L.C. G.I. 24/10/65.
Bsq. Low Life below Stairs; or, Transformations in Olympus. L.C. Cremorne, 8/6/67.
D. The Loyal Traitor. L.C. Grand, Southampton, 28/12/99.
D. Loyalty (Grand, Douglas, Isle of Man, 25/9/82).
Ca. Loyalty. L.C. P'cess. 30/9/87.
D. *£. s. d.*; or, Face to Face (Pav. 15/7/89). L.C. Alh. Barrow-in-Furness, 29/4/89.
F. Lucette's Husband; or, Jinks among the Breakers. L.C. S.W. 2/4/94.
Ext. Lucifer Matches; or, The Yankee (Adel. 25/9/56). L.C.
D. Lucille (Olym. 8/12/51).
F. Lucky Jemmy (Sur. 29/10/55).
D. The Lucky Stone (Brit. 16/7/77). L.C.
D.Sk. Lucky Walker; or, The Coster Girl. L.C. S.W. 8/8/95.
T. Lucretia Borgia, the Poisoner (Sur. 1/3/58). L.C.
D. Lucy Hatton (M'bone, 2/11/63).
D. Lucy of Lammermoor. L.C. Qns. 26/9/63.
Ext. Luna; or, Love in the Moon. L.C. Grand Pav. Blackpool, 5/7/92.
P. Lurline. L.C. Gai. Glasgow, 4/1/81.
P. Lurline; or, Sir Rupert the Reckless. L.C. Croydon, 24/12/74.
D. Lyddy Beale; or, Betrayed Innocence. L.C. Sur. 24/5/61.
D. Lynch Law; or, That Awful Yankee (Hull, 22/8/81).
D. Lynch Law; or, The Warden of Galway. L.C. Brit. 8/2/54.
D. Mabel Whyte, the Maid of Stratford. L.C. C.L. 24/11/51.
D. Mab's Mangle (Sefton, L'pool, 27/8/83).
Bsq. Macbeth. L.C. Grec. 28/5/57.
Bsq. Macbeth (R. Naval School, New Cross, 3/6/89).
F. The McTavish (P'cess. Glasgow, 5/10/96).
C. Madame Morensky. L.C. Lyc. 8/4/96.
Bal. Mad as a March Hare (Str. 6/4/57).
F. Mad as a March Hare. L.C. Roy. 10/4/79.
C.O. The Madcap Prince. L.C. M'bone, 9/9/84.
D. A Mad Crime. L.C. Goole, 29/3/95.
D. Madeleine. L.C. Sur. 1/7/51.
[The earliest performance I can find is St J. 21/6/55.]

D. Madeleine Dumas; or, The Child of the Foundling Hospital. L.C. P'cess. Leeds, 8/2/56.
D. Mademoiselle Fifi. L.C. Dumfries, 17/5/98.
Bsq. Mad-Fred. L.C. Sur. 13/11/63.
F. Madge's Adventure. L.C. Grec. 25/6/74.
D. The Mad Inventor. L.C. Alex. Brighouse, 31/12/95.
Bsq. The Mad Mother and her Lost Son (Scarborough, 21/4/84).
F. The Mad Painter (Alh. 6/10/79).
C.D. The Mad Woman through Love; or, The Child of the Island (Free Trade H. Manchester, 10/8/85).
D. Magawiska; or, The Indian Chief's Revenge. L.C. Pav. 5/6/51.
D. Maggie Lorme (Olym. 3/2/73). L.C.
Ent. Magic and Mystery (C.G. 25/12/55).
P. The Magic Axe; or, The Fairy of the Moss Rose Dell and the Fiend of the Whisper Valley. L.C. Vic. 16/12/59.
D. The Magic Bracelet. L.C. 4/10/51.
Ext. The Magic Branch of the Golden Glories of Fairy Land. (M'bone, 17/4/54). L.C.
Oa. The Magic Fife (Gai. 25/1/73).
P. The Magic Mistletoe; or, Harlequin Humbug and the Shams of London. L.C. Str. 22/12/56.
P. The Magic Moonstone (Brit. 26/12/99). L.C.
P. The Magic Rose; or, Harlequin Prince Progress and the Little Fairy Happiness. L.C. Var. 16/12/71.
Bsq. The Magic Shield. L.C. Gai. Dombwell, 21/12/96.
Ext. The Magic Wishing Cap. L.C. Brit. 22/5/65.
C.O. Magna Charta; or, A Romance of Runnymede (Athen. Lancaster, 12/1/88). L.C.
[Music by F. Dean.]
D. The Mahdi. L.C. H. 1/12/94.
O.Ext. The Maid and the Magpie. L.C. Vic. 2/8/52.
C.O. A Maiden Wife (Empire, 21/8/86). L.C.
[Music by A. Adam.]
F. The Maid of All Work (Grec. 25/7/61).
D. The Maid of Bonfleur. L.C. D.L. 14/2/55.
D. The Maid of Jersey (Sur. 6/3/54).
D. The Maid of Leyden. L.C. D.Y. 15/8/98.
M.C. The Maid of Mandalay. L.C. Metro. Devonport, 21/12/96.
D. The Maid of Mexico (Brit. 11/4/59).
D. The Maid of the Alps. L.C. P's. Preston, 12/9/95.
D. The Maid of the Ness. L.C. W.L. 31/3/93.
O. The Maid of Tokio. L.C. Drill H. Lyme Regis, 12/2/98.
Oa. Maids of Moscow. L.C. C.G. 27/11/74.
D. The Maintop Watch (Col. L'pool, 14/9/68).
F. The Major. L.C. Aquar. Brighton, 7/9/93.
C. The Major's Dilemma; or, Fine Feathers make Fine Birds (Jersey, 26/9/94).
D. Maladetta; or, The Spanish Maid and the Mountain of the Accursed (Brit. 1/6/63). L.C.
D. Malaeska. L.C. Warrington, 20/10/66.
Ext. Malala (Gai. 8/4/71). L.C.
D.Sk. Malice. L.C. S.W. 12/2/98.
F. Mamma's Opinions (St G. 31/1/93, *amat.*). L.C.
M.C. Mam'zelle Nitouche (Gai. 13/6/84). L.C.

D. Man; or, The Seven Steps to Ruin. L.C. Brit. 15/12/56.
C. The Manager in Love (H. 3/2/73). L.C. Bristol, 14/5/70.
F. The Manager at Home (Marionette, 5/7/52).
F. A Manager in Perplexities (S.W. 14/5/62). L.C.
Sk. The Manager's Room (Marionette, 12/1/52).
[See above, *The Manager at Home.*]
F. A Man and his Brother. L.C. Leicester, 30/3/72.
D. Man and his Master (People's O.H. Ashton, 16/7/83).
D. Man and Master. L.C. Woolwich, 31/8/94.
D. Man and Metal. L.C. Alh. Brighton, 12/6/94.
D. Man and Money (Sur. 7/5/60). L.C.
D. The Man and the Shadow. L.C. Alex. Bradford, 21/9/66.
F. Man and Woman; or, Slippers and Soothing Syrup. L.C. Leicester, 5/4/83.
D. The Man Cat. L.C. Vic. 29/5/71.
D. The Manchester Marriage (Stand. 17/2/59).
O. The Mandarin. L.C. Edinburgh, 21/10/96.
M.C. The Mandarin's Ghost. L.C. New, Walsingham, 30/3/97.
D. Mandrin (Sur. 28/11/64).
M.C. The Man from Borneo. L.C. Northampton, 20/6/98.
D. The Maniac Lover (Grec. 18/10/66).
D. The Man in Grey. L.C. Eff. 3/12/63.
D. The Man in the Iron Mask (Grec. 5/12/60).
P. The Man in the Moon. L.C. Portsmouth, 27/12/75.
P. The Man in the Moon. L.C. Cheltenham, 17/10/77.
D. The Manners and Customs of America (Sur. 26/8/57).
D. A Man of Iron (Gt Grimsby, 15/6/85).
F. The Man of Mystery; or, The Mysterious Waiter. L.C. Grec. 23/11/70.
D. The Man of the Red Mansion. L.C. Brit. 1/9/51.
F. The Man of Two Masters (Ast. 7/6/58).
D. A Man's a Man for a' that. L.C. Pav. 20/2/91.
F. The Man's Coming; or, Capillary Attraction. L.C. Grec. 10/6/50.
D. Man's Evil Spirit. L.C. Qns. 25/2/59.
D. Man's Folly; or, Drink. L.C. Var. 30/7/79.
D. Manuel of Spain; or, The Mounted Brigands of Valentia (Ast. 13/2/59). L.C.
D. The Man who couldn't die. L.C. St G. 20/6/95.
F.C. A Man with a Past (Str. 9/9/95, *copy.*). L.C.
D. The Man with a Past. L.C. Aven. 15/11/99.
D. The Marble Lover (Str. 6/7/54).
D. The Marble Maiden (Grec. 11/10/66). L.C.
D. The Marble Statue (Str. 18/8/56).
F. The Marble Statue. L.C. Var. 25/11/83.
D. Marcelle; or, A Woman's Work. L.C. Olym. 14/2/79.
D. The Marchioness of Brinvillion. L.C. C.L. 20/9/62.
D. March Winds and April Showers; or, The Old Folks at Home (M'bone, 21/5/60). L.C. Sheffield, 19/4/60.
D. Marco Schiarra (Grec. 12/7/60).
D. Marden Grange (Qns. 4/12/69).
D. Margot. L.C. Bradford, 24/7/79.
D. Marguerite. L.C. Grand H. Maidenhead, 7/12/91.
D. Marie; or, The Pearl of Chamouny (D.L. 5/2/55).

D. Marie Antoinette; or, The Queen's Necklace. L.C. Edinburgh, 27/2/58.
D. Marie de Meranie. L.C. Amphi. L'pool, 24/11/64.
D. Marie de Rohan. L.C. Qns. 12/8/62.
D. Marie de Roux; or, The Progress of Crime. L.C. Brit. 5/3/60.
T. Marie Stuart. L.C. H. 4/5/76.
D. The Mariner and the Delowar (Vic. 23/2/54).
D. The Mariner's Daughter. L.C. M'bone, 25/6/66.
D. Marinette; or, The Brigand's Daughter. L.C. Grec. 25/5/53.
D. Marion Delorme; or, The Cradle of Steam (Lyc. 3/1/59). L.C.
M.F. The Marionettes. L.C. P.W. L'pool, 30/9/76.
D. Marion Hazleton (Vic. 16/1/54).
D. Maritta. L.C. Grand, Croydon, 15/11/99.
D. Mark Jarrett's Dairy; or, The Wild Flower of Hazlebrook. L.C. Brit. 12/3/72.
D. The Mark of the Beast. L.C. Alex. Southend, 5/10/93.
D. Mark Ringwood: Two Chapters in the Life of a British Grenadier. L.C. Stand. 26/6/62.
D. Mark Winslow: A Tale of the Cornish Coast. L.C. Stand. 14/5/64.
D. The Maroon (Vic. 1/4/65). L.C.
D. The Marquis of Carabos. L.C. West, Albert H. 29/6/92.
Ca. Marriage à la Mode. L.C. P'cess. Edinburgh, 8/2/75.
D. Marriage Bells; or, The Cottage on the Cliff. L.C. Eff. 16/11/64.
Oa. A Marriage by Candlelight. L.C. Roy. 15/10/61.
Oa. Marriage by Licence; or, The Housekeeper's Elopement. L.C. Str. 17/2/58.
D. The Marriage Day; or, The Life Chase. L.C. Sur. 21/9/52.
C.O. The Marriage Eve. L.C. P.W. 24/4/91.
O. The Marriage of Figaro (Adel. 28/3/78).
C. The Marriage of Pride; or, The Marquis and the Cobbler (Grec. 21/6/60). L.C. Grec. 14/9/54.
F. The Married Bachelor (Str. 5/3/55).
F. Married Bachelors (Grec. 18/7/59).
Oa. Married in Spite of Himself. L.C. G.I. 21/9/65.
F. The Married Man. L.C. Park H. Camden Town, 14/4/90.
M.F. Married Moths. L.C. Booth's, Ashton-under-Lyne, 7/6/81.
F.C. Married Tomorrow (O.H. Chatham, 28/3/98). L.C.
C.D. A Married Woman. L.C. Pier Pav. Paignton, 29/9/99.
[This may be the play by F. Fenn, acted at Dundee, 30/10/1902, and at the Metropole, Camberwell, 24/11/1902.]
O. Martha (D.L. 11/11/55). L.C.
D. Martha; or, Richmond Market. L.C. Brit. 12/8/59.
D. Martha, the Factory Girl. L.C. Olym. 9/1/51.
D. Martyn Langton (Vic. 1/11/52).
M.D. The Martyr of Antioch (Lyc. Edinburgh, 25/2/98).
[Music by Sir Arthur Sullivan.]
D. The Martyr of Freedom (Coatbridge, 28/8/82).
Ext. The Marvels of Electricity (Amphi. Holborn, 28/12/68).
D. Mary Barton (Grec. 11/11/61). L.C.
D. Mary Barton; or, A Tale of Manchester Life. L.C. Vic. 18/6/50.
D. Mary Blane (Brit. 7/2/59).
D. Mary Clifford (Brit. 6/8/62).
D. Mary Graham (Grec. 8/12/62).
F. Mary Jones (Qns. 30/3/68). L.C.

P. Mary, Mary, Quite Contrary, how does you Garden grow? (Pav. 26/12/59).
D. Mary May; or, The Deceived One. L.C. Gar. 19/5/56.
D. Mary of the Lighthouse (Brit. 12/8/61).
D. Mary Price; or, The Adventures of a Servant Girl. L.C. C.L. 26/8/53. *French.*
D. Mary Price; or, The Memoirs of a Servant Girl. L.C. Bower, 1/11/52.
T. Mary Stuart. L.C. Dundee, 4/9/66.
D. Mary Stuart; or, The Castle of Lochleven (D.L. 18/3/50).
D.Sk. Mary Stuart, the Child of Misfortune (Str. 17/10/93).
F. Mary, the Maid of the Inn (Stand. 1/8/57).
Bsq. Masaniello. L.C. Com. 10/3/86.
D. Masked (Brit. 18/4/70). L.C.
F. The Masked Ball. L.C. S.W. 14/8/50.
D. The Masked Man; or, The Victim of the Star Chamber (Eff. 23/7/66). L.C.
D. The Mask of Bronze. L.C. Qns. 30/3/60.
D. Masks and Faces. L.C. Stand. 19/2/56.
[See *T. TAYLOR*, 1852.]
D.Sk. The Mason. L.C. Empress, 17/5/99.
C.O. The Mason and the Locksmith. L.C. St G. 14/7/79.
D. The Massacre of Glencoe; or, The Fate of the Macdonalds. L.C. Vic. 8/5/56.
F. Master Bell Blue (Brit. 22/10/60).
O. The Master Singers (Manchester, 16/4/96). L.C.
D. Master Walter (Soho, 21/3/59).
Ca. A Match for a Mother-in-Law. L.C. Ch.X. 17/2/70.
[See *W. REEVE*, 1859.]
F. Matching for Money; or, The Cobler's Stratagem. L.C. P's. Manchester, 19/12/68.
Bsq. Mathias; or, The Polish Jew polished off. L.C. Norwich, 20/2/83.
D. Mathilde. L.C. 25/4/50.
[The earliest performance I can find is Sur. 11/5/57.]
D. Mathilde; or, The Mulatto. L.C. Grec. 8/8/61.
C. Matrimonial (Nov. 9/6/91, *copy.*). L.C.
Ca. Matrimonial Advertisement; or, The Twelve P.P.s. L.C. P's. Glasgow, 30/9/63.
F. The Matrimonial Agent. L.C. St G. H. Canterbury, 20/6/98.
F. Matrimonial Bliss. L.C. Col. 31/10/88.
Oa. Matrimony; or, Six and Six when suited (Huddersfield, 14/5/83).
D. Maude Muller (Alex. Walsall, 1/11/83).
D. Maum Guinea (Brit. 22/9/62). L.C. as *M.G.; or, Life among the Slaves and Pirates of the Mississippi.*
D. Maurice the Woodcutter (Vic. 9/5/54). *French.*
D. Maxey's Money; or, The Fisher's Prize. L.C. Woolwich, 7/12/93.
Oa. May and December (Assembly R. Tunbridge Wells, 16/3/75).
D. May and December. L.C. P.W. Birmingham, 15/8/65.
D. May Blossom. L.C. Olym. 17/7/84.
D. May Dudley; or, The White Mask. L.C. Pav. 4/5/63.
D. May Myrtle (Dundee, 26/4/75).
Past. The May Queen. L.C. St J. 5/9/71.
O. The May Queen (C.P. 18/10/83).
[Music by Sir W. S. Bennett.]

C.O. The May Queen. L.C. O.C. 3/2/93.
Bal. The May Queen (Pal. Manchester, 19/12/98).
D. The May Queen; or, The Folly Fête (Leicester, 2/3/74).
Ca. A May Tempest. L.C. Edinburgh, 17/4/83.
D. The Maze of Life. L.C. Sur. 13/9/82.
Equest.D. Mazeppa (Ast. 7/7/51).
Bsq. Mazeppa. L.C. Vic. 16/2/66.
Bsq. Mazeppa. L.C. E.C. 29/9/80.
D. Mazeppa. L.C. Ast. 13/9/82.
Bsq. Mazeppa. L.C. Lincoln, 12/4/83.
O. Mazeppa (Com. Manchester, 27/8/88).
[Music by P. Tschaikowski.]
Equest.Sk. Mazeppa. L.C. N. Olym. 22/7/93.
D. The Mechanic; or, The Lights and Shades of Virtue and Vice. L.C. Eff. 8/4/59.
F. The Mechanical Babes in the Wood. L.C. M'bone, 21/6/82.
D. The Mechanic's Wife (Rotunda, L'pool, 13/8/83).
D. The Medal of Death (Eff. 19/11/66). L.C.
T. Medea (Olym. 3/3/83).
T. Medea (H. 1876). L.C.
Ca. The Media; or, Table Moving. L.C. Pav. 23/6/53.
O. Mefistofele (Gai. Dublin, 21/8/84).
[Music by Arrigo Boito.]
D.Sk. Meg. L.C. Empress, 11/9/99.
O. The Meistersingers [see *The Master Singers*].
Skit. Melodrama (Lyc. 2/5/99).
D. The Mendicant Son (Vic. 8/9/51).
D. Mephisto. L.C. Brit. 14/6/80.
Bsq. Mephistopheles. L.C. S.W. 27/10/94.
D. The Merchant of Paisley; or, The False Bride (Paisley, 7/11/70).
Ext. The Merchant of Venice. L.C. Assembly R. Preston, 4/6/96.
C. The Merchant Prince of Cornville. L.C. Nov. 18/12/96.
D. The Merchant's Daughter. L.C. Var. 10/12/84.
D. The Merciful Soul. L.C. H. 28/12/99.
D. Mercy's Choice; or, Shifting Scenes of a Workman's Life. L.C. Grec. 2/10/71.
D. Merely Players. L.C. P.W. 19/7/82.
Ca. Merely Players. L.C. Vic. H. Cowes, 12/2/98.
C.D. A Mere Scratch. L.C. Roy. 15/6/83.
Oa. A Merry Dell. L.C. R.A. Woolwich, 16/5/88.
Bal. The Merry Millers (Str. 2/10/54).
C.Oa. Merry Monte Carlo. L.C. E.C. 31/7/94.
C. A Merry Muddling World. L.C. Lyc. Edinburgh, 10/6/93.
P. The Merry Wives of Windsor; or, Harlequin and Sir John Falstaff (Sur. 26/12/50). L.C.
D. Mervyn Clitheroe; or, Many a Slip between the Cup and the Lip (Grec. 13/6/59). L.C.
[By *G. CONQUEST.*]
D. A Message from the Sea (P.W. Birmingham, 30/8/69).
D. A Message from the Sea (Sur. 1/2/73).
[This is probably the above, revised.]
D.Sk. A Message of Mercy. L.C. S.W. 20/6/98.
[Title altered to *The Martyrdom of Michael*, 17/4/1907.]
Ent. The Metamorphoses. L.C. Egyptian H. 6/5/67.

D. The Mexican Bandit; or, The Silver Digger of Perate. L.C. Pav. 26/10/63.
D. Mexico. L.C. Terry's, 12/9/95.
D. Michael Ceno; or, The Morning Star and the Gipsey's Brick (Vic. 5/6/54). L.C.
D. Michel Perrin. L.C. S.W. 17/9/50.
D. The Midnight Angel. L.C. Sur. 18/5/61.
M.D. The Midnight Spectre; or, The Fatal Deed. L.C. Adel. 3/9/61.
Bal.F. A Midsummer's Eve (Lyc. 1/10/61). L.C.
D. A Midsummer Jest. L.C. Athen. Hammersmith, 18/9/94.
Bsq. Mifistifix; or, The Evil Spirit of a Bit o' Love and a Revengeful Heart. L.C. St G. 26/12/70.
D. Might and Right (S.W. 8/12/52).
D. Mignon. L.C. T.H. Barnstaple, 1/5/86.
Bsq. The Miller and his Men. L.C. Crit. 22/3/83.
Bsq. The Miller and the Maid (Conservative Club, Cambridge, 4/5/98, *amat.*).
C.O. The Miller's Daughter (H. 15/5/65). L.C.
[Music by L. Williams.]
D. The Miller's Wife (Vic. 6/3/54).
C.Bal. The Mill in an Uproar (Ast. 31/5/61).
C. Milliners and Lifesguardsmen (Sur. 15/5/54).
D. Milliner to the King (H. 14/3/59). L.C. as *The King's Milliner; or, The Royal Salute.*
D. Millo' Taftie Annie. L.C. T.H. Inverness, 1888.
C. Mind your Points. L.C. P.W. Rochdale, 30/11/69.
F. Mind your Stops (Olym. 2/12/50). L.C.
Ext. Mine Friend and the Lake Fay. L.C. Vic. 6/4/52.
D. The Miner's Dog; or, The Murder at the Pit's Bank (Qns. Barnsley, 28/6/72).
D. Minnie Grey. L.C. C.L. 15/4/52.
D. Minnie Grey. L.C. Pav. 23/6/53.
D. Minnie Grey, the Gipsey Girl. L.C. Bower, 21/4/52.
D. The Minute Gun at Sea (Stand. 1/3/56).
F. A Miraculous Cure. L.C. C.G. 17/12/81.
Bal. Miranda (D.L. 25/6/55).
P. Mirka the Enchantress (Craig-y-Noo Castle, 22/7/95).
F. Mischievous Annie; or, A Lesson for Husbands (D.L. 12/5/56). L.C.
F. Misconstructions. L.C. P'cess. 2/4/62.
D. The Miser. L.C. Birmingham, 18/9/90.
D. The Miser of Eltham Green; or, The Last Man. L.C. Brit. 19/7/67.
D. The Miser of Tewkesbury (Vic. 17/4/54).
D. The Miser's Daughter. L.C. Var. 26/1/85.
D. Misplaced Affections. L.C. P'cess. 19/3/63.
D. Miss Betty. L.C. Lyc. 12/2/98.
D. Miss Formosa; or, The Road to Blue Ruin. L.C. Wigan, 1/6/70.
D. Miss Forrester. L.C. Scarborough, 6/76.
F. The Missing Link. L.C. Grand, Walsall, 11/3/93.
D. The Missing Mortgage (Sunderland, 3/9/83).
D. Missing Waterloo. L.C. Grec. 14/5/80.
F. A Missive from the Clouds (P'cess. 18/9/71). L.C.

Ext. Miss Leer; or, The Maid, the Marriage and the Malediction (Sur. 11/4/64). L.C.
Ca. Miss Macpherson. L.C. Albert H. Reading, 2/12/80.
D. Miss Multon (Duke's, 23/11/78). L.C.
F. Miss Prudentia Single's Soirée (St J. 31/5/58).
Bsq. Miss Red Riding Hood. L.C. Sur. 27/9/50.
D. Mist. L.C. West, Albert H. 10/6/93.
C.D. Mistaken. L.C. P'cess. Glasgow, 12/2/80.
Ca. A Mistaken Idea. L.C. T.H. Hulme, 29/11/98.
F.C. Mistakes will happen. L.C. Adel. 9/8/98.
D. The Mist before the Dawn (Amphi. Leeds, 31/8/68).
Bsq. The Mistletoe Bough; or, The Maiden that perished of a Pain in the Chest. L.C. Brit. 6/5/61.
M.C. Mistress Dorcas. L.C. Devonshire Park, Eastbourne, 14/1/95.
D. The Mistress of Hawk's Crag. L.C. Eff. 15/7/65.
D. Mistress Prynne. L.C. Olym. 4/6/88.
F.C. Misunderstandings. L.C. Albert H. Jarrow, 21/12/88.
Bsq. The Mixture. L.C. Cambridge, 24/2/93.
D.Sk. A Model in a Muddle. L.C. W.L. 23/3/95.
C. Modern Amazons. L.C. Toole's, 16/7/87.
P. Modern Babes in the Wood. L.C. Grand, Hull, 27/12/98.
P. The Modern Forty Thieves. L.C. Bradford, 31/12/95.
D. A Modern Godiva. L.C. Oldham, 13/7/86.
Bsq. The Modern Ingomar; or, Palaces and Peeresses. L.C. Str. 30/11/53.
D.Sk. A Modern Juliet; or, Romeo Revised (Terry's, 26/7/93, *mat.*). L.C. [as *Gentle Juliet.*]
F.C. A Modern Shrew. L.C. Croydon, 19/9/89.
P. The Modern Sinbad the Sailor. L.C. Morton's, Greenwich, 21/12/92.
D. Mohammed. L.C. Pav. 8/4/53.
D. The Mohicans of Paris (Brit. 14/7/73). L.C.
Ext. Mokanna. L.C. Lecture H. Mechanics' Institute, Nottingham, 20/2/91.
C.O. Molly. L.C. Canterbury, 17/9/84.
D. Molly Malone (Brit. 28/4/62).
Ba. Molly Maydew. L.C. P.W. Liverpool, 30/11/65.
D. Molly Sullivan; or, Poverty and Splendour (Brit. 14/11/59). L.C. 13/12/55.
D. The Moment of Terror (Grec. 9/6/62). L.C.
D. The Monarch of the World. L.C. Blyth, 21/8/85.
D.Sk. Mona's Dream. L.C. S.W. 12/9/95.
D. The Moneylender; or, The Life of a Vagrant. L.C. C.L. 13/8/61. [By *N. LEE, Jr.* Also played as *The Usurer.*]
D. Monte Carlo. L.C. Var. 4/5/87.
C. Monte Carlo. L.C. Terry's, 6/4/91.
D. Monte Cristo (Grec. 9/4/60). L.C.
R.D. Monte Cristo (Adel. 17/10/68; *revised*, Aven. 7/2/91). L.C. Adel. and Aven.
D. Monte Cristo (E.C. 20/10/88).
D. Monte Cristo (P.H. Woking, 6/2/99). L.C.
D. Monte Cristo. L.C. Blyth, 11/9/99.
D. Monte the Prisoner. L.C. Brit. 31/5/56.
F. A Month from Home (G.I. 27/4/57).

M.C. The Montilladios (T.H. Bedford, 18/1/97, *amat.*).
D. without words. Moonflowers: a Cobweb (Gai. 1/7/91, *mat.*).
[Music by Ivan Caryll.]
D. Moonlight Jack; or, The King of the Road. L.C. M'bone, 12/6/66.
D. Morality. L.C. Albert H. Nelson, Lancs. 5/10/82.
C.D. The Morays; or, A Lie for a Life (P.W. Blackpool, 24/6/84).
D. The Moreen and Sham Van Voght; or, Love's Young Dream. L.C. Pav. 23/7/62.
D. More Sinned against than Sinning. L.C. Blyth, 5/5/92.
Ext. Mormons. L.C. Folly, 6/5/81.
D. The Morning of Life. L.C. Grec. 2/2/52.
F. Mother and Child are doing well (Stand. 2/7/55).
D. Mother Brownrigg, the Painter's Wife of Fetter Lane; or, The Murder of Mary Clifford, the Foundling Apprentice Girl. L.C. Pav. 13/8/63.
P. Mother Goose. L.C. Torquay, 8/1/83.
P. Mother Goose. L.C. Grand, Leeds, 14/11/89.
P. Mother Goose. L.C. Alex. Sheffield, 26/11/91.
P. Mother Goose. L.C. P'cess. Glasgow, 19/12/92.
P. Mother Goose and the Sleeping Beauty. L.C. Manchester, 24/12/87.
P. Mother Hubbard. L.C. P'cess. Glasgow, 17/12/88.
P. Mother Red-Cap; or, Harlequin and Johnny Gilpin, his Ride to Islington (Adel. 27/12/58). L.C.
F.C. Mothers. L.C. Ladb. H. 27/5/84.
P. Mother Shipton's Prophecy, Seven Women to One Man; or, Don Giovanni and the Steam King. L.C. Brit. 17/12/55.
D. Moths (S.W. 4/9/82). L.C. Greenwich.
D. Moths. L.C. Torquay, 5/10/82.
D. The Motto on the Duke's Coat (Grec. 20/7/63). L.C.
[By *G. CONQUEST.*]
D. The Moulds of the Mould Manor. L.C. Sur. 30/8/56.
D. The Mountain Devil (Vic. 12/6/54).
[See *G. REEVES*, 1879.]
D. The Mountaineers' Dance (St J. 4/7/59).
D. The Mountain Flower; or, Unrequited Love. L.C. C.L. 15/10/64.
[By *W. TRAVERS.*]
D. The Mountain Guide. L.C. W.L. 31/1/95.
D. The Mountain Monarch; or, The Hero, the Champion and the Murderer. L.C. C.L. 27/9/55.
D. The Mountain Robbers; or, The Blind Sister. L.C. Vic. 3/3/63.
D. Mountain Torrents (Grec. 10/10/61).
D. The Mountebank. L.C. C.L. 15/1/51.
D. The Mousetrap. L.C. Edinburgh, 11/10/97.
D. Mowbray Chase (Brit. 26/9/59).
D. Moyra the Doomed (Vic. 2/5/54).
D. An M.P.'s Wife (O.C. 16/2/95). L.C.
P. Mr and Mrs Gulliver; or, Little Boy Blue, the Land of Lilliput and the Home of the Giants. L.C. Alex. Sheffield, 19/12/70.
F. Mr and Mrs White (Str. 15/5/54).
F. Mr Briggs in his Pleasures of House Keeping (Ast. 1/5/54).
C. Mr Flimsey's Family (P.W. Glasgow, 22/9/68).
Ca. Mr Hughes at Home (H. 2/7/56). L.C.
P. Mr Jarley at Court. L.C. Devonshire Park, Eastbourne, 28/12/99.

F. Mr Jolliboy's Conjugal Woes. L.C. Olym. 21/12/78.
F. Mr Pickwick's Little Mistake. L.C. Grand, Walsall, 24/9/92.
F. Mrs Chesterfield Thinskin. L.C. P'cess. 20/6/53.
M.Ent. Mrs Colonel Fitzsmythe's Bal Costumé. L.C. Birmingham, 19/11/50.
D. Mrs Daintree's Daughter. L.C. Ladb. H. 10/2/94.
D. Mrs Gardiner. L.C. St G. 9/4/88.
C. Mrs Gray's Secret. L.C. H. 18/12/96.
F. Mr Smith. L.C. Plymouth, 13/4/99.
Monol. Mrs Rawdon's Rehearsal. L.C. Court, 20/6/98.
D.Sk. Mrs Rip van Winkle. L.C. S.W. 30/11/99.
Oa. Mrs Speaker; or, Lady Legislators. L.C. Assembly R. Waterloo, Liverpool, 17/3/85.
F. Mr Webster's Company is requested at a photographic Soirée (Adel. 27/12/58).
Ca. The Mugwump (Court, 19/10/98). L.C.
D. The Mulatto Murderer; or, The Bridal Ring. L.C. C.L. 20/6/54.
D. Murder in Hoxton (Grec. 14/3/59).
Ca. The Murder in Leicester Square. L.C. Holb. 29/5/73.
D. Murder will out; or, The Fratricide. L.C. Leeds, 24/3/99.
F. Musical Bob; or, Sharps, Flats and Naturals. L.C. Bower, 31/5/56.
Oa. Musical Whist. L.C. Broom House, Fulham, 7/8/96.
D. The Musician's Daughter; or, The Lovers of Heidelberg. L.C. Sur. 24/7/50.
Ca. The Music Master. L.C. O.C. 5/8/92.
F. The Mustard Plaster. L.C. Mat. 30/3/98.
D. Must he die? L.C. H.M. Carlisle, 14/5/92.
C. My American Aunt; or, Dundreary in Difficulties. L.C. P'cess. Edinburgh, 4/8/64.
M.D. My Aunt (Vic. 10/9/64). L.C.
F. My Cook and Housekeeper (D.L. 9/3/54). L.C.
F. My Cousin Peppy (Stand. 16/4/61).
C. My Daughter-in-Law (Crit. 27/9/99). L.C.
M.D. My Dearest Anna Maria. L.C. Str. 3/7/51.
F. My Detective. L.C. Alb. 27/4/76.
D. My Fetch (Stand. 1/11/58).
F. My First Brief (S.W. 13/11/61). L.C.
F. My First Client. L.C. T.H. Brierley Hill, Staffs. 14/4/90.
F.C. My Friend from India. L.C. Gai. 18/11/96.
F. My Friend in the Straps (H. 24/10/50). L.C.
D. My Friend's Address. L.C. Rochdale, 10/9/85.
Bsq. My Gal at Tea. L.C. P.H. Sutton, Sur. 25/3/89.
Ca. My Husband's Secret. L.C. Soho, 2/6/58.
C. My Idiot. L.C. Ladb. H. 13/4/99.
D. My Jack. L.C. Albert Inst. Windsor, 7/1/95.
D. My Lady of Levenmore. L.C. Athen. Hammersmith, 18/9/94.
D. My Lady's Lord. L.C. D.Y. 22/12/99.
[By *H. V. ESMOND.*]
D. My Landlord. L.C. S.W. 20/8/94.
Ba. My Latest Opera (St. G. 24/11/94).
Ca. My Mice. L.C. Str. 22/12/90.
C. My Miser. L.C. O.C. 8/10/86.
F. My Mother's Maid (H. 18/11/58). L.C.

F. My Neighbour Brown. L.C. Gt Yarmouth, 9/9/84.
Ca. My New Maid (St G. 22/6/78).
F. My New Wife (Soho, 4/4/59).
M.F. My Noble Capting. L.C. Var. 10/9/83.
D. My Old Luck (S.W. 17/11/58). L.C.
F. My Poor Dog Tray (Vic. 15/6/54).
D. My Queen. L.C. Vaud. 8/4/89.
D. My Son Dick. L.C. Court, 25/2/74.
D. My Son-in-Law (Olym. 24/6/50). L.C.
D. The Mysteries of Audley Court (Ast. 11/8/66). L.C.
D. The Mysteries of Callow Abbey; or, Old Fidelity (L'pool, 15/5/76).
D. The Mysteries of Carrow (E.C. 6/10/88).
D. The Mysteries of Shoreditch; or, The Comb-seller of Victoria Park. L.C. C.L. 8/12/60.
D. The Mysteries of the Temple. L.C. Brit. 10/7/63.
D. The Mysteries of Wilton Hall. L.C. M'bone, 24/5/58.
F. A Mysterious Disappearance (St Andrew's H. Norwich, 11/5/69). L.C.
Ca. The Mysterious Letter. L.C. Leeds, 25/2/74.
D. The Mysterious Unknown (Brit. 19/12/59).
D. The Mystery (Sur. 19/9/63). L.C.
D. The Mystery of a Hansom Cab. L.C. Grand, Birmingham, 11/4/88.
[See *A. LAW*, 1888.]
D. The Mystery of Cloisterham. L.C. Sur. 26/10/71.
Bal. The Mystic Branch (Soho, 26/4/59).
D. Mystic Number VII; or, Withered Leaves. L.C. Grec. 12/11/72.
F. My Uncle's Card (Stand. 21/4/55).
Ca. My Uncle's Pet. L.C. Swansea, 24/3/60.
F. My Wife and my Umbrella. L.C. Grec. 30/10/57.
D. My Wife's Baby. L.C. Empress, 30/12/98.
F. My Wife's Cousin. L.C. Grec. 31/8/53.
M.F. My Wife's First Husband. L.C. Grec. 16/3/54.
F. My Wife shan't act (P'cess. 26/2/50). L.C.
F. My Wife's Lover (Sur. 25/4/59).
F. My Wife's Lovers. L.C. S.W. 30/8/99.
F. My Wig and my Wife's Shawl (M'bone, 19/2/55). L.C.
Oa. The Nabob. L.C. St G. 27/12/98.
Oa. The Nabob's Pickle. L.C. Aquar. Gt Yarmouth, 13/7/83.
D. Nadeshta, the Slave Girl; or, Russian Tyranny. L.C. Vic. 14/5/50.
D. Nameless; or, Philanthropy Rewarded. L.C. Temperance H. Gainsborough, 7/10/84.
Oa. Namouna. L.C. Lyr. Ealing, 23/10/82.
D. Nana Sahib; or, A Story of Aymere (Vic. 2/11/63). L.C.
F. Nap; or, A Comedy of Terrors. L.C. Shrewsbury, 10/5/81.
D. Napoleon. L.C. M'bone, 26/3/52.
D. Napoleon III (Str. 25/9/54).
D. Narcisse (Lyc. 17/2/68). L.C.
Bal. Nathalie; or, The Swiss Milkman (Grec. 7/58).
D. The Nation's Curse; or, The Effects of Drink. L.C. Dumfries, 24/11/79.
Ca. Nature and Philosophy (Lyc. 18/4/76).

D. Nature's Nobleman (Brit. 7/7/82).
[See *J. F. SCUDAMORE*, 1882.]
P. The Naughty Forty Thieves. L.C. P's. Bristol, 22/12/93.
Ca. A Naughty Novel. L.C. Ryde, 4/7/81.
D. Naulahka (O.C. 26/10/91, *copy*.). L.C.
C.O. The Naval Cadets (Glo. 27/3/80). L.C.
[Music by R. Genée.]
C. Naval Engagements (P.W. 25/9/65).
D. The Nazarenes. L.C. Nottingham, 23/9/93.
D. Nearly Stranded. L.C. Grec. 14/6/72.
D. The Necromancer; or, The Sixth Victim. L.C. Pav. 24/4/62.
D. Ned Dauntless. L.C. Vic. 2/12/50.
D. Ned Kelly; or, The Perils of the Bush. L.C. Brit. 23/10/80.
F. Needles and Pins (Brit. 7/2/60).
D. The Neglected Home; or, The Spirit Child's Prayer. L.C. C.L. 11/2/65.
F. A Neighbourly Action. L.C. Toole's, 12/3/85.
D. Nell. L.C. P.W. L'pool, 15/10/80.
F.C. Nelly Nightingale. L.C. Com. 20/4/85.
F. Nelly's Sister; or, She's a Man. L.C. Woolwich, 30/1/95.
D. Nelly, the Rag-gatherer. L.C. Vic. 19/10/52.
D. Nelson. L.C. Parkhurst, 11/6/92.
C.O. Nestor. L.C. Masonic H. Camberwell, 14/10/92.
F.C. Never Again (Birmingham, 4/10/97; Vaud. 11/10/97). L.C.
O. Never Despair (Adel. 25/7/59). L.C.
D. Never Despair (Norwich, 22/10/75).
[See *G. COMER*, 1887.]
F. Never Judge by Appearances (S.W. 21/3/57).
Oa. Never Judge by Appearances (Adel. 7/7/59). L.C.
F. Never Reckon your Chickens before they are Hatched (Grec. 7/6/58). L.C.
F. Never Satisfied. L.C. Mechanics' Inst. Swindon, 20/4/86.
D. Never too late to mend (Sur. 26/4/58). L.C.
D. Never too late to mend. L.C. Grec. 14/6/58.
D. Never too late to mend. L.C. Brit. 7/3/59.
P. A New Edition of the Fairy Tales of Mother Goose, with many Highly Coloured Illustrations (Adel. 9/4/55).
D. The New Endimion; or, Eastern Diplomacy (New P.H. Perth, 1/11/82). L.C. Music H. Inverness.
D. The New Fortune; or, The Gold Seekers of Carpentara. L.C. Qns. 24/6/53.
F. The New Hand. L.C. P.W. Southampton, 28/1/85.
D. New Lights (Sur. 25/4/64).
D. The New Magdalen. L.C. New Cross P.H. 12/4/84.
D.Sk. The New Model. L.C. Nov. 4/6/96.
D. The New Monte Cristo. L.C. Stratford, 14/7/92.
F. A New School for Scandal (Str. 29/1/53).
F.C. The New Secretary. L.C. P.H. New Cross, 20/2/88.
Bsq. A New Version of Uncle Tom's Cabin (M'bone, 26/1/57).
F. New Wags of Windsor (Str. 8/9/54). L.C.
D. New Year's Eve. L.C. Court, 14/10/73.
D. New Year's Eve; or, The Belle of the Season (Lyc. 1/4/61). L.C.
D.Sk. Next Department. L.C. Newcastle, 13/4/99.
Duol. Next Door. L.C. P.H. East Ham, 20/7/97.

F. Next Please. L.C. New, Richmond, 23/8/92.
D. Next Year's Morning. L.C. Norwich, 28/12/99.
Ca. A Nice Girl (Gai. 8/2/73). L.C.
F. A Nice Mince Pie. L.C. Col. Glasgow, 15/1/68.
D. Nicholas Nickleby (Amphi. L'pool, 28/8/75). L.C. Alb.
D. Nicholas Nickleby. L.C. Worcester, 1/9/76.
D. Nicholas Nickleby. (Str. 10/9/85).
D. Nicksey; or, Under the Star. L.C. M'bone, 28/7/80.
Oa. The Nigger's Opera; or, The Darkie that walked in her Sleep. L.C. Bijou, 12/3/61.
D. Nigg's Affinity. L.C. Bijou, 8/4/96.
D. Night; or, The Perils of the Alps (Pav. 26/1/63). L.C.
D. Night and Day; or, the Haunts of the Hunted Down (Pav. 3/10/68).
F. A Night at the Bal Masqué (Sur. 10/3/66). L.C.
F. A Night at the Widow's. L.C. Birmingham, 5/5/51.
D. A Night in a Churchyard; or, The Hag of the Hollow. L.C. Vic. 28/6/54.
Oa. A Nightingale at Home. L.C. Gai. 18/3/80.
F.C. A Night in Paris (Cheltenham, 3/10/89). L.C. as *A N. in P.; or, The Missing Duchess*.
Ent. A Night in Persia; or, The Shah's Festival (Ast. 9/6/51).
D. The Night Mail. L.C. Jubilee H. Weymouth, 27/7/93.
Ca. A Nightmare. L.C. Lyr. Ealing, 26/12/95.
D. The Night Porter; or, Dark Hearts (Grec. 14/11/61). L.C.
F. A Night Session (Glo. 1/11/97). L.C.
F. A Night with Burns. L.C. C.L. 8/3/53.
Ca. The Nincompoop. L.C. Crook, 30/3/98.
D. Ninety Days. L.C. Athenaeum H. Shepherd's Bush, 25/1/93.
Bsq. Nitocris; or, The Racketty Queen of Egypt (Str. 22/10/55). L.C.
[By *C. J. COLLINS*.]
Vaud. Nitouche (O.C. 12/5/84; Court, 1/6/96, *revised*). L.C.
D. No. L.C. Glo. 17/2/76.
[This was also entered as *Bleak House*.]
Ca. No Assets (County, St Albans, 17/5/98).
Sk. A Noble Deed (Oxford M.H. 6/11/99).
D. A Noble's Daughter. L.C. Constitution H. Oxford, 1/6/97.
Bsq. Nobody in Town; or, The Age of Wonders. L.C. Grec. 21/4/51.
D. Nobody's Son; or, Half a Loaf better than no Bread—A Night in the Workhouse (Eff. 12/2/66). L.C.
F. No Irish need apply (Str. 20/2/54). L.C.
F. Nomination Day; or, The Election at Rottenburgh (Greenock, 28/2/73).
F. No Misses; or, It's Two to One (L'pool, 25/8/73).
Int. The Nondescript. L.C. Str. 5/8/57.
C.O. Nora (Albert H. Edinburgh, 25/2/89).
D. Norah; or, Ireland by Night and Day. L.C. Woolwich, 5/1/94.
D. Norah Creina (Pav. 18/12/58).
F. No Risk, no Gain (Sur. 28/7/62).
D. The Normandy Sisters (Sur. 17/5/60).
P. The Northern Imp; or, Harlequin and the Spirit of Freedom. L.C. Gar. 4/12/55.

D. Not Dead Yet (Stand. 17/10/63). L.C.
D. Not Guilty. L.C. Var. 28/2/84.
D. Not Guilty; or, Wrong made Right (P.W. Warrington, 18/5/75).
C. Nothing but Nerves. L.C. Com. 23/5/90.
F. Nothing like it at the Zoo. L.C. Phil. 21/10/79.
F. Nothing to wear (H. 14/3/59).
Ext. The Nottingham Gazette. L.C. Nottingham, 27/9/73.
P. Noughts and Crosses; or, Harlequin Tit, Tat, Toe and the Magic Slate. L.C. Gar. 24/12/68.
F. Now in Rehearsal (Marionette, 12/4/52).
D.Sk. No. 5. L.C. S.W. 30/8/99.
Ba. No. 49 (St J. 5/3/60). L.C.
F. Number Ninety Nine; or, The Diamond Necklace (Gai. Glasgow, 16/3/82). L.C.
F. No. 70; or, Uneasy Shaving. L.C. H. 4/1/86.
F. Nos. 1, 2 and 3. L.C. Amphi. Ramsgate, 21/7/83.
F. No. 13; or, A Managing Director. L.C. Vic. 3/3/63.
D. The Nubian Captive; or, The Royal Slave. L.C. Margate, 15/6/57.
D. The Nuns of Minsk. L.C. Vic. 6/8/77.
D. Nurse Charity. L.C. Stourbridge, 7/11/94.
D. Nurse Dorothy (D.L. 26/1/55).
D. Nydia, the Blind Girl of Pompeii (Qns. Dublin, 18/10/69).
D. Oak Leaves and Emeralds; or, The Titled Grisette. L.C. Grec. 25/1/56.
D. The Oath and the Hour; or, The Venetian's Vengeance. L.C. Qns. 21/6/60.
M. Oberon; or, The Charmed Horn. L.C. Stand. 25/10/52.
C.O. Obstinate Bretons. L.C. Connaught, 1880.
D. Ocean Born; or, The Pirate Father: A Tale of the Southern Seas. L.C. Pav. 8/11/52.
D. The Ocean Knight; or, Golden Evidence. L.C. Brit. 10/11/62.
D. Oceola (Sur. 25/4/59). L.C.
F. The Oddities of the Olio (H. 28/5/60).
D. Odette (H. 25/4/82). L.C.
Bsq. O'Donoghue and the Princess. L.C. Manchester, 13/10/60.
M.D. Oello's Friends. L.C. Alfred, 11/7/71.
C. The Off Chance. L.C. Vic. H. 30/8/99.
M.Ca. Off to Algiers. L.C. Assembly R. Leytonstone, 16/4/94.
F. Oh dear! what can the matter be? (Soho, 28/3/53).
Bsq. Oily Collins. L.C. Soho, 18/7/61.
P. Okee Pokee Wangee Fum, how do you like your 'Taters done? or, Harlequin and the Gorilla King of the Cannibal Islands. L.C. Pav. 18/12/61.
Ca. Old and New. L.C. Montpelier Rotunda, Cheltenham, 17/11/92.
Duol. Old and Young. L.C. Grand, Fulham, 12/7/99.
D. Old Bishop's Gate (C.L. 25/8/51). L.C.
D. Old Booty (Brit. 9/7/60).
D. The Old Cherry Tree; or, The Orphan Cousins (Brit. 10/66). L.C. 25/8/66.
F.C. Old Chums. L.C. Athenaeum H. Shepherd's Bush, 10/6/84.
D. The Old Church Walls (M'bone, 29/11/52).
C. The Old Coat. L.C. Vaud. 31/12/97.
F. The Old Commodore (Sur. 5/5/64).
D. The Old Curiosity Shop. L.C. Grand, Walsall, 24/9/92.

P. Old Daddy Longlegs and Sir Regent Circus; or, The Race for the Golden Apples. L.C. Brit. 9/12/65.
P. Old Dame Trot. L.C. Sefton, L'pool, 8/1/83.
P. Old Dame Trot and her Comical Cat; or, Harlequin Little Boy Blue that lost his Sheep. L.C. Qns. 17/12/64.
F. The Oldest Inhabitant (Olym. 16/8/50). L.C.
D. The Old Folks (Stand. 28/5/64). [See *H. M. PAUL*, 1867.]
D. The Old Forge. L.C. Sur. 4/9/90.
Ca. Old Friends. L.C. O.C. 5/6/90.
[See *LADY VIOLET GREVILLE*, 1890.]
D. The Old House at Home (Grec. 1/3/60).
P. Old Isaak Walton; or, Tom Moore of Fleet Street, the Silver Trout and the Seven Sisters of Tottenham. L.C. S.W. 20/12/58.
D. The Old Ivy Tower. L.C. S.W. 26/12/95.
D. Old Kentucky. L.C. Bolton, 16/2/94.
P. Old King Coal. L.C. Circus of Varieties, Barnsley, 6/1/76.
P. Old King Cole. L.C. Corn Exchange, Maidstone, 28/12/86.
P. Old King Cole. L.C. Rotunda, L'pool, 8/1/97.
P. Old King Cole; or, Harlequin Hey Diddle Diddle the Cat and the Fiddle and the Four and Twenty Blackbirds baked in a Pie. L.C. Birmingham, 26/12/64.
D. The Old Lock Gate. L.C. New Foresters' H. Cambridge Road, 13/2/94.
D. Old London Bridge. L.C. Pav. 25/2/73.
M.D. Old London Bridge in the Days of Jack Sheppard and Jonathan Wilde (Stand. 12/3/94). L.C.
F. The Old Maid in a Winding Sheet; or, The Dream of a Coquette (Brit. 12/5/62). L.C.
P. The Old Man and his Ass; or, Robin Redbreast and his Eleven Hungry Brothers (Brit. 26/12/71). L.C.
D. An Old Man's Blessing (G.I. 13/6/68). L.C.
D. The Old Mill Stream. L.C. Qns. 16/9/50.
P. Old Mother Goose (Bower, 26/12/73).
P. Old Mother Goose. L.C. Qns. Manchester, 18/12/79.
P. Old Mother Goose. L.C. Corn Exchange, Maidstone, 24/12/91.
P. Old Mother Hubbard. L.C. Oldham, 16/12/80.
P. Old Mother Hubbard and her Wonderful Dog, Mother Shipton and her Comical Cat, Jack and Jill, and the Extraordinary Adventures of Master Tommy Tucker and Little Miss Muffet (S.W. 23/12/71).
Ca. Old Partners. L.C. St G. 2/12/80.
D. Old Phil Hardy; or, Family Troubles (Grec. 17/10/66). L.C. Grec. 28/8/63.
D. Old St Paul's (Soho, 14/5/59).
F. The Old School and the New (Sur. 1852). L.C. Bath and Bristol, 6/2/52.
D. Old Shadow; or, The Spirit of Conscience. L.C. Brit. 9/10/57.
D. The Old Story; or, A Life's Lesson. L.C. 3/1/81.
C.D. Old Times. L.C. P's. Bradford, 30/5/78.
D. Old Times. L.C. Var. 18/12/90.
D. The Old Toll House (M'bone, 30/9/61). L.C.
P. The Old Woman who lived in a Shoe; or, Harlequin Miller of the River Dee and the Fairies of the Barley Sugar Bowers. L.C. M'bone, 18/12/61.

D. The Old World and the New; or, British Pluck and Yankee Valour. L.C. M'bone, 18/2/61.
D. Olga. L.C. Lyc. Edinburgh, 8/10/83.
P. Oliver Cromwell; or, Charley over the Water (C.L. 26/12/51). L.C.
F. Oliver Cromwell's Sofa (Qns. 3/12/77). L.C.
D. Oliver Twist. L.C. Stand. 26/7/55.
D. Oliver Twist. L.C. Pav. 1/10/55.
D. Oliver Twist. L.C. Gar. 21/4/68.
D. Oliver Twist; or, The Parish Boy's Adventures. L.C. C.L. 11/8/55.
D. Olive Varcoe. L.C. Hanley, 5/8/81.
C.O. Olympus; or, Vulcan and Co., Ltd. L.C. W. Hartlepool, 30/6/97.
Ext. Olympus in a Muddle (H. 23/8/55). L.C. as *Olympus in an Uproar; or, Wrong People in the Wrong Place.*
F. The Omnibus (Str. 30/1/54).
D. On and Off (Vaud. 1/12/98). L.C. Devonshire Park, Eastbourne, 27/12/98.
Fancy. On an old Harpsichord (Brighton, 18/11/97).
Oa. Once too often (D.L. 20/1/62). L.C.
D. On Change. L.C. P.W. L'pool, 28/10/67.
D. On Chesil Beach. L.C. P.W. 10/12/94.
D. One False Step (Guernsey, 9/5/73).
D. The One Hundred Cuirassiers (Ast. 28/2/59). L.C.
Ca. £100 Reward. L.C. St G. 16/5/79.
D. One Hundred Pounds Reward—A Child Lost. L.C. Pav. 16/11/65.
D. One Hundred Years Old (Olym. 10/7/75). L.C.
C. One More. L.C. London Hotel Assembly R. Taunton, 22/12/99.
C.D. One of the Bravest (Brit. 2/12/95). L.C.
D. One Shade Deeper; or, Bond and Free (Eff. 16/2/63). L.C.
C. One Step from the King's Highway. L.C. Lyr. Ealing, 23/2/85.
Ca. One Summer Afternoon. L.C. Assembly R. Hanbury, 20/12/94.
F. One Thousand Napoleons (Brit. 21/7/62).
D. One Tree Square. L.C. Grec. 22/4/65.
D. One True Heart (Willington, 8/2/75).
D. One Witness. L.C. Brit. 21/8/50 (alterations in last act).
D. The One Word (Sur. 22/11/58).
D. On Foreign Service. L.C. Pleasure Gdns. Folkestone, 26/4/98.
D. Only a Boy. L.C. P.W. L'pool, 30/11/99.
D.Sk. Only a Common Sailor. L.C. Empire, Newcastle, 30/3/96.
D. Only a Dream. L.C. P.W. 17/3/94.
D.Sk. Only a Model (Vaud. 23/2/92, *mat.*). L.C.
F.C. Only an Actor. L.C. International, 22/2/84.
D. Only a Tramp. L.C. M'bone, 15/11/80.
D. Only a Vagabond. L.C. Connaught, 7/3/81.
O.C. Only a Waif; or, The Deadlock Mystery. L.C. Greenwich, 4/5/76.
D. Only for Life. L.C. Stand. 10/8/74.
F. The Only Jones. L.C. Var. 11/6/83.
F. The Only One. L.C. Ladb. H. 8/1/86.
Ca. On Shore from the Hercules (Greenock, 19/1/80).
M.F. On the Briny. L.C. Vic. H. Weston, 8/8/95.
[Title altered to *Miss Mite*, 1/10/1919.]

D. On the Sea Shore. L.C. Ladb. H. 29/7/91.
F. On the Spree. L.C. Huddersfield, 6/9/73.
D. On the Track (Bradford, 29/4/78).
D. On the Verge. L.C. M'bone, 17/10/85.
[See *E. S. FRANCE*, 1888.]
M.F. On Tour (T.H. Kilburn, 23/2/95).
Ext. Open Sesame (Adel. 9/7/55).
O. The Oracle; or, Christmas Eve. L.C. Vic. H. 21/2/65.
P. Oranges and Lemons, said the Bells of St Clement's; or, Harlequin and the Fairy of the New Year (Stand. 26/12/67). L.C.
C. The Order of the Bath. L.C. C.P. 30/12/98.
Bal. Orfa (H.M. 5/12/60).
D. The Organ Boy (Brit. 30/7/60).
M.D. Ormond the Unknown. L.C. Gar. 30/6/71.
T. Ornano. L.C. Birmingham, 27/7/54.
D. The Orphan of the Mine. L.C. Qns. 11/4/59.
D. The Orphans. L.C. Gt Yarmouth, 21/8/62.
D. The Orphans (Stand. 28/9/89).
Bsq. Orpheus and Eurydice. L.C. Str. 19/4/71.
Bsq. Orson the Great and Valentine the Small. L.C. Sur. 17/4/62.
D. Oscar the Dane. L.C. Brit. 5/8/52.
D. The Ostler's Vision (Grec. 15/8/60).
O. Othello (P's. Manchester, 8/10/92).
Bsq. Othello, the Moor and his Amour. L.C. Manchester, 23/4/61.
D. The Other Mr Brooks. L.C. Leicester, 26/11/59.
C.D. Ought we to visit her? L.C. Qns. 1/6/77.
[See *W. S. GILBERT*, 1874.]
M.Ext. Our Baby. L.C. Str. 10/12/78.
F. Our Colonial Relative (Tyne, Newcastle, 8/7/86). L.C.
C. Our Dear Boz. L.C. Scarborough, 24/10/78.
Ca. Our Elsie. L.C. T.H. Dover, 16/1/94.
D. Our English Admirals (Vic. 19/6/54).
F. Our Family Dentist (Stand. 18/10/58).
F. Our Family Jars. L.C. Empire, Burnley, 15/4/96.
Ent. Our Family Legend; or, Heads and Tales. L.C. G.I. 28/3/62.
D. Our Father. L.C. Vic. H. 30/11/97.
Ca. Our Female American Cousin (Adel. 30/4/60). L.C.
F.C. Our Flirt. L.C. P.H. New Cross, 30/11/97.
M.C. Our Girls. L.C. Middleton, 15/8/98.
M.C. Our Goblins; or, Fun on the Rhine (Circus Pav. Leamington, 18/9/82). L.C. Cheltenham.
D. Our Golden Wedding. L.C. P.W. L'pool, 16/6/76.
M.C. Our Greek Play. L.C. Ladb. H. 27/7/92.
F. Our Hussars. L.C. Qns. 11/3/62.
M.F. Our Irish Visitors. L.C. W. Hartlepool, 19/12/94.
D. Our Lady of the Willow (Vic. 11/3/54).
C. Our Lovers. L.C. Qns. Manchester, 20/10/81.
D. Our M.D.; or, Mad, Marred and Married. L.C. Grantham, 25/1/81.
F. Our National Defences (M'bone, 16/2/52). L.C.
Ca. Our New Lady's Maid (H. 17/7/52). L.C.
F. Our Nurse Dorothy (D.L. 25/1/55). L.C.
M.Ca. Our Opera; or, Before the Play. L.C. Assembly R. Bexhill, 16/11/93.

Bsq. Our Private Theatricals. L.C. Croydon, 18/7/94.
F.C. Our Three Hats; or, All Topsy Turvy. L.C. Eastbourne, 16/9/85.
Bsq. Our Traviata. L.C. (Sur. 14/9/57). L.C.
D. Our Victories in the Crimea. L.C. L'pool, 14/3/55.
F. Our Volunteers; or, Pressed into the Service. L.C. Sur. 11/6/62.
F. Our War Correspondent. L.C. Ch.X. 14/8/71.
Ba. Our War Correspondent (O.H. Leicester, 27/5/78).
C. Our Wives. L.C. Roy. 6/1/87.
[See *F. BLANCHARD*, 1885.]
D. The Outcast. L.C. Amph. L'pool, 16/4/66.
D. The Outcast. L.C. S.W. 31/7/94.
D. The Outcast Fortune Teller (Birkenhead, 18/12/82).
D. The Outcast of the Streets (C.L. 18/2/86).
D. The Outcasts (Eff. 6/2/64). L.C.
D. The Outcasts. L.C. Vic. 10/2/64.
D. The Outcasts. L.C. M'bone, 20/2/64.
D. Outcasts of Louisiana (Vic. 10/59).
F. Out for a Holiday (Northampton, 29/11/70).
D. Out of Evil cometh Good. L.C. Lyc. Sunderland, 3/8/67.
[Title altered and play revised as *The Priest and the Convict*, 4/6/94.]
F. Out of Place. L.C. Roy. 23/2/70.
F. Out of Sight, out of Mind (H. 4/8/59).
F.C. Out of Sorts (Windsor, 20/9/84).
C. Out of Town. L.C. Vic. Walthamstow, 21/10/96.
D. Outward Bound; or, Not Guilty (Col. L'pool, 17/5/75).
F. Outwitted. L.C. Holb. 15/5/84.
Ca. Outwitted at last. L.C. Ast. 30/6/64.
D. The Overland Mail (Soho, 26/10/58).
D. The Overlooker: A Tale of the Factories. L.C. 1/9/51.
Ent. Over the Border (Eyre Arms, St John's Wood, 16/11/70).
M.F. Over the Garden Wall again. L.C. M'bone, 27/5/82.
D. Ovingdean Grange. L.C. Vic. 5/1/63.
[See *F. F. COOPER*, 1851.]
F. Paddy's Ghost (M'bone, 11/5/63).
F. Paddy shooting the Moon (Str. 20/3/54).
F. Paddy's Portfolio (Str. 27/2/54).
Ca. A Page from a Novel. L.C. Gai. 24/5/81.
F. A Page from History. L.C. H. 22/11/50.
D. A Page from the Life of David Garrick. L.C. St G. H. Llandudno, 5/11/95.
D. Paid in Full; or, A Life's Repentance (Oldham, 3/11/73).
D. The Painter of Antwerp. L.C. H.M. 31/1/82.
D. The Painter of Terracina (D.L. 18/4/53).
F. A Pair of Boots (Olym. 4/10/73). L.C.
C. A Pair of Lovers. L.C. Com. 26/8/92.
C.D. A Pair of Red Heels. L.C. Kidderminster, 27/7/92.
C.D. Palladia. L.C. Vic. H. 26/5/98.
Ca. Palmistry. L.C. Edinburgh, 26/4/87.
[See *R. R. LUMLEY*, 1888.]
C.D. Pandemonium; or, The Student's Dream. L.C. Albion, 27/9/55.
M.Ca. Pandora. L.C. St G. 27/12/98.
Ca. Paradise Villa. L.C. Str. 28/9/81.

D. The Parish Waif (Vic. 19/2/66). L.C.
D. A Parisian Romance (Lyc. 1/10/88). L.C.
D. Paris in 1792 (Sur. 7/1/56).
F. The Parlour Maid. L.C. W.L. 30/11/97.
F. The Parrot. L.C. S.W. 20/6/95.
Ca. A Partial Eclipse. L.C. Market H. Red Hill, 9/12/92.
F. A Partner for Life (S.W. 6/11/58).
[See *H. J. BYRON*, 1871.]
F. The Pas de Fascination (S.W. 7/5/55).
Ca. Passing Fancies; or, Red and Blue. L.C. Sheffield, 6/2/67.
D. The Passing Hour (Southminster, Edinburgh, 13/12/73).
D. Passion and Pride (Sur. 18/4/53).
C. Passion and Principle. L.C. Olym. 17/6/61.
C.D. Passions. L.C. Grand, Croydon, 17/5/99.
D. The Passions of the Heart; or, Nature against the World (Albion, 26/6/76).
D. Passion's Penalty (New, Swansea, 16/4/84).
F. Past Midnight (Grec. 26/10/59). L.C. Grec. 24/3/55.
C.D. Pat. L.C. S.W. 6/3/88.
P. Pat a Cake, Pat a Cake, Baker's Man; or, Harlequin Bah-Bah, Black Sheep (Stand. 26/12/65). L.C.
C. The Patent of Gentility (Col. Glasgow, 6/2/69).
D. Pater Noster. L.C. Glo. 30/3/98.
T. Patience (S.W. 27/10/66). L.C. as *P.; or, The Purpose of Life.*
D. Patrick's Vow; or, A Rival's Revenge. L.C. E.C. 11/3/76.
[See *J. A. FRASER*, 1873.]
D. The Patriot. L.C. Stand. 31/5/61.
D. The Patriot Spy (Sur. 7/11/59). L.C.
D. Pat, the Irish Lancer (S.W. 12/3/88).
Oa. Patty; or, The Shipwright's Love (Bijou, 6/6/72).
D. Paul (Str. 8/11/52). L.C. as *P.; or, The Fortunate Slave.*
Bsq.O. Paul Clifford; or, The Ladies' Pet (Brit. 19/12/59). L.C.
Bal. Paulina; or, The Pupil of Nature (Marionette, 12/1/52).
D. Pauline. L.C. Edinburgh, 24/7/51.
[See *J. OXENFORD*, 1851.]
D.Sk. Pauline (Portman R. Baker Street, 16/5/92).
D. Pauline; or, The Chateau of Sevigny (Grec. 6/12/58).
D. Paul Periwinkle; or, The Horrors of the Press-gang. L.C. C.L. 31/10/54.
P. Paul Pry on Horseback; or, Harlequin and the Magic Horse-shoe. L.C. Ast. 19/12/56.
D. Paul the Poacher (Vic. 2/9/65).
D. Paul the Showman; or, The Dead Mother's Letter. L.C. Brit. 16/4/64.
D. The Pauper of Lambeth; or, The Tramp and the Treasure of the Seven Seas (Vic. 21/4/51). L.C.
R.D. Paying the Penalty. L.C. Barnard's, Woolwich, 26/5/98.
Ext. Peace; or, A Turkey and a Bear. L.C. Phil. 24/9/77.
D. The Peacemaker (P.H. Ipswich, 30/9/87).
M.Sk. Peace or War (Canterbury, 8/78).
Ca. A Peal of Belles. L.C. Bijou, 11/6/63.
P. The Pearl of Cyprus. L.C. Star, 2/1/79.
D. The Pearl of Rouen; or, Two in One. L.C. Manchester, 24/4/52.
D.Sk. The Pearl of Spain (St J. 11/6/59).

M.C. The Pearly Earl. L.C. T.H. Kilburn, 20/6/95.
Ext. Peek-a-boo. L.C. Oxford, 5/8/86.
F. Peeping Tom. L.C. Vic. H. 28/9/97.
Bsq. Peep of Day by a new (Lime) Light; or, Savourneen Delishus. L.C. L'pool, 19/3/63.
F. The Peerless Pool (Grec. 5/12/61).
D. Pemberton. L.C. St. J. 18/2/90.
C. Pentrobin. L.C. St G. 8/6/91.
Bsq. The People's William; or, Randy the (W)Reckless and the Grand Old Man of the Sea (Birkenhead, 12/5/84).
F. Pepper and Salt. L.C. S.W. 19/11/94.
D. Perequillo (Sur. 1/10/55).
D. Perfect Confidence (Olym. 10/7/54). L.C.
C.O. La Perichole (P'cess. 27/6/70; Alh. 9/11/78). L.C. Alh. 4/11/78. [Music by Offenbach.]
D. The Perilous Pass (Brit. 11/8/62).
D. Perils by Land and Wave (Sur. 11/1/58). L.C.
D. The Perils of Certain English Prisoners and their Treasure in Women, Children, Silver and Jewels. L.C. Brit. 14/1/58.
Bsq. Perola; or, The Jewel and the Duel (Rotherham, 19/3/83).
D. Persecution (Grec. 23/8/66).
D. Persecution; or, Man's Hate and Woman's Friendship. L.C. C.L. 11/4/64.
Ext. Perseus; or, A Rocky Road to travel. L.C. Qns. 21/3/64.
C.D. Pert. L.C. P.W. Birmingham, 6/8/86.
F. The Pet (Stand. 28/5/55).
O. The Pet Dove (C.P. 20/9/70). [Music by R. Gounod.]
Ext. Peter Monk's Dream of the Marble Heart; or, The Little Glass Man and the Fiend of the "Pinkiknoll". L.C. Brit. 12/3/51.
D. Peter's Pride. L.C. New Iron Hall, Eastbourne, 25/2/80.
C. Peter Stuyvesant. L.C. E.C. 15/11/99.
C.O. Peter the Shipwright (Gai. 15/4/71). L.C.
P. Peter Wilkins (Ast. 26/12/60). L.C.
P. Peter Wilkins. L.C. Corn Exchange, Maidstone, 24/12/83.
P. Peter Wilkins. L.C. P'cess. Glasgow, 12/12/89.
P. Peter Wilkins and the Flying Indians; or, The Wild Man of the Loadstone Islands. L.C. Grec. 21/12/57.
D. The Pet Heiress; or, The Gipsy's Secret. L.C. Eff. 25/9/64.
C.D. The Pet of the Public. L.C. Vaud. 10/11/97.
D. Petrolengro. L.C. Lyr. Hammersmith, 13/7/91.
Oa. Petruccio. L.C. C.G. 25/7/95.
F. The Pets of the Ballet (Str. 12/6/54).
D. The Phantom. L.C. Adel. 17/4/62.
D. The Phantom Captain (Grec. 28/9/64). L.C.
D. The Phantom Fight (Grec. 4/6/63).
D. A Phantom Love; or, A Woman's Whim. L.C. St G. 26/11/67.
D. The Phantom Lover (Sur. 23/6/60).
D. The Phantom of the Barque (Vic. 13/12/52).
F. The Phantom Wives (Str. 1/10/57). L.C. as *The Phantom Brides*.
D. Philippe del Turbillino; or, The Wreck and the Rescue. L.C. Qns. 21/5/63.
D. Phillip Quarl (Brit. 21/10/61).

Ca. Phobus' Fix (D.L. 28/2/70). L.C.
F. The Photograph (Sur. 21/9/61). L.C.
M.Ca. A Photographic Fog. L.C. P's. Kew Bridge, 12/2/98.
Ca. Photographs. L.C. Str. 13/2/84.
Ca. Photography. L.C. Star, Swansea, 30/1/76.
D. Phroso. L.C. D.Y. 30/12/98.
D. Phyllis Thorpe; or, The Cloud and the Silver Lining. L.C. C.L. 8/1/55.
F. Physic. L.C. Glo. 9/10/88.
D. The Physician's Wife (Grec. 4/10/58).
D. Picked up at Sea [see *Found at Sea*].
D. The Picklock of Paris (Eff. 27/10/66).
D. Pierre Brouillard; or, The Rats of the Seine. L.C. M'bone, 30/11/65.
Bal. Pierrot (Sur. 18/5/54).
Ext. Pierrot of the Minute. L.C. T.H. Chelsea, 16/11/92.
Oa. Piffardino. L.C. Lyr. Ealing, 23/10/82.
F.C. Pigeons and Hawks. L.C. Grec. 14/2/56.
D. Pigeonwiddy's Perils; or, The Spare Bed (Str. 1/5/54).
D. The Pilot's Son (Stand. 1/9/51).
D. Pinch (Sur. 18/9/58).
D. The Pioneers of America (Lyc. 22/10/60). L.C. as *Pioneers; or, The Maid of the Warpath.*
D. Piquillo Allegra; or, The Adventurer (Grec. 5/9/61). L.C.
O.D. The Pirate. L.C. T.H. Glasgow, 30/1/89.
D. The Pirate Queen; or, The Cataract of the Giant's Rock. L.C. Qns. 30/10/50.
D. The Pirate's Love; or, Ocean Birds of Prey (Grec. 6/9/60). L.C.
D. The Pirates of the Flowery Land. L.C. Pav. 19/10/64.
D. The Pirates of the Savannah (Stand. 13/5/61). L.C.
D. The Pirate's Wife (Tyne, Newcastle, 16/4/70).
Ext. The Piratical Pirate of the Precipitous Precipice (C.P. 1/8/63).
Ca. A Piscatorial Adventure. L.C. Dumfries, 27/5/87.
F. Pity the Poor Blind (Lyc. 8/5/58). L.C.
D. Pity the Sorrows of a Poor Old Man; or, Love Rules the World. L.C. C.L. 24/1/66.
Ext. Pizarro. L.C. D.L. 12/9/56.
Bsq. Pizarro, the Great Tyrant; or, The Little Wonder. L.C. Brit. 10/6/61.
D.Sk. A Plague o' both your Houses; or, The Double-barrelled Gun Trick (Str. 17/1/56). L.C.
C. The Plague of the Family. L.C. Grec. 31/1/54.
Ca. Planchette; or, The Happy Medium. L.C. Vic. H. 16/5/90.
D. The Planter's Wife. L.C. Darwen, 28/3/85.
F. Playing First Fiddle; or, Follow my Leader (Adel. 1/4/50). L.C.
Bsq. Playing with Water; or, Pearls of the Rhine. L.C. Bower, 6/2/62.
F. A Pleasant Time of it. L.C. Str. 2/2/58.
P. Plum Pudding and Roast Beef; or, Harlequin Ninepins and the Card King of the Island of Games. L.C. Stand. 20/12/53.
Duol. The Plunger. L.C. Empress, 13/4/99.
C.O. Poala. L.C. Roy. Chester, 2/5/89.
D. Poccahontas; or, The English Tar and the Indian Princess. L.C. Margate, 15/6/57.

F. The Poetess. L.C. Court, 5/7/92.
F. Poetry and Poison (Plymouth, 11/9/76).
D. The Poet's Slave (Olym. 25/2/50). L.C.
D. The Poisoned Mask. L.C. Qns. 16/4/64.
[By *W. E. SUTER*.]
D. The Poisoner of Venice. L.C. Qns. 5/12/60; additional act licensed Qns. 12/11/61.
C. A Political Woman. L.C. Com. 6/10/94.
F. Poll Practice (Marionette, 1/3/52).
C. Polly and Joe Stubbs. L.C. 3/9/76.
Bsq. Polly Middles. L.C. S.W. 8/3/92.
D. Pompeii (Stand. 25/4/58).
P. Poonowing Kewang; or, Harlequin Hokey Pokey and the King of the Cannibal Islands. L.C. Ashton-under-Lyne, 12/12/51.
D. Poor but honest. L.C. Bower, 11/2/70.
D. The Poor Carpenter and his Family (Brit. 3/10/59). L.C. as *A Poor Man's Trials*.
Ba. Poor Dick. L.C. Rotunda, L'pool, 5/5/90.
D. The Poor Girl. L.C. Eff. 8/7/63.
D. Poor Jack; or, The Wreck of the Vampyre (Gt Yarmouth, 26/4/75).
D.Sk. Poor Jack's Luck. L.C. S.W. 29/3/95.
M.D. Poor Joe of Horsemonger Lane; or, The Child of the Hempen Widow. L.C. C.L. 25/9/61.
D. Poor Little Jo (Park, 2/7/77).
D. A Poor Man's Trials. L.C. Oddfellows' H. Stalybridge, 4/3/80.
D. The Poor Needlewoman of London (M'bone, 14/6/58).
D. Poor Ray, the Drummer Boy. L.C. Brit. 1/7/69.
D. Poor Tom (Sur. 8/9/51).
F.C. Poor Tommy (O.H. Chatham, 26/4/97; Str. 6/12/97, as *The Triple Alliance*). L.C.
M.F. Poor Unlucky Bob. L.C. Var. 23/7/85.
F. Pop goes the Weasel (C.L. 23/5/53).
F. Pop goes the Weasel; or, The Adventures of the Weasel Family (Stand. 2/5/53). L.C.
F. Positive and Negative. L.C. York, 11/9/99.
F. A Possible Case. L.C. Stratford, 22/3/88.
F. A Possible Exception. L.C. 24/4/73.
F. The Postal Card (Edinburgh, 13/2/71).
O. The Postillion of Longjumeau (Lyc. Edinburgh, 10/12/92).
D. Post Office Frauds (Blackburn, 24/10/70).
F.C. The Potentate. L.C. Court, 30/3/98.
F.C. Pothooks; or, The Landlady. L.C. Cardiff, 11/6/83.
F. Potocatapelto. L.C. Gai. 10/1/77.
F. A Powerful Party (Olym. 18/8/62). L.C.
D. The Power of Gold (Vic. 19/6/65). L.C. as *The P. of G.; or, Honesty the Best Policy*.
[By *W. R. OSMAN*.]
D. The Power of Love. L.C. Park, 14/2/81.
[See *H. LINDLEY*, 1888.]
D. The Power of Truth (Sur. 4/5/61).
D. The Prairie Flower (Brit. 19/11/60). L.C.
C. Prawns and Pommery. L.C. Com. 3/1/84.
Bsq. Precious Little Crusoe. L.C. Baths, Worple Road, Wimbledon, 15/1/94.

Ext. The Prentice. L.C. Gai. Brighton, 18/3/95.

C.D. Pretence. L.C. Roy. 7/9/96.

Ext. Pretty Blue Belle and the Ugly Beast (M'bone, 24/12/60). L.C. as *The Pretty Princess and the Ugly Beast; or, Harlequin King of Corr Castle.*

F. The Pretty Gipsey and the Bullfighter (H. 17/9/55).

C. The Pretty Girls of Stilberg (Adel. 20/6/55).

P. The Pretty Princess and the Ugly Beast [see *Pretty Blue Bells*].

Ca. A Pretty Request. L.C. St G. 15/6/85.

C. The Preux Chevalier; or, The Peer and the Peasant. L.C. Sur. 12/4/53.

D. Pride and Patience (Pav. 24/1/59).

D. The Pride of Fallen Pine. L.C. S.W. 16/7/94.

R.C. The Pride of Jerrico. L.C. St J. 12/7/99.

D. The Pride of Life (Grec. 26/2/63).

D. The Priest and the Convict [see *Out of Evil cometh Good*].

C. The Prime Minister. L.C. Bradford, 30/11/87.

P. Prince Amabel, Mother Goose; or, Little Boy Blue and Jenny Wren. L.C. Bower, 26/12/73.

Oa. Prince and Peasant. L.C. Ladb. H. 16/11/81.

Bsq. The Prince and the Fairy. L.C. Vic. 27/5/57.

P. The Prince and the Lion King; or, Harlequin, the Invisible Cap and the Fairy Queen that was changed into a Frog. L.C. Stand. 24/12/63.

P. The Prince and the Ogre; or, Queen Grasshopper and the Glow-worms of Glow-worm Glade (Brit. 31/12/60). L.C.

P. Prince Blue Cap; or, Harlequin Mermaid and her Misty Mate. L.C. P's. Landport, 21/12/76.

P. Prince Brilliantino. L.C. Aquar. Brighton, 14/12/88.

C.D. Prince Carlo's Party. L.C. Nov. 14/2/87.

Ext. Prince Cherry and Princess Fair Star; or, The Jewelled Children of the Enchanted Isle (Str. 18/6/55). L.C.
[By *C. J. COLLINS.*]

P. Prince Fortune and Prince Fatal; or, The Queen Silverwing of the Butterfly Bower of Brilliants and Harlequin King Stony Batter. L.C. Vic. 21/12/54.

D. The Prince of Jerusalem. L.C. Grand, Fulham, 28/12/99.

Oa. The Prince of Madagascar. L.C. D.L. 28/5/84.

F. A Prince of Mischance (P.W. Southampton, 7/10/97, *copy.*). L.C.

P. The Prince of Pearls; or, Harlequin and Jane Shore the Queen of the Grapes (Sur. 24/12/55). L.C.

P. The Prince of the Peaceful Islands; or, Harlequin, the Magic Pearl and the Fairy Amazon (S.W. 26/12/63). L.C.

F. The Prince of Wales's Visit (Scarborough, 22/10/69).

P. Prince Peacock and the Queen of Spite; or, The Fountain of Eternal Youth (Brit. 1/1/59). L.C.

Ext. Prince Pigmy and Gorillacum (Grec. 20/3/62).

P. Prince Pippo and the Fair Mayde of Islington; or, Harlequin the Fairy Magpie and the Twelve Magic Spoons (Alex. 26/12/66). L.C.

Ext. Princess Badoura. L.C. Gai. Hastings, 27/5/87.

P. Princess Charming; or, The Lovebirds of Fairyland (R.A. Woolwich, 26/12/77).

D. Princess George (P's. 20/1/85). L.C.
Ext. The Princess of the Burning Eyes. L.C. Grec. 14/9/54.
P. The Princess of the Pearl Island; or, The Three Kingdoms of Pearl, Gold and Silver (Brit. 24/12/66). L.C.
Ext. Princess Pansy. L.C. P'cess. Glasgow, 11/12/91.
Ext. Princess Pocahontas. L.C. Corn Exchange, Maidstone, 19/12/94.
Ext. The Princess who lost her Head (Str. 24/12/57).
D.D. Principal and Interest. L.C. Brighton, 15/9/81.
F. Printers' Squabbles. L.C. Soho, 20/2/52.
Ca. Priscella; or, The Maid and the Monarch. L.C. Ladb. H. 25/4/89.
D. The Prisoner of Ham; or, The Sealed Packet. L.C. Brit. 19/10/55.
D. The Prisoner of Lyons (Vic. 17/5/54).
Oa. Prisoners at the Bar. L.C. Roy. 13/4/81.
[See *C. H. ROSS*, 1878.]
D. The Prisoners of the Ball; or, Honour's Test (Sur. 26/12/60). L.C.
D. The Prisoner's Daughter. L.C. Guildhall, Winchester, 3/2/87.
D. Private Life (Lyr. Ealing, 1/7/82).
D.Sk. Private Makeland. L.C. Bijou, 31/12/95.
F. The Prizes. L.C. Ladb. H. 25/8/91.
[See *O. BOOTH*, 1885.]
F. The Professor (Norwich, 12/3/68). L.C.
C. The Professor. L.C. P.W. L'pool, 23/4/83.
C.O. The Professor. L.C. Bradford, 10/10/91.
F. Professor—of what? (St J. 6/10/66). L.C.
M.F. Professor Sick War. L.C. St J. Wrexham, 10/10/98.
C.D. The Professor's Novel. L.C. T.H. Waterloo, L'pool, 8/4/96.
F. Professor Wiggles; or, A Tale of a Wig. L.C. Sur. 23/5/70.
D. A Profligate's Career (Brit. 8/9/62). L.C. as *Orlando the Outcast*.
D. The Progress of Crime (Brit. 26/3/68).
D. Promised in Pique (Gai. 16/4/85).
Ext. A Proper Fairy. L.C. Var. 17/10/83.
D. The Prophet. L.C. Manchester, 10/2/51.
O. The Prophet. L.C. Sur. 31/7/54.
O. The Prophet (Court, L'pool, 2/3/92).
Bsq. Prospero; or, The King of the Caliban Islands (Imp. 26/12/83). L.C.
Oa. Psychic Force; or, Singing in One Lesson. L.C. Gai. 1/5/72.
Ext. Puck (Lyr. Hammersmith, 17/11/90.
Ext. Punch à la Romaine (Marionette, 31/5/52).
P. Punch and Judy (St J. 24/12/59). L.C.
P. Punch and Judy; or, Harlequin and his Dog Toby. L.C. Brit. 19/12/53.
P. Punch and Judy; or, Harlequin Prince Valiant and Shallabilla, the Good Little Fairy of the Wood (Grec. 26/12/64). L.C.
F. Punch in Naples (Soho, 18/11/58).
F. Pup; or, A Dog in the Manger. L.C. P'cess. 16/7/83.
M.F. The Pupil of an Architect. L.C. 13/12/71.
F. The Puppet. L.C. O.H. Chatham, 28/9/97.
D.Sk. Puppet Town. L.C. S.W. 29/11/99.
R.C. The Puritan's Romance. L.C. Vaud. 11/10/97.
Ext. Puss; or, Metempsychosis (P'cess. 27/10/59). L.C.
P. Puss in Boots. L.C. C.G. 14/12/59.
P. Puss in Boots. L.C. Birmingham, 22/12/75.

P. Puss in Boots. L.C. Col. L'pool, 30/12/75.
P. Puss in Boots. L.C. Bradford, 6/12/76.
P. Puss in Boots. L.C. Newcastle, 7/1/76.
P. Puss in Boots. L.C. P'cess. Edinburgh, 11/12/77.
P. Puss in Boots. L.C. Bijou, Paignton, 18/1/78.
P. Puss in Boots. L.C. P's. Manchester, 6/12/78.
P. Puss in Boots. L.C. Corn Exchange, Maidstone, 21/12/78.
P. Puss in Boots. L.C. Glasgow, 27/12/78.
P. Puss in Boots. L.C. Alex. Sheffield, 17/12/79.
P. Puss in Boots. L.C. Dewsbury, 22/12/80.
P. Puss in Boots. L.C. Cardiff, 4/1/81.
P. Puss in Boots. L.C. M.H. Hastings, 22/12/81.
P. Puss in Boots. L.C. S. Shields, 17/1/82.
P. Puss in Boots. L.C. Greenock, 1/12/82.
P. Puss in Boots. L.C. Worcester, 30/12/82.
P. Puss in Boots. L.C. W. Bromwich, 22/12/84.
P. Puss in Boots. L.C. Grand, Birmingham, 16/12/89.
P. Puss in Boots. L.C. Glasgow, 31/12/97.
P. Puss in Boots. L.C. P's. Manchester, 31/12/97.
P. Puss in Boots. L.C. P.W. Birmingham, 30/12/98.
P. Puss in Boots. L.C. Tyne Newcastle, 30/12/98.
P. Puss in Boots. L.C. O.H. Cheltenham, 30/12/98.
P. Puss in Boots; or, Harlequin Ralph the Miller's Son. L.C. Brighton, 26/12/61.
P. Puss in Boots; or, Harlequin the Miller's Son and the Ogre. L.C. Qns. Edinburgh, 13/12/56.
Oa. Puss in Petticoats. L.C. St G. 18/12/67.
F. Puzzled and Pleased (Grec. 16/8/55).
Ext. Quack, Quack, Quack; or, Modern Practice (Grec. 6/10/51). L.C.
D. The Quadroon; or, The Sun Picture. L.C. Sur. 8/12/60.
D. The Quadroon, the Slave Bride. L.C. Vic. 15/10/57.
D. Quadroona; or, The Blot upon Humanity. L.C. Brit. 17/7/57.
D. Quadroona; or, The Man of Crime. L.C. Gar. 28/4/57.
F. Quarter Day (Stand. 20/3/55).
M.F. Quarter Day; or, How to Pay Rent without Money (Glo. 28/8/76).
C. Quarters. L.C. Scarborough Dramatic Club, 14/10/87.
Ba. The Queen and the Knave; or, The Rose of Castille. L.C. Vic. 17/2/62.
D. The Queen and the Yeoman (C.L. 19/1/62).
P. Queen Anne's Farthing and the Three Kingdoms of Copper, Silver and Gold; or, Harlequin and the Fairies of the Magic Mint (Stand. 1/1/59). L.C.
P. Queen Cock-a-doodle-do, the Dame who lost her Shoe; or, The Princess, the Tulip, the Page and the Peri of the Deep Sea Blue. L.C. Bower, 20/12/66.
T. Queen Elizabeth (Manchester, 29/11/69).
Ba. Queen Elizabeth's Visit to Reading. L.C. Reading, 22/5/62.
Ba. Queen Ellinor; or, The Matrimonial Noose. L.C. Dramatic Club, Hackney, 16/1/75.
P. Queen Lady Bird and her Children; or, Harlequin and a House on Fire (H. 26/12/60). L.C.
P. Queen Mab; or, Harlequin and the Golden Pippin. L.C. Birmingham, 23/10/50.

Oa. The Queen of a Day (H. 13/8/51). L.C.
[Music by E. Fitzwilliam.]
Ext. The Queen of Arts (Preston, 4/8/84).
C.D. The Queen of Connaught (Olym. 15/1/77). L.C.
P. The Queen of Hearts. L.C. Brighton, 8/12/83.
P. The Queen of Hearts. L.C. Birmingham, 24/12/83.
Bsq. The Queen of Hearts (Sanger's Amphi. Ramsgate, 14/7/84).
P. The Queen of Hearts. L.C. Cardiff, 10/12/84.
P. The Queen of Hearts. L.C. Qns. Manchester, 15/12/84.
C.D. The Queen of Hearts. L.C. Var. 24/3/94.
D. The Queen of May (Grec. 1/12/51).
M.D. The Queen of Spades (Grec. 27/12/52). L.C.
D. The Queen of the Moor (T.H. Stoke, 26/12/99). L.C.
M.D. The Queen of the Roses; or, The Sorcerer of Candahar (P'cess. 4/50). L.C.
D. The Queen of the Vintage and the Courier Prince. L.C. Brit. 9/9/54.
D. Queen o' May. L.C. Blackburn, 23/7/84.
D. The Queen's Page (Sur. 9/1/60).
F. The Queen's Rifles. L.C. Qns. 13/8/60.
O.C. Queen Topaze (H.M. 26/12/60). L.C.
C. A Question of Sleep. L.C. W.L. 17/5/98.
Bal. Quicksilver Dick. L.C. Adel. 8/4/71.
F. A Quiet Game at Football. L.C. Cambridge, 26/3/77.
F. Quiet Lodgings (P'cess. 13/11/65).
[See *F. J. STEIN*, 1872.]
C. Quite a Romance. L.C. Plymouth, 3/4/66.
M.F. Quite Cracked. L.C. O.C. 26/10/75.
D.Sk. Quits. L.C. Empress, 24/3/99.
D. Quywic; or, A Life of Shame. L.C. Var. 7/9/87.
D. Raby Rattler (Vic. 18/9/65).
F. A Race for a Cup. L.C. C.G. 3/11/73.
D. Rachel; or, The Hebrew Maid. L.C. Gar. 13/10/71.
D. Rachel's Choice. L.C. Manchester, 14/9/89.
F. A Raffle for an Elephant; or, The Lottery of Love (Str. 5/6/55). L.C.
D. Rail, River and Road. L.C. E.L. 12/9/68.
D. The Railroad of Life; or, A Parliamentary Express (Eff. 26/9/59). L.C.
D. The Railroad of Life; or, Danger on the Line. L.C. Phil. Cardiff, 28/10/78.
Bsq. The Railway King. L.C. Soho, 7/3/51.
Bsq. The Raiment and Agonies of that most Amiable Pair, Raimond and Agnes; or, The Crime-stained Bandit and the Bleeding Buzzum (Brit. 23/7/60). L.C.
Ent. The Raitchpoot, an Indian Puzzle. L.C. St G. 23/2/76.
D. The Rajah of Nagpore (Ast. 24/2/62).
D. Ralph Gaston; or, The Three Lives (Sur. 15/9/60). L.C.
D. The Ranache King. L.C. Grand, Plymouth, 30/6/91.
C.O. A Random Shot. L.C. Mat. 26/4/98.
C. Rank (Tyne, Newcastle, 20/11/71).
D. Raphelina; or, The Gipsy Mother (Dumfries, 13/10/79). L.C.
P. Rasselas, Prince of Abyssinia; or, Harlequin and the Happy Valley. L.C. Alex. Bradford, 24/12/64.

D. The Rat-catcher's Daughter. L.C. Pav. 23/5/55.
D. The Rat-catcher's Daughter. L.C. Qns. 26/9/55.
D. The Rathboys; or, Shadroch the Shingawn and Ailleen the Rose of Kilkenny. L.C. Sheffield, 27/3/63.
[See *R. BUCHANAN*, 1862.]
C.O. Raymonde. L.C. Halifax, 30/9/92.
C.D. The Ray of Light (Park, 14/10/76). L.C.
F. Ready and Willing. L.C. Margate, 19/7/80.
D. The Realities of Life; or, The Thief, the Artist, the Doctor and the Banker (Grec. 21/4/62). L.C.
C.D. The Real Mr Potter of Texas. L.C. Str. 21/4/90.
F. The Rear Admiral (St J. 12/4/66).
D. Rebecca of York. L.C. Amphi. L'pool, 25/11/74.
D. Rebecca, the Jewish Wanderer. L.C. Eff. 16/4/64.
D. The Rebel Rose. L.C. D.Y. 25/12/99.
D. The Rebel Spirits. L.C. St J. 31/12/94.
C.D. Reckless Temple. L.C. Aven. 22/10/90.
C.D. The Reckoning Day (Northampton, 1/85).
[See *The Spider's Web, infra.*]
D. The Recluse of the Forest (Grec. 20/4/63).
C.O. The Recruit. L.C. Tyne, Newcastle, 22/2/92.
D. The Red Bridge. L.C. Qns. 17/10/60.
D. The Red Brigade; or, Vice and its Consequences. L.C. Vic. 18/11/56.
D. The Red Buoy; or, The Tar of Trinidad and the Spirit of the Ocean. L.C. Stand. 6/2/51.
D. Red Dick (O.H. Bolton, 8/12/73).
D. The Red Dwarf; or, Love, Mystery and Revenge. L.C. Brit. 27/10/71.
D. The Red Dwarf; or, Mystery and Vengeance (E.C. 21/4/73).
D. Redemption. L.C. Vic. H. 30/11/97.
D. Redemption; or, Dark Turnings in Life. L.C. Pullan's Theatre of Varieties, Bradford, 28/9/82.
D. The Red Hand (Vic. 25/2/65). L.C. as *Cahill Euve Dha Rhug; or, He of the Red Hand.*
D. The Red Hand of Fontainebleau. L.C. Vic. 27/5/57.
D. The Red Hand of Justice. L.C. Grec. 26/9/78.
F. The Red House; or, A Crack Shot. L.C. M'bone, 12/2/50.
D. The Red Huntsman; or, The Phantom of the Black Valley. L.C. Vic. 20/5/58.
D. Red John the Daring; or, A Settler's Perils (Brit. 23/9/61). L.C.
D. The Red Lamp; or, The Dark Dens of the City. L.C. Pav. 17/4/62.
D. The Red Man and the Headsman. L.C. Vic. 1/3/57.
D. Redmond of the Hills; or, The Whisperer. L.C. Woolwich, 15/3/60.
D. The Red Ribbon; or, The Soldier's Motto "Life for Life". L.C. Brit. 18/7/61.
P. Red Riding Hood. L.C. Birmingham, 9/12/58. MS. Birmingham.
P. Red Riding Hood. L.C. St Helens, 20/12/76.
P. Red Riding Hood. L.C. Tyne, Newcastle, 15/1/80.
P. Red Riding Hood. L.C. Grand, Leeds, 8/12/81.
P. Red Riding Hood. L.C. P'cess. Glasgow, 15/12/82.
P. Red Riding Hood. L.C. Sefton, L'pool, 19/12/83.

P. Red Riding Hood. L.C. Bradford, 10/12/84.
P. Red Riding Hood. L.C. R.A. Woolwich, 18/12/84.
P. Red Riding Hood. L.C. Alex. Sheffield, 6/12/86.
P. Red Riding Hood. L.C. Com. Manchester, 12/1/87.
P. Red Riding Hood. L.C. Bury, 19/12/92.
P. Red Riding Hood. L.C. Nottingham, 24/12/94.
P. Red Riding Hood. L.C. Stratford, 31/12/95.
P. Red Riding Hood. L.C. Sheffield, 10/1/96.
P. Red Riding Hood. L.C. Shrewsbury, 26/12/96.
P. Red Riding Hood. L.C. P's. Bristol, 31/12/97.
P. Red Riding Hood. L.C. Mechanics' Institute, Eccleshill, Bradford, 27/12/98.
P. Red Riding Hood. L.C. Plymouth, 22/12/99.
P. Red Riding Hood; or, Little Bo-Peep. L.C. Alex. Sheffield, 26/11/94.
P. Red Riding Hood and Baron von Wolf; or, Harlequin Little Boy Blue and Old Gammer Gurton. L.C Brighton, 24/12/58.
D. Red Rob the Coiner (M'bone, 6/6/63).
Ext. Red Rufus; or, Harlequin Fact, Fiction and Fancy (Olym. 26/12/51).
D. Red Ruthven. L.C. Qns. 4/2/59.
D. Reds of the Midi. L.C. Roy. 7/9/96.
D. The Red Star (Ilkeston, 10/7/94). L.C.
D. Reflection; or, Honour before Wealth. L.C. Concert H. Maidstone, 1/2/77.
D. The Regent (D.L. 8/1/55).
F. The Registered Lodging House; or, Strange Arrivals in 1851. L.C. Sur. 29/4/51.
F. A Regular Scamp. L.C. Soho, 10/12/60.
F. The Regular Thing. L.C. O.H. Bury, Lancs. 14/9/86.
F. The Rehearsal. L.C. Cheltenham, 13/9/82.
Bsq. Rehearsalization. L.C. New, Aberdare, 12/7/99.
C. The Reign of Woman. L.C. T.H. Kilburn, 7/5/92.
D. Reinhard and Leonora. L.C. L'pool, 5/1/56.
D. The Released Convict; or, It is a long lane that has no turning. L.C. C.L. 10/2/57.
F. Remember the Grotto (M'bone, 20/11/54). L.C.
C. Renaissance (Daly's, 5/7/97). L.C.
D. Reparation (Gai. 16/5/82). L.C.
D. The Reprieve (Grec. 6/8/60).
D. The Reprobate. L.C. Athen. Lancaster, 15/12/91.
D. A Reprobate. L.C. Central H. Hanley, 8/4/96.
D. The Republican Duke (Pav. 6/7/60).
D. Resolution; or, The Trials of Youth. L.C. Vic. H. Salford, 23/12/89.
D. Respectability; or, Love and Duty. L.C. Croydon, 4/6/83.
C. The Respectable Man (Soho, 23/4/53). L.C.
Oa. Retained on Both Sides (P's. Manchester, 13/11/76).
D. Retaliation. L.C. Adel. 17/7/83.
[See *R. DIRCKS*, 1890.]
D. Retribution; or, The Gipsey's Revenge. L.C. Bristol, 7/10/59.
D. Retributive Justice; or, Maliel the Avenger (Vic. 5/1/63). L.C.
[By *E. G. BURTON*.]
F. The Return from the Baltic (Ast. 9/4/55).

F. Returned from India (Sur. 28/11/59).
D. The Return of a Ticket-of-Leave. L.C. Stand. 30/6/63.
D. Reuben Blight; or, Something to live for. L.C. Wolverhampton, 11/1/61.
D. Reunited (Athen. 24/7/88). L.C.
Ent. La Revanche des Cigales (Mat. 17/4/97). L.C.
Equest.D. Revolt in the East; or, The Fugitives and their Faithful Steed (Ast. 1/1/59). L.C.
D. The Revolutionist. L.C. St G. 21/6/82.
D. Rich and Poor; or, The Workman's Dream. L.C. S.W. 30/11/66.
D. Rich and Poor: A Story of Four Seasons. L.C. Brit. 30/4/66.
D. Rich and Poor: A Story of the Four Seasons. L.C. Eff. 21/5/66.
D. Rich and Poor: The Uphill Game of Life. L.C. Grec. 2/5/54.
D. Richard Savage. L.C. Vaud. 31/12/97.
[See *J. M. BARRIE*, 1891.]
Bsq. Richard III. L.C. Str. 20/4/54.
C. Richelieu. L.C. P'cess. 23/11/88.
D. Riches and Poverty; or, A Daughter's Sacrifice (Brit. 9/9/61). L.C.
F. Rich in Love but Poor in Pocket (Grec. 4/7/59). L.C. Grec. 13/7/55.
P. Ride-a-cock-horse to Banbury. L.C. Birmingham, 22/12/74. MS. Birmingham.
P. Ride-a-cock-horse to Banbury Cross (Sinclair and Crowe's Circus, 24/12/70).
D. The Riflemen (Sur. 3/3/60).
[Later as *Riflemen Beware* (Sur. 18/6/60). See *E. STIRLING*, 1859.]
D. Right and Might. L.C. S.W. 2/12/52.
D. Right and Wrong; or, Smiles and Tears (Sur. 8/2/58). L.C. as *R. and W.; or, A Tale of the Old and New Year.*
D. Right and Wrong; or, The Dream of Life (Col. L'pool, 2/11/68).
D. Right at Last. L.C. May's Dramatic Co. 1/4/87.
D. The Rightful Heir; or, The Dead Hand and the Hour of One (Swansea, 25/9/71).
F. The Right Man in the Right Place; or, Handy and Dandy (D.L. 12/3/60). L.C.
D. Rigoletti; or, The Malediction. L.C. Qns. 17/4/61.
Vaud. Rigolo (St J. 21/6/55). L.C.
D.Sk. The Ring. L.C. Str. 29/3/95.
Ent. Ringing the Changes (S.W. 24/5/62). L.C.
D. The Ring of Polycrates. L.C. Lyc. 15/7/90.
[See *J. H. McCARTHY*, 1892.]
Ca. Rings on her Fingers. L.C. Winter Gdns. Stockport, 18/11/96.
D. Rip Van Winkle. L.C. Norwich, 5/3/66.
D. Rip Van Winkle. L.C. Oldham, 23/3/66.
Bsq. Rip Van Winkle; or, Somnambulistic Knickerbockers. L.C. Newcastle, 13/3/66.
F. The Rising Generation (Brit. 24/4/61).
F. The Rising Sun. L.C. Bath Saloons, Torquay, 31/3/82.
Bal. The Rival Artisans (Ast. 19/6/54).
D. The Rival Fountains; or, The Spring of Life and the Spring of Death (Brit. 7/11/59). L.C.
F. Rival Lodgers. L.C. Var. 8/12/83.

Int. The Rival Poet. L.C. Grec. 28/6/71.
C.D. The Rivals. L.C. Var. 23/3/87.
F. The Rival's Rendezvous (S.W. 22/2/61).
D. Riven Clouds. L.C. Literary and Musical Society, Axminster, 2/12/80.
D. The Road to Ruin; or, The Victim of Drink. L.C. S.W. 30/11/97.
D. Roaring Dick and Co. L.C. Bijou, Bayswater, 7/9/96.
P. Robbing Robin Hood. L.C. M'bone, 26/12/90.
R.D. Robert Burns (Edinburgh, 28/5/96).
[Music by E. T. De Banzie.]
D. Robert Emmett, the Irish Patriot of 1803 (Octagon, Blyth, 14/2/73).
D. Robert La Grange (Grec. 12/8/61).
C.O. Robert Macaire. L.C. C.P. 20/9/87.
D. Robert Richborne; or, The Disputed Title (Col. L'pool, 31/7/71).
O. Robert the Devil (Court, L'pool, 8/2/88).
P. Robin Hood. L.C. D.L. 20/12/58.
Bsq. Robin Hood. L.C. Brit. 8/4/61.
P. Robin Hood (Alex. L'pool, 26/12/69).
P. Robin Hood. L.C. Star, Ashton-under-Lyne, 13/1/76.
Bsq. Robin Hood. L.C. Crit. 12/4/76.
P. Robin Hood. L.C. Bradford, 24/11/79.
P. Robin Hood. L.C. Alex. L'pool, 2/12/80.
P. Robin Hood. L.C. Margate, 22/12/81.
P. Robin Hood. L.C. R.A. Woolwich, 21/12/88.
P. Robin Hood. L.C. Glasgow, 26/12/96.
P. Robin Hood and his Merry Men; or, The Loves of Fayre Rosamond and King Henry (E.L. 26/12/67).
P. Robin Hood and Little John. L.C. Corn Exchange, Maidstone, 10/1/96.
P. Robin Hood, Little John and Friar Tuck; or, Harlequin and the Goblin of Mindestone Moor, with the Castle of 100 Gates. L.C. Birmingham, 11/12/54.
P. Robinson Crusoe. L.C. Birmingham, 26/12/67.
P. Robinson Crusoe. L.C. Dumfries, 4/1/76.
P. Robinson Crusoe. L.C. Manchester, 14/12/76.
P. Robinson Crusoe. L.C. P's. Bradford, 20/12/76.
P. Robinson Crusoe. L.C. Gai. Glasgow, 22/12/76.
P. Robinson Crusoe. L.C. Exeter, 8/1/77.
P. Robinson Crusoe. L.C. Bilston, 20/1/77.
P. Robinson Crusoe. L.C. H.M. Aberdeen, 14/12/77.
P. Robinson Crusoe. L.C. Dundee, 21/12/77.
P. Robinson Crusoe. L.C. Qns. Wigan, 21/12/77.
P. Robinson Crusoe. L.C. Worcester, 26/12/77.
P. Robinson Crusoe. L.C. P.W. Newport, 19/12/78.
P. Robinson Crusoe. L.C. Alex. L'pool, 21/12/78.
P. Robinson Crusoe. L.C. Birmingham, 27/12/78.
P. Robinson Crusoe. L.C. Cardiff, 2/1/79.
P. Robinson Crusoe. L.C. Peterborough, 11/1/79.
P. Robinson Crusoe. L.C. Star, Bury, 16/1/79.
P. Robinson Crusoe. L.C. Leeds, 11/12/79.
P. Robinson Crusoe. L.C. P'cess. Edinburgh, 13/12/79.
P. Robinson Crusoe. L.C. Sheffield, 17/12/79.

P. Robinson Crusoe. L.C. Wolverhampton, 15/1/80.
P. Robinson Crusoe. L.C. Corn Exchange, Derby, 14/12/80.
P. Robinson Crusoe. L.C. Victory, Aldershot, 14/12/80.
P. Robinson Crusoe. L.C. Hull, 28/11/81.
P. Robinson Crusoe. L.C. Greenock, 28/11/81.
P. Robinson Crusoe. L.C. Nottingham, 29/12/81.
P. Robinson Crusoe. L.C. Southport, 10/1/82.
P. Robinson Crusoe. L.C. York, 31/3/82.
P. Robinson Crusoe. L.C. Grand, Leeds, 8/12/82.
P. Robinson Crusoe. L.C. Plymouth, 20/12/82.
P. Robinson Crusoe. L.C. Edinburgh, 27/12/82.
P. Robinson Crusoe. L.C. Grand, Glasgow, 27/12/82.
P. Robinson Crusoe. L.C. P.W. L'pool, 8/1/83.
P. Robinson Crusoe. L.C. Leicester, 8/1/83.
P. Robinson Crusoe. L.C. Alex. Sheffield, 8/12/83.
P. Robinson Crusoe. L.C. N. Shields, 14/12/83.
P. Robinson Crusoe. L.C. Bolton, 10/1/84.
P. Robinson Crusoe. L.C. Preston, 10/12/84.
P. Robinson Crusoe. L.C. P'cess. Glasgow, 12/12/85.
P. Robinson Crusoe. L.C. Birmingham, 19/12/85.
P. Robinson Crusoe. L.C. Cardiff, 13/12/86.
P. Robinson Crusoe. L.C. Rotunda, L'pool, 20/12/86.
P. Robinson Crusoe. L.C. Leeds, 21/12/86.
P. Robinson Crusoe. L.C. Sheffield, 21/12/86.
P. Robinson Crusoe. L.C. Newcastle, 21/12/86.
P. Robinson Crusoe. L.C. Edinburgh, 29/12/86.
P. Robinson Crusoe. L.C. O.H. Northampton, 7/12/88.
P. Robinson Crusoe. L.C. P's. Bristol, 21/12/88.
P. Robinson Crusoe. L.C. Glasgow, 13/12/89.
P. Robinson Crusoe. L.C. Alex. Sheffield, 20/11/90.
P. Robinson Crusoe. L.C. P.W. L'pool, 5/12/90.
P. Robinson Crusoe. L.C. Bradford, 11/12/90.
P. Robinson Crusoe. L.C. Roy. Chester, 24/12/90.
P. Robinson Crusoe. L.C. Lyc. Edinburgh, 15/12/91.
P. Robinson Crusoe. L.C. Nottingham, 1/1/92.
Bsq. Robinson Crusoe. L.C. Hodson's Theatre of Varieties, Ossett, near Wakefield, 28/10/92.
P. Robinson Crusoe. L.C. R.A. Woolwich, 19/12/92.
P. Robinson Crusoe. L.C. Leeds, 8/12/93.
P. Robinson Crusoe. L.C. Aquar. Brighton, 16/12/93.
P. Robinson Crusoe. L.C. Stratford, 16/12/93.
P. Robinson Crusoe. L.C. Harte's Theatre of Varieties, Openshaw, 30/11/94.
P. Robinson Crusoe. L.C. Birmingham, 19/12/94. MS. Birmingham.
P. Robinson Crusoe. L.C. Grand, Glasgow, 26/12/95.
P. Robinson Crusoe. L.C. Metro. Camberwell, 31/12/95.
P. Robinson Crusoe. L.C. Leicester, 10/1/96.
P. Robinson Crusoe. L.C. P's. Manchester, 10/1/96.
P. Robinson Crusoe. L.C. Grand, Hull, 1/2/96.
P. Robinson Crusoe. L.C. Bradford, 21/12/96.
P. Robinson Crusoe. L.C. Stockport, 26/12/96.
P. Robinson Crusoe (Kilburn, 26/12/96).
P. Robinson Crusoe. L.C. P's. Bristol, 8/1/97.
P. Robinson Crusoe. L.C. Grand, Croydon, 8/1/97.

P. Robinson Crusoe. L.C. Edinburgh, 8/1/97.
P. Robinson Crusoe. L.C. Newcastle, 8/1/97.
P. Robinson Crusoe. L.C. Exeter, 9/2/97.
P. Robinson Crusoe. L.C. Lyc. Sheffield, 31/12/97.
P. Robinson Crusoe. L.C. Rotunda, L'pool, 31/12/97.
P. Robinson Crusoe. L.C. P'cess. Glasgow, 31/12/97.
P. Robinson Crusoe. L.C. Shrewsbury, 31/12/97.
P. Robinson Crusoe. L.C. O.H. Bury, 31/12/97.
P. Robinson Crusoe. L.C. Eden, Brighton, 31/12/97.
P. Robinson Crusoe. L.C. Cardiff, 31/12/97.
P. Robinson Crusoe. L.C. O.H. Leicester, 31/12/97.
P. Robinson Crusoe. L.C. Grand, Hull, 27/12/98.
P. Robinson Crusoe. L.C. Assembly R. Balham, 30/12/98.
P. Robinson Crusoe. L.C. Grand, Leeds, 30/12/98.
P. Robinson Crusoe. L.C. County, Reading, 30/12/98.
P. Robinson Crusoe. L.C. Grand, Birmingham, 30/12/98.
P. Robinson Crusoe. L.C. Mechanics' Institute, Eccleshall, 22/12/99.
P. Robinson Crusoe. L.C. Alex. Widnes, 22/12/99.
P. Robinson Crusoe. L.C. Glasgow, 28/12/99.
P. Robinson Crusoe. L.C. Preston, 28/12/99.
P. Robinson Crusoe; or Harlequin Man Friday and the King of the Cannibal Islands (New, Greenwich, 26/12/65).
Bsq. Robinson Crusoe; or, The Pirate Will, Pretty Poll and Captain Bill (Todmorden, 29/10/83).
P. Robinson Crusoe, Esq.; or, Koffe King of Ashantee. L.C. Alex. Sheffield, 8/12/74.
Bsq. Robinson Crusoe Rewigged. L.C. Greenwich, 19/2/78.
P. Robinson Crusoe up-to-date. L.C. County, Reading, 15/12/90.
D. Rob Roy (Ast. 9/2/57).
Bsq. Rob Roy, the Bold Outlaw. L.C. Brit. 19/5/64.
D. Robur Ragabas; or, 1792 (E.C. 8/3/73).
D. Rocco Salvioni; or, The Nightingale of the Mountain. L.C. Qns. 9/9/62.
T. Roderic. L.C. Birmingham, 26/8/53.
D. Roger O'Hare (Vic. 28/8/65). L.C.
F. The Rogue's Paradise. L.C. Ladb. H. 31/12/95.
Equest.Spec. Roland and his Steed; or, The Wild Boar of the Fens. L.C. Ast. 20/5/58.
Ca. The Rolling Stone. L.C. Str. 22/8/56.
D. The Rolling Stone. L.C. S.W. 20/7/96.
D. The Roll of the Drum. L.C. Woolwich, 2/3/94.
D. Romance and Reality. L.C. H. 4/10/60.
D. The Romance of a Poor Young Man (Brit. 30/6/62). L.C. as *The Disguised Nobleman; or, The R. of the P.Y.M.*
D. A Romantic Affair. L.C. Var. 31/8/92.
Bsq. Romantic Ruy Blas (Vaud. 3/1/73).
D. Romulus (St J. 1/6/54).
D. Rookwood. L.C. Grec. 14/10/59.
D. Rookwood; or, Turpin's Ride to York (Ast. 24/12/55).
D. The Root of All Evil (Guernsey, 12/6/76).
D. The Root of All Evil. L.C. Qns. 21/3/64.
D. Rosalia: A Tale of Algiers. L.C. Lyc. 1/11/60.
D. Rosalie; or, The Chain of Guilt (Ast. 28/3/64). L.C.
D. Rosalie Mortimer; or, Fate and its Victims. L.C. Brit. 6/6/57.

D. Rosalinde. L.C. Roy. 5/5/92.
D. The Rose and the Lily; or, The Fleur de Lis. L.C. Pav. 16/6/73.
D. Rose Brilliant. L.C. P's. Bristol, 15/11/99.
D. Rose Clinton (Vic. 20/3/54).
D. Rose Graham; or, The Lass of Gowrie. L.C. Swansea, 19/3/60.
O. The Rose of Ispahan. L.C. Bristol, 28/9/97.
D. The Rose of Killarney. L.C. S.W. 10/7/94.
Oa. The Rose of Salency. L.C. Roy. 22/3/66.
Oa. The Rose of St Fleur. L.C. Waterloo O.H. Edinburgh, 2/12/67.
D. The Rose of the Ferry (Brit. 9/4/60).
Bal. The Rose of the Village (H. 11/11/56).
Ent. The Rose Queen. L.C. P.H. Sydenham, 9/8/98.
D. Rose's Victory; or, A Game of Fortune. L.C. Brit. 17/2/71.
Bsq. Rosmer of Rosmersholm. A Drama...by a Respectful Student of the Works of Henrik Ibsen. 8° 1891.
D. Rosmersholm. L.C. Brighton, 31/8/93.
T. Rosmunda (Lyc. 27/6/56). L.C.
D. Rotherhithe in the Olden Time. L.C. Pav. 27/6/54.
D. Rouge et Noir (Lyc. 26/12/66). L.C.
F. Rough and Ready (Sur. 16/4/60).
D. Rough Hands and Honest Hearts (S. Shields, 31/3/73).
D. Roughly Woo'd and Gently Won (Lynn, 27/6/78).
D.Spec. Round the Globe in Eighty Days (Birmingham, 15/11/75).
D. Round the World in Eighty Days (P'cess, 15/3/75). L.C.
D. The Rover's Secret (Sur. 18/6/60).
F. A Row on the Premises. L.C. Adel. 26/10/59.
D. The Royal Escape; or, King Charles at Brighthelmstone. L.C. Brighton, 21/11/61.
D. The Royalist. L.C. S.W. 5/2/50.
D. The Royalist (Richmond, 4/4/79).
D. Royalist and Republican (Grec. 30/4/60). L.C. Grec. 14/3/55.
D. Rube the Showman. L.C. P'cess. Leeds, 19/2/62.
[See *C. CALVERT*, 1870.]
D. Rule Britannia. L.C. S.W. 23/12/95.
D. Rule Britannia; or, England expects every Man to do his Duty (Col. L'pool, 7/9/68).
Oa. Rumbelow. L.C. Lyr. Ealing, 31/10/88.
F. Rum'uns from Rome. L.C. Ast. 3/5/81.
F. A Runaway Match (S.W. 12/4/54).
C.O. A Runaway Match. L.C. C.P. 16/10/80.
Ca. The Runaways. L.C. Gar. 10/12/94.
[See *F. W. BROUGHTON*, 1880.]
Ca. A Run of Luck. L.C. Alex. L'pool, 10/4/77.
[See *H. PETTITT*, 1886.]
Ext. Russia against Turkey, now on Trial at Cook's Arena of Chivalry before Britannia assisted by immortal Punch (Ast. 26/6/54). L.C.
D. Russian Tyranny (M'bone, 14/10/84). L.C.
Oa. The Rustic Roses (L'pool, 24/11/73).
F.C. Ruth (Alex. Sheffield, 12/3/83).
M.F. Ruth's Lovers. L.C. Empire, L'pool, 10/10/98.
D. Ruy Blas. L.C. Adel. Sheffield, 12/12/60.
D. Ruy Blas. L.C. Grec. 7/1/61.
D. The Rye House Plot (Brit. 26/6/61).
F. The Rye House Plot. L.C. C.L. 14/10/65.

D. Sabbioneta. L.C. Bijou, 28/9/96.
D. Sacontala; or, The Fatal Ring. 8° 1870.
D. The Sacred Trust; or, The Field of Death. L.C. Vic. 24/1/61.
D. The Sacrifice; or, Love unto Death. L.C. Sur. 7/10/57.
D. Sail Ahoy! (Tyne, Newcastle, 29/9/74).
D. The Sailor's Sheet-Anchor; or, Friends at Sea and Foes on Shore. L.C. Pav. 13/4/65.
D. St Anne's Night (Sur. 8/11/62). L.C.
P. St George and the Dragon. L.C. Qns. 22/12/55.
P. St George and the Dragon. L.C. Plymouth, 21/12/57.
Ext. St George and the Dragon. L.C. C.G. 23/12/84.
P. St George and the Dragon. L.C. Corn Exchange, Maidstone, 26/12/88.
P. St George and the Dragon; or, The Seven Champions (Stand. 26/12/96).
P. St George and the Dragon, and the Seven Champions of Christendom (M'bone, 26/12/83). L.C.
P. St George and the Dragon; or, Harlequin and the Seven Champions of Christendom. L.C. Pav. 17/12/64.
Bsq. St George and the Dragon (Torquay, 6/8/83).
D. Sakuntala (Conservatory, Botanic Gdns. Regent's Park, 3/7/99).
T. Salammbo (Ladb. H. 11/11/85). L.C.
Bsq. Salammbo, the Lovely Queen of Carthage (Hol. 6/5/71). L.C.
D. Salem's Sorrow (Stockport, 25/11/72).
F. Sally Smart; or, The Clockmaker's Hat (Str. 14/5/55).
Bsq. Salthello Ovini (H. 26/7/75).
D. Salvator Rosa. L.C. P.W. L'pool, 17/11/66.
F. Sam Carr, the Man in Possession (Darlington, 21/6/72).
F. Sam Patch (Sur. 17/9/55).
D. Santuzza. L.C. Com. 3/9/97.
Bsq. Sappho (Stand. 11/6/66). L.C.
D. Sappho; or, The Idol of an Hour. L.C. Shakespeare, Clapham Junction, 18/10/98.
D. Sarah the Jewess (Grec. 10/7/61).
D. Satan; or, The Sorrows of Margaret Forster. L.C. E.C. 5/3/97.
Bsq. Saturnalia; or, The Rivals and the Revels. L.C. E.L. 28/8/73.
C. Saucy May; or, Love's Stratagem (S. Shields, 10/3/84).
M.F. Saucy Nabob. L.C. Var. 20/4/86.
D. The Savage and Civilization (Sur. 3/9/64).
D. The Savannah (D.L. 7/3/61). L.C.
D. Saved. L.C. Var. 28/1/89.
D. Saved from Sin. L.C. Gateshead, 13/11/91.
D. Saved from the Wreck; or, The Smuggler's Fate (Weymouth, 12/4/69).
D. Saved from the Yardarm. L.C. Var. Hoxton, 5/5/90.
D. Sawney Bean, the Cannibal. L.C. C.L. 20/4/64.
D. The Scales of Justice; or, Merit and Interest. L.C. Brit. 14/8/57.
D. The Scamps of London. L.C. Scarborough, 20/9/77.
Bsq. A Scandanavian Sketch. L.C. Str. 24/4/51.
D. The Scapegrace of Paris (Stand. 12/3/55).
D. The Scarlet Flower; or, The Token of Love, Faith and Death (Brit. 6/10/62). L.C.
D. The Scarlet Flower; or, The Token of Love, Faith and Death. L.C. Eff. 6/10/62.

D. Scattered Leaves (Grec. 12/9/61). L.C.
[By *R. H. LINGHAM.*]
F. A Scene in the Life of an Unprotected Female. L.C. Str. 26/1/50.
F.C. The Schemer (Aquar. Brighton, 14/5/94). L.C.
D. The School Drudge; or, The Modern Cinderella (Greenock, 5/9/81).
C. The School for Wits. L.C. Richmond, 1/10/60.
C. The School for Wives. L.C. Qns. 4/9/71.
D. The Schoolmaster of Lynn (M'bone, 23/8/79).
Ca. Science and Art. L.C. Gai. 17/8/81.
D. The Scotch Sisters: An Episode in the Life of Jeanie Deans. L.C. Roy. 17/2/63.
D. Scotland Yard. L.C. Nottingham, 7/3/95.
D. The Scribe (Grand, Boscombe, 12/5/99). L.C.
D. Sea Fruit. L.C. Gt Yarmouth, 20/7/87.
[See *H. MOSS*, 1893.]
D. Sealed; or, St Agnes' Eve. L.C. Albion, 16/6/76.
D. Sealed Lips. L.C. Hyde, 15/6/88.
F. The Sealed Sentence (Soho, 2/11/57).
D. The Seamstress and the Duchess; or, Pride, Poverty and Splendour. L.C. Vic. 1/11/56.
Bal. The Sea-nymph's Cave (Str. 22/5/54).
M.F. A Seaside Holiday. L.C. Var. 10/9/85.
F. Seaside Swells; or, The Prizefighter's Daughter. L.C. Middlesborough, 2/2/89.
D. Sebastopol, from Our Own Correspondent. L.C. M'bone, 17/10/54.
D. A Second Brutus (Stand. 28/3/55).
D. Second to None (Stand. 5/11/64). L.C.
C.O. The Secret Marriage. L.C. C.P. 10/12/77.
D. The Secret Marriage; or, The Soldier, the Monk and the Assassin. L.C. Vic. 29/2/60.
Ca. The Secret Mission. L.C. Leicester, 22/3/77.
D. The Secret Passion. L.C. M'bone, 7/2/58.
D. The Secrets of the Devil (Vic. 27/8/64). L.C.
D. The Secrets of War (Ast. 10/9/55).
D. The Secret Twelve; or, The Bridge of Baltaz. L.C. Vic. 25/5/55.
C. Seeing's Believing. L.C. Olym. 6/10/52.
F. Seeing's Not Believing. L.C. Vic. 23/4/61.
F. Seeing the Grecian Pantomime (Grec. 5/7/75). L.C.
D. Self. L.C. P.W. Warrington, 25/5/83.
[Title altered to *The Midnight London Express*, 30/6/1911.]
D. Self-condemned. L.C. Darlington, 22/6/76.
D.Sk. Selfishness; or, A Guilty Conscience (C.L. 9/2/56). L.C.
D. Self Made (St J. 18/1/62). L.C.
Ca. The Sensation Hunt. L.C. St G. 22/1/68.
D. Sentenced, but not Guilty (Col. L'pool, 18/12/76).
D.Sk. The Sentry-Go. L.C. S.W. 21/12/96.
D. Sequin the Scalp-hunter. L.C. C.L. 22/10/53.
D. The Serenade. L.C. St G. 2/3/94.
D. The Serpent on the Hearth; or, The Mulatto Nobleman (Grec. 12/8/61).
F. Servant or Suitor (Roy. 20/5/72).
O. Sesostris. L.C. Ladb. H. 13/4/99.

D. Seth Green; or, Struck Oil at Last (E.C. 25/10/84). L.C. M'bone, 9/7/84.
C. A Set of Rogues. L.C. Vic. Walthamstow, 12/7/99.
D. The Seven Ages of Man (Brit. 14/1/59).
P. The Seven Champions of Christendom; or, Harlequin Queen Diamond and the Realms of Gems and Jewels. L.C. Vic. 19/12/53.
D. The Seven Poor Travellers (Sur. 29/1/55). L.C.
D. Seven Poor Travellers. L.C. Vic. 2/2/55.
D. Seven Poor Travellers. L.C. Grec. 14/3/55.
D. Seven Poor Travellers; or, Life's Faults and Follies. L.C. Pav. 9/2/55.
D. Seven Steps to Ruin (Brit. 6/6/59).
D. The Seventh Hour; or, The Price of Life (Brit. 5/9/61). L.C. C.L. 25/1/60.
[This is probably the play by *B. HUGHES* and *A. FAUCQUEZ* (C.L. 10/4/61): see p. 792.]
D. Severed Ties. L.C. Lyr. Ealing, 6/3/89.
C.D. Severine (Gai. 6/5/85). L.C.
D. The Sexton of Stepney (Brit. 6/8/62).
D. The Sexton's Bird; or, The Orphan Peeress of Greymoor Abbey. L.C. C.L. 31/3/55.
D. Shades of the Night. L.C. Lyr. Hammersmith, 18/12/94.
[See *R. MARSHALL*, 1896.]
D. Shadowed; or, Day and Night. L.C. M'bone, 27/11/90.
D. The Shadow of Sin. L.C. Lyc. Blackburn, 23/7/84.
[See *F. JARMAN*, 1893.]
D. The Shadow of Wrong; or, Threat for Threat (Grec. 23/2/63). L.C.
D. The Shadow on the Hearth. L.C. Vic. 19/1/63.
D. The Shadows of Crime (Sur. 4/2/56). L.C.
D. The Shadows of Life (Adel. L'pool, 14/10/72).
D.Sk. The Shadows of the Past. L.C. S.W. 5/3/97.
D. Shadragh the Shingawn. L.C. Stand. 14/5/62.
D. Shaft No. 2 (Metro. Gateshead, 19/4/97). L.C. Newcastle.
F. Shake Hands (St J. 25/4/64). L.C.
M.C. The Sham Duke. L.C. Cambridge, 20/7/96.
C. Shares (Glasgow, 7/2/73).
Ca. A Shattered Idol (Col. Dudley, 18/10/95).
[See *CIMINO*, 1877.]
D. Shaw, the Lifeguardsman (Pav. 31/1/59).
C.O. The She Dragon of Irwell. L.C. Manchester, 3/11/75.
D. Shelah from Cork; or, The Spy in the Crimea (Brit. 8/5/56). L.C.
[By *W. SEAMAN*.]
D. Sherlock Holmes—Private Detective (Hanley, 15/12/94, *copy*.). L.C.
D. The Shield of David (W.L. 3/4/99). L.C.
D. The Shingawn; or, Ailleen the Rose of Killarney (Brit. 24/9/62). L.C.
D. The Shingawn; or, Ailleen the Rose of Killarney. L.C. St J. 23/2/69.
D. The Ship Boy (Vic. 12/8/54).
D. The Ship Launch; or, The Dumb Boy of Toulon. L.C. 4/10/51.
D. The Ship on Fire (Brit. 17/7/61).

Ext. Shooting Stars (Folly, 22/11/77). L.C.
D. Shot and Shell. L.C. Ast. 10/7/82.
F. The Shower Bath. L.C. Leamington, 16/4/87.
D. Show Folks; or, Punch and his Little Dog Toby (M'bone, 7/7/51). L.C.
Int. Shylock in 1851. L.C. S.W. 13/5/50.
Ca. The Shy Man. L.C. Norwich, 20/2/65.
C.D. Sidecraft. L.C. Imp. 10/9/83.
D. The Siege of Marby. L.C. Vic. H. 17/5/99.
D. The Siege of Sebastopol; or, The Horrors of War. L.C. Brit. 2/2/54.
Equest.Spec. The Siege of Silistria. L.C. Ast. 19/9/54.
Equest.Bsq. The Siege of Troy; or, The Miss-judgment of Paris (Ast. 28/8/54). L.C.
D. Sight and Sound (Brit. 20/11/76). L.C.
D. The Sightless Tyrant of Persia; or, The Hundredth Victim of the Shark's Cliff (Brit. 24/9/60). L.C. Brit. 12/3/51.
D. The Sight of St Paul's. L.C. Sur. 25/7/95.
D. Signal Dispatch. L.C. S.W. 15/11/88.
F. A Signal Mistake. L.C. Olym. 31/8/60.
D.Sk. A Signal Success. L.C. Parkhurst, 9/8/95.
D. The Signet Ring; or, The Heart Wreck. L.C. Sur. 28/6/50.
C.D. Signor Appiani (Plymouth, 22/10/97).
Lyric D. The Silent Curfew. L.C. Winter Gdns. Southport, 29/11/89.
D. The Silent Highway. L.C. S.W. 17/5/98.
D. The Silent Pool. L.C. W.L. 27/7/93.
D. The Silver Devil. L.C. Ast. 20/6/54.
D. The Silver Devil. L.C. Vic. 27/3/61.
C.O. The Silver Key. L.C. Portsmouth, 9/5/84.
D. The Silver Queen. L.C. Assembly R. Tenby, 26/2/86.
D. Silver Store Island; or, Pedro Mendez the South American Pirate. L.C. Vic. 17/2/58.
D. Silver Store Island; or, The British Flag of the South American Pirate. L.C. Str. 13/2/58.
D. Silvio. L.C. S.W. 2/3/94.
D. Simon the Tanner; or, The Maid of the Cherry-tree Garden of Bermondsey (Vic. 7/4/56). L.C.
D. Simon the Thief (Vic. 6/1/66). L.C.
Ca. Simply an Advertisement. L.C. Assembly R. Herne Bay, 8/8/63.
P. Sinbad the Sailor. L.C. Alex. L'pool, 21/12/75.
P. Sinbad the Sailor. L.C. Birkenhead, 23/12/75.
P. Sinbad the Sailor. L.C. Nottingham, 6/1/76.
P. Sinbad the Sailor. L.C. Alex. Sheffield, 12/12/76.
P. Sinbad the Sailor. L.C. P's. Manchester, 19/12/76.
P. Sinbad the Sailor. L.C. H.M. Aberdeen, 20/12/76.
P. Sinbad the Sailor. L.C. Birmingham, 21/12/76. MS. Birmingham.
P. Sinbad the Sailor. L.C. P's. Bradford, 18/12/77.
P. Sinbad the Sailor. L.C. Norwich, 26/1/78.
P. Sinbad the Sailor. L.C. Brighton, 13/12/78.
P. Sinbad the Sailor. L.C. O.H. Leicester, 19/12/78.
P. Sinbad the Sailor. L.C. Hull, 21/12/78.
P. Sinbad the Sailor. L.C. Bristol, 23/12/79.
P. Sinbad the Sailor. L.C. Rotunda, L'pool, 23/12/80.
P. Sinbad the Sailor. L.C. Worcester, 29/12/81.

Ext. Sinbad the Sailor. L.C. Roy. 5/4/82.
P. Sinbad the Sailor. L.C. Bradford, 5/12/82.
P. Sinbad the Sailor. L.C. P.W. Birmingham, 18/12/82.
P. Sinbad the Sailor. L.C. Lyc. Crewe, 18/12/82.
P. Sinbad the Sailor. L.C. Manchester, 20/12/82.
P. Sinbad the Sailor. L.C. Birmingham, 23/12/82.
P. Sinbad the Sailor. L.C. Sunderland, 30/12/82.
P. Sinbad the Sailor. L.C. S. Shields, 24/1/83.
P. Sinbad the Sailor. L.C. Cardiff, 8/12/83.
P. Sinbad the Sailor. L.C. P'cess. Glasgow, 12/12/83.
P. Sinbad the Sailor. L.C. Huddersfield, 31/12/83.
P. Sinbad the Sailor. L.C. Tyne, Newcastle, 2/1/84.
P. Sinbad the Sailor. L.C. Sheffield, 10/12/84.
P. Sinbad the Sailor. L.C. Corn Exchange, Maidstone, 23/12/85.
P. Sinbad the Sailor. L.C. P's. Bristol, 20/12/86.
P. Sinbad the Sailor. L.C. Alex. L'pool, 22/12/86.
P. Sinbad the Sailor. L.C. County, Reading, 9/12/87.
P. Sinbad the Sailor. L.C. Stratford, 21/12/88.
P. Sinbad the Sailor. L.C. P's. Manchester, 21/12/88.
P. Sinbad the Sailor. L.C. Stockport, 26/12/88.
P. Sinbad the Sailor. L.C. Sheffield, 5/12/89.
P. Sinbad the Sailor. L.C. Rotunda, L'pool, 12/12/89.
P. Sinbad the Sailor. L.C. Nottingham, 1/1/90.
P. Sinbad the Sailor. L.C. Cardiff, 15/12/90.
P. Sinbad the Sailor. L.C. Edinburgh, 16/12/90.
P. Sinbad the Sailor. L.C. Plymouth, 11/12/91.
P. Sinbad the Sailor. L.C. Birmingham, 13/1/92. MS. Birmingham.
P. Sinbad the Sailor. L.C. Alex. Sheffield, 8/12/92.
P. Sinbad the Sailor. L.C. Alex. Oldham, 8/12/92.
P. Sinbad the Sailor. L.C. Aldershot, 21/12/92.
P. Sinbad the Sailor. L.C. P'cess. Glasgow, 16/12/93.
P. Sinbad the Sailor. L.C. Bradford, 16/12/93.
P. Sinbad the Sailor. L.C. Qns. Manchester, 20/1/94.
P. Sinbad the Sailor. L.C. Plymouth, 18/12/94.
P. Sinbad the Sailor. L.C. Manchester, 18/12/94.
P. Sinbad the Sailor. L.C. S. Shields, 31/12/95.
P. Sinbad the Sailor. L.C. Glasgow, 10/1/96.
P. Sinbad the Sailor. L.C. Stockton-on-Tees, 26/12/96.
P. Sinbad the Sailor (Richmond, 26/12/98).
P. Sinbad the Sailor. L.C. P's. Bristol, 30/12/98.
P. Sinbad the Sailor. L.C. P's. Manchester, 30/12/98.
P. Sinbad the Sailor. L.C. Leeds, 28/12/99.
P. Sinbad the Sailor. L.C. Lyr. Hammersmith, 28/12/99.
P. Sinbad the Sailor. L.C. P'cess. Glasgow, 28/12/99.
P. Sinbad the Sailor. L.C. P.W. Birmingham, 28/12/99.
P. Sinbad the Sailor; or, Harlequin Old Man of the Sea, the Emperor, the Ogre, the Good Fairy and the Princess. L.C. Pav. 27/12/66.
P. Sinbad the Sailor; or, Harlequin the Demon of the Sea, the Seven Savages of Sage and the Onion Island. L.C. Bower, 30/12/72.
P. Sinbad the Sailor; or, King Diamond and the Fairies of the Golden Lake. L.C. Gar. 8/12/71.
P. Sing a Song of Sixpence. L.C. Brit. 21/12/57.
P. Sing a Song of Sixpence, a Pocket full of Rye, Four and Twenty Black Birds Baked in a Pie (C.L. 26/12/62). L.C.

P. Sir Bevis and Ascapart. L.C. Southampton, 19/12/77.
Bsq. Sir Giles Overreach; or, A New Way Old Debts to pay. L.C. St J. 24/3/59.
R.D. Sir Hilary's Wager. L.C. D.Y. 9/8/98.
D. Sir Jasper's Tenant. L.C. S.W. 22/11/65.
P. Sir Richard Whittington. L.C. Richmond, 31/12/95.
D. The Sisters. L.C. Cab. 29/2/64.
D. The Sisters. L.C. P.W. Birmingham, 23/4/75.
D. A Sister's Honour. L.C. Var. 11/12/89.
D. The Sisters of Segoria. L.C. Ladb. Grove, 5/2/79.
D. The Sister's Sacrifice (Lyc. 20/1/59). L.C.
D. A Sister's Wrongs; or, The Dark Hour before Dawn. L.C. Brit. 8/9/55.
Ca. Six and Eightpence (P's. 17/3/84). L.C.
D. The Six Degrees of Crime (Grec. 22/3/60).
C.O. Sixty-Six. L.C. Ch.X. 4/7/76.
D. Sixty Years Ago (Stand. 27/12/52).
F. A Skeleton in the Cupboard. L.C. Lyr. Ealing, 23/2/85.
D. The Skeleton of the Wave (Qns. 1/3/52).
D. The Skeleton Robber (Brit. 15/7/61).
Ent. Sketches in India (Str. 20/2/54).
Ca. A Sketch from the Louvre. L.C. Grec. 19/7/67.
Ca. A Skilful Practitioner. L.C. Windsor, 25/11/61.
Ca. A Skilful Practitioner. L.C. Canterbury, 2/7/68.
D. The Skipper of the Two Sisters. L.C. P.W. L'pool, 10/6/84.
D. The Skipper's Secret. L.C. Axminster Literary Society, 2/12/78.
D. Slander. L.C. 11/3/82.
D. The Slave Hunter and the Half Caste; or, Life in New Orleans (C.L. 6/8/66). L.C.
D. The Slave Lost. L.C. Adel. L'pool, 18/6/67.
D. The Slaves of Crime; or, Sowing the Whirlwind and Reaping the Storm. L.C. Brit. 9/7/64.
D. The Slaves of London; or, The Battle of the World. L.C. 11/10/51.
D. The Sledge Bells. L.C. Hull, 3/11/77.
P. The Sleeping Beauty. L.C. Brighton, 23/12/62.
P. The Sleeping Beauty. L.C. Wolverhampton, 13/1/76.
P. The Sleeping Beauty. L.C. Alex. L'pool, 28/11/76.
P. The Sleeping Beauty. L.C. Margate, 18/12/80.
P. The Sleeping Beauty. L.C. Portland H. Southsea, 22/12/86.
P. The Sleeping Beauty. L.C. Tyne, Newcastle, 8/1/97.
P. The Sleeping Beauty. L.C. Edinburgh, 31/12/97.
P. The Sleeping Beauty. L.C. P.W. Birmingham, 31/12/97.
P. The Sleeping Beauty. L.C. Corn Exchange, Maidstone, 30/12/98.
P. The Sleeping Beauty. L.C. Metro. Manchester, 29/12/99.
P. The Sleeping Beauty; or, The Darling Prince. L.C. Bower, 23/12/71.
P. The Sleeping Beauty; or, The Spirit of the Brook. L.C. Holte, Aston, Birmingham, 13/12/79.
P. The Sleeping Beauty in the Wood. L.C. P'cess. Edinburgh, 14/12/78.
P. The Sleeping Beauty in the Wood; or, Harlequin Prince Pretty and the Seven Fairy Godmothers (Stand. 26/12/61). L.C.

Oa. The Sleeping Queen. L.C. G.I. 31/8/64.
[By *H. B. FARNIE.*]

C. Slightly Touched; or, The Gentleman with a Bee in his Bonnet. L.C. Col. Glasgow, 22/9/68.

Oa. Slocum's Perplexities (Sur. Masonic H. 22/11/98).

Bsq. The Slumbering Beauty. L.C. The Slumbering Burlesque Co. 30/11/83.

F. Slumber my Darling. L.C. Str. 21/3/68.

D. The Slur of Slander; or, The Castlemont Mystery. L.C. Lyr. Hammersmith, 8/5/89.

M.F. Smiles and Kisses (Com. Manchester, 23/2/85; Olym. 27/6/85).

F. Smiles and Tears. L.C. Stockton, 10/3/84.

F. Smith. L.C. Alex. L'pool, 1/6/71.

F. The Smiths of Norwood (St J. 19/1/63). L.C.

Oa. The Smuggler's Daughter. L.C. Market H. Appleby, 26/4/98.

D. A Snake in the Grass. L.C. Grec. 6/6/56.

D. The Snake in the Grass (C.L. 8/11/58). L.C.

P. The Snake King and the Frog Prince; or, Harlequin and the Queen of the Water Lily. L.C. Manchester, 30/11/57.

D. Snapdragon (Grec. 3/4/62). L.C. as *The Heather Flower; or Snapdragon the Highwayman and the Mysteries of Grassdale Manor.*

O. Snefern the Second; or, The Land of Khem. L.C. St Andrew's H. Glasgow, 9/2/97.

D. Snowdrops. L.C. Regent Park Pav. Morecambe, 17/11/92.

D. Snowed Up. L.C. S.W. 25/9/94.

F. A Snug Investment. L.C. Alex. L'pool, 15/3/73.

D. The Social Reformer (Ladb. H. 17/6/92, *amat.*).

F.C. Social Sinners (Sunderland, 17/8/85).

C. Social Undertakers. L.C. S.W. 18/12/94.

F.C. A Society Beauty (Sturton T.H. Cambridge, 1/5/84). L.C. Leamington.

F. Sold. L.C. H.M. Aberdeen, 25/3/73.

F. Sold. L.C. Hull, 19/1/79.

Ca. Sold. L.C. St G. H. Canterbury, 20/6/98.

D. The Soldier's Bride (Vic. 9/1/54).

Oa. The Soldier's Legacy. L.C. G.I. 19/10/64.

D. The Soldier's Return. L.C. Var. 2/12/86.

D. The Soldier's Wife. L.C. Brit. 30/5/53.

D. The Soldier's Wife. L.C. Str. 17/11/54.

D. Solid Silver (Darlington, 17/5/80).

F. Solon Shingle (Adel. 3/7/65).

D. Some Bells that ring the Old Year out and a New One in (Brit. 15/12/62).

Ca. Something Forgotten. L.C. Leeds, 25/2/74.

D. Something like a Nugget (Norwich, 25/1/69). L.C.

Bal. Something of All Sorts. L.C. Alh. 31/5/71.

F. La Somnambula (Str. 2/1/54).

Bsq.O. The Sonambula. L.C. Brit. 16/11/59.

Oa. Son and Stranger (Guildhall School of Music, 23/12/96).

D. The Son of Night. L.C. Sunderland, 18/11/56.

D. The Son of Night. L.C. Manchester, 9/4/57.

D. The Son of Night. L.C. Vic. 27/5/57.

D. The Son of Night (S.W. 2/9/72).

D. The Son of the Sea (Grec. 5/9/66).
F. Sons and Systems (S.W. 7/11/59).
D. The Sons of Columbia: A Story of the American War (Brit. 10/3/62). L.C.
D. The Sons of Freedom (Grec. 5/7/66).
[See *A. FAUCQUEZ*, 1868.]
D. The Sorrows of Satan (Nottingham, 1/3/97; Shakespeare, Clapham, 12/4/97). L.C. S. Shields.
D. So the World goes. L.C. Eff. 27/5/60.
F. So very obliging (Str. 28/9/57). L.C.
D. The Sowers. L.C. St J. 8/1/97.
D. Spadra the Satirist (Sheffield, 18/11/69).
Bsq. Spanish Onions. L.C. Lyc. Crewe, 28/11/82.
Ent. The Spanish Page (Brit. 26/4/59).
D. Spare the Rod, Spoil the Child. L.C. C.L. 11/4/57.
D. The Spectre Bride. L.C. W.L. 12/11/94.
D. The Spectre of Conway Castle. L.C. M'bone, 12/9/63.
D. A Speedy Settlement. L.C. Barnard's, Woolwich, 7/9/96.
P. The Spider and the Fly (Ast. 26/12/62).
P. The Spider and the Fly; or, Harlequin Number Nip and the Magic Toys. L.C. Grec. 20/12/62.
D. The Spider's Web. L.C. Star, Swansea, 19/7/81.
[Title altered to *The Reckoning Day*, 3/12/84.]
F. Spindlepops (Sur. 15/10/54).
F. The Spinster. L.C. O.H. Stockport, 22/3/83.
[See *P. GWYNNE*, 1887.]
F. Spinsters Beware! L.C. Qns. 26/2/73.
D. The Spirit Bride; or, Children of the Earth. L.C. Vic. 26/3/50.
D. The Spirit Child's Prayer (C.L. 27/2/65).
F. A Spirit Medium (Roy. 29/4/62). L.C.
D. The Spirit of Death; or, Twelve O'Clock and the Midnight Angel. L.C. Stand. 24/5/61.
P. The Spirit of Liberty (Brit. 26/12/59). L.C. [as *Harlequin Needles and Pins; or, The S. of L. in Asia, Africa and America*].
D. The Spirit of Mercy. L.C. Qns. 26/10/63.
D. The Spirit of Revenge (Grec. 5/3/60).
D. The Spirit of the Haunted Room; or, The Dunmow Festival. L.C. Brit. 25/8/55.
F. Spirit Rapping and Table Moving (M'bone, 4/7/53).
F. Spirit Rapping and Table Moving (Grec. 18/7/53).
F. Spirit Rapping and Table Moving (Marionette, 25/7/53).
F. Spirit Rappings and Table Moving; or, The Mahogany Polka (C.L. 27/6/53). L.C.
D. The Spirits of Good and Evil. L.C. Brit. 31/10/57.
D. The Spirits of the Departed (Brit. 30/6/63).
D. The Spirit Trapper; or, The Rapparee's Mystery (Vic. 25/7/53). L.C.
F. The Spirit World (Worcester, 6/4/88). L.C.
Ca. Splendid Mrs Wichels. L.C. T.H. Brighton, 29/11/98.
F. A Spoilt Spree. L.C. Assembly R. Bognor, 16/11/92.
F. Sport. L.C. Var. 5/11/83.
F. Sporting Intelligence Extraordinary (Olym. 17/12/61).
F. Sporting in the Dark (Sur. 7/5/55).
D. The Sport of Fate. L.C. Consett, Durham, 31/5/95.

D.Sk. The Spouse Trap; or, The Kitchen Girl. L.C. Assembly R. Taunton, 30/11/99.
M.D. The Spring and Fall of Life (Grec. 21/5/66). L.C.
D. Spring-heeled Jack; or, The Felon's Wrongs (Grec. 4/6/63). L.C.
D. The Spy of Paris; or, A Struggle for Liberty. L.C. Brit. 29/4/58.
F. The Squeaker. L.C. Cambridge H. of Varieties, Bishopsgate, 5/6/94.
F. The Squeaker. L.C. W.L. 4/7/95.
D. The Standard of England; or, The Life of a Soldier (M'bone, 6/4/63). L.C.
Bal. The Star of Andalusia (H. 24/7/54).
D. The Star of Destiny. L.C. S.W. 10/10/98.
D. The Star of the Street (Adel. 26/3/60).
D. Starved to Death; or, High Crime and Low Crime (Adel. L'pool, 26/8/72).
D. The Station House (Adel. 9/10/54).
D. The Statue Lover (Str. 22/5/54).
D. The Statue of Clay. L.C. Parkhurst, 22/4/92.
D. Steel Hand and his Nine Thieves; or, The Fairy Pool of the Giant Mountain (Brit. 11/5/57). L.C.
C. Stella; or, Bauble and Co. L.C. P'cess. 24/8/52.
D. Stella Gordon. L.C. Gai. Hastings, 15/5/93.
D. Stella, the Female Pirate (Brit. 9/5/59).
D. Step by Step; or, The End will come. L.C. Qns. 25/3/62.
D. The Stepmother. L.C. Miss Marriot's Co. 13/9/82.
C. Stepmothers; or, A Broken Reed. L.C. Blackburn, 14/5/77.
D. Stolen; or, The Street Ballad Singer (S.W. 23/11/68).
D.Sk. Stolen Bonds; or, A London Sensation. L.C. S.W. 31/12/97.
M.D. The Stolen Diamonds; or, A Woman's Error. L.C. Miss Ida Glen's Dramatic Co. 20/3/76.
D. Stolen from Home; or, Human Hearts (S.W. 12/10/91).
F. The Stolen Kiss. L.C. Str. 18/10/56.
F. Stone Broke. L.C. S.W. 4/7/95.
D. The Stone Jug. L.C. Adel. 18/3/73.
F. The Stone Man. L.C. Adel. 14/11/54.
D.Sk. Stoney Broke. L.C. S.W. 30/3/97.
Ca. Stop for Dinner. L.C. Vic. R. Bridlington Quay, 8/2/94.
D. Storm and Sunshine (C.P. 24/7/89). L.C.
M.Ca. A Storm in a Teacup. L.C. Bijou, 13/2/75.
Equest.Spec. The Storming and Capture of Delhi (Ast. 23/11/57). L.C.
D. The Storm of Life. L.C. Moseley and Balsall Heath Inst. Moseley, 25/9/86.
D. The Storm Signal; or, Drifting to Seaward (Grec. 29/10/66). L.C.
D. The Storm Visitor; or, The Avenging Gift. L.C. Brit. 27/6/56.
D. The Story of a Night (Grec. 1/1/59).
D.Sk. A Story of Babylon. L.C. S.W. 30/3/98.
D. A Story of Procida (St J. 4/11/67). L.C.
D. A Story of the Heart; or, A Father's Love (Brit. 13/2/60). L.C.
F. A Straight Tip (D.L. 20/9/73). L.C.
D. Strange but True (Grec. 2/7/66). L.C. [as *One Crime; or, The Felon's Wife*].
Bsq. The Strange Case of a Hyde and Seekyll. L.C. Toole's, 18/5/86.

F.C. A Strange Legacy. L.C. Grand, Birmingham, 25/11/88.
F. A Stranger in a Strange Land. L.C. Terry's, 24/3/99.
F. The Straw Hat (P.W. L'pool, 13/12/73). L.C.
D. The Stricken Oak. L.C. P's. Glasgow, 31/8/63.
D. The Strike. L.C. Var. 5/1/85.
F. A Striking Widow (H. 16/6/58). L.C.
D. The String of Pearls (Grec. 6/6/61). L.C.
D. The String of Pearls; or, The Life and Death of Sweeny Tod. L.C. Eff. 11/7/62.
C.D. Stronger than Love. L.C. Bijou, 16/7/94.
C. Struck Oil; or, The Pennsylvania Dutchman (Adel. 17/4/76). L.C.
D. The Struggle for Gold and the Orphan of the Frozen Sea (M'bone, 20/2/54).
D. Struggles of the Poor; or, Love, Poverty and Wealth. L.C. C.L. 16/6/57.
D. The Students (Sur. 16/2/61). L.C.
Ca. A Subterfuge (Olym. 10/8/57). L.C.
Oa. A Suburban Spectre. L.C. T.H. Hounslow, 7/6/98.
Duol. A Successful Mission (P.W. 14/7/94). L.C.
D. Such is Life (E.C. 28/2/85).
D. Such is Life. L.C. Eff. 14/5/64.
Ca. A Sudden Attack (Lyc. 10/1/63). L.C.
D.Trifle. A Sudden Shower. L.C. King's Lynn, 31/5/95.
D. The Suicide's Tree; or, Lady Hatton and the Mystery of the Bleeding Heart. L.C. Pav. 9/9/63.
Ca. A Suitable Match. L.C. P's. Manchester, 2/4/79.
Oa. A Suitor at Sea. L.C. Greenwich, 18/2/70.
D. The Sulamite. L.C. Internat. 10/3/84.
D. The Sultan and the Tsar (Sur. 24/4/54).
Bal. The Sultan's Dream (Olym. 10/10/50).
Oa. A Summer Cloud (Str. 20/9/80). L.C.
C.D. A Summer Cloud. L.C. Empress, 30/8/99.
Oa. A Summer Festival. L.C. Surrey Gdns. 9/7/73.
Bal. Summer Flowers (Str. 1/5/54).
F. Summerland's Mistake (P.W. Wolverhampton, 10/3/73).
Bal. The Sun and the Wind (H. 1/10/60).
F. The Supper Party (Sur. 18/5/61).
D. A Supreme Moment. L.C. Court, 30/8/99.
D. Sure to Win (Gymnasium, Huddersfield, 2/5/76).
C. The Surprise. L.C. Crit. 22/12/99.
Ca. Susan's Lovers. L.C. Reading, 2/5/78.
D. Suspicion (Brit. 11/8/75).
D. The Swallows' Nest (M'bone, 25/5/63).
Ext. The Swan and Edgar; or, The Fairy Lake (St J. 16/11/59). L.C.
P. Sweet Cinderella. L.C. E.C. 20/12/89.
Ca. Sweet Seventeen. L.C. St G. H. Canterbury, 20/6/98.
D. Sweet Sorrow. L.C. Grand, Derby, 15/11/99.
F.C. The Swell Miss Fitzwell. L.C. Vaud. 11/10/97.
D. The Swiss Church (Brit. 12/12/59).
R.C. The Swiss Girl. L.C. Vic. H. Sudbury, 31/12/97.
F. Sworn to Secrecy. L.C. Sur. 15/5/73.
D. Sybyle; or, Weary of Bondage (Ch.X. 22/10/73).
Bal. The Sylph of the Glen. L.C. Alh. 8/7/71.

O. Sylvia; or, The Forest Flower (Roy. 17/2/66). L.C.
C.D. Sylvia's Exchange. L.C. Canterbury, 11/9/99.
Bsq. Sylvius; or, The Peril, the Pelf and the Pearl (H. 26/12/66). L.C.
F. Taffy's Triumph; or, Go Wyn Wyn Wyn. L.C. Olym. 24/1/76. [See *J. F. McARDLE*, 1874.]
P. Taffy was a Welchman; or, Harlequin and the Magic Marrowbone (Str. 20/11/54).
F. The Tailor's Strike (Sur. 25/4/59).
D. The Taint in the Blood; or, The Poisoned Pearl. L.C. Grec. 16/10/56.
D.Sk. Take back the Heart (Devonshire Park, Eastbourne, 31/5/86; Crit. 15/6/86, *mat.*). L.C.
F. Taking it easy (Toole's, 11/82). L.C.
Monol. Taking the Waters (St G. 1/11/86).
C. A Tale of a Coat (H. 6/11/58). L.C.
F. The Tale of a Copper. L.C. P'cess. 25/2/71.
F. A Tale of a Telegram. L.C. Glo. 9/11/88.
D. A Tale of Dartmoor. L.C. Parkhurst, 9/4/91.
F. A Tale of the Kitchen (Sur. 8/3/62). L.C. [as *Oh! Betsy!*].
D. A Tale of Troy (P's. H. 14/5/86).
D. Tales of the Holly Tree Inn. L.C. Brit. 13/1/56.
F. Talons and Claws. L.C. Woolwich, 27/11/86.
P. Tam o' Shanter (Qns. Edinburgh, 26/12/58).
Ba. Tam o' Shanter. L.C. O.H. Kilmarnock, 27/2/76.
Ext. Tam o' Shanter; or, The Brig o' Doon (Col. Glasgow, 1/6/68).
D. Tamworth in A.D. 670; or, The Pagan King, the Christian Bishop and the Princely Martyrs of Eagles' Hall (Eccleshall) (Pav. Tamworth, 22/8/94).
D. A Tangled Web. L.C. Assembly R. Bognor, 12/6/91.
O. Tannhäuser (H.M. 14/2/82). L.C.
D. The Tars of England (Stand. 3/5/52).
F. The Tasting Order. L.C. Str. 4/9/54.
C. Teddy O'Connor; or, An Irishman's Love. L.C. Portsmouth, 22/4/76.
Duol. Telegrams. L.C. St Martin's H. 29/3/95.
F. A Telegraphic Error. L.C. Stand. 23/11/68.
P. Tell Tale Tit; or, Harlequin Dickery Dickery Dock (Stand. 26/12/68). L.C.
D. Temptation. L.C. Pav. 4/4/55.
D. Temptation. L.C. Birmingham, 16/5/55.
D. Temptation and Atonement (Grec. 9/2/60). L.C.
D. The Tempter. L.C. C.L. 1/12/59.
D. The Tempter and the Disowned (Grec. 29/8/60).
F. A Tenant for Life (S.W. 1/11/58). L.C.
F. Tenants in Common. L.C. Ast. 23/7/85.
Oa. Ten Daughters and No Husband. L.C. O.C. 7/11/71.
Ent. Terpsichore (D.L. 5/6/55).
D. Tess of the D'Urbervilles. L.C. Grand, Blackpool, 29/12/99. [See *L. STODDARD*, 1897.]
D. Tested, Tried and True. L.C. Pav. 28/2/72.
D.Sk. A Texan's Revenge. L.C. S.W. 27/2/96.
Ent. Thalia. L.C. Lyc. Stafford, 15/7/78.
D. That Beautiful Wretch (Bijou, L'pool, 26/12/81). L.C.

F. That Boy Pete. L.C. Ast. 3/5/81.
F. That Dancing Dog (Sur. 27/3/55).
F. That Horrid Biggins (Roy. 27/1/66). L.C. Soho, 21/11/60.
C. That House in High Street (Str. 28/7/56). L.C.
Oa. That Mysterious Novel (Steinway H. 2/4/97).
[Music by Lila Jarratt.]
F. That Rascal Jack (Lyc. 4/3/61).
M.C. A Theatrical Duchess. L.C. Exeter, 28/9/96.
[Title altered to *The Chorus Girl*, 28/5/97.]
D. Theo. L.C. Athen. Hammersmith, 15/9/94.
D. Theodore of Ritzberg; or, The Dumb Boy of Vienna. L.C. Brit. 17/7/57.
D. There are Secrets in all Families; or, Clouds of Sorrow and Rays of Sunshine. L.C. S.W. 27/9/62.
C.D. There's nothing like a Friend at Court when a Man is in Search of Relations. L.C. Grec. 26/7/54.
Bsq. Theusia. L.C. Col. Dudley, 16/11/92.
Monol. They're all alike. L.C. Metro. 10/12/98.
F. They're both to blame (St J. 20/10/59).
D. They were Friends. L.C. Edin. 6/11/89.
F. Thieves! Thieves! (Olym. 12/3/57). L.C.
D. Third Class and First Class; or, The Career of the Widow's Son (Brit. 1/8/59). L.C.
D. The Thirteenth Chime (Soho, 11/5/59).
D. Thirteen Years' Labour Lost (Stand. 30/4/55).
Bsq. The Thirty Nine Thieves. L.C. Str. 31/3/63.
P. The Thirty Nine Thieves. L.C. Grimsby, 18/1/77.
D. This and the other Hand; or, Plague, Fire and Water. L.C. Eff. 27/5/63.
M.Ca. Thisbe and Pyramus. L.C. West, Albert H. 7/3/89.
Ent. This Horse will be sold to pay the Expenses, if not claimed within Fourteen Days (Ast. 5/6/54). L.C.
Ca. This Plot of Ground to let, a Capital Site for a Theatre (Alex. 26/1/74). L.C.
F. This Side Up. L.C. Stand. 2/4/74.
Ext. The Thistle and the Rampant Lion (O.H. Dundee, 11/3/72).
F. Those Horrid Garotters (Olym. 3/2/73). L.C.
F.C. Those Terrible Twins (Cardiff, 25/6/1900). L.C. Ladb. H. 22/12/99.
[Title altered to *Mabel's Twins*, 22/5/1922.]
D. Three and the Deuce (S.W. 1/3/62).
D. The Three Brothers of Brevannes (S.W. 3/3/63).
D. The Three Brothers of Mystery. L.C. Qns. 18/2/61.
D. The Three Brothers of Normandy; or, The Compact of Life and Death (Brit. 11/4/59). L.C. Brit. 7/4/57.
D. The Three Brothers of the Old Chateau (Grec. 29/10/60).
F. Three Black Smiths. *French*.
D. Three Cheers for Charity; or, A Night's Wonders. L.C. Grec. 2/7/53.
F. Three Dummies (Sur. 1/10/59). L.C.
D. The Three Fast Men; or, The Female Robinson Crusoes of America. L.C. Stand. 8/6/60.
D. Three-Fingered Jack (Brit. 10/9/60).
M.Ca. Three Flats. L.C. St G. 25/2/80.
Ca. The Three Graces. L.C. Lyr. 11/12/91.
[See *H. B. COLLINS*, 1898.]

C. Three Hundred a Year. L.C. Sheffield, 26/9/63.
P. The Three Jacks. L.C. Bristol, 8/1/83.
D. The Three Lives (Brit. 14/5/60). L.C.
O. The Three Musqueteers. L.C. Glasgow, 13/4/99.
F. Three of a Kind. L.C. S.W. 10/12/94.
F. Three Pairs of Lovers (Str. 22/3/52).
D. Three Shots from a Carbine; or, A Love's Revenge. L.C. Eff. 27/1/65.
[By *W. E. SUTER.*]
F. The Three Singles (Stand. 14/4/62).
D. The Three Thieves of Lambetti (Vic. 4/5/54).
M.Ca. Three to One. L.C. Lyr. Ealing, 8/12/93.
C.Vaud. Three to One; or, The Forget-me-not. L.C. Str. 16/4/53.
F. Three Turkish Razor Grinders (Str. 1/5/54).
D. The Three Women (Pav. 19/11/66).
D.Sk. Through Shot and Shell. L.C. S.W. 21/10/96.
P. Tib, Pat, Joe, the Three Butcher Boys all of a Row; or, Harlequin Mephistopheles and Old Father Thames. L.C. Eff. 16/12/58.
D. Ticket of Leave (Sur. 9/5/59). L.C.
D. Tickets. L.C. Harry Liton's Co. 11/3/82.
F. The Tiffins; or, Our Bachelor Friends. L.C. Newcastle, 7/12/58.
C.D. A Tiger's Claw. L.C. Adel. L'pool, 24/3/99.
D. The Tiger Slayer of the Savannah. L.C. Eff. 26/4/61.
D. Tiger Tom. L.C. E.C. 5/5/73.
C. A Tight Rein; or, A Home Ruler. L.C. P.W. Glasgow, 13/10/79.
D. Tilbury Fort; or, The Black Knight of Chelmsford. L.C. 17/10/51.
D. The Timely Warning; or, Past, Present and Future. L.C. Grec. 18/3/56.
D. Time's Revenge (Brit. 4/10/75). L.C.
D. Time's Triumph. L.C. P.W. 21/11/89.
D. Time the Avenger. L.C. Hanley, 8/11/77.
F. Timson's Little Holiday. L.C. D.L. 9/9/84.
F. Tinker's Holiday. L.C. Var. 2/3/86.
F. Tit for Tat. L.C. Lyc. 20/5/58.
F. Tit for Tat. L.C. S.W. 25/6/62.
Ent. Tobin and Nannette (St J. 27/6/59).
F. Toddles and Togg (Sur. 30/4/55). L.C.
M.C. Toledo. L.C. Empire, Aberdeen, 18/11/96.
F. The Tomboy. L.C. Burton-on-Trent, 9/4/88.
F. To meet Mr Stripling. L.C. Bijou, 23/12/95.
F. Tomkins the Troubadour (Qns. 31/8/68). L.C. *Lacy.*
D. Tommy Atkins. L.C. Sur. 31/5/95.
D. Tom Sheppard; or, The Bright Road of Honesty and the Dark Path of Crime (Grec. 31/5/66). L.C. Bower, 23/9/65.
F. Tom's Wife (Sur. 4/10/62). L.C.
P. Tom Tom the Piper's Son (Park, 26/12/76). L.C.
P. Tom Tom the Piper's Son. L.C. Lyc. Sunderland, 23/1/78.
P. Tom Tom the Piper's Son. L.C. Victory, Aldershot, 6/12/78.
P. Tom Tom the Piper's Son. L.C. R.A. Woolwich, 7/12/85.
P. Tom Tom the Piper's Son. L.C. Corn Exchange, Maidstone, 24/12/87.
P. Tom Tom the Piper's Son; or, Harlequin the Magic Thistle and the Fairy that lived in a Grotto. L.C. Eff. 19/12/60.
C.O. Tong-li-Too. L.C. Market H. Appleby, 13/4/99.

D. The Ton of Gold; or, A Woman keeps the Secret (Pav. 21/10/66). L.C.
C. Too Clever (Alex. L'pool, 2/4/76). L.C.
Vaud. Too Clever by Half; or, The Wild Irish Girl. L.C. M'bone, 24/6/68.
D. The Toodles. L.C. D.L. 18/6/62.
Ca. Too Fatiguing (Scarborough, 24/8/85).
D. Too Late. L.C. P.W. 25/9/68.
Ext. Toolooloo and Woolooloo; or, The Great Bear and the Two Kings (Sur. 5/4/58). L.C.
Oa. Too Many Cooks. (G.I. 31/8/64). L.C.
[By *G. REED*; music J. Offenbach.]
C. Too much Johnson (Gar. 18/4/98). L.C.
F. Topsy Turvy. L.C. Birkenhead, 15/1/85.
Ca. A Toss Up. L.C. Vestry H. Anerley, 31/12/97.
D.Sk. To the Front. L.C. S.W. 30/1/95.
F. Touch and Go. L.C. W.L. 16/12/93.
F. Touch and Take; or, Saturday Night and Sunday Morning (D.L. 4/1/55).
F. A Touching Story. L.C. Lyc. 30/4/53.
F. The Tour. L.C. Art Galleries, Newcastle, 11/4/93.
C. The Tour of a Perrywinkle. L.C. P'cess. Edinburgh, 23/1/86.
D.Sk. The Tower Bridge. L.C. S.W. 18/3/95.
Oa. The Toy Maker (C.G. 19/11/61). L.C.
Bsq. The Tragedy Queen (H. 6/7/55).
D. Traill the Anarchist. L.C. P.H. Erith, 15/4/96.
D. Traitor Doubts. L.C. Bath, 21/10/87.
F. Transferring a Licence. L.C. L'pool, 12/4/52.
D. The Transformed. (Sur 20/11/54). L.C.
D. Trapped. L.C. Var. 13/3/85.
D.Sk. Trapped (Mechanics' Inst. Stockport, 27/1/98).
D.Sk. Travellers. L.C. S.W. 31/12/97.
Oa. The Travellers' Rest. L.C. Ladb. H. 10/6/87.
O. La Traviata; or, The Blighted One (Sur. 8/6/57). L.C.
D. La Traviata, the Lost One. L.C. Brit. 27/6/57.
D. A Treaty of Peace. L.C. Swansea, 24/3/60.
D. The Trials of the Poor. L.C. Var. 14/12/87.
F. Trick and Trap (Sur. 21/11/59).
D. Tricks and Trials; or, Life as we find it in 1850 (Sur. 14/8/50). L.C.
D. Tricks of the Turf (Vic. 13/5/67).
D.Sk. Tried for Life; or, A Woman's Peril. L.C. S.W. 27/2/96.
F. Trifles light as Air. L.C. P'cess. 6/9/50.
D. Trilby. L.C. Darwen, 15/4/96.
D. Trilby. L.C. Eastbourne, 28/4/96.
D. Trilby the Model. L.C. Loughborough, 15/4/96.
F.C. The Triple Alliance (Str. 6/12/97).
[See *Poor Tommy, supra.*]
Ca. The Triple Dilemma; or, Our First Visitors. L.C. P's. Glasgow, 7/8/63.
F.C. A Trip to Blackpool. L.C. P.W. 15/11/99.
[Title altered to *A Naughty Husband*, 21/12/1918.]
M.F. A Trip to Chicago (Vaud. 5/8/93).
Ba. A Trip to Klondyke. L.C. Mechanics' Inst. Swindon, 31/12/97.

Ext. A Trip to Paris. L.C. Palace of Var. 3/12/92.
F. A Trip to Richmond (Grec. 19/9/61).
O. Tristan and Isolde (Court, L'pool, 15/4/98; Lyc. 3/2/99).
Spec. The Triumph of Peace; or, Honour to the Brave. L.C. Ast. 23/5/56.
D. The Triumph of the Standard; or, Ben and Bob, the British Bulldogs (Stand. 31/5/52). L.C.
D.Sk. Trixie's Trust (Bedford M.H. 3/4/99). L.C. Brixton.
Bal. Les trois Nymphes (Lyc. 16/5/55).
F. Trot's Troubles (S. Shields, 25/10/75). L.C.
D. The Troubadour; or, The Gipsey's Vengeance. L.C. C.L. 18/8/58.
Ent. Trouble at the Court of King Bulbous. L.C. Bijou, 1/2/96.
D. The Troubled Hearts. L.C. Alex. Bradford, 17/3/66.
D. Troubled Waters (Vic. 27/6/64). L.C.
Ca. Troubled Waters. L.C. St G. 16/5/78.
C. Troubled Waters. L.C. Ladb. H. 2/11/93.
D. True Woman. L.C. S.W. 3/5/83.
D. The Trump Card (Leicester, 25/2/78).
C. Trust. L.C. St G. 4/10/71.
C. Trust. L.C. Hackney, Clapham, 5/6/77.
C. The Trustee (Olym. 24/10/54). L.C.
D.Sk. The Turkish Bath; or, Turkish Delight. L.C. S.W. 10/11/97.
Spect. The Turkish War (Qns. 14/12/53).
P. Turn again, Whittington. L.C. Grand, Leeds, 31/12/95.
Ca. The Turn of the Lane. L.C. Albert Inst. Windsor, 29/12/99.
D. Turn Round (Vic. H. Newport, 29/10/70, *amat.*).
Equestr.D. Turpin's Ride to York; or, The Heir of Rookwood (Ast. 3/12/55). L.C.
F.C. The Turtle Doves (Booth's, Ashton-under-Lyne, 22/11/80). L.C. P's. Manchester [as *One of the Family*].
[See *G. CAPEL*, 1898.]
C.O. Twelve O'Clock. L.C. O.C. 26/6/84.
F. Twenty Minutes with an Impudent Puppy. L.C. C.G. 14/1/56.
F. Twenty Minutes with a Tiger (D.L. 29/10/55). *Lacy.*
F. Twenty Minutes with H. P. (Campden House, 4/6/60).
D. Twenty Straws. L.C. Brit. 5/2/65.
D. Twenty Straws. L.C. Eff. 7/3/65.
Ca. Twice Fooled (Gai. 23/7/95). L.C.
F. Twice Married (Roy. 11/5/65).
D. Twilight to Dawn (Lyc. Stafford, 8/10/85).
P. Twinkle, Twinkle, Little Star. L.C. Brighton, 22/12/75.
P. Twinkle, Twinkle, Little Star. L.C. Qns. Manchester, 25/12/75.
P. Twinkle, Twinkle, Little Star. L.C. Bradford, 30/12/98.
P. Twinkle, Twinkle, Little Star. L.C. Lyc. Sheffield, 29/12/99.
D. 'Twixt Gold and Love; or, A True Woman's Heart (Scarborough, 5/11/83).
Ca. Two can play at that Game. L.C. Plymouth, 15/4/57.
D. The Two Christmas Eves; or, The Old World and the New. L.C. C.L. 6/1/59.
D. Two College Friends (Sur. 23/3/57).
D. The Two Daughters. L.C. Alex. Walsall, 9/9/81.
Ba. The Two D's. L.C. S.W. 11/9/99.
Ca. The Two Georges. L.C. P.H. Urmston, 30/3/96.

F. The Two G's of P.P.P. (Sur. 10/5/60).
Ca. Two in One. L.C. Aven. 19/3/91.
F. Two Lodgers to one Lodging (Grec. 4/4/64).
F. Two Lovers too many (Sur. 15/10/55).
F. Two Mean Husbands. L.C. Barnard's, Woolwich, 18/7/94.
D. Two Men and a Woman. L.C. County, Kingston, 21/8/99.
M.D. Two of a Trade. L.C. Aven. 21/5/96.
C. Two Old Blokes (Portsmouth, 17/3/71).
C.D. Two Old Pals. L.C. Com. Manchester, 9/8/95.
D. The Two Orphan Girls. L.C. P's. Blackburn, 17/5/99.
D. The Two Orphans. L.C. Bristol, 7/2/83.
D. The Two Orphans of Paris. L.C. Gai. Burnley, 19/12/92.
D. The Two Orphans of Paris. L.C. Metro. Devonport, 14/9/97.
D. The Two Penitents. L.C. P.W. Birmingham, 5/3/94.
F. Two Precious Scoundrels (Str. 26/8/56). L.C.
F. Two Pretty Women (H. 17/6/55).
D. The Two Revolutions; or, The Brother's Destiny and the Early Crime. L.C. C.L. 23/9/54.
D. The Two Roads of Life; or, Right and Wrong (Swansea, 14/8/71). [See *E. R. CALLENDER*, 1875.]
D. The Two Shades of Life. L.C. Grantham, 25/7/88.
D. The Two Sisters (P.W. Warrington, 10/3/75).
D. The Two Students (Sur. 16/2/61).
M.F. Two to One, bar One. L.C. W.L. 18/10/94.
D. Two Winters; or, Frost at the Heart (M'bone, 8/3/59).
D.Sk. Two Women (Terry's, 17/6/95). L.C.
Ca. Two Young Wives. L.C. Crit. 18/5/92.
D. Tyranny: A Tale of the Press-gang of 1810 (Scarborough, 1/84).
D. An Ultramarine Retreat. L.C. P.W. L'pool, 21/5/65.
C.O. Ulysses. L.C. D.Y. 27/12/98.
D. The Umpire (Burnley, 31/1/87).
Bsq. Una (Qns. Dublin, 5/4/75).
D. Uncas; or, The Last of the Mohicans (Pav. 3/3/66). L.C.
Ba. An Unchartered Voyage. L.C. St G. 16/2/99.
Oa. Uncle Becker's Story. L.C. O.C. 7/11/71.
F. Uncle Benjamin's Hat. L.C. Alh. 13/1/80.
F. Uncle Bob (Sur. 12/5/55).
F. Uncle Bob. L.C. Parkhurst, 10/9/92.
F. Uncle Foozle (Olym. 28/10/51).
O.F. Uncle Jack. L.C. West Pier, Brighton, 11/9/99.
F. Uncle Jack's Legacy. L.C. Alh. 9/3/77.
D. Uncle Josh (Blackburn, 30/7/88). L.C.
D. Uncle Mark. L.C. S.W. 24/8/50.
F. Uncle's Jim. L.C. Lyr. 20/7/97.
P. Uncle Tom and Lucy Neal; or, Harlequin Liberty and Slavery. L.C. Pav. 27/12/52.
D. Uncle Tom's Cabin. L.C. Pav. 9/10/52.
D. Uncle Tom's Cabin (Living Marionettes, 8/11/52).
D. Uncle Tom's Cabin. L.C. C.L. 3/1/53.
D. Uncle Tom's Cabin. L.C. Stand. 13/9/82.
D. Uncle Tom's Cabin; or, Life among the Lowly (M'bone, 4/10/52). L.C.
D. Uncle Tom's Cabin; or, The Fugitive Slave (Vic. 20/9/52). L.C.
D. Uncle Tom's Cabin; or, The Negro Slave (Stand. 13/9/52). L.C

D. Uncle Tom's Cabin; or, The Negro Slave (Qns. 20/9/52).
D. Uncle True; or, Little Gerty (Albert, Portsmouth, 27/3/71).
Ca. The Undecided Voter. L.C. Qns. Manchester, 7/6/81.
D. Under a Cliff. L.C. Vic. H. 1/6/97.
D. Under a Cloud. L.C. Eff. 9/5/59.
D. Under a Cloud (Brit. 26/4/59). L.C.
D. Under a Cloud. L.C. St J. 2/1/63.
Oa. Under a Mask. L.C. Hengler's, 9/9/81.
D. Under Cover (K. X. 27/2/65).
F. Under Fire (Mary Street Schoolroom, W. Kensington, 16/4/88).
C.D. Under Suspicion. L.C. English's, Sebright H. Hackney Road, 5/6/94.
D. Under the Ban. L.C. Parkhurst, 23/3/95.
D. Under the Earth; or, The Sons of Toil (Ast. 22/4/67). L.C.
C. Under the Flag. L.C. Miss F. Sidley's Dramatic Co. 19/9/79.
D. Under the Gas Light. L.C. Alfred, 12/8/69.
[See *A. DALY*, 1868.]
D. Under the Lamps; or, The Gentlemen of the Night. L.C. Grec. 25/9/62.
D. Under the Red Robe. L.C. T.H. Beccles, 30/3/96.
D. Under the Red Robe (County, Kingston, 4/10/97).
D. Under the Shadow. L.C. Qns. Manchester, 10/4/84.
D. Under the Snow (Brit. 27/8/77). L.C.
D. Under the Tricolour. L.C. Swansea, 1/10/86.
D. Under the Union Jack. L.C. S.W. 28/9/97.
D. Under Two Flags. L.C. Bijou, Woolwich, 31/10/83.
D. Under Two Flags; or, A Race for Life through Flood and Flame. L.C. Sur. 12/5/69.
D. Under which Flag? L.C. S.W. 17/5/99.
Ext. Undine. L.C. Margate, 2/8/83.
Bsq. Undine (Gt Yarmouth, 13/8/83).
P. Undine; or, Harlequin and the Spirit of the Waters (H. 27/12/58). L.C.
Bsq. Undine Undone (Halifax, 21/4/73).
D. Unequally Sentenced (Ipswich, 27/3/76).
F. The Unexpected (Dublin, 28/11/70).
F. The Unfortunate Propensity. L.C. P'cess. 26/2/53.
D. United Service; or, The Lion of England and the Eagle of France (D.L. 19/1/55).
F. The United Service of England and France. L.C. Str. 21/7/54.
D. The Unknown (Sur. 12/3/59).
D. The Unknown and the Bayedere (Adel. 12/2/55).
D. The Unlucky Leap Year. L.C. Brit. 29/4/58.
F. An Unlucky Mortal (H. 4/6/63). L.C.
D. Unmasked. L.C. Gai. 6/3/86.
D. Unmasked. L.C. Albert H. Jarrow, 21/12/88.
F. Unstable as Water. L.C. Brighton, 22/12/99.
D. Until the Day Break. L.C. Blyth, 22/4/91.
Bsq. The Ups and Downs of Deal and Black-eyed Susan (M'bone, 10/6/67). L.C.
Ca. Upside Down. L.C. Brit. 29/11/64.
D.Sk. Upside Down. L.C. Empress, 11/9/99.
F.C. Up the Nile. L.C. Vaud. 30/10/94.
Bsq. Up to Dick. L.C. Swansea, 17/12/91.

Bsq. Up to Time. L.C. Temperance H. Batley, 19/9/91.
Ent. The Upturned Faces of the Roses. L.C. H.M. 30/8/99.
D. Uriel Acosta. L.C. Internat. 13/2/84.
D. The Use and Abuse of Drink (Ryde, 4/6/80).
Ca. The Usual Remedy. L.C. St G. 8/8/95.
D. Vacation Brief. L.C. P.W. 8/5/88.
D. The Vagabonds. L.C. Edmonton, 30/3/98.
D. The Vagabonds; or, Good out of Evil (Vic. 1/10/66). L.C.
D. The Vagabonds; or, On the Track. L.C. Var. 23/4/84.
D. The Vagrant and his Family (Grec. 27/10/59).
D. The Vain Heart. L.C. Eff. 27/1/62.
P. Valentine and Orson (Park, 26/12/74).
P. Valentine and Orson. L.C. Alex. 4/1/75.
P. Valentine and Orson; or, Harlequin King Pippin, Queen Butterfly and the Green Knight of Agramont. L.C. Grec. 20/12/59.
Bsq. Valentine and Orson "Hys Brother". L.C. Newcastle, 21/11/62.
P. Valentine's Day; or, Harlequin and the Fairy of the True Lover's Knot (H. 26/12/59). L.C.
D. Valerie Duclos; or, The Prisoner of Bordeaux. L.C. Brit. 30/9/52.
O. The Valkyrie (Gar. 3/2/97).
O. The Valley of Andoire. L.C. P'cess. 13/1/50.
D. The Valley of Andoire; or, The Peasant Girl of the Pyrenees. L.C. Vic. 16/2/50.
Ext. The Valley of Diamonds; or, The City of Stars. L.C. Qns. 19/9/50.
D. The Valley of Tears. L.C. C.L. 31/12/50.
D. Valmonde the Merchant of Calais. L.C. Amphi. L'pool, 17/9/60.
D. Vanity (Grec. 11/9/61).
D. Van the Virginian (St Helens, 11/8/79).
D. Variety; or, The Will and the Word. L.C. Sur. 22/11/50.
D. Varley the Vulture (Brit. 9/7/60).
C.O. Vedah. L.C. Portsmouth, 26/8/86.
D. Veemah Kareeda; or, The Fall of Delhi. L.C. Vic. 14/11/57.
F. The Vegetarians (Sur. 17/11/51). L.C.
D. The Vendetta. L.C. Sur. 30/3/58.
D. The Vendetta; or, The Book with the Iron Clasps (Croydon, 8/4/78). L.C.
D. The Vendetta; or, The Corsican Brothers (D.L. 27/2/54). L.C.
D. The Vendetta; or, Family Feud (Vic. 11/5/63). L.C.
D. The Vendetta; or, Life's Chances (Brit. 3/8/96). L.C.
D. Vengeance. L.C. Richmond, 27/7/81.
Ext. Venus and Adonis. L.C. D.L. 18/3/90.
F.C. Venus Bewildered (Cheltenham, 9/4/83).
C.D. Verdant Giles (Brit. 1/7/61).
M.F. Verdant Very Esq. L.C. Var. 30/4/85.
Ext. The Very Grand Dutch—s. L.C. St G. 9/2/69.
F. A Very Queer Lover. L.C. Stand. 10/4/84.
F. Vesta's Temple (Court, 14/11/72). L.C.
D. The Veteran and his Progeny (Lyc. 27/5/65).
D. The Veteran and his Son; or, France and Algeria (Sur. 15/9/60). L.C.
D. The Veteran Ashore (Vic. 10/11/51).
D. The Veterans. L.C. County, Reading, 21/10/88.
C.D. The Vicar of Wakefield. L.C. H. 3/4/50.

C.D. The Vicar of Wakefield. L.C. Stand. 27/3/50.
D. The Vicissitudes of Sir Roger Tichbourne (Trowbridge, 21/6/72).
D. A Victim of Delusion; or, Humble Origin (Brit. 5/6/65). L.C.
D. The Victory of the Heart (Grec. 16/10/61).
D. Vidocq (Brit. 10/12/60). L.C. as *The Thief-taker of Paris; or, V.*
D. Village Bells. L.C. Athen. 17/11/92.
D. The Village Blacksmith (Sur. 1/6/57).
Oa. The Village Coquette. L.C. Canterbury, 17/6/84.
Ent. A Village Festival (H. 31/7/55).
D. The Village Smithy. L.C. York Theatre of Varieties, Southampton, 10/2/94.
O. Le Villi; or, The Witch Dancers (Com. Manchester, 24/9/97).
F. Villikins and his Dinah. L.C. Pav. 6/3/54.
Bal. Violante (Vic. 18/4/64).
D. Violet's Perils; or, The False Mother and the Parent Guardian. L.C. Brit. 4/9/62.
D. Violette. L.C. Lincoln, 4/5/68.
D. Violette la Grande; or, The Life of an Actress. L.C. Grec. 9/11/53.
C.D. A Virginian Courtship. L.C. Vaud. 11/10/97.
F. The Virginian Mummy (Str. 23/1/54).
F. The Virginian Mummy. L.C. Alh. 3/6/72.
Bsq. Virginibus Puerisque. L.C. St. G. 28/5/94.
C. The Viscount of Létorières (Sur. 27/6/59). L.C. Kidderminster, 17/12/54.
C.D. The Visionary. L.C. St G. Llandudno, 7/9/86.
[Title altered to *Our Doctor*, 9/1887.]
F.Ent. Visions. L.C. Newcastle, 15/10/79.
Bal. La Vivandière (Str. 12/4/52).
D. Vive l'Empereur. L.C. Duchess, Balham, 28/12/99.
M.Sk. Le Voeu. L.C. P.W. 12/7/99.
D. A Voice from the Sea; or, The King's Casket (Brit. 16/2/59). L.C.
R.D. A Voice from the Silence. L.C. Vic. H. 1/6/97.
D. The Voice of Honour (Grec. 22/8/60). L.C. Grec. 13/7/58.
D. The Volcano of Italy; or, A Fugitive's Pearls. L.C. Brit. 7/4/65.
F. The Volunteer Corps (Ast. 13/6/59).
F.C. Vote for Griggs (Vaud. 12/5/92). L.C.
D. A Vow of Silence (Vic. 1/5/54).
D. A Vow of Vengeance. L.C. S.W. 28/9/97.
C. V.R. L.C. Cheswick H. Cheswick, 3/6/87.
Ext. Vulcan. L.C. Roy. 17/3/82.
D. The Vultures. L.C. S.W. 28/12/99.
Ca. The Wager; or, The Romance of an Hour. L.C. Sheffield, 23/2/67.
M.F. Wagner Mania. L.C. O.C. 27/5/84.
Bsq.O. Wagner Out-wagged. L.C. Ast. 3/5/81.
D. The Waif of the Streets (Pav. 19/5/77). L.C. S. Shields, 26/3/77.
C.D. Wait for a Year and a Day (P.W. L'pool, 22/1/76).
D. Wait for the End; or, Ursula's Bridegroom. L.C. Grec. 9/2/77.
D.Sk. Waiting (Edinburgh, 29/4/87). L.C. Tyne, Newcastle.
D. Waiting. L.C. Spa R. Harrogate, 28/12/99.
D. Waiting for Dead Men's Shoes. L.C. Alex. 14/8/75.

F. Waiting for the Underground (Str. 27/8/66). L.C.
Oa. A Waiting Game. L.C. Grand, Leeds, 3/3/91.
D. The Wallachian; or, The Passage of the Danube. L.C. Pav. 10/4/54.
D. Walter, the Mechanic (Vic. 27/3/54).
C. The Waltz (Spa, Scarborough, 8/7/95). L.C.
[By G. K. W.]
D. The Wanderer (H.M. Dundee, 25/12/93). L.C. S.W. 13/9/94.
D. The Wanderer; or, Restored to Reason. L.C. Qns. Keighley, 24/3/99.
D. Wandering Janet: A Story of the Dee (Aberdeen, 18/1/73).
D. The Wanderers (Alh. Pemberton, 6/7/85).
D. The Wanderer's Fortune (Grec. 26/3/63).
F. Wanted. L.C. H.M. Carlisle, 2/3/81.
[See *H. W. WILLIAMSON*, 1884.]
Oa. Wanted, a Curate. L.C. P.H. Croydon, 31/10/94.
F. Wanted, an Errand Boy; or, The Maid of All Work. L.C. Sur. 15/10/57.
F. Wanted, a Wife. L.C. St Mark's School, Rosherville, 31/12/97.
F. Wanted, a Wife and Child. L.C. Soho, 10/12/60.
[See *J. E. SODEN*, 1871.]
M.F. Wanted Immediately. L.C. Spa Concert R. Clifton, 5/4/95.
P. War and Peace; or, Harlequin and the Great Bear. L.C. Pav. 24/12/55.
D. The Warden (St J. 9/1/55).
D. A Ward of France. L.C. Vaud. 10/11/97.
D. The War in Abyssinia (M'bone, 11/5/68). L.C.
Spec. The War in Turkey; or, The Struggle for Liberty (Brit. 22/5/54). L.C.
Equest.D. The War in Zululand. L.C. Cooke's Circus, Manchester, 1/11/79.
F.C. Warm Members (Manor R. Hackney, 8/12/91).
D. A Warning Voice (C.L. 9/4/64).
F. Warranted. L.C. Str. 4/5/75.
Ca. A Warrior Bold. L.C. St G. 24/4/79.
D. War Time: A Tale of the Press Gang (S. Shields, 9/12/67).
Equest.Spect. The War Trail; or, The White Horse of the Prairie. L.C. Ast. 15/10/57.
D. Washed Ashore (Egremont Inst. L'pool, 6/10/94). L.C.
D. Was he the Man? A Secret of Twenty Years. L.C. Brit. 16/9/70.
D. Wasted Lives (Bishops Auckland, 29/1/75).
D. The Watchdog (Vic. 29/5/54).
D. The Watchers on the Longships (Central H. Penzance, 13/11/85).
D. The Watchman of New York (Vic. 24/3/56). L.C.
Ent. A Water Carnival. L.C. Sanger's, 11/12/90.
O. The Water Carrier (P'cess. 27/10/75).
D. The Watercress Girl (C.L. 14/10/65). L.C.
D. The Waterloo Cup (Amphi. Newcastle, 21/6/97).
D. The Waterman of Bankside; or, The Origin of Doggett's Coat and Badge (Vic. 4/8/79).
D. The Waters; or, Mildred's Choice. L.C. Vic. 9/11/63.
D. Waverley; or, A Rebel for Love (Edinburgh, 11/9/71).
Oa. The Waxwork Wooing. L.C. Aquar. Brighton, 23/6/84.
C. The Way of the World. L.C. Grec. 15/4/57.

C.D. The Way of the World. L.C. Var. Hoxton, 22/12/92.
D. Wealth and Poverty; or, The Trials of Life. L.C. Vic. 2/4/55.
T. The Wealth of Shylock, the Jew of Venice. L.C. 9/9/51.
C. Wedded. L.C. P.W. Blackpool, 7/10/84.
D. The Wedding Eve; or, The Traitor's Touch (Vic. 5/12/64). L.C.
F. A Wedding Present. L.C. New, Swansea, 23/9/81.
[See *A. ARTHUR*, 1888.]
D. Wee Curly (Greenock, 2/4/83). L.C. Qns. Glasgow, 26/4/98.
D. Welch Rabbits, Rarebits (Vic. 19/10/63). L.C.
Ca. Welcome Home (Soho, 22/5/60).
D.Sk. Welcome Little Stranger (Adel. 30/3/57). L.C.
Ca. A Welcome Messenger. L.C. Olym. 20/4/85.
C. The Weller Family. L.C. H.M. Aberdeen, 7/8/78.
D. Wellington; or, The Night after the Battle (Marionette, 22/11/52).
D. Wellington and Waterloo (M'bone, 27/12/52). L.C.
D. Wellington, Nelson and Napoleon (Stand. 13/12/52).
Ca. We'll Watch (Brit. 30/11/59).
C.D. The Welsh Girl (Olym. 30/4/55).
D. Wept-ton-no-Mah, the Indian Mail Carrier (Shakespeare, L'pool, 10/4/93; E.C. 11/9/93). L.C.
C. The West End. L.C. Shrewsbury, 15/2/88.
F. Weston, the Walker (P.W. Birmingham, 17/4/76).
D. We Too. L.C. Vaud. 20/2/91.
D. The Whalers (Vic. 5/12/63).
Int. What a Corporation! or, A Matrimonial Perplexity. L.C. Birmingham, 7/11/55.
F. What does he want? (C.G. 28/1/56).
D.Sk. What happened to Tommy. L.C. Duchess, Balham, 28/12/99.
F. What! No Cab on the Stand? (C.L. 8/11/53).
F. What's in a Name? L.C. Birmingham, 2/12/80.
D. What will he do with it? (Sur. 24/10/59). L.C.
Ca. What will my Aunt say? (P'cess. 17/5/50).
D. The Wheel of Life. L.C. Brit. 5/1/56.
D. Wheels within Wheels; or, A Wife's Atonement. L.C. Leeds, 4/7/73.
D. When Rogues fall out. L.C. S.W. 26/4/98.
Ca. Where have you been? L.C. Village H. Cobham, 9/4/88.
F. Where's Brown? or, An Hour's Romance. L.C. Newcastle, 1/2/59.
F. Where's Brown? or, Brown, Jones and Robinson at Brighton. L.C. Brighton, 9/2/59.
F. Where's Crevelli? (Str. 6/11/54). L.C.
F. Where's Mr Smith? L.C. Grec. 27/3/58.
F. Which is my Husband? (S.W. 28/10/61).
[See *Mrs DAVIDSON*, 1850.]
F. Which is which? L.C. Alh. 17/6/78.
C. Whiffin and Co. L.C. New Cross H. 20/1/93.
D. While the Snow is falling (P.W. Rochdale, 10/3/73).
D. The Whiskey Demon; or, The Dream of the Reveller (Pav. 9/11/67). L.C.
F. Whitebait at Cremorne (Ast. 24/4/65).
Play without words. The White Bear. L.C. H. 30/3/98.
D. The White Boys: A Tale of the Irish Rebellion of 1798 (Sur. 20/1/62).
D. The White Boys; or, Ireland in 1798. L.C. Vic. 30/1/62.

D. The White Chateau; or, Present, Past and Future (Grec. 14/10/61). L.C.
D. The White Chief; or, The Buffalo Hunter of the Death Prairies (Pav. 5/11/66). L.C.
F. The White Hat (Adel. 14/4/73).
D. The White Indian; or, The Renegade's Daughter. L.C. Vic. 2/4/60.
Ca. The White Lady (P.W. 28/7/92). L.C.
D. The White Lady. L.C. Durham, 27/1/93.
Ca. White Lies. L.C. Derby H. Baker Street, L'pool, 26/2/86.
F. White Lies (West, Albert H. 11/6/97). L.C. Swiss Gdns. Shoreham, 20/7/96.
D. The White Lily (Hanley, 31/8/91). L.C.
M.D. The White Palfrey; or, The Wild Boar of the Fens (Ast. 24/5/58).
D. The White Passport (Pav. 29/3/69).
D. The White Queen. L.C. P'cess. 7/8/89.
[See *J. W. BOULDING*, 1883.]
D. The White Scarf (Stand. 30/1/64).
D. The White Star. L.C. S. Shields, 30/5/91.
D. Whitsuntide; or, The Last Link of the Chain (Stand. 9/6/51).
P. Whittington. L.C. New, Edinburgh, 21/12/76.
P. Whittington. L.C. Edinburgh, 21/12/81.
P. Whittington and his Cat (M'bone, 17/4/65).
P. Whittington and his Cat. L.C. Qns. Manchester, 13/12/65.
P. Whittington and his Cat. L.C. Bradford, 13/12/70.
P. Whittington and his Cat. L.C. Ast. 14/12/77.
P. Whittington and his Cat. L.C. Alex. Sheffield, 8/12/81.
P. Whittington and his Cat. L.C. Alex. L'pool, 17/12/81.
P. Whittington and his Cat. L.C. D.L. 21/12/85.
P. Whittington and his Cat. L.C. Tyne, Newcastle, 21/12/86.
P. Whittington and his Cat. (Pav. 26/12/95). L.C.
F. Who'd be a Manager? (Qns. Dublin, 15/12/76).
D. Who did it? or, The Track of Crime (Brit. 18/12/67). L.C.
F. Who has seen Tommy Toddle? L.C. Vic. 22/11/50.
Ca. Who is he? L.C. Lyc. Sunderland, 25/3/73.
D.Sk. Who'll serve the Queen? (Str. 10/1/55).
F. Who lodges at No. 1? (Sur. 12/9/53).
Ca. Whom the Gods love. L.C. Gai. 13/9/82.
F. Who's a Traveller? (Str. 1/11/54). L.C.
M.F. Whose Baby? L.C. Var. 8/6/85.
Ca. Who's my Husband? (S.W. 28/10/61). L.C.
Ca. Who's to be Master? (Stratford, 29/3/86).
D. Who's to blame? L.C. Hackney, 13/1/80.
D. Who's to win? (Weymouth, 24/5/71; Adel. Glasgow, 29/4/78).
F. Who's who? (Str. 25/7/53).
F. Who's your Hatter? or, A Day's Adventure at Little Snuggleton. L.C. Pav. 10/10/55.
D. Who wins; or, The Outcast's Bride. L.C. P'cess. Edinburgh, 23/2/66.
F. Why didn't she marry? (Str. 27/3/54; Str. 3/3/56, as *Why don't she marry?*).
D. The Whyte Chapel Byrd Catchers (Stand. 7/7/51).
D. The Wicked Widow. L.C. Internat. 22/2/84.
D. A Wicked Woman. L.C. Nottingham, 23/11/71.

D. Wickerd, the Witcherer (Alex. O.H. Sheffield, 14/4/73).
D. The Wide Wide World. L.C. Stand. 18/8/56.
D. Widow and Orphans (Brit. 18/4/63).
Oa. The Widow Bewitched (G.I. 14/8/65). L.C.
D. The Widower's Victim (Str. 20/11/55).
Ca. The Widow's Choice. L.C. Glo. 1/6/97.
C.O. The Widow's Husband. L.C. Portsmouth, 20/11/88.
D. The Widow's Son (Brit. 13/11/61). L.C.
F. A Wife for a Day (Stand. 3/11/60).
D. The Wife of Scarli (P.W. Birmingham, 9/9/97). L.C.
D. Wife or Crown. L.C. Court, 10/10/78.
D.Sk. A Wife's Devotion. L.C. S.W. 12/2/98.
F. The Wife's First Lesson (Grec. 29/8/60).
D. A Wife's Redemption. L.C. St G. 10/3/70.
D. The Wife's Revenge; or, A Masked Rider (Sur. 23/11/57). L.C.
D. A Wife's Struggle. L.C. Darwen, 26/3/85.
D. A Wife's Terrors. L.C. Qns. 12/9/60.
D. A Wife's Vengeance. L.C. Var. 9/2/85.
C.D. A Wife's Victory (Amphi. L'pool, 28/3/79). L.C.
D. The Wild Duck (Roy. 5/5/94). L.C.
D. The Wild Flower of Mexico (Stand. 4/6/60).
D. The Wild Gipsy Girl; or, Dark Shadows and Sunshine. L.C. Vic. 7/4/57.
C.D. The Wild Primrose (Nov. 7/2/91). L.C.
D. The Wild Tribes of London. L.C. C.L. 31/5/56.
[By *C. H. HAZLEWOOD.*]
D. The Wild Woman (Soho, 17/5/59).
C.D. Wiles. L.C. West, Albert H 20/6/98.
D. Wilfred Ned; or, The Skeleton Crew (Brit. 19/12/66). L.C.
P. Wilfred of Ivanhoe. L.C. Colchester, 17/12/81.
D. The Will and the Way (M'bone, 16/5/53). L.C. Birmingham, 25/4/53.
D. The Will and the Way (Qns. 30/5/53).
D. The Will and the Word (Grec. 9/7/60).
D. William March; or, The Man of Genius. L.C. M'bone, 8/7/59.
Ext. William Tell. L.C. Alex. Walsall, 27/12/82.
Bsq.P. William Tell; or, The Strike of the Cantons. L.C. Lyc. 24/5/56.
Ext. William that married Susan; or, A Squall in the Downs (Brit. 24/12/61). L.C. Brit. 17/3/59.
D. Willie the Wanderer (M'bone, 6/8/66).
D. A Willing Sacrifice. See *Marguerite*.
D. The Will o' the Wisp (Brit. 22/2/59). L.C. as *W. o' the W.; or, The Morass of the Murdered.*
P. Will o' the Wisp. L.C. Alex. Pal. Walsall, 18/12/79.
Oa. Will o' the Wisp. L.C. Spa, Harrogate, 31/3/90.
D. Will o' the Wisp; or, The Doomed of Dyneley Chase. L.C. Eff. 25/2/59.
D. Will o' the Wisp; or, The Mystery of the Ruined Mill (Pottery, Hanley, 27/9/69).
D. The Willow Grove; or, Gipsy George the Outcast. L.C. C.L. 1/9/50.
D. The Willow Marsh (S.W. 8/10/62).

D. The Willow Pool; or, The Shadow of Death (Grec. 14/11/70). L.C.
D. Will Pontypridd (Cambrian, Merthyr Tydfil, 9/3/75).
D.Sk. Will Tell; or, True to the Core. L.C. S.W. 10/5/95.
F. Winkle's Waxworks. L.C. Var. 2/7/83.
D. The Winner. L.C. W.L. 31/7/94.
Int. Winning a Widow (Soho, 28/5/56). L.C.
Ca. Winning a Wife (Aquar. Gt Yarmouth, 12/11/88).
D. The Winning Post. L.C. Croydon, 17/10/85.
D. Winona, the Sioux Queen; or, The Death Shot and the Dog of the Prairie (Parkhurst, 2/2/81). L.C. Vic. Longton, Staffs. 30/8/80.
F. Winterbottoms (St J. 28/11/59).
D. A Winter in London; or, A Devilish Good Fellow. L.C. Grec. 8/4/54.
D. The Wishing Cup. L.C. P's. Manchester, 18/11/96.
D. The Wishing Gate; or, A Night in the Haunted Dell (Eff. 3/9/66). L.C.
D. The Wishing Glen; or, The Spirits of the Departed (Brit. 22/6/63). L.C.
D. The Witches' Weeds; or, Pride and Patience (Pav. 26/9/68).
D. The Witching Hour. L.C. Vic. H. 1/6/97.
P. The Witch of Hawley. L.C. 16/11/76.
D. Withered Daisies; or, A Midnight Marriage. L.C. C.L. 10/4/54.
D. The Withered Oak; or, A Gipsy Romance. L.C. W.L. 4/5/93.
D. A Withered Rose. L.C. Albert H. Jarrow, 21/12/88.
D. Within the Tombs. L.C. Willenhall, Staffs. 30/6/97.
F. Without Encumbrance. L.C. E.C. 18/3/95.
Duol. With Safety Pins. L.C. Grand, Fulham, 31/7/99.
D. The Witness from the Grave (Brit. 14/11/59).
F. The Wives of Whitechapel; or, Love in a Tub. L.C. Brit. 20/9/50.
F. The Wolf and the Lamb. L.C. Var. 11/12/77.
D. The Wolf of Hornsey Wood. L.C. 17/10/51.
D. Wolves (O.H. Blackburn, 16/3/70).
D. Woman and the Law (Hull, 28/7/84; Olym. 13/3/85, as *The Passion Flower*). L.C.
D. The Woman from the People (M.H. Hastings, 29/5/82).
F. A Woman in my Dust Hole. L.C. Str. 9/2/58.
D. The Woman in White (Sur. 3/11/60). L.C.
D. The Woman in White. L.C. Norwich, 11/1/61.
D. The Woman in White. L.C. S.W. 19/8/61.
F. The Woman in 1900. L.C. Richmond, 19/4/94.
D. The Woman of the World. L.C. Vic. 25/10/58.
D. The Woman of the World (Sur. 22/11/58). L.C.
D. Woman's Devotion (Brit. 23/2/63).
D. A Woman's Faith (Lyc. 2/11/55).
D. Woman's Fools. L.C. Lyr. 20/7/97.
D. Woman's Heart (Grec. 12/10/58).
D. Woman's Love. L.C. Newcastle, 25/7/81.
D. A Woman's Love. L.C. Roy. Walls End, 22/11/94.
Ca. A Woman's No. L.C. Terry's, 22/4/95.
D. A Woman's Reputation. L.C. Eden, Bishop Auckland, 2/4/94.
D. Woman's Revenge; or, The Plague and the Fire. L.C. Vic. 2/4/60.
D. Woman's Rights. L.C. Ch.X. 12/10/69.
D. Woman's War (Brit. 10/1/60).

D. Woman's Worth. L.C. Eff. 28/9/63.
D. The Women Three. L.C. Pav. 16/11/66.
D. Won by a Head; or, The Waterloo Cup. L.C. Star, Wolverhampton, 30/11/97.
D.D. Won by a Neck; or, A Living Lie. L.C. Gai. W. Hartlepool, 3/9/80.
C.O. Won by a Trick. L.C. Gai. 14/4/85.
Oa. The Wonderful Cousin (Brighton, 18/8/74).
Ent. Woodin's Carpet-bag and Sketchbook. L.C. Regent's Gallery, 31/1/54.
D. Woodleigh; or, On and Off the Stage (York, 9/2/83). L.C.
Equest.Spec. The Woodman's Horse; or, The False Knight (Ast. 21/2/54). L.C.
Ca. Wooing one's Wife. L.C. Lyc. 14/5/70.
[See *J. M. MORTON*, 1861.]
D. The Woolcomber's Progress. L.C. Pullan's, Bradford, 8/12/79.
F. Worcester Sauce; or, A Man and a Brother (Amat. Dramat. Club, Worcester, 26/4/72).
D. The Workgirls of London (Brit. 19/12/64). L.C.
D. The Workhouse, the Palace and the Grave (Brit. 6/12/58). L.C.
D. The Working Man; or, The Diamond and the Pearl. L.C. C.L. 29/3/52.
F. Working the Oracle (P'cess. 5/3/62).
C.D. The Workman's Wife (L'pool, 26/4/75).
D. The Workmen of Paris (Adel. 30/11/64). L.C.
D. The World's War; or, The Siege of Jerusalem (Vic. 17/4/54). L.C.
P. The World turned Upside Down (Regent, 26/12/73).
F. Worried to Death. L.C. Qns. R. Oxford, 11/9/85.
D. Wrath's Whirlwind; or, The Neglected Child, the Vicious Youth and the Degraded Man. L.C. Brit. 10/53 [licence refused].
D. Wreck and Rescue; or, The Labyrinth of Death. L.C. Grec. 23/3/63.
D. The Wreck at New Brighton (Birkenhead, 15/5/82).
Oa. The Wreckers. L.C. P.H. Sutton, 26/1/92.
D. The Wreck of the Golden Mary. L.C. Brit. 17/1/57.
D. The Wreck of the Golden Mary (Vic. 19/1/57).
D. The Wreck of the Golden Mary (Stand. 28/1/57).
D. The Wreck of the Golden Mary. L.C. C.L. 10/2/57.
D. The Wreck of the Golden Mary. L.C. Grec. 1/3/57.
Ca. Wretchedly Obstinate. L.C. O.H. Torquay, 25/5/83.
F. A Writing on the Shutters (D.L. 12/2/55). L.C.
Duol. The Wrong Address (D.Y. 5/10/95). L.C.
F. The Wrong Baby. L.C. Grec. 11/4/57.
C. The Wrong Box (Olym. 20/3/54). L.C.
F. The Wrong Box. L.C. Beaufort H. Walham Green, 29/6/65.
D. The Wrongs of Poland; or, The Patriots of 1863 (Vic. 11/2/65). L.C.
D. The Wrongs of the Lowly (Vic. 26/12/57).
D. The Wrongs of Twenty Years; or, Doomed to Slavery. L.C. C.L. 2/8/62.
F. The Wrong 'Un. L.C. S.W. 20/6/95.
F. Yankee Courtship; or, Away down East (Adel. 15/2/58). L.C.
F. The Yankee Housekeeper (D.L. 28/4/56). L.C.

F. The Yankee Legacy (D.L. 1/9/62). L.C.
F.C. Yankee Notions. L.C. Ladb. H. 9/7/89.
D. Yaromeer the Yager (Stand. 8/9/51).
D. A Year and a Day. L.C. Albion, 18/3/79.
P. Ye Childe of Hale. L.C. Sefton, L'pool, 18/12/80.
P. Ye Days of ye Good Queen Bess. L.C. W. Hartlepool, 18/12/79.
D. The Yell of Doom. L.C. Brit. 9/4/57.
Ext. The Yellow Boy (W. Hartlepool, 16/5/83). L.C.
P. The Yellow Dwarf. L.C. Greenock, 4/12/76.
P. The Yellow Dwarf. L.C. Cheltenham, 8/12/76.
P. The Yellow Dwarf. L.C. Tyne, Newcastle, 22/12/76.
P. The Yellow Dwarf. L.C. Manchester, 6/12/78.
P. The Yellow Dwarf. L.C. H.M. Aberdeen, 11/12/79.
P. The Yellow Dwarf. L.C. Shakespeare, L'pool, 6/12/88.
P. The Yellow Dwarf. L.C. Shakespeare, L'pool, 31/12/97.
P. The Yellow Dwarf. L.C. West Pier, Brighton, 30/12/98.
Ent. Ye Mysseltoe Boughe (Brit. 6/5/61).
M.D. Ye Signe of ye Golden Ship. L.C. Literary Soc. Axminster, 17/12/81.
Duol. Yes or No? (Portman R. Baker Street, 16/5/92).
[By *W. POEL.*]
Bal. Yolande. L.C. Alh. 14/8/77.
D. The Yorkshire Brothers. L.C. Stand. 4/5/52.
Int. The Young Actress. L.C. Adel. 31/8/60.
[See *D. BOUCICAULT*, 1856.]
D. Young America. L.C. Grantham, 11/8/97.
D. The Young Burglar (P'cess. of W. Kennington, 22/4/91).
C. The Young Couple (St J. 25/8/51). L.C.
P. Young Dick Whittington and his Cat. L.C. R.A. Woolwich, 21/12/89.
D. A Young Girl from the Country. L.C. C.L. 25/8/62.
D. A Young Girl from the Country; or, A Peep at the Vices and Virtues of Rustic and City Life. L.C. Pav. 23/7/60.
D. The Young King (H. 26/6/54).
D. The Young Man from the County (M'bone, 21/3/63).
D. The Young Man from the Country. L.C. Olym. 1/5/63.
C. The Young Pretender. L.C. Gai. Burnley, 20/8/87.
[See *B. WHITE*, 1890.]
Oa. The Young Recruit (Pav. 28/11/60). L.C.
Ca. The Young Scamp (St J. 15/10/51).
C.O. Young Shai, the Mandarin's Daughter. L.C. St G. 29/11/98.
F. You're another (D.L. 29/10/60).
D. Youth, Love and Folly (D.L. 1/3/55).
Play without Words. Yvette (Aven. 12/9/91). L.C.
Ext. Zac. L.C. Corn Exchange, Maidstone, 26/12/84.
O. Zaida, the Pearl of Granada. L.C. L'pool, 12/2/59.
O.D. Zampa (Gai. 8/10/70). L.C.
D. Zana; or, The Pride of the Alhambra (Brit. 19/9/70). L.C. Brit. 26/10/61.
D. Zanga (Vic. 22/8/77).
D. Zangride (Qns. Hull, 6/7/68).
Lyric D. The Zaporogues. L.C. Birmingham, 31/5/94.
D. Zappolyna the Moor (Vic. 16/11/52).

D. Zenobia. L.C. Vestry H. Hampstead, 16/2/99.
[Title altered to *A Skeleton in the Cupboard*, 4/5/1904.]

D. Zerago; or, The Wild Tribe of a Mountain Torrent (Tunbridge Wells, 24/5/69).

Ext. The Zig Zag Travels of Messrs Danube and Pruth (Adel. 6/12/54). L.C.

Ent. Zingarella (Brit. 6/5/61).

D. Zingaro, an Earnest Statue Maker (Coronet, 21/5/1900). L.C.

Ext. Zitella. L.C. Park, 6/12/77.

D. Zitella; or, The Guerilla Boy and the Spectre Sister. L.C. C.L. 20/7/53.

D. Zola; or, Stronger than Hate. L.C. Albert H. Jarrow, 17/10/87.
[Title altered to *Unmasked*, 1892.]

F. A Zulu Chief. L.C. Paisley, 19/7/82.

SUPPLEMENTARY NOTES

During the past few years not quite so much detailed attention has been given to the late nineteenth-century theatre as to earlier periods of stage activity; but such contributions as have appeared indicate that there is still a vast amount of work to be accomplished—particularly, perhaps, in the study of individual playwrights and of their writings. The "bibliography" of the period, and in especial the investigation of privately printed texts, obviously demands detailed exploration.

On the staging of the time, two books call for immediate notice, Richard Southern's *Changeable Scenery* (1952), the last chapter of which deals with the theatres of 1850–1900, and A. N. Vardac's *Stage to Screen* (Cambridge, Mass. 1949). The former discusses the methods by which new effects were being secured, and the latter presents an interesting thesis—that throughout the nineteenth century the stage was, as it were, groping its way unconsciously toward the cinema-to-be. Cinematic conventions, he points out, were introduced even in early melodramas, while in the later melodramas they ran riot, "spectacles" and realistic effects being aimed at of a kind difficult or impossible to realise satisfactorily in the theatre, although entirely proper to the world of the film. Besides these major contributions to our knowledge of the subject there are a few other shorter essays, such as J. H. McDowell's examination of the box set,[1] W. A. Armstrong's discussion of an early contribution by a certain Peter Nicholson on "Dramatic Machinery",[2] Richard Southern's notes on the picture-frame proscenium,[3] and, of peculiar importance, Armstrong's account of the material presented in T. W. Erle's *Letters from a Theatrical Scene-painter* (1880).[4]

At this present time, when local town councils and planners, with pickaxe-happy and insensate valiancy, are engaged in destroying so many ancient buildings, and among them interesting

[1] "The Historical Development of the Box Set" (*Theatre Annual*, 1945, pp. 65–83).

[2] "Peter Nicholson and the Scenographic Art" (*Theatre Notebook*, viii, 1954, 91–6).

[3] "The Picture-frame Proscenium of 1880" (*Theatre Notebook*, v, 1951, 59–61).

[4] "The Art of the Minor Theatres in 1860" (*Theatre Notebook*, x, 1956, 89–94).

relics of playhouses of the past, the work of the Society for Theatre Research is of prime value, and its organ, *Theatre Notebook*, has printed several articles, such as that by F. Grice on Worcester's Theatre Royal,[1] which will have enduring value as records of what is being irretrievably lost. Attention should also be drawn to a series of notes contributed by Gerald Morice and others on divers nineteenth-century stages and music-halls,[2] and to some essays on individual theatres, such as that by L. J. R. Bailey on the Royal West London Theatre[3] and that by Victor Glasstone on the Comedy Theatre.[4] It may here be noted that useful lists of theatres and music-halls, records of the destruction of playhouses by fire and estimates of audience attendance at music-halls (about 14,000,000 in 1892) are to be found in the *Report from the Select Committee on Theatres and Places of Entertainment* (1892).

A certain amount of research has also been devoted to the important subject of the change in acting styles during this period. Here, the considerable collection of articles by E. J. West is of special significance. Apart from one or two general surveys,[5] he has essays on Barry Sullivan,[6] the group of Robertsonians,[7] Ellen Terry,[8] Madge Kendal,[9] and that "last of the giants of tradition", Henry Irving.[10] An attempt to preserve a record of Irving's method is made in *We Saw Him Act: A Symposium on the Art of Sir Henry Irving*, edited by H. A. Saintsbury and Cecil Palmer (1939) and in

[1] "The Theatre Royal at Worcester" (*Theatre Notebook*, x, 1956, 83–6).

[2] "A Record of Some XIX-century Theatres" (*Notes and Queries*, Oct. 9, 1943, with following correspondence, Nov. 20 and Dec. 4, 1943, Feb. 26 and April 8, 1944). See also Sir St Vincent Troubridge, "Minor Victorian Playhouses" (*Notes and Queries*, Sept. 14, 1940).

[3] The Royal West London Theatre in the Nineteenth Century" (*Notes and Queries*, Oct. 21, 1944).

[4] "The Comedy Theatre" (*Theatre Notebook*, x, 1955, 17–20).

[5] "From a Player's to a Playwright's Theatre: The London Stage, 1870–1890" (*Quarterly Journal of Speech*, xxviii, 1942, 430–6); "The London Stage, 1870–1890" (*University of Colorado Studies*, Series B, ii, 1943, 31–84).

[6] "Barry Sullivan: Shavian and Actual" (*Educational Theatre Journal*, i, 1949, 14–58).

[7] "The Original Robertsonians" (*Speech Monographs*, xvi, 1949, 253–71).

[8] *Ellen Terry: Histrionic Enigma* (Colorado College Publications, 1940, pp. 39–62).

[9] "Actress between Two Schools: The Case of Madge Kendal" (*Speech Monographs*, xi, 1944, 105–14).

[10] "Henry Irving, 1870–1890" (*Studies in Speech and Drama in Honor of Alexander M. Drummond*, Ithaca, N.Y. 1944).

Laurence Irving's intimate study (1951). S. S. Allen strives to recapture the style of Samuel Phelps;[1] D. B. Pallette writes on "The English Actor's Fight for Respectability";[2] Lynton Hudson deals summarily with this period in *The English Stage, 1850–1950* (1951); while Tree and Alexander figure in Hesketh Pearson's *The Last Actor-Managers* (1950). Among these men, William Poel cannot be counted a great actor, yet he was a maker of actors; it is fitting that the invaluable list of his productions issued by the William Poel Portrait Committee should now be followed by a detailed chronicle of his achievements written by Robert Speaight (1954).

So far as the drama is concerned, there has been a not surprising tendency to deal rather with the colourful work of the minor theatres, the theatres specializing in musical comedy and the music-halls than with the "legitimate" stage. It is this world which figures most prominently in *Ring up the Curtain* (1938) by E. Short and A. Compton-Rickett; it is this world, too, which runs its course in M. Willson Disher's *Blood and Thunder: Mid-Victorian Melodrama and its Origins* (1950) and the same author's *Melodrama* (1954), and in a series of works by A. E. Wilson, such as *Penny Plain, Twopence Coloured* (1932), *Christmas Pantomime* (1934) and *East End Entertainment* (1954). The same world, of course, is that inhabited by Frances Fleetwood in her entertaining *Conquest* (1953).

One general study, George Rowell's *The Victorian Theatre* (1956), provides an excellent general survey of all kinds of dramatic activity. Starting with an account of dramatic conditions, he proceeds to examine the contributions of Lytton, Taylor, Reade and Boucicault and thence moves on, through Robertson, to Pinero and Jones. Particularly interesting are his comments on those qualities of the age which led to an almost total eclipse of comedy. J. P. McCormick seeks to blame these qualities for Browning's failure to become an outstanding dramatist;[3] from the start regarded as chief hope of the theatre, this poet, in his opinion, aimed at creating a new form, in which mood might dominate over action. The playwrights of the nineties have not received much attention, although one article by Marjorie Northend,[4] usefully stresses that

[1] "Samuel Phelps, Last of a Dynasty" (*Theatre Annual*, 1950, pp. 55–70).

[2] *Theatre Annual* (1948–9), pp. 27–34.

[3] "Robert Browning and the Experimental Drama" (*P.M.L.A.* lxviii, 1953, 982–91).

[4] "Henry Arthur Jones and the Development of Modern English Drama" (*Review of English Studies*, xviii, 1942, 448–63).

unswerving seriousness of purpose and unflagging perseverance which made H. A. Jones the chief exponent of the new ideals in dramatic authorship and Raymond Williams has an interesting essay on "Criticism into Drama 1888–1950",[1] which traces the modern movement from Hettner to Shaw. The impact of Goethe's *Faust* is well discussed by A. I. Frantz in *Half a Hundred Thralls to Faust* (Chapel Hill, 1949). C. R. Decker, equally usefully, has documented the early introduction of Ibsen to England, from Gosse's article of 1872 on to the Ibsen mania and phobia of 1890.[2]

On the other hand, renewed interest has been shown in the playwrights who stood behind Jones and Pinero. Winton Tolles has an illuminating book on *Tom Taylor and the Victorian Drama* (New York, 1940); Maynard Savin examines the work of *Thomas William Robertson* (Providence, R.I. 1950); and there are several studies of Reade's writings. Leone Rives has presented a general study of this author's career (Toulouse, 1940); a valuable bibliographical account appears in *Wilkie Collins and Charles Reade* (1940) by M. L. Parrish and Elizabeth V. Miller; D. H. MacMahor elucidates "The Composition and Early Stage History of *Masks and Faces*";[3] and K. J. Fielding discusses the fight waged by Reade and Dickens against piracy.[4] There is a general study of *Wilkie Collins* (1951) by K. Robinson. In an essay on Lytton and the censor, C. H. Shattuck comes to the conclusion that we must not put too much blame on the Lord Chamberlain's Office for interfering with the dramatists: "Public opinion and the Press...were as fussily intolerant" as the fussiest Reader of Plays.[5] Mention may also be made here of K. J. Fielding's study of the dramatisations of *Edwin Drood*,[6] and E. J. West's critical appreciation of the theatrical criticism of Henry Labouchere, the "Scrutator" of *Truth*.[7] Although concerned mainly with the American stage, Marvin Felheim's *The Theater of Augustin Daly* (Cambridge, Mass. 1956) has much of interest for students of the English drama of the time.

[1] *Essays in Criticism*, i, 1951, 120–38.

[2] "Ibsen's Literary Reputation and Victorian Taste" (*Studies in Philology*, xxxii, 1935, 632–45).

[3] *Research Studies of the State College of Washington*, xiv, 1946, 251–70.

[4] "Charles Reade and Dickens—A Fight against Piracy" (*Theatre Notebook*, x, 1956, 106–12).

[5] "E. L. Bulmer and Victorian Censorship" (*Quarterly Journal of Speech*, xxxiv, 1948, 65–72).

[6] "The Dramatisation of *Edwin Drood*" (*Theatre Notebook*, vii, 1953, 52–8).

[7] "An Unappreciated Victorian Dramatic Critic: Henry Labouchere" (*Quarterly Journal of Speech*, xxix, 1943, 321–8).

SUPPLEMENTARY NOTES TO THE HAND-LIST OF PLAYS, 1850–1900

The same symbols and methods used in the preceding volumes of this *History* are employed here, a + sign being employed to indicate authors and plays not recorded in the original list. As is indicated in the preface, it should be noted that, apart from the supplementary notes, numerous alterations and corrections have been made in the Hand-list itself. Once more, full and grateful acknowledgement is made for help generously given by Sir St Vincent Troubridge.

p. 234] *À BECKETT, G. ARTHUR*
L'Ombra. [Music F. von Flotow; libretto J. H. Vernoy de Saint-Georges (Paris, 7/7/70).]
Grimstone Grange. [Music King Hall.]
That Dreadful Boy. [Music Corney Grain.]

p. 235] *ACHURCH, J.*
+D. The Coming of Peace. 4° [1900: written in collaboration with *C. E. WHEELER*].

+*ADAMS, MERCER*
M.Sk. Society's Whims (P.W. 1/1897).

+*ADAMS, WILLIAM*
T. Zenobia; or, The Fall of Palmyra. 8° 1870.

ADDISON, H. R.
Locked in with a Lady. [+*Lacy*.]

p. 236] *AIDÉ, H.*
[+from *UA*: The Widow Bewitched.]
Die Fledermaus. [Music J. Strauss: libretto C. Haffner and R. Genée (Vienna, 5/4/74).]

p. 237] *ALBERY, J.*
[+from *UA*: The Golden Wreath.]
Doctor Davy. [*J. J. DILLEY* is also credited with collaborating in this play. See *How to Act* (*UA*), p. 694.]
+C. Fortune (Fifth Avenue, N.Y. 3/12/73).
[All his plays, including the unacted *The Jesuits* and *Genevieve* (*Fearns*), are printed in his *Dramatic Works*, ed. W. Albery, 2 vols., 1939.]

p. 238] *ALLEN, F.*
[+from *UA*: That Horrid Biggins.]

p. 239] *ALMAR, G.*
[+from *UA*: Born with a Caul.]

p. 240] *ANDERSON, J. R.*
[+from *UA*: Fast Friends up a Tree; The Republican Duke; The Savage and Civilisation (with *J. H. WILKINS*).]
+C. The Elder Brother (D.L. 11/3/50). [An adaptation from the "Beaumont and Fletcher" play.]

p. 241] *ANDERTON, J.*
+P. Bonnie Bo-Peep and Little Boy Blue. L.C. P.W. Birmingham, 30/11/93.

p. 242] *ARCHER, W. J.*
[+from *UA*: Hearts that Love Us; Marriage Bells.]
+Desmoro; or, The Red Hand (M'bone, 6/10/66).

ARCHER, WILLIAM
[See also under "*E. V. WARD*". Almost all the plays in the Hand-list are, of course, translations from Ibsen and Maeterlinck.]
+Australia; or, The Bushrangers (Grec. 16/4/81). See *A. G. STANLEY.*
+Hedda Gabler (Vaud. 20/4/91). See *Sir E. GOSSE.*

p. 243] *ARLON, F.* [A pseudonym for *A. A. DOWTY.*]

ARMBRUSTER, C.
The Children of the King. [Music E. Humperdinck.]

ARNOLD, H. T.
+P. Harlequin Humpty Dumpty (Lyc. 26/12/68). See *T. L. GREENWOOD.*

p. 247] +*BACHE, CONSTANCE*
[+from *UA*: Hansel and Gretel.]

+*BAGOT, A. E.*
Matches (Com. 17/1/99). See *C. GLENNEY.*

p. 251] *BARRIE, Sir J. M.*
+D. Bandelero the Bandit (Dumfries Academy, 29/12/77). MS. (sold at Sotheby's, 21/5/1957).
+Ca. Caught Napping. 8° [1883; Nottingham].
Ibsen's Ghost [+ 8° 1939 (*priv.*)].

p. 252] *BARTHOLEYNS, A. O'D.*
Military Manoeuvres. [Music F. Idle.]

p. 254] *BEATTY-KINGSTON, W.*
+C.O. The Poet's Dream (Roy. Glasgow, 18/2/98). L.C. [Music A. Thomas.]

p. 257] *BELLINGHAM, H.*
Bluebeard Re-paired. [Adapted from *Barbe-bleue*, libretto H. Meilhac and L. Halévy, music J. Offenbach (Paris, 5/2/66).]

p. 258] *BENNETT, JOSEPH*
Djamileh. [+Dublin, 10/9/92. Translation of the opera by L. Gallot, music G. Bizet (Paris, 22/5/72).]
+Philémon and Baucis (C.G. 26/4/94). [Translation of the opera by I. Barbier and M. Carré, music C. Gounod (Paris, 18/2/60).]

p. 259] *BERNARD, C.*
[+from *UA*: The Very Grand Dutch-s.]
+D. The Master of the Forge; or, A Midnight Marriage (Bath, 1/1/84).

+*BERTIN, W.*
[+from *UA*: The Divorce (C.L. 1859).]

p. 260] + *BERWICK, E. L. A.*
D. Win and Wear; or, The Lottery of Life (Dublin, 5/2/59).

p. 261] + "*BETA*"
D. Faust. The First Part. 8° 1895. [A translation of Goethe's drama.]

p. 262] + *BIRDS, JOHN ADELY*
D. Faust. 8° 1880 (Part I), 1889 (Part II).

BLAKE, T. G.
[+from *UA*: The Life Boat; My Poor Dog Tray.]

BLANCHARD, E. L.
[See also under "*FRANCISCO FROST*". +from *UA*: The Bridal of Beauty; Harlequin Hans and the Golden Goose (with *T. L. GREENWOOD*); Harlequin Jack Sprat (with *T. L. GREENWOOD*); Jack and the Beanstalk (D.L. 1859); Jack the Giant Killer (Birmingham, 1853); Robin Hood (D.L. 1858).]

p. 263] Jack and Jill. [+8° (1854).]
+Sk. The Seven Ages of Woman (St Martin's H. 10/12/55; S.W. 19/3/56).
The Fisherman and the Genie. [Attributed also to *T. L. GREENWOOD*.]
Little Jack Horner. [Music J. H. Tully.]
Cinderella. [+8° (1864).]
Hop o' my Thumb. [+8° (1864).]

p. 264] The Yellow Dwarf. [+8° (1875).]
The Forty Thieves. [The full title is *Harlequin and the Forty Thieves*.]
The White Cat. [+8° 1877.]
The Forty Thieves. [+8° 1886.]

p. 265] *BLOOD, J. J.*
[+from *UA*: The Forty Thieves (Birmingham, 1890).]

p. 266] + *BLUNT, ARTHUR CECIL*
[See under "*ARTHUR CECIL*".]

BOKER, G. H.
The Betrothal. [First performed at Philadelphia, 25/9/50.]

BOLTON, C.
[+ from *UA*: The Engineer; The Shadow on the Hearth.]

p. 267] *BONAWITZ, J. H.*
Irma. [Music by the author.]

BOUCICAULT, D.
[+from *UA*: The Phantom (Adel. 1862); Una.]
+D. L'Abbaye de Castro (Olym. 2/1851).
The Sentinel. [Music Stöpel.]

p. 268] Faust and Margaret. [This play was claimed by Boucicault in *Era*, 2/6/61.]
Dot. [Revived at Gai. 24/12/70 as *A Christmas Story*.]

p. 270] + *BOWEN, CHARLES HARTPOLE*
D. Faust. 8° 1878. [A translation of Goethe's drama.]

p. 273] *BRADDON, M. E.*
+Ca. The Model Husband (Sur. 28/9/68).
+*BRAEKSTAD, H. L.*
D. A Gauntlet. 8° 1890. [Translated from B. Bjørnson, *En Hanske* (1883).]
D. True Women. 8° (1890). [Translated from A. C. Edgren.]

p. 274] *BRANSON, W. S.*
[+from *UA*: Lillian Trafford.]
BRENNAN, J. C.
Don Giovanni. [This is the same as *Don Giovanni* (S.W. 17/11/64) in *UA*.]
BRIDGEMAN, J. V.
[+from *UA*: Little Red Riding Hood (C.G. 1858; with *H. S. EDWARDS*); The Major's Daughter; Puss in Boots (C.G. 1859).]

p. 275] Sunny Vale Farm. [Adapted from S. H. Mosenthal, *Der Sonnenwendhof*.]

p. 276] + *BRILL, P.*
D. Quentin Durward. 8° 1894.

p. 277] *BROOKFIELD, C. H. E.*
Poor Jonathan. [Adapted from *Der arme Jonathan*, libretto H. Wittmann and J. Bauer, music Millöcker (Vienna, 4/1/90).]
The Lucky Star. [Adapted from *The Merry Monarch*, libretto J. C. Goodwin and W. Morse, music arranged by Sousa (N.Y. 18/8/90), itself adapted from *L'Étoile*, libretto E. Leterrier and A. Vanloo, music E. Chabrier (Paris, 28/11/78).]
+*BROOKS, CHARLES TIMOTHY*
D. Faust. 16° 1856, 1857. [A translation of Goethe's drama.]
+*BROOME, FREDERICK NAPIER*
D. Poem. The Stranger of Seriphos. 8° 1869.

p. 278] *BROUGH, W.*
[+from *UA*: Ching-Chow-Hi (with *G. REED*); Kicks and Halfpence (with —. *FRANCK*); A Tale of a Coat (with —. *FRANCK*).]
How to make Home happy. [=Family Secrets (*UA*), p. 675.]

p. 279] Ye Belle Alliance. [In the bills this is attributed to *G. A. SALA*; music Loder.]
The Colleen Bawn settled at last. [+*Lacy*; *French*.]
King Arthur. [+*Lacy*.]

p. 280] *BROUGHAM, J.*
[+from *UA*: The Golden Dream; The Mysteries of Audley Court.]

p. 281] Nellie's Trials. [A revised version of *Might of Right; or, The Soul of Honour* (Ast. 30/1/64).]
Captain Cuttle. [+Burton's Theatre, N.Y. 14/1/50; Manchester, 1867.]
[A play called *The Spirit Warning* was announced in *Era*, 16/8/63, as ready for production, but I find no other record of it, unless it is *Bel Demonio*.]

p. 283] *BROWNE, M.*
+C.O. Così fan tutte. 8° 1890.
The Barber of Bagdad. [Translation of *Der Barbier von Bagdad*, music P. Cornelius (Weimar, 15/12/58). +8° 1891.]
+O. Fidelio. 8° 1891.

p. 284] *BRUTON, J.*
[+from *UA*: Clean your Boots.]

BUCHANAN, R.
The Rathboys. [Written in collaboration with *CHARLES GIBBON.*]

p. 286] *BUCKINGHAM, L. S.*
[+from *UA*: Drat that Comet; For the Benefit of the Playful Crocodile; The Gentleman Opposite; Harlequin Humbug; How it's to be done; An Impudent Puppy; The Phantom Wives; A Pleasant Time of it; So very obliging; Two Precious Scoundrels; A Woman in my Dust Hole; You're another.]
+Ca. Over the Way (Str. 1/12/56).
Jeannette's Wedding. [Music V. Massé.]

BUCKSTONE, J. B.
[+from *UA*: Undine (H. 1858); Valentine's Day.]

p. 287] +D. The Trafalgar Medal (C.L. 5/63).
Harlequin and the Three Bears. [Music E. Fitzwilliam.]
Little Bo-Peep. [+8° (1854).]

+*BURLEIGH, FRANCES*
F.C. Jones and Co. (Myddleton H. Islington, 30/11/93) L.C.

p. 288] *BURNAND, F. C.*
Dido. [+12° (n.d.).]
B.B. [+*Lacy.*]
A Volunteer's Ball. [Written in collaboration with *M. WILLIAMS.*]
Acis and Galatea. [+*Lacy.*]
L'Africaine. [+8° 1865.]

p. 289] Helen. [Version of *La belle Hélène*, libretto H. Meilhac and L. Halévy, music J. Offenbach (Paris, 17/12/64) +8° 1866.]
The Latest Edition of Blackeyed Susan. [+8° 1866.]
Guy Fawkes. [+8° 1866.]
Hit or Miss. [Version of *L'œil crevé*, libretto and music F. R. Hervé (Paris, 12/10/67) +8° 1868.]
The Rise and Fall of Richard III. [+8° 1868.]
The Frightful Hair. [+*or, Who Shot the Dog?* +8° 1868.]
Claude Duval. [+8° 1869.]
The Military Billy Taylor. [+8° 1869.]

p. 290] La Vie Parisienne in London. [Version of *La vie parisienne*, libretto M. Meilhac and L. Halévy, music J. Offenbach (Paris, 31/10/66).]
Kissi-Kissi. [Version of *L'île de Tulipatan*, libretto H. C. Chivot and A. Duru, music J. Offenbach (Paris, 30/9/68).]
The Beast and the Beauty. [+8° 1869.]

King Indigo. [Version of *Indigo und die vierzig Räuber*, libretto M. Steiner, music J. Strauss (Vienna, 10/2/71).]
The Red Rover. [+*or, I Believe You, My Busy!* 12° (1877).]

p. 291] Blue Beard. [+8° (1883).]

p. 292] La Cigale. [Version of *La Cigale et la Fourmi*, libretto H. C. Chivot and A. Duru, music E. Audran (Paris, 30/10/86).]
Miss Decima. [Version of *Miss Hélyett*, libretto M. Boucheron, music E. Audran (Paris, 12/11/90).]
+D. The Husband. 12° (Cambridge, n.d.). See *C. E. DONNE*.

BURNETT, Mrs F. H.
The Real Little Lord Fauntleroy. [+*French*.]
+C.D. The Showman's Daughter (Worcester, 12/10/91; Roy. 6/1/92). L.C.

BURNETT, H.
Out of the World. [This is also attributed to *LITA SMITH*.]

p. 294] *BURTON, E. G.*
[+from *UA*: Retributive Justice.]
+D. The Repentant; or, Ticket of Leave Man (M'bone, 10/8/63).

+*BUTLER, RICHARD*. [See under "*RICHARD HENRY*".]

p. 295] *BYRNE, C. A.*
Gabriella. [A performance was given the same day at Boston, in an Italian text by Byrne and F. Fulgonio, music Pizzi.]

p. 296] *BYRON, H. J.*
Puss in a New Pair of Boots. [+8° 1862 (Scarborough).]
Harlequin St George and the Dragon. [+8° (1863).]
Lady Belle Belle. [Music Riviere.]
The Lion and the Unicorn. [+8° (1864).]

p. 297] Princess Springtime. [+*Lacy*.]
+P. Harlequin Blue Beard (Amphi. L'pool, 26/12/66).
+P. Little Dick Whittington, Thrice Lord Mayor of London; or, Harlequin Hot Pot and the Fairies of the Elfin Grot (L'pool, 26/12/66).
+P. The Wonderful Travels of Gulliver (Manchester, 1867) 8° (1867; Manchester).
Robinson Crusoe. [+8° (1868).]
The Yellow Dwarf. [+8° (1869).]

p. 298] Blue Beard. [+8° (1871).]
La Fille de Mme Angot. [Version of the opera, libretto L. F. N. Clairville, P. Siraudin and V. Koning, music A. C. Lecocq (Brussels, 4/12/72).]
The Pretty Perfumeress. [Version of *La jolie parfumeuse*, libretto H. Crémieux and E. Blum, music J. Offenbach (Paris, 29/11/73).]

p. 299] The Crushed Tragedian. [Revised version of *The Prompter's Box* (Adel. 23/3/70).]

p. 300] *CALVERT, CHARLES*
[+from *UA*: The Hive of Life; The Island Home.]
+D. The Masked Mother; or, The Hidden Hand (Vic. 5/12/59).
+D. The Duke's Legacy (Qns. Manchester, 1863; Sur. 30/6/63).

p. 301] *CAMPBELL, A. V.*
[For his earlier plays see iv, 278–9. +from *UA*: One Thousand Napoleons; The Perilous Pass. At the Brit. 30/3/74 was performed, "the first time for 14 years", *England, the Home of the Free.*]

p. 306] *CAZAURAN, A. R.*
[+from *UA*: Miss Moulton; A Parisian Romance.]

p. 307] +*CHAMBERS, THOMAS*
P. Beauty and the Beast (Manchester, 26/12/61).
P. The House that Jack built (Manchester, 16/12/62).
P. The Sleeping Beauty (Manchester, 26/12/63). See *W. S. HYDE.*

+*CHAPMAN, JANE FRANCES*
D. Axel and Valborg. 12° 1851. [Translated from A. G. Oehlenschläger.]

+*CHAPMAN, JOHN*
D. Palnatoke. 12° 1855.
T. Lord William Russell. 12° 1858 (priv.). [Translated from A. Munch.]
T. Hakon Jarl. 12° 1875. [Translated from A. G. Oehlenschläger.]

p. 308] +*CHARLTON, W. H.*
D. The Son of the Desert. 8° 1859. [Translation of F. Halm, *Der Sohn der Wildnis.*]
D. The Gladiator of Ravenna. 8° 1861. [Translation of F. Halm, *Der Fechter von Ravenna.*]

+*CHATTERTON, Lady GEORGIANA*
D. Oswald of Deira. 8° 1867.

CHEATHAM, F. G. [Sometimes given as *CHEETHAM.*]
[+from *UA*: Cause and Effect; Jo, or, Love in a Fog; King Sillyninny; The Manchester Marriage; St George and the Dragon (Pav. 1864).]
+P. Harlequin Blue Beard; or, The Red Rover, the Fairy of the Golden Locks and the Genie of the Magic Key (Alex. 26/12/65).

+*CHEETHAM, T.*
[+from *UA*; The Graven Image.]

p. 310] *CHORLEY, H. F.*
White Magic. [Music Biletta.]
Dinorah. [Version of *Le pardon de Ploërmel*, libretto J. Barbier and M. Carré music, G. Meyerbeer (Paris, 4/4/59) +L.C.]
The Black Domino. [Version of *Le domino noir*, libretto A. E. Scribe, music D. F. E. Auber (Paris, 2/12/37).]

Faust. [Version of the opera, libretto J. Barbier and M. Carré, music C. Gounod (Paris, 19/3/59).]
+O. The Amber Witch (H.M. 28/2/61). [Music V. Wallace.]

+*CHUTE, J. H.*
P. Babes in the Wood (Bristol, 26/12/58).

+*CLAIR, GEORGE*
[+from *UA*: The Mechanic.]

p. 313] *CLARKE, H. S.*
Gillette. [Version of *Gillette de Narbonne*, libretto H. C. Chivot and A. Duru, music E. Audran (Paris, 11/11/82). +8° 1883.]

+*CLARKE, WILLIAM BARNARD*
D. Faust. 8° 1865. [A translation of Goethe's drama.]

+*CLAYTON, JOHN*
[+from *UA*: Bibb and Tucker.]

p. 314] *CLEMENTS, A.*
The Blind Beggars of Burlington Bridge. [Version of *Les deux aveugles*, libretto J. Moinaux, music J. Offenbach (Paris, 5/7/55).]

CLIFFORD, Mrs W. K.
[+from *UA*: A Supreme Moment.]

p. 315] *CLIFTON, L.*
[+from *UA*: Cousin Grace (with *J. DILLEY*).]
Marjorie. [+8° (1890).]

COAPE, H. C.
[+from *UA*: Flying Colours; Our New Lady's Maid. A play *Lavater*, is also attributed to him in a Lacy list.]
+F. Samuel in Search of Himself (P'cess, 5/4/58). See *J. S. COYNE*.

COATES, A.
[+from *UA*: The Borderer's Son.]
+D. Colonel Jack; or, The Miser of Clerkenwell (M'bone, 16/11/63).
Bitter Cold. [Acted at the Brit. before March 1863.]

+*COE, E. O.*
D. Angelo. 8° 1880. [Translation of the play (1835) by V. Hugo.]

p. 316] *COGHLAN, C. F.*
[+from *UA*: The Royal Escape.]

COLEMAN, J.
[A play of his, *Valjean*, was advertised in *Era Almanack*, 1879, as already produced in several provincial theatres.]

p. 317] *COLERIDGE, S.*
+T. Demetrius. 4° 1881.

COLLETTE, C.
+D. Micawber (Imp. 5/81).
Cryptoconchoidsyphonostomata. [Written in collaboration with *R. H. EDGAR*.]

+*COLLIER, JOSEPH*
P. Brighthelmstone; or, Harlequin the Devil, the Duke and the Doctor (Brighton, 26/12/53).

COLLINGHAM, G. G.
The Idol of an Hour. [=Sappho (*UA*), p. 746.]

COLLINS, C. J.
[+from *UA*: The Anti-garotte; City Friends; Good Queen Bess (Str. 1856); Harlequin Father Thames; King Queer and his Daughters Three (with *J. HALFORD*); Nitocris; Pizarro; Prince Cherry and Princess Fair Star; Punch and Judy (St. J. 1859).]

p. 318] *COLLINS, W. W.*
The Frozen Deep. [+8° 1866 (priv.).]
A Message from the Sea. [A piratical text, not by Collins.]
No Thoroughfare. [+8° 1867.]
No Name. [+8° 1863.]

+*COLLIS, —*
[+from *UA*: The Magic Branch.]

+*COLQUHOUN, W. H.*
D. Faust. 8° 1878.

p. 320] *CONQUEST, G.*
[+from *UA*: The Angel of Darkness; The Blue Bird of Paradise (with *H. SPRY*); Briarly Farm; The Buccaneer's Wife; Cora (Grec. 1865); Destiny (Grec. 1860); The Devil's Gap; The Fair One with the Locks of Gold (Grec. 1861; with *H. SPRY*); The Fall of the Avalanche (with *W. E. SUTER*); Forget and Forgive; Fugitives; The Ghost Hunter (Grec. 1862); The Hanged Man; Harlequin Guy Faux (with *H. SPRY*); Harlequin Valentine and Orson (with *H. SPRY*); The Hidden Light; The Home in the Heart; The House in the Valley; Mervyn Clitheroe; The Moment of Terror; The Motto on the Duke's Coat; Never Too Late to Mend (Grec. 1858); Peter Wilkins and the Flying Indians (with *H. SPRY*); The Phantom Captain; The Pirate's Love; The Realities of Life; Rookwood (Grec. 1859); The Shadow of Wrong; Temptation and Atonement; Where's Mr Smith?; The White Chateau.]
Harlequin Sun and Moon. [This is also attributed to *C. RICE*. +Grec. 26/12/55.]
Number Nip. [=The Spider and the Fly (Grec. 1862) in *UA*.]
Genevieve. [This is said to have been produced originally at the Grec. in 1855.]

p. 323] *CONQUEST, Mrs G.*
[+from *UA*: Flora and Zephyr (Grec. 31/3/52).]
+Bal. La fille mal gardée (Grec. 13/9/58).

+*COOK, —*
[+from *UA*: The Dove and the Serpent (with — *LITCHFIELD*).]

p. 324] *COOKE, W.*
[+from *UA*: Don Quixote and the Steed Rosinante.]

COOPER, F. F.

[+from *UA*: Garibaldi; Hard Times (Shr. 1854); Ivanhoe (Ast. 1859); Little Dorrit; The New Wags of Windsor (with *J. HOWARD*); Silver Store Island (Str. 1858); The Soldier's Wife (Str. 1854); Where's Crevelli (with *J. HOWARD*); Who's a Traveller? (with *J. HOWARD*).]

+D. The Christmas Carol (Str. 11/12/54).

+D. A Tale of Two Cities; or, The Incarcerated Victim of the Bastille (Vic. 7/7/60).

+P. Giovanni Redivivus; or, Harlequin in a Fox and Pantaloon on Horseback (Bower, 26/12/64).

p. 325] *CORDER, F.*

Nordisa. [Music by the author.]

+O. Tristan and Isolde. 8° 1882. [Written in collaboration with *H. CORDER*. Translation of the opera by R. Wagner (Munich, 10/6/65).]

+*COUPLAND, J. A.*

D. Louis XI. 8° 1889.

COURT, F. H.

[+from *UA*: The Irish Minstrel.]

p. 326] *COURTNEY, J.*

[+from *UA*: Harlequin and Cinderella; The Students.]

The Life Chase. [=The Marriage Day (*UA*), p. 716.]

+P. Undine; or, Albert the Reckless (Adel. L'pool, 26/12/57).

+P. Oberon, King of the Elves; or, Sir Huyon of Guyenne and the Fairy of the Magic Horn (Adel. L'pool, 26/12/58).

+D. The Two Homes; or, The Life of a Tradesman's Daughter (Eff. 15/8/59).

+D. Woman's Wrongs (C.L. 31/10/59).

+D. The Bandit of Sicily; or, The Mountain Haunt (M'bone, 10/60).

+D. The Battle with the World (C.L. 4/11/61).

+D. The Road to Transportation (Eff. 1/9/62).

[A play, *The Sailor of France*, is attributed to him in a Lacy list; there is a drama of this title by *J. B. JOHNSTONE*, see p. 438.]

p. 327] +*COX, SAMUEL ALFRED*

Ext. Shakespeare Converted into Bacon. 12° (1899).

COYNE, J. S.

[+from *UA*: The Vicar of Wakefield.]

p. 328] The Latest from New York. [A play of this title (D.L. 27/12/58) was attributed to *C. SELBY*.]

Samuel in Search of Himself. [Written in collaboration with *H. C. COAPE*.]

The Talking Fish. [Revised version of *Catching a Mermaid* (Olym. 20/10/55).]

+Sk. Shakespeare's House (Adel. 28/4/64).

+*CRAUFORD, Mrs W. R.*

[+from *UA*: Paul the Showman.]

CRAVEN, H. T.

[+from *UA*: Alonzo the Brave (Str. 1855). A play, *My Daughter's Debut*, appears in a Lacy list.]

p. 330] +*CROSLAND, Mrs NEWTON*

D. Hernani. 8° 1867. [Translation of the play (1830) by Victor Hugo.]

D. Ruy Blas. 8° 1887. [Translation of the play (1838) by Victor Hugo.]

"*CROWQUILL, A.*"

[For his earlier plays see iv, 287.]

p. 331] + *CUSNIE, W.*

P. Tit, Tat, Toe, the Three Jolly Butcher Boys All of a Row; or, Harlequin Mephistopheles and Old Father Thames (Eff. 26/12/58).

p. 332] "*DALE, FELIX.*" [See also under *H. C. MERIVALE.*]

+D. Time and the Hour (Qns. 29/6/68). See *J. P. SIMPSON.*

DALLAS, J.

+Oa. My Only Coat (Gai. 15/9/82). [Music W. Slaughter.]

p. 335] *DAM, H. J. W.*

The Coquette. [Version of *Le meunier d'Alcala*, libretto E. Garrida, music J. Clerice (Lisbon, 11/4/87).]

p. 336] *DANVERS, H.*

A Fascinating Individual. [+*Lacy.*]

D'ARCY, G.

+Bal. F. Dancing Dolls (Brit. 7/10/72).

+Bal. F. A Charming Plaything (Brit. 21/7/73). [Music J. Bernard.]

p. 338] *DAVEY, R.*

Marion Delorme. [Translation of the play (1831) by Victor Hugo.]

Lesbia. [Music W. H. Eayrens.]

+*DAVIES, JAMES.* [See under "*OWEN HALL.*"]

DAVIES, JOSEPH

Our Town. [+8° 1859 (Warrington).]

DAVIS, A.

+P. Nick of the Woods; or, The Avenging Spirit (Newcastle, 9/4/55).

+P. Valentine and Orson (Newcastle, 24/12/58).

+P. The King of the Peacocks (Newcastle, 26/12/60).

p. 339] +*DAVIS, HENRY*

D. Britons Abroad; or, The English in Algeria (Newcastle, 2/12/61).

+*DAVIS, JOHN D.*

[+from *UA*: The Zaporogues (with *E. L. LEVY*).]

DAVIS, S.

+D. The Will and the Way; or, The Mystery of Carrow Abbey (Newcastle, 9/1/54).

+D. The Lamplighter; or, The Guiding Star of Virtue (Newcastle, 15/1/55).

+D. Woman and her Master (Newcastle, 3/5/55).

+D. Minnie Gray; or, Gus and his Friend (Newcastle, 10/3/56).

+D. Dick Tarleton (Newcastle, 2/3/57).

p. 341] *DEFFELL, C.*
Christmas Eve. [This almost certainly = *The Oracle* (*UA*), p. 729.]

p. 342] +*DENNY, J.*
D. Stephen. 8° 1851.

p. 343] *DERRICK, J.*
[+from *UA*: The Little Stranger.]

DESPREZ, F.
[+from *UA*: La Perichole.]
Madame Angot. [Music A. C. Lecocq.]
Lurette. [=La Belle Lurette (Aven. 22/3/83) in *UA*.]

p. 344] +*DIANÉ*, —
[+from *UA*: Le Bouquet.]

+*DIBDIN, E. R. V.* [See "*E. V. WARD*".]

+*DIBDIN, T. C.*
Bal. Lord Bateman and the Fair Sophia (Cremorne, 24/5/58).

+*DICKS, J.*
D. A Year and a Day; or, The Trappers of the Mountains (C.L. 29/2/64).

+*DICKSON, C.*
[+from *UA*: Shatchem.]

p. 345] *DILLEY, J. J.*
[+from *UA*: Cousin Grace (with *L. CLIFTON*).]
+Doctor Davy (New, Greenwich, 6/2/65). See *J. ALBERY.*

p. 346] +*DOBLIN, H.*
[+from *UA*: Shatchem.]

p. 347] +*DONALD, J.*
[+from *UA*: The Dark Shadows.]

+*DONNE, C. E.*
D. The Husband. 12° (n.d. Cambridge). [Written in collaboration with *F. C. BURNAND.*]

+*DORRINGTON, W.*
P. Davy Jones, the Merman of the Sea (Plymouth, 26/12/58).

p. 348] *DOUGLASS, J. T.* [pseudonym "*JAMES WILLING*"].
[+from *UA*: The Assassins of the Roadside; The Brigand (Vic. 1865); Cora (Pav. 1861); Dame Durden; The Fireman and the Volunteer; First Impression's Everything; The Forty Thieves (Stand. 1864); The House on the Bridge of Notre Dame (Stand. 1861); I've beat all three; Jack the Giant Killer (Stand. 1869); Mark Winslow; Night; Oranges and Lemons; Pat a Cake (with *B. WRIGHT*); The Pirates of the Savannah; Tell Tale Tit.]
+D. The Midnight Angel (Stand. 1/5/61). [Some doubt is connected with this play; the title is also given to *W. E. SUTER* and *T. H. LACY*, and it appears, as at the Surrey, in *UA*.]
+D. The Savannah (Pav. 13/5/61).
+D. Louisiana; or, The Slave Daughter (Pav. 11/11/61).
+Bsq. The Brigand in a New Suit for Easter (Stand. 17/4/65). [This is the same as *The Brigand* (Vic. 1865) in *UA*.]

+D. £200 Reward (Pav. 20/11/65).
Guy Fawkes. [+8° (1870); music B. Isaacson.]
[In addition, the following titles are attributed to him in various lists: *The Man with the Pigeons*; *The Roadside Inn*; *Saved, or, the Innundation*; *The Sea-girt Cliff*; *A Child Lost*.]

p. 350] +*DOWTY, A. D.* [See under "*F. ARLON*".]

DOYLE, T. F.
[+from *UA*: Aladdin (Shakespeare, L'pool, 1891); Little Red Riding Hood (P.W. L'pool, 1880); The Yellow Dwarf (Shakespeare, L'pool, 1888).]
+P. Old Mother Hubberd (Shakespeare, L'pool, 21/12/89).

DRAYTON, H.
[+from *UA*: Diamond cut Diamond; Never Despair (Adel. 1859); Never Judge by Appearances (Adel. 1859).]

p. 352] *DU TERREAUX, L. H.*
[+from *UA*: Waiting for the Underground.]
La Fille de Madame Angot. [Music A. C. Lecocq.]
The Broken Branch. [Music G. Serpette.]

DUTNALL, M.
[+from *UA*: Harlequin Hey Diddle Diddle (Sur. 1861); Harlequin King Pumpkin.]
+Ext. Valentine the Great and Orson the Small (Sur. 21/4/62).

p. 353] *EAST, J. M.*
The Kitchen Girl. [=The Spouse Trap (*UA*), p. 754.]

EBSWORTH, J.
The Advocate and his Daughter. [Evidently the same as *The Advocate's Daughter* in *UA*.]

+*EBURNE, W. H.*
D. Phoebe Hersel; or, Eighty Years of a Woman's Life (Brighton, 2/60).

p. 354] *EDGAR, R. H.*
+F. Cryptoconchoidsyphonostomata (Roy. 8/12/75). See *C. COLLETTE*.

EDISON, J. H.
[For an earlier play see iv, 582.]

EDMUND, C.
The Maid of Athens. [Music F. Osmond Carr.]

+*EDOUIN, WILLIE*
M.C. A Dream (Aven. 16/7/83). See *N. CHILDS*.
C. Daughters (Portsmouth, 30/6/90). See *T. G. WARREN*.

p. 355] *EDWARDS, H. S.*
[+from *UA*: Little Red Riding Hood (C.G. 1858; with *J. V. BRIDGEMAN*); The Swan and Edgar (with *C. L. KENNEY*).]
Madame Cartouche. [Music L. Vasseur.]
+O. Eugene Onegin (Olym. 17/10/92). [Translation of the opera, libretto K. S. Shilovski, music P. I. Chaikovski (Moscow, 29/3/79).]

EDWARDS, OSMAN
A Gauntlet. [+8° 1894.]

p. 356] +*ELLIOTT, WILLIAM*

P. Tam O'Shanter, Cutty Sark, and Auld Mare Meg (Aberdeen, 12/57).

p. 358] *ELPHINSTONE, J.*

[+from *UA*: London Labour and London Poor.]

+D. Prince's Park and Scotland Row; or, Vice in Liverpool (Col. L'pool, 1/11/67).

ELTON, E.

[+from *UA*: The Mohicans of Paris (with *C. H. HAZLEWOOD*).]

EMDEN, W. S.

[+from *UA*: An Honest Attorney.]

The Head of the Family. [+*Lacy*.]

+F. Please to remember the Grotto (St J. 26/12/65). See *J. OXENFORD*.

p. 359] "*ESMOND, H. V.*"

[+from *UA*: My Lady's Lord.]

+*EVANS, FRED*

C. Bal. Skip Jack Joe (Brit. 30/3/74).

+*EVERETT, HENRY*

[+from *UA*: Roger O'Hare.]

+*FABER, M. A.*

D. Poem. The Child of the Wold. 8° 1867. [Translation of F. Halm, *Der Sohn des Wildniss*.]

+*FAIRCLOUGH, B.*

D. The King's Edict. 8° 1872. [Translation of V. Hugo, *Marion Delorme* (1831).]

p. 360] *FALCONER, E.*

[+from *UA*: The Leprechaun.]

Next of Kin. [This may=*A Day of Disasters* (*UA*), p. 664.]

p. 361] *FARJEON, B. L.*

+D. A Life's Revenge; or, The Days of the French Revolution (provinces, 1865).

FARNIE, H. B.

[+from *UA*: The Sleeping Queen.]

Le Petit Faust. [Version of the opera, libretto H. Crémieux and A. Jaime, music F. R. Hervé (Paris, 29/4/69).]

+Oa. The Rose of Auvergne (Gai. 8/11/69).

+Oa. Les deux aveugles (Gai. 15/4/71). [Version of the opera, libretto J. Moinaux, music J. Offenbach (Paris, 5/7/55).]

L'Oeil crevé. [Version of the opera, libretto and music F. R. Hervé (Paris, 12/10/67).]

Geneviève de Brabant. [Version of the opera, libretto A. Jaime and E. Tréfeu, music J. Offenbach (Paris, 19/11/59).]

Forty Winks. [Music J. Offenbach.]

Fleur de Lys. [Music L. Delibes.]

La Fille de Mme Angot. [Music A. C. Lecocq.]

+Oa. My New Maid (O.C. 18/3/74). [Music A. C. Lecocq.]

Madame l'Archiduc. [Version of the opera, libretto A. Millaud, music J. Offenbach (Paris, 31/10/74).]

Les Cloches de Corneville. [Version of the opera, libretto L. F. N. Clairville and C. Gabot, music R. Planquette (Paris, 19/4/77) +8° (1878).]

Madame Favart. [Version of the opera, libretto A. Duru and H. C. Chivot, music J. Offenbach (Paris, 28/12/78).]

Irene. [Version of *La reine de Saba*, libretto J. Barbier and M. Carré, music C. Gounod (Paris, 28/2/62).]

+O. Der Seekadett (Glo. 27/3/80). [Version of the opera, libretto F. Zell, music R. Genée (Vienna, 24/10/76).]

La Fille du tambour major. [Version of the opera, libretto H. C. Chivot and A. Duru, music J. Offenbach (Paris, 13/12/79).]

Olivette. [Version of *Les noces d'Olivette*, libretto H. C. Chivot and A. Duru, music E. Audran (Paris, 13/11/79). +8° (1880).]

Les Mousquetaires au Couvent. [Version of the opera, libretto P. Ferrier and J. Prével, music Varney (Paris, 16/3/80). +8° (1880).]

La Mascotte. [Version of the opera, libretto A. Duru and H. C. Chivot, music E. Audran (Paris, 28/12/80). +8° (1881).]

Manola. [+8° (1882).]

p. 363] Boccaccio. [Version of the opera, libretto F. Zell and R. Genée, music F. von Suppé (Vienna, 1/2/79).]

Rip van Winkle. [Version of the opera, libretto H. Meilhac and P. Gille, music R. Planquette. +8° 1883.]

The Grand Mogul. [Version of *Le gran Mogul*, libretto H. C. Chivot and A. Duru, music E. Audran (Marseilles, 24/3/77). +8° (1884).]

Paul Jones. [Music R. Planquette.]

FAUCIT, HENRY SAVILLE

[I have been unable satisfactorily to disentangle the Faucits and Savilles. For John Saville Faucit (who died in 1857) see iv, 311; he is probably the author of *The Amber Witch*. Henry Saville Faucit seems to have called himself also Henry Faucit Saville. As Henry Saville he was responsible for *Harlequin Christoval* (with *E. TOWERS*), *The Life and Adventures of Will Shakespeare*, and *London Vice and London Virtue* in *UA*.]

+D. Devilshoof; or, The Domino of Death (Vic. 9/6/62).

+P. Tom Thumb; or, Merlin the Magician and the Fairy in the Grotto of Silver Shells (Northampton, 26/12/62).

+P. Harlequin King Atlas and the Seven Princesses of the Stars; or, The Faye of the Fountain of Jewels (Nottingham, 26/12/64). 12° (1864; Nottingham).

+P. Harlequin and the Sleeping Beauty (Nottingham, 26/12/66).

+D. The Black Captain (1867). See *W. D. FISHER*.

FAUCQUEZ, A.

[+from *UA*: André the Miner; The Deserted Wife; The Forced Marriage; Lost and Found; The Sacred Trust; Woman's Devotion.]

+D. The Abyss of Thorns (Vic. 12/3/61).

+D. The Seventh Hour (C.L. 10/4/61). [Written in collaboration with *B. HUGHES*. This may be the play of the same name in *UA*.]
+D. The Leopard; or, Wild Doings in the South (Vic. 18/11/61).
+D. The Adventurer's Doom; or, The Murder of the Willow Marsh (Grec. 14/7/62). [This seems to be the same as *The Forced Marriage* and *The Willow Marsh* in *UA*.]
+D. The Lost Fortune (Grec. 24/7/65).

p. 365] *FENTON, F.*
[+from *UA*: Baron Munchausen (with *W. R. OSMAN*); Harlequin and Old Æsop (with *W. R. OSMAN*); The Kidnappers (with *W. R. OSMAN*); The Secrets of the Devil (with *W. R. OSMAN*).]

FERNALD, C. B.
[+from *UA*: The Ghetto.]

FIELD, J.
[+from *UA*: It was a Dream.]

FIELD, K.
[+from *UA*: Eyes Right.]

p. 367] +*FINLAYSON, —*
[+from *UA*: Love wins the Day.]

FISHER, D.
[+from *UA*: The Counterfeit.]

+*FISHER, WALTER D.*
D. The Black Captain (1867). [In collaboration with *H. S. FAUCIT*.]

FITZBALL, E.
[+from *UA*: Harlequin and Humpty Dumpty.]
Azael the Prodigal. [Version of *L'enfant prodigue*, libretto A. E. Scribe, music D. F. E. Auber (Paris, 6/12/50); music adapted for English production by H. Laurent. It is not certain whether this and *Azael* (Ast. 3/11/51) were the same.]

p. 368] Raymond and Agnes. [Music E. Loder.]
Pierette. [Music W. H. Montgomery.]
The Widow's Wedding. [+8° 1859.]
Christmas Eve. [+*Lacy*.]
She Stoops to Conquer. [+8° (1864).]

p. 370] +*FORMAN, A.*
O. Tristan and Isolde. 8° 1891. [Translation of Wagner's opera (Munich, 10/6/65).]

p. 371] *FORRESTER, A. H.*
[+from *UA*: The King of the Castle.]

p. 372] *FRANCE, E. S.*
[An advertisement by this author in 1878 lists *The Flag of Truce*, *John Darell's Dream*, *The Last Chime of Midnight* and *Wasted Lives*.]

+*FRANCK* or *FRANCKS, Dr*
[+from *UA*: Kicks and Halfpence (with *W. BROUGH*); A Tale of a Coat (with *W. BROUGH*).]

+*FRASER, W.*
[+from *UA*: Spare the Rod, Spoil the Child.]

p. 373] +*FRENCH, G. H.*
P. Red Riding Hood (Nottingham, 18/3/61). 12° 1861 (Northampton).

FRENCH, S.
[+from *UA*: The Sister's Sacrifice.]
A Friend in Need. [+*Lacy*.]

"*FROST, F.*" [*E. L. BLANCHARD*]
+P. Harlequin Friar Bacon; or, Great Grim John of Gaunt, and the Enchanted Lane of Robin Goodfellow (Ast. 26/12/63).
Tit, Tat, Toe. [=*The Fairy Elves* and *Harlequin Tit, Tat, Toe* in *UA*.]

p. 375] *GALEN, CHARLES*
[+from *UA*: Our Female American Cousin.]

GALER, E. J. N.
[+from *UA*: Folly Fête.]

+*GALVAN, JOHN*
D. Faust 8° 1860, 1862 (Dublin).

p. 377] *GEE, L.*
[+from *UA*: Slumber my Darling.]

GEORGE, G. H.
[+from *UA*: Harlequin Billy Taylor (Eff. 1857).]
+Ext. The Musical Mummy (Sur. 20/7/59).

p. 378] +*GIBBON, CHARLES*
D. The Rath Boys (Stand. 17/5/62). See *R. BUCHANAN*.

GIBNEY, S.
[+from *UA*: A Woman's No.]

+*GILBEIGH, —*
[+from *UA*: Abou Hassan (with *G. GRIMES*).]

p. 381] [*GILLETTE, W.*
[+from *UA*: Too Much Johnson.]

p. 382] *GLEN, I.*
A Woman's Error. [=The Stolen Diamonds (*UA*), p. 754.]

GLENNEY, C.
Matches. [Written in collaboration with *A. E. BAGOT*.]

+*GLOVER, HENRY*
[+from *UA*: Once too often.]

+*GLOVER, WILLIAM H.*
O. Ruy Blas (C.G. 24/10/61).

GLYNN, G.
[For his earlier plays see iv, 319.]

p. 384] *GOLDSWORTHY, A.*
The Blacksmith's Daughter. [Written in collaboration with *E. B. NORMAN*.]

+*GOMERSAL, E. W.*
D. Boraldi the Outlaw (Leeds, 21/10/62). [Music by Jackman.]

p. 385] *GORDON, W.*
[+from *UA*: Two can play at that Game.]
Home for a Holiday. [+*Lacy*.]

+*GRANT, JOHN WYNNIAT*
D. Faust 8° 1867.

p. 389] *GRATTAN, H. P.*
[For his earlier plays see iv, 320.]
[+from *UA*: The Fairy Circle; The White Boys (Sur. 1862).]
+The Game of Life; or, The Swallows of Paris (Sur. 16/11/63). [Written in collaboration with *H. VOLLAIRE*.]

GRAVES, CLOTILDE
[+from *UA*: Katharine Kavanagh; Puss in Boots (D.L. 1888).]
Rachel. [=*Death and Rachel* in *UA*.]

p. 390] *GREEN, F. W.*
[+from *UA*: Aladdin (Brighton, 1880); Froggy would a-wooing go; Jack in the Box; Little Red Riding Hood (Rotunda, L'pool, 1883); Twinkle, Twinkle, Little Star (Brighton, 1875).]
+P. Little Goody Two Shoes (Brighton, 26/12/71).
+P. Ali Baba and the Forty Thieves (Brighton, 26/12/72).

p. 392] *GREENBANK, H.*
The Scarlet Feather. [Version of *La petite mariée*, libretto A. Vanloo and L. Leterrier, music A. C. Lecocq (Paris, 21/12/75).]

p. 393] *GREENWOOD, T. L.*
[For his earlier plays see iv, 321.]
[+from *UA*: Harlequin and Old Izaac Walton; Harlequin and Puss in Boots; Harlequin and the House that Jack built; Harlequin Hans and the Golden Goose (with *E. L. BLANCHARD*); Harlequin Jack Sprat (with *E. L. BLANCHARD*); Harlequin Tom Tom the Piper's Son; Is it the King?]
The House that Jack built in 1851. [=Harlequin and the H.t.J.b. in 1851 (*UA*), p. 687.]
Harlequin and the Yellow Dwarf. [Music W. Montgomery.]
Dick Whittington and his Cat. [Music W. Montgomery.]
Harlequin and Tom Thumb. [Music W. Montgomery.]
+P. Harlequin Ali Baba and the Forty Thieves; or, Morgiana and the Arabian Nights (S.W. 26/12/54). [Music W. Montgomery.]
Harlequin and Beauty and the Beast. [See *Harlequin Beauty and the Beast* (*UA*), p. 688.]

p. 394] *GREGG, T. D.*
+D. Queen Elizabeth; or, The Origin of Shakespeare. 8° 1872.

+*GRIMES, G.*
[+from *UA*: Abou Hassan (Norwich, 1850); with —, *GILBEIGH.*]

+"*GRINN BROTHERS, THE*" [Pseudonym of *T. L. GREENWOOD AND E. L. BLANCHARD.*]

p. 395] *GRIST, WILLIAM*
[+from *UA*: The Bohemians (with *P. E. PINKERTON*).]
The Impresario. [Version of *Der Schauspieldirektor*, libretto G. Stephanie, music A. W. Mozart (Vienna, 7/2/1786).]
+O. Il Matrimonio Segreto (C.P. 13/12/77).
Ruy Blas. [Version of the opera, libretto C. D'Ormeville, music F. Marchetti (Milan, 3/4/69).]
At Santa Lucia [Version of *A Santa Lucia*, libretto E. Golisciani and G. Cagnetti, music Tasca (Berlin, 16/11/92).]

p. 396] +*GROVES, CHARLES*
Ca. A Golden Wedding (H. 30/11/98). See *E. PHILLPOTTS.*

GRUNDY, S.
La Cosaque. [Music F. R. Hervé.]

p. 397] *GUNTON, R. T.*
The Lancashire Witches. [For the production at the Court, L'pool, 10/9/81, this had a sub-title: *or, King Jamie's Frolic.*]

GURNEY, A. T. [For his earlier plays see iv, 322.]

p. 398] +*HAKE, T. G.*
D. The Serpent Play. 8° 1883.

HALE, W. P.
+Bsq. The Princess in the Tower (Olym. 2/9/50). See *F. TALFOURD.*

HALFORD, J.
[+from *UA*: The Carrier of London; The Cricket on the Hearth (Str. 1855); King Queer and his Daughters Three (with *C. J. COLLINS*); The Little Demon.]

p. 399] *HALL, F.*
+F. In and Out and Round About (M'bone, 16/11/63).

p. 403] *HARDWICKE, P.*
+Ca. A Whirligig (Vaud. 23/8/75).

p. 404] *HARRINGTON, N. H.*
[+from *VA*: Mr Webster's Company is requested at a Photographic Soirée (with *E. YATES*).]

HARRINGTON, R.
The Pedlar Boy. [This was apparently first produced at the Stand. 2/62.]

HARRIS, A. G.
[+from *UA*: The Fairy Page; Our Nurse Dorothy.]

p. 406] *HARRIS, Sir A. H. G.*
Basoche. [With *E. OUDIN*. Version of the opera, libretto A. Carré, music A. Messager (Paris, 30/5/90).]
Dick Whittington. [+8° 1894.]

HARRISON, W.
The Marriage of Georgette. [Version of *Les noces de Jeannette*, libretto J. Barbier and M. Carré, music F. M. V. Massé (Paris, 4/2/53).]

p. 409] +*HASTINGS, S.*
[+from *UA*: The Wrongs of Poland.]

HATTON, J.
No. 20. [+*or, The Bastille of Calvados.*]
+Birds of a Feather. 12° (n.d.).

p. 411] *HAY, F.*
+D. Flamma; or, The Child of the Fire (Brit. 6/6/70). See *EDITH SANDFORD.*

+*HAYDON, FLORENCE*
[+from *UA*: Jack of All Trades (with *H. NEVILLE*).]

p. 412] *HAZLETON, F.*
[+from *UA*: A Fiery Ordeal (Brit. 1862).]

HAZLEWOOD, C. H.
[+from *UA*: Auld Robin Gray; Belphegor, the Mountebank to any Amount of Property; The Black Gondola; The Black Statue; Carlo Leoni; The Champion of England; The Confederate's Daughter; The Dark King of the Black Mountains; Dirty Dick; Faith, Hope and Charity; The Farmer of Inglefield Forest; Goosey Goosey Gander; The Gorilla Hunt in the Forest of Gabon; Gratitude; Harlequin and the Little Mouse; The Hebrew Diamond; The Idolaters; Jeannie Deans (Stand. 1862); Jerry Abershaw; Jessie, the Morman's Daughter; The Jolly Dogs of London; The King of the Assassins; Laurette's Bridal; Life's Trials; Lyddy Beale; The Magic Wishing Cap; Mary Price; The Mohicans of Paris (with *E. ELTON*); Never Too Late to Mend (Brit. 1859); The Old Cherry Tree; Old Daddy Longlegs (with *D. JOHNSON*); The Old Maid in a Winding Sheet; The Old Toll House; Oliver Twist (C.L. 1855); Paul Clifford; Phyllis Thorpe; Pretty Blue Belle; Prince Pippo; The Princess of the Pearl Island; Rich and Poor; The Rival Fountains; The Romance of a Poor Young Man; The Sailor's Sheet-Anchor; The Slaves of Crime; Some Bells that Ring the Old Year Out and the New One In; The Spirit of Liberty; Struggles of the Poor; The Three Lives; La Traviata (Brit. 1857); Twenty Straws (Brit. 1865); Under a Cloud (Brit. 1859); Upside Down (Brit. 1864); The Volcano of Italy; The Wedding Eve; The Wild Tribes; The Workgirls of London.]
+P. Puss in Boots (Gravesend, 9/59).
The Chevalier of the Moulin Rouge. [Played at the M'bone, 9/9/67 as *The Man of the Red Château; or, The Days of Terror*.]
+D. Bessy Moore (C.L. 18/6/60).
+D. The Harvest Storm (Brit. 26/7/62). *Lacy.*
+D. The Jewess of the Temple (Brit. 23/11/63).

+P. Harlequin Bluebeard and his Seven Headless Wives (Pav. 21/12/65). [See *Bluebeard* in *UA*.]

p. 413] The Detective. [Played apparently at the Vic. 20/7/63.]

The False Mother. [It seems probable that this = *Violet's Perils* (*UA*), p. 764.]

+D. Nellie; or, The Companions of the Chair. [Acted before 8/65, when it was acquired by the M'bone.]

+P. Sinbad the Sailor; or, Harlequin, Old Man of the Sea, the Emperor, the Ogre, the Fairy and the Princess (Pav. 26/12/66).

+D. Abel Flint (Brit. 20/6/68).

p. 414] +D. The Mill of the Happy Valley (Brit. 17/10/70).

p. 415] Lady Audley's Secret. [+*Lacy*, which gives production Vic. 25/5/63; it certainly was performed at the Brit. 18/6/66.]

[Titles listed as his include: *Lilla the Lost One*; *Our Tea Party*; *Who's the Victim* (C.L. 1856). An O. Ba. called *Cinderella* was revived at the Brit. 4/5/72 and a Bsq. *Beauty and the Beast* at the same theatre, 11/5/74.]

p. 417] *HENRY, A.*

[+from *UA*: Little Red Riding Hood (Hengler's, 1874).]

"*HENRY, R.*"

Monte Cristo. [Music M. Lutz.]

p. 418] *HERAUD, J. A.*

[+from *UA*: Agnolo Diora.]

Videna. [+8° 1854.]

HERBERT, G. C.

Our Bitterest Foe. [+L.C.]

p. 419] *HERIOT, P.*

A Remarkable Cure. [+L.C.]

HERMAN, H.

For a Child's Sake. [+Sur. 4/12/99.]

HERSEE, H.

+O. The Merry Wives of Windsor (Adel. 11/2/78). [Music O. Nicolai.]

Carmen. [Version of the opera, libretto H. Meilhac and L. Halévy, music G. Bizet (Paris, 3/3/75).]

The Dragoons. [Version of *Les Dragons de Villars*, libretto J. P. Lockroy and E. Cormon, music L. Maillart (Paris, 19/9/56).]

p. 420] Aida. [Version of the opera, libretto A. Ghislanzoni, music G. Verdi (Cairo, 24/12/71).]

+O. I Promessi Sposi (Edin. 23/3/81). [Version of the opera, music A. Ponchielli (Cremona, 30/8/56).]

The Piper of Hamelin. [Version of *Der Rattenfänger von Hameln*, libretto F. Hofmann, music J. E. Nessler (Leipzig, 19/3/79).]

The Royal Ward. [Music Isadore de Lara.]

HEWSON, J. J.

[+from *UA*: Aladdin (P.W. L'pool, 1896); Cinderella (P.W. L'pool, 1899); Dick Whittington (P.W. L'pool, 1898); Little Red Riding Hood (P.W. L'pool, 1897); Sinbad the Sailor (Alex. L'pool, 1880, with *T. E. PEMBERTON*.]

+P. The Forty Thieves (Alex. L'pool, 26/12/87). See *T. E. PEMBERTON*.

p. 421] *HIGGIE, T. H.*

[+from *UA*: Harlequin King Holliday.]

Belphegor. [Written with *T. H. LACY*. +*Lacy*.]

p. 422] +*HILLIS, S.*

[+from *UA*: Ornano.]

HIPKINS, T. H.

+Is She His Daughter? [See *GASTON MURRAY*.]

p. 424] +*HOLLINGSWORTH, J.*

F. The Distracted Bachelor (Stand. 24/7/71).

HOLT, C.

[+from *UA*: Out of Evil cometh Good.]

+D. The Spirit Captain (New Zealand, *c.* 1860; C.L. 5/12/64).

+"*HOME, RISDEN*"

D. Nelson's Enchantress (Aven. 11/2/97). L.C.

p. 425] *HOOD, B.*

+Fairy D. Hans Anderson's Fairy Tales (Terry's 24/4/97). [Music W. Slaughter.]

p. 426] *HORNE, F. L.*

[=from *UA*: The Head of a Clan.]

p. 427] *HORSMAN, C.*

[+from *UA*: The Lost Bride of Garryowen]

+P. Sinbad the Sailor; or, The Old Man of the Sea (Qns. Manchester, 26/12/63).

HORTON, S. G.

[+from *UA*: Robin Hood (R.A. Woolwich, 1888), with *H. MILLS*.]

+*HOUGH, ALFRED JAMES*

Old Sarum; or, Hunted to Death by a Woman (Salisbury, 21/9/68).

p. 428] [*HOWARD, B.*

The Henrietta. [+Union Square, New York, 26/9/87.]

+*HOWARD, J.*

[+from *UA*: The New Wags of Windsor (with *F. F. COOPER*); Where's Crevelli? (with *F. F. COOPER*); Who's a Traveller? (with *F. F. COOPER*).]

HOWE, J. B.

[+from *UA*: The Necromancer; A Young Girl from the Country.]

+D. The Beggar Marquis (Eff. 17/8/63).

The Wedding Eve. [+*or, The Dream of Aileen and the Cave of Dunmore*.]

p. 430] *HUME, H.*
[+from *UA*: Troubled Waters (Vic. 1864).]

HUNT, G. W.
[Two plays, *Our Wedding Day* and *The World We Live In*, were advertised in the *Era Almanack*, 1879.]

p. 431] +*HUTH, ALFRED HENRY*
D. Faust. 8° 1889. [A version of Goethe's drama.]

+*HYDE, W. S.*
D. Blanche of Nevers; or, I am here (Manchester, 6/4/63).
P. The Sleeping Beauty (Manchester, 26/12/63). See *T. CHAMBERS.*

p. 432] *IRVING, L. S. B.*
[+from *UA*: A Christmas Story (Var. 1893); Godefroi and Yolande.]

+*IRWIN, E.*
P. Old Mother Goose (Qns. Dublin, 26/12/62). See *C. WEBB.*

JACKSON, J. P.
The Flying Dutchman. [Version of *Die fliegende Holländer*, music R. Wagner (Dresden, 2/1/43).]
The Golden Cross. [Version of *Das goldene Kreuz*, libretto S. H. Mosenthal, music I. Brüll (Berlin, 22/12/75).]
Rienzi. [Version of *Cola Rienzi*, music R. Wagner (Dresden, 20/10/42).]
Lohengrin. [Version of the opera, music R. Wagner (Weimar, 28/8/50).]

JACOBS, W. W.
The Grey Parrot. [With *CHARLES ROCK.*]

p. 433] *JAMES, C.*
The Honourable John. [*E. J. MALYON* also collaborated in this play.]

JAMES, H.
Guy Domville. [+8° 1894 (priv.).]
+The Ghost (Brede School House, 28/12/99, *amat.*). [Written in collaboration with nine others, including *GEORGE GISSING, RIDER HAGGARD, JOSEPH CONRAD, H. G. WELLS* and *A. E. W. MASON.* See J. D. Gordan, "The Ghost of Brede Place" (*Bulletin of the New York Public Library*, lvi, 1952, 591–5).]

p. 434] +*JAMESON, F.*
O. Tristan and Isolde. 8° 1886. [Translation of the opera, music R. Wagner (Munich, 10/6/65).]

+*JAMESON, R. W.*
T. Timoleon. L.C. Adel. Edinburgh, 9/3/52. 8° 1852 (Edinburgh).

JARVIS, J. H.
Fleur de Thé. [Music A. C. Lecocq.]

JAY, H.
[+from *UA*: The Queen of Connaught.]

p. 435] *JEFFERYS, C.*

+O. La Traviata (S.W. 24/5/58). [Version of the opera, music G. Verdi.]

The Gipsy's Vengeance. [Version of *Il trovatore*, libretto S. Cammarano, music G. Verdi (Rome, 19/1/53).]

Esmerelda. [Version of *Ermelinda*, libretto D. Bolognese, music V. Battista (Naples, 15/2/51).]

+O. Luisa Miller; or, Love and Intrigue. L.C. S.W. 27/5/58. [Music G. Verdi.]

p. 436] *JERROLD, D. W.*

+ D. The Heart of Gold (P'cess, 9/10/54).

JERROLD, M. W. B.

Beau Brummell. [+*Lacy*, as *B.B., the King of Calais.*]

p. 437] *JOHNSON, D.*

[+from *UA*: Old Daddy Longlegs (with *C. H. HAZLEWOOD*).]

JOHNSON, G. D.

[+from *UA*: In and Out of Place.]

p. 430] *JOHNSTONE, J. B.*

[+from *UA*: Avarice; Ellie Forester; Harlequin Green Beetle; The Holly Tree Inn; How We Live in the World of London; The Love Test; The Old Woman who lived in a Shoe; The Railroad of Life (Eff. 1859); St Anne's Night; The Seven Poor Travellers (Sur. 1855); Under a Cloud (Eff. 1859); The Will o' the Wisp (Eff. 1859).]

+D. Never Too Late to Mend (Qns. Manchester, 18/9/58).

+P. The King of the Busybodies; or, Harlequin Ruby and the Emerald Sprite (Woolwich, 26/12/58).

+D. The Sailor's Wife; or, Forty Years Ago (Eff. 23/5/59).

+D. Ingratitude; or, Highways and Holidays (Eff. 29/8/59).

+P. Harlequin Robin Readbreast and Prince Cocksparrow (Qns. Manchester, 26/12/59).

+D. Rougemont the French Robber; or, The Rats of the Rigmerole (Eff. 15/10/60).

+D. Aurora Floyd (M'bone, 5/63).

+D. The Poor of London (M'bone, 16/5/64).

The Coal Mine. [+*or, Life below the Earth.*]

+D. British Bull Dogs (M'bone, 27/3/68).

The Old Mint. [This seems to be a revised version of his *The Old Mint of Southwark* (Sur. 9/6/45).]

p. 439] +*JONES, DAVID H.*

D. Old Swansea Castle (Swansea, 25/8/58).

JONES, H. A.

Harmony Restored. [Apparently this play, *Harmony*, *The Organist* and *It's Only Round the Corner* were all one piece.]

p. 440] The Case of Rebellious Susan. [+8° 1894 (priv.).]

JONES J. S.

The Carpenter of Rouen. [This seems to be the same play as that listed under Jacob Jones in iv, 334.]

JONES J. W.

[+from *UA*: The Forty Thieves (Rotunda, L'pool, 1885.]

p. 441] +P. Humpty Dumpty (Shakespeare, L'pool, 26/12/90).
The Babes in the Wood. [+8° (1894) +*or, Robin Hood and his Foresters Good.*]

p. 442] +*KEATING, Miss*
[+from *UA*: Gosling the Great; Red Riding Hood (Birmingham, 1858).]
P. Little Red Riding Hood and Baron von Wolf (Brighton, 26/12/58).
P. The House that Jack built, ye Lord Lovell and ye Nancy Belle (Brighton, 27/12/59).

p. 443] *KENNEY, C. L.*
[+from *UA*: The Swan and Edgar (with *H. S. EDWARDS*).]
The Mock Doctor. [Version of *Le médecin malgré lui*, music C. Gounod (Paris, 15/1/58).]
L'Africaine. [Version of the opera, libretto A. E. Scribe, music G. Meyerbeer (Paris, 28/4/65).]
+C.O. Barbe Bleue (Stand. 13/12/69; Gai. 29/8/70, as *Bluebeard*). [Version of the opera, libretto H. Meilhac and L. Halévy, music J. Offenbach (Paris, 12/4/67).]
The Grand Duchess of Gerolstein. [Music J. Offenbach.]
The Princess of Trebizonde. [Version of the opera, libretto C. Nuitter and E. Tréfeu, music J. Offenbach (Baden-Baden, 31/7/69).]
La Belle Hélène. [Music J. Offenbach.]
The Wonderful Duck. [Music Emile Jones.]
+La Jolie Parfumeuse (Birmingham, 8/7/75). [Version of the opera, libretto H. Crémieux and E. Blum, music J. Offenbach (Paris, 29/11/73).]
The Mock Doctor. [The performance at the Grand in 1890 was a revision of the opera originally produced in 1865.]

p. 444] *KINGDOM, J. M.*
[+from *UA*: Love and Crime.]
+D. The High Road of Life; or, The Brigand Marquis (C.L. 23/3/57).

+*KINGSTON, LAWRENCE*
[+from *UA*: Angela.]

KINGSTON, W. B. [and see *W. BEATTY-KINGSTON*].
The Poet's Dream. [Version of *Le songe d'une nuit d'été*, libretto J. B. Rosier and A. de Leuven, music A. Thomas (Paris, 20/4/50).]
+C.O. Falstaff (Lyc. 11/12/96, as revised by *F. HART*). [Version of the opera, libretto A. Boito, music G. Verdi (Milan, 9/2/93).]

p. 445] [*KLEIN, C. H.*
El Capitan. [+originally produced Boston, 13/4/96.]

p. 446] +*KRASINSKI, Count HENRY*
Queen Hortensia's Shoe; and The Sultan, the Gardener, and the Odalisque, Two Melodramas. 8° 1857.

LACY, M. R.
[+from *UA*: The Blind Sister; The House on the Bridge of Notre Dame (Lyc. 1861).]

LACY, T. H.

D. Belphegor the Buffoon (Vic. 27/1/51). See *T. H. HIGGIE.*

C. John Bull; or, The Comedy of 1854. 8° (1854).

D. The Angel of Midnight (Grec. 20/5/61). See *W. E. SUTER.*

p. 448] +"*LANE, PRINGLE*"

P. Mother Goose; or, The Queen of Hearts who made some Tarts (P's. Manchester, 26/12/64).

LANGFORD, —

+C.D. A Border Marriage (Adel. 3/1/56). See *W. J. SORRELL.*

p. 449] *LAURI, E.*

+C.Ent. Ki-ki-ko-ko-oh-ki-key (Brit. 12/6/71). [Written in collaboration with *B. McCORMACK.*]

+*LAVALLIN, J. P.*

D. Helen in Egypt. 8° 1882 (Oxford).

p. 450] *LAW, A.*

A Strange Host [=A Happy New Year (*UA*), p. 687.]

p. 451] *LAWRENCE, F.*

[+from *UA*: No. 49.]

LAYTON, G. M.

Melusine the Enchantress. [Music F. R. Hervé.]

Liline and Valentin. [Music A. C. Lecocq.]

The Duke's Daughter. [Music L. Vasseur.]

"*LEADER, J.*"

+M.F. In Town (P.W. 15/10/92). [Written in collaboration with *ADRIAN ROSS.*]

p. 452] *LECLERCQ, P.*

[+from *UA*: All Hallow's Eve (H. 1859).]

LEE, NELSON.

[+from *UA*: Anne Boleyn; Birds, Beasts and Fishes; The Fox and the Grapes; Joe Miller; Oliver Cromwell.]

Harlequin Alfred the Great. [This appears also in *UA*: it is attributed in the Lacy text to *G. H. RODWELL.*]

LEE, NELSON, Jr.

[It is sometimes difficult to separate the pieces written by Nelson Lee and those written by Nelson Lee, Jr. The year 1857 seems to provide a dividing line.]

[+from *UA*: The Fallen Star; Harlequin Baron Munchausen; The Idiot of the Mountain (with *W. TRAVERS*); Johnny Gilpin's Ride; King Comet and Prince Quicksilver; The King of the Golden Valley; The Moneylender; Sing a Song of Sixpence (C.L. 1862); The Tempter.]

+D. Redman the Reckless (C.L. 18/7/59, "first time" at this theatre).

+D. The Returned Outcast; or, Crimes in High Life (C.L. 10/59).

+D. The Adventures of a Young Man (C.L. 29/10/60).

+F. Chaunting Ben of Spitalfields (C.L. 11/60).

+P. Fair Rosamond, and the Queen with the Dagger and the Bowl; or, The Fairy of the Enchanted Labyrinth (C.L. 26/12/60).
+P. Alonzo the Brave; or, Harlequin and the Fair Imogene (C.L. 26/2/61).
+F. Bob Ridley (C.L. 20/5/61).
+P. King Hal the Bluff, Anne Boleyne the Fair; or, Harlequin Herne the Hunter and the Good Little Fairies of the Silver Ferns (M'bone, 24/12/62).
+D. Life at the East End of London (C.L. 31/10/64).
+P. The Rose, Shamrock and Thistle (Crystal Palace, 26/12/65).

p. 453] +P. The Old Woman who lived in a Shoe and Little Bopeep who lost her Sheep; or, Harlequin Tom the Piper's Son and the Good Fairy of the Golden Mountains (Hull, 26/12/63).
Derby Day. [+*or, The Field against the Favourite.*]

+*LEE, SMYTHE*
[+from *UA*: A Great Sensation.]

+*LEGG, JAMES*
[+from *UA*: Has anybody seen Mr Brown?; Where's Brown? (Brighton, 1859).]

p. 454] *LEIGH, H. S.*
Falsacappa. [Version of *Les brigands*, libretto H. Meilhac and L. Halévy, music J. Offenbach (Paris, 10/12/69).]
The Bridge of Sighs. [Version of *Le port des soupirs*, libretto H. Crémieux and L. Halévy, music J. Offenbach (Paris, 23/3/61).]
Fatinitza. [Version of the opera, libretto F. Zell and R. Genée, music F. von Suppé (Vienna, 5/1/76).]
The Great Casimir. [Music A. C. Lecocq.]
Prince Methuselem. [Version of the opera, libretto K. Treumann, music J. Strauss (Vienna, 3/1/77).]
Suzanne. [Music M. Paladilke.]

LEIGHTON, Sir B.
Day Dreams. [+8[c] 1875 (*priv.*) as *Kate of Coventry.*]

p. 455] *LEMON, M.*
[+from *UA*: Welcome Little Stranger.]
Keeley worried by Buckstone. [In a revised form this was given at L'pool, 3/9/52, as *Baker worried by Buckstone.*]

LENNARD, H.
D. The Old Curiosity Shop (L'pool, 3/81). See *J. MACKAY*.
Lalla Rookh. [+Music P. Bucalossi.]
The Babes in the Wood and Bold Robin Hood. [+8° (1892).]
Cinderella. [Music O. Barrett.]
Blue Beard. [+8° 1894.]
Santa Claus. [Music O. Barrett.]
Robinson Crusoe. [Music O. Barrett.]

LEON, HUGO
[+from *UA*: Lovers at Play.]

p. 457] *LESLIE, H. T.*
[+from *UA*: Rouge et noir.]

p. 458] *LEVY, E. L.*
[+from *UA*: The Zaporogues (+*J. DAVIS*).]

LEWES, G. H. [pseudonym "*FRANK CHURCHILL*"]
The Noble Heart. [+8° 1850.]
Taking by Storm. [Under pseudonym "*FRANK CHURCHILL*". +L.C. *Lacy*.]

p. 459] +*LINDERS, G.*
D. The Avenger's Vow (Nottingham, 1863).

p. 460] +*LINDSAY, Sir COUTTS*
T. Boadicea. 8° 1857 (*priv.*).

+*LINGHAM, R. H.*
[+from *UA*: Scattered Leaves.]

LINLEY, G.
[+from *UA*: Queen Topaze; The Toy Maker.]

p. 461] +*LITCHFIELD, CHARLES*
[+from *UA*: The Dove and the Serpent; The Heart of Old Ireland.]

p. 462] *LOCKE, F.*
[+from *UA*: Little Bo Peep (Rotunda, L'pool, 1892); Little Red Riding Hood (Birmingham, 1893); Robinson Crusoe (Birmingham, 1894).]
+P. The Babes in the Wood (P.W. L'pool, 26/12/86).

LODGE, A.
Won, not wooed. [+8° 1874.]

+*LOGAN, W. H.*
P. Cinderella and the Sensation Slipper (Qns. Edinburgh, 26/12/61).
+P. Red Riding Hood (Qns. Dublin, 26/12/61).
P. Cinderella; or, The Silver Slipper and Harlequin in the Land of Dreams (Aberdeen, 26/12/63).

p. 463] *LONGMUIR, ANDREW*
Deception. [+L.C.]

LORNE, The Marquis of. [*J. G. CAMPBELL.*]

LOVER, S.
Barney the Baron. [+*Dicks.*]

p. 466] *LYTTON, BARON*
Walpole. [+*or, Every Man has his Price.*]

McARDLE, J. F.
[+from *UA*: Babes in the Wood (Court, L'pool, 1881); Beauty and the Beast (P.W. L'poool, 1883 +*F. J. STIMSON*); Robin Hood (Alex. L'pool, 1880); Sinbad the Sailor (Rotunda, L'pool, 1880).]
+P. Cinderella (Rotunda, L'pool, 27/12/75).

p. 467] *McCARTHY, J. H.*
François the Radical. [Music F. Bernicot and A. Messager.]

p. 468] +*McCORMACK, B.*
C.M. Ki-ki-ko-ko-oh-ki-key (Brit. 12/6/71). See *E. LAURI.*

MACDERMOTT, G. H. [Pen-name of *G. H. FARRELL.*]

p. 469] *MACFARREN, G. A.*
Jessy Lea. [Written in collaboration with *J. OXENFORD.*]

MACKAY, H.
[+from *UA*: Iron Latch Farm.]

MACKAY, J.
+D. The Old Curiosity Shop (L'pool, 3/81). See *H. LENNARD.*

p. 471] *MACNAIR, A.*
+D. The Way of the World (Glasgow, 4/5/60).

p. 472] *MADDOX, J. M.*
[+from *UA*: Peter the Shipwright.]

+MAITLAND, FRANK
P. The Invisible Prince; or Harlequin King Noodle (Qns. Manchester, 26/12/62).

MAJOR, H. A.
+Ca. A Sketch from the Louvre (Soho, 28/7/60). [This title appears also in *UA*, possibly a revision of the earlier play.]

MALET, Sir EDWARD
Harold. [+*or, The Norman Conquest.*]

p. 473] *+MALONE, —*
Bsq. Macbeth Travestie (Str. 18/4/53).
Bsq. King Richard III, according to Act of Parliament (Str. 17/4/54).

MALYON, E. J.
The Lady Burglar. [=In a Fit of Abstraction (*UA*), p. 695.]
Honourable John. [*C. JAMES* also collaborated in this play.]

p. 474] *+MANLEY, JOHN*
D. Rip Van Winkle, a Tale of the Catskill Mountains (Brit. 14/8/71).

MANSELL, H.
Vert Vert. [Translation of the opera, libretto H. Meilhac and C. Nuitter, music J. Offenbach (Paris, 10/3/69).]

p. 475] *MARCHANT, F.*
[+from *UA*: Abou Hassan (Brit. 1862); Barrington; The Blue Dwarf; A Dark Night's Work; The Devil's Compact; The Idle Apprentice; The King of the Cures; Kynge Lear and his Faythfull Foole; The Mistletoe Bough; The Old Man and his Ass; Pizarro, the Great Tyrant; The Prince and the Ogre; The Raiment and Agonies of that most Amiable Pair Raimond and Agnes; Vidocq.]
+D. The Convict's Escape; or, The Fatal Resemblance (C.L. 13/6/64).
+D. The Summer and Winter of Life; or, A Story of Country Lanes and London Streets (M'bone, 30/8/64; Eff. 17/10/64, as *Summer and Winter*).
+Bal. The Gorillas (Brit. 29/3/69).

p. 478] *MARSHALL, F.*
[A *Lacy* list includes another play: ***Briganzio the Brigand.***]

MARSTON, J. W.
The Wife's Portrait. [+*Lacy.*]

p. 479] *MARTIN, Sir THEODORE*

+D. Faust 8° 1865, 1866 (Pt. I); 1886 (Pt. II).

+T. The Gladiator of Ravenna. 8° 1885 (*priv.*). [Translated from F. Halm, *Der Fechter von Ravenna.*]

p. 480] +*MARZIALS, THEO.*

[+from *UA*: Mefistofele.]

+Lyric D. Esmeralda (D.L. 26/3/83). L.C. [Written in collaboration with *A. RANDEGGER*: music A. G. Thomas.]

MATHEWS, —

R.D. The Puritans; or, The Dogs of the Far West (Brit. 10/3/56).

MATHEWS, C. J.

[+from *UA*: Milliner to the King; Nothing to Wear; The Savannah.]

The Adventures of a Love Letter. [Also acted as *The A. of a Billet-Doux.*]

p. 481] *MATTHISON, A.*

[+from *UA*: Keep your Door Locked.]

Ten of 'em. [Version of *Zehn Mädchen und kein Mann*, libretto K. Treumann, music F. von Suppé (Vienna, 25/10/62).]

+O. Mignon (H.M. 13/1/80). [Version of the opera, libretto J. Barbier and M. Carré, music A. Thomas (Paris, 17/11/66).]

MATTOS, A. T. DE

The Heirs of Rabourdin. [Translated from Emile Zola. +8° 1894.]

MAURICE, W.

Ready Money Mortiboy. [=My Son Dick (*UA*), p. 723.]

p. 483] *MAYHEW, A.*

Christmas Boxes. [+*Lacy.*]

+*MAYNARD, MARY*

Ca. Shakespeare's Dream; or, A Night in Fairy Land (Sur. 7/9/61). [Version of L. Tieck, *Die Sommernacht*; music B. Gilbert.]

MEAD, T.

[+from *UA*: The Cloud of Life; The Heart's Victory; The Serpent on the Hearth; The Story of a Night; The Three Brothers of Brevannes; Under the Lamps.]

p. 485] +*MENDEZ, CATULLE*

M.C. The Old Clo Man (H.M. 8/3/97).

+*MEREWEATHER, Rev. Cavaliere*

D. Bacchus and Ariadne. 8° 1891.

MERION, C.

+Ca. Fascination (Brit. 10/8/71).

MERITT, P. [Real name P. Maetzger.]

Sid. [The first production was at Doncaster, 1870.]

p. 487] *MERIVALE, H. C.*

+D. Time and the Hour (Qns. 29/6/68). See *J. P. SIMPSON.*

p. 489] *MILLS, H.*

[+from *UA*: Robin Hood (R.A. Woolwich, 1888: in collaboration with *S. G. HORTON*).]

MILLWARD, C.

[+from *UA*: Dick Whittington (Rotunda, L'pool, 1879); The Fair One with the Golden Locks (P.W. L'pool, 1877).]

+P. Ye Siege of Liverpool; or, Harlequin Prince Rupert and ye Fayre Mayde of Toxteth (Park, L'pool, 26/12/52).

+P. Ormshead the Great; or, Harlequin and Jenny Jones, the Flower of Snowdon (Park, L'pool, 26/12/53).

+P. Little Red Riding Hood; or, Harlequin Dickey Sam and the Wolf of Toxteth (Park, L'pool, 26/12/57).

+P. The Jolly Miller of the Dee; or, Harlequin Bluff King Hal and the Fair Maid of Leasowe (Birkenhead, 26/12/64).

p. 490] *MILTON, A.*

[+from *UA*: Aladdin (Grand, Birmingham, 1897: in collaboration with *P. MILTON*.]

MILTON, P.

[+from *UA*: Aladdin (Grand, Birmingham, 1897: in collaboration with *A. MILTON*); Dick Whittington (Shakespeare, L'pool, 1898).]

MOLLOY, J. L.

+Oa. A Students' Frolic (St J. Hall, 24/5/64).

p. 492] *MOORE, A.*

Change of Name. [Also called *Mr Scroggins*. +*Lacy*.]

+*MOORE, JOHN*

[+from *UA*: The Fringe of Society.]

MORDAUNT, J.

[+from *UA*: Holly Bush Hall (Stand. 1860).]

p. 494] *MORTIMER, J.*

Heartsease. [Version of A. Dumas, *La dame aux Camélias*.]

p. 495] *MORTON, J. M.*

[+from *UA*: Harlequin and the Maid and the Magpie.]

Harlequin Hogarth. [+*Lacy*.]

p. 496] The Pascha of Pimlico. [+*Lacy*.]

Catch a Weazel. [+*Lacy*.]

The Alabama. [+*Lacy*.]

p. 497] +My Bachelor Days, etc. 8° 1883.

p. 498] *MOSS, H.*

Bootle's Baby. [+L.C. Roy. 8/2/88.]

MOUILLOT, F.

The Honourable John. [Written in collaboration with *C. JAMES* and *E. J. MALYON*.]

MOWBRAY, T.

[+from *UA*: Don't you wish you may get it?; Harlequin Billy Taylor (Soho, 1859); Harlequin Master Walter.]

+Bsq. Life in Olympus (Soho, 20/2/60).

+Bsq. Billy Taylor, the Gay Young Fellow (Soho, 1/4/61).

p. 499] *MURRAY, A.*
[+from *UA*: Périchole.]

p. 500] La Béarnaise. [Version of the opera, libretto E. Leterrier and A. Vanloo, music A. Messager (Paris, 12/12/85).]

MURRAY, GASTON
+D. Grimaldi; or, The Street Juggler (M'bone, 25/11/61). See *T. H. HIPKINS*.
+F. A Nice Quiet Day (Roy. 26/12/61). See *T. H. HIPKINS*.
[An undated *Lacy* list gives to him: *Beaujolais the Necromancer*, which seems to be an alternative title of *Is She His Daughter?* (in collaboration with *T. H. HIPKINS*).]

p. 501] +*NATION, W. H. C.*
[+from *UA*: Under the Earth.]

p. 502] *NEVILLE, H.*
[+from *UA*: Jack of All Trades (in collaboration with *FLORENCE HAYDON*).]

p. 503] +*NEWTON, H. C.*
[+from *UA*: Mazeppa (Ast. 1882).]

+*NEWTON, J.*
F. My Last Resource (M'bone, 9/11/63).

NICHOLS, H.
Robinson Crusoe. [+8° 1893.]

p. 504] *NIGHTINGALE, J. H.*
D. Off to the Diggings (Amphi. L'pool, 15/10/52).

p. 506] +*OAKLEY, Rev. FREDERICK*
D. The Christian's Cross (Roy. Chester, 7/4/97; Qns. Langton, 19/11/97; Sur. 1/8/98, as *From Cross to Crown*). L.C. Portsmouth, 30/3/98, as *The Christian's Cross and Martyr's Crown*. [Revised by *C. CLAYPOLE*.]

O'BRYAN, C.
Lugarto the Mulatto. [+*Lacy*.]

OGILVIE, G. S.
[+from *UA*: Knowledge.]

p. 507] *O'NEIL, J. R.*
+F. An Optical Delusion. *Lacy*.
+Ent. Ali Baba; or, A Night with the Forty Thieves. 12° 1852.
+D. The Sham Van Voght (Pav. 28/7/62).
[Other titles given to him are: *Aladdin, The Corsican Brothers, The Golden Pippin* and *The Prince and the Peri*.]

+*O'ROURKE, E.*
D. Ruy Blas. *Lacy* (?1861).

p. 508] +*OSBORN, H.*
D. Fame. 8° 1850.

OSMAN, W. R.
[+from *UA*: Baron Munchausen (in collaboration with *F. FENTON*); Harlequin and Old Æsop (in collaboration with *F. FENTON*); Harlequin Cock Robin (Vic. 1866); The Kidnappers (in collaboration with *F. FENTON*); Life in Lambeth; The Secrets of the Devil (in collaboration with *F. FENTON*).]
The Power of Gold. [This is in *UA* (Vic. 19/6/65).]

p. 509] +*OWENS, JOHN E.*
[+from *UA*: Solon Single.]

OXENFORD, E.
This House to let. [Probably the same as *In Ladbroke Square* in *UA*.]

OXENFORD, J.
[+from *UA*: Ariadne (Olym. 1850); A Case of Conscience; Der Freischutz; The Girl I left behind me; It's an Ill Wind that blows Nobody Good; Lara.]
Only a Half-penny. [+*Lacy*.]
A Family Failing. [+*Lacy*.]
The Porter's Knot. [+*Lacy*.]
Retained for the Defence. [+*Lacy*.]
p. 510] Uncle Zachary. [+*Lacy*.]
A Legal Impediment. [+*Lacy*.]
The Lily of Killarney. [Music J. Benedict.]
The World of Fashion. [+*Lacy*; *French*.]
I couldn't help it. [+*Lacy*.]
Bristol Diamonds. [+*Lacy*.]
Beauty or the Beast. [+*Lacy*.]
+Oa. Jessy Lea (G.I. 2/11/63). See *G. A. MACFARREN*.
Please to remember the Grotto. [Written in collaboration with *W. S. EMDEN*.]
p. 511] The Porter of Havre. [Version of *Papà Martin*, libretto A. Ghislanzoni, music A. Cagnoni (Genoa, 4/3/71).]

PALMER, F. G.
+P. Sinbad the Sailor; or, The Wreck, the Roc, and the Recreant, and the Wicked Old Man of the Sea (Leicester, 1885). See *G. THORNE*.

p. 512] +*PANTON, JOSEPH*
[+from *UA*: Reuben Blight; or, Something to live for (+C.L. 25/2/61).]

PARKE, W.
Manteaux Noirs. [Written in collaboration with *H. PAULTON*.]

p. 514] *PARLEY, P.*
[+from *UA*: Taffy was a Welchman.]

p. 515] *PARSELLE, J.*
[+from *UA*: The Changed Heart; The Kettledrum of the Surrey.]

+*PATTERSON, R. H.*
D. Robespierre. 8° 1877.

+*PAUL, CHARLES KEGAN*
D. Faust. 8° 1873.

[*PAUL, H. M.*
The Queen of Aragon. [+*Lacy*.]
p. 516] A Lucky Hit. [+S.W. 26/6/54.]
The Bronze Horse. [Music D. F. E. Auber.]

PAULTON, H.
+C.O. Manteaux Noirs (Aven. 3/6/82). See *W. PARKE*.

p. 519] *PEMBERTON, T. E.*

[+from *UA*: Sinbad the Sailor (Alex. L'pool, 1886, in collaboration with *J. J. HEWSON*).]

+P. The Forty Thieves (Alex. L'pool, 26/12/87). See *J. J. HEWSON*.

p. 522] +*PHELPS, W.*

[+from *UA*: A Tenant for Life.]

PHILLIPS, A. R.

Crazed. [+Glo. 14/3/87.]

PHILLIPS, F. L.

[+from *UA*: Ambition (Sur. 1857); The Artist and his Family; Clinton; The Dead Guest; The Patriot Spy; What will he do with it?]

A Bird in the Hand. [+*Lacy*.]

+D. Sixtus the Fifth (C.L. 23/7/60).

A Tramp's Adventure. [=The Dying Gift (*UA*), p. 671.]

p. 523] *PHILLIPS, L.*

Marianne Duval. [+*Lacy*.]

+*PHILLIPS, R.*

[+from *UA*: Manuel of Spain; The One Hundred Cuirassiers.]

p. 524] *PHILLPOTTS, E.*

+Ca. A Golden Wedding (H. 30/11/98). L.C. [Written in collaboration with *C. GROVES*.]

PILGRIM, J.

[For his earlier plays see iv, 372.]

p. 525] *PINERO, Sir A. W.*

The Squire. [+8° 1881.]

The Benefit of the Doubt. [+8° 1895 (*priv.*).]

The Princess and the Butterfly. [+8° 1896 (*priv.*).]

Trelawny of the "Wells". [+8° 1897 (*priv.*).]

The Gay Lord Quex. [+8° 1899 (*priv.*).]

PINKERTON, P.

At the Harbour Side. [Written in collaboration with *W. GRIST*.]

PITT, C.

[+from *UA*: Captain Firebrand; The Forger and his Victim; Hidden Crime; Poor Ray (in collaboration with *W. H. PITT*).]

+D. The Maison de Santé; or, Adventures of a Cockney (Brit. 18/6/60).

+D. The Deer Slayers (Brit. 16/12/70). See *W. H. PITT*.

[Other titles credited to him are: *Black Rollo* and *The Wild Boys of London*.]

p. 526] *PITT, G. D.*

[+from *UA*: Belinda Seagrave; The Corporal's Daughter; Diogenes in Search of a Contented Man; Lady Hatton (Brit. 1859); Molly Sullivan.]

+D. The Great Fire of London (Brit. 19/8/61). [This was not a new play in 1861 but I have no record of its first performance.]

p. 527] *PITT, W. H.*
[+from *UA*: In the Holly; The Lord and the Lout; Poor Ray (in collaboration with *C. PITT*).]
The Deer Slayers. [Written in collaboration with *C. PITT.*]
+D. The Lady of the Lake; or, The Maniac Bride (Brit. 9/12/72).

PLANCHÉ, J. R.
The Prince of Happy Land. [+8° 1851.]
Orpheus in the Haymarket. [Version of *Orphée aux Enfers*, libretto H. Crémieux and L. Halévy, music J. Offenbach (Paris, 21/10/58).]
+F. Peter Spyk (Gai. 22/8/70). [A revision of *The Loan of a Lover* (Olym. 29/9/34).]

+*PLUMMER, JOHN.* [See "*ARTHUR RUSHTON*".]

+*PLUNKETT, H. G.* [*H. P. GRATTAN.*]
[For his earlier plays see iv. 383. +from *UA*: The White Boys.]

p. 529] *POEL, W.*
[+from *UA*: Called to the Bar; Chiromancy; Debts of Honour; The King and the Countess; Laura; Mamma's Opinions; Yes or No?]
The Man of Forty. [+*French.*]
+Episode. Don Quixote de la Mancha (provinces, 9/2/80).
+Ca. The Wayside Cottage (provinces, 26/2/81).
+Charade. The Lost Bag (provinces, 18/12/83).
Lady Jane Gray. [+provinces, 18/12/83].
Absence of Mind. [+*French.*]
Adelaide. [+provinces, 29/12/85.]
Mrs Weakly's Difficulty. [+provinces, 20/2/86.]

+*POOLE, S. WORDSWORTH*
D. Drummond; or, Dishonour's Due. 12° [1870].

p. 530] *PRATT, F. W.*
[+from *UA*: Aladdin (P.W. L'pool, 1889); Ali Baba (P.W. L'pool, 1892); Robinson Crusoe (P.W. L'pool, 1890).]

PREST, T. P. [Full name *THOMAS PECKETT PREST.*]
[+from *UA*: There's nothing like a Friend at Court.]
The Miser of Shoreditch. [+*Lacy.*]
[Other titles credited to him in a *Lacy* list are: *Gallant Tom* and *Morna of the Glen.*]

p. 531] "*PRICE, M.*"
+Oa. All's Fair in Love and War (S.W. 21/4/62).
[This probably is a revision of the play by *J. BROUGHAM.*]

+*PRITCHARD, —*
D. Chevalier de Maison Rouge and Marie Antoinette; or, The Days of Terror (Hull, 10/10/59).

p. 532] *RAE, C. M.*
Our Diva. [Music V. Roger.]

p. 533] *RAE, L.*
[+from *UA*: This Side Up.]

p. 534] +*RAMSAY, CECIL*
[+from *UA*: Only a Model.]
+*RANDEGGER, A.*
Lyric D. Esmeralda (D.L. 26/3/83). See *T. MARZIALS.*
RANGER, —
+F. Never Despair (Str. 18/2/56).

p. 535] +*RAY, CATHERINE*
D. Emperor and Galilean. 8° 1876. [Translated from H. Ibsen.]
RAYMOND, KATE. [=*CATHERINE FRANCES MALONE.*]
[For her earlier plays see iv, 388.]
RAYNER, ALFRED
[+from *UA*: Fate and its Wonders; The Ostler's Vision; The Three Brothers of the Old Chateau.]
+D. The Three Brothers of Paris (M'bone, 27/9/58). [This would seem to be an earlier version of *The T. B. of the Old Chateau*, above.]
+D. The Foundling of the Sea; or, The Outcast Son (Vic. 1/59). [Evidently the same as *Ben Lighterware* (*UA*), p. 648.]
+*RAYNER, R.*
[+from *UA*: Jibbenainosey.]

p. 536] *READE, C.*
The Robust Invalid. [First produced Chestnut Street, Philadelphia, 29/11/69, as *The Saucy Housemaid.*]
An Actress by Daylight. [A revised version of *Art* (St J. 17/2/55).]
The Scuttled Ship. [A revised version of *Foul Play* (Holborn, 28/5/58). In 1874 it was toured as *Our Seamen.*]
Drink. [Version of the play, based on E. Zola's *L'assommoir*, dramatised by W. Busnach and O. Gastineau (Paris, 19/1/79).]
+Double Faces (Edinburgh, Nov. 1883).
[Other plays said to have been written by him are *The Way Things Turn, The Dangerous Path, The Lost Sisters, Marguerite, Lucrezia Borgia, A Lady's Oath, Christie Johnstone.*]

p. 537] *REECE, R.*
Ulf the Minstrel. [This was printed 12° (n.d. Cheltenham) as by *W. F. MARSHALL*, with the sub-title, *or, Change for a Sovereign.*]
+P. The Farewell of the Fairies (Edinburgh, 12/67).
Honeydove's Troubles. [+Manchester, 19/9/67.]
The Ambassadress. [Music D. F. E. Auber.]
Chilperic. [Version of the opera, libretto and music F. R. Hervé (Paris, 24/10/68).]
Little Robin Hood. [+*Lacy.*]

p. 538] The Island of Bachelors. [Version of *Les cent vierges*, libretto H. C. Chivot, A. Duru and L. F. N. Clairville, music A. C. Lecocq (Brussels, 16/3/72).]
The Half-crown Diamonds. [Music C. Dubois.]

The Creole. [+Folly, 15/9/77; Aven. 10/5/86, as *The Commodore*. Version of the opera, libretto A. Millaud, H. Meilhac and L. Halévy, music J. Offenbach (Paris, 3/11/75).]
La Petite Mademoiselle. [Music A. C. Lecocq.]
Jeanne, Jeanette and Jeanneton. [Version of the opera, libretto L. F. N. Clairville and A. Delacour, music Lacome (Paris, 10/10/76).]
The Merry War. [Version of *Der lustige Krieg*, libretto F. Zell and R. Genée, music J. Strauss (Vienna, 25/11/81).]
The Yellow Dwarf. [Music A. Mora.]
The Commodore. [See *The Creole*, above.]
Girouette. [Music A. Coedès.]

p. 540] *REED, G.*
[+from *UA*: Ching-Chow-Hi (in collaboration with *W. BROUGH*); Too many Cooks.]

REEVE, W.
[+from *UA*: Little Red Riding Hood (Sheffield, 1862).]

p. 541] +*REID, Captain MAYNE*
[+from *UA*: The Maroon.]

RENNELL, C. R.
+F. Thompkins in North-street (Qns. Dublin, 9/65).

+*REUSS, T.*
O. Die Feen. [Translation of opera, libretto and music R. Wagner (Munich, 29/6/88); lyrics by *A. V. SINCLAIR*.]

p. 542] +*REYNOLDSON, T. H.*
[+from *UA*: The Confession (Sur. 1858). The Gitano Boy; Home Truths; La Traviata (Sur. 1857).]
The Barrister. [=Home Truths (*UA*), p. 693.]
+O. Martha (D.L. 11/10/58). [A version of *Martha, oder der Markt von Richmond* (Vienna, 25/11/1847), libretto W. Friedrich, music F. von Flotow.]

RHYS, Captain H. [="*MORTON PRICE*".]
[+from *UA*: Everyday Occurrences; Leonie.]
+Ca. A Double Courtship; or, Before and After Luncheon (S.W. 27/9/62).

RICE, C.
[+from *UA*: The Man of the Red Mansion.]
The Three Musketeers. [+*Lacy*.]
The Merchant and the Mendicant. [+Glasgow, 4/58.]
+D. The Life, Trial and Execution of the Wretched Homicide Rush (Vic. 27/10/60).
[Other titles given to him in a *Lacy* list are: *The Bride, Koh-i-noor, The Painter of Rome* and *St Catharine's Eve*.]

p. 543] *RIGHTON, E.* [Another of his pseudonyms was "*H. GIRNOT*".]
+P. Blaza the Beautiful; or, Harlequin Bird of Paradise, the Great King of the Little Goldfishes, and the Prettiest Princess that ever was seen (Amphi. Leeds, 26/12/64).]

p. 544] *RISQUE, W. H.*
[+from *UA*: Bluebeard (Shakespeare, L'pool, 1892).]

+*RIVERS, H.*
[A play called *A Tale of Two Cities* was advertised in 1861.]

ROBERTS, G.
Under the Rose. [+*Lacy.*]
Cousin Tom. [+*Lacy.*]

+*ROBERTS, Mrs VALENTINE*
[+from *UA*: Jack Mingo; The Young Recruit.]

p. 546] *ROBERTSON, T. W.*
Ernestine. [See under *Clarisse* in *UA*.]

p. 547] *ROBINSON, N.*
+P. Little Red Riding Hood and Harlequin Blue Boy; or, The Wolf, the Wizard and the Fairies (Dublin, 26/12/68).

+*ROCK, CHARLES*
D. The Grey Parrot (Str. 6/11/99). See *W. W. JACOBS.*

+*ROCKINGHAM, Sir CHARLES*
Dramatic Sketches. 8° 1866 and 1867 (Worksop, *priv.*). [Acted by amateurs at Thomastown Castle.]

ROE, J. E. [Full name *JOHN E. ROE.*]
+P. The Queen of Hearts (Brighton, 26/12/63).
+P. Jack the Giant Killer (Brighton, 26/12/65).
+P. Beauty and the Beast (Brighton, 26/12/66).
+P. Valentine and Orson (Brighton, 26/12/67).
+P. The Yellow Dwarf; or, Harlequin Meliodorus, the King of the Gold Mines and the Good Fairies of the Golden Groves (Brighton, 26/12/68).
+P. Babes in the Wood (Brighton, 26/12/70).

+*ROGERS, FELIX*
[+from *UA*: Willie the Wanderer.]

p. 549] *ROGERS, T. S.*
[+from *UA*: Babes in the Wood (Rotunda, L'pool, 1884); Robinson Crusoe (Rotunda, L'pool, 1897).]

ROGERS, W.
[For his earlier plays see iv, 396. +from *UA*: Darby and Joan; Frank the Ploughman; The Gipsy and the Showman.]
+D.D. The Dying Flower; or, Fond Hearts Blighted (Brit. 4/9/71).

+*ROSCOE, WILLIAM CALDWELL*
[For an earlier play see iv, 609.]
+T. Violenza. 8° 1851.

p. 550] *ROSE, GEORGE*
[See "*ARTHUR SKETCHLEY*".]

p. 551] *ROSS, A.*
In Town. [Written in collaboration with *J. LEADER.*]

ROTHERY, W. G.
+D. The Fate of Derwentwater. 8° 1865.
The Judgment of Paris. [Music Costé.]

p. 552] +*ROUSBY, WYBERT*
D. The Motto of Nevers (Northampton, 1863).

p. 553] *RUBENSTEIN, A.*

The Demon. [Apparently this was given in Russian; Rubenstein was the composer.]

p. 554] *ST LEGER, E. W.*

Cigarette. [+8° 1892 (Cardiff).]

SALA, G. A.

+Ye Belle Alliance (C.G. 25/12/55). See *W. BROUGH.*

Wat Tyler, M.P. [+8° 1869.]

p. 555] +*SAMUEL, SYDNEY*

O. Piccolino (Gai. Dublin, 4/1/79; H.M. 29/1/79). [Version of the opera, libretto V. Sardou and C. Nuitter, music G. Giraud (Paris, 11/4/76); L.C. Rotunda, L'pool, 14/12/78.]

SANDFORD, EDITH

+D. Flamma; or, The Child of the Fire (Brit. 6/6/70). [Written in collaboration with *F. HAY.*]

p. 556] *SAUNDERS, J.*

Love's Martyrdom. [+8° 1855.]

+*SAVILLE, HENRY FAUCIT*

[+from *UA*: The Life and Adventures of Will Shakespeare.]

SAWYER, W.

Garibaldi in Sicily. [Music J. L. Hatton and J. G. Calcott.]

+*SCHOFIELD, W. M.*

[+from *UA*: Britomarte (M'bone, 1866).]

[*SCHONBERG, J.*

Narcisse. [+*Lacy*.]

+*SCHULER, F.*

D. Fanchon the Cricket (Strand, 9/2/63).

SCOTT, C. W.

[+from *UA*: Odette.]

The Little Duke. [Version of *Le petit duc*, libretto H. Meilhac and L. Halévy, music A. C. Lecocq (Paris, 25/1/78).]

Odette. [See under *UA*.]

p. 559] *SEAMAN, W.*

[+from *UA*: Annie Monksworth; Barber, Barber, Shave the Cat; The Daughter of Night; The Dead Duchess; Holly Bush Hall (Eff. 1860); Shelah from Cork; Third Class and First Class; The Will o' the Wisp (Brit. 1859); The Workhouse, the Palace and the Grave.]

+D. Shoals and Quicksands; or, Dark Deeds and Doings in London (Vic. 4/6/60).

+The Fate of Forgery (Eff. 13/10/62).

+P. Humpty Dumpty (Qns. Manchester, 26/12/64).

[In 1872 another play, *The Death Kiss*, was attributed to him.]

p. 560] *SELBY, C.*

[+from *UA*: Harlequin and the Loves of Cupid and Psyche.]

[Another title attributed to him in a *Lacy* list is: *The Tutor's Assistant*: this is presumably *The Court Guide* listed in iv, 446.]

Paris and Pleasure. [+*Lacy*.]

p. 561] *SELLMAN, R.*
Dagobert. [Music F. R. Hervé.]

SEYMOUR, F.
+P. Beauty and the Beast (Bath, 12/1/85). See *F. J. STIMSON.*

+*SHARP, R. FARQUHARSON*
D. Hernani. 8° 1898. [Translation of the play by V. Hugo (1830).]

p. 562] +*SHAW, W. B.*
P. Beauty and the Beast; or, Harlequin Snow King and the Fairy of the Floral Isles (Prince's, Glasgow, 26/12/60).

+*SHELLEY, —*
[+from *UA*: Arrah-No-Brogue.]

p. 563] *SHIELD, H.*
+P. The Fairies' Frolic; or, Harlequin the Enchanted Princess and the Spirit of Mischief (Newcastle, 26/12/63). L.C.

p. 565] +*SIDNEY, —*
D. A Sailor's Trials (Sunderland, 12/11/60).

p. 566] +*SIEG, WILLIAM*
D. Griseldis. 8° 1871 (Edinburgh). [Translation of the play by F. Halm.]

p. 567] +*SIMPSON, CHARLES*
F. Robert Macaire (St J. 23/3/67). [Written in collaboration with *J. P. SIMPSON.*]

SIMPSON, J. P.
+Prison and Palace. [Originally produced at Thurloe Place, West Brompton. +12° 1853 (*priv.*).]
Romance. [Music H. Leslie.]
+F. Robert Macaire (St J. 23/3/67). See *C. SIMPSON.*

p. 568] Time and the Hour. [Written in collaboration with *H. MERIVALE.*]
Letty. [Music M. W. Balfe.]
[In a *Lacy* list appears another title: *Too Happy by Half.*]

p. 570] "*SKETCHLEY, A.*"
[+from *UA*: The Golden Wedding.]
The Dark Cloud. [+*Lacy.*]

p. 571] *SLOUS, A. R.*
The Templar. [+8° 1850.]
+D. Waldeck. 8° 1852.
+D. The King's Diversion. 8° 1887. [Translation of V. Hugo, *Le roi s'amuse.*]

p. 572] *SMITH, A. R.*
+Ext. La Tarantula; or, The Spider King (Adel. 26/12/50). See *F. TALFOURD.*

SMITH, H. B.
Maid Marian. [Revision of *Robin Hood,* music De Koven (Chicago, 9/6/90).]

SMITH, LITA

+Out of the World. [See under *H. BURNETT* in supplementary notes.]

p. 573] *SMITH, V.*

A King for a Day. [Version of *Si j'étais roi*, libretto A. P. d'Ennery and J. Brésil, music A. Adam (Paris, 4/9/52).]

SMITHYES, G.

+D. The Sons of Neptune; or, The Sailor and the Landsman (Eff. 6/9/58).

+*SNAGG, THOMAS W.*

F. Very Embarrassing. 8° 1861 (Dresden).

SNOW, W. R.

[+from *UA*: Hamlet the Hysterical.]

SODEN, J. E.

F. A Photographic Fright (P'cess, 12/81).

p. 574] *SOMERSET, C. A.*

[+from *UA*: King Bluster Bubble: The Ship on Fire.]

SOMERSET, C. W.

[+from *UA*: The French in Algiers.]

p. 575] *SOUTAR, R.*

[+from *UA*: The Bronze Horse (M'bone, 1864); Fayre Rosamond (M'bone, 1865); Harlequin Dick Whittington and his Cat; Harlequin Little Jack Horner; Puss in Boots (Brighton, 1861); The Sleeping Beauty (Brighton, 1862).]

The Fast Coach. [This seems to have been first acted Olym. 9/6/51.]

+P. Harlequin Ralph the Miller's Son, Old King Cole! the Cat! the Ogre-ella, Diabolocadabra; or, the Fairies of the Silver Lilies (Brighton, 26/12/61).

[In 1869 a play *The Chinese Giant* was attributed to him.]

p. 576] *SPICER, H.*

+T. White-hands. 8° 1856.

+*SPINK, WILLIAM*

Lesled, Lord of the Isles. 8° 1890. [In *Autocrat in the Greenroom.*]

SPRY, H.

[+from *UA*: The Blue Bird of Paradise (with *G. CONQUEST*); The Fair One with the Locks of Gold (Grec. 1861; with *G. CONQUEST*); Harlequin Guy Faux (with *G. CONQUEST*); Harlequin Valentine and Orson (with *G. CONQUEST*); Peter Wilkins and the Flying Indians (with *G. CONQUEST*).]

p. 578] +*SQUIRES, JOHN*

D. Home, Out and Home; or, The Spanish Bride (Vic. 10/3/62).

STALMAN, A.

[+from *UA*: The Countess of Argentine.]

p. 581] *STEPHENS, W.*

The Mystery of Edwin Drood. [=The Mystery of Cloisterham (*UA*), p. 723.]

p. 582] *STEPHENSON, B. C.*
The Bold Recruit. [Music F. Clay.]
Dorothy. [+8° (1886).]

p. 583] *STEWART, D.*
[+from *UA*: Spring-heeled Jack.]

p. 584] +*STEWART, Miss E. M.*
D. The Rival Knights (C.L. 21/8/66).

+*STIMSON, FRED, J.*
[+from *UA*: Beauty and the Beast (P.W. L'pool, 1882; with *J. F. McARDLE*).]

STIRLING, E.
[+from *UA*: The Latch Key; Sir Jasper's Tenant; The Struggle for Gold; The United Service of England and France.]
The Reapers. [+*Lacy*.]
A Pair of Pigeons. [+*Lacy*.]
A Lucky Hit. [+*Lacy*.]
+Ext. The Fairy and the Golden Dove (Vic. 4/58).
The Spy of the Republic. [+Birmingham, 5/12/61.]

p. 585] *STOCQUELER, J. H.*
[+from *UA*: The Battle of the Alma (Ast. 1854); The Bombardment and Capture of Canton.]

STONES-DAVIDSON, T. W.
Taradiddles. [=White Lies (*UA*), p. 767.]

+*STORER, S.*
D. The O'Donohue of the Lakes (Dublin, 1/58).

STRACHAN, W., Jr.
[+from *UA*: Rip Van Winkle (Newcastle, 1866).]

STRAUSS, FERNAND
[+from *UA*: Cartouche (Soho, 1860).]

STUART, M.
[+from *UA*: That House in High Street.]

p. 586] *STURGESS, A.*
La Poupée. [Version of the opera, libretto M. Ordonneau, music E. Audran (Paris, 21/10/96).]

STURGIS, J.
+Little Comedies, Old and New. 8° 1882.

p. 587] +*SUMMERS, OLIVER*
[+from *UA*: Zaida.]

[*SUMMERS, W. J.*
[+from *UA*: Aladdin (Court, L'pool, 1898); The Babes in the Wood (Court, L'pool, 1899).]

SUTER, W. E.
[+from *UA*: Bibbins and Figgins; The Broken Chain; The Children in the Wood (Qns. 1860); The Cries of London; Emmeline; The Fall of the Avalanche (with *G. CONQUEST*); Harlequin Blue Beard (Qns. 1859); Harlequin, Hey Diddle Diddle (Eff. 1861); The High Ways and By Ways of Life; I beg you wouldn't mention it; The Iron

Arm; King Teapot the Great; The Miller's Daughter; My Wife's First Husband; Never Reckon your Chickens before they are Hatched; The Orphan of the Mine; The Poisoned Mask; The Red Bridge; The Spirit of Revenge; The Three Brothers of Mystery; Three Shots from a Carbine; Tom, Tom the Piper's Son (Eff. 1860); The Voice of Honour; The White Palfrey (=Roland and his Steed).]

The Life of an Actress. [=Violette la Grande (*UA*), p. 764.]

Dred. [+*Lacy*.]

+F. The Serious Youth (Sur. 16/3/57).

A Life's Revenge. [+*Lacy*.]

Holly Bush Hall. [+*Lacy*.]

+Ext. Blue Beard, his Blue chamber and Fatal Curiosity (Eff. 9/4/60).

p. 588] +D.D. It's a long lane that has no turning (Eff. 11/6/60).

The Pirates of the Savannah. [+*Lacy*; *French*.]

The Angel of Midnight. [+*Lacy*. Written in collaboration with *T. H. LACY*. Acted at the Stand. 1/6/61 as *The Midnight Angel; or Twelve O'Clock and the Spirit of Death*. =The Spirit of Death (*UA*), p. 753.]

Dick Turpin. [+*Lacy*, as *The Adventure of D. T. and Tom King*.]

Whom shall I marry? [+*Lacy*, as *Which shall I marry?*]

+D. Idleness the Root of Evil (Qns. 26/3/64).

Brother Bill and Me. [The *Lacy* text gives Aug. 1858 as the date of first performance.]

The Test of Truth. [+Eff. 11/6/60.]

[Other titles attributed to him in *Lacy* lists are: *Double Dealing; or, The Rifle Volunteer, My Daughter's Intended, The Old House on the Bridge of Notre Dame, The Prisoner of Piguerolles*.]

p. 589] *SWANBOROUGH, W. H.*

[+from *UA*: The Wrong Box.]

+*SWANWICK, ANNA*

The Dramatic Works of Goethe 8° 1850 (Faust, Iphigenia in Tauris, Torquato Tasso, Egmont).

+*SWANWICK, CATHERINE*

D. The Talisman. 8° 1864.

p. 590] *TALFOURD, F.*

[+from *UA*: The Anonymous Letter; Harlequin Black-eyed Sue; Jones the Avenger.]

Alcestis. [+8° 1850.]

The Princess in the Tower. [+*Lacy*: In collaboration with *W. P. HALE*.]

+D. Alvarez; or, The Heart Wreck (Stand. 23/9/50).

La Tarantula. [In collaboration with *A. SMITH*.]

Pluto and Proserpine. [=King Pluto (*UA*), p. 703.]

[Another title attributed to him in a *Lacy* list is: *Number* 1 A.]

p. 591] +*TAYLOR, Rev. —*

[+from *UA*: The Lady of the Lake.]

+*TAYLOR, EDGAR*
P. Aladdin and the Wonderful Lamp (Brighton, 26/12/56).

+*TAYLOR, Mrs FRANK*
C. Newmarket (P's. Manchester, 22/6/96). See *E. B. JONES*.
F. No Credit (Str. 12/7/98).

+*TAYLOR, Sir HENRY*
D. The Virgin Widow. 8° 1850.
D. St Clement's Eve. 8° 1862.

TAYLOR, J. G.
[+from *UA*: A Happy Family.]
+Oa. Do-Re-Mi-Fa (Gai. 2/11/73). [Music J. Offenbach.]

+*TAYLOR, ROBERT*
D. Faust 8° 1871 (Pt. I), 1872 (Pt. II).

p. 592] *TAYLOR, TOM*
[+from *UA*: Little Red Riding Hood (Adel. 1851); Narcisse. Add also from *UA* in vol. iv: Friends at Court; The Enchanted Horse.]
Cinderella. [This appears wrongly under *T. P. TAYLOR* in iv, 411.]
To Parents and Guardians. [+*Lacy*.]
Novelty Fair. [*Lacy*.]
Masks and Faces. [Played also as *Peg Woffington*.]

p. 593] An Unequal Match. [+8° 1874 (Manchester).]
The Fool's Revenge. [Adapted from V. Hugo, *Le roi s'amuse*.]
Joan of Arc. [Played also as *Jeanne Darc*.]

p. 594] *TEMPLE, R.*
+O. Le Roi l'a dit (P.W. 13/12/94, *amat.*). [Version of the opera, libretto E. Gondinet, music L. Delibes (Paris, 24/5/73).]

p. 596] +*THOMAS, W. MOY*
[+from *UA*: A Nice Girl.]

p. 597] "*THOMPSON, A.*"
[+from *UA*: Zampa.]
Columbus. [+8° 1869.]
Linda of Chamouni. [+8° (1869).]
The King's Pleasure. [+8° 1870.]
Aladdin the Second. [Music F. R. Hervé. = *Aladdin the Third* (*UA*), p. 640.]
+P. Harlequin Blackbeard; or, The Honey, the Money and the Dainty Dish (P's. Manchester, 26/12/70).
Cinderella the Younger. [Music E. Jones.]
Calypso. [+8° 1874.]

p. 598] *THOMSON, A.*
Sunshine and Shadow. [Music D. F. E. Auber.]

"*THORNE, G.*"
[+from *UA*: Cinderella (P.W. L'pool, 1893).]
+P. Sinbad the Sailor; or, The Wreck, the Roc and the Wicked Old Man of the Sea (Leicester, 26/12/85). [Written in collaboration with *F. G. PALMER*.]

p. 599] +P. Babes in the Wood (P.W. L'pool, 22/12/94).
+P. Robinson Crusoe (P.W. L'pool, 21/12/95).

p. 600] *TOWERS, E.*
[+from *UA*: Claribel's Mystery; Colonel Jack; Desolation; Destiny (Vic. 1860); Edith the Captive; The Enchanted Horn; The Four Knaves and the Pack; Harlequin Christoval (with *H. SAVILLE*); Harlequin Goody Two Shoes; Harlequin King Peewit; The Magic Axe; The Medal of Death; The Mistress of Hawk's Craig; The White Boys (Vic. 1862); The White Indian.]
+D. Red Bob the Coiner; or, First and Second Love (Eff. 16/3/63).
+D. The Black Hand (Eff. 29/8/64).
+D. All-Hallows' Eve; or Truth Will Out (Eff. 28/8/65).
Carynthia. [+*or, The Legend of the Black Rock.*]
Ready and Willing. [+*or, A Working Man's Story.*]
+D. The Battle of the Season (C.L. 2/6/67—not first performance).

p. 602] +*TOWNLEY, CHARLES* (see "*G. THORNE*").

TOWNSEND, W. T.
[+from *UA*: The Battle of Bothwell Brig; Found Drowned; Harlequin King Humpty Dumpty; The Iron Clasp; The King's Mail; The Life Raft; The Lion Conqueror; Mary Burton (Grec. 1861); One Witness; The Vain Heart; The War Trail.]
+D. Quadroona (M'bone, 4/57).
+D. A Mendicant's Revenge; or, The Last of the Moors of Granada (Eff. 11/8/62).
+P. Harlequin and the Enchanted Prince; or, the Fairies of the Magic Grove and the Three Rummy Brothers of Bagdad (Eff. 26/12/62).

TRAILL, F. T.
Glaucus. [Music J. H. Tully.]

TRAVERS, W.
[+from *UA*: Benliel; The Boy Pirate; Captain Macheath; Cartouche (C.L. 1859); The Dead Hand; The Deformed; The Demon of Darkness; The Fortune-teller; The Gipsy Girl of Granada; Jessie Farleigh (with *N. LEE*, Jr.); Life for a Life; The Life of a Beggar; Moonlight Jack; The Mountain Flower; The Neglected Home; Okee Pokee Wangee Fum; Perils by Land and Wave; Poor Joe of Horsemonger-Lane; The Red Lamp; The Reprieve; The Spirit Child's Prayer; The Storm Visitor; The Troubadour; The Watercress Girl.]
+D. First Love; or, A Heart's Devotion (C.L. 12/9/59).
+D. The Night Birds (Vic. 7/11/59—not first performance). [Apparently the same as *George Barrington: or, The N. B. of Hounslow Heath* (Pav. 14/11/61).]
+D. Dinorah (Str. 10/4/60).
+D. The Champion's Belt; or, This Side of the Water (Vic. 5/60).

+D. The Child of Chance; or, Esperance, the French Foundling (M'bone, 2/7/60).
+D. Atlantic Jack; or, The Friend of the Family (1/9/60).
+D. The Crimes of Twenty Years (Pav. 23/6/62—not first performance).
+D. Voices across the Waters; or, The Old Village Bells (C.L. 6/4/63).
+D. Lost Rosabel; or, A Page from Woman's History (C.L. 7/3/64).
+D. Oceola; or, The Son of the Wilderness (Eff. 22/8/64).
+D. Bravado the Swindler (M'bone, 3/10/64).
+D. Conrad, the Ghost Lover; or, The Last Words at Parting (Eff. 20/2/65).
+D. The Daughter of the Wolf (C.L. 24/7/65).

p. 603] The Infanticide. [+in collaboration with *N. LEE, Jr.*]

p. 604] +*TROUTBECK, Rev. J.*
O. Taming of the Shrew (D.L. 26/10/78).

+*TULLY, J.*
[+from *UA*: Jack the Giant Killer (N. Shields, 1882).]

TULLY, J. H.
Which is it? [Music by the author.]

p. 605] +*TURVEY, GEORGE F.*
D. Duplicity. 8° (Dunoon, *c.* 1870; *priv.*).

p. 606] *VANDENHOFF, H.*
[+from *UA*: The Captain of the Vulture.]

VANDERVELL, W. F.
[+from *UA*: Our Traviata.]
+P. Queen Mab; or, Harlequin Romeo and Juliet (Sur. 26/12/57).

+*VICKERY, S.*
P. Ye Evil Spirits and Dickie Sam; or, Harlequin Birkie Ned and the Beautiful Docksa (Birkenhead, 26/12/58).

VILLIERS, EDWIN
Oa. A Mere Blind (Gai. 29/4/71). [Music J. Offenbach.]

p. 609] +*VINING, GEORGE*
[+from *UA*: Self Made.]

+*VOLLAIRE, JOHN*
D. The Duke's Bequest (Pav. 6/4/63).

p. 610] +*WADDIE, JOHN*
R.C. The Maid of Norway. 8° 1859.

+*WADE, WILLIAM*
[+from *UA*: Jack and Jill (Rotunda, L'pool, 1893).]

p. 611] *WALKER, G. R.*
Coming Home. [=*Sithors to Grind*, p. 611.]

p. 613] +*WARD,* —
P. Little Tom Tucker (Edinburgh, 24/12/64).

p. 614] *WARDROPER, W.*
The Miraculous Doll. [Version of *La poupée de Nuremberg*, libretto A. de Leuven and L. L. Brunswick, music A. Adam (Paris, 21/2/52).]

+*WARE, J. M.*
[+from *UA*: The Woman in White (Sur. 1860).]

p. 617] *WEBB, C.*
[+from *UA*: Belphegor the Mountebank (Sur. 1856); The Physician's Wife.]
+D. The Royalists of Paris; or, The Flower Girl of the Temple (Vic. 6/10/62).

+*WEBB, THOMAS E.*
D. Faust. 8° 1880 (London and Dublin).

WEBB, T. H.
[+from *UA*: The Seven Ages of Man.]

WEBSTER, A.
+D. Disguises. 8° 1879.

p. 618] *WEBSTER, B.*
[+from *UA*: The Pretty Girls of Stilberg.]

+*WEBSTER, B. J.*
[+from *UA*: The Legend of the Headless Man.]

p. 620] +*WHEELER, C. E.*
The Coming of Peace. 4° [1900]. See *J. ACHURCH*.

+*WHIGHTWICK, G.*
D. Henry II. 8° 1851.
C. The Flirts (Plymouth, 4/10/66).

p. 622] *WIGAN, H.*
Taming the Truant. [Adapted from V. Sardou, *Le Papillon.*]

WILKINS, J. H.
[+from *UA*: The Battle of the Heart: A Broken Home; The Huguenots (C.G. 1851); Jericho Jack; The Savage and Civilisation (with *J. ANDERSON*); The Widow's Son.]
+D. Laelia, the Queen of the Hills; or, The Corsican Maid (Vic. 4/58).
+D. Old Finsbury; or, Edith Lester the Wronged (C.L. 2/9/60).
+D. The Scalp Hunters (C.L. 20/5/61—not first performance).

WILKS, T. E.
How's your Uncle. [+*Lacy*.]
The Miller of Whetstone. [+*Lacy.*]
Eily O'Connor. [+*Lacy.*]

p. 624] +*WILLIAMS, FRED*
D. The Blue Ribbon of the Turf (Halifax, 28/4/67).

+*WILLIAMS, G. H.*
D. Sesostris. 8° 1853.

WILLIAMS, M.
+F. A Volunteer's Ball (Str. 19/7/60). See *F. C. BURNAND.*
A Fair Exchange. [+*Lacy.*]
The Isle of St Tropez. [+*Lacy.*]
Carte de Visite. [+*Lacy.*]

p. 625] *WILLIAMS, T. J.*
[+from *UA*: The Belle and the Boor; La Locandiera.]
A Race for a Widow. [+*Lacy.*]
Truth and Fiction. [Written in collaboration with *A. G. HARRIS.*]
The Silent System. [+*Lacy.*]
Jack's Delight. [+*Lacy.*]
[Other titles attributed to him in *Lacy* lists are: *Francesco di Rimini, Maria Stuarda, Pia di Tolomei* and *Rosamunda.*]

p. 627] *WILLS, W. G.*
Hinko. [+8° 1871.]
Olivia. [+4° (1878, *priv.*).]
Ninon. [+8° 1864, as *St Cyr.*]
Faust. [+4° (1887).]

p. 628] *WILSON, J. C.*
My Knuckleduster. [Revised version of *The Antigarotte* by *C. J. COLLINS.*]
[Another title attributed to him in a *Lacy* list is: *Jonathan Oldakre.*]

WILSON, S.
[+from *UA*: Won by a Trick.]

p. 630] +*WOOD, J. HICKORY*
[from *UA*: Cinderella (Shakespeare, L'pool, 1899).]
+P. Puss in Boots (Gar. 26/12/99).

p. 632] *WOOLER, J. P.*
[+from *UA*: The Language of Flowers.]
A Model Husband. [+*Lacy.*]
Did I Dream it? [+*Lacy.*]
Old Phil's Birthday. [+*French.*]
Orange Blossoms. [+*French.*]
Blonde or Brunette. [Music W. M. Lutz.]
The Ring and the Keeper. [Music W. H. Montgomery.]
Marriage at any Price. [+*Lacy.*]

[*WOOLF, B. E.*
Alcantara. [This was first presented at Boston, 7/4/62, as *The Doctor of Alcantara.* The Connaught production had the title, *The Village Doctor.*]

+*WOOLFE, J. H.*
[+from *UA*: Babes in the Wood (Shakespeare, L'pool, 1896); Little Bo Peep (Shakespeare, L'pool, 1894); The Yellow Dwarf (Shakespeare, L'pool 1897).]
+P. Blue Beard (Lyr. L'pool, 26/12/97).

p. 633] *WRIGHT B.*
[+from *UA*: Pat a Cake (with *J. T. DOUGLASS*).]

WYCOMBE, MAGDELINE
Cloris. [+L.C.]

p. 634] *WYNDHAM, Sir C.*
[+from *UA*: The Fringe of Society; Her Ladyship's Guardian.]

YARDLEY, W.
Beauty and the Beast. [+8° 1890.]

p. 635] *YATES, E.*
[+from *UA*: Mr Webster's Company is requested at a Photographic Soirée (with *N. H. HARRINGTON*).]
Double Dummy. [+*Lacy*.]

+*YELLAND, W. H.*
[+from *UA*: A Midsummer's Eve.]

p. 636] +*YOUNG, E.*
P. King Diamond; or, High Low, Jack and the Game (Sheffield, 26/12/64).

YOUNG, H.
[+from *UA*: Harlequin Prince Love the Day; Ida May (M'bone, 1857); Keereda and Nana Sahib (=Veemah Kareeda); Silver Store Island (Vic. 1858).]
+D. It's never too late to mend (Eff. 7/5/60).
+D. The Lady in Black (Eff. 17/9/60—not first performance).
+D. The Slave Bride; or, The Quadroon and the Secret Tree Cavern (Pav. 1/4/61).
+D. The New World; or, The Life of an Emigrant (Eff. 9/12/61—not first performance). [This may=The Gold Diggings of Australia (*UA*), p. 684.]
+D. The Prodigal Son (Eff. 7/3/64). [Advertised also as *Azael; or, The P.S.*]

YOUNG, Mrs H.
[+from *UA*: Catherine Hayes the Murderess (Eff. 1864); The Dark Woman; Fair Lilias; The Fatal Shadow; Jessie Ashton; Left Alone; The Life and Adventures of George Barrington; The String of Pearls (Eff. 1862); Twenty Straws (Eff. 1865).]
+D. Jenny Vernon; or, A Barmaid's Career (Vic. 17/11/62).
+D. The Gipsy's Bride (Pav. 16/11/63—not first performance).

p. 637] +*YOUNG, Mrs W. S.*
[+from *UA*: The Black Band (Pav. 1861).]

YOUNGE, A.
[+from *UA*: Michel Perrin; Uncle Mark.]

YOUNGE, W.
Little Bo Peep. [+8° 1881.]

ZOBLINSKY, Mme.
Annie of Thorau. [Version of *Aennchen von Thorau*, libretto R. Feils, music Hofmann (Hamburg, 6/11/78).]

SUPPLEMENTARY NOTES TO THE LIST OF UNKNOWN AUTHORS

p. 638] Abou Hassan (Norwich). [=— *GILBEIGH* and *G. GRIMES.*]
Abou Hassan (Brit.). [=*F. MARCHANT.*]
The Adventurer. [=The Fiend's Mountain (*UA*), p. 677.]
+Bal. The Adventures of a Night; or, Mistakes in the Dark (Str. 30/9 50).
The Advocate's Daughter. [=*J. EBSWORTH, The Advocate and his Daughter.*]

p. 639] Agnolo Diora. [=*J. A. HERAUD.*]
Aladdin (Brighton, 1880). [=*F. W. GREEN.*]
Aladdin (P.W. L'pool, 1889). [=*F. W. PRATT.*]

p. 640] Aladdin (Shakespeare, L'pool, 1891). [=*T. F. DOYLE.*]
Aladdin (P. W. L'pool, 1896). [=*J. J. HEWSON.*]
Aladdin (Grand, Birmingham, 1897). [=*A.* and *P. MILTON.*]
Aladdin (Court, L'pool, 1898). [=*W. SUMMERS.*]
Aladdin the Third. [= *A. THOMPSON, Aladdin the Second* (Gai. 24/12/70).]

p. 641] Ali Baba (P.W. L'pool, 1892). [=*F. W. PRATT.*]
+P. Ali Baba; or, A Night with the Forty Thieves (Exeter, 26/12/50).
+P. Ali Baba and the Forty Thieves; or, Harlequin and the Magic Donkey (Alex. L'pool, 26/12/68).
Alice in Wonderland. [This probably=the play by *H. S. CLARKE.*]
All Hallows' Eve (H. 1859). [=*P. LECLERCQ.*]
+Spec. The Amazonian Warriors (Amphi. Leeds, 30/9/61).
Ambition (Sur. 1857). [=*F. L. PHILLIPS.*]
Amy Arlington. [=*D. STEWART.*]

p. 642] André the Miner. [=*A. FAUCQUEZ.* +Brit. 21/10/61.]
Angela. [=*L. KINGSTON.*]
The Angel of Darkness. [=*G. CONQUEST.*]
Anne Boleyn. [=*N. LEE.*]
Annie Monksworth. [=*W. SEAMAN.*]
The Anonymous Letter. [=*F. TALFOURD.*]
The Anti-garotte. [=*C. J. COLLINS. My Knuckleduster* is a revised version by *J. C. WILSON.*]
Archy Moore. [=*H. YOUNG.*]
Ariadne (Olym. 1850). [=*J. OXENFORD.* Originally performed M'bone, 2/1849.]
Arrah-No-Brogue. [=— *SHELLEY.*]
The Artisan's Triumph. [=*A. WOOD.*]
The Artist and his Family. [=*F. L. PHILLIPS.*]

p. 643] The Assassins of the Roadside. [=*J. T. DOUGLASS.*]
Auld Robin Gray. [=*C. H. HAZLEWOOD.*]
Avarice. [This may=*Avarice; or, The Miser's Daughter*, by *J. B. JOHNSTONE*, revived Brit. 9/10/71.]
+P. The Babes in the Wood (Glasgow, 26/12/57).
+P. The Babes in the Wood (Bath, 26/12/58).

+P. The Babes in the Wood (Swansea, 26/12/59).
+P. The Babes in the Wood (Oldham, 26/12/60).
+P. The Babes in the Wood (Rotunda, L'pool, 26/12/72).

p. 644] The Babes in the Wood (Court, L'pool, 1881). [=*J. F. McARDLE.*]
The Babes in the Wood (Rotunda, L'pool, 1884). [=*T. S. ROGERS.*]
+P. The Babes in the Wood (Newcastle, 26/12/87).
+P. The Babes in the Wood (Tyne, Newcastle, 26/12/89).
The Babes in the Wood (Shakespeare, L'pool, 1896). [=*J. H. WOOLFE.*]

p. 645] The Babes in the Wood (Court, L'pool, 1899). [=*W. J. SUMMERS.*]
+P. The Babes in the Wood (Rotunda, L'pool, 26/12/99).
+P. The Babes in the Wood; or, Harlequin Cock Robin and the Forest Fays (Qns. Edinburgh, 26/12/59).
+P. The Babes in the Wood; or, Harlequin King of the Fairies and the Cruel H'Uncle (Birmingham, 26/12/55).
+F. A Barbarous Idea; or, Two Ghosts in One House (Str. 26/5/57).
Barber, Barber, Shave the Cat. [=*W. SEAMAN.*]
+Bal. Le Barbier de Cadiz (Str. 2/4/55).

p. 646] Baron Munchausen. [=*F. FENTON* and *W. R. OSMAN.*]
Barrington. [= *F. MARCHANT.*]
The Bartons of Barton Wold. [=*B. S. MONTGOMERY.*]
The Battle of Bothwell Brig. [=*W. T. TOWNSEND.*]
The Battle of the Heart. [=*J. H. WILKINS.*]
+Bal. The Beauties of the Harem (Alh. 24/4/71).
+P. Beauty and the Beast (P'cess. Leeds, 26/12/57).
+P. Beauty and the Beast (Glasgow, 26/12/60).

p. 647] Beauty and the Beast (P.W. L'pool. 1883). [=*J. F. McARDLE* and *F. J. STIMSON.*]
+P. Beauty and the Beast (Tyne, Newcastle, 26/12/91).
+P. Beauty and the Brigand; or, Harlequin Fra Diavolo and the Fairies of the Silver Lake (Southampton, 26/12/58).
+Masque. Beauty's Awakening (Guildhall, 29/6/99). 8° 1899.
Belinda Seagrave. [=*G. D. PITT.*]
Belinda the Blind. [This is probably a revival of the play by *G. D. PITT* (see iv, 373) and=*Belinda Seagrave.*]
The Belle and the Boor. [=*T. J. WILLIAMS.*]
La Belle Lurette (Avon. 1883). [=*F. DESPREZ* and *A. MURRAY*, *Lurette*, p. 343.]
The Belle of the Season. [Probably by *MATILDA HERON* (Winter Garden, N.Y. 12/3/62).]
Belphegor the Mountebank (S.W.). [=*C. WEBB.*]
Belphegor the Mountebank (Brit.). [=*C. H. HAZLEWOOD.*]

p. 648] Ben Child. [=*Mrs H. YOUNG*=The Swallow's Nest (*UA*), p. 755.]
Ben Hur. [This is probably the American drama by *W. YOUNG.*]
Benliel (C.L. 1857). [=*W. TRAVERS.*]
+T. Bertha. 12° 1851 (Cambridge).

Bibb and Tucker. (=*J. CLAYTON*.]
Bibbins and Figgins. [=*W. E. SUTER*.]
Birds, Beasts and Fishes. [=*N. LEE*.]
+P. The Birth of the New Year (Adel. Sheffield, 1/60).

p. 649] The Black Band (Pav.). [=*Mrs W. S. YOUNG*.]
The Black Gondola. [=*C. H. HAZLEWOOD*.]
The Black Statue. [=*C. H. HAZLEWOOD*.]
The Blind Sister. [=*M. R. LACY*: see iv, 434, 621.]

p. 650] +P. Bluebeard (Manchester, 26/12/59).
Bluebeard (Pav. 1865). [=*C. H. HAZLEWOOD*. The title should read *Harlequin Bluebeard and his Seven Headless Wives*.]
+P. Bluebeard (Birmingham, 26/12/69).
+P. Bluebeard (L'pool, 26/12/70).
Bluebeard (Shakespeare, L'pool, 1892). [=*W. H. RISQUE*.]

p. 651] +P. Bluebeard; or, The Great Bashaw (Portsmouth, 26/12/58).
The Blue Bird of Paradise. [=*G. CONQUEST* and *H. SPRY*.]
The Blue Dwarf. [=*F. MARCHANT*.]
Blue Skin. [=*F. MARCHANT*.]
The Bohemians. [=*W. GRIST* and *P. E. PINKERTON*. Version of *La Bohème*, libretto G. Giacosa and L. Illico, music G. Puccini (Turin, 1/2/96).]
The Bombardment and Capture of Canton. [=*J. H. STOCQUELER*.]

p. 652] Born with a Caul. [=*G. ALMAR*. +*or, The Personal Adventures of David Copperfield*.]
The Bottle Imp. [=*G. CONQUEST* and *H. SPRY*.]
Le Bouquet. [=—*DIANÉ*.]
Bow Bells. [=*J. B. JOHNSTONE*.]
The Boy Pirate. [=*W. TRAVERS*.]
Bravin's Brow. [=*J. S. FOX*.]
The Bravoes of London. [=*Mrs H. YOUNG*.]

p. 653] Briarly Farm. [=*G. CONQUEST*.]
The Bridal of Beauty. [=*E. L. BLANCHARD*.]
The Bridal Phantom. [=*G. CONQUEST*.]
+D. The Bride of Everton; or, Liverpool in the Olden Time (Adel. L'pool, 5/4/52).
+D. The Bride of Milton and the Merchant of Gravesend (Gravesend, 15/8/59).
The Brigand. [=*J. T. DOUGLASS*. The full title is *The Brigand in a New Suit for Easter* (Stand. 15/4/65).]
The Brigand of London. [=*W. TRAVERS*.]
Britomarte. [=*W. M. SCHOFIELD*.]
Briton and Boer. [=*F. COOKE*.]
The Broken Chain. [=*W. E. SUTER*.]
A Broken Home. [=*J. H. WILKINS*.]
The Bronze Horse (M'bone). [=*R. SOUTAR*.]

p. 654] The Buccaneer's Wife. [=*G. CONQUEST*. +*or, The Siege of Dunkerque*.]
+Bal. The Bull-fighter (Str. 6/8/55).
+P. The Butterfly's Ball and the Grasshopper's Feast; or, Harlequin and the Genius of Spring (L'pool, 26/12/53).

p. 655] Called to the Bar. [=*W. POEL.*]
The Cameronians. [=*W. SUTER.*]
Captain Firebrand. [=*C. PITT.*]
Captain Macheath. [=*W. TRAVERS.* +*or, Life on the Road.*]
The Captain of the Vulture (Vic. 1864). [=*H. VANDENHOFF.*]
+Bal. The Captives; or, A Night in the Alhambra (H. 29/9/55—59th time).
Carlo Leoni. [=*C. H. HAZLEWOOD.*]

p. 656] The Carrier of London. [=*J. HALFORD.*]
Cartouche (Soho, 1860). [=*F. STRAUSS.*]
Cartouche (C.L. 1859). [=*W. TRAVERS.*]
A Case of Conscience. [=*J. OXENFORD.*]
Catherine Hayes. [=*Mrs H. YOUNG.* Full title, *Catherine Hayes the Murderess.*]
Cause and Effect. [=*F. G. CHEATHAM.*]
The Champion of England. [=*C. H. HAZLEWOOD.*]
The Changed Heart. [=*J. PARSELLE.*]

p. 657] A Charming Cottage. [=*A. HALLIDAY.*]
Cheek and Plant. [=*F. FENTON.* Full title: *The Adventures of Cheek and Plant.*]
+Bal. Le chien du zouave (Str. 17/11/56).
The Children in the Wood (Qns. 1860). [=*W. E. SUTER.*]
The Chimes. [=*W. TRAVERS.*]

p. 658] Ching-Chow-Hi. [=*W. BROUGH* and *G. REED.* Music J. Offenbach.]
+F. Choose your own path. 8° 1857.
Christine. [Music H. Gadsby.]
Christmas Story (Var. 1893). [=*L. S. B. IRVING.*]
+P. Cinderella (Bradford, 26/12/58).
+P. Cinderella (Manchester, 26/12/60).
+P. Cinderella (Newcastle, 26/12/79).

p. 659] +P. Cinderella (Tyne, Newcastle, 26/12/93).
Cinderella (P.W. L'pool, 1893). [=*G. THORNE.*]
+P. Cinderella (Newcastle, 26/12/95).
+P. Cinderella (Court, L'pool, 26/12/96).
+P. Cinderella (Empire, L'pool, 26/12/97).
+P. Cinderella (Lyr. L'pool, 24/12/97).

p. 660] Cinderella (P.W. L'pool, 1899). [=*J. J. HEWSON.*]
Cinderella (Shakespeare, L'pool, 1899). [=*J. H. WOOD.*]
+P. Cinderella and her Cruel Sisters; or, The Prince, the Fairy and the Little Glass Slipper (New, Birmingham, 26/12/61).
+P. Cinderella; or, The Fairy of the Chrystal Fountain (Adel. L'pool. 26/12/54).
City Friends. [=*C. J. COLLINS.*]
+Ba. The City Prison; or, The Queen's Secret (C.L. 3/6/61).
Claribel's Mystery. [=*E. TOWERS.*]
Clarisse (St J. 1855). [=*T. W. ROBERTSON*; a revised version of *Ernestine.*]
Clean Your Boots. [=*J. BRUTON.*]
Clergy. [=Unequally Sentenced (*UA*), p. 762.]
Clinton. [=*F. L. PHILLIPS.*]
The Cloud of Life. [=*T. MEAD.*]

Colonel Jack. [=*E. TOWERS.* +Vic. 26/11/60.]
+Ext. A Comedy of Terrors; or, Who is to Marry Princess Royal? 12° 1855 (Boscombe).

p. 661] The Confederate's Daughter. [=*C. H. HAZLEWOOD.*]
The Confession. [=*T. H. REYNOLDSON.*]
+P. Conrad the Corsair; or, Harlequin and the Good Little Fairy at the Bottom of the Sea (Preston, 26/12/58).
The Corporal's Daughter. [=*G. D. PITT.*]
The Counterfeit. [=*D. FISHER.*]

p. 662] The Countess d'Argentine. [=*A. STALMAN.*]
Cousin Grace. [=*J. J. DILLEY* and *L. CLIFTON.*]
The Cricket on the Hearth (Str. 1855). [=*J. HALFORD.*]
The Cries of London. [=*W. E. SUTER.*]

p. 663] The Cruel Brother. [=*W. TRAVERS.*]
The Danites. [This was probably the American play by Bronson Howard and given by a touring company.]
Darby and Joan. [=*W. ROGERS.*]
The Dark King of the Black Mountains. [=*C. H. HAZLEWOOD.*]
A Dark Night's Work. [=*F. MARCHANT.*]
The Dark Shadows. [=*J. DONALD.*]
The Dark Woman. [=*Mrs H. YOUNG.*]
The Daughter of Midnight. [=*F. MARCHANT.*]
The Daughter of Night. [=*W. SEAMAN.* +Brit. 31/7/56.]

p. 665] The Dead Duchess. [=*W. SEAMAN.*]
The Dead Guest. [=*F. L. PHILLIPS.*]
The Dead Hand. [=*W. TRAVERS.* +M'bone, 16/8/61.]
The Dead Woman's Secret. [A play of this name by *J. COURTNEY* was revived M'bone, 16/2/52; but the title is attributed to *W. T. TOWNSEND* in a *Lacy* list.]
+T. Death's Waiting Room. 8° 1851.
Debo-Lear. [=*C. H. HAZLEWOOD.*]
Deborah. [=*G. CONQUEST.*]
Debts of Honour. [=*W. POEL.* +Bijou, 21/7/93.]
The Deformed. [=*W. TRAVERS.*]
The Demon of Darkness. [=*W. TRAVERS.* +*or, The Three Temptations.*]

p. 666] The Deserted Wife. [=*A. FAUCQUEZ.*]
Desolation. [=*E. TOWERS.*]
Destiny (Vic. 1860). [=*E. TOWERS.*]
Destiny (Grec. 1860). [=*G. CONQUEST.*]
+Bal. Les deux dominos (Str. 23/9/50).
The Devil in Town. [=*J. B. JOHNSTONE.*]
The Devil's Compact. [=*F. MARCHANT.*]
The Devil's Gap. [=*G. CONQUEST.*]
Diamond cut Diamond. [=*H. DRAYTON.*]
+P. Dick Whittington (Rotunda, L'pool, 26/12/70).
Dick Whittington (Rotunda, L'pool, 1879). [=*C. MILLWARD.*]

p. 667] +P. Dick Whittington (Newcastle, 26/12/82).
+P. Dick Whittington (Alex, L'pool, 26/12/88).
+P. Dick Whittington (Newcastle, 24/12/93).
+P. Dick Whittington (Court, L'pool, 26/12/95).

p. 668] Dick Whittington (Shakespeare, L'pool, 1898). [=*P. MILTON.*]
Dick Whittington (P.W. L'pool, 1898). [=*J. J. HEWSON.*]
Dick Whittington and his Wonderful Cat. [=*F. MARCHANT.*]
+D. The Digger's Bride (Gar. 19/9/59).
Dirty Dick. [This is probably by *C. H. HAZLEWOOD.*]
The Divorce (C.L. 1859). [=*W. BERTIN.*]

p. 669] +D. The Dogs of the Dark Blue Waters (Qns. 28/2/59).
Dolly. [Version of *La poupée de Nuremberg*, libretto A. de Leuven and L. L. Brunswick, music A. Adam (Paris, 21/2/52).]
Don Giovanni (S.W. 17/11/64). [=*J. C. BRENNAN.* This is presumably the same as the *D.G.* recorded on p. 274, and is probably =*D.G. Jr.* on p. 669.]
Don Quixote (Ast. 1857). [=*W. COOKE.*]
Don't you wish you may get it? = [— *MOWBRAY*].

p. 670] The Dove and the Serpent. [=*C. LITCHFIELD* and — *COOK.*]
Drat that Comet. [=*L. S. BUCKINGHAM.* +Str. 13/7/57.]
Drip, drop, Drip drop. [=*Mrs H. YOUNG.*]

p. 671] The Duke's Device. [Revised version by *H. NEVILLE* of *JOHN BROUGHAM*, *The Duke's Motto.*]
The Dying Gift. [=*F. L. PHILLIPS*, *A Tramp's Adventure*, p. 522.]

p. 672] Egypt Three Thousand Years Ago. [=*W. ROGERS.*]
+Ent. Eigenwillig; or, The Self-willed. 8° 1870.
Eleanor's Victory. [=*J. B. JOHNSTONE.*]
An Eligible Villa. [Version of *L'opéra aux fenêtres*, libretto L. Halévy, music M. Gastenel (Paris, 5/5/57).]
Ellie Forester. [=*J. B. JOHNSTONE.*]

p. 673] Emmeline. [=*W. E. SUTER.*]
+Oa. The Emperor's Gift (Str. 20/6/53).
The Enchanted Horn. [=*E. TOWERS.*]
The Enchanted Lake (Newcastle, 1856). [=*J. F. BAIRD.*]
+P. The Enchanted Lake; or, The King of the Mist and the Spell-bound Princess (Exeter, 26/12/68).
The Engineer. [=*C. BOLTON.* +*or, England's Pride and Glory.*]

p. 674] Esperanza. [=*G. CONQUEST.*]
+Bal. L'Etoile; or, The Spirit of the Air (Str. 17/3/56).
+Bal. The Evening Fête (Str. 6/4/57).
Every-Day Occurrences. [=*H. RYHS.*]
Evil Hands. [=*C. H. HAZLEWOOD.*]
Eyes Right. [=*K. FIELD.*]
Fair Lilias. [=*Mrs H. YOUNG.*]
The Fair One with the Golden Locks (P.W. L'pool, 1877). [=*C. MILLWARD.*]
The Fair One with the Locks of Gold. [=*G. CONQUEST* and *H. SPRY.*]
The Fairy Circle. [=*H. P. GRATTAN.*]
The Fairy Elves. [="*F. FROST.*" This is the same as *Tit, Tat, Toe*: see p. 374.]
+P. The Fairy Fawn (Birmingham, 26/12/72).

The Fairy Page. [=*A. G. HARRIS.*]
Faith, Hope and Charity. [=*C. H. HAZLEWOOD.* This was also called *The Clergyman's Widow and her Orphans* and *Widow and Orphans* (for which see p. 768).]
The Fallen Star (C.L. 1859). [=*N. LEE.*]
The Fallen Star (Eff. 1864). [=*Mrs H. YOUNG.*]
The Fall of the Avalanche. [=*G. CONQUEST* and *W. E. SUTER.*]
Family Secrets. [=*W. BROUGH, How to make Home happy,* p. 279.]
+D. Family Ties; or, Uncle Josh's Will (Str. 22/10/56).
Fanchette. [=*W. C. LEVEY.*]

p. 676] The Farmer of Inglefield Forest. [=*C. H. HAZLEWOOD.*]
Fast Friends up a Tree. [=*J. R. ANDERSON.*]
The Fatal Shadow. [=*Mrs H. YOUNG.*]
Fate and its Wonders. [=*A. RAYNER.*]

p. 677] +Bal. Fays of the Forest; or, The Enchanted Woodman (Str. 2/9/50).
+Bal. Une Fête à Lisbon (Str. 31/3/56).
+Bal. Une Fête dansante (Str. 21/4/56).
+Bal. La Fête orientale (Str. 19/9/53).
The Fiend's Mountain. [=The Adventurer (*UA*), p. 638.]
A Fiery Ordeal (Brit. 1862). [=*F. HAZLETON.*]
A Fight for Life. [=*CLARA DILLON.* Apparently in error, this was attributed to *F. A. SCUDAMORE* when it was given at the Surrey on 8/7/95.]
The Fireman and the Volunteer. [=*J. T. DOUGLASS.*]

p. 678] First Impression's Everything. [=*J. T. DOUGLASS.*]
The Flirt. [This was probably a revival of the play by *G. D. PITT*; see iv, 375.]
Flora and Zephyr. [=*Mrs G. CONQUEST.* Originally produced Grec. 31/3/52.]
Flying Colours. [=*H. C. COAPE.*]

p. 679] Folly Fête. [=*E. J. N. GALER.*]
Forbidden Fruit. [=What will my Aunt say? (*UA*), p. 766.]
The Forced Marriage. [=*A. FAUCQUEZ.* Apparently the same as *The Adventurer's Doom* and *The Willow Marsh* (see p. 768).]
The Forger and his Victim. [=*C. PITT.*]
Forget and Forgive. [=*G. CONQUEST.*]
For the Benefit of the Playful Crocodile. [=*L. S. BUCKINGHAM.*]
+P. Fortunatus; or, The Magic Wishing Cap (Col. L'pool, 26/12/66).
The Fortune-teller [=*W. TRAVERS.*]
The Forty Thieves (Lyc. 1860). [Written by "members of the Savage Club".]
The Forty Thieves (Strand. 1864). [=*J. T. DOUGLASS.*]

p. 680] The Forty Thieves (Rotunda, L'pool, 1885). [=*J. W. JONES.*]
The Forty Thieves (Birmingham, 1890). [=*J. J. BLOOD.*]
+P. The Forty Thieves; or, Harlequin Ali Baba and the Fairy Ardinella (Qns. 26/12/58).

Found at Sea. [=*T. G. CHETHAM.*]
Found Drowned. [=*W. T. TOWNSEND.*]
The Four Knaves and the Pack. [=*E. TOWERS.*]
The Four-leaved Shamrock. [=*W. TRAVERS.*]

p. 681] The Fox and the Grapes. [=*N. LEE.*]
Frank the Ploughman. [=*W. ROGERS.* Originally produced 1849: see iv, 396.]
Der Freischutz. [=*J. OXENFORD.* +Ast. 2/4/66. +*Lacy.*]
The French in Algiers. [=*C. W. SOMERSET.*]
The Freshman. [=*H. ELLIS.*]
The Fringe of Society. [=*Sir C. WYNDHAM* and *J. MOORE.*]
Froggy would a-wooing go. [=*F. W. GREEN.*]
Fugitives. [=*G. CONQUEST.*]

p. 682] Galatea. [=*F. A. SCHWAB.* Version (Philadelphia, 20/11/86) of *Galatée*, libretto J. Barbier and M. Carré, music F. M. V. Massé (Paris, 14/4/52).]
+Ganymede and Galatea (Gai. 20/1/72). [Version of *Die schöne Galatée*, libretto Kohl von Kohlenegg, music F. von Suppé (Berlin, 30/6/65).]
Garibaldi. [+*F. F. COOPER.* Full title, *Garibaldi the Italian Liberator.*]
The Gentleman Opposite. [=*L. S. BUCKINGHAM.*]

p. 683] The Ghetto. [=*C. B. FERNALD.* Adaptation of H. Heijermans, *Ghetto* (1899).]
The Ghost Hunter (Grec. 1862). [=*G. CONQUEST.*]
The Gipsy and the Showman. [=*W. ROGERS.*]
The Gipsy Girl of Granada. [=*W. TRAVERS.*]
The Gipsy Showman. [Apparently this=*W. TRAVERS, The Gipsy and the Showman.*]
Giselle and the Phantom Night Dancers. [=*F. FENTON* and *W. R. OSMAN.*]
The Gitano Boy. [=*T. H. REYNOLDSON.*]
Godefroi and Yoland. [=*L. S. B. IRVING.*]

p. 684] The Golden Dream. [=*J. BROUGHAM.*]
A Golden Wedding. [=*A. SKETCHLEY.* Music J. Parry Cole.]
The Golden Wreath. [=*J. ALBERY.* +Alh. 20/5/78.]
Good Queen Bess (Str. 1856). [=*C. J. COLLINS.*]

p. 685] Goosey Goosey Gander. [=*C. H. HAZLEWOOD.*]
The Gorilla Hunt. [=*C. H. HAZLEWOOD.*]
Gratitude. [=*C. H. HAZLEWOOD.*]
The Graven Image. [=*T. CHEATHAM.*]
A Great Sensation. [=*S. LEE.*]

p. 686] +Guy Fawkes (Sheffield, 26/12/60).
+Ext. Hamlet, according to Act of Parliament (Str. 7/11/53).
Hamlet the Hysterical. [=*W. R. SNOW.*]
The Hand of Cards. [=*E. STIRLING.* Apparently a revised version of his play of 1846.]

p. 687] The Hanged Man. [=*G. CONQUEST.*]
Hansel and Gretel. [=*CONSTANCE BACHE.* Version of *Hänsel und Gretel*, libretto Adelaide Wette, music E. Humperdinck (Weimar, 1893).]

A Happy family. [=*J. G. TAYLOR.*]
+C. Oa. The Happy Village (Gai. 12/3/70).
Hard Times (Str. 1854). [=*F. F. COOPER.*]
Harlequin and Cinderella. [=*J. COURTNEY.*]
Harlequin and Humpty Dumpty. [=*E. FITZBALL.*]
+P. Harlequin and O'Donoghue (Grec. Birmingham, 26/12/60).
Harlequin and Old Æsop. [=*F. FENTON* and *W. R. OSMAN.*]
Harlequin and Old Izaak Walton. [=*T. L. GREENWOOD.*]
Harlequin and Puss in Boots. [=*T. L. GREENWOOD.*]
+P. Harlequin and the Babes in the Wood; or, Cock Robin and the Cruel Uncle (Bradford, 26/12/59).
+P. Harlequin and the Child of Hale; or, The King of the Red Noses and the Liver Queen (L'pool, 26/12/50).
Harlequin and the House that Jack Built in 1851 = *T. L. GREENWOOD, The House that Jack built in 1851* [see p. 393].
+P. Harlequin and the Little Black Hen (L'pool, 26/12/60).
Harlequin and the Little Mouse. [=*C. H. HAZLEWOOD* = *The Little Mouse* (*UA*), p. 709.]
Harlequin and the Loves of Cupid and Psyche. [=*C. SELBY.*]
+P. Harlequin and the Magic Wreath; or All that glitters is not gold (Vine, L'pool, 26/12/63).
Harlequin and the Maid and the Magpie. [=*J. M. MORTON.*]

p. 688] +P. Harlequin and the Three Bears; or, Little Golden Hair and the Fairies (L'pool, 26/12/62).
+P. Harlequin and Tim Bobbin; or, The Lancashire Witches (Bell's Circus, L'pool, 26/12/62).
Harlequin Baron Munchausen. [=*N. LEE, Jr.*]
Harlequin Beauty and the Beast. [=*T. L. GREENWOOD, Harlequin and Beauty and the Beast* (see p. 393). Music Cohen.]
Harlequin Billy Taylor (Eff. 1857). [=*G. H. GEORGE.*]
Harlequin Billy Taylor (Soho, 1859). [=*T. MOWBRAY.*]
Harlequin Black-eyed Sue. [=*F. TALFOURD.*]
Harlequin Blue Beard (C.L. 1863). [=*N. LEE, Jr.*]
Harlequin Blue Beard (Qns. 1859). [=*W. E. SUTER.*]
+P. Harlequin Blue Beard (Sunderland, 28/12/57).
+P. Harlequin Blue Beard and his Seven Headless Wives (Pav. 21/12/65). [=*C. H. HAZLEWOOD* = *Bluebeard* (*UA*), p. 650.]
Harlequin Cock Robin (Vic. 1866). [=*W. R. OSMAN.*]
Harlequin Dick Whittington. [=*R. SOUTAR.*]
Harlequin Father Thames. [=*C. J. COLLINS.*]
Harlequin Goody Two Shoes. [=*E. TOWERS.*]
Harlequin Green Beetle. [=*J. B. JOHNSTONE.*]

p. 689] Harlequin Gulliver. [Full title, *Peter Parley's Pantomime, Harlequin Gulliver, or The Clown in Lilliput.*]
Harlequin Guy Faux. [=*G. CONQUEST* and *H. SPRY.*]
Harlequin Hans. [=*T. L. GREENWOOD* and *E. L. BLANCHARD.*]
Harlequin Hey diddle Diddle (Eff. 1861). [=*W. E. SUTER.*]
Harlequin Hey-diddle-diddle (Sur. 1861). [=*M. DUTNALL*; music B. Isaacson.]
Harlequin Humbug. [=*L. S. BUCKINGHAM* = *Magic Mistletoe* (*UA*), p. 714.]

Harlequin Humpty Dumpty = *W. T. TOWNSEND.* [The title should be *Harlequin King Humpty Dumpty.*]
Harlequin Jack Sprat. [= *E. L. BLANCHARD* and *T. L. GREENWOOD* = *Jack Sprat* (*UA*), p. 699.]
Harlequin King Crystal. [= *E. TOWERS.*]
Harlequin King Holliday. [= *T. H. HIGGIE.*]
Harlequin King Peewit. [= *E. TOWERS.*]
Harlequin King Pumpkin. [= *M. DUTNALL.*]
+P. Harlequin King Rufus (Blackburn, 26/12/58).
+P. Harlequin Little Goody Two Shoes and the Fairies of the Chrystal Lake; or, Gaffer Goosecap and the Demons of Fire (Preston, 14/1/61).
Harlequin Little Jack Horner. [= *R. SOUTAR.*]
Harlequin Master Walter. [= *T. MOWBRAY.*]

p. 690] +P. Harlequin O'Donoghue; or, The Fairy White Horse of Killarney (Cirque, Birkenhead, 26/12/59).
Harlequin Old King Cole. [= *M. DUTNALL.*]
+P. Harlequin Paddy Carey and the Fairies of the Silver Forest (Southampton, 2/2/59).
Harlequin Prince Love the Day. [= *H. YOUNG.*]
+P. Harlequin Prince Primrose and Cinderella; or, Goody Two Shoes, her Twelve Fairy Daughters and the Little Magic Glass Slipper (Adel. L'pool, 26/12/67).
+P. Harlequin Red Riding Hood (Manchester, 26/12/58).
+P. Harlequin Robin Hood (Manchester, 26/12/58).
Harlequin Robinson Crusoe. [= *G. CONQUEST* and *H. SPRY.*]
+P. Harlequin Sinbad the Sailor (Qns. Hull, 26/12/57).
+P. Harlequin Steam; or, The Old Swan and the Knotty Ash (L'pool, 26/12/55).
Harlequin Tit Tat Toe. [= "*F. FROST*" = *The Fairy Elves of the Fourth Estate* (*UA*), pp. 374, 675.]
Harlequin Tom Moody. [= *N. LEE, Jr.*]
Harlequin Tom, Tom. [= *T. L. GREENWOOD.* +8° (1865).]
Harlequin Valentine and Orson (Grec. 1859). [= *G. CONQUEST* and *H. SPRY.*]
Has anybody seen Mr Brown? [= *J. LEGG.* Probably = *Where's Brown?* (Brighton, 1859) (see p. 766).]

p. 691] The Head of a Clan. [= *F. L. HORNE.*]
+Head Quarters. 8° 1853.
The Heart of Midlothian (Vic. 1863). [= *W. R. OSMAN.*]
The Heart of Old Ireland. [= *C. LITCHFIELD.*]
Hearts that Love us. [= *W. J. ARCHER.*]
The Heart's Victory. [= *T. MEAD.*]
The Hebrew Diamond. [= *C. H. HAZLEWOOD.*]
The Heir of Ellangowan. [= *C. BOLTON.*]
Her Ladyship's Guardian. [= *Sir C. WYNDHAM.*]

p. 692] Hickory Dickory Dock. [= *C. H. HAZLEWOOD.*]
Hidden Crime. [= *C. PITT.*]
Hidden Light. [= *G. CONQUEST.* Full title, *The H.L.*]
High Ways and By Ways of Life. [= *W. E. SUTER.* Full title, *The H.W. and B.W. of L.*]
+O. Bsq. Hints to the Curious; or, Blue Beard, according to Act of Parliament (Str. 27/6/53).

p. 693] The Hive of Life. [=*C. CALVERT.*]
Holly Bush Hall (Stand. 1860). [=*J. MORDAUNT.*]
Holly Bush Hall (Eff. 1860). [=*W. SEAMAN.*]
The Holly Tree Inn. [=*J. B. JOHNSTONE.*]
Homage to Flora. [This may be the same as a ballet by *J. MILANO* (Roy. 10/3/60).]
The Home in the Heart. [=*G. CONQUEST.*]
Home Truths. [=*T. H. REYNOLDSON.*]
An Honest Attorney. [+Str. 20/6/55, as *The Honest Lawyer*=*W. S. EMDEN.*]
Honi Soit. [=A Modern Godiva (*UA*), p. 720.]

p. 694] The Horse of the Cavern. [=Carlo Brunari (*UA*), p. 655.]
The House in the Valley. [=*G. CONQUEST.*]
The House on the Bridge of Notre Dame (Lyc. 1861). [=*M. R. LACY.*]
The House on the Bridge of Notre Dame. (Stand. 1861). [=*J. T. DOUGLASS.*]
+P. The House that Jack built (Plymouth, 26/12/60).
+P. The House that Jack built (Rotunda, L'pool, 26/12/71).
+P. The House that Jack built (Empire, L'pool, 26/12/97).
How it's to be done. [=*L. S. BUCKINGHAM.*]

p. 695] How we live in the World of London. [=*J. B. JOHNSTONE.*]
The Huguenots (C.G. 1851). [=*J. H. WILKINS.*]
+P. Humpty Dumpty (Tyne, Newcastle, 26/12/92).
+P. Humpty Dumpty Crook-a-back Dick and Jane Shore; or, Harlequin Pearl Prince and the Grape Queen (Sheffield, 26/12/57).
I beg you wouldn't mention it. [=*W. E. SUTER.*]
+P. The Ice Witch; or, The Frozen Hand (Rotherham, 26/12/60).
Ida Lee. [=*Mrs H. YOUNG.*]
Ida May (M'bone, 1857). [=*H. YOUNG.*]
+D. The Idiot of the Mill; or, The Hidden Treasure (Qns. 28/2/59).
The Idiot of the Mountain. [=*N. LEE, Jr.*]
The Idle Apprentice. [Probably=*The I. A.; or, The Orphan of the Storm* (Brit. 5/10/62) by *F. MARCHANT.*]
The Idolaters. [=*C. H. HAZLEWOOD.*]
An Impudent Puppy. [=*L. S. BUCKINGHAM.*]
In and Out of Place. [Probably an American drama by *G. D. JOHNSON.*]

p. 696] In Ladbroke Square [see *E. OXENFORD*, *This House to Let*, p. 509].
In the Holly. [=*W. H. PITT.*]
In the Wrong Box. [=*W. H. SWANBOROUGH.*]
Ireland as it is. [Presumably this was a revision of the play by *J. H. AMHERST*, noted in iv, 254.]

p. 697] The Irish Minstrel (Cheltenham, 1867). [=*F. H. COURT.*]
The Iron Arm. [=*W. E. SUTER.*]
Iron Clasp. [=*W. T. TOWNSEND.* Full title, *The I.C.*]
Iron Latch Farm. [=*H. MACKAY.*]
Is it the King? [=*T. L. GREENWOOD.*]

The Island Home. [=*C. CALVERT.*]
It's an Ill Wind. [=*J. OXENFORD.*]
+D. It's never too late to mend (Soho, 3/61).
It was a Dream. [=*J. FIELD.*]
Ivanhoe (Ast. 1859). [=*F. F. COOPER.* Also called *The Lists of Ashby; or, The Conquests of Ivanhoe.*]
Ivanhoe (Qns. 1863). [=*W. E. SUTER.*]
I've beat all three. [=*J. T. DOUGLASS.*]

p. 698] Jack and Jill (Rotunda, L'pool, 1893). [=*W. WADE.*]
+P. Jack and the Bean Stalk (Leicester, 26/12/57).
+P. Jack and the Bean Stalk (Yarmouth, 26/12/57).
Jack and the Beanstalk (D.L. 1859). [=*E. L. BLANCHARD.* +8° (1859), with sub-title, *or, Harlequin Leap Year, and the Merry Pranks of the Good Little People.*]
+P. Jack and the Bean Stalk (Tyne, Newcastle, 26/12/84).
+P. Jack and the Bean Stalk (Tyne, Newcastle, 26/12/90).
Jack in the Box. [=*F. W. GREEN.*]
Jack Mingo. [=*VALENTINE ROBERTS.*]

p. 699] Jack of All Trades. [=*H. NEVILLE* and *FLORENCE HAYDON.*]
Jack Sprat. [=*T. L. GREENWOOD*=*Harlequin Jack Sprat* (*UA*), p. 689.]
+P. Jack the Giant Killer (Bradford, 26/12/60).
+P. Jack the Giant Killer (Dublin, 26/12/60).
+P. Jack the Giant Killer (Bristol, 26/12/61).
+P. Jack the Giant Killer (Rotunda, L'pool, 26/12/69).
Jack the Giant Killer (N. Shields, 1882). [=*J. TULLY.*]
Jack the Giant Killer (Birmingham, 1853). [=*E. L. BLANCHARD.*]
Jack the Giant Killer (Stand. 1869). [=*J. T. DOUGLASS.*]
+P. Jack the Giant Killer; or, Harlequin King Arthur and ye Knights of ye Round Table (Bolton, 18/11/61).
+D. Jane of Liverpool; or, The Licensed Victualler's Daughter (Adel. L'pool, 21/7/62).

p. 700] Jeannie Deans (Stand, 1862). [=*C. H. HAZLEWOOD.*]
Jericho Jack. [=*J. H. WILKINS.*]
Jerry Abershaw. [=*C. H. HAZLEWOOD.*]
Jessie Ashton. [=*Mrs H. YOUNG.*]
Jessie Farleigh. [=*W. TRAVERS* and *N. LEE, Jr.* +*or, The Trial for Infanticide.*]
Jessie, the Mormon's Daughter. [=*C. H. HAZLEWOOD.*]
Jibbenainosay. [=*R. RAYNER.*]
Joe Miller. [=*N. LEE.*]
Johnny Gilpin's Ride. [=*N. LEE, Jr.* This is a P. and full title is, *J. G. R. to Edmonton.*]

p. 701] The Jolly Dogs of London. [=*C. H. HAZLEWOOD.*]
+P. Jolly Jock (Empire, L'pool, 26/12/99).
Jolly King Christmas. [=*F. MARCHANT.*]
Jones the Avenger. [=*F. TALFOURD.*]
Jo; or, Love in a Fog. [=*F. G. CHEATHAM.*]
+Bal. Le Jour de Fête (Str. 14/4/56).

p. 702] Katharine Kavanagh. [=*C. GRAVES.*]
Keep Your Door Locked. [=*A. MATTHISON.*]
Keereda and Nana Sahib. [=*H. YOUNG*=*Veemah Kareeda* (*UA*), p. 763.]
+P. Kenilworth (Newcastle, 26/12/59).
Kerim=*G. D. PITT.* Probably the play of 1847; see iv, 487 and 630; full title *K. the Pearl Diver; or, The Fiend of the Whirlpool.*
The Kettle-drum of the Surrey. [=*J. PARSELLE.*]
Kicks and Halfpence. [=*W. BROUGH* and — *FRANCK.*]
Kiddle-a-wink (Vic. 1864). [=*B. HILL.*]
Kiddle-a-wink (C.L. 1864). [=*W. TRAVERS.*]
The Kidnappers. [=*W. R. OSMAN* and *F. FENTON.*]
The King and the Countess. [=*W. POEL.* A version of *Edward III*, originally produced Steinway H. 2/5/90: printed as *Love's Constancy* (1906).]
King Comet. [=*N. LEE, Jr.*]

p. 703] The King of the Assassins. [=*C. H. HAZLEWOOD.*]
The King of the Castle. [="*A. CROWQUILL.*"]
The King of the Cures. [=*F. MARCHANT.*]
The King of the Golden Valley. [=*N. LEE.*]
King Pluto. [=*F. TALFOURD, Pluto and Proserpine*, p. 590.]
King Queer. [=*J. HALFORD* and *C. J. COLLINS.*]
The King's Butterfly. [=— *BELLEW.*]
King Sillyninny. [=*F. G. CHEATHAM.*]
The King's Mail. [=*W. T. TOWNSEND.*]
King Teapot the Great. [=*W. E. SUTER.*]
Kiss Me Quick. [=A Trip to Klondyke (*UA*), p. 759.]
Knowledge. [=*G. S. OGILVIE.*]

p. 704] Lady Hatton (Brit. 1859). [=*G. D. PITT.*]
The Lady of the Camelias (Vaud. 1852). [+*Lacy.*]
The Lady of the Lake. [=*R. W. TAYLOR.*]

p. 705] Lara. [=*J. OXENFORD.* Version of the opera, libretto E. Cormon and M. Carré, music L. Maillart (Paris, 21/3/64).]
Lashed to the Helm. [=*C. H. HAZLEWOOD.*]
The Latch Key. [= *E. STIRLING.* +*or, Our Street.*]
Laura. [=*W. POEL.* Also called *The Faithful Heart, The Faithful Lover* and *The Queen's Lieutenant.*]
Laurette's Bridal. [=*C. H. HAZLEWOOD.*]

p. 706] Left Alone. [=*Mrs H. YOUNG.*]
Left Handed Marriages. [=*C. H. HAZLEWOOD.*]
The Legend of the Headless Man. [=*B. J. WEBSTER.*]
The Leprechaun. [=*E. FALCONER.*]
A Lesson for Husbands. [=Mischievous Annie (*UA*), p. 719.]
The Life and Adventures of George Barrington. [=*Mrs H. YOUNG.*]
The Life and Adventures of Will Shakespeare. [=*H. F. SAVILLE.*]

p. 707] The Life Boat (Pav. 1850). [=*T. G. BLAKE.*]
Life for a Life. [=*W. TRAVERS*=*The Reprieve* (*UA*), p. 740.]
Life in Lambeth. [=*W. R. OSMAN.*]
The Life of a Beggar. [=*W. TRAVERS.*]

The Life of a Miner. [=*A. FAUCQUEZ*. +or, *The Fatal Fire Damp*. This play was presented, as new, both at the Eff. 10/3/62 and at the M'bone, 16/2/67.]

The Life Raft. [=*W. T. TOWNSEND*.]

Life's Trials. [=*C. H. HAZLEWOOD*.]

Lillian Trafford. [=*W. S. BRONSON*.]

The Lion Conqueror. [=*W. T. TOWNSEND*. +*or, The Jungle Death*.]

The Lion of England and the Eagle of France. [=United Service (*UA*), p. 762. Under the first title it was presented on 17/1/55; two days later the second title was used.]

p. 708] Lion's Love [=*G. CONQUEST*.]

+Oa. Lischen and Fritzchen (C.G. 27/12/69). [Music J. Offenbach.]

+P. Little Bo Peep (Amphi. L'pool, 26/12/60).

+P. Little Bo Peep (Adel. L'pool, 26/12/73).

+P. Little Bo Peep (Tyne, Newcastle, 24/12/81).

+P. Little Bo Peep (Newcastle, 26/12/92).

Little Bo Peep (Rotunda, L'pool, 1892). [=*F. LOCKE*.]

Little Bo Peep (Shakespeare, L'pool, 1894). [=*J. H. WOOLFE*.]

+P. Little Bo Peep; or, Harlequin and the Girl that Lost her Sheep (Edinburgh, 26/12/57).

+P. Little Boy Blue (Newcastle, 26/12/63).

The Little Busy Bee. [=*C. H. HAZLEWOOD*.]

The Little Demon. [=*J. HALFORD*.]

p. 709] Little Dorothy. [=*R. THORNE*].

Little Dorrit. [=*F. F. COOPER*.]

+P. Little Jack Horner and his Christmas Pie (Qns. Leeds, 26/12/58).

The Little Mouse [=*C. H. HAZLEWOOD*=Harlequin and the Little Mouse (*UA*), p. 687.]

Little Red Riding Hood (C.G. 1858). [=*J. V. BRIDGEMAN* and *H. S. EDWARDS*.]

Little Red Riding Hood (Hengler's, 1874). [=*A. HENRY*.]

+P. Little Red Riding Hood (P'cess, Leeds, 26/12/59).

+P. Little Red Riding Hood (Qns. Hull, 26/12/60).

+P. Little Red Riding Hood (Lyc. Sunderland, 26/12/60).

+P. Little Red Riding Hood (Rotunda, L'pool, 26/12/73).

p. 710] Little Red Riding Hood (P.W. L'pool, 1880). [=*T. F. DOYLE*.]

Little Red Riding Hood (Rotunda, L'pool, 1883). [=*F. W. GREEN*. +*or Harlequin Boy Blue, the Good Fairy and the Naughty Wolf*.]

Little Red Riding Hood (Birmingham, 1893). [=*F. LOCKE*; music F. W. Humphreys.]

Little Red Riding Hood (P.W. L'pool, 1897). [=*J. J. HEWSON*.]

Little Red Riding Hood (Sheffield, 1860). [=*W. REEVE*.]

+P. Little Red Riding Hood; or, Harlequin Hop o' my Thumb and the Ogre with the Seven League Boots (Nottingham, 26/12/57).

+P. Little Red Riding Hood; or, Harlequin the Wolf Wizard and the Magic Rose (Glasgow, Dec. 1860).

The Little Stranger. [=*J. DERRICK*.]

p. 711] La Locandiera. [=*T. J. WILLIAMS.*]
London Labour and London Poor. [=*J. ELPHINSTONE.*]
+D. The London Mechanic; or, Drink, Poverty and Crime (Qns. 10/10/59).
London Vice and London Virtue. [=*H. SAVILLE.*]
The Lord and the Lout. [=*W. H. PITT.*]
Lost and Found. [=*A. FAUCQUEZ.*]
The Lost Bride of Garryowen. [This seems to be by *C. HORSMAN*, first produced Qns. Manchester, 19/11/60.]

p. 712] Lovers at Play. [=*H. LEON.*]

p. 713] The Love Test. [=*J. B. JOHNSTONE.*]
Love wins the Day. [=— *FINLAYSON.*]
+Bsq. O. Lucy Did-Lub-Him-More! (Str. 25/2/57).
Lyddy Beale. [=*C. H. HAZLEWOOD.*]

p. 714] Mad-Fred. [=*M. DUTNALL.*]
The Magic Axe. [=*E. TOWERS.* Full title, *Harlequin and the Magic Axe*; music T. Harris.]
The Magic Branch. [=— *COLLIS.*]
The Magic Fife. [Music J. Offenbach.]
+P. The Magic Horse; or, Harlequin Fortunio and his Seven Gifted Servants (Qns. Dublin, 26/12/58).
The Magic Mistletoe. [=*L. S. BUCKINGHAM*=*Harlequin Humbug* (*UA*), p. 689.]
The Magic Wishing Cap. [=*C. H. HAZLEWOOD.*]
Malala. [Music J. Offenbach.]
Mamma's Opinions. [=*W. POEL.*]

p. 715] The Manchester Marriage. [=*F. G. CHEATHAM.*]
The Man in Grey. [=*J. B. HOWE.*]
+P. The Man in the Moon. (Amphi. L'pool, 10/11/79).
The Man of the Red Mansion. [=*C. RICE.*]
Manuel of Spain. [=*R. PHILLIPS.*]
+D. Marianne de Lancy; or, The Double Marriage (Str. 27/4/54).

p. 716] Mark Winslow. [=*J. T. DOUGLASS.*]
The Maroon. [=*M. REID.*]
Marriage Bells. [=*W. J. ARCHER.* +Eff. 12/11/64.]
Marriage by Candlelight. [Version of *Le mariage aux lanternes*, libretto M. Carré and L. Battu, music J. Offenbach (Paris, 10/10/57).]
The Marriage Day. [=*J. COURTNEY*, *The Life Chase*, p. 326.]
Mary Barton (Grec. 1861). [=*W. T. TOWNSEND.* +*or, The Weaver's Distress.*]

p. 717] +P. Mary, Mary, Quite Contrary; or, Harlequin Leap Year and the Fairy Sunlight (Leeds, 26/12/60).
Mary Price. [=*C. H. HAZLEWOOD.*]
The Master Singers. [Version of *Die Meistersinger von Nürnberg*, music R. Wagner (Munich, 21/6/68).]
+P. May and December; or, Harlequin June and his Magic Tune (Halifax, 26/12/58).
May Blossom. [This is probably the American drama by *D. BELASCO.*]
May Dudley. [=*F. MARCHANT.*]

p. 718] Mazeppa (Ast. 1882). [=*H. C. NEWTON*; music W. H. Brinkworth.]
The Mechanic. [=*G. CLAIR.*]
The Medal of Death. [=*E. TOWERS.*]
Mefistofele. [=*T. MARZIALS.*]
The Mendicant Son. [Probably this is the play (1845) by *E. STIRLING*; see iv, 408.]
+D. The Merchant's Honour; or, The Plebeian Daughter (Qns. Manchester, 18/9/58).
Mervyn Clitheroe. [=*G. CONQUEST.*]

p. 719] The Mexican Bandit. [=*Mrs H. YOUNG.*]
Michel Perrin. [=*A. YOUNGE.*]
A Midsummer's Eve. [=*W. H. YELLAND.*]
Might and Right. [Music W. Montgomery.]
The Miller's Daughter. [=*W. E. SUTER.*]
Milliner to the King. [=*C. J. MATHEWS.*]
+D. The Minister and the Favourite (Str. 14/4/56).
Mischievous Annie. [=A Lesson for Husbands (*UA*), p. 706.]

p. 720] Miss Lear. [=*M. DUTNALL* and *A. C. SHELLEY.*]
Miss Multon. [This seems to be the American drama by *A. R. CAZAURAN.*]
The Mistletoe Bough. [=*F. MARCHANT.*]
The Mistress of Hawk's Crag. [=*E. TOWERS.*]
A Modern Godiva. [=Honi Soit (*UA*), p. 693.]
The Mohicans of Paris. [=*E. ELTON* and *C. H. HAZLEWOOD.*]
Molly Sullivan. [=*G. D. PITT.*]
The Moment of Terror. [=*G. CONQUEST.*]

p. 721] Moonlight Jack. [=*W. TRAVERS.*]
+D. Mordecai. 8° 1851.

p. 722] Mr Webster's Company is requested. [=*E. YATES* and *N. H. HARRINGTON.*]

p. 723] My New Maid. [This is apparently the Oa. by *H. B. FARNIE.* (O.C. 18/3/74).]
My Poor Dog Tray. [=*T. G. BLAKE.* +*or, The Green Hills of Shannon.*]
My Son Dick. [=*W. MAURICE, Ready Money Mortiboy*, p. 482.]
The Mysteries of Audley Court. [=*J. BROUGHAM.*]
The Mystery of Cloisterham. [=*W. STEPHENS, The Mystery of Edwin Drood.*]
My Wife's First Husband. [=*W. E. SUTER.*]
Nana Sahib. [=*F. FENTON* and *W. R. OSMAN.*]
Narcisse. [=*T. TAYLOR.*]

p. 724] The Necromancer. [=*J. B. HOWE.*]
The Neglected Home. [=*W. TRAVERS*=*The Spirit Child's Prayer* (*UA*), p. 753.]
+M.F. Netley Abbey (Southampton, 8/58).
Never Despair (Adel. 1859). [=*H. DRAYTON*; music F. J. Duggan.]
Never Judge by Appearances (Adel. 1859). [=*H. DRAYTON*; music E. J. Loder.]

Never Reckon Your Chickens. [=*W. E. SUTER.*]
Never too late to mend (Grec. 1858). [=*G. CONQUEST, Jr.*]
Never too late to mend (Brit. 1859). [=*C. H. HAZLEWOOD.* +Brit. 9/5/59.]
Newcastle in an Uproar; or, The Errors and Repentance of Mr Ralfus Stucko. 8° 1851 (Newcastle). [Ascribed to *RALPH DODDS.*]
The New Wags of Windsor. [=*J. HOWARD* and *F. COOPER.*]

p. 725] A Nice Girl. [=*W. M. THOMAS.*]
Night. [=*J. T. DOUGLASS.*]
+D. Noemi, the Village Orphan (Qns. 10/10/59).

p. 726] Not Guilty. [This is probably=*Outward Bound* (*UA*), p. 730.]
Nothing to wear. [=*C. J. MATHEWS.* A version of *Number One round the Corner*, by *W. BROUGH.*]
No. 13. [=*W. T. TOWNSEND.* Also called *The Managing Director.* +Vic. 16/3/63.]
No. 49. [=*F. LAWRENCE.*]
+Masque. Oberon's Empire. 8° 1858.
+P. The Ocean Queen; or, Harlequin Harold, King of the Sea, and the Fairies of the Frozen Zone (Grimsby, 26/12/58).
Odette. [=*C. W. SCOTT* and *B. C. STEPHENSON.*]
Okee Pokee. [=*W. TRAVERS.*]
The Old Cherry Tree. [=*C. H. HAZLEWOOD.*]

p. 727] Old Daddy Longlegs. [=*C. H. HAZLEWOOD* and *D. JOHNSON.*]
Old Isaak Walton. [=*T. L. GREENWOOD*=*Harlequin and Old Izaac W.* (*UA*), p. 687.]
Old King Cole (Birmingham, 1864). [=*M. DUTNALL.*]
The Old Maid in a Winding Sheet. [=*C. H. HAZLEWOOD.*]
The Old Man and his Ass. [=*F. MARCHANT*; music H. Hope.]
Old Phil Hardy. [=*G. CONQUEST.* Originally produced Grec. 30/8/63.]
The Old Toll House. [=*C. H. HAZLEWOOD.*]
The Old Woman who lived in a Shoe. [=*J. B. JOHNSTONE*; music L. Giorgi.]
+P. The Old Woman who lived in a Shoe; or, Harlequin Child of Childwall and the Choice Spirits of Dingle Dell (Amphi. L'pool, 26/12/61).

p. 728] Oliver Cromwell. [=*N. LEE.*]
Oliver Twist (C.L. 1855). [=*C. H. HAZLEWOOD.*]
Once too often. [=*H. GLOVER.*]
The One Hundred Cuirassiers. [=*R. PHILLIPS.*]
One Thousand Napoleons. [=*A. CAMPBELL.* +*or, The Golden Pheasant.*]
One Witness. [=*W. T. TOWNSEND.*]
Only a Model. [=*CECIL RAMSAY.*]
The Oracle. [Almost certainly=*C. DEFFELL* and *M. BROWNE, Christmas Eve*, p. 341.]

p. 729] Oranges and Lemons. [=*J. T. DOUGLASS.*]
Ornano. [=*S. HILLIS.*]
The Orphan of the Mine. [=*W. E. SUTER.*]

The Ostler's Vision. [=*A. RAYNER.*]
Othello the Moor and his Amour. [+12^{n} 1856 (Liverpool).]
Our Female American Cousin. [=*C. GALEN.*]
Our New Lady's Maid. [=*H. C. COAPE.*]
Our Nurse Dorothy. [=*A. G. HARRIS.*]

p. 730] Our Traviata. [=*W. F. VANDERVELL.*]
The Outcasts (Vic. 1864). [=*C. H. HAZLEWOOD.*]
Out of Evil cometh Good. [=*C. HOLT.*]
Outward Bound. [Probably=*Not Guilty* (*UA*), p. 726.]
+P. Paddy Carey; or, Harlequin Dan and the Good Fairies of Everton Hill (P'cess, L'pool, 26/12/60).

p. 731] A Parisian Romance. [=*A. R. CAZAURAN.*]
+Sk. Passing Clouds. 8° 1854.
Pat a Cake. [=*J. T. DOUGLASS* and *B. WRIGHT.*]
The Patriot Spy. [=*F. L. PHILLIPS.*]
Paul Clifford. [=*C. H. HAZLEWOOD.*]
Paul the Showman. [=*Mrs W. R. CRAUFORD.*]

p. 732] Perichole. [=*F. DESPREZ.* Version of the opera, libretto H. Meilhac and L. Halévy, music J. Offenbach (Paris, 6/10/68).]
The Perilous Pass. [=*A. V. CAMPBELL.* +*or, The Maid of Aosta.*]
Perils by Land and Wave. [=*W. TRAVERS.*]
+Bal. Perpetual Motion (Str. 15/12/55).
Perseus. [=*W. E. SUTER.*]
+P. Peter Parley's Pantomime [see under *Harlequin Gulliver*, p. 689.]
Peter the Shipwright. [Version of *Czaar und Zimmermann*, music A. Lortzing (Leipzig, 22/12/37).]
Peter Wilkins and the Flying Indians. [=*H. SPRY* and *G. CONQUEST.*]
The Phantom. [=*D. BOUCICAULT.*]
The Phantom Captain. [=*G. CONQUEST.*]
The Phantom Wives. [=*L. S. BUCKINGHAM.*]

p. 733] Phyllis Thorpe. [=*C. H. HAZLEWOOD* (ascribed).]
The Physician's Wife. [=*C. WEBB.*]
Piquillo Allegra. [=*C. WEBB.*]
+P. The Pirate's Bride; or, Harlequin Conrad and Medora (Southampton, 27/12/57).
The Pirate's Love. [=*G. CONQUEST.*]
The Pirates of the Savannah. [=*J. T. DOUGLASS.*]
Pizarro. [=*C. J. COLLINS.*]
Pizarro, the Great Tyrant. [=*F. MARCHANT.* A revised version appeared Brit. 27/7/74 as *Pizarro, the Rolla-King Spanish Tyrant.*]
A Pleasant Time of it. [=*L. S. BUCKINGHAM.*]
The Poor Girl. [=*Mrs H. YOUNG.*]
Poor Joe of Horsemonger Lane. [=*W. TRAVERS.* Acted M'bone, 14/10/61 as *Horsemonger-Lane Joe.*]
Poor Ray. [=*C. PITT* and *W. H. PITT.*]

p. 735] Pretty Blue Belle. [=*C. H. HAZLEWOOD.*]
The Pretty Girls of Stilberg. [=*B. WEBSTER.*]
The Prince and the Lion King. [=*W. E. SUTER.*]

The Prince and the Ogre. [=*F. MARCHANT.*]
The Prince of the Peaceful Islands. [=*F. G. CHEATHAM.*]
+P. Prince Peerless; or, Harlequin and the Good Fairy of the Golden Branch (Adel. L'pool, 26/12/60).
Prince Pippo. [=*C. H. HAZLEWOOD.*]
+P. Princess Fairlocks, or, Harlequin Prince Honourbright and the Battle of the Giant and the Dwarf (Newcastle, 26/12/57).

p. 736] The Princess of the Pearl Island. [=*C. H. HAZLEWOOD.*]
The Prisoner of Lyons. [This seems to be by *H. YOUNG*; revived at M'bone, 14/3/60.]
+Ba. The Prisoner of Rochelle; or, Inns and Outs (Str. 4/2/56).
The Prophet (Sur. 1854). [+Sur. 7/8/54.]
Punch and Judy (St J. 1859). [=*C. J. COLLINS.*]
Punch and Judy (Grec. 1864). [=*G. CONQUEST* and *H. SPRY.*]
+Bal. Punch in Paris; or, The Well and the Treasure (M'bone, 4/8/51).
+P. Puss in Boots (L'pool, 26/12/57).
+P. Puss in Boots (Exeter, 26/12/57).
+P. Puss in Boots (Oldham, 26/12/59).
+P. Puss in Boots (South Shields, 26/12/59).
Puss in Boots (C.G. 1859). [=*J. V. BRIDGEMAN.*]
+P. Puss in Boots (Bristol, 26/12/60).
+Puss in Boots (Birmingham, 26/12/62).
+P. Puss in Boots (Newcastle, 24/12/75).
Puss in Boots (D.L. 1888). [=*C. GRAVES.*]

p. 737] +P. Puss in Boots (Tyne, Newcastle, 12/88).
Puss in Boots; or, Harlequin Ralph. [=*R. SOUTAR.*]
+P. Puss in Boots; or, The Princess Fair, the Ogre Rat, the Miller's Merry Son and the Little Manx Cat (Rotunda, L'pool, 26/12/74).
+P. Puss in Boots, the King, Princess and Ogre (Leicester, 26/12/58).
+P. The Queen Bee; or, Harlequin Prince Golden Land, Jack Frost, and the Lazy Drones of the Enchanted Valley (L'pool, 26/12/69).
+P. Queen Mab (Belfast, 2/60).
+P. Queen Mab; or, Harlequin in the Magic Pippin and the Peri of the Pearly Lake (Grec. 26/12/51).
Queen of Connaught. [=*H. JAY.*]
+D. The Queens Musketeers (Str. 24/11/56).

p. 738] Queen Topaze. [=*G. LINLEY.* Version of *La Reine Topaze*, libretto J. P. Lockroy and L. Battu, music F. M. V. Massé (Paris, 27/12/57).]
+D. Quendryth, a Legend of the Heptarchy. 12° 1877.
+D. The Rabbi of York. 8° 1852.
The Railroad of Life (Eff. 1859). [=*J. B. JOHNSTONE.*]
The Raiment and Agonies. [=*F. MARCHANT.*]

p. 739] The Realities of Life. [=*G. CONQUEST.*]
Rebecca, the Jewish Wanderer. [=*FANNY GARTHWAITE.*]
The Red Bridge. [=*W. E. SUTER.*]

The Red Hand. [=*T. LYON*. Variously acted as *He of the Red Hand* and *Cahill Euve*.]
The Red Lamp. [=*W. TRAVERS*.]
Red Riding Hood (Birmingham, 1858). [=*Miss KEATING*.]
+P. Red Riding Hood (Swansea, 26/12/60).

p. 740] The Reprieve. [=*W. TRAVERS*. This was later called *Life for a Life*, and as such it appears in *UA*, p. 707.]
The Republican Duke. [=*J. R. ANDERSON*. +*or, The Revolt of Genoa*. First acted Amphi. L'pool, 4/50 as *Fiesco*.]

p. 741] Reuben Blight. [=*J. PANTON*.]
Rich and Poor (Brit. 1866). [=*C. H. HAZLEWOOD*.]
+P. Richard Coeur de Lion taking in Wolverhampton on his Road to Palestine (Wolverhampton, 26/12/57).
Rip Van Winkle (Newcastle, 1866). [=*W. STRACHAN, Jr*.]
The Rival Fountains. [=*C. H. HAZLEWOOD*.]

p. 742] Robin Hood (D.L. 1858). [=*E. L. BLANCHARD*; music J. H. Tully.]
Robin Hood (Alex. L'pool, 1880). [=*J. F. McCARDLE*.]
Robin Hood (R.A. Woolwich, 1888). [=*H. MILLS* and *S. G. HORTON*; music A. Mills and B. J. Hancock.]
+P. Robin Hood; or, Harlequin Friar Tuck and the Merry Men of Sherwood Forest (Nottingham, 26/12/59).
+P. Robinson Crusoe (Manchester, 26/12/57).
+P. Robinson Crusoe (Newcastle, 12/78).

p. 743] Robinson Crusoe (P.W. L'pool, 1890). [=*F. W. PRATT*.]
Robinson Crusoe (Birmingham, 1894). [=*F. LOCKE*; music W. Humphreys.]
+P. Robinson Crusoe (Tyne, Newcastle, 12/94).
+P. Robinson Crusoe (Court, L'pool, 26/12/97).
Robinson Crusoe (Rotunda L'pool, 1897). [=*T. S. ROGERS*.]
+P. Robinson Crusoe (Lyr. L'pool, 23/12/99).

p. 744] Rob Roy, the Bold Outlaw. [=*C. H. HAZLEWOOD*.]
Roger O'Hare. [=*H. EVERETT*. +*or, The Lost Will*.]
Roland and his Steed. [=*W. E. SUTER*=*The White Palfrey* (*UA*), p. 767.]
The Romance of a Poor Young Man. [=*C. H. HAZLEWOOD*.]
+D. The Romantic Widow (Str. 28/1/56).
Rookwood (Grec. 1859). [=*G. CONQUEST*.]

p. 745] Rose Clinton. [This is probably a revised version of the play by *J. COURTNEY* (1848); see iv, 284.]
Rouge et Noir. [=*H. T. LESLIE*.]
The Royal Escape. [=*C. F. COGHLAN*.]
+D. The Ruby Ring; or, The Murder in Piper's Row in 1672 (Wolverhampton, 27/5/58).
+D. Russian Tyranny; or, The Fatal Snow Storm (Str. 20/3/54).

p. 746] The Sacred Trust. [=*A. FAUCQUEZ*.]
The Sailor's Sheet-Anchor. [=*C. H. HAZLEWOOD*.]
St Anne's Night. [=*J. B. JOHNSTONE*. +*or, The Smuggler of the Abbey*.]

+P. St George and the Dragon (Qns. Edinburgh, 26/12/57).
+P. St George and the Dragon (Plymouth, 26/12/57).
St George and the Dragon (Pav. 1864). [=*F. G. CHEATHAM.*]
Sappho. [=*G. G. COLLINGHAM*, *The Idol of an Hour*, p. 317.]
The Savage and Civilization. [This probably=*The Huron Chief; or, the S. and C.* (Brit. 7/5/60) by *J. H. WILKINS* and *J. R. ANDERSON*; see also *Civilization* (C.L. 10/11/52), p. 623.]
The Savannah. [=*C. J. MATHEWS.*]

p. 747] The School Drudge. [This probably=*H. F. HYDE*, *Success*, p. 431.]
+Bal. The Sculptor of Frankfort (M'bone. 11/2/50).
Second to None. [+*or, The Lady of the Lone House.*]
The Secrets of the Devil. [=*W. R. OSMAN* and *F. FENTON.*]
Self Made. [=*G. VINING.*]

p. 748] The Seven Ages of Man. [=*T. H. WEBB.*]
The Seven Poor Travellers (Sur. 1855). [=*J. B. JOHNSTONE.*]
The Seventh Hour. [This is apparently the play by *B. HUGHES* and *A. FAUCQUEZ* (C.L. 10/4/61).]
The Shadow of Wrong. [=*G. CONQUEST.*]
The Shadow on the Hearth. [=*C. BOLTON.*]
Shake Hands. [=*L. S. BUCKINGHAM.*]
Shelah from Cork. [=*W. SEAMAN.*]
The Ship on Fire. [This is probably *The Ocean Monarch; or, The Ship on Fire*, recorded as by *C. A. SOMERSET* and it may=*The Loss of the Monarch; or, The Ship on Fire* (Brit. 27/9/48).]

p. 749] Shooting Stars. [Music F. R. Hervé.]
Silver Store Island (Vic. 1858). [=*H. YOUNG.*]
Silver Store Island (Str. 1858). [=*F. F. COOPER.*]
+P. Sinbad the Sailor (Norwich, 26/12/57).
+P. Sinbad the Sailor (Tyne, Newcastle, 12/71).
+P. Sinbad the Sailor (Newcastle, 12/80).
Sinbad the Sailor (Rotunda, L'pool, 1880). [=*J. F. McARDLE.*]
+P. Sinbad the Sailor (P.W. L'pool, 26/12/84).
Sinbad the Sailor (Alex. L'pool, 1886). [=*T. E. PEMBERTON* and *J. J. HEWSON.*]
+P. Sinbad the Sailor (Newcastle, 12/88).

p. 750] Sing a Song of Sixpence (C.L. 1862). [=*N. LEE, Jr.*]

p. 751] Sir Jasper's Tenant. [=*E. STIRLING.*]
The Sister's Sacrifice. [=*S. FRENCH.* +*or, The Orphans of Valneige.*]
A Sketch from the Louvre. [This is probably a revised version of the play by *H. A. MAJOR* (Soho, 28/7/60).]
The Slaves of Crime. [=*C. H. HAZLEWOOD.*]
The Sleeping Beauty (Brighton, 1862). [=*R. SOUTAR.*]
+P. The Sleeping Beauty; or, Harlequin of the Emerald Isle (Adel. L'pool, 26/12/55).
+P. The Sleeping Beauty in the Wood (Dublin, 26/12/58).
+P. The Sleeping Beauty in the Wood (Norwich, 26/12/58).
+P. The Sleeping Beauty in the Wood (Glasgow, 26/12/59).

p. 752] Slumber my Darling. [=*L. GEE.*]
The Soldier's Wife (Str. 1854). [=*F. F. COOPER.* +*or, The Heights of Alma.*]
Solon Shingle. [=*J. E. OWENS.* A revision of an American play, *The People's Lawyer*, by *J. S. JONES.*]
Some Bells that ring the Old Year out. [=*C. H. HAZLEWOOD.*]
+Oa. The Song of Fortunio (Gai. 10/1/76). [Music J. Offenbach.]

p. 753] So very obliging. [=*L. S. BUCKINGHAM.*]
Spare the Rod. [=*W. FRASER.*]
The Spider and the Fly (Grec. 1862). [=*G. CONQUEST* and *H. SPRY.*=*Number Nip*, p. 320.]
The Spirit Child's Prayer. [=*W. TRAVERS*=*The Neglected Home* (*UA*), p. 724.]
The Spirit of Death. [=*W. E. SUTER*=*The Angel of Midnight*, p. 588.]
The Spirit of Liberty. [=*C. H. HAZLEWOOD.*]
The Spirit of Revenge. [=*W. E. SUTER.*]
Spirits of the Departed. [=*The Wishing Glen* (*UA*), p. 769.]

p. 754] The Spouse Trap. [=*J. M. EAST, The Kitchen Girl*, p. 353.]
Spring-heeled Jack. [=*D. STEWART.*]
The Standard of England. [=*H. YOUNG.*]
+Bal. The Star of the Rhine (Str. 12/10/53).
+Bal. La Statue Blanche; or, Pierrot in a Fix (Str. 6/2/56).
The Stolen Diamonds. [=*I. GLEN, A Woman's Error*, p. 382.]
+P. The Storm King's Dream; or, Harlequin Rainbow and the Fairy of the Sunlit City of the Sea (Bolton, 11/60).
The Storm Visitor. [=*W. TRAVERS.*]
The Story of a Night. [=*T. MEAD.*]

p. 755] The String of Pearls (Eff. 1862). [=*Mrs H. YOUNG.*]
The Struggle for Gold. [=*E. STIRLING.*]
Struggles of the Poor. [=*C. H. HAZLEWOOD.*]
The Students. [=*J. COURTNEY.*]
Such is Life (Eff. 1864). [=*H. YOUNG.*]
The Suicide's Tree. [=*F. MARCHANT.* Played also under sub-title.]
+P. The Sultan of Mocha (P.W. L'pool, 26/12/76).
A Supreme Moment. [=*Mrs W. K. CLIFFORD.*]
The Swallow's Nest. [=*Mrs H. YOUNG*=*Ben Child* (*UA*), p. 648.]
The Swan and Edgar. [=*H. S. EDWARDS* and *C. KENNEY.*]
+D. The Switzer's Curse; or, The Maniac of the Torrent (Qns. 28/2/59).

p. 756] Taffy was a Welchman. [="*P. PARLEY*".]
A Tale of a Coat. [=*W. BROUGH* and — *FRANCKS.*]
+D. A Tale of Two Cities; or, The Horrors of the Bastille (Southampton, 6/2/60).
Tell Tale Tit. [=*J. T. DOUGLASS.*]
Temptation and Atonement. [=*G. CONQUEST.*]
The Tempter. [=*N. LEE, Jr.*]
A Tenant for Life. [=*W. PHELPS.*]
Tess of the D'Urbervilles. [=*H. MOUNTFORD.*]

p. 757] That Horrid Biggins. [=*F. ALLEN.*]
That House in High Street. [=*M. STUART.*]
That Rascal Jack. [Apparently a revision of the play by *T. L. GREENWOOD* (S.W. 2/43); see iv, 321.]
There's nothing like a Friend at Court. [=*T. P. PREST.*]
Third Class and First Class. [=*W. SEAMAN.*]
+F. 1395 (Str. 28/11/55).
This Side Up. =[*L. RAE.*]
+C. The Three Bachelors. 8° 1862.
The Three Brothers of Brevannes. [=*T. MEAD.*]
The Three Brothers of Mystery. [=*W. E. SUTER.*]
The Three Brothers of the Old Chateau. [=*A. RAYNER.*]
+Bsq. The Three Graces (Qns. Dublin, 17/3/59).

p. 758] +P. Three Legs, King of Man; or, Harlequin Lord Stanlie and the Eagle and Child (L'pool, 26/12/53).
The Three Lives. [=*C. H. HAZLEWOOD.*]
+C. Three to One. 4° 1850.
Tom Tom the Piper's Son (Eff. 1860). [=*W. E. SUTER.*]

p. 759] Too Many Cooks. [=*G. REED*; music J. Offenbach.]
Too much Johnson. [=*W. GILLETTE.* +New Stand. N.Y. 26/11/94.]
The Toy Maker. [=*G. LINLEY.* Version of *La poupée de Nuremberg*, libretto A. de Leuven and L. L. Brunswick, music A. Adam (Paris, 21/2/52).]
The Tragedy Queen. [=*J. OXENFORD.*]
+Bal. The Transformed Lover (Str. 8/10/50).
La Traviata (Sur. 1857). [=*T. H. REYNOLDSON.* Version of the opera, libretto F. M. Piave, music G. Verdi (Venice, 6/3/53).]
La Traviata (Brit. 1857). [=*C. H. HAZLEWOOD.*]
A Trip to Klondyke. [=Kiss Me Quick (*UA*), p. 703.]

p. 760] Tristan and Isolde. [Version of the opera, music R. Wagner (Munich, 10/6/65).]
The Triumph of Peace. [=The Festival of Peace (*UA*), p. 677.]
The Troubadour. [=*W. TRAVERS.*]
Troubled Waters (Vic. 1864). [=*H. HUME.* +*or, The Family Secret.*]
Twenty Straws (Brit. 1865). [*C. H. HAZLEWOOD.*]
Twenty Straws (Eff. 1865). [=*Mrs H. YOUNG.*]
Twinkle, Twinkle, Little Star (Brighton, 1875). [=*F. W. GREEN.*]
Two can play at that Game. [=*W. GORDON.*]

p. 761] Two Precious Scoundrels. [=*L. S. BUCKINGHAM.*]
Una. [=*D. BOUCICAULT.*]
Uncle Mark. [=*A. YOUNGE.*]

p. 762] Under a Cloud (Eff. 1859). [=*J. B. JOHNSTONE.*]
Under a Cloud (Brit. 1859). [*C. H. HAZLEWOOD.*]
Under the Earth. [=*W. H. C. NATION.*]
Under the Lamps. [=*T. MEAD.*]
Undine (H. 1858). [*J. B. BUCKSTONE.*]
Unequally Sentenced. [=Clergy (*UA*), p. 660.]

The United Service of England and France. [=*E. STIRLING* +Str. 10/7/54.]
Upside Down (Brit. 1864). [=*C. H. HAZLEWOOD.*]
p. 763] The Vain Heart. [=*W. T. TOWNSEND.*]
+P. Valentine and Orson (Portsmouth, 26/12/60).
Valentine's Day. [=*J. B. BUCKSTONE.* +8° 1859.]
+Bal. The Valley of Sweet Waters (Str. 30/9/50).
Veemah Kareeda. [=*H. YOUNG*=*Keereda and Nana Sahib* (*UA*), p. 702.]
The Vendetta. [=*F. G. CHEETHAM.*]
The Very Grand Dutch—s. [=*C. BERNARD.*]
The Vicar of Wakefield. [=*J. S. COYNE.*]
p. 764] Vidocq. [=*F. MARCHANT.*]
+C.Bal. The Village Torment (Brit. 7/3/70).
Violette la Grande. [=*W. E. SUTER, The Life of an Actress*, p. 587.]
The Voice of Honour. [=*W. E. SUTER.*]
+Bal. Vol-au-Vent; or, Love on Ladders (Cheltenham, 7/1/61).
The Volcano of Italy. [=*C. H. HAZLEWOOD.*]
Waiting for the Underground. [=*L. H. DU TERREAUX.*]
p. 765] +D. Walpurgis Night; or, The Demon Hunter of the Hartzburg (M'bone, 10/59).
A Warning Voice. [=*N. LEE, Jr.*]
The War Trail. [=*W. T. TOWNSEND.*]
+D. The Watch Tower; or, The Sons of Altona (Brit. 8/59).
The Watercress Girl. [=*W. TRAVERS.*]
p. 766] The Wedding Eve. [=*C. H. HAZLEWOOD.*]
Welch Rabbits. [=*J. B. JOHNSTONE.*]
Welcome Little Stranger. [=*M. LEMON.*]
What will he do with it? [=*F. L. PHILLIPS.*]
What will my Aunt say? [=Forbidden Fruit (*UA*), p. 679.]
Where's Brown? (Brighton, 1859). [=*J. LEGG.*]
Where's Crevelli? [=*J. HOWARD* and *F. F. COOPER.*]
Where's Mr Smith? [=*G. CONQUEST.*]
+F. Whiskey and Water; or, Paddy's Dream (Str. 30/3/54). [Possibly=*Whisky and Water* by *G. W. SHANDS*: see p. 561.]
The White Boys (Sur. 1862). [=*H. G. PLUNKETT.*]
The White Boys (Vic. 1862). [=*E. TOWERS.*]
p. 767] +D. The White Chateau. 8° 1852.
The White Chateau (Grec. 1861). [=*G. CONQUEST.*]
The White Indian. [=*E. TOWERS.*]
White Lies (West, Albert H. 1897). [=*T. W. STONES-DAVIDSON, Taradiddles*, p. 585.]
The White Palfrey. [=*W. E. SUTER*=*Roland and his Steed* (*UA*), p. 744.]
Whitsuntide. [This seems to be a revised version of *E. R. LANCASTER, Whitsun Eve*; see iv, 553, 643.]
+P. Whittington and his Cat (Greenock, 16/1/59).
Who's a Traveller? [=*J. HOWARD* and *F. F. COOPER.*]
The Whyte Chapel Byrd Catchers. [Apparently a revision of the play by *E. R. LANCASTER*; see iv, 593.]

p. 768] Widow and Orphans. [=*C. H. HAZLEWOOD*=*Faith, Hope and Charity* (*UA*), p. 675.]
The Widow Bewitched. [=*H. AIDÉ*; music Virginia Gabriel.]
The Widow's Son. [=*J. H. WILKINS*. +*or, The Merchant of Brussels.*]
Wilfred Ned. [=*C. H. HAZLEWOOD*=*The Skeleton Crew* (*UA*), p. 768.]
Willie the Wanderer. [=*F. ROGERS*. +*or, The Life of a Policeman.*]
The Will o' the Wisp (Brit. 1859). [=*W. SEAMAN*.]
The Will o' the Wisp (Eff. 1859). [=*J. B. JOHNSTONE*.]
The Willow Marsh. [=*A. FAUCQUEZ*. Apparently=*The Forced Marriage; or, The W.M.* (see p. 679) and *The Adventurer's Doom; or, The Murder of the W.M.* (Grec. 14/7/62).]
The Wishing Glen. [=Spirits of the Departed (*UA*), p. 753.]

p. 769] A Woman in my Dust Hole. [=*L. S. BUCKINGHAM*. +Str. 8/2/58.]
The Woman in White (Sur. 1860). [=*J. M. WARE*.]
Woman's Devotion. [=*A. FAUCQUEZ*.]
A Woman's No. [=*S. GIBNEY*.]

p. 770] Woman's Worth. [=*J. B. HOWE*.]
Won by a Trick. [=*S. WILSON*; music M. Lutz.]
The Workgirls of London. [=*C. H. HAZLEWOOD*.]
The Workhouse, the Palace and the Grave. [=*W. SEAMAN*.]
+Spec. The Wounded Horse; or, The Leap of Death (New Ampi. Leeds, 30/7/61).
Wreck and Rescue. [=*T. MEAD*.]
The Wrongs of Poland. [=*S. HASTINGS*.]

p. 771] +P. The Yellow Dwarf (Southampton, 26/12/60).
The Yellow Dwarf (Shakespeare, L'pool, 1888). [=*T. F. DOYLE*.]
The Yellow Dwarf (Shakespeare, L'pool, 1897). [=*J. H. WOOLFE*.]
+P. The Yellow Dwarf; or, Harlequin King of the Golden Mines and the Beautiful Mermaid with the Golden Hair (Amphi. L'pool, 26/12/65).
+D. The Yellow Frigate (Dundee, 29/4/61).
A Young Girl from the Country (Pav. 1860). [=*J. B. HOWE*.]
The Young Recruit. [=*Mrs V. ROBERTS*.]
You're another. [=*L. S. BUCKINGHAM*.]
Zaida. [=*O. SUMMERS*; music M. Lutz.]
Zampa. [=*A. THOMPSON*; music F. Hérold.]
The Zaporogues. [=*J. D. DAVIS* and *E. L. LEVY*.]

p. 772] +Bal. La Zitanella (Str. 3/12/55).

INDEX

54-2